THE CONSTITUTIONAL AND LEGAL RIGHTS OF WOMEN

Fourth Edition

LESLIE F. GOLDSTEIN
Morris Professor Emerita of Political Science
University of Delaware

JUDITH A. BAER
Professor Emerita of Political science
Texas A&M University

COURTENAY W. DAUM
Professor of Political Science
Colorado State University

TERRI SUSAN FINE
Professor of Political Science
University of Central Florida

WEST ACADEMIC PUBLISHING

The publisher is not engaged in rendering legal or other professional advice, and this publication is not a substitute for the advice of an attorney. If you require legal or other expert advice, you should seek the services of a competent attorney or other professional.

© 2019 LEG, Inc. d/b/a West Academic
444 Cedar Street, Suite 700
St. Paul, MN 55101
1-877-888-1330

West, West Academic Publishing, and West Academic are trademarks of West Publishing Corporation, used under license.

Printed in the United States of America

ISBN: 978-1-64020-125-5

This volume is dedicated to Justice Ruth Bader Ginsburg, in gratitude for her achievements on behalf of women's rights, first as an advocate and then as a judge.

Table of Contents

TABLE OF CASES XIII

Introduction 1

Chapter 1. Women Seek Constitutional Equality 21
Women and U.S. Law Before the Fourteenth Amendment 21
The Privileges or Immunities Clause: The *Slaughterhouse Cases* (1873) 22
Access to the Bar: *Myra Bradwell v. State of Illinois* (1873) 27
    Brief of Bradwell's Counsel for *Bradwell v. Illinois* (1873) 28
    Myra Bradwell v. State of Illinois 31
Women's Suffrage and the Fourteenth Amendment Debates 34
    Elizabeth Cady Stanton to the Editor, 'This Is the Negro's Hour,' *National Anti-Slavery Standard,* New York, 26 December 1865 35
    Minor v. Happersett 37
Women and Modern Citizenship, Part One: The Vote by Constitutional Amendment 43
Liberty of Contract: *Lochner v. New York* (1905) 49
    Lochner v. New York 50
    Protection for Women as Wedge into Liberty of Contract 61
        Muller v. Oregon (1908) 61
            Muller v. Oregon 62
        Bunting v. Oregon (1917) 65
            Bunting v. Oregon 66
        Adkins v. Children's Hospital (1923) 67
            Adkins v. Children's Hospital 69
    Protecting Women by Limiting Their Freedom: *Radice v. New York* (1924) 81
    Capitulation on Minimum Wages for Women: *West Coast Hotel v. Parrish* (1937) and *U.S. v. Darby* (1941) 84
Equal Protection Clause 87
    A Century of "Ordinary Scrutiny" of Sex-Based Classifications 96
        Goesaert v. Cleary (1948) 98
            Goesaert et al. v. Cleary et al., Liquor Control Commission 99
        Hoyt v. Florida (1961) 101
            Hoyt v. Florida 103

Chapter 2. Women Attain (?) Constitutional Equality 111
Almost Strict Scrutiny 111
    Doctrinal and Political Setting 111
    Reed v. Reed (1971) 115
        Reed v. Reed 115
    Frontiero v. Richardson (1973) 118
        Sharron and Joseph Frontiero v. Elliot Richardson, Sec'y of Defense 119
    Court Bides Its Time 131
        Kahn v. Shevin (1974) 131
        Schlesinger v. Ballard (1975) 132

   Weinberger v. Wiesenfeld (1975) 134
Officially Intermediate Scrutiny: *Craig v. Boren* (1976) 136
  Craig v. Boren 138
Sex Discrimination Post-*Craig*... 149
  Statutory Rape: *Michael M. v. Sonoma County* (1981) 150
   Michael M. v. Sonoma County, CA 151
Women and Modern Citizenship Part Two: Jury Service, Military Service, and
  Conferring Citizenship 168
  Systematic Exclusion from Juries: *Taylor v. Louisiana* (1975) 168
   Billy Taylor v. Louisiana 170
  Serving in the Military 180
   The Draft: *Rostker v. Goldberg* (1981) 180
   Post-*Rostker* Reform: Women in Combat 182
Interlude: Doctrinal Development on the Clinton Court.. 186
Conferring Citizenship: Female Versus Male Parents 187
 Miller v. Albright (1998) 187
 Tuan Anh Nguyen v. INS (2001) 190
 Sessions v. Morales-Santana (2017) 192
  Sessions v. Morales-Santana 192
When Is Discrimination Not Discrimination? *Personnel Administrator v. Feeney*
 (1979) 201
  Personnel Administrator of Massachusetts v. Feeney 202
Rights in Conflict.. 211
  First Amendment Freedoms Versus Equal Opportunity: *Pittsburgh Press v.*
   Human Relations Commission (1973), *Hishon v. King & Spaulding* (1984), and
   Roberts v. U.S. Jaycees (1984) 211
  Equality for Women vs. States' Rights 215
Conclusion 216

Chapter 3. Women and Employment 221
Kimberlé Crenshaw, "Demarginalizing the Intersection of Race and Sex: A Black
 Feminist Critique of Antidiscrimination Doctrine, Feminist Theory and
 Antiracist Politics" 223
Equal Pay and Comparable Worth 224
  Transition to Equal Pay: *Corning Glass Works v. Brennan* (1974) 225
  Pensions 227
  Comparable Worth 228
Title VII and the BFOQ Exemption 230
  Women's Labor Legislation.. 230
  Weeks v. Southern Bell (1969) 231
   Weeks v. Southern Bell 231
  Rosenfeld v. Southern Pacific (1971) 236
   Rosenfeld v. Southern Pacific Company 237
"Sex Plus" Discrimination 241
  Phillips v. Martin-Marietta (1971) 241
   Phillips v. Martin-Marietta Corp. 241
Sexual Harassment as Sex Discrimination.. 244
  Supreme Court Guidelines: *Meritor Savings Bank v. Vinson* (1986) 244
  Lower Court Innovation: *Ellison v. Brady* (1991) 247
   Kerry Ellison v. Nicholas F. Brady, Sec'y of the Treasury 247

Table of Contents

  Supreme Court Response: *Harris v. Forklift* (1993) 258
    Harris v. Forklift Systems, Inc. 260
  Same-Sex Harassment: *Oncale v. Sundowner* (1998) 263
    Joseph Oncale v. Sundowner Offshore Services et al. 264
  Suing a Sitting President: *Jones v. Clinton* (1998) 268
    Jones v. Clinton 269
  Employer Liability Revisited 271
    Burlington Industries, Inc. v. Ellerth 271
Gender Stereotyping and the Workplace: *Price Waterhouse v. Hopkins* (1989) 278
  Price Waterhouse v. Hopkins 281
Title VII and Gender Discrimination 294
  Smith v. City of Salem 295
  Mia Macy v. Eric Holder 297
The Civil Rights Act of 1991 298
BFOQ and Disparate Impact 303
  E. C. Dothard et al. v. Dianne Rawlinson et al. 306
The Worker as Mother 314
  Mandatory Maternity Leaves 315
    Cleveland Bd. of Education et al. v. Lafleur et al. 316
  Protection of the Fetus vs. Opportunity for Women: *UAW v. Johnson Controls* (1991) 321
    United Autoworkers v. Johnson Controls Inc. 324
  Pregnancy and Benefits 338
    The PDA and Protective Laws for Pregnant Workers: *Cal Fed v. Guerra* (1987) 339
      California Federal S. & L. Assn. v. Guerra 342
    The Family and Medical Leave Act: *Nevada v. Hibbs* (2003) 358
  Sex-Based Affirmative Action: *Johnson v. Transportation Agency* (1987) 360
    Johnson v. Transportation Agency 364
  Time Limits: *Ledbetter v. Goodyear Tire & Rubber Co.* (2007) 388
    Lilly M. Ledbetter v. Goodyear Tire & Rubber Company 389
Conclusion 399

Chapter 4. Women and Reproductive Freedom 407
Legal Context: Implied Constitutional Rights 407
Sterilization 412
  Buck v. Bell (1927) 412
    From Stephen Jay Gould, "Carrie Buck's Daughter" 412
    Buck v. Bell 415
  Skinner v. Oklahoma (1942) 416
    Skinner v. Oklahoma 417
  After *Skinner*: The Paradox of Sterilization Policy 422
  Stump v. Sparkman (1978) 423
  Sterilization Reform 424
Feminists and Contraception: A Mixed History 424
  Griswold v. Connecticut (1965) 425
    Griswold v. Connecticut 427
  Eisenstadt v. Baird (1972) 440
    Eisenstadt v. Baird 442

Legalizing Abortion 453
   Roe v. Wade (1973) and *Doe v. Bolton* (1973) 456
      Roe v. Wade and Doe v. Bolton 458
   Post-*Roe* Restrictions on Abortion 481
      Constitutional Framework 481
         Planned Parenthood v. Danforth (1976) 481
            Planned Parenthood v. Danforth 483
         Bellotti v. Baird (1976) 498
      Refinements of the Framework: 1979–1989 498
   Shifting Judicial Consensus, 1989–1991 506
      Background: Restrictions on Abortion Funding, 1977–1980 507
      Obituary for *Roe v. Wade*? *Webster v. Reproductive Health Services* (1989) 511
      Six Votes Against *Roe*? *Rust v. Sullivan* (1991) 521
   Reprieve and Reset on *Roe v. Wade*: *Planned Parenthood v. Casey* (1992) 526
      Planned Parenthood of Southeastern PA. v. Casey 529
Restricting Abortion Technique 571
   Stenberg v. Carhart (2000) 571
Constitutional Law Changes with Judicial Personnel 575
   Gonzales v. Carhart 578
Securing Access to Abortion: RICO Lawsuits and Buffer Zones 596
   Hill v. Colorado (2000) 602
      Leila Jeanne Hill et al. v. Colorado et al. 602
   Scheidler v. NOW (2003) 622
   Legislation Against Abortion Clinics: *Whole Woman's Health v. Hellerstedt* (2016) 625
      Whole Woman's Health v. Hellerstedt 627
Religious Freedom Versus Reproductive Rights 643
   Burwell v. Hobby Lobby Stores 644
Pregnant Women's Privacy 664
   Coerced Caesareans: *In re A.C.* (1990) 664
      In re A.C. 667
   Criminalizing Pregnant Behavior: *Ferguson v. Charleston, S.C.* (2001) 681
      Ferguson et al. v. City of Charleston et al. 683
   Update on Criminalizing Behavior During Pregnancy 694
Reproductive Technology and the Law 694
   The *Baby M* Case (1988) 694
      In the Matter of Baby M 696
   Policy Issues on Surrogate Motherhood 705
   Surrogacy Perspectives 706
   Policy Issues on Surrogate Motherhood 707
   After *Baby M* 707
Whose Property Are Frozen Embryos? 708
   Davis v. Davis (1992) 708
   A.Z. v. B.Z. (2000) 709
Posthumous Procreation: *Woodward v. Commissioner of Social Security* (2002) 710
Conclusion 710

Chapter 5. Gender and Family Law 719
What Is Marriage? 719
   Gay Rights and Marriage 719

Table of Contents

   The U.S. Supreme Court Changes the Definition of Marshall.................724
    U.S. v. Windsor (2013)..725
     U.S. v. Windsor..726
    Obergefell v. Hodges (2015)...736
     Obergefell v. Hodges..738
   The Future Family?...756
  Legal History of Marriage...758
   Eighteenth- and Nineteenth-Century Perspectives...............................759
    William Blackstone, *Commentaries on the Laws of England* (1776).......759
    Charles Dickens, *Oliver Twist*, Chapter 51 (1837)........................760
   Remnants of Coverture: *U.S. v. Yazell* (1966)..761
    United States v. Yazell..761
   Sex Discrimination: *Stanton v. Stanton* (1975).......................................763
    Stanton v. Stanton..764
   Revolutionizing Marriage..768
    Orr v. Orr (1979)..768
     Orr v. Orr..769
    Kirchberg v. Feenstra (1981)...773
     Kirchberg v. Feenstra..773
  The Traditional Family...776
   The Wife as Husband's Property—*Tinker v. Colwell* (1904).................776
    Tinker v. Colwell..776
   A Married Woman's Surname: *Rago* and *Palermo* Cases.....................779
   Asymmetrical Reciprocity: *McGuire v. McGuire* (1953) and *Borelli v. Brousseau*
    (1993)...780
    McGuire v. McGuire..780
    Borelli v. Brousseau..785
  Divorce...791
   Arizona Revised Statutes...792
  Parents' Rights and Child Custody...795
   Paternal Custody and Its Limits..795
    James Kent, *Commentaries on American Law*, 4th ed. (1840)..............795
    Joseph Story, *Commentaries on Equity Jurisprudence*, Sec. 1341 (1836).....796
   "Tender Years" Doctrine: *Long v. Long* (1955)....................................796
    Ethel Long v. Herbert Long..797
   The Best Interests of the Child: Gender-Neutral? *Salk v. Salk* (1975)......801
    Kerstin Salk v. Lee Salk..801
   Race and "Best Interest of the Child": *Palmore v. Sidoti* (1984)...............808
   The Primary Caregiver Standard..808
   Unfaithful Spouses and Child Custody: Comparative Cases...................808
    Louis A. Bunim v. Ethel Bunim..809
    Jacqueline Jarrett v. Walter Jarrett..810
    David M. v. Margaret M...816
   The Future of Child Custody..826
    Linda Tetreault v. Mark Tetreault..826
    In re Marriage of Culbertson..828
  Rights of Unmarried Fathers..832
   Stanley v. Illinois (1972)..833
    Peter Stanley v. Illinois..834
   Follow-up to Stanley: *Fiallo v. Bell* and *Quilloin v. Walcott*.....................843

Caban v. Mohammed (1979) 844
  Abdiel Caban v. Kazim and Maria Mohammed 845
Parham v. Hughes (1974) 858
Lehr v. Robertson (1983) 859
  Lehr v. Robertson 861
 The "Baby Richard" Case 870
  In re Petition of Doe 871
"Adulterous Fathers": *Michael H. v. Gerald D.* (1989) 873
 Michael H. v. Gerald D. 876
Parents Versus Grandparents 893
 Painter v. Bannister (1966) 893
 Pamela Kay Bottoms v. Sharon Bottoms (1995) 894
 Troxel v. Granville (2000) 896
  Troxel v. Granville 897
Parents' Rights Versus Community Rights: Native Americans and Family Law 899
 Santa Clara Pueblo v. Martinez (1978) 899
  Santa Clara Pueblo et al. v. Martinez et al. 900
 Mississippi Choctaw v. Holyfield (1989) 907
  Mississippi Band of Choctaw Indians v. Holyfield 909
 Adoptive Couple v. Baby Girl (2013) 916
  Adoptive Couple v. Baby Girl 917
Parents' Rights Versus Human Rights 925
Conclusion 927

Chapter 6. Women and Education 935
Single-Sex Public Schools: Separate but Equal? 936
 Alice de Rivera, "On De-Segregating Stuyvesant High" 938
 Janice Bray et al. v. Joseph Lee et al. 939
 Susan L. Vorchheimer v. School District of Philadelphia 942
Higher Education 952
 From Edward H. Clarke, M.D., *Sex in Education; or, a Fair Chance for the Girls* 952
 From Lynn White, *Educating Our Daughters: A Challenge to the Colleges* 953
 Texas A&M Cases: *Heaton v. Bristol* (1958) and *Allred v. Heaton* (1960) 955
 Kirstein v. Rector and Visitors of the University of Virginia (1970) 956
  Kirstein v. Rector and Visitors of the University of Virginia 956
 Williams v. McNair (1970) 957
  Williams v. McNair 957
 Mississippi University for Women v. Hogan (1982) 959
  Mississippi University for Women v. Hogan 960
 Women in the Military Academies: *U.S. v. Virginia* (1996) 972
  United States v. Virginia 975
Title IX and Educational Equality 1002
 Grove City College v. Bell (1984) 1003
 Title IX and College Sports: *Cohen v. Brown U.* (1996) 1005
Title IX and Sexual Harassment 1007
 Franklin v. Gwinnett County (1992) 1007
 Gebser v. Lago Vista (1998) 1008
  Gebser v. Lago Vista Independent School District 1009
  From Stephen Schulhofer, *Unwanted Sex* (1998) 1021

Table of Contents

Davis v. Monroe County (1999) 1022
    Davis v. Monroe County Board Of Education et al. 1022
Title IX and Retaliation 1041
Title IX and Gender Identity 1042
Conclusion 1043

Chapter 7. Women and Crime 1047

Spouse Abuse 1048
  The Old Days: Three Cases 1048
    Joyner v. Joyner (1862) 1048
      Joyner v. Joyner 1048
    State v. Rhodes (1868) 1051
      State v. A. B. Rhodes 1051
    State v. Richard Oliver (1874) 1054
      State v. Richard Oliver 1055
  From Wife Beating to Domestic Violence 1056
  Police Responsibility 1056
    Thurman v. Torrington (1984) 1056
      Tracey Thurman et al. v. City of Torrington et al. 1057
    Navarro v. Block (1995) 1061
      Navarro v. Block, Sheriff of Los Angeles County 1061
      Fajardo, Guardian Ad Litem for Navarro Minors [Navarro] v.
      [Block, Sheriff of] County of Los Angeles 1066
  The Victim Who Strikes Back: Wife Abuse and Husband Homicide 1073
    From Lenore E. A. Walker, *The Battered Woman Syndrome* 1073
    From Donald A. Downs, *More Than Victims: Battered Women, the Syndrome
    Society, and the Law* 1074
    State v. Kelly (1984) 1075
      State v. Kelly 1075
    State v. Stewart (1988) 1085
      State v. Stewart 1085
Rape 1099
  From Camille Paglia, *Sex, Art, and American Culture* 1100
  From Susan Estrich, *Real Rape* 1101
  Emily Doe, *Victim Impact Statement in People of the State of California v. Brock
  Allen Turner* (2016) 1102
  Force and Consent: *Goldberg v. State of Maryland* (1978) 1104
    Randy Jay Goldberg v. State of Maryland 1105
  Resistance 1112
    State v. Rusk (1981) 1112
      State v. Rusk 1114
    In the Interest of M.T.S. (1992) 1120
      In the Interest of M.T.S. 1121
      From Stephen J. Schulhofer, *Unwanted Sex: The Culture of Intimidation
      and the Failure of Law* 1132
  Marital Rape 1133
    From Lisa Eskow, "The Ultimate Weapon? Demythologizing Spousal
    Rape..." 1133

  Kelly C. Connerton, "Comment: The Resurgence of the Marital Rape Exemption: The Victimization of Teens by Their Statutory Rapists" 1134
Feminists Divide over Pornography 1135
 Catharine A. MacKinnon, from *Only Words* 1136
 Nadine Strossen, from *Defending Pornography* 1137
 Obscenity Doctrine: *American Booksellers Association v. Hudnut* 1138
  American Booksellers Assoc. v. Hudnut 1141
 Hate Speech and the Future of Pornography Laws: *R.A.V. v. St. Paul* (1992) ... 1145
 Restitution for Child Pornography Victims: *Paroline v. United States* (2014) 1148
The Violence Against Women Act: *United States v. Morrison and Brzonkala v. Morrison* (2000) 1150
 United States v. Antonio J. Morrison et al. and Christy Brzonkala v. Antonio J. Morrison et al. 1154
Women and Sexual Violence on Campus 1180
Women Criminals 1182
 Prostitution 1182
  Unequal Enforcement—Does It Take Two to Tango? 1182
   In the Matter of [Dora] P. 1182
  Feminists Divide: Modern Remnant of Slavery Versus Just Another Job 1185
  Sexual Slavery: *U.S. v. Footman* (1999) 1188
   U.S. v. Troy Footman 1189
Conclusion 1194

Chapter 8. Conclusions 1199

GLOSSARY 1205

INDEX 1209

Table of Cases

A. B. Rhodes, State v., 1051
A.C., In re, 667, 717
Abdiel Caban v. Kazim and Maria Mohammed, 845
Abele v. Markle, 474
Ada v. Guam, 715
Adair v. United States, 69
Adams v. City of Milwaukee, 128
Adams v. Tanner, 438
Adamson v. California, 531
Adarand v. Pena, 387
Adkins v. Children's Hospital, 67, **69,** 438
Adoptive Couple v. Baby Girl, 916, **917**
Akron v. Akron Center for Reproductive Health (Akron I), 713
Albemarle Paper v. Moody, 398, 404
Alexander v. Gardner-Denver Co., 392
Alexander v. Louisiana, 208, 217
Allgeyer v. Louisiana, 51, 56, 63, 69, 108
American Booksellers Assoc. v. Hudnut, 1141, 1147, 1196
American Pipe & Constr. Co. v. Utah, 392
American Steel Foundries v. Tri-City Central Trades Council, 605
American Sugar Refining Co. v. Louisiana, 83
American Trucking Assns., Inc., United States v., 345
Anderson v. Anderson, 823
Anderson v. Celebrezze, 543
Anderson, United States v., 716
Andrews v. City of Philadelphia, 256
Ankenbrandt v. Richards, 728
Anthony v. Commonwealth, 207
Antonio J. Morrison et al., United States v., 1154
Apodaca v. Oregon, 172, 175
Appletree v. City of Hartford, 1060
Aptheker v. Secretary of State, 465, 473, 712
Argersinger v. Hamlin, 714
Arizona Governing Committee v. Norris, 330, 334
Arkansas Natural Gas Co. v. Railroad Commission, 83
Arlington Heights v. Metropolitan Housing Dev. Corp., 203, 207, 208, 1065
Armstrong v. Manzo, 867
Arnold v. Board of Education of Escambia County, Ala., 536
Ashcroft v. ACLU, 1196
Ashwander v. Tennessee Valley Authority, 449, 476
Atkin v. Kansas, 57, 59

Aurelia Davis v. Monroe County Board of Education, 1197
Avery v. County of Burke, 536
Ayotte v. Planned Parenthood of Northern New Eng., 586, 641
B.B., Matter of, 932
Baby Girl, L.J., In the matter of, 717
Baby M, In the Matter of, 696
Baehr v. Lewin, 721
Baggett v. Bullitt, 428
Baird, Commonwealth v., 442, 448
Baker v. Carr, 770
Baker v. Nelson, 741
Baldwin v. Missouri, 516
Balistreri v. Pacifica Police Department, 1065
Ballard v. United States, 102, 171, 173, 217
Barbier v. Connolly, 56, 109, 116
Barenblatt v. United States, 428
Barnes v. City of Cincinnati, 294
Barnes v. Moore, 715
Bates v. Little Rock, 434
Batista v. Rodriguez, 1060
Batson v. Kentucky, 179
Bazemore v. Friday, 394
Beal v. Doe, 157, 714
Bell v. Burson, 837
Bellotti v. Baird, 551, 713
Berkelman v. San Francisco Unified School District, 945
Bernstein v. Aetna Life & Cas., 335
Bess, State v., 1076
Biediger v. Quinnipiac University, 1006
Billy Taylor v. Louisiana, 170
Black v. Cutter Laboratories, 964
Blake v. McClung, 472
Board of Education v. Barnette, 428
Board of Trustees of Univ. of Ala. v. Garrett, 405
Boddie v. Connecticut, 109, 714
Boerne v. Flores, 1159
Bolling v. Sharpe, 91, 125, 216, 473, 729
Borelli v. Brousseau, 785
Bosley v. McLaughlin, 79, 80, 83
Bottoms v. Bottoms, 932
Bowe v. Colgate-Palmolive Co., 239
Bowers v. Hardwick, 452, 560, 720, 740, 929
Boy Scouts of America v. Dale, 219, 720
Boyd v. United States, 429, 464
Boyd, In re, 672
Bradwell v. Illinois, 31, 108, 122, 354, 552, 593, 964, 998
Brandenburg v. Ohio, 1141

Bray v. Alexandria Women's Health Clinic, 715, 716
Bray v. Lee, 945
Breard v. Alexandria, 429
Breed v. Jones, 486
Breedlove v. Suttles, 97, 110
Brimmer v. Rebman, 55
Bromage v. Prosser, 777
Brooks v. Brooks, 786, 789
Brown v. Allen, 171, 177
Brown v. Board of Education, 19, 203, 539, 945, 948, 1044
Brown v. Buhman, 749
Brown v. Louisiana, 447
Brown, State v., 1123
Bruno v. Codd, 1059
Buck v. Bell, 415, 420, 421, 465
Bunting v. Oregon, 66, 71
Burlington Industries, Inc. v. Ellerth, 271, 403
Burnet v. Coronado Oil & Gas Co., 563
Burns v. Ohio, 714
Burrus, In re, 728
Burson v. Freeman, 611
Burwell v. Hobby Lobby Stores, 643, **644**
Butchers' Union Co. v. Crescent City Co., 69
Caban v. Mohammed, 196, 203, 210, 348, 355, 863, 960
Cafeteria Workers v. McElroy, 836
Califano v. Goldfarb, 150, 167, 204, 209, 593, 976
Califano v. Webster, 150, 152, 154, 156, 209, 770, 771, 772, 962, 976
Califano v. Westcott, 348
California Federal S. & L. Assn. v. Guerra, 335, **342**, 976
California v. Greenwood, 690
California v. LaRue, 101, 143
Callister's Estate, In re, 788, 789
Cannon v. University of Chicago, 1045
Canterbury v. Spence, 668
Cantwell v. Connecticut, 465, 711
Carey v. Brown, 606, 611, 613
Carey v. Population Services International, 157, 453, 532, 554
Carhart v. Ashcroft, 595
Cariddi v. Kansas City Chiefs Football Club, 403
Carolene Products, United States v., 420, 711
Carrington v. Rash, 124, 216, 473
Carroll v. Greenwich Insurance Co., 84
Carter v. Jury Comm'n, 171, 177
Caspar Weinberger v. Stephen Wiesenfeld, 134
Castaneda v. Partida, 208
Castle Rock v. Gonzalez, 1195
Castleman, United States v., 1099, 1195
Catholic Charities of Sacramento, Inc. v. Superior Court, 656
Cessna, People v., 813
Chandler v. Miller, 684, 685, 687
Chaplinsky v. New Hampshire, 1144, 1196

Chardon v. Fernandez, 390
Cherokee Intermarriage Cases, 904
Chevron Oil Co. v. Huson, 856
Chicago, Milwaukee and St. Paul Railway v. Minnesota, 108
Child of Indian Heritage, In re Adoption of, 912
Christenson v. Iowa, 402
Church of the Holy Trinity v. United States, 345, 383
City Bank Farmers Trust Co. v. McGowan, 672
Civil Rights Cases, 401, 1154, 1160, 1177, 1197
Clark v. Jeter, 993
Cleveland Bd. of Education et al. v. Lafleur et al., 139, **316**
Cleveland v. United States, 930
Clinton v. Jones, 403
Cohen v. Brown University, 1006
Cohen v. California, 604
Cohen v. Chesterfield County Bd. of Education, 404
Coker v. Georgia, 1195
Colautti v. Franklin, 713
College Savings Bank v. Florida Prepaid Postsecondary Ed. Expense Bd., 405
Collin v. Smith, 1141
Collins v. Texas, 583
Compston v. Borden, 403
Conroy, In re, 668
Consolidated Rail v. Darrone, 1045
Cooper v. Aaron, 715, 1164
Cooper v. Southern Co., 393
Coppage v. Kansas, 69, 438
Corning Glass Works v. Brennan, 225, 284
Cort v. Ash, 905
Cox v. Louisiana, 611
Coyle v. Smith, 929
Craig v. Boren, 138, 151, 157, 161, 167, 194, 199, 203, 209, 355, 770, 771, 845, 865, 961, 969, 988, 993, 994, 1059
Craig, In re Marriage of, 831
Crain v. Allison, 668
Cramer v. United States, 207
Crandall v. Nevada, 712
Crisonino v. New York City Housing Auth., 270
Crouse Irving Memorial Hospital v. Paddock, 670, 717
Crowell v. Benson, 584
Crowley v. Christensen, 51
Cruikshank, United States v., 1161
Cruzan v. Director, Mo. Dept. of Health, 535, 552
Culbertson v. Culbertson, 828
Curran v. Mount Diablo Council of Boy Scouts, 219
Cutter v. Wilkinson, 660
Dandridge v. Williams, 121, 128
Daniels v. Williams, 530
Darby, United States v., 1170

Table of Cases

David M. v. Margaret M., 816
Davis v. Monroe County Board Of Education et al., **1022**
Davis v. Monsanto Chemical Co., 256, 263, 275
Dege, United States v., 762
DeGrace v. Rumsfeld, 275
DeJonge v. Oregon, 428, 711, 1141
Dennis v. Cty. of Fairfax, 275
Department of Agriculture v. Moreno, 729
Derby, Matter of Marriage of, 823
DeShaney v. Winnebago Cty. Soc. Servs. Dept., 1068
Diaz v. Pan-American World Airways, 404
Dillon v. Frank, 296
District of Columbia v. Carter, 1162
Doe v. Bolton, **458**, 543
Doe v. Kelley, 717
Doe v. Rampton, 714
Doe v. Rose, 714
Doe v. Trump, 186
Doe v. University of Illinois, 1026
Doe v. Westby, 714
Doe v. Wohlgemuth, 714
Doe, In re Petition of, **871**
Dora P., In the Matter of, 1197
Dothard v. Rawlinson, 284, 325, 332, 404
Douglas v. California, 109, 216, 714
Duncan v. Louisiana, 171, 172, 177, 217, 740
Dunn v. Palermo, 930
E. C. Dothard et al. v. Dianne Rawlinson et al., **306**
E.C. Knight, United States v., 1197
Earle v. Earle, 782
Edwards v. California, 109, 216, 712, 714
EEOC v. Commercial Office Products Co., 392
Eisenstadt v. Baird, 316, **442**, 458, 464, 465, 474, 485, 532, 543, 552, 740, 744, 931
Electrical Workers v. Robbins & Myers, Inc., 392
Elizabeth Hishon v. King & Spaulding, 212
Ellison v. Brady, **247**, 403
English v. General Electric Co., 335
Erznoznik v. Jacksonville, 604, 615, 619
Ethel Long v. Herbert Long, **797**
Everton v. Everton, 1049
Fabian v. Hosp. of Central Conn., 294, 298
Faragher v. City of Boca Raton, 403
Faulkner v. Jones, 1044
Fay v. New York, 174, 175, 176
FCC v. Pacifica Foundation, 1144
Feeney v. Massachusetts, 207
Ferguson et al. v. Charleston, 717
Ferguson v. Charleston, **683**, 717
Ferguson v. Skrupa, 473
Fiallo v. Bell, 187, 196, 217, 931
Finley v. California, 418
Firefighters Institute for Racial Equality v. St. Louis, 403
Firefighters v. Cleveland, 366, 371
Fisher v. University of Texas, 388

Fitzpatrick v. Bitzer, 1159
Flemming v. Nestor, 121
Florida Lime & Avocado Growers, Inc. v. Paul, 329, 343, 347
Florida Prepaid Postsecondary Ed. Expense Bd. v. College Savings Bank, 1163
Florida Star v. B.J.F., 676
Forbush v. Wallace, 930
Frank v. Maryland, 429
Franklin v. Gwinnett County Public Schools, 1016
Freche, In re, 778
Frisby v. Schultz, 604, 605, 610, 611, 612
Frontiero v. Laird, 126
Frontiero v. Richardson, 109, 138, 144, 203, 332, 961, 962, 975
Fullilove v. Klutznick, 360
Funk v. United States, 762
G.E v. Gilbert, 338
Gaines v. Canada, 419
Garcia v. Elf Atochem North America, 265
Garcia v. San Antonio Metropolitan Transit Authority, 561, 563, 1164, 1171, 1176, 1197
Garger v. New Jersey, 536
Garrett v. Board of Education of School District of Detroit, 1001, 1044
Garska v. McCoy, 816
Gaston County, United States v., 125
Gault, In re, 486
Gebser v. Lago Vista Independent School District, **1009**
Geduldig v. Aiello, 338
General Electric Co. v. Gilbert, 342, 345, 405
German Alliance Insurance Co. v. Lewis, 80
Gibbons v. Ogden, 712, 1164
Giboney v. Empire Storage Co., 428
Gibson v. Gibson, 789
Gideon v. Wainwright, 714
Gillette v. Delmore, 1063
Ginsberg v. New York, 486
Gitlow v. New York, 711
Glasser v. United States, 171, 176, 177
Glona v. American Guarantee and Liability Insurance, 216, 837
Godfrey v. Spano, 733
Goesaert v. Cleary, **99**, 110, 194, 975
Gomez v. Perez, 857
Gomillion v. Lightfoot, 203
Gonzales v. Carhart, 576, **578**, 633
Goodridge et al. v. Commissioner of Public Health, 753, 929
Goodwin v. General Motors Corp., 395
Goss v. Lopez, 486, 1034
Grace, United States v., 611, 617
Gratz v. Bollinger, 388
Gray v. Greyhound Lines, East, 403
Gray, State v., 1089, 1090
Grayned v. City of Rockford, 611
Griffin v. Illinois, 109, 216, 714
Griffin v. Wisconsin, 687
Griggs v. Duke Power Co., 240, 252, 306, 346, 350, 372, 386, 404

Griswold v. Connecticut, 316, **427**, 442, 444, 448, 450, 458, 464, 465, 473, 485, 535, 554, 564, 740, 748, 836, 931
Grobart v. Grobart, 1123
Grote v. Sebelius, 658
Grove City College v. Bell, 1045
Grutter v. Bollinger, 109, 388
Guardians' Assn. v. Civil Service, 1045
Gudbrandson v. Genuine Parts Co., 402
Guest, United States v., 473, 1161, 1197
Guinn v. United States, 203
H.L. v. Matheson, 713
Haddock v. Haddock, 728
Hall, State v., 107
Halloway, In re Adoption of, 913, 915
Harlow v. Fitzgerald, 971
Harper v. Board of Elections, 109, 110, 216, 714
Harris v. Forklift Systems, Inc., 260, 265, 275
Harris v. McRae, 157, 543, 562, 714
Harris, State v., 1124
Harris, United States v., 1154, 1160, 1177, 1197
Hawker v. New York, 418
Hawley v. Walker, 80
Hazel v. State, 1109, 1110, 1112, 1114
Hazelwood School District v. United States, 364, 375
Heart of Atlanta Motel, Inc. v. United States, 1155, 1167, 1175
Heath and Milligan v. Worst, 108, 109
Heaton v. Bristol, 1044
Heckler v. Mathews, 200, 994
Heffron v. International Soc. for Krishna Consciousness, Inc., 609, 610, 612
Henson v. Dundee, 252, 403
Hernandez v. Commissioner, 651
Hernandez v. Texas, 104
Hernandez, People v., 163
Hewitt v. Hewitt, 812, 813
Higgins v. New Balance Athletic Shoe, Inc., 295
Hill v. Thomas, 611
Hill, State v., 1089, 1092, 1093
Hines v. Davidowitz, 343
Hipplewith, State v., 1081
Hirabayashi v. United States, 91
Hishon v. Spaulding, 403
Hodel v. Irving, 194
Hodel v. Virginia Surface Mining & Reclamation Assn., 1165
Hodges, State v., 1090, 1091, 1097
Hodgson v. Minnesota, 561, 715
Hoffa v. United States, 691
Hogan v. Mississippi University for Women, 960
Holden v. Hardy, 52, 56, 60, 63
Holloway v. Arthur Andersen & Co., 403
Hope Clinic v. Ryan, 594, 716
Hopkins v. Price Waterhouse, 403
Horne, State v., 1089

Hoyt v. Florida, 103, 173, 176, 177, 194, 553
Hudnut v. American Booksellers' Association, 1138
Hundley, State v., 1089, 1090, 1092, 1096, 1097
Indianapolis v. Edmond, 686
Industrial Union Dept. v. American Petroleum Institute, 335
Isbister v. Boys' Club of Santa Cruz, 219
J. E. B. v. Alabama ex rel. T. B., 179, 194, 199, 975, 994
Jackson v. Birmingham Board of Education, 1045
Jackson v. Virginia, 1116
Jacobson v. Massachusetts, 57, 60, 415, 446, 465, 536, 583, 669, 717
Jacqueline Jarrett v. Walter Jarrett, 810
Jahnke v. State, 1091
Jamaica Hospital, In re, 670, 717
James v. Strange, 109
James v. Valtierra, 109
James v. Wallace, 307
Janice Bray et al. v. Joseph Lee et al., 939
Jarrett v. Jarrett, 813
Jay Burns Baking Co. v. Bryan, 438
Jefferson v. Griffin Spalding County Hospital Authority, 668
Jefferson v. Hackney, 121
Johnson v. Bunny Bread Co., 275
Johnson v. Transportation Agency, Santa Clara Cty., 265, **364**
Jones v. Alfred Mayer, 401
Jones v. Clinton, 269
Jones v. Rath Packing Co., 343
Jones v. United States, 583
Joseph Oncale v. Sundowner Offshore Services et al., 264
Joyner v. Joyner, 1048
Kaemmerling v. Lappin, 658
Kahn v. Shevin, 131, 140, 149, 152, 217, 771, 945
Kansas v. Hendricks, 583
Katz v. United States, 464, 475, 477
Katzenbach v. McClung, 1167, 1175
Katzenbach v. Morgan, 964, 1159
Kelly, State v., 1075
Kemmler, In re, 51
Kent v. Dulles, 473, 712
Keokee Coke Co. v. Taylor, 84, 419
Kerstin Salk v. Lee Salk, 801
Kimel v. Florida Bd. of Regents, 405
Kirchberg v. Feenstra, 773, 960, 976
Kirstein v. Rector and Visitors of the University of Virginia, 956, 978
Kitchen v. Herbert, 745
Klein v. Nassau County Medical Center, 714
Korematsu v. United States, 91, 109, 714
Kovacs v. Cooper, 434, 609, 612, 836
Kowalski v. Tesmer, 194
Kowalski, Guardianship of, 929
Kramer v. Union Free School District, 216, 465

Table of Cases

xvii

Kras, United States v., 714
Kubrick, United States v., 392
Labine v. Vincent, 109
LaFleur v. Cleveland Bd. of Education, 404
Lambert v. Yellowley, 583
Lane v. Brown, 216
Lane v. Wilson, 203
Lanza v. New York, 429
Lassiter v. Department of Social Services, 867
Lau v. Nichols, 347
Lavinia Goodell, In re, 988
Lawrence v. Texas, 592, 720, 729, 730, 732, 740, 744, 929
Lawton v. Steele, 57
Lebron v. Washington Metropolitan Area Transit Authority, 1141
Ledbetter v. Goodyear Tire, 389, 405
Lee v. Weisman, 715
Lehr v. Robertson, 860, **861**
Leicester v. Hoadley, 778
Leila Jeanne Hill et al. v. Colorado et al., 602
Lemons v. Denver, 402
Leopando, In re Marriage of, 823
Levy v. Louisiana, 109, 216, 836
Lewis v. High Point Regional Health Sys., 294
Lincoln Union v. Northwestern Co., 427
Linda R. S. v. Richard D., 770
Linda Tetreault v. Mark Tetreault, 826
Lindsley v. Natural Carbonic Gas Co., 109, 116
Lipsett v. University of Puerto Rico, 251
Little Sisters of the Poor v. Sebelius, 654
Little v. Streater, 867
Littleton v. Prange, 757
Liverpool, New York & Philadelphia S. S. Co. v. Commissioners of Emigration, 476, 767
Lochner v. New York, 50, 62, 69, 427, 438, 711
Long v. District Court, 216, 714
Lopez v. River Oaks Imaging & Diagnostic Group, Inc., 294
Lopez, United States v., 1154, 1197
Lorelyn Pinero Miller v. Madeleine Albright, Secretary of State, 188, 194, 196, 200, 218
Los Angeles Dept. of Water and Power v. Manhart, 285, 324, 331, 347
Louis A. Bunim v. Ethel Bunim, 809
Louisiana v. United States, 982
Loving v. Virginia, 109, 316, 446, 464, 474, 531, 568, 741, 881, 929
Lowe v. Lowe, 783
Lyman v. People, 815
M.C., In re, 931
M.L.B. v. S.L.J., 216, 744
M.T.S., In the Interest of, 1121
Macy v. Department of Justice, 403
Madsen v. Women's Health Center, Inc., 604, 613, 619, 716
Maher v. Roe, 157, 543, 713, 714
Maine v. Thiboutot, 385
Malone v. White Motor Corp., 343, 344, 345

Malpica-Orsini, In re, 846
Mapp v. Ohio, 429
Marshall v. United States, 583
Martin v. Struthers, 428
Martin v. Wilks, 404
Mary Ann Turner v. Department of Employment Security of Utah, 321
Maryland Savings-Share Insurance Corp., United States v., 127
Maryland v. Louisiana, 343
Massachusetts Bd. of Retirement v. Murgia, 203
Massachusetts Maritime Academy, United States v., 1044
Massachusetts v. Secretary of Health and Human Services, 715
Masterpiece Cakeshop v. Colorado Civil Rights Commission, 756
Mathews v. Eldridge, 867
Mathews v. Lucas, 210, 1065
May v. Anderson, 836
Mayer v. Chicago, 714
Maynard v. Hill, 485, 743, 929
Mazurek v. Armstrong, 583
McCulloch v. Maryland, 20, 57
McDonald v. Board of Election Commissioners of Chicago, 109, 116, 216
McDonald v. Santa Fe Trail Transportation Co., 370, 372, 373
McDonnell Douglas Corp. v. Green, 282, 289, 291, 292, 309
McGowan v. Maryland, 121, 144
McGuire v. McGuire, 780
McLaughlin v. Florida, 109, 203, 434
McLaurin v. Oklahoma State Regents, 1044
McLean v. Arkansas, 418
McMillan v. Massachusetts Soc. for the Prevention of Cruelty to Animals, 395
Medical Soc. v. Department of Law & Pub. Safety, 1122
Medtronic, Inc. v. Lohr, 604
Meritor Savings Bank v. Vinson, 262, 265, 403, 404, 1036
Meyer v. Nebraska, 316, 431, 433, 438, 464, 473, 836, 862, 930, 931
Mia Macy v. Eric Holder, 297
Michael H. v. Gerald D., 531, 560, **876**, 877, 993
Michael M. v. Sonoma County, CA, 151
Mieth v. Dothard, 404
Miller v. California, 1196
Miller v. Johnson, 1164
Miller v. Wilson, 79, 80, 83, 418
Milliken v. Bradley, 982
Mills v. Habluetzel, 993
Minnesota v. Barber, 55, 57
Minor v. Happersett, 37
Miranda v. Arizona, 687, 691
Mississippi Band of Choctaw Indians v. Holyfield, 909
Mississippi University for Women v. Hogan, 195, 200, **960**

Mitchell v. Axcan Scandipharm, Inc., 294
Mitchell v. W.T. Grant Co., 538
Mobile County v. Kimball, 108
Mohasco Corp. v. Silver, 392
Monell v. New York City Department of Social Services, 384, 385, 1060, 1062
Monmouth County v. Wissell, 1122
Monroe v. Pape, 384, 385, 429
Moore v. East Cleveland, 531, 877, 931
Moore v. Missouri, 418
Moose Lodge v. Irvis, 476
Morehead v. New York ex rel Tipaldo, 109
Morey v. Doud, 471, 631, 841
Morrison v. California, 420
Morrison, United States v., 1197
Moss v. State, 1124, 1125
Mt. Healthy City Bd. of Ed. v. Doyle, 284, 288
Mugler v. Kansas, 51, 57, 530
Muller v. Oregon, 19, **62**, 69, 78, 354, 593, 1045
NAACP v. Alabama, 428, 430, 712
NAACP v. Button, 212, 428, 617
Nale v. Nale, 824
Nashville Gas Co. v. Satty, 345
National Abortion Federation v. Ashcroft, 588, 595
National Abortion Federation v. Gonzales, 588, 595
National Endowment for Arts v. Finley, 612
National League of Cities v. Usery, 1197
National Mutual Ins. Co. v. Tidewater Transfer Co., 474
National Org. For Women (NOW) et al. v. Operation Rescue, et al., 716, 1173
National Railroad Passenger Corporation v. Morgan, 390, 394
Navarro v. Block, **1061**, **1066**, 1068
Near v. Minnesota, 711
Nevada Dept. of Human Resources v. Hibbs, 196
New Jersey v. T. L. O., 684, 1026
New York City Transit Authority v. Beazer, 865
New York Life Insurance Co. v. Dodge, 69
New York State Club Association v. City of New York, 219
New York Times Co. v. Sullivan, 1143
New York Times Co. v. United States, 1143
New York v. Sullivan, 715
Newport News Shipbuilding & Dry Dock Co. v. EEOC, 265, 324, 339, 345, 348, 352
NLRB v. Baptist Hospital, Inc., 604, 609
NLRB v. Friedman-Harry Marks Clothing Co., 1197
NLRB v. Jones & Laughlin Steel, 1170, 1197
NLRB v. Transportation Management Corp., 283
Norman v. Reed, 543
Norman, State v., 1090
North Carolina Board of Education v. Swann, 109

Norwood v. Harrison, 213
O'Brien, United States v., 155, 612, 732
Obergefell v. Hodges, 195, 724, 736, **738**, 930
Occidental Life Ins. Co. of Cal. v. EEOC, 392
Ohio v. Akron Center for Reproductive Health (Akron II), 529, 561, 565, 566
Olmstead v. United States, 464, 604, 615
Olsen v. Nebraska, 427
Oncale v. Sundowner Offshore Services, 403, 1037
Operation Rescue, et al v. Women's Health Center, et al., 716
Orr v. Orr, 154, 155, 204, 209, 210, **769**, 775, 960, 964, 969
Ortman v. Ortman, 771
Osbey, State v., 1097
Osborne, In re, 674
Owens v. Haas, 1060
P., In the Matter of, **1182**
Pacific Gas & Electric Co. v. State Energy Comm'n, 346
Painter v. Bannister, 932
Palko v. Connecticut, 433, 464, 562
Palmore v. Sidoti, 20, 931
Parents Involved in Community Schools v. Seattle School District, No. 1, 109, 388, 405
Parham v. Hughes, 152, 156, 858
Parham v. J.R., 930
Paris Adult Theater v. Slaton, 1196
Paroline v. United States, 1196
Patsone v. Pennsylvania, 83, 419
Patterson v. McLean Credit Union, 404, 534
Payne v. Tennessee, 561
Pembaur v. City of Cincinnati, 1063
Pennhurst v. Halderman, 1030
Pennsylvania State Police v. Suders, 277
Perez v. United States, 1155, 1174
Perry Ed. Assn. v. Perry Local Educators' Assn., 614
Personnel Administrator of Mass. v. Feeney, **202**, 219, 775, 960, 1064
Peter Stanley v. Illinois, **834**
Peters v. Kiff, 170, 172, 217
Phillips v. Martin-Marietta Corp., **241**, 307, 311, 347
Pierce v. Society of Sisters, 316, 432, 433, 438, 464, 473, 711, 742, 862, 930, 931
Pierce, People v., 789
Pikula v. Pikula, 823
Pittsburgh Press v. Human Relations Commission, 211
Planned Parenthood Ass'n v. Chicago Transit Authority, 1144
Planned Parenthood Federation of America v. Sullivan, 715
Planned Parenthood of Central Mo. v. Danforth, **483**, 516, 546, 551, 565, 566, 584, 587, 857
Planned Parenthood of Southeastern Pa. v. Casey, **529**, 586, 619, 638, 655

Table of Cases

Planned Parenthood of Wis., Inc. v. Schimel, 628, 633
Planned Parenthood of Wis., Inc. v. Van Hollen, 628
Planned Parenthood Southeast, Inc. v. Strange, 628
Planned Parenthood v. Ashcroft, 588, 713, 930
Playboy Entertainment Group, Inc., United States v., 611, 614
Plessy v. Ferguson, 19, 948
Plyler v. Doe, 216
Poe v. Ullman, 474, 531, 712, 740
Poelker v. Doe, 157, 542, 714
Police Dept. of Chicago v. Mosley, 611, 614, 1141
Powell v. Alabama, 432
Powers v. Ohio, 194
Presbyterian Church in U.S. v. Mary Elizabeth Blue Hull Memorial Presbyterian Church, 651
President and Directors of Georgetown College, In re, 670, 717
Price Waterhouse v. Hopkins, 281, 333, 398, 403
Prince v. Massachusetts, 316, 432, 434, 464, 474, 486, 532, 660, 836, 862
Public Utilities Comm'n v. Pollak, 429
Quilloin v. Walcott, 844, 923
Quinlan, In re, 536
Quong Wing v. Kirkendall, 80, 96, 110
R.A.V. v. City of St. Paul, Minnesota, 611, 1147, 1196
Rabidue v. Osceola Refining Co., 250, 403
Radice v. New York, 81
Rago, People ex rel. v. Lipsky, 930
Railroad Telegraphers v. Railway Express Agency, Inc., 392
Railway Express Agency v. New York, 116, 446
Railway Mail Association v. Corsi, 213
Raines, United States v., 449
Raleigh-Fitkin Paul Morgan Hospital v. Anderson, 670, 717
Randy Jay Goldberg v. State of Maryland, 1105
Rawlins v. Georgia, 174
Reed v. Reed, 114, **115**, 120, 125, 129, 130, 141, 143, 145, 203, 209, 446, 770, 771, 839, 845, 949, 960, 961, 975, 980
Regents of California v. Bakke, 109, 360, 367, 369
Reitman v. Mulkey, 152, 155
Reno v. ACLU, 1196
Republican Party of Minn. v. White, 750
Reynolds v. Sims, 216, 711
Reynolds v. United States, 929, 930
Rhodes, State v., 1195
Rice v. Santa Fe Elevator Corp., 343
Richard Oliver, State v., 1055
Richardson v. Belcher, 121
Richmond, City of v. J. A. Croson Co., 256

Riggins v. Nevada, 535
Riley v. Massachusetts, 79, 80
Rinaldi v. Yeager, 128, 152
Ritchie v. White, 788
Roberts v. Clark County School District, 298
Roberts v. LaVallee, 109, 216, 714
Roberts v. Louisiana, 712
Roberts v. U.S. Jaycees, 213
Robinson, United States ex rel. v. York, 958
Rochin v. California, 531, 535, 676
Roe v. Wade, 19, 316, 457, **458**, 483, 485, 494, 497, 515, 529, 540, 545, 554, 558, 586, 627
Roff v. Burney, 904
Rogers v. EEOC, 274, 403
Romer v. Evans, 720, 728, 929
Rosa v. Park West Bank & Trust Co., 295
Rosenfeld v. Southern Pacific Co., 233, **237**, 402
Rosenthal v. New York, 419
Rostker v. Goldberg, 217
Rotary International v. Rotary Club of Duarte, 219
Roth v. United States, 1196
Rowan v. Post Office Dept., 605
Royster Guano Co. v. Virginia, 109, 116, 443, 765
Rundlett v. Oliver, 154
Runyon v. McCrary, 213, 370
Rusk, State v., 1114, 1195
Russell v. Russell, 771
Rust v. Sullivan, 715
Rutan v. Republican Party of Ill., 993
Saffron v. Wilson, 1061
Sail'er Inn v. Kirby, 216, 312
Salerno, United States v., 565
Salve Regina College v. Russell, 590
San Antonio Independent School District v. Rodriguez, 109, 216, 1057
Santa Clara Pueblo et al. v. Martinez et al., 900
Sapp v. Superior Court, 786
Scheidler v. NOW, 622, 625, 716
Schenck v. Pro-Choice Network of Western N. Y., 611, 619, 716
Schenck v. United States, 1196
Schlesinger v. Ballard, 133, 138, 140, 152, 156, 771, 850, 851, 961, 969
Schmerber v. California, 669
Schneider v. Rusk, 125
Schneider v. State, 711
Schroeder v. City of New York, 868
Schroer v. Billington, 294
Schware v. Board of Bar Examiners, 434, 473
Scott v. Sears, Roebuck & Co., 250
Searls v. People, 815
Seminole Tribe of Fla. v. Florida, 405, 1000
Sessions v. Morales-Santana, 192
Settler v. O'Hara, 109
Shapiro v. Thompson, 124, 125, 130, 216, 446, 465, 472, 473

Sharron and Joseph Frontiero v. Elliot Richardson, Sec'y of Defense, 119
Shaw v. Delta Air Lines, Inc., 343, 344, 348
Sheet Metal Workers v. EEOC, 366
Sheil v. Sheil, 803
Shelley v. Kraemer, 1160
Shelton v. Tucker, 317, 434
Sherbert v. Verner, 465
Shreveport Rate, Cases, 1155
Shultz v. First Victoria Nat'l Bank, 239
Sierra Club v. Morris, 476
Silkwood v. Kerr-McGee Corp., 335
Simon & Schuster, Inc. v. Members of N. Y. State Crime Victims Bd., 611
Simon, State v., 1091, 1092
Singleton v. Wulff, 194
Sinn v. Sinn, 782
Skinner v. Oklahoma, 216, 316, 317, **417**, 429, 434, 446, 464, 474, 491, 719, 744, 836, 931
Skinner v. Railway Labor Executives' Assn., 684, 687
Slaughterhouse Cases, 22, 107, 108
Smith v. Bennett, 714
Smith v. City of Salem, 295, 403
Smith v. Organization of Foster Families, 863, 864
Smith v. Texas, 171
Smith v. Wayne Probate Judge, 419
Snell v. Suffolk Cty., 275
Snyder v. Massachusetts, 431, 432, 478, 562, 878
Sonnicksen, Estate of, 786
Soto v. Flores, 1071
Southern R. Co. v. United States, 1155
Spaulding v. University of Washington, 402
Spencer v. World Vision, Inc., 662
Splunge v. Shoney's, Inc., 269
Stanley v. Georgia, 445, 464, 1196
Stanley v. Illinois, 124, 138, 139, 148, 318, 491, 494, 552, 564, 856
Stanton v. Stanton, 136, 138, 139, 140, 145, 209, **764**, 769, 770, 976
Stenberg v. Carhart, 574, 578, 586
Stewart, State v., 1085
Strauder v. West Virginia, 104, 109, 176
Street v. New York, 478
Stromberg. v. California, 447
Sturgis v. Attorney General, 442
Sugarman v. Dougall, 108
Superior Court (Hartway), People v., 1184
Surrogate Parenting v. Commonwealth ex rel. Armstrong, 717
Susan L. Vorchheimer v. School District of Philadelphia, 942, 964
Swann v. Charlotte-Mecklenburg Board of Education, 204
Sweatt v. Painter, 945, 985, 1044
Sweezy v. New Hampshire, 428
Swift & Co. v. Wickham, 534
Taft v. Taft, 670

Takahashi v. Fish and Game Commission, 108, 110
Talton v. Mayes, 902
Tanghe v. Tanghe, 823
Taylor v. Georgia, 420
Taylor v. Louisiana, 139
Teamsters v. United States, 364, 390, 395, 397
Terry v. Ohio, 464
Terry, State v., 1124
Texas Dept. of Community Affairs v. Burdine, 283, 289, 291, 292
Thiel v. Southern Pacific, 102, 173
Thompson v. City of Los Angeles, 1063
Thornburgh v. American College of Obstetricians and Gynecologists, 619, 713
Thornhill v. Alabama, 605
Tigner v. Texas, 100
Tileston v. Ullman, 712
Tillman v. Wheaton-Haven Recreation Association, 401
Tinker v. Colwell, 776
Tinker v. Des Moines School District, 486, 1026
Title Ins. & Trust Co., United States v., 534
Tobias D., In re Adoption of, 923
Toomer v. Witsell, 472
Tot v. United States, 129
Tracey Thurman et al. v. City of Torrington et al., 1057
Train v. Colorado Public Interest Research Group, Inc., 345
Trammel v. United States, 762
Trans World Airlines, Inc. v. Hardison, 657
Trans World Airlines, Inc. v. Thurston, 325
Traux v. Raich, 108, 109
Treasury Employees v. Von Raab, 684, 687
Trimble v. Gordon, 775
Tronetti v. TLC HealthNet Lakeshore Hospital, 294
Troxel v. Granville, 897, 932
Troy Footman, United States v., 1189
Truax v. Raich, 473
Tuan Anh Nguyen et al. v. INS, 190, 195, 196, 200, 218
Turner Broadcasting System, Inc. v. FCC, 993, 1167
Turner v. Fouche, 714
Turner v. Safley, 741, 748, 881
UAW v. Johnson Controls, 324, 405
Udall v. Tallman, 242
Ulane v. Eastern Airlines, Inc., 403
Union Pacific R. Co. v. Botsford, 464, 669
United Jewish Organizations v. Carey, 206
United Steelworkers of America, AFL-CIO-CLC v. Marshall, 335
United Steelworkers v. Weber, 341, 345, 350, 360, 364, 370, 372, 382
Vasquez v. Hillery, 518
Vernonia School Dist. 47J v. Acton, 684, 685, 687, 1026, 1035
Virginia v. Rives, 1160

Table of Cases

Virginia, Commonwealth of, United States v., 996, 1045
Virginia, Ex parte, 964
Virginia, United States v., 194, 593, **975**, 1044, 1045
Vlandis v. Kline, 318
Voisine v. United States, 1099, 1195
Vorchheimer v. School Dist. of Philadelpha, 947
Vuitch, United States v., 467, 475, 713
Ward v. Maryland, 472
Ward v. Rock Against Racism, 606, 611, 612
Wards Cove Packing v. Atonio, 398, 404
Warth v. Seldin, 193
Washington v. Davis, 203, 206, 208, 211, 219
Washington v. Glucksberg, 748, 753
Washington v. Harper, 531, 535
Watson v. Fort Worth Bank & Trust, 390
Weber v. Aetna, 109, 122
Webster v. Reproductive Health Services, 511, 542, 566, 583, 714
Weeks v. Southern Bell, **231**, 238, 239, 306, 328, 333, 402
Weinberger v. Stephen Wiesenfeld, 138, 149, 152, 199, 203, 209, 217, 771, 961, 976
Wengler v. Druggists Mutual Ins. Co., 198, 348, 355, 961, 969, 994
West Coast Hotel v. Parrish, 85, 427, 711
West Virginia Bd. of Ed. v. Barnette, 745, 1141
Western Air Lines, Inc. v. Criswell, 325, 332
Whalen v. Roe, 547, 687, 692
Whitner v. South Carolina, 717
Whitney v. California, 530
Whole Woman's Health v. Hellerstedt, **627**, 716
Whole Woman's Health v. Lakey, 641
Wickard v. Filburn, 1165, 1197
Wieman v. Updegraff, 428
Williams v. Florida, 172
Williams v. Illinois, 109
Williams v. McNair, 946, **957**
Williamson v. Lee Optical, Co., 144, 428, 444, 477, 547, 564, 1173
Wilson v. State, 1123
Wimberly v. Labor and Industrial Relations Commission, 357
Windsor, United States v., 724, **726**, 753
Winston v. Lee, 531, 669
Wisconsin v. Mitchell, 1196
Wisconsin v. Yoder, 864, 930
Wolf v. Schroering, 488
Woodson v. North Carolina, 712
Woodward v. Commissioner of Social Security, 710
Worcester v. Georgia, 902
Wulff v. Singleton, 714
Wygant v. Jackson Board of Education, 374, 375, 381
Yarborough v. Yarborough, 912
Yates v. Avco Corp., 256
Yazell, United States v., **761**, 862

Yick Wo v. Hopkins, 108, 109, 203, 418, 434, 478
Young v. American Mini Theatres, Inc., 1144
Young v. United Parcel Service, 358
Zablocki v. Redhail, 741
Zemel v. Rusk, 434
Zhuang v. Datacard Corp., 393
Zipes v. Trans World Airlines, Inc., 396
Zubik v. Burwell, 663

THE CONSTITUTIONAL AND LEGAL RIGHTS OF WOMEN

Fourth Edition

Introduction

There are several reasons for studying women's rights from the perspective of American law. First, it is an area of law in which rapid and substantial change has taken place within the past seventy-five years. The U.S. Supreme Court has reversed itself, for example, explicitly altering the meaning of the U.S. Constitution within a mere 14 years, *Hoyt v. Florida* [1961] overruled by *Taylor v. Louisiana* [1975]. The Court has initiated profound and controversial social change by announcing that a woman's right to have an abortion is a right secured to her by the Constitution, *Roe v. Wade* and *Doe v. Bolton* [1973]. The Court has grappled with the dilemma of knowing that a particular constitutional amendment (the Equal Rights Amendment) that had been overwhelmingly adopted by Congress, rapidly attained ratification from two-thirds of state legislatures, and supported in opinion polls in the remaining states, did not meet the formal requirements for a constitutional amendment. Yet, several members of the Court believed that the content of the new amendment was already implicit in the Constitution.

Second, during this period, women's rights organizations successfully mobilized to prompt Congress to create a number of new statutory rights for women, including, for instance, the right to sue persons who subject them to "gender-motivated violence," immunity from pregnancy-based discrimination by employers, and equal access to programs (such as school sports) that receive federal funds. A number of these statutes have provoked not only controversy but also court challenges. Thus, the arena of women's rights provides a nearly ideal laboratory for examining the way courts both initiate and respond to social change. The role that legal argument plays in this process, the role of changing societal mores and assumptions, and perhaps even the role of political pressures can all be explored, as teacher and student analyze these cases together.

Third, these cases provide a stage on which abstract legal terms such as *suspect classification, minimum rationality scrutiny, substantive due process, reasonable woman,* and *best interest of the child* take on concrete meaning, as students see them applied to live controversies of topical interest. Moreover, students will be able to trace the roots of these doctrines back to their legal-historical origins. They can witness the twists and turns of the substantive due process doctrine, for example, as it evolves from the solid roots of *Lochner v. New York* (1905) to apparent withering in *West*

Coast Hotel v. Parrish (1937) and *U.S. v. Darby* (1941), and then to the surprise sprouting of a vigorous new branch in *Griswold v. Connecticut* (1965).

A fourth reason for studying these cases is the sheer value of knowing the standing law, especially on important questions of public policy, as this one surely is. For example, knowledge of the existing constitutional law is an essential prerequisite for deciding whether we really do need the Equal Rights Amendment (ERA) to the Constitution. Or, are the Supreme Court's decisions on the legal rights of women as protected under the Equal Protection Clause over the latter third of the twentieth century sufficient to guarantee women equal rights? Acquaintance with current law is indispensable for evaluating the need for future law.

Finally, these cases provide an opportunity for the student to ponder serious and perennial normative questions, questions ultimately linked to the core issue of what constitutes the good society. Some of these questions relate particularly to women's rights as such. For example, is it permissible, and not a violation of the idea of fairness implied in the phrase "equal protection of the law," for society to provide a special tax advantage to widows that it denies to widowers? (See *Kahn v. Shevin* [1974]). If it is permissible to have special protective legislation for women, where is the line to be drawn between protecting women and depriving them of important legal and political rights? (See *Bradwell. v. State* [1873], *Hoyt y. Florida,* and *Taylor v. Louisiana*). At what point does well-intentioned protective legislation for women become unfair discrimination against men? (Compare *Kahn v. Shevin* or *Califano v. Webster* [1977] to *Weinberger v. Wiesenfeld* [1975] or *Califano v. Goldfarb* [1977]). Other normative questions arising out of these cases reach far beyond women's issues as such. The *Adkins v. Children's Hospital* (1923)/*West Coast Hotel v. Parrish* (1937) line of cases presents the eternally problematic question of how far an individual's liberty may be hindered for the sake of societal welfare. A great many of these cases pose the general question of whether some sectors of society may be singled out by the law for special treatment, and the subsidiary but more difficult question of how one decides at what point such special treatment becomes unjust to the rest of society. Of particular importance to the American regime, but also of importance to all other would-be democratic regimes, is the question posed with particular force by the abortion cases: as a body of unaccountable and unelected decision makers, set purposefully above political pressures because of their assumed superior wisdom on the law, how far can the Supreme Court distance itself from prevailing public opinion? Does too much distance tend toward the destruction of the very democratic quality that makes the Constitution worth protecting in the first place? Throughout this book, the questions asked at the end of each case attempt to stimulate the exploration of some of these issues. Yet, the most important question in every case has actually been omitted; how would you have decided this case?

Before proceeding to a discussion of cases, it may be helpful to define what we mean by "women's rights." The term actually has three usages in this text. First, it refers to women's right to be treated by the government *the same as men*. Women have a right to "equal protection of the law," and equal treatment in this sense is commanded by the Constitution. In other words, the Constitution directly forbids statutes denying this kind of equality of treatment (e.g., a hypothetical statute saying that robbery of women will not be prosecuted).

Second, the term can refer to women's rights to be treated *differently from men*—in other words, favored or "protected" by the law. When used in this sense, the word *right* does not mean that the Constitution *requires* such treatment (contra our first usage), but it does mean that the Constitution *permits* such difference of treatment. Another way of stating this idea is to say that men's right to "equal protection of the law" does not mean they shall in every way be treated the same as women. The courts recognize that not all groups in society are "similarly situated" and that to compensate for dissimilar societal situations, it may be appropriate to allow unequal treatment by the law in order to attain "equal protection of the law." The Fourteenth Amendment has been read as sometimes permitting (but not as commanding) such unequal treatment of women.

Finally, "women's rights" can refer to rights that are common to all American citizens but affect women in particularly strong ways, or that affect only women, for reasons that are biological rather than legal. The constitutional right to choose birth control or abortion is in a real sense a woman's right because women are the ones who give birth and have abortions. (Of course, men share in the right to use birth control, and in a certain sense share in the right to terminate a pregnancy involving their own offspring. Clearly, however, the potential mother is more drastically and directly affected by the denial or the granting of these rights.)

In earlier editions, the term "woman" was uncontested, and was used to refer to biological females. While the terms sex and gender are often used interchangeably, one's biological sex (i.e. female) may or may not correlate with one's gender expression (i.e. a female may present as masculine or feminine). As such, a biological female may find that she is discriminated against on the basis of her sex (e.g. a policy that prohibits women from working as a prison guard in a male facility, see *Dothard v. Rawlinson* [1977]) or that she is discriminated against on the basis of her gender expression (e.g. a woman is denied a promotion because she is perceived as being unfeminine, see *Price Waterhouse v. Hopkins* [1989]). In recent years, however, growing scientific, socio-cultural and legal awareness about the intricacies of sex and gender have introduced new complexity to the terms woman, sex, and gender, and this edition now contains sections elaborating on these complexities as they relate to the law.

Recognizing that binary and fixed conceptions of sex (female-male), gender identity (woman-man), and gender expression (masculine-feminine) are oversimplified and inaccurate, the growing trans rights movement seeks to challenge laws, policies, and practices that discriminate against transgender and gender non-conforming individuals. At the national level, litigation has focused on whether or not Title VII of the 1964 Civil Rights Act's prohibitions on sex discrimination in the workplace include protections for individuals who are targeted for differential treatment because they are transgender or gender non-conforming as discussed in Chapter 3, and on whether Title IX of the 1972 Education Amendments' prohibitions on sex discrimination in education include protections for transgender and gender non-conforming students as discussed in Chapter 6.

Women and Law

Women and the Law, with variations, is the title of many books. A title like *Men and the Law* sounds absurd. The male is the norm, the female the exception because white men make up the dominant, advantaged group in society. Yet, male supremacy is illogical on its face. Domination and subjection are typically defended by arguments that the subject group is inferior to the dominant group in some way. Where slavery has existed, proponents have alleged that slaves were less intelligent, less virtuous, or less responsible than free people. The inferior legal status of children relative to adults is defended by arguments that children are less capable of governing themselves. Reproduction is an essential function for the survival of any species. Women can bear children; men cannot. Yet throughout human history, women's reproductive function has been the primary justification for denying them equal treatment with men. More than a hundred years ago, a unanimous Supreme Court opinion declared that "woman's physical structure and the performance of maternal functions" justified restrictions on "her exercise of contractual powers" that would be unconstitutional if imposed on men.[1]

Consigning to inferior status a group that has a useful ability that the top group lacks seems counterintuitive, but that is just what male supremacist societies do. In fact, this book shows that American law has punished, and continues to punish, both the women who assume traditional roles and the women who reject them. Physical differences between the sexes do not explain male supremacy. The statement in the same Supreme Court opinion that man "established his control at the outset by superior physical strength" may be a better historical explanation. Women's childbearing function did not cause their inferior status; it has been a post hoc justification of this status. Women's reproductive function is natural. Male supremacy is not.

This book is concerned with one manifestation of male supremacy: the legal status of women. Applied to a group, the term "legal status" can have any one of several meanings. Members of a group may share a generalized inferior status relative to others, as slaves did, as children do now, and as women did before the 1920s. Legal status may involve specific, limited burdens or restrictions that do not add up to a general inferiority, such as laws that limited women's working hours or denied them access to certain occupations. Restrictions may affect only women in certain roles. Married woman, for example, once had legal obligations that neither men nor single women had.

The legal status of many women is affected by their membership in other groups. Laws that single out racial minorities, LGBQT individuals, immigrants or disabled people obviously affect women in these groups, and the intersectional identities of many women render them more vulnerable to oppression and discrimination than other women. On the other hand, the granting of a benefit to one of these subgroups has sometimes excluded women; the wording of the Fifteenth Amendment assured that Black men but not Black women would get the vote, since it was still permitted for states to exclude women qua women.

Laws that are gender-neutral on their face often have a disproportionate impact on women. A minimum height requirement for police officers will exclude more women than men, since the average woman is shorter than the average man. Laws that confer benefits or prohibit discrimination, such as family leave or civil rights laws, also help determine a person's legal status.

Law is only part of a society; it does not explain or control everything. We do not look to law books alone for information about people's lives. In the United States today, the law says that virtually all jobs are open to anyone, regardless of sex. Yet, labor statistics show that the working world is divided into "men's" and "women's" occupations and that about half of women workers are concentrated in a "job ghetto" of low-paying, low-status clerical, sales, technical support, and service occupations, and this segregation is exacerbated for women of color.[2] In addition, lesbians and transwomen are not explicitly protected from workplace discrimination by federal law on the basis of sexual orientation or gender identity, and this fact makes these women vulnerable to economic discrimination and exploitation.

Many factors other than law affect people's lives, and some of the most radical changes in American women's status have resulted from forces outside of the law including war (which gets women into the workplace as men enter military service and later draws women into the service and combat), access to higher education (which brings women onto college campuses, exposing many of them to feminist ideas), innovations in birth control (which control family size), and labor-saving devices (which lighten the burden of housework). The decline of the "family wage," with which one male full-time worker could support a household (due in large part to the waning of labor unions), has resulted in a drastic decrease in the number of full-time homemakers and a corresponding increase in the number of gainfully employed wives and mothers. Technological advancements ranging from reliable contraceptives to in vitro fertilization and artificial insemination to oocyte cryopreservation (egg freezing) have increased women's control over their fertility. The divorce rate, which has hovered at 50 percent since 1980, also renders marriage an unreliable source of lifetime financial support, and this fact pushes women to take their career options more seriously.

Some experts have insisted that law cannot change society. In the nineteenth century, the idea that "folkways" were impervious to law was an article of faith among scholars and judges. "Legislation is powerless to eradicate social differences," wrote the Supreme Court in a decision upholding segregation in public accommodation. "If the two races are to meet on terms of social equality, it must be as a result of natural affinities, a mutual appreciation of each other's merits and a voluntary consent of individuals."[3] These attitudes persisted well into the twentieth century. "You can't legislate morality," said President Dwight D. Eisenhower in 1957, as he stood beside a Southern governor who refused to enforce the Supreme Court's ruling in *Brown v. Board of Education*.[4]

The failure of Prohibition, government's attempt to end the sale and consumption of alcoholic beverages, is a warning to all who would rely on law to change behavior. Enacted by the Eighteenth Amendment and repealed by the Twenty-first, Prohibition failed to discourage either the drinking or the selling of alcohol; both may have actually increased between 1918 and 1933. Law cannot do everything, but it does not follow that law can do nothing. How can the races develop "natural affinities" if the law keeps them apart? A decision that the railroad cars in Louisiana must be integrated might have brought about the association that could change attitudes.

The end of *de jure* school segregation in 1954 resulted in a dramatic increase over a 20-year period in the percentage of Black public school students going to school with any whites in the South. The figure jumped from .001 percent in

1954–1955 to 91.3 percent in 1972–1973.[5] The Voting Rights Act of 1965 led to the election of many Black officials in the South and doubled the number of Black voters in the 11 southern states between the 1964 and 1968 presidential elections. The number of women law students in the United States tripled after Title IX of the Education Amendments Act of 1972 went into effect.[6] Law is not separate and distinct from social forces; it is one of many social forces.

Historical Overview

Someone whose only knowledge of women's legal status came from the original text of the U.S. Constitution would not know that America was a male supremacist society. The document always refers to "persons," not to "men," or uses the passive voice: "no person" under the age of 30 may be a U.S. senator; "no bill of attainder or *ex post facto* law shall be passed." The recognition of individual rights, the regulation of marriage and the family, and the protection of public welfare, were considered the purview of each state, not the federal government. Even the Bill of Rights was largely motivated by the goal of ensuring state sovereignty by limiting the power of the federal government.

The people eligible to vote for the House of Representatives—the only federal officeholders then chosen by direct popular vote—"shall have the qualifications requisite for electors of the most numerous branch of the state legislature." At the time, a few communities and the state of New Jersey gave the vote to all property owners, male or female, but all had excluded women from the franchise within 20 years after ratification.[7]

But the authors of the Constitution ensured, intentionally or not, that women would have access to the political process. The fact that the Constitution uses the word "person" rather than "man" in its common generic sense made it impossible for anyone to claim that constitutional rights do not apply to women. The First Amendment guarantees of freedom of expression and association, which are essential for any sort of political activity, have been available to women who wished to promote change. And there has never been a question of women's eligibility for the federal offices that would give them power to pursue their goals. Although the original Constitution was silent on the issue of sexual equality, its gender-neutral provisions did encourage women to try to change the situation.

The denial of the vote was not the only limitation that state laws imposed on women in the founding period. The original states adopted the English common law doctrine of *coverture*, which provided that, in William Blackstone's words, "husband and wife are one, and that one is the husband" (see Chapters 1 and 5).

Unmarried women had none of the legal disabilities imposed on wives; they could dispose of property and controlled their own earnings. The fact that few women could support themselves on their own earnings made marriage an attractive alternative. Most single women lived with family members and shared homemaking responsibilities. The law made the situation of spinsters and widows better than it might have been. Single women could not only inherit property but also use it as they wished, in contrast to married women whose property (and children) belonged to their husbands. One feature of English law that did not make it across the Atlantic was the right of primogeniture, by which a landholder's estate passed to the oldest son. Americans could will their property as they wished, except for a widow's entitlement; in the absence of a will, inheritance was determined by consanguinity, not gender. Many men had no estate to bequeath, and fathers often favored their sons over their daughters, but by the mid-1800s, enough American women were privileged by class, leisure, and education to reflect critically on their status.

The first American feminists came from the abolitionist movement. Women joined with men to oppose slavery, but they were not always welcomed as partners in the struggle. At the World Anti-Slavery Convention in London in 1840, no woman was allowed to address the gathering. Two silenced Americans, Lucretia Mott and Elizabeth Cady Stanton, returned home determined to change things. Their efforts culminated in a Women's Rights Convention in Seneca Falls, New York in 1848. The signers of the convention's "Declaration of Sentiments and Resolutions" pledged their support for reforms in property and child custody law, women's access to higher education, and the right to vote. The same year, Mrs. Stanton's home state, New York, passed the Married Women's Property Act.[8]

The battle for women's suffrage was long, difficult, and divisive, but it ultimately succeeded (see Chapter 1). By the time the Nineteenth Amendment to the Constitution was ratified in 1920, several states had already given women the vote, wives controlled their property and earnings, and child custody law favored mothers rather than fathers. (This last change was no doubt facilitated by the transition from an agrarian to an industrial economy; children's labor was no longer an economic asset for most men.) But even after 1920, many laws remained that treated men and women differently. The husband still had the right to determine his family's domicile, or legal residence. Most states required women to take their husbands' last names after marriage. The husband was still obligated to support the wife, and she retained full responsibility for domestic duties even when she earned an income. All the states had special labor laws applying only to women, "protective" labor legislation such as the law the Supreme Court upheld in 1908.[9] This issue produced a division within the women's rights movement that persists to the present day. Some feminists supported laws limiting women's working hours or barring them from certain occupations on the grounds that women needed special protection because of physical differences between the sexes, especially reproductive function. Feminist opponents of protective legislation insisted that limiting women workers would hinder them in competing for good jobs currently held by men. By the 1920s, most of these policies had the latter effect.[10]

By the 1980s, all of these policies had changed. The Civil Rights Act of 1964 forbade sex discrimination in employment. Within 10 years, federal courts had used this law to invalidate virtually all labor laws applying only to women. Other laws and executive orders have prohibited wage discrimination and gender differences in educational benefits. Courts have also struck down many discriminatory laws as unconstitutional. One of the most dramatic, far-reaching changes has been the enhancement of reproductive choice. The Supreme Court recognized a right to abortion in 1973 in the landmark case of *Roe v. Wade*.[11] But full equality remains a goal, not a fact. Women do not enjoy constitutional equality with men. The Equal Rights Amendment, which would have forbidden the denial of "equality of rights" on the basis of sex, was not ratified. Nor have courts interpreted the Constitution to extend quite the same protection to women that the Equal Protection Clause of the Fourteenth Amendment gives to racial minorities.

Since the election of Donald Trump to the Presidency, efforts to revive the ERA have picked up steam. In 2017 Nevada became the 36th state to ratify the Amendment, and a half dozen other states are considering adopting their own state version of it.[12]

The civil rights laws have not ended gender stereotyping and segregation in the job market. Although the Equal Pay Act of 1963 forbade wage discrimination where men and women hold the same jobs, the law's effect was limited by the fact that men and women usually hold different jobs. Comparable worth—a policy in which women's jobs would pay as well as men's jobs that are equally complex and difficult—has not been established in this country (see Chapter 3).

Efforts to overrule *Roe v. Wade* are ongoing and while opponents of *Roe* have not succeeded, reproductive choice has been limited. Laws prohibiting the use of public funds for abortions have put the procedure beyond the reach of many poor women, most states have enacted laws requiring parental or judicial permission before minors may get abortions, and acts of violence against abortion providers (including eleven murders resulting from attacks on individuals or clinics since 1993) constitute further threats to the availability of abortions.

Worse still, some contemporary legal innovations threaten women's interests. Changes in divorce law have left many ex-wives in poverty or threatened mothers with loss of child custody. State laws and court decisions favorable to single fathers have given them leverage over both natural and adoptive mothers. The discovery that many substances used in the workplace can harm unborn infants led to rules that excluded all women of childbearing age, pregnant or not, from certain jobs. Some states have tried to criminalize the use of alcohol or drugs during pregnancy.[13]

Although the relationship between legal status and socioeconomic conditions is complex, the situation of women shows that actual equality lags even behind legal equality. Women earned 82 cents to a male's dollar in 2016, which means that the median salary for a woman was $38,948 and for a man it was $47,580.[14] The wage gap is even larger for women of color. While one study reported that white women earn 79 percent of what men earn on an annual basis, Black women earned 62.5 percent and Latinas earned 54.4 percent of what white men earned in a given year.[15] The Institute for Women's Policy Research estimates that women will achieve pay parity in 2059, but it will take Black women until 2124 and Latina women until 2233 to do so.[16] This gap is largely attributable to the fact that many of the jobs occupied by women have lower wages than jobs held by men, but across nearly all jobs women on average earn less than men for doing the same work.[17] Sex discrimination and implicit biases interact with racism to exacerbate the wage gap. Despite significant advancements, white men retain a monopoly on the best-paying and most influential jobs.[18]

In 2018, women make up almost twenty percent of the members of the United States Senate and House of Representatives. While these statistics are much better than they were in 1991 when Congress was only 5 percent female, these figures compare badly with the fact that women make up just more than half of the U.S. population. Only six state governors are women in 2018, and only three of the nine justices of the U.S. Supreme Court are women. No woman has ever been president.[19]

The United States remains a male-dominated society. Men hold power. Though not all men have equal amounts of power, virtually all men have some power over at least some women. Maleness still confers power and privilege. But it would be incorrect to say that men hold all the power and women have none. Women can exercise all the rights and privileges of adult U.S. citizens. While women do not vote in a bloc or agree on every issue, their aggregate power is a force no government can ignore. Politics and society are very different today from what they would be if women did not vote, get educations, or hold office.

Structure and Process in American Law

Common Law, Statutes, and the Federal System

The United States is a federal system. The Constitution makes it clear that the federal government is supreme, but the states elect their own officials and make their own laws. The national Congress has the powers specified in Article 1, Section 8 of the Constitution, and all powers that are implied by the specified powers.[20] All other legislative powers belong to the states (and may be delegated by those states to their local governments).[21] The implications of federalism for the study of law are that some laws are made by the national government and others—the majority—by the individual states. Federal courts may invalidate a state law by ruling that it violates the U.S. Constitution. Congress may pass laws, such as the Civil Rights Act of 1964, that preempt any contrary state laws. Some federal laws become binding at the state level only by state option, such as the Uniform Gift to Minors Act. Congress may also exercise its power of the purse to withhold federal funds from the states if they refuse to do what Congress wants them to. Although Congress could not force the states to raise the drinking age to 21, it accomplished that goal by making federal highway funds contingent on so doing. All 50 states have complied. But most of the time states pass laws on their own.

Since the founding, the balance of power between the federal government and the states has decisively shifted in favor of the former. This change is attributable to three factors: the Civil War, the Industrial Revolution, and the enormous financial advantage of the federal government vis-a-vis the states. The Civil War and the three amendments that resulted from it overrode state power over slavery, suffrage, and individual rights. During Reconstruction, Congress used its enforcement powers under the Thirteenth, Fourteenth, and Fifteenth Amendments to enact legislation giving individuals the right to sue states for rights violations. The Industrial Revolution led to the establishment of federal agencies such as the Interstate Commerce Commission to oversee nationwide industries like railroads. The ratification of the Sixteenth Amendment in 1913 gave the federal government a vast source of revenue by empowering Congress to levy taxes on individual incomes. The federal treasury grew exponentially in the last century.

Traditionally, states hold two kinds of power that have significant effects on women. The police power—the power to protect public health, safety, welfare, and morals—includes labor legislation and abortion laws, for instance. The law of domestic relations—of marriage, family, and divorce—is also state law. The presumption that family law is the province of the states is so powerful that the Supreme Court only rarely reviews decisions involving divorce and child custody.[22]

Another important distinction, besides that between state and federal law, is the difference between statutes and common law. *Statute* is another word for what we usually mean when we speak of a law: an act passed by a legislative body. *Common law* is an old term for case law: decisions made by judges expected to be binding on later judges. Case law existed before there were any legislatures; judges had to decide disputes among citizens and between citizens and the government. Most of the common law of the United States originated in England, where judges were deciding cases by ostensibly applying the customs of the community, before Parliament was established in the thirteenth century. Much of our family law and criminal law began as common law. State legislatures may change this law or adopt it by statute, but they need not. Common law spells out in detail the reciprocal rights and duties of husband and wife; states have varied in how much of this law they have enacted.

Constitutional law supersedes both statutory and common law. Not all governments have written constitutions, but the federal government and each of the 50 states do. A written constitution is paramount, fundamental law, superior to all existing law where it is binding. If any law—state or federal, case or statute—conflicts with the U.S. Constitution, the law is void. Article VI makes federal law "the supreme law of the land"; any state law, even a constitutional provision, is void if it conflicts with any federal law. Judges have the task of deciding these conflicts.

These distinctions are important because these three types of law have different kinds and degrees of effect on actual practice. Statutes may go unenforced, but they usually describe what public policy is to be. If people disobey them, they may suffer civil or criminal sanctions. Common law, particularly the common law of domestic relations, may bear little resemblance to actual practice. For example, under common law, the husband was obliged to support the family, and the wife to keep the home. But there were many families where both spouses earned money, and there were some where the husband went to school and the wife was both breadwinner and homemaker. Were these arrangements illegal? Not if both spouses were satisfied with them. Courts became concerned with such arrangements only when the relationship broke down and one party sought dissolution through annulment or divorce. Under common law, a divorce was a lawsuit: the "innocent" spouse obtained a settlement from the "guilty" party. In that situation, courts had to determine the legality of private arrangements. But states now have no-fault divorce laws; either partner may dissolve the marriage without proving the other's "guilt." Moreover, as Chapters 2 and 5 will show, some Supreme Court decisions negated these common law doctrines.

How the Supreme Court Operates

Jurisdiction. The Constitution mandates the establishment of a Supreme Court and grants this court jurisdiction over all "cases and controversies" involving diplomatic personnel, legal clashes on the seas, clashes between citizens or governments of different states, legal disputes between Americans and foreigners, and all cases "arising under" any of the three forms of national law: federal statutes, treaties, or clauses of the Constitution. This grant of power in a variety of ways imposes limits on the Court's powers.

First, no legal dispute that is wholly an in-state matter may go to the federal courts. If the clash involves only the state law (and the bulk of laws affecting our daily lives are state laws), and the parties to the dispute all live within that state, no federal court may intervene. The federal courts may be brought in only if some element of federal law is at issue, such as, for example, the prohibition within the federal Constitution against unreasonable searches and seizures. (If a party in a local trial wishes to appeal the case later to a federal court, that party must raise the issue of federal law at the initial trial. People are not permitted to wait until they lose at the local level and then try to dream up new "federal" issues so that they can keep appealing to the federal courts.)

Second, the federal courts will hear only genuine, live "controversies"—that is, cases in which the court's ruling will settle someone's pending claim. The federal courts will not hand out "advisory opinions," or general opinions as to a law's merits or its constitutionality that do not settle actual live disputes between concrete individuals or groups. For this reason, the Supreme Court avoids "moot" cases—those in which the resolution of the initial legal claim has (usually by the passage of time) somehow been taken out of the power of the court. A mother who objects to prayers in public school but whose children have graduated from school by the time her case gets to the highest court would be one example of someone whose case had been "mooted" by the passage of time.

By inference from the "cases and controversies" phrase, the Supreme Court requires that the parties who present cases have an actual, tangible stake in the outcome. This requirement that the parties involved must somehow stand to gain or lose directly from the outcome of the case is called the "standing" requirement.

The federal courts apply it with a certain flexibility; it is one way for them to bow out tactfully from politically "hot" cases. For cases that the justices want to decide, they occasionally bend the rules of standing.

In all cases involving diplomatic personnel and in those where one state government is opposing another government or an out-of-state citizen, the Constitution gave the Supreme Court original jurisdiction. That means that the Supreme Court may hear the case on the initial round, before any other judicial body hears it. (Only about 150 cases in the entire history of the Supreme Court have been handled in this way.) The rest of the Supreme Court's jurisdiction is appellate (cases come to it on appeal from the decision of lower courts, both state and federal). The Constitution gives Congress the power to make exceptions to these rules of jurisdiction and to create lower federal courts to supplement the work of the Supreme Court.

Congress also has the power to alter the number of justices on the Supreme Court, and it has done so on a number of occasions. The official size of the Supreme Court has remained steadily at nine for more than a century.

The Supreme Court's appellate jurisdiction is now entirely discretionary. The Supreme Court exercises this discretion to select for decision only those cases of importance to the legal system of the country as a whole. In other words, the Supreme Court is more likely to accept a case for decision if that case presents a legal issue of national importance than if one of the parties in the case simply happened to receive unfair treatment.

Structure and Workload of the Federal Courts. The vast majority of legal cases in the United States are handled in the state court system. (This system includes county and municipal courts.) In addition, about 150,000 cases each year are initiated in the federal court system at the level of the district courts.

The United States is divided into 89 judicial districts, and the District of Columbia, Puerto Rico, Guam, the Northern Mariana Islands, and the Virgin Islands, each constitutes an additional district. Each has its own federal district court. There are 663 seats for federal district judges. The district courts have original jurisdiction for cases arising under federal laws. They also have appellate jurisdiction to hear cases from the state courts in which a convicted criminal claims that his conviction process was in some way unconstitutional. Generally, district judges hear cases as individuals, but if a case presents a major constitutional issue, a panel of three district judges will hear it.

Anyone who loses at the district court level has a right to appeal to the one of the 12 U.S. circuit courts of appeals whose circuit includes the district of the original case. The courts of appeals must hear cases appealed to them. Roughly 10 percent of cases heard in district courts are taken to the circuit courts of appeals. There are 167 seats for circuit court judges plus an additional twelve judges on the Court of Appeals for the Federal Circuit as well as numerous other judges that serve on special courts for customs and patent cases, military appeals, and tax cases. At the circuit level the use of three-judge panels to decide cases is much more typical than in the district courts. The number of court of appeals judges per circuit varies according to the size of the circuit. Whenever possible, the three-judge panels are designed to include at least two judges from states other than the one where the case arose. Very rarely (for the purpose of avoiding differing decisions by three-judge panels) all the judges of a circuit will hear a case together, or *en banc*.

Federal court opinions are printed in the *Federal Supplement* (F. Supp.) or the *Federal Reporter* (F. 2d); state supreme court decisions are reprinted by region in collections such as *Northwest Reporter* (N.W.) or *Northeast Reporter Second Series* (N.E. 2d) or are published in state collections such as *Idaho Reports* (Idaho).

Supreme Court Proceedings. Approximately 7,000 to 8,000 cases each year are appealed to the Supreme Court.[23] Some of these come from state supreme courts and a few come directly from federal district courts, but the majority come from the circuit courts of appeals and often reflect splits (or disagreements) between circuits on similar issues.[24] Each year approximately 80 cases are accepted for full argument at the Supreme Court, and this reflects a significant decrease from the 100–150 cases the Justices used to decide per year.[25] As such, the overwhelming majority of appeals for Supreme Court review are rejected outright. In addition, each term, a few hundred cases are disposed of in "summary" proceedings, in which no further argument is presented to the Supreme Court. Sometimes a summary disposition will have no explanatory opinion at all; the Supreme Court can just announce a summary affirmance or reversal. Often summary proceedings include very brief (three or four sentences) *per curiam* opinions authored anonymously for the Court as a group.

To be accepted for review by the Court, a case must garner the votes of four of the nine justices in favor of its petition for review. (These petitions officially are requesting a "writ of certiorari," a document that agrees to hear the case. Issuing the writ is called "granting cert.") Petitions arrive throughout the year, and are read by the justices (or their clerks), and any single justice can suggest that a particular petition be discussed at the next available conference. Seventy percent of the petitions never garner such a suggestion and are, therefore, rejected without any discussion.

The Supreme Court session begins on the first Monday in October and lasts until early July. The Court's session consists of alternating two-week periods in which the justices first hear oral arguments and then spend time drafting and redrafting opinions to explain their decisions for the cases they have heard argued.

Fridays are set aside for conferences. These conferences begin at 9:30 AM with a series of handshakes between every justice and each of the other eight justices. The proceedings are kept completely secret. No one else is present. Only the chief justice takes notes (and these are not made public). If any books or papers are needed, the most "junior" justice (based on the date of appointment to the Court) goes to the door and hands a message to the bailiff, who is always waiting there.

The chief justice starts the discussion of each case, and the other justices then comment in order of descending seniority. When each justice speaks he or she indicates a tentative vote on the case, or on the petition for review. Once all nine have spoken, an official vote is taken, this time in reverse order of seniority. In other words, the chief justice can see how everyone else has voted before casting his or her vote. Any petition for review that obtains four votes in this process is then scheduled for full briefing and oral argument, usually several months hence.

The attorneys on both sides of cases accepted by the Court then submit written "briefs" (often hundreds of pages long), detailing their legal arguments. In addition, other parties (individuals, groups, or government agencies) who feel they have a stake in the outcome of the case often request the opportunity to submit *amicus curiae* ("friend of the court") briefs, supplementing the original brief with arguments presenting their own perspective on the case. These briefs may be submitted either by permission of both parties or by permission of the Supreme Court.

Once the Supreme Court justices have read the briefs and have had time, with the help of their (four per justice) law clerks (generally people who recently graduated at the top of their law school class) to research the cases further, they then hear oral argument. Oral argument is usually limited to 30 minutes for each side. The process of oral argument is a rather awesome spectacle. All nine justices sit in a row of high-backed chairs on an elevated platform behind a long table. They all wear black robes, and the solicitor general, who argues cases for the federal government, dons a formal morning coat. The attorney stands facing the justices (with back to the small audience) and begins his or her argument. He or she generally manages no more than a few sentences before the justices begin to pepper him or her with questions. The rest of the "argument" then consists of a lively interchange between justices and attorney. Audio recordings and transcripts of oral arguments are made available to the public on the U.S. Supreme Court's website www.supremecourt.gov.

On the Friday following oral argument, the case is again discussed in conference. The justices follow the same procedures of speaking and voting, and, of course, a majority (rather than a vote of four) is now decisive. If the chief justice votes with the majority, he assigns the job of writing the "Court" opinion. If the chief justice is in the minority, the most senior of the associate justices in the majority assigns the Court opinion. Some effort is made to distribute the opinion-writing responsibility evenly around the Court, but attention is paid to areas of expertise and the numbers of opinions written per year may vary among the justices. Once the selected justice has drafted the intended majority opinion, he or she circulates this rough version to every other justice. At this point the other justices jot down various suggestions for changing the draft; a justice in the original minority, for example, may offer to change sides if a particular point is added or deleted, strengthened or weakened. Likewise, an original member of the majority may threaten to break ranks if the opinion is not modified to his or her specifications. Meanwhile, if the vote on the case was non-unanimous (as most are), a dissenting opinion will also be circulating. Occasionally, a dissent is so persuasive, or a majority opinion so unpersuasive, that the initial dissent becomes a majority opinion before the consulting process has ended. These opinion drafts are frequently revised several times, and any justice is free to change sides until the official decision is announced in open court. Any justice who wants to may also write his or her own concurring or dissenting opinion.

Opinions are "read aloud" in Court, often on Mondays and Tuesdays. These days, justices generally summarize their main arguments and read only selected portions of an opinion. On occasion, a dissenting Justice will opt to read her or his dissenting opinion aloud from the bench to signal his or her dismay with the majority decision in a given case. When the opinion is announced, complete copies are distributed to the news media, litigants and the lower courts involved, and made available to the public online.

While the Supreme Court opinions are easily accessed online, they continue to be reprinted every week in a journal called *U.S. Law Week: Supreme Court Section* (abbreviated U.S.L.W. or L. W.), which is available in and/or accessible online from every law library. All law schools have law libraries, as do all county seats. Eventually the opinions also are reprinted in each of three edited series: *United States Supreme Court Reports* (abbreviated U.S.), the official version of the Government Printing Office; *The Supreme Court Reporter* (abbreviated S. Ct.), and *United States Supreme Court, Lawyers' Edition* (abbreviated L. Ed.), both published by

West Publishing, a private company. At least one of these editions is always available in law libraries.

Court cases use a legal notation form for citing cases. For example, in the citation 198 U.S. 45, 47, the letters U.S. are the abbreviation of the title of the collection in which the case can be found (in this instance, *United States Supreme Court Reports*), the first number, 198, refers to the volume number in that collection; the second number, 45, refers to the page on which the case begins; the third number, 47, refers to the page on which the particular quotation is found. For other forms of citation and further help, see a legal handbook or *A Uniform System of Citation*.

Scope of the Book

Women's rights under the law in fact vary from state to state because we live under 50 different state legal systems. When Congress exercises its (Section 5) power to enforce the Fourteenth Amendment by passing statutes that assure women equal treatment within particular contexts (e.g., hiring and firing for jobs in the private sector), Congress is rendering such treatment a legal right of women that applies nationwide. Similarly, any Supreme Court interpretation of women's rights under the Constitution applies nationwide. By contrast, judicial or legislative interpretations, issued by state authorities, of rights under state constitutions, although they may affect the lives of millions of people, are limited in their impact to the jurisdiction of that one state. The same applies to rulings of particular federal district or circuit courts; their interpretations of federal law are binding only within their own districts or circuits.

In addition to Supreme Court opinions, this book includes a number of state- and lower federal-level cases. It does so in order to illustrate difficult or pressing issues concerning women's rights that confront policymakers across the land. Not every policy question concerning women's rights is structured by guidance from the U.S. Supreme Court, and our inclusion of some of these sub-Supreme-Court cases allows the student to grapple with these problems even as policy makers are attempting to craft appropriate solutions for them. Of necessity, we have shrunk excerpts of some of the older cases and reduced others to summary format in order to present a more detailed picture of the contemporary Court in action.

Chapters 1 and 2 of this book deal exclusively with constitutional law. Most of Chapter 2 deals with due process and equal protection, the constitutional guarantees that have had the greatest impact on women's rights. The next five chapters include many constitutional law cases but include a greater balance of statutory construction and lower-court case law. Chapter 3 explores the

Introduction

legitimization of protective labor laws in the early twentieth century, the preemption of most of these laws by antidiscrimination laws enacted in the 1960s and 1970s, and the reappearance of protective policies in the form of fetal protection rules. The chapter also deals with such recurring issues as affirmative action, pregnancy policies, sexual harassment, and discrimination on the basis of gender identity. Chapter 4 examines the cluster of complex legal issues relating to reproduction, including fertility control, the right to be a mother and the right not to be one, and the government's role in regulating the behavior of pregnant women. Chapter 5 discusses the law of sexuality, domestic partnership, marriage, childrearing, divorce, and widowhood. The final two chapters deal with legal topics of particular concern to women: Chapter 6 with equal educational opportunity, and Chapter 7 with women-centric crimes: spousal assault, sexual assault, pornography, and prostitution.

---

[1] *Muller v. Oregon,* 208 U.S. 412 (1908).

[2] "Employed Persons by Sex, Race, and Occupation, 1983 and 1999," Table 669, in *2000 Statistical Abstract of the United States* (U.S. Department of Commerce, Bureau of the Census, *Employment and Earnings,* monthly issues), 416–418.

[3] *Plessy v. Ferguson,* 163 U.S. 537, 552 (1896).

[4] *New York Times,* September 15, 1957; 347 U.S. 483 (1954).

[5] Lawrence Baum, *The Supreme Court,* 4th ed. (Washington, DC: CQ Press, 1993), 216.

[6] Lynn Hecht Schafran, "Practicing Law in a Sexist Society," in Laura L. Crites and Winifred L. Hepperle, eds., *Women, the Courts, and Society* (Newbury Park, Calif: Sage Publications, 1987), 191–194; "First Professional Degrees Earned in Selected Professions, 1970 to 1997," in *2000 Statistical Abstract of the United States* (U.S. Department of Commerce, Bureau of the Census, 2000), Table 322.

[7] Marlene Stein Wortman, ed., *Women in American Law* (New York, NY: Holmes & Meier, 1985), vol. 1, 62. See also Chapter 1 of this book and Leslie F. Goldstein, *Constitutional Rights of Women,* 2nd ed. (Madison, WI: University of Wisconsin Press, 1988), 74–75.

[8] See Betty Friedan, *The Feminine Mystique* (New York, NY: W.W. Norton, 1963), chap. 4; Eleanor Flexner, *Century of Struggle,* rev. ed. (New York, NY: Atheneum, 1971).

[9] *Muller v. Oregon*, 208 U.S. 412 (1908).

[10] See Judith A. Baer, *The Chains of Protection* (Westport, CT: Greenwood Press, 1978).

[11] 410 U.S. 113.

[12] Stephanie Ebbert, "Welcome to the Way Back Machine: The Equal Rights Amendment is on the Table," *Boston Globe*, August 27, 2017. (Available at: https://www.bostonglobe.com/metro/2017/08/27/welcome-wayback-machine-the-equal-rights-amendment-table/pslRCKVjJKXpxmgtBGyKXL/story.html, accessed April 10, 2018).

[13] See "Pregnant Woman is Charged with Child Abuse," *The New York Times*, January 22, 1990; Kristen Gwynne, "How Marijuana Legalization Leaves Mothers and Pregnant Women Behind," *Rewire.News*, May 12, 2014. (Available at: https://rewire.news/article/2014/05/12/marijuana-legalization-leaves-mothers-pregnant-women-behind/, accessed April 19, 2018).

[14] Bureau of Labor Statistics, U.S. Department of Labor, The Economics Daily, Women's and Men's Earnings by Age in 2016. (Available at: https://www.bls.gov/opub/ted/2017/womens-and-mens-earnings-by-age-in-2016.htm, accessed April 12, 2018).

[15] Institute for Women's Policy Research, "Five Ways to Win an Argument about the Gender Wage Gap (updated 2017)," September 16, 2017. (Available at: https://iwpr.org/publications/five-ways-to-win-an-argument-about-the-gender-wage-gap/, accessed March 9, 2018).

[16] Institute for Women's Policy Research, "Pay Equity and Discrimination," 2018. (Available at: https://iwpr.org/issue/employment-education-economic-change/pay-equity-discrimination/, accessed March 9, 2018).

[17] Ibid. Also, see Judith A. Baer, *Women in American Law: The Struggle for Equality from the New Deal to The Present*, 3rd ed. (New York, NY: Holmes & Meier, 2002), p. 118.

The six states with comparable worth policies as of 2002 were Iowa, New York, Oregon, Wisconsin, Minnesota, and Washington. Mark R. Killingsworth, "Comparable Worth and Pay Equity: Recent Developments in the United States," *Canadian Public Policy* Vol. XXVIII S. 1 (May 2002): 171–186. (Available at: http://economics.ca/cgi/jab?journal=cpp&view=v28s1/Killingsworth_Chap.pdf, accessed September 15, 2004). An additional fourteen states have implemented some partial pay equity style adjustments. (Ibid.) See also Debra Stewart, "State Initiatives in the Federal System: The Politics and Policy of Comparable Worth," *Publius* 15 (Summer 1985): 81–95.

[18] Bureau of Labor Statistics, "Women's and men's earnings by age in 2016," August 25, 2017 https://www.bls.gov/opub/ted/2017/womens-and-mens-earnings-by-age-in-2016.htm accessed Sept.21, 2018.

[19] Center for American Women and Politics, Eagleton Institute of Politics, Rutgers University, "Women in Statewide Elective Executive Office 2018." (Available at: http://www.cawp.rutgers.edu/women-statewide-elective-executive-office-2018, accessed March 4, 2018).

[20] See *McCulloch v. Maryland,* 4 Wheaton (17 U.S.) 316 (1819).

[21] U.S. Constitution, Amendment X.

[22] See Eva Rubin, *The Supreme Court and the American Family* (Westport, CT: Greenwood Press, 1986). *Palmore v. Sidoti,* 466 U.S. 429 (1984), was an important exception to this generalization. Here, a unanimous Supreme Court reversed Florida's custody award of a white child to her father after her mother married a Black man. For additional exceptions see unmarried fathers' rights section in Chapter 5.

[23] Supreme Court of the United States, "The Justices' Caseload," 2018. (Available at: https://www.supremecourt.gov/about/justicecaseload.aspx, accessed May 8, 2018).

[24] Adam Feldman, "Looking Back to Make Sense of the Court's (Relatively) Light Workload," January 9, 2018. (Available at: https://empiricalscotus.com/2018/01/09/light-workload/, accessed May 8, 2018).

[25] Supreme Court of the United States, "The Justices' Caseload," 2018. (Available at: https://www.supremecourt.gov/about/justicecaseload.aspx, accessed May 8, 2018).

CHAPTER 1

Women Seek Constitutional Equality

WOMEN AND U.S. LAW BEFORE THE FOURTEENTH AMENDMENT

The nineteenth-century women's movement began with the first Women's Rights Convention in Seneca Falls, New York in 1848. At this time, the legal and social obstacles discussed in the Introduction were pervasive in every state of the union. The nineteenth-century women's rights movement (assisted by allies with a variety of motivations) succeeded in attaining state legislative elimination of the vast majority of the married women's property restrictions between 1850 and 1900. (For a discussion of Supreme Court amelioration of late-twentieth-century remnants, see *Orr v. Orr* [1979] and *Kirchberg v. Feenstra* [1981] in Chapter 5.) The Fourteenth Amendment and the democratic process eventually made it possible to remove other obstacles, but the change came slowly and with much travail.

Many Americans assume that any statute that strikes them as fundamentally unjust must be somehow unconstitutional; indeed, their chances of convincing federal judges on the point have increased dramatically since the nineteenth century. That increase would not have been possible without three specific developments of the post-Civil War period: the Thirteenth (1865), Fourteenth (1868), and Fifteenth (1870) amendments to the U.S. Constitution. Before those amendments were adopted, although the federal government was hemmed in by various clauses, including the Bill of Rights (the first 10 amendments to the Constitution), state governments were left almost entirely unfettered by the Constitution.[1] Most of the legislation affecting our daily lives is state legislation, and state governments were originally free to infringe on freedom of speech, to establish religions, to try people without giving them lawyers, and to treat various groups of persons—including women—as unequally as they pleased. During the nineteenth century, state governments did all these things and many others that seem equally shocking to us in our twenty-first-century notions of the Constitution.

The post-Civil War amendments changed this situation, placing the shield of the national Constitution between the basic citizen rights of individuals and the potentially tyrannical government of their own states. The Thirteenth Amendment freed the slaves, and the Fifteenth Amendment prohibited states from depriving persons of the right to vote on the grounds of race or previous servitude. The Fourteenth Amendment cast its net more broadly, encompassing what might be viewed as the fundamental rights of citizenship, or even the fundamental rights of life within a free and just society. It contains three clauses that together shouldered the burden of most of the important constitutional litigation of the twentieth century:

1. No state shall make or enforce any law which shall abridge the privileges or immunities of citizens of the United States;

2. nor shall any state deprive any person of life, liberty, or property without due process of law;

3. nor deny to any person within its jurisdiction the equal protection of the laws.

Reference is made to these three clauses so frequently that they are called simply (1) the privileges or immunities clause, (2) the due process clause, and (3) the equal protection clause. Although the privileges or immunities clause seems to sweep the most broadly of the three, its efficacy was drastically undermined in early Fourteenth Amendment litigation. This left to the two remaining clauses the job of protecting civil rights and civil liberties against state governmental interference. Indeed, the task of protecting women's rights, as well as of protecting virtually all other constitutional rights, has fallen on the due process clause and the equal protection clause.

THE PRIVILEGES OR IMMUNITIES CLAUSE: THE *SLAUGHTERHOUSE CASES* (1873)

Women's rights litigation is about as old as Fourteenth Amendment litigation. The first women's rights case, *Bradwell v. State of Illinois* (1873) (see below), was decided by the Supreme Court in 1873 on the day after the Court had handed down its first Fourteenth Amendment decision in the *Slaughterhouse Cases*, 83 U.S. 36 (1873). In the *Slaughterhouse Cases*, the Court laid down the basic rules of the game for future Fourteenth Amendment litigation—rules effective, to some extent, today. The basic impact of those cases was to decimate the privileges or immunities clause as a potential grounds for attacking state statutes.

The cases arose out of challenges by a number of butchers to a Louisiana statute that granted to a single corporation located in a prescribed area a 25-year monopoly for maintaining "slaughterhouses, landings for cattle and stockyards" within the metropolitan area surrounding and including New Orleans. Under this 1869 statute, butchers who wanted to continue to carry on their trade in the New Orleans area had to rent facilities from the monopoly at rates regulated by the state. Louisiana's rationale for passing the law was to protect the general population from the unpleasant fumes, sounds, and other disturbances associated with the slaughtering of animals by limiting those activities to a single, narrowly circumscribed area of town. The butchers argued that this law should be voided on several constitutional grounds; they claimed that it established "involuntary servitude" in violation of the Thirteenth Amendment and that in violation of the Fourteenth Amendment it abridged their "privileges or immunities" of American citizenship, took their liberty and property without due process of law, and denied them equal protection of law.

The Thirteenth Amendment argument did not impress the Court. The majority simply dismissed as implausible the claim that a law restricting the slaughtering of cattle to a single part of the city, even if it did grant monopoly privileges to some, somehow placed the non-monopolists in a state of servitude. To answer the Fourteenth Amendment privileges or immunities argument, the Court had to work a little harder. An 1823 federal circuit court case had interpreted the words *privileges and immunities* rather broadly, although the precedent involved not the Fourteenth Amendment but the privileges and immunities clause of Article IV (which calls for granting to out-of-staters "the privileges and immunities of citizens of the several states"). *Corfield v. Coryell* (1823) had established that this phrase referred to

> those privileges and immunities which are fundamental; which belong of right to the citizens of all free governments, and which have at all times been enjoyed by citizens of the several states which compose this Union, from the time of their becoming free, independent, and sovereign. What these fundamental principles are, it would be more tedious than difficult to enumerate. They may all, however, be comprehended under the following general heads: protection by the government, with the right to acquire and possess property of every kind, and to pursue and obtain happiness and safety, subject nevertheless, to such restraints as the government may prescribe for the

general good of the whole; the right of a citizen of one State to pass through, or reside in, any other State for purposes of trade, agriculture, professional pursuits, or otherwise; to claim the benefit of the writ of habeas corpus; to institute and maintain actions of any kind in the courts of the State; to take hold, and dispose of property, either real or personal; and an exemption from higher taxes or impositions than are paid by the other citizens of the State, may be mentioned as some of the particular privileges and immunities of citizens which are clearly embraced by the general description of privileges deemed to be fundamental.[2]

The four dissenters in *Slaughterhouse* argued that *Corfield* and later Supreme Court cases established that one's right to pursue a livelihood, and all other privileges that are so basic that they "belong of right to the citizens of all free governments," were now to be shielded by the Fourteenth Amendment from any harm one's own state government might attempt upon them. In other words, all those protections that the Article IV privileges and immunities clause created for citizens traveling into new states, the Fourteenth Amendment privileges or immunities clause now provided for citizens vis-a-vis their home-state governments. State governments would no longer be allowed to create and abolish civil rights according to their whims; civil rights of Americans would become truly nationalized. This was a radical shift in the governmental structure of the United States (although its being radical is not surprising if one recalls that the country had just fought a protracted and bloody Civil War over the states' rights question). It was such a radical shift that the Supreme Court majority in *Slaughterhouse* refused to acknowledge that it had taken place.

Instead, Justice Miller wrote for the majority that the language of the Fourteenth Amendment privileges or immunities clause had not unequivocally signaled an intent to impose such a radical change on the governmental structure:

> When, as in the case before us, these consequences are so serious, so far-reaching and pervading, so great a departure from the structure and spirit of our institutions; when the effect is to fetter and degrade the state governments . . . in the exercise of powers heretofore universally conceded to them of the most ordinary and fundamental character; when in fact it radically changes the whole theory of the relations of the State and Federal governments to each other and of both these governments to the people; . . . in the absence of language which expresses such a purpose too clearly to admit of doubt we must reject the "radical" interpretation.[3]

What, then, did Justice Miller make of the privileges or immunities clause? The answer is a simple one: not much. He argued that the Fourteenth Amendment phrase "privileges or immunities of citizens *of the United States*" meant something different from the notion of fundamental civic rights expressed in the Article IV phrase "privileges and immunities of citizens *of the several states*." The Fourteenth Amendment, he maintained, safeguarded only the rights of *national* citizenship (a collection he very narrowly circumscribed). The basic civil rights described in *Corfield v. Coryell* he placed in the category of *state* citizenship rights, and these, he claimed, lay out of reach of the Fourteenth Amendment.

As for the content of those national citizenship rights, he explained that they were the special rights accorded to Americans by virtue of our living in a single united nation under a national constitution. For example, as national citizens we have a right of free access to all American seaports. This right derives from the clause that gives to Congress (rather than to the states) authority to regulate foreign commerce. The strange thing about Justice Miller's interpretation is that all the rights he places under the shield of the Fourteenth Amendment privileges or immunities clause were already protected by the national Constitution before the Fourteenth Amendment was adopted. He rendered the privileges or immunities clause a virtual nullity. And such it has remained to this day.

What did not endure from Justice Miller's *Slaughterhouse* opinion was the limited scope that he also tried to impose on the due process and equal protection clauses. In answer to the argument that a lawfully adopted statute regulating the property of butchers could be viewed as having deprived them of "property without due process of law," Miller took his bearings by the well-established meaning of the due process clause of the Fifth Amendment, which restrained the national government in words identical to those restraining the states in the Fourteenth. Miller said simply that "under no construction of that provision that we have ever seen, or any that we deem admissible" could such a property regulation be viewed as unlawful (83 U.S., at 81). Justice Miller was following the well-entrenched idea that "due process of law" referred simply to the proper legal procedures or processes that had to accompany any taking of life, liberty, or property. He could not treat seriously enough even to design a counterargument the claim that the due process clause regulated the *substantive* qualities of laws. He did not frame any real response to the novel viewpoint of dissenters Swayne and Bradley that if a law, in its substance, took away liberty or property to a degree that was not "fair" or "just," it violated the due process clause.[4] (As becomes apparent in *Lochner v. New York* [1905] below, it took roughly 30 years for what was a new viewpoint in 1873 to become the official law of the land.)

Finally, Justice Miller's majority opinion disposed of the equal protection clause argument with two sentences:

> We doubt very much whether any action of a State not directed by way of discrimination against the Negroes as a class, or on account of their race, will ever be held to come within the purview of this provision. It is so clearly a provision for that race and that emergency, that a strong case would be necessary for its application to any other.[5]

Miller did not unconditionally reject the possibility that the equal protection clause might be used to protect nonracial groups, such as women, but he expressed deep skepticism that a strong enough case would ever be presented to convince the Court to depart from the specific historical intention of the Fourteenth Amendment.

Miller's predictions concerning the restricted application of the equal protection clause proved considerably more durable than his expectations on the due process clause.[6] Although the reach of the clause fairly quickly stretched beyond "Negroes as a class" to strike down legislation that discriminated against the Chinese (a nationality group but of a non-Caucasian race),[7] the clause did remain, until the mid-twentieth century, almost exclusively a prohibition on *racial* discrimination. This exclusive application, although not following the strict words of Miller's *Slaughterhouse* opinion, certainly seems to have been guided by its spirit of a narrow interpretation based on historic intent.

The only extension beyond the racial-discrimination concept of the equal protection clause that the Supreme Court ventured before the 1940s occurred in an area closely related to that of racial discrimination. In 1915 the Court used the equal protection clause to strike down a law that blatantly discriminated against aliens.[8] Alienage, especially in that era of frankly race-based restrictions on who could become a naturalized citizen, was closely tied conceptually to race. The logical heritage, then, from the *Slaughterhouse Cases* version of the equal protection clause endured more or less intact well into the twentieth century.

Nevertheless, this narrow application of the Fourteenth Amendment was accompanied historically by a series of cases that gave lip service, but only lip service, to an equal protection standard of much more far-reaching potential. That standard was the rule that whenever the law "classified" different groups of persons, or treated them unequally, the classification had to have some "reasonable" relationship to promoting the public good. In other words, laws could treat people unequally if (but only if) there was some reasonable basis for doing so. In practice, however, this standard was all bark and no bite. An honest acknowledgment of its toothlessness is provided in one of the Court opinions from this period: "A classification may not be merely arbitrary, but necessarily *there must be great freedom of discretion, even though it result in 'ill-advised, unequal and oppressive legislation.'* "⁹

The legacy of the *Slaughterhouse Cases* was as follows: (1) the privileges or immunities clause was emptied of any real meaning; (2) the idea that the due process clause might create a limit on the substance of legislation, requiring that the mandate of a statute be "fair," was summarily rejected—so summarily that the majority opinion devoted virtually no discussion to determining what the due process clause did mean; (3) the equal protection clause was interpreted to focus narrowly on the evil of racial discrimination. Although the Court soon began to give lip service to the idea that the equal protection clause had a considerably more general impact, in practice it continued to follow the lead of the *Slaughterhouse Cases* until the mid-twentieth century.

ACCESS TO THE BAR: *MYRA BRADWELL V. STATE OF ILLINOIS* (1873)

The first case challenging a sex-based classification as a violation of the Fourteenth Amendment was *Myra Bradwell v. State of Illinois* (1873).¹⁰ In fact, *Bradwell v. Illinois* appears to have been the first Supreme Court case to present a Fourteenth Amendment challenge to any legislation. Although *Bradwell* was argued at the Supreme Court two weeks before the *Slaughterhouse Cases* were argued, the Supreme Court handed down the *Slaughterhouse Cases* decision one day in advance of the *Bradwell* decision. This timing rendered the *Slaughterhouse Cases* the historic first official interpretation of the Fourteenth Amendment. For this reason, the Court presented much more thorough and detailed arguments in the *Slaughterhouse Cases* than the justices presented in the *Bradwell* decision. In deciding Myra Bradwell's fate, they could simply announce, in effect, that they were following the Fourteenth Amendment principles they had explicated the day before. By this twist of fate, a case involving a few butchers who resented geographic limitations on their trade became the "landmark" constitutional law case—included in virtually every constitutional law course and casebook—whereas the case of Myra Bradwell, who in 1869 had been forbidden to practice law for no reason other than that she was a married woman, which actually reached the Court first with the same arguments, gathered dust in the proverbial bin of history.

Illinois officials did not even send a lawyer to Washington to present their side of the case. In fact, the Illinois legislature, apparently unbeknownst to the

U.S. Supreme Court, had adopted a law in 1872 *forbidding* the barring of employment to any person on the basis of sex.[11] (A Court decision in her favor therefore would not have altered Illinois law but could protect women's job access in other states.) The Supreme Court opinion does complain, "The record [of what transpired at Myra Bradwell's earlier hearing in the Illinois Supreme Court] is not very perfect" (83 U.S., at 137). The lack of a properly presented case may partially explain why the Supreme Court did not wish to use Myra Bradwell's case for making constitutional history.

Myra Bradwell had trained for the Illinois bar under the tutelage of her husband, an attorney. By the time she passed the state bar exam, she had already attained respect in legal circles for her editorship of *The Chicago Legal News*, a journal that provided up-to-date case summaries of current legal developments. Her application to the Illinois bar was not unprecedented. In 1869 the Iowa judiciary admitted Arabella Mansfield, who had passed the bar exam with high honors, to the bar of that state, despite an explicit reference to males in the Iowa statutes on bar eligibility.[12]

The arguments of Mrs. Bradwell's attorney, Senator Matthew Hale Carpenter, are in fact more interesting than the Supreme Court's opinion. He had to grapple seriously with the meaning of the Fourteenth Amendment, because the *Slaughterhouse Cases*, explicating the clauses of that amendment, had yet to be handed down. Apparently, Senator Carpenter viewed the equal protection and due process clauses as clauses about the way laws should be applied rather than about limits on the content of laws. He viewed the privileges or immunities clause as the really forceful clause of the Fourteenth Amendment, as the one that shields the basic civil rights of Americans against potentially oppressive state legislation. The wording of the three important clauses of the Fourteenth Amendment makes it difficult to disagree with his implicit ranking of them. After the Supreme Court had disagreed with him, however, knocking all meaning out of the privileges or immunities clause in its *Slaughterhouse Cases* decision, the very claims that Carpenter made about the privileges or immunities clause were eventually applied to the equal protection clause. His argument serves as a model for future equal protection litigation. The relevant portion follows.

BRIEF OF BRADWELL'S COUNSEL FOR *BRADWELL V. ILLINOIS* (1873)

The conclusion is irresistible that the profession of the law, like the clerical profession and that of medicine, is an avocation open to every citizen of the United States. And while the legislature may prescribe qualifications for entering upon this pursuit, it cannot, under the guise of fixing qualifications, exclude a class of citizens from admission to the bar. The legislature may say at what age candidates shall be admitted; may elevate or depress the standard of learning required. But a qualification to which a whole class of citizens can never attain is not a regulation of admission to the bar, but is, as to such citizens, a prohibition. For instance, a state legislature could not, in enumerating the qualifications, require the candidate to be a white citizen. I presume it will be admitted that such an act would be void. The only provision in the Constitution of the United States which secures to colored male citizens the privilege of admission to the bar, or the pursuit of the other ordinary avocations of life is the provision that "No state shall make or enforce any law which shall abridge the privileges or immunities of the citizens." If this provision protects the colored citizen, then it protects every citizen, black or white, male or female.

Why may a colored citizen buy, hold and sell land in any state of the Union? Because he is a citizen of the United States, and that is one of the privileges of a citizen. Why may a colored citizen be admitted to the bar? Because he is a citizen, and that is one of the avocations open to every citizen, and no state can abridge his right to pursue it. Certainly no other reason can be given.

Now, let us come to the case of Myra Bradwell. She is a citizen of the United States and of the state of Illinois, residing therein. She has been judicially ascertained to be of full age, and to possess the requisite character and learning. Indeed, the court below in its opinion found in the record says: "Of the ample qualifications of the applicant we have no doubt." Still, admission to the bar was denied the petitioner; not upon the ground that she was not a citizen; not for. . . reasonable regulations prescribed by the legislature; but upon the sole ground that inconvenience would result from permitting her to enjoy her legal rights in this, to wit: that her clients might have difficulty in enforcing the contracts they might make with her as their attorney, because of her being a married woman.

Now, with entire respect to that court, it is submitted that this argument *ab inconvenienti*, which might have been urged with whatever force belongs to it against adopting the Fourteenth Amendment in the full scope of its language, is utterly futile to resist its full and proper operation, now that it has been adopted.

I maintain that the Fourteenth Amendment opens to every citizen of the United States, male or female, black or white, married or single, the honorable

> professions as well as the servile employments of life; and that no citizen can be excluded from anyone of them. Intelligence, integrity and honor are the only qualifications that can be prescribed as conditions precedent to an entry upon any honorable pursuit or profitable avocation, and all the privileges and immunities which I vindicate to a colored citizen, I vindicate to our mothers, our sisters and our daughters. . . .

Justice Miller in the Supreme Court opinion that follows does not address the arguments of Bradwell's counsel at all. Relying on the distinction drawn in his *Slaughterhouse Cases* opinion, Miller simply asserts that the opportunity to enter the legal profession, if it is a "privilege or immunity" of citizenship, pertains only to state citizenship. As he explained in *Slaughterhouse*, the Fourteenth Amendment protects only the privileges and immunities of national citizenship, and because the opportunity to become a lawyer does not fall into that category (except for practice in the federal courts, which was not directly at issue here), Mrs. Bradwell's plight is unaffected by the Fourteenth Amendment. As is also evident, the Court's opinion is totally silent concerning the equal protection clause. That is at least a bit puzzling in light of the combination of Miller's statements in *Slaughterhouse* and the Bradwell attorney's argument here. Miller made clear in his *Slaughterhouse Cases* opinion that he agrees with Senator Carpenter in the conclusion that anti-Black legislation is prohibited by the Fourteenth Amendment. Whereas Carpenter finds this prohibition in the privileges or immunities clause, Miller finds it in the equal protection clause. The counsel's argument, then, has not been met: he claims, in effect, that if the generally worded commands of the Fourteenth Amendment prohibit discrimination on account of race (i.e., exclusion of a whole class of people irrespective of their individual strengths), they implicitly prohibit it on account of sex. Because the equal protection clause contains the same degree of generality in its wording as the privileges or immunities clause, Senator Carpenter's claim, as it would apply to the equal protection clause, seems to deserve a response. Justice Miller's *Slaughterhouse Cases* opinion reveals that he believed the equal protection clause applied only to racial discrimination and not to other forms of discrimination. He did not repeat the point here, but perhaps he believed that his reference to his *Slaughterhouse Cases* opinion of the preceding day was adequate explanation.

The four dissenters of the *Slaughterhouse Cases* do take these arguments more seriously than Miller does, apparently because they take the privileges or immunities clause itself more seriously. Only Chief Justice Chase, however, was willing to accept the full implications of the views on the privileges or immunities clause with which he had aligned himself the day before. He dissented here without opinion, but the lines of his reasoning are not difficult to surmise. He had concurred with the dissent in the *Slaughterhouse Cases* that had argued that "equality of right, among citizens in the pursuit of the ordinary avocations of life. . . with exemption from all disparaging and partial enactments. . . is the distinguishing privilege of citizens of the United States."[13] Because the first clause of the Fourteenth Amendment granted citizenship to "all persons" born in the United States, and because women were clearly persons, the validity of Mrs. Bradwell's claim would seem to be the obvious conclusion.

Justice Bradley viewed it differently; he explained on behalf of the two other dissenters of yesterday why they now concurred with Justice Miller. Justice Bradley's own *Slaughterhouse Cases* dissent, just 24 hours earlier, had included the following statement: "If my views are correct with regard to what are the privileges and immunities of citizens, it follows conclusively that any law. . . depriving a large class of citizens of the privilege of pursuing a lawful employment does abridge the privileges of those citizens."[14] Is his explanation here in *Bradwell v. Illinois* a convincing explanation for treating women as a "peculiar" case?

MYRA BRADWELL V. STATE OF ILLINOIS
83 U.S. 130 (1873)

[Material omitted from court opinions is marked by ellipses, except for omissions of footnotes or repetitious or tangential case citation material. Brackets indicate material added by the book authors, except when the bracket is inside an internal quotation or parentheses. Footnotes are those from the Court opinions, except when marked "AU."—AU.]

MR. JUSTICE MILLER delivered the opinion of the Court.

[In the official recitation of the facts of the case that preceded Miller's opinion, the U.S. Reports note the Illinois Supreme Court denied her application on the grounds that she is a married woman, so not obligated by contracts. 83 U.S. 131] In regard to [the Fourteenth] Amendment counsel for the plaintiff. . . says that there are certain privileges and immunities which belong to a citizen of the United States as such. . . and he proceeds to argue that admission to the bar of a state, of a person who possesses the requisite learning and character, is one of those which a state may not deny.

. . .[W]e are not able to concur. . . . We agree with him that there are privileges and immunities belonging to citizens of the United States. . . and that it is these. . . which a state is forbidden to abridge. But the right to admission to practice in the courts of a state is not one of them. This right in no sense depends on citizenship of the United States.... [Many] distinguished lawyers have been admitted to practice, both in the state and Federal courts, who were not citizens.... But, on whatever basis this right may be placed, so far as it can have any relation to citizenship at all, it would seem that, as to the courts of the state, it would relate to citizenship of the state, and as to Federal courts, it would relate to citizenship of the United States. The opinion just delivered in the *Slaughterhouse Cases*, from Louisiana, renders elaborate argument in the present case unnecessary; for, unless we are wholly and radically mistaken in the principle on which those cases are decided, the right to control and regulate the granting of license to practice law in the courts of a state is one of those powers which are not transferred for its protection to the Federal government, and its exercise is in no manner governed or controlled by citizenship of the United States in the party seeking such license.

It is unnecessary to repeat the argument on which the judgment in those cases is founded. It is sufficient to say, they are conclusive of the present case. The judgment of the State Court is, therefore *Affirmed*.

MR. JUSTICE BRADLEY:

I concur in the judgment of the Court... but not for the reasons specified in the opinion just read.

The claim of the plaintiff, who is a married woman, to be admitted to practice as an attorney and counselor at law, is based upon the supposed right of every person, man or woman, to engage in any lawful employment for a livelihood. The supreme court of Illinois denied the application on the ground that, by the common law, which is the basis of the laws of Illinois, only men were admitted to the bar... The court, however, regarded itself as bound by at least two limitations. One was that it should establish such terms of admission as would promote the proper administration of justice, and the other that it should not admit any persons or class of persons not intended by the legislature to be admitted, even though not expressly excluded by statute. In view of this latter limitation the court felt compelled to deny the application of females to be admitted as members of the bar. Being contrary to the rules of the common law and the usages of Westminster Hall from time immemorial, it could not be supposed that the legislature had intended to adopt any different rule.

It certainly cannot be affirmed, as a historical fact, that this has ever been established as one of the fundamental privileges and immunities of the sex. On the contrary, the civil law, as well as nature herself, has always recognized a wide difference in the respective spheres and destinies of man and woman.

Man is, or should be, woman's protector and defender. The natural and proper timidity and delicacy which belongs to the female sex evidently unfits it for many of the occupations of civil life. The constitution of the family organization, which is founded in the divine ordinance, as well as in the nature of things, indicates the domestic sphere as that which properly belongs to the domain and functions of womanhood. The harmony, not to say identity, of interests and views which belong or should belong to the family institution, is repugnant to the idea of a woman adopting a distinct and independent career from that of her husband. So firmly fixed was this sentiment in the founders of the common law that it became a maxim of that system of jurisprudence that a woman had no legal existence separate from her husband, who was regarded as her head and representative in the social state; and, notwithstanding some recent modification of this civil status, many of the special rules of law flowing from and dependent upon this cardinal principle still exist in full force in most states. One of these is, that a married woman is incapable, without her husband's consent, of making contracts which shall be binding on her or him. This very incapacity was one circumstance which the supreme court of Illinois deemed important in rendering a married woman incompetent fully to perform the duties and trusts that belong to the office of an attorney and counselor.

It is true that many women are unmarried and not affected by any of the duties, complications, and incapacities arising out of the married state, but these are exceptions to the general rule. The paramount destiny and mission of woman are to fulfill the noble and benign offices of wife and mother. This is the law of the Creator. And the rules of civil society must be adapted to the general constitution of things, and cannot be based upon exceptional cases.

The humane movements of modern society, which have for their object the multiplication of avenues for woman's advancement, and of occupations adapted to her condition and sex, have my heartiest concurrence. But I am not prepared to say that it is one of her fundamental rights and privileges to be admitted into every office and position, including those which require highly special qualifications and demanding special responsibilities. In the nature of things it is not every citizen of every age, sex, and condition that is qualified for every calling and position. It is the prerogative of the legislator to prescribe regulations founded on nature, reason, and experience for the due admission of qualified persons to professions and callings demanding special skill and confidence. This fairly belongs to the police power of the state; and, in my opinion in view of the peculiar characteristics, destiny, and mission of woman, it is within the province of the legislature to ordain what offices, positions, and

> callings shall be filled and discharged by men, and shall receive the benefits of those energies and responsibilities, and that decision and firmness which are presumed to predominate in the sterner sex.
>
> For these reasons I think that the laws of Illinois now complained of are not obnoxious to the charge of abridging any of the privileges and immunities of citizens of the United States.
>
> **Mr. Justice Field and Mr. Justice Swayne:**
>
> We concur in the opinion of Mr. Justice Bradley
>
> **Dissenting, Mr. Chief Justice Chase.**

Case Questions

1. Is Justice Miller admitting that the opportunity to enter the bar for federal courts is a privilege or immunity of "citizens of the United States" and that therefore states may not abridge that opportunity on the basis of gender?

2. Justice Miller in the *Slaughterhouse Cases* characterized "the privileges and immunities of the citizens of the United States," as rights "which owe their existence to the Federal government, its National character, its Constitution, or its laws." Since the 1870s, women have not used the privileges or immunities clause for challenges to gender-based discrimination. Are there arguments that might render the clause useful in such challenges?

3. Bradwell's lawyer, Senator Carpenter, argued, in effect, for a "reasonableness" test as a standard for the privileges or immunities clause. Had he convinced the court as to that standard, would Mrs. Bradwell have won a favorable result?

Case note: Myra Bradwell applied again, this time successfully, to the Illinois bar in 1890, and in 1892 she was admitted to the U.S. Supreme Court bar.[15]

WOMEN'S SUFFRAGE AND THE FOURTEENTH AMENDMENT DEBATES

Although the Fourteenth Amendment included three clauses that inspired much helpful women's rights litigation, the amendment also contained a clause that was anathema to a large segment of the early women's suffrage movement.[16] Section two of the amendment puts the word *male* into the U.S. Constitution, and suffragists fought hard but unsuccessfully to keep that from happening. Now that slavery had been outlawed in the Thirteenth Amendment, the section in question first gets rid of the old three-fifths rule for counting non-free persons for representation in Congress and then adds: "But when the right to vote [for federal or state officials] . . . is denied to any of the male inhabitants of [a]. . . state, being twenty-one years of age, and citizens of the United States, or in any way abridged, except for participation in rebellion, or other crime, the basis of representation [in Congress for that state shall be proportionately]. . . reduced."

The suffragists' argument was straightforward: If the right to vote was to be granted to men of all races, they argued, why not to both sexes? The congressional debates on the amendments give the impression that Congress never took this idea as seriously as the feminists did. Nor did abolitionist leaders back the women up. Even Frederick Douglass, long a supporter of women's suffrage in principle, insisted that the timing was not right, in a piece titled "This Is the Negro's Hour." The suffragists and abolitionists, once partners, became increasingly estranged. Elizabeth Cady Stanton's response to Douglass's words, which Douglass published in his own newspaper, helped widen the breach.

> ### ELIZABETH CADY STANTON TO THE EDITOR, 'THIS IS THE NEGRO'S HOUR,' *NATIONAL ANTI-SLAVERY STANDARD,* NEW YORK, 26 DECEMBER 1865
>
> Sir, by an amendment of the Constitution, ratified by three-fourths of the loyal States, the black man is declared free. The largest and most influential political party is demanding Suffrage for him throughout the Union, which right in many of the States is already conceded. Although this may remain a question for politicians to wrangle over for five or ten years, the black man is still, in a political point of view, far above the educated women of the country.
>
> The representative women of the nation have done their uttermost for the last thirty years to secure freedom for the negro, and so long as he was lowest in the scale of being we were willing to press *his* claims; but now, as the celestial gate to civil rights is slowly moving on its hinges, it becomes a serious question whether we had better stand aside and see "Sambo" walk into the kingdom first.
>
> As self-preservation is the first law of nature, would it not be wiser . . . when the Constitutional door is open, [to] avail ourselves of the strong arm and blue uniform of the black soldier to walk in by his side, and thus make the gap so wide that no privileged class could ever again close it against the humblest citizen of the Republic?
>
> "This is the negro's hour." Are we sure that he, once entrenched in all his inalienable rights, may not be an added power to hold us at bay? Have not

> "black male citizens" been heard to say they doubted the wisdom of extending the right of Suffrage to women? Why should the African prove more just and generous than his Saxon compeers?
>
> If the two millions of Southern black women are not to be secured in their rights of person, property, wages, and children, their emancipation is but another form of slavery. In fact, it is better to be the slave of an educated white man, than of a degraded, ignorant black one. We who know what absolute power the statute laws of most of the States give man, in all his civil, political, and social relations, do demand that in changing the status of the four millions of Africans, the women as well as the men should be secured in all the rights, privileges, and immunities of citizens.
>
> . . .The struggle of the last thirty years has not been merely on the black man as such, but on the broader ground of his humanity. Our Fathers, at the end of the first revolution, in their desire for a speedy readjustment of all their difficulties, and in order to present to Great Britain, their common enemy, a united front, accepted the compromise urged on them by South Carolina, and a century of wrong, ending in another revolution, has been the result of their action.
>
> This is our opportunity to retrieve the errors of the past and mold anew the elements of Democracy. The nation is ready for a long step in the right direction; party lines are obliterated, and all men are thinking for themselves. If our rulers have the justice to give the black man Suffrage, woman should avail herself of that new-born virtue to secure her rights; if not, she should begin with renewed earnestness to educate the people into the idea of universal suffrage.

Despite the efforts of the early suffragists, both the Fourteenth and Fifteenth Amendments did attain ratification without explicit inclusion of women. Efforts then turned to the courts. Virginia Minor and 149 other female suffragists just went to the polls on the national election day, 1872, in 10 states and D.C. Four had their votes counted, most were arrested, and Virginia Minor simply had her request to register refused. Her husband, an attorney, appealed all the way to the Supreme Court.[17]

MINOR V. HAPPERSETT
88 U.S. 162 (1875)

MR. CHIEF JUSTICE WAITE delivered the opinion of the Court:

The question is presented in this case, whether, since the adoption of the Fourteenth Amendment, a woman, who is a citizen of the United States and of the State of Missouri, is a voter in that State, notwithstanding the provision of the constitution and laws of the States, which confine the right of suffrage to men alone. . . .

It is contended that the provisions of the Constitution and laws of the State of Missouri which confine the right of suffrage and registration therefor to men, are in violation of the Constitution of the United States and, therefore, void. The argument is, that as a woman, born and naturalized in the United States and subject to the jurisdiction thereof, is a citizen of the United States and of the State in which she resides, she has the right of suffrage as one of the privileges and immunities of her citizenship, which the State cannot by its laws or Constitution abridge.

There is no doubt that women may be citizens. They are persons, and by the Fourteenth Amendment "All persons born or naturalized in the United States and subject to the jurisdiction thereof" are expressly declared to be "citizens of the United States and of the State wherein they reside." But, in our opinion, it did not need this Amendment to give them that position. Before its adoption, the Constitution of the United States did not in terms prescribe who should be citizens of the United States or of the several States, yet there were necessarily such citizens without such provision. There cannot be a nation without a people. The very idea of a political community, such as a nation is, implies an association of persons for the promotion of their general welfare. Each one of the persons associated becomes a member of the nation formed by the association. He owes it allegiance and is entitled to its protection. Allegiance and protection are, in this connection, reciprocal obligations. The one is a compensation for the other; allegiance for protection and protection for allegiance.

For convenience it has been found necessary to give a name to this membership. . . . For this purpose the words "subject," "inhabitant," and "citizen" have been used, and the choice between them is sometimes made to depend upon the form of the government. Citizen is now more commonly employed, however, and as . . . better suited to the description of one living under a republican government, it was adopted by nearly all of the States upon their separation from Great Britain, and was afterwards adopted in the Articles of Confederation and in the Constitution of the United States. When used in this sense it is understood as conveying the idea of membership of a nation, and nothing more.

To determine, then, who were citizens of the United States before the adoption of the Amendment, it is necessary to ascertain what persons originally associated themselves together to form the nation, and what were afterwards admitted to membership.

[Here followed a lengthy documentation of the conclusion that state and federal law have treated women as citizens since the beginning. The opinion referred to naturalization laws, laws that limited inheritance to citizens, homesteading laws that did the same, and access to federal courts in controversies between "citizens" of two different states.—AU.] . . . [S]ex has never been made one of the elements of citizenship in the United States. In this respect men have never had an advantage over women. The same laws precisely apply to both. The Fourteenth Amendment did not affect the citizenship of women any more than it did of men. In this particular, therefore, the rights of Mrs. Minor do not depend upon the Amendment. She has always been a citizen from her birth, and entitled to all the privileges and immunities of citizenship. The Amendment prohibited the State, of which she is a citizen from abridging any of her privileges and immunities as a citizen of the United States; but it did not confer citizenship on her. That she had before its adoption.

If the right of suffrage is one of the necessary privileges of the citizen of the United States, then the Constitution and laws of Missouri confining it to men are in violation of the Constitution of the United States. . . . The direct question is, therefore, presented whether all citizens are necessarily voters.

The Constitution does not define the privileges and immunities of citizens. For that definition we must look elsewhere. In this case we need not determine what they are, but only whether suffrage is necessarily one of them.

It certainly is nowhere made so in express terms. The United States has no voters in the States of its own creation. The elective officers of the United States are all elected directly or indirectly by state voters. The members of the House of Representatives are to be chosen by the people of the States, and the electors in each State must have the qualifications requisite for electors of the most numerous branch of the State Legislature. Const, art. I, § 2. Senators are to be chosen by the Legislatures of the States, and necessarily the members of the Legislature required to make the choice are elected by the voters of the State. Const, art. I, § 3. Each State must appoint, in such manner as the Legislature thereof may direct, the electors to elect the President and Vice-President. Const, art. II, § 2. The times, places and manner of holding elections for Senators and Representatives are to be prescribed in each State by the Legislature thereof: but Congress may at any time, by law, make or alter such regulations, except as to the place of choosing Senators. Const, art. I, § 4. . . .The power of the State in this particular is . . . supreme until Congress acts.

The Amendment did not add to the privileges and immunities of a citizen. It simply furnished an additional guaranty for the protection of such as he already had. [Emphasis added—AU.] No new voters were necessarily made by it. Indirectly it may have had that effect, because it may have increased the number of citizens entitled to suffrage under the Constitution and laws of the States, but it operates for this purpose, if at all, through the States and the state laws. . .

It is clear . . . that the Constitution has not added the right of suffrage to the privileges and immunities of citizenship as they existed at the time it was adopted. This makes it proper to inquire whether suffrage was coextensive with the citizenship of the States at the time of its adoption. If it was, then it may with force be argued that suffrage was one of the rights which belonged to citizenship. . . .

. . .Upon an examination of [the original thirteen state] Constitutions we find that in no State were all citizens permitted to vote. Each State determined for itself who should have that power. [Here followed the suffrage requirements of the first thirteen states.—AU.]

In this condition of the law in respect to suffrage in the several states, it cannot for a moment be doubted that if it had been intended to make all citizens of the United States voters, the framers of the constitution would not have left it to implication. So important a change in the condition of citizenship as it actually existed, if intended, would have been expressly declared. But if further proof is necessary to show that no such change was intended, it can easily be found both in and out of the Constitution. By Article IV, § 2, it is provided that "The citizens of each State shall be entitled to all the privileges and immunities of citizens in the several States." If suffrage is necessarily a part of citizenship, then the citizens of each State must be entitled to vote in the several States precisely as their citizens are. This is more than asserting that they may change their residence and become citizens of the State and thus be voters.

It goes to the extent of insisting that while retaining their original citizenship they may vote in any State. This, we think, has never been claimed. And again, by the very terms of the Amendment we have been considering (the Fourteenth), "Representatives shall be apportioned among the several States according to their respective numbers, counting the whole number of persons in each State, excluding Indians not taxed. But when the right to vote at any election for the choice of electors for President and Vice-President of the United States, representatives in Congress, the executive and judicial officers of a State, or the members of the Legislature thereof, is denied to any of the male inhabitants of such State, being twenty-one years of age and citizens of the United States, or in any way abridged, except for participation in rebellion, or other crimes, the basis of representation therein shall be reduced in the proportion which the number of such male citizens shall bear to the whole number of male citizens twenty-one years of age in such State." Why this, if it was not in the power of the Legislature to deny the right of suffrage to some male inhabitants? ... Women and children are, as we have seen, "persons." They are counted in the enumeration upon which the appropriation is to be made, but if they were necessarily voters because of their citizenship unless clearly excluded, why inflict the penalty for the exclusion of males alone? Clearly, no such form of words would have been selected to express the idea here indicated, if suffrage was the absolute right of all citizens.

And still again; after the adoption of the Fourteenth Amendment, it was deemed necessary to adopt a fifteenth, as follows: "The right of citizens of the United States to vote shall not be denied or abridged by the United States, or by any State, on account of race, color or previous condition of servitude." The Fourteenth Amendment had already provided that no State should make or enforce any law which should abridge the privileges or immunities of citizens of the United States. If suffrage was one of these privileges or immunities, why amend the Constitution to prevent its being denied on account of race, etc.? ...

It is true that the United States guaranties to every State a republican form of a government. Const, art. IV, § 4. Also ... no State can pass a bill of attainder, Const, art. I, § 10, and no person can be deprived of life, liberty or property without due process of law. Const, amend. V.

All these several provisions of the Constitution must be construed in connection with the other parts of the instrument, and in the light of the surrounding circumstances. The guaranty is of a republican form of government. No particular government or form of government ... is designated as republican. Here, as in other parts of the instrument, we are compelled to resort elsewhere to ascertain what was intended.

The guaranty necessarily implies a duty on the part of the States themselves to provide such a government. All the States had governments when the Constitution was adopted. In all, the people participated to some extent, through their representatives elected in the manner specially provided. These governments the Constitution did not change. They were accepted precisely as they were, and it is, therefore, to be presumed that they were such as it was the duty of the States to provide. Thus we have unmistakable evidence of what was republican in form, within the meaning of that term as employed in the Constitution.

As has been seen, all the citizens of the States were not invested with the right of suffrage. In all, save perhaps New Jersey, this right was only bestowed upon men and not upon all of them. Under these circumstances it is certainly now too late to contend that a government is not republican, within the meaning of this guaranty in the Constitution, because women are not made voters.

The same may be said of the other provisions just quoted. Women were excluded from suffrage in nearly all the States by the express provision of their Constitution and laws. If that had been equivalent to a bill of attainder, certainly its abrogation would not have been left to implication. Nothing less than express language would have been employed to effect so radical a change. So, also, of the Amendment which declares that no person shall be deprived of life, liberty or property without due process of law, adopted as it was as early as 1791. If suffrage was intended to be included within its obligations language better adapted to express that intent would most certainly have been employed. The right of suffrage, when granted, will be protected. He who has it can only be deprived of it by due process of law, but in order to claim protection he must first show that he has the right.

But we have already sufficiently considered the proof found upon the inside of the Constitution. That upon the outside is equally effective. The Constitution was submitted to the States for adoption in 1787, and was ratified by nine States in 1790. Vermont was the first new State admitted to the union, and it came in under a Constitution which conferred the right of suffrage only upon men of the full age of twenty-one years, having resided in the State for the space of one whole year next before the election, and who were of quiet and peaceable behavior. This was in 1791. [The Court gave two more, similar examples.—AU.] . . .No new State has ever been admitted to the Union which has conferred the right of suffrage upon women, and this has never been considered a valid objection to her admission. . . . Since then the governments of the insurgent States have been reorganized under a requirement that before their representatives could be admitted to seats in Congress they must have adopted new Constitutions, republican in form. In no one of these Constitutions was suffrage conferred upon women, and yet the States have all been restored to their original position as States in the Union.

Besides this, citizenship has not in all cases been made a condition precedent to the enjoyment of the right of suffrage. Thus, in Missouri, persons of foreign birth, who have declared their intention to become citizens of the United States, may under certain circumstances vote. The same provision is to be found in the Constitutions of Alabama, Arkansas, Florida, Georgia, Indiana, Kansas, Minnesota and Texas.

Certainly, if the courts can consider any question settled, this is one. For nearly ninety years the people have acted upon the idea that the constitution, when it conferred citizenship, did not necessarily confer the right of suffrage. If uniform practice, long continued, can settle the construction of so important an instrument as the Constitution of the United States confessedly is, most certainly it has been done here. Our province is to decide what the law is, not to declare what it should be.

. . . If the law is wrong, it ought to be changed; but the power for that is not with us. The arguments addressed to us bearing upon such a view of the subject may, perhaps, be sufficient to induce those having the power to make the alteration but they ought not to be permitted to influence our judgment in determining the present rights of the parties now litigating before us. Nor argument as to woman's need of suffrage can be considered. We can only act upon her rights as they exist. It is not for us to look at the hardship of withholding. Our duty is at an end if we can find it is within the power of a State to withhold.

Being unanimously of the opinion that the Constitution of the United States does not confer the right of suffrage upon anyone, and that the Constitutions and laws of the several States which commit that important trust to men alone are not necessarily void, we *Affirm* the judgment of the court below.

Case Questions

1. Does it seem puzzling that persons not allowed to vote could be considered "citizens"? Are American-born persons under the age of 18 considered "citizens"?

2. What portion of the "citizen" privileges cited by Justice Waite are what could be called economic, as distinguished from political or legal, rights? Is a certain level of economic participation implied by the word *citizen*? If there is no intrinsic connection between citizenship and voting, why is it the custom that "republican governments" say "citizens" in contexts where other kinds of government say "subjects"?

3. In the light of the italicized statement about the privileges or immunities clause, can one conclude that the Court believed that the clause added nothing to the Constitution? (N.B. the phrase "additional guaranty.")

4. The members of the Court say that their "province is to decide what the law is, not to declare what it should be." Do they always follow this maxim? Should they? Should the words of the Constitution always mean what they meant to people in 1790? Always mean what the authors of the words intended?

CASE NOTE

The Supreme Court's rejection of the Minors' privileges or immunities clause argument in this case had two decisive effects on the women's movement. First, the Court's emphatic denial that the privileges or immunities clause added any new civil rights to the Constitution motivated women's rights litigants to turn their attention to other clauses of the Constitution in subsequent cases. Second, this decision made it clear that an additional constitutional amendment would be required if women were ever to gain nationwide suffrage at a single stroke. Litigation efforts on the basis of the existing Constitution offered no hope for the suffragists. Within three years, the eventual Nineteenth Amendment was introduced into Congress for the first time by Senator Aaron Sargent of California.[18] It was to be 42 years before that amendment obtained ratification.

WOMEN AND MODERN CITIZENSHIP, PART ONE: THE VOTE BY CONSTITUTIONAL AMENDMENT

While most books on constitutional law do not discuss the political process by which formal constitutional amendments are obtained, a discussion of women's constitutional rights would be incomplete without the story of the successful battle for the Nineteenth Amendment. That account has meaning not only because it fills in the picture of the costs of Virginia Minor's failure at the Supreme Court but also because a second constitutional amendment to expand the legal rights of women came within inches of ratification in the late twentieth century. Today, if women's equal rights advocates begin to lose consistently in the halls of the Supreme Court, they will have no choice but to renew their political campaign for the Equal Rights Amendment (ERA). It is possible that women today will find it necessary to follow the lessons of those who in the past labored for decades to gain in the Constitution's own words what one of their allies failed to gain by judicial interpretation.

In the aftermath of the Minors' failure at the Supreme Court, it was not immediately obvious to the suffragists that amending the national Constitution was the surest route to victory. At that time there were two nationwide suffragist organizations: the American Woman Suffrage Association, led by Susan B. Anthony and Elizabeth Cady Stanton, and the National Woman Suffrage Association, led by Lucy Stone and Julia Ward Howe. The former lobbied Congress steadily from 1878 to 1893 for passage of what came to be known as the Anthony Amendment.[19] The latter, for decades, focused its efforts on persuading the states, on a one-by-one basis, to grant women the vote. The suffragists' variegated and often uncoordinated efforts were summed up by one of the veterans of the campaign as follows:

> To get the word "male" in effect out of the Constitution cost the women of the country fifty-two years of pauseless campaign. . . . During that time they were forced to conduct 56 campaigns of referenda to male voters; 480 campaigns to get [state] legislatures to submit suffrage amendments to voters; 47 campaigns to get state constitutional conventions to write woman suffrage into state constitutions; 277 campaigns to get state party conventions to include woman suffrage planks; 30 campaigns to get presidential party conventions to adopt woman suffrage planks in party platforms; and 19 campaigns with 19 successive Congresses.[20]

In short, it was a long and arduous struggle, in which millions of dollars and millions of hours of labor were expended on many fronts: in political organizing, propagandizing, petitioning, speech making, parading, lobbying, and picketing. The story includes a cast ranging from prominent socialites to immigrant factory workers, former slaves, and their daughters. Before the struggle ended, it was also to include mob violence, jail sentences, hunger strikes in jail accompanied by brutal forced feedings, and legislative votes so close that partisans were carried in on stretchers.[21]

In 1893 the two suffragist armies decided to combine forces into the National American Woman Suffrage Association (NAWSA). Despite the protestations of Susan B. Anthony, the NAWSA decided to de-emphasize the lobbying effort for a constitutional amendment. As a result of this decision, the amendment stopped receiving favorable committee reports in Congress in 1893, and after 1896 it did not even manage to get out of committee for a floor vote. The amendment remained a dead issue until it was stirred back into life by a new women's suffrage group, the Congressional Union for Woman Suffrage, that formed under the leadership of Alice Paul in 1913.

One factor that weakened the suffrage movement was its exclusiveness. The breach between the white feminists and the abolitionists created by the controversy over the Fourteenth Amendment widened and intensified. For the rest of her life, Stanton made public references to "Sambo" and unfavorably compared the status of American women with the enfranchisement of "Africans, Chinese, and all the ignorant foreigners the moment they touch our shores."[22]

Black women refused to allow this racist rhetoric to keep them out of the struggle. They were active on their own, often at the price of opposition and condescension from the African-American press. The Chicago-based Negro Fellowship League, under the leadership of Ida B. Wells-Barnett, played a major role in the successful campaign in Illinois. But at the 1913 suffrage parade in Washington, D.C. (described below in the paragraph on 1913–1915), Wells-Barnett and her group were relegated to the rear of the march; when her protest against this "jim-crowing" failed, she joined the Illinois delegation at the head.[23]

By the twentieth century, class exclusiveness, too, limited the feminist constituency. Nineteenth-century leaders Stanton, Anthony, and their colleagues, women from privileged backgrounds, had nevertheless welcomed trade union women as allies. The second generation of leaders, women like Carrie Chapman Catt and Rachel Foster Avery, rebuffed working-class women.[24]

During the period from 1893 to 1913, the NAWSA exhausted its energies in hundreds of state campaigns. By 1910 it had won only four victories: Wyoming (in 1890) and Utah (in 1896) each entered the Union retaining the women's suffrage they had adopted while still territories, and Colorado (in 1893) and Idaho (in 1896) each adopted women's suffrage in state referenda. All four states were sparsely populated and lacked significant political impact.

Toward the end of this period, from 1910 to 1913, NAWSA efforts did take on some added vigor. The association was stimulated by newly forming suffrage groups led by women who had participated in the more militant British suffragist movement; these groups introduced more flamboyant tactics into the American campaign. This period added outdoor ("protest") meetings, street parades, automobile tours, and trolley tours to the women's movement. Also, the new groups introduced the political organizing tactics often associated with political party machines: the keeping of file cards on all voters on a precinct basis, careful voter canvassing, and the appointment of thousands of election district "captains" whose job it was to mobilize voters in their own districts.[25] With this new style of campaigning, by 1911 the NAWSA managed to win victories in state referenda in two western states: Washington and California. In 1912, they brought in three more victories, in Arizona, Kansas, and Oregon.

Although by this time women had the vote in nine states with a total of 45 electoral votes, a discouraging pattern was emerging. Women were winning in some state referenda, but they were losing in many others. And the ones in which they lost were the more industrialized, more populated, more politically powerful states of the Midwest and East. Liquor interests, fearing that women would favor Prohibition, and other conservative business interests funded massive antisuffrage campaigns, which included the plying of legislators with liquor and blatant frauds at the ballot box. It was apparent by 1913 that the bigger and more important the state, the more impressive the antisuffrage campaign would be. This pattern continued through 1915. Out of a total of 11 state referenda, in 1914 and 1915, the suffragists managed to win only in the two least populated states, Montana and Nevada. They lost both of the Dakotas, Nebraska, Missouri, Ohio, New York, Pennsylvania, New Jersey, and Massachusetts.[26]

The period 1913–1915, however, brought a number of crucial changes to the American women's suffrage effort. The first was the rise to prominence of Alice Paul. Ms. Paul, who had worked in the militant British suffrage movement, returned to the United States in 1910 and began chairing the NAWSA's Congressional Committee in 1912. For her first major contribution, Ms. Paul organized a suffrage parade; 5,000 women marched through Washington, D.C., on the day before Woodrow Wilson's inauguration in 1913. The paraders were physically harassed by crowds of hostile onlookers, and for some reason the police ignored the problem. Along parts of the route full-scale rioting broke out, and the National Guard was finally called in to restore order.[27] This incident produced tremendous publicity and stimulated a variety of pro-suffrage pilgrimages to Washington. In April 1913, Ms. Paul organized the Congressional Union (soon to become the Women's Party), which aimed at a single-minded campaign for a constitutional amendment. Within the year, Ms. Paul left the NAWSA, whose leadership still felt that the time was not ripe for an all-out drive for the federal amendment.[28]

The next two important changes involved the leadership of the NAWSA. In late 1914 it received $2 million in the form of a personal bequest from Miriam F. Leslie (a wealthy publisher) to Carrie Chapman Catt with instructions that the money be used "to the furtherance of the cause of woman suffrage."[29] Then, in December 1915, Ms. Catt was drafted for the presidency of the NAWSA. The combination of Ms. Catt's organizational genius, the NAWSA's newfound prosperity, the militant tactics of the Congressional Union, and the undeniably major role that women played in the World War I economy eventually proved too powerful even for the wealthy anti-suffrage forces.

The lobbying pressures of the Congressional Union brought the suffrage amendment to the floor of Congress for the first time since 1896. It was voted down in the Senate in March 1914 and in the House in January 1915.[30] Whereas the Congressional Union took the approach of castigating "the party in power" for failure to pass the amendment, the NAWSA developed close ties to President Wilson, inviting him to their 1916 convention, where their leaders believed he was converted to their cause. At that same convention, Carrie Chapman Catt propounded a secret plan for a concerted six-year drive for the federal amendment.[31] It succeeded in four.

The drama of the long quest for women's suffrage reached its climax in the 13-month stretch from January 1917 through January 1918. In January 1917, Alice Paul's organization, now called the Women's Party, initiated a new tactic: it stationed silent picketers outside the White House, as a constant reminder of women's demands. The picket signs and banners carried messages that grew more strident as the United States entered World War I. When American "patriots" saw such statements as "Democracy Should Begin at Home" and derogatory references to "Kaiser Wilson," fights broke out between onlookers and the women picketers. Beginning in June, the police started arresting picketers for obstructing the sidewalks. Their attackers were never arrested. At their trials the women refused to address the charges against them; they either stood mute or delivered speeches for the suffrage cause. They also refused to pay fines, claiming that such payment would imply admission of guilt. When given the "option," they chose jail instead of paying fines. One spokeswoman described their feelings as follows: "As long as the government and the representatives of the government prefer to send women to jail on petty and technical charges, we will go to jail. Persecution has always advanced the cause of justice."[32] The earliest arrestees were dismissed without jail sentences. As the picketing and violence continued, jail sentences of a few days, then a few weeks, and finally six months were imposed. By the time the first session of Congress ended, a total of 218 women from 26 states had been arrested, and 97 women had gone to prison.[33]

Once in prison, these women drew added attention to their cause by demanding to be treated as political prisoners rather than as common criminals. To dramatize this complaint, the women went on hunger strikes. Police administrators resorted to brutal forced feedings. This sequence of events drew continuous and nationwide media attention. The forced feedings, in particular, produced newspaper stories replete with gory details. The public outcry grew so intense that the Wilson administration ordered the unconditional release of all picketers on November 27 and 28.[34]

Although it publicly disavowed any connection with the militant picketers, the NAWSA took advantage of the sympathetic atmosphere generated by the intense publicity about the women prisoners. The NAWSA membership campaigned tirelessly all around the country, buttonholing legislators, canvassing precincts, petitioning congressmen. Major political successes finally began to accumulate. In 1917 the first congresswoman took her seat, Jeannette Rankin of Montana. In New York, women finally won a referendum for suffrage in a heavily populated eastern state. Six state legislatures avoided the difficulties of a referendum by taking advantage of Article II, section 1, of the Constitution, which states that presidential electors are to be appointed "in such manner as the Legislature thereof may direct." Thus North Dakota, Ohio, Indiana, Rhode Island, Nebraska, and Michigan joined Illinois (which had done so in 1913) in granting women presidential suffrage. And the Arkansas state legislature, in March 1917, granted women the primary vote, which in the then one-party Democratic South was as meaningful as the vote in northern general elections.[35]

In December 1917, just two weeks after the picketers had been released from jail, the House of Representatives set January 10, 1918, as the date for voting on the suffrage amendment. The drama of that vote was unsurpassed by any in American history. Women in the galleries watched anxiously as four of the determining votes for the amendment came in literally from sickbeds. Congressman T. W. Sims of Tennessee had a broken arm and shoulder but refused to have them set, lest he miss the crucial vote. Despite the excruciating pain, he stayed on to the end, trying to persuade those colleagues who were ambivalent. The Republican House Leader, James Mann of Illinois, deathly pale and barely able to stand, came to the session straight from a six-month stint in the hospital. Representative Robert Crosser of Ohio also came in ill. And Henry Barnhart of Indiana was actually carried in on a stretcher for the last roll call. One congressman, Frederick Hicks of New York, even left his wife's deathbed to come to Washington for the vote. Mrs. Hicks, a dedicated suffragist, died just before he left; after the vote, he returned home for her funeral. The amendment passed the House with no votes to spare; it attained exactly the number needed for the required two-thirds majority, 274–136.[36]

Although the amendment just missed the needed two-thirds majority in the Senate that year, and although in 1918 there were more pickets, more jailings, and more hunger strikes,[37] the tide had turned. The later stages of victory were somewhat anticlimactic. Steady campaigning by the NAWSA and their allies increased the prosuffrage majority in the Senate to within one vote of two thirds in the February 1919 (lame-duck) session. The newly elected 66th Congress finally passed the amendment in May 1919 by exactly two-thirds in the Senate and by 304–89 in the House.[38] Ratification in three-fourths of the state legislatures came remarkably quickly. By August 26, 1920, American women had obtained the vote as a matter of explicit constitutional right.

LIBERTY OF CONTRACT: *LOCHNER V. NEW YORK* (1905)

Women's efforts to attain equal legal treatment via the privileges or immunities clause of the Fourteenth Amendment, as explained above, did not succeed. The suffragists turned their attention eventually to amending the Constitution to gain suffrage, but long before they obtained the Nineteenth Amendment, women again came to the attention of the Supreme Court in a number of cases concerning workplace reform legislation challenged under the Fourteenth Amendment's due process clause.

As they had for the butchers in Louisiana in 1873, corporate lawyers continued for years to hammer away at state economic regulations, using the Fourteenth Amendment as their principal weapon. The most effective section of that weapon proved to be the due process clause, interpreted so as to limit the substance of legislation (not just the procedures by which the legislation was adopted or enforced). Toward the end of the nineteenth century, the Court turned away from the deferential attitude toward state legislative authority that had characterized the *Slaughterhouse Cases* and started declaring various pieces of state economic legislation unconstitutional on the grounds that they clashed with the due process clause. The first apogee of this new trend was reached in *Lochner v. New York*.[39] The Court saw itself in this era as protecting the citizen rights of the individual against government power; the civil "rights" that they defended were economic or "property" rights. The particular economic "right" receiving attention in *Lochner* is one that the Court dubbed "freedom of contract."

Ironically, this first protection of citizen rights, in one sense, evolved into an inhibition of women's rights, in a second sense. As indicated in the discussion of the various meanings of "women's rights" in the Introduction, "rights" can refer to a "thou-shalt-not-infringe" statement to the legislature, but the term can also refer to a "thou-may-provide-special-protection-for" statement to the legislature. The economic rights (in the thou-shalt-not-sense) of the individual that the Supreme Court enshrined in *Lochner v. New York* eventually (in *Adkins v. Children's Hospital* [1923]) were applied so as to undercut women's right to be accorded special protection in economics legislation.

This abstract discussion of concepts of rights takes on more concrete meaning in the actual circumstances of the *Lochner* case. As a public welfare measure, the state of New York had enacted a statute that prohibited bakery employees from working any longer than a 10-hour day or a 60-hour week. While many people might think of this statute in terms of the public's (or legislature's) "right" to protect its health by regulating labor conditions in food-producing establishments, and while some might conceptualize it in terms of the right of the economically powerless to be protected by special legislation, the Supreme Court viewed it differently. They focused on the individual's right to be "free" (in the sense of unrestrained by regulatory legislation) in deciding how long to employ, or be employed by, another individual. In other words, while the Supreme Court majority saw themselves as guarding the working man's "right" to work as long as he "wanted," many people viewed the Court as destroying the working man's "right" to protect himself, by legislation, against demands from his employer that he work cruelly long hours. The Supreme Court was reading the due process clause as though it commanded the following to the legislature: thou shalt not interfere with the right of freedom of contract on the mere pretext that workers need protection against their bosses. Only special circumstances, such as widespread agreement that particular forms of labor are extraordinarily unhealthy (e.g., coal mining), could justify interference with liberty of contract.

LOCHNER V. NEW YORK
198 U.S. 45 (1905)

MR. JUSTICE PECKHAM delivered the opinion of the Court:

The indictment, it will be seen, charges that the plaintiff in error violated . . . the labor law of the State of New York, in that he wrongfully and unlawfully required and permitted an employee working for him to work more than sixty hours in one week.... It is assumed that the word ["required"] means nothing more than the requirement arising from voluntary contract for such labor in excess of the number of hours specified in the statute....

The employee may desire to earn the extra money, which would arise from his working more than the prescribed time, but this statute forbids the employer from permitting the employee to earn it.

The statute necessarily interferes with the right of contract between the employer and employees, concerning the number of hours in which the latter may labor in the bakery of the employer. The general right to make a contract in relation to his business is part of the liberty of the individual protected by the Fourteenth Amendment of the Federal Constitution. *Allgeyer v. Louisiana*, 165 U.S. 578. Under that provision no State can deprive any person of life, liberty or property without due process of law. The right to purchase or to sell labor is part of the liberty protected by this amendment, unless there are circumstances which exclude the right. There are, however, certain powers, existing in the sovereignty of each State in the Union, somewhat vaguely termed police powers, the exact description and limitation of which have not been attempted by the courts. Those powers, broadly stated and without, at present, any attempt at a more specific limitation, relate to the safety, health, morals and general welfare of the public. Both property and liberty are held on such reasonable conditions as may be imposed by the governing power of the State in the exercise of those powers, and with such conditions the Fourteenth Amendment was not designed to interfere, *Mugler v. Kansas*, 123 U.S. 623; *In re Kemmler*, 136 U.S. 436; *Crowley v. Christensen*, 137 U.S. 624.

The State, therefore, has power to prevent the individual from making certain kinds of contracts, and in regard to them the Federal Constitution offers no protection. If the contract be one which the State, in the legitimate exercise of its police power, has the right to prohibit, it is not prevented from prohibiting it by the Fourteenth Amendment. Contracts in violation of a statute, either of the Federal or state government, or a contract to let one's property for immoral purposes, or to do any other unlawful act, could obtain no protection from the Federal Constitution, as coming under the liberty of person or of free contract.... [W]hen the State, by its legislature, in the assumed exercise of its police powers, has passed an act which seriously limits the right to labor or the right of contract ... it becomes of great importance to determine which shall prevail—the right of the individual to labor for such time as he may choose, or the right of the State to prevent the individual from laboring or from entering into any contract to labor beyond a certain time prescribed by the State.

This court has recognized the existence and upheld the exercise of the police powers of the States in many cases which might fairly be considered as border ones. . . . Among the later cases where the state law has been upheld by this court is that of *Holden v. Hardy,* 169 U.S. 366. A . . . Utah act limiting the employment of workmen in all underground mines or workings, to eight hours per day. . . was held a valid exercise of the police powers of the State. . . . It was held that the kind of employment, mining, smelting, etc., and the character of the employees in such kinds of labor, were such as to make it reasonable and proper for the State to interfere to prevent the employees from being constrained by the rules laid down by the proprietors in regard to labor. . . . There is nothing in *Holden v. Hardy* which covers the case now before us.

It must, of course, be conceded that there is a limit to the valid exercise of the police power. . . . Otherwise the Fourteenth Amendment would have no efficacy and the legislatures of the States would have unbounded power, and it would be enough to say that any piece of legislation was enacted to conserve the morals, the health or the safety of the people; such legislation would be valid, no matter how absolutely without foundation the claim might be. The claim of the police power would be a mere pretext—become another and delusive name for the supreme sovereignty of the State to be exercised free from constitutional restraint. . . . [T]he question necessarily arises: Is this a fair, reasonable and appropriate exercise of the police power of the State, or is it an unreasonable, unnecessary and arbitrary interference with the right of the individual to his personal liberty or to enter into those contracts in relation to labor which may seem to him appropriate or necessary for the support of himself and his family? . . .

This is not a question of substituting the judgment of the court for that of the legislature. If the act be within the power of the State it is valid, although the judgment of the court might be totally opposed to the enactment of such a law. But the question would still remain: Is it within the police power of the State?, and that question must be answered by the court.

The question whether this act is valid as a labor law, pure and simple, may be dismissed in a few words. There is no reasonable ground for interfering with the liberty of person or the right of free contract, by determining the hours of labor, in the occupation of a baker. There is no contention that bakers as a class are not equal in intelligence and capacity to men in other trades or manual occupations, or that they are not able to assert their rights and care for themselves without the protecting arm of the State, interfering with their independence of judgment and of action. They are in no sense wards of the State. Viewed in the light of a purely labor law, with no reference whatever to the question of health, we think that a law like the one before us involves neither the safety, the morals nor the welfare of the public, and that the interest of the public is not in the slightest degree affected by such an act. The law must be upheld, if at all, as a law pertaining to the health of the individual engaged in the occupation of a baker. It does not affect any other portion of the public than those who are engaged in that occupation. Clean and wholesome bread does not depend upon whether the baker works but ten hours per day or only sixty hours a week....

It is a question of which of two powers or rights shall prevail—the power of the State to legislate or the right of the individual to liberty of person and freedom of contract. The mere assertion that the subject relates though but in a remote degree to the public health does not necessarily render the enactment valid. The act must have a more direct relation, as a means to an end, and the end itself must be appropriate and legitimate, before an act can be held to be valid which interferes with the general right of an individual to be free ... in his power to contract in relation to his own labor.

* * *

We think the limit of the police power has been reached and passed in this case. There is, in our judgment, no reasonable foundation for holding this to be necessary or appropriate as a health law to safeguard the public health or the health of the individuals who are following the trade of a baker. If this statute be valid .... there would seem to be no length to which legislation of this nature might not go....

We think that there can be no fair doubt that the trade of a baker, in and of itself, is not an unhealthy one to that degree which would authorize the legislature to interfere with the right to labor, and with the right of free contract on the part of the individual.... In looking through statistics regarding all trades and occupations, it may be true that the trade of a baker does not appear to be as healthy as some other trades, and is also vastly more healthy than still others.... There must be more than the mere fact of the possible existence of some small amount of unhealthiness to warrant legislative interference with liberty.... [A]lmost any kind of business, would all come under the power of the legislature, on this assumption. No trade, no occupation, no mode of earning one's living, could escape this all-pervading power, and the acts of the legislature in limiting the hours of labor in all employments would be valid, although such limitation might seriously cripple the ability of the laborer to support himself and his family. . . .

It is also urged, pursuing the same line of argument, that it is to the interest of the State that its population should be strong and robust, and therefore any legislation which may be said to tend to make people healthy must be valid as health laws, enacted under the police power. If this be a valid argument and a justification for this kind of legislation, it follows that the protection of the Federal Constitution from undue interference with liberty of person and freedom of contract is visionary. . . . Not only the hours of employees, but the hours of employers, could be regulated, and doctors, lawyers, scientists, all professional men, as well as athletes and artisans, could be forbidden to fatigue their brains and bodies by prolonged hours of exercise, lest the fighting strength of the State be impaired. We mention these extreme cases because the contention is extreme. We do not believe in the soundness of the views which uphold this law. On the contrary, we think that such a law as this, although passed in the assumed exercise of the police power, and as relating to the public health, or the health of the employees named, is not within that power, and is invalid. The act is not, within any fair meaning of the term, a health law, but is an illegal interference with the rights of individuals, both employers and employees, to make contracts regarding labor upon such terms as they may think best, or which they may agree upon with the other parties to such contracts. Statutes of the nature of that under review, limiting the hours in which grown and intelligent men may labor to earn their living, are mere meddlesome interferences with the rights of the individual, and they are not saved from condemnation by the claim that they are passed in the exercise of the police power and upon the subject of the health of the individual whose rights are interfered with, unless there be some fair ground, reasonable in and of itself, to say that there is material danger to the public health or to the health of the employees, if the hours of labor are not curtailed. If this be not clearly the case the individuals ... are under the protection of the Federal Constitution. . . . A prohibition to enter into any contract of labor in a bakery for more than a certain number of hours a week, is, in our judgment, so wholly beside the matter of a proper, reasonable and fair provision, as to run counter to that liberty of person and of free contract provided for in the Federal Constitution.

It was further urged on the argument that restricting the hours of labor in the case of bakers was valid because it tended to cleanliness on the part of the workers, as a man was more apt to be cleanly when not overworked, and if cleanly then his "output" was also more likely to be so.... We do not admit the reasoning to be sufficient to justify the claimed right of such interference. The State in that case would assume the position of a supervisor, or *pater familias*, over every act of the individual... In our judgment it is not possible in fact to discover the connection between the number of hours a baker may work in the bakery and the healthful quality of the bread made by the workman. The connection, if any exists, is too shadowy and thin to build any argument for the interference of the legislature. If the man works ten hours a day it is all right, but if ten and a half or eleven his health is in danger and his bread may be unhealthful, and, therefore, he shall not be permitted to do it. This, we think, is unreasonable and entirely arbitrary. When assertions such as we have adverted to become necessary in order to give, if possible, a plausible foundation for the contention that the law is a "health law," it gives rise to at least a suspicion that there was some other motive dominating the legislature than the purpose to subserve the public health or welfare.

This interference on the part of the legislatures of the several States with the ordinary trades and occupations of the people seems to be on the increase....

It is impossible for us to shut our eyes to the fact that many of the laws of this character, while passed under what is claimed to be the police power for the purpose of protecting the public health or welfare, are, in reality, passed from other motives. We are justified in saying so when, from the character of the law and the subject upon which it legislates, it is apparent that the public health or welfare bears but the most remote relation to the law. The purpose of a statute must be determined from the natural and legal effect of the language employed; and whether it is or is not repugnant to the Constitution of the United States must be determined from the natural effect of such statutes when put into operation, and not from their proclaimed purpose. *Minnesota v. Barber,* 136 U.S. 313; *Brimmer v. Rebman,* 138 U.S. 78.

It is manifest to us that the limitation of the hours of labor as provided for... has no such direct relation to and no such substantial effect upon the health of the employee, as to justify us in regarding the section as really a health law. It seems to us that the real object and purpose were simply to regulate the hours of labor between the master and his employees. Under such circumstances the freedom of master and employee to contract with each other in relation to their employment, and in defining the same, cannot be prohibited or interfered with, without violating the Federal Constitution.

* * *

Reversed.

MR. JUSTICE HARLAN, with whom MR. JUSTICE WHITE and MR. JUSTICE DAY concurred, dissenting:

While this court has not attempted to mark the precise boundaries of what is called the police power of the State, the existence of the power has been uniformly recognized, both by the Federal and state courts.

All the cases agree that this power extends at least to the protection of the lives, the health and the safety of the public against the injurious exercise by any citizen of his own rights. . . . .

[This court said] in *Barbier v. Connolly,* 113 U.S. 27: "But neither the [14th] Amendment—broad and comprehensive as it is—nor any other Amendment was designed to interfere with the power of the State, sometimes termed its police power, to prescribe regulations to promote the health, peace, morals, education, and good order of the people."

Speaking generally, the State in the exercise of its powers may not unduly interfere with the right of the citizen to enter into contracts that may be necessary and essential in the enjoyment of the inherent rights belonging to everyone, among which rights is the right "to be free in the enjoyment of all his faculties; to be free to use them in all lawful ways; to live and work where he will; to earn his livelihood by any lawful calling; to pursue any livelihood or avocation." This was declared in *Allgeyer v. Louisiana,* 165 U.S. 578, 589. But in the same case it was conceded that the right to contract in relation to persons and property or to do business, within a State, may be "regulated and sometimes prohibited, when the contracts or business conflict with the policy of the State as contained in its statutes" (p. 591).

So, as said in *Holden v. Hardy,* 169 U.S. 366, 391:

This right of contract, however, is itself subject to certain limitations which the State may lawfully impose in the exercise of its police powers. While this power is inherent in all governments, it has doubtless been greatly expanded in its application during the past century, owing to an enormous increase in the number of occupations which are dangerous, or so far detrimental to the health of the employees as to demand special precautions for their well-being and protection, or the safety of adjacent property. . . . [T]he police power. . . may be lawfully resorted to for the purpose of preserving the public health, safety or morals, or the abatement of public nuisances, and a large discretion "is necessarily vested in the legislature to determine not only what the interests of the public require, but what measures are necessary for the protection of such interests." *Lawton v. Steele,* 152 U.S. 133, 136.

Referring to the limitations placed by the State upon the hours of workmen, the court in the same case said (p. 395): "These employments, when too long pursued, the legislature has judged to be detrimental to the health of the employees, and, so long as there are reasonable grounds for believing that this is so, its decision upon this subject cannot be reviewed by the Federal courts."

Granting then that there is a liberty of contract which cannot be violated even under the sanction of direct legislative enactment, but assuming, as according to settled law we may assume, that such liberty of contract is subject to such regulations as the State may reasonably prescribe for the common good and the well-being of society, what are the conditions under which the judiciary may declare such regulations to be in excess of legislative authority and void? Upon this point there is no room for dispute; for, the rule is universal that a legislative enactment, Federal or state, is never to be disregarded or held invalid unless it be, beyond question, plainly and palpably in excess of legislative power. In *Jacobson v. Massachusetts,* 197 U.S. 11, we said that the power of the courts to review legislative action in respect of a matter affecting the general welfare exists only "when that which the legislature has done comes within the rule that if a statute purporting to have been enacted to protect the public health, the public morals or the public safety, has no real or substantial relation to those objects, or is beyond all question, a plain, palpable invasion of rights secured by the fundamental law"—citing *Mugler v. Kansas,* 123 U.S. 623, 661; *Minnesota v. Barber,* 136 U.S. 313, 320; *Atkin v. Kansas,* 191 U.S. 207, 223. If there be doubt as to the validity of the statute, that doubt must therefore be resolved in favor of its validity, and the courts must keep their hands off, leaving the legislature to meet the responsibility for unwise legislation. If the end which the legislature seeks to accomplish be one to which its power extends, and if the means employed to that end, although not the wisest or best, and yet not plainly and palpably unauthorized by law, then the court cannot interfere. In other words, . . . the burden of proof. . . is upon those who assert it to be unconstitutional. *McCulloch v. Maryland,* 4 Wheat. 316, 421.

* * *

It is plain that this statute was enacted in order to protect the physical well-being of those who work in bakery and confectionery establishments. It may be that the statute had its origin, in part, in the belief that employers and employees in such establishments were not upon an equal footing, and that the necessities of the latter often compelled them to submit to such exactions as unduly taxed their strength. Be this as it may, the statute must be taken as expressing the belief to the people of New York that... labor in excess of sixty hours during a week in such establishments may endanger the health of those who thus labor. Whether or not this be wise legislation it is not the province of the court to inquire. Under our systems of government the courts are not concerned with the wisdom or policy of legislation. So that in determining the question of power to interfere with liberty of contract, the court may inquire whether the means devised by the State are germane to an end which may be lawfully accomplished and have a real or substantial relation to the protection of health.... I find it impossible, in view of common experience, to say that there is here no real or substantial relation between the means employed by the State and the end sought to be accomplished by its legislation. *Mugler v. Kansas*... Therefore I submit that this court will transcend its functions if it assumes to annul the statute of New York. It must be remembered that this statute... applies only to work in bakery and confectionery establishments, in which, as all know, the air constantly breathed by workmen is not as pure and healthful as that to be found in some other establishments or out of doors.

Professor Hirt in his treatise on the "Diseases of the Workers" has said:

The labor of the bakers is among the hardest and most laborious imaginable, because it has to be performed under conditions injurious to the health of those engaged in it. It... requires a great deal of physical exertion in an overheated workshop and during unreasonably long hours, [and the baker must].... perform the greater part of his work at night, thus depriving him of an opportunity to enjoy the necessary rest and sleep, a fact which is highly injurious to his health.

Another writer says: "The constant inhaling of flour dust causes inflammation of the lungs and of the bronchial tubes...." [Other scientific references were cited here.—AU.]

We judicially know that the question of the number of hours during which a workman should continuously labor has been, for a long period, and is yet, a subject of serious consideration among civilized peoples, and by those having special knowledge of the laws of health. Suppose the statute prohibited labor in bakery and confectionery establishments in excess of eighteen hours each day. No one, I take it, could dispute the power of the State to enact such a statute. But the statute before us does not embrace extreme or exceptional cases. It may be said to occupy a middle ground in respect of the hours of labor. What is the true ground for the State to take between legitimate protection, by legislation, of the public health and liberty of contract is not a question easily solved, nor one in respect of which there is or can be absolute certainty. . . .

* * *

. . .It is enough for the determination of this case, and it is enough for this court to know, that the question is one about which there is room for debate and for an honest difference of opinion. There are many reasons of a weighty, substantial character, based upon the experience of mankind, in support of the theory that, all things considered, more than ten hours' steady work each day, from week to week, in a bakery or confectionery establishment, may endanger the health, and shorten the lives of the workmen, thereby diminishing their physical and mental capacity to serve the State, and to provide for those dependent upon them.

If such reasons exist that ought to be the end of this case, for the State is not amenable to the judiciary, in respect of its legislative enactments, unless such enactments are plainly, palpably, beyond all questions, inconsistent with the Constitution of the United States. We are not to presume that the State of New York has acted in bad faith. Nor can we assume that its legislature acted without due deliberation, or that it did not determine this question upon the fullest attainable information, and for the common good. We cannot say that the State has acted without reason nor ought we to proceed upon the theory that its action is a mere sham. . .

. . .No evils arising from such legislation could be more far-reaching than those that might come to our system of government if the judiciary, abandoning the sphere assigned to it by the fundamental law, should enter the domain of legislation, and upon grounds merely of justice or reason or wisdom annul statutes that had received the sanction of the people's representatives. . . . *Atkin v. Kansas,* 191 U.S. 207, 223.

The judgment in my opinion should be affirmed.

MR. JUSTICE HOLMES dissenting:

I regret sincerely that I am unable to agree with the judgment in this case, and that I think it my duty to express my dissent.

> This case is decided upon an economic theory which a large part of the country does not entertain. If it were a question whether I agreed with that theory, I should desire to study it further and long before making up my mind. But I do not conceive that to be my duty, because I strongly believe that my agreement or disagreement has nothing to do with the right of a majority to embody their opinions in law. It is settled by various decisions of this court that state constitutions and state laws may regulate life in many ways which we as legislators might think as injudicious or if you like as tyrannical as this, and which equally with this interfere with the liberty to contract. Sunday laws and usury laws are ancient examples. A more modern one is the prohibition of lotteries. The liberty of the citizen to do as he likes so long as he does not interfere with the liberty of others to do the same, which has been a shibboleth for some well-known writers, is interfered with by school laws, by the Post Office, by every state or municipal institution which takes his money for purposes thought desirable, whether he likes it or not. The Fourteenth Amendment does not enact Mr. Herbert Spencer's *Social Statics*. The other day we sustained the Massachusetts vaccination law. *Jacobson v. Massachusetts,* 197 U.S. 11. . . . The decision sustaining an eight hour law for miners is still recent. *Holden v. Hardy,* 169 U.S. 366. Some of these laws embody convictions or prejudices which judges are likely to share. Some may not. But a constitution is not intended to embody a particular economic theory, whether of paternalism and the organic relation of the citizen to the State or of *laissez faire*.
>
> . . .Every opinion tends to become a law. I think that the word liberty in the Fourteenth Amendment is perverted when it is held to prevent the natural outcome of a dominant opinion, unless it can be said that a rational and fair man necessarily would admit that the statute proposed would infringe fundamental principles as they have been understood by the traditions of our people and our law. It does not need research to show that no such sweeping condemnation can be passed upon the statute before us. A reasonable man might think it a proper measure on the score of health. Men whom I certainly could not pronounce unreasonable would uphold it as a first installment of a general regulation of the hours of work. Whether in the latter aspect it would be open to the charge of inequality I think it unnecessary to discuss.

Case Questions

1. How convincing are the following assertions from the majority opinion?

    a. "This is not a question of substituting the judgment of the court for that of the legislature."

b. "Clean and wholesome bread does not depend upon whether the baker works but ten hours per day or sixty hours per week."

c. "There is . . . no reasonable foundation for holding this to be necessary or appropriate as a health law to safeguard the public health or the health of individuals who are following the trade of a baker."

2. The "police power" (general legislating power) of the state is, as the Court puts it, the power to promote "the safety, health, morals, and general welfare of the public." Even if one were to concede that this is not a "health" regulation, is it plausible to argue that maximum-hours labor regulations might have a "direct relation, as a means to an end," to one or more of the other goals within the police power?

3. The majority builds part of its case on the premise that bakers are "grown and intelligent men" and "able to assert their rights and care for themselves without the protecting arm of the State, interfering with their independence of judgment and of action. They are in no sense wards of the State." If the Supreme Court would permit 10-hour-day legislation for women workers only if the Court were convinced that women do need to be, in a sense, wards of the state, would you advise women to forgo the legislation rather than stoop to such an argument?

Protection for Women as Wedge into Liberty of Contract

Muller v. Oregon (1908)

In 1908, a young lawyer named Louis D. Brandeis (the same Brandeis who later became a Supreme Court justice) presented to the Court a radically new form of legal argument. The case of *Muller v. Oregon* involved a challenge to an Oregon maximum-hours statute forbidding the employment of women in factories, laundries, or other "mechanical establishments" for any longer than 10 hours a day. In response to the *Lochner* majority's assertion that it was not "reasonable" to believe that maximum-hours legislation promoted public health, Oregon's lawyer, Brandeis, devoted over 100 pages of his brief to subject matter that theretofore had not been viewed as part of a "legal" argument: a heavily statistical discussion of the relationship between hours of labor and the health and morals of women, including cross-cultural analysis of American and European factory legislation. (The actual research of gathering these statistics was performed by prominent women reformists Josephine Goldmark and Florence Kelly.) Only two pages of the brief followed the traditional pattern of explaining American legal precedents as they related to the case.

Brandeis's new approach was a huge success. He won a unanimous opinion in behalf of the statute's constitutionality. As the following excerpt reveals, however, the assumptions about the "nature" of women that brought about this "victory" may leave contemporary feminists more than a little uncomfortable.

MULLER V. OREGON
208 U.S. 412 (1908)

MR. JUSTICE BREWER wrote for the Court:

The single question is the constitutionality of the statute under which the defendant was convicted, so far as it affects the work of a female in a laundry. . . .

It is the law of Oregon that women, whether married or single, have equal contractual and personal rights with men. . . .

It thus appears that, putting to one side the elective franchise, in the matter of personal and contractual rights they stand on the same plane as the other sex. Their rights in these respects can no more be infringed than the equal rights of their brothers. We held in *Lochner v. New York,* 198 U.S. 45, that a law providing that no laborer shall be required or permitted to work in bakeries more than sixty hours in a week or ten hours in a day was not, as to men, a legitimate exercise of the police power of the state, but an unreasonable, unnecessary, and arbitrary interference with the right and liberty of the individual to contract in relation to his labor, and as such was in conflict with, and void under [the Fourteenth Amendment of] the Federal Constitution. That decision is invoked by plaintiff in error as decisive of the question before us. But this assumes that the difference between the sexes does not justify a different rule respecting a restriction of the hours of labor.

. . . It may not be amiss, in the present case, before examining the constitutional question, to notice the course of legislation, as well as expressions of opinion from other than judicial sources. In the brief filed by Mr. Louis D. Brandeis for the defendant in error is a very copious collection of all these matters, an epitome of which is found in the margin.

[Here followed a footnote by the Court citing sections of the statutory codes of 19 states that contained restrictions on women's labor and references to similar statutes in the laws of seven European nations. The court then concluded its summary of the brief as follows—AU.] . . . Then follow extracts for over ninety [governmental] reports . . . to the effect that long hours of labor are dangerous for women, primarily because of their special physical organization. The matter is discussed in these reports in different aspects, but all agree as to the danger.... Following them are extracts from similar reports discussing the general benefits of short hours from an economic aspect of the question.... Perhaps the general scope and character of all these reports may be summed up in what an inspector for Hanover says: 'The reasons for the reduction of the working day to ten hours—(a) the physical organization of women, (b) her maternal functions, (c) the rearing and education of her children, (d) the maintenance of the home—are all so important and so far-reaching that the need for such reduction need hardly be discussed.'

The legislation and opinions referred to in the margin may not be, technically speaking, authorities, and in them is little or no discussion of the constitutional question presented to us for determination, yet they are significant of a widespread belief that woman's physical structure, and the functions she performs in consequence thereof, justify special legislation restricting or qualifying the conditions under which she should be permitted to toil. Constitutional questions, it is true, are not settled by even a consensus of present public opinion, for it is the peculiar value of a written constitution that it places in unchanging form limitations upon legislative action, and thus gives a permanence and stability to popular government which otherwise would be lacking. At the same time, when a question of fact is debated and debatable, and the extent to which a special constitutional limitation goes is affected by the truth in respect to that fact, a widespread and long-continued belief concerning it is worthy of consideration. We take judicial cognizance of all matters of general knowledge.

It is undoubtedly true, as more than once declared by this court, that the general right to contract in relation to one's business is part of the liberty of the individual, protected by the Fourteenth Amendment to the Federal Constitution; yet it is equally well settled that this liberty is not absolute.... Without stopping to discuss at length the extent to which a state may act in this respect, we refer to the following cases in which the question has been considered: *Allgeyer v. Louisiana,* 165 U.S. 578, *Holden v. Hardy,* 169 U.S. 366, *Lochner v. New York.*

That woman's physical structure and the performance of maternal functions place her at a disadvantage in the struggle for subsistence is obvious. This is especially true when the burdens of motherhood are upon her. Even when they are not, by abundant testimony of the medical fraternity continuance for a long time on her feet at work, repeating this from day to day, tends to injurious effects upon the body, and, as healthy mothers are essential to vigorous offspring, the physical well-being of woman becomes an object of public interest and care in order to preserve the strength and vigor of the race.

Still again, history discloses the fact that woman has always been dependent upon man. He established his control at the outset by superior physical strength, and this control in various forms, with diminishing intensity, has continued to the present. As minors, though not to the same extent, she has been looked upon in the courts as needing especial care that her rights may be preserved. Education was long denied her, and while now the doors of the schoolroom are opened and her opportunities for acquiring knowledge are great, yet even with that and the consequent increase of capacity for business affairs it is still true that in the struggle for subsistence she is not an equal competitor with her brother. Though limitations upon personal and contractual rights may be removed by legislation, there is that in her disposition and habits of life which will operate against a full assertion of those rights. She will still be where some legislation to protect her seems necessary to secure a real equality of right. Doubtless there are individual exceptions, and there are many respects in which she has an advantage over him; but looking at it from the viewpoint of the effort to maintain an independent position in life, she is not upon an equality. Differentiated by these matters from the other sex, she is properly placed in a class by herself, and legislation designed for her protection may be sustained, even when like legislation is not necessary for men, and could not be sustained. It is impossible to close ones eyes to the fact that she still looks to her brother and depends upon him. Even though all restrictions on political, personal, and contractual rights were taken away, and she stood, so far as statutes are concerned, upon an absolutely equal plane with him, it would still be true that she is so constituted that she will rest upon and look to him for protection: that her physical structure and a proper discharge of her maternal functions—having in view not merely her own health, but the well-being of the race—justify legislation to protect her from the greed as well as the passion of man. The limitations which this statute places upon her contractual powers, upon her right to agree with her employer as to the time she shall labor, are not imposed solely for her benefit, but also largely for the benefit of all. Many words cannot make this plainer. The two sexes differ in structure of body, in the functions to be performed by each, in the amount of physical strength, in the capacity for long-continued labor, particularly when done standing, the influence of vigorous health upon the future well-being of the race, the self-reliance which enables one to assert full rights, and in the capacity to maintain the struggle for subsistence. This difference justifies a

> difference in legislation, and upholds that which is designed to compensate for some of the burdens which rest upon her.
>
> * * *
>
> For these reasons, and without questioning in any respect the decision in *Lochner v. New York,* we are of the opinion that it cannot be adjudged that the act in question is in conflict with the Federal Constitution,. . . and the judgment of the Supreme Court of Oregon is
>
> *Affirmed.*

Case Questions

1. If *Lochner* had really established a constitutional right to "freedom of contract," does *Muller v. Oregon* amount to a statement that women have fewer constitutional rights than men?

2. Does this decision hinge on women's physical weakness? Could an employer who tests all his women employees for physical endurance before hiring them claim that he should be exempted from the statute?

3. Does this decision hinge on women's supposed psychological dependence on men? On women's unique capacity to bear future generations? If physical weakness and psychological dependence were scientifically disproved, would women's birth-giving, fetus-carrying role continue to justify special treatment by society?

4. The Court refuses to question the *Lochner* ruling: Is it saying here that maintaining healthy mothers is legitimately an "object of public interest" but that having healthy fathers is not?

Bunting v. Oregon (1917)

In a sense, the combination *of Lochner* (with its acceptance of the *Holden v. Hardy* precedent allowing an 8-hour day for miners) and *Muller* amounted to a rule that liberty of contract could be restricted only for exceptionally dangerous occupations (like mining) or exceptionally weak people (like women). Only nine years later, in the case of *Bunting v. Oregon*, the Supreme Court again changed the rules, upholding a 10-hour-day statute that applied to workers in milling or manufacturing establishments of every kind.

By the time this case was argued, Brandeis had already been nominated to the Supreme Court (although he did not take his seat in time to participate in the decision). Oregon's counsel this time was another future Supreme Court justice,

Felix Frankfurter, who again presented what was by now called a "Brandeis brief" to defend the rationality of the statute. By this time, the rationality of maximum-hours legislation as a health measure appeared so obvious that the Supreme Court devoted most of its argument to an ancillary part of the statute that dealt with overtime pay requirements—to rebutting the contention that this law was a wage regulation in disguise. They tersely laid to rest the somewhat decayed corpse of the *Lochner* approach to hours legislation, giving the whole subject no more than one paragraph (reprinted below), and managing to avoid any explicit reference to *Lochner*.

BUNTING V. OREGON
243 U.S. 426 (1917)

MR. JUSTICE MCKENNA delivered the opinion of the court:

The consonance of the Oregon law with the Fourteenth Amendment is the question in the case, and this depends upon whether it is a proper exercise of the police power of the state, as the supreme court of the state decided that it is.

That the police power extends to health regulations is not denied, but it is denied that the law has such purpose or justification. . . .

Section 1 of the law expresses the policy that impelled its enactment to be the interest of the state in the physical well-being of its citizens and that it is injurious to their health for them to work "in any mill, factory or manufacturing establishment" more than ten hours in any one day. . . .

There is a contention made that the law, even regarded as regulating hours of service, is not either necessary or useful "for preservation of the health of employees in mills, factories, and manufacturing establishments." The record contains no facts to support the contention, and against it is the judgment of the legislature and the supreme court, which said: "In view of the well-known fact that the custom in our industries does not sanction a longer service than ten hours per day, it cannot be held, as a matter of law, that the legislative requirement is unreasonable or arbitrary as to hours of labor. Statistics show that the average daily working time among workingmen in different countries, is, in Australia, 8 hours; in Britain, 9; in the United States, 9 3/4; in Denmark, 9 3/4; in Norway, 10; Sweden, France, and Switzerland, 10 1/2; Germany, 10 1/4; Belgium, Italy, and Austria, 11; and in Russia, 12 hours."

Further discussion we deem unnecessary.

> Judgment *affirmed*.
>
> THE CHIEF JUSTICE, MR. JUSTICE VAN DEVANTER, and MR. JUSTICE MCREYNOLDS, dissent.
>
> [without written opinion].

Adkins v. Children's Hospital (1923)

By this time, the strategy for liberals who wanted social welfare legislation seemed obvious. They needed only (1) to restrict their social welfare legislation at first to women, (2) use the weaker-sex rationale to convince the Court to accept the protective legislation as "reasonable," and (3) then, having obtained this concession, enact the same reasonable measures to protect the men of the community as well. Nevertheless, at the next plateau of social welfare legislation, minimum-wage statutes, this three-step strategy collapsed at step two.

The first minimum-wage case settled by the Supreme Court was *Adkins v. Children's Hospital*, 261 U.S. 525 (1923).[40] It involved a District of Columbia statute that created a minimum-wage board with authority to set minimum wages for child labor and to establish for women workers minimum wages geared to "the necessary cost of living" and adequate to maintain those workers "in good health and to protect their morals." Although this case presented a usual challenge, one from a thwarted employer, the Children's Hospital, the Court's opinion also contained the decision for an unusual companion case, *Adkins v. Lyons*, in which objection to the minimum-wage law came from a dissatisfied female employee. This woman worked at the Congress Hall Hotel for $35 a month and two free meals a day. She claimed that these wages were the best she was capable of earning, and if she were not permitted to settle for these, she would have to go without work. In other words, she believed that her labor skills were not worthy of the minimum wage and that if the law were enforced she would be fired and would not be able to find a new job.

Once again, Felix Frankfurter argued the case for the statute, and once again Justice Brandeis refrained from participating in the decision. Justice Brandeis's daughter Elizabeth was secretary of the District of Columbia Minimum Wage Board, and the appearance of conflict of interest had to be avoided. Because the case came from the District rather than from a state, the constitutional clause at issue was the Fifth Amendment due process clause, which commands the federal government, rather than the Fourteenth Amendment due process clause, which is addressed to the states. Because the two clauses contain identical wording, however, what the Court said about the due process clause here also applied to the states. And what they said was that minimum-wage laws constitute "undue" interferences with the "liberty of contract." Justice Sutherland's majority opinion (the Court divided 5–3) contained a number of surprises. One was that he relied heavily on the *Lochner v. New York* precedent, even though that case appeared to have been silently overruled by *Bunting v. Oregon*. (With an uncanny ability to look in two opposite directions at once, Sutherland faced *Bunting* long enough to admit that it established the constitutionality of maximum-hours legislation—just what *Lochner* had denied—and simultaneously looked to *Lochner* to find the precedent that created and rendered virtually inviolable the right to freedom of contract.)

A second surprise was Sutherland's assertion that the Nineteenth Amendment (giving women the vote) nullified the constitutional basis to single out women for special protection; Americans had transcended the myth of "the ancient inequality of the sexes" and had brought the "civil and political" differences between the sexes "to the vanishing point," he claimed (at 261 U.S., 553). Sutherland's argument was that although hours legislation properly took gender into account, because of women's physical weakness, wage legislation was premised on an assumption of women's incapacity to fend for themselves in the economy. Now that women had the vote, as well as the legal right to make contracts, Sutherland believed that there was no longer any justification for putting further "restrictions" on women's "freedom." He made these assertions notwithstanding the undisputed evidence that then, as now, women's earnings were, on the average, at the bottom of the pay scale (e.g., within every racial group, women earn less per year than men).

Nonetheless, Sutherland's views did have contemporaneous support from Alice Paul, leader of the decidedly militant branch of the women's suffragist movement, who had been rallying her forces, since 1913, behind the slogan "Equality Not Protection." Not satisfied with the success of the suffrage amendment effort in 1920, Ms. Paul and her Women's Party within three years had drafted and submitted to Congress the Equal Rights Amendment, to prohibit unequal treatment of men and women by legislation (The legal import of the Equal Rights Amendment, or ERA, is detailed in Chapter 2.) This was the same year that *Adkins v. Children's Hospital* was handed down.

ADKINS V. CHILDREN'S HOSPITAL
261 U.S. 525 (1923)

MR. JUSTICE SUTHERLAND wrote for the Court:

...The judicial duty of passing upon the constitutionality of an act of Congress is one of great gravity and delicacy. The ... legislative branch of the government,... by enacting it, has affirmed its validity; and that determination must be given great weight. This Court ... has steadily adhered to the rule that every possible presumption is in favor of the validity of an act of Congress until overcome beyond rational doubt. But if by clear and indubitable demonstration a statute be opposed to the Constitution we have no choice but to say so. The Constitution, by its own terms, is the supreme law of the land, emanating from the people, the repository of ultimate sovereignty under our form of government. A congressional statute, on the other hand, is the act of an agency of this sovereign authority and if it conflict with the Constitution must fall; for that which is not supreme must yield to that which is. To hold it invalid (if it be invalid) is a plain exercise of the judicial power—that power vested in courts to enable them to administer justice according to law. From the authority to ascertain and determine the law in a given case, there necessarily results, in case of conflict, the duty to declare and enforce the rule of the supreme law and reject that of an inferior act of legislation which, transcending the Constitution, is of no effect and binding on no one. This is not the exercise of a substantive power to review and nullify acts of Congress, for no such substantive power exists. It is simply a necessary concomitant of the power to hear and dispose of a case or controversy properly before the court, to the determination of which must be brought the test and measure of the law.

The statute now under consideration is attacked upon the ground that it authorizes an unconstitutional interference with the freedom of contract included within the guaranties of the due process clause of the Fifth Amendment. That the right to contract about one's affairs is a part of the liberty of the individual protected by this clause, is settled by the decisions of this Court and is no longer open to question. *Allgeyer v. Louisiana,* 165 U.S. 578, 591; New *York Life Insurance Co. v. Dodge,* 246 U.S. 357, 373–374; *Coppage v. Kansas,* 236 U.S. 1, 10, 14; *Adair v. United States,* 208 U.S. 161; *Lochner v. New York,* 198 U.S. 45; *Butchers' Union Co. v. Crescent City Co.,* 111 U.S. 746; *Muller v. Oregon,* 208 U.S. 412, 421. Within this liberty are contracts of employment of labor. In making such contracts, generally speaking, the parties have an equal right to obtain from each other the best terms they can as the result of private bargaining....

In *Coppage v. Kansas* (p. 14), this Court, speaking through Mr. Justice Pitney, said:

> Included in the right of personal liberty and the right of private property—partaking of the nature of each—is the right to make contracts for the acquisition of property. Chief among such contracts is that of personal employment, by which labor and other services are exchanged for money or other forms of property. If this right be struck down or arbitrarily interfered with, there is a substantial impairment of liberty in the long-established constitutional sense. The right is as essential to the laborer as to the capitalist, to the poor as to the rich; for the vast majority of persons have no other honest way to begin to acquire property, save by working for money.

An interference with this liberty so serious as that now under consideration, and so disturbing of equality of right, must be deemed to be arbitrary, unless it be supportable as a reasonable exercise of the police power of the State.

There is, of course, no such thing as absolute freedom of contract. It is subject to a great variety of restraints. But freedom of contract is, nevertheless, the general rule and restraint the exception; and the exercise of legislative authority to abridge it can be justified only by the existence of exceptional circumstances. Whether these circumstances exist in the present case constitutes the question to be answered. It will be helpful to this end to review some of the decisions where the interference has been upheld and consider the grounds upon which they rest.

1. *Those dealing with statutes fixing rates and charges to be exacted by businesses impressed with a public interest....*

2. *Statutes relating to contracts for the performance of public work....* These cases sustain such statutes as depending... upon the right of the government to prescribe the conditions upon which it will permit work of a public character to be done for it.... We may, therefore... dismiss these... as inapplicable.

3. *Statutes prescribing the character, methods and time for payment of wages....* In none of the statutes thus sustained, was the liberty of employer or employee to fix the amount of wages... interfered with. Their tendency and purpose was to prevent unfair and perhaps

fraudulent methods in the payment of wages and in no sense can they be said to be, or to furnish a precedent for, wage-fixing statutes.

4. *Statutes fixing hours of labor.* It is upon this class that the greatest emphasis is laid in argument and therefore, and because such cases approach most nearly the line of principle applicable to the statute here involved, we shall consider them more at length. In some instances the statute limited the hours of labor for men in certain occupations and in others it was confined in its application to women. No statute has thus far been brought to the attention of this Court which by its terms, applied to all occupations....

[Here followed two pages of quotes from *Lochner* to the effect that legislative interferences with liberty of contract may not be "arbitrary" or "unreasonable."—AU.]

Subsequent cases in this Court have been distinguished from that decision, but the principles therein stated have never been disapproved.

In *Bunting v. Oregon,* 243 U.S. 426, a state statute forbidding the employment of any person in any mill, factory or manufacturing establishment more than ten hours in any one day, and providing payment for overtime not exceeding three hours in any one day at the rate of time and a half of the regular wage, was sustained on the ground that, since the state legislature and State Supreme Court had found such a law necessary for the preservation of the health of employees in these industries, this Court would accept their judgement, in the absence of facts to support the contrary conclusion. The law was... sustained as a reasonable regulation of hours of service....

In the *Muller Case* the validity of an Oregon statute, forbidding the employment of any female in certain industries more than ten hours during any one day was upheld. The decision proceeded upon the theory that the difference between the sexes may justify a different rule respecting hours of labor in the case of women than in the case of men. It is pointed out that these consist in differences of physical structure, especially in respect of the maternal functions, and also in the fact that historically woman has always been dependent upon man, who has established his control by superior physical strength.... But the ancient inequality of the sexes, otherwise than physical, as suggested in the *Muller* Case (p. 421) has continued "with diminishing intensity." In view of the great—not to say revolutionary—changes which have taken place since that utterance, in the contractual, political and civil status of women, culminating in the Nineteenth Amendment, it is not unreasonable to say that these differences have now come almost, if not quite, to the vanishing point. In this aspect of the matter, while the physical differences must be recognized in appropriate cases, and legislation fixing hours or conditions of work may properly take them into account, we cannot accept the doctrine that women of mature age, *sui juris*, require or may be subjected to restrictions upon their liberty of contract which could not lawfully be imposed in the case of men under similar circumstances. To do so would be to ignore all the implications to be drawn from the present day trend of legislation, as well as that of common thought and usage, by which woman is accorded emancipation from the old doctrine that she must be given special protection or be subjected to special restraint in her contractual and civil relationships. In passing, it may be noted that the instant statute applies in the case of the woman employer contracting with a woman employee as it does when the former is a man.

The essential characteristics of the statute now under consideration, which differentiate it from the laws fixing hours of labor, will be made to appear as we proceed. It is sufficient now to point out that the latter... deal with incidents of the employment having no necessary effect upon the heart of the contract, that is, the amount of wages to be paid and received. A law forbidding work to continue beyond a given number of hours leaves the parties free to contract about wages and thereby equalize whatever additional burdens may be imposed upon the employer as a result of the restrictions as to hours, by an adjustment in respect of the amount of wages. Enough has been said to show that the authority to fix hours of labor cannot be exercised except in respect of those occupations where work of long continued duration is detrimental to health. This Court has been careful in every case where the question has been raised, to place its decision upon this limited authority of the legislature to regulate hours of labor and to disclaim any purpose to uphold the legislation as fixing wages, thus recognizing an essential difference between the two. It seems plain that these decisions afford no real support for any form of law establishing minimum wages.

...[This] is simply and exclusively a price-fixing law, confined to adult women (for we are not now considering the provisions relating to minors), who are legally as capable of contracting for themselves as men. It forbids two parties having lawful capacity—under penalties as to the employer—to freely contract with one another in respect of the price for which one shall render service to the other in a purely private employment where both are willing, perhaps anxious, to agree, even though the consequence may be to oblige one to surrender a desirable engagement and the other to dispense with the services of a desirable employee.[1] The price fixed by the board need have no relation to the capacity or earning power of the employee, the number of hours which may happen to constitute the day's work, the character of the place where the work is to be done, or the circumstances or surroundings of the employment; and, while it has no other basis to support its validity than the assumed necessities of the employee, it takes no account of any independent resources she may have. It is based wholly on the opinions of the members of the board and their advisers—perhaps an average of their opinions, if they do not precisely agree—as to what will be necessary to provide a living for a woman, keep her in health and preserve her morals. It applies to any and every occupation in the District, without regard to its nature or the character of the work.

The standard furnished by the statute for the guidance of the board is so vague as to be impossible of practical application with any reasonable degree of accuracy. What is sufficient to supply the necessary cost of living for a woman worker and maintain her in good health and protect her morals is obviously not a precise or unvarying sum—not even approximately so. The amount will depend upon a variety of circumstances: the individual temperament, habits of thrift, care, ability to buy necessaries intelligently, and whether the woman lives alone or with her family. To those who practice economy, a given sum will afford comfort, while to those of contrary habit the same sum will be wholly inadequate. The cooperative economies of the family group are not taken into account though they constitute an important consideration in estimating the cost of living, for it is obvious that the individual expense will be less in the case of a member of a family than in the case of one living alone. The relation between earnings and morals is not capable of standardization. It cannot be shown that well paid women safeguard their morals more carefully than those who are poorly paid. Morality rests upon other considerations than wages; and there is, certainly, no such prevalent connection between the two as to justify a broad attempt to adjust the latter with reference to the former. As a means of safeguarding morals the attempted classification, in our opinion, is without reasonable basis. No distinction can be made between women who work for others and those who do not; nor is there ground for distinction between women and men, for, certainly, if women require a minimum wage to preserve their morals men require it to preserve their honesty. For these reasons, . . . the inquiry in respect of the necessary cost of living and of the income necessary to preserve health and morals. . . must be answered for each individual considered by herself and not by a general formula prescribed by a statutory bureau.

***

The law takes account of the necessities of only one party to the contract. It ignores the necessities of the employer by compelling him to pay not less than a certain sum, not only whether the employee is capable of earning it, but irrespective of the ability of his business to sustain the burden, generously leaving him, of course, the privilege of abandoning his business as an alternative for going on at a loss. Within the limits of the minimum sum, he is precluded, under penalty of fine and imprisonment, from adjusting compensation to the differing merits of his employees. It compels him to pay at least the sum fixed in any event, because the employee needs it, but requires no service of equivalent value from the employee. . . . The law is not confined to the great and powerful employers but embraces those whose bargaining power may be as weak as that of the employee. It takes no account of periods of stress and business depression, of crippling losses, which may leave the employer himself without adequate means of livelihood. To the extent that the sum fixed exceeds the fair value of the services rendered, it amounts to a compulsory exaction from the employer for the support of a partially indigent person, for whose condition there rests upon him no peculiar responsibility, and therefore, in effect, arbitrarily shifts to his shoulders a burden which, if it belongs to anybody, belongs to society as a whole.

The feature of this statute which, perhaps more than any other, puts upon it the stamp of invalidity is that it exacts from the employer an arbitrary payment for a purpose and upon a basis having no causal connection with his business, or the contract or the work the employee engages to do. . . . The ethical right of every worker, man or woman, to a living wage may be conceded. One of the declared and important purposes of trade organizations is to secure it. And with that principle and with every legitimate effort to realize it in fact, no one can quarrel; but the fallacy of the proposed method of attaining it is that it assumes that every employer is bound at all events to furnish it. The moral requirement implicit in every contract of employment, viz, that the amount to be paid and the service to be rendered shall bear to each other some relation of just equivalence, is completely ignored. The necessities of the employee are alone considered and these arise outside of the employment, are the same when there is no employment, and as great in one occupation as in another. Certainly the employer by paying a fair equivalent for the service rendered, though not sufficient to support the employee, has neither caused nor contributed to her poverty. On the contrary, to the extent of what he pays he has relieved it. In principle, there can be no difference between the case of selling labor and the case of selling goods. If one goes to the butcher, the baker or grocer to buy food, he is morally entitled to obtain the worth of his money but he is not entitled to more. . . . A statute requiring an employer to pay. . . the value of the services rendered, even to pay with fair relation to the extent of the benefit obtained from the service, would be understandable. But a statute which prescribes payment without regard to any of these things. . . is so clearly the product of a naked, arbitrary exercise of power that it cannot be allowed to stand under the Constitution of the United States.

We are asked, upon the one hand, to consider the fact that several States have adopted similar statutes, and we are invited, upon the other hand, to give weight to the fact that three times as many States presumably as well informed and as anxious to promote the health and morals of their people, have refrained from enacting such legislation. We have also been furnished with a large number of printed opinions approving the policy of the minimum wage, and our own reading has disclosed a large number to the contrary. These are all proper enough for the consideration of the lawmaking bodies, since their tendency is to establish the desirability or undesirability of the legislation; but they reflect no legitimate light upon the question of its validity, and that is what we are called upon to decide. The elucidation of that question cannot be aided by counting heads.

It is said that great benefits have resulted from the operation of such statutes, not alone in the District of Columbia but in the several States, where they have been in force. A mass of reports, opinions of special observers and students of the subject, and the like, has been brought before us in support of this statement, all of which we have found interesting but only mildly persuasive. . . .

Finally, it may be said that if, in the interest of the public welfare, the police power may be invoked to justify the fixing of a minimum wage, it may, when the public welfare is thought to require it, be invoked to justify a maximum wage. The power to fix high wages connotes, by like course of reasoning, the power to fix low wages. If, in the face of the guaranties of the Fifth Amendment, this form of legislation shall be legally justified, the field for the operation of the police power will have been widened to a great and dangerous degree. . . . . . A wrong decision does not end with itself: it is a precedent, and, with the swing of sentiment, its bad influence may run from one extremity of the arc to the other.

It has been said that legislation of the kind now under review is required in the interest of social justice, for whose ends freedom of contract may lawfully be subjected to restraint. The liberty of the individual to do as he pleases, even in innocent matters, is not absolute. It must frequently yield to the common good, and the line beyond which the power of interference may not be pressed is neither definite nor unalterable but may be made to move, within limits not well defined, with changing need and circumstance. Any attempt to fix a rigid boundary would be unwise as well as futile. But, nevertheless, there are limits to the power, and when these have been passed, it becomes the plain duty of the courts in the proper exercise of their authority to so declare. . . . [T]he good of society as a whole cannot be better served than by the preservation against arbitrary restraint of the liberties of its constituent members.

. . . The act in question passes the limit prescribed by the Constitution, and, accordingly, the decrees of the court below are

Affirmed.

Opinion Footnote

1 This is the exact situation in the *Lyons case* as is shown by the statement in the first part of this opinion.

MR. CHIEF JUSTICE TAFT, dissenting:

I regret much to differ from the Court in these cases.

The boundary of the police power beyond which its exercise becomes an invasion of the guaranty of liberty under the Fifth and Fourteenth Amendments to the Constitution is not easy to mark. Our Court has been laboriously engaged in pricking out a line in successive cases. We must be careful, it seems to me, to follow that line as well as we can and not to depart from it by suggesting a distinction that is formal rather than real.

Legislatures in limiting freedom of contract between employee and employer by a minimum wage proceed on the assumption that employees, in the class receiving least pay, are not upon a full level of equality of choice with their employer and in their necessitous circumstances are prone to accept pretty much anything that is offered. They are peculiarly subject to the overreaching of the harsh and greedy employer. The evils of the sweating system and of the long hours and low wages which are characteristic of it are well known. Now, I agree that it is a disputable question . . . how far a statutory requirement of maximum hours or minimum wages may be useful . . ., and whether it may not make the case of the oppressed employee worse. . . . But it is not the function of this Court to hold congressional acts invalid simply because they are passed to carry out economic views which the Court believes to be unwise or unsound.

Legislatures which adopt a requirement of maximum hours or minimum wages may be presumed to believe that when sweating employers are prevented from paying unduly low wages by positive law they will continue their business, abating that part of their profits, which were wrung from the necessities of their employees, and will concede the better terms required by the law; and that while in individual cases hardship may result, the restriction will inure to the benefit of the general class of employees in whose interest the law is passed and so to that of the community at large.

The right of the legislature under the Fifth and Fourteenth Amendments to limit the hours of employment on the score of the health of the employee . . . has been firmly established. . . . *Bunting v. Oregon* . . . sustained a law limiting the hours of labor of any person, whether man or woman working in any mill, factory or manufacturing establishment to ten hours a day. . . . The law covered the whole field of industrial employment and certainly covered the case of persons employed in bakeries. Yet the opinion in the *Bunting* case does not mention the *Lochner* case. No one can suggest any constitutional distinction between employment in bakery and one in any other kind of a manufacturing establishment which should make a limit of hours in the one invalid, and the same limit in the other permissible. It is impossible for me to reconcile the *Bunting* case and the *Lochner* case and I have always supposed that the *Lochner* case was thus overruled *sub silentio*. Yet the opinion of the Court herein in support of its conclusion quotes from the opinion in the *Lochner* case as one which has been sometimes distinguished but never overruled. Certainly there was no attempt to distinguish it in the *Bunting* case.

However, the opinion herein does not overrule the *Bunting* case . . . and therefore I assume that the conclusion in this case rests on the distinction between a minimum of wages and a maximum of hours in the limiting of liberty to contract. I regret to be at variance with the Court as to the substance of this distinction. In absolute freedom of contract the one term is as important as the other, for both enter equally into the consideration given and received. . . . One is the multiplier and the other the multiplicand.

If it be said that long hours of labor have a more direct effect upon the health of the employee than the low wage, there is very respectable authority from close observers, disclosed in the record and . . . quoted at length in the briefs, that they are equally harmful in this regard. Congress took this view and we cannot say it was not warranted in so doing.

With deference to the very able opinion of the Court and my brethren who concur in it, it appears to me to exaggerate the importance of the wage term of the contract of employment as more inviolate than its other terms. Its conclusion seems influenced by the fear that the concession of the power to impose a minimum wage must carry with it a concession of the power to fix a maximum wage. This, I submit, is a *non sequitur*. A line of distinction like the one under discussion in this case is, as the opinion elsewhere admits, a matter of degree and practical experience and not of pure logic. Certainly [there is a]... wide difference between prescribing a minimum wage and a maximum wage....

Moreover, there are decisions by this Court which have sustained legislative limitations in respect to the wage term in contracts of employment.... While these did not impose a minimum on wages, they did take away from the employee the freedom to agree as to how they should be fixed, in what medium they should be paid, and when they should be paid, all features that might affect the amount or the mode of enjoyment of them.... In *Bunting v. Oregon,* employees in a mill, factory or manufacturing establishment were required if they worked over a ten hours a day to accept for the three additional hours permitted not less than fifty per cent more than their usual wage. This was sustained as a mild penalty imposed on the employer to enforce the limitation as to hours; but it necessarily curtailed the employee's freedom to contract to work for the wages he saw fit to accept during those three hours. I do not feel, therefore, that either on the basis of reason, experience or authority, the boundary of the police power should be drawn to include maximum hours and exclude a minimum wage.

Without, however, expressing an opinion that a minimum wage limitation can be enacted for adult men, it is enough to say that the case before us involves only the application of the minimum wage to women. If I am right in thinking that the legislature can find as much support in experience for the view that a sweating wage has as great and as direct a tendency to bring about an injury to the health and morals of workers, as for the view that long hours injure their health, then I respectfully submit that *Muller v. Oregon,* 208 U.S. 412, controls this case. The law which was there sustained forbade the employment of any female in any mechanical establishment or factory or laundry for more than ten hours. This covered a pretty wide field in women's work and it would not seem that any sound distinction between that case and this can be built upon the fact that the law before us applies to all occupations of women with power in the board to make certain exceptions. [T]he Court in *Muller v. Oregon,* based its conclusion on the natural limit to women's physical strength and the likelihood that long hours would therefore injure her health, and we have had since a series of cases [limiting the employment of women] which may be said to have established a rule of decision. *Riley v. Massachusetts,* 232 U.S. 671; *Miller v. Wilson,* 236 U.S. 373; *Bosley v. McLaughlin,* 236 U.S. 385. . . .

I am not sure from a reading of the opinion whether the court thinks the authority of *Muller v. Oregon* is shaken by the adoption of the Nineteenth Amendment. The Nineteenth Amendment did not change the physical strength or limitations of women upon which the decision in *Muller v. Oregon* rests. . . . I don't think we are warranted in varying constitutional construction based on physical differences between men and women, because of the Amendment.

But for my inability to agree with some general observations in the forcible opinion of MR. JUSTICE HOLMES who follows me, I should be silent and merely record my concurrence in what he says. . . .

I am authorized to say that MR. JUSTICE SANFORD concurs in this opinion.

MR. JUSTICE HOLMES, dissenting:

The question in this case is the broad one, whether Congress can establish minimum rates of wages for women in the District of Columbia with due provision for special circumstances, or whether we must say that Congress has no power to meddle with the matter at all. To me, notwithstanding the deference due to the prevailing judgment of the Court, the power of Congress seems absolutely free from doubt. The end, to remove conditions leading to ill health, immorality and the deterioration of the race, no one would deny to be within the scope of constitutional legislation. The means are means that have the approval of Congress, of many States, and of those governments from which we have learned our greatest lessons. When so many intelligent persons, who have studied the matter more than any of us can, have thought that the means are effective and are worth the price, it seems to me impossible to deny that the belief reasonably may be held by reasonable men. . . . [I]n the present in stance the only objection that can be urged is found within the vague contours of the Fifth Amendment, prohibiting the depriving any person of liberty or property without due process of law. To that I turn.

The earlier decisions upon the same words in the Fourteenth Amendment began within our memory and went no farther than an unpretentious assertion of the liberty to follow the ordinary callings. Later that innocuous generality was expanded into the dogma, Liberty of Contract. Contract is not specially mentioned in the text that we have to construe. It is merely an example of doing what you want to do, embodied in the word liberty. But pretty much all law consists in forbidding men to do some things that they want to do, and contract is no more exempt from law than other acts. Without enumerating all the restrictive laws that have been upheld I will mention a few that seem to me to have interfered with liberty of contract quite as seriously and directly as the one before us. Usury laws prohibit contracts by which a man receives more than so much interest for the money that he lends. Statutes of frauds restrict many contracts to certain forms. Some Sunday laws prohibit practically all contracts during one-seventh of our whole life. Insurance rates may be regulated. *German Alliance Insurance Co. v. Lewis,* 233 U.S. 389. [Several precedents on contractual limits follow here.—AU.]...Finally women's hours of labor may be fixed; *Muller v. Oregon*; *Riley v. Massachusetts,* 232 U.S. 671, 679; *Hawley v. Walker,* 232 U.S. 718; *Miller v. Wilson,* 236 U.S. 373; *Bosley v. McLaughlin,* 236 U.S. 385; and the principle was extended to men with the allowance of a limited overtime to be paid for "at the rate of time and one-half of the regular wage," in *Bunting v. Oregon.*

I confess that I do not understand the principle on which the power to fix a minimum for the wages of women can be denied by those who admit the power to fix a maximum for their hours of work. I fully assent to the proposition that here as elsewhere the distinctions of the law are distinctions of degree, but I perceive no difference in the kind or degree of interference with liberty, the only matter with which we have any concern, between the one case and the other. The bargain is equally affected whichever half you regulate.... It will need more than the Nineteenth Amendment to convince me that there are no differences between men and women, or that legislation cannot take those differences into account. I should not hesitate to take them into account if I thought it necessary to sustain this act. *Quong Wing v. Kirkendall,* 233 U.S. 59, 63. But after *Bunting v. Oregon,* I had supposed that it was not necessary, and that *Lochner v. New York* would be allowed a deserved repose.

This statute does not compel anybody to pay anything. It simply forbids employment at rates below those fixed as the minimum requirement of health and right living. It is safe to assume that women will not be employed at even the lowest wages allowed unless they earn them, or unless the employer's

> business can sustain the burden. In short the law in its character and operation is like hundreds of so-called police laws that have been upheld. . . .
>
> The criterion of constitutionality is not whether we believe the law to be for the public good. We certainly cannot be prepared to deny that a reasonable man reasonably might have that belief in view of the legislation of Great Britain, Victoria and a number of the States of this Union. The belief is fortified by a very remarkable collection of documents submitted on behalf of the appellants, material here, I conceive, only as showing that the belief reasonably may be held. . . . If a legislature should adopt. . . the doctrine that "freedom of contract is a misnomer as applied to a contract between an employer and an ordinary individual employee," 29 *Harv. Law Rev.* 13, 25, I could not pronounce an opinion with which I agree impossible to be entertained by reasonable men. . . .
>
> I am of opinion that the statute is valid and that the decree should be reversed.

Case Questions

1. When the Court majority says that the minimum-wage statute is *arbitrary,* what do they mean by that term? Does it mean that it is irrational to think that a minimum wage will raise living standards (and thereby improve health)? That it is irrational to think that a woman's earning power affects her "morals" (i.e., sexual behavior)? That it is unfair to employers? As you read the due process clause, does it seem to prohibit taking property or liberty by "unfair" laws? By foolish laws?

2. If one agrees with Sutherland that women are not less able to fend for themselves than men, how might one otherwise explain the pattern of their being systematically lower paid than men, then as now?

3. Everyone on the Court except Holmes (and Brandeis, who was silent) assumes that a maximum-wage law would be clearly unconstitutional. Would it? Even as a "wage price stabilization act" to control inflation?

Protecting Women by Limiting Their Freedom: *Radice v. New York* (1924)

The case of *Radice v. New York,* 264 U.S. 292 (1924), decided only months after *Adkins,* illustrates more clearly than the latter why Alice Paul and her pro-ERA followers opposed legislation aimed at protecting women in the economic arena. Although minimum-wage laws do discernibly promote public health to the degree that (in a pre-food-stamp era) they prevent the paying of literally starvation wages, the relationship between public welfare and the statute challenged by Mr. Radice, a Buffalo, New York, restaurateur, was not all that obvious.

The part of the New York statute that *Radice* was contesting prohibited employing women between the hours of 10:00 PM and 6:00 AM in restaurants or "in connection with any restaurant" in large cities. (Other parts of the statute, not under challenge, established maximums of the 9-hour day and a 54-hour week for women in restaurant work.) The statute was riddled with exceptions: it did not apply to restaurants in small cities or towns, it did not apply to "singers and performers of any kind," it did not apply to cloakroom and restroom attendants, it did not apply to hotel-related restaurants and their kitchens, and it did not apply to employees-only eating establishments operated by employers for their workers. In short, it meant that women in major cities could not work as waitresses or cooks or hostesses in most restaurants after 10:00 at night, but they could work in the same restaurants in other capacities (e.g., as a coat checker), and they could even work as waitresses, cooks, or hostesses in small cities. Although the statute was challenged by an employer, it is not hard to see that this law had the impact of stamping certain jobs as "men only." These were the same jobs that women were permitted to do during daylight hours or in smaller towns.

How did nine Supreme Court justices convince themselves that this complex combination of permissions and prohibitions was "reasonably" related to the promotion of public health or welfare? They simply "assumed" certain beliefs to be facts—beliefs about the "more delicate organism" of women, which were alleged in the state's defense of its statute. Justice Sutherland's opinion provides no satisfactory explanation why the Court continued to assume that beliefs alleged by legislators in behalf of wage legislation (such as the law voided in *Adkins*) had no basis in reality, but that beliefs alleged in relation to what hour of the night a person worked did have such a basis.

Another curious aspect of Sutherland's opinion is the disparity in his treatment of the due process challenge to the statute and the equal protection challenge to it. Supposedly, "reasonableness" was to be the test for applying either clause. Just as liberty was not to be limited unless that limitation bore a rational relationship to promoting public welfare, so statutory classifications differentiating groups of people were to be based on a reasonable connection to the public good. The reason Sutherland identified for prohibiting women from these particular night jobs in big cities was the goal of protecting women from what he termed "the dangers and menaces incident to night life in large cities." Sutherland actually proffers no reason, however, why working at night as a waitress in a hotel-related or employee-service restaurant would have a less harsh impact on women's health or welfare than working at the same job in a non-hotel restaurant. Here is what he said about the equal protection challenge to the statutory exceptions (at 264 U.S., 296–298):

> The limitation of the legislative prohibition to cities of the first and second class does not bring about an unreasonable and arbitrary classification. Nor is there substance in the contention that the exclusion of restaurant employees of a special kind, and of hotels and employees' lunch rooms, renders the statute obnoxious to the Constitution. The statute does not present a case where some persons of a class are selected for special restraint from which others of the same class are left free; but a case where all in the same class of work, are included in the restraint. Of course, the mere fact of classification is not enough to put a statute beyond the reach of the equality provision of the Fourteenth Amendment. Such classification must not be "purely arbitrary, oppressive or capricious." *American Sugar Refining Co. v. Louisiana,* 179 U.S. 89, 92. But the mere production of inequality is not enough. Every selection of persons for regulation so results, in some degree. The inequality produced, in order to encounter the challenge of the Constitution, must be "actually and palpably unreasonable and arbitrary." *Arkansas Natural Gas Co. v. Railroad Commission,* 261 U.S. 379, 384, and cases cited. . . . Directly applicable are recent decisions of this Court sustaining hours of labor for women in hotels but omitting women employees of boarding houses, lodging houses, etc., *Miller v. Wilson* [236 U.S. 373 (1915)], at p. 382; and limiting the hours of labor of women pharmacists and student nurses in hospitals but excepting graduate nurses. *Bosley v. McLaughlin* [236 U.S. 385 (1915)], at pp. 394–96. The opinion in the first of these cases was delivered by Mr. Justice Hughes, who, after pointing out that in hotels women employees are for the most part chambermaids and waitresses; that it cannot be said that the conditions of work are the same as those which obtain in the other establishments; and that it is not beyond the power of the legislature to recognize the differences, said (pp. 383–84):
>
>> The contention as to the various omissions. . . ignores the well-established principle that the legislature is not bound, in order to support the constitutional validity of its regulation, to extend it to all cases which it might possibly reach. Dealing with practical exigencies, the legislature may be guided by experience. *Patsone v. Pennsylvania,* 232 U.S. 138, 144. It is free to recognize degrees of

harm, and it may confine its restrictions to those classes of cases where the need is deemed to be clearest. As has been said, it may "proceed cautiously, step by step," and "if an evil is specially experienced in a particular branch of business" it is not necessary that the prohibition "should be couched in all-embracing terms." *Carroll v. Greenwich Insurance Co.,* 199 U.S. 401, 411. If the law presumably hits the evil where it is most felt, it is not to be overthrown because there are other instances to which it might have been applied. *Keokee Coke Co. v. Taylor,* 234 U.S. 224, 227. Upon this principle which has had abundant illustration in the decisions cited below, it cannot be concluded that the failure to extend the act to other and distinct lines of business, having their own circumstances and conditions, or to domestic service, created an arbitrary discrimination as against the proprietors of hotels.

In short, the Court's "one step at a time" doctrine for equal protection seemed to permit states to carve out exceptions to statutes when there was little more explanation for the exception than the political strength of some lobby favoring the exemption.

Capitulation on Minimum Wages for Women: *West Coast Hotel v. Parrish* (1937) and *U.S. v. Darby* (1941)

Despite its concessions for hours legislation, the Court continued its opposition to minimum-wage legislation through the Great Depression and through the first administration of Franklin D. Roosevelt (FDR). As late as 1936, the justices invalidated a women's minimum-wage law of the State of New York,[41] again essentially on the grounds that the due process clause forbids laws that in their substance constitute unfair (in the Court's eyes) regulations of property. (This notion has come to be known as the doctrine of "economic substantive due process.") Using other legal doctrines, they also invalidated a great many other social welfare measures, including the bulk of Roosevelt's New Deal. An infuriated FDR, after his overwhelming electoral victory of 1936, introduced into Congress his famous (or notorious) Court-packing plan. By adding six judges to the Court, all his own appointments, FDR would have been able to transform the 6–3 and 5–4 decisions against his programs into, at worst, 9–6 decisions in his favor.

Just as the debate on this plan was taking place in Congress, the Supreme Court dramatically reversed itself on a number of legal issues, including minimum wages for women and various central planks of the New Deal platform. Although

Roosevelt lost his Court-packing plan, he "won the war." After the crucial doctrinal switch in 1937, which evidently discouraged his four most die-hard opponents on the Court, and after new Congressional legislation that allowed Supreme Court justices to retire at full pay, Roosevelt had the opportunity to replace retirements with seven new justices between 1937 and 1941. By the time Roosevelt died, he had appointed eight of the nine justices on the Court (the ninth was Roberts).

The Court's reversal on minimum wages for women occurred in the case of *West Coast Hotel v. Parrish,* 300 U.S. 379 (1937). At issue was a statute of the State of Washington that paralleled in every major respect the District of Columbia statute that the Supreme Court had voided in *Adkins*. It created a board to establish minimum wages for women and children, specifying that in the case of women workers, the wage be adequate "for the decent maintenance of women" and "not detrimental to health and morals." One interesting variation in this case involves the original plaintiff. The person who initiated the lawsuit was one Elsie Parrish, an employee who, unlike the woman employee in the companion case to *Adkins v. Children's Hospital,* wanted this law *enforced*. Elsie Parrish was suing her employer, the West Coast Hotel, for back pay owed her to bring her wages up to the legal minimum of $14.50 a week (for 48 hours of work).

This time the Supreme Court openly and explicitly overruled its own precedent. First, the Court majority (of five) pointedly noted the following about the "freedom of contract" claim that the employer was making (and that had driven this whole series of cases since *Lochner*) (at 391):

> What is this freedom? The Constitution does not speak of freedom of contract. It speaks of liberty and prohibits the deprivation of liberty without due process of law.... [T]he Constitution does not recognize an absolute and uncontrollable liberty.... [T]he liberty safeguarded is liberty in a social organization which requires the protection of law against the evils which menace the health, safety, morals and welfare of the people. Liberty under the Constitution is thus necessarily subject to the restraints of due process, and regulation which is reasonable in relation to its subject and is adopted in the interests of the community is due process.

Next the Court simply reiterated the logic of the *Adkins* dissent to explain what was reasonable about minimum wage laws for women and children the lowest-paid workers. It supplemented these arguments by reference to the current, extraordinarily harsh economic conditions of the Great Depression. Finally, as was traditional for nonracial discrimination in this time period, it gave short shrift to the equal protection claim, citing many of the same precedents cited in *Radice*. It addressed the equal protection claim with the following brief discussion (at 400):

> The argument that the legislation in question constitutes an arbitrary discrimination, because it does not extend to men, is unavailing. This Court has frequently held that the legislative authority, acting within its proper field, is not bound to extend its regulation to all cases which it might possibly reach. The legislature "is free to recognize degrees of harm and it may confine its restrictions to those classes of cases where the need is deemed to be clearest." If "the law presumably hits the evil where it is most felt, it is not to be overthrown because there are other instances to which it might have been applied." . . . This familiar principle has repeatedly been applied to legislation which singles out women, and particular classes of women, in the exercise of the State's protective power. . . . Their relative need in the presence of the evil, no less than the existence of the evil itself, is a matter for the legislative judgment. [Citations omitted.]

Although the *West Coast* majority opinion did not directly address the question of the constitutionality of potential minimum-wage laws that would apply to workers in general, it was not too long before the Court squarely faced that question. In the 1941 case of *United States v. Darby*, the Court confronted the issue of the constitutionality of the national Fair Labor Standards Act (or Wages and Hours Act) of 1938. This act established minimum wages and maximum hours for all workers producing goods intended for interstate commerce. As in *Adkins v. Children's Hospital*, the Court here dealt with the Fifth Amendment due process clause (because national legislation was involved), but presented arguments that applied equally to the Fourteenth Amendment due process clause.

The parallels between the *West Coast Hotel v. Parrish/United States v. Darby* pattern and the earlier *Muller v. Oregon/Bunting v. Oregon* pattern are striking. As with the hours legislation pattern, this minimum-wage acceptance pattern presented a piece of general welfare legislation to the Supreme Court within a few years after the same kind of legislation on a protection-of-women basis had been acknowledged as reasonable by that Court. The proponents of social welfare legislation, once again having used the need to protect women as the cutting edge of their argument, were widening its wedge so as to shelter all members of society behind the same rationale.

The second striking similarity between the two patterns involves the relative amounts of attention devoted to due process clause arguments between the first and the second cases in each series. Like *Muller v. Oregon*, *West Coast Hotel v. Parrish* was largely devoted to the due process question, and the weight of the argument in both cases rested largely on the assumption of the special needs and/or weaknesses of women. Similarly, like the *Bunting* sequel to *Muller*, the *Darby* sequel to *West Coast Hotel* spent little time on the due process question, devoting the rest of a rather lengthy opinion to other legal issues. (In *Darby*, those questions involved the constitutional relationship between national and state legislative power.) In other words, once the constitutionality of women's legislation had been seriously debated, the due process question for similar legislation of *general* applicability was again simply assumed to have been already settled.

The repeated success of the *Muller/Bunting* and *West Coast Hotel/Darby* approach to obtaining societal acceptance of social welfare legislation via the women-and-children-first technique renders understandable why veterans of social welfare legislation battles, such as the AFL-CIO, for years prior to the mid-1960s opposed the Equal Rights Amendment. Those groups were reluctant to potentially negate protective legislation given its utility as a mechanism for advancing broader protections for all workers. Even as of the twenty-first century, the Supreme Court has not declared unconstitutional all laws that treat men differently from women, so this issue has not entirely disappeared.

EQUAL PROTECTION CLAUSE

After failing twice in pleas based on the privileges or immunities clause, women's rights litigants themselves shifted their attention to the Fourteenth Amendment's equal protection clause. That "no state shall deny to any person within its jurisdiction the equal protection of the law" is a command, like most of those in the Constitution, with more than one possible interpretation. Obviously, it means at least that all shall be equal "in the eyes of the law," that is, that the law as written shall be applied evenhandedly to all persons without regard to wealth or station. Although even this minimal meaning of the clause establishes a worthy (but, sadly, too often unattained) goal for the legal system, judges and legislators recognized from the start that the clause surely requires something more. That extra something in the way of "equal protection" refers to a certain measure of equality in the content of the laws themselves.

All laws treat different people differently. Some of them, one recognizes intuitively, do not violate the idea of "equal protection": A person who kills another under circumstances of self-defense may go free; a person who kills without those circumstances must go to prison. A murderer with a history of three prior criminal convictions receives a more severe penalty than a murderer with no prior convictions. Fifteen-year-olds who commit murder receive a lesser sentence than 30-year-olds who commit the same act. Persons who are certifiably insane and commit murder are sent to a hospital; legally "sane" murderers are sent to prison. All these inequalities of treatment are mandated by statute law, and none of them violates the equal protection clause. Nonetheless, certain kinds of legal categorizations do violate that clause, as that clause has always been understood.

It is much easier to itemize the classifications forbidden by the equal protection clause than it is to explicate the principle underlying that prohibition. Everyone understood, as shown in the *Slaughterhouse Cases*, that the equal protection clause was intended to outlaw the Black Codes, or Slave Codes, which then prevailed throughout the South. These codes prohibited all Black persons or all persons who had once been slaves from owning property, from entering certain occupations, from attending schools, and so forth. In the phrase "equal protection of the law," Congress and the states that ratified the amendment[42] were announcing the rule that laws denying rights on the basis of race or previous condition of servitude were henceforth unconstitutional. While this is not a suitable context for exploring the anomalies of the separate-but-equal approach to this rule, which distorted it from 1896 to 1954, it is nonetheless true that laws depriving Black individuals of rights granted to white persons were widely understood to have been rendered unconstitutional by the equal protection clause. Thus, as early as 1880, a law excluding Black individuals from jury duty was declared invalid by the Supreme Court.[43]

This prohibition on racial discrimination by overt legal mandate was soon broadened to cover the example of a law that, as applied, resulted in excluding virtually all persons of Chinese origin from entering certain occupations.[44] Not long after that, the prohibition was further extended to cover the case of laws that discriminated against aliens without good reason.[45]

This sort of race or nationality discrimination, when it has no other basis than majority dislike of a minority group, is termed "invidious discrimination" by the Supreme Court and is banned by the equal protection clause.

Not every racial classification in laws is banned, however. Instead of creating a ban on racial classifications, the equal protection clause imposes a heavy burden of justification on those classifications. In situations of extreme public need, where a "compelling" or "overriding" governmental need can be demonstrated, the Court will permit legislative lines to be drawn on the basis of race. The busing of schoolchildren and the racially-oriented gerrymandering of school district lines for desegregation in the 1960s and 1970s are examples of these justified exceptions. Instead of being forbidden classifications, then, race and nationality are said to be "suspect classifications." They are suspected (or assumed) to be "invidious" (based on unreasoned group antagonisms) until proven to be justified by a "compelling legislative purpose."

The historical circumstances surrounding the adoption of the Fourteenth Amendment provide a ready explanation for labeling racial classifications as "suspect" by virtue of the equal protection clause. When one notices that the original case treating nationality discrimination as suspect involved Chinese individuals,[46] that is, a non-Caucasian group who were at the time not permitted to become naturalized (in effect, condemned to be permanently aliens), the conceptual connection between racial and nationality classifications takes on even more concrete reality.

In the 1960s, the Supreme Court appeared to be extending the label "suspect" to classifications based on poverty as well. This further extension of the category is not as readily explainable, but did look solidly entrenched by the early 1970s.[47] By 1969, Chief Justice Earl Warren was referring to lines "drawn on the basis of wealth or race" as involving "two factors which independently render a classification highly suspect."[48]

What characteristics race, nationality, and poverty have in common that would render them equally suspect as "invidious" are not easy to determine, and, indeed, the Court since the early 1970s has largely backed away from treating poverty this way. But during the early 1970s, whatever those characteristics were, other discriminated-against groups were litigating in an effort to claim a share in them and thus to gather shelter from the suspect classification umbrella. Most prominent among such groups were women.[49]

An understanding of the way that the suspect classification doctrine operates is absolutely crucial for understanding how the U.S. Constitution does and does not protect women's rights. For one thing, sex may yet be declared a suspect classification under the existing Fourteenth Amendment equal protection clause. In 1973, in the case of *Frontiero v. Richardson*[50] the Court came bewilderingly close to doing just that. Although at present it looks as if the Court will continue to refrain from taking that step, the possibility nonetheless remains that the Court will someday declare gender to be a suspect classification on the basis of the equal protection clause alone.

At the same time, however, growing awareness about the complexities of sex and gender challenge the correlation between these two characteristics and further complicate this debate. As discussed in Chapters 3 and 6, existing legislative prohibitions on sex discrimination have been interpreted at times to include protections for transgender and gender non-conforming individuals, but the U.S.

Supreme Court has yet to decide a case involving the equal protection clause and gender identity. Thus, it is not clear if and when the justices will embrace the contemporary understanding of sex and/or gender: one that acknowledges the mutability of these characteristics. Such an acknowledgment would have consequences for the level of scrutiny applied to future Fourteenth Amendment equal protection claims alleging sex and/or gender discrimination.

Second, if the Equal Rights Amendment, which missed being added to the Constitution by only three states in the 1970s, is ever adopted, the need to understand the legal ramifications of suspect classifications will no longer rest on a hypothetical possibility. For it is certain that, just as the historical circumstances surrounding the adoption of the equal protection clause rendered it a pronouncement that racial classifications in the law would be "suspect," so the wording of the ERA would cause it to be interpreted as rendering sex-based classifications "suspect." An examination of a sample of the Court's treatment of racial classifications will thus provide an accurate estimate of the degree of justification that would be required before a sex-based classification could be upheld under an ERA.

Although many racial exclusions had earlier been struck down by the Court, the grounding of such a move in the rule that racial classifications are "suspect" under the equal protection clause occurred for the first time in the case of *McLaughlin v. Florida* in 1964.[51] The case involved a Florida statute making it a crime for a "Negro man and a white woman or a white man and Negro woman" to "occupy in the nighttime the same room." Both members of the couple could receive up to one year in jail. No proof of fornication was required to prove guilt. Florida had additional statutes punishing fornication, adultery, and "lewd cohabitation," all of which required proof of sexual intercourse to determine guilt, so this statute clearly concerned a "crime" based solely on the race of the "offenders." Florida argued that this law's purpose derived from its support for another Florida statute—the law against miscegenation. The Supreme Court's unanimous reply was that, even assuming for the sake of argument that the anti-miscegenation statute was constitutional (three years later, they were to make clear that it was not),[52] and that this statute in fact aided its enforcement, such justification was simply not enough. Here are their own words concerning the degree of justification needed to support racial classification in the law (at 379 U.S., 192–196, emphasis added):

> The central purpose of the Fourteenth Amendment was to eliminate racial discrimination emanating from official sources in the States. This strong policy renders racial classifications "constitutionally suspect,"

Bolling v. Sharpe, 347 U.S. 497, 499; and subject to the "most *rigid scrutiny*," *Korematsu v. United States*, 323 U.S. 214, 216; and "in most circumstances irrelevant" to any constitutionally acceptable legislative purpose, *Hirabayashi v. United States*, 320 U.S. 81, 100. . . .Our inquiry, therefore, is whether there clearly appears in the relevant materials *some overriding statutory purpose* requiring the proscription of the specified conduct when engaged in by a white person and a Negro, but not otherwise. Without such justification the racial classification contained in § 798.05 is reduced to an invidious discrimination forbidden by the Equal Protection Clause...[L]egislative discretion to employ the piecemeal approach stops short of permitting a State to narrow statutory coverage to focus on a racial group. Such classifications *bear a far heavier burden of justification*. . . . There is involved here an exercise of the state police power which trenches upon the constitutionally protected freedom from invidious official discrimination based on race. Such a law, even though [we might assume that it was] enacted pursuant to a valid state interest, *bears a heavy burden of justification*, as we have said, and will be upheld only if it is *necessary, and not merely rationally related, to* the accomplishment of a *permissible state policy*.

As the Court stated in *McLaughlin,* and as we emphasized in italics, the constitutional test for any suspect classification is that it must be proved "necessary" for the accomplishment of some "overriding" legislative purpose. What, then, is an "overriding" purpose? It means, in general, a weighty or important purpose, so important as to outweigh the constitutional condemnation of racial discrimination; sometimes the adjective "compelling" has been used by the Court in place of "overriding." Two overriding purposes held adequate to justify racial classifications have been (1) national defense during wartime, which was used to justify the evacuation and incarceration of Japanese Americans residing on the West Coast after Japan attacked the U.S. during World War II,[53] and (2) the need, in the late twentieth century, to eliminate *de jure* school segregation in communities where decades of governmentally forced segregation had an inevitable and enduring effect on shaping school attendance habits and neighborhood residential patterns.

The Court not only permitted racial classifications to be used for desegregation purposes, but also declared unconstitutional a law forbidding such classifications. The North Carolina Anti-Busing Law stated, "No student shall be assigned or compelled to attend any school on account of race, creed, color, or national origin." In 1971, the Supreme Court unanimously struck down the statute, explaining that "state policy must give way when it operates to hinder vindication of federal constitutional guarantees."[54] The constitutional guarantee of which they were speaking was the fundamental right of children (under earlier decisions interpreting the equal protection clause) to equal educational opportunity. If any community had a "dual," or two-race, school system in the past, its constitutional obligation was to disestablish, or desegregate, that dual system to provide equal educational opportunity, and such rectification required looking at student race. When they were essential in this way, racial classifications were not only permitted but even required.[55]

More recently, however, the Court has indicated that in its imposition of the strict scrutiny test, it draws a sharp distinction between governmental action to undo segregation where it was forced upon people initially and governmental action to integrate communities or schools segregated due to other-than-governmental forces. For the latter, sometimes it upholds the government action and sometimes not.[56]

If sex were to become officially a suspect classification, some circumstances would surely arise, parallel to those of the busing situation, that still required sex-based distinctions in the law. (This matter receives further consideration in the case note following *Frontiero v. Richardson* in Chapter 2.)

Because the equal protection clause speaks in general terms without specific mention of race, at least in principle the clause soon acquired a general content with implications reaching far beyond its specific prohibition (or near-prohibition) of racial (or suspect) classifications. These implications comprised an alternative constitutional doctrine available to women's rights litigants as long as the "suspect classification" label eluded their grasp. It is important to examine this alternative equal protection approach in order both to understand the legal context that stimulated the ERA campaign of the 1970s and to grasp the significance of the changes in constitutional law wrought by the Supreme Court since the time of that campaign,[57] changes that likely contributed to the failure of the amendment to attain ratification. This general approach, or "ordinary" equal protection scrutiny, in the century before 1970 presented a partly cloudy/partly sunny picture of opportunity for litigants attacking sex discrimination.

The clouds in this picture were the first part to develop. The *Slaughterhouse Cases*, with the statement that the equal protection clause probably applied only to racial discrimination, forecast difficulty in expanding the equal protection clause beyond race, and the Supreme Court made only minor adjustments to this rule until the mid-twentieth century. Those minor adjustments were shaped by broad statements of principle that the Court applied with such a light touch that for the first 50 years the impact of these statements was barely perceptible. Still, they did create at least a small opening in the precedent law to which later litigants could eventually appeal with much more noticeable success.

By 1886 the Supreme Court had acknowledged that "the equal protection of the laws is a pledge of the protection of equal laws."[58] "Equal laws," however, did not mean laws that affected all members of society equally. As explained above, all laws affect different people with differing impacts. What "equal laws" *did* mean was that the equal protection clause, in addition to denoting racial classifications suspect, created a certain standard of fairness against which all legislative classifications would have to be measured.

At first that standard of fairness was stated only in the vaguest, and therefore most unenforceable, of terms. In 1885 the Court explained the equal protection clause as though it were little (if anything) more than a guideline of legislative convenience:

> Special burdens are often necessary for general benefits. . . . Regulations for these purposes may press with more or less weight upon one than upon another, but they are [acceptable if] designed, not to impose unequal or *unnecessary* restrictions upon anyone, but to promote, with *as little inconvenience as possible*, the general good. [Emphasis added.][59]

By "unnecessary" here the Court meant utterly groundless. Thus, the justices read the equal protection clause as stating that legislatures could not penalize particular groups of people in whimsical or "purely arbitrary" ways: equal protection required that there be some point to any classification that a legislature enacted into law. But what legislature would bother to enact a law that had absolutely no purpose? If this seems an exaggerated depiction of the turn-of-the-century Court's nonrule of equal protection, consider the following explanation of it in the Court's own words in a 1911 case:

> 1. The equal protection clause of the Fourteenth Amendment does not take from the State the power to classify in the adoption of police laws, but admits of a wider scope of discretion in that regard, and avoids what is done *only when it is without any reasonable basis and therefore is purely arbitrary*. 2. A classification having *some* reasonable basis does not offend against the clause merely because it is not made with mathematical nicety or because in practice it results in some inequality. 3. When the classification in such a law is called in question, *if any state of facts reasonably can be conceived that would sustain it, the existence of the state of facts must be assumed*. 4. One who assails the classification in such a law must carry

the *burden of showing that it does not rest upon any reasonable basis but is essentially arbitrary.* [Emphases added.][60]

The italics, of course, stress the interpretation compatible with our point; we note that the requirement that classifications have a "reasonable" basis is one of the most accordion-like standards of the American legal system. Thus the Court's oft-quoted 1920 statement that equal protection required that classifications "be reasonable, not arbitrary and . . . rest upon some ground of difference having a fair and substantial relation to the object of the legislation, so that all persons similarly circumstanced shall be treated alike"[61] can be read in a variety of ways. It looks like it means that legislative classifications must be in fact sensibly related to the public welfare purpose at which the law is aiming. This full-blown version would stress the "fair and substantial relation" phrase in the standard. Nevertheless, if the Court wanted to stress the word *some* (reading, "classifications. . . must rest upon *some* ground of difference") and wanted to interpret "object of the legislation" in a narrow way, the justices could collapse the reasonableness accordion into almost invisible size.

For example, a law that prohibited women from entering the state bar to become lawyers, by the expanded, or rigorous, reasonableness standard could be said to have no "fair and substantial" relation to the legislative objective of providing well-qualified lawyers to serve the public (the broad objective of bar admissions standards). But using the same 1920 statement as a guide, the Court could say of the same law that there is some ground for excluding women from the bar and that the (narrow) legislative objective of keeping women at home to care for their children does have a reasonable relationship to the legislative practice of excluding them from all paid professions.

The "reasonableness" standard for the equal protection clause provided the Court, one might say, with a hammer that it could wield with whatever strength it desired. Wielded by a strong arm, the hammer could be used to strike down much, even most, legislation—depending on how substantial the "substantial relation" had to be and the breadth of the "object of the legislation" on which the Court chose to focus. Wielded by a gentle hand, the reasonableness hammer could strike so lightly as to make no impression. Not needing the equal protection hammer for striking down economic legislation—the task that preoccupied the Court in the first few decades of the century, the era of *Lochner v. New York*, and for which the sledgehammer of economic substantive due process was more than adequate—the Supreme Court allowed the equal protection hammer to lie dormant, wielding it with only the gentlest of kid gloves during this period. *Radice v. New York* (above) provides a good period example of the Court's disparate treatment of these two clauses. While the Court took the due process argument seriously there, its response to the equal protection argument was relatively cavalier: the legislature, the Court said, may proceed "step by step" (letting women work certain jobs at night but not others); "it is not necessary that the prohibition . . . be all-embracing [e.g., cover men and women workers equally]" (264 U.S., at 298). This is standard logic under ordinary equal protection scrutiny.

Thus, for several decades this "reasonableness" equal protection principle received no more than lip service from the Court. The justices openly admitted that the principle, as they interpreted it, permitted laws to be "ill-advised, unequal," and even "oppressive."[62] In other words, they were willing to view as "reasonable" any law for which the legislature, or legislature's counsel, could conjure up any rationale, even if unpersuasive or implausible.

This accordion-like "reasonableness" test for applying the equal protection clause, because it is the one applied in the common case—as contrasted with the "suspect classification" approach, which occurs only in the rare case—is often called the "ordinary scrutiny" approach to equal protection. Ordinarily, when a particular legislative classification is challenged as a denial of equal protection of the laws, the justices simply ask themselves whether this classification bears some "reasonable" or "rational" relationship to some valid legislative purpose. In the race case, *McLaughlin v. Florida*, the Court referred to the need to subject suspect classifications not to "ordinary scrutiny" but rather to "the most rigid scrutiny." The general rule then, circa 1970, was that suspect classifications received "strict scrutiny" (i.e., must be shown to be necessary for the attainment of a compelling governmental interest), whereas all other classifications receive merely "ordinary scrutiny," or—because the accordion is generally kept in its collapsed state— "minimal scrutiny" (i.e., need only bear some logical or "rational" relationship to any legitimate governmental purpose).[63]

The direction of, as well as the obstacles along, women's alternative to the suspect classification route should now be clear. Women's rights litigants could venture along the ordinary scrutiny path in challenging sex-discriminatory legislation as a violation of equal protection of the laws. To reach their goal of having those laws declared void, the litigants would need to surmount the obstacle of having to demonstrate that the laws had no rational relationship to promoting a valid legislative purpose. This task of demonstration would vary in difficulty according to the rigor with which the Court chose to apply the reasonableness test.

A Century of "Ordinary Scrutiny" of Sex-Based Classifications

Early-Twentieth-Century Cases. By the early 1900s, the principle that the equal protection clause broadly limited the content of legislation, according to the rationality standard described in the preceding section, was firmly established. As long as the Court followed the four guidelines for applying the reasonableness test quoted above, the chances were almost nil that a challenger could successfully prove that a law embodied an "unreasonable" classification. In short, as applied during the early twentieth century, the rule simply accorded every conceivable benefit of doubt to the side of the statute under attack.

The earliest equal protection clause challengers to gender discrimination were men rather than women, and they were attacking legislation that singled out women for special benefit. Whether legislation ostensibly protective of women helps them more than it hurts them is, of course, a subject of controversy.[64] But that it hurts men is often intuitively obvious, and "men's rights" advocates were quick to assert their claims in court.

Within a few years of *Muller v. Oregon*, the Supreme Court received a case, *Quong Wing v. Kirkendall*, 223 U.S. 59 (1912), that challenged on sex discrimination grounds a law providing special economic benefits to women. Quong Wing, a male Chinese American[65] who operated a hand laundry in Lewis and Clark County, Montana, challenged a Montana law that imposed a 10-dollar "license tax" on all operators of hand laundries. The statute explicitly exempted steam laundries from this tax, and it also exempted women who ran laundries employing no more than two women. Quong Wing challenged both exemptions as a violation of the equal protection clause of the Fourteenth Amendment.

The Supreme Court's response to Quong Wing's challenge is illustrative of two prevalent tendencies in equal protection clause analysis of this early period. First, it illustrates in stark colors the Court's willingness to swallow any argument in defense of legislation providing special treatment to women. Justice Oliver Wendell Holmes devotes all of one sentence to the matter of the "reasonableness" of this sex-based occupational tax: "If Montana deems it advisable to put a lighter burden upon women than upon men with regard to an employment that our people commonly regard as more appropriate for the former, the Fourteenth Amendment does not interfere by creating a fictitious equality where there is a real difference."[66] Second, the Holmes majority opinion illustrates the bifurcated approach to equal protection scrutiny that had already developed by this time. Racial discrimination was scrutinized with far more care than "ordinary" classifications were. Justice Holmes indicates the Court's grounds for suspecting that this sex discrimination law may be a race discrimination law in disguise; he notes that many Chinese men but virtually no men "of our race" operate hand laundries. If it were a matter of race discrimination, Justice Holmes admits, it "would be a discrimination that the Constitution does not allow."[67] Holmes's defense of the constitutionality of this law offered no hints why the equal protection clause would forbid the same discrimination against Chinese-American men that it would permit against men in general.

The Supreme Court's cavalier approach to male complaints about sex discrimination continued long after Justice Holmes left the Court. In 1937, in *Breedlove v. Suttles*, 302 U.S. 277 (1937), the Court again, and this time unanimously, rejected the constitutional arguments of a man complaining about sex-based discrimination in tax laws.

The state of Georgia required all males (except the blind) between the ages of 21 and 60 to pay a $1 annual tax. This tax was called a "poll tax," evidently because it was collected when people tried to register to vote and because they were not allowed to vote if their poll taxes were not paid in full. Despite the label, however, alien males, who were not permitted to vote, had to pay the tax, and elderly males who did vote were excused from the tax on the basis of age. Women in the 21–60 age group, regardless of their marital status, had to pay the tax only if they registered to vote.

A 28-year-old man named Nolan Breedlove tried to register to vote without having paid his poll taxes. When the registrars turned him away, he initiated a suit in the local courts to have these tax laws declared unconstitutional on the grounds that they conflicted with the equal protection clause, the privileges or immunities clause, and the Nineteenth Amendment. The county court and the state supreme court both rejected his claims, and Breedlove appealed to the U.S. Supreme Court.

The Supreme Court paid little attention to Breedlove's privileges or immunities argument. Justice Butler's opinion followed the old *Minor v. Happersett* ruling that the right to vote was not a privilege of national citizenship.

The Court opinion took the Nineteenth Amendment argument only slightly more seriously. Because members of both sexes, if they wanted to vote, had to pay the tax, the Court saw no plausibility in the claim that this tax tended to abridge the right to vote "on account of sex." The Court buttressed this reasoning with the observation that requiring "the payment of poll taxes as a prerequisite to voting" was a widely accepted practice in the American states. (Eventually, in

1966, the Supreme Court did declare poll taxes a violation of equal protection of the laws.)⁶⁸

The Court gave the most weight to Breedlove's equal protection argument. Beginning with the reminder, "The equal protection clause does not require absolute equality," Justice Butler first justified exempting minors and the elderly from the tax. The young do not generally support themselves, so taxing them would usually result just in extra taxes on their parents. And the old are excused from a variety of public duties, such as jury duty and service in the militia. Justice Butler reasoned that this tax exemption did not differ to a "substantial" degree from those other exemptions for the elderly. His arguments aimed at justifying the tax discrimination between nonvoting women and nonvoting men were as follows:

> The tax being upon the person, women may be exempted on the basis of special considerations to which they are naturally entitled. In view of burdens necessarily borne by them for the preservation of the race, the State may reasonably exempt them from poll taxes. [Case citations omitted.] The laws of Georgia declare the husband to be the head of the family and the wife to be subject to him. To subject her to the levy would be to add to his burden. Moreover, Georgia poll taxes are laid to raise money for education purposes, and it is the father's duty to provide for education of the children.
>
> Discrimination in favor of all women being permissible, appellant may not complain because the tax is laid only upon some or object to the registration of women without payment of taxes for previous years.⁶⁹

Goesaert v. Cleary (1948)

When legislation purporting to protect women blatantly cut them off from certain job opportunities, they, too, took complaints to court. As the *Radice v. New York* case made evident, due process challenges to such laws generally foundered on the *Muller v. Oregon* precedent. Eventually, women tried asserting their rights under the equal protection clause. Confronting the Court's any-rationalization-is-reasonable approach to "ordinary scrutiny," these women fared no better than the men's rights litigants.

The 1948 case of *Goesaert v. Cleary*⁷⁰ provides a typical sampling of the Court's approach to "ordinary" equal protection scrutiny by the mid-twentieth century. Ms. Goesaert was challenging a Michigan statute that prohibited a woman from serving liquor as a bartender unless she was "the wife or daughter of the male owner" of a licensed liquor establishment. In marked historical contrast to the *Bradwell* case, Ms. Goesaert's case was argued at the Supreme Court by a woman lawyer. Nevertheless, Ms. Goesaert fared no better than Myra Bradwell had.

Justice Frankfurter, who writes the majority opinion here, had served as lawyer on the *Bunting v. Oregon* and the *Adkins v. Children's Hospital* cases, in which he had argued that the Fourteenth Amendment does not prohibit states from enacting social welfare legislation that gives special protection to women. While his conclusions in *Goesaert v. Cleary* are obviously consistent with his previous advocacy role, one can argue that he did not take seriously the question whether a principled distinction can be drawn between hours and wage legislation protective of women, on the one hand, and legislation barring some women from certain trades, on the other. What is the answer to that question?

GOESAERT ET AL. V. CLEARY ET AL., LIQUOR CONTROL COMMISSION
335 U.S. 464 (1948)

MR. JUSTICE FRANKFURTER delivered the opinion of the Court:

...The claim, denied below, one judge dissenting, 74 F. Supp. 735, and renewed here, is that Michigan cannot forbid females generally from being barmaids and at the same time make an exception in favor of the wives and daughters of the owners of liquor establishments. Beguiling as the subject is, it need not detain us long. To ask whether or not the Equal Protection of the Laws Clause of the Fourteenth Amendment barred Michigan from making the classification the State has made between wives and daughters of owners of liquor places and wives and daughters of non-owners, is one of those rare instances where to state the question is in effect to answer it.

...[R]egulation of the liquor traffic is one of the oldest and most untrammeled of legislative powers. Michigan could, beyond question, forbid all women from working behind a bar. This is so despite the vast changes in the social and legal position of women. The fact that women may now have achieved the virtues that men have longed claimed as their prerogatives and now indulge in vices that men have long practiced, does not preclude the States from drawing a sharp line between the sexes, certainly in such matters as the regulation of the liquor traffic. See the Twenty-First Amendment....The Constitution does not require legislatures to reflect sociological insight, or shifting social standards, any more than it requires them to keep abreast of the latest scientific standards.

While Michigan may deny to all women opportunities for bartending, Michigan cannot play favorites among women without rhyme or reason. The Constitution in enjoining the equal protection of the laws upon States precludes irrational discrimination as between persons or groups of persons in the incidence of a law. But the Constitution does not require situations "which are different in fact or opinion to be treated in law as though they were the same." *Tigner v. Texas,* 310 U.S. 141, 147. Since bartending by women may, in the allowable legislative judgment, give rise to moral and social problems against which it may devise preventive measures, the legislature need not go to the full length of prohibition if it believes that as to a defined group of females other factors are operating which either eliminate or reduce the moral and social problems otherwise calling for prohibition. Michigan evidently believes that the oversight assured through ownership of a bar by a barmaid's husband or father minimizes hazards that may confront a barmaid without such protecting oversight. This Court is certainly not in a position to gainsay such belief by the Michigan legislature. If it is entertainable, as we think it is, Michigan has not violated its duty to afford equal protection of its laws. We cannot cross-examine either actually or argumentatively the mind of Michigan legislators nor question their motives. Since the line they have drawn is not without a basis in reason, we cannot give ear to the suggestion that the real impulse behind this legislation was an unchivalrous desire of male bartenders to try to monopolize the calling.

* * *

Nor is it unconstitutional for Michigan to withdraw from women the occupation of bar-tending because it allows women to serve as waitresses where liquor is dispensed. The District Court has sufficiently indicated the reasons that may have influenced the legislature in allowing women to be waitresses in a liquor establishment over which a man's ownership provides control. . . .

Judgment *Affirmed*.

MR. JUSTICE RUTLEDGE, with whom MR. JUSTICE DOUGLAS and MR. JUSTICE MURPHY join, dissenting:

While the equal protection clause does not require a legislature to achieve "abstract symmetry" or to classify with "mathematical nicety," that clause does requires lawmakers to refrain from invidious distinctions of the sort drawn by the statute challenged in this case.

The statute arbitrarily discriminates between male and female owners of liquor establishments. A male owner, although he himself is always absent from

> his bar, may employ his wife and daughter as barmaids. A female owner may neither work as a barmaid herself nor employ her daughter in that position, even if a man is always present in the establishment to keep order.... Since there could be no... conceivable justification for such discrimination against women owners of liquor establishments, the statute should be held invalid as a denial of equal protection.

Case Questions

1. To what extent does Justice Frankfurter's opinion rely on the Twenty-first Amendment? In *California v. LaRue*, 410 U.S. 948 (1972), the Supreme Court held that a state's right to regulate liquor traffic under the Twenty-first Amendment overrode even some of the rights of free expression implied by the First Amendment. If the ERA were to be ratified, would the Twenty-first Amendment nonetheless keep this Michigan statute constitutional?

2. Just what is the "basis in reason" that Frankfurter finds for keeping women from behind the bar? For making an exception of wives and daughters of male bar owners? For not making an additional exception for female owners and their daughters "even if a man is always present to keep order"?

3. If the Michigan legislature altered the statute to comply with the dissenters' objections concerning an exemption for female bar owners, would the law still violate the equal protection clause? Would it violate an ERA?

Hoyt v. Florida (1961)

As is evident by now, in the name of ordinary equal protection scrutiny, the Supreme Court has allowed the flimsiest of "reasons" to support statutes challenged as denials of equal protection. This pattern continued to cloud the efforts of women's rights litigants even into the 1960s, a period when the Court was thought of as generally "liberal." And the case in question, *Hoyt v. Florida*, concerned what might be thought of as another basic citizen right besides voting, the right to serve on juries.

This 1960s example of the Court's acceptance of unreasoned "reasons" for denials to women of equal treatment involved an incident within that sanctuary of family life, the home. One Mrs. Hoyt of Florida assaulted and killed her husband with a baseball bat during a "marital upheaval," as the Court put it. Mrs. Hoyt not only suspected her husband of adultery, but had the further motivation that he rejected her when she said she was willing to forgive and take him back. She pleaded "temporary insanity" and was convicted of second-degree murder by an all-male jury.

Florida law provided that no female could serve on a jury unless she had personally made a trip down to the circuit court office and specifically requested to be put on the jury list. Because men did not have to make such efforts, the law naturally produced an enormous disproportion of male to female jurors, which almost always produced all-male juries, like Mrs. Hoyt's. (Of some 10,000 persons on her local jury list of eligibles, only 10 were women.) Mrs. Hoyt claimed that this statute denied her equal protection of the law because (as Justice Harlan put it, at p.59) "women jurors would have been more understanding or compassionate than men in assessing the quality of [her] act and her defense of 'temporary insanity.'"

In deciding *Hoyt,* as is often the situation, the Court had available to it alternative lines of precedents that pointed in opposed directions. On one hand (against Mrs. Hoyt) were the equal protection cases presented above. On the other hand was a line of trial-by-jury cases that *might* have been used to infer the rule that impartiality in jury trials was a necessary element of equal protection and that impartiality required a fair cross-section of the community.

In its role as supervisor of the federal courts, in the 1940s the U.S. Supreme Court had outlawed the systematic exclusion of daily wage earners from federal juries with an argument that the "American tradition of trial by jury" demands "an impartial jury drawn from a cross-section of the community," and that this implied that jurors must be selected "without systematic and intentional exclusion of any [economic, social, religious, racial, political or geographical] groups" (*Thiel v. Southern Pacific*, 328 U.S. 217, 220).

The Court had also ruled in the 1946 case *Ballard v. U.S.*, 329 U.S. 187, that three elements of the Congressional statute governing federal jury selection (Judicial Code § 275, 28 U.S.C. § 411) "reflect a design to make the jury 'a cross-section of the community' and truly representative of it." Those three elements in the statute were (a) a prohibition on racial exclusion, (b) a command that jurors be chosen "without regard to party affiliation," and (c) a rule that jurors be selected from such parts of the district as to make most likely an impartial jury and not unduly burden the citizens of any one part of the district. (Note that it is not at all obvious that these three rules imply more strongly than does the phrase "equal protection of the laws" the rule that juries must be chosen from a representative cross-section of the community.) Having arrived at the representative cross-section rule in *Ballard,* the Court then used it to guide the interpretation of the federal statute requiring that jurors in federal trials be chosen according to state juror selection rules. California in 1946 (unlike 40 percent of the states) did make women eligible for jury duty. But as a matter of state practice women were not called to serve. Federal courts in California, in a good faith effort to obey federal law, had been following state practice rather than the letter of state statute. The Supreme Court in *Ballard* held this federal practice in the particular state of California to be a "departure from the federal scheme Congress adopted" and to be an error to be corrected by the Court's power "over the administration of justice in the federal courts." In ordering this correction, the Supreme Court reasoned as follows:

> It is said, however, that an all-male panel drawn from the various groups within a community will be as truly representative as if women were included. The thought is that the factors which tend to influence the action of women are the same as those which influence the action of men—personality, background, economic status—and not sex. Yet it is not enough to say that women when sitting as jurors neither act nor tend to act as a class. Men likewise do not act as a class. But, if the shoe were on the other foot, who would claim that a jury was truly representative of the community if all men were intentionally and systematically excluded from the panel? The truth is that the two sexes are not fungible; a community made up exclusively of one is different from a community composed of both; the subtle interplay of influence one [has] on the other is among the imponderables. To insulate the courtroom from either may not in a given case make an iota of difference. Yet a flavor, a distinct quality is lost if either sex is excluded. The exclusion of one may indeed make the jury less representative of the community than would be true if an economic or racial group were excluded.

It was Justice Douglas who wrote these words in 1946 regarding federal trials in one state. In *Hoyt v. Florida*, a case concerning state trials in a different state 15 years later, he shows no sign of remembering his own arguably relevant logic.

HOYT V. FLORIDA
368 U.S. 57 (1961)

MR. JUSTICE HARLAN delivered the opinion of the Court:

...Of course [Mrs. Hoyt's] premises misconceive the scope of the right to an impartially selected jury assured by the Fourteenth Amendment. That right does not entitle one accused of crime to a jury tailored to the circumstances of the particular case, whether relating to the sex or other condition of the defendant, or to the nature of the charges to be tried. It requires only that the jury be indiscriminately drawn from among those eligible in the community for jury service, untrammeled by any arbitrary and systematic exclusions. See *Fay v. New York,* 332 U.S. 261, 284–85, and the cases cited therein. The result of this appeal must therefore depend on whether such an exclusion of women from jury service has been shown.

I

We address ourselves first to appellant's challenge to the statute on its face.

Several observations should initially be made. We of course recognize that the Fourteenth Amendment reaches not only arbitrary class exclusions from jury service based on race or color, but also all other exclusions which "single out" any class of persons "for different treatment not based on some reasonable classification." *Hernandez v. Texas*, 347 U.S. 475, 478. We need not, however, accept appellant's invitation to canvass in this case the continuing validity to this Court's dictum in *Strauder v. West Virginia*, 100 U.S. 303, 310, to the effect that a State may constitutionally "confine" jury duty "to males." This constitutional proposition has gone unquestioned for more than eighty years in the decisions of the Court, see *Fay v. New York*, at 289–90, and had been reflected, until 1957, in congressional policy respecting jury service in the federal courts themselves.[2] Even were it to be assumed that this question is still open to debate, the present case tenders narrower issues.

Manifestly, Florida's § 40.1 (1) does not purport to exclude women from state jury service. Rather, the statute "gives to women the privilege to serve but does not impose service as a duty.". . . This is not to say, however, that what in form may be only an exemption of a particular class of persons can in no circumstances be regarded as an exclusion of that class. Where, as here, an exemption of a class in the community is asserted to be in substance an exclusionary device, the relevant inquiry is whether the exemption itself is based on some reasonable classification and whether the manner in which it is exercisable rests on some rational foundation.

In the selection of jurors Florida has differentiated between men and women in two respects. It has given women an absolute exemption from jury duty based solely on their sex, no similar exemption obtaining as to men. And it has provided for its effectuation in a manner less onerous than that governing exemptions exercisable by men: women are not to be put on the jury list unless they have voluntarily registered for such service; men, on the other hand, even if entitled to an exemption, are to be included on the list unless they have [annually] filed a written claim of exemption. . . .

In neither respect can we conclude that Florida's statute is not "based on some reasonable classification," and that it is thus infected with unconstitutionality. Despite the enlightened emancipation of women from the restrictions and protections of bygone years, and their entry into many parts of community life formerly considered to be reserved to men, woman is still regarded as the center of home and family life. We cannot say that it is constitutionally impermissible for a State, acting in pursuit of the general welfare, to conclude that a woman should be relieved from the civic duty of jury service unless she herself determines that such service is consistent with her own special responsibilities.

Florida is not alone in so concluding. Women are now eligible for jury service in all but three States of the Union. Of the forty-seven States where women are eligible, seventeen besides Florida, as well as the District of Columbia, have accorded women an absolute exemption based solely on their sex, exercisable in one form or another. In two of these States, as in Florida, the exemption is automatic, unless a woman volunteers for such service. It is true, of course, that Florida could have limited the exemption, as some other States have done, only to women who have family responsibilities. But we cannot regard it as irrational for a state legislature to consider preferable a broad exemption, whether born of the State's historic public policy or of a determination that it would not be administratively feasible to decide in each individual instance whether the family responsibilities of a prospective female juror were serious enough to warrant an exemption.

Likewise we cannot say that Florida could not reasonably conclude that full effectuation of this exemption made it desirable to relieve women of the necessity of affirmatively claiming it, while at the same time requiring of men an assertion of the exemptions available to them. Moreover, from the standpoint of its own administrative concerns the State might well consider that it was "impractical to compel large numbers of women, who have an absolute exemption, to come to the clerk's office for examination since they so generally assert their exemption."

Appellant argues that whatever may have been the design of this Florida enactment, the statute in practical operation results in an exclusion of women from jury service, because women, like men, can be expected to be available for jury service only under compulsion. . . .

This argument, however, is surely beside the point. Given the reasonableness of the classification involved in § 40.01 (1), the relative paucity of women jurors does not carry the constitutional consequence appellant would have it bear. "Circumstances or chance may well dictate that no persons in a certain class will serve on a particular jury or during some particular period." *Hernandez v. Texas* at 482.

We cannot hold this statute as written offensive to the Fourteenth Amendment.

II

Appellant's attack on the statute as applied in this case fares no better. . . .

This case in no way resembles those involving race or color in which the circumstances shown were found by this Court to compel a conclusion of purposeful discriminatory exclusions from jury service [citations omitted.] There is present here neither the unfortunate atmosphere of ethnic or racial prejudices which underlay the situations depicted in those cases, nor the long course of discriminatory administrative practice which the statistical showing in each of them evinced.

In the circumstances here depicted, it indeed "taxes our credulity," *Hernandez v. Texas* at 482, to attribute to these administrative officials a deliberate design to exclude the very class whose eligibility for jury service the state legislature, after many years of contrary policy, had declared only a few years before. [Women became "eligible" for Florida juries in 1948.]

. . . We must sustain the judgment of the Supreme Court of Florida.

Opinion Footnote

2   From the First Judiciary Act of 1798, § 29, 1 Stat. 73,88, to the Civil Rights Act of 1957,71 Stat. 634, 638, 28 U.S.C. § 1861—a period of 168 years—the inclusion or exclusion of women on federal juries depended upon whether they were eligible for jury service under the law of the State where the federal tribunal sat.

By the Civil Rights Act of 1957 Congress made eligible for jury service "Any citizen of the United States," possessed of specific qualifications, 28 U.S.C. § 1861, thereby for the first time making. . . women eligible for federal jury service even though ineligible under state law. There is no indication that such congressional action was impelled by constitutional consideration.

THE CHIEF JUSTICE, MR. JUSTICE BLACK and MR. JUSTICE DOUGLAS, concurring:

We cannot say from this record that Florida is not making a good faith effort to have women perform jury duty without discrimination on the ground

> of sex. Hence, we concur in the result, for the reasons set forth in Part II of the Court's opinion.

Case Questions

1. What "reason" justifies excluding single women from jury duty?

2. Should the fact that a particular classification appears in the statutes of a large number of states be treated as evidence that there is a reasonable basis for the classification?

3. Does the three-judge concurring opinion imply that those judges would view an across-the-board ineligibility for women jurors as unconstitutional? If statistics can be used to show that Blacks are purposely being kept off juries and that these purposeful acts are unconstitutional, why should a system that yields only 10 women in every 10,000 jurors not be unconstitutional even if one cannot show that it is being purposely manipulated by someone?

4. Is it likely that an all-male jury has certain biases not shared by women? That persons who earn less than $20,000 a year have biases not shared by those who earn over $40,000? That Democrats have biases not shared by Republicans? That persons over 60 have biases not shared by persons under 30? Should communities be required to have laws that do not produce systematic jury bias in any of these directions?

Case note: As recently as 1968 the Court refused to reconsider the issue settled in *Hoyt* (*State v. Hall*, 385 U.S. 98).

---

[1] A few limits were placed on state governments. In regard to individual rights, states are forbidden from passing "bills of attainder" (laws that label named individuals as criminals, regardless of whether they have committed any illegal acts), "*ex post facto* laws" (statutes that declare punishments for past actions that, at the time they were committed, were legal), and laws "impairing the obligation of contracts" (for example, a law saying that particular debts would not have to be paid, thereby depriving the lender of his property right). (See Art. I, sec. 10, of the Constitution.) The states had to provide a "republican form of government" (Art. IV, sec. 4) and to refrain from granting titles of nobility (Art. I, sec. 10). States were ordered to give cognizance to property rights recognized by other states (Art. IV, sec. 1), including the property right in runaway "persons held to service or labor" (Art. IV, sec. 2). Finally, states had to grant "all privileges and immunities of citizens in the several states" to the citizens of each state. This confusingly worded clause (Art. IV, sec. 2) simply meant that states were not allowed to discriminate against out-of-staters in basic legal rights, such as access to the courts, the rights to buy and sell, or the right to be hired for a job.

[2] 4 Washington's Circuit Court 380, cited in *Slaughterhouse Cases*, 83 U.S. 36, 117.

[3] 83 U.S., at 78.

[4] Swayne dissent, 83 U.S., at 127.

[5] 83 U.S., at 81

[6] A classic analysis of the Fourteenth Amendment suggests that this is due to the "primacy of the American concern with liberty over equality" (Joseph Tussman and Jacobus ten Broek, "The Equal Protection of the Laws," 37 *California Law Review* 341 [1949]). The tremendous upsurge in equal protection litigation in the post-World War II era (desegregation, state legislative reapportionment, welfare rights, nonmarital

children's rights, prisoners' rights, in addition to the subject of this book) indicates that equality, as against liberty, took on increased importance in American political ideology.

7   *Yick Wo v. Hopkins*, 118 U.S. 356 (1886).

8   *Traux v. Raich*, 235 U.S. 33 (1915). A later case supporting the same principle was *Takahashi v. Fish and Game Commission*, 334 U.S. 410 (1948). Even into the 1970s, the late Chief Justice Rehnquist (at the time still an Associate Justice) would have limited the condemned classification doctrine to racial classifications. See his dissent in *Sugarman v. Dougall*, 413 U.S. 634 (1973).

9   *Heath and Milligan v. Worst*, 207 U.S. 338, 354 (1907), emphasis added. The interior quote is from *Mobile County v. Kimball*, 102 U.S. 691 (1881).

10 83 U.S. 130.

11 Joan Hoff, *Law, Gender & Injustice* (New York, NY: New York University Press, 1991), 169.

12 Edward James, *Notable American Women, 1607–1950* 3 vols. (Cambridge, MA: Belknap Press, 1971), 1:223–25, 2:492–93.

13 83 U.S. 36, 109–10.

14 83 U.S. 36, 122.

15 Hoff, *Law, Gender, & Injustice*, 169.

16 Indeed, the women's suffrage movement split in two over this issue. The branch that supported the Fourteenth Amendment was headed by Lucy Stone and Julia Ward Howe. See discussion of the suffrage movement in the section that follows *Minor v. Hapersett*.

17 Eleanor Flexner, *Century of Struggle* (New York, NY: Atheneum, 1970), 165; Anne F. Scott and Andrew Scott, *One Half the People: The Fight for Woman Suffrage* (Philadelphia, PA: J.B. Lippincott, 1975), 19–20.

18 Scott and Scott, *One Half the People*, 20. A women's suffrage amendment with different wording had been introduced unsuccessfully as early as 1868. Flexner, *Century of Struggle*, 173.

19 Flexner, *Century of Struggle*, 173–75, 220–22.

20 Carrie Chapman Catt and Nettie Rogers Shuler, *Woman Suffrage and Politics* (New York, NY: Charles Scribner's Sons, 1923), 107. The description is Ms. Catt's.

21 Flexner, *Century of Struggle*, 291. The Flexner book contains the fullest account of the suffragist effort that can be found in a single volume. The five-volume *The History of Woman Suffrage* by Elizabeth Cady Stanton, Susan B. Anthony, Matilda Joslyn Gage, and Ida Husted Harper is more complete but not as well organized.

22 Ibid., 144.

23 Patricia A. Schechter, *Ida B. Wells-Barnett and American Reform, 1880–1930* (Chapel Hill, NC: University of North Carolina Press, 2001), Chapter 5, 200.

24 Flexner, *Century of Struggle*, 219.

25 Ibid. 248–257.

26 *Id*. 254–268.

27 *Id*. 264.

28 *Id*. 265

29 *Id*. 272–273.

30 *Id*. 269.

31 *Id*. 279.

32 Doris Stevens, *Jailed for Freedom* (New York, NY: Boni & Liveright, 1920), 102.

33 Flexner, *Century of Struggle*, 285.

34 *Id*. 286.

35 *Id*. 290.

36 *Id*. 290.

37 *Id*. 291–292.

38 Flexner, *Century of Struggle*, 312–314.

39 See *Chicago, Milwaukee and St. Paul Railway v. Minnesota*, 134 U.S. 418 (1890); *Allgeyer v. Louisiana*, 165 U.S. 578 (1898).

⁴⁰ The Supreme Court did hear arguments on Oregon's minimum-wage law for women in 1916 (*Settler v. O'Hara*, 243 U.S. 629) but then tied 4–4, leaving the lower court decision in place.

⁴¹ *Morehead v. New York ex rel Tipaldo*, 298 U.S. 587. An attorney for the National Consumers League, Dorothy Kenyon, submitted an *amicus* (friend of the court) brief endorsing the constitutionality of New York's women-only minimum-wage law. The same attorney in 1961 presented the Supreme Court case against Florida's women-only automatic jury exemption (see *Hoyt v. Florida* below). Ms. Kenyon also presented an *amicus* brief in the 1971 *Phillips v. Martin-Marietta* employment discrimination case (see Chapter 3). For the latter two cases, Ms. Kenyon was in the employ of the American Civil Liberties Union.

⁴² The Southern states were pressured into ratifying the Fourteenth Amendment by a set of congressional requirements that, for the decision-making process, enfranchised Blacks and disfranchised participants in the rebellion, and that also made ratification a precondition for regaining representation in Congress. A. Kelly and W. Harbison, *The American Constitution*, 4th ed. (New York, NY: W.W. Norton, 1970), 465–473.

⁴³ *Strauder v. West Virginia*, 100 U.S. 303 (1880).

⁴⁴ *Yick Wo v. Hopkins*, 118 U.S. 356 (1886).

⁴⁵ *Traux v. Raich*, 239 U.S. 33 (1915). Although the law involved here (as well as various later ones that discriminated against aliens) was declared unconstitutional, the equal protection clause does allow some "discrimination" against aliens, e.g., the limitation of suffrage rights to American citizens. For the explanation of what is considered good enough "reason" to deprive aliens of certain privileges, see the text below.

⁴⁶ *Yick Wo v. Hopkins*, 118 U.S. 356 (1886).

⁴⁷ See *Edwards v. California*, 314 U.S. 160 (1941); *Griffin v. Illinois*, 351 U.S. 12 (1956); *Douglas v. California*, 372 U.S. 353 (1963); *Roberts v. LaVallee*, 389 U.S. 40 (1967); *Harper v. Board of Elections*, 383 U.S. 663 (1966); *Williams v. Illinois*, 399 U.S. 235 (1970); *Boddie v. Connecticut*, 401 U.S. 371 (1971); *James v. Strange*, 407 U.S. 128 (1972). But contrast *James v. Valtierra*, 402 U.S. 137 (1971); and *San Antonio Independent School District v. Rodriguez*, 411 U.S. 1 (1973).

⁴⁸ *McDonald v. Board of Election Commissioners*, 394 U.S. 802, 807 (1969).

⁴⁹ Attorneys for persons born out of wedlock ("illegitimates") met with mixed success during this period in asserting claims that "illegitimacy" should be a suspect classification. See *Levy v. Louisiana*, 391 U.S. 68 (1968); *Labine v. Vincent*, 401 U.S. 532 (1971); and *Weber v. Aetna*, 406 U.S. 164 (1972).

⁵⁰ 411 U.S. 677.

⁵¹ *McLaughlin v. Florida*, 379 U.S. 184 (1964).

⁵² *Loving v. Virginia*, 388 U.S. 1 (1967).

⁵³ *Korematsu v. United States*, 323 U.S. 214 (1944). Three unusually bitter dissents were recorded for that case, and the majority opinion upholding the incarceration remains controversial to this day.

⁵⁴ *North Carolina Board of Education v. Swann*, 402 U.S. 43 (1971).

⁵⁵ *Id.*

⁵⁶ See *Parents Involved in Community Schools v. Seattle School District No. 1*, 551 U.S. 701 (2007); *Grutter v. Bollinger*, 539 U.S. 306 (2003); *Regents of Univ. of Cal. v. Bakke*, 438 U.S. 265 (1978).

⁵⁷ The ERA was "proposed" by well over the minimum two-thirds of both houses of Congress on March 22, 1972. Congress set a seven-year limit for ratification. On October 6, 1978, Congress, by majority vote, extended the ratification deadline to June 30, 1982. By this deadline, the proposed amendment had attained ratification in only 35 of the needed 38 states (70 percent instead of 75 percent). After that, the ERA became bogged down in politics around abortion and could not attain the needed two-thirds of Congress for re-proposal.

⁵⁸ *Yick Wo v. Hopkins*, 118 U.S. 356, 369 (1886).

⁵⁹ *Barbier v. Connolly*, 113 U.S. 27, 31–32 (1885).

⁶⁰ *Lindsley v. Natural Carbonic Gas*, 220 U.S. 61, 78 (1911).

⁶¹ *Royster Guano v. Virginia*, 253 U.S. 412, 415 (1920).

⁶² *Heath and Milligan v. Worst*, 207 U.S. 338, 354 (1907).

⁶³ In discussions of the due process clause, where fundamental rights are at stake, the terms "strict scrutiny" and "rigid scrutiny" are also used, and where no such right is involved, "ordinary" or "minimal scrutiny" is used.

64 See, for example, Judith Baer, *The Chains of Protection* (Westport, CT: Greenwood Press, 1978).

65 He was a permanent resident of the USA and was of Chinese descent. No person born in China was permitted to become a naturalized American citizen until 1943, when China was our wartime ally. Natives of India, the Philippines, and Japan were barred from citizenship until even later. See discussion in *Takahashi v. Fish and Game Comm.*, 334 U.S. 410 (1948).

66 *Quong Wing v. Kirkendall,* 223 U.S. 59, 63 (1912).

67 *Id.*, at 63.

68 *Harper v. Virginia Board of Elections*, 383 U.S. 663 (1966).

69 *Breedlove v. Suttles, Tax Collector*, 302 U.S. 277, 282 (1937).

70 335 U.S. 464.

CHAPTER 2

Women Attain (?) Constitutional Equality

ALMOST STRICT SCRUTINY

Doctrinal and Political Setting

Hoyt v. Florida was the last case involving women's rights that the Supreme Court decided by the traditional "ordinary equal protection scrutiny" approach. The Court did, in many kinds of cases, continue to follow its old-fashioned minimal scrutiny standard; for instance, in a 1969 prisoners' rights case, they announced that statutory classifications challenged under the equal protection clause need bear no more than "some rational relationship to a legitimate state end and will be set aside as violative of the equal protection clause *only if based on reasons totally unrelated to the pursuit of that goal . . . only if no grounds can be conceived to justify them*" (emphasis added).[1] By 1969, however, ordinary equal protection scrutiny was, if not consistently rejected, disregarded with increasing frequency at the Supreme Court level. By the end of the 1960s the Court had transformed the equal protection clause from a toothless restraint on state legislation into one with considerable bite for certain sorts of cases.

The transformation of the equal protection clause into a more potent weapon for litigants challenging discriminatory statutes developed along two different doctrinal paths. The first was the suspect classification/strict scrutiny path. The Court not only expanded the suspect classification category beyond its traditional race-nationality-alienage bounds so that poverty was often treated as a suspect basis of discrimination,[2] but also extended the strict scrutiny approach, formerly reserved to those classifications, to another kind of discrimination: discrimination involving restraints on fundamental rights.

The extension of the strict scrutiny approach to infringements of "fundamental rights" had its roots in the 1940s with President Franklin Delano

Roosevelt's appointed Supreme Court and did not attain its growth into a full-blown statement of constitutional principle until the Warren Court of the 1960s. The justices first used "fundamental rights" language to strike down a statute under an equal protection challenge in 1942. They declared a sterilization statute unconstitutional, saying that it affected "one of the basic civil rights of man" and that therefore it must be subjected to "strict scrutiny."[3] By the end of the 1960s, other fundamental rights had joined procreation in the equal protection/strict scrutiny arsenal;[4] they included the right to vote[5] and the right to travel freely among the states.[6]

If discriminated-against groups could neither gain the designation of "suspect" nor find a "fundamental right" that had been infringed, to invoke the strict scrutiny test by which to invalidate a statute, they still need not despair: In the late 1960s a second doctrinal path opened up to them. In two cases involving laws that penalized children born out-of-wedlock,[7] the Court took an unusual step, a step that broke through the roadblock previously hampering ordinary scrutiny equal protection challenges. The Court used ordinary equal protection reasonableness language but applied it with bite.[8] Thus, instead of asking, "Is there any *conceivable* reason for this classification?" the Court began asking, in effect, "Now, is this classification *really* reasonable?" Nuances of the latter question proved much more likely than those of the former to result in holdings that particular classifications are "unreasonable." Thus the Court majority claimed in these two decisions that there was "no possible rational basis" for the statutes, even though three Supreme Court justices, in dissent, argued that reasoned justification for the statutes was "obvious." Unless we conclude that three Supreme Court justices can be viewed as wholly irrational, we must conclude that something very new indeed was going on.

Although they still spoke in terms of ordinary versus strict scrutiny, the Court was beginning to use a third standard of equal protection scrutiny, looser than that in suspect classification or fundamental rights cases, but stricter than that of minimal ordinary scrutiny. The Court in these "third standard" cases continued to insist that it is looking merely for some reasonable basis for the statute, but its practice belied its words. Once the Court began applying scrutiny that was semi-strict in practice though "ordinary" in label, the future prospects of women's rights litigants became much brighter. By 1971, perhaps influenced by the various political developments that we summarize below, and under the leadership of Chief Justice Warren Burger, the Supreme Court added women to non-marital children, as groups for whom the statutory denial of benefits would be treated as at least semi-suspect. The justices, however, did not admit that they were using this new doctrine for sex discrimination until December of 1976, in the case of *Craig v. Boren*,[9] when they acknowledged in retrospect that they had been doing so for six years.

When the Supreme Court in 1971 began to enforce the reasonableness standard "with bite" for women's equal protection challenges, it initiated a new epoch in women's rights litigation. No single cause can explain why the Court began to apply this new form of equal protection scrutiny to women's rights cases within a decade of its blithe dismissal of the women's discrimination claim in *Hoyt v. Florida*. A multiplicity of political and societal changes took place in the intervening decade, which supplemented the impact of the legal developments in equal protection doctrine summarized above.

In 1961, President Kennedy, at the suggestion of Esther Peterson, director of the Women's Bureau, established a national Commission on the Status of Women. In partial response to the commission's report, which documented the ongoing discrimination experienced by women and advocated measures to improve the situation, fifty such state commissions were formed in 1963. In July 1962, President Kennedy by executive order barred sex discrimination within the federal civil service. Also in 1963, Betty Friedan's *The Feminine Mystique*, calling for drastic changes in societal roles for women, was published. The scientific development and subsequent widespread popularity of the birth-control pill further contributed to demographic and cultural changes during the decade. Increasing numbers of women were attending college and entering the labor force. The draining of young men from the labor force that resulted from the Vietnam war (1964–1973) substantially increased job opportunities for women. The percentage of working women in the United States by the 1970s doubled that of the 1920s. By the end of the 1960s a genuine "women's movement" flourished along two fronts: (1) National organizations appealed, in general, to middle-class professional women, such as the National Organization for Women (formed in 1966), the National Federation of Business and Professional Women,[10] the National Women's Political Caucus, and the Women's Equity Action League, and (2) hundreds of small, ill-organized, more radical groups, with a generally younger clientele than the national organizations, seemed to draw in women who were veterans of, but frustrated by the sexism within, the civil rights and antiwar movements.[11]

Meanwhile, legislative changes took place, but for reasons that varied substantially as the decade wore on. In 1963 Congress passed the Equal Pay Act, requiring for women equal pay for equal work. Evidently a response to findings of blatantly antifemale discrimination reported by the Commission on the Status of Women, and to consequent pressure from organized labor, the act nonetheless bore important signs of being tokenism. The act contained no viable enforcement mechanisms; moreover, its reach excluded executive, administrative, and professional employees. Title VII of the Civil Rights Act of 1964 forbade sex discrimination in employment. However, many of the members of Congress who voted to add sex discrimination to the bill's list of forbidden kinds of discrimination (race, color, national origin, and religion) were southern opponents of the bill who viewed the language prohibiting sex discrimination as a combination joke/political tactic designed to ensure the Civil Rights Act's failure. Although Title VII successfully passed into law with the rest of the bill, its enforcement agency (Equal Employment Opportunity Commission or EEOC) was for several years given no power beyond that of conciliation (bringing employer and discriminated-against employee together to talk). By 1967, however, women began to make substantial advances on the enforcement front. In that year President Johnson (in Executive Order 11375) prohibited sex discrimination by employers under federal contract or subcontract. In 1972, in a continuation of this trend, the Equal Employment Opportunity Commission acquired the power to sue discriminating employers in federal courts.

Finally, trends within the legal profession during this decade created certain pressures upon the Court. By 1971 a number of law school journals had published articles or even symposia on women's rights questions.[12] In May 1971, the California Supreme Court did what the U.S. Supreme Court would not do and declared sex classifications to be "suspect" under their state constitution, and to require, therefore, "compelling justification."[13]

Perhaps most significant, in August, 1970 by a margin of greater than ten to one (350–15), the House of Representatives voted to amend the U.S. Constitution on behalf of sex equality. The proposed Equal Rights Amendment (ERA) stated:

> Equality of rights under the law shall not be denied or abridged by the United States or by any state on account of sex. The Congress shall have the power to enforce, by appropriate legislation, the provisions of this article. The amendment shall take effect two years after the date of ratification.

The Senate did not vote on it during this session. In the new Congress, in October 1971 the House again overwhelmingly endorsed the ERA, 354–24. *Reed v. Reed*, 404 U.S. 71, was handed down on November 22, 1971. In March, 1972 the Senate was to vote for the ERA, 84–8.

Reed v. Reed (1971)

We recapitulate these events leading up to the Court's shift of approach, if not of language, in *Reed v. Reed* in November 1971, not to imply that the Court succumbed to political pressure but, rather, to provide relevant context. Possibly the shift would have occurred simply on the basis of the late-1960s shifts in constitutional doctrine outlined above. Nevertheless, the Supreme Court does not operate in a political vacuum. Serious and positive debate on the ERA was going on in Congress by 1971, the President was issuing executive orders barring sex discrimination, and the Supreme Court moved in the same direction. This combination is probably not pure coincidence.

For whatever reason, the Court definitely did begin a new wave in interpretations of the equal protection clause vis-à-vis women with the 1971 case of *Reed v. Reed*. This case and the women's rights cases that followed in its wake make clear that for such cases the Court does not plan to return to the any-rationalization-is-reasonable approach of *Hoyt v. Florida*.

Reed v. Reed again took the Supreme Court into the precincts of a marital dispute. Mr. and Mrs. Reed, who were separated, were competing for the legal appointment as administrator of their deceased son's estate. According to the Idaho statute § 15–314, if other qualifications for being administrator of a particular estate are equal (such as, here, the qualification of being a parent), then "males must be preferred to females." The probate judge appointed Cecil Reed the administrator, citing no grounds other than the command of this statute. Sally Reed appealed the decision. After the District Court ruled it unconstitutional, the Idaho Supreme Court, on further appeal, upheld Cecil Reed's appointment.

In a unanimous opinion the U.S. Supreme Court held that, although both the Idaho legislature and the Idaho Supreme Court judged it reasonable to classify women in this way, it was nonetheless "arbitrary;" that is, not reasonable. The Court explained:

REED V. REED
404 U.S. 71 (1971)

MR. CHIEF JUSTICE BURGER delivered the opinion of the Court.

...Having examined the record and considered the briefs and oral arguments of the parties, we have concluded that the arbitrary preference established in favor of males by § 15–314 of the Idaho Code cannot stand in the face of the Fourteenth Amendment's command that no state deny the equal protection of the laws to any person within its jurisdiction.

Idaho does not, of course, deny letters of administration to women altogether. Indeed, under § 15–312, a woman whose spouse dies intestate has a preference over a son, father, brother, or any other male relative of the decedent. Moreover, . . . in this country, presumably due to the greater longevity of women, a large proportion of estates, both intestate and under wills of decedents, are administered by surviving widows.

Section 15–314 is restricted in its operation to those situations where competing application for letters of administration have been filed by both male and female members of the same entitlement class . . . [and] provides that different treatment be accorded to the applicants on the basis of their sex; it thus establishes a classification subject to scrutiny under the Equal Protection Clause.

In applying that clause, this Court has consistently recognized that the Fourteenth Amendment does not deny to States the power to treat different classes of persons in different ways. *Barbier v. Connolly*, 113 U.S. 27 (1885); *Lindsley v. Natural Carbonic Gas Co.*, 220 U.S. 61 (1911); *Railway Express Agency v. New York*, 336 U.S. 106 (1949); *McDonald v. Board of Election Commissioners*, 394 U.S. 802 (1969). The Equal Protection Clause of that amendment does, however, deny to States the power to legislate that different treatment be accorded to persons placed by a statute into different classes on the basis of criteria wholly unrelated to the objective of that statute. A classification "must be reasonable, not arbitrary, and must rest upon some ground of difference having a fair and substantial relation to the object of the legislation, so that all persons similarly circumstanced shall be treated alike." *Royster Guano Co. v. Virginia*, 253 U.S. 412, 415 (1920). The question presented by this case, then, is whether a difference in the sex of competing applicants for letters of administration bears a rational relationship to a state objective that is sought to be advanced by the operation of § 15–312 and § 15–314.

In upholding the latter section, the Idaho Supreme Court concluded that its objective was to eliminate one area of controversy when two or more persons, equally entitled under § 15–312, seek letters of administration and thereby present the probate court "with the issue of which one should be named." The court also concluded that where such persons are not of the same sex, the elimination of females from consideration "is neither an illogical nor arbitrary method devised by the legislature to resolve an issue that would otherwise require a hearing as to the relative merits. . .of the two or more

> petitioning relatives. . . ." 93 Idaho, at 514, 465 P. 2d, at 638. ["Idaho" refers to the published collection of Idaho state cases, and "P. 2d" refers to Pacific Reporter Second Series, another published collection of cases.—AU.]
>
> . . . [T]he objective of reducing the workload on probate courts by eliminating one class of contests is not without some legitimacy. The crucial question, however, is whether § 15–314 advances that objective in a manner consistent with the command of the Equal Protection Clause. We hold that it does not. To give a mandatory preference to members of either sex over members of the other, merely to accomplish the elimination of hearings on the merits, is to make the very kind of arbitrary legislative choice forbidden by the Equal Protection Clause of the Fourteenth Amendment; and whatever may be said as to the positive values of avoiding intrafamily controversy, the choice in this context may not lawfully be mandated solely on the basis of sex.
>
> . . .The objective of § 15–312 clearly is to establish degrees of entitlement of various classes of persons in accordance with their varying degrees and kinds of relationship to the intestate. Regardless of their sex, persons within any one of the enumerated classes of that section are similarly situated with respect to that objective. By providing dissimilar treatment for men and women who are thus similarly situated, the challenged section violates the Equal Protection Clause. *Royster Guano Co. v. Virginia.*
>
> The judgment of the Idaho Supreme Court is reversed and the case remanded for further proceedings not inconsistent with this opinion.
>
> *Reversed and remanded.*

Case Questions

1. Is it fair to say that a preference for males over females as estate administrators is an "arbitrary legislative choice"? More arbitrary than, say, spouse over father?

2. Was it utterly unreasonable in 1971 to believe that, as a general category, men would be more competent than women as a general category in the task of administering an estate?

3. Recall the language of *Hoyt v. Florida* where the Court justified a jury exemption for all women on the grounds that some have special family responsibilities (Emphasis added):

> But *we cannot regard it as irrational* for a state legislature to consider preferable a broad exemption [even if it were]. . .born of a determination that *it would not be*

administratively feasible to decide in each individual instance whether the family responsibilities of a prospective juror were serious enough to warrant an exemption.

Has the Court's rejection in *Reed* of the administrative convenience rationale for sex-based classifications indicated that the rule of *Hoyt* would no longer be good law?

Frontiero v. Richardson (1973)

During the year and a half that elapsed between *Reed v. Reed* and the next case that involved discrimination against women, *Frontiero v. Richardson*, the Equal Rights Amendment to the Constitution (ERA) made considerable progress through the legislative labyrinth. Introduced in every session of Congress since 1923, it finally won the needed two-thirds majority in each house on March 22, 1972 (four months after *Reed*[14] was decided).

By January 1973, when Sharron Frontiero's lawyers were presenting her case to the Supreme Court, twenty-two state legislatures of the thirty-two that had held sessions after the ERA was proposed had ratified it.

Sally Reed's lawyers had argued that the equal protection clause of the Fourteenth Amendment on its own rendered sex classifications suspect, but Chief Justice Burger's Court opinion for *Reed* sidestepped her argument and instead used language of the ordinary scrutiny arbitrariness-versus-reasonableness approach. The justices' opinions in the *Frontiero* decision focus directly on the suspect classification approach urged by Sally Reed's lawyers and now again by Sharron Frontiero's and on the pending ERA, which (they say) would write that approach into the Constitution. The Court divides almost in half, however, over the question of how it should respond to congressional approval of the ERA. Justice Brennan cites it as grounds for treating sex as a suspect classification; Justice Powell, for doing the contrary. Both justices, writing for a total of seven, express the view that the ERA would make sex classifications suspect.

Sharron Frontiero and her husband, Joseph, were pressing a claim under the due process clause of the Fifth Amendment, rather than the Fourteenth Amendment. The two clauses are identical except that the Fifth applies to the federal government (as do all parts of the Constitution that do not explicitly mention the states) whereas the Fourteenth applies to state governments. The Frontieros' arguments referred to the Fifth Amendment because their complaint involved a federal statute, but the Court was fully aware that whatever it said about the due process clause of the Fifth would also apply to the due process clause of the Fourteenth and thereby limit all the state governments. Furthermore, it was a long-standing rule that the due process clause of the Fifth implied the command of "equal protection of the law" spelled out in the Fourteenth.[15] Thus, equal protection arguments figured prominently in this decision. The parties involved realized that equal protection precedents established here would apply to state laws in future cases.

Joseph Frontiero was a veteran receiving a monthly GI benefit of $205 while he attended college full-time. Sharron Frontiero was a lieutenant in the U.S. Air Force. Under federal law,[16] males in the "uniformed services" (Army, Navy, Air Force, Marine Corps, Coast Guard, Environmental Science Services Administration, and the public health services) *automatically* received an extra housing allowance and extra medical benefits if they had a wife. To receive the same housing and medical benefits for a husband, a woman in the same uniformed services had to prove that she paid more than one-half of her husband's living costs. Joseph Frontiero's living costs were $354 a month. Because his veterans benefits were $205 a month, Sharron Frontiero could claim to be paying no more than three-sevenths of his living costs—just under half. Thus, she could not obtain the extra spousal benefits that would have been automatically available to any male in her position.

Eight of the nine justices judged this situation so unfair that it violated "due process of law." But they are persuaded by differing reasons, and those differences were of decisive importance for future women's rights litigants. There is no majority agreement on a legal rationale here, and thus no "Court opinion," only a number of opinions expressing the respective views of various fractions of the Court.

> ### SHARRON AND JOSEPH FRONTIERO V. ELLIOT RICHARDSON, SEC'Y OF DEFENSE
> 411 U.S. 677 (1973)
>
> MR. JUSTICE BRENNAN announced the judgment of the Court and an opinion in which MR. JUSTICE DOUGLAS, MR. JUSTICE WHITE, and MR. JUSTICE MARSHALL join.
>
> ...[T]he question is whether this difference in treatment constitutes an unconstitutional discrimination against servicewomen in violation of the Due Process Clause of the Fifth Amendment. A three-judge District Court for the Middle District of Alabama, one judge dissenting,...sustained the constitutionality of the provisions of the statutes making this distinction. 341 F. Supp. 201 (1972)....We reverse.

I

...Appellants [contend] that ... the statutes unreasonably discriminate on the basis of sex in violation of the Due Process Clause of the Fifth Amendment.[5] In essence, appellants asserted that the discriminatory impact of the statutes is two-fold: first, as a procedural matter, a female member is required to demonstrate her spouse's dependency, while no such burden is imposed upon male members; and second, as a substantive matter, a male member who does not provide more than one-half of his wife's support receives benefits while a similarly situated female member is denied such benefits. Appellants therefore sought a permanent injunction against the continued enforcement of these statutes and an order directing the appellees to provide Lieutenant Frontiero with the same housing and medical benefits that a similarly situated male member would receive.

Although the legislative history...sheds virtually no light on the purposes underlying the differential treatment..., a majority of the three-judge District Court surmised that Congress might have reasonably concluded that, since the husband in our society is generally the "breadwinner"...and the wife "dependent"..."it would be more economical to require married female members claiming husbands to prove actual dependency than to extend the presumption of dependency to such members." 341 F.Supp., at 207. Indeed, given the fact that approximately 99 percent of all members of the uniformed services are male, the District Court speculated that such differential treatment might conceivably lead to a "considerable saving...."

II

[A]ppellants contend that classifications based upon sex, like classifications based upon race, alienage, and national origin are inherently suspect and must therefore be subjected to close judicial scrutiny. We agree and, indeed, find at least implicit support for such an approach in our unanimous decision only last term in *Reed v. Reed*, 404 U.S. 71 (1971).

In *Reed*, the Court considered the constitutionality of an Idaho statute providing that, when two individuals are otherwise equally entitled to appointment as administrator of an estate, the male applicant must be preferred to the female....

The Court noted that the Idaho statute "provides that different treatment be accorded to the applicants on the basis of their sex; it thus establishes a classification subject to scrutiny under the Equal Protection Clause." 404 U.S. at 75. Under "traditional" equal protection analysis, a legislative classification must be sustained unless it is "patently arbitrary" and bears no rational relationship to a legitimate governmental interest. See *Jefferson v. Hackney*, 406 U.S. 535, 546 (1972); *Richardson v. Belcher*, 404 U.S. 78, 81 (1971); *Flemming v. Nestor*, 363 U.S. 603, 611 (1960); *McGowan v. Maryland*, 366 U.S. 420, 426 (1961); *Dandridge v. Williams*, 397 U.S. 471, 485 (1970).

In an effort to meet this standard, appellee contended that the statutory scheme was a reasonable measure designed to reduce the workload on probate courts by eliminating one class of contests. Moreover, appellee argued that the mandatory preference for male applicants was in itself reasonable since "men [are] as a rule more conversant with business affairs than...women." Indeed, appellee maintained that "it is a matter of common knowledge, that women still are not engaged in politics, the professions, business or industry to the extent that men are." And the Idaho Supreme Court, in upholding the constitutionality of this statute, suggested that the Idaho Legislature might reasonably have "concluded that in general men are better qualified to act as an administrator than are women."

Despite these contentions, however, the Court held the statutory preference for male applicants unconstitutional. In reaching this result, the court implicitly rejected appellee's apparently rational explanation of the statutory scheme, and concluded that, by ignoring the individual qualifications of particular applicants, the challenged statute provided "dissimilar treatment for men and women who are...similarly situated." *Reed v. Reed* at 77. The Court therefore held that, even though the State's interest in achieving administrative efficiency "is not without some legitimacy," "[t]o give a mandatory preference to members of either sex over members of the other, merely to accomplish the elimination of hearings on the merits, is to make the very kind of arbitrary legislative choice forbidden by the [Constitution]...." Id., at 76. This departure from "traditional" rational basis analysis with respect to sex-based classifications is clearly justified.

There can be no doubt that our Nation has had a long and unfortunate history of sex discrimination. Traditionally, such discrimination was rationalized by an attitude of "romantic paternalism" which, in practical effect, put women not on a pedestal, but in a cage. Indeed, this paternalistic attitude became so firmly rooted in our national consciousness that, exactly 100 years ago, a distinguished member of this Court was able to proclaim:

> Man is, or should be, woman's protector and defender. The natural and proper timidity and delicacy which belongs to the female sex evidently unfits it for many of the occupations of civil life. The

constitution of the family organization, which is founded in the divine ordinance, as well as in the nature of things, indicates the domestic sphere as that which properly belongs to the domain and functions of womanhood. The harmony, not to say identity, of interests and views which belong, or should belong to the family institution is repugnant to the ideas of a woman adopting a distinct and independent career from that of her husband....

...The paramount destiny and mission of woman are to fulfil the noble and benign offices of wife and mother. This is the law of the Creator. *Bradwell v. Illinois*, 83 U.S. 130, 141 (1873) (Bradley, J., concurring).

As a result of notions such as these, our statute books gradually became laden with gross, stereotypical distinctions between the sexes and, indeed, throughout much of the 19th century the position of women in our society was, in many respects, comparable to that of blacks under the pre-Civil War slave codes. Neither slaves nor women could hold office, serve on juries, or bring suit in their own names, and married women traditionally were denied the legal capacity to hold or convey property or to serve as legal guardians of their own children. See generally. L. Kanowitz. *Women and the Law: The Unfinished Revolution* 5-6 (1969); G. Myrdal, *An American Dilemma* 1073 (2d ed. 1962). And although blacks were guaranteed the right to vote in 1870, women were denied even that right—which is itself "preservative of other basic civil and political rights"—until adoption of the Nineteenth Amendment half a century later.

It is true, of course, that the position of women in America has improved markedly in recent decades. Nevertheless, it can hardly be doubted that, in part because of the high visibility of the sex characteristic,[16] women still face pervasive, although at times more subtle, discrimination in our educational institutions, on the job market and, perhaps most conspicuously, in the political arena.[17] See generally, K. Amundsen, *The Silenced Majority: Women and American Democracy* (1971); The President's Task Force on Women's Rights and Responsibilities, *A Matter of Simple Justice* (1970).

Moreover, since sex, like race and national origin, is an immutable characteristic determined solely by the accident of birth, the imposition of special disabilities upon the members of a particular sex because of their sex would seem to violate "the basic concept of our system that legal burdens should bear some relationship to individual responsibility...." *Weber v. Aetna Casualty & Surety Co.*, 406 U.S. 164, 175 (1972). And what differentiates sex from such nonsuspect statutes as intelligence or physical disability, and aligns it with the recognized suspect criteria, is that the sex characteristic frequently bears no relation to ability to perform or contribute to society. As a result, statutory distinctions between the sexes often have the effect of invidiously relegating the entire class of females to inferior legal status without regard to the actual capabilities of its individual members.

We might also note that, over the past decade, Congress has itself manifested an increasing sensitivity to sex-based classifications. In Title VII of the Civil Rights Act of 1964, for example, Congress expressly declared that no employer, labor union, or other organization subject to the provisions of the Act shall discriminate against any individual on the basis of "race, color, religion, sex, or national origin." Similarly, the Equal Pay Act of 1963 provides that no employer covered by the Act "shall discriminate...between employees on the basis of sex." And § 1 of the Equal Rights Amendment, passed by Congress on March 22, 1972, and submitted to the legislatures of the States for ratification, declares that "[e]quality of rights under the law shall not be denied or abridged by the United States or by any State on account of sex."[21] Thus, Congress has itself concluded that classifications based upon sex are inherently invidious, and this conclusion of a coequal branch of Government is not without significance to the question presently under consideration.

The sole basis of the classification established in the challenged statutes is the sex of the individuals involved. Thus, under [them] a female member of the uniformed services seeking to obtain housing and medical benefits for her spouse must prove his dependency in fact, whereas no such burden is imposed upon male members. In addition, the statutes operate so as to deny benefits to a female member, such as appellant Sharron Frontiero, who provides less than one-half of his spouse's support. Thus, to this extent at least, it may fairly be said that these statutes command "dissimilar treatment for men and women who are... similarly situated." *Reed v. Reed*, at 77.

With these considerations in mind, we can only conclude that classifications based upon sex, like classifications based upon race, alienage, or national origin, are inherently suspect, and must therefore be subjected to strict judicial scrutiny. Applying the analysis mandated by that stricter standard of review, it is clear that the statutory scheme now before us is constitutionally invalid.

Moreover, the Government concedes that the differential treatment accorded men and women under these statutes serves no purpose other than mere "administrative convenience." In essence, the Government maintains that, as an empirical matter, wives in our society frequently are dependent upon their husbands, while husbands rarely are dependent upon their wives. Thus, the Government argues that Congress might reasonably have concluded that it would be both cheaper and easier simply conclusively to presume that wives of male members are financially dependent upon their husbands, while burdening female members with the task of establishing dependency in fact.[22]

The Government offers no concrete evidence, however, tending to support its view that such differential treatment in fact saves the Government any money. In order to satisfy the demands of strict judicial scrutiny, the Government must demonstrate, for example, that it is actually cheaper to grant increased benefits with respect to all male members, than it is to determine which male members are in fact entitled to such benefits and to grant increased benefits only to those members whose wives actually meet the dependency requirement. Here, however, there is substantial evidence that, if put to the test, many of the wives of male members would fail to qualify for benefits.[23]

And in light of the fact that the dependency determination with respect to the husbands of female members is presently made solely on the basis of affidavits, rather than through the more costly hearing process the Government's explanation of the statutory scheme is, to say the least, questionable.

In any case, our prior decisions make clear that, although efficacious administration of governmental programs is not without some importance, "the Constitution recognizes higher values than speed and efficiency." *Stanley v. Illinois*, 405 U.S. 645, 656 (1972). And when we enter the realm of "strict judicial scrutiny," there can be no doubt that "administrative convenience" is not a shibboleth, the mere recitation of which dictates constitutionality. See *Shapiro v. Thompson*, 394 U.S. 618 (1969); *Carrington v. Rash*, 380 U.S. 89 (1965). On the contrary, any statutory scheme which draws a sharp line between the sexes, *solely* for the purpose of achieving administrative convenience, necessarily commands "dissimilar treatment for men and women who are ...similarly situated," and therefore involves the "very kind of arbitrary legislative choice forbidden by the [Constitution]...." *Reed v. Reed*, at 77, 76. We therefore conclude that, by according differential treatment to male and female members of the uniformed services for the sole purpose of achieving administrative convenience, the challenged statutes violate the Due Process Clause of the Fifth Amendment insofar as they require a female member to prove the dependency of her husband.

Reversed.

Opinion Footnotes

5 [W]hile the Fifth Amendment contains no equal protection clause, it does forbid discrimination that is "so unjustifiable as to be violative of due process." *Schneider v. Rusk*, 377 U.S. 163, 168 (1964); see Shapiro v. Thompson, 394 U.S. 618, 641–642 (1969); *Bolling v. Sharpe*, 347 U.S. 497 (1954).

16 See, e.g., "Note, Sex Discrimination and Equal Protection: Do We Need a Constitutional Amendment?" 84 *Harv. L. Rev.* 1499, 1507 (1971).

17 It is true... that... women do not constitute a small and powerless minority. Nevertheless, in part because of past discrimination, women are vastly underrepresented in this Nation's decisionmaking councils. There has never been a female President, nor a female member of this Court. Not a single woman presently sits in the United States Senate, and only 14 women hold seats in the House of Representatives. And, as appellants point out, this underrepresentation is present throughout all levels of our State and Federal government. See Joint Reply Brief of Appellants and American Civil Liberties Union (*Amicus Curiae*) 9.

21 H.J. Res. No. 208, 92nd Cong., 2d Sess. (1972). In conformity with these principles, Congress in recent years has amended various statutory schemes similar to those presently under consideration so as to eliminate the differential treatment of men and women. [Here followed a list of four amended laws—AU.].

22 It should be noted that these statutes are not in any sense designed to rectify the effects of past discrimination against women. On the contrary, these statutes seize upon a [group—women—who have historically suffered discrimination in employment, and rely on the effects of this past discrimination as a justification for heaping on additional economic disadvantages. Cf. *United States v. Gaston County*, 395 U.S. 285, 296–97 (1969).

23 In 1971, 43% of all women over the age of 16 were in the labor force, and 18% worked full-time 12 months per year. See U.S. Women's Bureau, Dept. of Labor, *Highlights of Women's Employment & Education* 1 (W.B. Pub. No. 71–191, March 1972). Moreover, 41.5% of all married women are employed. See U.S. Bureau of Labor Statistics, Dept. of Labor. Work Experience of the Population in 1971 4 (Summary Special Labor Force Report, August 1972)....

MR. JUSTICE STEWART concurs in the judgment, agreeing that the statutes before us work an invidious discrimination in violation of the Constitution. *Reed v. Reed*, 404 U.S. 71.

MR. JUSTICE POWELL, with whom THE CHIEF JUSTICE and MR. JUSTICE BLACKMUN join, concurring in the judgment.

I agree that the challenged statutes constitute an unconstitutional discrimination against service women in violation of the Due Process Clause of the Fifth Amendment, but I cannot join the opinion of MR. JUSTICE BRENNAN, which would hold that all classifications based upon sex, "like classifications based upon race, alienage, and national origin," are "inherently suspect and must therefore be subject to close judicial scrutiny."

It is unnecessary for the Court in this case to characterize sex as a suspect classification, with all of the far-reaching implications of such a holding. *Reed v. Reed*, 404 U.S. 71 (1971), which abundantly supports our decision today, did not add sex to the narrowly limited group of classifications which are inherently suspect. [W]e . . . should decide this case on the authority of *Reed* and reserve for the future any expansion of its rationale.

There is another, and I find compelling, reason for deferring a general categorizing of sex classifications as invoking the strictest test of judicial scrutiny. The Equal Rights Amendment, which if adopted will resolve the substance of this precise question, has been approved by the Congress and submitted for ratification by the States. If this Amendment is duly adopted, it will represent the will of the people accomplished in the manner prescribed by the Constitution. By acting prematurely and unnecessarily, . . . the Court has assumed a decisional responsibility at the very time when state legislatures, functioning within the traditional democratic process, are debating the proposed Amendment. . . .This reaching out to pre-empt by judicial action a major political decision which is currently in process of resolution does not reflect appropriate respect for duly prescribed legislative processes.

There are times when this Court, under our system, cannot avoid a constitutional decision on issues which normally should be resolved by the elected representatives of the people. But democratic institutions are weakened, and confidence in the restraint of the Court is impaired, when we appear unnecessarily to decide sensitive issues of broad social and political importance at the very time they are under consideration within the prescribed constitutional processes.

MR. JUSTICE REHNQUIST dissents for the reasons stated by Judge Rives in his opinion for the District Court, *Frontiero v. Laird*, 341 F. Supp. 201 (1972).

[Excerpts from Judge Rives' opinion are provided here.—AU.]

. . .Plaintiffs point out that a male member may claim his wife without proving her actual dependency, while a female member must prove such in order to claim her husband. At first blush, then, the statute seems to draw a classification entirely on the basis of sex. Such is not the case. . . .[W]e must examine the over-all statutory scheme. A conclusive presumption of dependency is extended in the following instances:

1. *To male members* claiming spouses and unmarried, legitimate, minor children; and

2. *to female members* claiming unmarried, legitimate, minor children for purposes of medical and dental benefits.

On the other hand, dependency in fact must be shown:

1. *By male members* claiming adult children, parents, and parents-in-law; and

2. *by female members* claiming anyone other than an unmarried, legitimate, minor child for medical and dental benefits.

Thus, on the whole the availability of the presumption does not turn exclusively on the basis of the member's sex but rather on the nature of the relationship between the member and the claimed dependent....

Yet even if we were to view this case in the narrow context invited by plaintiffs' approach, viz., the different treatment accorded a male member claiming his wife as a dependent and a female member claiming her husband, we would uphold the statute. Before moving to that discussion however, it is necessary to clarify the standards by which we judge the statute.

An Act of Congress carries with it a strong presumption of constitutionality and places the burden upon the challenging party to prove the unconstitutionality of the statute at issue....The Due Process Clause of the Fifth Amendment, on which this challenge is based, bars federal legislation embodying a baseless classification.

...Undoubtedly there is much similarity between the equal protection test which courts employ in determining the validity of a state statute and the due process test which is utilized in evaluating a federal statute.

Thus, in determining the constitutionality of the statutory scheme which plaintiffs attack, this Court must ask whether the classification established in the legislation is reasonable and not arbitrary and whether there is a rational connection between the classification and a legitimate governmental end.[2] In making that judgment, the statute must be upheld "if any state of facts rationally justifying it is demonstrated to *or perceived by* the courts." *United States v. Maryland Savings-Share Insurance Corp.*, 400 U.S. 4 (1970) [challenge to a federal tax statute] (emphasis supplied).

The Supreme Court has recently enunciated the test for determining whether a classification squares with the Equal Protection Clause of the Fourteenth Amendment:

> In the area of economics and social welfare, a State does not violate the Equal Protection Clause merely because the classifications made by its laws are imperfect. If the classification has some "reasonable basis," it does not offend the Constitution simply because the

classification "is not made with mathematical nicety or because in practice it results in some inequality." ...."The problems of government are practical ones and may justify, it they do not require, rough accommodations—illogical, it may be, and unscientific." . . ."A statutory discrimination will not be set aside if any state of facts reasonably may be conceived to justify it. . ." *Dandridge v. Williams*, 397 U.S. 471, 485 (1970).

In summary, the law is well-settled that a statutory classification, challenged as an unlawful discrimination, should be upheld if it has a rational basis.

The defendants contend that the statutory provisions here at issue do no more than establish a conclusive presumption that a married male member of the uniformed services has a dependent wife while requiring a married female member of the uniformed services to prove the dependency of her husband, a distinction which, they say, does no more than take account of facts which the courts and statistical studies evidence in no way discriminate against females, as such. It seems clear that the reason Congress established a conclusive presumption in favor of married service men was to avoid imposing on the uniformed services a substantial administrative burden of requiring actual proof from some 200,000 male officers and over 1,000,000 enlisted men that their wives were actually dependent upon them. The question presented here then is whether the price for enjoying this administrative benefit fails to justify the different treatment of married service women.

. . .The classification which establishes a conclusive presumption in favor of married service men claiming wives allows the uniformed services to carry out the statutory purposes with a considerable saving of administrative expense and manpower. Congress apparently reached the conclusion that it would be more economical to require married female members claiming husbands to prove actual dependency than to extend the presumption of dependency to such members. Such a presumption. . . does not violate the equal protection guarantee of the Constitution if it does not unduly burden or oppress one of the classes upon which it operates. See *Adams v. City of Milwaukee*, 228 U.S. 572. (1913). "[L]egislation may impose special burdens upon defined classes in order to achieve permissible ends." *Rinaldi v. Yeager*, 384 U.S. 305, 309 (1966). Nothing in the instant statutory classification jeopardizes the ability of a female member to obtain the benefits intended to be bestowed upon her by the statutes. The classification is burdensome for a female member who is not actually providing over one-half the support for her claimed husband only to the extent that were she a man she could receive dependency benefits in spite of the fact that her spouse might not be actually dependent, as that term has been defined by Congress. In other words, the alleged injustice of the distinction lies in the possibility that some married service men are getting "windfall" payments, while married service women are denied them. Sharron Frontiero is one of the service women thus denied a windfall.

...[W]e are of the opinion that the incidental bestowal of some undeserved benefits on male members of the uniformed services does not so unreasonably burden female members that the administrative classification should be ruled unconstitutional. Under...a contrary finding...[t]he Court would be faced with a Hobson-like choice in fashioning a remedy: either strike down the conclusive presumption in favor of married service men, forcing the services to invest the added time and expense necessary to administer the law accurately, or require the presumption to be applied to both male and female married members, thereby abandoning completely the concept of dependency in fact upon which Congress intended to base the extension of benefits.

...

This is not to say that if plaintiffs could prove that the rational basis—administrative and economic convenience—did not exist due process would nevertheless be satisfied. (*Tot v. United States*, 319 U.S. 463 [1943]). But the plaintiffs here have not come close to proving such a state of facts. There is no evidence before this Court proving that so many male members are in fact dependent on their wives as to make it advisable to deny male members the presumption of dependency. Nor is there proof that so many female members have dependent husbands as to justify extending the benefit of the presumption to them....

Moreover, the result we here reach is clearly in harmony with ... *Reed v. Reed*, 404 U.S. 71 (1971), [striking] down, as violative of the Equal Protection Clause of the Fourteenth Amendment, an Idaho statute which discriminated against women....

...[W]hile there is arguably some similarity between the administrative advantage of avoiding probate hearing and the administrative benefit of not having to determine the actual dependency of over a million service wives, there is a significant qualitative distinction. In *Reed* there was a statutory presumption which had no relation to the statutory purpose of selecting the best qualified administrator. The effect was to exclude certain qualified females from serving as administrators, whereas the classification presented here does not exclude qualified female members. They merely have to show actual dependency.

... There is no reason to believe that the Congress would not respond to a significant change in the practical circumstances presumed by the statutory classification or that the present statutory scheme is merely a child of Congress' "romantic paternalism" and "Victorianism."

Opinion Footnote

2 In *Reed v. Reed* 404 U.S. 71 (1971), the Supreme Court was faced with a challenge to a state law which allegedly discriminated on the basis of sex. In stating the test by which to judge that statute the Court did not require that it meet the compelling interest test, see *Shapiro v. Thompson* 394 U.S. 618 (1969), but rather that it satisfy the rational connection standard. Similarly in this case we would be remiss in applying the compelling interest test.

Case Questions

1. How many of the nine justices conclude that sex classifications in statutes are inherently suspect and can be constitutional only when they are supported by "compelling justification"? How many judges conclude that sex classifications can be constitutional only when they are simply not "arbitrary" or "invidious"—i.e., as long as they bear some "rational" relation to a valid legislative purpose? As of 1973, is sex a suspect classification?

2. Does the four-judge Brennan opinion rely primarily on case precedents (previous Supreme Court statements about the meaning of the Constitution) or on other sources? What other kinds of authority besides legal precedents appear in Brennan's reasoning? Are there particular strengths or weaknesses inherent in the use of these kinds of authority by Supreme Court judges?

3. Does Brennan's opinion imply that he and those who concur with him deceived the American public in the *Reed v. Reed* case? That they did not realize what they were saying? Is either a desirable implication?

4. After comparing the opinions of the Court majority to those of the Judge Rives opinion, which Justice Rehnquist endorsed, are you convinced that the discrimination in this statute "bears no rational relationship to a legitimate governmental interest"?

5. Whose version of *Reed v. Reed* do you find most convincing: Brennan's, Powell's, or Rives's?

6. In note 22 Brennan distinguishes this statute from laws *protective* of women. Does his general line of reasoning lead you to believe that he would uphold such legislation?

Case note: While seven justices indicated here that the ERA would make sex a suspect classification and the other two express no disagreement on the point, it is worth noting that the amendment's legal impact was explained somewhat differently both by official Congressional reports and by an influential *Yale Law Journal* article often cited by ERA proponents. Both of the latter stated that the ERA would ban all legislative sex discrimination except for two kinds: [1] laws designed to take into account actual physiological differences of reproductive function, such as those involving separate bathrooms, rape, wet-nurses, sperm-donors, costs of giving birth, or determinations of paternity;[17] and [2] laws designed to compensate women for the impact of societal discrimination against them.[18] While the Supreme Court has never specifically endorsed this two-exceptions-only approach to sex-discriminatory laws, both of these concerns have shaped the kind of exceptions to the rule of sex equality that the Supreme Court was willing to permit after 1971.

Court Bides Its Time

Kahn v. Shevin (1974)

Frontiero brought the principle that sex is a semi-suspect classification into the open. The frank admission by four justices that the *Reed* result would have been different if the Supreme Court had followed the reasonableness test it was espousing indicated that the Court was examining sex classifications with something other than this test. The implicit claim by Justices Stewart, Powell, Blackmun, and Burger that the armed forces' denial of spousal benefits to women like Sharron Frontiero was arbitrary and had no reasonable basis, in the face of Judge Rives's elaborate defense of the reasons underlying the statute, amounts to a similar admission couched in different terms. What the justices seem to be saying is this: "When it comes to sex discrimination in the law, not just *any* reason, such as administrative convenience, will pass the 'reasonableness' test. There has to be a pretty good reason before we will hold that sex discrimination is justified, although we are not willing at this time to go so far as to say that it must be a 'compelling' reason." The Court, however, waited a few years before stating this implication as official doctrine. Meanwhile, by five votes to four, the official doctrine was still the "reasonableness" test.

The justices soon revealed that they could in fact be convinced of the existence of one such justification. They did so the very next year in a case involving a women's-right-to-special-benefit, or, conversely, a men's rights case, *Kahn v. Shevin*, 416 U.S. 351. *Kahn v. Shevin* presented a challenge by Mr. Kahn, a widower, to a Florida statute that gave to widows but not widowers an automatic $500 annual property-tax exemption. Kahn's appeal was presented to the U.S.

Supreme Court by two well-known women's rights attorneys, Ruth Bader Ginsburg and Melvin Wulf, the same attorneys who had worked on the Court briefs for the successful *Reed v. Reed* and *Frontiero v. Richardson* plaintiffs.[19] In *Kahn v. Shevin*, they were not so successful. The U.S. Supreme Court upheld the Florida Supreme Court's decision that the widows-only property tax exemption did not violate the equal protection clause.

The grounds on which the Court did so are difficult to locate. First, the Court majority recapitulated both the "fair and substantial" relation language of *Reed* and the old minimal scrutiny "reasonableness" test from which it originated and stated that this statute met that standard. The Court majority went on to say that in matters of tax legislation the "reasonableness" test is the one that should apply, and that this law was "well within" the bounds of reasonableness.[20] Most puzzling, Justice Douglas, who had been a member of the four-judge group in *Frontiero* who had argued that sex classifications are suspect and therefore should require compelling justification, was the author of this *Kahn* majority opinion endorsing the reasonableness test! (His three former allies from *Frontiero* did have the consistency to dissent in this case.) Douglas pointed out that over the prior twenty years the earnings of women fulltime workers averaged only about sixty percent that of male workers and concluded that this widows' tax break, which dated from 1855, was "reasonably designed to further the state policy of cushioning the financial impact of spousal loss upon the sex for which that loss imposes a disproportionately heavy burden" (at 355).

The Court majority's repeated use in *Kahn* of such terms as "reasonably," "reasonable," and "not arbitrary" seemed to imply that the "fair and substantial relationship" test of *Reed* had been reduced back down to its earlier meaning as a mere synonym for "reasonableness." This, of course, would have undercut the momentum of the *Reed* and *Frontiero* steps toward declaring sex classifications suspect. It did not become clear until later cases whether (1) this was what was happening in *Kahn*, (2) the Court was simply carving out a special exception for taxing and welfare policy, or (3) the Court majority believed that laws discriminating against men were not as "suspect" as laws discriminating against women.

Schlesinger v. Ballard (1975)

By a change of his vote in the next case brought by a male plaintiff complaining of unfair sex discrimination, Justice Douglas, at least, seemed to demonstrate that the middle of these three possibilities best explained his own view of the *Kahn v. Shevin* decision. Even without his vote, however, the *Kahn* majority held five votes, and these produced the majority in *Schlesinger v. Ballard* 419 U.S. 498 (1975) to uphold again the statutory benefit to women being challenged by a man.

The Schlesinger of the case was (then) Secretary of Defense James Schlesinger. He was appealing a U.S. District Court decision that naval regulations 10 U.S.C. § 6382(a) and 10 U.S.C. § 6401 were unconstitutional as violations of the concept of equal protection implied by the Fifth Amendment due process clause. Section 6382(a) mandated that any lieutenant in the U.S. Navy or captain in the U.S. Marine Corps who is twice passed over for promotion shall receive an honorable discharge in the year of his second failure to be promoted. The section did not apply to women officers. Women Navy lieutenants and Marine Corps captains were given a minimum of thirteen years of officer service duty according to § 6401, before they could be forced out of the corps by such a discharge.

Lieut. Robert Ballard had initiated this lawsuit because, pursuant to § 6382(a), he was ordered discharged from the Navy after only nine years of service as an officer. He contended that this rule amounted to sheer sex discrimination because, had he been female, he would have been allowed thirteen years of officer service. In his particular case, this time disparity had substantial financial repercussions; if he were allowed to stay in the service for four more years, he would have been entitled to a lifetime pension (since he had put in seven additional years as an enlisted man).

The Supreme Court overruled the District Court's conclusion that under the precedents of *Frontiero* and *Reed* this differential treatment was unconstitutional. The five-justice majority found that the statutes promoted more substantial goals than administrative or fiscal convenience. This majority employed the language of a "rationality" test in discussing this sex-based distinction, yet their acknowledgments that "administrative convenience" and "archaic generalizations" would be inadequate to justify sex discrimination suggested a test stiffer than the mere "rationality" test. In short, this case did little to clarify the doctrinal confusion wrought by *Reed, Frontiero,* and *Kahn.*

What swayed the majority was that, as in *Kahn,* they perceived the purpose of the law as compensating women officers for a disadvantage they faced. Unlike men, women could not enhance their military record by combat service, so they needed extra time to accumulate an impressive resume.

Weinberger v. Wiesenfeld (1975)

Within days of the *Schlesinger* ruling, the Supreme Court overturned its *Hoyt* decision. That case, *Taylor v. Louisiana*, is covered in a later section of this chapter dealing with jury duty. It bears mention here, however, that in the course of rejecting the woman's-place-is-home argument for keeping women off jury lists, the *Taylor* majority, instead of simply saying that this was not a compelling justification (which might have been expected since the Court there was using a fundamental rights analysis), said that in this day and age the argument was not even a "reasonable" one. To assume that all women fit a mold that applied now only to a minority was, to use their word, "untenable." This shift was major. The kinds of justifications for depriving women of legal rights that had been found "reasonable" in such cases as *Bradwell*, *Goesaert*, and *Hoyt* had always relied almost entirely on the premise that there is "a wide difference in the respective spheres and destinies of man and woman."[21] The rejection of this premise in *Taylor v. Louisiana* had to mean that the "reasonableness" test as applied to sex-based discrimination would look different from its 1961 *Hoyt v. Florida* configuration. Perhaps the change wrought by *Taylor* was to lay bare the unwritten premise that had been silently undergirding the majority justices' reasoning ever since the 1971 *Reed v. Reed* decision. Conceivably, the Court majority had viewed the statutes of *Reed* and *Frontiero* as unreasonable because those statutes made assumptions about all women that were now true of only about half or even fewer than half of women.

Two months later, the Supreme Court for the first time declared void (strictly on the grounds of sex discrimination) a statute arguably discriminating against males. The case was *Caspar Weinberger v. Stephen Wiesenfeld,* 420 U.S. 636 (1975); and as in *Reed v. Reed*, the first case to strike down anti-female sex discrimination, the result was a unanimous one (except that Justice Douglas did not participate.) This was the first unanimous decision to declare void a sex discrimination statute since Justice Rehnquist joined the Court (He joined after *Reed* and dissented in *Frontiero*, and *Taylor*.) Once again the case was argued by those specialists in women's rights law, Ruth Bader Ginsburg and Melvin Wulf. *Weinberger v. Wiesenfeld* added one more to their string of victories against sex discrimination, which had begun with *Reed* and *Frontiero*.[22]

In drafting the Court opinion, Justice Brennan sidestepped the doctrinal rift between the reasonableness faction of Justices Stewart, Blackmun, Powell, Burger, and Rehnquist, and the compelling-interest faction of White, Marshall and himself. Justice Douglas, a usual member of the latter faction (except in the *Kahn* decision), was seriously ill during this period. (He officially retired in November

1975 and was replaced by Justice Stevens in December.) Brennan managed to bind seven of the eight justices to his majority opinion[23] by avoiding any references to either a reasonableness test or to an "overriding interest" test for sex discrimination.[24] Instead, he termed the discrimination both "unjustifiable" and "irrational" in relation to the government's professed versus its actual legislative purpose. His conclusion was based on the long-standing but conveniently vague rule (cited as well in *Reed* and *Frontiero*) that legislation may not provide "dissimilar treatment for men and women who are. . .similarly situated."[25]

This case was initiated on the complaint of Stephen C. Wiesenfeld. He married Paula Polatschek, a schoolteacher, in 1970. She had been working full-time for five years by then, and she continued to work after their marriage. In each of these years, the maximum Social Security percentage was deducted from her income. During the two and one-half years of their married life, Paula was the main economic supporter of the couple. In 1970 and 1971, she earned about $10,000 a year to Stephen's $2000–$3000 a year. In 1972, she earned $7000 a year to Stephen's $2500. On June 5, 1972, she died in childbirth, leaving an infant son, Jason.

After her death, Stephen applied for Social Security benefits for his son and himself. For his son, he received about $250 a month.[26] For himself, he received nothing, even though statute 42 U.S.C. § 402(g), would have awarded him $250 a month for himself had he been an unemployed female surviving parent. Had he been a woman and chosen to go to work under these circumstances, he would have lost, out of the $3000 a year, $1 for every $2 earned above $2400 a year.

Although the plaintiff was male, both the federal District Court and the U.S. Supreme Court analyzed the law as a discrimination against women wage-earners. The ambiguity arises because the Social Security statute under challenge discriminated against male (husband) beneficiaries of the Social Security contributions of deceased female workers. From the perspective that looks at who earned the denied benefits, the law discriminates against women. But from the perspective that looks at the one who actually suffers by failure to receive benefits (benefits that would be received, were he a woman), the victim of the discrimination is male—the surviving husband.

The U.S. Supreme Court agreed unanimously that Wiesenfeld should receive the benefits; that the law discriminated unconstitutionally. Justice Brennan for seven justices said this was because its discrimination did not have a valid purpose; it was based on an "archaic and overbroad generalization," the assumption that men were breadwinners and wives stayed home to do childcare. "Such a gender-based generalization cannot suffice to justify the denigration of the efforts of women who do work and whose earnings contribute significantly to their families' support."27 Mrs. Wiesenfeld had paid Social Security taxes and the Fifth Amendment required that she get the same protection for her son's surviving parent as a man would have received upon his death.

Justice Rehnquist agreed on the result, but explained his thinking differently: "It is irrational to distinguish between mothers and fathers when the sole question is whether a child of a deceased contributing worker should have the opportunity to receive the full-time attention of the only parent remaining to it."28

OFFICIALLY INTERMEDIATE SCRUTINY: *CRAIG V. BOREN* (1976)

The Court decided its fourth sex equality case of 1975 that April, *Stanton v. Stanton*, 421 U.S. 7. Again the Court sided with the women's rights plaintiff against sex discrimination, and again it forestalled announcing any new constitutional rule for sex discrimination. This case dealt with the age at which children of divorce cease receiving obligatory child support, and it is included in Chapter 5.

By the end of 1976, the death knell of the ERA could be heard. The rush of its early popularity continued until March 22, 1973, the anniversary of Congressional adoption. During January, February, and March of 1973, eight additional states ratified. Then, however, the pace dramatically slowed. Three more ratifications came in 1974, bringing the total to 33 (66%), and one more in 1975. March of 1976 was the fourth anniversary of Congressional action, and no previous successful Constitutional amendment had taken longer than four years for ratification.29 By the end of 1976 no additional states ratified. One more ratification came in 1977, and it was to be the last, bringing the total to 35 (70%), three states short. As of December 1976, more than two-thirds of the states had ratified an amendment proposed by near-unanimity in each house of Congress, and public opinion surveys showed majorities favoring the amendment even in the non-ratifying states. Yet the ratification process seemed to have become derailed in part due to the coordinated resistance of the STOP ERA campaign led by conservative female activist Phyllis Schlafly. At this point, the U.S. Supreme Court abandoned its reticence about the principles that had been guiding its thinking on sex discrimination since *Reed*, and openly propounded a new rule of constitutional law.

In the case of *Craig v. Boren*, in December 1976 a majority of the Supreme Court for the first time announced that sex-based discriminations were quasi-suspect. The Court finally laid its doctrinal cards on the table with a clear statement that to comport with the constitutional requirement of equal protection, *"classifications by gender must serve important governmental objectives and must be substantially related to achievement of those objectives."* Justice Brennan's opinion, which announced this rule, had the adherence of five other justices, for a total majority of six. This marked the first time since *Reed v. Reed* (1971) that any more than four justices had agreed on a general standard for judging the constitutionality of sex-based discriminations.

As often happens in constitutional adjudication, the seed for this momentous decision sprouted in the soil of a trivial set of facts. Two young Oklahoma men, Mark Walker and Curtis Craig, objected to a state law permitting women to purchase beer containing 3.2% alcohol once they turned eighteen but prohibiting men from making such purchases until they turned twenty-one.

Oklahoma, in response to the Supreme Court's *Reed v. Reed* decision and to a federal court decision relying upon it, had eliminated most of the sex differences in the state's age-of-majority statutes. Before 1972, for example, girls but not boys had been held criminally responsible for crimes as "adults" once they turned sixteen. All such differences in both civil law and criminal law were eliminated in 1972, except for the age difference for legal permission to buy "3.2 beer."

Oklahoma defended its beer rules with an argument based on traffic safety. The state presented documents in Court proving that (1) more than ten times as many males as females between the ages of eighteen and twenty were arrested for drunk driving; (2) roughly ten times as many males as females in that age bracket were arrested for public drunkenness; (3) a slightly greater percentage (84 percent as against 77 percent) of male drivers than female drivers under age twenty-one preferred beer to other alcoholic beverages. The federal District Court found these statistics adequate to establish constitutionality under *Reed*. The U.S. Supreme Court, acknowledged, "*Reed*. . .is controlling," but disagreed with the lower court as to whether this law met the standard established by *Reed*.

The Court majority claims things about *Reed*, however, that do not match what it said in 1971. In effect, the Court made new law in *Craig*, but claimed this new rule of law was as old as *Reed*.

Craig v. Boren
429 U.S. 190 (1976)

Mr. Justice Brennan delivered the opinion of the Court.

...The question to be decided is whether such a gender-based differential constitutes a denial to males 18–20 years of age of the Equal Protection of the Laws in violation of the Fourteenth Amendment...

...Analysis may appropriately begin with the reminder that *Reed v. Reed*, emphasized that statutory classifications that distinguish between males and females are "subject to scrutiny under the Equal Protection Clause." 404 U.S., at 75. *To withstand constitutional challenge, previous cases establish that classifications by gender must serve important governmental objectives and must be substantially related to achievement of those objectives.* [Emphasis added.—AU.] Thus, in *Reed*, the objectives of "reducing the workload on probate courts," *id.*, at 76, and "avoiding intrafamily controversy," *id.*, at 77, were deemed of insufficient importance to sustain use of an overt gender criterion in the appointment of intestate administrators. Decisions following *Reed* similarly have rejected administrative ease and convenience as sufficiently important objectives to justify gender-based classifications. See, e.g., *Stanley v. Illinois*, 405 U.S. 645, 656 (1972); *Frontiero v. Richardson*, 411 U.S. 677, 690 (1973); cf. *Schlesinger v. Ballard*, 419 U.S. 498, 506–507 (1975). And only two terms ago, *Stanton v. Stanton*, 421 U.S. 7 (1975), expressly stating that *Reed v. Reed* was "controlling," *id.*, at 13, held that *Reed* required invalidation of a Utah differential age-of-majority statute, notwithstanding the statute's coincidence with and furtherance of the State's purpose of fostering "old notions" of roletyping and preparing boys for their expected performance in the economic and political worlds. *Id.*, at 14–15.[6]

Reed v. Reed has also provided the underpinning for decisions that have invalidated statutes employing gender as an inaccurate proxy for other, more germane bases of classification. Hence, "archaic and overbroad" generalizations, *Schlesinger v. Ballard*, 419 U.S., at 508, concerning the financial position of servicewomen, *Frontiero v. Richardson*, 411 U.S. at 689 n. 3, and working women *Weinberger v. Wiesenfeld*, 420 U.S. 636, 643 (1975), could not justify use of a gender line in determining eligibility for certain governmental entitlements. Similarly increasingly outdated misconceptions concerning the role of females in the home rather than in the "marketplace and world of ideas" were rejected as loose-fitting characterizations incapable of supporting state statutory schemes that were premised upon their accuracy. *Stanton v. Stanton*;

Taylor v. Louisiana, 419 U.S. 522, 535 n. 17 (1975). In light of the weak congruence between gender and the characteristic or trait that gender purported to represent, it was necessary that the legislatures choose either to realign their substantive laws in a gender-neutral fashion, or to adopt procedures for identifying those instances where the sex-centered generalization actually comported to fact. See, e.g., *Stanley v. Illinois*, 405 U.S. at 658; cf. *Cleveland Board of Educ. v. LaFleur*, 414 U.S. 632, 650 (1974).

In this case too, "*Reed* we feel, is controlling. . . ." *Stanton v. Stanton* 421 U.S., at 13. We turn then to the question whether, under *Reed*, the difference between males and females with respect to the purchase of 3.2% beer warrants the differential in age drawn by the Oklahoma statute. We conclude that it does not.

The District Court . . . found the requisite important governmental objective in the traffic-safety goal proferred by the Oklahoma Attorney General. It then concluded that the statistics introduced by the appellees established that the gender-based distinction was substantially related to achievement of that goal.

We accept for purposes of discussion the District Court's identification of the objective underlying § 241 and § 245 as the enhancement of traffic safety. Clearly, the protection of public health and safety represents an important function of state and local governments. However, appellees' statistics in our view cannot support the conclusion that the gender-based distinction closely serves to achieve that objective and therefore the distinction cannot under *Reed* withstand equal protection challenge.

The appellees introduced a variety of statistical surveys.

. . .

Even were this statistical evidence accepted as accurate, it nevertheless offers only a weak answer to the equal protection question presented here. The most focused and relevant of the statistical surveys, arrests of 18–20-year-olds for alcohol-related driving offenses, exemplifies the ultimate unpersuasiveness of this evidentiary record. Viewed in terms of the correlation between sex and the actual activity that Oklahoma seeks to regulate—driving while under the influence of alcohol—the statistics broadly establish that 0.18% of females and 2% of males in that age group were arrested for that offense. While such a disparity is not trivial in a statistical sense, it hardly can form the basis for employment of a gender line as a classifying device. Certainly if maleness is to serve as a proxy for drinking and driving, a correlation of 2% must be considered an unduly tenuous "fit." Indeed, prior cases have consistently rejected the use of sex as a decision making factor even though the statutes in question certainly rested on far more predictive empirical relationships than this.[13] Moreover, the statistics exhibit a variety of other shortcomings . . . . Setting aside . . . methodological problems,[14] the surveys do not adequately justify the salient features of Oklahoma's gender-based traffic-safety law. None purports to measure the use and dangerousness of 3.2% beer as opposed to alcohol generally, a detail that is of particular importance since, in light of its low alcohol level, Oklahoma apparently considers the 3.2% beverage to be "non-intoxicating." 37 Okla. Stat. § 163.1 (1971). . . .

There is no reason to belabor this . . . . Proving broad sociological propositions by statistics . . . inevitably is in tension with the normative philosophy that underlies the Equal Protection Clause. Suffice to say that the showing offered by the appellees does not satisfy us that sex represents a legitimate, accurate proxy for the regulation of drinking and driving. In fact, when it is further recognized that Oklahoma's statute prohibits only the selling of 3.2% beer to young males and not their drinking the beverage once acquired (even after purchase by their 18–20-year-old female companions), the relationship between gender and traffic safety becomes far too tenuous to satisfy *Reed*'s requirement that the gender-based difference be substantially related to achievement of the statutory objective.

We hold, therefore, that under *Reed*, Oklahoma's 3.2% beer statute invidiously discriminates against males 18–20 years of age [and]. . . constitutes a denial of the Equal Protection of the Laws.

[Discussion of Twenty-first Amendment omitted.] . . . *Reverse*.

Opinion Footnotes

6   *Kahn v. Shevin*, 416 U.S. 351 (1974) and *Schlesinger v. Ballard*, 419 U.S. 498 (1975), upholding the use of gender-based classifications, rested upon the Court's perception of the laudatory purposes of those laws as remedying disadvantageous conditions suffered by women in economic and military life. See 416 U.S., at 353–354; 419 U.S., at 508. Needless to say, in this case (such compensation is not at issue). . .

13   For example, we can conjecture that in *Reed*, Idaho's apparent premise that women lacked experience in formal business matters (particularly compared to men) would have proved to be accurate in substantially more than 2% of all cases. And in both *Frontiero* and *Wiesenfeld*, we expressly found the government's empirical defense of mandatory dependency tests for men but not women to be unsatisfactory, even though we recognized that husbands still are far less likely to be dependent on their wives than vice versa. See, e.g., 411 U.S., at 688–90.]

14   The very social stereotypes that find reflection in age differential laws, see *Stanton v. Stanton*, 421 U.S., at 114–15, are likely substantially to distort the accuracy of these comparative statistics. Hence "reckless" young men who drink and drive are transformed into arrest statistics, whereas their female counterparts are chivalrously escorted home. See, e.g., W. Reckless & B. Kay, *The Female Offender* 4, 7, 13, 16–17. . .

MR. JUSTICE POWELL, concurring.

I join the opinion of the Court as I am in general agreement with it. I do have reservations as to some of the discussion concerning the appropriate standard for equal protection analysis and the relevance of the statistical evidence. Accordingly, I add this concurring statement.

With respect to the equal protection standard, I agree that *Reed v. Reed*, is the most relevant precedent. But I find it unnecessary, in deciding this case, to read that decision as broadly as some of the Court's language may imply. *Reed* and subsequent cases involving gender-based classifications make clear that the Court subjects such classifications to a more critical examination than is normally applied when "fundamental" constitutional rights and "suspect classes" are not present.*

I view this as a relatively easy case. No one questions the legitimacy or importance of the asserted governmental objective: the promotion of highway safety. . . .[T]he case turns on whether the state legislature, by the classification it has chosen, has adopted a means that bears a "fair and substantial relation" to this objective. *Reed v. Reed*, 404 U.S. at 76, quoting *Royster v. Guano*.

It seems to me that the statistics offered by the State and relied upon by the District Court do tend generally to support the view that young men drive more, possibly are inclined to drink more, and—for various reasons—are involved in more accidents than young women. Even so, I am not persuaded that these facts and the inferences fairly drawn from them justify this classification based on a three-year age differential between the sexes, and especially one that is so easily circumvented as to be virtually meaningless. Putting it differently, this gender-based classification does not bear a fair and substantial relation to the object of the legislation.

Opinion Footnote

* As is evident from our opinion, the Court has had difficulty in agreeing upon a standard of equal protection analysis that can be applied consistently to the wide variety of legislative classifications. There are valid reasons for dissatisfaction with the "two-tier" approach that has been prominent in the Court's decisions in the past decade. Although viewed by many as a result-oriented substitute for more critical analysis, that approach—with its narrowly limited "upper-tier"—now has substantial precedential support. As has been true of *Reed* and its progeny, our decision today will be viewed by some as a "middle-tier" approach. While I would not endorse that characterization and would not welcome a further subdividing of equal protection analysis, candor compels the recognition that the relatively deferential "rational basis" standard of review normally applied takes on a sharper focus when we address a gender-based classification. So much is clear from our recent cases. . . .

MR. JUSTICE STEVENS, concurring.

There is only one Equal Protection Clause. It requires every State to govern impartially. It does not direct the courts to apply one standard of review in some cases and a different standard in other cases. Whatever criticism may be levelled at a judicial opinion implying that there are at least three such standards applies with the same force to a double standard.

I am inclined to believe that what has become known as the two-tiered analysis of equal protection claims does not describe a completely logical method of deciding cases, but rather is a method the Court has employed to explain decisions that actually apply a single standard in a reasonably consistent fashion. I also suspect that a careful explanation of the reasons motivating particular decisions may contribute more to an identification of that standard than an attempt to articulate it in all-encompassing terms. It may therefore be appropriate for me to state the principal reasons which persuaded me to join the Court's opinion.

In this case, the classification is not as obnoxious as some the Court has condemned,[1] nor as inoffensive as some the Court has accepted. It is objectionable because it is based on an accident of birth, because it is a mere remnant of the now almost universally rejected tradition of discriminating against males in this age bracket,[3] and because, to the extent it reflects any physical difference between males and females, it is actually perverse.[4] The question then is whether the traffic safety justification put forward by the State is sufficient to make an otherwise offensive classification acceptable.

The classification is not totally irrational. For the evidence does indicate that there are more males than females in this age bracket who drive and also more who drink. Nevertheless, there are several reasons why I regard the justification as unacceptable. It is difficult to believe that the statute was actually intended to cope with the problem of traffic safety,[5] since it has only a minimal effect on access to a not-very-intoxicating beverage and does not prohibit its consumption. Moreover, the empirical data submitted by the State accentuates the unfairness of treating all 18–21-year-old males as inferior to their female counterparts. The legislation imposes a restraint on one hundred percent of the males in the class allegedly because about 2% of them have probably violated one or more laws relating to the consumption of alcoholic beverages. It is unlikely that this law will have a significant deterrent effect either on that 2% or on the law-abiding 98%. But even assuming some such slight benefit, it does not seem to me that an insult to all of the young men of the State can be justified by visiting the sins of the 2% on the 98%. . .

Opinion Footnotes

1 Men as a general class have not been the victims of the kind of historic, pervasive discrimination that has disadvantaged other groups.

3 Apparently, Oklahoma is the only State to permit this narrow discrimination to survive the elimination of the disparity between the age of majority for males and females.

4 Because males are generally heavier than females, they have a greater capacity to consume alcohol without impairing their driving ability than do females.

5 There is no legislative history to indicate that this was the purpose, and several features of the statutory scheme indicate the contrary. The statute exempts license holders who dispense 3.2 beer to their own children, and a related statute makes it unlawful for 18-year old men (but not women), to work in establishments in which 3.2 beer accounts for over 25% of gross sales. 37 Okla. Stat. §§ 241, 243, 245. There is, of course, no way of knowing what actually motivated this discrimination, but I would not be surprised if it represented nothing more than the perpetuation of a stereotyped attitude about the relative maturity of the members of the two sexes in this age bracket. If so, the following comment is relevant: "[A] traditional classification is more likely to be used without pausing to consider its justification than is a newly created classification. Habit, rather than analysis, makes it seem acceptable and natural to distinguish between male and female, alien and citizen, legitimate and illegitimate; for too much of our history there was the same inertia in distinguishing between black and white. But that sort of stereotyped reaction may have no rational relationship—other than purely prejudicial discrimination—to the stated purpose for which the classification is being made." Matthews v. Lucas (STEVENS, J., dissenting).

MR. JUSTICE STEWART, concurring [in the judgment].

I. . . concur in the Court's judgment on the merits of the constitutional issue before us.

Every State has broad power under the Twenty-first Amendment to control the dispensation of alcoholic beverages within its borders. [citations omitted] But "[t]his is not to say that the Twenty-first Amendment empowers a State to act with total irrationality or invidious discrimination in controlling the dispensation of liquor. . . ." *California v. LaRue*, 409 U.S. 109, at 120 n.*(concurring opinion).

The disparity created by these Oklahoma statutes amounts to total irrationality. For the statistics upon which the state now relies, whatever their other shortcomings, wholly fail to prove or even suggest that 3.2 beer is somehow more deleterious when it comes into the hands of a male aged 18–20 than of a female of like age. The disparate statutory treatment of the sexes here, without even a colorably valid justification or explanation, thus amounts to invidious discrimination. See *Reed v. Reed*, 404 U.S. 71.

MR. CHIEF JUSTICE BURGER, dissenting.

I am in general agreement with MR. JUSTICE REHNQUIST'S dissent. . . .

. . .

...[T]hough today's decision does not go so far as to make gender-based classifications "suspect," it makes gender a disfavored classification. Without an independent constitutional basis supporting the right asserted or disfavoring the classification adopted, I can justify no substantive constitutional protection other than the normal *McGowan v. Maryland*, 366 U.S. 420, at 425–26, protection afforded by the Equal Protection Clause.

The means employed by the Oklahoma Legislature to achieve the objectives sought may not be agreeable to some judges, but since eight members of the Court think the means not irrational, I see no basis for striking down the statute as violative of the Constitution simply because we find it unwise, unneeded, or possibly even a bit foolish.

MR. JUSTICE REHNQUIST, dissenting.

The Court's disposition of this case is objectionable on two grounds. First is its conclusion that men challenging a gender-based statute which treats them less favorably than women may invoke a more stringent standard of judicial review than pertains to most other types of classifications. Second is the Court's enunciation of this standard, without citation to any source, as being that "classifications by gender must serve *important* governmental objectives and must be *substantially* related to achievement of those objectives." (emphasis added). The only redeeming feature of the Court's opinion, to mind, is that it apparently signals a retreat by those who joined the plurality opinion in *Frontiero v. Richardson*, 411 U.S. 677 (1973), from their view that sex is a "suspect" classification for purposes of equal protection analysis. I think the Oklahoma statute challenged here need pass only the "rational basis" equal protection analysis expounded in cases such as *McGowan v. Maryland*, 366 U.S. 420 (1961), and *Williamson v. Lee Optical Co.*, 348 U.S. 483 (1955), and I believe that it is constitutional under that analysis.

In *Frontiero v. Richardson*, the opinion for the plurality sets forth the reasons of four Justices for concluding that sex should be regarded as a suspect classification for purposes of equal protection analysis. These reasons center on our Nation's "long and unfortunate history of sex discrimination," *id.*, at 684, which has been reflected in a whole range of restrictions on the legal rights of women, not the least of which have concerned the ownership of property and participation in the electoral process. . . .[T]he plurality rested its invocation of strict scrutiny largely upon the fact that "statutory distinctions between the sexes often have the effect of invidiously relegating the entire class of females to inferior legal status without regard to the actual capabilities of its individual members." *Id.*, at 686–687. See *Stanton v. Stanton*, 421 U.S. 7, 14–15 (1975).

Subsequent to *Frontiero*, the Court had declined to hold that sex is a suspect class, *Stanton v. Stanton*, at 13. . . . However, the Court's application here of an elevated or "intermediate" level scrutiny, like that invoked in cases dealing with discrimination against females, raises the question of why the statute here should be treated any differently than countless legislative classifications unrelated to sex.

Most obviously unavailable to support any kind of special scrutiny in this case, is a history or pattern of past discrimination, such as was relied on by the plurality in *Frontiero* to support its invocation of strict scrutiny. There is no suggestion in the Court's opinion that males in this age group are in any way peculiarly disadvantaged, subject to systematic discriminatory treatment, or otherwise in need of special solicitude from the courts.

. . .It is true that a number of our opinions contain broadly phrased dicta implying that the same test should be applied to all classifications based on sex, whether affecting females or males. E.g., *Frontiero v. Richardson*, at 688; *Reed v. Reed*, 404 U.S. 71, 76. However, before today, no decision of this Court has applied an elevated level of scrutiny to invalidate a statutory discrimination harmful to males, except where the statute impaired an important personal interest protected by the Constitution.[1] There being no such interest here, and there being no plausible argument that this is a discrimination against females,[2] the Court's reliance on our previous sex-discrimination cases is ill-founded. It treats gender classification as a talisman which—without regard to the rights involved or the person affected—calls into effect a heavier burden of judicial review.

The Court's conclusion that a law which treats males less favorably than females "must serve important governmental objectives and must be substantially related to achievement of those objectives" apparently comes out of thin air. The Equal Protection Clause contains no such language, and none of our previous cases adopt that standard, I would think we have had enough difficulty with the two standards of review which our cases have recognized—the norm of "rational basis," and the "compelling state interest" required where a "suspect classification" is involved—so as to counsel weightly against the insertion of still another "standard" between those two. How is this Court to divine what objectives are important? How is it to determine whether a particular law is "substantially" related to the achievement of such objective, rather than related in some other way to its achievement? Both of the phrases used are so diaphanous and elastic as to invite subjective judicial preferences or prejudices relating to particular types of legislation, masquerading as judgments whether such legislation is directed at "important" objectives or, whether the relationship to those objectives is "substantial" enough.

I would have thought that if this Court were to leave anything to decision by the popularly elected branches of the Government, where no constitutional claim other than that of equal protection is invoked, it would be the decision as to what governmental objectives to be achieved by law are "important," and which are not. As for the second part of the Court's new test, the Judicial Branch is probably in no worse position than the Legislative or Executive Branches to determine if there is any rational relationship between a classification and the purpose which it might be thought to serve. But the introduction of the adverb "substantially" requires courts to make subjective judgments as to operational effects, for which neither their expertise nor their access to data fits them. And even if we manage to avoid both confusion and the mirroring of our own preferences in the development of this new doctrine, the thousands of judges in other courts who must interpret the Equal Protection Clause may not be so fortunate.

. . .Our decisions indicate that the application of the Equal Protection Clause in a context not justifying an elevated level of scrutiny does not demand "mathematical nicety" or the elimination of all inequality. Those cases recognize that the practical problems of government may require rough accommodations of interests, and hold that such accommodations should be respected unless no reasonable basis can be found to support them. *Dandridge v. Williams*, at 485. Whether the same ends might have been better or more precisely served by a different approach is no part of the judicial inquiry under the traditional minimum rationality approach. *Richardson v. Belcher*, at 84.

The Court "accept[s] for purposes of discussion" the District Court's finding that the purpose of the provisions in question was traffic safety, and proceeds to examine the statistical evidence in the record in order to decide if "the gender-based distinction *closely* serves to achieve that objective" (emphasis added). (Whether there is a difference between laws which "closely serve" objectives and those which are only "substantially related" to their achievement, we are not told.) I believe that a more traditional type of scrutiny is appropriate in this case. . . . One need not immerse oneself in the fine-points of statistical analysis . . . to see the weaknesses in the Court's attempted denigration of the evidence at hand.

One survey of arrest statistics assembled in 1973 indicated that males in the 18–20 age group were arrested for "driving under the influence" almost 18 times as often as their female counterparts, and for "drunkenness" in a ratio of almost ten-to-one. Accepting, as the Court does, appellants' comparison of the total figures with 1973 Oklahoma census data, this survey indicates a 2% arrest rate among males in the age group, as compared to a 0.18% rate among females.

Other surveys indicated (1) that over the five-year period from 1967 to 1972, nationwide arrests for drunken driving increased 138%, and that 93% of all persons arrested for drunken driving were male; (2) that youths in the 17–21 age group were overrepresented among those killed or injured in Oklahoma traffic accidents, that male casualties substantially exceeded female, and that deaths in this age group continued to rise while overall traffic deaths declined; (3) that over 3/4 of the drivers under 20 in the Oklahoma City area are males, and that each of them, on average, drives half again as many miles per year as their female counterpart; (4) that 4/5 of male drivers under 20 in the Oklahoma City area state a drink preference for beer, while about 3/5 of female drivers of that age state the same preference; and (5) that the percentage of male drivers under 20 admitting to drinking within two hours of driving was half again larger than the percentage for females, and that the percentage of male drivers of that age group with a blood alcohol content greater than .01% was almost half again larger than for female drivers.

The Court's criticism of the statistics relied on by the District Court conveys the impression that a legislature in enacting a new law is to be subjected to the judicial equivalent of a doctoral examination in statistics. Legislatures . . . are entitled to draw factual conclusions on the basis of the determination of probable cause which an arrest by a police officer normally represents. In this situation, they could reasonably infer that the incidence of drunk driving is a good deal higher than the incidence of arrest.

And while, as the Court observes. . .such statistics may be distorted as a result of stereotyping, the legislature is not required to prove before a court that its statistics are perfect. In any event, if stereotypes are as pervasive as the Court suggests, they may in turn influence the conduct of the men and women in question, and cause the young men to conform to the wild and reckless image which is their stereotype.

. . .[T]he State of Oklahoma—and certainly this Court for purposes of equal protection review—can surely take notice of the fact that drunkenness is a significant cause of traffic casualties, and that youthful offenders have participated in the increase of the drunk driving problem. On this latter point, the survey data indicating increased driving casualties among 18–21-year-olds, while overall casualties dropped, is not irrelevant.

Nor is it unreasonable to conclude from the expressed preference for beer by 4/5 of the age group males that that beverage was a predominant source of their intoxication-related arrests. . . . [T]he state could reasonably bar those males from any purchases of alcoholic beer, including that of the 3.2% variety. This Court lacks the expertise or the data to evaluate the intoxicating properties of that beverage, and in that posture our only appropriate course is to defer to the reasonable inference supporting the statute—that taken in sufficient quality this beer has the same effect as any alcoholic beverage. . . .

The rationality of a statutory classification for equal protection purposes does not depend upon the statistical "fit" between the class and the trait sought to be singled out. It turns on whether there may be a sufficiently higher incidence of the trait within the included class than in the excluded class to justify different treatment. Therefore the present equal protection challenge to this gender-based discrimination poses only the question whether the incidence of drunk driving among young men is sufficiently greater than among young women to justify differential treatment. Notwithstanding the Court's critique of the statistical evidence, that evidence suggests clear differences between the drinking and driving habits of young men and women. Those differences are grounds enough for the State reasonably to conclude that young males pose by far the greater drunk driving hazard, both in terms of sheer numbers and in terms of hazard on a per-driver basis. The gender-based difference in treatment in this case is therefore not irrational.

The Court's argument that a 2% correlation between maleness and drunk driving is constitutionally insufficient therefore does not pose an equal protection issue concerning discrimination between males and females. The clearest demonstration of this is the fact that the precise argument made by the Court would be equally applicable to a flat bar on such purchases by anyone, male or female, in the 18–20 age group. . . . Under the appropriate rational basis test for equal protection, it is neither irrational nor arbitrary to bar [18–20-year-old males] from making purchases of 3.2% beer, which purchases might in many cases be made by a young man who immediately returns to his vehicle with the beverage. . . .

Opinion Footnotes

1 In *Stanley v. Illinois*, 405 U.S. 645 (1972), the Court struck down a statute allowing separation of illegitimate children from a surviving father but not a surviving mother, without any showing of parental unfitness. The Court stated that "the interest of a parent in the companionship, care, custody, and

> management of his or her children 'come[s] to this Court with a momentum for respect lacking when appeal is made to liberties which derive merely from shifting economic arrangements.'"
>
> In *Kahn v. Shevin*, 416 U.S. 351 (1974), the Court upheld Florida's $500 property tax exemption for widows only. The opinion of the Court appears to apply a rational basis test, and is so understood by the dissenters. *Id.*, at 355, 357.
>
> In *Weinberger v. Wiesenfeld*, 420 U.S. 636 (1975), the Court invalidated § 202(g) of the Social Security Act, which allowed benefits to mothers but not fathers of minor children, who survive the wage earner. This statute was treated, in the opinion of the Court, as discrimination against female wage earners, on the ground that it minimizes the financial security which their work efforts provide for their families. *Id.*, at 645.
>
> 2 I am not unaware of the argument from time to time advanced, that all discriminations between the sexes ultimately redound to the detriment of females, because they tend to reinforce "old notions" restricting the roles and opportunities of women. As a general proposition . . ., I believe that this argument was implicitly found to carry little weight in our decisions upholding [antimale] gender-based differences. See *Schlesinger v. Ballard*; *Kahn v. Shevin*. Seeing no assertion that it has special applicability to the situation at hand, I believe it can be dismissed as an insubstantial consideration.

Case Questions

1. Justice Rehnquist charges that the new *Craig v. Boren* rule that gender classifications "must serve important governmental objectives and must be substantially related to the achievement of those objectives" does not come from any precedential source and was pulled "out of thin air." The Court majority claims that this rule was in fact guiding the Court's thinking in sex discrimination cases dating back to 1971. Who is right?

2. Rehnquist insists that the new *Craig* standard is more likely than the old "rational basis" test to invite the imposition of "subjective judicial preferences or prejudices." Yet even using the rational-basis test, Justice Stewart cannot agree with Justices Burger and Rehnquist on the rationality of this statute. If the standard were still rationality, would you uphold this law?

3. Justice Stevens says that the Court has all along been employing one basic guideline: that states must govern impartially. Does his description fit the sex discrimination cases up to 1976?

SEX DISCRIMINATION POST-*CRAIG*

Once the *Craig* rule of intermediate scrutiny became official, the Court did not simply strike down all sex discrimination in the laws. Instead, the Court seemed to follow the guidelines that prominent ERA proponents (see Case note to *Frontiero*) had said the ERA would produce if ratified. Laws that distinguished between the sexes for reasons linked to differences of reproductive physiology and laws that struck the Court as designed to compensate women for societal discrimination continued to be upheld. Others were declared void as violations of equal protection.

Two Social Security cases of 1977 are illustrative of the compensatory concern. The first *Califano v. Goldfarb*, 430 U.S. 199, declared unconstitutional a provision that permitted all widows to receive surviving spouse benefits if their husbands' Social Security payments were greater than those they would receive from their own earnings, but permitted this benefit to widowers only if they could prove actual dependency. The "swing" (or tiebreaking) vote in the case was that of Justice Stevens who wrote that it did not make sense to give this benefit to non-dependent widows but not non-dependent widowers; he considered this combination therefore "not the product of a conscious purpose to redress the legacy of economic discrimination against females" but rather "the accidental byproduct of a traditional way of thinking about females" (at 221). He suggested that *Kahn v. Shevin* had been silently overruled by *Weinberger v. Wiesenfeld*, and that he was following the latter.

By contrast, in the second case, *Califano v. Webster*, 430 U.S. 313, the Court upheld by a unanimous "per curiam" (i.e., unsigned) opinion a Social Security provision that gave all women who had retired before 1975 a more generous way to calculate Social Security benefits from their earnings than was available to men. The Court explained that in this instance, "[T]he legislative history is clear that the differing treatment...was deliberately enacted to compensate for particular economic disabilities suffered by women" (at 320).

As cases in some later chapters will show, the Court was willing to deploy the *Craig* rule to make dramatic changes in American law, both on the traditional law of marriage and on state-run single-sex colleges. But when the Court believed a particular discrimination dealt sensibly with biological sex differences, it stopped short of interfering with the legislative judgment, as exemplified in the case of "Michael M." below.

Statutory Rape: *Michael M. v. Sonoma County* (1981)

The feminist movement in the decade of the 1970s made considerable progress in reforming those aspects of traditional rape law that made rape a particularly difficult crime to prosecute successfully. These are detailed in Chapter 7. Some reformers wanted to go beyond these changes and render all rape laws gender-neutral. A particularly likely target was "statutory rape" legislation. Most states had laws punishing males for sex with females deemed too young to give informed consent to sexual intercourse. In California the age of such consent was 18. A 17 1/2 year old male, Michael M., was prosecuted in Sonoma County for sex with a 16 1/2 year old female, Sharon, in June 1978. He challenged the proceedings on the grounds that California's statutory rape law denied him equal protection, in violation of the Fourteenth Amendment. The California Supreme Court, *even using a strict-scrutiny-compelling-interest test*, as required by their own reading of their state constitution, nonetheless upheld the law (as had two lower courts). Using the *Craig* test, the U.S. Supreme Court also upheld the law.

Although this case was prosecuted as consensual intercourse, the facts revealed in Justice Blackmun's opinion indicated that it was arguably a forcible rape (although Blackmun seems to think otherwise). Statutory rape laws function not infrequently as a practical, back-up alternative for prosecutors for these cases where forcible rape convictions appear to have uncertain chances of success. This need comprised one of California's arguments on behalf of the statute.

> ### MICHAEL M. V. SONOMA COUNTY, CA
> 450 U.S. 464 (1981)
>
> **JUSTICE REHNQUIST announced the judgment of the Court and delivered an opinion, in which THE CHIEF JUSTICE, JUSTICE STEWART, and JUSTICE POWELL joined.** [In the 1980–81 term, the U.S. Supreme Court Reports stopped inserting "Mr." in front of "Justice." On August 19, 1981, Pres. Reagan nominated Sandra Day O'Connor to the Court and the Senate confirmed on September 21, 1981.—AU.]
>
> The question presented in this case is whether California's "statutory rape" law, § 261.5 of the Cal. Penal Code Ann., violates the Equal Protection Clause of the Fourteenth Amendment. Section 261.5 defines unlawful sexual intercourse as "an act of sexual intercourse accomplished with a female not the wife of the perpetrator, where the female is under the age of 18 years." The statute thus makes men alone criminally liable for the act of sexual intercourse.
>
> . . .
>
> . . .Unlike the California Supreme Court, we have not held that gender-based classifications are "inherently suspect" and thus we do not apply so-called "strict scrutiny" to those classifications. Our cases have held, however, that the traditional minimum rationality test takes on a somewhat "sharper focus" when gender-based classifications are challenged. See *Craig v. Boren*, 429 U.S. 190, 210 n.[*] (1976) (POWELL, J., concurring). In . . . *Craig v. Boren*, at 197, the Court restated the test to require the classification to bear a "substantial relationship" to "important governmental objectives."
>
> Underlying these decisions is the principle that a legislature may not "make overbroad generalizations based on sex which are entirely unrelated to any

differences between men and women or which demean the ability or social status of the affected class." *Parham v. Hughes*, 441 U.S. 347, 354 (1979) (plurality opinion of STEWART, J.). But because the Equal Protection Clause does not "demand that a statute necessarily apply equally to all persons" or require " 'things which are different in fact . . . to be treated in law as though they were the same,' " *Rinaldi v. Yeager*, 384 U.S. 305, 309 (1966). . ., this Court has consistently upheld statutes where the gender classification is not invidious, but rather realistically reflects the fact that the sexes are not similarly situated in certain circumstances. *Parham v. Hughes*; *Califano v. Webster*, 430 U.S. 313 (1977); *Schlesinger v. Ballard*, 419 U.S. 498 (1975); *Kahn v. Shevin*, 416 U.S. 351 (1974). As the Court has stated, a legislature may "provide for the special problems of women." *Weinberger v. Wiesenfeld*, 420 U.S. 636, 653 (1975).

Applying those principles to this case, the fact that the California Legislature criminalized the act of illicit sexual intercourse with a minor female is a sure indication of its intent or purpose to discourage that conduct. Precisely why the legislature desired that result is of course somewhat less clear. . . . Here, for example, the individual legislators may have voted for the statute for a variety of reasons. Some legislators may have been concerned about preventing teenage pregnancies, others about protecting young females from physical injury or from the loss of "chastity," and still others about promoting various religious and moral attitudes towards premarital sex.

The justification for the statute offered by the State, and accepted by the Supreme Court of California, is that the legislature sought to prevent illegitimate teenage pregnancies. That finding, of course, is entitled to great deference. *Reitman v. Mulkey*, 387 U.S. 369, 373–374 (1967). And although our cases establish that the State's asserted reason for the enactment of a statute may be rejected, if it "could not have been a goal of the legislation," *Weinberger v. Wiesenfeld*, at 648, n. 16, this is not such a case.

We are satisfied not only that the prevention of illegitimate pregnancy is at least one of the "purposes" of the statute, but also that the State has a strong interest in preventing such pregnancy. At the risk of stating the obvious, teenage pregnancies, which have increased dramatically over the last two decades,[3] have significant social, medical, and economic consequences for both the mother and her child, and the State.[4] Of particular concern to the State is that approximately half of all teenage pregnancies end in abortion. And of those children who are born, their illegitimacy makes them likely candidates to become wards of the State.[6]

We need not be medical doctors to discern that young men and young women are not similarly situated with respect to the problems and the risks of sexual intercourse. Only women may become pregnant, and they suffer disproportionately the profound physical, emotional, and psychological consequences of sexual activity. The statute at issue here protects women from sexual intercourse at an age when those consequences are particularly severe.[7]

The question thus boils down to whether a State may attack the problem of sexual intercourse and teenage pregnancy directly by prohibiting a male from having sexual intercourse with a minor female. We hold that such a statute is sufficiently related to the State's objectives to pass constitutional muster.

Because virtually all of the significant harmful and inescapably identifiable consequences of teenage pregnancy fall on the young female, a legislature acts well within its authority when it elects to punish only the participant who, by nature, suffers few of the consequences of his conduct. It is hardly unreasonable for a legislature acting to protect minor females to exclude them from punishment. Moreover, the risk of pregnancy itself constitutes a substantial deterrence to young females. No similar natural sanctions deter males. A criminal sanction imposed solely on males thus serves to roughly "equalize" the deterrents on the sexes.

We are unable to accept petitioner's contention that the statute is impermissibly underinclusive and must, in order to pass judicial scrutiny, be broadened so as to hold the female as criminally liable as the male. It is argued that this statute is not necessary to deter teenage pregnancy because a gender-neutral statute, where both male and female would be subject to prosecution, would serve that goal equally well. . . .

. . .[W]e cannot say that a gender-neutral statute would be as effective as the statute California has chosen to enact. The State persuasively contends that a gender-neutral statute would frustrate its interest in effective enforcement. Its view is that a female is surely less likely to report violations of the statute if she herself would be subject to criminal prosecution. In an area already fraught with prosecutorial difficulties, we decline to hold that the Equal Protection Clause requires a legislature to enact a statute so broad that it may well be incapable of enforcement.[10]

We similarly reject petitioner's argument that § 261.5 is impermissibly overbroad because it makes unlawful sexual intercourse with prepubescent females, who are, by definition, incapable of becoming pregnant. Quite apart from the fact that the statute could well be justified on the grounds that very young females are particularly susceptible to physical injury from sexual intercourse, see *Rundlett v. Oliver*, 607 F.2d 495 (CA1 1979), it is ludicrous to suggest that the Constitution requires the California Legislature to limit the scope of its rape statute to older teenagers and exclude young girls.

There remains only petitioner's contention that the statute is unconstitutional as it is applied to him because he, like Sharon, was under 18 at the time of sexual intercourse. Petitioner argues that the statute is flawed because it presumes that as between two persons under 18, the male is the culpable aggressor. We find petitioner's contentions unpersuasive. Contrary to his assertions, the statute does not rest on the assumption that males are generally the aggressors. It is instead an attempt by a legislature to prevent illegitimate teenage pregnancy by providing an additional deterrent for men. The age of the man is irrelevant since young men are as capable as older men of inflicting the harm sought to be prevented.

In upholding the California statute we also recognize that this is not a case where a statute is being challenged on the grounds that it "invidiously discriminates" against females. To the contrary, the statute places a burden on males which is not shared by females. But we find nothing to suggest that men, because of past discrimination or peculiar disadvantages, are in need of the special solicitude of the courts. Nor is this a case where the gender classification. . . rests on "the baggage of sexual stereotypes" as in *Orr v. Orr*, 440 U.S., at 283. As we have held, the statute instead reasonably reflects the fact that the consequences of sexual intercourse and pregnancy fall more heavily on the female than on the male.

Accordingly the judgment of the California Supreme Court is

Affirmed.

Opinion Footnotes

3 In 1976 approximately one million 15-to-19-year-olds became pregnant, one-tenth of all women in that age group. Two-thirds of the pregnancies were illegitimate. Illegitimacy rates for teenagers (births per 1,000 unmarried females ages 14 to 19) increased 75% for 14-to-17-year-olds between 1961 and 1974 and 33% for 18-to-19-year-olds. Alan Guttmacher Institute, *11 Million Teenagers* 10, 13 (1976); C. Chilman, *Adolescent Sexuality In a Changing American Society* 195 (NIH Pub. No. 80-1426, 1980).

4 The risk of maternal death is 60% higher for a teenager under the age of 15 than for a woman in her early twenties. The risk is 13% higher [450 U.S. 464, 471] for 15-to-19-year-olds. The statistics further show that most teenage mothers drop out of school and face a bleak economic future. . .

6 . . .Subsequent to the decision below, the California Legislature . . .rejected proposals to render § 261.5 gender neutral, thereby ratifying the judgment of the California Supreme Court. That is enough to answer petitioner's contention that the statute was the " 'accidental by-product of a traditional way of thinking about females.' " *Califano v. Webster*, 430 U.S. 313, 320 (1977). . . . Certainly this decision of the California Legislature is as good a source as is this Court in deciding what is "current" and what is "outmoded". . .

7 Although petitioner concedes that the State has a "compelling" interest in preventing teenage pregnancy, he contends that the "true" purpose of § 261.5 is to protect the virtue and chastity of young women. As such, the statute is unjustifiable because it rests on archaic stereotypes. What we have said above is enough to dispose of that contention. . . . [T]he only question under the Federal Constitution is whether the legislation violates the Equal Protection Clause of the Fourteenth Amendment, not whether its supporters may have endorsed it for reasons no longer generally accepted. Even if the preservation of female chastity were one of the motives of the statute, and even if that motive be impermissible, petitioner's argument must fail because "[i]t is a familiar practice of constitutional law that this court will not strike down an otherwise constitutional statute on the basis of an alleged illicit legislative motive." *United States v. O'Brien*, 391 U.S. 367, 383 (1968). In *Orr v. Orr*, 440 U.S. 268 (1979), for example, the Court rejected one asserted purpose as impermissible, but then considered other purposes to determine if they could justify the statute. . . .

10 The question whether a statute is substantially related to its asserted goals is at best an opaque one. It can be plausibly argued that a gender-neutral statute would produce fewer prosecutions than the statute at issue here. See STEWART, J., concurring, at 481, n. 13. JUSTICE BRENNAN'S dissent argues, . . ."even assuming that a gender-neutral statute would be more difficult to enforce, . . . [c]ommon sense . . . suggests that a gender-neutral statutory rape law is potentially a greater deterrent of sexual activity than a gender-based law, for the simple reason that a gender-neutral law subjects both men and women to criminal sanctions and thus arguably has a deterrent effect on twice as many potential violators," at 493–494. Where such differing speculations as to the effect of a statute are plausible, we think it appropriate to defer to the decision of the California Supreme Court, "armed as it was with the knowledge of the facts and circumstances concerning the passage and potential impact of [the statute], and familiar with the milieu in which that provision would operate." *Reitman v. Mulkey*, 387 U.S. 369, 378–379 (1967).

JUSTICE STEWART, concurring.

. . .The petitioner contends that this state law, which punishes only males for the conduct in question, violates his Fourteenth Amendment right to the equal protection of the law. The Court today correctly rejects that contention.

At the outset, it should be noted that the statutory discrimination, when viewed as part of the wider scheme of California law, is not as clearcut as might at first appear. Females are not freed from criminal liability in California for engaging in sexual activity that may be harmful. It is unlawful, for example, for any person, of either sex, to molest, annoy, or contribute to the delinquency of anyone under 18. . . All persons are prohibited from committing "any lewd or lascivious act," including consensual intercourse, with a child under 14. And members of both sexes may be convicted for engaging in deviant sexual acts with anyone under 18. Finally, females may be brought within the proscription of § 261.5 itself, since a female may be charged with aiding and abetting its violation.

Section 261.5 is thus but one part of a broad statutory scheme that protects all minors from the problems and risks attendant upon adolescent sexual activity. To be sure, § 261.5 creates an additional measure of punishment for males who engage in sexual intercourse with females between the ages of 14 and 17. The question then is whether the Constitution prohibits a state legislature from imposing this additional sanction on a gender-specific basis.

The Constitution is violated when government, state or federal, invidiously classifies similarly situated people on the basis of the immutable characteristics with which they were born. Thus, detrimental racial classifications by government always violate the Constitution, for the simple reason that, so far as the Constitution is concerned, people of different races are always similarly situated. [citations omitted] By contrast, while detrimental gender classifications by government often violate the Constitution, they do not always do so, for the reason that there are differences between males and females that the Constitution necessarily recognizes. In this case we deal with the most basic of these differences: females can become pregnant as the result of sexual intercourse; males cannot.

As was recognized in *Parham v. Hughes*, 441 U.S. 347, 354, "a State is not free to make overbroad generalizations based on sex which are entirely unrelated to any differences between men and women or which demean the ability or social status of the affected class.". . . But we have recognized that in certain narrow circumstances men and women are not similarly situated; in these circumstances a gender classification based on clear differences between the sexes is not invidious, and a legislative classification realistically based upon those differences is not unconstitutional. See *Parham v. Hughes*; *Califano v. Webster*, 430 U.S. 313, 316–317; *Schlesinger v. Ballard*, 419 U.S. 498. . .

. . .Young women and men are not similarly situated with respect to the problems and risks associated with intercourse and pregnancy, and the statute is realistically related to the legitimate state purpose of reducing those problems and risks.

As the California Supreme Court's catalog shows, the pregnant unmarried female confronts problems more numerous and more severe than any faced by her male partner.[7] She alone endures the medical risks of pregnancy or abortion. She suffers disproportionately the social, educational, and emotional consequences of pregnancy. Recognizing this disproportion, California has attempted to protect teenage females by prohibiting males from participating in the act necessary for conception.

. . .Experienced observation confirms the common sense notion that adolescent males disregard the possibility of pregnancy far more than do adolescent females. . .

. . .

In short, the Equal Protection Clause does not mean that the physiological differences between men and women must be disregarded. . . .

> **Opinion Footnote**
>
> 7 ...[F]rom 1971 through 1976, 83.6% of the 4,860 children born to girls under 15 in California were illegitimate, as were 51% of those born to girls 15 to 17. The court also observed that while accounting for only 21% of California pregnancies in 1976, teenagers accounted for 34.7% of legal abortions...

JUSTICE BLACKMUN, concurring in the judgment.

It is gratifying that the plurality recognizes that "...teenage pregnancies ... have increased dramatically..." and "have significant ... consequences." There have been times when I have wondered whether the Court was capable of this perception, particularly when it has struggled with the different but not unrelated problems that attend abortion issues. See, for example, the opinions (and the dissenting opinions) in *Beal v. Doe*, 432 U.S. 438 (1977); *Maher v. Roe*, 432 U.S. 464 (1977); *Poelker v. Doe*, 432 U.S. 519 (1977); *Harris v. McRae*, 448 U.S. 297 (1980)....

I ... cannot vote to strike down the California statutory rape law, for I think it is a sufficiently reasoned and constitutional effort to control the problem at its inception. For me, there is an important difference between this state action and a State's adamant and rigid refusal to face, or even to recognize, the "significant ... consequences"—to the woman—of a forced or unwanted conception. I have found it difficult to rule constitutional, for example, state efforts to block, at that later point, a woman's attempt to deal with the enormity of the problem confronting her, just as I have rejected state efforts to prevent women from rationally taking steps to prevent that problem from arising. See, e.g., *Carey v. Population Services International*, 431 U.S. 678 (1977). In contrast, I am persuaded that, although a minor has substantial privacy rights in intimate affairs connected with procreation, California's efforts to prevent teenage pregnancy are to be viewed differently from Utah's efforts to inhibit a woman from dealing with pregnancy once it has become an inevitability.

Craig v. Boren, 429 U.S. 190 (1976), was an opinion which ... I joined.... I vote to affirm the judgment of the Supreme Court of California and to uphold the State's gender-based classification on that test ...

I note, also, that § 261.5 of the California Penal Code is just one of several California statutes intended to protect the juvenile. JUSTICE STEWART, in his concurring opinion, appropriately observes that § 261.5 is "but one part of a broad statutory scheme that protects all minors..."

I think, too, that it is only fair, with respect to this particular petitioner, to point out that his partner, Sharon, appears not to have been an unwilling participant in at least the initial stages of the intimacies that took place the night of June 3, 1978.* Petitioner's and Sharon's nonacquaintance with each other before the incident; their drinking; their withdrawal from the others of the group; their foreplay, in which she willingly participated and seems to have encouraged; and the closeness of their ages (a difference of only one year and 18 days) are factors that should make this case an unattractive one to prosecute at all, and especially to prosecute as a felony, rather than as a misdemeanor chargeable under § 261.5. But the State has chosen to prosecute in that manner, and the facts, I reluctantly conclude, may fit the crime.

Opinion Footnote

> * Sharon at the preliminary hearing testified as follows:
>
> "Q. [by the Deputy District Attorney]. On June the 4th, at approximately midnight—midnight of June the 3rd, were you in Rohnert Park?
>
> "A. [by Sharon]. Yes.
>
> "Q. Is that in Sonoma County?
>
> "A. Yes.
>
> "Q. Did anything unusual happen to you that night in Rohnert Park?
>
> "A. Yes.
>
> "Q. Would you briefly describe what happened that night? Did you see the defendant that night in Rohnert Park?
>
> "A. Yes.
>
> "Q. Where did you first meet him?
>
> "A. At a bus stop.
>
> "Q. Was anyone with you?
>
> "A. My sister.
>
> "Q. Was anyone with the defendant?
>
> "A. Yes.
>
> "Q. How many people were with the defendant?
>
> "A. Two.
>
> "Q. Now, after you met the defendant, what happened?
>
> "A. We walked down to the railroad tracks.
>
> "Q. What happened at the railroad tracks?
>
> "A. We were drinking at the railroad tracks and we walked over to this bush and he started kissing me and stuff, and I was kissing him back, too, at first. Then, I was telling him to stop—
>
> "Q. Yes.
>
> "A. —and I was telling him to slow down and stop. He said, 'Okay, okay.' But then he just kept doing it. He just kept doing it and then my sister and two other guys came over to where we were and my sister said—told me to get up and come home. And then I didn't—
>
> "Q. Yes.
>
> "A. —and then my sister and—
>
> "Q. All right.
>
> "A. —David, one of the boys that were there, started walking home and we stayed there and then later—
>
> "Q. All right.
>
> "A. —Bruce left Michael, you know.
>
> "The Court: Michael being the defendant?

"The Witness: Yeah. We was laying there and we were kissing each other, and then he asked me if I wanted to walk him over to the park; so we walked over to the park and we sat down on a bench and then he started kissing me again and we were laying on the bench. And he told me to take my pants off.

"I said, 'No,' and I was trying to get up and he hit me back down on the bench and then I just said to myself, 'Forget it,' and I let him do what he wanted to do and he took my pants off and he was telling me to put my legs around him and stuff.

. . . .

"Q. Did you have sexual intercourse with the defendant?
"A. Yeah.
"Q. He did put his penis into your vagina?
"A. Yes.
"Q. You said that he hit you?
"A. Yeah.
"Q. How did he hit you?
"A. He slugged me in the face.
"Q. With what did he slug you?
"A. His fist.
"Q. Where abouts in the face?
"A. On my chin.
"Q. As a result of that, did you have any bruises or any kind of an injury?
"A. Yeah.
"Q. What happened?
"A. I had bruises.
"The Court: Did he hit you one time or did he hit you more than once?
"The Witness: He hit me about two or three times.

. . . .

"Q. Now, during the course of that evening, did the defendant ask you your age?
"A. Yeah.
"Q. And what did you tell him?
"A. Sixteen.
"Q. Did you tell him you were sixteen?
"A. Yes.
"Q. Now, you said you had been drinking, is that correct?
"A. Yes.
"Q. Would you describe your condition as a result of the drinking?
"A. I was a little drunk."

CROSS-EXAMINATION

"Q. Did you go off with Mr. M. away from the others?
"A. Yeah.
"Q. Why did you do that?
"A. I don't know. I guess I wanted to.
"Q. Did you have any need to go to the bathroom when you were there.
"A. Yes.
"Q. And what did you do?
"A. Me and my sister walked down the railroad tracks to some bushes and went to the bathroom.
"Q. Now, you and Mr. M., as I understand it, went off into the bushes, is that correct?

"A. Yes.

"Q. Okay. And what did you do when you and Mr. M. were there in the bushes?

"A. We were kissing and hugging.

"Q. Were you sitting up?

"A. We were laying down.

"Q. You were lying down. This was in the bushes?

"A. Yes.

"Q. How far away from the rest of them were you?

"A. They were just bushes right next to the railroad tracks. We just walked off into the bushes; not very far.

. . . .

"Q. So your sister and the other two boys came over to where you were, you and Michael were, is that right?

"A. Yeah.

"Q. What did they say to you, if you remember?

"A. My sister didn't say anything. She said, 'Come on, Sharon, let's go home.'

"Q. She asked you to go home with her?

"A. (Affirmative nod.)

"Q. Did you go home with her?

"A. No.

"Q. You wanted to stay with Mr. M.?

"A. I don't know.

"Q. Was this before or after he hit you?

"A. Before.

. . . . .

"Q. What happened in the five minutes that Bruce stayed there with you and Michael?

"A. I don't remember.

"Q. You don't remember at all?

"A. (Negative head shake.)

"Q. Did you have occasion at that time to kiss Bruce?

"A. Yeah.

"Q. You did? You were kissing Bruce at that time?

"A. (Affirmative nod.)

"Q. Was Bruce kissing you?

"A. Yes.

"Q. And were you standing up at this time?

"A. No, we were sitting down.

. . . .

"Q. Okay. So at this point in time you had left Mr. M. and you were hugging and kissing with Bruce, is that right?

"A. Yeah.

"Q. And you were sitting up.

"A. Yes.

"Q. Was your sister still there then?

"A. No. Yeah, she was at first.

"Q. What was she doing?

"A. She was standing up with Michael and David.

"Q. Yes. Was she doing anything with Michael and David?
"A. No, I don't think so.
"Q. Whose idea was it for you and Bruce to kiss? Did you initiate that?
"A. Yes.
"Q. What happened after Bruce left?
"A. Michael asked me if I wanted to go walk to the park.
"Q. And what did you say?
"A. I said, 'Yes.'
"Q. And then what happened?
"A. We walked to the park.
. . . .
"Q. How long did it take you to get to the park?
"A. About ten or fifteen minutes.
"Q. And did you walk there?
"A. Yes.
"Q. Did Mr. M. ever mention his name?
"A. Yes."

JUSTICE BRENNAN, with whom JUSTICES WHITE and MARSHALL join, dissenting.

It is disturbing to find the Court so splintered on a case that presents such a straightforward issue: Whether the admittedly gender-based classification in Cal. Penal Code Ann. § 261.5 bears a sufficient relationship to the State's asserted goal of preventing teenage pregnancies to survive the "mid-level" constitutional scrutiny mandated by *Craig v. Boren*, 429 U.S. 190 (1976). Applying the analytical framework provided by our precedents, I am convinced that there is only one proper resolution of this issue: the classification must be declared unconstitutional. I fear that the plurality opinion and JUSTICES STEWART and BLACKMUN reach the opposite result by placing too much emphasis on the desirability of achieving the State's asserted statutory goal—prevention of teenage pregnancy—and not enough emphasis on the fundamental question of whether the sex-based discrimination in the California statute is substantially related to the achievement of that goal.

After some uncertainty as to the proper framework for analyzing equal protection challenges to statutes containing gender-based classifications this Court settled upon the proposition that a statute containing a gender-based classification cannot withstand constitutional challenge unless the classification is substantially related to the achievement of an important governmental objective. *Kirchberg v. Feenstra* (1981); *Wengler v. Druggists Mutual Ins. Co.* (1980); *Califano v. Westcott* (1979); *Caban v. Mohammed* (1979); *Orr v. Orr* (1979); *Califano v. Goldfarb* (1977); *Califano v. Webster* (1977); *Craig v. Boren*. This analysis applies whether the classification discriminates against males or against females. *Caban v. Mohammed*, at 394; *Orr v. Orr*, at 278–279; *Craig v. Boren*, at 204. The burden is on the government to prove both the importance of its asserted objective and the substantial relationship between the classification and that objective. See *Kirchberg v. Feenstra*, at 461; *Wengler v. Druggists Mutual Ins. Co.*, at 151–152; *Caban v. Mohammed*, at 393; *Craig v. Boren*, at 204. And the State cannot meet that burden without showing that a gender-neutral statute would be a less effective means of achieving that goal. *Wengler v. Druggists Mutual Ins. Co.*, at 151–152; *Orr v. Orr*, at 281, 283.

The State of California vigorously asserts that the "important governmental objective" to be served by § 261.5 is the prevention of teenage pregnancy. . . . But even assuming that prevention of teenage pregnancy is . . . in fact an objective. . ., California still has the burden of proving that there are fewer teenage pregnancies under its gender-based statutory rape law than there would be if the law were gender neutral. . . .

The plurality . . . accepts the State's assertion that "a female is surely less likely to report violations of the statute if she herself would be subject to criminal prosecution.". . .

. . . [T]here are at least two serious flaws in the State's assertion that law enforcement problems created by a gender-neutral statutory rape law would make such a statute less effective than a gender-based statute in deterring sexual activity.

First, the experience of other jurisdictions, and California itself, belies the plurality's conclusion that a gender-neutral statutory rape law "may well be incapable of enforcement." There are now at least 37 States that have enacted gender-neutral statutory rape laws. Although most of these laws protect young persons (of either sex) from the sexual exploitation of older individuals, the laws of Arizona, Florida, and Illinois permit prosecution of both minor females and minor males for engaging in mutual sexual conduct. California has introduced no evidence that those States have been handicapped by enforcement problems. . . Surely, if those States could provide such evidence, we might expect that California would have introduced it.

. . .

The second flaw in the State's assertion is that even assuming that a gender-neutral statute would be more difficult to enforce, the State has still not shown that those enforcement problems would make such a statute less effective than a gender-based statute in deterring minor females from engaging in sexual intercourse. Common sense, however, suggests that a gender-neutral statutory rape law is potentially a greater deterrent of sexual activity than a gender-based law, for the simple reason that a gender-neutral law subjects both men and women to criminal sanctions and thus arguably has a deterrent effect on twice as many potential violators. Even if fewer persons were prosecuted under the gender-neutral law . . . it would still be true that twice as many persons would be subject to arrest. The State's failure to prove that a gender-neutral law would be a less effective deterrent than a gender-based law, like the State's failure to prove that a gender-neutral law would be difficult to enforce, should have led this Court to invalidate § 261.5.

Until very recently, no California court or commentator had suggested that the purpose of California's statutory rape law was to protect young women from the risk of pregnancy. Indeed, the historical development . . . demonstrates that the law was initially enacted on the premise that young women, in contrast to young men, were to be deemed legally incapable of consenting to an act of sexual intercourse. Because their chastity was considered particularly precious, those young women were felt to be uniquely in need of the State's protection.[10] In contrast, young men were assumed to be capable of making such decisions for themselves; the law therefore did not offer them any special protection.

. . .[T]he State has not shown that Cal. Penal Code § 261.5 is any more effective than a gender-neutral law would be in deterring minor females from engaging in sexual intercourse. It has therefore not met its burden of proving that the statutory classification is substantially related to the achievement of its asserted goal.

I would hold that § 261.5 violates the Equal Protection Clause. . .

Opinion Footnote

10 Past decisions of the California courts confirm that the law was designed to protect the State's young females from their own uninformed decisionmaking. . . .As recently as 1964, the California Supreme Court decided People v. Hernandez, 61 Cal. 2d, at 531, 393 P.2d, at 674, in which it stated that the underage female is presumed too innocent and naive to understand . . .her act. . . . The law's concern with her capacity . . . to so understand is explained in part by a popular conception of the social, moral and personal values which are preserved by the abstinence from sexual indulgence on the part of a young woman. An unwise disposition of her sexual favor is deemed to do harm both to herself and the social mores by which the community's conduct patterns are established. Hence the law of statutory rape intervenes in an effort to avoid such a disposition.

In . . . Michael M. . . . the California Supreme Court decided, for the first time in the 130-year history of the statute, that pregnancy prevention had become one of the purposes of the statute.

JUSTICE STEVENS, dissenting.

Local custom and belief—rather than statutory laws of venerable but doubtful ancestry—will determine the volume of sexual activity among unmarried teenagers. The empirical evidence cited by the plurality demonstrates the futility of the notion that a statutory prohibition will significantly affect the volume of that activity or provide a meaningful solution to the problems created by it. Nevertheless, as a matter of constitutional power, I would have no doubt about the validity of a state law prohibiting all unmarried teenagers from engaging in sexual intercourse. The societal interests in reducing the incidence of venereal disease and teenage pregnancy are sufficient, in my judgment, to justify a prohibition of conduct that increases the risk of those harms.

My conclusion that a nondiscriminatory prohibition would be constitutional does not help me answer the question whether a prohibition applicable to only half of the joint participants in the risk-creating conduct is also valid. It cannot be true that the validity of a total ban is an adequate justification for a selective prohibition; otherwise, the constitutional objection to discriminatory rules would be meaningless. The question in this case is whether the difference between males and females justifies this statutory discrimination based entirely on sex.[4]

. . .[T]he plurality is quite correct in making the assumption that the joint act that this law seeks to prohibit creates a greater risk of harm for the female than for the male. But the plurality surely cannot believe that the risk of pregnancy confronted by the female—any more than the risk of venereal disease confronted by males as well as females—has provided an effective deterrent to voluntary female participation in the risk-creating conduct. Yet the plurality's decision seems to rest on the assumption that the California Legislature acted on the basis of that rather fanciful notion.

In my judgment, the fact that a class of persons is especially vulnerable to a risk that a statute is designed to avoid is a reason for making the statute applicable to that class. The argument that a special need for protection provides a rational explanation for an exemption is one I simply do not comprehend.

In this case, the fact that a female confronts a greater risk of harm than a male is a reason for applying the prohibition to her—not a reason for granting her a license to use her own judgment on whether or not to assume the risk. Surely, if we examine the problem from the point of view of society's interest in preventing the risk-creating conduct from occurring at all, it is irrational to exempt 50% of the potential violators. See dissent of JUSTICE BRENNAN. And, if we view the government's interest as that of a *parens patriae* seeking to protect its subjects from harming themselves, the discrimination is actually perverse. Would a rational parent making rules for the conduct of twin children of opposite sex simultaneously forbid the son and authorize the daughter to engage in conduct that is especially harmful to the daughter? That is the effect of this statutory classification.

If pregnancy or some other special harm is suffered by one of the two participants in the prohibited act, that special harm no doubt would constitute a legitimate mitigating factor in deciding what, if any, punishment might be appropriate in a given case. But from the standpoint of fashioning a general preventive rule—or, indeed, in determining appropriate punishment when neither party in fact has suffered any special harm—I regard a total exemption for the members of the more endangered class as utterly irrational.

In my opinion, the only acceptable justification for a general rule requiring disparate treatment of the two participants in a joint act must be a legislative judgment that one is more guilty than the other. The risk-creating conduct that this statute is designed to prevent requires the participation of two persons—one male and one female. In many situations it is probably true that one is the aggressor and the other is either an unwilling, or at least a less willing, participant in the joint act. If a statute authorized punishment of only one participant and required the prosecutor to prove that participant had been the aggressor, I assume that the discrimination would be valid. Although the question is less clear, I also assume, for the purpose of deciding this case, that it would be permissible to punish only the male participant, if one element of the offense were proof that he had been the aggressor, or at least in some respects the more responsible participant in the joint act. The statute at issue in this case, however, requires no such proof. The question raised by this statute is whether the State, consistently with the Federal Constitution, may always punish the male and never the female when they are equally responsible or when the female is the more responsible of the two.

It would seem to me that an impartial lawmaker could give only one answer to that question. The fact that the California Legislature has decided to apply its prohibition only to the male may reflect a legislative judgment that in the typical case the male is actually the more guilty party. Any such judgment must, in turn, assume that the decision to engage in the risk-creating conduct is always—or at least typically—a male decision. If that assumption is valid, the statutory classification should also be valid. But what is the support for the assumption? It is not contained in the record of this case or in any legislative history or scholarly study that has been called to our attention. I think it is supported to some extent by traditional attitudes. . . . But the possibility that such a habitual attitude may reflect nothing more than an irrational prejudice makes it an insufficient justification for discriminatory treatment that is otherwise blatantly unfair. For, as I read this statute, it requires that one, and only one, of two equally guilty wrongdoers be stigmatized by a criminal conviction.

I cannot accept the State's argument that the constitutionality of the discriminatory rule can be saved by an assumption that prosecutors will commonly invoke this statute only in cases that actually involve a forcible rape, but one that cannot be established by proof beyond a reasonable doubt.[8] That assumption implies that a State has a legitimate interest in convicting a defendant on evidence that is constitutionally insufficient. Of course, the State may create a lesser-included offense that would authorize punishment of the more guilty party, but surely the interest in obtaining convictions on inadequate proof cannot justify a statute that punishes one who is equally or less guilty than his partner.

Nor do I find at all persuasive the suggestion that this discrimination is adequately justified by the desire to encourage females to inform against their male partners. Even if the concept of a wholesale informant's exemption were an acceptable enforcement device, what is the justification for defining the exempt class entirely by reference to sex rather than by reference to a more neutral criterion such as relative innocence? Indeed, if the exempt class is to be composed entirely of members of one sex, what is there to support the view that the statutory purpose will be better served by granting the informing license to females rather than to males? If a discarded male partner informs on a promiscuous female, a timely threat of prosecution might well prevent the precise harm the statute is intended to minimize.

Finally, even if my logic is faulty and there actually is some speculative basis for treating equally guilty males and females differently, I still believe that any such speculative justification would be outweighed by the paramount interest in evenhanded enforcement of the law. A rule that authorizes punishment of only one of two equally guilty wrongdoers violates the essence of the constitutional requirement that the sovereign must govern impartially.

I respectfully dissent.

> ## Opinion Footnotes
>
> **4** Equal protection analysis is often said to involve different "levels of scrutiny." It may be more accurate to say that the burden of sustaining an equal protection challenge is much heavier in some cases than in others. Racial classifications, which are subjected to "strict scrutiny," are presumptively invalid because there is seldom, if ever, any legitimate reason for treating citizens differently because of their race. On the other hand, most economic classifications are presumptively valid because they are a necessary component of most regulatory programs. In cases involving discrimination between men and women, the natural differences between the sexes are sometimes relevant and sometimes wholly irrelevant. If those differences are obviously irrelevant, the discrimination should be treated as presumptively unlawful in the same way that racial classifications are presumptively unlawful. Cf. *Califano v. Goldfarb*, 430 U.S. 199, 223 (STEVENS, J., concurring in judgment). But if, as in this case, there is an apparent connection between the discrimination and the fact that only women can become pregnant, it may be appropriate to presume that the classification is lawful. This presumption, however, may be overcome by a demonstration that the apparent justification for the discrimination is illusory or wholly inadequate. Thus, instead of applying a "mid-level" form of scrutiny in all sex discrimination cases, perhaps the burden is heavier in some than in others. Nevertheless, as I have previously suggested, the ultimate standard in these, as in all other equal protection cases, is essentially the same. See *Craig v. Boren*, 429 U.S. 190, 211–212 (STEVENS, J., concurring). . . .[We ask] "whether the harm done to the disadvantaged class by the legislative classification is disproportionate to the public purposes the measure is likely to achieve." Cox, Book Review, 94 *Harv. L. Rev.* 700, 706 (1981).
>
> **8** According to the [brief of] State of California: "The statute is commonly employed in situations involving force, prostitution, pornography or coercion due to status relationships, and the state's interest in these situations is apparent." The State's interest in these situations is indeed apparent and certainly sufficient to justify statutory prohibition of forcible rape, prostitution, pornography, and nonforcible, but nonetheless coerced, sexual intercourse. However, it is not at all apparent to me how this state interest can justify a statute not specifically directed to any of these offenses.

Case Questions

1. If laws against sex with minors were written in a gender-neutral way but only males prosecuted, would a defendant be likely to argue that they were unconstitutional *as applied*? If laws against sex between minors were written in such a way as to punish only the aggressor or initiator of the sex, might courts confront insurmountable problems of proof? (e.g., What act defines the "initiation" of sexual intercourse? Is the definition provable "beyond a reasonable doubt"?)

2. Do laws like this one help or hurt females?

3. What do you suppose Justice Stevens has in mind when he mentions in note 8 "nonforcible but nonetheless coerced, sexual intercourse"?

WOMEN AND MODERN CITIZENSHIP PART TWO: JURY SERVICE, MILITARY SERVICE, AND CONFERRING CITIZENSHIP

Systematic Exclusion from Juries: *Taylor v. Louisiana* (1975)

As *Hoyt v. Florida* revealed, the obtaining of suffrage by women did not immediately entail the attainment of all other responsibilities and privileges of citizenship. Only gradually over the course of the twentieth century did individual states accord women access to the jury box, and this access did not become a matter of constitutional right until 1975. A week after the *Schlesinger v. Ballard* decision, the Court produced a re-examination of the issue it had dealt with in *Hoyt v. Florida*. This time the state involved was Louisiana and the person complaining about the no-women jury was a man, Billy Taylor; but the state law at issue was identical to the one that the Supreme Court had upheld only fourteen years earlier in *Hoyt*. An all-male jury had found Billy Taylor guilty of aggravated kidnapping. Every woman in Louisiana was excluded from jury duty unless she filed a written affidavit declaring her desire to serve. As of 1970, Louisiana was the only state that still retained this kind of statute; Florida had abandoned its "volunteers only" approach to jury duty for women back in 1967.[30]

Only three years earlier, in 1972, the Supreme Court had refused to reconsider the *Hoyt* precedent in a Louisiana case similar to Taylor's; at that time they had explained, "Nothing in past adjudication [indicates] that [a male] petitioner has been denied equal protection by the alleged exclusion of women from grand jury service."[31] But after that, both *Frontiero* and an important jury decision, *Peters v. Kiff*,[32] were handed down. So in *Taylor* the Court admits that "past adjudications" had indeed changed the law since 1961.

It may seem strange that a man would complain about the absence of women on a jury, and, indeed, it would seem stranger to people familiar with the law than to laypeople. For there is a longstanding rule that only parties who have a personal stake in the outcome of a particular decision—who actually stand to gain or lose, depending on what the judge says—are allowed to challenge laws in the federal courts. This status of having a stake in the decision is called "standing," and one might well wonder whether Billy Taylor had standing, as a man, to challenge the exclusion of women from juries.

Fortunately for Billy Taylor, a couple of years before his case reached the Supreme Court, the Court had held that a white man had standing to challenge the exclusion of black individuals from juries. Still, the message of that precedent, *Peters v. Kiff,* as it would apply to males challenging female jury exclusion was not clear; the six-judge majority of *Peters* had split in half over the reasons why a white person could challenge the exclusion of black people from juries. Three of the justices[33] based their decision on the narrow grounds that it was a federal crime for any official, even a state or local one, to exclude black persons from juries; they concluded, therefore, that to convict anyone in such an illegal trial procedure would violate "due process of law." Because no comparable statute made it a crime to exclude women from juries, this line of reasoning would help neither the women of Louisiana nor Billy Taylor. The other three justices of the *Peters* majority, however, espoused a line of reasoning that directly and explicitly applied to people in Billy Taylor's situation.

When the Court majority divides into two plurality opinions, as it did in *Peters,* there is no official "opinion of the Court," and neither plurality opinion has the binding force that it would if a majority of justices concurred in it. Still, the reasoning provides a line of argument that can be cited by future courts who want to hark back to it for the tone of legitimacy it provides. And the *Taylor v. Louisiana* majority cites the three-justice opinion from *Peters* more than once.

This opinion from *Peters,* authored by Justice Marshall, had announced an all but open break with the viewpoint of the *Hoyt* decision. Marshall stated, first, "The exclusion of a discernible class from jury service injures not only those defendants who belong to the excluded class, but other defendants as well, in that it destroys the possibility that the jury will reflect a representative cross section of the community."[34] He went on to argue that the Fourteenth Amendment's guarantee of due process of law includes trial by a competent and impartial tribunal.[35] This protection is so important that even the appearance of bias or partiality in the tribunal is forbidden.[36] This list of premises laid the groundwork for Marshall's conclusion in *Peters,* that the systematic exclusion of a "substantial and identifiable class of citizens" from jury service creates so much appearance of bias and probability of bias that such exclusion is forbidden by the due process clause.

Impartiality in trials has long been viewed as essential to due process. One additional change since the *Hoyt* decision was that whereas Hoyt had challenged all-male juries with the claim that such juries conflicted with the generally worded guarantees of "due process of law" and "equal protection of the law," a 1968 case, *Duncan v. Louisiana,*[37] had established that "due process of law" (required of the states by the Fourteenth Amendment), itself implies the *specific* idea of the right to trial by an impartial jury in any criminal prosecution. (This idea is spelled out in the Sixth Amendment, but as written there it applies only to the federal government.) In the 1975 case of *Taylor v. Louisiana*, then, the Supreme Court was interpreting not just the general phrases "due process" and "equal protection," but also the more precise term "an impartial jury." Whether this difference was substantial enough to explain the Court's explicit overruling of *Hoyt* is a question better addressed after a reading of the Court's discussion of it.

Another remarkable aspect of this decision is the *Taylor* Court's surprising rediscovery of *Ballard v. United States*.[38] That case predated *Hoyt* by fifteen years and had been completely ignored by all the *Hoyt* justices. Suddenly, it was unearthed to become a major building block in Justice White's reasoning, used to establish that juries cannot be representative cross-sections of the community if women are excluded from them.

Billy Taylor's appeal of his conviction on the grounds that the Louisiana jury system was unconstitutional had been rejected by two state courts before it reached the U.S. Supreme Court.

BILLY TAYLOR V. LOUISIANA
419 U.S. 522 (1975)

MR. JUSTICE WHITE delivered the opinion of the Court.

...[T]he Louisiana jury selection system deprived appellant of his Sixth and Fourteenth Amendment right to an impartial jury trial....In consequence, appellant's conviction must be reversed.

The Louisiana jury selection system does not disqualify women from jury service, but in operation its conceded systematic impact is that only a very few women, grossly disproportionate to the number of eligible women in the community, are called for jury service. In this case, no women were on the venire from which the petit jury was drawn. The issue we have, therefore, is whether a jury selection system which operates to exclude from jury service an identifiable class of citizens constituting 53% of eligible jurors in the community comports with the Sixth and Fourteenth Amendments.

...Taylor's claim is that he was constitutionally entitled to a jury drawn from a venire constituting a fair cross section of the community and that the jury that tried him was not such a jury by reason of the exclusion of women. Taylor was not a member of the excluded class; but there is no rule that claims such as Taylor presents may be made only by those defendants who are members of the group excluded from jury service. *Peters v. Kiff,* 407 U.S. 493 (1972)....

The background against which this case must be decided includes our holding in *Duncan v. Louisiana*, 391 U.S. 145 (1968), that the Sixth Amendment's provision for jury trial is made binding on the States by virtue of the Fourteenth Amendment. Our inquiry is whether the presence of a fair cross section of the community on . . . lists from which petit juries are drawn is essential to the fulfillment of the Sixth Amendment's guarantee of an impartial jury trial in criminal prosecutions.

The Court's prior cases are instructive. Both in the course of exercising its supervisory powers over trials in federal courts and *in the constitutional context, the Court has unambiguously declared that the American concept of the jury trial contemplates a jury drawn from a fair cross section of the community* [emphasis added.] A unanimous Court stated in *Smith v. Texas*, 311 U.S. 128, 130 (1940), that "[i]t is part of the established tradition in the use of juries as instruments of public justice that the jury be a body truly representative of the community." To exclude racial groups from jury service was said to be "at war with our basic concepts of a democratic society and a representative government." A state jury system that resulted in systematic exclusion of Negroes as jurors was therefore held to violate the Equal Protection Clause of the Fourteenth Amendment. *Glasser v. United States*, 315 U.S. 60, 85 (1942), in the context of a federal criminal case and the Sixth Amendment's jury trial requirement, stated that "our notions of what a proper jury is have developed in harmony with our basic concepts of a democratic system and representative government," and repeated the Court's understanding that the jury "be a body truly representative of the community. . .and not the organ of any special group or class."

A federal conviction by a jury from which women had been excluded, although eligible for service under state law, was reviewed in *Ballard v. United States*, 329 U.S. 187 (1946). Noting the federal statutory "design to make a jury a cross section of the community" and the fact that women had been excluded, the Court exercised its supervisory powers over the federal courts and reversed the conviction. In *Brown v. Allen*, 344 U.S. 443, 474 (1953), the Court declared that "[o]ur duty to protect the federal constitutional rights of all does not mean we . . . should impose on states our conception of the proper source of jury lists, so long as the source reasonably reflects a cross-section of the population suitable in character and intelligence for that civic duty."

Some years later in *Carter v. Jury Comm'n*, 396 U.S. 320, 330 (1970), the Court observed that the exclusion of Negroes from jury service because of their race "contravenes the very idea of a jury—'a body truly representative of the community. . . .'" (Quoting from *Smith v. Texas*.) At about the same time it was contended that the use of six-man juries in noncapital criminal cases violated the Sixth Amendment for failure to provide juries drawn from a cross section of the community, *Williams v. Florida*, 399 U.S. 78 (1970). In the course of rejecting that challenge, we said that the number of persons on the jury should "be large enough to promote group deliberation, free from outside attempts at intimidation, and to provide a fair possibility for obtaining a representative cross-section of the community." *Id.*, at 100. In like vein, in *Apodaca v. Oregon*, 406 U.S. 404, 410–11 (1970) (plurality opinion), it was said that "a jury will come to such a [commonsense] judgment as long as it consists of a group of laymen representative of a cross section of the community who have the duty and the opportunity to deliberate...on the question of a defendant's guilt." Similarly, three Justices in *Peters v. Kiff*, 407 U.S., at 500, observed that the Sixth Amendment comprehended a fair possibility for obtaining a jury constituting a representative cross section of the community.

The unmistakable import of this Court's opinions, at least since 1941, *Smith v. Texas*, and not repudiated by intervening decisions, is that the selection of a petit jury from a representative cross section of the community is an essential component of the Sixth Amendment right to a jury trial [emphasis added]. Recent federal legislation governing jury selection within the federal court system has a similar thrust....

We accept the fair cross-section requirement as fundamental to the jury trial guaranteed by the Sixth Amendment and are convinced that the requirement has solid foundation. The purpose of a jury is to guard against the exercise of arbitrary power—to make available the commonsense judgment of the community as a hedge against the overzealous or mistaken prosecutor and in preference to the professional or perhaps over-conditioned or biased response of a judge. *Duncan v. Louisiana*, 391 U.S., at 155–56. This prophylactic vehicle is not provided if the jury pool is made up of only special segments of the populace or if large, distinctive groups are excluded from the pool. Community participation in the administration of the criminal law, moreover, is not only consistent with our democratic heritage but is also critical to public confidence in the fairness of the criminal justice system. Restricting jury service to only special groups or excluding identifiable segments playing major roles in the community cannot be squared with the constitutional concept of jury trial. "Trial by jury presupposes a jury drawn from a pool broadly representative of the community as well as impartial in a specific case.... The broad representative character of the jury should be maintained, partly as assurance of a diffused impartiality and partly because sharing in the administration of justice is a phase of civic responsibility." *Thiel v. Southern Pacific Co.*, 328 U.S. 217, 227 (1946) (Frankfurter, J., dissenting).

We are also persuaded that the fair cross section requirement is violated by the systematic exclusion of women, who in the judicial district involved here amounted to 53% of the citizens eligible for jury service. This conclusion necessarily entails the judgment that women are sufficiently numerous and distinct from men that if they are systematically eliminated from jury panels, the Sixth Amendment's fair cross section requirement cannot be satisfied. This very matter was debated in *Ballard v. United States*. Positing the fair cross-section rule—there said to be a statutory one—the Court concluded that the systematic exclusion of women was unacceptable. The dissenting view that an all-male panel drawn from various groups in the community would be as truly representative as if women were included, was firmly rejected

The thought is that the factors which tend to influence the action of women are the same as those which influence the action of men—personality, background, economic status—and not sex. Yet it is not enough to say that women when sitting as jurors neither act nor tend to act as a class. But, if the shoe were on the other foot, who would claim that a jury was truly representative of the community if all men were intentionally and systematically excluded from the panel? The truth is that the two sexes are not fungible; a community made up exclusively of one is different from a community composed of both; the subtle interplay of influence one on the other is among the imponderables. To insulate the courtroom from either may not in a given case make an iota of difference. Yet a flavor, a distinct quality is lost if either sex is excluded. The exclusion of one may indeed make the jury less representative of the community than would be true if an economic or racial group were excluded (*Ballard v. U.S.*, 329 U.S., at 193–94[12].)

In this respect, we agree with the Court in *Ballard*: If the fair cross-section rule is to govern the selection of juries, as we have concluded it must, women cannot be systematically excluded from jury panels from which petit juries are drawn. This conclusion is consistent with the current judgment of the country, now evidenced by legislative or constitutional provisions in every State and at the federal level qualifying women for jury service.[13]

There remains the argument that women as a class serve a distinctive role in society and that jury service would so substantially interfere with that function that the State has ample justification for excluding women from service unless they volunteer, even though the result is that almost all jurors are men. It is true that *Hoyt v. Florida*, 368 U.S. 57 (1961), held that such a system did not deny due process of law or equal protection of the laws because there was a sufficiently rational basis for such an exemption.[15] But *Hoyt* did not involve a defendant's Sixth Amendment right to a jury drawn from a fair cross section of the community and the prospect of depriving him of that right if women as a class are systematically excluded. The right to a proper jury cannot be overcome on merely rational grounds.[16] There must be weightier reasons if a distinctive class representing 53% of the eligible jurors is for all practical purposes to be excluded from jury service. No such basis has been tendered here.

The States are free to grant exemptions from jury service to individuals in case of special hardship or incapacity and to those engaged in particular occupations the uninterrupted performance of which is critical to the community's welfare. *Rawlins v. Georgia*, 201 U.S. 638 (1906). It would not appear that such exemptions would pose substantial threats that the remaining pool of jurors would not be representative of the community. A system excluding all women, however, is a wholly different matter. It is untenable to suggest these days that it would be a special hardship for each and every woman to perform jury service or that society cannot spare any women from their present duties.[17] This may be the case with many, and it may be burdensome to sort out those who should not be exempted from those who should serve. But that task is performed in the case of men, and the administrative convenience in dealing with women as a class is insufficient justification for diluting the quality of community judgment represented by the jury in criminal trials.

Although this judgment may appear a foregone conclusion from the pattern of some of the Court's cases over the past 30 years, as well as from legislative developments at both federal and state levels, it is nevertheless true that until today no case had squarely held that the exclusion of women from jury venires deprives a criminal defendant of his Sixth Amendment right to trial by an impartial jury drawn from a fair cross section of the community. . . . [F]ederal juries in criminal cases were all-male . . . until the Civil Rights Act of 1957, 71 Stat. 634, 638, 28 U.S.C. § 1861 [when] Congress itself provided that all citizens, with limited exceptions, were competent to sit on federal juries. Until that time, federal courts were required by statute to exclude women from jury duty in those States where women were disqualified. . . . Moreover, *Hoyt v. Florida* . . . has stood for the proposition that, even if women as a group could not be constitutionally disqualified from jury service, there was ample reason to treat all women differently from men for the purpose of jury service and to exclude them unless they volunteered.[19]

Accepting as we do, however, the view that the Sixth Amendment affords the defendant in a criminal trial the opportunity to have the jury drawn from venires representative of the community, we think it is no longer tenable to hold that women as a class may be excluded or given automatic exemptions based solely on sex if the consequence is that criminal jury venires are almost totally male. To this extent we cannot follow the contrary implications of the prior cases, including *Hoyt v. Florida*. If it was ever the case that women were unqualified to sit on juries or were so situated that none of them should be required to perform jury service, that time has long since passed. If at one time it could be held that Sixth Amendment juries must be drawn from a fair cross section of the community but that this requirement permitted the almost total exclusion of women, this is not the case today. Communities differ at different times and places. What is a fair cross section at one item or place is not necessarily a fair cross section at another time or a different place. Nothing persuasive has been presented to us in this case suggesting that all-male venires in the parishes involved here are fairly representative of the local population otherwise eligible for jury service.

Our holding does not augur or authorize the fashioning of detailed jury selection codes by federal courts. The fair cross-section principle must have much leeway in application. The States remain free to prescribe relevant qualifications for their jurors and to provide reasonable exemptions. . . .

. . . Defendants are not entitled to a jury of any particular composition, *Fay v. New York*, 332 U.S. 261, 284 (1947); *Apodaca v. Oregon*, 406 U.S., at 413 (plurality opinion); but the jury . . . pools of names . . . from which juries are drawn must not systematically exclude distinctive groups in the community and thereby fail to be reasonably representative thereof.

The judgment of the Louisiana Supreme Court is *reversed* and the case remanded to that court for further proceedings not inconsistent with this opinion.

Opinion Footnotes

12 . . .Controlled studies of the performance of women as jurors conducted subsequent to the Court's decision in *Ballard* have concluded that women bring to juries their own perspectives and values that influence both jury deliberation and result. See generally Rudolph, Women on Juries—Voluntary or Compulsory?, 44 *J. Amer. Jud. Soc* 206 (1961); 55 *J. Sociology & Social Research* 442 (1971); 3 *J. Applied Soc. Psych.* 267 (1973); 19 *Sociometry* 3 (1956).

13 This is a relatively modern development. Under the English common law, women, with the exception of the trial of a narrow class of cases, were not considered to be qualified for jury service by virtue of the doctrine of *propter defectum sexus*, a "defect of sex." 3 W. Blackstone, *Commentaries* 362 (Lewis ed. 1897). This common law rule was made statutory by Parliament in 1870. . ., and then rejected by Parliament in 1919. . . . In this country women were disqualified by state law to sit as jurors until the end of the 19th century. They were first deemed qualified for jury service by a State in 1898, 35 Utah Rev.Stat.Ann. § 1297. Today, women are qualified as jurors in all the States. The jury service . . . rules of most States do not on their face extend to women the type of exemption presently before the Court, although the exemption provisions of some States do appear to treat men and women differently in certain respects.

15 The state interest, as articulated by the Court, was based on the assumption that "woman is still regarded as the center of home and family life." *Hoyt v. Florida*, 368 U.S., at 62. Louisiana makes a similar argument here, stating that its grant of an automatic exemption from jury service to females involves only the State's attempt "to regulate and provide stability to the state's own idea of family life."

16 In *Hoyt*, the Court determined both that the underlying classification was rational and that the State's proffered rationale for extending this exemption to females without family responsibilities was justified by administrative convenience. 386 U.S., at 62–63.

17 In *Hoyt v. Florida* the Court placed some emphasis on the notion, advanced by the State there and by Louisiana here in support of the rationality of its statutory scheme, that "woman is still regarded as the center of home and family life." 368 U.S., at 62. Statistics compiled by the Department of Labor indicate that in October 1974, 54.2% of all women between 18 and 64 years of age were in the labor force. United States Dept. of Labor, *Women in the Labor Force* (Oct. 1974). Additionally, in March 1974, 45.7% of women with children under the age of 18 were in the labor force; with respect to families containing children between the ages of six and 17, 67.3% of mothers who were widowed, divorced or separated were in the work force, while 51.2% of the mothers whose husbands were present in the household were in the work force. Even in family units in which the husband was present and which contained a child under three years old, 31% of the mothers were in the work force. United States Dept. of Labor, *Marital and Family Characteristics of the Labor Force*, Table F (March 1974). While these statistics perhaps speak more to the evolving nature of the structure of the family unit in American society than to the nature of the role played by women who happen to be members of a family unit, they certainly put to rest the suggestion that all women should be exempt from jury service based solely on their sex and the presumed role in the home.

19 *Hoyt v. Florida*, as had *Fay v. New York*, 332 U.S. 261, 289–90 (1947), also referred to the historic view that jury service could constitutionally be confined to males: "We need not, however, accept appellant's invitation to canvass in this case the continuing validity of this Court's dictum in *Strauder v. West Virginia*, 100 U.S. 303, 310, to the effect that a State may constitutionally 'confine' jury duty 'to males.' This constitutional proposition has gone unquestioned for more than eighty years in the decisions of the Court, see *Fay v. New York*, at 289–90, and had been reflected, until 1957, in congressional policy respecting jury service in the federal courts themselves." . . . See also *Glasser v. United States*, 315 U.S., at 60, 64–65, 85–86 (1942). . . .

MR. JUSTICE REHNQUIST, dissenting.

The Court's opinion reverses a conviction without a suggestion, much less a showing, that the appellant has been unfairly treated or prejudiced in any way by the manner in which his jury was selected. In so doing, the Court invalidates a jury selection system which it approved by a substantial majority only 12 years ago. I disagree with the Court and would affirm the judgment of the Supreme Court of Louisiana.

The majority opinion . . .[relies]. . .on carefully chosen quotations. . . . Fairly read, the only "unmistakable import" of those cases is that due process and equal protection prohibit jury selection systems which are likely to result in biased or partial juries. *Smith v. Texas*, concerned the equal protection claim of a Negro who was indicted by a grand jury from which Negroes had been systematically excluded. *Glasser v. United States*, 315 U.S. 60 (1942), dealt with allegations that the only women selected for jury service were members of a private organization which had conducted pro-prosecution classes for prospective jurors. *Brown v. Allen*, 344 U.S. 443 (1953), rejected the equal protection and due process contentions of several black defendants that members of their race had been discriminatorily excluded from their juries. *Carter v. Jury Comm'n*, 396 U.S. 320 (1970), similarly dealt with equal protection challenges to a jury selection system, but the persons claiming such rights were blacks who had sought to serve as jurors.

In *Hoyt v. Florida*, 368 U.S. 57 (1961), this Court gave plenary consideration to contentions that a system such as Louisiana's deprived a defendant of equal protection and due process. These contentions were rejected, despite circumstances which were much more suggestive of possible bias and prejudice than are those here. . . .

The first determinative event, in the Court's view, is *Duncan v. Louisiana*, 391 U.S. 145 (1968). Because the Sixth Amendment was there held applicable to the States, the Court feels free to dismiss *Hoyt* as a case which dealt with entirely different issues—even though in fact it presented the identical problem. But *Duncan*'s rationale is a good deal less expansive than is suggested by the Court's present interpretation of that case. Duncan rests on the following reasoning.

> . . .*Because we believe that trial by jury in criminal cases is fundamental to the American scheme of justice*, we hold that the Fourteenth Amendment guarantees a right of jury trial in all criminal cases. . . .(391 U.S., at 148–49; emphasis added)

[This] is a sturdy test, one not readily satisfied by every discrepancy between federal and state practice. . . .

In explaining the conclusion that a jury trial is fundamental to our scheme of justice, and therefore should be required of the States, the Court pointed out that jury trial was designed to be a defense "against arbitrary law enforcement," 391 U.S., at 156, and "to prevent oppression by the Government." *Id.*, at 155. The Court stated its belief that jury trial for serious offenses is "essential for preventing miscarriages of justice and for assuring that fair trials are provided for all defendants." *Id.*, at 158.

I cannot conceive that today's decision is necessary to guard against oppressive or arbitrary law enforcement, or to prevent miscarriages of justice and to assure fair trials. Especially is this so when the criminal defendant involved makes no claims of prejudice or bias. The Court ... fails ... to provide any satisfactory explanation of the mechanism by which the Louisiana system undermines the prophylactic role of the jury, either in general or in this case. The best it can do is to posit "a flavor, a distinct quality," which allegedly is lost if either sex is excluded. However, this "flavor" is not of such importance that the Constitution is offended if any given petit jury is not so enriched. This smacks more of mysticism than of law. The Court does not even purport to practice its mysticism in a consistent fashion—presumably doctors, lawyers, and other groups, whose frequent exemption from jury service is endorsed by the majority, also offer qualities as distinct and important as those at issue here.

In *Hoyt,* this Court considered a stronger due process claim than is before it today, but found that fundamental fairness had not been offended. I do not understand how our intervening decision in *Duncan* can support a different result. . . .

The second change since *Hoyt* that appears to undergird the Court's turnabout is societal in nature, encompassing both our higher degree of sensitivity to distinctions based on sex, and the "evolving nature of the structure of the family unit in American society." Op., at n. 17. These are matters of degree, and it is perhaps of some significance that in 1962 Mr. Justice Harlan saw fit to refer to the "enlightened emancipation of women from the restrictions and protections of bygone years, and their entry into many parts of community life formerly considered to be reserved to men." *Hoyt,* 368 U.S., at 61–62. Nonetheless, it may be fair to conclude that the Louisiana system is in fact an anachronism, inappropriate at this "time or place." But surely constitutional adjudication is a more canalized function than enforcing as against the States this Court's perception of modern life.

Absent any suggestion that appellant's trial was unfairly conducted, or that its result was unreliable, I would not require Louisiana to retry him (assuming the State can once again produce its evidence and witnesses) in order to impose on him the sanctions which its laws provide.

Case Questions

1. Is Justice White being accurate when he says that the Court's prior cases have *unambiguously* declared that a jury trial requires a "fair cross-section of the community," and that this is the *unmistakable import* of past cases? How did Justice Rehnquist manage to mistake their import? What motivation might White have for exaggerating?

2. In that part of his opinion accompanying footnote 17, White points out that it would be untenable to claim that "society cannot spare any women from their present duties" (since over 54 percent of women of working age were in the labor force in 1974). Had *Hoyt* rested on that now-untenable assumption? (In 1960 the portion in the labor force of women 16 to 65 was 38 percent.)

3. In your view, which of the following changes since *Hoyt* most influenced the Court's turnabout?

    a. The enlarged portion of women in the labor force

    b. The abandonment of automatic jury exemptions for women by all other state legislatures by 1975

    c. The decision in *Duncan v. Louisiana* that the right to trial by jury is a required part of "due process"

    d. The *Frontiero* and *Reed* decisions (which the Court does not mention)

    e. Changed attitudes toward women on the part of Supreme Court justices

4. Consider Justice Rehnquist's argument that exempting lawyers and doctors from juries removes a "distinct quality" or "flavor" from jury deliberations in the same way as exempting women does. Is it persuasive?

CASE NOTE: PEREMPTORY JURY STRIKES OF WOMEN: *J.E.B. V. ALABAMA* (1994)

Eleven years after *Taylor v. Louisiana* (1975), the Supreme Court ruled in *Batson v. Kentucky*, 476 U.S. 79 (1986), that demonstrable discrimination on the basis of race in the selection of jurors violates the equal protection clause, even when it is done in the group that an attorney is free to exclude from the jury by "peremptory strikes"—that is, without having to explain the reason to a judge. Traditionally, in Anglo-American law, there was no limit at all on these strikes, other than the sheer number of them, which, naturally, had to be equal on both sides.

After the Court ruled in *Batson*, defense lawyers then raised the issue of sex discrimination in peremptory strikes. In 1994 the Supreme Court ruled in *J.E.B. v. Alabama*, 511 U.S. 127 (1994) that like race, sex discrimination also is forbidden, because the state cannot demonstrate that permitting purposeful sex discrimination in peremptory strikes "substantially furthers" (as required by the *Craig* rule) the state's important interest in securing a fair and impartial jury. Therefore, it violates the constitutional requirement of equal protection of the laws. (The discrimination in the *J.E.B.* case, incidentally, had been against males.)

Serving in the Military

The Draft: *Rostker v. Goldberg* (1981)

Another aspect of citizenship, service in the military, remained officially closed to women until the twentieth century, and highly restricted after that.[39] Until 1967, for instance, women's enlistment in the military remained capped at two percent. Service in the military often enhances civilian job opportunities, and for this reason, as well as out of concern for abstract fairness, a number of feminists opposed women's exclusion from the military draft, and from combat requirements (or combat "opportunities," as career military personnel might think of them, since combat enhances promotion; see *Schlesinger v. Ballard* above). The military issue was not feminists' favorite topic,[40] and even the ERA hearings were ambiguous about the combat question under an ERA. The hearings seemed to imply that with an ERA women would be drafted but could still fall under a blanket exclusion from combat, although certainly many ERA proponents thought that the amendment would require lifting the ban on women's combat role. Toward the end of the ERA ratification period, with the ERA politically dead in its tracks, the question of a males-only military draft reached the Supreme Court.

By this time the *Craig* rule for interpreting the equal protection clause was clearly indicated in relevant precedents. On the other hand, a 1977 case *Fiallo v. Bell*[41] served as a signpost toward another route the Court might follow. *Fiallo* had posed the question of the constitutionality of a preference for unwed mothers as compared to unwed fathers in the context of a statutory right to obtain preferred immigrant status for one's own, under-21 children born outside the United States. Unwed mothers who were citizens or lawful residents had this right, as did married or divorced parents, but unwed fathers did not (unless the father legitimated any children before they turned 18). In deciding *Fiallo*, even in a situation where the fundamental right of fatherhood might have otherwise evoked strict scrutiny, the Court pointed to the foreign relations context and found the need for deference to Congressional flexibility to be compelling (and deference then meant a minimal rationality test, which meant upholding the statute).[42]

In this draft case, *Rostker v. Goldberg*,[43] the Court majority followed the same path of yielding to Congress's foreign relations power. However, Rehnquist, writing for the Court, camouflaged this path by, in effect, claiming that it overlaps the *Craig v. Boren* path. In other words Rehnquist, argued *both* that great deference is due to Congress on military matters *and* that this sex-based discrimination survives *Craig*-level scrutiny because Congressional flexibility in raising armies is an important governmental interest. The Supreme Court justices were divided over how to interpret the factual record, and that division swayed the votes of two of the dissenters.

This case began in 1971 when several men liable to be drafted into the Vietnam War had objected to males-only conscription, on the basis of a Fifth Amendment equal protection (due process clause) argument. The case remained in a kind of legal limbo for several years while the draft was discontinued, and then the case was reactivated in 1980 when President Carter re-instituted Selective Service registration. There was still no conscription; the military remained all-volunteer. Goldberg brought a lawsuit on behalf of himself and all males similarly situated; Rostker was director of the Selective Service System. On July 18, 1980, three days before registration was to begin, a federal District Court declared the Military Selective Service Act[44] unconstitutional on the grounds of its sex discrimination, and the court enjoined the Government from requiring registration under it. Rostker immediately appealed for a stay of the injunction pending appeal, and Justice Brennan granted it. Registration began on time. The Supreme Court handed down its decision a year later.

As the justices framed the issue, the question was whether the Constitution, as a matter of the equal protection implied in the Fifth Amendment due process clause, required that Congress make women register, along with men, for the draft even though women would never serve in combat roles. As so framed, the question was decided 6–3 against forcing Congress to require the registration of women. Rehnquist for the majority interpreted the Congressional testimony of the top military brass as meaning that the military via the volunteer process obtained as many women as it could use, even if the U.S. were to develop the need to draft men because of an increase in the need for combat troops.

White dissented, arguing that the testimony had not been clear on this point and that more hearings should be required to answer the question whether women could be usefully drafted into non-combat roles to free up men to fight. Marshall also dissented, arguing that registration served the purpose of providing information on the inventory of available personnel, and it could prove helpful to know how many women were available in the event of unanticipatable emergency. The military might believe now that adequate forces could be obtainable as volunteers for non-combat personnel, but in some future situation the military might develop a shortage in non-combat staff and then need to draft women. In this scenario, having women already registered would prove useful. Justice Brennan concurred in each of these dissents. Not a single justice in 1981 was willing to suggest that equal protection required the U.S. government to put women into combat.

As of 2019 men continue to register for Selective Service at age 18. Women do not. The military remains all-volunteer. What has changed is the combat situation.

Post-*Rostker* Reform: Women in Combat

Military policy concerning women in combat remained essentially unchanged until 1988, when the Department of Defense adopted the "risk rule." This policy barred women only from situations where the "risk of exposure to direct combat, hostile fire, or capture is equal to or greater than that experienced by associated combat units in the same theater of operations." The risk rule opened up 30,000 new positions for women.[45]

The 1991 Persian Gulf War demonstrated the effects of the risk rule. Over 40,000 women, 7% of military personnel involved in the war, served in Iraq. Their assignments included, but were not limited to, nursing, intelligence and communications, and service on aircraft ground crews. In addition, women worked as military police and helicopter pilots—activities as dangerous as combat. Iraqi SCUD missiles pushed the boundaries of combat hundreds of miles behind the front lines, deep into territory where women performed a wide variety of tasks. One soldier said, "You're no longer a female here—you're a soldier, like everyone else." After this war, Congress rescinded its prohibitions on women's engaging in combat missions. By 1994, the year Defense Secretary Les Aspin rescinded the risk rule, the Navy and the Air Force had already made women eligible for over 95% of all positions.

All services further reduced restrictions on women after Aspin's directive. The military action in Afghanistan and Iraq following the terrorist attacks of September 11, 2001, provided the first opportunity to test the Aspin policies. At the time of Operation Iraqi Freedom, approximately 1 in 7 military personnel were female, numbering around 200,000. While still barred from infantry, armor, field artillery, Special Forces, Navy SEALS and on submarines, women were now able to pilot gun ships and fighter planes, operate helicopters, and launch missiles. The Pentagon has even gone so far as to say that the military is dependent on women, who in early 2003 made up 15.5 percent of the Army, 18.3 percent of the Air Force, 13.3 percent of the Navy, and 6 percent of the Marines. In 2016, Ashton B. Carter, President Obama's Secretary of Defense, opened all combat roles to women.

The integration of women into the Armed Forces has raised concerns about the effects of these policies on both military and family life. A 1997 RAND Corporation study found no significant impact on unit readiness, unit cohesion, or unit morale. In both Iraq wars, many women sent overseas left young children at home. At the time of the second Gulf War, nearly 10% of active-duty service members were either single parents or were married to other active-duty members. Most military families deal with this situation by placing children temporarily with friends or relatives. In general, women and their families have dealt with these conflicting demands without permanent ill effects, just as men have done.

Sexual assault and harassment by male co-workers have been no less prevalent in the military than in civilian life. U.S. military bases and the service academies have had widely publicized scandals. The openness of the military to women throughout the 1990s encouraged many women to speak out on experiences of sexual harassment and sexual assault in the service. But many women who file complaints have been ignored; worse, some have been blamed for the incidents and even hounded out of the service. The Department of Defense has struggled to develop strategies that would effectively neutralize the tension and change the climate under which men and women serve, but the abuse continues.

Apart from sexual assault and sexual harassment, women in the military also face other forms of sex discrimination. Revelations that over 30,000 military persons, mostly U.S. Marines, formed a Facebook group that distributed and shared nude photos of military women without their consent, have resulted in new and updated social media and behavior guidelines that military personnel are expected to follow.[46]

Congress has become more involved than in the past by holding more oversight hearings, protecting accusers from retaliation, and tying sexual assault prevention and other reforms to the military budget outlined in the annual National Defense Authorization Act. Since 2013, Senator Kirsten Gillibrand has regularly introduced the Military Justice Improvement Act (MJIA), a piece of legislation intended to change the way that the military handles sexual assault allegations and cases by moving these decisions out of the chain-of-command in favor of an independent and professional system of reporting and prosecution.[47]

To provide context, the number of women serving active duty in the military has fluctuated around 200,000 since 2010.[48] And it is not clear whether the number of women experiencing sexual assault has increased in the military or whether there has been an increase in the number of reports. In 2012, for example, there were 3,604 sexual assault cases reported while in 2016 that number increased to 6,172. Yet the U.S. Department of Defense Sexual Assault and Prevention Response Office reported in May 2017 that sexual assault in the military decreased from 2014 to 2016. The apparent contradiction is explained as "Pentagon officials have called the increase [in reports] a sign that more victims are willing to come forward and trust the military to help them."[49]

Still, the number of reported sexual assault cases is far lower than the estimated number of service members experiencing sexual assault; the Department of Defense "estimates that about 14,900 Service members experienced some kind of sexual assault in 2016... down from an estimated 20,300 active duty members experiencing a sexual assault in 2014."[50] Fear of retaliation may explain the difference between the number of victims reporting sexual assault and the number of estimated victims; almost 60% of military sexual assault survivors report that they experienced retaliation after they reported crimes committed against them.[51]

Sexual assault and sexual harassment against women in the military has become a "front and center" issue to many members of Congress, especially among women with military backgrounds. These women are seeking and securing leadership roles on armed forces committees, utilizing their platforms to shape military policy on sexual harassment and sexual assault, and attempting to link budgetary appropriations to implementation of these policies.[52]

The federal government has also expanded opportunities and protections for LGBTQ (lesbian, gay, bisexual, transgender or queer) individuals to serve in the military. These opportunities have included lifting bans on military participation for members of these groups and establishing protocols to protect these persons from discrimination and harassment.

The U.S. military first banned homosexuals during the American Revolutionary war. Individuals who were found to be homosexual, whether or not they engaged in homosexual acts, faced various punishments including court-martial, dishonorable discharge, and other consequences.[53] During World War II, individuals who were identified as homosexuals would be examined by psychiatrists in military hospitals after which they were discharged.[54] Questions about the ban on homosexuals in the military percolated during the gay rights movement of the 1960s and 1970s although there was no policy change in response to those questions.[55]

The tide changed in 1992 when Arkansas Governor Bill Clinton campaigned for president. One of Clinton's campaign promises was to allow gays and lesbians to serve openly in the military. It was an open secret that homosexuals served in the military although fear of dishonorable discharge, court-martial, harassment, violence or bullying, prevented these persons from coming out from the shadows. Clinton met sharp resistance from congressional and military leaders. To fulfill his promise, Clinton took a compromise position that became known as "Don't Ask, Don't Tell" (DADT). DADT established that military recruits would not be asked their sexual orientation, or whether they had engaged in homosexual conduct, and gays and lesbians were prohibited from informing others of their sexual orientation. The U.S. Department of Defense issued Directive 1304.25 on December 21, 1993, and it took effect the following February.[56] This directive required that gays, lesbians and bisexual persons refrain from disclosing their sexual orientation or engaging in homosexual acts, on pain of military punishments that could include discharge.

Concerns about DADT continued because its marginalization of gays and lesbians perpetuated the stigma against them, despite expert determinations that sexual orientation did not hinder ability to serve in the military. For example, the American Psychological Association reported in 2004, "Empirical evidence fails to show that sexual orientation is germane to any aspect of military effectiveness including unit cohesion, morale, recruitment and retention."[57]

President Barack Obama reversed DADT in 2010.[58] The repeal allowed gays, lesbians and bisexuals to serve openly in the military, be protected from intimidation and harassment, and avoid punishment for their sexual orientations.

The decision to reverse DADT had no effect on the military experience of transgender persons. Various regulations have been in place regarding transgender military service. For example, until 2016, military persons had to present as a member of their biological sex which meant that they could not serve in a manner consistent with their (trans) gender identity.[59] Transgender persons have been subject to additional scrutiny compared with cis-gender persons (those persons whose gender identity correlates with their biological sex as assigned at birth) such as with claims that medical expenses are higher for transgender persons, and that units that included transgender persons compromised unit cohesion and effectiveness.[60] In essence, transgender persons have been subject to claims that they are unfit to serve in the military because they compromise morale and it costs more to provide them with medical care. Questions have also arisen as to whether the military is obligated to provide and pay for sex reassignment surgery.[61]

On June 30, 2016, President Obama's Secretary of Defense Ashton Carter announced that gender identity would no longer serve as a stand-alone basis for discharging or denying military enlistment opportunities to individuals.[62] The announcement also stated that discrimination or harassment based on gender identity would be deemed acts of sex discrimination and prosecuted within the military accordingly. The memo also required that, in the following months, various systems would be put in place to support transgender individuals including those seeking to transition from one gender to the other.[63] Hormone treatment and behavioral health services would be provided to persons seeking to transition although the costs of sex reassignment surgery would not be covered by the U.S. military. The memo also affirmed that advancement opportunities would be open to transgender individuals in the same manner that such opportunities were available to cisgender persons.

The Trump Administration, however, has taken steps to exclude transgender individuals from the military. In July 2017, President Trump announced via Twitter that he was going to negate the Obama Administration guidance and move to exclude all transgender individuals from military service. Legal advocacy organizations such as GLBTQ Legal Advocates and Defenders (GLAD) and the National Center for Lesbian Rights (NCLR) immediately challenged the eventual Trump directive in federal court, and in October 2017 the U.S. District Court for the District of Columbia enjoined the ban on transgender individuals in the military (*Doe v. Trump*, 288 F.Supp.3d 1045 (2017) Civil Action No. 17-1597 (CKK)). In March 2018, President Trump issued a revised ban on transgender individuals in the military that mandates that individuals serving in the military present in a manner consistent with their gender as assigned at birth explaining, "Transgender persons who require or have undergone gender transition are disqualified from military service,"[64] but allowing the military to make exceptions. Secretary of Defense James Mattis announced that current members of the military will be allowed to serve out their terms of duty.[65] This latest ban is likely to be the subject of a legal challenge, and the issues surrounding transgender persons serving in the military likely will continue to be debated through political, partisan and gendered lenses for some time to come.

INTERLUDE: DOCTRINAL DEVELOPMENT ON THE CLINTON COURT

As president, William Clinton appointed two justices to the U.S. Supreme Court, both with a link to women's issues. His first appointee, Ruth Bader Ginsburg, already mentioned in some case introductions, was such an eminent women's rights advocate that she was known in some circles as the "Thurgood Marshall of the women's movement." His second appointee, Steven J. Breyer, had, while serving as a federal appeals court judge in Boston, joined in an opinion declaring unconstitutional a "gag rule" on abortion counseling.[66] He replaced

Justice Harry Blackmun, and Ruth Bader Ginsburg replaced Justice Byron White. Shortly after their ascent to the Court, the justices recommenced declaring unconstitutional certain statutes on sex equity grounds, something the Court had not done from 1982 until 1994. The first such case, *J.E.B. v. Alabama* (1994), concerned the use of peremptory challenges to strike members of one sex from a jury, and for this reason is included in the discussion of jury service above.

The next case that applied the *Craig* test of intermediate scrutiny was *U.S. v. Virginia* (the VMI, or Virginia Military Institute, case) (1996), and was decided in the first Court opinion written by Justice Ruth Bader Ginsburg. Her opinion noted more than once that sex-based classifications require, "exceedingly persuasive justification," a phrase that Justice Sandra Day O'Connor had deployed also in her first opinion for the Court, *Mississippi University for Women v. Hogan* (1982). (Both cases deal with single-sex state-run colleges and appear in Chapter 6.) The phrase had originated in the 1979 *Feeney* case (see below) and also had been used in *Kirchberg v. Feenstra* (1980) (see Chapter 5), but had not been much noticed. In *U.S. v. Virginia*, however, the phrase received considerable discussion, and commentators off the Court speculated whether it was a signal of some new level of scrutiny. It also recurs in the two citizenship cases that follow here.

CONFERRING CITIZENSHIP: FEMALE VERSUS MALE PARENTS

Miller v. Albright (1998)

Whether the Court's repeated invocation of the talismanic "exceedingly persuasive justification," really meant that the Court majority was intensifying the level of scrutiny to apply to sex-based classifications, as Justice Scalia charged in the VMI case, did not immediately become clear. Two years after the VMI case, the Court took up the first of three constitutional challenges to a federal law that gave automatic citizenship to all offspring of mothers who were American citizens (so long as those mothers had resided for at least one year in the U.S.), even if those offspring were born abroad, but did not give it to nonmarital children of citizen fathers unless the father or a court took special steps to establish paternity before the child turned eighteen. Technically, this law involved not immigration but the definition of citizenship, so it was not precisely covered by the precedent of *Fiallo v. Bell*, 430 U.S. 787 (1977), which had relied on Congress' plenary power over foreign relations to uphold a similar discrimination on preferred immigrant status.

The first case, *Lorelyn Pinero Miller v. Madeleine Albright, Secretary of State*, 523 U.S. 420 (1998), was brought by Lorelyn Pinero, who had been born and lived all her life in the Philippines with her unmarried, Filipino mother. When Lorelyn was 21, she applied for U.S. citizenship and was turned down. A few months later, her father, Charles Miller, who had lived all this time in Texas, went to court and obtained certification of his paternity of Lorelyn Pinero, who, now, at the age of 22, took on his last name. She then reapplied, asking that she be declared a citizen on the basis of her parentage. Her application was denied, since his paternity declaration came after she had turned eighteen. Both the federal District and Circuit Court of Appeals turned down her complaint against the State Department, and so did the U.S. Supreme Court. Three of the justices dissented (Souter, Breyer, and Ginsburg), and the other six divided 2 to 2 to 2. As a result, there was not even a plurality opinion in favor of the majority vote to affirm the lower court.

Her father's effort to be a co-litigant in her case had been rejected at the district court level. This fact affected two of the votes within the six-justice majority in a way that seemed to offer hope for a future, better-situated litigant. Kennedy and O'Connor, in an opinion authored by O'Connor, refused to judge this law's mistreatment of Pinero's father on the grounds that only he himself could have standing to challenge the law on this basis. (He would have to bring his own lawsuit, if he really cared, they opined.) From the perspective of the offspring, the law did not discriminate on the basis of gender, but only on the basis of parentage, so they applied the rational basis test and voted to uphold. But Justice O'Connor took pains to state clearly, "I do not share [fellow majority] Justice Stevens' assessment that the provision withstands heightened scrutiny..."[67] Thus, it appeared likely that O'Connor and Kennedy, once a father did bring a lawsuit against this provision, would vote with the three dissenters to rule that under the "heightened scrutiny" [*Craig*] test for gender discrimination, this discrimination against unwed fathers was unconstitutional.

The other four in the majority divided into a Scalia-Thomas pair and a Stevens-Rehnquist pair. Scalia reasoned that only Congress can grant citizenship, so the Court should not take this case. Even if the Court ruled the discrimination unconstitutional, Congress would be free to deny citizenship to offspring of both unwed parents leaving Lorelyn Pinero with no beneficial result, and thus she should be denied standing (since she does not "stand" to gain necessarily by the outcome).

Stevens wrote a lengthy opinion defending the reasonableness of the discrimination, along lines similar to those of *Fiallo v. Bell*. As he put it here,

> The blood relationship to the birth mother is immediately obvious and is typically established by hospital records and birth certificates; the relationship to the unmarried father may often be undisclosed and unrecorded in any contemporary public record. Thus, the requirement that the father make a timely written acknowledgment under oath, or that the child obtain a court adjudication of paternity, produces the rough equivalent of the documentation that is already available to evidence the blood relationship between the mother and the child. . . .[Justice Stevens presumed that birth certificates were required everywhere, and therefore went on to argue,] Surely the fact that the statute allows 18 years in which to provide evidence that is comparable to what the mother provides immediately after birth cannot be viewed as discriminating against the father or his child.
>
> . . .
>
> [The law] serves two other important purposes. . .: the interest in encouraging the development of a healthy relationship between the citizen parent and the child while the child is a minor; and the related interest in fostering ties between the foreign-born child and the United States.[68]

Stevens noted the nine-month gap between conception and birth that causes many a father to lack awareness of the existence of his child, and reasoned that these Congressional efforts to adapt to this fact both served "strong governmental interests" and were "well-tailored to serve those interests"(at 440).

The three dissenters produced two opinions in which all three joined, one by Ruth Bader Ginsburg and one by Stephen Breyer. Justice Ginsburg traced the history of gender discrimination in U.S. immigration and citizenship laws, demonstrating that until fairly recently the practice had generally been to prefer fathers rather than mothers as the conveyers of citizenship to foreign-born offspring. The presumption appears to have been that women generally followed their mate into the country of his choice, while American men decided their own fate, so could choose to bring their (in-wedlock or legitimated) children back to the U.S. without having to deal with the hurdle of naturalization proceedings. (Moreover, American women who married foreigners lost their citizenship, while American men could marry whom they pleased without any such cost.) This paternal preference ended in 1934, replaced by equal treatment of male and female parents. A mere six years later Congress adopted a maternal preference for out-of-wedlock children, conferring U.S. citizenship on them subject to the requirement that the mother have previously resided in the U.S. Having reviewed this history, Justice Ginsburg then pointed out the obvious: If Congress wanted simply to reward close parent-child ties, it could have based the classification on a demonstrated bond between parent and child, rather than upon gender stereotypes, and for this reason she would judge the law unconstitutional under the *Craig* test.

Justice Breyer's dissent noted the precedents that had established that citizenship is a fundamental right, as is the right to "care and custody" of one's child. Since both are implicated here, as well as gender discrimination, the argument for heightened scrutiny was especially strong. The law was based on an over-generalized image of parenthood—some single mothers abandon their children; some single fathers raise their children. In an age where DNA testing made the identity of fathers certain, there was no good reason for the law to be relying on outmoded stereotypes.

Tuan Anh Nguyen v. INS (2001)

Three years later, when a case came to the Court launched by a father who *had* raised his child in this country, it seemed that this statute was facing its demise—the votes of Kennedy and O'Connor had been all but promised to the Breyer-Ginsburg-Souter group of dissenters, as explained above. But even Supreme Court justices can change their minds, and Kennedy evidently did. He wrote the 5–4 majority opinion, in the case of *Tuan Anh Nguyen et al. v. INS*, 533 U.S. 53 (2001), upholding the constitutionality of this law that gave automatic citizenship to offspring of citizen mothers born abroad and refused it to offspring of nonmarital children of citizen fathers, unless the father or a court took special steps to establish paternity before the child turned eighteen. In this instance, Tuan Anh Nguyen's American father, Joseph Boulais, obtained a court order of parentage when Nguyen was already 28 in order to prevent his son, whom he had raised in the United States since the boy was six, from being deported as an undesirable alien (Six years earlier, Nguyen had been convicted of sexual assault on a child and three years after that the INS had initiated deportation proceedings). Nguyen appealed the deportation, claiming U.S. citizenship. Because the father waited until after Nguyen turned eighteen to obtain the order, despite incontrovertible DNA evidence of Boulais' fatherhood, the law did not permit the parental relationship to prevent the deportation. Had Joseph Boulais, the American parent, been female rather than male, Tuan Anh Nguyen would have been an American citizen and not deportable, despite his foreign birthplace, his having one foreign parent, and his criminal record.

After acknowledging that the law under challenge "imposes a set of requirements on the children of citizen fathers born abroad and out of wedlock to a noncitizen mother that are not imposed under like circumstances when the citizen parent is the mother," Justice Kennedy for the majority noted, "All concede the requirements of § 1409 (a) (4), relating to a citizen father's acknowledgment of a child while he is under 18, were not satisfied in this case." He went on to cite the *Craig* test and to point out that the statute gives the father eighteen years to do one of three things that would make the offspring a citizen: "legitimation; a declaration of paternity under oath by the father; or a court order of paternity." The court majority saw two important governmental interests being served by this requirement of action from the father: First, it "assur[ed] that a biological parent-child relationship [with the father] exists." In the case of female parents, Kennedy wrote, "the relation is verifiable from the birth itself." "Here, the use of gender specific terms takes into account a biological difference between the parents." He added, "The second important governmental interest furthered in a substantial manner by § 1409 (a) (4) is the determination to ensure that the child and the citizen parent have some demonstrated opportunity or potential to develop not just a relationship that is recognized, as a formal matter, by the law, but one that consists of the real, everyday ties that provide a connection between child and citizen parent and, in turn, the United States."[69]

Justice Kennedy's opinion went on to observe that Americans traveled frequently to other countries, 59 million visits in 1999 alone, and stayed outside the U.S. an average of 15 days. He surmised that, in light of these huge numbers, American males may father a great many children abroad, of whose existence they are not even aware. He saw this statute as substantially furthering the likelihood that an American father who claimed citizenship of his foreign-born offspring would have an actual parental relationship with the growing child. Such a relationship, he argued, was more important than a mere DNA connection and Congress had a right to give preference to such relationships.[70]

Justice Sandra Day O'Connor, speaking for herself, Justice Ruth Bader Ginsburg, and Justices Souter and Breyer, wrote a lengthy dissent accusing the majority of being confused about what the *Craig* rule required and therefore misapplying it. Among other criticisms, she offered several possible sex-neutral alternatives that could achieve the goals Justice Kennedy posited—e.g., requiring that the American parent provide proof of having been present at the birth of their children or of having acted in a caregiving role toward the children prior to their adulthood. She noted that the date when the proof was provided to authorities is irrelevant toward determining whether the parenting took place, as this case itself demonstrated. It was undisputed that Joseph Boulais had raised his son in Texas from age 6 until adulthood. The fact that numerous sex-neutral options were available to Congress for achieving the goals posited in this sex-discriminatory statute convinced the dissenters that this law did not meet the *Craig* test and should have been declared unconstitutional.[71]

Sessions v. Morales-Santana (2017)

In 2017, the Supreme Court was asked to revisit similar issues in the case *Sessions v. Morales-Santana,* 137 S. Ct. 1678 (2017). In this case, Morales-Santana challenged the discrepancies between the duration of residency requirements necessary to convey citizenship on non-marital, foreign-born children of U.S. citizen mothers as compared to citizen fathers. To confer citizenship on their children, American fathers had to have resided in the U.S. for five years after reaching age fourteen, whereas American mothers only had to reside in the U.S. for one continuous year at any age. Morales-Santana argued that the shorter residency requirements for women in comparison to the longer requirements for men violated the equal protection implicitly guaranteed by the Fifth Amendment due process clause. In a 6–2 decision (newly confirmed, Trump-appointed, Justice Neil Gorsuch did not participate in this case), the Justices ruled that the different residency requirements violated the guarantees of equal protection.

SESSIONS V. MORALES-SANTANA
137 S. Ct. 1678 (2017)

JUSTICE GINSBURG delivered the opinion of the Court:

* * *

I.B

Respondent Luis Ramón Morales-Santana moved to the United States at age 13, and has resided in this country most of his life. Now facing deportation, he asserts U.S. citizenship at birth based on the citizenship of his biological father, José Morales, who accepted parental responsibility and included Morales-Santana in his household.

José Morales was born in Guánica, Puerto Rico, on March 19, 1900. Puerto Rico was then, as it is now, part of the United States. . .After living in Puerto Rico for nearly two decades, José left his childhood home on February 27, 1919, 20 days short of his 19th birthday, therefore failing to satisfy § 1401(a)(7)'s requirement of five years' physical presence after age 14. He did so to take up employment as a builder-mechanic for a U.S. company in the then-U.S.-occupied Dominican Republic.

By 1959, José attested in a June 21, 1971 affidavit presented to the U.S. Embassy in the Dominican Republic, he was living with Yrma Santana Montilla, a Dominican woman he would eventually marry. In 1962, Yrma gave birth to their child, respondent Luis Morales-Santana. While the record before us reveals little about Morales-Santana's childhood, the Dominican archives disclose that Yrma and José married in 1970, and that José was then added to Morales-Santana's birth certificate as his father.... In 1975, when Morales-Santana was 13, he moved to Puerto Rico, and by 1976, the year his father died, he was attending public school in the Bronx, a New York City borough.[5]

C

In 2000, the Government placed Morales-Santana in removal proceedings based on several convictions for offenses under New York State Penal Law, all of them rendered on May 17, 1995. Morales-Santana ranked as an alien despite the many years he lived in the United States, because, at the time of his birth, his father did not satisfy the requirement of five years' physical presence after age 14. An immigration judge rejected Morales-Santana's claim to citizenship derived from the U.S. citizenship of his father, and ordered Morales-Santana's removal to the Dominican Republic. In 2010, Morales-Santana moved to reopen the proceedings, asserting that the Government's refusal to recognize that he derived citizenship from his U.S.-citizen father violated the Constitution's equal protection guarantee....

II

Because § 1409 treats sons and daughters alike, Morales-Santana does not suffer discrimination on the basis of *his* gender. He complains, instead, of gender-based discrimination against his father, who was unwed at the time of Morales-Santana's birth and was not accorded the right an unwed U.S.-citizen mother would have to transmit citizenship to her child. Although the Government does not contend otherwise, we briefly explain why Morales-Santana may seek to vindicate his father's right to the equal protection of the laws.

Ordinarily, a party "must assert his own legal rights" and "cannot rest his claim to relief on the legal rights ... of third parties." *Warth* v. *Seldin*, 422 U.S. 490, 499 (1975). But we recognize an exception where, as here, "the party asserting the right has a close relationship with the person who possesses the right [and] there is a hindrance to the possessor's ability to protect his own interests." *Kowalski* v. *Tesmer*, 543 U.S. 125, 130 (2004) (quoting *Powers* v. *Ohio*, 499 U.S. 400, 411 (1991)). José Morales' ability to pass citizenship to his son, respondent Morales-Santana, easily satisfies the "close relationship" requirement. So, too, is the "hindrance" requirement well met. José Morales' failure to assert a claim in his own right "stems from disability," not "disinterest," *Miller* v. *Albright*, 523 U.S. 420, 450 (1998) (O'Connor, J., concurring in judgment), for José died in 1976, Record 140, many years before the current controversy arose. See *Hodel* v. *Irving*, 481 U.S. 704–712, 723, n. 7 (1987) (children and their guardians may assert Fifth Amendment rights of deceased relatives). Morales-Santana is thus the "obvious claimant," see *Craig* v. *Boren*, 429 U.S. 190, 197 (1976), the "best available proponent," *Singleton* v. *Wulff*, 428 U.S. 106, 116 (1976), of his father's right to equal protection.

III

Sections 1401 and 1409, we note, date from an era when the lawbooks of our Nation were rife with overbroad generalizations about the way men and women are. See, *e.g.*, *Hoyt* v. *Florida*, 368 U.S. 57, 62 (1961) (women are the "center of home and family life," therefore they can be "relieved from the civic duty of jury service"); *Goesaert* v. *Cleary*, 335 U.S. 464, 466 (1948) (States may draw "a sharp line between the sexes"). Today, laws of this kind are subject to review under the heightened scrutiny that now attends "all gender-based classifications." *J. E. B.* v. *Alabama ex rel. T. B.*, 511 U.S. 127, 136 (1994); see, *e.g.*, *United States* v. *Virginia*, 518 U.S. 515–556 (1996) (state-maintained military academy may not deny admission to qualified women).

Laws granting or denying benefits "on the basis of the sex of the qualifying parent," our post-1970 decisions affirm, differentiate on the basis of gender, and therefore attract heightened review under the Constitution's equal protection guarantee...

Prescribing one rule for mothers, another for fathers, § 1409 is of the same genre as the classifications we declared unconstitutional in *Reed*, *Frontiero*, *Wiesenfeld*, *Goldfarb*, and *Westcott*. As in those cases, heightened scrutiny is in order. Successful defense of legislation that differentiates on the basis of gender, we have reiterated, requires an "exceedingly persuasive justification." *Virginia*, 518 U.S., at 531...

A

The defender of legislation that differentiates on the basis of gender must show "at least that the [challenged] classification serves important governmental objectives and that the discriminatory means employed are substantially related to the achievement of those objectives." *Virginia*, 518 U.S., at 533 (quoting *Mississippi Univ. for Women* v. *Hogan*, 458 U.S. 718, 724 (1982); alteration in original); see *Tuan Anh Nguyen* v. *INS*, 533 U.S. 53, 60, 70 (2001). Moreover, the classification must substantially serve an important governmental interest *today*, for "in interpreting the [e]qual [p]rotection [guarantee], [we have] recognized that new insights and societal understandings can reveal unjustified inequality ... that once passed unnoticed and unchallenged." *Obergefell* v. *Hodges*, 576 U.S. ___, ___ (2015). Here, the Government has supplied no "exceedingly persuasive justification," *Virginia*, 518 U.S., at 531. . .

1

* * *

This unwed-mother-as-natural-guardian notion renders § 1409's gender-based residency rules understandable. Fearing that a foreign-born child could turn out "more alien than American in character," the administration believed that a citizen parent with lengthy ties to the United States would counteract the influence of the alien parent. [See Hearings on H. R. 6127 before the House Committee on Immigration and Naturalization, 76th Cong., 1st Sess., 43 (1940)], at 426–427. Concern about the attachment of foreign-born children to the United States explains the treatment of unwed citizen fathers, who, according to the familiar stereotype, would care little about, and have scant contact with, their nonmarital children. For unwed citizen mothers, however, there was no need for a prolonged residency prophylactic: The alien father, who might transmit foreign ways, was presumptively out of the picture. See *id.*, at 431; Collins, *Illegitimate Borders* 2203 (in "nearly uniform view" of U.S. officials, "almost invariably," the mother alone "concern[ed] herself with [a nonmarital] child" (internal quotation marks omitted)).

2

For close to a half century, as earlier observed, this Court has viewed with suspicion laws that rely on "overbroad generalizations about the different talents, capacities, or preferences of males and females." *Virginia*, 518 U.S., at 533; see *Wiesenfeld*, 420 U.S., at 643, 648. In particular, we have recognized that if a "statutory objective is to exclude or 'protect' members of one gender" in reliance on "fixed notions concerning [that gender's] roles and abilities," the "objective itself is illegitimate." *Mississippi Univ. for Women*, 458 U.S., at 725.

In accord with this eventual understanding, the Court has held that no "important [governmental] interest" is served by laws grounded, as § 1409(a) and (c) are, in the obsolescing view that "unwed fathers [are] invariably less qualified and entitled than mothers" to take responsibility for nonmarital children. *Caban* v. *Mohammed*, 441 U.S. 380, 382, 394 (1979). Overbroad generalizations of that order, the Court has come to comprehend, have a constraining impact, descriptive though they may be of the way many people still order their lives.[13] Laws according or denying benefits in reliance on "[s]tereotypes about women's domestic roles," the Court has observed, may "creat[e] a self-fulfilling cycle of discrimination that force[s] women to continue to assume the role of primary family caregiver." *Nevada Dept. of Human Resources* v. *Hibbs*, 538 U.S. 721, 736 (2003). Correspondingly, such laws may disserve men who exercise responsibility for raising their children. See *ibid*. In light of the equal protection jurisprudence this Court has developed since 1971, see *Virginia*, 518 U.S., at 531–534, § 1409(a) and (c)'s discrete duration-of-residence requirements for unwed mothers and fathers who have accepted parental responsibility is stunningly anachronistic.

B

In urging this Court nevertheless to reject Morales-Santana's equal protection plea, the Government cites three decisions of this Court: *Fiallo* v. *Bell*, 430 U.S. 787 (1977); *Miller* v. *Albright*, 523 U.S. 420; and *Nguyen* v. *INS*, 533 U.S. 53. None controls this case.

The 1952 Act provision at issue in *Fiallo* gave special immigration preferences to alien children of citizen (or lawful-permanent-resident) mothers, and to alien unwed mothers of citizen (or lawful-permanent-resident) children. . . .This case, however, involves no entry preference for aliens. Morales-Santana claims he is, and since birth has been, a U.S. citizen. . .

The provision challenged in *Miller* and *Nguyen* as violative of equal protection requires unwed U.S.-citizen fathers, but not mothers, to formally acknowledge parenthood of their foreign-born children in order to transmit their U.S. citizenship to those children. See § 1409(a)(4) (2012 ed.). . . .

Unlike the paternal-acknowledgment requirement at issue in *Nguyen* and *Miller*, the physical-presence requirements now before us relate solely to the duration of the parent's prebirth residency in the United States, not to the parent's filial tie to the child. As the Court of Appeals observed in this case, a man needs no more time in the United States than a woman "in order to have assimilated citizenship-related values to transmit to [his] child." 804 F. 3d, at 531. And unlike *Nguyen*'s parental-acknowledgment requirement, § 1409(a)'s age-calibrated physical-presence requirements cannot fairly be described as "minimal." 533 U.S., at 70.

C

Notwithstanding § 1409(a) and (c)'s provenance in traditional notions of the way women and men are, the Government maintains that the statute serves two important objectives: (1) ensuring a connection between the child to become a citizen and the United States and (2) preventing "statelessness," *i.e.*, a child's possession of no citizenship at all. Even indulging the assumption that Congress intended § 1409 to serve these interests, neither rationale survives heightened scrutiny.

1

We take up first the Government's assertion that § 1409(a) and (c)'s gender-based differential ensures that a child born abroad has a connection to the United States of sufficient strength to warrant conferral of citizenship at birth...

An unwed mother, the Government urges, is the child's only "legally recognized" parent at the time of childbirth. Brief for Petitioner. An unwed citizen father enters the scene later, as a second parent. A longer physical connection to the United States is warranted for the unwed father, the Government maintains, because of the "competing national influence" of the alien mother. *Id.* Congress, the Government suggests, designed the statute to bracket an unwed U.S.-citizen mother with a married couple in which both parents are U.S. citizens, and to align an unwed U.S.-citizen father with a married couple, one spouse a citizen, the other, an alien.

Underlying this apparent design is the assumption that the alien father of a nonmarital child born abroad to a U.S.-citizen mother will not accept parental responsibility. For an actual affiliation between alien father and nonmarital child would create the "competing national influence" that, according to the Government, justifies imposing on unwed U.S.-citizen fathers, but not unwed U.S.-citizen mothers, lengthy physical-presence requirements. Hardly gender neutral, see *id.*, that assumption conforms to the long-held view that unwed fathers care little about, indeed are strangers to, their children. Lump characterization of that kind, however, no longer passes equal protection inspection. See *supra*, and n. 13.

Accepting, *arguendo*, that Congress intended the diverse physical-presence prescriptions to serve an interest in ensuring a connection between the foreign-born nonmarital child and the United States, the gender-based means scarcely serve the posited end. The scheme permits the transmission of citizenship to children who have no tie to the United States so long as their mother was a U.S. citizen continuously present in the United States for one year at any point in her life *prior* to the child's birth. The transmission holds even if the mother marries the child's alien father immediately after the child's birth and never returns with the child to the United States. At the same time, the legislation precludes citizenship transmission by a U.S.-citizen father who falls a few days short of meeting § 1401(a)(7)'s longer physical-presence requirements, even if the father acknowledges paternity on the day of the child's birth and raises the child in the United States.[19] One cannot see in this driven-by-gender scheme the close means-end fit required to survive heightened scrutiny. See, *e.g.*, *Wengler* v. *Druggists Mut. Ins. Co.*, 446 U.S. 142–152 (1980) (holding unconstitutional state workers' compensation death-benefits statute presuming widows' but not widowers' dependence on their spouse's earnings); *Westcott*, 443 U.S., at 88–89.

2

The Government maintains that Congress established the gender-based residency differential in § 1409(a) and (c) to reduce the risk that a foreign-born child of a U.S. citizen would be born stateless. Brief for Petitioner. This risk, according to the Government, was substantially greater for the foreign-born child of an unwed U.S.-citizen mother than it was for the foreign-born child of an unwed U.S.-citizen father. *Ibid.* But there is little reason to believe that a statelessness concern prompted the diverse physical-presence requirements. Nor has the Government shown that the risk of statelessness disproportionately endangered the children of unwed mothers.

* * *

In sum, the Government has advanced no "exceedingly persuasive" justification for § 1409(a) and (c)'s gender-specific residency and age criteria. Those disparate criteria, we hold, cannot withstand inspection under a Constitution that requires the Government to respect the equal dignity and stature of its male and female citizens.[21]

IV

While the equal protection infirmity in retaining a longer physical-presence requirement for unwed fathers than for unwed mothers is clear, this Court is not equipped to grant the relief Morales-Santana seeks, *i.e.*, extending to his father (and, derivatively, to him) the benefit of the one-year physical-presence term § 1409(c) reserves for unwed mothers.

V

The gender-based distinction infecting §§ 1401(a)(7) and 1409(a) and (c), we hold, violates the equal protection principle, as the Court of Appeals correctly ruled. For the reasons stated, however, we must adopt the remedial course Congress likely would have chosen "had it been apprised of the constitutional infirmity." *Levin*, 560 U.S., at 427. Although the preferred rule in the typical case is to extend favorable treatment, see *Westcott*, 443 U.S., at 89–90, this is hardly the typical case. Extension here would render the special treatment Congress prescribed in § 1409(c), the one-year physical-presence requirement for U.S.-citizen mothers, the general rule, no longer an exception. Section 1401(a)(7)'s longer physical-presence requirement, applicable to a substantial majority of children born abroad to one U.S.-citizen parent and one foreign-citizen parent, therefore, must hold sway. Going forward, Congress may address the issue and settle on a uniform prescription that neither favors nor disadvantages any person on the basis of gender. In the interim, as the Government suggests, § 1401(a)(7)'s now-five-year requirement should apply, prospectively, to children born to unwed U.S.-citizen mothers.

* * *

The judgment of the Court of Appeals for the Second Circuit is affirmed in part and reversed in part, and the case is remanded for further proceedings consistent with this opinion.

It is so ordered.

Opinion Footnotes

5 There is no question that Morales-Santana himself satisfied the five-year residence requirement that once conditioned a child's acquisition of citizenship under § 1401(a)(7). See § 1401(b).

13 Even if stereotypes frozen into legislation have "statistical support," our decisions reject measures that classify unnecessarily and overbroadly by gender when more accurate and impartial lines can be drawn. *J. E. B.* v. *Alabama ex rel. T. B.*, 511 U.S. 127, 139, n. 11 (1994); see, *e.g.*, *Craig* v. *Boren*, 429 U.S. 190–199 (1976); *Weinberger* v. *Wiesenfeld*, 420 U.S. 636, 645 (1975). In fact, unwed fathers assume responsibility for their children in numbers already large and notably increasing. See Brief for Population and Family Scholars as *Amici Curiae* (documenting that nonmarital fathers "are [often] in a parental role at the time of their child's birth," and "most . . . formally acknowledge their paternity either at the hospital or in the birthing center just after the child is born"); Brief for American Civil Liberties Union et al. as *Amici Curiae* (observing, *inter alia*, that "[i]n 2015, fathers made up 16 percent of single parents with minor children in the United States").

19 Brief for Respondent, presents this example: "Child A is born in Germany and raised there by his U.S.-citizen mother who spent only a year of her life in the United States during infancy; Child B is born in Germany and is legitimated and raised in Germany by a U.S.-citizen father who spent his entire life in the United States before leaving for Germany one week before his nineteenth birthday. Notwithstanding the fact that Child A's 'legal relationship' with his U.S.-citizen mother may have been established 'at the moment of birth,' and Child B's 'legal relationship' with his U.S.-citizen father may have been established

a few hours later, Child B is more likely than Child A to learn English and assimilate U.S. values. Nevertheless, under the discriminatory scheme, only Child A obtains U.S. citizenship at birth." . . .

21 Justice Thomas, joined by Justice Alito, sees our equal protection ruling as "unnecessary," *post*, given our remedial holding. But, "as we have repeatedly emphasized, discrimination itself . . . perpetuat[es] 'archaic and stereotypic notions' " incompatible with the equal treatment guaranteed by the Constitution. *Heckler* v. *Mathews*, 465 U.S. 728, 739 (1984) (quoting *Mississippi Univ. for Women* v. *Hogan*, 458 U.S. 718, 725 (1982)).

JUSTICE THOMAS, with whom JUSTICE ALITO joins, concurring in the judgment in part.

The Court today holds that we are "not equipped to" remedy the equal protection injury that respondent claims his father suffered under the Immigration and Nationality Act (INA) of 1952. *Ante*. I agree with that holding. As the majority concludes, extending 8 U.S.C. § 1409(c)'s 1-year physical presence requirement to unwed citizen fathers (as respondent requests) is not, under this Court's precedent, an appropriate remedy for any equal protection violation. See *ante*. Indeed, I am skeptical that we even have the "power to provide relief of the sort requested in this suit—namely, conferral of citizenship on a basis other than that prescribed by Congress." *Tuan Anh Nguyen* v. *INS*, 533 U.S. 53, 73 (2001) (Scalia, J., joined by Thomas, J., concurring) (citing *Miller* v. *Albright*, 523 U.S. 420, 452 (1998) (Scalia, J., joined by Thomas, J., concurring in judgment)).

The Court's remedial holding resolves this case. Because respondent cannot obtain relief in any event, it is unnecessary for us to decide whether the 1952 version of the INA was constitutional, whether respondent has third-party standing to raise an equal protection claim on behalf of his father, or whether other immigration laws (such as the current versions of §§ 1401(g) and 1409) are constitutional. I therefore concur only in the judgment reversing the Second Circuit.

Case Questions

1. Since there are often if not always witnesses to the birth of non-marital children but no witnesses to the act that gave rise to fatherhood, what would be the most equitable arrangement for honoring the rights of American nonmarital fathers whose children are born outside the country? Should they simply be allowed to announce fatherhood at any time? Should a DNA test be required? Should any residence period in the U.S.A. be required of the father? Of the mother? Why or why not?

2. Have non-marital fathers changed so much by this time that there should be zero difference between fathers and mothers in how parenthood by a U.S. citizen confers citizenship on foreign-born, non-marital children?

WHEN IS DISCRIMINATION NOT DISCRIMINATION? *PERSONNEL ADMINISTRATOR V. FEENEY* (1979)

The *Craig* rule could tell the Court how to deal with sex discrimination but it provided no guidelines for deciding whether sex discrimination was present in non-obvious cases. One type of law that gave the Court difficulty in this regard was legislation that disfavored pregnancy. The Court's difficulty with such statutes is detailed in Chapter 3. A second type of law that put in question the very presence of gender discrimination was the sort of law that greatly favors one sex over the other in its *impact*, although the statute itself makes no mention of sex or gender. (This silence is referred to as "facial neutrality.") The Court had dealt with similar difficulties in examining laws with racially disproportionate impacts. Although its record in the racial context was not without inconsistency,[72] the Court by 1976, in *Washington v. Davis*[73] came up with a firm rule: If a law, neutral on its face, had a racially disparate impact, the Court would treat it as racial discrimination (and thus apply strict scrutiny) only if the challenges to the law could prove that some racial discrimination had been *intentional*.

In 1979 the Supreme Court, in *Personnel Administrator v. Feeney*,[74] chose to apply a similar test for deciding whether to invoke *Craig*-level-scrutiny for laws that hurt one sex more than another but are neutral on their face. The justices unanimously agreed on the test for locating sex discrimination in facially neutral statutes: the criterion must be evidence of an intent to discriminate. They disagreed, however, on how this test applied to the facts before them. Seven justices found no purposeful discrimination, whereas two justices claimed to find some. One reason for their differing conclusions is that the majority would place the burden of proof on the plaintiff; the dissenters, on the defendant.

Helen Feeney brought this case to challenge Massachusetts laws that provided an absolute preference of military veterans for state civil service jobs. Vets who applied for such a job, as long as they passed the civil service exam, automatically were granted a higher eligibility rank than any non-veteran applicant. (Among competing veterans, those with the higher score obtained the higher rank.) For any particular job the top three ranking candidates were eligible. Helen Feeney, a 12-year civil service employee, competed for a number of jobs, and scored well on the civil service tests (e.g., second or third highest in the state). But each time several veterans were ranked ahead of her. She initiated the suit in 1975 in federal District Court. She won a declaration of unconstitutionality there, but the U.S. Supreme Court had sent the case back down to the district level for reconsideration after *Washington v. Davis*. The District Court had reaffirmed its judgment and the case went back to the U.S. Supreme Court, who reversed the judgment, as they explain here:

> ### PERSONNEL ADMINISTRATOR OF MASSACHUSETTS V. FEENEY
> 442 U.S. 256 (1979)
>
> **MR. JUSTICE STEWART delivered the opinion of the Court.**
>
> ...The veterans' hiring preference in Massachusetts, as in other jurisdictions, has traditionally been justified as a measure designed to reward veterans for the sacrifice of military service, to ease the transition from military to civilian life, to encourage patriotic service, and to attract loyal and well-disciplined people to civil service occupations.
>
> . . .
>
> The first Massachusetts veterans' preference statute defined the term "veterans" in gender-neutral language. . . . Women who have served in official United States military units during wartime, then, have always been entitled to the benefit of the preference. In addition, Massachusetts, through a 1943 amendment to the definition of "wartime service," extended the preference to women who served in unofficial auxiliary women's units. 1943 Mass. Acts, ch. 194.
>
> . . .
>
> Notwithstanding the apparent attempts by Massachusetts to include as many military women as possible within the scope of the preference, the statute today benefits an overwhelmingly male class. This is attributable in some measure to the variety of federal statutes, regulations, and policies that have restricted the number of women who could enlist in the United States Armed Forces,[21] and largely to the simple fact that women have never been subjected to a military draft. See generally Binkin and Bach 4–21.
>
> When this litigation was commenced, then, over 98% of the veterans in Massachusetts were male; only 1.8% were female. And over one-quarter of the Massachusetts population were veterans. During the decade between 1963 and 1973 when the appellee was actively participating in the State's merit selection

system, 47,005 new permanent appointments were made in the classified official service. Forty-three percent of those hired were women, and 57% were men. Of the women appointed, 1.8% were veterans, while 54% of the men had veteran status. A large unspecified percentage of the female appointees were serving in lower paying positions for which males traditionally had not applied. . . .The impact of the veterans' preference law upon the public employment opportunities of women has thus been severe [and]. . .lies at the heart of the appellee's federal constitutional claim.

The sole question for decision on this appeal is whether Massachusetts, in granting an absolute lifetime preference to veterans, has discriminated against women in violation of the Equal Protection Clause of the Fourteenth Amendment.

The equal protection guarantee of the Fourteenth Amendment does not take from the States all power of classification. *Massachusetts Bd. of Retirement v. Murgia*, 427 U.S. 307, 314. Most laws classify, and many affect certain groups unevenly, even though the law itself treats them no differently from all other members of the class described by the law. When the basic classification is rationally based, uneven effects upon particular groups within a class are ordinarily of no constitutional concern. . . .

Certain classifications, however, in themselves supply a reason to infer antipathy. Race is the paradigm. A racial classification, regardless of purported motivation, is presumptively invalid and can be upheld only upon an extraordinary justification. *Brown v. Board of Education*, 347 U.S. 483; *McLaughlin v. Florida*, 379 U.S. 184. This rule applies as well to a classification that is ostensibly neutral but is an obvious pretext for racial discrimination. *Yick Wo v. Hopkins*, 118 U.S. 356; *Guinn v. United States*, 238 U.S. 347; cf. *Lane v. Wilson*, 307 U.S. 268; *Gomillion v. Lightfoot*, 364 U.S. 339. But, as was made clear in *Washington v. Davis*, 426 U.S. 229, and *Arlington Heights v. Metropolitan Housing Dev. Corp.*, 429 U.S. 252, even if a neutral law has a disproportionately adverse effect upon a racial minority, it is unconstitutional under the Equal Protection Clause only if that impact can be traced to a discriminatory purpose.

Classifications based upon gender, not unlike those based upon race, have traditionally been the touchstone for pervasive and often subtle discrimination. *Caban v. Mohammed*, 441 U.S. 380, 398 (STEWART, J., dissenting). This Court's recent cases teach that such classifications must bear a close and substantial relationship to important governmental objectives, *Craig v. Boren*, 429 U.S. 190, 197, and are in many settings unconstitutional. *Reed v. Reed*, 404 U.S. 71; *Frontiero v. Richardson*, 411 U.S. 677; *Weinberger v. Wiesenfeld*, 420 U.S. 636; *Craig v. Boren*, *supra*; *Califano v. Goldfarb*, 430 U.S. 199; *Orr v. Orr*, 440 U.S. 268; *Caban v. Mohammed*. Although public employment is not a constitutional right, *Massachusetts Bd. of Retirement v. Murgia*, and the States have wide discretion in framing employee qualifications, these precedents dictate that any state law overtly or covertly designed to prefer males over females in public employment would require an exceedingly persuasive justification to withstand a constitutional challenge under the Equal Protection Clause of the Fourteenth Amendment.

The cases of *Washington v. Davis* and *Arlington Heights v. Metropolitan Housing Dev. Corp.* recognize that when a neutral law has a disparate impact upon a group that has historically been the victim of discrimination, an unconstitutional purpose may still be at work. But those cases signaled no departure from the settled rule that the Fourteenth Amendment guarantees equal laws, not equal results. Davis upheld a job-related employment test that white people passed in proportionately greater numbers than Negroes, for there had been no showing that racial discrimination entered into the establishment or formulation of the test. Arlington Heights upheld a zoning board decision that tended to perpetuate racially segregated housing patterns, since, apart from its effect, the board's decision was shown to be nothing more than an application of a constitutionally neutral zoning policy. Those principles apply with equal force to a case involving alleged gender discrimination.

When a statute gender-neutral on its face is challenged on the ground that its effects upon women are disproportionably adverse, a twofold inquiry is thus appropriate. The first question is whether the statutory classification is indeed neutral in the sense that it is not gender based. If the classification itself. . .is not based upon gender, the second question is whether the adverse effect reflects invidious gender-based discrimination. See *Arlington Heights v. Metropolitan Housing Dev. Corp.* In this second inquiry, impact provides an "important starting point," 429 U.S., at 266, but purposeful discrimination is "the condition that offends the Constitution." *Swann v. Charlotte-Mecklenburg Board of Education*, 402 U.S. 1, 16.

. . .Against this background . . .we consider the . . . case.

. . .The appellee has conceded that ch. 31, § 23, is neutral on its face. She has also acknowledged that state hiring preferences for veterans are not per se invalid, for she has limited her challenge to the absolute lifetime preference that Massachusetts provides to veterans. The District Court made two central findings that are relevant here: first, that ch. 31, § 23, serves legitimate and worthy purposes; second, that the absolute preference was not established for the purpose of discriminating against women. The appellee has thus acknowledged and the District Court has thus found that the distinction between veterans and nonveterans drawn by ch. 31, § 23, is not a pretext for gender discrimination. The appellee's concession and the District Court's finding are clearly correct.

. . .

The distinction made by ch. 31, § 23, is, as it seems to be, quite simply between veterans and nonveterans, not between men and women.

The dispositive question, then, is whether the appellee has shown that a gender-based discriminatory purpose has, at least in some measure, shaped the Massachusetts veterans' preference legislation. As did the District Court, she points to two basic factors which in her view distinguish ch. 31, § 23, from the neutral rules at issue in the *Washington v. Davis* and *Arlington Heights* cases. The first is the nature of the preference, which is said to be demonstrably gender-biased in the sense that it favors a status reserved under federal military policy primarily to men. The second concerns the impact of the absolute lifetime preference upon the employment opportunities of women, an impact claimed to be too inevitable to have been unintended. The appellee contends that these factors, coupled with the fact that the preference itself has little if any relevance to actual job performance, more than suffice to prove the discriminatory intent required to establish a constitutional violation.

The contention that this veterans' preference is "inherently nonneutral" or "gender-biased" presumes that the State, by favoring veterans, intentionally incorporated into its public employment policies the panoply of sex-based and assertedly discriminatory federal laws that have prevented all but a handful of women from becoming veterans. There are two serious difficulties with this argument. First, it is wholly at odds with the District Court's central finding that Massachusetts has not offered a preference to veterans for the purpose of discriminating against women. Second, it cannot be reconciled with the assumption made by both the appellee and the District Court that a more limited hiring preference for veterans could be sustained. Taken together, these difficulties are fatal.

. . .

The appellee's ultimate argument rests upon the presumption, common to the criminal and civil law, that a person intends the natural and foreseeable consequences of his voluntary actions. Her position was well stated in the concurring opinion in the District Court:

"Conceding... that the goal here was to benefit the veteran, there is no reason to absolve the legislature from awareness that the means chosen to achieve this goal would freeze women out of all those state jobs actively sought by men. To be sure, the legislature did not wish to harm women. But the cutting-off of women's opportunities was an inevitable concomitant of the chosen scheme—as inevitable as the proposition that if tails is up, heads must be down. Where a law's consequences are that inevitable, can they meaningfully be described as unintended?" 451 F. Supp., at 151

This rhetorical question implies that a negative answer is obvious, but it is not. The decision to grant a preference to veterans was of course "intentional." So, necessarily, did an adverse impact upon nonveterans follow from that decision. And it cannot seriously be argued that the Legislature of Massachusetts could have been unaware that most veterans are men....

"Discriminatory purpose," however, implies more than intent as volition or intent as awareness of consequences. See *United Jewish Organizations v. Carey*, 430 U.S. 144, 179 (concurring opinion).[24] It implies that the decisionmaker, in this case a state legislature, selected or reaffirmed a particular course of action at least in part "because of," not merely "in spite of," its adverse effects upon an identifiable group. Yet nothing in the record demonstrates that this preference for veterans was originally devised or subsequently re-enacted because it would accomplish the collateral goal of keeping women in a stereotypic and predefined place in the Massachusetts Civil Service.

To the contrary...[w]hen the totality of legislative actions establishing and extending the Massachusetts veterans' preference are considered, see *Washington v. Davis*, 426 U.S., at 242, the law remains what it purports to be: a preference for veterans of either sex over nonveterans of either sex, not for men over women.

... The substantial edge granted to veterans by ch. 31, § 23, may reflect unwise policy. The appellee, however, has simply failed to demonstrate that the law in any way reflects a purpose to discriminate on the basis of sex.

The judgment is reversed, and the case is remanded for further proceedings consistent with this opinion.

Opinion Footnotes

21 The Army Nurse Corps, created by Congress in 1901, was the first official military unit for women, but its members were not granted full military rank until 1944. See Binkin and Bach *Women and the Military* 4–21(1977); M. Treadwell, *The Women's Army Corps* 6 (Dept. of Army 1954) (hereinafter Treadwell). During World War I, a variety of proposals were made to enlist women for work as doctors, telephone operators, and clerks, but all were rejected by the War Department. See *ibid.* The Navy, however, interpreted its own authority broadly to include a power to enlist women as Yeoman F's and Marine F's. About 13,000 women served in this rank, working primarily at clerical jobs. These women were the first in the United States to be admitted to full military rank and status. See *id.*, at 10.

Official military corps for women were established in response to the massive personnel needs of World War II...The authorizations for the women's units during World War II were temporary. The Women's Armed Services Integration Act of 1948, 62 Stat. 356, established the women's services on a permanent basis. Under the Act, women were given regular military status. However, quotas were placed on the numbers who could enlist, 62 Stat. 357, 360–361 (no more than 2% of total enlisted strength), eligibility requirements were more stringent than those for men, and career opportunities were limited. Binkin and Bach 11–12. During the 1950's and 1960's, enlisted women constituted little more than 1% of the total force. In 1967, the 2% quota was lifted, 1 (9) (E), 81 Stat. 375, 10 U.S.C. 3209 (b), and in the 1970's many restrictive policies concerning women's participation in the military have been eliminated or modified. See generally Binkin and Bach. In 1972, women still constituted less than 2% of the enlisted strength. *Id.*, at 14. By 1975, when this litigation was commenced, the percentage had risen to 4.6%. *Ibid.*

24 Proof of discriminatory intent must necessarily usually rely on objective factors, several of which were outlined in *Arlington Heights v. Metropolitan Housing Dev. Corp.*, 429 U.S. 252, 266. The inquiry is practical. What a legislature or any official entity is "up to" may be plain from the results its actions achieve, or the results they avoid. Often it is made clear from what has been called, in a different context, "the give and take of the situation." *Cramer v. United States*, 325 U.S. 1, 32–33 (Jackson, J.).

Mr. Justice Stevens, with whom Mr. Justice White joins, concurring.

...I concur in the Court's opinion....[F]or me the answer is largely provided by the fact that the number of males disadvantaged by Massachusetts' veterans' preference (1,867,000) is sufficiently large—and sufficiently close to the number of disadvantaged females (2,954,000)—to refute the claim that the rule was intended to benefit males as a class over females as a class.

Mr. Justice Marshall, with whom Mr. Justice Brennan joins, dissenting.

Although acknowledging that in some circumstances, discriminatory intent may be inferred from the inevitable or foreseeable impact of a statute, the Court concludes that no such intent has been established here. I cannot agree. In my judgment, Massachusetts' choice of an absolute veterans' preference system evinces purposeful gender-based discrimination. And because the statutory scheme bears no substantial relationship to a legitimate governmental objective, it cannot withstand scrutiny under the Equal Protection Clause.

The District Court found that the "prime objective" of the Massachusetts veterans' preference statute, Mass. Gen. Laws Ann., ch. 31, § 23, was to benefit individuals with prior military service. *Anthony v. Commonwealth*, 415 F. Supp. 485, 497 (Mass. 1976). See *Feeney v. Massachusetts*, 451 F. Supp. 143, 145 (Mass. 1978). Under the Court's analysis, this factual determination "necessarily compels the conclusion that the State intended nothing more than to prefer 'veterans.' Given this finding, simple logic suggests than an intent to exclude women from significant public jobs was not at work in this law." I find the Court's logic neither simple nor compelling.

That a legislature seeks to advantage one group does not, as a matter of logic or of common sense, exclude the possibility that it also intends to disadvantage another. Individuals in general and lawmakers in particular frequently act for a variety of reasons. . . . Thus, the critical constitutional inquiry is not whether an illicit consideration was the primary or but-for cause of a decision, but rather whether it had an appreciable role in shaping a given legislative enactment. Where there is "proof that *a* discriminatory purpose has been a motivating factor in the decision, . . . judicial deference is no longer justified." *Arlington Heights v. Metropolitan Housing Dev. Corp.*, at 265–266 (emphasis added).

Moreover, since reliable evidence of subjective intentions is seldom obtainable, resort to inference based on objective factors is generally unavoidable. To discern the purposes underlying facially neutral policies, this Court has therefore considered the degree, inevitability, and foreseeability of any disproportionate impact as well as the alternatives reasonably available. [Citations omitted.]

In the instant case, the impact of the Massachusetts statute on women is undisputed. Any veteran with a passing grade on the civil service exam must be placed ahead of a nonveteran, regardless of their respective scores. The District Court found that, as a practical matter, this preference supplants test results as the determinant of [all] upper level civil service appointments. 415 F. Supp., at 488–489. Because less than 2% of the women in Massachusetts are veterans, the absolute-preference formula has rendered desirable state civil service employment an almost exclusively male prerogative. 451 F. Supp., at 151 (Campbell, J., concurring).

As the District Court recognized, this consequence follows foreseeably, indeed inexorably, from the long history of policies severely limiting women's participation in the military.[1] Although neutral in form, the statute is anything but neutral in application. It inescapably reserves a major sector of public employment to "an already established class which, as a matter of historical fact, is 98% male." *Ibid.* Where the foreseeable impact of a facially neutral policy is so disproportionate, the burden should rest on the State to establish that sex-based considerations played no part in the choice of the particular legislative scheme. Cf. *Castaneda v. Partida*, 430 U.S. 482 (1977); *Washington v. Davis*, 426 U.S. 229, 241 (1976); *Alexander v. Louisiana*, 405 U.S. 625, 632 (1972); see generally Brest, "*Palmer v. Thompson*: An Approach to the Problem of Unconstitutional Legislative Motive," 1971 *Sup. Ct. Rev.* 95, 123.

Clearly, that burden was not sustained here. The legislative history of the statute reflects the Commonwealth's patent appreciation of the impact the preference system would have on women, and an equally evident desire to mitigate that impact only with respect to certain traditionally female occupations. Until 1971, the statute and implementing civil service regulations exempted from operation of the preference any job requisitions "especially calling for women." . . .In practice, this exemption, coupled with the absolute preference for veterans, has created a gender-based civil service hierarchy, with women occupying low-grade clerical and secretarial jobs and men holding more responsible and remunerative positions. 415 F. Supp., at 488; 451 F. Supp., at 148 n. 9.

Thus, for over 70 years, the Commonwealth has maintained, as an integral part of its veterans' preference system, an exemption relegating female civil service applicants to occupations traditionally filled by women. Such a statutory scheme both reflects and perpetuates precisely the kind of archaic assumptions about women's roles which we have previously held invalid. See *Orr v. Orr*, 440 U.S. 268 (1979); *Califano v. Goldfarb*, 430 U.S. 199, 210–211 (1977); *Stanton v. Stanton*, 421 U.S. 7, 14 (1975); *Weinberger v. Wiesenfeld*, 420 U.S. 636, 645 (1975). Particularly when viewed against the range of less discriminatory alternatives available to assist veterans, Massachusetts' choice of a formula that so severely restricts public employment opportunities for women cannot reasonably be thought gender-neutral. Cf. *Albemarle Paper Co. v. Moody*, at 425. The Court's conclusion to the contrary—that "nothing in the record" evinces a "collateral goal of keeping women in a stereotypic and predefined place in the Massachusetts Civil Service,"—displays a singularly myopic view of the facts established below.[3]

To survive challenge under the Equal Protection Clause, statutes reflecting gender-based discrimination must be substantially related to the achievement of important governmental objectives. See *Califano v. Webster*, 430 U.S. 313, 316–317 (1977); *Craig v. Boren*, 429 U.S. 190, 197 (1976); *Reed v. Reed*, 404 U.S. 71, 76 (1971). Appellants here advance three interests in support of the absolute-preference system: (1) assisting veterans in their readjustment to civilian life; (2) encouraging military enlistment; and (3) rewarding those who have served their country. Although each of those goals is unquestionably legitimate, the "mere recitation of a benign, compensatory purpose" cannot of itself insulate legislative classifications from constitutional scrutiny. *Weinberger v. Wiesenfeld*, at 648. And in this case, the Commonwealth has failed to establish a sufficient relationship between its objectives and the means chosen to effectuate them.

With respect to the first interest, facilitating veterans' transition to civilian status, the statute is plainly overinclusive. By conferring a permanent preference, the legislation allows veterans to invoke their advantage repeatedly, without regard to their date of discharge....

Nor is the Commonwealth's second asserted interest, encouraging military service, a plausible justification for this legislative scheme. In its original and subsequent re-enactments, the statute extended benefits retroactively to veterans who had served during a prior specified period. If the Commonwealth's "actual purpose" is to induce enlistment, this legislative design is hardly well suited to that end....Moreover, even if such influence could be presumed, the statute is still grossly overinclusive in that it bestows benefits on men drafted as well as those who volunteered.

Finally, the Commonwealth's third interest, rewarding veterans, does not "adequately justify the salient features" of this preference system. *Craig v. Boren*, at 202–203. See *Orr v. Orr*, at 281. Where a particular statutory scheme visits substantial hardship on a class long subject to discrimination, the legislation cannot be sustained unless " 'carefully tuned to alternative considerations.' " *Trimble v. Gordon*, at 772. See *Caban v. Mohammed*, 441 U.S. 380, 392–393, n. 13 (1979); *Mathews v. Lucas*, 427 U.S. 495 (1976). Here, there are a wide variety of less discriminatory means by which Massachusetts could effect its compensatory purposes. For example, a point preference system, such as that maintained by many States and the Federal Government, or an absolute preference for a limited duration, would reward veterans without excluding all qualified women from upper level civil service positions. Apart from public employment, the Commonwealth, can, and does, afford assistance to veterans in various ways, including tax abatements, educational subsidies, and special programs for needy veterans....Unlike these and similar benefits, the costs of which are distributed across the taxpaying public generally, the Massachusetts statute exacts a substantial price from a discrete group of individuals who have long been subject to employment discrimination, and who, "because of circumstances totally beyond their control, have [had] little if any chance of becoming members of the preferred class." 415 F. Supp., at 499. See n. 1, *supra*.

Given the range of alternatives available, this degree of preference is not constitutionally permissible.

> I would affirm the judgment of the court below.
>
> ### Opinion Footnotes
>
> **1** See 415 F. Supp. 485, 490, 495–499 (Mass. 1976); 451 F. Supp. 143, 145, 148 (Mass.1978). In addition to the 2% quota on women's participation in the Armed Forces, n. 21, enlistment and appointment requirements have been more stringent for females than males with respect to age, mental and physical aptitude, parental consent, and educational attainment. M. Binkin & S. Bach, *Women and the Military* (1977) (hereinafter Binkin and Bach); "Note, The Equal Rights Amendment and the Military," 82 *Yale L. J.* 1533, 1539 (1973). Until the 1970's, the Armed Forces precluded enlistment and appointment of women, but not men, who were married or had dependent children. . . .
>
> Thus, unlike the employment examination in *Washington v. Davis*, 426 U.S. 229 (1976), which the Court found to be demonstrably job related, the Massachusetts preference statute incorporates the results of sex-based military policies irrelevant to women's current fitness for civilian public employment. See 415 F. Supp., at 498–499.
>
> **3** Although it is relevant that the preference statute also disadvantages a substantial group of men (STEVENS, J., concurring), it is equally pertinent that 47% of Massachusetts men over 18 are veterans, as compared to 0.8% of Massachusetts women. Given this disparity, and the indicia of intent noted *supra*, the absolute number of men denied preference cannot be dispositive, especially since they have not faced the barriers to achieving veteran status confronted by women. See n. 1, *supra*.

Case Questions

1. Are state legislators likely to admit publicly that they have unconstitutional intentions? How else can their intentions be discovered?

2. Is the fact that the legislature purposely exempted many low-level, clerical type jobs from the veterans' preference, so that women could have them, itself evidence that the legislators intended the veterans' preference to favor males?

RIGHTS IN CONFLICT

First Amendment Freedoms Versus Equal Opportunity: *Pittsburgh Press v. Human Relations Commission* (1973), *Hishon v. King & Spaulding* (1984), and *Roberts v. U.S. Jaycees* (1984)

The Fourteenth Amendment protects values of liberty (in its due process clause) and values of equality (in its equal protection clause). Sooner or later, in many areas of American politics these values bump into each other and limit each other at the edges. Anti-discrimination law is one example. Several cases that posed conflicts between prohibitions on sex discrimination and First Amendment freedoms have already been resolved by the Supreme Court, and others continue to wind their way through the lower courts.

The first of these occurred relatively early in the Court's history of enforcing anti-discrimination law. In 1973, in *Pittsburgh Press v. Human Relations Commission*,

413 U.S. 376, the Supreme Court sustained a municipal administrative order forbidding *Pittsburgh Press* to run sex-designated help wanted ads, such as "Help Wanted—Female" or "Help Wanted—Male" (which used to be common advertisements in American newspapers). The Court's logic was that since sex discrimination in hiring was a federal offense, to forbid the press to be an "accessory before the fact" posed no constitutional problem. Four justices dissented, however, on the grounds that federal law did permit a narrow category of jobs for which sex was a "bona fide occupational qualification." They argued that it should be left to the editorial judgment of the press to decide which ads might lawfully qualify rather than let the government ban them all in advance. This group of dissenters drew support from the traditional interpretation of the freedom of press clause, which places particularly strong condemnation on any government censorship *prior* to publication. Despite that tradition, however, the Court majority found the Congressional ban on sex discrimination to be the more weighty concern here, and upheld the Human Relations Commission order.

Another sort of First Amendment clash with equal protection concerns exposed the tension between freedom of association (a well-established, implied right, derived from the combination of the explicit rights of speech and assembly) and the right of equality of opportunity. The case of *Elizabeth Hishon v. King & Spaulding*, 467 U.S. 69 (1984) presented just such a clash. Elizabeth Hishon had been hired by the King & Spaulding law firm as an associate in 1972, and she alleged that part of the firm's recruitment policy had been the assurance that satisfactory job performance would yield promotion to partner status within five or six years. She further alleged that the firm then refused to consider women for partnership promotion on a "fair and equal basis," but instead discriminated against them on the basis of sex. The law firm countered with the argument that Title VII did not apply to selections of partners, and both the federal District Court and Circuit Court of Appeals court accepted that argument. The U.S. Supreme Court was unanimous in its reversal.

The Supreme Court insisted that opportunity for promotion in a law firm to partner status was indisputably a "term, condition, or privilege of employment," within the meaning of Title VII. It tersely disposed of King & Spaulding's First Amendment argument as follows:

> [R]espondent argues that application of Title VII in this case would infringe constitutional rights of expression or association. Although we have recognized that the activities of lawyers may make a "distinctive contribution...to the ideas and beliefs of our society," *NAACP v. Button*, 371 U.S. 415, 431 (1963), respondent has not shown how its

ability to fulfill such a function would be inhibited by a requirement that it consider petitioner for partnership on her merits. Moreover, as we have held in another context, "[i]nvidious private discrimination may be characterized as a form of exercising freedom of association protected by the First Amendment, but it has never been accorded affirmative constitutional protections." *Norwood v. Harrison*, 413 U.S. 455, 470 (1973). There is no constitutional right, for example, to discriminate in the selection of who may attend a private school or join a labor union. *Runyon v. McCrary*, 427 U.S. 160 (1976); *Railway Mail Association v. Corsi*, 326 U.S. 88, 93–94 (1945).

Justice Powell authored a lone separate concurrence in which he made three points: (1) First Amendment rights of association are very much implicated by decisions to admit someone to partnership in a law firm, since the partnership is the managing body of the firm. (2) Here, King & Spaulding have no First Amendment defense because they voluntarily contracted (orally at the time of hiring) to consider Hishon on a "fair and equal basis" for partnership. (They cannot have a First Amendment right to renege on their contracts with only female employees, and an attempt to do so would put them in violation of Title VII.) (3) It is beneficial to society and the law if law firms refrain from discrimination on the basis of sex. Justice Powell left unclear whether in his view the combination of Title VII and the First Amendment would permit a law firm to hire associates with an explicit understanding that women could never be promoted to partnership, but the combination of his arguments seems to suggest that he would find such an arrangement lawful. On the other hand, the import of his third argument may be that anti-discrimination laws serve an interest compelling enough to override the First Amendment claim.

Two months after *Hishon*, the Supreme Court handed down a decision rejecting a challenge by the national Jaycees organization to a civil rights law of the state of Minnesota, *Roberts v. U.S. Jaycees*, 468 U.S. 609 (1984). The Jaycees (Junior Chamber of Commerce) is a civic organization that at the time was open only to males aged 18–35. Authorities in Minnesota had ruled that the Jaycees constituted a "place of public accommodation" within the meaning of their civil rights law, and had ordered the organization to stop discriminating on the basis of sex. Minnesota argued that since the Jaycees were not selective in their membership in any way other than age and sex, the organization's claims of First Amendment rights of association rang hollow. The U.S. Supreme Court (in a unanimous judgment in which Burger and Blackmun did not participate, and with which O'Connor concurred in a separate opinion and Rehnquist concurred with no opinion) found this argument persuasive.

The Jaycees presented a freedom of expression argument that gave the Court a bit more trouble. The claim was that admitting women would alter the message the Jaycees could express. The Court opinion resolved this claim with the compelling interest test, reasoning that even if the Jaycees' expressive freedom suffered "some incidental abridgement," that abridgement was no greater than the amount necessary for attaining the state's compelling interest in assuring women equal opportunity to participate fully in the public life of society. Justice O'Connor wrote separately to argue that this freedom of expression analysis was inappropriate since the Jaycees were essentially a commercial operation rather than "an expressive association" and consequently should be accorded only the most minimal of First Amendment rights.

The Supreme Court then essentially applied the Jaycees reasoning in two later cases to uphold state laws creating equal access to public accommodations that clashed with, first, Rotary Clubs International, and, second, the New York State Club Association.[75] The first concerned a group whose membership was basically non-selective, open to any male person of decent ethical standards who worked in the business world, and the second applied to genuinely selective clubs whose major purpose was to facilitate doing business.

In cases involving organizations for boys rather than men, courts have produced less uniform results. One Boys' Club organization that ran a swimming pool and gymnasium recreational facility open to all boys who wished to join was ordered by the California courts to abide by an open-public-accommodations law, which required allowing access to girls.[76] The same California courts, however, decided differently with respect to the Boy Scouts of America (BSA), in a case brought by a twelve year old straight "A" student, Katrina Yeaw in 1995.

Katrina's attorney, Lisa Bloom, described that case as follows:

Katrina Yeaw, who wanted the right to join the Boy Scouts of America to experience what her twin brother had—the chance to practice hiking, canoeing, camping, and to learn the leadership and outdoor skills that would enable her to earn the prestigious Eagle Scout honor. (In the Girl Scouts, she told me, she was mostly selling cookies.)[77]

Katrina's case became entangled in gay rights issues. Timothy Curran, an openly gay Eagle Scout attempted, against the wishes of the BSA but claiming protection from the state civil rights laws, to become an assistant BSA troop leader in California. The California Supreme Court ruled that the BSA was an essentially private organization "whose primary function is the inculcation of a specific set of values in its youth members,"[78] and, having done so, then dismissed Katrina's case as having been settled by its ruling.[79] The U.S. Supreme Court then faced the same gay rights issue in a case brought by a former assistant-scoutmaster who had lost his membership after the Boy Scouts became aware that he was gay. In *Boy Scouts of America v. Dale* he challenged his ouster, relying on New Jersey's public accommodations law. The U.S. Supreme Court, like the one in California, ruled on the side of the BSA's rights of expressive association, concluding that the BSA need not admit gay members.[80]

Notably, the BSA rescinded this prohibition on gay scouts. Effective January 1, 2014 membership became open to all eligible males regardless of sexual orientation. More recently, in 2017, the BSA opened membership first to transgender boy scouts and then to girls as well.[81]

Yet another variant of the clash between First Amendment freedoms and equality for women arises for many people who believe that pornography shapes the public mind in ways that ultimately damage women's equality of opportunity. While the Supreme Court has always ruled that "obscenity" is a category of publication unprotected by the First Amendment, the category "pornography" defined somewhat differently from "obscenity" by activists Catharine MacKinnon and the late Andrea Dworkin, did not attain the same treatment at the U.S. Supreme Court. Cases on this subject are covered in detail in Chapter 7.

Equality for Women vs. States' Rights

In the 1990s the U.S. Congress enacted two laws designed to enhance women's equality. The first, in 1993, the Family and Medical Leave Act (FMLA), promoted equality of opportunity for women by stipulating that anyone who stayed home to care for a new baby or a close family member who was ill would be entitled as a matter of federal law to a leave of up to three months in duration. In other words, while the law did not grant such people—people who were usually although not necessarily women—any pay for this period, it assured that they could not be fired for staying home under these circumstances. The second, in 1994, the Violence against Women Act (VAWA), aimed literally to enhance "equal protection of the law" for women by making it a federal crime to cross state lines with the intent of committing violence against a woman on the ground of some gender-based animus. The U.S. Supreme Court took up challenges to both these laws in the 21st century, which were brought by litigants who argued that these laws interfered with states' rights to independence from certain kinds of federal control. The Court upheld the FMLA, but struck down a piece of the VAWA.

The latter decision is presented in detail in Chapter 7, and the former in Chapter 3.

CONCLUSION

This chapter has directed attention to a variety of ways in which the U.S. Supreme Court in the last three decades of the twentieth century fundamentally altered the relation between women and the U.S. Constitution, opening up dimensions of citizenship that had previously been closed off to American women. Some of those dimensions then received further enhancement at the hands of the U.S. Congress or even the U.S. military. The Court itself also initiated a series of lines of precedent that continue to unfold in the ensuing chapters. For this reason, any further "conclusion" for this chapter would be premature.

---

1 *McDonald v. Board of Election Commissioners of Chicago,* 394 U.S. 802 (1969), 809.

2 Ibid.; plus *Edwards v. California,* 314 U.S. 160 (1941); *Griffin v. Illinois,* 351 U.S. 12 (1956); *Douglas v. California,* 372 U.S. 353 (1963); *Lane* v. Brown, 372 U.S. 477 (1963); *Long v. District Court,* 385 U.S. 192 (1966); *Roberts v. LaVallee,* 389 U.S. 40 (1967); *Harper v. Board of Elections,* 383 U.S. 663 (1966). But for a clarification, or narrowing, of this principle, see *San Antonio Independent School District v. Rodriguez,* 411 U.S. 1 (1973, which in turn was clarified in *Plyler v. Doe,* 457 U.S. 202 (1992) and *M.L.B. v. S.L.J.,* 519 U.S. 102 (1996).

3 *Skinner v. Oklahoma,* 316 U.S. 535.

4 For post-*Skinner* developments concerning procreation, see Chapter 4.

5 *Reynolds v. Sims,* 377 U.S. 533 (1964); *Carrington v. Rash,* 380 U.S. 89 (1965); *Harper* v. Board of Elections, 383 U.S. 663 (1966); *Kramer v. Union Free School District,* 395 U.S. 621 (1969).

6 *Shapiro v. Thompson,* 394 U.S. 618 (1969). This case, too, had roots in *Edwards v. California;* see note 2 above.

7 *Levy v. Louisiana,* 391 U.S. 68 (1968); *Glona v. American Guarantee and Liability Insurance,* 391 U.S. 73 (1968).

8 The term "rationality with bite" comes from Gerald Gunther, *American Constitutional Law* (9th ed.; Mineola, N.Y.: Foundation Press, 1975), p. 758.

9 429 U.S. 190.

10 This organization submitted a brief as "friend of the court" (or *amicus curiae,* in the official Latin), arguing the women's rights position, in the 1971 case of *Reed v. Reed.* Presenting the brief for them at the Supreme Court was U.S. Senator Birch Bayh (Dem.-IN, 1963–1981).

11 Jo Freeman, *The Politics of Women's Liberation* (New York: David McKay, 1975), gives an account of these two developments.

12 *Rutgers Law Review* (1970), *Harvard Civil Rights-Civil Liberties Law* Review (1971), *Women's Law Journal* (1971), *Valparaiso Law Review* (1971), *New York Law Forum* (1971), and *Journal of Family Law* (1971).

13 *Sail'er Inn v. Kirby,* 485 P. 2d. 529.

14 For a detailed look at Congressional ERA politics, see Gilbert Steiner, *Constitutional Inequality* (Washington, D.C.: The Brookings Institution, 1985).

15 *Bolling v. Sharpe,* 347 U.S. 497 (1954).

16 37 U.S.C. Sect. 401 (1); 10 U.S.C. Sect. 1072 (A). U.S.C. is the abbreviation for United States Code.

17 *Equal Rights for Men and Women 1972,* Senate Report #92-689, 92d Cong., 2d Sess. 1972, pp. 12, 16, 20; *Equal Rights for Men and Women 1971,* House of Representatives Report #92-359, 92d Cong., 1st Sess., 1971, p.7; *Equal Rights 1970,* Hearings Before the Senate Committee on the Judiciary, 91st Cong., 2d Sess., Sept. 9, 10, 11, 15, 1970, pp. 183, 299, 303; Barbara Brown, Thomas Emerson, et al., "The Equal Rights Amendment: A Constitutional Basis for Equal Rights for Women," 80 *Yale Law Journal* 871, at 893–4.

18 Brown, Emerson, et al., ibid. pp. 904–5.

19 In the latter case, they had filed briefs only as *amicus curiae* representing the American Civil Liberties Union.

20 *Kahn v. Shevin*, 416 U.S. 351, 356 (1974).

21 The quote is from Justice Bradley's concurring opinion in *Bradwell v. Illinois* (1873).

22 The reader will recall, however, that they did not achieve victory in *Kahn v. Shevin*.

23 Justice Rehnquist concurred only in the result.

24 He does, however, employ the overriding or compelling interest test in terms of the father's constitutional right to the companionship and care of his children. In other words, he uses it on the grounds of a fundamental right rather than suspect classification.

25 This is a very time-honored equal protection rule, but in the traditional formulation, the phrase is "persons similarly situated" rather than "men and women similarly situated."

26 Between June and September 1972, the amount was somewhat less: about $200.

27 *Weinberger v. Wiesenfeld*, 420 U.S. 636, 645 (1975).

28 *Id.*, at 655.

29 Janet Boles, *The Politics of the Equal Rights Amendment* (New York: Longman, 1979), pp. 63–4. Since this time, however, the 27th Amendment was added to the Constitution in 1992. It had been proposed by Congress in 1789, thus taking 203 years for ratification.

30 The Louisiana legislature actually ended this practice, two weeks before the Supreme Court handed down its decision. The Supreme Court went ahead because the legislative change did not affect people already in prison, like Taylor. And, of course, the Court decision affects any state that might in the future consider re-instituting the practice.

31 *Alexander v. Louisiana,* 405 U.S. 625, 633 (1972).

32 407 U.S. 493 (1972).

33 Justice White wrote the opinion, and Justice Powell and Brennan concurred.

34 407 U.S., at 500.

35 407 U.S., at 501–2.

36 407 U.S., at 503.

37 391 U.S. 145.

38 329 U.S. 187 (1946).

39 For details see n.21 of *Personnel Administrator v. Feeney*.

40 For a discussion of its divisiveness See Jane Mansbridge, "Who's in Charge Here? Decision by Accretion and Gatekeeping in the Struggle for the ERA," *Politics and Society* 13 (1984): 343–382.

41 430 U.S. 787.

42 The reasonableness of the distinction, said the majority, lay in possible difficulties of proving paternity as contrasted with the generally known identity of mothers (although for the specific litigants, there was no doubt as to paternal identity).

43 453 U.S. 57 (1981).

44 Military Selective Service Act, 50 U.S.C. App. 451 et seq.,

45 Sources for the following four paragraphs of text are as follows: Jane Gross, "Standoff in the Gulf: Needs of Family and Country Clash in Persian Gulf Mission," *The New York Times*, December 9, 1990; Margaret C. Harrell and Laura L. Miller, "New Opportunities for Military Women: Effects upon Readiness, Cohesion, and Morale," (RAND, 1997) (Available at: https://www.rand.org/pubs/monograph_reports/MR896.html, accessed May 27, 2018); Andrea Harter, "1993 Rule Change put Women Closer to Front: Up to 1 in 7 Now in War Zone a Woman," *Arkansas Democrat-Gazette*, April 3, 2003; Jon Nordheimer, "Women's Role in Combat: The War Resumes," *The New York Times,* May 26, 1991; Eric Schmitt, "War Puts U.S. Servicewomen Closer Than Ever to Combat," *The New York Times,* January 22, 1991.

46 Matthew Cox, "After Marine Photo Scandal, Services Issue Social Media Guidelines," Military.com, March 20, 2017. (Available at: https://www.military.com/daily-news/2017/03/20/marine-photo-scandal-services-issue-social-media-guidelines.html, accessed May 1, 2018).

47 Rebecca Kheel, "Gillibrand: Military sexual assault 'as pervasive as ever'," *The Hill*, September 7, 2017. (Available at: http://thehill.com/policy/defense/349672-dem-senator-military-sexual-assault-as-pervasive-as-ever, accessed February 28, 2018).

48 *Women Veterans Report: The Past, Present, and Future of Women Veterans*. National Center for Veterans Analysis and Statistics, Department of Veterans Affairs, Washington, DC, February 2017, p. 17.

49 Craig Whitlock, "In the Military, Trusted Officers have Become Alleged Assailants in Sex Crimes," *The Washington Post*, October 19, 2017.

50 "Fiscal Year 2016 Annual Report on Sexual Assault in the Military," Sexual Assault Prevention and Response Office, U.S. Department of Defense, May 2017 (Available at: http://sapr.mil/public/docs/reports/FY16_Annual/FY16_SAPRO_Annual_Report.pdf, accessed May 27, 2018).

51 Ibid., p. 35.

52 Rebecca Kheel, "Gillibrand: Military sexual assault 'as pervasive as ever,' " note 47 above.

53 Randy Shilts, *Conduct Unbecoming: Gays & Lesbians in the U.S. Military* (New York: St. Martin's Press), 1994, p. 11.

54 Alan Bérubé, *Coming Out Under Fire: The History of Gay Men and Women in World War Two* (New York: The Free Press, 1990), pp. 10–18.

55 National Defense Research Institute, *Sexual Orientation and U.S. Military Personnel Policy: An Update of RAND's 1993 Study*. Santa Monica, CA: RAND Corporation, 2010, p. 7 (Available at: https://www.rand.org/pubs/monographs/MG1056.html, accessed May 27, 2018).

56 Les Aspin, "Qualification Standards for Enlistment, Appointment, and Induction (DoD Directive 1304.26). Washington, DC: Department of Defense (Available at: https://biotech.law.lsu.edu/blaw/dodd/corres/html2/d130426x.htm, accessed May 27, 2018).

57 R.U. Paige, "Proceedings of the American Psychological Association for the Legislative Year 2004: Minutes of the Annual Meeting of the Council of Representatives, July 28 and 30, 2004, Honolulu, Hawaii," *American Psychologist*, 60, no. 5 (2005): 436.

58 Don't Ask, Don't Tell Repeal Act of 2010 (H.R. 2965, S. 4023).

59 Allison Ross, "The Invisible Army: Why the Military Needs to Rescind its Ban on Transgender Service Members," *Southern California Interdisciplinary Law Journal* 23 (2014): 185.

60 Agnes Gereben Schaefer et al., *Assessing the Implications of Allowing Transgender Personnel to Serve Openly*. Santa Monica, CA: RAND Corporation, 2016 (Available at: https://www.rand.org/pubs/research_reports/RR1530.html, accessed May 27, 2018).

61 Brandon Alford and Shawna J. Lee, "Toward Complete Inclusion: Lesbian, Gay, Bisexual, And Transgender Military Service Members After Repeal of Don't Ask, Don't Tell," *Social Work* 61, no. 3 (2016): 258–265.

62 "Secretary of Defense Ash Carter Announces Policy for Transgender Service Members" (Press release). Department of Defense. June 30, 2016 (Available at: https://www.defense.gov/News/News-Releases/News-Release-View/Article/821675/secretary-of-defense-ash-carter-announces-policy-for-transgender-service-members/, accessed May 27, 2018); see also Army Directive 2016–35 (Army Policy on Military Service of Transgender Soldiers), Secretary of the Army, October 7, 2016 (Available at: https://www.army.mil/e2/c/downloads/453704.pdf, accessed May 27, 2018).

63 "In-service Transition for Transgender Service Members," DoD Instruction 1300.28, Office of the Under Secretary of Defense for Personnel and Readiness, U.S. Department of Defense, June 30, 2016 Available at: https://dod.defense.gov/Portals/1/features/2016/0616_policy/DoD-Instruction-1300.28.pdf (accessed November 8, 2018).

64 Helene Cooper and Thomas Gibbons-Neff, "Trump Approves New Limits on Transgender Troops in the Military," *The New York Times*, March 25, 2018.

65 Ibid.

66 Paul Bedard, "Clinton Ends Wait, Names Breyer to Supreme Court; Concerns about Babbitt, Arnold Led to Decision," *The Washington Times*. May 14, 1994, Part A; Pg. A1.

67 *Miller v. Albright*, 523 U.S., at 436–43.

68 *Miller v. Albright*, 523 U.S., at 451.

69 *Tuan Anh Nguyen et al. v. INS*, 533 U.S. 53, 59–73 (2001).

70 Ibid.

71 Ibid., at 74–97.

72 For a review of these cases, see Gayle Binion, " 'Intent' and Equal Protection: A Reconsideration," *Supreme Court Review* 1983 (1983): 397–457.

73 426 U.S. 229.

74 442 U.S. 256.

75 *Rotary International v. Rotary Club of Duarte*, 481 U.S. 537 (1987) and *New York State Club Association v. City of New York*, 487 U.S. 1 (1988).

76 *Isbister v. Boys' Club of Santa Cruz*, 707 P.2d 212 (1985).

77 Lisa Bloom, "Aligning Equal Pay With The Power Of The Internet," (Available at: https://www.forbes.com/sites/forbeswomanfiles/2012/06/27/aligning-equal-pay-with-the-power-of-the-internet/#4ceff8444033, accessed May 16, 2018).

78 *Curran v. Mount Diablo Council of Boy Scouts*, 952 P.2d 218 (1998).

79 Lisa Bloom, "Aligning Equal Pay With The Power Of the Internet," above note 77.

80 530 U.S. 640 (2000).

81 "BSA Addresses Gender Identity," January 30, 2017. (Available at https://www.scoutingnewsroom.org/press-releases/bsa-addresses-gender-identity, accessed May 1, 2018).

CHAPTER 3

Women and Employment

Women have always worked, but they have not always been gainfully employed. This was true not only for slaves, indentured servants, and homemakers, but also in situations where adult males were paid. When the U.S. was an agrarian society, women shared the farm chores and worked in farm-related family businesses; husbands and fathers had no obligation to pay their wives and daughters. "Woman's place is in the home," that venerable antifeminist slogan, made sense only after the Industrial Revolution separated the home from the workplace for the majority of men. Women rarely worked for pay unless they had to for their own and their families' economic survival. The sex segregation of the working world began at this time. The jobs available to women were generally separate from and worse than the men's. Women's hours were even longer, their pay even lower, and their working conditions even less healthy.

The laundry workers of *Muller v. Oregon* were typical of women workers in the 1900s. They were in no danger of being displaced by men who could work longer hours, because men commanded better conditions in the labor market. The bartenders who initiated *Goesaert v. Cleary*, were better off before the ruling than most women workers in 1948. Many women had held similar well-paying blue-collar jobs in World War II, but the vast majority had either quit or been fired after the men came home.[1] Those who needed to work were forced back into the "female job ghetto" of clerical work and unskilled labor. *Goesaert* consigned the women bartenders in Detroit to the same fate. No laws like these exist today. They were either repealed or superseded by federal laws. Although some federal laws contain huge potential loopholes, most courts have interpreted the statutes in reasonably good faith. Sex discrimination in the workplace, once required by state law and accepted by federal law, is now illegal throughout the United States. This is not to suggest that sex discrimination within the work place has ceased to exist—in fact, sexual harassment, wage inequities, and other forms of bias continue to be obstacles—but the fact that it is prohibited as a matter of law provides victims of discrimination with recourse that previously did not exist.

Anti-discrimination law antedates the second wave of feminism. The first federal civil rights laws were enacted during Reconstruction, to protect the rights of former slaves. As we shall see, these laws remain in force today, although the post-Reconstruction Supreme Court weakened them (for about 85 years) by ruling that the Fourteenth Amendment did not give Congress the power to regulate private racial discrimination.[2] The first labor law prohibiting sex discrimination, the Equal Pay Act of 1963, was an amendment to the Fair Labor Standards Act of 1938 FLSA. This law mandated equal pay for "equal work" in order to protect male workers from being replaced by less expensive women workers. Title VII of the historic Civil Rights Act of 1964, the first federal statute since Reconstruction to provide strong legal remedies for racial discrimination, forbade employment discrimination on the basis of "race, color, religion, sex, or national origin." The word "sex" was inserted into the bill by its Southern Democratic opponents in an effort to get it defeated. The amendment provoked derisive laughter on the floor of Congress, but a group of liberal Democrats and moderate Republicans (including the few women serving in the House) got it passed. Since 1964, Congress has passed several civil rights laws broadening the coverage of Title VII, extending the right to sue, and reversing Supreme Court decisions that had allowed differential treatment of employees by sex (see below).[3] Anti-discrimination laws do not enforce themselves, but feminists were quick to see the potential of these laws for improving women's job opportunities, and litigants and government agencies have kept up the pressure on reluctant and resistant employers. The laughter stopped long ago.

While civil rights laws have not brought about sex equality in the workplace, many women have benefited from these laws. At the same time, however, the complexity of individuals' identities is not always easily accommodated by Title VII and/or the courts adjudicating these cases. On the one hand, the cases below demonstrate that a diverse group of women assumed the burden of challenging discriminatory treatment in the workplace: e.g., Mechelle Vinson and Lillian Garland, the successful plaintiffs in two widely publicized Title VII cases, are Black women.[4]

On the other hand, judicial rulings also demonstrate limits to Title VII. The statute focuses on single characteristics, such as race *or* sex, which makes it difficult to deploy for women facing intersectional discrimination—e.g. Black women alleging racialized sex discrimination. As Kimberlé Crenshaw makes clear, the practice of understanding sex discrimination on a single categorical axis (e.g., male-female) privileges some while simultaneously erasing the distinctive experiences and disadvantages of others.[5]

Kimberlé Crenshaw, "Demarginalizing the Intersection of Race and Sex: A Black Feminist Critique of Antidiscrimination Doctrine, Feminist Theory and Antiracist Politics"[6]

In *DeGraffenreid*, five Black women brought suit against General Motors, alleging that the employer's seniority system perpetuated the effects of past discrimination against Black women. Evidence adduced at trial revealed that General Motors simply did not hire Black women prior to 1964 and that all of the Black women hired after 1970 lost their jobs in a seniority-based layoff during a subsequent recession. The district court granted summary judgment for the defendant, rejecting the plaintiffs' attempt to bring a suit not on behalf of Blacks or women, but specifically on behalf of Black women. The court stated:

> [P]laintiffs have failed to cite any decisions which have stated that Black women are a special class to be protected from discrimination. The Court's own research has failed to disclose such a decision. The plaintiffs are clearly entitled to a remedy if they have been discriminated against. However, they should not be allowed to combine statutory remedies to create a new 'super-remedy' which would give them relief beyond what the drafters of the relevant statutes intended. Thus, this lawsuit must be examined to see if it states a cause of action for race discrimination, sex discrimination, or alternatively either, but not a combination of both.

Although General Motors did not hire Black women prior to 1964, the court noted that "General Motors has hired . . .female employees for a number of years prior to the enactment of the Civil Rights Act of 1964." Because General Motors did hire women—albeit *white women*—during the period that no Black women were hired, there was, in the court's view, no sex discrimination that the seniority system could conceivably have perpetuated.

After refusing to consider the plaintiffs' sex discrimination claim, the court dismissed the race discrimination complaint and recommended its consolidation with another case alleging race discrimination against the same employer. The plaintiffs responded that such consolidation would defeat the purpose of their suit since theirs was not purely a race claim, but an action brought specifically on behalf of Black women alleging race *and* sex discrimination. The court, however, reasoned:

> The legislative history surrounding Title VII does not indicate that the goal of the statute was to create a new classification of 'black women' who would have greater standing than, for example, a black male. The prospect of the creation of new classes of protected minorities, governed only by the mathematical principles of permutation and combination, clearly raises the prospect of opening the hackneyed Pandora's box.
>
> Thus, the Court apparently concluded that Congress either did not contemplate that Black women could be discriminated against as "Black women" or did not intend to protect them when such discrimination occurred. The court's refusal in *DeGraffenreid* to acknowledge that Black women encounter combined race and sex discrimination implies that the boundaries of sex and race discrimination doctrine are defined respectively by white women's and Black men's experiences. Under this view, Black women are protected only to the extent that their experiences coincide with those of either of the two groups. Where their experiences are distinct, Black women can expect little protection as long as approaches, such as that in *DeGraffenreid*, which completely obscures problems of intersectionality prevail.

As explained by Crenshaw, anti-discrimination laws are silent about the possibility that a worker can be subjected to a combination of sex and racial discrimination, and effectively exclude many intersectionally-burdened women workers from their coverage. Similarly, other aspects of labor legislation impose disproportionate harms on women of color. New Deal legislation specifically exempted domestic workers from its protective coverage, and Title VII's exemption for employers with fewer than 15 workers achieves the same result for virtually all domestic workers in private homes. Similarly, the lack of legal protection for migrant workers also has a disproportionate effect on racial and ethnic minorities.

EQUAL PAY AND COMPARABLE WORTH

The Equal Pay Act (1963)[7] requires that employers pay equal wages to all employees without regard to their sex "for equal work on jobs the performance of which requires equal skill, effort, and responsibility, and which are performed under similar working conditions." When a violation of the act is alleged, the burden of proof falls on the Department of Labor to show that this command has been disobeyed. Then the accused employer has the opportunity of showing that the unequal pay in question is justified by at least one of four specified exceptions to the equal pay requirement: "(i) a seniority system; (ii) a merit system; (iii) a system which measures earnings by quantity or quality of production; or (iv) a differential based on any factor other than sex." At this point, the burden of proof falls on the accused employer. The Department of Labor has authority to seek court injunctions against discriminatory practices and to seek back-pay restitution for workers subjected to such treatment. A case resulting from such an action reached the Supreme Court in 1974.

Transition to Equal Pay: *Corning Glass Works v. Brennan* (1974)

Corning Glass Works v. Brennan (417 U.S. 188), arose out of a complex situation. The case had its roots in a New York State law dating back to 1927. This law prohibited the employment of women between 10 p.m. and 6 a.m. Before 1925, Corning had operated only a day shift, and all of its inspector jobs were filled by women. After that date, technological changes made a night shift feasible; to fill the night inspector jobs, men were hired. Women day inspectors earned twenty to thirty cents an hour; men night inspectors received fifty-three cents an hour. During this same period, persons who worked at night received no special bonus for night work (what is called a "shift differential"); a day-shift worker in other jobs in the plant earned the same wage as his night-shift counterpart. Beginning in 1944, a labor union agreement forced Corning Glass to pay a shift differential to night workers. This differential (by 1974, sixteen cents an hour extra for night work) did not replace the wage difference between men night inspectors and women day inspectors; rather, it was superimposed on top of the preexisting difference. The male-female wage gap was thus exacerbated.

In 1953 it became legal throughout New York State for women to work at night, and in 1964 the Equal Pay Act became effective at Corning Glass (Congress had permitted a one-year grace period before the act took effect). Corning made no effort to comply with the Equal Pay Act until June 1966. The company's first effort at compliance took the form of opening up night-shift inspector jobs to females. As vacancies occurred, females could now compete with males, on a company seniority basis, for the higher-paying night inspector jobs.

The facts of this case were further complicated in January 1969, at which time Corning Glass made equal the pay of all starting inspector positions—day and night. This new wage meant a substantial raise for the previous day inspectors. Previous night inspectors, however, received the regular (company-wide) 8% raise of their base wage. This made their base pay higher than that of all new inspectors, day or night; and they were allowed to remain (by virtue of what is called a "red circle" provision) at this higher wage. In other words, as of 1969, all persons who had been inspectors before 1969 remained in a two-track wage system. The pre-1969 night inspectors continued to earn a higher base wage than the pre-1969 day inspectors, even though all new inspectors would receive a single base wage (equal to that now received by the pre-1969 day inspectors).

When the case arrived at the Supreme Court, the Justices had to answer two questions about this complicated situation. First, did working the night shift constitute a difference in "working conditions"? If it did, then Corning was paying unequal pay for unequal work and would not be in violation of the statute. Second, could the extra pay for the job of night inspector be justified on the grounds of a "factor other than sex," such as the additional stress attendant to nighttime employment? Two different federal circuit courts had given opposite answers to the first of these questions.

The Supreme Court's answer to both questions was negative; the justices held further that the changes implemented by Corning in 1966 and 1969 were inadequate remedies to the illegal situation. Justice Marshall wrote the opinion for the majority of five, and it consisted essentially of a detailed legislative history of the Equal Pay Act, with particular attention to deciphering Congress's meaning in regard to the phrases "working conditions" and "factor other than sex." Their conclusions are summarized in the following excerpts from Marshall's opinion:

> While laymen might well assume that time of day worked reflects one aspect of a job's "working conditions," the term has a different and much more specific meaning in the language of industrial relations. As Corning's own representative testified at the hearings, the element working conditions encompasses two subfactors: "surroundings" and "hazards." "Surroundings" measures the elements, such as toxic chemicals or fumes, regularly encountered by a worker, their intensity, and their frequency. "Hazards" takes into account the physical hazards regularly encountered, their frequency, and the severity of injury they can cause. This definition of "working conditions" is not only manifested in Corning's own job evaluation plans but is also well accepted across a wide range of American industry.
>
> Nowhere in any of these definitions is time of day worked mentioned as a relevant criterion. The fact of the matter is that the concept of "working conditions," as used in the specialized language of job evaluation systems, simply does not encompass shift differentials. . . .

This does not mean, of course, that there is no room in the Equal Pay Act for nondiscriminatory shift differentials. Work on a steady night shift no doubt has psychological and physiological impacts making it less attractive than work on a day shift. The Act contemplates that a male night worker may receive a higher wage than a female day worker, just as it contemplates that a male employee with 20 years' seniority can receive a higher wage than a woman with two years' seniority. Factors such as these play a role under the Act's four exceptions-the seniority differential under the specific seniority exception, the shift differential under the catchall exception for differentials "based on any other factor other than sex."

The question remains, however, whether Corning carried its burden of proving that the higher rate paid for night inspection work, until 1966 performed solely by men, was in fact intended to serve as compensation for night work, or rather constituted an added payment based upon sex. We agree that the record amply supports the District Court's conclusion that Corning had not sustained its burden of proof. As its history revealed, "the higher night rate was in large part the product of the generally higher wage level of male workers and the need to compensate them for performing what were regarded as demeaning tasks." 474 F. 2d, at 233. . . . That the company took advantage of such a situation may be understandable as a matter of economics, but its differential nevertheless became illegal once Congress enacted into law the principle of equal pay for equal work.

. . . .[T]he issue before us is not whether the company, in some abstract sense, can be said to have treated men the same as women after 1966. Rather, the question is whether the company remedied the specific violation of the Act which the Secretary proved. We agree with the Second Circuit, as well as with all other circuits that have had occasion to consider this issue, that the company could not cure its violation except by equalizing the base wages of female day inspectors[, which it has not done]. . . .[8]

Pensions

Sex-based pay differentials are prohibited both by the Equal Pay Act and by Title VII of the Civil Rights Act of 1964. Because women on the average live longer than men, however, employers often required women to make larger contributions than men to their pension funds or paid them less in benefits after they retired. *Los Angeles Department of Water and Power v. Manhart* (1978) applied Title VII to what was essentially an equal pay case. The statutory clause at issue was § 703[a][1], which forbade sex discrimination "with respect to...compensation, terms, conditions, or privileges of employment." The Supreme Court ruled, 6–2, that it amounted to illegal sex discrimination to require female employees to deduct from their salaries larger monthly pension fund contributions than male employees. Five years later, *Arizona Governing Committee v. Norris* invalidated sex discrimination in monthly (post-retirement) pension payments.

Comparable Worth

"Comparable worth" (sometimes called "pay equity"), was often called the civil rights issue of the 1980s. The term refers generally to a program of providing equal (or "comparable") pay for jobs involving comparable overall effort, skill, responsibility, and working conditions. Although the wage gap between men and women has narrowed considerably since the 1960s, according to the U.S. Census Bureau, women working full time earned 80.5 cents to a man's dollar in 2016: the median salary for a woman was $41,544 and for a man it was $51,640. The wage gap is even larger for women of color. While white women earn 79 percent of what men earn on an annual basis, Black women earned 62.5 percent and Latinas earned 54.4 percent of what white men earned in a given year.[9] The Institute for Women's Policy Research estimates that women will achieve pay parity in 2059, but it will take Black women until 2124 and Latina women until 2248 to do so.[10] This gap is largely attributable to the fact that many of the jobs occupied largely by women have lower wages than jobs held largely by men, but across nearly all jobs women on average earn less than men for doing the same work.[11] Sex discrimination and implicit biases interact with racism to exacerbate the wage gap.

Neither the history nor the language of the Equal Pay Act provides support for a "comparable worth" interpretation. The idea of setting workers' pay by comparing occupations did not exist in 1963. The law's exemption of any differential based on a "factor other than sex" suggests that "equal work" meant "work in the same jobs." When sex discrimination was added to the list of discriminations forbidden by Title VII, an amendment, 42 U.S.C. § 2000e–2(h), provided that "it shall not be an unlawful employment practice...for an employer to differentiate upon the basis of sex in determining...wages or compensation...if such differentiation is authorized by" the Equal Pay Act. In *Washington County v. Gunther* (1981), the U.S. Supreme Court decided that the requirement of precisely "equal work" from the Equal Pay Act had not been incorporated into Title VII, but the Court went out of its way to deny that it was endorsing "the controversial theory of comparable worth."

Thus, the women in Washington County, hired for the job of guard in the women's jail, even though the job had been ruled not "substantially equal" to men's jail guard (because there were so many fewer prisoners in the former), and even though no males were ever hired for the job of guard in the women's jail, still could bring a Title VII lawsuit, the Supreme Court ruled. The women claimed that the county administrators had evaluated the women's job as worth 95% of the men's and had then downgraded the women's salary to 70% of the men's because they knew that women will work for less than men. In other words, the allegation was that the women's wages had been lowered well below the degree appropriate for non-comparability of the work, on the basis of sheer sex discrimination. The Court reasoned that this was a valid Title VII claim and sent it back to the lower courts for hearings as to proof of the allegation. In 1986, the state and the major employees' union agreed on a multi-million dollar pay equity pact.

Some comparable worth advocates took encouragement from this outcome. They hoped they could convince courts of the weakness of employers' claims that paying lower wages for women-dominated jobs is simply a response to market forces, which fit into the "factor other than sex" exception. The counter-argument to this assertion is that sex discrimination pervades the market and thus shapes the market forces; therefore, market forces cannot be a "factor other than sex." Several states have adopted a comparable worth policy for state employees, either by legislative mandate or executive initiative.[12] But the federal government has consistently rejected comparable worth. All five EEOC (Equal Opportunity Employment Commission) commissioners voted against it in 1985, and so has every federal appellate court that has heard a relevant case.[13]

Studies of states where it was adopted showed little improvement in women's wages. Explanations of that fact ranged from blaming compromises built into the programs (such as agreements on not lowering anyone's wages, but only upgrading, such that all lowest-paid workers ended up with raises, not only women) to the assertion that fewer women could get hired once the pay had been raised.[14]

Since the 1980s, much less has been heard about comparable worth. Although a comparable worth act was introduced into every Congress beginning in 1993, these acts made little headway.[15] For instance, Representative Rosa DeLauro (D-CT) introduced the Paycheck Fairness Act in 1997 where it was referred to the House Committee on Education and the Workforce and died in committee.[16] The bill was reintroduced for the next several years, failing each time in both the House and Senate[17] until 2009 when the bill passed 256–163 in the House.[18] Senator Hillary Clinton introduced the bill in the Senate on January 8, 2009 although no vote was taken after the Health, Education, Labor, and Pensions Committee held hearings on the bill. Since then, the Paycheck Fairness Act has been re-introduced in every congressional session without passage.[19]

An amendment to the FLSA and the Equal Pay Act, this bill would limit "factors other than sex" for justifying pay differentials to bona fide factors, such as education, training, or experience, and would require that one of these factors account for "the entire differential in compensation at issue" in order to validate this defense.[20] It also prohibits employer retaliation against employees who disclose their wages to their coworkers and/or discuss company compensation policies. This type of transparency is necessary in order for individuals to determine if there are unjust and illegal variations in employee compensation as demonstrated by the Lilly Ledbetter case to be discussed below. As such, the Paycheck Fairness Act would close a number of the loopholes that exist under the Equal Pay Act and work to remedy ongoing issues of pay discrimination on the basis of sex in the workplace.

TITLE VII AND THE BFOQ EXEMPTION

The prohibition against employment discrimination based on race is absolute. Sex, religion, or national origin, however, may be a "bona fide occupational qualification reasonably necessary to the normal operation of that particular business or enterprise" (BFOQ), and as such can justify a refusal to hire someone. Unlike Equal Protection Clause cases, Title VII claims do not require a finding of intent to discriminate. Employers defending a sex discrimination case either deny that any such discrimination occurred or claim a "BFOQ" exception. Since the employer determines what is reasonably necessary, BFOQ is a potentially huge loophole. But federal courts have not interpreted it that way.

Women's Labor Legislation

Most states still had protective legislation on the books when the Civil Rights Act of 1964 became law. The contradiction between a law prohibiting sex-based employment discrimination and, say, a law forbidding women to work in certain jobs is as obvious as the rule for resolving conflicts between federal and state law is unambiguous. Since federal law is "the supreme law of the land," the federal law pre-empts the state law.[21] By 1968, federal district courts had decided three cases, all involving state laws limiting the amount of weight women could lift.

Women and Employment

Georgia and Minnesota courts had upheld the state laws as meeting the BFOQ exemption, but a California court ruled that Title VII negated that state's law.[22]

Weeks v. Southern Bell (1969)

Weeks v. Southern Bell, the Georgia case, was the first to reach the federal Court of Appeals. This ruling by a unanimous three-judge panel of the Fifth Circuit resolved the case in favor of Title VII and against special rules for women.

Like many of the occupations involved in Title VII litigation, the position for which Lorena Weeks had applied—telephone switchman—was among the better-paying and higher-status skilled blue-collar jobs once held exclusively by men. Switchmen were required to maintain equipment and make repairs in both the office and out in the field. Weeks had already worked at Southern Bell for 19 years as a telephone operator. These workers, virtually all of whom were women in the U.S., worked in conditions that resembled sweatshops, closely crowded into small quarters under heavy supervision. The telephone company had earned a reputation as "the nation's largest oppressor of women."[23] When Southern Bell rebuffed Weeks's application, she filed a charge of discrimination with the EEOC.

WEEKS V. SOUTHERN BELL
408 F.2d 228 (1969)

II.

Turning to the merits we observe that there is no dispute that Mrs. Weeks was denied the switchman's job because she was a woman, not because she lacked any qualifications as an individual. The job was awarded to the only other bidder for the job, a man who had less seniority than Mrs. Weeks. Under the terms of the contract between Mrs. Weeks' Union and Southern Bell, the senior bidder is to be awarded the job if other qualifications are met. Southern Bell, in effect, admits a prima facie violation of § 703(a) of the Civil Rights Act of 1964, 42 U.S.C. § 2000e–2(a), which provides in pertinent part:

"(a) Employer practices.

It shall be an unlawful employment practice for an employer—(1) to fail or refuse to hire or to discharge any individual, or otherwise to discriminate against any individual with respect to his compensation, terms, conditions, or privileges of employment, because of such individual's . . . sex . . ."

Southern Bell's answer, however, asserts by way of affirmative defense that the switchman's position fits within the exception to the general prohibition of discrimination against women set forth in § 703(e)(1), 42 U.S.C. § 2000e–2(e)(1), which provides in pertinent part:

"(e) Notwithstanding any other provision of this subchapter, (1) it shall not be an unlawful employment practice for an employer to hire and employ employees, . . . on the basis of his . . . sex, . . . in those certain instances where . . . sex, . . . in a *bona fide occupational qualification* reasonably necessary to the normal operation of that particular business or enterprise, . . ." (Emphasis added.)

The job description of the post of switchman reads as follows:

"Engaged in the maintenance and operation of dial central office equipment, test, power, frame, switch, and other telephone equipment, including the locating and correcting of faults; making adjustments, additions, repairs, and replacements; performing routine operation tests, etc., and working with test-desk, field, and other forces connected with central office work. Also operates and maintains, including adjusting and making repairs to or replacement of, air conditioning equipment, and performing other work as assigned in accordance with local circumstances and the current needs of the business."

We think it is clear that the burden of proof must be on Southern Bell to demonstrate that this position fits within the "bona fide occupational qualification" exception. The legislative history indicates that this exception was intended to be narrowly construed. This is also the construction put on the exception by the Equal Employment Opportunity Commission. Finally, when dealing with a humanitarian remedial statute which serves an important public purpose, it has been the practice to cast the burden of proving an exception to the general policy of the statute upon the person claiming it.

The more important question that must be decided here, however, is the extent of the showing required to satisfy that burden. In the court below, Southern Bell contended that a bona fide occupational qualification was created whenever reasonable state protective legislation prevented women from occupying certain positions. Southern Bell relied upon Rule 59, promulgated by the Georgia Commissioner of Labor pursuant to § 54–122(d) of the Georgia Code, which provides: "*Lifting.* For women and minors, not over 30 pounds.

Less depending on physical condition of women or minors. Minor as used here means anyone under 18 years of age, male or females."

The Commission has recognized that reasonable state protective legislation may constitute a bona fide occupational qualification. Thus, § 1604.1(3) of the Commission's guidelines provides:

> The Commission does not believe that Congress intended to disturb such laws and regulations which are intended to, and have the effect of, protecting women against exploitation and hazard. Accordingly, the Commission will consider qualifications set by such state laws or regulations to be bona fide occupational qualifications, and thus not in conflict with Title VII ... so, for example, restrictions on lifting will be honored except where the limit is set at an unreasonably low level which could not endanger women.

Mrs. Weeks does not dispute on appeal that the position of switchman occasionally requires lifting of weights in excess of 30 pounds. She has consistently contended that the Georgia limit is unreasonably low and that the Georgia Commissioner of Labor's Rule 59 does not have the intent or effect of protecting women from hazard. She also contends that the rule is arbitrary in violation of the equal protection clause of the Fourteenth Amendment and that it is contrary to Title VII and thus in violation of the supremacy clause, art. 6, cl. 2 of the Constitution. In this regard, it may be noted that a United States District Court has recently held that provisions of the California Labor Code restricting lifting by women to weights of 25 pounds and under is a restriction set at an unreasonably low level within the meaning of the Commission's guidelines and that even if 25 pounds did not constitute an unreasonably low level within the meaning of those guidelines, such restrictions are still contrary to Title VII of the Civil Rights Act and must yield. *Rosenfeld v. Southern Pacific Co.*, 293 F. Supp. 1219 (C.D. Cal. 1968).

We need not decide the reasonableness or the constitutionality of Rule 59, however, because effective August 27, 1968, Georgia repealed Rule 59. In its place, the Georgia Commissioner of Labor has promulgated a rule which reads: Weights of loads which are lifted or carried manually shall be limited so as to avoid strains or undue fatigue."

The decision to repeal the specific weight limit seems to have been at least partially motivated by, and is in conformity with, the recommendations of the Task Force on Labor Standards of the Citizens' Advisory Council on the Status of Women. The President's Commission pointed out: "Restrictions that set fixed maximum limits upon weights women are allowed to lift do not take account of individual differences, are sometimes unrealistic, and always rigid. They should be replaced by flexible regulations applicable to both men and women and set by appropriate regulatory bodies."

Because the new, flexible rule does not in terms necessarily prevent all women from performing the duties of switchman, the issue of protective state legislation disappears from the case. We are left with the question whether Southern Bell, as a private employer, has satisfied its burden of proving that the particular requirements of the job of switchman justify excluding women from consideration.

In ruling for Southern Bell, the District Court relied primarily on the effect of Rule 59. It did, however, make some additional findings of fact which Southern Bell contends are sufficient to satisfy its burden:

> At the trial of the case, the evidence established that a switchman is required to routinely and regularly lift items of equipment weighing in excess of thirty (30) pounds. Additionally, the evidence established that there is other strenuous activity involved in this job....The evidence established that a switchman is subject to call out 24 hours a day and is, in fact, called out at all hours and is sometimes required to work alone during late night hours, including the period from midnight to 6 a. m. In the event of an emergency or equipment failure, the switchman would be required to lift items of equipment weighing well in excess of thirty (30) pounds.

Southern Bell puts principal reliance on the fact that the District Court found the job to be "strenuous." That finding is extremely vague. We note, moreover, that Southern Bell introduced no evidence that the duties of a switchman were so strenuous that all, or substantially all, women would be unable to perform them. Nor did the District Court make a finding on this more concrete and meaningful statement of the issue. The Commission in its investigation, on the other hand, rejected Southern Bell's contention "that the switchman job at this location requires weight lifting or strenuous exertion which could not be performed by females." In addition, Mrs. Weeks produced testimony to the effect that she was capable of performing the job, that a woman in New York had been hired as a switchman and that seven others were performing the job of frameman, the duties of which were essentially indistinguishable from those of a switchman.

In examining the record carefully to interpret the finding that the duties of a switchman were "strenuous," we have observed that although Southern Bell attempted to connect a switchman's duties with various pieces of heavy equipment, only a 31-pound item called a "relay timing test set" was used "regularly and routinely" by a switchman. The testimony at trial and the Commission's investigation reveal that in actually using the set the normally accepted practice is to place the test set on the floor or on a rolling step-ladder and that very little lifting of it was required. Thus, while there would be a basis for finding that a switchman's job would require lifting technically in excess of a 30-pound weight limitation, the infrequency of the required lifting would permit quibbling over just how "strenuous" the job is. But we do not believe courts need engage in this sort of quibbling. Labeling a job "strenuous" simply does not meet the burden of proving that the job is within the bona fide occupational qualification exception.

As indicated above, the Commission appeared in *Rosenfeld v. Southern Pacific Co.*, to urge that the California weight limitation legislation be struck down. In so doing, the Commission successfully contended that this broad construction of the bona fide occupational qualification exception should not be followed. The Commission's amicus brief there stated that it has consistently interpreted its regulations as being incompatible with the idea that privately-imposed weight limitations on women are within the bona fide occupational qualification exception. It has taken that position on a case involving a 35-pound weight limit. The Commission relied upon its guidelines found in 29 C.F.R. Sec. 1601.1(a):

> (1) The Commission will find that the following situations do not warrant the application of the bona fide occupational qualification exception: (i) the refusal to hire a woman because of her sex, based on assumptions of the comparative employment characteristics of women in general.... (ii) the refusal to hire an individual based on stereotyped characterizations of the sexes....

It may be that where an employer sustains its burden in demonstrating that it is impossible or highly impractical to deal with women on an individualized basis, it may apply a reasonable general rule.

Southern Bell has clearly not met that burden here. They introduced no evidence concerning the lifting abilities of women. Rather, they would have us "assume," on the basis of a "stereotyped characterization" that few or no women can safely lift 30 pounds, while all men are treated as if they can. While one might accept, *arguendo*, that men are stronger on the average than women, it is not clear that any conclusions about relative lifting ability would follow. This is because it can be argued tenably that technique is as important as strength in determining lifting ability. Technique is hardly a function of sex. What does seem clear is that using these class stereotypes denies desirable positions to a great many women perfectly capable of performing the duties involved.

Southern Bell's remaining contentions do not seem to be advanced with great seriousness. The emergency work which a switchman allegedly must perform consists primarily in the handling of a 34-pound extinguisher in the event of fire. A speculative emergency like that could be used as a smoke screen by any employer bent on discriminating against women. It does seem that switchmen are occasionally subject to late hour call-outs. Of course, the record also reveals that other women employees are subject to call after midnight in emergencies. Moreover, Title VII rejects just this type of romantic paternalism as unduly Victorian and instead vests individual women with the power to decide whether or not to take on unromantic tasks. Men have always had the right to determine whether the incremental increase in remuneration for strenuous, dangerous, obnoxious, boring or unromantic tasks is worth the candle. The promise of Title VII is that women are now to be on equal footing. We cannot conclude that by including the bona fide occupational qualification exception Congress intended to renege on that promise.

Having concluded that Southern Bell has not satisfied its burden of proving that the job of switchman is within the bona fide occupational qualification exception, we must reverse the District Court on this issue and hold that Southern Bell has violated 42 U.S.C. § 2000e–2(a).

Case Questions

1. If "all or substantially all women" cannot perform a task, how does Title VII affect an exceptional woman who can perform it?

2. One section of Title VII provides that "Nothing in this title shall be deemed to exempt or relieve any person from any liability...or punishment provided by any present or future law of any State,...other than any such law which purports to require or permit the doing of any act which would be an unlawful employment practice under this title." What do you think Congress meant by this provision?

Rosenfeld v. Southern Pacific (1971)

Two years after *Weeks*, a federal appeals court ruled outright that Title VII pre-empted protective labor legislation.

ROSENFELD V. SOUTHERN PACIFIC COMPANY
444 F.2d 1219 (9th Cir. 1971)

HAMLEY, CIRCUIT JUDGE.

Leah Rosenfeld brought this action against Southern Pacific Company pursuant to § 706(f) of Title VII of the Civil Rights Act of 1964 (Act), 42 U.S.C. § 2000e–5(f). Plaintiff, an employee of the company, alleged that in filling the position of agent-telegrapher at Thermal, California, in March, 1966, Southern Pacific discriminated against her solely because of her sex, by assigning the position to a junior male employee.

On the merits, Southern Pacific argues that it is the company's policy to exclude women, generically, from certain positions. The company restricts these job opportunities to men for two basic reasons: (1) the arduous nature of the work-related activity renders women physically unsuited for the jobs; (2) appointing a woman to the position would result in a violation of California labor laws and regulations which limit hours of work for women and restrict the weight they are permitted to lift. Positions such as that of agent-telegrapher at Thermal fall within the ambit of this policy. The company concludes that effectuation of this policy is not proscribed by Title VII of the Civil Rights Act due to the exception created by the Act for those situations where sex is a "bona fide occupational qualification."

While the agent-telegrapher position at Thermal is no longer in existence, the work requirements which that position entailed are illustrative of the kind of positions which are denied to female employees under the company's labor policy described above. During the harvesting season, the position may require work in excess of ten hours a day and eighty hours a week. The position requires the heavy physical effort involved in climbing over and around boxcars to adjust their vents, collapse their bunkers and close and seal their doors. In addition, the employee must lift various objects weighing more than twenty-five pounds and, in some instances, more than fifty pounds.

The critical question presented by this argument is whether, consistent with Title VII of the Civil Rights Act of 1964, the company may apply such a labor policy. The pertinent provision of Title VII is § 703(a) of the Act, 42 U.S.C. § 2000e–2(a). [See *Weeks* above, for text of its subsection (1).]...Southern Pacific's employment policy under which, for example, it has denied Mrs. Rosenfeld an employment assignment on the ground that women, considered generically, are not physically or biologically suited for such work, results in distinguishing employees, thus discriminating against some because of sex, within the meaning of subsection (1) of this provision. It also [violates subsection (2) which forbids employers "to limit, segregate, or classify . . . employees or applicants for employment in a[ ] way which would deprive or tend to deprive an[ ] individual of employment opportunities . . . because of such individual's . . . sex. . . ."]

There is therefore no doubt that the type of discrimination against women broadly prohibited by Title VII occurs under Southern Pacific's personnel policy. However, appellants contend that § 703(e) of the Act, 42 U.S.C. § 2000e–2(e), provides specific authority for Southern Pacific's described employment policy. This subsection reads:

> (e) . . . it shall not be an unlawful employment practice for an employer to hire and employ [an employee]. . . on the basis of his religion, sex, or national origin in those certain instances where religion, sex, or national origin is a bona fide occupational qualification reasonably necessary to the normal operation of that particular business or enterprise. . .

We deal first with Southern Pacific's argument that the strenuous physical demands of the position, both as to the hours of work and the physical activity required, render sex "a bona fide occupational qualification reasonably necessary to the normal operation of that particular business or enterprise, . . ." The company contends that under the formulation put forward by the Fifth Circuit in *Weeks v. Southern Bell Tel. & Tel. Co.*, 408 F.2d 228 (5th Cir. 1969), if Southern Pacific could prove it "had . . . a factual basis for believing, that all or substantially all women would be unable to perform safely and effectively the duties of the job involved," *Id.* at 235, it could properly rely on the BFOQ exception as a legal basis for excluding women generically from positions such as that of agent-telegrapher at Thermal. Southern Pacific contends that it should not have been denied the opportunity to present such proof by the mechanism of summary judgment.

In the case before us, there is no contention that the sexual characteristics of the employee are crucial to the successful performance of the job, as they would be for the position of a wet-nurse, nor is there a need for authenticity or genuineness, as in the case of an actor or actress. 29 C.F.R. § 1604.1(a)(2). Rather, on the basis of a general assumption regarding the physical capabilities of female employees, the company attempts to raise a commonly accepted characterization of women as the "weaker sex" to the level of a BFOQ. The personnel policy of Southern Pacific here in question is based on "characteristics generally attributed to the group" of exactly the same type that the Commission has announced should not be the basis of an employment decision. 29 C.F.R. § 1604.1(a)(1)(ii). Based on the legislative intent and on the Commission's interpretation, sexual characteristics, rather than characteristics that might, to one degree or another, correlate with a particular sex, must be the basis for the application of the BFOQ exception. *See* "Developments in the Law—Title VII," 84 *Harv. L. Rev.* 1109, 1178–1179 (1971). Southern Pacific has not, and could not allege such a basis here, and § 703(e) thus could not exempt its policy from the impact of Title VII. There was no error in the granting of summary judgment. . . .

The premise of Title VII, the wisdom of which is not in question here, is that women are now to be on equal footing with men. *Weeks v. Southern Bell Tel. & Tel. Co.*, 408 F.2d 228, 236 (5th Cir. 1969). The footing is not equal if a male employee may be appointed to a particular position on a showing that he is physically qualified, but a female employee is denied an opportunity to demonstrate personal physical qualification. Equality of footing is established only if employees otherwise entitled to the position, whether male or female, are excluded only upon a showing of individual incapacity. See *Bowe v. Colgate-Palmolive Co.*, 416 F.2d 711, 718 (7th Cir. 1969). This alone accords with the Congressional purpose to eliminate subjective assumptions and traditional stereotyped conceptions regarding the physical ability of women to do particular work. See *Weeks v. Southern Bell Tel. & Tel. Co.*, at 235–236 (5th Cir. 1969); *Bowe v. Colgate-Palmolive Co.*, at 717 (7th Cir. 1969). See also, *Shultz v. First Victoria Nat'l Bank*, 420 F.2d 648, 656 (5th Cir. 1969) (interpreting the Equal Pay Act of 1963, 29 U.S.C. § 206(d)(1)).

But the company points out that, apart from its intrinsic merit, its policy is compelled by California labor laws. . . .Not only would the repeated lifting of weights in excess of twenty-five pounds violate the state's Industrial Welfare Order No. 9-63, but for her to lift more than fifty pounds as required by the job would violate § 1251 of the California Labor Code. Likewise, the peak-season days of over ten hours would violate § 1350 of the California Labor Code.

It would appear that these state law limitations upon female labor run contrary to the general objectives of Title VII of the Civil Rights Act of 1964, as reviewed above, and are therefore, by virtue of the Supremacy Clause, supplanted by Title VII. However, appellants again rely on § 703(e) and argue that since positions such as the Thermal agent-telegrapher required weight-lifting and maximum hours in excess of those permitted under the California statutes, being a man was indeed a bona fide occupational qualification. This argument assumes that Congress, having established by Title VII the policy that individuals must be judged as individuals, and not on the basis of characteristics generally attributed to racial, religious, or sex groups, was willing for this policy to be thwarted by state legislation to the contrary.

We find no basis in the statute or its legislative history for such an assumption. Section 1104 of the Act, 42 U.S.C. § 2000h–4, provides that nothing contained in the Act should be construed as indicating an intent to occupy the field in which the Act operates, to the exclusion of State laws or the same subject matter, nor be construed as invalidating any provision of state law ". . . unless such provision is inconsistent with any of the purposes of this Act, or any provision thereof." This section was added to the Act to save state laws aimed at preventing or punishing discrimination, and as the quoted words indicate, not to save inconsistent state laws. (H.R. Rep. No. 914, 88th Cong. 1st Sess. 1963 additional views of Hon. George Meader).

Still more to the point is § 708 of the Act, 42 U.S.C. § 2000e–7, which provides that nothing in Title VII shall be deemed to exempt or relieve any person from any liability. . .or punishment provided by any present or future state law ". . . other than any such law which purports to require or permit the doing of any act which would be an unlawful employment practice under this title." This section was designed to preserve the effectiveness of state antidiscrimination laws (110 Cong. Rec. 7243, 12721 1964, comments of Senators Case and Humphrey).

The Commission, created by the provisions of Title VII of the Act, through its published Guidelines and Policy Statements has, albeit after considerable hesitation, taken the position that state "protective" legislation, of the type in issue here, conflicts with the policy of non-discrimination manifested by Title VII of the Act. On August 19, 1969, the Commission revoked a portion of its Guidelines on Discrimination because of Sex, formerly appearing as 29 C.F.R. § 1604.1(a)(3), (b) and (c), and inserted a new subsection. It is implicit in this Commission pronouncement that state labor laws inconsistent with the general objectives of the Act must be disregarded. The Supreme Court has recently observed that the administrative interpretation of the Act by the enforcing agency "is entitled to great deference." *Griggs v. Duke Power Co.*, 401 U.S. 424 (1971).

Affirmed.

"SEX PLUS" DISCRIMINATION

Phillips v. Martin-Marietta (1971)

In the case of *Phillips v. Martin-Marietta Corp.*, the U.S. Supreme Court began to implement the sex discrimination provisions of Title VII of the 1964 Civil Rights Act. The Equal Employment Opportunity Commission (EEOC), the enforcement agency for this act, still had no effective mechanism for enforcing the act. Suit against *Martin-Marietta Corporation*, therefore, was brought by a private individual, Ida Phillips. Ms. Phillips had tried to apply for a job with *Martin-Marietta* and had met with the response that the company did not accept job applications from women with pre-school-age children. Ms. Phillips viewed this practice as discrimination based on sex, and she sued in federal court to obtain an order that she be hired.

As noted above, Title VII makes it unlawful for an employer "to refuse to hire...any individual...because of such individual's race, color, religion, sex, or national origin" except where "religion, sex, or national origin is a bona fide occupational qualification reasonably necessary to the normal operation of that particular business." *Martin-Marietta* did hire men with pre-school-age children. However, in the job slot for which Ms. Phillips tried to apply, assembly trainee, 70–75 percent of the applicants, and 75–80 percent of the persons hired for the job, were women.

Because of these figures, the federal district court granted **summary judgment** (judgment without a full formal hearing) in favor of the corporation, stating that a pattern of "bias against women as such" had not been presented. The Circuit Court of Appeals upheld the District Court. The Supreme Court in **per curiam** opinion (one authored anonymously for the Court as a group) sent the case back to the court of appeals to reconsider, as follows:

PHILLIPS V. MARTIN-MARIETTA CORP.
400 U.S. 542 (1971)

PER CURIAM.

* * *

Section 703(a) of the Civil Rights Act of 1964 requires that persons of like qualifications be given employment opportunities irrespective of their sex. The Court of Appeals therefore erred in reading this section as permitting one hiring policy for women and another for men—each having pre-school-age children. The existence of such conflicting family obligations, if demonstrably more relevant to job performance for a woman than for a man, could arguably be a basis for distinction under § 703(e) of the Act. But that is a matter of evidence tending to show that the condition in question "is a bona fide occupational qualification reasonably necessary to the normal operation of that particular business or enterprise." The record before us, however, is not adequate for resolution of these important issues. Summary judgment was therefore improper and we remand for fuller development of the record and for further consideration.

Vacated and remanded.

MR. JUSTICE MARSHALL, concurring.

While I agree that this case must be remanded for a full development of the facts, I cannot agree with the Court's indication that a "bona fide occupational qualification reasonably necessary to the normal operation of" Martin-Marietta's business could be established by a showing that some women, even the vast majority, with pre-school-age children have family responsibilities that interfere with job performance and that men do not usually have such responsibilities. Certainly, an employer can require that all of his employees, both men and women, meet minimum performance standards, and he can try to insure compliance by requiring parents, both mothers and fathers, to provide for the care of their children so that job performance is not interfered with.

But the Court suggests that it would not require such uniform standards. I fear that in this case, where the issue is not squarely before us, the Court has fallen into the trap of assuming that the Act permits ancient canards about the proper role of women to be a basis for discrimination. Congress, however, sought just the opposite result.

By adding the prohibition against job discrimination based on sex to the 1964 Civil Rights Act Congress intended to prevent employers from refusing "to hire an individual based on stereotyped characterizations of the sexes." EEOC Guidelines on Discrimination Because of Sex, 29 CFR § 1604.1(a)(i)(iii). . . . Even characterizations of the proper domestic roles of the sexes were not to serve as predicates for restricting employment opportunity. The exception for a "bona fide occupational qualification" was not intended to swallow the rule.

That exception has been construed by the EEOC, whose regulations are entitled to "great deference," *Udall v. Tallman*, 380 U.S. 1, 16, to be applicable only to job situations that require specific physical characteristics necessarily possessed by only one sex.[1] Thus the exception would apply where necessary "for the purpose of authenticity or genuineness" in the employment of actors or actresses, fashion models and the like. If the exception is to be limited as Congress intended, the Commission has given it the only possible construction.

When performance characteristics of an individual are involved, even when parental roles are concerned, employment opportunity may be limited only by employment criteria that are neutral as to the sex of the applicant.

Opinion Footnote

1 The Commission's regulations provide:

"Sex as a bona fide occupational qualification.

"(a) The Commission believes that the bona fide occupational qualification exception as to sex should be interpreted narrowly. Labels 'Men's jobs' and 'Women's jobs' tend to deny employment opportunities unnecessarily to one sex or the other.

"(1) The Commission will find that the following situations do not warrant the application of the bona fide occupational qualification exception:

"(i) The refusal to hire a woman because of her sex, based on assumption of the comparative employment characteristics of women in general. For example, the assumption that the turnover rate among women is higher than among men.

"(ii) The refusal to hire an individual based on stereotyped characterizations of the sexes. Such stereotypes include, for example, that men are less capable of assembling intricate equipment; that women are less capable of aggressive salesmanship. The principle of non-discrimination requires that individuals be considered on the basis of individual capacities and not on the basis of any characteristics generally attributed to the group.

* * *

"(b)(1) Many States have enacted laws or promulgated administrative regulations with respect to the employment of females. Among these laws are those which prohibit or limit the employment of females, e.g., the employment of females in certain occupations, in jobs requiring the lifting or carrying of weights exceeding certain prescribed limits, during certain hours of the night, or for more than a specified number of hours per day or per week.

"(2) The Commission believes that such State laws and regulations, although originally promulgated for the purpose of protecting females, have ceased to be relevant to our technology or to the expanding role of the female worker in our economy. The Commission has found that such laws and regulations do not take into account the capacities, preferences, and abilities of individual females and tend to discriminate rather than protect. Accordingly. . .such laws and regulations conflict with Title VII of the Civil Rights Act of 1964 and will not be considered a defense to an otherwise established unlawful employment practice or as a basis for the application of the bona fide occupational qualification exception." 29 CFR § 1604.1.

Case Questions

1. How do you respond to Justice Marshall's fear that when the Court says that "conflicting family obligations" must be demonstrated by evidence in court before "a woman" is refused a job on that basis, the Court really means that proof need only be presented regarding "some women" or most women? If his prediction were correct, would this approach undermine the spirit of Title VII?

2. The EEOC guidelines quoted in Marshall's footnotes suggest that state labor legislation intended to be protective of women, which singles them out for special treatment as a group, is no longer valid, because it conflicts with Title VII. Would it be preferable to read Title VII as permitting such legislation?

Case note: Only in March 1972, after the Supreme Court had begun in the *Phillips* case to take a really searching look at sex discrimination, did Congress provide the EEOC with the power to sue discriminating employers in court. That weapon provided the commission with the clout to back up its conciliation efforts; now that the commission could threaten court action, the possibilities for generous out-of-court settlements were considerably broadened. In January 1973, the EEOC obtained its first really substantial out-of-court settlement. The American Telephone and Telegraph Company (AT&T) consented to pay $15 million in back pay to thousands of discriminated-against female employees.[24]

SEXUAL HARASSMENT AS SEX DISCRIMINATION

Supreme Court Guidelines: *Meritor Savings Bank v. Vinson* (1986)[25]

As early as 1971[26] federal courts were reading the 1964 Civil Rights Act's prohibition on race discrimination in the "terms, conditions, or privileges of employment" to contain an implied prohibition on racial harassment in the workplace. In a series of decisions in the 1970s,[27] federal courts made clear that employee behavior such as placing drawings of caricatured Blacks being lynched by Klansmen on the desk or locker door of Black employees was forbidden by the statute and that employers who did not take steps to halt such behavior would be actionable under the law, just as though they had openly discriminated against their Black employees. Placing severe psychological pressure on employees, on racial grounds, to quit their jobs was close enough to firing the employees on racial grounds that the law would treat them as similar. This principle treating discriminatory harassment as discrimination under the law was also applied in those years to harassment based on religion[28] and national origin.[29]

Sometimes employee harassment of women on the job took a form that was directly analogous to that to which racial or ethnic minorities were exposed, as when, for instance, firemen angry at including women in their ranks tried to pressure them into quitting. More often, however, sexual harassment of women took a different form. This other form, *unwelcome sexual advances*, sometimes took the extreme form of **quid pro quo** exchanges—e.g. "if you do not have sex with me I will fire you" or "if you have sex with me I will promote you." More often, however, the harassment subjected recipients to sexual advances, which may or may not have been innocent. While the perpetrator may have intended friendliness or romantic affection, the recipient may have experienced the advances as hostile or threatening or, at a minimum, as a source of psychic discomfort in the workplace. As Catharine MacKinnon explained:

> Less clear, and undoubtedly more pervasive, is the situation in which sexual advances, made simply because she has a woman's body, can be a daily part of a woman's work life. She may be constantly felt or pinched, visually undressed and stared at, surreptitiously kissed, commented upon, manipulated into being alone, and generally taken advantage of at work—but never promised or denied anything explicitly connected with her job...Never knowing if it will ever stop or if escalation is imminent, a woman can put up with it or leave. Most women hardly choose to be confronted by "the choice of putting up with being manhandled, or being out of work." Most women are coerced into tolerance.[30]

In this way, MacKinnon argued that when female employees are subjected to a form of harassment and discomfort to which other employees are not subjected, this behavior constitutes discrimination on the basis of sex. Both the EEOC and several (but not all) federal courts[31] agreed that it was, and in 1986, the U.S. Supreme Court added its voice to this chorus of disapproval.

In the case that went to the Supreme Court, Mechelle Vinson, an African-American woman, complained that her supervisor at the bank where she worked subjected her to four years of sexual harassment. Shortly after her probationary period as a teller-trainee had ended, he had started dating her. Her description of the situation, as paraphrased in Justice Rehnquist's opinion for the Supreme Court went as follows:

> [H]e invited her out to dinner and during the course of the meal, suggested that they go to a motel and have sexual relations. At first she refused, but out of what she described as fear of losing her job she eventually agreed. According to respondent, Taylor [the supervisor] thereafter made repeated demands upon her for sexual favors, usually at the branch, both during and after business hours; she estimated that over the next several years she had sexual intercourse with him some 40 or 50 times. In addition, respondent testified that Taylor fondled her in front of other employees, followed her into the women's restroom when she went there alone, exposed himself to her, and even forcibly raped

her on several occasions. These activities ceased after 1977 . . . when she started going with a steady boyfriend. [Taylor denied that there had ever been a sexual relationship between them or that he had ever asked her for sexual favors.]

The federal district court that had heard Mechelle Vinson's complaint had rejected it on the grounds that the relationship she described struck that court as "voluntary" and that sexual compliance had never been made an explicit condition for her to keep her job or get a promotion. Both the Circuit Court of Appeals and the U.S. Supreme Court rejected this narrow view of the kind of sexual harassment that was prohibited.

Instead, they reasoned that, in addition to *quid pro quo* harassment, also forbidden was "[s]exual harassment which creates a hostile or offensive environment for members of one sex."[32] Such harassment, the Supreme Court ruled, would be actionable whenever it was "sufficiently severe or pervasive 'to alter the conditions of [the victim's] employment and create an abusive working environment.'"[33] The Court endorsed the EEOC rule that "employees have a right to work in an environment free from discriminatory intimidation, ridicule and insult."[34] The Supreme Court also specifically disapproved of the District Court's basing its decision on Vinson's technical consent to the sexual relationship; Justice Rehnquist reasoned that the central issue was not whether she were forced into sex against her will but rather whether the on-the-job advances were "unwelcome." Finally, the U.S. Supreme Court agreed with the Circuit Court that company management is liable for sexual harassment carried on by its employees and is responsible for adopting policies aimed at checking such harassment. The high Court, however, declined to issue "definitive" guidelines as to employer liability because of the sparseness of the record in the particular case before it. (It is worth noting that Title VII does not make sexual harassment criminal; if employers can assure that the harassment ceases, they are not obligated to fire or otherwise penalize the offender. The legal obligation is simply to rid the workplace of the offending behavior.)

Once the Supreme Court issues a ruling like this, it then must be applied by private employers, federal executive branch officials, and lower federal courts. In any application of a set of rules, there is some discretionary leeway. The following Circuit Court of Appeals decision from 1991 is presented to illustrate the kind of innovation that can take place at the hands of a court that is ostensibly "implementing" rules from a higher court; it is presented also in order to encourage the reader to consider the substantive issue that separates the dissenter from the majority.

Lower Court Innovation: *Ellison v. Brady* (1991)[35]

This Ninth Circuit Court of Appeals decision is much discussed by legal scholars because of its endorsement of a "reasonable woman" test for deciding whether there has or has not been sexual harassment. Indeed, that endorsement is precisely what provoked discussion from the dissenting judge in the same case. Because the outcome of the case is so fact-dependent, the excerpt presented below reprints the facts, virtually verbatim, as the Circuit Court majority described them.

KERRY ELLISON V. NICHOLAS F. BRADY, SEC'Y OF THE TREASURY

924 F.2d 872 (9th Cir. 1991)

ROBERT BEEZER, CIRCUIT JUDGE, wrote the opinion:

I

Kerry Ellison worked as a revenue agent for the Internal Revenue Service in San Mateo, California. During her initial training in 1984 she met Sterling Gray, another trainee, who was also assigned to the San Mateo office. The two co-workers never became friends, and they did not work closely together.

Gray's desk was twenty feet from Ellison's desk, two rows behind and one row over. Revenue agents in the San Mateo office often went to lunch in groups. In June of 1986 when no one else was in the office, Gray asked Ellison to lunch. She accepted. Gray had to pick up his son's forgotten lunch, so they stopped by Gray's house. He gave Ellison a tour of his house.

Ellison alleges that after the June lunch Gray started to pester her with unnecessary questions and hang around her desk. On October 9, 1986, Gray asked Ellison out for a drink after work. She declined, but she suggested that they have lunch the following week. She did not want to have lunch alone with him, and she tried to stay away from the office during lunch time. One day during the following week, Gray dressed in a three-piece suit and asked Ellison out for lunch. Again, she did not accept.

On October 22, 1986 Gray handed Ellison a note he wrote on a telephone message slip which read: "I cried over you last night and I'm totally drained today. I have never been in such constant term oil (sic). Thank you for talking with me. I could not stand to feel your hatred for another day."

When Ellison realized that Gray wrote the note, she became shocked and frightened and left the room. Gray followed her into the hallway and demanded that she talk to him, but she left the building.

Ellison later showed the note to Bonnie Miller, who supervised both Ellison and Gray. Miller said "this is sexual harassment." Ellison asked Miller not to do anything about it. She wanted to try to handle it herself. Ellison asked a male co-worker to talk to Gray, to tell him that she was not interested in him and to leave her alone. The next day, Thursday, Gray called in sick.

Ellison did not work on Friday, and on the following Monday, she started four weeks of training in St. Louis, Missouri. Gray mailed her a card and a typed, single-spaced, three-page letter. She describes this letter as "twenty times, a hundred times weirder" than the prior note. Gray wrote, in part:

> I know that you are worth knowing with or without sex. . . . Leaving aside the hassles and disasters of recent weeks. I have enjoyed you so much over these past few months. Watching you. Experiencing you from O so far away. Admiring your style and elan. . . . Don't you think it odd that two people who have never even talked together, alone, are striking off such intense sparks . . . I will [write] another letter in the near future.[1]

Explaining her reaction, Ellison stated: "I just thought he was crazy. I thought he was nuts. I didn't know what he would do next. I was frightened."

She immediately telephoned Miller. Ellison told her supervisor that she was frightened and really upset. She requested that Miller transfer either her or Gray because she would not be comfortable working in the same office with him. Miller asked Ellison to send a copy of the card and letter to San Mateo.

Miller then telephoned her supervisor, Joe Benton, and discussed the problem. That same day she had a counseling session with Gray. She informed him that he was entitled to union representation. During this meeting, she told Gray to leave Ellison alone

At Benton's request, Miller apprised the labor relations department of the situation. She also reminded Gray many times over the next few weeks that he must not contact Ellison in any way. Gray subsequently transferred to the San Francisco office on November 24, 1986. Ellison returned from St. Louis in late November and did not discuss the matter further with Miller.

After three weeks in San Francisco, Gray filed union grievances requesting a return to the San Mateo office. The IRS and the union settled the grievances in Gray's favor, agreeing to allow him to transfer back to the San Mateo office provided that he spend four more months in San Francisco and promise not to bother Ellison. On January 28, 1987, Ellison first learned of Gray's request in a letter from Miller explaining that Gray would return to the San Mateo office. The letter indicated that management decided to resolve Ellison's problem with a six-month separation, and that it would take additional action if the problem recurred.

After receiving the letter, Ellison was "frantic." She filed a formal complaint alleging sexual harassment on January 30, 1987 with the IRS. She also obtained permission to transfer to San Francisco temporarily when Gray returned.

Gray sought joint counseling. He wrote Ellison another letter which still sought to maintain the idea that he and Ellison had some type of relationship [although it is unclear in the trial record whether Ellison received this one.]

The IRS employee investigating the allegation agreed with Ellison's supervisor that Gray's conduct constituted sexual harassment. In its final decision, however, the Treasury Department rejected Ellison's complaint because it believed that the complaint did not describe a pattern or practice of sexual harassment covered by the EEOC regulations. After an appeal, the EEOC affirmed the Treasury Department's decision on a different ground. It concluded that the agency took adequate action to prevent the repetition of Gray's conduct.

Ellison filed a complaint in September of 1987 in federal district court. The court granted the government's motion for summary judgment on the ground that Ellison had failed to state a prima facie case of sexual harassment due to a hostile working environment. Ellison appeals.

III

The parties ask us to determine if Gray's conduct, as alleged by Ellison, was sufficiently severe or pervasive to alter the conditions of Ellison's employment and create an abusive working environment. The district court, with little Ninth Circuit case law to look to for guidance, held that Ellison did not state a prima facie case of sexual harassment due to a hostile working environment. It believed that Gray's conduct was "isolated and genuinely trivial." We disagree.

. . . The Supreme Court in *Meritor* explained that courts may properly look to guidelines issued by the Equal Employment Opportunity Commission (EEOC) for guidance when examining hostile environment claims of sexual harassment. 477 U.S. at 65. The EEOC guidelines describe hostile environment harassment as "conduct [which] has the purpose or effect of unreasonably interfering with an individual's work performance or creating an intimidating, hostile, or offensive working environment." 29 C.F.R. § 1604.11(a)(3). The EEOC, in accord with a substantial body of judicial decisions, has concluded that "Title VII affords employees the right to work in an environment free from discriminatory intimidation, ridicule, and insult." 477 U.S. at 65.

The Supreme Court cautioned, however, that not all harassment affects a "term, condition, or privilege" of employment within the meaning of Title VII. For example, the "mere utterance of an ethnic or racial epithet which engenders offensive feelings in an employee" is not, by itself, actionable under Title VII. *Id.* at 67. To state a claim under Title VII, sexual harassment "must be sufficiently severe or pervasive to alter the conditions of the victim's employment and create an abusive working environment." *Id.*

. . .

Although *Meritor* and our previous cases establish the framework for the resolution of hostile environment cases, they do not dictate the outcome of this case. Gray's conduct falls somewhere between forcible rape and the mere utterance of an epithet. 477 U.S. at 60, 67.

The government asks us to apply the reasoning of other courts which have declined to find Title VII violations on more egregious facts. In *Scott v. Sears, Roebuck & Co.*, 798 F.2d 210, 212 (7th Cir. 1986), the Seventh Circuit analyzed a female employee's working conditions for sexual harassment. It noted that she was repeatedly propositioned and winked at by her supervisor. When she asked for assistance, he asked "what will I get for it?" Co-workers slapped her buttocks and commented that she must moan and groan during sex. The court examined the evidence to see if "the demeaning conduct and sexual stereotyping caused such anxiety and debilitation to the plaintiff that working conditions were 'poisoned' within the meaning of Title VII." *Id.* at 213. The court did not consider the environment sufficiently hostile. *Id.* at 214.

Similarly, in *Rabidue v. Osceola Refining Co.*, 805 F.2d 611 (6th Cir. 1986), *cert. denied*, 481 U.S. 1041 (1987), the Sixth Circuit refused to find a hostile environment where the workplace contained posters of naked and partially dressed women, and where a male employee customarily called women "whores," "cunt," "pussy," and "tits," referred to plaintiff as "fat ass," and specifically stated, "All that bitch needs is a good lay." Over a strong dissent, the majority held that the sexist remarks and the pin-up posters had only a *de minimis* effect and did not seriously affect the plaintiff's psychological well-being.

We do not agree with the standards set forth in *Scott* and *Rabidue*,[6] and we choose not to follow those decisions Neither *Scott's* search for "anxiety and debilitation" sufficient to "poison" a working environment nor *Rabidue's* requirement that a plaintiff's psychological well-being be "seriously affected" follows directly from language in *Meritor*. . . . Surely, employees need not endure sexual harassment until their psychological well-being is seriously affected to the extent that they suffer anxiety and debilitation. . . . Title VII's protection of employees from sex discrimination comes into play long before the point where victims of sexual harassment require psychiatric assistance.

We have closely examined *Meritor* and our previous cases, and we believe that Gray's conduct was sufficiently severe and pervasive to alter the conditions of Ellison's employment and create an abusive working environment. We first note that the required showing of severity or seriousness of the harassing conduct varies inversely with the pervasiveness or frequency of the conduct. . . .

Next, we believe that in evaluating the severity and pervasiveness of sexual harassment, we should focus on the perspective of the victim. If we only examined whether a reasonable person would engage in allegedly harassing conduct, we would run the risk of reinforcing the prevailing level of discrimination. Harassers could continue to harass merely because a particular discriminatory practice was common, and victims of harassment would have no remedy.

We therefore prefer to analyze harassment from the victim's perspective. A complete understanding of the victim's view requires, among other things, an analysis of the different perspectives of men and women. Conduct that many men consider unobjectionable may offend many women. *See, e.g., Lipsett v. University of Puerto Rico*, 864 F.2d 881, 898 (1st Cir. 1988) ("A male supervisor might believe, for example, that it is legitimate for him to tell a female subordinate that she has a 'great figure' or 'nice legs.' The female subordinate, however, may find such comments offensive"). . . .

We realize that there is a broad range of viewpoints among women as a group, but we believe that many women share common concerns which men do not necessarily share. For example, because women are disproportionately victims of rape and sexual assault, women have a stronger incentive to be concerned with sexual behavior. Women who are victims of mild forms of sexual harassment may understandably worry whether a harasser's conduct is merely a prelude to violent sexual assault. Men, who are rarely victims of sexual assault, may view sexual conduct in a vacuum without a full appreciation of the social setting or the underlying threat of violence that a woman may perceive.

In order to shield employers from having to accommodate the idiosyncratic concerns of the rare hyper-sensitive employee, we hold that a female plaintiff states a prima facie case of hostile environment sexual harassment when she alleges conduct which a reasonable woman would consider sufficiently severe or pervasive to alter the conditions of employment and create an abusive working environment. . . .

We adopt the perspective of a reasonable woman primarily because we believe that a sex-blind reasonable person standard tends to be male-biased and tends to systematically ignore the experiences of women. The reasonable woman standard does not establish a higher level of protection for women than men. . . . Instead, a gender-conscious examination of sexual harassment enables women to participate in the workplace on an equal footing with men. By acknowledging and not trivializing the effects of sexual harassment on reasonable women, courts can work towards ensuring that neither men nor women will have to "run a gauntlet of sexual abuse in return for the privilege of being allowed to work and make a living." *Henson v. Dundee*, 682 F.2d 897, 902 (11th Cir. 1982).

We note that the reasonable victim standard we adopt today classifies conduct as unlawful sexual harassment even when harassers do not realize that their conduct creates a hostile working environment. Well-intentioned compliments by co-workers or supervisors can form the basis of a sexual harassment cause of action if a reasonable victim of the same sex as the plaintiff would consider the comments sufficiently severe or pervasive to alter a condition of employment and create an abusive working environment. That is because Title VII is not a fault-based tort scheme. "Title VII is aimed at the consequences or effects of an employment practice and not at the . . . motivation" of co-workers or employers. *Rogers*, 454 F.2d at 239; *see also Griggs v. Duke Power Co.*, 401 U.S. 424, 432 (1971) (the absence of discriminatory intent does not redeem an otherwise unlawful employment practice). To avoid liability under Title VII, employers may have to educate and sensitize their workforce to eliminate conduct which a reasonable victim would consider unlawful sexual harassment. . . .

The facts of this case illustrate the importance of considering the victim's perspective. Analyzing the facts from the alleged harasser's viewpoint, Gray could be portrayed as a modern-day Cyrano de Bergerac wishing no more than to woo Ellison with his words. There is no evidence that Gray harbored ill will toward Ellison. He even offered in his "love letter" to leave her alone if she wished. Examined in this light, it is not difficult to see why the district court characterized Gray's conduct as isolated and trivial.

Ellison, however, did not consider the acts to be trivial. Gray's first note shocked and frightened her. After receiving the three-page letter, she became really upset and frightened again. She immediately requested that she or Gray be transferred. Her supervisor's prompt response suggests that she too did not consider the conduct trivial. When Ellison learned that Gray arranged to return to San Mateo, she immediately asked to transfer, and she immediately filed an official complaint.

We cannot say as a matter of law that Ellison's reaction was idiosyncratic or hyper-sensitive. We believe that a reasonable woman could have had a similar reaction. After receiving the first bizarre note from Gray, a person she barely knew, Ellison asked a co-worker to tell Gray to leave her alone. Despite her request, Gray sent her a long, passionate, disturbing letter. He told her he had been "watching" and "experiencing" her; he made repeated references to sex; he said he would write again. Ellison had no way of knowing what Gray would do next. A reasonable woman could consider Gray's conduct, as alleged by Ellison, sufficiently severe and pervasive to alter a condition of employment and create an abusive working environment.

Sexual harassment is a major problem in the workplace.[15] Adopting the victim's perspective ensures that courts will not "sustain ingrained notions of reasonable behavior fashioned by the offenders." *Lipsett*, 864 F.2d at 898, quoting, *Rabidue*, 805 F.2d at 626 (Keith, J., dissenting). Congress did not enact Title VII to codify prevailing sexist prejudices. To the contrary, "Congress designed Title VII to prevent the perpetuation of stereotypes and a sense of degradation which serve to close or discourage employment opportunities for women." *Andrews*, 895 F.2d at 1483. We hope that over time both men and women will learn what conduct offends reasonable members of the other sex. When employers and employees internalize the standard of workplace conduct we establish today, the current gap in perception between the sexes will be bridged.

IV

We next must determine what remedial actions by employers shield them from liability under Title VII for sexual harassment by co-workers....

. . .

We. . .believe that remedies should be reasonably calculated to end the harassment. Employers should impose sufficient penalties to assure a workplace free from sexual harassment. . . .In essence. . .we think that the reasonableness of an employer's remedy will depend on its ability to stop harassment by the person who engaged in harassment. In evaluating the adequacy of the remedy, the court may also take into account the remedy's ability to persuade potential harassers to refrain from unlawful conduct. Indeed, meting out punishments that do not take into account the need to maintain a harassment-free working environment may subject the employer to suit by the EEOC.

. . .

We decline to accept the government's argument that its decision to return Gray to San Mateo did not create a hostile environment for Ellison because the government granted Ellison's request for a temporary transfer to San Francisco. Ellison preferred to work in San Mateo over San Francisco. We strongly believe that the victim of sexual harassment should not be punished for the conduct of the harasser. We wholeheartedly agree with the EEOC that a victim of sexual harassment should not have to work in a less desirable location as a result of an employer's remedy for sexual harassment.

Ellison maintains that the government's remedy was insufficient because it did not discipline Gray and because it allowed Gray to return to San Mateo after only a six-month separation. Even though the hostile environment had been eliminated when Gray began working in San Francisco, we cannot say that the government's response was reasonable under Title VII. The record on appeal suggests that Ellison's employer did not express strong disapproval of Gray's conduct, did not reprimand Gray, did not put him on probation, and did not inform him that repeated harassment would result in suspension or termination. Apparently, Gray's employer only told him to stop harassing Ellison. Title VII requires more than a mere request to refrain from discriminatory conduct. . . .If Ellison can prove on remand that Gray knew or should have known that his conduct was unlawful and that the government failed to take even the mildest form of disciplinary action, the district court should hold that the government's initial remedy was insufficient under Title VII. At this point, genuine issues of material fact remain concerning whether the government properly disciplined Gray.

Ellison further maintains that her employer's decision to allow Gray to transfer back to the San Mateo office after a six-month cooling-off period rendered the government's remedy insufficient. She argues that Gray's *mere presence* would create a hostile working environment.

...To avoid liability under Title VII for failing to remedy a hostile environment, employers may even have to remove employees from the workplace if their mere presence would render the working environment hostile. Once again, we examine whether the mere presence of a harasser would create a hostile environment from the perspective of a reasonable woman.

The district court did not reach the issue of the reasonableness of the government's remedy. Given the scant record on appeal, we cannot determine whether a reasonable woman could conclude that Gray's mere presence at San Mateo six months after the alleged harassment would create an abusive environment....[W]e do not know how often Ellison and Gray would have to interact at San Mateo.

Moreover, it is not clear to us that the six-month cooling-off period was reasonably calculated to end the harassment or assessed proportionately to the seriousness of Gray's conduct. There is evidence in the record which suggests that the government intended to transfer Gray to San Francisco permanently and only allowed Gray to return to San Mateo because he promised to drop some union grievances. We do know that the IRS did not request Ellison's input or even inform her of the proceedings before agreeing to let Gray return to San Mateo. This failure to even attempt to determine what impact Gray's return would have on Ellison shows an insufficient regard for the victim's interest in avoiding a hostile working environment. On remand, the district court should fully explore the facts concerning the government's decision to return Gray to San Mateo.

V

We reverse the district court's decision that Ellison did not allege a prima facie case of sexual harassment due to a hostile working environment, and we remand for further proceedings consistent with this opinion. Although we have considered the evidence in the light most favorable to Ellison because the district court granted the government's motion for summary judgment, we, of course, reserve for the district court the resolution of all factual issues.

Opinion Footnotes

1 In the middle of the long letter Gray did say "I am obligated to you so much that if you want me to leave you alone I will.... If you want me to forget you entirely, I can not do that."

6 We note that the Sixth Circuit has called *Rabidue* into question in at least two subsequent opinions. In *Yates v. Avco Corp.*, 819 F.2d 630, 637 (6th Cir. 1987), a panel of the Sixth Circuit expressly adopted one of the main arguments in the *Rabidue* dissent, that sexual harassment actions should be viewed from the victim's perspective. In *Davis v. Monsanto Chemical Co.*, 858 F.2d 345, 350 (6th Cir. 1988), *cert. denied*, 490 U.S. 1110 (1989), the Sixth Circuit once again criticized *Rabidue*'s limited reading of Title VII. *See also Andrews v. City of Philadelphia*, 895 F.2d 1469, 1485 (3d Cir. 1990)(explicitly rejecting *Rabidue* and holding that derogatory language directed at women and pornographic pictures of women serve as evidence of a hostile working environment).

15 Over 40 percent of female federal employees reported incidents of sexual harassment in 1987, roughly the same number as in 1980. United States Merit Systems Protection Board, *Sexual Harassment in the Federal Government: An Update* 11 (1988). Victims of sexual harassment "pay all the intangible emotional costs inflicted by anger, humiliation, frustration, withdrawal, dysfunction in family life," as well as medical expenses, litigation expenses, job search expenses, and the loss of valuable sick leave and annual leave. *Id.* at 42. Sexual harassment cost the federal government $267 million from May 1985 to May 1987 for losses in productivity, sick leave costs, and employee replacement costs. *Id.* at 39.

ALBERT L. STEPHENS, JR. DISTRICT JUDGE, dissenting:

This case comes to us on appeal in the wake of the granting of a summary judgment motion. There was no trial, therefore no opportunities for cross examination of the witnesses. In addition, there are factual gaps in the record...Consequently, I believe that it is an inappropriate case with which to establish a new legal precedent which will be binding in all subsequent cases of like nature in the Ninth Circuit. I refer to the majority's use of the term "reasonable woman," a term I find ambiguous and therefore inadequate.

Nowhere in § 2000e of Title VII, the section under which the plaintiff in this case brought suit, is there any indication that Congress intended to provide for any other than equal treatment in the area of civil rights. The legislation is designed to achieve a balanced and generally gender neutral and harmonious workplace which would improve production and the quality of the employees' lives. In fact, the Supreme Court has shown a preference against systems that are not gender or race neutral, such as hiring quotas. *See City of Richmond v. J. A. Croson Co.*, 488 U.S. 469 (1989). While women may be the most frequent targets of this type of conduct that is at issue in this case, they are not the only targets. I believe that it is incumbent upon the court in this case to use terminology that will meet the needs of all who seek recourse under this section of Title VII. Possible alternatives that are more in line with a gender neutral approach include "victim," "target," or "person."

The term "reasonable man" as it is used in the law of torts, traditionally refers to the average adult person, regardless of gender, and the conduct that can reasonably be expected of him or her. For the purposes of the legal issues that are being addressed, such a term assumes that it is applicable to all persons. Section 2000e of Title VII presupposes the use of a legal term that can apply to all persons and the impossibility of a more individually tailored standard. It is clear that the authors of the majority opinion intend a difference between the "reasonable woman" and the "reasonable man" in Title VII cases on the assumption that men do not have the same sensibilities as women. This is not necessarily true. . . .[C]ircumstances faced by women and their effect upon women can be and in given circumstances may be expected to be understood by men.

. . .Application of the "new standard" presents a puzzlement which is born of the assumption that men's eyes do not see what a woman sees through her eyes. I find it surprising that the majority finds no need for evidence on any of these subjects. I am not sure whether the majority also concludes that the woman and the man in question are also reasonable without evidence . . .[T]he workplace itself should be examined as affected, among other things, by the conduct of the people working there as to whether the workplace as existing is conducive to fulfilling the goals of Title VII. In any event, these are unresolved factual issues which preclude summary judgment.

. . .

It is my opinion that the case should be reversed with instructions to proceed to trial. This would certainly lead to filling in the factual gaps left by the scanty record. . .

The creation of the proposed "new standard" which applies only to women will not necessarily come to the aid of all potential victims of the type of misconduct that is at issue in this case. I believe that a gender neutral standard would greatly contribute to the clarity of this and future cases in the same area.

Case Questions

1. In the *Rabidue*[36] case, which the majority cites with disapproval (and which had since been disavowed even in its own circuit, as explained in footnote 6), extremely vulgar language (as quoted by the *Ellison* majority) had been judged not a violation of Title VII on the grounds that such language had been a part of "the lexicon of obscenity that pervaded the environment of the workplace both before and after the [female] plaintiff" went to work there, and that Title VII was not "designed to bring about a magical transformation in the social mores of American workers."[37] Is that a wrong-headed view of Title VII? Is it plausible, as the dissenter in *Ellison* argues, that any reasonable *person* (male or female) can figure out that certain terms are offensive to women and should not be addressed to them in a work setting? Should a woman who knowingly enters a work environment where "sexual jokes, sexual conversations and girlie magazines . . . abound" be prepared to tolerate such

things, as long as they are not addressed to her in a harassing way (e.g., by the placing of pornographic photos on *her* locker door, etc.)?

2. Does the "reasonable woman" standard espoused here mean that conduct which *some* reasonable women *might* find intimidating is now forbidden in the workplace, or only that conduct which *every* reasonable woman *would* so find is now forbidden? Even from a woman's point of view, does being pestered with questions, asked out for a drink (once), asked out for lunch (once), and being sent a card, two lovenotes (one long and one short, and one of which agrees to stop writing if so requested), and then another letter after the sender has promised "not to bother" the recipient again, add up to "a gauntlet of sexual abuse"? An "intimidating" environment? Suppose that in response to this decision, the employer put Gray on probation with the warning that any further communication addressed to Ellison would get him suspended or fired, but still let him work two rows behind her where he could stare at her all day. If Ellison insisted that this response was inadequate because she still felt great discomfort in his presence, would her demand that he be transferred out of her office be something the employer had to honor under a "reasonable woman" standard? Under a reasonable person standard?

3. Do men and women in fact have different sensibilities? Even if they do, does that make what is "reasonable" for one differ from what is "reasonable" for the other? Is a unisex standard, as advocated by the dissent, impossible? Undesirable? The majority granted (in a footnote omitted from this excerpt) that if a man were claiming harassment of himself, then a "reasonable man" standard would apply. Is there really a difference between what a male victim would find harassing and what a female victim would find harassing? If your imagination fails you in conceiving of a man truly not wanting someone's sexual attention, try imagining that he is being harassed by a gay supervisor. Would a man who received these lovenotes from such a supervisor have good cause for complaint? Does a judge really need the "reasonable woman" standard to decide these cases fairly?

4. Do the judges in this case seem insufficiently attentive to First Amendment freedom of speech concerns (which may conflict with the prohibition on sexual harassment, as the judges interpret it)?

Supreme Court Response: *Harris v. Forklift* (1993)

As the lower courts began to apply the reasoning of the *Meritor Savings* decision, new issues arose. Several of these concerned dimensions of the question: how bad does sexual harassment have to be in order to amount to job discrimination? Some lower courts ruled that complainants had to demonstrate some sort of injury in order to prevail in their lawsuits; a mere feeling of annoyance or distress would not suffice.[38]

Others, such as *Ellison v. Brady* above, ruled that, when a judge examines a sexual harassment complaint, in order to determine whether workplace "conduct was sufficiently severe and pervasive to alter the conditions of employment," the judge should apply not the traditional "reasonable person" standard but rather the standard of a reasonable member of the victim group, i.e., "the reasonable woman."

The Supreme Court addressed both of these rulings in 1993 when it decided *Harris v. Forklift Systems*. The federal district court below, following the reigning precedent of its circuit court, had ruled in this case that sex-based remarks at the workplace could not count as discrimination unless they were pervasive and severe enough to cause serious psychological harm.[39] The American Psychological Association filed an *amicus curiae* brief urging the Supreme Court to replace the "reasonable person" standard with a "reasonable woman" standard.

According to the account in Justice O'Connor's opinion, Teresa Harris, who worked as manager for two and a half years at Forklift Systems, initiated this lawsuit after the following sequence of events. The president of the company frequently insulted her with vulgar sexual innuendos or gender-based put-downs in the presence of other employees. These included, "You're a woman, what do you know"; "We need a man as the rental manager"; and "[You're] a dumb ass woman." Also in front of others, he suggested that the two of them "go to the Holiday Inn to negotiate [Harris'] raise." This man on more than one occasion asked Harris and other female employees to get coins from his front pants pocket; threw objects on the ground in front of Harris and other women, and then asked them to pick the objects up; and also remarked with sexual innuendo about Harris' and other women's clothing. After two years of such treatment, Harris complained to him about his conduct. He expressed surprise that Harris was offended, claimed he was only joking, promised to stop, and apologized. But six months later he began anew: While Harris was arranging a deal with one of Forklift's customers, he asked her, again in front of other employees, "What did you do, promise the guy . . . some [sex] Saturday night?" Harris quit after getting her next paycheck. She then sued Forklift, claiming that his conduct had created an abusive work environment for her because of her sex.

HARRIS V. FORKLIFT SYSTEMS, INC.
517 U.S. 17 (1993)

JUSTICE O'CONNOR delivered the opinion of the Court.

In this case, we consider the definition of a discriminatorily "abusive work environment" (also known as a "hostile work environment") under Title VII of the Civil Rights Act of 1964...

The United States District Court for the Middle District of Tennessee... found this to be "a close case," but held that [company president] Hardy's conduct did not create an abusive environment. The court found that some of Hardy's comments "offended [Harris], and would offend the reasonable woman," but that they were not "so severe as to be expected to seriously affect [Harris'] psychological wellbeing. A reasonable woman manager under like circumstances would have been offended by Hardy, but his conduct would not have risen to the level of interfering with that person's work performance. [Nor did Harris] suffer[ ] injury."

...

We granted certiorari to resolve a conflict among the Circuits on whether conduct, to be actionable as "abusive work environment" harassment (no quid pro quo harassment issue is present here), must "seriously affect [an employee's] psychological wellbeing" or lead the plaintiff to "suffe[r] injury." [Citations to circuit court cases omitted.]

II

Title VII of the Civil Rights Act of 1964 makes it "an unlawful employment practice for an employer... to discriminate against any individual with respect to his compensation, terms, conditions, or privileges of employment, because of such individual's ...sex...." 42 U.S.C.§ 2000e–2(a)(1). As we made clear in *Meritor*, this language "is not limited to "economic" or "tangible" discrimination. The phrase "terms, conditions, or privileges of employment" evinces a congressional intent "to strike at the entire spectrum of disparate treatment of men and women" in employment," which includes requiring people to work in a discriminatorily hostile or abusive environment. *Id.*, at 64. When the workplace is permeated with "discriminatory intimidation, ridicule, and insult," 477 U.S., at 65, that is "sufficiently severe or pervasive to alter the conditions of the victim's employment and create an abusive working environment," *id.*, at 67, Title VII is violated.

This standard, which we reaffirm today, takes a middle path between making actionable any conduct that is merely offensive and requiring the conduct to cause a tangible psychological injury. As we pointed out in *Meritor*, "mere utterance of an . . . epithet which engenders offensive feelings in an employee," does not sufficiently affect the conditions of employment to implicate Title VII. Conduct that is not severe or pervasive enough to create an objectively hostile or abusive work environment—an environment that a reasonable person would find hostile or abusive—is beyond Title VII's purview. . . .

But Title VII comes into play before the harassing conduct leads to a nervous breakdown. A discriminatorily abusive work environment, even one that does not seriously affect employees' psychological wellbeing, can and often will detract from employees' job performance, discourage employees from remaining on the job, or keep them from advancing in their careers. Moreover, even without regard to these tangible effects, the very fact that the discriminatory conduct was so severe or pervasive that it created a work environment abusive to employees because of their race, gender, religion, or national origin offends Title VII's broad rule of workplace equality. . . .

We therefore believe the District Court erred in relying on whether the conduct "seriously affect[ed] plaintiff's psychological wellbeing" or led her to "suffe[r] injury." Such an inquiry may needlessly focus the factfinder's attention on concrete psychological harm, an element Title VII does not require. Certainly Title VII bars conduct that would seriously affect a reasonable person's psychological wellbeing, but the statute is not limited to such conduct. So long as the environment would reasonably be perceived, and is perceived, as hostile or abusive, *Meritor*, at 67, there is no need for it also to be psychologically injurious.

This is not, and by its nature cannot be, a mathematically precise test. We need not answer today all the potential questions it raises, nor specifically address the EEOC's new regulations on this subject. . . . But we can say that whether an environment is "hostile" or "abusive" can be determined only by looking at all the circumstances. These may include the frequency of the discriminatory conduct; its severity; whether it is physically threatening or humiliating, or a mere offensive utterance; and whether it unreasonably interferes with an employee's work performance. The effect on the employee's psychological wellbeing is, of course, relevant to determining whether the plaintiff actually found the environment abusive. But, while psychological harm, like any other relevant factor, may be taken into account, no single factor is required.

III

Forklift, while conceding that a requirement that the conduct seriously affect psychological wellbeing is unfounded, argues that the District Court nonetheless correctly applied the *Meritor* standard. We disagree. Though the District Court did conclude that the work environment was not "intimidating or abusive to [Harris]," it did so only after finding that the conduct was not "so severe as to be expected to seriously affect plaintiff's psychological well-being," and that Harris was not "subjectively so offended that she suffered injury." The District Court's application of these incorrect standards may well have influenced its ultimate conclusion, especially given that the court found this to be a "close case."

We therefore reverse the judgment of the Court of Appeals, and remand the case for further proceedings consistent with this opinion.

Justice Scalia, concurring.

Meritor Savings Bank v. Vinson, 477 U.S. 57 (1986), held that Title VII prohibits sexual harassment that takes the form of a hostile work environment. The Court stated that sexual harassment is actionable if it is "sufficiently severe or pervasive 'to alter the conditions of [the victim's] employment and create an abusive work environment.'" Today's opinion elaborates that the challenged conduct must be severe or pervasive enough "to create an objectively hostile or abusive work environment—an environment that a reasonable person would find hostile or abusive."

"Abusive" (or "hostile," which in this context I take to mean the same thing) does not seem to me a very clear standard . . . . Be that as it may, I know of no alternative to the course the Court today has taken. One of the factors mentioned in the Court's nonexhaustive list—whether the conduct unreasonably interferes with an employee's work performance—would, if it were made an absolute test, provide greater guidance to juries and employers. But I see no basis for such a limitation in the language of the statute. Accepting *Meritor*'s interpretation of the term "conditions of employment" as the law, the test is not whether work has been impaired, but whether working conditions have been discriminatorily altered. I know of no test more faithful to the inherently vague statutory language than the one the Court today adopts. For these reasons, I join the opinion of the Court.

> **JUSTICE GINSBURG, concurring.**
>
> Today the Court reaffirms the holding of *Meritor*...: "[A] plaintiff may establish a violation of Title VII by proving that discrimination based on sex has created a hostile or abusive work environment." The critical issue, Title VII's text indicates, is whether members of one sex are exposed to disadvantageous terms or conditions of employment to which members of the other sex are not exposed....The adjudicator's inquiry should center, dominantly, on whether the discriminatory conduct has unreasonably interfered with the plaintiff's work performance. To show such interference, "the plaintiff need not prove that his or her tangible productivity has declined as a result of the harassment." *Davis v. Monsanto Chemical Co.*, 858 F.2d 345, 349 (CA6 1988). It suffices to prove that a reasonable person subjected to the discriminatory conduct would find, as the plaintiff did, that the harassment so altered working conditions as to "ma[k]e it more difficult to do the job." *Ibid*.... The Court's opinion, which I join, seems to me in harmony with the view expressed in this concurring statement.

Case Questions

1. Would a "reasonable woman" in fact judge sex-related conversation and behavior differently from how a "reasonable man" would?

2. Is it possible for any two people living within the same culture to agree on how to judge a situation "objectively...as a reasonable person"? As the U.S. becomes increasingly multi-cultural, does the question become more difficult?

Same-Sex Harassment: *Oncale v. Sundowner* (1998)

A few years after *Harris v. Forklift Systems*, the Supreme Court finally took up the question of whether same-sex harassment (e.g., male on male) was forbidden by Title VII's prohibition on sex-based discrimination. The Court's answer was a unanimous, "Yes," but the arguments by which the Court came to this conclusion may prove of limited utility in future cases. It involved harassment possibly on the basis of perceived sexual orientation, although Joseph Oncale who brought the lawsuit was married with two children, and described himself as "far from gay," and the harassers in question also said they are not gay.[40]

The specific allegations that led to the lawsuit were so offensive that the Supreme Court omitted them from its opinion, "for the sake of dignity." The Circuit Court decision had described them as follows:[41]

Oncale alleges that the harassment included Pippen and Johnson restraining him while Lyons placed his penis on Oncale's neck, on one occasion, and on Oncale's arm, on another occasion; threats of homosexual rape by Lyons and Pippen; and the use of force by Lyons to push a bar of soap into Oncale's anus while Pippen restrained Oncale as he was showering on Sundowner premises. Oncale alleges both quid pro quo and hostile work environment sexual harassment. Oncale quit his job at Sundowner soon after the shower incident.

After noting these facts, the Circuit Court ruled that same-sex harassment did not offend the words of Title VII that forbid discrimination in an individual's "conditions of employment . . .because of race, color, religion, sex, or national origin." Oncale appealed to the U.S. Supreme Court. After this Court ruling he and his employer reached an out-of-court financial settlement, of which neither side would disclose the terms.[42]

JOSEPH ONCALE V. SUNDOWNER OFFSHORE SERVICES ET AL.
523 U.S. 75 (1998)

JUSTICE SCALIA delivered the opinion of the Court.

This case presents the question whether workplace harassment can violate Title VII's prohibition against "discriminat[ion] . . . because of . . . sex," 42 U.S.C. § 2000e2(a)(1), when the harasser and the harassed employee are of the same sex.

I

The District Court having granted summary judgment for respondent, we must assume the facts to be as alleged by petitioner Joseph Oncale. The precise details are irrelevant to the legal point we must decide, and in the interest of both brevity and dignity we shall describe them only generally. In late October 1991, Oncale was working for respondent Sundowner Offshore Services on a[n] oil platform. He was employed as a roustabout on an eight-man crew which included respondents John Lyons, Danny Pippen, and Brandon Johnson. Lyons, the crane operator, and Pippen, the driller, had supervisory authority. On several occasions, Oncale was forcibly subjected to sex-related, humiliating actions against him by Lyons, Pippen and Johnson in the presence of the rest of the crew. Pippen and Lyons also physically assaulted Oncale in a sexual manner, and Lyons threatened him with rape.

Oncale's complaints to supervisory personnel produced no remedial action; in fact, the company's Safety Compliance Clerk, Valent Hohen, told Oncale that Lyons and Pippen "picked [on] him all the time too," and called him a name suggesting homosexuality. Oncale eventually quit—asking that his pink slip reflect that he "voluntarily left due to sexual harassment and verbal abuse." When asked at his deposition why he left Sundowner, Oncale stated "I felt that if I didn't leave my job, that I would be raped or forced to have sex."

Oncale filed a complaint against Sundowner in the United States District Court. . ., alleging that he was discriminated against in his employment because of his sex. Relying on the Fifth Circuit's decision in *Garcia v. Elf Atochem North America*, 28 F. 3d 446, 451–452 (CA5 1994), the district court held that "Mr. Oncale, a male, has no cause of action under Title VII for harassment by male co-workers". . .[A] panel of the Fifth Circuit. . .affirmed. 83 F. 3d 118 (1996). . . .

II

Title VII of the Civil Rights Act of 1964 provides, in relevant part, that "[i]t shall be an unlawful employment practice for an employer ... to discriminate against any individual with respect to his compensation, terms, conditions, or privileges of employment, because of such individual's . . .sex. . ." 78 Stat. 255, as amended, 42 U.S.C. § 2000e–2(a)(1). We have held that this not only covers "terms" and "conditions" in the narrow contractual sense, but "evinces a congressional intent to strike at the entire spectrum of disparate treatment of men and women in employment." *Meritor Savings Bank, FSB v. Vinson*, 477 U.S. 57, 64 (1986). "When the workplace is permeated with discriminatory intimidation, ridicule, and insult that is sufficiently severe or pervasive to alter the conditions of the victim's employment and create an abusive working environment, Title VII is violated." *Harris v. Forklift Systems, Inc.*, 510 U.S. 17, 21 (1993).

Title VII's prohibition of discrimination "because of ... sex" protects men as well as women, *Newport News Shipbuilding & Dry Dock Co.* v. EEOC, 462 U.S. 669, 682 (1983). . . . In *Johnson v. Transportation Agency, Santa Clara Cty.*, 480 U.S. 616 (1987), a male employee claimed that his employer discriminated against him because of his sex when it preferred a female employee for promotion. Although we ultimately rejected the claim on other grounds, we did not consider it significant that the supervisor who made that decision was also a man. See *id.*, at 624–625. If our precedents leave any doubt on the question, we hold today that nothing in Title VII necessarily bars a claim of discrimination "because of ... sex" merely because the plaintiff and the defendant...are of the same sex. Courts have had little trouble with that principle in cases like *Johnson*, where an employee claims to have been passed over for a job or promotion. But when the issue arises in the context of a "hostile environment" sexual harassment claim, the state and federal courts have taken a bewildering variety of stances. Some, like the Fifth Circuit in this case, have held that same-sex sexual harassment claims are never cognizable under Title VII. Other decisions say that such claims are actionable only if the plaintiff can prove that the harasser is homosexual (and thus presumably motivated by sexual desire). Still others suggest that workplace harassment that is sexual in content is always actionable, regardless of the harasser's sex, sexual orientation, or motivations. [Citations omitted.]

We see no justification in the statutory language or our precedents for a categorical rule excluding same-sex harassment claims from the coverage of Title VII. As some courts have observed, male-on-male sexual harassment in the workplace was assuredly not the principal evil Congress was concerned with when it enacted Title VII. But statutory prohibitions often go beyond the principal evil to cover reasonably comparable evils, and it is ultimately the provisions of our laws rather than the principal concerns of our legislators by which we are governed. Title VII prohibits "discriminat[ion] . . . because of . . . sex" in the "terms" or "conditions" of employment. Our holding that this includes sexual harassment must extend to sexual harassment of any kind that meets the statutory requirements.

Respondents and their *amici* contend that recognizing liability for same-sex harassment will transform Title VII into a general civility code for the American workplace. But that risk is no greater for same-sex than for opposite-sex harassment, and is adequately met by careful attention to the requirements of the statute. Title VII does not prohibit all verbal or physical harassment in the workplace; it is directed only at "discriminat[ion] . . . because of . . . sex." We have never held that workplace harassment, even harassment between men and women, is automatically discrimination because of sex merely because the words used have sexual content or connotations. "The critical issue, Title VII's text indicates, is whether members of one sex are exposed to disadvantageous terms or conditions of employment to which members of the other sex are not exposed." *Harris*, at 25 (GINSBURG, J., concurring).

Courts and juries have found the inference of discrimination easy to draw in most male-female sexual harassment situations, because the challenged conduct typically involves explicit or implicit proposals of sexual activity; it is reasonable to assume those proposals would not have been made to someone of the same sex. The same chain of inference would be available to a plaintiff alleging same-sex harassment, if there were credible evidence that the harasser was homosexual. But harassing conduct need not be motivated by sexual desire to support an inference of discrimination on the basis of sex. A trier of fact might reasonably find such discrimination, for example, if a female victim is harassed in such sex-specific and derogatory terms by another woman as to make it clear that the harasser is motivated by general hostility to the presence of women in the workplace. A same-sex harassment plaintiff may also, of course, offer direct comparative evidence about how the alleged harasser treated members of both sexes in a mixed-sex workplace. Whatever evidentiary route the plaintiff chooses to follow, he or she must always prove that the conduct at issue was not merely tinged with offensive sexual connotations, but actually constituted "discrimina[tion] . . . because of . . . sex."

And there is another requirement that prevents Title VII from expanding into a general civility code: As we emphasized in *Meritor* and *Harris*, the statute does not reach genuine but innocuous differences in the ways men and women routinely interact with members of the same sex and of the opposite sex. The prohibition of harassment on the basis of sex requires neither asexuality nor androgyny in the workplace; it forbids only behavior so objectively offensive as to alter the "conditions" of the victim's employment. "Conduct that is not severe or pervasive enough to create an objectively hostile or abusive work environment—an environment that a reasonable person would find hostile or abusive—is beyond Title VII's purview." *Harris*, 510 U.S., at 21, citing *Meritor*, 477 U.S. at 67. We have always regarded that requirement as crucial, and as sufficient to ensure that courts and juries do not mistake ordinary socializing in the workplace—such as male-on-male horseplay or intersexual flirtation—for discriminatory "conditions of employment."

We have emphasized, moreover, that the objective severity of harassment should be judged from the perspective of a reasonable person in the plaintiff's position, considering "all the circumstances." *Harris*, at 23. In same-sex (as in all) harassment cases, that inquiry requires careful consideration of the social context in which particular behavior occurs and is experienced by its target. A professional football player's working environment is not severely or pervasively abusive, for example, if the coach smacks him on the buttocks as he heads onto the field—even if the same behavior would reasonably be experienced as abusive by the coach's secretary (male or female) back at the office. The real social impact of workplace behavior often depends on a constellation of surrounding circumstances, expectations, and relationships

> which are not fully captured by a simple recitation of the words used or the physical acts performed. Common sense, and an appropriate sensitivity to social context, will enable courts and juries to distinguish between simple teasing or roughhousing among members of the same sex, and conduct which a reasonable person in the plaintiff's position would find severely hostile or abusive.
>
> ### III
>
> Because we conclude that sex discrimination consisting of same-sex sexual harassment is actionable under Title VII, the judgment of the Court of Appeals for the Fifth Circuit is reversed, and the case is remanded for further proceedings consistent with this opinion.
>
> **JUSTICE THOMAS, concurring.**
>
> I concur because the Court stresses that in every sexual harassment case, the plaintiff must plead and ultimately prove Title VII's statutory requirement that there be discrimination "because of . . . sex."

Case Questions

1. All nine justices agree that the key guideline is as follows: "The critical issue, Title VII's text indicates, is whether members of one sex are exposed to disadvantageous terms or conditions of employment to which members of the other sex are not exposed." *Harris*, at 25 (GINSBURG, J., concurring). As you read the facts of this case, are you convinced that men as a group are being subjected to this degree of sexual humiliation? If only certain men are being singled out, should the question then be whether a woman at the same job would have been similarly mistreated? Whether a woman who exhibited traits similar to those exhibited by effeminate men would be similarly mistreated?

2. If the record shows that, e.g., only men who frequent gay bars are mistreated in this way, has Title VII been violated?

Suing a Sitting President: *Jones v. Clinton* (1998)

The controversy over the notorious encounter between Paula Corbin Jones and Bill Clinton took seven years to resolve in court. When Jones filed her sexual harassment suit, Clinton asked the federal courts to dismiss the case on the grounds that a sitting president could not be sued. The Supreme Court rejected this claim in *Clinton v. Jones* (1997).[43]

In May 1991, Paula Corbin worked for the Arkansas Industrial Development Commission (AIDC). She was working at a conference the AIDC was sponsoring at a Little Rock hotel the same day then-Governor Clinton was speaking there. A state trooper invited Jones to meet the governor. She went to Clinton's suite, was admitted, and found herself alone with him. At this point, their stories diverge. In a lawsuit filed against the ex-governor and the trooper in May 1994, after she had married, resigned her job, and moved out of state, and Clinton had become President, Paula Corbin Jones alleged that Clinton had taken her hand, pulled her closer to him, and made suggestive remarks. When she tried to distract him, Clinton lowered his trousers, exposed his erect penis, and asked her to kiss it. She fled, as Clinton told her he would "take care of it" if she got into trouble at work, and, "advised" her, "You are smart. Let's keep this to ourselves." Clinton denied all Jones's allegations.

By the time the case was resolved, other women had come forward with stories similar to Jones'. And, partly as a result of an investigation by Independent Counsel Ken Starr into the Jones case, Clinton became embroiled in the Monica Lewinsky scandal, which eventually led to impeachment charges against him. Jones alleged that Clinton had engaged in both kinds of sexual harassment: *quid pro quo* because he made veiled threats and promises; hostile environment because she was frightened that he would retaliate against her. In 1998, Federal District Judge Susan Webber Wright issued a summary judgment for the defendants on the grounds that Jones had not made a prima facie case that either kind of harassment occurred. She explained as follows.

JONES V. CLINTON
990 F. Supp. 657 (W.D. Arkansas 1998)

JUDGE WEBBER WRIGHT:

It is plaintiff's burden to come forward with "specific facts" showing that there is a genuine issue for trial, and the Court finds that her testimony on this point, being of a most general and non-specific nature (and in some cases contradictory to the record), simply does not suffice to create a genuine issue of fact regarding any tangible job detriment as a result of her having allegedly been discouraged from seeking more attractive jobs and reclassification. Cf. *Splunge v. Shoney's, Inc.*, 874 F. Supp. 1258, 1271 (M.D.Ala. 1994.)

First [...plaintiff alleged] that her rejection of the President's alleged advances caused her to suffer adverse employment actions, including being transferred to a position that had no responsible duties for which she could be adequately evaluated to earn advancement and failing to receive raises and merit increases. In this regard, the Court determined that the "totality" of the

> allegations alleged in this case were such that they could be said to have altered the conditions of plaintiff's employment and created an abusive work environment. However, development of the record has now established that plaintiff's allegations of adverse employment actions are without merit. . . .
>
> Plaintiff received every merit increase and cost-of-living allowance for which she was eligible during her nearly two-year tenure with the AIDC, her job was upgraded from Grade 9 to Grade 11 (thereby increasing her salary), she consistently received satisfactory job evaluations, and her job responsibilities upon her return from maternity leave were not significantly different from prior to her taking leave and did not cause her any materially significant disadvantage. These facts are clearly established by the record and dispel the notion that she was subjected to a hostile work environment. . .
>
> While the alleged incident in the hotel, if true, was certainly boorish and offensive, the Court has already found that the Governor's alleged conduct does not constitute sexual assault. This is thus not one of those exceptional cases in which an incident of sexual harassment, such as an assault, was deemed sufficient to state a claim of hostile work environment sexual harassment. Cf. *Crisonino v. New York City Housing Auth.*, 985 F. Supp. 385 (S.D.N.Y. 1997) (supervisor called plaintiff a "dumb bitch" and "shoved her so hard that she fell backward and hit the floor, sustaining injuries from which she has yet to fully recover"). . .
>
> Considering the totality of the circumstances, it simply cannot be said that the conduct to which plaintiff was allegedly subjected was frequent, severe, or physically threatening, and the Court finds that defendants' actions as shown by the record do not constitute the kind of sustained and nontrivial conduct necessary for a claim of hostile work environment.

Just as the *Clinton v. Jones* Supreme Court ruling opened the way for civil suits against a sitting president, which in turn uncovered evidence then used by the special prosecutor that was later cited as grounds for impeachment, so history seems to be repeating itself as this book goes to press. President Donald Trump is currently being sued by some women for libelous defamation (because he described as lies their accusations of his sexual misconduct) and by the Democratic National Committee for collusion with a foreign power (Russia) to unlawfully tamper with the U.S. electoral process. The Special Counsel Robert Mueller may well use the information revealed in these court cases for his investigation into White House wrongdoing.

Employer Liability Revisited

Meritor v. Vinson was not the Court's last word on employer liability. In 1997, the EEOC adopted a "knew or should have known" standard: an employer is liable for co-worker harassment if it "knows or should have known of the conduct, unless it can show that it took immediate and appropriate corrective action."[44] It took only a year for the Court to have occasion to apply the new rule. Kimberly Ellerth, a Burlington Industries salesperson in Chicago, and Beth Ann Faragher, a lifeguard for the city of Boca Raton, Florida, received similar treatment in their respective jobs. Ellerth worked in a two-person office with her immediate supervisor. *His* immediate supervisor, Ted Slowik, was a Burlington vice president based in New York. Slowik subjected Ellerth to "repeated boorish and offensive remarks and gestures." Some of these remarks "could be construed as threats to deny the worker tangible job benefits, but these threats were not carried out, and the worker, despite knowing that the company had a policy against sexual harassment, did not inform anyone with authority about the vice president's conduct." The remarks made by Faragher's three supervisors included one man's declaration that he would never promote a woman to the rank of lieutenant, and, from a different man, "Date me or clean the toilets for a year." Faragher complained to her training captain, who had told one of several women with similar complaints that "the City just doesn't care." Like Ellerth, Faragher did not invoke the city's complaint procedure. Hounded out of their jobs, both Ellerth and Faragher filed sexual harassment charges against their employers.[45] In neither case were the facts in dispute; employer liability was the only issue by the time the Supreme Court heard the cases, which the Supreme Court handed down together on the same day.

BURLINGTON INDUSTRIES, INC. V. ELLERTH
524 U.S. 742 (1998)

JUSTICE KENNEDY delivered the opinion of the Court.

We decide whether, under Title VII of the Civil Rights Act of 1964. . ., an employee who refuses the unwelcome and threatening sexual advances of a supervisor, yet suffers no adverse, tangible job consequences, can recover against the employer without showing the employer is negligent or otherwise at fault for the supervisor's actions.

Summary judgment was granted for the employer, so we must take the facts alleged by the employee to be true.

The disagreement revealed in the careful opinions of the judges of the Court of Appeals reflects the fact that Congress has left it to the courts to determine controlling agency law principles in a new and difficult area of federal law. We granted certiorari to assist in defining the relevant standards of employer liability....

II

...We must decide...whether an employer has vicarious liability when a supervisor creates a hostile work environment by making explicit threats to alter a subordinate's terms or conditions of employment, based on sex, but does not fulfill the threat. We turn to principles of agency law, for the term "employer" is defined under Title VII to include "agents." 42 U.S.C. § 2000e(b); see *Meritor*, at 72. In express terms, Congress has directed federal courts to interpret Title VII based on agency principles. Given such an explicit instruction, we conclude a uniform and predictable standard must be established as a matter of federal law.

...[T]he Restatement (Second) of Agency (1957) (hereinafter Restatement), is a useful beginning point for a discussion of general agency principles. 477 U.S. at 72. Since our decision in *Meritor*, federal courts have explored agency principles, and we find useful instruction in their decisions, noting that "common-law principles may not be transferable in all their particulars to Title VII." *Ibid*. The EEOC has issued Guidelines governing sexual harassment claims under Title VII, but they provide little guidance on the issue...See 29 CFR § 1604.11(c) (1997) (vicarious liability for supervisor harassment turns on "the particular employment relationship and the job functions performed by the individual")...

D

When a supervisor makes a tangible employment decision, there is assurance the injury could not have been inflicted absent the agency relation. A tangible employment action in most cases inflicts direct economic harm. As a general proposition, only a supervisor, or other person acting with the authority of the company, can cause this sort of injury. A co-worker can break a co-worker's arm as easily as a supervisor, and anyone who has regular contact with an employee can inflict psychological injuries by his or her offensive conduct. But one co-worker (absent some elaborate scheme) cannot dock another's pay, nor can one co-worker demote another. Tangible employment actions fall within the special province of the supervisor. The supervisor has been empowered by the company as a distinct class of agent to make economic decisions affecting other employees under his or her control.

Tangible employment actions are the means by which the supervisor brings the official power of the enterprise to bear on subordinates. A tangible employment decision requires an official act of the enterprise, a company act. . . .The supervisor often must obtain the imprimatur of the enterprise and use its internal processes. . . .For these reasons, a tangible employment action taken by the supervisor becomes for Title VII purposes the act of the employer. . .

In order to accommodate the agency principles of vicarious liability for harm caused by misuse of supervisory authority, as well as Title VII's equally basic policies of encouraging forethought by employers and saving action by objecting employees, we adopt the following holding in this case and in *Faragher v. Boca Raton,* also decided today. An employer is subject to vicarious liability to a victimized employee for an actionable hostile environment created by a supervisor with immediate (or successively higher) authority over the employee. When no tangible employment action is taken, a defending employer may raise an affirmative defense to liability or damages, subject to proof by a preponderance of the evidence, see Fed. Rule Civ. Proc. 8(c). The defense comprises two necessary elements: (a) that the employer exercised reasonable care to prevent and correct promptly any sexually harassing behavior, and (b) that the plaintiff employee unreasonably failed to take advantage of any preventive or corrective opportunities provided by the employer or to avoid harm otherwise. While proof that an employer had promulgated an anti-harassment policy with complaint procedure is not necessary in every instance as a matter of law, the need for a stated policy suitable to the employment circumstances may appropriately be addressed in any case when litigating the first element of the defense. And while proof that an employee failed to fulfill the corresponding obligation of reasonable care to avoid harm is not limited to showing any unreasonable failure to use any complaint procedure provided by the employer, a demonstration of such failure will normally suffice to satisfy the employer's burden under the second element of the defense. No affirmative defense is available, however, when the supervisor's harassment culminates in a tangible employment action, such as discharge, demotion, or undesirable reassignment.

IV

Relying on existing case law which held out the promise of vicarious liability for all *quid pro quo* claims, Ellerth focused all her attention in the Court of Appeals on proving her claim fit within that category. Given our explanation that the labels *quid pro quo* and hostile work environment are not controlling for purposes of establishing employer liability, Ellerth should have an adequate opportunity to prove she has a claim for which Burlington is liable.

Although Ellerth has not alleged she suffered a tangible employment action at the hands of Slowik, which would deprive Burlington of the availability of the affirmative defense, this is not dispositive. In light of our decision, Burlington is still subject to vicarious liability for Slowik's activity, but Burlington should have an opportunity to assert and prove the affirmative defense to liability.

For these reasons, we will affirm the judgment of the Court of Appeals, reversing the grant of summary judgment against Ellerth. On remand, the District Court will have the opportunity to decide whether it would be appropriate to allow Ellerth to amend her pleading or supplement her discovery.

JUSTICE THOMAS, with whom JUSTICE SCALIA joins, dissenting.

The Court today manufactures a rule that employers are vicariously liable if supervisors create a sexually hostile work environment, subject to an affirmative defense that the Court barely attempts to define. This rule applies even if the employer has a policy against sexual harassment, the employee knows about that policy, and the employee never informs anyone in a position of authority about the supervisor's conduct. As a result, employer liability under Title VII is judged by different standards depending upon whether a sexually or racially hostile work environment is alleged. The standard of employer liability should be the same in both instances: An employer should be liable if, and only if, the plaintiff proves that the employer was negligent in permitting the supervisor's conduct to occur.

I

... [After] ... the landmark case *Rogers* v. *EEOC*, 454 F.2d 234 (1971), cert. denied, 406 U.S. 957 (1972), a plaintiff claiming employment discrimination based upon race could assert a claim for a racially hostile work environment, in addition to the classic claim of so-called "disparate treatment." A disparate treatment claim required a plaintiff to prove an adverse employment consequence and discriminatory intent by his employer. See 1 B. Lindemann & P. Grossman, *Employment Discrimination Law* 10–11 (3d ed. 1996). A hostile environment claim required the plaintiff to show that his work environment was so pervaded by racial harassment as to alter the terms and conditions of his employment. See, *e.g., Snell* v. *Suffolk Cty.*, 782 F.2d 1094, 1103 (CA2 1986) ("To establish a hostile atmosphere, . . . plaintiffs must prove more than a few isolated incidents of racial enmity"); *Johnson* v. *Bunny Bread Co.*, 646 F.2d 1250, 1257 (CA8 1981) (no violation of Title VII from infrequent use of racial slurs). This is the same standard now used when determining whether sexual harassment renders a work environment hostile. See *Harris* v. *Forklift Systems, Inc.*, 510 U.S. 17, 21 (1993) (actionable sexual harassment occurs when the workplace is "*permeated* with discriminatory intimidation, ridicule, and insult") (emphasis added).

In race discrimination cases, employer liability has turned on whether the plaintiff has alleged an adverse employment consequence, such as firing or demotion, or a hostile work environment. If a supervisor takes an adverse employment action because of race, causing the employee a tangible job detriment, the employer is vicariously liable for resulting damages. This is because such actions are company acts that can be performed only by the exercise of specific authority granted by the employer, and thus the supervisor acts as the employer. If, on the other hand, the employee alleges a racially hostile work environment, the employer is liable only for negligence: that is, only if the employer knew, or in the exercise of reasonable care should have known, about the harassment and failed to take remedial action. See, *e.g., Dennis* v. *Cty. of Fairfax*, 55 F.3d 151, 153 (CA4 1995); *Davis* v. *Monsanto Chemical Co.*, 858 F.2d 345, 349 (CA6 1988), cert. denied, 490 U.S. 1110 (1989). Liability has thus been imposed only if the employer is blameworthy in some way. See, *e.g., Davis* v. *Monsanto Chemical Co.*, 858 F.2d at 349; *Snell* v. *Suffolk Cty.*, at 1104; *DeGrace* v. *Rumsfeld*, 614 F.2d 796, 805 (CA1 1980).

This distinction applies with equal force in cases of sexual harassment. When a supervisor inflicts an adverse employment consequence upon an employee who has rebuffed his advances, the supervisor exercises the specific authority granted to him by his company. His acts, therefore, are the company's acts and are properly chargeable to it. See 123 F.3d 490, 514 (1997) (Posner, C. J., dissenting.) . . .

If a supervisor creates a hostile work environment, however, he does not act for the employer. As the Court concedes, a supervisor's creation of a hostile work environment is neither within the scope of his employment, nor part of his apparent authority. Indeed, a hostile work environment is antithetical to the interest of the employer. In such circumstances, an employer should be liable only if it has been negligent. That is, liability should attach only if the employer either knew, or in the exercise of reasonable care should have known, about the hostile work environment and failed to take remedial action.

Sexual harassment is simply not something that employers can wholly prevent without taking extraordinary measures—constant video and audio surveillance, for example—that would revolutionize the workplace in a manner incompatible with a free society. See 123 F.3d 490, 513 (Posner, C.J., dissenting). Indeed, such measures could not even detect incidents of harassment such as the comments Slowick allegedly made to respondent in a hotel bar. The most that employers can be charged with, therefore, is a duty to act reasonably under the circumstances. . . .

Under a negligence standard, Burlington cannot be held liable for Slowick's conduct. Although respondent alleged a hostile work environment, she never contended that Burlington had been negligent in permitting the harassment to occur, and there is no question that Burlington acted reasonably under the circumstances. The company had a policy against sexual harassment, and respondent admitted that she was aware of the policy but nonetheless failed to tell anyone with authority over Slowick about his behavior. Burlington therefore cannot be charged with knowledge of Slowick's alleged harassment or with a failure to exercise reasonable care in not knowing about it.

Rejecting a negligence standard, the Court instead imposes a rule of vicarious employer liability, subject to a vague affirmative defense, for the acts of supervisors who wield no delegated authority in creating a hostile work environment. This rule is a whole-cloth creation that draws no support from the legal principles on which the Court claims it is based. Compounding its error, the Court fails to explain how employers can rely upon the affirmative defense, thus ensuring a continuing reign of confusion in this important area of the law. . . .

The Court's decision is also in considerable tension with our holding in *Meritor* that employers are not strictly liable for a supervisor's sexual harassment. Although the Court recognizes an affirmative defense—based solely on its divination of Title VII's *gestalt*—it provides shockingly little guidance about how employers can actually avoid vicarious liability. Instead, it issues only Delphic pronouncements and leaves the dirty work to the lower courts.

. . . The Court's holding does guarantee one result: There will be more and more litigation to clarify applicable legal rules in an area in which both practitioners and the courts have long been begging for guidance. It thus truly

> boggles the mind that the Court can claim that its holding will effect "Congress' intention to promote conciliation rather than litigation in the Title VII context." All in all, today's decision is an ironic result for a case that generated eight separate opinions in the Court of Appeals on a fundamental question, and in which we granted certiorari "to assist in defining the relevant standards of employer liability."

Case Questions

1. If a plaintiff alleges that he or she avoided internal grievance procedures out of fear of retaliation, and the employer insists this fear is unjustified, what will judges have to know to resolve the contradiction? How might employer and employee best present their respective cases?

2. When Justice Thomas refers to "extraordinary measures—constant video and audio surveillance, for example—that would revolutionize the workplace in a manner incompatible with a free society," he is employing a logical device called *reductio ad absurdum*. Describe less extreme measures that would be compatible with both a free society and a reasonable degree of employer responsibility.

Case note: In *Pennsylvania State Police v. Suders*, 124 S. Ct. 2342 (2004), the Supreme Court ruled that a "hostile environment" plaintiff complaining of "constructive discharge" must show "harassing behavior 'sufficiently severe or pervasive to alter the conditions of [their] employment.' " To establish "constructive discharge," she:

> must show that the abusive working environment became so intolerable that her resignation qualified as a fitting response. An employer may defend against such a claim by showing both (1) that it had installed a readily accessible and effective policy for reporting and resolving complaints of sexual harassment, and (2) that the plaintiff unreasonably failed to avail herself of that employer-provided preventive or remedial apparatus. This affirmative defense will not be available to the employer, however, if the plaintiff quits in reasonable response to an employer-sanctioned adverse action officially changing her employment status or situation, for example, a humiliating demotion, extreme cut in pay, or transfer to a position in which she would face unbearable working conditions.

GENDER STEREOTYPING AND THE WORKPLACE: *PRICE WATERHOUSE V. HOPKINS* (1989)

One of the clauses of Title VII of the 1964 Civil Rights Act forbids discrimination "with respect to . . . compensation, terms, conditions or privileges of employment because of [an] individual's race, color, religion, sex, or national origin," and another makes it unlawful to "classify . . . employees . . . in any way which would deprive or tend to deprive any individual of equal employment opportunities because of such individual's race . . . sex . . .[etc.]."[46] In a 1984 case, *Hishon v. Spaulding*,[47] the Supreme Court ruled that eligibility to be promoted to partnership in a law firm was properly viewed as a "term, condition, or privilege of employment," and First Amendment rights of association of the partners in the firm did not override this statutory right of employees of the firm. The decision was widely understood as applying to analogous sorts of professional partnerships such as those of large accounting firms.

A case involving such a firm, the Price Waterhouse company, came before the Supreme Court in 1988–89, but with a new twist.[48] The discrimination alleged was not discrimination against women as such but was discrimination against a particular woman for behaving in an insufficiently feminine manner. The facts of this case highlight a problem with the Supreme Court's (and Congress's) practice of using the terms "sex discrimination" and "gender discrimination" interchangeably. Sociologists, by contrast, distinguish "sex" from "gender" by using "sex" to describe biological categories and "gender" to describe the expectations that society attaches to a biological sex group.

The Price Waterhouse case, in sociological terms, involved a corporate decision against promoting a female employee on the grounds of her gender non-conformity. The U.S. Supreme Court glided right past this innovative aspect of the case (analyzing it as just another example of sex discrimination), but the dissenter in the federal circuit court of appeals did raise the issue, and this Supreme Court ruling has become a significant precedent for individuals alleging discrimination on the basis of gender identity.

The facts of the case contained ample examples of what the Supreme Court called "sex stereotyping" in remarks made by supervisory personnel at Price Waterhouse who were examining the candidacy of Ann B. Hopkins for promotion to partnership. The general picture of her, from both supporters and critics, showed a mix. She combined a stellar record of acquiring lucrative contracts for the firm as well as an outstanding number of billable hours, excellent integrity, communication skills, and intelligence, with some problems in the area of interpersonal skills. Those problems include being sometimes "overly aggressive, unduly harsh, impatient with staff, and very demanding." These personality traits proved the fertile ground for the sex-stereotyped remarks. One of the opponents of her promotion (in his written evaluation) suggested that what she needed was a "course at charm school." A member of the Admissions Committee (which plays a pivotal role in the promotion process) specifically investigated a complaint in Hopkins's personnel file that she used profane language and testified that her use of profanity had been regarded by "several ... partners" as "one of the negatives." One of her supporters for promotion specifically responded to this issue by noting (in a written evaluation), "Many male partners are worse than Ann (language and tough personality)," and added that others were concerned about her profanity only "because she is a lady using foul language." Another of her supporters tried to head off this line of criticism by saying that she "had matured from a tough-talking, somewhat masculine, hard-nosed mgr. to an authoritative, formidable, but much more appealing lady partner candidate." After the firm voted to postpone Ms. Hopkins' promotion decision for a year, she met with the head partner of her own division, a firm supporter of her candidacy. He, Thomas Beyer, advised her (in sincerity) that the best avenue for improving her chances of promotion would be "to walk more femininely, dress more femininely, wear make-up, have her hair styled, and wear jewelry." Once her case was in court, Hopkins also presented some evidence of sex stereotyping in evaluations of candidates from previous years, including a comment from one partner the year prior to her own candidacy that he could never seriously consider a woman candidate for partner and believed women were not even capable of functioning as senior managers (the job Ann Hopkins already had.) His evaluation and vote in that year had been counted in the process just like that of the other partners, even though his practice was clearly unlawful, because it introduced sex-discriminatory bias into the process. While there was no evidence that he personally had participated in Ann Hopkins's evaluation, his comments were introduced to show the general atmosphere at the company.

Ann Hopkins was denied promotion at Price Waterhouse the second year as well as the first. She then resigned and sued the company for violating her rights under Title VII. At the District Court level, the judge ruled that she had persuasively demonstrated that the presence of "stereotyped assumptions about women" in the selection process at Price Waterhouse meant that its evaluation system was "subject to sex bias" in the "double standard" being applied to partner candidates; this stereotyping violated Title VII. Similarly, because the company failed to show "by clear and convincing evidence" that its decision to deny

Hopkins the promotion based on her lack of interpersonal skills would be the same absent the discrimination, the court awarded to Hopkins appropriate economic relief.[49] Both sides appealed (Hopkins, because she wanted a more substantial award of damages).

At the federal Circuit Court of Appeals, the three-judge panel upheld all of the district court rulings, by a two to one vote. The majority commented that Hopkins had "made a substantial showing of the role . . . sexual stereotyping played in the selection system" and that such stereotyping had "played a significant role in blocking plaintiff's admission to partnership."[50] The circuit court acknowledged that the other circuits divided over what should follow, once a plaintiff has demonstrated that "discriminatory animus played a significant or substantial role in the contested employment decision." Some let the employer prove simply by the preponderance of evidence that the decision would have been the same even without any discrimination, but others agreed with the district court below that the appropriate level of proof to be required was "clear and convincing evidence."[51] This circuit court (the D.C. Circuit) agreed with the district court that the appropriate standard was "clear and convincing evidence," and it is this aspect of the decision to which the U.S. Supreme Court directed its attention.

The U.S. Supreme Court totally neglected the host of questions that might be raised about the basic assumption that requiring gender conformity itself amounts to sex discrimination. Circuit Court Judge Stephen Williams, in dissent, had suggested this line of questions, but his suggestion was ignored by even the dissenters on the Supreme Court. He had complained: "Dismissal of a male employee because he routinely appeared for work in skirts and dresses would surely reflect a form of sexual stereotyping, but it would not, merely on that account, support Title VII liability. . . . The court makes no effort to delineate the theory, to draw a line between permissible and impermissible."[52] Here is what the Supreme Court did say:

PRICE WATERHOUSE V. HOPKINS
490 U.S. 228 (1989)

JUSTICE BRENNAN announced the judgment of the Court and delivered an opinion, in which **JUSTICE MARSHALL, JUSTICE BLACKMUN,** and **JUSTICE STEVENS** join.

. . .

II

The specification of the standard of causation under Title VII is a decision about the kind of conduct that violates that statute. According to Price Waterhouse, an employer violates Title VII only if it gives decisive consideration to an employee's gender, race, national origin, or religion in making a decision that affects that employee. On Price Waterhouse's theory, even if a plaintiff shows that her gender played a part in an employment decision, it is still her burden to show that the decision would have been different if the employer had not discriminated. In Hopkins' view, on the other hand, an employer violates the statute whenever it allows one of these attributes to play any part in an employment decision. Once a plaintiff shows that this occurred, according to Hopkins, the employer's proof that it would have made the same decision in the absence of discrimination can serve to limit equitable relief but not to avoid a finding of liability. We conclude that, as often happens, the truth lies somewhere in between.

A

In passing Title VII, Congress made the simple but momentous announcement that sex, race, religion, and national origin are not relevant to the selection, evaluation, or compensation of employees.[3] . . .

. . . In now-familiar language, the statute forbids an employer to "fail or refuse to hire or to discharge any individual, or otherwise to discriminate with respect to his compensation, terms, conditions, or privileges of employment," or to "limit, segregate, or classify his employees or applicants for employment in any way which would deprive or tend to deprive any individual of employment opportunities or otherwise adversely affect his status as an employee, *because of* such individual's . . . sex." 42 U.S.C. § 2000e–2(a)(1), (2) (emphasis added). We take these words to mean that gender must be irrelevant to employment decisions. To construe the words "because of" as colloquial shorthand for "but-for causation," as does Price Waterhouse, is to misunderstand them.

But-for causation is a hypothetical construct. In determining whether a particular factor was a but-for cause of a given event, we begin by assuming that that factor was present at the time of the event, and then ask whether, even if that factor had been absent, the event nevertheless would have transpired in the same way. The present, active tense of the operative verbs of § 703(a)(1) ("to fail or refuse"), in contrast, turns our attention to the actual moment of the event in question, the adverse employment decision. The critical inquiry, the one commanded by the words of § 703(a)(1), is whether gender was a factor in the employment decision at the moment it was made. Moreover, since we know that the words "because of" do not mean "solely because of," we also know that Title VII meant to condemn even those decisions based on a mixture of legitimate and illegitimate considerations. When, therefore, an employer considers both gender and legitimate factors at the time of making a decision, that decision was "because of" sex and the other, legitimate considerations—even if we may say later, in the context of litigation, that the decision would have been the same if gender had not been taken into account.

. . .

We need not leave our common sense at the doorstep when we interpret a statute. It is difficult for us to imagine that, in the simple words "because of," Congress meant to obligate a plaintiff to identify the precise causal role played by legitimate and illegitimate motivations in the employment decision she challenges. We conclude, instead, that Congress meant to obligate her to prove that the employer relied upon sex-based considerations in coming to its decision.

. . .To say that an employer may not take gender into account is not, however, the end of the matter, for that describes only one aspect of Title VII. The other important aspect of the statute is its preservation of an employer's remaining freedom of choice. We conclude that the preservation of this freedom means that an employer shall not be liable if it can prove that, even if it had not taken gender into account, it would have come to the same decision regarding a particular person. The statute's maintenance of employer prerogatives is evident from the statute itself and from its history, both in Congress and in this Court. . . .

. . . . And our emphasis. . . on "legitimate, nondiscriminatory reason[s]" in disparate-treatment cases, see *McDonnell Douglas Corp. v. Green*, 411 U.S. 792,

802 (1973); *Texas Dept. of Community Affairs v. Burdine*, 450 U.S. 248 (1981), results from our awareness of Title VII's balance between employee rights and employer prerogatives. . . .

When an employer ignored the attributes enumerated in the statute, Congress hoped, it naturally would focus on the qualifications of the applicant or employee. The intent to drive employers to focus on qualifications rather than on race, religion, sex, or national origin is the theme of a good deal of the statute's legislative history. An interpretive memorandum entered into the Congressional Record by Senators Case and Clark, co-managers of the bill in the Senate, is representative of this general theme. According to their memorandum, Title VII "expressly protects the employer's right to insist that any prospective applicant, Negro or white, must meet the applicable job qualifications. Indeed, the very purpose of title VII is to promote hiring on the basis of job qualifications, rather than on the basis of race or color."[9] (110 Cong.Rec. 7247 1964). . .

Our holding casts no shadow on *Burdine*, in which we decided that, even after a plaintiff has made out a prima facie case of discrimination under Title VII, the burden of persuasion does not shift to the employer to show that its stated legitimate reason for the employment decision was the true reason. 450 U.S., at 256–258. We stress, first, that neither court below shifted the burden of persuasion to Price Waterhouse on this question, and in fact, the District Court found that Hopkins had not shown that the firm's stated reason for its decision was pretextual. 618 F. Supp., at 1114–1115. Moreover, since we hold that the plaintiff retains the burden of persuasion on the issue whether gender played a part in the employment decision, the situation before us is not the one of "shifting burdens" that we addressed in *Burdine*. Instead, the employer's burden is most appropriately deemed an affirmative defense: the plaintiff must persuade the factfinder on one point, and then the employer, if it wishes to prevail, must persuade it on another. See *NLRB v. Transportation Management Corp.*, 462 U.S. 393, 400 (1983).[11]

Price Waterhouse's claim that the employer does not bear any burden of proof (if it bears one at all) until the plaintiff has shown "substantial evidence that Price Waterhouse's explanation for failing to promote Hopkins was not the 'true reason' for its action" merely restates its argument that the plaintiff in a mixed-motives case must squeeze her proof into *Burdine*'s framework. Where a decision was the product of a mixture of legitimate and illegitimate motives, however, it simply makes no sense to ask whether the legitimate reason was "*the* 'true reason'" (emphasis added) for the decision—which is the question asked by *Burdine*. See *Transportation Management*, at 400, n. 5. Oblivious to this last point, the dissent would insist that *Burdine*'s framework perform work that it was never intended to perform. It would require a plaintiff who challenges an adverse employment decision in which both legitimate and illegitimate considerations played a part to pretend that the decision, in fact, stemmed from a single source . . .

B

In deciding as we do today, we do not traverse new ground. We have in the past confronted Title VII cases in which an employer has used an illegitimate criterion to distinguish among employees, and have held that it is the employer's burden to justify decisions resulting from that practice. When an employer has asserted that gender is a BFOQ within the meaning of § 703(e), for example, we have assumed that it is the employer who must show why it must use gender as a criterion in employment. See *Dothard v. Rawlinson*, 433 U.S. 321, 332–337 (1977). In a related context, although the Equal Pay Act expressly permits employers to pay different wages to women where disparate pay is the result of a "factor other than sex," see 29 U.S.C. 206(d)(1), we have decided that it is the employer, not the employee, who must prove that the actual disparity is not sex linked. See *Corning Glass Works v. Brennan*, 417 U.S. 188, 196 (1974). . . . As these examples demonstrate, our assumption always has been that if an employer allows gender to affect its decision-making process, then it must carry the burden of justifying its ultimate decision. We have not in the past required women whose gender has proved relevant to an employment decision to establish the negative proposition that they would not have been subject to that decision had they been men, and we do not do so today.

We have reached a similar conclusion in other contexts where the law announces that a certain characteristic is irrelevant to the allocation of burdens and benefits. In *Mt. Healthy City Bd. of Ed. v. Doyle*, 429 U.S. 271 (1977), the plaintiff claimed that he had been discharged as a public school teacher for exercising his free-speech rights under the First Amendment. Because we did not wish to "place an employee in a better position as a result of the exercise of constitutionally protected conduct than he would have occupied had he done nothing," *id.*, at 285, we concluded that such an employee "ought not to be able, by engaging in such conduct, to prevent his employer from assessing his performance record and reaching a decision not to rehire on the basis of that record." Id., at 286. We therefore held that once the plaintiff had shown that his constitutionally protected speech was a "substantial" or "motivating factor" in the adverse treatment of him by his employer, the employer was obligated to prove "by a preponderance of the evidence that it would have reached the same decision as to [the plaintiff] even in the absence of the protected conduct." Id., at 287. A court that finds for a plaintiff under this standard has effectively concluded that an illegitimate motive was a "but-for" cause of the employment decision. . .

In *Transportation Management*, we upheld the NLRB's interpretation of 10(c) of the National Labor Relations Act [using similar reasoning]. . . .462 U.S., at 403.

We have, in short, been here before. Each time, we have concluded that the plaintiff who shows that an impermissible motive played a motivating part in an adverse employment decision has thereby placed upon the defendant the burden to show that it would have made the same decision in the absence of the unlawful motive. Our decision today treads this well-worn path.

C

In saying that gender played a motivating part in an employment decision, we mean that, if we asked the employer at the moment of the decision what its reasons were and if we received a truthful response, one of those reasons would be that the applicant or employee was a woman. In the specific context of sex stereotyping, an employer who acts on the basis of a belief that a woman cannot be aggressive, or that she must not be, has acted on the basis of gender.

Although the parties do not overtly dispute this last proposition, the placement by Price Waterhouse of "sex stereotyping" in quotation marks throughout its brief seems to us an insinuation either that such stereotyping was not present in this case or that it lacks legal relevance. We reject both possibilities. As to the existence of sex stereotyping in this case, we are not inclined to quarrel with the District Court's conclusion that a number of the partners' comments showed sex stereotyping at work. As for the legal relevance of sex stereotyping, we are beyond the day when an employer could evaluate employees by assuming or insisting that they matched the stereotype associated with their group, for "[i]n forbidding employers to discriminate against individuals because of their sex, Congress intended to strike at the entire spectrum of disparate treatment of men and women resulting from sex stereotypes." *Los Angeles Dept. of Water and Power v. Manhart*, 435 U.S. 702, 707, n. 13. An employer who objects to aggressiveness in women but whose positions require this trait places women in an intolerable and impermissible catch 22: out of a job if they behave aggressively and out of a job if they do not. Title VII lifts women out of this bind.

Remarks at work that are based on sex stereotypes do not inevitably prove that gender played a part in a particular employment decision. The plaintiff must show that the employer actually relied on her gender in making its decision. In making this showing, stereotyped remarks can certainly be evidence that gender played a part. . .

As to the employer's proof, in most cases, the employer should be able to present some objective evidence as to its probable decision in the absence of an impermissible motive. Moreover, proving "that the same decision would have been justified . . . is not the same as proving that the same decision would have been made." *Givhan*, 439 U.S., at 416. An employer may not, in other words, prevail in a mixed-motives case by offering a legitimate and sufficient reason for its decision if that reason did not motivate it at the time of the decision. Finally, an employer may not meet its burden in such a case by merely showing that at the time of the decision it was motivated only in part by a legitimate reason. The very premise of a mixed-motives case is that a legitimate reason was present, and indeed, in this case, Price Waterhouse already has made this showing by convincing Judge Gesell that Hopkins' interpersonal problems were a legitimate concern. The employer instead must show that its legitimate reason, standing alone, would have induced it to make the same decision.

III

The courts below held that an employer who has allowed a discriminatory impulse to play a motivating part in an employment decision must prove by clear and convincing evidence that it would have made the same decision in the absence of discrimination. We are persuaded that the better rule is that the employer must make this showing by a preponderance of the evidence.

Conventional rules of civil litigation generally apply in Title VII cases, . . . and one of these rules is that parties to civil litigation need only prove their case by a preponderance of the evidence. . . .

. . .Since the lower courts required Price Waterhouse to make its proof by clear and convincing evidence, they did not determine whether Price Waterhouse had proved by a preponderance of the evidence that it would have placed Hopkins' candidacy on hold even if it had not permitted sex-linked evaluations to play a part in the decision-making process. Thus, we shall remand this case so that that determination can be made.

IV

...Price Waterhouse disputes both that stereotyping occurred and that it played any part in the decision to place Hopkins' candidacy on hold. In the firm's view, in other words, the District Court's factual conclusions are clearly erroneous. We do not agree.

.... It takes no special training to discern sex stereotyping in a description of an aggressive female employee as requiring "a course at charm school." Nor, turning to Thomas Beyer's memorable advice to Hopkins, does it require expertise in psychology to know that, if an employee's flawed "interpersonal skills" can be corrected by a soft-hued suit or a new shade of lipstick, perhaps it is the employee's sex and not her interpersonal skills that has drawn the criticism.

Price Waterhouse appears to think that we cannot affirm the factual findings of the trial court without deciding that, instead of being overbearing and aggressive and curt, Hopkins is, in fact, kind and considerate and patient. If this is indeed its impression, petitioner misunderstands the theory on which Hopkins prevailed. The District Judge acknowledged that Hopkins' conduct justified complaints about her behavior as a senior manager. But he also concluded that the reactions of at least some of the partners were reactions to her as a woman manager. Where an evaluation is based on a subjective assessment of a person's strengths and weaknesses, it is simply not true that each evaluator will focus on, or even mention, the same weaknesses. Thus, even if we knew that Hopkins had "personality problems," this would not tell us that the partners who cast their evaluations of Hopkins in sex-based terms would have criticized her as sharply (or criticized her at all) if she had been a man. It is not our job to review the evidence and decide that the negative reactions to Hopkins were based on reality; our perception of Hopkins' character is irrelevant. We sit not to determine whether Ms. Hopkins is nice, but to decide whether the partners reacted negatively to her personality because she is a woman.

V

We hold that when a plaintiff in a Title VII case proves that her gender played a motivating part in an employment decision, the defendant may avoid a finding of liability only by proving by a preponderance of the evidence that it would have made the same decision even if it had not taken the plaintiff's gender into account. Because the courts below erred by deciding that the defendant must make this proof by clear and convincing evidence, we reverse the Court of Appeals' judgment against Price Waterhouse on liability and remand the case to that court for further proceedings.

Opinion Footnotes

3 We disregard, for purposes of this discussion, the special context of affirmative action.

9 Many of the legislators' statements, such as the memorandum quoted in text, focused specifically on race . . .but instead we take them as general statements on the meaning of Title VII. . . .By the same token, our specific references to gender throughout this opinion, and the principles we announce, apply with equal force to discrimination based on race, religion, or national origin.

11 Given that both the plaintiff and defendant bear a burden of proof in cases such as this one, it is surprising that the dissent insists that our approach requires the employer to bear "the ultimate burden of proof." It is, moreover, perfectly consistent to say both that gender was a factor in a particular decision when it was made and that, when the situation is viewed hypothetically and after the fact, the same decision would have been made even in the absence of discrimination. Thus, we do not see the "internal inconsistency" in our opinion that the dissent perceives. Finally, where liability is imposed because an employer is unable to prove that it would have made the same decision even if it had not discriminated, this is not an imposition of liability "where sex made no difference to the outcome." In our adversary system, where a party has the burden of proving a particular assertion and where that party is unable to meet its burden, we assume that that assertion is inaccurate. . . .

JUSTICE WHITE, concurring in the judgment.

In my view, to determine the proper approach to causation in this case, we need look only to the Court's opinion in *Mt. Healthy City Bd. of Ed. v. Doyle*, 429 U.S. 274 (1977). . . .

Because the Court of Appeals required Price Waterhouse to prove by clear and convincing evidence that it would have reached the same employment decision in the absence of the improper motive, rather than merely requiring proof by a preponderance of the evidence as in *Mt. Healthy*, I concur in the judgment reversing this case in part and remanding. With respect to the employer's burden, however, . . .[i]n my view . . .there is no special requirement that the employer carry its burden by objective evidence. In a mixed-motives case, where the legitimate motive found would have been ample grounds for the action taken, and the employer credibly testifies that the action would have been taken for the legitimate reasons alone, this should be ample proof.

JUSTICE O'CONNOR, concurring in the judgment.

I agree with the plurality that, on the facts presented in this case, the burden of persuasion should shift to the employer to demonstrate by a preponderance of the evidence that it would have reached the same decision concerning Ann Hopkins' candidacy absent consideration of her gender. I further agree that this burden shift is properly part of the liability phase of the litigation. I thus concur in the judgment of the Court. My disagreement stems from the plurality's conclusions concerning the substantive requirement of causation under the statute and its broad statements regarding the applicability of the allocation of the burden of proof applied in this case. The evidentiary rule the Court adopts today should be viewed as a supplement to the careful framework established by our unanimous decisions in *McDonnell Douglas Corp. v. Green*, 411 U.S. 792 (1973), and *Texas Dept. of Community Affairs v. Burdine*, 450 U.S. 248 (1981), for use in cases such as this one where the employer has created uncertainty as to causation by knowingly giving substantial weight to an impermissible criterion. I write separately to explain why I believe such a departure from the *McDonnell Douglas* standard is justified in the circumstances presented by this and like cases, and to express my views as to when and how the strong medicine of requiring the employer to bear the burden of persuasion on the issue of causation should be administered. . . .

II

The dissent's summary of our individual disparate treatment cases to date is fair and accurate, and amply demonstrates that the rule we adopt today is at least a change in direction from some of our prior precedents. We have indeed emphasized in the past that in an individual disparate treatment action the plaintiff bears the burden of persuasion throughout the litigation. . . . *McDonnell Douglas* and *Burdine* assumed that the plaintiff would bear the burden of persuasion . . . and we clearly depart from that framework today. Such a departure requires justification, and its outlines should be carefully drawn.

First, *McDonnell Douglas* itself dealt with a situation where the plaintiff presented no direct evidence that the employer had relied on a forbidden factor under Title VII in making an employment decision. . . . I do not think that the employer is entitled to the same presumption of good faith where there is direct evidence that it has placed substantial reliance on factors whose consideration is forbidden by Title VII . . .

Second, the facts of this case, and a growing number like it decided by the Courts of Appeals, convince me that the evidentiary standard I propose is necessary to make real the promise of *McDonnell Douglas* that "[i]n the implementation of [employment] decisions, it is abundantly clear that Title VII tolerates no . . . discrimination, subtle or otherwise." 411 U.S., at 801 . . .

At this point Ann Hopkins had taken her proof as far as it could go. She had proved discriminatory input into the decisional process, and had proved that participants in the process considered her failure to conform to the stereotypes credited by a number of the decisionmakers had been a substantial factor in the decision. . . . [O]ne would be hard pressed to think of a situation where it would be more appropriate to require the defendant to show that its decision would have been justified by wholly legitimate concerns.

Moreover, there is mounting evidence in the decisions of the lower courts that respondent here is not alone in her inability to pinpoint discrimination as the precise cause of her injury, despite having shown that it played a significant role in the decisional process. Many of these courts, which deal with the evidentiary issues in Title VII cases on a regular basis, have concluded that placing the risk of nonpersuasion on the defendant in a situation where uncertainty as to causation has been created by its consideration of an illegitimate criterion makes sense as a rule of evidence and furthers the substantive command of Title VII.... Particularly in the context of the professional world, where decisions are often made by collegial bodies on the basis of largely subjective criteria, requiring the plaintiff to prove that any one factor was the definitive cause of the decisionmakers' action may be tantamount to declaring Title VII inapplicable to such decisions....

Finally, I am convinced that a rule shifting the burden to the defendant where the plaintiff has shown that an illegitimate criterion was a "substantial factor" in the employment decision will not conflict with other congressional policies embodied in Title VII....

I believe there are significant differences between shifting the burden of persuasion to the employer in a case resting purely on statistical proof as in the disparate impact setting and shifting the burden of persuasion in a case like this one, where an employee has demonstrated by direct evidence that an illegitimate factor played a substantial role in a particular employment decision....

Requiring that the plaintiff demonstrate that an illegitimate factor played a substantial role in the employment decision identifies those employment situations where the deterrent purpose of Title VII is most clearly implicated. As an evidentiary matter, where a plaintiff has made this type of strong showing of illicit motivation, the factfinder is entitled to presume that the employer's discriminatory animus made a difference to the outcome, absent proof to the contrary from the employer. Where a disparate treatment plaintiff has made such a showing, the burden then rests with the employer to convince the trier of fact that it is more likely than not that the decision would have been the same absent consideration of the illegitimate factor.

...In this case, I agree with the plurality that petitioner should be called upon to show that the outcome would have been the same if respondent's professional merit had been its only concern. On remand, the District Court should determine whether Price Waterhouse has shown [this] by a preponderance of the evidence. . . .

JUSTICE KENNEDY, with whom THE CHIEF JUSTICE and JUSTICE SCALIA join, dissenting.

Today the Court manipulates existing and complex rules for employment discrimination cases in a way certain to result in confusion. Continued adherence to the evidentiary scheme established in *McDonnell Douglas Corp. v. Green*, 411 U.S. 792 (1973), and *Texas Dept. of Community Affairs v. Burdine*, 450 U.S. 248 (1981), is a wiser course than creation of more disarray in an area of the law already difficult for the bench and bar, and so I must dissent.

Before turning to my reasons for disagreement with the Court's disposition of the case, it is important to review the actual holding of today's decision. I read the opinions as establishing that in a limited number of cases Title VII plaintiffs, by presenting direct and substantial evidence of discriminatory animus, may shift the burden of persuasion to the defendant to show that an adverse employment decision would have been supported by legitimate reasons. The shift in the burden of persuasion occurs only where a plaintiff proves by direct evidence that an unlawful motive was a substantial factor actually relied upon in making the decision.

Where the plaintiff makes the requisite showing, the burden that shifts to the employer is to show that legitimate employment considerations would have justified the decision without reference to any impermissible motive. [See] opinion of WHITE, J. [and] opinion of O'CONNOR, J.. The employer's proof on the point is to be presented and reviewed just as with any other evidentiary question: the Court does not accept the plurality's suggestion that an employer's evidence need be "objective" or otherwise out of the ordinary. ([See] opinion of WHITE, J.).

In sum, the Court alters the evidentiary framework of *McDonnell Douglas* and *Burdine* for a closely defined set of cases. Although JUSTICE O'CONNOR advances some thoughtful arguments for this change, I remain convinced that it is unnecessary and unwise. . . .

I

. . .[T]he import of today's decision is. . .that in certain cases it is not the plaintiff who must prove the presence of causation, but the defendant who must prove its absence.

II

We established the order of proof for individual Title VII disparate-treatment cases in *McDonnell Douglas Corp. v. Green*, 411 U.S. 792 (1973), and reaffirmed this allocation in *Texas Dept. of Community Affairs v. Burdine*, 450 U.S. 248 (1981). Under *Burdine*, once the plaintiff presents a prima facie case, an inference of discrimination arises. The employer must rebut the inference by articulating a legitimate nondiscriminatory reason for its action. The final burden of persuasion, however, belongs to the plaintiff. *Burdine* makes clear that the "ultimate burden of persuading the trier of fact that the defendant intentionally discriminated against the plaintiff remains at all times with the plaintiff." *Id.*, at 253. . . . I would adhere to this established evidentiary framework, which provides the appropriate standard for this and other individual disparate-treatment cases. . . .

III

. . . I think it important to stress that Title VII creates no independent cause of action for sex stereotyping. Evidence of use by decisionmakers of sex stereotypes is, of course, quite relevant to the question of discriminatory intent. The ultimate question, however, is whether discrimination caused the plaintiff's harm.

. . . In this case, Hopkins plainly presented a strong case both of her own professional qualifications and of the presence of discrimination in Price Waterhouse's partnership process. Had the District Court found on this record that sex discrimination caused the adverse decision, I doubt it would have been reversible error. That decision was for the finder of fact, however, and the District Court made plain that sex discrimination was not a but-for cause of the decision to place Hopkins' partnership candidacy on hold. . . .

IV

. . . . Here the District Court found that . . . "[b]ecause plaintiff has considerable problems dealing with staff and peers, the Court cannot say that she would have been elected to partnership if the Policy Board's decision had not been tainted by sexually based evaluations," 618 F.Supp., at 1120. Hopkins thus failed to meet the requisite standard of proof after a full trial. I would remand the case for entry of judgment in favor of Price Waterhouse.

Case Questions

1. If firing a woman for failing to wear make-up or feminine jewelry or certain colors of clothing is illegal sex discrimination, would it be similarly illegal to fire a man for

    a. Wearing obvious make-up—say, heavy lipstick and eye shadow?

    b. Wearing skirts to work? Wearing men's suits but in the color of red or pink (say, to a law office)?

    c. Wearing long, dangling earrings and prominent necklaces?

2. In a state that did not explicitly ban sexual-orientation discrimination, would it be illegal for a company to fire a lesbian who appeared at a company picnic holding hands with her female partner? A gay male who did the same with a male companion? Could a company fire a woman for failure to remove or cover up a large and prominently dark mustache? In Ann Hopkins's case, testimony was unanimous that she excelled at garnering business for the firm. Would the situation be different if some of the hypothetical practices suggested in question 1 as to a male employee could be shown to have cost a company its clients? (Note that under Title VII such a client-costing argument would not be treated as valid justification for a blanket refusal to hire women or Black persons.[53]) Does the answer change if the employee is in the process of transitioning to another gender?

3. Is the requirement that the employer prove that it would have had (and acted upon) sufficient legitimate motives for firing someone in Ann Hopkins' position akin to treating the employer as guilty until proven innocent? Would requiring Ann Hopkins to prove that she would not have been fired if the employers did not harbor views that certain behavior was especially inappropriate for women, impose on her an impossible burden of proof?

Case note: The four justice plurality proposed a rule that shifts the burden of proof of innocent motive to the employer once the employee shows that a forbidden motive, such as racial or gender bias, "played a motivating part in an employment decision." Justices White and O'Connor, either of whose vote is needed to make a majority, argue that the language from precedents such as *Mt. Healthy* establishes that the phrase "motivating factor" should be interpreted to mean "substantial factor," and thus they stressed that courts should require evidence that the forbidden motive played a "substantial" role in the employment decision before requiring that the employer prove a legitimate, alternative motive. The Civil Rights Act of 1991, further discussed below, adopted into law the explicit rule: "[A]n unlawful employment practice is established when the complaining party demonstrates that race, color, religion, sex, or national origin was a motivating factor for any employment practice, even though other factors also motivated the practice."[54]

TITLE VII AND GENDER DISCRIMINATION

In the years following the *Price Waterhouse* decision, this precedent proved to be a powerful tool for both males and females challenging discriminatory sex stereotyping in the workplace. More recently, litigants have successfully deployed it to protect transgender men and women who alleged violations of Title VII's prohibitions on sex discrimination by employers mistreating them for their failure to conform to sex and gender stereotypes. Prior to *Price Waterhouse*, the federal courts ruled that transgender individuals have no legal recourse to challenge employment discrimination under Title VII because "a prohibition against discrimination based on an individual's sex is not synonymous with a prohibition against discrimination based on an individual's sexual identity disorder or discontent with the sex into which they were born."[55] *Price Waterhouse*, however, signaled that sex discrimination encompasses gender discrimination, and resulted in a series of court decisions that expanded Title VII to protect transgender individuals from sex stereotyping in the workplace.

These cases include instances in which an employer rescinded a job offer upon learning that an individual is transgender (*Lopez v. River Oaks Imaging & Diagnostic Group, Inc.*, 542 F. Supp. 2d 653 (S.D. Tex. 2008); *Schroer v. Billington*, 577 F. Supp. 2d 293 (D.D.C. 2008)) or when an employer refused to extend an employment offer to a transgender individual (*Lewis v. High Point Regional Health Sys.*, 79 F. Supp. 3d 588 (E.D.N.C. 2015), *Fabian v. Hosp. of Central Conn.*, 172 F. Supp. 3d 509 (D. Conn. 2016)). Other cases implicate questions related to how employers treat their current transgender employees. For example, in *Barnes v. City of Cincinnati* (401 F.3d 729), the Sixth Circuit Court of Appeals ruled that a police officer who alleged that they were demoted because of their failure to conform to sex stereotypes—they presented as a male at work but lived as a woman in their private time—had a legitimate sex discrimination claim under Title VII. In other instances, the courts have ruled that if an employee is terminated for transitioning and/or undergoing sex reassignment surgery they have an actionable Title VII sex discrimination claim (*Tronetti v. TLC HealthNet Lakeshore Hospital*, No. 03-cv-375E (W.D.N.Y. 2003), *Mitchell v. Axcan Scandipharm, Inc.*, No. 05-243 (W.D. Pa. 2006)).

For example, Jimmie L. Smith was a lieutenant in the Salem, Ohio fire department when he initiated the transition from male to female at which point Smith's "co-workers began questioning him about his appearance and commenting that his appearance and mannerisms were not 'masculine enough.'"[56] Smith contacted his immediate supervisor to complain, and the latter informed the Chief of the Fire Department who reached out to the city's legal counsel to investigate how to terminate Smith. Via a leak, Smith learned of the city's plans, and initiated legal proceedings with the EEOC. When the city discovered Smith's legal actions, he was suspended from work for a twenty-four hour shift for allegedly violating city policy. Once local proceedings were exhausted, Smith filed suit in federal district court alleging employment discrimination and retaliation in violation of Title VII. The district court ruled in favor of the City of Salem, but Smith appealed. In *Smith v. City of Salem*, the U.S. Court of Appeals for the Sixth Circuit relied on *Price Waterhouse* to overturn the lower court decision.

SMITH V. CITY OF SALEM
378 F.3d 566 (6th Cir. 2004)

Before COLE and GILMAN, CIRCUIT JUDGES; SCHWARZER, SENIOR DISTRICT JUDGE:

* * *

II.A.1

...After *Price Waterhouse*, an employer who discriminates against women because, for instance, they do not wear dresses or makeup, is engaging in sex discrimination because the discrimination would not occur but for the victim's sex. It follows that employers who discriminate against men because they do wear dresses and makeup, or otherwise act femininely, are also engaging in sex discrimination, because the discrimination would not occur but for the victim's sex. See, e.g., *Nichols*, 256 F.3d 864 (Title VII sex discrimination and hostile work environment claim upheld where plaintiff's male co-workers and supervisors repeatedly referred to him as "she" and "her" and where co-workers mocked him for walking and carrying his serving tray "like a woman"); *Higgins v. New Balance Athletic Shoe, Inc.*, 194 F.3d 252, 261 n. 4 (1st Cir. 1999) ("[J]ust as a woman can ground an action on a claim that men discriminated against her because she did not meet stereotyped expectations of femininity, a man can ground a claim on evidence that other men discriminated against him because he did not meet stereotypical expectations of masculinity." (internal citation omitted)); see also *Rosa v. Park West Bank & Trust Co.*, 214 F.3d 213 (1st Cir. 2000) (applying *Price Waterhouse* and Title VII jurisprudence to an Equal Credit Opportunity Act claim and reinstating claim on behalf of biologically male plaintiff who alleged that he was denied an opportunity to apply for a loan because was dressed in "traditionally feminine attire").

Yet some courts have held that this latter form of discrimination is of a different and somehow more permissible kind. For instance, the man who acts

> in ways typically associated with women is not described as engaging in the same activity as a woman who acts in ways typically associated with women, but is instead described as engaging in the different activity of being a transsexual (or in some instances, a homosexual or transvestite). Discrimination against the transsexual is then found not to be discrimination "because of sex," but rather, discrimination against the plaintiff's unprotected status or mode of self-identification. In other words, these courts superimpose classifications such as "transsexual" on a plaintiff, and then legitimize discrimination based on the plaintiff's gender non-conformity by formalizing the non-conformity into an ostensibly unprotected classification. See, e.g., *Dillon v. Frank*, No. 90-2290, 1992 WL 5436 (6th Cir. Jan. 15, 1992).
>
> Such was the case here: [ ]despite the fact that Smith alleges that Defendants' discrimination was motivated by his appearance and mannerisms, which Defendants felt were inappropriate for his perceived sex, the district court expressly declined to discuss the applicability of *Price Waterhouse*. The district court therefore gave insufficient consideration to Smith's well-pleaded claims concerning his contra-gender behavior, but rather accounted for that behavior only insofar as it confirmed for the court Smith's status as a transsexual, which the district court held precluded Smith from Title VII protection.
>
> Such analyses cannot be reconciled with *Price Waterhouse*, which does not make Title VII protection against sex stereotyping conditional or provide any reason to exclude Title VII coverage for non sex-stereotypical behavior simply because the person is a transsexual. As such, discrimination against a plaintiff who is a transsexual—and therefore fails to act and/or identify with his or her gender—is no different from the discrimination directed against Ann Hopkins in *Price Waterhouse*, who, in sex-stereotypical terms, did not act like a woman. Sex stereotyping based on a person's gender non-conforming behavior is impermissible discrimination, irrespective of the cause of that behavior; a label, such as "transsexual," is not fatal to a sex discrimination claim where the victim has suffered discrimination because of his or her gender non-conformity. Accordingly, we hold that Smith has stated a claim for relief pursuant to Title VII's prohibition of sex discrimination.

While the Sixth Circuit recognized that Smith could pursue litigation under Title VII, the Court's opinion suggests that Smith is protected because *he* is a gender non-conforming male. At the time of the litigation, Smith was in the early stages of transition and still identified as a male in the workplace.[57] Yet, the Court's positioning of transgender women as gender non-conforming men is legally significant, and for transgender individuals it may be personally and emotionally challenging to be vindicated in this manner.

As Diane Schroer, the plaintiff in *Schroer v. Billington* (2008)—an employment discrimination case in which the D.C. Circuit Court of Appeals ruled that Title VII prohibitions on workplace discrimination "because of sex" are analogous to those "because of religion," and just as an employer cannot rescind a job offer if someone converts from one religion to another an employer cannot do so if one changes sex—told her lawyer, "I haven't gone through all this only to have a court vindicate my rights as a gender non-conforming man."[58] Put another way, Diane Schroer identifies herself as a woman, and she wanted to be recognized as a woman under the law. This type of recognition requires judges to adjust their traditional conception of sex in order to move beyond a biological binary—male-female—towards a more multifaceted and complicated understanding of sex in both science and the law.[59]

In all of the aforementioned cases, the courts considered whether or not the transgender employees in question were being penalized for their failure to comply with traditional gender norms or sex stereotypes similar to the type of discrimination experienced by Hopkins in the *Price Waterhouse* case. In 2012, the EEOC went a step further and determined that discrimination against transgender individuals in workplaces covered by Title VII is sex discrimination regardless of whether or not it is based on gender or sex stereotypes. In *Macy v. Holder*, the EEOC ruled that when the Bureau of Alcohol, Tobacco, Firearms and Explosives halted the hiring process for Mia Macy upon receiving notification that she had transitioned from man to woman, she had the right to seek recourse under Title VII procedures.

MIA MACY V. ERIC HOLDER

U.S. Equal Employment Opportunity Commission, Appeal No. 0120120821 (2012)

. . .

Thus, a transgender person who has experienced discrimination based on his or her gender identity may establish a prima facie case of sex discrimination through any number of different formulations. These different formulations are not, however, different claims of discrimination that can be separated out and investigated within different systems. Rather, they are simply different ways of describing sex discrimination.

> For example, Complainant could establish a case of sex discrimination under a theory of gender stereotyping by showing that she did not get the job as an NIBIN ballistics technician at Walnut Creek because the employer believed that biological men should consistently present as men and wear male clothing.
>
> Alternatively, if Complainant can prove that the reason she did not get the job at Walnut Creek is that the Director was willing to hire her when he thought she was a man, but was not willing to hire her once he found out that she was now a woman—she will have proven that the Director discriminated on the basis of sex. Under this theory, there would actually be no need, for purposes of establishing coverage under Title VII, for Complainant to compile any evidence that the Director was engaging in gender stereotyping.

The EEOC's conclusion "that intentional discrimination against a transgender individual because that person is transgender is, by definition, discrimination 'based on...sex,' and such discrimination therefore violates Title VII" erases the distinction between complaints based on gender stereotyping and complaints based on one's transgender identity alone.[60] In effect, this means that employers cannot take transgender individuals' gender or sex into account when making employment decisions without running afoul of Title VII.

As the federal agency charged with implementing Title VII, the EEOC has the power to interpret the law for purposes of enforcement, and to date a few courts cases have cited the *Macy* holding to substantiate that discrimination against transgender employees in the workplace is sex discrimination in violation of Title VII (*Roberts v. Clark County School District,* No. 2:15-cv-00388-JAD-PAL (D. Nev. Oct. 4, 2016), *Fabian v. Hospital of Central Connecticut,* 172 F. Supp. 3d 509 (D. Conn. 2016)). As litigation in this area increases it will be interesting to see if the EEOC position as articulated in *Macy* prevails. In order to be able to avoid problematic reliance on Title VII's prohibition on sex discrimination, proponents of LGBT rights and their allies have pushed for congressional legislation that would explicitly prohibit discrimination in the workplace on the basis of gender identity or sexual orientation (see, e.g. the Employment Non-Discrimination Act and the Equality Act).[61]

THE CIVIL RIGHTS ACT OF 1991

In addition to its implications for workplace discrimination on the basis of gender identity, the Court's decision in *Price Waterhouse* prompted new congressional legislation. Dissenting Justice Kennedy's frequent reference to the absence of a statutory mandate for the standards of proof that the Court was establishing in the *Price Waterhouse* case was met head on by a Congressional response; the Civil Rights Act of 1991 codified the language from the plurality's opinion into explicit statutory mandate (as described in the Case note above.) In addition to a direct Congressional response to divisions within the *Price Waterhouse* Court, the Act modified three 1989 Supreme Court rulings on equal employment opportunity.

This Congressional reply to these Court decisions took as long as it did because Congress's initial response, the Civil Rights Act of 1990, was vetoed by President George Herbert Walker Bush (Bush I) on the ostensible grounds that the legislation would, despite Congress's expressed intention to the contrary, pressure employers into hiring on the basis of affirmative "quotas." Congress then repassed quite similar legislation as the Civil Rights Act of 1991. This time, faced with an election only one year away, and with many women voters who were angered by the Anita Hill/Clarence Thomas hearings, President Bush I agreed to sign the Act, and did so on November 21, 1991.[62]

The first of the three 1989 decisions altered by this law, *Wards Cove Packing v. Atonio*,[63] concerned the clause in the 1964 Civil Rights Act that made it unlawful to "classify...applicants for employment in any way which would deprive *or tend to deprive* any individual of equal employment opportunities...because of such individual's race...or sex" (emphasis added).[64] In a number of cases involving employment practices that operated with a disproportionately negative *impact* on women or on racial minorities, the Supreme Court by 1989 had evolved certain procedural rules for applying this clause.[65]

If a plaintiff wants to claim that a particular job requirement, which looks neutral (nondiscriminatory) on the surface, in fact has a *tendency* to discriminate against one sex (or one race), the plaintiff can present general statistical evidence on the disproportionate impact that the particular requirement has on one sex (or one race). In other words, if approximately 98 percent of males meet a particular job requirement, but only 2 percent of females meet the requirement, clear evidence of a sex-lined disproportionate impact of the requirement would be present.

Once such evidence has been presented, however, the Court's work has only begun. This evidence creates what is called a "prima facie" case of sex discrimination. This means that the job requirement in question is then presumed to be discriminatory, until proven otherwise. The burden of proof then shifts from the plaintiff to the defendant-employer. If the employer can prove that the requirement reflects "business necessity" and bears "a manifest relation to the employment in question,"[66] or that the requirement is "essential to effective job performance,"[67] the employer can succeed in shifting the burden of proof back to the plaintiff. At this point the plaintiff must show that other, nondiscriminatory (or less discriminatory) selection devices are available that would achieve the same goal as the discriminatory one. If the plaintiff can do this, the Court is supposed to strike down the discriminatory requirement.

What happened in the *Ward's Cove* case is that the 5–4 majority opinion by Justice White appeared to water down some of the language from these rules in a way that made it more difficult for plaintiff-employees to prevail against defendant-employers. Instead of requiring from the employer "proof" of "business necessity," the Court majority said that the employer had only to "produce evidence" that the "challenged practice serves, in a significant way, the legitimate employment goals of the employer."[68] Congress's 1991 corrective to this judicial decision was the rule that the respondent must "demonstrate that the challenged practice is job related for the position in question and consistent with business necessity."[69] (If the employer succeeds in this, the employees can still prevail if they can prove that there is an alternative available with a less discriminatory impact that still achieves the same business purpose.)

The second 1989 judicial decision that prompted Congressional reversal was handed down, again 5–4,[70] in *Martin v. Wilks*.[71] There the majority had permitted some white firefighters to bring a lawsuit challenging a "consent decree" to which two groups of Black plaintiff employees, the federal government, and the employer had all consented as a way of settling a job discrimination lawsuit. Consent decrees have for a long time been an important weapon in the arsenal of women fighting employment discrimination. For instance, in January 1973, the American Telephone and Telegraph Company (AT&T) consented to pay $15 million in back pay to thousands of discriminated-against female employees.[72]

The lawsuit that led to the decree challenged in *Martin v. Wilks* had been initiated by the federal government in combination with the two groups of Black employees in 1974 and 1975. After the employer had been found guilty of discrimination in hiring and promotions, the various parties to the case and the federal District Court had approved the negotiated "consent decree," which specified an affirmative hiring plan for people of color. After granting provisional approval to the plan, the District Court had ordered that "all interested parties" be notified of it and of their right to file objections to it. Two months later, the District Court had held a fairness hearing, at which both white and Black employees had presented objections (from different directions) to the plan. The District Court had then overruled the objections and put the plan into effect in

1981. Within several months, various groups of white firefighters, believing that less meritorious Black firefighters were starting to receive promotions ahead of them, began bringing a series of legal actions against the consent decree. These various legal actions were consolidated in the District Court, and settled by it in a 1985 opinion, rejecting the various challenges to the Consent Decree. This decision was then appealed, and by the time it reached the U.S. Supreme Court the issue had narrowed down to the question of which parties are free to challenge a remedial Title VII consent decree after it has gone into effect. Five justices answered that question in a way that the four dissenters found much too expansive of the previous limits on challenges to affirmative action consent decrees.

Congress then turned around in 1991 and legislated explicitly what the dissenters had claimed were the pre-existing rules on the subject: Persons are forbidden to challenge a remedial consent decree "that resolves a claim of employment discrimination under the Constitution or Federal civil rights laws" if such persons prior to the effective date of the decree have already had available to them "actual notice of the proposed . . . order sufficient to apprise such person[s] that such . . . order might adversely affect the interests and legal rights of such person[s] and that an opportunity was available to present objections to such . . . order by a future date certain," and "a reasonable opportunity to present objections to [the] . . . order."[73] In other words, Congress stepped in to eliminate the specter, provoked by the majority decision in *Martin v. Wilks*, of a "never-ending stream of litigation" against remedial consent decrees.[74]

The third Supreme Court decision overturned in the 1991 Civil Rights Act was *Patterson v. McLean Credit Union*.[75] *Patterson* is a case that brought to light anomalies in federal anti-discrimination law, anomalies that Congress was willing to correct, up to a point. Brenda Patterson, a Black woman, worked as a teller and file coordinator until she was laid off after ten years. She alleged a consistent pattern of on-the-job race-based harassment; she was subjected to racial slurs, given more work than white fellow employees, denied promotion, assigned to the most demeaning tasks, and singled out for scrutiny and criticism. Patterson brought her claim not under Title VII but under a much older law, the Civil Rights Act of 1866. Specifically, § 1981 of this law mandated, "All persons . . . shall have the same right . . . to make and enforce contracts . . . as is enjoyed by white citizens."[76] Brenda Patterson had several reasons for preferring a § 1981 lawsuit to a Title VII one. Title VII limited back pay awards to two years and did not allow extra compensatory and punitive damages; § 1981 does not impose these limits. (Also, § 1981 covers all employers, including those who have fewer than fifteen employees, whereas Title VII exempts this 15% of the workforce from its coverage.)

The Supreme Court had ruled in 1986 that race-based or sex-based harassment which is sufficiently severe or pervasive to "create an abusive working environment" must be viewed as affecting a "condition of employment" under Title VII.[77] While the Supreme Court was unanimous in *Patterson* in its willingness to apply this "same right to make contracts" language of § 1981 to an initial hiring contract or to an employment contract signed pursuant to a promotion, a majority of five[78] refused to extend this § 1981 language to cover racial disparities in the "terms or conditions" of employment (which disparities would be forbidden, as to either race or gender, under Title VII). The Civil Rights Act of 1991 amended § 1981 to correct what Congress considered an erroneous judicial interpretation.

When civil rights lobbyists went to work in Congress against the *Patterson* Court decision, they did not keep their attack within the narrow confines of the terms of § 1981. Instead, they urged that all the sorts of discrimination condemned by Title VII be rendered just as punishable (through civil suits) as race discrimination in hiring and promotions. They succeeded up to a point. The Civil Rights Act of 1991 did amend § 1981 so that it covers "the enjoyment of all benefits, privileges, terms, and conditions of the contractual relationship."[79] In other words, on-the-job *racial* harassment is now actionable even for employers of fewer than fifteen individuals and without the limits on damages awards contained in Title VII. Section 1981 was also amended to allow compensatory and punitive damages for victims of the other kinds of intentional discrimination forbidden by Title VII (i.e. non-racial ones); this change allows victims of sex-based (or religion-based) job discrimination (including harassment) to sue for punitive and compensatory damages.[80] These damages are limited, however, by the rule that firms of fewer than fifteen employees are still exempted from coverage; firms of 15–100 employees have a damage ceiling of $50,000; firms of 101–200 employees, a ceiling of $100,000; firms of 201–500 employees, a ceiling of $200,000; and firms of more than 500 employees, a ceiling of $300,000.[81] In short, as a matter of explicit federal law, employers who engage in sex-based discrimination are at less financial risk than employers who engage in race-based discrimination.

This difference between the penalties for racist discrimination and for sexist discrimination was opposed by Congressional Democrats and added to the bill in order to overcome Republican President Bush's determination to veto the bill if some limits were not imposed. The resulting limits were the most significant sense in which the bill was a compromise, since President Bush had argued for a

$150,000 limit and the Democrats had opposed all limits on the grounds that the two kinds of discrimination should be equally punishable.[82]

Overall, one can conclude from the pattern exhibited in the judicial-legislative dialogue of 1988–1991, especially in light of the precedent for that pattern that took place between the judicial *Grove City College* decision of 1984[83] and the Congressional Civil Rights Restoration Act of 1987, that the 1980s and early 1990s showed the Congresses of these years to have been more staunchly dedicated to protecting the rights of racial minorities and of women than was the U.S. Supreme Court. This pattern runs contrary to the prediction by Alexander Hamilton in Federalist No.78 that the Supreme Court, because justices could not be voted out of office, would prove to be the special protector of rights of "the minor party" and of individuals against "the oppressions" that a majority might otherwise impose. The pattern of the 1980s obviously has something to do with the judicial appointing power of Republican presidents Reagan and Bush I and with the evidently effective position of racial minorities and women (or of their supporters) in the electoral coalition that backs Congressional Democrats. (The effective role that minorities can play in national majority coalitions was itself predicted in another of the *Federalist Papers* of 1787, Number 10, by James Madison).

This pattern of the 1980s is not necessarily a pattern for all times; the Supreme Court that produced the school desegregation decisions of the 1950s was more protective of racial minorities than were the political branches (i.e., Congress and the President) of that era, and it was the Supreme Court, not Congress, that legalized abortion nationwide in the 1970s. Still, one can infer from the experience of the 1980s and early '90s that the institutional pattern predicted by Alexander Hamilton (with its special role for the Supreme Court) for protecting individual and minority rights in the United States does not always prevail.

BFOQ AND DISPARATE IMPACT

In some Title VII cases, sex discrimination is not obvious because the policies under challenge do not explicitly target males or females for differential treatment. Dianne Rawlinson was excluded from a "correctional counselor" (prison guard) job by the Alabama Board of Corrections (headed by E.C. Dothard) not specifically on the basis of sex, but rather on the basis of height and weight requirements. Dianne Rawlinson contended that the 5'2" height minimum and the 120-pound weight minimum had a tendency to exclude otherwise qualified women.[84]

The Supreme Court by 1977 had already handed down two decisions interpreting the "tend to" discriminate clause of Title VII; both cases had presented allegations of racial rather than sex discrimination,[85] but they did establish procedural precedents that would apply likewise to claims of sex discrimination. If a plaintiff wants to claim that a particular job requirement, which looks neutral (nondiscriminatory) on the surface, in fact *tends* to discriminate against one sex (or one race), the plaintiff, as explained in the previous section, can present general statistical evidence on the disproportionate impact that the particular requirement has on one sex (or one race). Once this has been shown, the burden of proof then shifts from the plaintiff to the defendant-employer who gets the chance to prove (in the phrases legally operative as of the 1970s) that the requirement bears "a manifest relation to the employment in question,"[86] or that the requirement is reasonably necessary to avoid undermining "the essence of the business operation."[87] If successful, this shifts the burden of proof to the plaintiff, who gets the chance to prove that other, nondiscriminatory selection devices are available that would achieve the same goal as the discriminatory one. If the plaintiff can do so, the Court is supposed to strike down the discriminatory requirement.

In attacking the height and weight requirements, Dianne Rawlinson had no trouble demonstrating their disproportionate impact on women. More than 99 percent of American men were taller than 5 feet 2 inches and weighed more than 120 pounds. Only 59 percent of American women met those physical requirements. The disproportion was obvious.

At the district court level, where Ms. Rawlinson first took her case,[88] the Alabama Corrections Board argued that the height and weight requirements achieved a certain level of physical strength in their prison guards. They presented no evidence to support their assumption, and they offered no argument why a direct strength test could not be substituted for the height and weight rule. After hearing both sides, the district court concluded that the height and weight requirements for Alabama prison guards violated Title VII of the Civil Rights Act.

While Ms. Rawlinson's case was pending at the district court, the Alabama Board of Corrections adopted a new regulation, Number 204, which established a same-sex rule for all correctional counselors (prison guards) working in "contact positions" within maximum-security institutions. Contact positions are those requiring continual close physical proximity to prisoners. Like most states, Alabama operated separate prisons for men and for women. Since more prisoners in maximum-security jails are men, this meant that more prison guard jobs would be available to men. More precisely, this new rule closed off access for women to all but 25 percent of the prison guard jobs in the State of Alabama. When Regulation 204 was adopted, Dianne Rawlinson amended her complaint to include a protest against it, too, as a violation of Title VII. The district court decided in her favor on this point, too.

A description of conditions in these maximum-security prisons is useful for assessing the needfulness of the same-sex guard requirement. In these institutions in Alabama, living quarters are arranged by large dormitories, with communal showers and toilets that are open to view from the dormitories and hallways. In two of the male penitentiaries, because of their farming operations, "strip searches" of prisoners to look for contraband were frequent. In American prisons, "strip searches" not uncommonly include anal inspections and, in the case of women prisoners, vaginal inspections.

In Alabama's non-maximum security prisons, women did work in "contact positions" among male prisoners. Women guards performed most of the usual duties, including inspections of shower-room and toilet areas, but they did not engage in searches and frisks of nude male prisoners. In the two male maximum-security institutions where strip searches were frequent, only 25–33% of the guards actually were involved in the task of conducting strip searches. The possibility that maximum security prisons, too, could assign male guards to perform this particular task and could nonetheless employ female guards to perform other tasks had figured prominently in the district court's decision that Regulation 204 amounted to arbitrary sex discrimination.[89]

The U.S. Supreme Court split three ways over this decision. A majority of six justices, headed by Justice Stewart, agreed with the district court that the height and weight requirement violated Title VII, but they disagreed as to Regulation 204. They held that Alabama had bona-fide job-related reasons for excluding women guards from contact jobs within male maximum-security penitentiaries. Two justices, Brennan and Marshall, dissented on the Regulation 204 question; they agreed with the district court. Justice White dissented entirely, because he believed that Rawlinson had never made a valid statistical demonstration of prima facie discrimination, and that therefore the case should simply have been thrown out of court. Three of the six justices in the majority—Rehnquist, Burger, and Blackmun—indicated in a separate opinion that they might be more willing to uphold height and weight requirements in future cases. Nonetheless, this left a clear five-judge majority on record against height and weight requirements, at least for the job of prison guard. The reasons proffered by each group of justices follows.

E. C. Dothard et al. v. Dianne Rawlinson et al.
433 U.S. 321 (1977)

Mr. Justice Stewart delivered the opinion of the Court.

....We turn...to the appellants' argument that they have rebutted the prima facie case of discrimination by showing that the height and weight requirements are job related. These requirements, they say, have a relationship to strength, a sufficient but unspecified amount of which is essential to effective job performance as a correctional counselor. In the district court, however, the appellants produced no evidence correlating the height and weight requirements with the requisite amount of strength thought essential to good job performance. Indeed, they failed to offer evidence of any kind in specific justification of the statutory standards.

If the job-related quality that the appellants identify is bona fide, their purpose could be achieved by adopting and validating a test for applicants that measures strength directly. Such a test, fairly administered, would fully satisfy the standards of Title VII because it would be one that "measure[s] the person for the job and not the person in the abstract." *Griggs v. Duke Power Co.,* 401 U.S., at 436. But nothing in the present record even approaches such a measurement.

For the reasons we have discussed, the District Court was not in error in holding that Title VII of the Civil Rights Act of 1964, as amended, prohibits application of the statutory height and weight requirements to Rawlinson and the class she represents.

III

Unlike the statutory height and weight requirements, Regulation 204 explicitly discriminates against women on the basis of their sex. In defense of this overt discrimination, the appellants rely on § 703e of Title VII, which permits sex-based discrimination "in those certain instances where...sex...is a bona fide occupational qualification reasonably necessary to the normal operation of that particular business or enterprise."

The District Court rejected the bona fide occupational qualification (bfoq) defense, relying on the virtually uniform view of the federal courts that § 703e provides only the narrowest of exceptions to the general rule requiring equality of employment opportunities. This view has been variously formulated. In.....an earlier case, *Weeks v. Southern Bell Telephone and Telegraph Co.,* 408 F.2d 228, 235, the [5th Cir. Court of Appeals] said that an employer could rely on the bfoq exception only by proving "that he had reasonable cause to believe, that is, a factual basis for believing, that all or substantially all women would be unable to perform safely and efficiently the duties of the job involved." See also *Phillips v. Martin-Marietta Corp.*, 400 U.S. 542. But whatever the verbal formulation, the federal courts have agreed that it is impermissible under Title VII to refuse to hire an individual woman or man on the basis of stereotyped characterizations of the sexes, and the District Court in the present case held in effect that Regulation 204 is based on just such stereotypical assumptions.

We are persuaded—by the restrictive language of § 703e, the relevant legislative history, and the consistent interpretation of the EEOC that the bfoq exception was in fact meant to be an extremely narrow exception to the general prohibition of discrimination on the basis of sex. In the particular factual circumstances of this case, however, we conclude that the District Court erred in rejecting the State's contention that Regulation 204 falls within the narrow ambit of the bfoq exception.

The environment in Alabama's penitentiaries is a peculiarly inhospitable one for human beings of whatever sex. Indeed, a federal district court has held that the conditions of confinement in the prisons of the State, characterized by "rampant violence" and a "jungle atmosphere," are constitutionally intolerable. *James v. Wallace*, 406 F.Supp. 318, 325 (MD Ala.). The record in the present case shows that because of inadequate staff and facilities, no attempt is made in the four maximum security male penitentiaries to classify or segregate inmates according to their offense or level of dangerousness—a procedure that, according to expert testimony, is essential to effective penological administration. Consequently, the estimated 20% of the male prisoners who are sex offenders are scattered throughout the penitentiaries' dormitory facilities.

In this environment of violence and disorganization, it would be an oversimplification to characterize Regulation 204 as an exercise in "romantic paternalism." In the usual case, the argument that a particular job is too dangerous for women may appropriately be met by the rejoinder that it is the purpose of Title VII to allow the individual woman to make that choice for herself. More is at stake in this case, however, than an individual woman's decision to weigh and accept the risks of employment . . . .

The essence of a correctional counselor's job is to maintain prison security. A woman's relative ability to maintain order in a male, maximum security, unclassified penitentiary of the type Alabama now runs could be directly reduced by her womanhood. There is a basis in fact for expecting that sex offenders who have criminally assaulted women in the past would be moved to do so again if access to women were established within the prison. There would also be a real risk that other inmates, deprived of a normal heterosexual environment, would assault women guards because they were women.[22] In a prison system where violence is the order of the day, where inmate access to guards is facilitated by dormitory living arrangements, where every institution is understaffed, and where a substantial portion of the inmate population is composed of sex offenders mixed at random with other prisoners, there are few visible deterrents to inmate assaults on women custodians.

The plaintiffs' own expert testified that dormitory housing for aggressive inmates poses a greater security problem than single-cell lock-ups, and further testified that it would be unwise to use women as guards in a prison where even 10% of the inmates had been convicted of sex crimes and were not segregated from the other prisoners.[23] The likelihood that inmates would assault a woman because she was a woman would pose a real threat not only to the victim of the assault but also to the basic control of the penitentiary and protection of its inmates and the other security personnel. The employee's very womanhood would thus directly undermine her capacity to provide the security that is the essence of a correctional counselor's responsibility.

There was substantial testimony from experts on both sides of the litigation that the use of women as guards in "contact" positions under the existing conditions in Alabama maximum security male penitentiaries would pose a substantial security problem, directly linked to the sex of the prison guard. On . . .that evidence, we conclude that the District Court was in error in ruling that being male is not a bfoq for the job of correctional counselor in a "contact" position in an Alabama male maximum security penitentiary.[24]

The judgment is accordingly affirmed in part and reversed in part. . . .

Opinion Footnotes

[22] The record contains evidence of an attack on a female clerical worker in an Alabama prison, and of an incident involving a woman student who was taken hostage during a visit to one of the maximum security institutions.

[23] Alabama's penitentiaries are evidently not typical. The appellees' two experts testified that in a normal, relatively stable maximum security prison—characterized by control over the inmates, reasonable living conditions, and segregation of dangerous offenders—women guards could be used effectively and beneficially. Similarly, an *amicus* brief filed by the State of California attests to that State's success in using women guards in all-male penitentiaries.

[24] The record shows by contrast, that Alabama's minimum security facilities, such as work-release centers, are recognized by their inmates as privileged confinement situations not to be lightly jeopardized

by disobeying applicable rules of conduct. Inmates assigned to these institutions are thought to be the "cream of the crop" of the Alabama prison population.

MR. JUSTICE REHNQUIST, with whom THE CHIEF JUSTICE and MR. JUSTICE BLACKMUN join, concurring in the result and concurring in part.

I agree with, and join, Parts I and III of the Court's opinion in this case and with its judgment. While I also agree with the Court's conclusion in Part II of its opinion, holding that the District Court was "not in error" in holding the statutory height and weight requirements in this case to be invalidated by Title VII, the issues with which that part deals are bound to arise so frequently that I feel obliged to separately state the reasons for my agreement with its result. I view affirmance of the District Court in this respect as essentially dictated by the peculiarly limited factual and legal justifications offered below by appellants on behalf of the statutory requirements. For that reason, I do not believe—and do not read the Court's opinion as holding—that all or even many of the height and weight requirements imposed by States on applicants for a multitude of law enforcement agency jobs are pretermitted by today's decision.

I agree that the statistics relied upon in this case are sufficient, absent rebuttal, to sustain a finding of a prima facie violation of § 703(a)(2), in that they reveal a significant discrepancy between the numbers of men, as opposed to women, who are automatically disqualified by reason of the height and weight requirements. . . .

Appellants, in order to rebut the prima facie case under the statute, had the burden placed on them to advance job-related reasons for the qualification. *McDonnell Douglas Corp. v. Green*, 411 U.S. 792, at 802 (1973). . . . The District Court was confronted. . .with only one suggested job-related reason for the qualification—that of strength. Appellants argued only the job-relatedness of actual physical strength; they did not urge that an equally job-related qualification for prison guards is the appearance of strength. As the Court notes, the primary job of correctional counselor in Alabama prisons "is to maintain security and control of the inmates. . . ." a function that I at least would imagine is aided by the psychological impact on prisoners of the presence of tall and heavy guards. If the appearance of strength had been urged upon the District Court here as a reason for the height and weight minima, I think that the District Court would surely have been entitled to reach a different result than it did. . . . As appellants did not even present the "appearance of strength" contention to the District Court as an asserted job-related reason for the qualification requirements, I agree that their burden was not met. . . .

MR. JUSTICE MARSHALL, with whom MR. JUSTICE BRENNAN joins, concurring in part and dissenting in part.

I agree entirely with the Court's analysis of Alabama's height and weight requirements for prison guards, and with its finding that these restrictions discriminate on the basis of sex in violation of Title VII. Accordingly, I join Parts I and II of the Court's opinion. I also agree with much of the Court's general discussion in Part III of the bfoq exception contained in § 703(e) of Title VII. The Court is unquestionably correct when it holds "that the bfoq exception was in fact meant to be an extremely narrow exception to the general prohibition of discrimination on the basis of sex." I must, however, respectfully disagree with the Court's application of the bfoq exception in this case.

The Court properly rejects two proffered justifications for denying women jobs as prison guards. It is simply irrelevant here that a guard's occupation is dangerous and that some women might be unable to protect themselves adequately. Those themes permeate the testimony of the state officials below, but as the Court holds, "the argument that a particular job is too dangerous for women" is refuted by the "purpose of Title VII to allow the individual woman to make that choice for herself." Some women, like some men, undoubtedly are not qualified and do not wish to serve as prison guards, but that does not justify the exclusion of all women from this employment opportunity. . . .

What would otherwise be considered unlawful discrimination against women is justified by the Court, however, on the basis of the "barbaric and inhumane" conditions in Alabama prisons, conditions so bad that state officials have conceded that they violate the Constitution. To me, this analysis sounds distressingly like saying two wrongs make a right. It is refuted by the plain words of § 706(e). The statute requires that a bfoq be "reasonably necessary to the normal operation of that particular business or enterprise." But no governmental "business" may operate "normally" in violation of the constitution. Every action of government is constrained by constitutional limitations. While those limits may be violated more frequently than we would wish, no one disputes that the "normal operation" of all government functions takes place within them. A prison system operating in blatant violation of the Eighth Amendment is an exception that should be remedied with all possible speed, as Judge Johnson's comprehensive order in *James v. Wallace*, is designed to do. In the meantime, the existence of such violations should not be legitimatized by calling them "normal." Nor should the Court accept them as justifying conduct that would otherwise violate a statute intended to remedy age-old discrimination.

The Court's error in statutory construction is less objectionable, however, than the attitude it displays toward women. Though the Court recognizes that possible harm to women guards is an unacceptable reason for disqualifying women, it relies instead on an equally speculative threat to prison discipline supposedly generated by the sexuality of female guards. There is simply no evidence in the record to show that women guards would create any danger to security in Alabama prisons significantly greater than already exists. All of the dangers—with one exception discussed below—are inherent in a prison setting whatever the gender of the guards.

The Court first sees women guards as a threat to security because "there are few visible deterrents to inmate assaults on women custodians." In fact, any prison guard is constantly subject to the threat of attack by inmates....No prison guard relies primarily on his or her ability to ward off an inmate attack to maintain order. Guards are typically unarmed and sheer numbers of inmates could overcome the normal complement. Rather, like all other law enforcement officers, prison guards must rely primarily on the moral authority of their office and the threat of future punishment for miscreants. As one expert testified below, common sense, fairness, and mental and emotional stability are the qualities a guard needs to cope with the dangers of the job. Well qualified and properly trained women, no less than men, have these psychological weapons at their disposal.

The particular severity of discipline problems in the Alabama maximum security prisons is also no justification for the discrimination sanctioned by the Court. The District Court found in *James v. Wallace* that guards "must spend all their time attempting to maintain control or to protect themselves." 406 F. Supp., at 325. If male guards face an impossible situation, it is difficult to see how women could made the problem worse, unless one relies on precisely the type of generalized bias against women that the Court agrees Title VII was intended to outlaw. For example much of the testimony of appellants' witnesses ignores individual differences among members of each sex and reads like "ancient canards about the proper role of women." *Phillips v. Martin-Marietta Corp.*, 400 U.S., at 545. The witnesses claimed that women guards are not strict disciplinarians; that they are physically less capable of protecting themselves and subduing unruly inmates; that inmates take advantage of them as they did their mothers, while male guards are strong father figures who easily maintain discipline, and so on. Yet the record shows that the presence of women guards has not led to a single incident amounting to a serious breach of security in any Alabama institution.[3] . . .

It appears that the real disqualifying factor in the Courts view is "[t]he employee's very womanhood." The Court refers to the large number of sex offenders in Alabama prisons, and to "the likelihood that inmates would assault a woman because she was a woman." In short, the fundamental justification for the decision is that women as guards will generate sexual assaults. With all respect, this rationale regrettably perpetuates one of the most insidious of the old myths about women—that women, wittingly or not, are seductive sexual objects. The effect of the decision, made I am sure with the best of intentions, is to punish women because their very presence might provoke sexual assault. It is women who are made to pay the price in lost job opportunities for the threat of depraved conduct by prison inmates. Once again, "[t]he pedestal upon which women have been placed has. . . .upon closer inspection, been revealed as a cage." *Sail'er Inn, Inc. v. Kirby*, 5 Cal. 3d 1, 20, 485 P. 2d 529, 541 (1971). It is particularly ironic that the cage is erected here in response to feared misbehavior by imprisoned criminals.

. . . .[T]he danger in this emotionally laden context is that common sense will be used to mask the "romantic paternalism" and persisting discriminatory attitudes that the Court properly eschews. To me [it is clear] that the incidence of sexually motivated attacks on guards will be minute compared to the "likelihood that inmates will assault" a guard because he or she is a guard.

The proper response to inevitable attacks on both female and male guards is not to limit the employment opportunities of law-abiding women who wish to contribute to their community, but to take swift and sure punitive action against the inmate offenders. . . . To deprive women of job opportunities because of the threatened behavior of convicted criminals is to turn our social priorities upside down.[5]

Although I do not countenance the sex discrimination condoned by the majority, it is fortunate that the Court's decision is carefully limited to the facts before it. I trust the lower courts will recognize that the decision was impelled by the shockingly inhuman conditions in Alabama prisons. . .

Opinion Footnotes

3   The Court refers to two incidents involving potentially dangerous attacks on women in prisons, at n. 22. But these did not involve trained corrections officers. . . .

5   The appellants argue that restrictions on employment of women are also justified by consideration of inmates' privacy. It is strange indeed to hear state officials who have for years been violating the most basic principles of human decency in the operation of their prisons suddenly become concerned about inmate privacy. It is stranger still that these same officials allow women guards in contact positions in a number of nonmaximum security institutions, but strive to protect inmates' privacy in the prisons where personal freedom is most severely restricted. I have no doubt on this record that appellants' professed concern is nothing but a feeble excuse for discrimination.

Women and Employment

> As the District Court suggested, it may well be possible, once constitutionally adequate staff is available, to rearrange work assignments so that legitimate inmate privacy concerns are respected without denying jobs to women. Finally, if women guards behave in a professional manner at all times they will engender reciprocal respect from inmates, who will recognize that their privacy is being invaded no more than if a woman doctor examines them. The suggestion implicit in the privacy argument that such behavior is unlikely on either side is an insult to the professionalism of guards and the dignity of inmates.
>
> ### MR. JUSTICE WHITE, dissenting.
>
> ...I am unwilling to believe that the percentage of women applying or interested in applying for jobs as prison guards in Alabama approximates the percentage of women either in the national or state population...I am not now convinced that a large percentage of the actual women applicants, or of those who are seriously interested in applying, for prison guard positions would fail to satisfy the height and weight requirements. Without a more satisfactory record on this issue, I cannot conclude that appellee has made out a prima facie case for the invalidity of the restrictions....

Case Questions

1. Justice Marshall argues that it is unpersuasive to use sexual attacks on a female clerical worker and female student as evidence that the presence of female prison guards would provoke sexual assaults. Suppose there had been two sexual assaults on women guards in the male penitentiary over the past five years; would that change Marshall's position? Ten sexual assaults? What would be the best response by prison officials, already hard-pressed for operating funds, to a situation where women guards in a male penitentiary were being victimized by sexual assaults? To a situation where sexual assaults on women guards are increasing the total of already too-frequent disruptions of prison security and order?

2. Suppose that state officials, in a sincere effort to promote the privacy and dignity of prison inmates, ordered that all guards whose jobs placed them in view of shower and toilet areas be of the same sex as inmates. Suppose further that because so many more prisoners are male than female, this order denied women access to 80 percent of prison guard jobs? Would this be a violation of Title VII? Consider Marshall's suggestion in footnote 5 that prisoners should view the situation of exposure to opposite-sex guards as similar to being examined by a doctor of the opposite sex. Are there other significant differences between the two situations?

3. Justice Rehnquist, joined by Justices Burger and Blackmun, suggests that it would be reasonable for prison administrators to desire the *appearance* of physical strength in prison guards. Does a man who is 5'3" tall and who weighs 130 pounds look very strong? Does a woman who is 5'6" and weighs 150 pounds? Might "appearance" of strength be affected by sex-based prejudices of the observer? Is

Rehnquist's reasonableness argument undermined by the fact that women guards have been used successfully in California's all-male maximum security prisons?

Case note: The long term outcome of *Dothard v. Rawlinson* created opportunities for women to secure positions as prison guards in environments where they had previously been denied opportunities. An emerging concern that is now getting the attention of the courts is the sexual harassment of female security guards by male prisoners. It is an interesting twist in that the persons without power, the prisoners, are creating a hostile work environment and sexually harassing the women who guard them while male supervisors have been reluctant to help.

In February 2016, over 500 female prison employees won a $20 million settlement against the Coleman Federal Correctional Complex in Wildwood, Florida. "One of the largest class-action sexual harassment settlements in U.S. history,"[90] the women were subjected to lewd comments, catcalls, gestures and rape threats by inmates. There were occasions when the inmates would masturbate in front of the female guards or show the guards their penises through the food slots in their cells. Supervisors questioned whether the actions against these women constituted sexual harassment since the power dynamic between the prisoners and the guards was not consistent with supervisors' understanding of what constituted sexual harassment.

In 2016, 10 female corrections officers filed suit against the City and County of Denver Sheriff Department in federal district court claiming that they were victims of sexual harassment under Title VII because they were subject to aggressive sexual gestures and statements by prisoners. According to the complaint, jail supervisors did not intervene on behalf of the corrections officers. Several of these corrections officers expressed fear that prisoners, upon their release, will make good on their threats.[91]

These female corrections officers experienced a work environment that contrasted with what one might typically classify as sexual harassment. As corrections officers, these women were the "superiors" (and not the subordinates) of the inmates doing the harassing. However, arguably the prison supervisors who served as superiors to the corrections officers bore legal culpability for having neglected to intervene to protect their underlings from sexual harassment at the hands of the prisoners.

THE WORKER AS MOTHER

Prohibitions on contraception and abortions, or refusals to fund them (all discussed in Chapter 4), have not been the only state policies that restricted women's freedom in matters of childbearing. Indirect techniques of control have included (1) firing women from state jobs once they become visibly pregnant, (2) refusing to fund maternity-related medical costs in state-operated medical disability insurance programs, (3) denying unemployment compensation to unemployed pregnant women, and (4) allowing employers to exclude women from jobs involving exposure to substances that might harm fetuses.

From the point of view of the women litigants who challenged these regulations, all imposed penalties by which the state or the employer restricted these women's freedom of choice. From the opposite point of view, however, not all these laws were aimed at penalizing individual childbearing choices. Mandatory pregnancy leaves, at least in the eyes of some legislators, aimed at promoting maternal health. The exclusion of maternity benefits from employee health insurance plans and the denial of unemployment compensation to pregnant women were perceived as money-saving measures. (By contrast, state or national government decisions to eliminate abortion funding from Medicaid programs, while providing funding for childbirth expenses, were in fact attempts to penalize the abortion decision and to encourage its alternative.)

The Supreme Court's variegated responses to these differing governmental constraints on the constitutional "right of privacy" were not readily predictable from cases like *Roe v. Wade*. Indeed, the question of the consistency between those responses and the earlier precedents provoked controversy in the legal commentary.

The assertion that these statutes infringe on the right of privacy has not been the only basis on which legal challenges to them have been mounted. Governmental and private employee insurance plans that excluded maternity costs from the surgical and hospitalization benefits available to workers have also been challenged as instances of sex discrimination. These challenges have relied on the equal protection clause for the case of state-run programs (*Geduldig v. Aiello*), on Title VII of the Civil Rights Act for the case of private employers' programs (*General Electric v. Gilbert* and *UAW v. Johnson Controls*), and finally on the Pregnancy Discrimination Act amendment to Title VII (*Newport News Shipbuilding v. EEOC*). All of these cases are discussed below. Challenges to denials of Medicaid funds for abortions have also relied in part on the equal protection clause. Of these antidiscrimination challenges to funding arrangements, only the challenge based on Congress's own Pregnancy Discrimination Act met with success at the Supreme Court.

Mandatory Maternity Leaves

In settling the earliest challenges to a state-imposed penalty on a childbearing decision, the Supreme Court did not apply an Equal Protection Clause analysis, even though an equal protection violation had been the basis of holdings of unconstitutionality in the lower courts.[92] Instead, the Court majority focused on the degree of state infringement into the right of privacy, which had been announced in *Griswold v. Connecticut* in 1965 (discussed in Chapter 4), and on the quality of the state's justification for that infringement. The challengers to the law emerged victorious.

Two statutes were at issue in this first challenge: the Cleveland, Ohio, Board of Education had a rule requiring pregnant teachers to take an unpaid leave five months in advance of the expected date of childbirth and to stay away from the job until the semester that began after the baby was three months old; the Chesterfield County, Virginia, School Board had a rule requiring pregnant teachers to leave work at least four months before the expected birth and to stay away from the job until the beginning of a semester following a physician's certification of post-childbirth fitness. Two separate lawsuits challenging these rules had been launched by pregnant schoolteachers early in 1971. Jo Carol LaFleur and Ann Elizabeth Nelson attacked the Cleveland rule, and Susan Cohen attacked the Chesterfield rule. The U.S. Supreme Court consolidated the two suits into *Cleveland Bd. of Ed. et al. v. LaFleur et al.* and handed down its decision in January 1974, one year after the groundbreaking abortion decisions *Roe* and *Doe*.

CLEVELAND BD. OF EDUCATION ET AL. V. LAFLEUR ET AL.
414 U.S. 632 (1974)

MR. JUSTICE STEWART delivered the opinion of the Court.

* * *

These cases call upon us to decide the constitutionality of the school boards' rules. . . .

II

This Court has long recognized that freedom of personal choice in matters of marriage and family life is one of the liberties protected by the Due Process Clause of the Fourteenth Amendment. *Roe v. Wade*, 410 U.S. 113; *Loving v. Virginia*, 388 U.S. 1, 12; *Griswold v. Connecticut*, 381 U.S. 479; *Pierce v. Society of Sisters*, 268 U.S. 510; *Meyer v. Nebraska*, 262 U.S. 390. See also *Prince v. Massachusetts*, 321 U.S. 158; *Skinner v. Oklahoma*, 316 U.S. 535. As we noted in *Eisenstadt v. Baird*, 405 U.S. 438, 453, there is a right "to be free from unwarranted governmental intrusion into matters so fundamentally affecting a person as the decision whether to bear or beget a child."

By acting to penalize the pregnant teacher for deciding to bear a child, overly restrictive maternity leave regulations can constitute a heavy burden on the exercise of these protected freedoms. Because public school maternity leave rules directly affect "one of the basic civil rights of man," *Skinner v. Oklahoma*, at 541, the Due Process Clause of the Fourteenth Amendment requires that such rules must not needlessly, arbitrarily, or capriciously impinge upon this vital area of a teacher's constitutional liberty. The question before us in these cases is whether the interests advanced in support of the rules of the Cleveland and Chesterfield County School Boards can justify the particular procedures they have adopted.

The school boards in these cases have offered two essentially overlapping explanations for their mandatory maternity leave rules. First, they contend that the firm cutoff dates are necessary to maintain continuity of classroom instruction, since advance knowledge of when a pregnant teacher must leave facilitates the finding and hiring of a qualified substitute. Secondly, the school boards seek to justify their maternity rules by arguing that at least some teachers become physically incapable of adequately performing certain of their duties during the latter part of pregnancy. By keeping the pregnant teacher out of the classroom during these final months, the maternity leave rules are said to protect the health of the teacher and her unborn child, while at the same time assuring that students have a physically capable instructor in the classroom at all times.[9]

...Continuity of instruction is a significant and legitimate educational goal. Regulations requiring pregnant teachers to provide early notice of their condition to school authorities undoubtedly facilitate administrative planning toward the important objective of continuity. But... the absolute requirements of termination at the end of the fourth or fifth month of pregnancy are not [rationally related to this objective].... [because] the fifth or sixth month of pregnancy will obviously begin at different times in the school year for different teachers....

The question remains as to whether the cutoff dates at the beginning of the fifth and sixth months can be justified on the other [legitimate] ground advanced...—the necessity of keeping physically unfit teachers out of the classroom... Despite... conflicting medical testimony..., we can assume...that at least some teachers become physically disabled from effectively performing their duties during the latter stages of pregnancy.

...The question is whether the rules sweep too broadly. See *Shelton v. Tucker*, 364 U.S. 479. That question must be answered in the affirmative, for the provisions amount to a conclusive presumption that every pregnant teacher who reaches the fifth or sixth month of pregnancy is physically incapable of continuing. There is no individualized determination by the teacher's doctor—or the school board's—as to any particular teacher's ability to continue at her job. The rules contain an irrebuttable presumption of physical incompetency, and that presumption applies even when the medical evidence as to an individual woman's physical status might be wholly to the contrary. . . . *Vlandis v. Kline*, 412 U.S. 441, 446; *Stanley v. Illinois*, 405 U.S. 645.

The school boards have argued that the mandatory termination dates serve the interest of administrative convenience, since there are many instances of teacher pregnancy, and the rules obviate the necessity for case-by-case determinations. Certainly, the boards have an interest in devising prompt and efficient procedures to achieve their legitimate objectives in this area. But, as the Court stated in *Stanley v. Illinois*, at 656:

> [T]he Constitution recognizes higher values than speed and efficiency. Indeed, one might fairly say of the Bill of Rights in general, and the Due Process Clause in particular, that they were designed to protect the fragile values of a vulnerable citizenry from the overbearing concern for efficiency and efficacy that may characterize praiseworthy government officials no less, and perhaps more, than mediocre ones. . . .

While it might be easier for the school boards to conclusively presume that all pregnant women are unfit to teach past the fourth or fifth month, of pregnancy, administrative convenience alone is insufficient to make valid what otherwise is a violation of due process of law.[13] The Fourteenth Amendment requires the school boards to employ alternative administrative means, which do not so broadly infringe upon basic constitutional liberty, in support of their legitimate goals.

We conclude, therefore, that neither the necessity for continuity of instruction nor the state interest in keeping physically unfit teachers out of the classroom can justify the[se] . . . sweeping mandatory leave regulations . . .[T]hey cannot pass muster under the Due Process Clause of the Fourteenth Amendment.

III

In addition to the mandatory termination provisions, both the Cleveland and Chesterfield County rules contain limitations upon a teacher's eligibility to return to work after giving birth. Again, the school boards offer two justifications for the return rules—continuity of instruction and the desire to be certain that the teacher is physically competent when she returns to work. As is the case with the leave provisions, the question is not whether the school board's goals are legitimate, but rather whether the particular means chosen to achieve those objectives unduly infringe upon the teacher's constitutional liberty. . . . The provisions concerning a medical certificate or supplemental physical examination are narrowly drawn methods of protecting the school board's interest in teacher fitness; these requirements allow an individualized decision as to the teacher's condition, and thus avoid the pitfalls of the presumptions inherent in the leave rules. Similarly, the provision limiting eligibility to return to the semester following delivery is a precisely drawn means of serving the school board's interest in avoiding unnecessary changes in classroom personnel during any one school term.

The Cleveland rule, however, does not simply contain these reasonable medical and next-semester eligibility provisions. In addition, the school board requires the mother to wait until her child reaches the age of three months before the return rules begin to operate. The school board has offered no reasonable justification for this supplemental limitation, and we can perceive none. . . . The presumption, moreover, is patently unnecessary, since the requirement of a physician's certificate or a medical examination fully protects the school's interests in this regard. . . .

Thus, we conclude that the Cleveland return rule, insofar as it embodies the three month age provision, is wholly arbitrary and irrational, and hence violates the Due Process Clause of the Fourteenth Amendment. The age limitation serves no legitimate state interest, and unnecessarily penalizes the female teacher for asserting her right to bear children.

Opinion Footnotes

9 The records in these cases suggest that the maternity leave regulations may have originally been inspired by other, less weighty, considerations. For example, Dr. Mark C. Schinnerer,. . .Superintendent of Schools in Cleveland at the time,. . .testified in the District Court that the rule had been adopted in part to save pregnant teachers from embarrassment at the hands of giggling schoolchildren; the cutoff date at the end of the fourth month was chosen because this was when the teacher "began to show." Similarly, at least several members of the Chesterfield County School Board thought a mandatory leave rule was justified in order to insulate schoolchildren from the sight of conspicuously pregnant women. One . . . thought that it was "not good for the school system" for student to view pregnant teachers, "because some of the kids say, my teacher swallowed a watermelon, things like that.". . .

13 This is not to say that the only means for providing appropriate protection for the rights of pregnant teachers is an individualized determination in each case and in every circumstance. We are not dealing in these cases with maternity leave regulations requiring a termination of employment at some firm date during the last few weeks of pregnancy. We therefore have no occasion to decide whether such regulations might be justified by considerations not presented in these records—for example, widespread medical consensus about the "disabling" effect of pregnancy on a teacher's job performance during these

latter days, or evidence showing that such firm cutoffs were the only reasonable method of avoiding the possibility of labor beginning while some teacher was in the classroom. . . .

Mr. Justice Douglas concurs in the result.

Mr. Justice Powell, concurring in the result.

. . .It seems to me that equal protection analysis is the appropriate frame of reference. . . .

The records before us abound with proof that a principal purpose behind the adoption of the regulations was to keep visibly pregnant teachers out of the sight of schoolchildren. The boards do not advance this today as a legitimate objective, yet its initial primacy casts a shadow over these cases. Moreover, most of the after-the-fact rationalizations proposed by these boards are unsupported in the records. The boards emphasize teacher absenteeism, classroom discipline, the safety of schoolchildren, and the safety of the expectant mother and her unborn child. No doubt these are legitimate concerns. But the boards have failed to demonstrate that these interests are in fact threatened by the continued employment of pregnant teachers.

To be sure, the boards have a legitimate and important interest in fostering continuity of teaching. And, even a normal pregnancy may at some point jeopardize that interest. But the classifications chosen by these boards, so far as we have been shown, are either counterproductive or irrationally overinclusive even with regard to this significant, nonillusory goal. Accordingly, in my opinion these regulations are invalid under rational-basis standards of equal protection review. . . .

Mr. Justice Rehnquist, with whom The Chief Justice joins, dissenting.

The Court rests its invalidation of the school regulations involved in these cases on the Due Process Clause of the Fourteenth Amendment, rather than on any claim of sexual discrimination under the Equal Protection Clause of that Amendment. . . . .

If legislative bodies are to be permitted to draw a general line anywhere short of the delivery room, I can find no judicial standard of measurement which says the ones drawn here were invalid. I therefore dissent.

Case Questions

1. When the Court describes a statute as overly broad, it is using a scrutiny level more strict than the rationality test. The date of this case preceded the *Craig* rule

for gender discrimination. Is Justice Powell convincing in his claim that none of these rules has any rational connection to a legitimate goal?

2. Does Justice Rehnquist's dissent (joined by Justice Burger) suggests that a mandatory leave even for women only one or two months pregnant would be constitutional?

Case note: Late in 1975, the Supreme Court handed down a brief per curiam opinion in a 5–3 summary judgment for the case of *Mary Ann Turner v. Department of Employment Security of Utah* (423 U.S. 44). As in *Cleveland v. LaFleur*, the challenger to the legislative penalty on a childbearing decision prevailed. *Turner v. Department of Employment* was similar to *Cleveland v. LaFleur* in reasoning as well as result. It was the only other challenge to a penalty on a childbearing decision in which the litigants managed to persuade the Court majority to examine the statute from a perspective that acknowledged and focused on the statute's clash with the right of familial privacy.[93]

The Supreme Court in *Turner* noted that "freedom of personal choice in matters of marriage and family life is one of the liberties protected by the due process clause" and that any infringement on such "basic human liberties" must be imposed by carefully "individualized means" instead of by sweeping categorical presumptions. In this instance the presumption at issue was Utah's belief that women in the last three months of pregnancy and the first six weeks after childbirth are unfit for gainful employment and therefore should be denied unemployment compensation. The Court declared such a presumption an unconstitutional infringement on the right of familial privacy.

Protection of the Fetus vs. Opportunity for Women: *UAW v. Johnson Controls* (1991)

In March of 1991, the Supreme Court relied on Title VII to strike down employment practices that were even more restrictive than mandatory maternity leaves. The Johnson Controls company, a lead battery manufacturing enterprise, barred from all "jobs involving lead exposure or which could expose them to lead through . . . transfer or promotion" any women workers who could not provide medical documentation certifying that they were sterile. This description covered all industrial jobs at the company.

Essentially the Johnson Controls case turned on the Court's understanding of the meaning of the "BFOQ" rule (see *Dothard v. Rawlinson*, above.) For *Johnson Controls*, an additional clause of Title VII also bore some relevance: in 1978 in the Pregnancy Discrimination Act, Congress had amended Title VII to say that the phrases "because of sex" and "on the basis of sex," which referred to forbidden job discrimination "include but are not limited to, because of or on the basis of pregnancy, childbirth, or related medical conditions; and women affected by pregnancy, childbirth, or related medical conditions shall be treated the same for all employment-related purposes . . . as other persons not so affected but similar in their ability or inability to work."[94]

The Johnson Controls company had a history of clear-cut sex discrimination. Before the 1964 Civil Rights Act, the company employed no women in any battery-manufacturing job, its main business activity. Finally, in June of 1977,[95] Johnson Controls changed its approach. The company announced, with regard to the employment of women in jobs where they would be exposed to the lead used in making batteries,

> [P]rotection of the health of the unborn child is the immediate and direct responsibility of the prospective parents. While the medical profession and the company can support them in the exercise of this responsibility, it cannot assume it for them without simultaneously infringing their rights as persons. . . .
>
> . . . .Since not all women who can become mothers wish to become mothers (or will become mothers), it would appear to be illegal discrimination to treat all who are capable of pregnancy as though they will become pregnant.

Johnson supplemented this announcement with a written warning to its women employees stating that there was evidence "that women exposed to lead have a higher rate of abortion" but that this evidence was "not as clear . . . as the relationship between cigarette smoking and cancer," and that, still, it was "medically speaking, just good sense not to run that risk if you want children and do not want to expose the unborn child to risk, however small. . . ." Any woman who wished to be considered for employment at Johnson Controls thereafter had to sign a statement indicating that she had read this warning.

Five years later the company changed from a policy of warning to one of prohibition. The federal Occupational Safety and Health Administration (OSHA) indicates that blood lead levels in excess of 30 micrograms per deciliter are dangerous for women who are pregnant (but also that such levels endangered the reproductive capacity of men).[96] Johnson Controls adopted this standard and said that any work station where over the past year an employee had registered a blood lead level in this range[97] would henceforth be off-limits to any woman capable of pregnancy. (In general, about one third of the workers at these stations registered at this level; careful washing after work could minimize lead risk, and some workers protected themselves better than others. In the years from 1979 to 1983, eight employees became pregnant with blood lead levels in this range. Only one of the babies born to this group later was shown to have this elevated blood lead level.)

In response to the 1982 prohibition, a lawsuit was initiated against Johnson Controls in 1984 by a group of its employees and their union. Two of the employees were female; one had become sterilized in order to keep her job, and the other had suffered a pay cut as a result of a transfer pursuant to the new policy. A third was a male who had tried, and failed, to get the company to give him a leave of absence from a high lead-exposure job because he wanted to lower his blood lead level in preparation for conceiving a child.

The federal District Court issued a summary judgment siding with the employer on the grounds that there was ample expert opinion that exposure to lead is much more dangerous to a fetus than to an adult, and that concern for protecting the safety of the fetus was a legitimate business consideration of the company. This court treated the company policy as one of disparate impact and ruled that Johnson Controls had satisfactorily demonstrated a "business necessity" for it. The Circuit Court of Appeals affirmed in a 7–4 vote, ruling that whether business necessity were the test or whether it were BFOQ, either way the company had an adequate basis for its policy of excluding fertile women from these jobs. Both courts reasoned essentially that lead exposure of pregnant women presents a substantial health risk to the fetus, and there is no "less discriminatory alternative" available that can protect the fetus from this hazard. They both found avoidance of this health risk to be a legitimate business concern, and one essential enough to count as either "business necessity" or "bona fide occupational qualification." The Circuit Court dissenters presented a number of arguments that were reiterated by the U.S. Supreme Court and that show up below. One that was not mentioned by the Supreme Court, however, was Judge Easterbrook's description of the drastic impact that fetal protection policies of a blanket exclusionary nature (like this one) would have on women's job opportunities if universally adopted in the United States: More than twenty million jobs would be closed to most women workers.

On appeal, the U.S. Supreme Court reversed unanimously but with three different factions utilizing three different lines of reasoning. The various opinions appear below:

UNITED AUTOWORKERS V. JOHNSON CONTROLS INC.
499 U.S. 187 (1991)

JUSTICE BLACKMUN delivered the opinion of the Court.

III

The bias in Johnson Controls' policy is obvious. Fertile men, but not fertile women, are given a choice as to whether they wish to risk their reproductive health for a particular job. Section 703(a) of the Civil Rights Act of 1964...prohibits sex-based classifications in terms and conditions of employment, in hiring and discharging decisions, and in other employment decisions that adversely affect an employee's status.

...Respondent does not seek to protect the unconceived children of all its employees. Despite evidence in the record about the debilitating effect of lead exposure on the male reproductive system, Johnson Controls is concerned only with the harms that may befall the unborn offspring of its female employees.... Johnson Controls' policy is facially discriminatory, because it requires only a female employee to produce proof that she is not capable of reproducing.

Our conclusion is bolstered by the Pregnancy Discrimination Act of 1978 (PDA).... "The Pregnancy Discrimination Act has now made clear that, for all Title VII purposes, discrimination based on a woman's pregnancy is, on its face, discrimination because of her sex." *Newport News Shipbuilding & Dry Dock Co. v. EEOC*, 462 U.S. 669, 684 (1983). In its use of the words "capable of bearing children" in the 1982 policy statement as the criterion for exclusion, Johnson Controls explicitly classifies on the basis of potential for pregnancy. Under the PDA, such a classification must be regarded, for Title VII purposes, in the same light as explicit sex discrimination...

We concluded above that Johnson Controls' policy is not neutral, because it does not apply to the reproductive capacity of the company's male employees in the same way as it applies to that of the females....

In sum, Johnson Controls' policy "does not pass the simple test of whether the evidence shows 'treatment of a person in a manner which, but for that person's sex, would be different.' " *Los Angeles Dept. of Water & Power v. Manhart*, 435 U.S. 702, 711 (1978).... We hold that Johnson Controls' fetal-protection policy is sex discrimination forbidden under Title VII unless respondent can establish that sex is a "bona fide occupational qualification."

IV

Under § 703(e)(1) of Title VII, an employer may discriminate on the basis of "religion, sex, or national origin in those certain instances where religion, sex, or national origin is a bona fide occupational qualification reasonably necessary to the normal operation of that particular business or enterprise." 42 U.S.C.§ 2000e–2(e)(1)...

The BFOQ defense is written narrowly, and this Court has read it narrowly. See, e.g., *Dothard v. Rawlinson*, 433 U.S. 321, 332–337 (1977); *Trans World Airlines, Inc. v. Thurston*, 469 U.S. 111, 122–125(1985)....*Western Air Lines, Inc. v. Criswell*, 472 U.S. 400 (1985). Our emphasis on the restrictive scope of the BFOQ defense is grounded on both the language and the legislative history of § 703. The wording of the BFOQ defense contains several terms of restriction that indicate that the exception reaches only special situations. The statute thus limits the situations in which discrimination is permissible to "certain instances" where sex discrimination is "reasonably necessary" to the "normal operation" of the "particular" business. Each one of these terms—certain, normal, particular—prevents the use of general subjective standards and favors an objective, verifiable requirement. But the most telling term is "occupational"; this indicates that these objective, verifiable requirements must concern job-related skills and aptitudes.

The concurrence defines "occupational" as meaning related to a job. According to the concurrence, any discriminatory requirement imposed by an employer is "job-related" simply because the employer has chosen to make the requirement a condition of employment....This reading of "occupational" renders the word mere surplusage.... By modifying "qualification" with "occupational," Congress narrowed the term to qualifications that affect an employee's ability to do the job.

Johnson Controls argues that its fetal-protection policy falls within the so-called safety exception to the BFOQ. Our cases have stressed that discrimination on the basis of sex because of safety concerns is allowed only in narrow circumstances. In *Dothard v. Rawlinson*, this Court indicated that danger to a woman herself does not justify discrimination. 433 U.S., at 335 ... We there allowed the employer to hire only male guards in contact areas of maximum-security male penitentiaries only because more was at stake than the "individual woman's decision to weigh and accept the risks of employment." *Ibid*. We found sex to be a BFOQ inasmuch as the employment of a female guard would create real risks of safety to others if violence broke out because the guard was a woman. Sex discrimination was tolerated because sex was related to the guard's ability to do the job—maintaining prison security. . . .

Similarly, some courts have approved airlines' layoffs of pregnant flight attendants at different points during the first five months of pregnancy on the ground that the employer's policy was necessary to ensure the safety of passengers. . .

We considered safety to third parties in *Western Airlines, Inc. v. Criswell*, in the context of the Age Discrimination in Employment Act. . . . We focused upon "the nature of the flight engineer's tasks," and the "actual capabilities of persons over age 60" in relation to those tasks. 472 U.S., at 406. Our safety concerns were not independent of the individual's ability to perform the assigned tasks, but rather involved the possibility that, because of age-connected debility, a flight engineer might not properly assist the pilot, and might thereby cause a safety emergency. Furthermore, although we considered the safety of third parties in *Dothard* and *Criswell*, those third parties were indispensable to the particular business at issue. In *Dothard*, the third parties were the inmates; in *Criswell*, the third parties were the passengers on the plane. We stressed that, in order to qualify as a BFOQ, a job qualification must relate to the "essence," *Dothard*, 433 U.S., at 333, or to the "central mission of the employer's business," *Criswell*, 472 U.S., at 413.

The concurrence ignores the "essence of the business" test, and so concludes that "protecting fetal safety while carrying out the duties of battery manufacturing is as much a legitimate concern as is safety to third parties in guarding prisons (*Dothard*) or flying airplanes (*Criswell*)." By limiting its discussion to cost and safety concerns and rejecting the "essence of the business" test that our case law has established, [it]. . . seeks to expand what is now the narrow BFOQ defense. Third-party safety considerations properly entered into the BFOQ analysis in *Dothard* and *Criswell* because they went to the core of the employee's job performance. Moreover, that performance involved the central purpose of the enterprise. *Dothard*, 433 U.S., at 335 ("The essence of a correctional counselor's job is to maintain prison security"); *Criswell*, 472 U.S., at 413 (the central mission of the airline's business was the safe transportation of its passengers). JUSTICE WHITE attempts to transform this case into one of customer safety. The unconceived fetuses of Johnson Controls' female employees, however, are neither customers nor third parties whose safety is essential to the business of battery manufacturing. No one can disregard the possibility of injury to future children; the BFOQ, however, is not so broad that it transforms this deep social concern into an essential aspect of battery-making.

Our case law, therefore, makes clear that the safety exception is limited to instances in which sex or pregnancy actually interferes with the employee's ability to perform the job. This approach is consistent with the language of the BFOQ provision itself, for it suggests that permissible distinctions based on sex must relate to ability to perform the duties of the job. Johnson Controls suggests, however, that we expand the exception to allow fetal-protection policies that mandate particular standards for pregnant or fertile women. We decline to do so. Such an expansion contradicts not only the language of the BFOQ and the narrowness of its exception, but the plain language and history of the Pregnancy Discrimination Act.

The PDA's amendment to Title VII contains a BFOQ standard of its own: unless pregnant employees differ from others "in their ability or inability to work," they must be "treated the same" as other employees "for all employment-related purposes." 42 U.S.C. § 2000e(k). This language clearly sets forth Congress' remedy for discrimination on the basis of pregnancy and potential pregnancy. Women who are either pregnant or potentially pregnant must be treated like others "similar in their ability . . . to work." *Ibid.* In other words, women as capable of doing their jobs as their male counterparts may not be forced to choose between having a child and having a job.

. . .The concurrence . . .[ignores] the second clause of the Act, which states that "women affected by pregnancy, childbirth, or related medical conditions shall be treated the same for all employment-related purposes . . . as other persons not so affected but similar in their ability or inability to work." . . .

The legislative history confirms what the language of the Pregnancy Discrimination Act compels. The Senate Report [on the PDA] states that employers may not require a pregnant woman to stop working at any time during her pregnancy unless she is unable to do her work. Employment late in pregnancy often imposes risks on the unborn child, see Chavkin, *Walking a Tightrope: Pregnancy, Parenting, and Work, in Double Exposure* 196, 196–202 (W. Chavkin ed. 1984), but Congress indicated that the employer may take into account only the woman's ability to get her job done. See Becker, "From Muller v. Oregon to Fetal Vulnerability Policies," 53 *U.Chi.L.Rev.* 1219, 1255–1256 (1986). With the PDA, Congress made clear that the decision to become pregnant or to work while being either pregnant or capable of becoming pregnant was reserved for each individual woman to make for herself. . . .

V

We have no difficulty concluding that Johnson Controls cannot establish a BFOQ. Fertile women, as far as appears in the record, participate in the manufacture of batteries as efficiently as anyone else. Johnson Controls' professed moral and ethical concerns about the welfare of the next generation do not suffice to establish a BFOQ of female sterility. Decisions about the welfare of future children must be left to the parents who conceive, bear, support, and raise them, rather than to the employers who hire those parents. Congress has mandated this choice through Title VII, as amended by the PDA. Johnson Controls has attempted to exclude women because of their reproductive capacity. Title VII and the PDA simply do not allow a woman's dismissal because of her failure to submit to sterilization.

Nor can concerns about the welfare of the next generation be considered a part of the "essence" of Johnson Controls' business. Judge Easterbrook in this case pertinently observed: "It is word play to say that 'the job' at Johnson [Controls] is to make batteries without risk to fetuses in the same way 'the job' at Western Air Lines is to fly planes without crashing." 886 F.2d, at 913.

. . . .[I]t perhaps is worth noting. . .that Johnson Controls has shown no "factual basis for believing that all or substantially all women would be unable to perform safely and efficiently the duties of the job involved." *Weeks v. Southern Bell Tel. & Tel. Co.*, 408 F.2d 228, 235 (CA5 1969), quoted with approval in *Dothard*, 433 U.S., at 333. . . . .Of the eight pregnancies reported among the female employees, it has not been shown that any of the babies have birth defects or other abnormalities. The record does not reveal the birth rate for Johnson Controls' female workers, but national statistics show that approximately nine percent of all fertile women become pregnant each year. The birthrate drops to two percent for blue collar workers over age 30. See Becker, 53 *U.Chi.L.Rev.*, at 1233. Johnson Controls' fear of prenatal injury, no matter how sincere, does not begin to show that substantially all of its fertile women employees are incapable of doing their jobs.

VI

A word about tort liability and the increased cost of fertile women in the workplace is perhaps necessary. One of the dissenting judges in this case expressed concern about an employer's tort liability, and concluded that liability for a potential injury to a fetus is a social cost that Title VII does not require a company to ignore. 886 F.2d, at 904–905. It is correct to say that Title VII does not prevent the employer from having a conscience. The statute, however, does prevent sex-specific fetal-protection policies. These two aspects of Title VII do not conflict.

More than 40 States currently recognize a right to recover for a prenatal injury based either on negligence or on wrongful death. . . . According to Johnson Controls, however, the company complies with the lead standard developed by OSHA and warns its female employees about the damaging effects of lead. It is worth noting that OSHA gave the problem of lead lengthy consideration, and concluded that "there is no basis whatsoever for the claim that women of childbearing age should be excluded from the workplace in order to protect the fetus or the course of pregnancy." 43 Fed.Reg. 52952, 52966 (1978). See also id., at 54354, 54398. Instead, OSHA established a series of mandatory protections which, taken together, "should effectively minimize any risk to the fetus and newborn child." Id., at 52966. See 29 CFR 1910.125(k)(ii) (1989). Without negligence, it would be difficult for a court to find liability on the part of the employer. If, under general tort principles, Title VII bans sex-specific fetal-protection policies, the employer fully informs the woman of the risk, and the employer has not acted negligently, the basis for holding an employer liable seems remote, at best.

Although the issue is not before us, the concurrence observes that "it is far from clear that compliance with Title VII will preempt state tort liability." The cases relied upon . . . to support its prediction, however, are inapposite. . . . When it is impossible for an employer to comply with both state and federal requirements, this Court has ruled that federal law preempts that of the States. See, e.g., *Florida Lime & Avocado Growers, Inc. v. Paul*, 373 U.S. 132, 142–143 (1963).

. . .

If state tort law furthers discrimination in the workplace and prevents employers from hiring women who are capable of manufacturing the product as efficiently as men, then it will impede the accomplishment of Congress' goals in enacting Title VII. Because Johnson Controls has not argued that it faces any costs from tort liability, not to mention crippling ones, the preemption question is not before us. We therefore say no more than that the concurrence's speculation appears unfounded, as well as premature.

. . . Title VII plainly forbids illegal sex discrimination as a method of diverting attention from an employer's obligation to police the workplace. Second, the spectre of an award of damages reflects a fear that hiring fertile women will cost more. The extra cost of employing members of one sex, however, does not provide an affirmative Title VII defense for a discriminatory refusal to hire members of that gender. See *Manhart*, 435 U.S., at 716–718, and n. 32. Indeed, in passing the PDA, Congress considered at length the considerable cost of providing equal treatment of pregnancy and related conditions, but made the "decision to forbid special treatment of pregnancy despite the social costs associated therewith." *Arizona Governing Committee v. Norris*, 463 U.S. 1073, 1084, n. 14 (1983) (opinion of MARSHALL, J.).

We, of course, are not presented with, nor do we decide, a case in which costs would be so prohibitive as to threaten the survival of the employer's business. We merely reiterate our prior holdings that the incremental cost of hiring women cannot justify discriminating against them.

VII

It is no more appropriate for the courts than it is for individual employers to decide whether a woman's reproductive role is more important to herself and her family than her economic role. Congress has left this choice to the woman as hers to make.

The judgment of the Court of Appeals is reversed, and the case is remanded for further proceedings consistent with this opinion.

JUSTICE WHITE, with whom THE CHIEF JUSTICE and JUSTICE KENNEDY join, concurring in part and concurring in the judgment.

The Court properly holds that Johnson Controls' fetal protection policy overtly discriminates against women, and thus is prohibited by Title VII unless it falls within the bona fide occupational qualification (BFOQ) exception, set forth at 42 U.S.C.§ 2000e–2(e). The Court erroneously holds, however, that the BFOQ defense is so narrow that it could never justify a sex-specific fetal protection policy. I nevertheless concur in the judgment of reversal because, on the record before us, summary judgment in favor of Johnson Controls was improperly entered by the District Court and affirmed by the Court of Appeals.

I

In evaluating the scope of the BFOQ defense, the proper starting point is the language of the statute . . . . [T]herefore, the policy must be "reasonably necessary" to the "normal operation" of making batteries, which is Johnson Controls' "particular business."

. . .[A] fetal protection policy would be justified under the terms of the statute if, for example, an employer could show that exclusion of women from certain jobs was reasonably necessary to avoid substantial tort liability.

Common sense tells us that it is part of the normal operation of business concerns to avoid causing injury to third parties, as well as to employees, if for no other reason than to avoid tort liability and its substantial costs. This possibility of tort liability is not hypothetical; every State currently allows children born alive to recover in tort for prenatal injuries caused by third parties, see W. Keeton et al., *Prosser and Keeton on Law of Torts* § 55 p. 368 (5th ed. 1984), and an increasing number of courts have recognized a right to recover even for prenatal injuries caused by torts committed prior to conception.

The Court dismisses the possibility of tort liability by no more than speculating. . . .Such speculation will be small comfort to employers. First, it is far from clear that compliance with Title VII will preempt state tort liability, and the Court offers no support for that proposition.[2] Second, although warnings may preclude claims by injured employees, they will not preclude claims by injured children, because the general rule is that parents cannot waive causes of action on behalf of their children, and the parents' negligence will not be imputed to the children. Finally, although state tort liability for prenatal injuries generally requires negligence, it will be difficult for employers to determine in advance what will constitute negligence. Compliance with OSHA standards, for example, has been held not to be a defense to state tort or criminal liability. . . . Moreover, it is possible that employers will be held strictly liable, if, for example, their manufacturing process is considered "abnormally dangerous." See *Restatement (Second) of Torts* § 869, comment b (1979).

Relying on *Los Angeles Dept. of Water and Power v. Manhart*, 435 U.S. 702 (1978), the Court contends that tort liability cannot justify a fetal protection policy because the extra costs of hiring women is not a defense under Title VII. This contention misrepresents our decision in *Manhart*. There, we held that a requirement that female employees contribute more than male employees to a pension fund, in order to reflect the greater longevity of women, constituted discrimination against women under Title VII because it treated them as a class, rather than as individuals. 435 U.S., at 708. We did not in that case address in any detail the nature of the BFOQ defense, and we certainly did not hold that cost was irrelevant to the BFOQ analysis. Rather, we merely stated in a footnote that "there has been no showing that sex distinctions are reasonably necessary to the normal operation of the Department's retirement plan." *Id.*, at 716, n. 30. We further noted that, although Title VII does not contain a "cost justification defense comparable to the affirmative defense available in a price discrimination suit," "no defense based on the total cost of employing men and women was attempted in this case." *Id.*, at 716–717, and n. 32.

Prior decisions construing the BFOQ defense confirm that the defense is broad enough to include considerations of cost and safety of the sort that could form the basis for an employer's adoption of a fetal protection policy. In *Dothard v. Rawlinson*, 433 U.S. 321 (1977), the Court held that being male was a BFOQ for "contact" guard positions in Alabama's maximum security male penitentiaries. The Court first took note of the actual conditions of the prison environment: "In a prison system where violence is the order of the day, where inmate access to guards is facilitated by dormitory living arrangements, where every institution is understaffed, and where a substantial portion of the inmate population is composed of sex offenders mixed at random with other prisoners, there are few visible deterrents to inmate assaults on women custodians." *Id.*, at 335–336. The Court also stressed that "[m]ore [was] at stake" than a risk to individual female employees: "The likelihood that inmates would assault a woman because she was a woman would pose a real threat not only to the victim of the assault but also to the basic control of the penitentiary and protection of its inmates and the other security personnel." *Ibid.* Under those circumstances, the Court observed that "it would be an oversimplification to characterize [the exclusion of women] as an exercise in "romantic paternalism." Cf. *Frontiero v. Richardson*, 411 U.S. 677, 684." *Id.*, at 335.

We revisited the BFOQ defense in *Western Air Lines, Inc. v. Criswell*, 472 U.S. 400 (1985), this time in the context of the Age Discrimination in Employment Act of 1967 (ADEA). There, we endorsed the two-part inquiry for evaluating a BFOQ defense. . . . First, the job qualification must not be "so peripheral to the central mission of the employer's business" that no discrimination could be "reasonably *necessary* to the normal operation of the particular business." 472 U.S., at 413. Although safety is *not* such a peripheral concern, *id.*, at 413, 419, the inquiry "adjusts to the safety factor"—"[t]he greater the safety factor, measured by the likelihood of harm and the probable severity of that harm in case of an accident, the more stringent may be the job qualifications," *id.*, at 413. Second, the employer must show either that all or substantially all persons excluded "would be unable to perform safely and efficiently the duties of the job involved," or that it is "impossible or highly impractical" to deal with them on an individual basis. 472 U.S., at 414. We further observed that this inquiry properly takes into account an employer's interest in safety—"[w]hen an employer establishes that a job qualification has been carefully formulated to respond to documented concerns for public safety, it will not be overly burdensome to persuade a trier of fact that the qualification is 'reasonably necessary' to safe operation of the business." 472 U.S., at 419:

> *Dothard* and *Criswell* make clear that avoidance of substantial safety risks to third parties is *inherently* part of both an employee's ability to perform a job and an employer's "normal operation" of its business. Indeed, in both cases, the Court approved the statement in *Weeks v. Southern Bell Telephone & Telegraph Co.*, 408 F.2d 228 (CA5 1969), that an employer could establish a BFOQ defense by showing that "all or substantially all women would be unable to perform *safely* and *efficiently* the duties of the job involved." *Id.*, at 235 (emphasis added). See *Criswell*, 472 U.S., at 414; *Dothard*, 433 U.S., at 333. The Court's statement in this case that "the safety exception is limited to instances in which sex or pregnancy actually interferes with the employee's ability to perform the job," therefore adds no support to its conclusion that a fetal protection policy could never be justified as a BFOQ. On the facts of this case, for example, protecting fetal safety while carrying out the duties of battery manufacturing is as much a legitimate concern as is safety to third parties in guarding prisons (*Dothard*) or flying airplanes (*Criswell*).[5]

> *Dothard* and *Criswell* also confirm that costs are relevant in determining whether a discriminatory policy is reasonably necessary for the normal operation of a business. In *Dothard*, the safety problem that justified exclusion of women from the prison guard positions was largely a result of inadequate staff and facilities. See 433 U.S., at 335. If the cost of employing women could not be considered, the employer there should have been required to hire more staff and restructure the prison environment, rather than exclude women. Similarly, in *Criswell*, the airline could have been required to hire more pilots and install expensive monitoring devices, rather than discriminate against older employees. The BFOQ statute, however, reflects "Congress' unwillingness to require employers to change the very nature of their operations." *Price Waterhouse v. Hopkins*, 490 U.S. 228, 242 (1989) (plurality opinion).

> The PDA, contrary to the Court's assertion, did not restrict the scope of the BFOQ defense. The PDA was only an amendment to the "Definitions" section of Title VII, 42 U.S.C.§ 2000e, and did not purport to eliminate or alter the BFOQ defense. Rather, it merely clarified Title VII to make it clear that pregnancy and related conditions are included within Title VII's antidiscrimination provisions. As we have already recognized, "the purpose of the PDA was simply to make the treatment of pregnancy consistent with

general Title VII principles." *Arizona Governing Committee . . . v. Norris*, 463 U.S. 1073, 1085, n. 14 (1983).

. . .The Court's narrow interpretation of the BFOQ defense in this case, however, means that an employer cannot exclude even pregnant women from an environment highly toxic to their fetuses. It is foolish to think that Congress intended such a result, and neither the language of the BFOQ exception nor our cases require it.[8]

II

Despite my disagreement with the Court concerning the scope of the BFOQ defense, I concur in reversing the Court of Appeals because that court erred in affirming the District Court's grant of summary judgment in favor of Johnson Controls. First, the Court of Appeals erred in failing to consider the level of risk-avoidance that was part of Johnson Controls' "normal operation." Although the court did conclude that there was a "substantial risk" to fetuses from lead exposure in fertile women, 886 F.2d 871, 879–883, 898 (CA7 1989), it merely meant that there was a high risk that some fetal injury would occur absent a fetal protection policy. That analysis, of course, fails to address the extent of fetal injury that is likely to occur. If the fetal protection policy insists on a risk-avoidance level substantially higher than other risk levels tolerated by Johnson Controls, such as risks to employees and consumers, the policy should not constitute a BFOQ.[10]

Second, even without more information about the normal level of risk at Johnson Controls, the fetal protection policy at issue here reaches too far. This is evident both in its presumption that, absent medical documentation to the contrary, all women are fertile regardless of their age, see *id.*, at 876, n. 8, and in its exclusion of presumptively fertile women from positions that might result in a promotion to a position involving high lead exposure, *id.*, at 877. There has been no showing that either of those aspects of the policy is reasonably necessary to ensure safe and efficient operation of Johnson Controls' battery-manufacturing business. Of course, these infirmities in the company's policy do not warrant invalidating the entire fetal protection program.

Third, it should be recalled that, until 1982, Johnson Controls operated without an exclusionary policy, and it has not identified any grounds for believing that its current policy is reasonably necessary to its normal operations. Although it is now more aware of some of the dangers of lead exposure, *id.*, at 899, it has not shown that the risks of fetal harm or the costs associated with it have substantially increased. Cf. *Manhart*, 435 U.S., at 716, n. 30, in which we rejected a BFOQ defense because the employer had operated prior to the discrimination with no significant adverse effects.

Finally, the Court of Appeals failed to consider properly petitioners' evidence of harm to offspring caused by lead exposure in males. The court considered that evidence only in its discussion of the business necessity standard, in which it focused on whether petitioners had met their burden of proof. 886 F.2d, at 889–890. The burden of proving that a discriminatory qualification is a BFOQ, however, rests with the employer. See, e.g., *Price Waterhouse*, 490 U.S., at 248; *Dothard*, 433 U.S., at 333. Thus, the court should have analyzed whether the evidence was sufficient for petitioners to survive summary judgment in light of respondent's burden of proof to establish a BFOQ. Moreover, the court should not have discounted the evidence as "speculative," 886 F.2d, at 889, merely because it was based on animal studies. We have approved the use of animal studies to assess risks, see *Industrial Union Dept. v. American Petroleum Institute*, 448 U.S. 607, 657, n. 64 (1980), and OSHA uses animal studies in establishing its lead control regulations, see *United Steelworkers of America, AFL-CIO-CLC v. Marshall*, 647 F.2d 1189, 1257, n. 97 (1980), cert. denied, 453 U.S. 913 (1981).

Opinion Footnotes

2 Cf. *English v. General Electric Co.*, 496 U.S. 72 (1990) (state law action for intentional infliction of emotional distress not preempted by Energy Reorganization Act of 1974); *California Federal Savings and Loan Assn. v. Guerra*, 479 U.S. 272, 290–292 (1987) (state statute requiring the provision of leave and pregnancy to employees disabled by pregnancy not preempted by the PDA); *Silkwood v. Kerr-McGee Corp.*, 464 U.S. 238, 256 (1984) (state punitive damage claim not preempted by federal laws regulating nuclear power plants); *Bernstein v. Aetna Life & Cas.*, 843 F.2d 359, 364–365 (CA9 1988) ("It is well-established that Title VII does not preempt state common law remedies"); see also 42 U.S.C.§ 2000e–7.

5 I do not, as the Court asserts, reject the "essence of the business" test. Rather, I merely reaffirm the obvious—that safety to third parties is part of the "essence" of most if not all businesses. Of course, the BFOQ inquiry "adjusts to the safety factor." *Criswell*, 472 U.S., at 413. As a result, more stringent occupational qualifications may be justified for jobs involving higher safety risks, such as flying airplanes. But a recognition that the importance of safety varies among businesses does not mean that safety is completely irrelevant to the essence of a job such as battery manufacturing.

8 The Court's cramped reading of the BFOQ defense is also belied by the legislative history of Title VII, in which three examples of permissible sex discrimination were mentioned—a female nurse hired to care for an elderly woman, an all-male professional baseball team, and a masseur. See 110 Cong.Rec. 2718 (1964) (Rep. Goodell); *id.*, at 7212–7213 (interpretive memorandum introduced by Sens. Clark and Case); *id.*, at 2720 (Rep. Multer). In none of those situations would gender "actually interfer[e] with the employee's ability to perform the job," as required today by the Court.

The Court's interpretation of the BFOQ standard also would seem to preclude considerations of privacy as a basis for sex-based discrimination, since those considerations do not relate directly to an employee's physical ability to perform the duties of the job. The lower federal courts, however, have consistently recognized that privacy interests may justify sex-based requirements for certain jobs.

10 It is possible, for example, that alternatives to exclusion of women, such as warnings combined with frequent blood testings, would sufficiently minimize the risk such that it would be comparable to other risks tolerated by Johnson Controls.

JUSTICE SCALIA, concurring in the judgment.

I generally agree with the Court's analysis, but have some reservations, several of which bear mention.

First, I think it irrelevant that there was "evidence in the record about the debilitating effect of lead exposure on the male reproductive system." Even without such evidence, treating women differently "on the basis of pregnancy" constitutes discrimination "on the basis of sex," because Congress has unequivocally said so. Pregnancy Discrimination Act of 1978, 92 Stat. 2076, 42 U.S.C.§ 2000e(k).

Second, the Court points out that "Johnson Controls has shown no factual basis for believing that all or substantially all women would be unable to perform safely . . . the duties of the job involved," In my view, this is . . .entirely irrelevant. By reason of the Pregnancy Discrimination Act, it would not matter if all pregnant women placed their children at risk in taking these jobs, just as it does not matter if no men do so. As Judge Easterbrook put it in his dissent below, "Title VII gives parents the power to make occupational decisions affecting their families. A legislative forum is available to those who believe that such decisions should be made elsewhere." 886 F.2d 871, 915 (CA7 1989) (Easterbrook, J., dissenting).

Third, I am willing to assume, as the Court intimates, that any action required by Title VII cannot give rise to liability under state tort law. That assumption, however, does not answer the question whether an action is required by Title VII (including the BFOQ provision) even if it is subject to liability under state tort law. It is perfectly reasonable to believe that Title VII has accommodated state tort law through the BFOQ exception. However, all that need be said in the present case is that Johnson has not demonstrated a substantial risk of tort liability—which is alone enough to defeat a tort-based assertion of the BFOQ exception.

Last, the Court goes far afield, it seems to me, in suggesting that increased cost alone—short of "costs . . . so prohibitive as to threaten survival of the employer's business"—cannot support a BFOQ defense. I agree with JUSTICE WHITE's concurrence, that nothing in our prior cases suggests this, and, in my view, it is wrong. I think, for example, that a shipping company may refuse to hire pregnant women as crew members on long voyages because the

> on-board facilities for foreseeable emergencies, though quite feasible, would be inordinately expensive. In the present case, however, Johnson has not asserted a cost-based BFOQ.
>
> I concur in the judgment of the Court.

Case Questions

1. Compare the majority's description of the *Dothard v. Rawlinson* decision with Justice White's description of the same case. Who seems to be persuasive as to whether considerations of cost were or were not implicit in the resolution of that case?

2. Four justices grant that genuine necessity for avoiding substantial tort liability should count in determining what is a BFOQ. The other five justices reject that assertion but admit that the analysis might be different if "cost would be so prohibitive as to threaten the survival of the employer's business." Does this acknowledgment undermine the rest of their logic on tort liability?

3. The majority and Justice Scalia reject the argument that employer concerns about the safety of to-be-born babies is a legitimate consideration in deciding what is a BFOQ, although they do grant that financial threat to the employer (see Question 2) is a legitimate consideration. Is there anything troubling about a statutory scheme that honors an employer's pocketbook but not his/her conscience?

4. Are the six justices who do not concur with Justice White correct in their belief that he is ignoring the basic thrust of the Pregnancy Discrimination Act?

5. If a child is born deformed as a result of its mother's exposure to toxic chemicals in the workplace, but the mother and father knowingly worked there, is it the parents who should be liable for damages in a lawsuit? Why should the company be liable if it gave ample warning to potential parents of the dangers at work? Should it be an adequate corporate defense in such cases that the parents could have taken a leave from work until their blood lead levels subsided to a safe point for creating a pregnancy?

6. Why do you suppose this conscience-stricken company ignored the OSHA safety levels for the reproductive systems of male employees?

7. If a toxic industrial chemical were discovered that could not be shown to be harmful to adults or to their reproductive systems but that was highly toxic to fetuses, causing, say, cancer in two-thirds of the children born to women who had been exposed to the chemical at close range for more than twenty hours per week during pregnancy, should this degree of harm be viewed as a BFOQ eliminating pregnant workers from those close range jobs?

Pregnancy and Benefits

The Pregnancy Discrimination Act of 1978 figured prominently in the resolution of the *Johnson Controls* case. But before there was such an act, there were two Supreme Court decisions that provoked widespread outrage among advocates for women, enough outrage to mobilize Congress to adopt this law.

The first of these presented a challenge to a state government as an employer. As such, the state was obliged to follow the Equal Protection Clause. The *Craig* rule had not yet been adopted. Still, the year was 1974, and the Court had begun to show some hostility to governmental sex discrimination as early as *Reed v. Reed* in 1971 (see Chapter 2). Encouraged by decisions like *Reed* and *Frontiero*, employees of the state of California in *Geduldig v. Aiello*, 417 U.S. 484 (1974) sued their employer for violating the Equal Protection Clause by giving unequal benefit packages to males versus females.

This state paid medical disability and hospital benefits to its workers out of a fund created by deducting one percent of those workers' wages. Normal pregnancies, unlike other occasions for hospitalization, were specifically excluded from coverage. All physiological problems unique to males that could result in a hospitalization of eight days or longer were included in coverage, e.g. prostatectomy or testicular cancer. All other voluntary or quasi voluntary causes of an 8-day or longer hospitalization were covered—e.g. plastic surgery, attempted suicide, ski accident. Only pregnancy, unique to women, was categorically excluded.

Against three dissents that insisted that this program amounted to unjustified sex-based discrimination, the majority argued that no sex discrimination was involved. Justice Stewart for the Court claimed that the program did not favor men over women; rather it favored "non-pregnant persons" over "pregnant women."[98]

Against the potentially vague Equal Protection Clause, *Geduldig* attracted relatively little attention, but in 1976, female employees of General Electric company brought a suit alleging that a similar benefit package violated Title VII's specific and clear ban on sex discrimination in the terms or conditions of employment. In this case, *G.E v. Gilbert*, 429 U.S. 125 (1976), the majority reiterated the logic of *Geduldig*, to the effect that no sex discrimination was present. The insurance package that the males received, on average, was worth just as much as the insurance package of the females. It was not the employer's duty to give women extra compensation just because being female during the employable years cost more in medical expenses due to the potential for pregnancy. The dissenters pointed out the obvious: "The program has the intent and effect of providing that 'only women [employees are subjected] to a substantial risk of total loss of income because of temporary medical disability.' "[99]

The dissenters' point of view prevailed politically, if not at the Supreme Court. By 1977, in response to fierce reaction against *G.E. v. Gilbert* by feminist groups, the Senate voted overwhelmingly (75–11) for the Pregnancy Discrimination Act (PDA), a bill that specifically amended Title VII by defining pregnancy discrimination by employers as a type of forbidden sex discrimination. Because of conflicts over how to treat employee abortion costs, the bill did not become law until October 1978.

Once it received this loud and clear signal from Congress, the Court went even further than the bare terms of the PDA requirements. Whereas the PDA addressed the situation of "pregnant employees," the Supreme Court in *Newport News Shipbuilding v. EEOC*, 462 U.S. 669 (1983), ruled 7–2 that employers who provide medical expenses for *spouses* of their employees must include equal coverage for the medical expenses of maternity care for employees' wives. Building out the language of the statute, the Court reasoned that now the very concept of sex discrimination had been reshaped and henceforth included all pregnancy discrimination in employee benefits.

The PDA and Protective Laws for Pregnant Workers: *Cal Fed v. Guerra* (1987)

Just as the most prominent women activists of the early twentieth century were divided over whether the Constitution should permit legislatures to single out women employees for special protection, a similar controversy erupted in the late 1980s. Feminists and activists favoring special treatment disagreed with those favoring equal treatment, specifically over whether or not the PDA constituted a floor or a ceiling for benefits for pregnant employees. In the 1920s the pro-special-treatment women's activists had more prestige, numbers, and political influence. In the 1970s the equal-treatment feminists were predominant. By the late 1980s prominent feminist advocates of special treatment became increasingly influential, as new cases presented in new contexts this old issue.

In 1987, the U.S. Supreme Court decided a case that pitted certain self-proclaimed feminists (including some attorneys) against such feminist strongholds as the National Organization for Women, the National Women's Political Caucus, the American Civil Liberties Union, and the League of Women Voters. The case, *California Federal Savings & Loan v. Guerra*, began when Lillian Garland attempted after four months maternity leave in 1982 to return to the receptionist job that she had held for several years. The bank refused to rehire her, relying on its stated policy reserving such right of refusal for any employee on any leave of absence. The bank was defying California's Fair Employment and Housing Act, § 12945(b)(2), which required employers to grant pregnancy disability leave of up to four months. Specifically, the law said:

> It shall be an unlawful employment practice unless based upon a bona fide occupational qualification:
>
> . . .
>
> (b) For any employer to refuse to allow a female employee affected by pregnancy, childbirth or related medical conditions. . . .
>
> . . .
>
> (2) To take a leave on account of pregnancy for a reasonable period of time, provided such period shall not exceed four months. . . .Reasonable period of time means that period during which the female employee is disabled on account of pregnancy, childbirth, or related medical conditions. . . .
>
> An employer may require any employee who plans to take a leave pursuant to this section to give reasonable notice of the date such leave shall commence and the estimated duration of such leave.

Federal law (always supreme in case of a conflict, according to Article VI, Section 2 of the Constitution) forbids employers to discriminate on the basis of sex and states in the Pregnancy Discrimination Act (PDA) (42 U.S.C. § 2000e[k]):

> The terms . . . "on the basis of sex" include, but are not limited to, because of or on the basis of pregnancy, childbirth, or related medical conditions; and women affected by pregnancy, childbirth, or related medical conditions, shall be treated the same for all employment-related purposes, including receipt of benefits under fringe benefit programs, as other persons not so affected but similar in their ability or inability to work, and nothing in § 2000e–2(h) of this title shall be interpreted to permit otherwise.

The district court judge declared that this federal law negated California's law. The federal circuit court of appeals reversed, stating that the federal law was intended to enhance, not diminish, women's employment opportunities. This court interpreted the PDA as intended "to construct a floor beneath which pregnancy disability benefits may not drop—not a ceiling above which they may not rise" (758 F.2d, at 396). The Supreme Court took the appeal from this decision and a number of interest groups submitted additional *amicus* briefs. The American Civil Liberties Union's brief, submitting on the side of the bank, argued:

> Protectionist laws reflect an ideology which values women most highly for their childbearing and nurturing roles. Such laws reinforce stereotypes about women's inclinations and abilities; they deter employers from hiring women of childbearing age or funnel them into less responsible positions; and they make women *appear* to be more expensive, less reliable employees.

Professor Lucinda Finley of Yale Law School argued publicly to the contrary: "Pretending men and women are the same is not equality. . . . The equal treatment argument, carried to the extreme, tries to defy social reality, particularly among poor women. The social reality is that there are a lot of women out there in need." The news article from which these quotes are taken[100] points out that related potential future legislation that might be barred by an overly rigid approach to equality includes requirements of paid maternity leave or time off during the workday for breastfeeding. It also noted that women were 45% of the U.S. workforce in 1986 and 90% of them had or would have children. More than 60% of these women workers had no guarantees that the jobs they left for childbirth would be available to them when they were ready to return to work.

The Supreme Court decided this case on January 13, 1987, and it was the first of the cases in this text where "chief justice" referred to Rehnquist, Burger having retired from a tenure that began in 1969. The vacancy left by Burger's retirement was filled by Justice Scalia, who sides here with the majority of six, but for reasons of his own, which he explains below.

Justice Stevens, too, differs from the majority's reasoning in part. He is influenced by a 1979 precedent, *United Steelworkers v. Weber*, 443 U.S. 193, which had upheld private employer affirmative action programs for Black employees. The particular program upheld there had set aside 50% of the slots in an in-plant craft training program for qualified Black workers. This program was upheld by the Court against a challenge by a white worker shut out of the program despite his seniority (the basic qualifying factor), which was superior to that of many of the accepted Black applicants. He had based his challenge on Title VII of the Civil Rights Act, which prohibited, among other things, "any employer, labor organization, or joint labor-management committee," from discriminating "against any individual because of his race, color, religion, sex, or national origin in admission [to] any program established to provide apprenticeship or other training." The other justices barely mention this precedent that Justice Stevens found so compelling.

CALIFORNIA FEDERAL S. & L. ASSN. V. GUERRA
479 U.S. 272 (1987)

JUSTICE MARSHALL delivered the opinion of the Court.

The question presented is whether Title VII of the Civil Rights Act of 1964, as amended by the Pregnancy Discrimination Act of 1978, pre-empts a state statute that requires employers to provide leave and reinstatement to employees disabled by pregnancy.

I

Respondent Fair Employment and Housing Commission, the state agency authorized to interpret the FEHA, has construed § 12945(b)(2) to require California employers to reinstate an employee returning from such pregnancy leave to the job she previously held, unless it is no longer available due to business necessity. In the latter case, the employer must make a reasonable, good-faith effort to place the employee in a substantially similar job. The statute does not compel employers to provide paid leave to pregnant employees. Accordingly, the only benefit pregnant workers actually derive from § 12945(b)(2) is a qualified right to reinstatement.

Title VII of the Civil Rights Act of 1964 . . . prohibits various forms of employment discrimination, including discrimination on the basis of sex. However, in *General Electric Co. v. Gilbert,* 429 U.S. 125 (1976), this Court ruled that discrimination on the basis of pregnancy was not sex discrimination under Title VII. In response to the *Gilbert* decision, Congress passed the Pregnancy Discrimination Act of 1978 (PDA), 42 U.S.C. § 2000e (k). The PDA specifies that sex discrimination includes discrimination on the basis of pregnancy.[6]

II

Petitioner California Federal Savings & Loan Association (Cal Fed) is a federally chartered savings and loan association based in Los Angeles; it is an employer covered by both Title VII and § 12945(b)(2). Cal Fed has a facially neutral leave policy that permits employees who have completed three months of service to take unpaid leaves of absence for a variety of reasons, including disability and pregnancy. Although it is Cal Fed's policy to try to provide an employee taking unpaid leave with a similar position upon returning, Cal Fed expressly reserves the right to terminate an employee who has taken a leave of absence if a similar position is not available.

. . .

[W]e now affirm [the Court of Appeals ruling].

III

A

In determining whether a state statute is pre-empted by federal law and therefore invalid under the Supremacy Clause of the Constitution, our sole task is to ascertain the intent of Congress. See *Shaw v. Delta Air Lines, Inc.*, 463 U.S. 85, 95 (1983); *Malone v. White Motor Corp.*, 435 U.S. 497, 504 (1978). Federal law may supersede state law in several different ways. First, when acting within constitutional limits, Congress is empowered to pre-empt state law by so stating in express terms. E. g., *Jones v. Rath Packing Co.*, 430 U.S. 519, 525 (1977). Second, congressional intent to pre-empt state law in a particular area may be inferred where the scheme of federal regulation is sufficiently comprehensive to make reasonable the inference that Congress "left no room" for supplementary state regulation. *Rice v. Santa Fe Elevator Corp.*, 331 U.S. 218, 230 (1947). Neither of these bases for pre-emption exists in this case. . . .

As a third alternative, in those areas where Congress has not completely displaced state regulation, federal law may nonetheless pre-empt state law to the extent it actually conflicts with federal law. Such a conflict occurs either because "compliance with both federal and state regulations is a physical impossibility," *Florida Lime & Avocado Growers, Inc. v. Paul*, 373 U.S. 132, 142–143 (1963), or because the state law stands "as an obstacle to the accomplishment and execution of the full purposes and objectives of Congress." *Hines v. Davidowitz*, 312 U.S. 52, 67 (1941). [Other citations omitted.] Nevertheless, pre-emption is not to be lightly presumed. See *Maryland v. Louisiana*, 451 U.S. 725, 746 (1981).

This third basis for pre-emption is at issue in this case. In two sections of the 1964 Civil Rights Act, § 708 and § 1104, Congress has indicated that state laws will be pre-empted only if they actually conflict with federal law. Section 708 of Title VII provides:

> Nothing in this title shall be deemed to exempt or relieve any person from any liability, duty, penalty, or punishment provided by any present or future law of any State or political subdivision of a State, other than any such law which purports to require or permit the doing of any act which would be an unlawful employment practice under this title. 42 U.S.C. § 2000e–7.

Section 1104 of Title XI, applicable to all titles of the Civil Rights Act, establishes the following standard for pre-emption:

> Nothing contained in any title of this Act shall be construed as indicating an intent on the part of Congress to occupy the field in which any such title operates to the exclusion of State laws on the same subject matter, nor shall any provision of this Act be construed as invalidating any provision of State law unless such provision is inconsistent with any of the purposes of this Act, or any provision thereof. 42 U.S.C. § 2000h–4.

Accordingly, there is no need to infer congressional intent to pre-empt state laws from the substantive provisions of Title VII; these two sections provide a "reliable indicium of congressional intent with respect to state authority" to regulate employment practice. *Malone v. White Motor Corp.*, at 505.

Sections 708 and 1104 severely limit Title VII's preemptive effect. Instead of pre-empting state fair employment laws, § 708 " 'simply left them where they were before the enactment of title VII.' " *Shaw v. Delta Air Lines*, Inc., at 103, n. 24. Similarly, § 1104 was intended primarily to "assert the intention of Congress to preserve existing civil rights laws." 110 Cong. Rec. 2788 (1964) (remarks of Rep. Meader). See also H. R. Rep. No. 914, 88th Cong., 1st Sess., 59 (1963) (additional views of Rep. Meader).[12] The narrow scope of preemption available under § 708 and § 1104 reflects the importance Congress attached to state antidiscrimination laws in achieving Title VII's goal of equal employment opportunity. [Citations omitted.] The legislative history of the PDA also supports a narrow interpretation of these provisions, as does our opinion in *Shaw v. Delta Air Lines, Inc.*[15]

In order to decide whether the California statute requires or permits employers to violate Title VII, as amended by the PDA, or is inconsistent with the purposes of the statute, we must determine whether the PDA prohibits the States from requiring employers to provide reinstatement to pregnant workers, regardless of their policy for disabled workers generally.

B

Petitioners argue that the language of the federal statute itself unambiguously rejects California's "special treatment" approach to pregnancy discrimination, thus rendering any resort to the legislative history unnecessary. They contend that the second clause of the PDA forbids an employer to treat pregnant employees any differently than other disabled employees. Because "[t]he purpose of Congress is the ultimate touchstone' " of the pre-emption inquiry, *Malone v. White Motor Corp.*, 435 U.S., at 504, however, we must examine the PDA's language against the background of its legislative history and historical context. As to the language of the PDA, "[i]t is a 'familiar rule, that a thing may be within the letter of the statute and yet not within the statute, because not within its spirit, nor within the intention of its makers.'" *Steelworkers v. Weber*, 443 U.S. 193, 201 (1979) (quoting *Church of the Holy Trinity v. United States*, 143 U.S. 457, 459 (1892)). See *Train v. Colorado Public Interest Research Group, Inc.*, 426 U.S. 1, 10 (1976); *United States v. American Trucking Assns., Inc.*, 310 U.S. 534, 543–544 (1940).

It is well established that the PDA was passed in reaction to this Court's decision in *General Electric Co. v. Gilbert*, 429 U.S. 125 (1976). . . .*Newport News Shipbuilding & Dry Dock Co. v. EEOC*, 462 U.S., at 678. By adding pregnancy to the definition of sex discrimination prohibited by Title VII, the first clause of the PDA reflects Congress' disapproval of the reasoning in *Gilbert. Newport News*, at 678–679, and n. 17 (citing legislative history). Rather than imposing a limitation on the remedial purpose of the PDA, we believe that the second clause was intended to overrule the holding in *Gilbert* and to illustrate how discrimination against pregnancy is to be remedied. Cf. 462 U.S., at 678, n. 14 Accordingly, subject to certain limitations,[17] we agree with the Court of Appeals' conclusion that Congress intended the PDA to be "a floor beneath which pregnancy disability benefits may not drop—not a ceiling above which they may not rise." 758 F.2d, at 396.

The context in which Congress considered the issue of pregnancy discrimination supports this view of the PDA. Congress had before it extensive evidence of discrimination against pregnancy, particularly in disability and health insurance programs like those challenged in *Gilbert* and *Nashville Gas Co. v. Satty*, 434 U.S. 136 (1977).[18] The Reports, debates, and hearings make abundantly clear that Congress intended the PDA to provide relief for working women and to end discrimination against pregnant workers.[19] In contrast to the thorough account of discrimination against pregnant workers, the legislative history is devoid of any discussion of preferential treatment of pregnancy,[20] beyond acknowledgments of the existence of state statutes providing for such preferential treatment. Opposition to the PDA came from those concerned with the cost of including pregnancy in health and disability-benefit plans and the application of the bill to abortion[21], not from those who favored special accommodation of pregnancy.

In support of their argument that the PDA prohibits employment practices that favor pregnant women, petitioners and several *amici* cite statements in the legislative history to the effect that the PDA does not require employers to extend any benefits to pregnant women that they do not already provide to other disabled employees. For example, the House Report explained that the proposed legislation "does not require employers to treat pregnant employees in any particular manner.... H. R. 6075 in no way requires the institution of any new programs where none currently exist."[22] We do not interpret these references to support petitioners' construction of the statute. On the contrary, if Congress had intended to prohibit preferential treatment, it would have been the height of understatement to say only that the legislation would not require such conduct. It is hardly conceivable that Congress would have extensively discussed only its intent not to require preferential treatment if in fact it had intended to prohibit such treatment.

We also find it significant that Congress was aware of state laws similar to California's but apparently did not consider them inconsistent with the PDA. In the debates and Reports on the bill, Congress repeatedly acknowledged the existence of state antidiscrimination laws that prohibit sex discrimination on the basis of pregnancy.[23] Two of the States mentioned then required employers to provide reasonable leave to pregnant workers.[24] After citing these state laws, Congress failed to evince the requisite "clear and manifest purpose" to supersede them. See *Pacific Gas & Electric Co. v. State Energy... Comm'n,* 461 U.S. 190, 206 (1983). To the contrary, both the House and Senate Reports suggest that these laws would continue to have effect under the PDA.[25]

Title VII, as amended by the PDA, and California's pregnancy disability leave statute share a common goal. The purpose of Title VII is "to achieve equality of employment opportunities and remove barriers that have operated in the past to favor an identifiable group of ... employees over other employees." *Griggs v. Duke Power Co.*, 401 U.S. 424, 429–430 (1971). [Additional citations omitted.] Rather than limiting existing Title VII principles and objectives, the PDA extends them to cover pregnancy. As Senator Williams, a sponsor of the Act, stated: "The entire thrust ... behind this legislation is to guarantee women the basic right to participate fully and equally in the workforce, without denying them the fundamental right to full participation in family life." 123 Cong. Rec. 29658 (1977).

Section 12945(b) (2) also promotes equal employment opportunity. By requiring employers to reinstate women after a reasonable pregnancy disability leave, § 12945(b) (2) ensures that they will not lose their jobs on account of pregnancy disability.[27] California's approach is consistent with the dissenting opinion of JUSTICE BRENNAN in *General Electric Co. v. Gilbert*, which

Congress adopted in enacting the PDA. Referring to *Lau v. Nichols*, 414 U.S. 563 (1974), a Title VI decision, JUSTICE BRENNAN stated:

> [D]iscrimination is a social phenomenon encased in a social context and, therefore, unavoidably takes its meaning from the desired end products of the relevant legislative enactment, end products that may demand due consideration of the uniqueness of the 'disadvantaged' individuals. A realistic understanding of conditions found in today's labor environment warrants taking pregnancy into account in fashioning disability policies. 429 U.S., at 159.

By "taking pregnancy into account," California's pregnancy disability-leave statute allows women, as well as men, to have families without losing their jobs.

We emphasize the limited nature of the benefits § 12945 (b) (2) provides. The statute is narrowly drawn to cover only the period of *actual physical disability* on account of pregnancy, childbirth, or related medical conditions. Accordingly, unlike the protective labor legislation prevalent earlier in this century, § 12945(b) (2) does not reflect archaic or stereotypical notions about pregnancy and the abilities of pregnant workers. A statute based on such stereotypical assumptions would, of course, be inconsistent with Title VII's goal of equal employment opportunity. See, e. g., *Los Angeles Dept. of Water and Power v. Manhart*, 435 U.S. 702, 709 (1978); *Phillips v. Martin Marietta Corp.*, 400 U.S. 542, 545 (1971) (MARSHALL, J., concurring).

C

Moreover, even if we agreed with petitioners' construction of the PDA, we would nonetheless reject their argument that the California statute requires employers to violate Title VII. Section 12945(b) (2) does not prevent employers from complying with both the federal law (as petitioners construe it) and the state law. This is not a case where "compliance with both federal and state regulations is a physical impossibility," *Florida Lime & Avocado Growers, Inc. v. Paul*, 373 U.S., at 142–143, or where there is an "inevitable collision between the two schemes of regulation." *Id.*, at 143.[30] Section 12945(b) (2) does not compel California employers to treat pregnant workers *better* than other disabled employees; it merely establishes benefits that employers must, at a minimum, provide to pregnant workers. Employers are free to give comparable benefits to other disabled employees, thereby treating "women affected by pregnancy" no better than "other persons not so affected but similar in their ability or inability to work." Indeed, at oral argument, petitioners conceded that compliance with both statutes "is theoretically possible."

Petitioners argue that "extension" of the state statute to cover other employees would be inappropriate in the absence of a clear indication that this is what the California Legislature intended. They cite cases in which this Court has declined to rewrite underinclusive state statutes found to violate the Equal Protection Clause. See, e.g., *Wengler v. Druggists Mutual Insurance Co.*, 446 U.S. 142, 152–153 (1980); *Caban v. Mohammed*, 441 U.S. 380, 392–393, n. 13 (1979). This argument is beside the point. Extension is a remedial option to be exercised by a court once a statute is found to be invalid.[31] See, e. g., *Califano v. Westcott*, 443 U.S. 76, 89 (1979).

IV

Thus, petitioners' facial challenge to § 12945(b) (2) fails. The statute is not pre-empted by Title VII, as amended by the PDA, because it is not inconsistent with the purposes of the federal statute, nor does it require the doing of an act which is unlawful under Title VII.[32]

The judgment of the Court of Appeals is *Affirmed*.

Opinion Footnotes

6 The PDA added subsection (k) to 701, the definitional section of Title VII. Subsection (k) provides, in relevant part: "The terms 'because of sex' or 'on the basis of sex' include, but are not limited to, because of or on the basis of pregnancy, childbirth, or related medical conditions; and women affected by pregnancy, childbirth, or related medical conditions shall be treated the same for all employment-related purposes, including receipt of benefits under fringe benefit programs, as other persons not so affected but similar in their ability or inability to work, and nothing in § 703(h) of this title shall be interpreted to permit otherwise." The legislative history of the PDA reflects Congress' approval of the views of the dissenters in *Gilbert*. See *Newport News Shipbuilding & Dry Dock Co. v. EEOC*, 462 U.S. 669, 678–679, and nn. 15–17 (1983) (citing legislative history).

12 Representative Meader, one of the sponsors of the 1964 Civil Rights Act, proposed the precursor to § 1104 as an amendment to the Civil Rights Act, see 110 Cong. Rec. 2788 (1964), because he feared that § 708 and similar provisions in other titles were "wholly inadequate to preserve the validity and force of State laws aimed at discrimination." H. R. Rep. No. 914, 88th Cong., 1st Sess., 59 (1963) (additional views of Rep. Meader). His version provided that state laws would not be pre-empted "except to the extent that there is a direct and positive conflict between such provisions so that the two cannot be reconciled or consistently stand together." 110 Cong. Rec. 2787 (1964). The version ultimately adopted by Congress was a substitute offered by Representative Mathias without objection from Representative Meader. Id., at 2789. There is no indication that this substitution altered the basic thrust of § 1104.

15 In *Shaw v. Delta Air Lines, Inc.*, 463 U.S., at 100–104, we concluded that Title VII did not pre-empt a New York statute which proscribed discrimination on the basis of pregnancy as sex discrimination at a time when Title VII did not equate the two.

17 For example, a State could not mandate special treatment of pregnant workers based on stereotypes or generalizations about their needs and abilities.

18 See *Discrimination on the Basis of Pregnancy*, 1977, Hearings on S. 995 before the Subcommittee on Labor of the Senate Committee on Human Resources, 95th Cong., 1st Sess., 31–33 (1977) (statement of Vice Chairman, Equal Employment Opportunity Commission, Ethel Bent Walsh); id., at 113–117 (statement of Wendy W. Williams); id., at 117–121 (statement of Susan Deller Ross); id., at 307–310 (statement of Bella S. Abzug). See also *Legislation to Prohibit Sex Discrimination on the Basis of Pregnancy*, Hearings on H. R. 5055 and H. R. 6075 before the Subcommittee on Employment Opportunities of the House Committee on Education and Labor, 95th Cong., 1st Sess. (1977).

19 See, e. g., 123 Cong. Rec. 8144 (1977) (remarks of Sen. Bayh) (legislation "will end employment discrimination against pregnant workers"); 124 Cong Rec. 21440 (1978) (remarks of Rep. Chisholm) (bill "affords some 41 percent of this Nation's labor force some greater degree of protection and security without fear of reprisal due to their decision to bear children"); id., at 21442 (remarks of Rep. Tsongas) (bill "would put an end to an unrealistic and unfair system that forces women to choose between family and career—clearly a function of sex bias in the law"); id., at 36818 (remarks of Sen. Javits) (the "bill represents only basic fairness for women employees"); id., at 38574 (remarks of Rep. Sarasin) (Subcommittee "learned of the many instances of discrimination against pregnant workers, as we learned of the hardships this discrimination brought to women and their families").

20 The statement of Senator Brooke, quoted in the dissent, merely indicates the Senator's view that the PDA does not itself require special disability benefits for pregnant workers. It in no way supports the conclusion that Congress intended to prohibit the States from providing such benefits for pregnant workers. . . .

21 See, e.g., S.Rep. No. 95-331, p. 9 (1977), Leg.Hist. 46 (discussing cost objections); H.R.Conf.Rep. No. 95-1786, pp. 3–4 (1978), Leg.Hist. 196–197 (application of the PDA to abortion).

Leg.Hist. 41; 123 Cong.Rec. 7540 (1977) (remarks of Sen. Williams); id. at 10582 (remarks of Rep. Hawkins); id. at 29387 (remarks of Sen. Javits); id. at 29664 (remarks of Sen. Brooke).

22 H.R.Rep. No. 95-948, p. 4 (1978), Leg.Hist. 150. See also S.Rep. No. 95-331, supra, at 4.

23 See, e. g., id., at 29387 (remarks of Sen. Javits), Leg. Hist. 67 ("[S]everal state legislatures . . . have chosen to address the problem by mandating certain types of benefits for pregnant employees"). See also S. Rep. No. 95-331, at 3, Leg. Hist. 40; H. R. Rep. No. 95-948, at 10–11, Leg. Hist. 156–157; 123 Cong. Rec. 29648 (1977) (list of States that require coverage for pregnancy and pregnancy-related disabilities); id., at 29662 (remarks of Sen. Williams).

24 See, e. g., Conn. Gen. Stat. § 31–126(g) (1977), now codified at § 46a–60(a)(7) (1985); Mont. Rev. Codes § 41–2602 (Smith Supp. 1977), now codified at Mont. Code Ann. § 49–2–310 and § 49–2–311 (1986). . . . See also Mass. Gen. Laws ch.149: § 105D (1985) (providing up to eight weeks maternity leave).

25 For example, the Senate Report states: "Since title VII does not preempt State laws which would not require violating title VII . . ., these States would continue to be able to enforce their State laws if the bill were enacted." S. Rep. No. 95-331, at 3, n. 1, Leg. Hist. 40.

27 As authoritatively construed by respondent Commission, the provision will "insure that women affected by pregnancy, childbirth or related medical conditions have equal employment opportunities as persons not so affected." California Fair Employment and Housing Commission's Proposed Regulation.

30 Indeed, Congress and the California Legislature were each aware in general terms of the regulatory scheme adopted by the other when they enacted their legislation. California recognized that many of its provisions would be pre-empted by the PDA and, accordingly, exempted employers covered by Title VII from all portions of the statute except those guaranteeing unpaid leave and reinstatement to pregnant workers. Congress was aware that some state laws mandated certain benefits for pregnant workers, but did not indicate that they would be pre-empted by federal law.

31 We recognize that, in cases where a state statute is otherwise invalid, the Court must look to the intent of the state legislature to determine whether to extend benefits or nullify the statute. By arguing that extension would be inappropriate in this case, however, and citing this as a basis for pre-emption, the dissent simply ignores the pre-requisite of invalidity.

32 Because we conclude that in enacting the PDA Congress did not intend to prohibit all favorable treatment of pregnancy, we need not decide and therefore do not address the question whether § 12945(b)(2) could be upheld as a legislative response to leave policies that have a disparate impact on pregnant workers.

JUSTICE STEVENS, concurring in part and concurring in the judgment.

The Pregnancy Discrimination Act of 1978 (PDA) does not exist in a vacuum. As JUSTICE WHITE recognizes in his dissent, Congress did not intend to "put pregnancy in a class by itself within Title VII," and the enactment of the PDA "did not mark a departure from Title VII principles." But this realization does not lead me to support JUSTICE WHITE's position; rather, I believe that the PDA's posture as part of Title VII compels rejection of his argument that the PDA mandates complete neutrality and forbids all beneficial treatment of pregnancy.[1]

In *Steelworkers v. Weber*, 443 U.S. 193 (1979), the Court rejected the argument that Title VII prohibits all preferential treatment of the disadvantaged classes that the statute was enacted to protect. The plain words of Title VII, which would have led to a contrary result, were read in the context of the statute's enactment and its purposes.[2] In this case as well, the language of the Act seems to mandate treating pregnant employees the same as other employees. I cannot, however, ignore the fact that the PDA is a definitional section of Title VII's prohibition against gender-based discrimination. Had *Weber* interpreted Title VII as requiring neutrality, I would agree with JUSTICE WHITE that the PDA should be interpreted that way as well. But since the Court in *Weber* interpreted Title VII to draw a distinction between discrimination against members of the protected class and special preference in favor of members of that class, I do not accept the proposition that the PDA requires absolute neutrality.

I therefore conclude that JUSTICE MARSHALL's view, which holds that the PDA allows some preferential treatment of pregnancy, is more consistent with our interpretation of Title VII than JUSTICE WHITE's view is. This is not to say, however, that all preferential treatment of pregnancy is automatically beyond the scope of the PDA.[3] Rather, as with other parts of Title VII, preferential treatment of the disadvantaged class is only permissible so long as it is consistent with "accomplish[ing] the goal that Congress designed Title VII to achieve." *Weber*, at 204. That goal has been characterized as seeking "to achieve equality of employment opportunities and to remove barriers that have operated in the past to favor an identifiable group of . . . employees over other employees." *Griggs v. Duke Power Co.*, 401 U.S. 424, 429–430 (1971).

It is clear to me, as it is to the Court, and was to the Court of Appeals, that the California statute meets this test. Thus, I agree that a California employer would not violate the PDA were it to comply with California's statute without affording the same protection to men suffering somewhat similar disabilities.

Opinion Footnotes

1 Because I agree with the Court that the California statute does not conflict with the purposes of the PDA, and does not purport to "require or permit" action inconsistent with the PDA, I do not reach the question whether § 1104 of the Civil Rights Act of 1964, 42 U.S.C. § 2000h–4, is applicable to Title VII, or whether, as JUSTICE SCALIA suggests, § 708, 42 U.S.C. § 2000e–7, is the only provision governing Title VII's pre-emptive scope. . . .Since Part **III-A** of JUSTICE MARSHALL's opinion does not make clear whether it decides this issue, or whether it only assumes for the purposes of the decision that § 1104 applies, I do not join that section. I do, however, join the remainder of the Court's opinion. . . .

2 There is a striking similarity between the evidence about the enactment of Title VII that was available in *Steelworkers v. Weber* and the evidence available regarding the enactment of the PDA. First, the plain language in both cases points to neutrality, see 443 U.S., at 201, although, if anything, that language was even less equivocal in *Weber* than it is here. Second, in both cases the records are replete with indications that Congress' goal was to bar discrimination against the disadvantaged class or classes at issue. See 443 U.S., at 201–204. Third, in neither case was there persuasive evidence that Congress considered the ramifications of a rule mandating complete neutrality. See 443 U.S., at 204. Finally, there were statements in the legislative histories of both provisions stressing that Congress did not intend to require preferential treatment, statements that undermine the conclusion that Congress indeed intended to prohibit such treatment. See 443 U.S., at 204–206.

3 I do not read the Court's opinion as holding that Title VII presents no limitations whatsoever on beneficial treatment of pregnancy. Although the opinion does make some mention of the "floor" but "not a ceiling" language employed by the Court of Appeals, the Court also points out that there are limitations on what an employer can do, even when affording "preferential" treatment to pregnancy. See n. 17 [and last paragraph of **III-B**].

JUSTICE SCALIA, concurring in the judgment.

The only provision of the Civil Rights Act of 1964 whose effect on pre-emption need be considered in the present case is § 708 of Title VII, 42 U.S.C. § 2000e–7. Although both that section and § 1104, 42 U.S.C. § 2000h–4, are described by the majority as pre-emption provisions, they are more precisely anti-pre-emption provisions, prescribing that nothing in Title VII (in the case of § 708) and nothing in the entire Civil Rights Act (in the case of § 1104) shall be deemed to pre-empt state law unless certain conditions are met. The exceptions set forth in the general § 1104 ban on pre-emption ("inconsisten[cy] with any of the purposes of this Act, or any provision thereof") are somewhat broader than the single exception set forth in the Title VII § 708 ban. Because the Pregnancy Disability Act (PDA) is part of Title VII, the more expansive prohibition of pre-emption particularly applicable to that Title applies. If that precludes pre-emption of Cal. Govt. Code Ann. § 12945(b)(2) (West 1980), it is unnecessary to inquire whether § 1104 would do so.

Section 708 narrows the pre-emptive scope of the PDA so that it pre-empts only laws which "purpor[t] to require or permit the doing of any act which would be an unlawful employment practice" under the Title 42 U.S.C. § 2000e–7. Thus, whether or not the PDA prohibits discriminatorily favorable disability treatment for pregnant women, § 12945(b)(2) of the California Code cannot be pre-empted, since it does not remotely purport to require or permit any refusal to accord federally mandated equal treatment to others similarly situated. No more is needed to decide this case.

. . .

I am fully aware that it is more convenient for the employers of California and the California Legislature to have us interpret the PDA prematurely. It has never been suggested, however, that the constitutional prohibition upon our rendering of advisory opinions is a doctrine of convenience. I would affirm the judgment of the Court of Appeals on the ground that § 12945(b) (2) of the California Code does not purport to require or permit any act that would be an unlawful employment practice under any conceivable interpretation of the PDA, and therefore, by virtue of § 708, cannot be pre-empted.

JUSTICE WHITE, with whom THE CHIEF JUSTICE and JUSTICE POWELL join, dissenting.

I disagree with the Court that Cal. Govt. Code Ann. § 12945(b) (2) (West 1980) is not pre-empted by the Pregnancy Discrimination Act of 1978 (PDA), 42 U.S.C. § 2000e(k), and § 708 of Title VII. Section 703(a) of Title VII, 42 U.S.C. § 2000 e–2 (a), forbids discrimination in the terms of employment on the basis of race, color, religion, sex, or national origin. The PDA gave added meaning to discrimination on the basis of sex:

> The terms 'because of sex' or 'on the basis of sex' [in § 703(a) of this Title] include, but are not limited to, because of or on the basis of pregnancy, childbirth or related medical conditions; and women affected by pregnancy, childbirth, or related medical conditions shall be treated the same for all employment-related purposes, including receipt of benefits under fringe benefit programs, as other persons not so affected but similar in their ability or inability to work . . . . § 2000e(k).

The second clause quoted above could not be clearer: it mandates that pregnant employees "shall be treated the same for all employment-related purposes" as nonpregnant employees similarly situated with respect to their ability or inability to work. This language leaves no room for preferential treatment of pregnant workers. The majority would avoid its plain meaning by misapplying our interpretation of the clause in *Newport News Shipbuilding & Dry Dock Co. v. EEOC*, 462 U.S. 669, 678, n. 14 (1983). The second clause addresses only female employees and was not directly implicated in *Newport News* because the pregnant persons at issue in that case were spouses of male employees. . . .

Contrary to the mandate of the PDA, California law requires every employer to have a disability leave policy for pregnancy even if it has none for any other disability. An employer complies with California law if it has a leave policy for pregnancy but denies it for every other disability. On its face, § 12945(b) (2) is in square conflict with the PDA and is therefore pre-empted. Because the California law permits employers to single out pregnancy for preferential treatment and therefore to violate Title VII, it is not saved by § 708 which limits pre-emption of state laws to those that require or permit an employer to commit an unfair employment practice.[1]

The majority nevertheless would save the California law on two grounds. First, it holds that the PDA does not require disability from pregnancy to be treated the same as other disabilities; instead, it forbids less favorable, but permits more favorable, benefits for pregnancy disability. The express command of the PDA is unambiguously to the contrary, and the legislative history casts no doubt on that mandate.

The legislative materials reveal Congress' plain intent not to put pregnancy in a class by itself within Title VII, as the majority does with its "floor . . . not a ceiling" approach. The Senate Report clearly stated:

> By defining sex discrimination to include discrimination against pregnant women, the bill rejects the view that employers may treat pregnancy and its incidents as *sui generis*, without regard to its functional comparability to other conditions. Under this bill, the treatment of pregnant women in covered employment must focus not on their condition alone but on the actual effects of that condition on their ability to work. Pregnant women who are able to work must be permitted to work on the same conditions as other employees; and when they are not able to work for medical reasons, they must be accorded the same rights, leave privileges and other benefits, as other workers who are disabled from working.[2]

The House Report similarly stressed that the legislation did not mark a departure from Title VII principles:

> It must be emphasized that this legislation, operating as part of Title VII, prohibits only discriminatory treatment. Therefore, it does not require employers to treat pregnant employees in any particular manner with respect to hiring, permitting them to continue working, providing sick leave, furnishing medical and hospital benefits, providing disability benefits, or any other matter. H. R. 6075 in no

way requires the institution of any new programs where none currently exist. The bill would simply require that pregnant women be treated the same as other employees on the basis of their ability or inability to work.³

The majority correctly reports that Congress focused on discrimination against, rather than preferential treatment of, pregnant workers. There is only one direct reference in the legislative history to preferential treatment. Senator Brooke stated during the Senate debate: "I would emphasize most strongly that S. 995 in no way provides special disability benefits for working women. They have not demanded, nor asked, for such benefits. They have asked only to be treated with fairness, to be accorded the same employment rights as men."⁴ Given the evidence before Congress of the widespread discrimination against pregnant workers, it is probable that most Members of Congress did not seriously consider the possibility that someone would want to afford preferential treatment to pregnant workers. The parties and their *amici* argued vigorously to this Court the policy implications of preferential treatment of pregnant workers. In favor of preferential treatment it was urged with conviction that preferential treatment merely enables women, like men, to have children without losing their jobs. In opposition to preferential treatment it was urged with equal conviction that preferential treatment represents a resurgence of the 19th-century protective legislation which perpetuated sex-role stereotypes and which impeded women in their efforts to take their rightful place in the workplace. See, e. g., *Muller v. Oregon*, 208 U.S. 412, 421–423 (1908); *Bradwell v. Illinois*, 16 Wall. 130, 141 (1873) (Bradley, J., concurring). It is not the place of this Court, however, to resolve this policy dispute. Our task is to interpret Congress' intent in enacting the PDA. Congress' silence in its consideration of the PDA with respect to preferential treatment of pregnant workers cannot fairly be interpreted to abrogate the plain statements in the legislative history, not to mention the language of the statute, that equality of treatment was to be the guiding principle of the PDA.

Congress' acknowledgment of state antidiscrimination laws does not support a contrary inference. The most extensive discussion of state laws governing pregnancy discrimination is found in the House Report.⁵ It was reported that six States, Alaska, Connecticut, Maryland, Minnesota, Oregon, and Montana, and the District of Columbia specifically included pregnancy in their fair employment practices laws. In 12 additional States, Illinois, Indiana, Iowa, Kansas, Massachusetts, Michigan, Missouri, New York, Pennsylvania, South Dakota, Washington, and Wisconsin, the prohibition on sex discrimination in the state fair employment practices law had been interpreted, either by a state court or the state enforcement agency, to require equal treatment of pregnant workers. Finally, five States, California, Hawaii, New Jersey, New York, and Rhode Island, had included pregnancy in their temporary disability laws under which private employers are required to provide partial wage replacement for temporary disabilities. The Report noted, however, that whereas California, New Jersey, and New York covered complications from pregnancy on the same basis as other disabilities, California, New Jersey, New York, and Rhode Island set maximum limits on the coverage required for disability associated with normal childbirth. The Report did not in any way set apart the Connecticut and Montana statutes, on which the majority relies, from the other state statutes. The House Report gave no indication that these statutes required anything more than equal treatment. Indeed, the state statutes were considered, not in the context of pre-emption, but in the context of a discussion of health insurance costs. . . .

Nor does anything in the legislative history from the Senate side indicate that it carefully considered the state statutes, including those of Connecticut and Montana, and expressly endorsed their provisions. The Senate Report noted that "25 States presently interpret their own fair employment practices laws to prohibit sex discrimination based on pregnancy and childbirth," and Senator Williams presented during the Senate debate a list of States which required coverage for pregnancy and pregnancy-related disabilities, but there was no analysis of their provisions.[7]

The Court's second, and equally strange, ground is that even if the PDA does prohibit special benefits for pregnant women, an employer may still comply with both the California law and the PDA: it can adopt the specified leave policies for pregnancy and at the same time afford similar benefits for all other disabilities. This is untenable. California surely had no intent to require employers to provide general disability leave benefits. It intended to prefer pregnancy and went no further. Extension of these benefits to the entire work force would be a dramatic increase in the scope of the state law and would impose a significantly greater burden on California employers. That is the province of the California Legislature. See *Wengler v. Druggists Mutual Insurance Co.*, 446 U.S. 142, 152–153 (1980); *Caban v. Mohammed*, 441 U.S. 380, 392–393, n. 13 (1979); *Craig v. Boren*, 429 U.S. 190, 210, n. 24 (1976). Nor can § 12945(b)(2) be saved by applying Title VII in tandem with it, such that employers would be required to afford reinstatement rights to pregnant workers as a matter of state law but would be required to afford the same rights to all other workers as a matter of federal law. The text of the PDA does not speak to this question but it is clear from the legislative history that Congress did not intend for the PDA to impose such burdens on employers. As recognized by the majority, opposition to the PDA came from those concerned with the cost of including pregnancy in health and disability benefit plans. The House Report acknowledged these concerns and explained that the bill "in no way requires the institution of any new programs where none currently exist."[9] The Senate Report gave a similar assurance.[10] In addition, legislator after legislator stated during the floor debates that the PDA would not require an employer to institute a disability benefits program if it did not already have one in effect.[11] Congress intended employers to be free to provide any level of disability benefits they wished—or none at all—as long as pregnancy was not a factor in allocating such benefits. The conjunction of § 12945(b) (2) and the PDA requires California employers to implement new minimum disability leave programs. Reading the state and federal statutes together in this fashion yields a result which Congress expressly disavowed.

In sum, preferential treatment of pregnant workers is prohibited by Title VII, as amended by the PDA. Section 12945(b) (2) of the California Government Code, which extends preferential benefits for pregnancy, is therefore pre-empted. It is not saved by 708 because it purports to authorize employers to commit an unfair employment practice forbidden by Title VII.[12]

Opinion Footnotes

1 The same clear language preventing preferential treatment based on pregnancy forecloses respondents' argument that the California provision can be upheld as a legislative response to leave policies that have a disparate impact on pregnant workers. Whatever remedies Title VII would otherwise provide for victims of disparate impact, Congress expressly ordered pregnancy to be treated in the same manner as other disabilities.

2 S. Rep. No. 95-331, p. 4 (1977), *Legislative History of the Pregnancy Discrimination Act of 1978* (Committee Print prepared for the Senate Committee on Labor and Human Resources), p. 41 (1980) (*Leg. Hist.*).

3 H. R. Rep. No. 95-948, p. 4 (1978), *Leg. Hist.* 150 (emphasis added). The same theme was also expressed repeatedly in the floor debates. Senator Williams, for example, the Chairman of the Senate Committee on Labor and Human Resources and a sponsor of the Senate bill. . .: "The central purpose of the bill is to require that women workers be treated equally with other employees on the basis of their ability or inability to work. The key to compliance in every case will be equality of treatment. In this way, the law will protect women from the full range of discriminatory practices which have adversely affected their status in the work force." 123 Cong. Rec. 29385 (1977), *Leg. Hist.* 62–63.

4 123 Cong. Rec. 29664 (1977), *Leg. Hist.* 135.

5 H. R. Rep. No. 95-948, at 10–11, *Leg. Hist.* 156–157.

7 S. Rep. No. 95-331, at 3, *Leg. Hist.* 40; 123 Cong. Rec. 29648 (1977), *Leg. Hist.* 91.

9 H. R. Rep. No. 95-948, at 4, *Leg. Hist.* 150.

10 S. Rep. No.95-331, at 4 (1977, *Leg. Hist.* 41.

11 123 Cong. Rec. 7541 (1977), *Leg. Hist.* 8 (remarks of Sen. Brooke) ("[T]he bill being introduced would not mandate compulsory disability coverage"); 123 Cong. Rec., at 8145, *Leg. Hist.* 19 (remarks of

Sen. Bayh) ("Under the provisions of our legislation, only those companies which already voluntarily offer disability coverage would be affected"); 123 Cong. Rec., at 10582, *Leg. Hist.* 25 (remarks of Rep. Hawkins) ("[A]n employer who does not now provide disability benefits to his employees will not have to provide such benefits to women disabled due to pregnancy or childbirth"); 123 Cong. Rec., at 29386, *Leg. Hist.* 64 (remarks of Sen. Williams) ("[T]his legislation does not require that any employer begin to provide health insurance where it is not presently provided"); 123 Cong. Rec., at 29388, *Leg. Hist.* 71 (remarks of Sen. Kennedy) ("This amendment does not require all employers to provide disability insurance plans; it merely requires that employers who have disability plans for their employees treat pregnancy-related disabilities in the same fashion that all other temporary disabilities are treated with respect to benefits and leave policies"); 123 Cong. Rec., at 29663, *Leg. Hist.* 131 (remarks of Sen. Cranston) ("[S]ince the basic standard is comparability among employees, an employer who does not provide medical benefits at all, would not have to pay the medical costs of pregnancy or child birth"); 123 Cong. Rec., at 29663, *Leg. Hist.* 133 (remarks of Sen. Culver) ("The legislation before us today does not mandate compulsory disability coverage").

12 Section 12945(b) (2) does not *require* employers to treat pregnant employees better than other disabled employees; employers are free voluntarily to extend the disability leave to all employees. But if this is not a statute which "purports to . . . permit the doing of any act which would be an unlawful employment practice" under Title VII, I do not know what such a statute would look like. . .

Neither is § 12945(b) (2) saved by § 1104 of the Civil Rights Act since it is inconsistent with the equal-treatment purpose and provisions of Title VII.

Case Questions

1. The dissenters in their n. 3 cite a statement from the PDA's sponsor to the effect that "the key to compliance . . . will be equality of treatment." The majority argue that § 12945(b)(2) promotes equality because: "By taking pregnancy into account, California's pregnancy disability leave statute allows women, as well as men, to have families without losing their jobs." Which side has the sounder comprehension of "equality"? Gives the more persuasive account of Congressional intent? Should Congressional intent be decisive?

2. How convincing is Justice Stevens's argument that the *Weber* precedent should settle this case? Why might the other justices be ignoring that precedent?

Case note: One week later, the Supreme Court added a coda to the *Guerra* reasoning by an 8–0 decision in *Wimberly v. Labor and Industrial Relations Commission*, 479 U.S. 511. There, in an opinion by Justice O'Connor, the Court affirmed a ruling of the Missouri Supreme Court to the effect that there was no conflict between Missouri's law that denied unemployment benefits to all workers who leave their jobs voluntarily and the 1976 Federal Unemployment Compensation Amendments which provided that states may not deny unemployment compensation "solely on the basis of pregnancy or termination of pregnancy." Justice O'Connor ruled that Missouri, pursuant to its statute, denied unemployment compensation to a woman who left work to have a baby, and who then could not get her job back when she tried three months later, did not transgress the federal law. This was because Missouri imposed only a "neutral rule" that treated pregnancy the same as other voluntary reasons for leaving work including "other types of temporary disabilities."[101] The federal rule prohibiting discrimination against pregnancy here was read as not *requiring* preferential treatment of pregnancy. In *Guerra*, a similar rule was read as not *forbidding* preferential treatment.

Not all pregnant workers can afford to take a leave from their jobs. In a recent twist on the application of the PDA, a woman sued her employer, United Parcel Service (UPS) because it refused to give her a less physically burdensome job during the months of her advanced pregnancy, even though the company did make such accommodations for employees injured on the job, employees with permanent disabilities (covered by the Americans with Disabilities Act), and employees who due to illness or injury (or for other reasons) lost their certification to drive trucks. In a 2015 decision the U.S. Supreme Court ruled 6–3 that if a company is making this kind of accommodation for large numbers of other employees "similar in their inability to work" (the second clause of § 2000e(k)), then it must do so for its pregnant employees who are similar in their inability to perform the job for which they are requesting an accommodation. *Young v. United Parcel Service*, 575 U.S. ___ (2015).

The Family and Medical Leave Act: *Nevada v. Hibbs* (2003)

In 1993, after nearly ten years of effort by feminist lobbyists, the Family and Medical Leave Act (FMLA)[102] was signed into law by the new president, Bill Clinton, as he had promised in his campaign. Congress had twice voted to adopt the law under the administration of George Bush I, but he had vetoed it on the grounds that it interfered too much with the freedom of business owners. This bill largely obviated the issue that the Court faced in *Cal Fed v. Guerra* (1987); now all covered workers, male and female, received a guarantee that their jobs would be held for them if they took a leave, up to twelve weeks in any one year, in order to deal with a new baby, whether from their own conception or through adoption. Moreover, this law allowed workers to take a leave to care for a close family member (parent, child or spouse) facing "a serious health condition," or to take a medically necessary leave for themselves. The act applies to firms of fifty or more employees and to all state and federal government agencies, including schools. This bill had been intensely opposed by business organizations and by some states' rights advocates (since these issues are generally left to state law).[103] A 2012 report commissioned by the U.S. Department of Labor reports that 44 percent of employees taking FMLA leave are males, and the majority of males and of females use the leave for their own health needs.[104]

Congressional power to enact this law was basically non-controversial; Congress is clearly given the power to regulate the national economy in Article I, Section 8, clause 3. However, the law contained an enforcement clause that permitted aggrieved workers to sue employers for back pay and reinstatement if the employer violated the law. State and local governments together employ about nineteen million people.[105] This lawsuit authorization as applied to (unconsenting) state governments would have posed no problem prior to 1995, but in 1996 the Supreme Court began to hand down a series of decisions striking down this application of such clauses in other federal laws.[106] Each of these occurred via a five-four vote. Five of the justices—Rehnquist, Scalia, Thomas, O'Connor, and Kennedy—believed in a version of federalism rejected in long and emphatic dissents by the other four.

William Hibbs invoked this law to sue his employer, the State of Nevada Human Resources Department, claiming the employer had not allotted him his full twelve weeks of leave to care for his wife who had been in a car accident and underwent neck surgery. Although the case is neither a "women's rights" nor a gender equity case strictly speaking, but deals rather with Congress's constitutional powers vis à vis the states, nonetheless, there was in the justices' opinions a good deal of discussion of gender equity.

Justices Rehnquist and O'Connor broke ranks with their allies in the "federalist five" to argue (in the Court opinion by Chief Justice Rehnquist) that this legal provision, as a corrective to state discrimination, is authorized under the enforcement clause of the Fourteenth Amendment, and as such it forms a legitimate exception to the recent precedents (see note 106 above) narrowly constraining Congressional power to authorize private lawsuits against the states. The Rehnquist opinion noted a long history of state laws discriminating against women in employment opportunities and reinforcing the stereotype that women put home and family duties first, and work second. This stereotype then fosters discrimination against women workers by both state and private employers. The opinion pointed out that discrimination in parental leave arrangements (i.e., providing them for women but not men) persisted long after Congress enacted Title VII (forbidding sex discrimination in employment), and created the need for this additional legislation as a prophylactic measure.

Justice Kennedy dissented for himself, Scalia and Thomas, arguing essentially that Congress should have been limited (in providing the private lawsuit remedy against states) to just those states for which there was specific evidence that the state agents had discriminated in parental (or family medical care) leave policies.

The combined effect of *Hibbs* and the prior rulings discussed in this section is that people can now sue state or local government employers for violations of the Family and Medical Leave Act (which requires sex-neutral provision of three months leave for family care obligations) but they may not sue such government employers for violating the federal prohibitions on discriminating on the basis of age[107] or disability.[108]

Sex-Based Affirmative Action: *Johnson v. Transportation Agency* (1987)

At least since the early 1970s it has been clear that the federal courts were willing to employ race-conscious remedies to counteract the still-ongoing effects of prior illegal or unconstitutional racial discrimination. In the context of elementary and secondary public schools, such remedies often included court-ordered busing, and for employment discrimination, such remedies have included group awards of back pay, or temporary affirmative hiring quotas to bring a workforce into line with where it would have been "but for" the illegal discrimination.

In addition to remedies for specific wrongdoing, the U.S. Supreme Court in 1980 (*Fullilove v. Klutznick*, 448 U.S. 448) upheld a mandate by Congress that federal public works contracts had to be awarded in such a way that at least 10% of the contracts went to businesses owned by members of designated racial minorities. The Court interpreted this law as a remedy imposed by Congress to a long history of racial discrimination in the contracting industries and upheld it within that broadly remedial framework.

Where, however, race-conscious affirmative action efforts have been taken by employers or university admissions personnel outside of a specific remedial context—i.e., without proof or confession of previous wrongdoing by the party implementing affirmative action—the Supreme Court has issued decidedly mixed messages about the legality of such voluntary affirmative action. (Details are provided below.)

For sex-based discrimination, courts similarly permitted or ordered stringent corrective remedies to compensate for prior, demonstrated illegal employment discrimination. However, before 1987 the Supreme Court had been utterly silent about the legality of voluntary affirmative efforts to increase percentages of women in jobs or educational programs from which they had previously been excluded or discouraged by society at-large, albeit not by the particular party offering the affirmative action program.

In the matter of voluntary race-conscious affirmative action programs, the two leading Supreme Court precedents as of the time of the sex-based affirmative action case, *Johnson v. Transportation Agency*, were *Regents of California v. Bakke*, 438 U.S. 265 (1978) and *United Steelworkers v. Weber*, 443 U.S. 193 (1979). In the former, the majority (of five) ruled that the prohibition on race discrimination by educational institutions receiving federal funds, which comprises Title VI of the 1964 Civil Rights Act, forbade fixed racial quotas in university admissions, however benevolently motivated. On the other hand, the majority said that Title VI did permit taking minority racial status into account as a "plus" factor in the admission decision as a way of attaining diversity, a goal that is "compelling" for state universities due to its connection to First Amendment values.

In the *Weber* case decided just a year later, a majority of five ruled that Title VII, which bans discrimination on the basis of race in hiring and promotion, did permit rigid racial quotas of an affirmative nature. (It was Justice Stewart who switched sides from the *Bakke* majority.) If an employer wished to implement such quotas voluntarily, in order "to eliminate conspicuous racial imbalance in traditionally segregated job categories,"[109] Title VII, despite its language to the contrary, would permit it. Justice Brennan writing for the majority, explained that sometimes what appears to contradict the letter of the law fulfills its spirit, and that the goal of the Civil Rights Act was to enhance economic opportunity for those races that had previously suffered discrimination. Justice Blackmun wrote a concurring opinion in which he took pains to explain that a "traditionally segregated job category" meant one where there had been "a societal history of purposeful exclusion of blacks from the job category, resulting in a persistent disparity between the proportion of blacks in the labor force and the proportion . . . who hold jobs within the category."[110] Thus, the *Weber* majority appeared to view permissible voluntary affirmative action programs as remedial measures, even if not as remedies specifically for discrimination perpetrated by the particular employer and union adopting the program.

These two cases, *Bakke* and *Weber*, framed the legal background for the decision on March 25, 1987 of *Paul Johnson v. Transportation Agency of Santa Clara*, the Supreme Court's first statement on the legality of voluntary sex-based affirmative action. And since *Johnson v. Agency* arose in an employment context, *Weber* is accorded great prominence in the debate between the majority, led by Justice Brennan, and the dissenters, led by Justice Scalia. Justice Scalia, (Burger's replacement on the Court) argues forcefully that *Weber* should be overruled.

The *Johnson* case began when Paul Johnson was passed over in a competition for the job of road dispatcher for Santa Clara County, California. The County chose instead to promote into the position another of its employees, Diane Joyce. The County acknowledged that this selection occurred pursuant to its Affirmative Action Plan, adopted in December 1978, with the goal of remedying "the effects of past practices and. . .[attaining] an equitable representation of minorities, women and handicapped persons."[111] The Plan indicated that in making appointments for "a traditionally segregated job classification in which women have been significantly underrepresented, the Agency is authorized to consider as one factor the sex of a qualified applicant."[112] The Plan described traditionally segregated jobs as ones for which women "had not been strongly motivated to seek training or employment 'because of the limited opportunities that have existed in the past for them to work in such classifications.' "[113] (Justice Brennan quoting the Plan, 480 U.S. 616, at 621.) The Plan set no fixed quotas; it aimed ultimately at attaining proportions of women in each job that would match those in the local labor force, but acknowledged that more realistic annual goals should be geared to proportions of women in the labor force who possess relevant job qualifications. (The Plan said similar things about racial minorities and the handicapped, but those were not specifically at issue in the *Johnson* case.)

When the vacancy for road dispatcher was announced, twelve county employees applied for it, including Diane Joyce and Paul Johnson. Nine of those, again including Joyce and Johnson, were deemed qualified for the job on the basis of such criteria as work experience, and were then interviewed by a two-person committee. Applicants were scored on the basis of the interview; a 70 was passing, and seven people earned passing scores. The highest score given was an 80, Johnson ranked next with 75 and Joyce ranked next with 73. All seven thereby judged qualified were then scheduled for a second interview by a board of three Agency supervisors.

Because Diane Joyce had previously clashed with two of the three scheduled interviewers, in incidents some of which apparently reflected gender prejudice, she at this point (encouraged to do so by the Director of the Santa Clara County Commission on the Status of Women, Rina Rosenberg) contacted the County's Affirmative Action Office to express fear that she would receive biased treatment in her second interview. The Supreme Court's description of her previous difficulties with these men is as follows:

> Joyce testified that she had had disagreements with two of the three members of the second interview panel. One had been her first supervisor when she began work as a road maintenance worker. In performing arduous work in this job, she had not been issued coveralls, although her male co-workers had received them. After ruining her pants, she complained to her supervisor, to no avail. After three other similar incidents, ruining clothes on each occasion, she filed a grievance, and was issued four pairs of coveralls the next day. Joyce had dealt with a second member of the panel for a year and a half in her capacity as

chair of the Roads Operations Safety Committee, where she and he "had several differences of opinion on how safety should be implemented." In addition, Joyce testified that she had informed the person responsible for arranging her second interview that she had a disaster preparedness class on a certain day the following week. By this time about 10 days had passed since she had notified this person of her availability, and no date had yet been set for the interview. Within a day or two after this conversation, however, she received a notice setting her interview at a time directly in the middle of her disaster preparedness class. This same panel member had earlier described Joyce as a "rebel-rousing, skirt-wearing person." (480 U.S. 616, 624, n.5)

The Coordinator of the Affirmative Action Office, whose job includes apprising the Director of the Agency of qualified women, members of racial minorities and handicapped individuals for particular openings, then recommended that Joyce receive the promotion to road dispatcher. At the time, no women had ever held that job.

The Director of the Agency, James Graebner, then received a recommendation from the second interview panel to hire Paul Johnson. Technically authorized to select any of the seven, Graebner chose Diane Joyce. He later explained that he had taken into account "the whole picture"[114]—both persons' experience, background, expertise, test scores, and "affirmative action matters." He indicated further that he viewed both Johnson and Joyce as "well-qualified" and that the difference between test scores of 75 and 73 on an interview was insignificant.

After Joyce's appointment Paul Johnson went to federal court with a complaint that sex had been "the determining factor" in Diane Joyce's selection over him, and the District Court was persuaded by his argument that this violated Title VII. The Circuit Court of Appeals reversed, and Johnson appealed to the U.S. Supreme Court.

At the Supreme Court, the Reagan Administration Justice Department submitted an amicus brief. In 1986, the Justice Department had argued in three different cases that all voluntary affirmative action violates the law and the Constitution, and that even affirmative action remedies to illegal discrimination should be limited to proven individual victims of the discrimination. Rebuffed by the Supreme Court in all three cases, the Justice Department in *Johnson v. Agency* had modified its position, but still insisted that the Santa Clara plan swept too broadly and had invaded Paul Johnson's legal rights. The Supreme Court again rejected the Department's arguments.

JOHNSON V. TRANSPORTATION AGENCY
480 U.S. 616 (1987)

JUSTICE BRENNAN delivered the opinion of the Court.

. . .

[Here the Court reviewed relevant precedents and said in footnote 7 about the *Weber* precedent, "Congress has not amended the statute to reject our construction, *nor have any such amendments even been proposed*, and we therefore may assume that our interpretation was correct." Emphasis added.—AU.] . . .

In reviewing the employment decision at issue in this case, we must first examine whether that decision was made pursuant to a plan prompted by concerns similar to those of the employer in *Weber*. Next, we must determine whether the effect of the Plan on males and non-minorities is comparable to the effect of the plan in that case.

The first issue is therefore whether consideration of the sex of applicants for Skilled Craft jobs was justified by the existence of a "manifest imbalance" that reflected underrepresentation of women in "traditionally segregated job categories." In determining whether an imbalance exists that would justify taking sex or race into account, a comparison of the percentage of minorities or women in the employer's work force with the percentage in the area labor market or general population is appropriate in analyzing jobs that require no special expertise, see *Teamsters v. United States*, 431 U.S. 324 (1977) (comparison between percentage of blacks in employer's work force and in general population proper in determining extent of imbalance in truck driving positions), or training programs designed to provide expertise, see *Steelworkers v. Weber*, 443 U.S. 193 (1979) (comparison between proportion of blacks working at plant and proportion of blacks in area labor force appropriate in calculating imbalance for purpose of establishing preferential admission to craft training program). Where a job requires special training, however, the comparison should be with those in the labor force who possess the relevant qualifications. See *Hazelwood School District v. United States*, 433 U.S. 299 (1977) (must compare percentage of blacks in employer's work ranks with percentage of qualified black teachers in area labor force in determining underrepresentation in teaching positions). The requirement that the "manifest imbalance" relate to a "traditionally segregated job category" provides assurance both that sex or race will be taken into account in a manner consistent with Title VII's purpose of eliminating the effects of employment discrimination, and that the interests of those employees not benefiting from the plan will not be unduly infringed.

A manifest imbalance need not be such that it would support a prima facie case against the employer, as suggested in JUSTICE O'CONNOR's concurrence, since we do not regard as identical the constraints of Title VII and the Federal Constitution on voluntarily adopted affirmative action plans. Application of the "prima facie" standard in Title VII cases would be inconsistent with *Weber*'s focus on statistical imbalance, and could inappropriately create a significant disincentive for employers to adopt an affirmative action plan. See *Weber*, at 204 (Title VII intended as a "catalyst" for employer efforts to eliminate vestiges of discrimination). A corporation concerned with maximizing return on investment, for instance, is hardly likely to adopt a plan if in order to do so it must compile evidence that could be used to subject it to a colorable Title VII suit.

It is clear that the decision to hire Joyce was made pursuant to an Agency plan that directed that sex or race be taken into account for the purpose of remedying underrepresentation. The Agency Plan acknowledged the "limited opportunities that have existed in the past," for women to find employment in certain job classifications "where women have not been traditionally employed in significant numbers."[12] As a result, observed the Plan, women were concentrated in traditionally female jobs in the Agency, and represented a lower percentage in other job classifications than would be expected if such traditional segregation had not occurred. Specifically, 9 of the 10 Para-Professionals and 110 of the 145 Office and Clerical Workers were women. By contrast, women were only 2 of the 28 Officials and Administrators, 5 of the 58 Professionals, 12 of the 124 Technicians, none of the Skilled Craft Workers, and 1—who was Joyce—of the 110 Road Maintenance Workers. The Plan sought to remedy these imbalances through "hiring, training and promotion of . . . women throughout the Agency in all major job classifications where they are underrepresented."

As the Agency Plan recognized, women were most egregiously underrepresented in the Skilled Craft job category, since none of the 238 positions was occupied by a woman. In mid-1980, when Joyce was selected for the road dispatcher position, the Agency was still in the process of refining its short-term goals for Skilled Craft Workers in accordance with the directive of the Plan. This process did not reach fruition until 1982, when the Agency established a short-term goal for that year of 3 women for the 55 expected openings in that job category—a modest goal of about 6% for that category.

...The Agency's Plan emphasized that the long-term goals were not to be taken as guides for actual hiring decisions, but that supervisors were to consider a host of practical factors in seeking to meet affirmative action objectives, including the fact that in some job categories women were not qualified in numbers comparable to their representation in the labor force.

By contrast, had the Plan simply calculated imbalances in all categories according to the proportion of women in the area labor pool, and then directed that hiring be governed solely by those figures, its validity fairly could be called into question. This is because analysis of a more specialized labor pool normally is necessary in determining underrepresentation in some positions. If a plan failed to take distinctions in qualifications into account in providing guidance for actual employment decisions, it would dictate mere blind hiring by the numbers, for it would hold supervisors to "achievement of a particular percentage of minority employment or membership ... regardless of circumstances such as economic conditions or the number of available qualified minority applicants...." *Sheet Metal Workers v. EEOC*, 478 U.S. 421, 495 (1986) (O'CONNOR, J., concurring in part and dissenting in part).

The Agency's Plan emphatically did not authorize such blind hiring. It expressly directed that numerous factors be taken into account in making hiring decisions, including specifically the qualifications of female applicants for particular jobs....

... Given the obvious imbalance in the Skilled Craft category, and given the Agency's commitment to eliminating such imbalances, it was plainly not unreasonable for the Agency to determine that it was appropriate to consider as one factor the sex of Ms. Joyce in making its decision. The promotion of Joyce thus satisfies the first requirement enunciated in *Weber*, since it was undertaken to further an affirmative action plan designed to eliminate Agency work force imbalances in traditionally segregated job categories.

We next consider whether the Agency Plan unnecessarily trammeled the rights of male employees or created an absolute bar to their advancement. In contrast to the plan in *Weber*, which provided that 50% of the positions in the craft training program were exclusively for blacks, and to the consent decree upheld last Term in *Firefighters v. Cleveland*, 478 U.S. 501 (1986), which required the promotion of specific numbers of minorities, the Plan sets aside no positions for women. The Plan expressly states that "[t]he 'goals' established for each Division should not be construed as 'quotas' that must be met." Rather, the Plan merely authorizes that consideration be given to affirmative action concerns when evaluating qualified applicants. As the Agency Director testified, the sex of Joyce was but one of numerous factors he took into account in arriving at his decision. The Plan thus resembles the "Harvard Plan" approvingly noted by JUSTICE POWELL in *Regents of University of California v. Bakke*, 438 U.S. 265, 316–319 (1978), which considers race along with other criteria in determining admission to the college. As JUSTICE POWELL observed: "In such an admissions program, race or ethnic background may be deemed a 'plus' in a particular applicant's file, yet it does not insulate the individual from comparison with all other candidates for the available seats." Id., at 317. Similarly, the Agency Plan requires women to compete with all other qualified applicants. No persons are automatically excluded from consideration; all are able to have their qualifications weighed against those of other applicants.

In addition, petitioner had no absolute entitlement to the road dispatcher position. Seven of the applicants were classified as qualified and eligible, and the Agency Director was authorized to promote any of the seven. Thus, denial of the promotion unsettled no legitimate, firmly rooted expectation on the part of petitioner. Furthermore, while petitioner in this case was denied a promotion, he retained his employment with the Agency, at the same salary and with the same seniority, and remained eligible for other promotions.

Finally, the Agency's Plan was intended to attain a balanced work force, not to maintain one. The Plan contains 10 references to the Agency's desire to "attain" such a balance, but no reference whatsoever to a goal of maintaining it.

. . .Express assurance that a program is only temporary may be necessary if the program actually sets aside positions according to specific numbers. See, e. g., *Firefighters*, at 510 (4-year duration for consent decree providing for promotion of particular number of minorities); *Weber*, 443 U.S., at 199 (plan requiring that blacks constitute 50% of new trainees in effect until percentage of employer work force equal to percentage in local labor force). This is necessary both to minimize the effect of the program on other employees, and to ensure that the plan's goals "[are] not being used simply to achieve and maintain . . . balance, but rather as a benchmark against which" the employer may measure its progress in eliminating the underrepresentation of minorities and women. *Sheet Metal Workers*, 478 U.S., at 477–478. In this case, however, substantial evidence shows that the Agency has sought to take a moderate, gradual approach to eliminating the imbalance in its work force, one which establishes realistic guidance for employment decisions, and which visits minimal intrusion on the legitimate expectations of other employees. Given this fact, as well as the Agency's express commitment to "attain" a balanced work force, there is ample assurance that the Agency does not seek to use its Plan to maintain a permanent racial and sexual balance.

III

In evaluating the compliance of an affirmative action plan with Title VII's prohibition on discrimination, we must be mindful of "this Court's and Congress' consistent emphasis on 'the value of voluntary efforts to further the objectives of the law.'" *Wygant*, 476 U.S., at 290 (O'CONNOR, J., concurring in part and concurring in judgment) (quoting *Bakke*, at 364). The Agency in the case before us has undertaken such a voluntary effort, and has done so in full recognition of both the difficulties and the potential for intrusion on males and nonminorities. The Agency has identified a conspicuous imbalance in job categories traditionally segregated by race and sex. It has made clear from the outset, however, that employment decisions may not be justified solely by reference to this imbalance, but must rest on a multitude of practical, realistic factors. It has therefore committed itself to annual adjustment of goals so as to provide a reasonable guide for actual hiring and promotion decisions. The Agency earmarks no positions for anyone; sex is but one of several factors that may be taken into account in evaluating qualified applicants for a position.[17] As both the Plan's language and its manner of operation attest, the Agency has no intention of establishing a work force whose permanent composition is dictated by rigid numerical standards.

We therefore hold that the Agency appropriately took into account as one factor the sex of Diane Joyce in determining that she should be promoted to the road dispatcher position. The decision to do so was made pursuant to an affirmative action plan that represents a moderate, flexible, case-by-case approach to effecting a gradual improvement in the representation of minorities and women in the Agency's work force. Such a plan is fully consistent with Title VII, for it embodies the contribution that voluntary employer action can make in eliminating the vestiges of discrimination in the workplace. Accordingly, the judgment of the Court of Appeals is

Affirmed.

Opinion Footnotes

12 For instance, the description of the Skilled Craft Worker category, in which the road dispatcher position is located, is as follows:

> Occupations in which workers perform jobs which require special manual skill and a thorough and comprehensive knowledge of the process involved in the work which is acquired through on-the-job training and experience or through apprenticeship or other formal training programs. Includes: mechanics and repairmen; electricians, heavy equipment operators, stationary

engineers, skilled machining occupations, carpenters, compositors and typesetters and kindred workers.

As the Court of Appeals said in its decision below, "A plethora of proof is hardly necessary to show that women are generally underrepresented in such positions and that strong social pressures weigh against their participation." 748 F.2d, at 1313.

17 JUSTICE SCALIA's dissent predicts that today's decision will loose a flood of "less qualified" minorities and women upon the work force, as employers seek to forestall possible Title VII liability. The first problem with this projection is that it is by no means certain that employers could in every case necessarily avoid liability for discrimination merely by adopting an affirmative action plan. Indeed, our unwillingness to require an admission of discrimination as the price of adopting a plan has been premised on concern that the potential liability to which such an admission would expose an employer would serve as a disincentive for creating an affirmative action program. See n. 8, *supra*.

A second, and more fundamental, problem with JUSTICE SCALIA's speculation is that he ignores the fact that

> [i]t is a standard tenet of personnel administration that there is rarely a single, 'best qualified' person for a job. An effective personnel system will bring before the selecting official several fully-qualified candidates who each may possess different attributes which recommend them for selection. Especially where the job is an unexceptional, middle-level craft position, without the need for unique work experience or educational attainment and for which several well-qualified candidates are available, final determinations as to which candidate is 'best qualified' are at best subjective. Brief for the American Society for Personnel Administration as *Amicus Curiae*.

This case provides an example of precisely this point. Any differences in qualifications between Johnson and Joyce were minimal, to say the least. The selection of Joyce thus belies JUSTICE SCALIA'S contention that the beneficiaries of affirmative action programs will be those employees who are merely not "utterly unqualified."

JUSTICE STEVENS, concurring.

While I join the Court's opinion, I write separately to explain my view of this case's position in our evolving antidiscrimination law and to emphasize that the opinion does not establish the permissible outer limits of voluntary programs undertaken by employers to benefit disadvantaged groups.

I

...As a shield, an antidiscrimination statute can also help a member of a protected class by assuring decisionmakers in some instances that, when they elect for good reasons of their own to grant a preference of some sort to a minority citizen, they will not violate the law. The Court properly holds that the statutory shield allowed respondent to take Diane Joyce's sex into account in promoting her to the road dispatcher position.

Prior to 1978 the Court construed the Civil Rights Act of 1964 as an absolute blanket prohibition against discrimination which neither required nor permitted discriminatory preferences for any group, minority or majority. The Court unambiguously endorsed the neutral approach, first in the context of gender discrimination[1] and then in the context of racial discrimination against a white person.[2] As I explained in my separate opinion in *Regents of University of California v. Bakke*, 438 U.S. 265, 412–418 (1978), and as the Court forcefully stated in *McDonald v. Santa Fe Trail Transportation Co.*, 427 U.S. 273, 280 (1976), Congress intended " 'to eliminate all practices which operate to disadvantage the employment opportunities of any group protected by Title VII, including Caucasians' " (citations omitted). If the Court had adhered to that construction of the Act, petitioner would unquestionably prevail in this case. But it has not done so.

In the *Bakke* case in 1978 and again in *Steelworkers v. Weber*, 443 U.S. 193 (1979), a majority of the Court interpreted the antidiscriminatory strategy of the statute in a fundamentally different way. The Court held in the Weber case that an employer's program designed to increase the number of black craftworkers in an aluminum plant did not violate Title VII.[3] It remains clear that the Act does not require any employer to grant preferential treatment on the basis of race or gender, but since 1978 the Court has unambiguously interpreted the statute to permit the voluntary adoption of special programs to benefit members of the minority groups for whose protection the statute was enacted. . . .Thus, as was true in *Runyon v. McCrary*, 427 U.S. 160, 189 (1976) (STEVENS, J., concurring), the only problem for me is whether to adhere to an authoritative construction of the Act that is at odds with my understanding of the actual intent of the authors of the legislation. I conclude without hesitation that I must answer that question in the affirmative, just as I did in *Runyon. Id.*, at 191–192.

Bakke and *Weber* have been decided and are now an important part of the fabric of our law. This consideration is sufficiently compelling for me to adhere to the basic construction of this legislation that the Court adopted in *Bakke* and in *Weber*. There is an undoubted public interest in "stability and orderly development of the law." 427 U.S., at 190.

The logic of antidiscrimination legislation requires that judicial constructions of Title VII leave "breathing room" for employer initiatives to benefit members of minority groups. If Title VII had never been enacted, a private employer would be free to hire members of minority groups for any reason that might seem sensible from a business or a social point of view. The Court's opinion in *Weber* reflects the same approach; the opinion relied heavily on legislative history indicating that Congress intended that traditional management prerogatives be left undisturbed to the greatest extent possible. See 443 U.S., at 206–207. As we observed last Term, " 'It would be ironic indeed if a law triggered by a Nation's concern over centuries of racial injustice and intended to improve the lot of those who had "been excluded from the American dream for so long" constituted the first legislative prohibition of all voluntary, private, race-conscious efforts to abolish traditional patterns of racial segregation and hierarchy.'" *Firefighters v. Cleveland*, 478 U.S. 501, 516 (1986) (quoting *Weber*, 443 U.S., at 204). In *Firefighters*, we again acknowledged Congress' concern in Title VII to avoid "undue federal interference with managerial discretion." 478 U.S., at 519.[5]

. . .

As construed in *Weber* and in *Firefighters*, the statute does not absolutely prohibit preferential hiring in favor of minorities; it was merely intended to protect historically disadvantaged groups against discrimination and not to hamper managerial efforts to benefit members of disadvantaged groups that are consistent with that paramount purpose. The preference granted by respondent in this case does not violate the statute as so construed; the record amply supports the conclusion that the challenged employment decision served the legitimate purpose of creating diversity in a category of employment that had been almost an exclusive province of males in the past. Respondent's voluntary decision is surely not prohibited by Title VII as construed in *Weber*.

II

Whether a voluntary decision of the kind made by respondent would ever be prohibited by Title VII is a question we need not answer until it is squarely presented. Given the interpretation of the statute the Court adopted in *Weber*, I see no reason why the employer has any duty, prior to granting a preference to a qualified minority employee, to determine whether his past conduct might constitute an arguable violation of Title VII. Indeed, in some instances the employer may find it more helpful to focus on the future. Instead of retroactively scrutinizing his own or society's possible exclusions of minorities in the past . . .—in many cases the employer will find it more appropriate to consider other legitimate reasons to give preferences to members of underrepresented groups. Statutes enacted for the benefit of minority groups should not block these forward-looking considerations.

> Public and private employers might choose to implement affirmative action for many reasons other than to purge their own past sins of discrimination. . . .[:] improving their services to black constituencies, averting racial tension over the allocation of jobs in a community, or increasing the diversity of a work force, to name but a few examples. Or they might adopt affirmative action simply to eliminate from their operations all de facto embodiment of a system of racial caste . . .— Sullivan, "The Supreme Court—Comment, Sins of Discrimination:

Last Term's Affirmative Action Cases," 100 *Harv. L. Rev.* 78, 96 (1986).

The Court today does not foreclose other voluntary decisions based in part on a qualified employee's membership in a disadvantaged group. Accordingly, I concur.

Opinion Footnotes

1 "Discriminatory preference for any group, minority or majority, is precisely and only what Congress has proscribed. What is required by Congress is the removal of artificial, arbitrary, and unnecessary barriers to employment when the barriers operate invidiously to discriminate on the basis of racial or other impermissible classification." *Griggs v. Duke Power Co.*, 401 U.S. 424, 431 (1971).

2 "Similarly the EEOC, whose interpretations are entitled to great deference, [401 U.S.,] at 433–434, has consistently interpreted Title VII to proscribe racial discrimination in private employment against whites on the same terms as racial discrimination against nonwhites, holding that to proceed otherwise would 'constitute a derogation of the Commission's Congressional mandate to eliminate all practices which operate to disadvantage the employment opportunities of any group protected by Title VII, including Caucasians.' EEOC Decision No. 74-31, 7 FEP Cases 1326, 1328 (1973)." "This conclusion is in accord with uncontradicted legislative history to the effect that Title VII was intended to 'cover white men and white women and all Americans,' 110 Cong. Rec. 2578 (1964) (remarks of Rep. Celler), and create an 'obligation not to discriminate against whites,' *id.*, at 7218 (memorandum of Sen. Clark). See also *id.*, at 7213 (memorandum of Sens. Clark and Case); *id.*, at 8912 (remarks of Sen. Williams). We therefore hold today that Title VII prohibits racial discrimination against the white petitioners in this case upon the same standards as would be applicable were they Negroes and Jackson white." *McDonald v. Santa Fe Trail Transportation Co.*, 427 U.S. 273, 279–280 (1976) . . .

3 Toward the end of its opinion, the Court mentioned certain reasons why the plan did not impose a special hardship on white employees or white applicants for employment. *Steelworkers v. Weber*, 443 U.S., at 208. I have never understood those comments to constitute a set of conditions that every race-conscious plan must satisfy in order to comply with Title VII.

5 As JUSTICE BLACKMUN observed in *Weber*, 443 U.S., at 209, 214–215 (concurring opinion): "Strong considerations of equity support an interpretation of Title VII that would permit private affirmative action to reach where Title VII itself does not. The bargain struck in 1964 with the passage of Title VII guaranteed equal opportunity for white and black alike, but where Title VII provides no remedy for blacks, it should not be construed to foreclose private affirmative action from supplying relief. . . ."

JUSTICE O'CONNOR, concurring in the judgment.

In *Steelworkers v. Weber*, 443 U.S. 193 (1979), this Court held that § 703(d) of Title VII does not prohibit voluntary affirmative action efforts if the employer sought to remedy a "manifest . . . imbalanc[e] in traditionally segregated job categories." *Id.*, at 197. As JUSTICE SCALIA illuminates with excruciating clarity, § 703 has been interpreted by *Weber* and succeeding cases to permit what its language read literally would prohibit. (STEVENS, J., concurring). Section 703(d) prohibits employment discrimination "against any individual because of his race, color, religion, sex, or national origin." 42 U.S.C. § 2000e–2(d) (emphasis added). The *Weber* Court, however, concluded that voluntary affirmative action was permissible in some circumstances because a prohibition of every type of affirmative action would " 'bring about an end completely at variance with the purpose of the statute.'" 443 U.S., at 202. This purpose, according to the Court, was to open employment opportunities for blacks in occupations that had been traditionally closed to them.

None of the parties in this case have suggested that we overrule *Weber* and that question was not raised, briefed, or argued in this Court or in the courts below. If the Court is faithful to its normal prudential restraints and to the principle of *stare decisis* we must address once again the propriety of an affirmative action plan under Title VII in light of our precedents, precedents that have upheld affirmative action in a variety of circumstances. This time the question posed is whether a public employer violates Title VII by promoting a qualified woman rather than a marginally better qualified man when there is a statistical imbalance sufficient to support a claim of a pattern or practice of discrimination against women under Title VII.

I concur in the judgment of the Court in light of our precedents. I write separately, however, because the Court has chosen to follow an expansive and ill-defined approach to voluntary affirmative action by public employers despite the limitations imposed by the Constitution and by the provisions of Title VII, and because JUSTICE SCALIA'S dissent rejects the Court's precedents and addresses the question of how Title VII should be interpreted as if the Court were writing on a clean slate. The former course of action gives insufficient guidance to courts and litigants; the latter course of action serves as a useful point of academic discussion, but fails to reckon with the reality of the course that the majority of the Court has determined to follow.

In my view, the proper initial inquiry in evaluating the legality of an affirmative action plan by a public employer under Title VII is no different from that required by the Equal Protection Clause. In either case, consistent with the congressional intent to provide some measure of protection to the interests of the employer's nonminority employees, the employer must have had a firm basis for believing that remedial action was required. An employer would have such a firm basis if it can point to a statistical disparity sufficient to support a prima facie claim under Title VII by the employee beneficiaries of the affirmative action plan of a pattern or practice claim of discrimination.

In *Weber*, this Court balanced two conflicting concerns in construing § 703(d): Congress' intent to root out invidious discrimination against any person on the basis of race or gender, *McDonald v. Santa Fe Transportation Co.*, 427 U.S. 273 (1976), and its goal of eliminating the lasting effects of discrimination against minorities. Given these conflicting concerns, the Court concluded that it would be inconsistent with the background and purpose of

Title VII to prohibit affirmative action in all cases. As I read *Weber*, however, the Court also determined that Congress had balanced these two competing concerns by permitting affirmative action only as a remedial device to eliminate actual or apparent discrimination or the lingering effects of this discrimination.

Contrary to the intimations in JUSTICE STEVENS' concurrence, this Court did not approve preferences for minorities "for any reason that might seem sensible from a business or a social point of view." Indeed, such an approach would have been wholly at odds with this Court's holding in *McDonald* that Congress intended to prohibit practices that operate to discriminate against the employment opportunities of nonminorities as well as minorities. Moreover, in *Weber* the Court was careful to consider the effects of the affirmative action plan for black employees on the employment opportunities of white employees. 443 U.S., at 208. Instead of a wholly standardless approach to affirmative action, the Court determined in *Weber* that Congress intended to permit affirmative action only if the employer could point to a "manifest . . . imbalanc[e] in traditionally segregated job categories." *Id.*, at 197. This requirement both "provides assurance . . . that sex or race will be taken into account in a manner consistent with Title VII's purpose of eliminating the effects of employment discrimination," and is consistent with this Court's and Congress' consistent emphasis on the value of voluntary efforts to further the antidiscrimination purposes of Title VII. *Wygant v. Jackson Board of Education*, 476 U.S. 267, 290 (1986) (O'CONNOR, J., concurring in part and concurring in judgment).

The *Weber* view of Congress' resolution of the conflicting concerns of minority and nonminority workers in Title VII appears substantially similar to this Court's resolution of these same concerns in *Wygant v. Jackson Board of Education*, which involved the claim that an affirmative action plan by a public employer violated the Equal Protection Clause. In *Wygant*, the Court was in agreement that remedying past or present racial discrimination by a state actor is a sufficiently weighty interest to warrant the remedial use of a carefully constructed affirmative action plan. The Court also concluded, however, that "[s]ocietal discrimination, without more, is too amorphous a basis for imposing a racially classified remedy." *Id.*, at 276. Instead, we determined that affirmative action was valid if it was crafted to remedy past or present discrimination by the employer. Although the employer need not point to any contemporaneous findings of actual discrimination, I concluded in *Wygant* that the employer must point to evidence sufficient to establish a firm basis for believing that remedial action is required, and that a statistical imbalance sufficient for a Title VII prima facie case against the employer would satisfy this firm basis requirement...

The *Wygant* analysis is entirely consistent with *Weber*....Here, however, the evidence of past discrimination is more complex. The number of women with the qualifications for entry into the relevant job classification was quite small. A statistical imbalance between the percentage of women in the work force generally and the percentage of women in the particular specialized job classification, therefore, does not suggest past discrimination for purposes of proving a Title VII prima facie case. See *Hazelwood School District v. United States*, 433 U.S. 299, 308, and n. 13 (1977).

Unfortunately, the Court today gives little guidance for what statistical imbalance is sufficient to support an affirmative action plan. Although the Court denies that the statistical imbalance need be sufficient to make out a prima facie case of discrimination against women, the Court fails to suggest an alternative standard. Because both *Wygant* and *Weber* attempt to reconcile the same competing concerns, I see little justification for the adoption of different standards for affirmative action under Title VII and the Equal Protection Clause.

While employers must have a firm basis for concluding that remedial action is necessary, neither *Wygant* nor *Weber* places a burden on employers to prove that they actually discriminated against women or minorities. Employers are "trapped between the competing hazards of liability to minorities if affirmative action is not taken to remedy apparent employment discrimination and liability to nonminorities if affirmative action is taken." *Wygant v. Jackson Board of Education*, 476 U.S., at 291 (O'CONNOR, J., concurring in part and concurring in judgment). Moreover, this Court has long emphasized the importance of voluntary efforts to eliminate discrimination. *Id.,* at 290. Thus, I concluded in *Wygant* that a contemporaneous finding of discrimination should not be required because it would discourage voluntary efforts to remedy apparent discrimination. A requirement that an employer actually prove that it had discriminated in the past would also unduly discourage voluntary efforts to remedy apparent discrimination....Evidence sufficient for a prima facie Title VII pattern or practice claim against the employer itself suggests that the absence of women or minorities in a work force cannot be explained by general societal discrimination alone and that remedial action is appropriate.

In applying these principles to this case, it is important to pay close attention to both the affirmative action plan, and the manner in which that plan was applied to the specific promotion decision at issue in this case. . . .

The long-term goal of the plan was "to attain a work force whose composition in all job levels and major job classifications approximates the distribution of women . . . in the Santa Clara County work force." If this long-term goal had been applied to the hiring decisions made by the Agency, in my view, the affirmative action plan would violate Title VII. "[I]t is completely unrealistic to assume that individuals of each [sex] will gravitate with mathematical exactitude to each employer . . . absent unlawful discrimination." *Sheet Metal Workers*, 478 U.S., at 494 (O'CONNOR, J., concurring in part and dissenting in part). Thus, a goal that makes such an assumption, and simplistically focuses on the proportion of women and minorities in the work force without more, is not remedial. Only a goal that takes into account the number of women and minorities qualified for the relevant position could satisfy the requirement that an affirmative action plan be remedial. This long-range goal, however, was never used as a guide for actual hiring decisions. Instead, the goal was merely a statement of aspiration wholly without operational significance . . . [T]he plan provided for the development of short-term goals, which alone were to guide respondents, and the plan cautioned that even these goals "should not be construed as 'quotas' that must be met." Instead, these short-term goals were to be focused on remedying past apparent discrimination, and would "[p]rovide an objective standard for use in determining if the representation of minorities, women and handicapped persons in particular job classifications is at a reasonable level in comparison with estimates of the numbers of persons from these groups in the area work force who can meet the educational and experience requirements for employment."

. . .

As JUSTICE SCALIA views the record in this case, the Agency Director made the decision to promote Joyce rather than petitioner solely on the basis of sex and with indifference to the relative merits of the two applicants. In my view, however, the record simply fails to substantiate the picture painted by JUSTICE SCALIA. The Agency Director testified that he "tried to look at the whole picture, the combination of [Joyce's] qualifications and Mr. Johnson's qualifications, their test scores, their experience, their background, affirmative action matters, things like that." Contrary to JUSTICE SCALIA'S suggestion, the Agency Director knew far more than merely the sex of the candidates and that they appeared on a list of candidates eligible for the job. The Director had spoken to individuals familiar with the qualifications of both applicants for the promotion, and was aware that their scores were rather close. Moreover, he testified that over a period of weeks he had spent several hours making the promotion decision, suggesting that Joyce was not selected solely on the basis of her sex. Additionally, the Director stated that had Joyce's experience been less than that of petitioner by a larger margin, petitioner might have received the promotion. As the Director summarized his decision to promote Joyce, the underrepresentation of women in skilled craft positions was only one element of a number of considerations that led to the promotion of Ms. Joyce. While I agree with JUSTICE SCALIA'S dissent that an affirmative action program that automatically and blindly promotes those marginally qualified candidates falling within a preferred race or gender category, or that can be equated with a permanent plan of "proportionate representation by race and sex," would violate Title VII, I cannot agree that this is such a case. Rather, as the Court demonstrates, Joyce's sex was simply used as a "plus" factor.

In this case, I am also satisfied that respondents had a firm basis for adopting an affirmative action program. Although the District Court found no discrimination against women in fact, at the time the affirmative action plan was adopted, there were no women in its skilled craft positions. Petitioner concedes that women constituted approximately 5% of the local labor pool of skilled craft workers in 1970. Thus, when compared to the percentage of women in the qualified work force, the statistical disparity would have been sufficient for a prima facie Title VII case brought by unsuccessful women job applicants. See Teamsters, 431 U.S., at 342, n. 23 ("[F]ine tuning of the statistics could not have obscured the glaring absence of minority line drivers. . . . [T]he company's inability to rebut the inference of discrimination came not from a misuse of statistics but from 'the inexorable zero' ").

In sum, I agree that respondents' affirmative action plan as implemented in this instance with respect to skilled craft positions satisfies the requirements of *Weber* and of *Wygant*. Accordingly, I concur in the judgment of the Court.

JUSTICE WHITE, dissenting.

I agree with Parts I and II of JUSTICE SCALIA'S dissenting opinion. Although I do not join Part III, I also would overrule *Weber*. My understanding of *Weber* was, and is, that the employer's plan did not violate Title VII because it was designed to remedy the intentional and systematic exclusion of blacks by the employer and the unions from certain job categories. That is how I understood the phrase "traditionally segregated jobs" that we used in that case.

The Court now interprets it to mean nothing more than a manifest imbalance between one identifiable group and another in an employer's labor force. As so interpreted, that case, as well as today's decision, as JUSTICE SCALIA so well demonstrates, is a perversion of Title VII. I would overrule *Weber* and reverse the judgment below.

JUSTICE SCALIA, with whom THE CHIEF JUSTICE joins, and with whom JUSTICE WHITE joins in Parts I and II, dissenting.

With a clarity which, had it not proven so unavailing, one might well recommend as a model of statutory draftsmanship, Title VII of the Civil Rights Act of 1964 declares:

It shall be an unlawful employment practice for an employer—

(1) to fail or refuse to hire or to discharge any individual, or otherwise to discriminate against any individual with respect to his compensation, terms, conditions, or privileges of employment, because of such individual's race, color, religion, sex, or national origin; or

(2) to limit, segregate, or classify his employees or applicants for employment in any way which would deprive or tend to deprive any individual of employment opportunities or otherwise adversely affect his status as an employee, because of such individual's race, color, religion, sex, or national origin.—42 U.S.C. § 2000e–2(a).

The Court today completes the process of converting this from a guarantee that race or sex will not be the basis for employment determinations, to a guarantee that it often will.

I

Several salient features of the plan should be noted. Most importantly, the plan's purpose was assuredly not to remedy prior sex discrimination by the Agency. It could not have been, because there was no prior sex discrimination to remedy. The majority . . . neglects to mention the District Court's finding that the Agency "has not discriminated in the past, and does not discriminate in the present against women in regard to employment opportunities in general and promotions in particular." This finding was not disturbed by the Ninth Circuit.

Not only was the plan not directed at the results of past sex discrimination by the Agency, but its objective was . . . to mirror the racial and sexual composition of the entire county labor force, not merely in the Agency work force as a whole, but in each and every individual job category at the Agency.... Quite obviously, the plan did not seek to replicate what a lack of discrimination would produce, but rather imposed racial and sexual tailoring that would, in defiance of normal expectations and laws of probability, give each protected racial and sexual group a governmentally determined "proper" proportion of each job category.

That the plan was not directed at remedying or eliminating the effects of past discrimination is most clearly illustrated by its description of what it regarded as the "Factors Hindering Goal Attainment"—i.e., the existing impediments to the racially and sexually representative work force that it pursued. The plan noted that it would be "difficult," to attain its objective of across-the-board statistical parity in at least some job categories, because:

a. Most of the positions require specialized training and experience. Until recently, relatively few minorities, women and handicapped persons sought entry into these positions. Consequently, the number of persons from these groups in the area labor force who possess the qualifications required for entry into such job classifications is limited.

. . .

c. Many of the Agency positions where women are underrepresented involve heavy labor; e. g., Road Maintenance Worker. Consequently, few women seek entry into these positions.

. . .

f. Many women are not strongly motivated to seek employment in job classifications where they have not been traditionally employed because of the limited opportunities that have existed in the past for them to work in such classifications.

That is, the qualifications and desires of women may fail to match the Agency's Platonic ideal of a work force. The plan concluded from this, of course, not that the ideal should be reconsidered, but that its attainment could not be immediate.

Finally, the one message that the plan unmistakably communicated was that concrete results were expected, and supervisory personnel would be evaluated on the basis of the affirmative-action numbers they produced....As noted earlier, supervisors were reminded of the need to give attention to affirmative action in every employment decision, and to explain their reasons for failing to hire women and minorities whenever there was an opportunity to do so.

The petitioner in the present case, Paul E. Johnson, had been an employee of the Agency since 1967, coming there from a private company where he had been a road dispatcher for 17 years. He had first applied for the position of Road Dispatcher at the Agency in 1974, coming in second. Several years later, after a reorganization resulted in a down-grading of his Road Yard Clerk II position, in which Johnson "could see no future," he requested and received a voluntary demotion from Road Yard Clerk II to Road Maintenance Worker, to increase his experience and thus improve his chances for future promotion. When the Road Dispatcher job next became vacant, in 1979, he was the leading candidate—and indeed was assigned to work out of class full time in the vacancy, from September 1979 until June 1980. There is no question why he did not get the job.

The fact of discrimination against Johnson is much clearer, and its degree more shocking, than the majority and JUSTICE O'CONNOR'S concurrence would suggest—largely because neither of them recites a single one of the District Court findings that govern this appeal, relying instead upon portions of the transcript which those findings implicitly rejected, and even upon a document (favorably comparing Joyce to Johnson), that was prepared after Joyce was selected. Worth mentioning, for example, is the trier of fact's determination that, if the Affirmative Action Coordinator had not intervened, "the decision as to whom to promote . . . would have been made by [the Road Operations Division Director]," who had recommended that Johnson be appointed to the position. Likewise, the even more extraordinary findings that James Graebner, the Agency Director who made the appointment, "did not inspect the applications and related examination records of either [Paul Johnson] or Diane Joyce before making his decision," and indeed "did little or nothing to inquire into the results of the interview process and conclusions which [were] described as of critical importance to the selection process." In light of these determinations, it is impossible to believe (or to think that the District Court believed) Graebner's self-serving statements relied upon by the majority and JUSTICE O'CONNOR'S concurrence, such as the assertion that he "tried to look at the whole picture. . ." It was evidently enough for Graebner to know that both candidates (in the words of Johnson's counsel, to which Graebner assented) "met the M.Q.'s, the minimum. Both were minimally qualified." When asked whether he had "any basis," for determining whether one of the candidates was more qualified than the other, Graebner candidly answered, "No. . . . As I've said, they both appeared, and my conversations with people tended to corroborate, that they were both capable of performing the work."

After a 2-day trial, the District Court concluded that Diane Joyce's gender was "the determining factor," in her selection for the position. Specifically, it found that "[b]ased upon the examination results and the departmental interview, [Mr. Johnson] was more qualified for the position of Road Dispatcher than Diane Joyce," that "[b]ut for [Mr. Johnson's] sex, male, he would have been promoted to the position of Road Dispatcher," and that "[b]ut for Diane Joyce's sex, female, she would not have been appointed to the position . . . ." The Ninth Circuit did not reject these factual findings as clearly erroneous, nor could it have done so on the record before us. We are bound by those findings under Federal Rule of Civil Procedure 52(a).

II

The most significant proposition of law established by today's decision is that racial or sexual discrimination is permitted under Title VII when it is intended to overcome the effect, not of the employer's own discrimination, but of societal attitudes that have limited the entry of certain races, or of a particular sex, into certain jobs. Even if the societal attitudes in question consisted exclusively of conscious discrimination by other employers, this holding would contradict a decision of this Court rendered only last Term. *Wygant v. Jackson Board of Education*, 476 U.S. 267 (1986), held that the objective of remedying societal discrimination cannot prevent remedial affirmative action from violating the Equal Protection Clause. See *id.*, at 276; *id.*, at 288 (O'CONNOR, J., concurring in part and concurring in judgment); *id.*, at 295 (WHITE, J., concurring in judgment). While Mr. Johnson does not advance a constitutional claim here, it is most unlikely that Title VII was intended to place a lesser restraint on discrimination by public actors than is established by the Constitution. . . . Because, therefore, those justifications (e. g., the remedying of past societal wrongs) that are inadequate to insulate discriminatory action from the racial discrimination prohibitions of the Constitution are also inadequate to insulate it from the racial discrimination prohibitions of Title VII; and because the portions of Title VII at issue here treat race and sex equivalently; *Wygant*, which dealt with race discrimination, is fully applicable precedent, and is squarely inconsistent with today's decision.[4]

. . .

Today's decision goes well beyond merely allowing racial or sexual discrimination in order to eliminate the effects of prior societal discrimination. The majority opinion often uses the phrase "traditionally segregated job category" to describe the evil against which the plan is legitimately (according to the majority) directed. As originally used in *Steelworkers v. Weber*, 443 U.S. 193 (1979), that phrase described skilled jobs from which employers and unions had systematically and intentionally excluded black workers—traditionally segregated jobs, that is, in the sense of conscious, exclusionary discrimination. But that is assuredly not the sense in which the phrase is used here. It is absurd to think that the nationwide failure of road maintenance crews, for example, to achieve the Agency's ambition of 36.4% female representation is attributable primarily, if even substantially, to systematic exclusion of women eager to shoulder pick and shovel. It is a "traditionally segregated job category" not in the *Weber* sense, but in the sense that, because of longstanding social attitudes, it has not been regarded by women themselves as desirable work. Or as the majority opinion puts the point, quoting approvingly the Court of Appeals: " 'A plethora of proof is hardly necessary to show that women are generally underrepresented in such positions and that strong social pressures weigh against their participation.' " At n. 12. Given this meaning of the phrase, it is patently false to say that "[t]he requirement that the 'manifest imbalance' relate to a 'traditionally segregated job category' provides assurance . . . that sex or race will be taken into account in a manner consistent with Title VII's purpose of eliminating the effects of employment discrimination." . . . . [The] social attitudes which cause women themselves to avoid certain jobs and to favor others are [not the same as] exclusionary discrimination. . . .[i]t is the alteration of social attitudes, rather than the elimination of discrimination, which today's decision approves as justification for state-enforced discrimination. This is an enormous expansion, undertaken without the slightest justification or analysis.

III

[U]ntil today the applicability of *Weber* to public employers remained an open question. . .*Weber* rested in part on the assertion that the 88th Congress did not wish to intrude too deeply into private employment decisions. See 443 U.S., at 206–207. See also *Firefighters v. Cleveland*, at 519–521. Whatever validity that assertion may have with respect to private employers (and I think it negligible), it has none with respect to public employers or to the 92d Congress that brought them within Title VII. See Equal Employment Opportunity Act of 1972, Pub. L. 92–261, 2, 86 Stat. 103, 42 U.S.C.§ 2000e(a). Another reason for limiting *Weber* to private employers is that state agencies, unlike private actors, are subject to the Fourteenth Amendment. As noted earlier, it would be strange to construe Title VII to permit discrimination by public actors that the Constitution forbids.

In truth, however, the language of 42 U.S.C. § 2000e–2 draws no distinction between private and public employers, and the only good reason for creating such a distinction would be to limit the damage of *Weber*. It would be better, in my view, to acknowledge that case as fully applicable precedent, and to use the Fourteenth Amendment ramifications—which *Weber* did not address and which are implicated for the first time here—as the occasion for reconsidering and overruling it. It is well to keep in mind just how thoroughly *Weber* rewrote the statute it purported to construe. The language of that statute, as quoted at the outset of this dissent, is unambiguous: [here Scalia repeats the statute] . . . *Weber* disregarded the text of the statute, invoking instead its " 'spirit,' " 443 U.S., at 201 (quoting *Holy Trinity Church v. United States*, 143 U.S. 457, 459 (1892)), and "practical and equitable [considerations] only partially perceived, if perceived at all, by the 88th Congress," 443 U.S., at 209 (BLACKMUN, J., concurring). It concluded, on the basis of these intangible guides, that Title VII's prohibition of intentional discrimination on the basis of race and sex does not prohibit intentional discrimination on the basis of race and sex, so long as it is "designed to break down old patterns of racial [or sexual] segregation and hierarchy," "does not unnecessarily trammel the interests of the white [or male] employees," "does not require the discharge of white [or male] workers and their replacement with new black [or female] hirees," "does [not] create an absolute bar to the advancement of white [or male] employees," and "is a temporary measure . . . not intended to maintain racial [or sexual] balance, but simply to eliminate a manifest racial [or sexual] imbalance." *Id.*, at 208. In effect, *Weber* held that the legality of intentional discrimination by private employers against certain disfavored groups or individuals is to be judged not by Title VII but by a judicially crafted code of conduct, the contours of which are determined by no discernible standard, aside from (as the dissent convincingly demonstrated) the divination of congressional "purposes" belied by the face of the statute and by its legislative history. . . .

The majority's response to this criticism of *Weber* [in its n.7] . . . asserts that, since "Congress has not amended the statute to reject our construction,. . .we. . .may assume that our interpretation was correct." This assumption, which frequently haunts our opinions, should be put to rest. It is based, to begin with, on the patently false premise that the correctness of statutory construction is to be measured by what the current Congress desires, rather than by what the law as enacted meant. To make matters worse, it assays the current Congress' desires with respect to the particular provision in isolation, rather than (the way the provision was originally enacted) as part of a total legislative package containing many quids pro quo. Whereas the statute as originally proposed may have presented to the enacting Congress a question such as "Should hospitals be required to provide medical care for indigent patients, with federal subsidies to offset the cost?" the question theoretically asked of the later Congress, in order to establish the "correctness" of a judicial interpretation that the statute provides no subsidies, is simply "Should the medical care that hospitals are required to provide for indigent patients be federally subsidized?" Hardly the same question—and many of those legislators who accepted the subsidy provisions in order to gain the votes necessary for enactment of the care requirement would not vote for the subsidy in isolation, now that an unsubsidized care requirement is, thanks to the judicial opinion, safely on the books. But even accepting the flawed premise that the intent of the current Congress, with respect to the provision in isolation, is determinative, one must ignore rudimentary principles of political science to draw any conclusions regarding that intent from the failure to enact legislation. The "complicated check on legislation," *The Federalist* No. 62, p. 378 (C. Rossiter ed. 1961), erected by our Constitution creates an inertia that makes it impossible to assert with any degree of assurance that congressional failure to act represents (1) approval of the status quo, as opposed to (2) inability to agree upon how to alter the status quo, (3) unawareness of the status quo, (4) indifference to the status quo, or even (5) political cowardice. It is interesting to speculate on how the principle that congressional inaction proves judicial correctness would apply to another issue in the civil rights field, the liability of municipal corporations under § 1983. In 1961, we held that that statute did not reach municipalities. See *Monroe v. Pape*, 365 U.S. 167, 187 (1961). Congress took no action to overturn our decision, but we ourselves did, in *Monell v. New York City Dept. of Social Services*, 436 U.S. 658, 663 (1978). On the majority's logic, *Monell* was wrongly decided, since Congress' 17 years of silence established that *Monroe* had not "misperceived the political will," and one could therefore "assume that [*Monroe*'s] interpretation was correct." On the other hand, nine years have now gone by since *Monell*, and Congress again has not amended § 1983. Should we now "assume that [*Monell*'s] interpretation was correct"? Rather, I think we should admit that vindication by congressional inaction is a canard.

JUSTICE STEVENS' concurring opinion emphasizes the "undoubted public interest in 'stability and orderly development of the law,'" that often requires adherence to an erroneous decision.... For a number of reasons, *stare decisis* ought not to save *Weber*. First, this Court has applied the doctrine of *stare decisis* to civil rights statutes less rigorously than to other laws. See *Maine v. Thiboutot*, 448 U.S. 1, 33 (1980) (POWELL, J., dissenting); *Monroe v. Pape*, at 221–222 (Frankfurter, J., dissenting in part). Second, as JUSTICE STEVENS acknowledges in his concurrence, *Weber* was itself a dramatic departure from the Court's prior Title VII precedents, and can scarcely be said to be "so consistent with the warp and woof of civil rights law as to be beyond question." *Monell v. New York City Dept. of Social Services*, at 696. Third, *Weber* was decided a mere seven years ago, and has provided little guidance to persons seeking to conform their conduct to the law, beyond the proposition that Title VII does not mean what it says. Finally, "even under the most stringent test for the propriety of overruling a statutory decision . . .—'that it appear beyond doubt . . . that [the decision] misapprehended the meaning of the controlling provision,'" 436 U.S., at 700 (quoting *Monroe v. Pape*, at 192 (Harlan, J., concurring)), *Weber* should be overruled.

The majority emphasizes, as though it is meaningful, that "No persons are automatically excluded from consideration; all are able to have their qualifications weighed against those of other applicants." *Ibid.* . . . Johnson was indeed entitled to have his qualifications weighed against those of other applicants—but more to the point, he was virtually assured that, after the weighing, if there was any minimally qualified applicant from one of the favored groups, he would be rejected.

Similarly hollow is the Court's assurance that we would strike this plan down if it "failed to take distinctions in qualifications into account" . . . [W]hat the Court means by "taking distinctions in qualifications into account" consists of no more than eliminating from the applicant pool those who are not even minimally qualified for the job. Once . . . the promoting officer assures himself that all the candidates before him are "M.Q.'s" (minimally qualifieds), he can then ignore, as the Agency Director did here, how much better than minimally qualified some of the candidates may be, and can proceed to appoint from the pool solely on the basis of race or sex. . .

Today's decision does more, however, than merely reaffirm *Weber*, and more than merely extend it to public actors. It is impossible not to be aware that the practical effect of our holding is to accomplish de facto what the law—in language even plainer than that ignored in *Weber*, see 42 U.S.C. § 2000e–

2(j)—forbids anyone from accomplishing de jure: in many contexts it effectively requires employers, public as well as private, to engage in intentional discrimination on the basis of race or sex. This Court's prior interpretations of Title VII, especially the decision in *Griggs v. Duke Power Co.*, 401 U.S. 424 (1971), subject employers to a potential Title VII suit whenever there is a noticeable imbalance in the representation of minorities or women in the employer's work force. Even the employer who is confident of ultimately prevailing in such a suit must contemplate the expense and adverse publicity of a trial, because the extent of the imbalance, and the "job relatedness" of his selection criteria, are questions of fact to be explored through rebuttal and counterrebuttal of a "prima facie case" consisting of no more than the showing that the employer's selection process "selects those from the protected class at a 'significantly' lesser rate than their counterparts." B. Schlei & P. Grossman, *Employment Discrimination Law* 91 (2d ed. 1983). If, however, employers are free to discriminate through affirmative action, without fear of "reverse discrimination" suits by their nonminority or male victims, they are offered a threshold defense against Title VII liability premised on numerical disparities. Thus, after today's decision the failure to engage in reverse discrimination is economic folly, and arguably a breach of duty to shareholders or taxpayers, wherever the cost of anticipated Title VII litigation exceeds the cost of hiring less capable (though still minimally capable) workers. (This situation is more likely to obtain, of course, with respect to the least skilled jobs—perversely creating an incentive to discriminate against precisely those members of the nonfavored groups least likely to have profited from societal discrimination in the past.) It is predictable, moreover, that this incentive will be greatly magnified by economic pressures brought to bear by government contracting agencies upon employers who refuse to discriminate in the fashion we have now approved. A statute designed to establish a color-blind and gender-blind workplace has thus been converted into a powerful engine of racism and sexism, not merely permitting intentional race- and sex-based discrimination, but often making it, through operation of the legal system, practically compelled.

. . .[The] losers in the process are the Johnsons of the country, for whom Title VII has been not merely repealed but actually inverted. The irony is that these individuals—predominantly unknown, unaffluent, unorganized—suffer this injustice at the hands of a Court fond of thinking itself the champion of the politically impotent. I dissent.

> **Opinion Footnote**
>
> 4 JUSTICE O'CONNOR'S concurrence at least makes an attempt to bring this Term into accord with last. Under her reading of Title VII, an employer may discriminate affirmatively, so to speak, if he has a "firm basis" for believing that he might be guilty of (nonaffirmative) discrimination under the Act, and if his action is designed to remedy that suspected prior discrimination. This is something of a halfway house between leaving employers scot-free to discriminate against disfavored groups, as the majority opinion does, and prohibiting discrimination, as do the words of Title VII. In the present case, although the District Court found that in fact no sex discrimination existed, JUSTICE O'CONNOR would find a "firm basis" for the agency's belief that sex discrimination existed in the "inexorable zero": the complete absence, prior to Diane Joyce, of any women in the Agency's skilled positions. There are two problems with this: First, even positing a "firm basis" for the Agency's belief in prior discrimination, as I have discussed above the plan was patently not designed to remedy that prior discrimination, but rather to establish a sexually representative work force. Second, even an absolute zero is not "inexorable." While it may inexorably provide "firm basis" for belief in the mind of an outside observer, it cannot conclusively establish such a belief on the employer's part, since he may be aware of the particular reasons that account for the zero. That is quite likely to be the case here, given the nature of the jobs we are talking about, and the list of "Factors Hindering Goal Attainment" recited by the Agency plan. The question is in any event one of fact, which, if it were indeed relevant to the outcome, would require a remand to the District Court rather than an affirmance.

Case Questions

1. In the majority's depiction of the facts, Diane Joyce and Paul Johnson were about equally qualified for the job. In Justice Scalia's version Johnson was clearly more qualified and lost the job only because he was a male. Which version of the facts is more convincing? Does it matter which version is accurate?

2. The majority argues that Congress's acceptance of the Court's *Weber* reading of Title VII (as permitting voluntary affirmative action) is convincing evidence of Congressional intent. Justice Scalia replies that what Congress intends now is irrelevant; what counts is what the people in Congress wanted when they enacted Title VII, 23 years ago. Has Justice Scalia turned the theory of representative democracy on its head? Should Congress be allowed to let the meaning of statutes evolve in order to reflect current (rather than past) moral sentiments?

3. Does the Court's description of Diane Joyce's clashes with her supervisors make it appear that she has suffered actual sex discrimination, as distinguished from mere "social pressure"? Should federal law penalize sex-based preferential hiring by private employers who would like to engage in affirmative efforts to counteract social pressures that have limited women's opportunities? What about similar hiring by government employers?

Case note: In the years following the Court's decision in *Johnson v. Transportation Agency*, the Court has taken a stricter position on race-based affirmative action. In *Adarand v. Pena*, 515 U.S. 200 (1995), the Court ruled 5–4 that all government-enacted, race-based affirmative action programs must be evaluated using strict scrutiny. The Justices have imposed similar restrictions on race-based affirmative action in publicly subsidized higher education. See *Gratz v. Bollinger*, 539 U.S. 244 (2003); *Grutter v. Bollinger*, 539 U.S. 306 (2003); *Fisher v. University of Texas*, 579 U.S. ___ (2016). In 2007, for the first time, the U.S. Supreme Court required strict scrutiny review for voluntary elementary and secondary school programs designed to increase racial integration of public schools in *Parents Involved in Community Schools v. Seattle School District, No. 1*, 551 U.S. 701 (2007). In *Parents Involved in Community Schools*, Chief Justice Roberts (appointed by Bush II) quipped, "[t]he way to stop discrimination on the basis of race is to stop discriminating on the basis of race."[115]

However, similar opposition has not coalesced around sex-based affirmative action programs. Instead, the circuit courts are divided on whether to apply intermediate scrutiny or strict scrutiny as the required standard in cases alleging that affirmative action programs favoring women or women-owned businesses violate the equal protection clause; the Roberts Court has yet to rule decisively on this issue.[116] Not surprisingly, in those instances where the courts utilize intermediate scrutiny, such programs tend to be accepted as constitutional. This fact, fortified by the *Johnson v. Transportation Agency* precedent, means that affirmative action policies favoring women are more viable than those seeking to favor racial and ethnic minorities.

Time Limits: *Ledbetter v. Goodyear Tire & Rubber Co.* (2007)[117]

In 2007, the Supreme Court took up Title VII's 180-day deadline for bringing charges of employment discrimination. Lilly Ledbetter was an employee at the Goodyear Tire and Rubber Company's plant in Gadsden, Alabama for nearly twenty years (1979–1998). Ledbetter worked in a male-dominated field as an area manager, and by 1997 she was the only woman employed in this job. At that time, the pay discrepancy between Ledbetter and the 15 male managers was, in Justice Ginsburg's terms, "stark": Ledbetter's salary was $3,727 per month; the lowest paid male area manager's salary was $4,286 per month; the highest paid, $5,236. Upon learning of the discrepancy, Ledbetter initiated litigation.

In a 5–4 decision, the justices not only dismissed Lilly Ledbetter's claim against the plant where she had worked for almost 20 years, but effectively barred claims by workers who did not discover their unlawfully discriminatory treatment before the 180-day deadline; a conclusion that gave employers an incentive to conceal their practices. "The ball is in Congress's court," Justice Ginsburg wrote in dissent, calling on the legislative branch to "correct this Court's parsimonious reading of Title VII."[118]

LILLY M. LEDBETTER V. GOODYEAR TIRE & RUBBER COMPANY

550 U.S. 618 (2007)

JUSTICE ALITO delivered the opinion of the Court.

. . .

I

. . .

The Court of Appeals for the Eleventh Circuit reversed, holding that a Title VII pay discrimination claim cannot be based on any pay decision that occurred prior to the last pay decision that affected the employee's pay during the EEOC charging period. 421 F. 3d 1169, 1182–1183 (2005). The Court of Appeals then concluded that there was insufficient evidence to prove that Goodyear had acted with discriminatory intent in making the only two pay decisions that occurred within that time span, namely, a decision made in 1997 to deny Ledbetter a raise and a similar decision made in 1998. Id., at 1186–1187.

Ledbetter filed a petition for a writ of certiorari but did not seek review of the Court of Appeals' holdings regarding the sufficiency of the evidence in relation to the 1997 and 1998 pay decisions. Rather, she sought review of the following question:

"Whether and under what circumstances a plaintiff may bring an action under Title VII of the Civil Rights Act of 1964 alleging illegal pay discrimination when the disparate pay is received during the statutory limitations period, but is the result of intentionally discriminatory pay decisions that occurred outside the limitations period." Pet. for Cert.

. . .

II

Title VII of the Civil Rights Act of 1964 makes it an "unlawful employment practice" to discriminate "against any individual with respect to his compensation . . . because of such individual's . . . sex." 42 U.S.C. § 2000e–2(a)(1). An individual wishing to challenge an employment practice under this provision must first file a charge with the EEOC. § 2000e–5(e)(1). Such a charge must be filed within a specified period (either 180 or 300 days, depending on the State) "after the alleged unlawful employment practice occurred," *ibid.*, and if the employee does not submit a timely EEOC charge, the employee may not challenge that practice in court, § 2000e–5(f)(1).

In addressing the issue whether an EEOC charge was filed on time, we have stressed the need to identify with care the specific employment practice that is at issue. [*National Railroad Passenger Corporation v.*] *Morgan*, 536 U.S., at 110–111. Ledbetter points to two different employment practices as possible candidates. Primarily, she urges us to focus on the paychecks that were issued to her during the EEOC charging period (the 180-day period preceding the filing of her EEOC questionnaire), each of which, she contends, was a separate act of discrimination. Alternatively, Ledbetter directs us to the 1998 decision denying her a raise, and she argues that this decision was "unlawful because it carried forward intentionally discriminatory disparities from prior years." . . . Both of these arguments fail because they would require us in effect to jettison the defining element of the legal claim on which her Title VII recovery was based.

Ledbetter asserted disparate treatment, the central element of which is discriminatory intent. See *Chardon* v. *Fernandez*, 454 U.S. 6, 8 (1981) (per curiam); *Teamsters* v. *United States*, 431 U.S. 324, n. 15 (1977); *Watson* v. *Fort Worth Bank & Trust*, 487 U.S. 977, 1002 (1998) (Blackmun, J., joined by Brennan, and Marshall, JJ., concurring in part and concurring in judgment) ("[A] disparate-treatment challenge focuses exclusively on the intent of the employer"). However, Ledbetter does not assert that the relevant Goodyear decisionmakers acted with actual discriminatory intent either when they issued her checks during the EEOC charging period or when they denied her a raise in 1998. Rather, she argues that the paychecks were unlawful because they would have been larger if she had been evaluated in a nondiscriminatory manner *prior to* the EEOC charging period. . .Similarly, she maintains that the 1998 decision was unlawful because it "carried forward" the effects of prior, uncharged discrimination decisions. . . .In essence, she suggests that it is sufficient that discriminatory acts that occurred prior to the charging period had continuing effects during that period. . . . ("[E]ach paycheck that offers a woman less pay than a similarly situated man because of her sex is a separate violation of Title VII with its own limitations period, regardless of whether the paycheck simply implements a prior discriminatory decision made outside the limitations period"). . . .This argument is squarely foreclosed by our precedents.

. . .

Our most recent decision in this area confirms this understanding. In *Morgan*, we explained that the statutory term "employment practice" generally refers to "a discrete act or single 'occurrence'" that takes place at a particular point in time. 536 U.S., at 110–111. We pointed to "termination, failure to promote, denial of transfer, [and] refusal to hire" as examples of such "discrete" acts, and we held that a Title VII plaintiff "can only file a charge to cover discrete acts that 'occurred' within the appropriate time period." *Id.*, at 114.

The instruction provided by [*United Airlines v.*] *Evans*, [*Delaware State College v.*] *Ricks*, *Lorance* [*v. AT & T Technologies*], and *Morgan* is clear. The EEOC charging period is triggered when a discrete unlawful practice takes place. A new violation does not occur, and a new charging period does not commence, upon the occurrence of subsequent nondiscriminatory acts that entail adverse effects resulting from the past discrimination. But of course, if an employer engages in a series of acts each of which is intentionally discriminatory, then a fresh violation takes place when each act is committed. See *Morgan*, *supra*, at 113.

Ledbetter's arguments here—that the paychecks that she received during the charging period and the 1998 raise denial each violated Title VII and triggered a new EEOC charging period—cannot be reconciled with *Evans*, *Ricks*, *Lorance*, and *Morgan*. Ledbetter, as noted, makes no claim that intentionally discriminatory conduct occurred during the charging period or that discriminatory decisions that occurred prior to that period were not communicated to her. Instead, she argues simply that Goodyear's conduct during the charging period gave present effect to discriminatory conduct outside of that period. . . . But current effects alone cannot breathe life into prior, uncharged discrimination; as we held in *Evans*, such effects in themselves have "no present legal consequences." 431 U.S., at 558. Ledbetter should have filed an EEOC charge within 180 days after each allegedly discriminatory pay decision was made and communicated to her. She did not do so, and the paychecks that were issued to her during the 180 days prior to the filing of her EEOC charge do not provide a basis for overcoming that prior failure.

In an effort to circumvent the need to prove discriminatory intent during the charging period, Ledbetter relies on the intent associated with other decisions made by other persons at other times. . . .

Ledbetter's attempt to take the intent associated with the prior pay decisions and shift it to the 1998 pay decision is unsound. It would shift intent from one act (the act that consummates the discriminatory employment practice) to a later act that was not performed with bias or discriminatory motive. The effect of this shift would be to impose liability in the absence of the requisite intent.

. . .

Not only would Ledbetter's argument effectively eliminate the defining element of her disparate-treatment claim, but it would distort Title VII's "integrated, multistep enforcement procedure." *Occidental Life Ins. Co. of Cal.* v. *EEOC,* 432 U.S. 355, 359 (1977). We have previously noted the legislative compromises that preceded the enactment of Title VII, *Mohasco Corp.* v. *Silver,* 447 U.S. 807, 819–821 (1980); *EEOC* v. *Commercial Office Products Co.,* 486 U.S. 107, 126 (1988) (Stevens, J., joined by Rehnquist, C. J., and Scalia, J., dissenting). Respectful of the legislative process that crafted this scheme, we must "give effect to the statute as enacted," *Mohasco, supra,* at 819, and we have repeatedly rejected suggestions that we extend or truncate Congress' deadlines. See, *e.g., Electrical Workers* v. *Robbins & Myers, Inc.,* 429 U.S. 229, 236–240 (1976) (union grievance procedures do not toll EEOC filing deadline); *Alexander* v. *Gardner-Denver Co.,* 415 U.S. 36, 47–49 (1974) (arbitral decisions do not foreclose access to court following a timely filed EEOC complaint).

Statutes of limitations serve a policy of repose. *American Pipe & Constr. Co.* v. *Utah,* 414 U.S. 538, 554–555 (1974). They "represent a pervasive legislative judgment that it is unjust to fail to put the adversary on notice to defend within a specified period of time and that 'the right to be free of stale claims in time comes to prevail over the right to prosecute them.'" *United States* v. *Kubrick,* 444 U.S. 111, 117 (1979) (quoting *Railroad Telegraphers* v. *Railway Express Agency, Inc.,* 321 U.S. 342, 349 (1944)).

The EEOC filing deadline "protect[s] employers from the burden of defending claims arising from employment decisions that are long past." *Ricks, supra,* at 256–257. Certainly, the 180-day EEOC charging deadline, 42 U.S.C. § 2000e–5(e)(1), is short by any measure, but "[b]y choosing what are obviously quite short deadlines, Congress clearly intended to encourage the prompt processing of all charges of employment discrimination." *Mohasco, supra,* at 825. This short deadline reflects Congress' strong preference for the prompt resolution of employment discrimination allegations through voluntary conciliation and cooperation. *Occidental Life Ins., supra,* at 367–368; *Alexander, supra,* at 44.

A disparate-treatment claim comprises two elements: an employment practice, and discriminatory intent. Nothing in Title VII supports treating the intent element of Ledbetter's claim any differently from the employment practice element. If anything, concerns regarding stale claims weigh more heavily with respect to proof of the intent associated with employment practices than with the practices themselves. For example, in a case such as this in which the plaintiff's claim concerns the denial of raises, the employer's challenged acts (the decisions not to increase the employee's pay at the times in question) will almost always be documented and will typically not even be in dispute. By contrast, the employer's intent is almost always disputed, and evidence relating to intent may fade quickly with time. In most disparate-treatment cases, much if not all of the evidence of intent is circumstantial. Thus, the critical issue in a case involving a long-past performance evaluation will often be whether the evaluation was so far off the mark that a sufficient inference of discriminatory intent can be drawn. See *Watson*, 487 U.S., at 1004 (Blackmun, J., joined by Brennan and Marshall, JJ., concurring in part and concurring in judgment) (noting that in a disparate-treatment claim, the *McDonnell Douglas* factors establish discrimination by inference). See also, *e.g.*, *Zhuang* v. *Datacard Corp.*, 414 F. 3d 849 (CA8 2005) (rejecting inference of discrimination from performance evaluations); *Cooper* v. *Southern Co.*, 390 F. 3d 695, 732–733 (CA11 2004) (same). This can be a subtle determination, and the passage of time may seriously diminish the ability of the parties and the factfinder to reconstruct what actually happened.⁴

Ultimately, "experience teaches that strict adherence to the procedural requirements specified by the legislature is the best guarantee of evenhanded administration of the law." *Mohasco*, 447 U.S., at 826. By operation of §§ 2000e–5(e)(1) and 2000e–5(f)(1), a Title VII "claim is time barred if it is not filed within these time limits." *Morgan*, 536 U.S., at 109; *Electrical Workers*, 429 U.S., at 236. We therefore reject the suggestion that an employment practice committed with no improper purpose and no discriminatory intent is rendered unlawful nonetheless because it gives some effect to an intentional discriminatory act that occurred outside the charging period. Ledbetter's claim is, for this reason, untimely.

. . .

Opinion Footnote

4 The dissent dismisses this concern, post, but this case illustrates the problems created by tardy lawsuits. Ledbetter's claims of sex discrimination turned principally on the misconduct of a single Goodyear supervisor, who, Ledbetter testified, retaliated against her when she rejected his sexual advances during the early 1980's, and did so again in the mid-1990's when he falsified deficiency reports about her work. His misconduct, Ledbetter argues, was "a principal basis for [her] performance evaluation in 1997."...Yet, by

the time of trial, this supervisor had died and therefore could not testify. A timely charge might have permitted his evidence to be weighed contemporaneously.

JUSTICE GINSBURG, with whom JUSTICE STEVENS, JUSTICE SOUTER, and JUSTICE BREYER join, dissenting.

The Court's insistence on immediate contest overlooks common characteristics of pay discrimination. Pay disparities often occur, as they did in Ledbetter's case, in small increments; cause to suspect that discrimination is at work develops only over time. Comparative pay information, moreover, is often hidden from the employee's view. Employers may keep under wraps the pay differentials maintained among supervisors, no less the reasons for those differentials. Small initial discrepancies may not be seen as meet for a federal case, particularly when the employee, trying to succeed in a nontraditional environment, is averse to making waves.

Pay disparities are thus significantly different from adverse actions "such as termination, failure to promote, . . . or refusal to hire," all involving fully communicated discrete acts, "easy to identify" as discriminatory. See *National Railroad Passenger Corporation* v. *Morgan*, 536 U.S. 101, 114 (2002). It is only when the disparity becomes apparent and sizable, *e.g.*, through future raises calculated as a percentage of current salaries, that an employee in Ledbetter's situation is likely to comprehend her plight and, therefore, to complain. Her initial readiness to give her employer the benefit of the doubt should not preclude her from later challenging the then current and continuing payment of a wage depressed on account of her sex.

On questions of time under Title VII, we have identified as the critical inquiries: "What constitutes an 'unlawful employment practice' and when has that practice 'occurred'?" *Id.*, at 110. Our precedent suggests, and lower courts have overwhelmingly held, that the unlawful practice is the *current payment* of salaries infected by gender-based (or race-based) discrimination—a practice that occurs whenever a paycheck delivers less to a woman than to a similarly situated man. See *Bazemore* v. *Friday*, 478 U.S. 385, 395 (1986) (Brennan, J., joined by all other Members of the Court, concurring in part).

. . .

I
B

The realities of the workplace reveal why the discrimination with respect to compensation that Ledbetter suffered does not fit within the category of singular discrete acts "easy to identify." A worker knows immediately if she is denied a promotion or transfer, if she is fired or refused employment. And promotions, transfers, hirings, and firings are generally public events, known to co-workers. When an employer makes a decision of such open and definitive character, an employee can immediately seek out an explanation and evaluate it for pretext. Compensation disparities, in contrast, are often hidden from sight. It is not unusual, decisions in point illustrate, for management to decline to publish employee pay levels, or for employees to keep private their own salaries. See, *e.g.*, *Goodwin* v. *General Motors Corp.*, 275 F. 3d 1005, 1008–1009 (CA10 2002) (plaintiff did not know what her colleagues earned until a printout listing of salaries appeared on her desk, seven years after her starting salary was set lower than her co-workers' salaries); *McMillan* v. *Massachusetts Soc. for the Prevention of Cruelty to Animals*, 140 F. 3d 288, 296 (CA1 1998) (plaintiff worked for employer for years before learning of salary disparity published in a newspaper). Tellingly, as the record in this case bears out, Goodyear kept salaries confidential; employees had only limited access to information regarding their colleagues' earnings. . .

The problem of concealed pay discrimination is particularly acute where the disparity arises not because the female employee is flatly denied a raise but because male counterparts are given larger raises. Having received a pay increase, the female employee is unlikely to discern at once that she has experienced an adverse employment decision. She may have little reason even to suspect discrimination until a pattern develops incrementally and she ultimately becomes aware of the disparity. Even if an employee suspects that the reason for a comparatively low raise is not performance but sex (or another protected ground), the amount involved may seem too small, or the employer's intent too ambiguous, to make the issue immediately actionable—or winnable.

Further separating pay claims from the discrete employment actions identified in *Morgan*, an employer gains from sex-based pay disparities in a way it does not from a discriminatory denial of promotion, hiring, or transfer. When a male employee is selected over a female for a higher level position, someone still gets the promotion and is paid a higher salary; the employer is not enriched. But when a woman is paid less than a similarly situated man, the employer reduces its costs each time the pay differential is implemented. Furthermore, decisions on promotions, like decisions installing seniority systems, often implicate the interests of third-party employees in a way that pay differentials do not. Cf. *Teamsters* v. *United States*, 431 U.S. 324, 352–353 (1977) (recognizing that seniority systems involve "vested . . . rights of employees" and concluding that Title VII was not intended to "destroy or water down" those rights). Disparate pay, by contrast, can be remedied at any time solely at the expense of the employer who acts in a discriminatory fashion.

. . .

II

The Court asserts that treating pay discrimination as a discrete act, limited to each particular pay-setting decision, is necessary to "protec[t] employers from the burden of defending claims arising from employment decisions that are long past.". . . (quoting *Ricks*, 449 U.S., at 256–257). But the discrimination of which Ledbetter complained is *not* long past. As she alleged, and as the jury found, Goodyear continued to treat Ledbetter differently because of sex each pay period, with mounting harm. Allowing employees to challenge discrimination "that extend[s] over long periods of time," into the charge-filing period, we have previously explained, "does not leave employers defenseless" against unreasonable or prejudicial delay. *Morgan*, 536 U.S., at 121. Employers disadvantaged by such delay may raise various defenses. *Id.*, at 122. Doctrines such as "waiver, estoppel, and equitable tolling" "allow us to honor Title VII's remedial purpose without negating the particular purpose of the filing requirement, to give prompt notice to the employer." *Id.*, at 121 (quoting *Zipes v. Trans World Airlines, Inc.*, 455 U.S. 385, 398 (1982)); see 536 U.S., at 121 (defense of laches may be invoked to block an employee's suit "if he unreasonably delays in filing [charges] and as a result harms the defendant"); EEOC Brief 15 ("[I]f Ledbetter unreasonably delayed challenging an earlier decision, and that delay significantly impaired Goodyear's ability to defend itself . . . Goodyear can raise a defense of laches. . . .").

In a last-ditch argument, the Court asserts that this dissent would allow a plaintiff to sue on a single decision made 20 years ago "even if the employee had full knowledge of all the circumstances relating to the . . . decision at the time it was made.". . . It suffices to point out that the defenses just noted would make such a suit foolhardy. No sensible judge would tolerate such inexcusable neglect. See *Morgan*, 536 U.S., at 121 ("In such cases, the federal courts have the discretionary power . . . to locate a just result in light of the circumstances peculiar to the case.").

. . .

III

To show how far the Court has strayed from interpretation of Title VII with fidelity to the Act's core purpose, I return to the evidence Ledbetter presented at trial. Ledbetter proved to the jury the following: She was a member of a protected class; she performed work substantially equal to work of the dominant class (men); she was compensated less for that work; and the disparity was attributable to gender-based discrimination.

Specifically, Ledbetter's evidence demonstrated that her current pay was discriminatorily low due to a long series of decisions reflecting Goodyear's pervasive discrimination against women managers in general and Ledbetter in particular. Ledbetter's former supervisor, for example, admitted to the jury that Ledbetter's pay, during a particular one-year period, fell below Goodyear's minimum threshold for her position...Although Goodyear claimed the pay disparity was due to poor performance, the supervisor acknowledged that Ledbetter received a "Top Performance Award" in 1996. *Id.,*... The jury also heard testimony that another supervisor—who evaluated Ledbetter in 1997 and whose evaluation led to her most recent raise denial—was openly biased against women. *Id.,*... And two women who had previously worked as managers at the plant told the jury they had been subject to pervasive discrimination and were paid less than their male counterparts. One was paid less than the men she supervised. *Id.,*...Ledbetter herself testified about the discriminatory animus conveyed to her by plant officials. Toward the end of her career, for instance, the plant manager told Ledbetter that the "plant did not need women, that [women] didn't help it, [and] caused problems." *Id.,*...After weighing all the evidence, the jury found for Ledbetter, concluding that the pay disparity was due to intentional discrimination.

Yet, under the Court's decision, the discrimination Ledbetter proved is not redressable under Title VII. Each and every pay decision she did not immediately challenge wiped the slate clean. Consideration may not be given to the cumulative effect of a series of decisions that, together, set her pay well below that of every male area manager. Knowingly carrying past pay discrimination forward must be treated as lawful conduct. Ledbetter may not be compensated for the lower pay she was in fact receiving when she complained to the EEOC. Nor, were she still employed by Goodyear, could she gain, on the proof she presented at trial, injunctive relief requiring, prospectively, her receipt of the same compensation men receive for substantially similar work. The Court's approbation of these consequences is totally at odds with the robust protection against workplace discrimination Congress intended Title VII to secure. See, *e.g., Teamsters* v. *United States,* 431 U.S., at 348 ("The primary purpose of Title VII was to assure equality of employment opportunities and to eliminate ... discriminatory practices and

> devices...." (internal quotation marks omitted)); *Albemarle Paper Co.* v. *Moody*, 422 U.S. 405, 418 (1975) ("It is ... the purpose of Title VII to make persons whole for injuries suffered on account of unlawful employment discrimination.").
>
> This is not the first time the Court has ordered a cramped interpretation of Title VII, incompatible with the statute's broad remedial purpose.... .See also *Wards Cove Packing Co.* v. *Atonio*, 490 U.S. 642 (1989) (superseded in part by the Civil Rights Act of 1991); *Price Waterhouse* v. *Hopkins*, 490 U.S. 228 (1989) (plurality opinion) (same); 1 B. Lindemann & P. Grossman, Employment Discrimination Law 2 (3d ed. 1996) ("A spate of Court decisions in the late 1980s drew congressional fire and resulted in demands for legislative change[,]" culminating in the 1991 Civil Rights Act (footnote omitted)). Once again, the ball is in Congress' court. As in 1991, the Legislature may act to correct this Court's parsimonious reading of Title VII.
>
> * * *
>
> For the reasons stated, I would hold that Ledbetter's claim is not time barred and would reverse the Eleventh Circuit's judgment.

Case Questions

1. If a woman is hired at a starting pay of $100/week and a man in the same period is hired at $110/week, and each afterward, per company policy, received percentage-based raises, say 10% each year, in their fifth years of employment, the man would be receiving $161 per week to the woman's $146 per week. Each worker in that fifth year, as in the prior years had received identical 10% raises. In your opinion, did Ledbetter's employer nonetheless discriminate against her during that fifth year, in violation of Title VII's prohibition on sex discrimination?

2. Are you persuaded by Justice Alito's argument that Ledbetter's individual paychecks (in which she was paid less than her male peers) fail to constitute a "discrete unlawful practice" in violation of Title VII? Is his interpretation of the 180-day statutorily specified period for filing an employment discrimination complaint unreasonable? Is it just to deny Ledbetter legal recourse simply because she filed a "tardy lawsuit"? How could Ledbetter file a claim until she knew about the pay discrepancy?

3. Justice Ginsburg's dissent draws attention to the fact that some employers intentionally keep employee compensation confidential. Can you see any valid reasons that employers may wish to do this? Is this likely to be more problematic for some employees (e.g. women, people of color) than others?

4. How is pay discrimination different from other types of employment discrimination such as termination or demotion?

Case note: It took two years and a new presidential administration for Congress to supersede this ruling. The Lilly Ledbetter Fair Pay Act (opposed by Bush II) was introduced in the House of Representatives a month after the Court's decision. This bill restarts the 6-month clock every time a worker gets a paycheck. The House passed it easily, but Senate Republicans prevented it from coming up for a vote. When the 111th Congress met in January 2009, the Democratic Senators had enough votes to end debate. The bill was re-introduced and passed in both houses. On January 29, President Obama signed the bill, making it the first federal law of his administration.[119]

CONCLUSION

Employment law provides an excellent illustration of both the effectiveness and the limits of law in a changing society. Law did not create the division of gainful employment into men's jobs and women's jobs. That division was the product of cultural and socioeconomic forces. The relationship between law and social practice has undergone a fundamental change since the mid-nineteenth century. Decisions like *Bradwell*, *Muller*, and *Goesaert* (see Chapters 1 and 2) reveal how American law once reinforced and legitimized the sex segregation of the workplace. This chapter has shown how civil rights legislation has transformed the law into a tool for ameliorating this gendered division of labor.

Readers of this book may be surprised to learn that newspapers once divided classified ads into "Help Wanted-Male" and "Help Wanted-Female." The Civil Rights Act of 1964 (assisted by a friendly reading of the First Amendment by the Supreme Court in 1973)[120] ended this practice. But the law could not eradicate social attitudes that associate jobs with either men or women. Many state and federal laws forbid sex-based employment discrimination, but rarely does a job have a male-female ratio approximating that of the adult population. Whatever the want ads say, men's jobs and women's jobs still exist—and the higher the status of the occupation, the greater the imbalance in favor of men. What antidiscrimination law can do is to provide some protection against employers' reluctance to hire and promote those women who overcome social barriers to traditionally male jobs by ignoring social disapproval and acquiring the necessary education and training. By construing Title VII broadly and the BFOQ exception narrowly, courts and administrative agencies have entrenched antidiscrimination law as a powerful counterweight to social attitudes. These attitudes, too, have changed since the 1960s as more workplaces become integrated. American society is diverse and pluralistic enough so that many women can choose traditionally male occupations without negative feedback.

That being said, because women are now able to access a broader array of jobs does not mean that all women have equal access to those jobs and/or that women's experiences in the workplace are free from discrimination. Women of color continue to confront the combined effects of racialized sex discrimination and sexualized racial discrimination, which limit employment opportunities. Transgender women and lesbians are vulnerable to employment discrimination because (without a definitive pronouncement from the Supreme Court) Title VII does not prohibit workplace discrimination on the basis of gender identity or sexual orientation. Many poor and immigrant women work in hourly-wage jobs that are paid off of the books, which practice makes them vulnerable to economic exploitation and job insecurity.

In the workplace, sexual harassment continues to be a major issue, and the #MeToo movement of 2017–2018 highlights the extent to which sexual harassment and abuse continue unabated in many places of employment. In addition to continuing wage disparities, the EEOC reports that one in four women experience harassment in the workplace and many are still disinclined to report this illegal treatment.[121]

Too many women continue to be paid less for doing the same job as their male counterparts like Lilly Ledbetter and too many women continue to be segregated into "women's" jobs which pay less than traditional "men's" jobs. Furthermore, the EEOC reports that "women also continue to face persistent pregnancy discrimination"[122] resulting in thousands of claims being filed with the EEOC each year.[123]

The reality is that anti-discrimination laws can do relatively little to eradicate the gendered division of labor that occurred prior to, and reinforces, the gendered workplace: the fact that women have disproportionate responsibility for home and family. Once, this coin had another side: men were responsible for earning a living for their families. The disappearance of the "family wage," which enabled one adult (male, middle-class) worker to support a family, has forced wives and mothers into gainful employment while doing nothing to mitigate their domestic duties. Most if not all jobs, especially high-status, well-paid jobs, presume an "ideal worker" to whom the job is the first priority. "Day one of taking gender into account," wrote Catharine MacKinnon, "was the day the job was structured with the expectation that the worker would have no child care responsibilities."[124] Court decisions on "sex plus motherhood" discrimination and mandatory maternity leaves show how Title VII and the Constitution provide grounds for limiting employers' license to act on the assumption that work and motherhood are incompatible. The large number of pregnancy discrimination claims filed with the EEOC[125] each year indicate that women continue to navigate gendered assumptions about mothers in the workplace.

Similarly, while Congress has taken positive steps to address workers' roles as parents and caregivers beginning with the passage of the PDA in response to the Supreme Court's refusal to classify pregnancy discrimination as sex discrimination, there is still much to be done. The Family and Medical Leave Act of 1993 took a significant step by establishing a sex-neutral policy that facilitates childcare by persons of either sex. At the same time, however, the FMLA covers only 59% of employees, and it guarantees only unpaid leave. This means that almost half of American workers are unable to take leave under FMLA, and for others unpaid leave is not an option; in particular, the latter imposes a huge burden on lower income mothers and families.[126] In effect, this means that many individuals who need to take leave are unable to do so. According to the National Partnership for Women & Families, reporting on the year 2012, "Women made up 64 percent of those who needed but did not take leave. Hispanic workers, workers who are not white, workers with earnings below $35,000 per year and unmarried workers were more likely than their counterparts to need leave they didn't take."[127] Finally, when individuals are able to take leave, statistics demonstrate that women still take more leave than men, and the stigmas associated with paternity leave continue to affect new fathers.[128] While there was talk from the 2016 Trump campaign of changing the FMLA to have it require paid leave, not merely a guarantee of a return to the job, as this book goes to press, no move has been made to introduce such a bill in Congress.

---

[1] See Judith A. Baer, *The Chains of Protection: The Judicial Response to Women's Labor Legislation* (Westport, CT: Greenwood Press, 1978), chap. 4.

[2] *Civil Rights Cases*, 109 U.S. 3 (1883); *Jones v. Alfred Mayer*, 392 U.S. 409 (1968); *Tillman v. Wheaton-Haven Recreation Association*, 410 U.S. 431 (1973).

[3] Equal Pay Act: 29 U.S.C. § 206(d)(1); Civil Rights Act of 1964: 42 U.S.C. § 2000e § 703. See Caroline Bird, *Born Female: The High Cost of Keeping Women Down*, rev. ed. (New York: David McKay, 1973), pp. 4–5.

[4] See Serena Mayeri, *Reasoning from Race: Feminism, Law, and the Civil Rights Revolution* (Cambridge, MA: Harvard University Press, 2011).

[5] Kimberlé Crenshaw, "Demarginalizing the Intersection of Race and Sex: A Black Feminist Critique of Antidiscrimination Doctrine, Feminist Theory and Antiracist Politics," *University of Chicago Legal Forum*, Volume 1989 (1), Article 8: 139–167.

[6] Ibid.

[7] Equal Pay Act: 29 U.S.C. § 206(d)(1).

[8] The three dissenters, Burger, Rehnquist, and Blackmun, simply stated that they endorsed the contrary opinion of Judge Adams of the Circuit Court of Appeals. He had argued that extra pay for night time work was properly interpreted as compensation for a more stressful working condition, and he, too, had based his argument on his reading of the legislative history.

⁹ U.S. Census Bureau, Current Population Survey. 2017. "Historical Income Tables: Table P-38. Full-Time, Year-Round Workers by Median Earnings and Sex: 1987 to 2016." Available at: https://www.census.gov/data/tables/time-series/demo/income-poverty/historical-income-people.html (accessed May 3, 2018). See also Anna Brown and Eileen Patton, "The Narrowing, but Persistent, Gender Gap in Pay," Pew Research Center, April 3. 2017. Available at: https://medium.com/@pewresearch/the-narrowing-but-persistent-gender-gap-in-pay-30777d55876e (accessed May 22, 2018).

¹⁰ Ariane Hegewisch and Emma Williams-Baron, "The Gender Wage Gap: 2017 Earnings Differences by Race and Ethnicity," Institute for Women's Policy Research, March 7, 2018. Available at: https://iwpr.org/publications/gender-wage-gap-2017-race-ethnicity/ (accessed May 22, 2018); "If Current Trends Continue, Hispanic Women Will Wait 232 Years for Equal Pay; Black Women Will Wait 108 Years," Institute for Women's Policy Research, October 31, 2016. Available at: https://iwpr.org/publications/if-current-trends-continue-hispanic-women-will-wait-232-years-for-equal-pay-black-women-will-wait-108-years/ (accessed May 22, 2018).

¹¹ Heidi Hartmann et al., "Five Ways to Win an Argument about the Gender Wage Gap," Institute for Women's Policy Research, September 16, 2016. Available at: https://iwpr.org/publications/five-ways-to-win-an-argument-about-the-gender-wage-gap/ (accessed May 22, 2018). See also Judith A. Baer, *Women in American Law: The Struggle for Equality from the New Deal to the Present*, 3rd ed. (New York: Holmes & Meier, 2002), p. 118.

¹² The six states with comparable worth policies as of 2002 were Iowa, New York, Oregon, Wisconsin, Minnesota, and Washington. Mark R. Killingsworth, "Comparable Worth and Pay Equity: Recent Developments in the United States," *Canadian Public Policy* Vol. XXVIII S. 1 (May 2002): 171–186; available at: http://economics.ca/cgi/jab?journal=cpp&view=v28s1/Killingsworth_Chap.pdf (accessed September 15, 2004). An additional fourteen states have implemented some partial pay equity style adjustments, Ibid. See also Debra Stewart, "State Initiatives in the Federal System: The Politics and Policy of Comparable Worth," *Publius* 15 (Summer 1985): 81–95.

¹³ The EEOC ruling is discussed in Robert Pear, "Equal Pay Is Not Needed for Jobs of Comparable Worth," *The New York Times*, June 18, 1985, p. A12. The Administration's role in the Illinois comparable worth case was reported by Pear, "Court Cases Reveal New Inequalities in Women's Pay," *The New York Times*, August 21, 1985, pp. C1, C6. The court decisions are *Spaulding v. University of Washington*, 740 F. 2d 686 (9th Cir. 1984); *cert. denied* 469 U.S. 1036 (1984); *Lemons v. Denver*, 620 F. 2d 228 (10th Cir. 1980); *Christenson v. Iowa*, 563 F. 2d 353 (8th Cir. 1977). See also Debra Stewart, "State Initiatives in the Federal System: The Politics and Policy of Comparable Worth," *Publius* 15 (Summer 1985): 81–95.

¹⁴ Linda Levine, "The Gender Wage Gap and Pay Equity: Is Comparable Worth the Next Step?" Congressional Research Service, June 5, 2001, at 16–24. Available at: https://digitalcommons.ilr.cornell.edu/cgi/viewcontent.cgi?article=1026&context=key_workplace (accessed April 23, 2018).

¹⁵ Ibid.

¹⁶ H.R.2023—105th Congress (1997–1998).

¹⁷ See H.R. 541, H.R. 2397, S. 74—106th Congress (1999–2000), H.R. 781—107th Congress (2001–2002), H.R. 1688—108th Congress (2003–2004), H.R. 1687—109th Congress (2005–2006), H.R. 1338—110th Congress (2007–2008).

¹⁸ H.R. 12—111th Congress (2009–2010).

¹⁹ H.R. 1518—112th Congress (2011–2012), H.R. 377—113th Congress (2013–2014), H.R. 1619 (2015–2016), H.R. 1869 (2017–2018).

²⁰ H.R. 1869 "To amend the Fair Labor Standards Act of 1938 to provide more effective remedies to victims of discrimination in the payment of wages on the basis of sex, and for other purposes," 115th Congress, First Session, introduced April 4, 2017.

²¹ There have been occasions where the issue of federal preemption has involved a state which appears to be a step or two ahead of Congress, rather than the other way around. See, for example, *California Federal v. Guerra*, below.

²² Respectively, *Weeks v. Southern Bell*, 277 F. Supp. 117 (S.D. Ga. 1967); *Gudbrandson v. Genuine Parts Co.*, 297 F. Supp. 134 (D. Minn. 1968); *Rosenfeld v. Southern Pacific Co.*, 293 F. Supp. 1219 (C.D. Cal. 1968).

²³ Susan Brownmiller, "Looking Back," *The Women's Review of Books* (Center for Research on Women at Wellesley College, June 2003).

24 A detailed account of this settlement can be found in Lisa Cronin Wohl, "Liberating Ma Bell," *Ms.*, November 1973, p. 52.

25 477 U.S. 57.

26 *Rogers v. EEOC*, 454 F.2d 234 (5th Cir.1971), cert. denied, 406 U.S. 957 (1972).

27 *Firefighters Institute for Racial Equality v. St. Louis*, 549 F.2d 506, 514–515 (8th Cir.)(1977); *Gray v. Greyhound Lines, East*, 545 F.2d 169, 176 (1976).

28 *Compston v. Borden*, 424 F.Supp. 157 (S.D. Ohio 1976).

29 *Cariddi v. Kansas City Chiefs Football Club*, 568 F.2d 87, 88 (8th Cir.) (1977).

30 Catharine MacKinnon, *Sexual Harassment of Working Women: A Case of Sex Discrimination* (New Haven, CT: Yale University Press, 1979), 40.

31 E.g., *Henson v. Dundee*, 682 F.2d 897, 902 (1982).

32 *Meritor Savings v. Vinson*, Section II, quoting *Henson v. Dundee*, 682 F.2d 897, at 902.

33 *Meritor Savings*, Section II, quoting *Henson*, 682 F.2d, at 904.

34 *Meritor Savings*, Section II.

35 *Ellison v. Brady*, 924 F.2d 872 (9th Cir. 1991).

36 *Rabidue v. Osceola Refining*, 805 F.2d 611 (6th Cir. 1986).

37 Ibid., at 620–21.

38 *Rabidue v. Osceola Refining Co.*, 805 F.2d 611, 620 (CA6 1986).

39 Neither the opinion of the United States District Court for the Middle District of Tennessee nor the affirmance by its Circuit Court of Appeals was published.

40 John Cloud, "Harassed or Hazed? Why the Supreme Court Ruled That Men Can Sue Men for Sex Harassment," *TIME*, March 16, 1998, 55.

41 *Oncale v. Sundowner Offshore Services*, 83 F 3rd 118, at 118–119 (1996).

42 Mary Judice, "LA. Offshore Worker Settles Sex Suit; Harassment Case Made History in Supreme Court," *Times-Picayune* (New Orleans, LA), October 24, 1998.

43 520 U.S. 681.

44 29 CFR § 1604.11(d.).

45 These details are found in the respective syllabi of the cases: *Burlington Industries, Inc. v. Ellerth*, 524 U.S. 742, and *Faragher v. City of Boca Raton*, 524 U.S. 775.

46 42 U.S.C. § 2000e–2(a)(1) and (2).

47 *Hishon v. Spaulding*, 467 U.S. 69 (1984).

48 *Price Waterhouse v. Hopkins*, 490 U.S. 228 (1989).

49 *Ann B. Hopkins v. Price Waterhouse*, 618 F.Supp. 1109 (1985).

50 *Hopkins v. Price Waterhouse*, 825 F.2d 458, at 468–69 (1987).

51 See citations described in *Hopkins*, 825 F.2d 458, at 471.

52 Ibid, at 474.

53 42 U.S.C. § 2000e–2(k)(2). In § 105(a) of the Civil Rights Act of 1991, at 105 Stat. 1075.

54 P.L. 102–166, 105 Stat. 1071, Sec. 107(a), which became 42 U.S.C. § 2000e–2(m), or § 703(m) of the 1964 Civil Rights Act.

55 *Ulane v. Eastern Airlines, Inc.*, 742 F.2d 1081 (7th Circ.1984). See also, *Holloway v. Arthur Andersen & Co.*, 566 F.2d 659, 661–63 (9th Cir.1977).

56 *Smith v. City of Salem*, 378 F.3d 566 (6th Cir. 2004), 568.

57 Sharon M. McGowan, "Working with Clients to Develop Compatible Visions of What it Means to 'Win' a Case: Reflections on *Schroer v. Billington*," *Harvard Civil Rights-Civil Liberties Law Review*, Vol 45 (2010): 205–245, p. 205.

58 Ibid.

59 Ibid., at 236.

60 *Macy v. Department of Justice*, EEOC Appeal No. 0120120821 (April 20, 2012).

61 H.R.2015—Employment Non-Discrimination Act of 2007, 110th Congress (2007–2008).

⁶² The president insisted that the 1991 law was a compromise product that took into account his most important concerns. News analysis generally viewed this claim as mostly a face-saving gesture. See, e.g., "The Compromise on Civil Rights," *The New York Times*, October 26, 1991, p.7, col. 3. See also 42 U.S.C. Section 1981 (b), amendment from Section 101 of Civil Rights Act of 1991, 105 Stat. 1071–72.

⁶³ 490 U.S. 642 (1989).

⁶⁴ 42 U.S.C. Section 2000e–2(a)(2).

⁶⁵ *Griggs v. Duke Power*, 401 U.S. 424 (1971) and *Albemarle Paper v. Moody*, 422 U.S. 405 (1975) concerned disparate impact by race; *Dothard v. Rawlinson*, 433 U.S. 321 (1977) concerned disparate impact by gender.

⁶⁶ *Griggs*, 401 U.S., at 431 and 432.

⁶⁷ *Dothard v. Rawlinson*, 433 U.S. 321, 331.

⁶⁸ 490 U.S., at 658–60.

⁶⁹ 42 U.S.C. Section 2000e–2 (k)(1)(A)(i). Section 105(a) of Civil Rights Act of 1991.

⁷⁰ The dissenters in both this case and *Ward's Cove* were Stevens, Blackmun, Brennan and Marshall.

⁷¹ 490 U.S. 755 (1989).

⁷² Lisa Cronin Wohl, "Liberating Ma Bell," *Ms.*, November, 1973, p. 52.

⁷³ 42 U.S.C. Section 2000e–2(n) (1)(B)(i)(I)–(II). Amendment contained in Section 108 of Civil Rights Act of 1991, 105 Stat. 1076.

⁷⁴ The quote is from Section III of Justice Stevens's dissenting opinion.

⁷⁵ 491 U.S. 164 (1989).

⁷⁶ Now 42 U.S.C. Section 1981.

⁷⁷ *Meritor Savings v. Vinson*, 477 U.S. 57 (1986). See next section.

⁷⁸ Again the dissenters were Stevens, Blackmun, Marshall, and Brennan.

⁷⁹ 42 U.S.C. Section 1981 (b), amendment from Section 101 of Civil Rights Act of 1991, 105 Stat. 1071–72.

⁸⁰ Similar changes were adopted to allow damage awards for victims of discrimination against disabled persons, which discrimination is prohibited by the Americans with Disabilities Act of 1990 and by Section 501 of the Rehabilitation Act of 1973.

⁸¹ 42 U.S.C. Section 1981a(a) and (b). Amendment contained in Section 102 of Civil Rights Act of 1991, 105 Stat. 1072–73.

⁸² "The Compromise on Civil Rights," note 62 above.

⁸³ 465 U.S. 555 (1984).

⁸⁴ Ms. Rawlinson herself was 5'3" tall and weighed 115 pounds. She was a 22-year-old college graduate who had majored in Correctional Psychology.

⁸⁵ *Griggs v. Duke Power*, 401 U.S. 424 (1971) and *Albemarle Paper v. Moody*, 422 U.S. 405 (1975).

⁸⁶ *Griggs*, 401 U.S., at 432.

⁸⁷ *Diaz v. Pan-American World Airways*, 442 F.2d 385, 388.

⁸⁸ Ms. Rawlinson brought suit as a class action on behalf of herself and other women similarly situated.

⁸⁹ *Mieth v. Dothard*, 418 F.Supp. 1169, 1184–85.

⁹⁰ Alysia Santo, "The Unique Sexual Harassment Problem Female Prison Workers Face," *The Marshall Project*, November 9, 2017. Available at https://www.themarshallproject.org/2017/11/09/the-unique-sexual-harassment-problem-female-prison-workers-face (accessed May 3, 3018).

⁹¹ *Terri Eddy et al., v. City and County of Denver, Denver Sheriff Department*, United States District Court for the District of Colorado, filed June 29, 2016. See also Kirk Mitchell, "10 Female Denver Deputies Sue Jail, Saying Sexual Harassment by Inmates Goes Unpunished," *The Denver Post*, June 30, 2016. Available at: https://www.denverpost.com/2016/06/30/denver-jail-female-deputies-sue-sexual-harassment/ (accessed May 11, 2018).

⁹² *LaFleur v. Cleveland Bd. of Education*, 465 F.2d 1184; and *Cohen v. Chesterfield County Bd. of Education*, 326 F.Supp. 1159.

⁹³ In the 1977 abortion funding decisions, the Court did acknowledge the centrality of the fundamental right of privacy. But, rejecting the non-funding-as-penalty argument, it then concluded that a state's decision

Women and Employment

to refuse to fund abortions through Medicaid does not "impinge on the fundamental right recognized in *Roe*," and it bluntly denied that such a law "penalizes the exercise of that right." See discussion of *Maher v. Roe* (1977) in Chapter 4.

94 42 U.S.C. § 2000e(k).

95 While sex discrimination in employment was officially prohibited in 1964, it was not until 1972 that a federal agency, the EEOC (Equal Employment Opportunity Commission) was given power to take employers to court for violations. Coincidentally (perhaps), 1977 was also the year that the U.S. Senate voted 75–11 for the Pregnancy Discrimination Act. (The concurrence of the House of Representatives was not obtained until 1978.)

96 OSHA 1910.1025 App C—Medical surveillance guidelines https://www.osha.gov/laws-regs/regulations/standardnumber/1910/1910.1025AppC (accessed October 11, 2018). Males at the higher levels risked lowered sperm count, decreased sperm motility, increased danger of malformed sperm, and impotence. *UAW v. Johnson Controls*, 886 F.2d 871, at 918–919.

97 The company also declared that work stations where the air level showed lead in excess of 30 micrograms per cubic meter were off-limits to women.

98 "The program divides potential recipients into two groups—pregnant women and non-pregnant persons. While the first group is exclusively female, the second includes members of both sexes," 417 U.S., at 496–97, n. 20.

99 *G.E v. Gilbert*, 429 U.S. 125, 147 (quoting EEOC brief) (1976).

100 Kai Bird and Max Holland, "Capitol Letter," *The Nation* (July 5/12, 1986), p.8.

101 479 U.S. 516.

102 29 U.S.C Chapter 28.

103 *The New York Times*, Feb.3, 1987, p. A-18, col. 4.

104 Jacob Alex Klerman, Kelly Daley and Alyssa Pozniak, *Family and Medical Leave in 2012: Technical Report*, September 7, 2012, Revised April 18, 2014, p. 60. Available at: https://www.dol.gov/asp/evaluation/fmla/FMLA-2012-Technical-Report.pdf (accessed May 22, 2018).

105 Lisa Jessie and Mary Tarleton, *2012 Census of Governments: Employment Summary Report*, Government Division Briefs, March 6, 2014, p. 2. Available at: https://www2.census.gov/govs/apes/2012_summary_report.pdf (accessed May 22, 2018).

106 *Board of Trustees of Univ. of Ala. v. Garrett*, 531 U.S. 356, 363 (2001); *Kimel v. Florida Bd. of Regents*, 528 U.S. 62, 72–73 (2000); *College Savings Bank v. Florida Prepaid Postsecondary Ed. Expense Bd.*, 527 U.S. 666, 669–670 (1999); and *Seminole Tribe of Fla. v. Florida*, 517 U.S. 44, 54 (1996).

107 *Kimel v. Florida Bd. of Regents*, 528 U.S. 62, 72–73 (2000).

108 *Board of Trustees of Univ. of Ala. v. Garrett*, 531 U.S. 356, 363 (2001).

109 443 U.S., at 209.

110 443 U.S., at 212.

111 480 U.S. 616, 620.

112 480 U.S., at 621.

113 Justice Brennan quoting the Plan, 480 U.S. 616, at 621.

114 480 U.S., at 625.

115 *Parents Involved in Community Schools v. Seattle School District No. 1*, 551 U.S. 701, 748 (2007).

116 Rosalie Berger Levinson, "Gender-based Affirmative Action and Reverse Gender Bias: Beyond *Gratz, Parents Involved*, and *Ricci*," *Harvard Journal of Law and Gender*, Vol. 34 (2011): 1–36.

117 *Ledbetter v. Goodyear Tire*, 550 U.S. 618 (2007).

118 Ibid., p. 661.

119 P.L. 111–2, 123 Stat. 5.

120 See discussion of *Pittsburgh Press v. Human Relations Commission* (1973) in Chapter 2.

121 "Select Task Force on the Study of Harassment in the Workplace Report of Co-Chairs Chai R. Feldblum & Victoria A. Lipnic," Equal Employment Opportunity Commission, June 2016, p. 8. Available at: https://www.eeoc.gov/eeoc/task_force/harassment/report.cfm (accessed May 3, 2018).

[122] "American Experiences versus American Expectations: An Updated Look at Private Sector Employment for Women, African Americans, Hispanics, Asian Americans and American Indians/Alaskan Natives in Celebration of the EEOC's 50th Anniversary," *U.S. Equal Employment Opportunity Commission*, July 2015. Available at: https://www.eeoc.gov/eeoc/statistics/reports/american_experiences/ (accessed May 22, 2018).

[123] Ibid.

[124] "Difference and Dominance: On Sex Discrimination," in *Feminism Unmodified* (Cambridge, Mass.: Harvard University Press, 1987), 37. See also Joan Williams, *Unbending Gender: Why Family and Work Conflict and What to Do About it* (New York: Oxford University Press, 2000).

[125] "Women in the American Workforce," Equal Employment Opportunity Commission. Available at https://www.eeoc.gov/eeoc/statistics/reports/american_experiences/women.cfm (accessed May 3, 2018).

[126] "A Look at the U.S. Department of Labor's 2012 Family and Medical Leave Act Employee and Worksite Surveys," National Partnership for Women & Families. Available at: http://www.nationalpartnership.org/research-library/work-family/fmla/dol-fmla-survey-key-findings-2012.pdf (accessed April 24, 2018).

[127] Ibid.

[128] Ibid.

CHAPTER 4

Women and Reproductive Freedom

LEGAL CONTEXT: IMPLIED CONSTITUTIONAL RIGHTS

The political controversy over a woman's right to have an abortion did not cease in 1973 when the Supreme Court "found" that right in the Constitution, and the controversy does not seem to be waning. The fact that women are lined up on both sides of the abortion issue does not remove the issue from the category of women's rights. There are women who oppose the Equal Rights Amendment, too.

That the abortion question is a matter precisely of women's rights is abundantly demonstrated in the case of *Planned Parenthood v. Danforth* (1976), which addressed the specific question of whether the father of a fetus could stop its mother from obtaining an abortion. Was the right to abort a right only of the unified parental couple or a right of the mother? If it were the former, the potential father would have absolute veto power over the potential mother's decision. The Supreme Court's answer was clear: abortion is a woman's right.

This right derives from the constitutional right of privacy. One cannot find "the right of privacy" anywhere in the letter of the Constitution; it is one of a small group of implied rights that the Supreme Court has found or invented or inferred or imagined somewhere in the spirit of that document. For the reader to decide whether the Court should be engaging in this business of inferring or discovering or inventing "constitutional" rights, a review of the history of other implied constitutional rights may be helpful.

Chapter 1 dealt with cases in which a constitutional right called "liberty of contract" was said to be at issue. "Liberty of contract" is mentioned nowhere in the Constitution. Nevertheless, conservative Supreme Court majorities, beginning with the *Lochner v. New York* (1905) case, found it lurking somewhere in the shadows of the due process clauses of the Fifth and Fourteenth Amendments.

Those clauses command that "liberty" shall not be taken "without due process of law." These justices inferred from that brief command that certain specific liberties, such as the right to contract freely in lawful business matters, were so fundamental to the American way of life that "due process" required extraordinarily strong justification before any restriction on them could be upheld.[1] For example, the dangers to health attendant to working in a coal mine (*Holden v. Hardy*, 1898) constituted strong enough justification to uphold an hours limit on the working day of miners; but the dangers to health, public or private, attendant to working long hours in a bakery (*Lochner v. New York*, 1905) did not constitute, according to five Supreme Court justices, a "reasonable ground for interfering with...the right of free contract" to the extent of imposing a 10-hour per day maximum on working hours for bakery employees.

This use of the due process clause to strike down statutes on the basis of *substantive* or *content* considerations (i.e., on the basis of the substantive question of which liberty was being restricted) became known as substantive due process. Specifically with regard to cases involving liberty of contract, it became known as economic substantive due process. This doctrine has been thoroughly discredited since the late 1940s and has been abandoned doctrine in American law.

Economic substantive due process was criticized on at least three grounds. First, liberal partisans condemned it for policy reasons: The doctrine was used repeatedly to strike down statutes that liberal legislative majorities (and, probably, popular majorities), attempting to redress the imbalance of power between employers and workers, believed to be in the public interest.

Second, it was condemned because, in introducing the notion of unwritten constitutional rights into American jurisprudence, it turned judges into nonelected legislators-nay, nonelected Founders. By releasing the Supreme Court from the written text of the Constitution, the concept of implied rights unleashes subjective prejudices to reshape the Constitution in whatever direction the prevailing winds of judicial prejudices tended to push it. Justice Holmes expressed this criticism of economic substantive due process as follows: "A constitution is not intended to embody a particular economic theory, whether of paternalism and the organic relation of the citizen to the State, or of *laissez faire*."[2]

A third criticism was closely related to the second. In implicitly postulating that some rights are more fundamental to the American system than others,[3] economic substantive due process introduced an additional subjective element into American jurisprudence. Who was to decide which parts of "liberty" were fundamental, and by what test? The due process clause mentions "life, liberty, and property"; it does not rank some liberties above others. Yet the Supreme Court majority of the early twentieth century seemed to be engaging in just such a ranking of liberties, and that majority provided no explanation of why the "right to labor or the right of contract" happened to rank near the top of their list.

It was during the heyday of economic substantive due process that the Supreme Court began to infer additional substantive liberties into the due process clause—some of which liberties have textual referents in the First Amendment, but others of which can be found nowhere in the text of the Constitution. In 1923 in *Meyer v. Nebraska* (a case where the legislature had tried to ban the study of German), the Court majority announced that the word "liberty" in the due process clause protects, among other things, "the right of the individual to ... marry, establish a home and bring up children, to worship God according to the dictates of his own conscience. . ." The litany of implied rights offered in that case also included the right of pupils "to acquire knowledge" and of parents "to control the education of their own." Building on *Meyer*, in 1925 the Court in *Pierce v. Society of Sisters*[4] unanimously struck down an Oregon law that required all children to attend public rather than parochial schools: The Supreme Court reaffirmed here "the liberty of parents. . .to direct the upbringing and education of children under their control." The Constitution nowhere mentions such a right, and yet not a single justice dissented. By this time both the doctrine of substantive due process and the concept of implied rights were securely fixed in the American constitutional firmament.

During the 1920s and 1930s the Supreme Court gradually added to the barrel of substantive-due-process-protected liberties each of the freedoms mentioned in the First Amendment: freedom of speech[5] and of the press,[6] right to peaceable assembly,[7] freedom for free exercise of religion,[8] and freedom from establishment of religion.[9] Nevertheless, during the 1930s and 1940s, the liberty-of-contract apples in that same barrel had begun to smell noticeably rotten. The aforementioned legal criticisms of economic substantive due process were gaining additional adherents under the economic pressures of the Great Depression and the political pressures stemming from electoral victories of the New Dealers.

Although the policy-oriented condemnation of economic substantive due process did not necessarily extend to substantive due process decisions involving civil liberties, the two other criticisms of substantive due process did present problems. In abandoning the old rule that there was a constitutional right to "freedom of contract," the 1937 Court majority said bluntly: "What is this freedom? The Constitution does not speak of freedom of contract."[10] Yet the Court never addressed a similar critique to the other unmentioned freedoms that it had begun to protect: freedom to acquire knowledge, to marry, to establish a home, and to guide the education of one's children. The Supreme Court retained these other implied freedoms even as it abandoned the one no-longer-implied freedom that had carved out the path for these others.

The addition of the specifically itemized First Amendment freedoms into the substantive due process barrel provided its own answer to the question, why single out some parts of liberty for special treatment when the Fourteenth Amendment itself refers only to "liberty" in general and subjects all liberty to the same phrase, "due process of law"? The Constitution, after all, had singled out the First Amendment liberties, had included them at the head of the Bill of Rights, and had girded their walls with language among the most emphatic in the Constitution ("Congress shall make no law...abridging"). Thus, special protection for *these* freedoms had a textual basis that was lacking in such claims as the assertion that one has a constitutional "right" to pressure employees to work a 12-hour day.

In an attempt to develop a more comprehensive explanation why the Court should retain the doctrine of substantive due process, and its related strict scrutiny approach, in matters of civil liberties while rejecting them in economic matters, Justice Harlan Fiske Stone produced the most famous footnote in Supreme Court history. In it he suggested that something more than mere "reasonableness" was demanded by "due process" when (1) "legislation appears on its face to be within one of the specific prohibitions of the Bill of Rights," and such extra justification also might be demanded when (2) legislation restricts those political processes essential to the functioning of a democratic law-making process (e.g., the right to vote), and when (3) legislation seems to attack "discrete and insular minorities" such as racial or religious groups.[11] To Justice Stone, and to the post-1937 Supreme Court majority, *due process* meant those liberties essential to a *democratic political process*. Stone's explanation made no reference to the marriage and childrearing rights established in the early 1920s. Whether those were dead letters in American legal history was not to become clear for another few decades.[12]

Before the Supreme Court returned to the matter of constitutional rights involving family life, the Court found a few more implied rights in the Constitution. Some, such as the right to vote[13] and the right of political association,[14] were closely linked, or linkable, to specific phrases in the Constitution. One, the right to travel, has no visible basis in the text of the Constitution.

The Articles of Confederation had provided that "the people of each State shall have free ingress and regress to and from any other State," but the Constitution contains no such statement. Nonetheless, in 1868 the Supreme Court invalidated a Nevada tax on passengers leaving the state via commercial transportation.[15] Such legislation violated either the implied message of the Commerce Clause[16] that the states may not impose undue burdens on the free flow of commerce among the states or else the implied message of the national structure of government: that all citizens of the nation may travel freely within the nation.[17] From the perspective of the individual citizen, the implication of these messages was that every person had a right to be free from undue, state-imposed burdens on his or her travel among the states.

In 1941 the Supreme Court based a decision squarely on this implication when it declared unconstitutional California's anti-Okie law, which barred entry into the state by "indigent" migrants.[18] Four of the justices in that decision, not comfortable with basing a personal right to travel on Congress's commerce power, urged (in a concurring opinion by Justice Jackson) that the right of free interstate travel should be viewed as one of the privileges and immunities of national citizenship protected by the privileges or immunities clause of the Fourteenth Amendment. Additional indirect textual support for a constitutional right of free interstate travel can be found in the Article IV, section 2, clause 1 command that out-of-state citizens must be entitled to the "privileges and immunities" of in-state citizens upon arriving in a new state.

The Commerce Clause justification for claiming a "right to travel" can restrict state legislation that interferes with travel, but naturally it cannot be the basis for restricting Congress's own power to regulate travel (which is a part of commerce). Nonetheless, the Supreme Court has ruled that even Congress must observe constitutional constraints in regulating the travel of Americans. In 1958, in a case involving the denial of passports to American leftists, the Court announced that the "right to travel" is a "constitutional right" protected not only against state abridgment but also, via the Fifth Amendment due process clause, against congressional abridgment.[19] The Court majority opinion for that case traced the right all the way back to the Magna Carta and asserted that it is "basic in our scheme of values."

In a more fully developed discussion of the right to travel, in a 1964 case[20] the Supreme Court declared that when statutes swept "*unnecessarily* broadly ...[into] the area of protected freedoms," they must be declared void (emphasis added).[21] The Court thereby struck down a congressional prohibition on foreign travel by American communists. This "necessity" test was just another formulation of the strict scrutiny test: Legislation that interferes with a fundamental right, if it is to be upheld, must be necessitated by (not just reasonably related to) an overriding governmental interest. By 1964, then, at least five justices on the Court were still willing to use substantive due process to strike down statutes, and to use it even for *unwritten* "constitutional" rights. The only explanation offered by the Court for according this strong protection to the right to travel was the brief statement that "freedom of travel is a constitutional liberty closely related to rights of free speech and association."[22]

STERILIZATION

Buck v. Bell (1927)

Meanwhile, those other unwritten constitutional rights that had been established in the early 1920s—the right to marry, establish a home, and rear children as one sees fit—remained shrouded in silence for a 40-year period. Even as the Supreme Court (in 1927 and in 1942) confronted the question of compulsory sterilization statutes—which certainly affected the right to marry and bring up children—the judges continued to ignore these precedents.

Buck v. Bell (1927) concerned a Virginia law mandating the sterilization of inmates of state institutions for the "feeble-minded." The law itself contained the conclusion that "experience has shown that heredity plays an important part in the transmission of insanity, imbecility, etc." The statute then provided that a superintendent at one of the state institutions for such people, when he or she believed "that it is for the best interests of the patients and of society," could order the sexual sterilization of any inmate who "was afflicted with hereditary forms of insanity, imbecility, etc."

Various procedural "safeguards" were provided in the statute. The superintendent had to petition the board of directors of the hospital or "colony" for permission for the operation. The would-be victim of the sterilization was given notice of the hearing and was permitted to attend it, as was his or her guardian; if the inmate was a minor, his or her parents were also notified of the hearing. All evidence presented at the hearing was to be put in writing and could be made the basis of an appeal to the circuit court of the county. Further appeal, before the operation would take place, was also available to the Virginia Supreme Court of Appeals.

> **FROM STEPHEN JAY GOULD, "CARRIE BUCK'S DAUGHTER"**[23]
>
> When we understand why Carrie Buck was committed in January 1924, we can finally comprehend the hidden meaning of her case and its message for us today. The silent key, again and as always, is her daughter Vivian, born on March 28, 1924, and then but an evident bump on her belly. Carrie Buck was

one of several illegitimate children borne by her mother, Emma. She grew up with foster parents, J.T. and Alice Dobbs, and continued to live with them, helping out with chores around the house. She was apparently raped by a relative of her foster parents, then blamed for her resultant pregnancy. Almost surely, she was (as they used to say) committed to hide her shame (and her rapist's identity), not because enlightened science had just discovered her true mental status. In short, she was sent away to have her baby. Her case never was about mental deficiency; it was always a matter of sexual morality and social deviance. The annals of her trial and hearing reek with the contempt of the well-off and well-bred for poor people of "loose morals." Who really cared whether Vivian was a baby of normal intelligence; she was the illegitimate child of an illegitimate woman. Two generations of bastards are enough. Harry Laughlin began his "family history" of the Bucks by writing: "These people belong to the shiftless, ignorant and worthless class of anti-social whites of the South."

We come then to the crux of the case, Carrie's daughter, Vivian. What evidence was ever adduced for her mental deficiency? This and only this: At the original trial in late 1924, when Vivian Buck was seven months old, a Miss Wilhelm, social worker for the Red Cross, appeared before the court. She began by stating honestly the true reason for Carrie Buck's commitment: "Mr. Dobbs, who had charge of the girl, had taken her when a small child had reported to Miss Duke [the temporary secretary of Public Welfare for Albemarle County] that the girl was pregnant and...he wanted to have her committed somewhere—to have her sent to some institution." Miss Wilhelm then rendered her judgment of Vivian Buck by comparing her with the normal granddaughter of Mrs. Dobbs, born just three days earlier:

> It is difficult to judge probabilities of a child as young as that, but it seems to me not quite a normal baby. In its appearance—I should say that perhaps my knowledge of the mother may prejudice me in that regard, but I saw the child at the same time as Mrs. Dobbs' daughter's baby, which is only three days older than this one, and there is a very decided difference in the development of the babies. That was about two weeks ago. There is a look about it that is not quite normal, but just what it is, I can't tell.

This short testimony, and nothing else, formed all the evidence for the crucial third generation of imbeciles. Cross-examination revealed that neither Vivian nor the Dobbs grandchild could walk or talk, and that "Mrs. Dobbs' daughter's baby is a very responsive baby. When you play with it or try to attract its attention—it is a baby that you can play with. The other baby is not. It seems very apathetic and not responsive." Miss Wilhelm then urged Carrie Buck's sterilization: "I think," she said, "it would at least prevent the propagation of her kind." Several years later, Miss Wilhelm denied that she had ever examined Vivian or deemed the child feebleminded.

When Buck v. Bell resurfaced in 1980, it immediately struck me that Vivian's case was crucial and that evidence for the mental status of a child who died at age 8 might best be found in report cards. I have therefore been trying to track down Vivian Buck's school records for the past four years and have finally succeeded. (They were supplied to me by Dr. Paul A. Lombardo, who also sent other documents, including Miss Wilhelm's testimony, and spent several hours answering my questions by mail and Lord knows how much time playing successful detective in re: Vivian's school records...)

Vivian Buck was adopted by the Dobbs family, who had raised (but later sent away) her mother, Carrie. As Vivian Alice Elaine Dobbs, she attended the Venable Public Elementary School of Charlottesville for four terms, from September 1930 until May 1932, a month before her death. She was a perfectly normal, quite average student, neither particularly outstanding nor much troubled.... This offspring of "lewd and immoral" women excelled in deportment and performed adequately, although not brilliantly, in her academic subjects.

In short, we can only agree with the conclusion that Dr. Lombardo has reached in his research on *Buck v. Bell*—there were no imbeciles, not a one, among the three generations of Bucks. I don't know that such correction of cruel but forgotten errors of history counts for much, but it is at least satisfying to learn that forced eugenic sterilization, a procedure of such dubious morality, earned its official justification (and won its most quoted line of rhetoric) on a patent falsehood.

In appealing the decision of Superintendent Bell of the State Colony of Epileptics and Feeble Minded to have her sterilized, Carrie Buck did not contest the procedural arrangements of the statute. Her attorney argued instead that in its substance it violated "her constitutional right of bodily integrity," thereby violating the substantive implications of the due process clause. None of the courts, including the U.S. Supreme Court, were persuaded by her arguments. In an opinion supported by a total of eight Supreme Court justices, here is how Justice Oliver Wendell Holmes responded to Carrie Buck's plea that she not be sterilized.

BUCK V. BELL
274 U.S. 200 (1927)

MR. JUSTICE HOLMES delivered the opinion of the Court.

* * *

Carrie Buck is a feeble minded white woman who was committed to the State Colony above mentioned in due form. She is the daughter of a feeble minded mother in the same institution, and the mother of an illegitimate feeble-minded child. She was eighteen years old at the time of the trial of her case. . .in the latter part of 1924.

. . .It seems to be contended that in no circumstances could such an order be justified. It certainly is contended that the order cannot be justified upon the existing grounds. The judgment finds the facts that have been recited and that Carrie Buck "is the probable potential parent of socially inadequate offspring, likewise afflicted, that she may be sexually sterilized without detriment to her general health and that her welfare and that of society will be promoted by her sterilization," and thereupon makes the order. In view of the general declarations of the legislature and the specific findings of the Court, obviously we cannot say as matter of law that the grounds do not exist, and if they exist they justify the result. We have seen more than once that the public welfare may call upon the best citizens for their lives. It would be strange if it could not call upon those who already sap the strength of the State for these lesser sacrifices, often not felt to be such by those concerned, in order to prevent our being swamped with incompetence. It is better for all the world, if instead of waiting to execute degenerate offspring for crime, or to let them starve for their imbecility, society can prevent those who are manifestly unfit from continuing their kind. The principle that sustains compulsory vaccination is broad enough to cover cutting the Fallopian tubes. *Jacobson v. Massachusetts*, 197 U.S. 11. Three generations of imbeciles are enough. . . .

[Holmes then rejected the argument that it denied equal protection to sterilize only feeble-minded inmates of state institutions rather than all feeble-minded persons.]

MR. JUSTICE BUTLER dissents.

[No written opinion.]

Case Questions

1. Are there differences of constitutional dimension between a statute that orders smallpox vaccinations and a statute that orders sterilization? Should there be?

2. Could Justice Holmes's reasoning have been used to sustain compulsory sterilization of all persons whose IQs were below 90 because certain scientists have asserted that IQ is largely hereditary? Could it be used to sustain compulsory sterilization of any second-generation "welfare mother"? It is easy to argue that such programs would be morally wrong (even abhorrent), but is there anything in the Constitution itself that forbids them? Is the phrase due process of law really broad enough to forbid all immoral laws? Might coerced sterilization of an innocent person be sensibly viewed as "cruel and unusual punishment," forbidden in the Eighth Amendment?

3. If a particular mental disability were known to be 90 percent genetically transmissible, would that justify state sterilization? 50 percent?

Skinner v. Oklahoma (1942)

Once the Supreme Court had declared that the "socially inadequate" could be forcibly sterilized, it certainly seemed plausible to state legislatures that the Court would also uphold forced sterilizations of persons convicted of serious crimes. In 1935 Oklahoma adopted the Habitual Criminal Sterilization Act. That act defined "habitual criminals" as persons who were convicted three times of "felonies involving moral turpitude" and ordered that such criminals be sexually sterilized on request of the state's attorney general. A court hearing (including the right of jury trial) in advance of the operation was required, but the only "defenses" available to the potential sterilization victim were that (1) his or her "general health" would suffer from the operation or that (2) he or she did not meet the state's legal definition of "habitual criminal." Certain felonies were expressly excluded from the "moral turpitude" category: tax evasion, embezzlement, political offenses, or violations of Prohibition.

Jack T. Skinner (a white man) was convicted on three occasions for crimes of "moral turpitude": chicken stealing in 1926, armed robbery in 1929, and armed robbery again in 1934. The state instituted sterilization proceedings against him in 1935, and he appealed the jury's pro-vasectomy decision to the Oklahoma Supreme Court. That court upheld the decision by 5–4, and he tried again at the U.S. Supreme Court. This time the Court (only 15 years after turning deaf ears to Carrie Buck's pleas) unanimously agreed that the sterilization statute was unconstitutional.

It is worth noting that at the time of the *Skinner v. Oklahoma* (1942) decision, the United States was engaged in a declared war against the combined forces of world fascism. The Court was not unaware of the popularity of eugenics theories among our enemies. However, the Court, despite its kind treatment of Mr. Skinner, did not go so far as to overrule *Buck v. Bell*. Instead, *Buck v. Bell* is still cited as a viable precedent by every justice who authored an opinion in the *Skinner* case.

The Supreme Court's opinion in the *Skinner* case relied not on the morally abhorrent implications of compulsory sterilization but rather on the equal protection problems raised by sterilizing some criminals and not others. It is extremely uncommon for the Court to interfere with state decisions about the severity of criminal penalties and even less common for the Court to interfere with them on the basis of the equal protection clause. "Equal protection of the laws" has never been read as requiring that a state impose the same sentence on all perpetrators of a particular criminal offense.[24] Yet the basis of this decision was the premise that the equal protection clause forbade Oklahoma to impose substantially different penalties for substantially similar crimes. This level of interference with the state's basic police power is incomprehensible without reference to the Court's obvious revulsion for compulsory sterilization.

That revulsion is evident in both the Douglas majority opinion and the Stone and Jackson concurring opinions. All three imply that laws affecting "one of the basic civil rights of man"—"the right to have offspring"—will be subjected to strict scrutiny (whether under the equal protection clause, the due process clause, or both). Yet none of the opinions suggests any desire to overrule *Buck v. Bell*. Why they don't remains something of a mystery.

SKINNER V. OKLAHOMA
316 U.S. 535 (1942)

MR. JUSTICE DOUGLAS delivered the opinion of the Court.

This case touches a sensitive and important area of human rights. Oklahoma deprives certain individuals of a right which is basic to the perpetuation of a race—the right to have offspring.

. . .[T]here is a feature of the Act which clearly condemns it. That is, its failure to meet the requirements of the equal protection clause of the Fourteenth Amendment.

We do not stop to point out all of the inequalities in this Act. A few examples will suffice. In Oklahoma, grand larceny is a felony. Okla. Stat. Ann. Tit. 21 § 1705, 5. Larceny is grand larceny when the property taken exceeds $20 in value. Embezzlement is punishable "in the manner prescribed for feloniously stealing property of the value of that embezzled." *Id.* § 1462. Hence, he who embezzles property worth more than $20 is guilty of a felony. A clerk who appropriates over $20 from his employer's till (*id.* § 1456) and a stranger who steals the same amount are thus both guilty of felonies. If the latter repeats his act and is convicted three times, he may be sterilized. But the clerk is not subject to the pains and penalties of the Act no matter how large his embezzlement nor how frequent his convictions.

[I]f we had here only a question as to a State's classification of crimes, such as embezzlement or larceny, no substantial federal question would be raised. See *Moore v. Missouri*, 159 U.S. 673; *Hawker v. New York*, 170 U.S. 189; *Finley v. California*, 222 U.S. 28; *Patsone v. Pennsylvania*. For a State is not constrained in the exercise of its police power to ignore experience which marks a class of offenders or a family of offenses for special treatment. Nor is it prevented by the equal protection clause from confining "its restrictions to those classes of cases where the need is deemed to be clearest." *Miller v. Wilson*, 236 U.S. 373, 384. And see *McLean v. Arkansas*, 211 U.S. 539....

But the instant legislation runs afoul of the equal protection clause, though we give Oklahoma that large deference which the rule of the foregoing cases requires. We are dealing here with legislation which involves one of the basic civil rights of man. Marriage and procreation are fundamental to the very existence and survival of the race. The power to sterilize, if exercised, may have subtle, far-reaching and devastating effects. In evil or reckless hands it can cause races or types which are inimical to the dominant group to wither and disappear. There is no redemption for the individual whom the law touches. Any experiment which the State conducts is to his irreparable injury. He is forever deprived of a basic liberty. We mention these matters not to reexamine the scope of the police power of the States. We advert to them merely in emphasis of our view that strict scrutiny of the classification which a State makes in a sterilization law is essential, lest unwittingly, or otherwise, invidious discriminations are made against groups or types of individuals in violation of the constitutional guaranty of just and equal laws. The guaranty of "equal protection of the laws is a pledge of the protection equal laws." *Yick Wo v. Hopkins*, 118 U.S. 356, 369. When the law lays an unequal hand on those who have committed intrinsically the same quality of offense and sterilizes one and not the other, it has made as invidious a discrimination as if it had selected a particular race or nationality for oppressive treatment. *Yick Wo v. Hopkins*; *Gaines v. Canada*, 305 U.S. 337. Sterilization of those who have thrice committed grand larceny, with immunity for those who are embezzlers, is a clear, pointed, unmistakable discrimination. Oklahoma makes no attempt to say that he who commits larceny by trespass or trick or fraud has biologically inheritable traits which he who commits embezzlement lacks....

We have not the slightest basis for inferring that line has any significance in eugenics, nor that the inheritability of criminal traits follows the neat legal distinctions which the law has marked between those two offenses. In terms of fines and imprisonment, the crimes of larceny and embezzlement rate the same under the Oklahoma code. Only when it comes to sterilization are the pains and penalties of the law different. The equal protection clause would indeed be a formula of empty words if such conspicuously artificial lines could be drawn. See *Smith v. Wayne Probate Judge*, 231 Mich. 409, 420–21, 204 N.W. 40. In *Buck v. Bell* the Virginia statute was upheld though it applied only to feeble-minded persons in institutions of the State. But it was pointed out that "so far as the operations enable those who otherwise must be kept confined to be returned to the world, and thus open the asylum to others, the equality aimed at will be more nearly reached." 274 U.S., at 208. Here there is no such saving feature. Embezzlers are forever free. Those who steal or take in other ways are not.

Reversed.

MR. CHIEF JUSTICE STONE, concurring:

I concur in the result, but I am not persuaded that we are aided in reaching it by recourse to the equal protection clause.

If Oklahoma may resort generally to the sterilization of criminals on the assumption that their propensities are transmissible to future generations by inheritance, I seriously doubt that the equal protection clause requires it to apply the measure to all criminals in the first instance, or to none. See *Rosenthal v. New York* 226 U.S. 260, 271; *Keokee Coke Co. v. Taylor*, 234 U.S. 224, 227; *Patsone v. Pennsylvania*, 232 U.S. 138, 144.

Moreover, if we must presume that the legislature knows—what science has been unable to ascertain—that the criminal tendencies of any class of habitual offenders are transmissible regardless of the varying mental characteristics of its individuals, I should suppose that we must likewise presume that the legislature, in its wisdom, knows that the criminal tendencies of some classes of offenders are more likely to be transmitted than those of others. And so I think the real question we have to consider is not one of equal protection, but whether the wholesale condemnation of a class to such an invasion of personal liberty without opportunity to any individual to show that his is not the type of case which would justify resort to it, satisfies the demands of due process.

There are limits to the extent to which the presumption of constitutionality can be pressed, especially where the liberty of the person is concerned (see *United States v. Carolene Products Co.*, 304 U.S. 144, 152, n. 4) and where the presumption is resorted to only to dispense with a procedure which the ordinary dictates of prudence would seem to demand for the protection of the individual from arbitrary action. Although petitioner here was given a hearing to ascertain whether sterilization would be detrimental to his health, he has given none to discover whether his criminal tendencies are of an inheritable type. Undoubtedly a state may, after appropriate inquiry, constitutionally interfere with the personal liberty of the individual to prevent the transmission by inheritance of his socially injurious tendencies. *Buck v. Bell*, 274 U.S. 200. But until now we have not been called upon to say that it may do so without giving him a hearing and opportunity to challenge the existence as to him of the only facts which could justify so drastic a measure.

Science has found and the law has recognized that there are certain types of mental deficiency associated with delinquency which are inheritable. But the State does not contend—nor can there be any pretense—that either common knowledge or experience, or scientific investigation, has given assurance that the criminal tendencies of any class of habitual offenders are universally or even generally inheritable. In such circumstances, inquiry whether such is the fact in the case of any particular individual cannot rightly be dispensed with. Whether the procedure by which a statute carries its mandate into execution satisfies due process is a matter of judicial cognizance. A law which condemns, without hearing, all the individuals of a class to so harsh a measure as the present because some or even many merit condemnation, is lacking in the first principles of due process. *Morrison v. California*, 291 U.S. 82, 90, and cases cited; *Taylor v. Georgia*, 315 U.S. 25. And so, while the state may protect itself from the demonstrably inheritable tendencies of the individual which are injurious to society, the most elementary notions of due process would seem to require it to take appropriate steps to safeguard the liberty of the individual by affording him, before he is condemned to an irreparable injury in his person, some opportunity to show that he is without such inheritable tendencies. . . .

> **MR. JUSTICE JACKSON concurring:**
>
> I join the CHIEF JUSTICE in holding that the hearings provided are too limited in the context of the present Act to afford due process of law. I also agree with the opinion of MR. JUSTICE DOUGLAS that the scheme of classification set forth in the Act denies equal protection of the law. I disagree with the opinion of each in so far as it rejects or minimizes the grounds taken by the other....
>
> I also think the present plan to sterilize the individual in pursuit of a eugenic plan to eliminate from the race characteristics that are only vaguely identified and which in our present state of knowledge are uncertain as to transmissibility presents other constitutional questions of gravity. This Court has sustained such an experiment with respect to an imbecile, a person with definite and observable characteristics, where the condition had persisted through three generations and afforded grounds for the belief that it was transmissible and would continue to manifest itself in generations to come. *Buck v. Bell*, 274 U.S. 200.
>
> There are limits to the extent to which a legislatively represented majority may conduct biological experiments at the expense of the dignity and personality and natural powers of a minority—even those who have been guilty of what the majority define as crimes. But this Act falls down before reaching this problem, which I mention only to avoid the implication that such a question may not exist because not discussed. On it I would also reserve judgment.

Case Questions

1. If Oklahoma were to reenact this statute after restructuring its criminal penalties so that the jail sentence for grand larceny were twice as long as that for embezzlement, would that vitiate the Court majority's objection to this statute? If Oklahoma were to reenact this statute after removing the exemption clause for tax criminals, Prohibition criminals, political criminals, and embezzlers, would that vitiate the majority's objection?

2. Suppose that social scientists concurred that a tendency to commit violent crime was hereditary in this sense: 1 in 1,000 people are convicted of violent crimes but 1 in 100 of the offspring of those convicted of violent crimes (even when adopted and raised by noncriminals) eventually are convicted of violent crimes. Is a tendency ten times that of the normal population, but only likely to strike 1% of the target population, grounds to prevent the birth of that entire target population?

3. When Justice Douglas refers to "invidious discriminations... against groups or types of individuals" that might be made by sterilization laws, is he suggesting that classifications for the purpose of sterilization have intrinsically racial implications and therefore should be considered "suspect" (because racial classifications are suspect)?

4. When Justice Jackson reserves judgment on the "problem" of how far a legislative majority may go in conducting "biological experiments at the expense of the dignity and personality and natural powers of a minority," is he implying that *Buck v. Bell* may have overstepped the line? That the line is somewhere between *Buck v. Bell* and *Skinner v. Oklahoma*?

5. Is it preposterous to suggest that the all-male Supreme Court was more sensitive to the preciousness of the right of procreation when it was a male whose procreative capacities were being threatened?

6. If the right to bear children is a fundamental civil right, should the state not need more compelling justification for overriding it than the state had in *Buck v. Bell*? If so, why does every justice cite *Buck* with apparent approval?

Case note: When the Court ignored the early 1920s *Meyer* and *Pierce* precedents on the rights of family life in handing down *Buck v. Bell*, the omission may have been conscious. The results in the former were not entirely compatible with the results in the latter; because of this, silence had certain face-saving functions.[25] The Court's silence about these precedents in *Skinner* is more difficult to explain. This is true because *Meyer*'s assertion of constitutional safeguards for the right to marry, establish a home, and rear children would have helped to buttress Justice Douglas's announcement in *Skinner* that the right to procreate is a fundamental civil right. Perhaps the Court's silence in *Skinner* can be explained by the following consideration: The year in which *Skinner* was decided, 1942, was in the midst of the period when Supreme Court disapproval of economic substantive due process was at its peak. The Court at this time was dominated by Roosevelt appointees, for whom such doctrines (because they had been used to thwart liberal economic programs) were a definite sore point. The historical and doctrinal linkages between the *Meyer* and *Pierce* cases and the economic substantive due process cases may have rendered these 1920s precedents tainted in the eyes of the 1942 Court. This could explain this Court's silence regarding a precedent whose potential utility seems, at least in retrospect, obvious.

After *Skinner:* The Paradox of Sterilization Policy

Skinner v. Oklahoma did not end involuntary sterilization in the United States. The ruling applied only to punishment for crime and had no impact on the status of *Buck v. Bell.* Sterilization abuse, which "occurs when people are subjected to the procedure without their consent or full understanding," was commonplace for women—but not men—in prison, in institutions, on Native American reservations, and on public assistance until late in the twentieth century.[26] Poor, disabled, and minority women were the primary victims of this abuse. When these women were not coerced, they were manipulated: denied counseling in their native language; told they needed a different procedure such as an appendectomy; threatened with loss of benefits; and so on. The "Mississippi appendectomy" was infamous among poor Black women; it was a hysterectomy.[27]

At the same time, voluntary sterilization was routinely denied to women. The American College of Obstetrics and Gynecology instituted the "rule of 120": a woman should be sterilized only if her age multiplied by the number of living children she had borne added up to that number. This rule was not binding, but many doctors and hospitals used it as a guideline even after ACOG changed its policy in the late 1960s. Vasectomy, by contrast, was available to any adult male who requested it.[28]

Stump v. Sparkman (1978)

One case of sterilization abuse reached the Supreme Court. In 1971, 15-year-old Linda Kay Spitler went into the hospital for what she thought was an appendectomy. Linda didn't know that her mother had obtained a court order from Indiana circuit court judge Harold D. Stump authorizing a tubal ligation, after filing a petition stating that Linda was sexually active and "mildly retarded." Linda had never been so diagnosed; the judgment is questionable in light of the fact that she was at grade level for her age and of her subsequent behavior. Confronted with a court order, Dr. John Hines performed the operation. When Linda married Leo Sparkman, they tried and failed to conceive a child. After consulting a physician, Linda learned for the first time that she had been surgically sterilized. The Sparkmans sued the mother, the doctor, and the judge, alleging that they had violated Linda's due process rights.

The federal District Court threw out the suit because the plaintiff had not shown that the issuing of the court order constituted state action and because the judge had judicial immunity. The appellate court reversed on the grounds that Judge Stump had forfeited his immunity by acting outside his jurisdiction; no law specifically authorized a judge to order surgery for minors at the request of their parents. Indiana law permitted court-ordered sterilization only for inmates of institutions. The Supreme Court agreed with the District Court: "Because Judge Stump performed the type of act normally performed only by judges and because he did so in his capacity as a Circuit Court Judge, we find no merit to respondents' argument that the informality with which he proceeded rendered his action nonjudicial and deprived him of his absolute immunity." No one was liable; this wrong went without a remedy.

Sterilization Reform

The decade between 1969 and 1979 represented the high point of sterilization abuse. The federal government officially approved the use of sterilization as a form of birth control in 1969, effectively giving itself a license to do what it had already been doing. Feminists took up the cause of sterilization abuse in the 1970s, bringing it to national attention. They insisted that protecting the right to abortion was not enough; preserving women's right to procreate was equally important. CARASA (the Committee for Abortion Rights and Against Sterilization Abuse) was a prominent activist organization in the 1970s. Lawsuits, protests, and reports of abuse finally led the Department of Health, Education, and Welfare (now Health and Human Services) to ban involuntary sterilization in 1979. These new regulations included mandatory informed consent after counseling in the woman's native language, prohibition of the use of hysterectomy as a method of sterilization, and a ban on procuring "consent" by threatening the woman with the loss of benefits. But since most sterilizations are funded by state programs, the states have become the focus of controversy on this issue.[29]

FEMINISTS AND CONTRACEPTION: A MIXED HISTORY

The women who attended the 1848 Women's Rights Convention (see the Introduction) could not have envisioned the availability, reliability, and variety of artificial contraception that exist now. But it is unlikely that the early feminists would have welcomed today's choices had they been available. Their preferred method of birth control was abstinence: "Voluntary motherhood," as it came to be called, meant that women had sex only when they wanted to conceive. Most nineteenth-century feminists believed that artificial birth control would make women more vulnerable to men's sexual demands than they already were. This attitude reflected the dominant view of the time in the United States, which neither expected nor wanted women to enjoy sex.[30]

By the early twentieth century, new cultural perspectives and enhanced knowledge had enabled more women to experience sexual pleasure. Many twentieth-century feminists, most notably Emma Goldman and her fellow socialists, welcomed birth control as a means for women to enjoy sex without risking pregnancy. Margaret Sanger, the founder of the American Birth Control League (now the Planned Parenthood Federation of America) was among the first to recognize the importance of birth control for the poor. She became a prominent, and often imprisoned, activist. An excerpt from her autobiography reveals the gravity of the situation she sought to remedy. Sanger recounted an episode where she cared for a woman who nearly died from a self-induced abortion:

> [Sadie Sachs] finally voiced her fears. "Another baby will finish me, I suppose?"
>
> "It's too early to talk about that," I temporized.
>
> But when the doctor came to make his last call, I drew him aside. "Mrs. Sachs is terribly worried about having another baby."
>
> "She may well be," replied the doctor.... He laughed good naturedly. "You want to have your cake and eat it too, do you? Well, it can't be done."
>
> Then picking up his hat and bag to depart he said, "Tell Jake to sleep on the roof."
>
> I glanced quickly at Mrs. Sachs. Even through my sudden tears I could see stamped on her face an expression of absolute despair.
>
> ... The telephone rang one evening three months later, and Jake Sachs' agitated voice begged me to come at once; his wife was sick again and from the same cause.... Mrs. Sachs was in a coma and died within ten minutes.[31]

Some of Sanger's associates—and, briefly, Sanger herself—had less compassionate reasons for supporting birth control for the poor. The birth control movement attracted eugenics adherents whose views were similar to those expressed by Justice Holmes in *Buck v. Bell*. Disenchanted with the eugenics sympathies of some ABCL leaders, Sanger resigned from the league in 1928.[32] It was not until the resurgence of feminism in the 1960s and 1970s that advocates of reproductive choice committed themselves to choice for all women, whatever their circumstances. By then, the Supreme Court had given privacy the status of a fundamental right.

Griswold v. Connecticut (1965)

By 1965, the judicial practice of using substantive due process to protect implied liberties was not so tainted in the eyes of liberals as it had been in the days of *Skinner v. Oklahoma*. By this time the Supreme Court had established an implied right to travel, an implied right of association, and an implied right to vote, and the Court had repeatedly applied a strict scrutiny approach (clearly derivative from substantive due process) in examining statutory limitations on these rights. Thus, in 1965, when the Court finally did announce that there is a right of privacy in matters of marital intimacy, it freely made reference to these 1920s precedents.

The 1965 case that occasioned this announcement was *Griswold v. Connecticut*. Estelle Griswold, executive director of the Planned Parenthood League of Connecticut, and Lee Buxton, a physician who served as medical director of the league's public clinic in New Haven, Connecticut, had been arrested in November 1961. Their crime was having given information to married persons about available contraceptive devices. Connecticut law made it a crime, punishable by 60 days to one year in jail or a 50 dollar fine, to use "any drug. . .or instrument for the purpose of preventing conception." To aid, abet, or advise someone else to commit a crime was in Connecticut, as elsewhere, itself a crime (the crime of being an "accessory"). Griswold and Dr. Buxton were each fined $100 as accessories to married couples whom they advised to commit the crime of using birth control. Their conviction had been upheld by two appeals courts within Connecticut before it reached the U.S. Supreme Court.

On two previous occasions[33] this statute had been challenged at the U.S. Supreme Court. Evidently unwilling to provide the "not unconstitutional" stamp of approval and yet unable to find a specific constitutional clause that condemned the statute, the Court had twice ducked the constitutional issue, using legal technicalities to avoid deciding the cases.[34] The Court's hope was clearly that Connecticut would either choose never to enforce this statute, letting it die a quiet death of disuse, or else repeal it through the legislative process. The Court did not reckon with the political power of the Roman Catholic vote in Connecticut. Neither of the sensible options carried the day. Instead, *Griswold v. Connecticut* brought this statute back to the Supreme Court for the third time within 18 years. And this time seven members of the Court found something in the Constitution that implied a right, at least for married couples, to use birth control.

The majority split into three factions over the question of which dark corner of the Constitution had contained this right to use birth control for so many years. One faction (Justices Harlan and White) chose to illuminate the due process clause itself, arguing that it sheltered all the fundamental liberties of Americans, of which the right of marital privacy was certainly one. Another faction (Justices Douglas and Clark) engaged in a valiant effort to find the right of marital privacy in the shadows, or "penumbras," as Douglas put it, of various guarantees of the Bill of

Rights, which (Douglas implies) are incorporated into the Fourteenth Amendment phrase "due process of law" as restraints upon the state governments.[35] A third faction (Justices Goldberg, Warren, and Brennan) agreed with both groups: several Bill of Rights amendments do imply a right of marital privacy, and even if they did not, the due process clause would imply the right as a basic liberty in our society. This third group specifically addressed the question of the legitimacy of inferring unwritten rights into the Constitution, and they offered the Ninth Amendment as justification for that practice.

In addition, *Griswold v. Connecticut* brought the whole substantive due process question out of the historical closet. Douglas (in the Court opinion) denied that he was using the doctrine; he carefully attempted to dissociate this decision from *Lochner v. New York* (1905) and its economic substantive due process bedfellows. (He did cite both *Meyer* and *Pierce* in defense of his argument; he transformed them, however, to First Amendment incorporation decisions, ignoring the fact that the First Amendment was not mentioned in either of them.)[36] Harlan, White, and Goldberg (with Brennan and Warren concurring) defended the validity of a substantive due process approach. And Stewart and Black attacked the substantive due process approach, with Black noting pointedly that the M*eyer* and *Pierce* precedents, cited by majority justices, were based on "long-discredited decisions." Black fought a career-long war against this approach, but the *Griswold* battle seems to have indicated a decisive turning point in the direction of his opponents' victory in that war.

GRISWOLD V. CONNECTICUT

381 U.S. 479 (1965)

MR. JUSTICE DOUGLAS delivered the opinion of the Court.

* * *

We think that appellants have standing to raise the constitutional rights of the married people with whom they had a professional relationship.... Certainly the accessory should have standing to assert that the offense which he is charged with assisting is not, or cannot constitutionally be, a crime....

Coming to the merits, we are met with a wide range of questions that implicate the Due Process Clause of the Fourteenth Amendment. Overtones of some arguments suggest that *Lochner v. New York*, 198 U.S. 45, should be our guide. But we decline that invitation as we did in *West Coast Hotel Co. v. Parrish*, 300 U.S. 379; *Olsen v. Nebraska*, 313 U.S. 236; *Lincoln Union v. Northwestern Co.*,

335 U.S. 525; *Williamson v. Lee Optical Co.*, 348 U.S. 483; *Giboney v. Empire Storage Co.*, 336 U.S. 490 [All these rejected economic substantive due process arguments.—AU.].

We do not sit as a super-legislature to determine the wisdom, need, and propriety of laws that touch economic problems, business affairs, or social conditions. This law, however, operates directly on an intimate relation of husband and wife and their physician's role in one aspect of that relation.

The association of people is not mentioned in the Constitution nor in the Bill of Rights. The right to educate a child in a school of the parent's choice—whether public or private or parochial—is also not mentioned. Nor is the right to study any particular subject or any foreign language. Yet the First Amendment has been construed to include certain of those rights.

By *Pierce v. Society of Sisters*, the right to educate one's children as one chooses is made applicable to the State by the force of the First and Fourteenth Amendments. By *Meyer v. Nebraska*, the same dignity is given the right to study the German language in a private school. In other words, the State may not, consistently with the spirit of the First Amendment, contract the spectrum of available knowledge. The right of freedom of speech and press includes not only the right to utter or to print, but the right to distribute, the right to receive, the right to read (*Martin v. Struthers*, 319 U.S. 141, 143) and freedom of inquiry, freedom of thought, and freedom to teach (see *Wieman v. Updegraff*, 344 U.S. 183, 195)—indeed the freedom of the entire university community. *Sweezy v. New Hampshire*, 354 U.S. 234, 249–50, 261–63; *Barenblatt v. United States*, 360 U.S. 109, 112; *Baggett v. Bullitt*, 377 U.S. 360, 369. Without those peripheral rights the specific rights would be less secure. And so we reaffirm the principle of the *Pierce* and the *Meyer* cases.

In *NAACP v. Alabama*, 357 U.S. 449, 462, we protected the "freedom to associate and privacy in one's associations," noting that freedom of association was a peripheral First Amendment right. . . . In other words, the First Amendment has a penumbra where privacy is protected from governmental intrusion. In like context, we have protected forms of "association" that are not political in the customary sense but pertain to the social, legal, and economic benefit of the members. *NAACP v. Button*, 371 U.S. 415, 430–31. . . .

Those cases involved more than the "right of assembly"—a right that extends to all irrespective of their race or ideology. *De Jonge v. Oregon*, 299 U.S. 353. The right of "association," like the right of belief (*Board of Education v. Barnette*, 319 U.S. 624), is more than the right to attend a meeting; it includes the right to express one's attitudes or philosophies by membership in a group or by affiliation with it or by other lawful means. Association in that context is a form of expression of opinion; and while it is not expressly included in the First Amendment its existence is necessary in making the express guarantees fully meaningful.

The foregoing cases suggest that specific guarantees in the Bill or Rights have penumbras, formed by emanations from those guarantees that help give them life and substance. Various guarantees creates zones of privacy. The right of association contained in the penumbra of the First Amendment is one, as we have seen. The Third Amendment in its prohibition against the quartering of soldiers "in any house" in time of peace without the consent of the owner is another facet of that privacy. The Fourth Amendment explicitly affirms the "right of the people to be secure in their persons, houses, papers, and effects, against unreasonable searches and seizures." The Fifth Amendment in its Self-Incrimination Clause enables the citizen to create a zone of privacy which government may not force him to surrender to his detriment. The Ninth Amendment provides: "The enumeration in the Constitution, of certain rights, shall not be construed to deny or disparage others retained by the people."

The Fourth and Fifth Amendments were described in *Boyd v. United States*, 116 U.S. 616, 630, as protection against all governmental invasions "of the sanctity of a man's home and the privacies of life."* We recently referred in *Mapp v. Ohio*, 367 U.S. 643, 656, to the Fourth Amendment as creating a "right to privacy, no less important than any other right carefully and particularly reserved to the people."

We have had many controversies over these penumbral rights of "privacy and repose." See, e.g., *Breard v. Alexandria*, 341 U.S. 622, 626, 644; *Public Utilities Comm'n v. Pollak*, 343 U.S. 451; *Monroe v. Pape*, 365 U.S. 167; *Lanza v. New York*, 370 U.S. 139; *Frank v. Maryland*, 359 U.S. 360; *Skinner v. Oklahoma*, 316 U.S. 535, 541. These cases bear witness that the right of privacy which presses for recognition here is a legitimate one.

The present case, then, concerns a relationship lying within the zone of privacy created by several fundamental constitutional guarantees. And it concerns a law which, in forbidding the use of contraceptives rather than regulating their manufacture or sale, seeks to achieve its goals by means having a maximum destructive impact upon that relationship. Such a law cannot stand in light of the familiar principle, so often applied by this Court, that a "governmental purpose to control or prevent activities constitutionally subject to state regulation may not be achieved by means which sweep unnecessarily broadly and thereby invade the area of protected freedoms." *NAACP v. Alabama*, 377 U.S. 288, 307. Would we allow the police to search the sacred precincts of marital bedrooms for telltale signs of the use of contraceptives? The very idea is repulsive to the notions of privacy surrounding the marriage relationship.

We deal with the right of privacy older than the Bill of Rights—older than our political parties, older than our school system. Marriage is a coming together for better or for worse, hopefully enduring, and intimate to the degree of being sacred. It is an association that promotes a way of life, not causes; a harmony in living, not political faiths; a bilateral loyalty, not commercial or social projects. Yet it is an association for as noble a purpose as any involved in our prior decisions.

Reversed.

Opinion Footnote

* The Court said...[there]: "The principles laid down in this opinion [of Lord Candem's in the 1765 case, Entick v. Carrington, 19 How. St. Tr. 1029] affect the very essence of constitutional liberty and security. They...apply to all invasions on the part of the government and its employees of the sanctity of a man's home and the privacies of life.

MR. JUSTICE GOLDBERG, whom THE CHIEF JUSTICE and MR. JUSTICE BRENNAN join, concurring.

I agree with the Court that Connecticut's birth-control law unconstitutionally intrudes upon the right of marital privacy, and I join in its opinion and judgment. Although I have not accepted the view that "due process" as used in the Fourteenth Amendment incorporates all of the first eight Amendments, I do agree that the concept of liberty protects those personal rights that are fundamental, and is not confined to the specific terms of the Bill of Rights. My conclusion that the concept of liberty is not so restricted and that it embraces the right of marital privacy though that right is not mentioned explicitly in the Constitution is supported both by numerous decisions of this Court, referred to in the Court's opinion, and by the language and history of the Ninth Amendment. In reaching the conclusion that the right of marital privacy is protected, as being within the protected penumbra of specific guarantees of the Bill of Rights, the Court refers to the Ninth Amendment. I add these words to emphasize the relevance of that Amendment to the Court's holding.

The Court stated many years ago that the Due Process Clause protects those liberties that are "so rooted in the traditions and conscience of our people as to be ranked as fundamental." *Snyder v. Massachusetts*, 291 U.S. 97, 105....And, in *Meyer v. Nebraska*, 262 U.S. 390, 399, the Court, referring to the Fourteenth Amendment, stated:

> While this Court has not attempted to define with exactness the liberty thus guaranteed, the term has received much consideration and some of the included things have been definitely stated. Without doubt, it denotes not merely freedom from bodily restraint but also [for example,] the right...to marry, establish a home and bring up children....

This Court, in a series of decisions, has held that the Fourteenth Amendment absorbs and applies to the States those specifics of the first eight amendments which express fundamental personal rights. The language and history of the Ninth Amendment reveal that the Framers of the Constitution believed that there are additional fundamental rights, protected from governmental infringement, which exist alongside those fundamental rights specifically mentioned in the first eight constitutional amendments.

The Ninth Amendment reads, "The enumeration in the Constitution, of certain rights, shall not be construed to deny or disparage others retained by the people."...To hold that a right so basic and fundamental and so deep-rooted in our society as the right of privacy in marriage may be infringed because that right is not guaranteed in so many words by the first eight amendments to the Constitution is to ignore the Ninth Amendment and to give it no effect whatsoever. Moreover, a judicial construction that this fundamental right is not protected by the Constitution because it is not mentioned in explicit terms by one of the first eight amendments or elsewhere in the Constitution would violate the Ninth Amendment, which specifically states that "[t]he enumeration in the Constitution, of certain rights, shall not be *construed* to deny or disparage others retained by the people." (Emphasis added.)...[T]he Ninth Amendment shows a belief of the Constitution's authors that fundamental rights exist that are not expressly enumerated in the first eight amendments and an intent that the list of rights included there not be deemed exhaustive...[and] that other fundamental personal rights should not be denied...protection or disparaged in any other way simply because they are not specifically listed in the first eight constitutional amendments....I do not see how this broadens the authority of the Court; rather it serves to support what this Court has been doing in protecting fundamental rights.

Nor am I turning somersaults with history in arguing that the Ninth Amendment is relevant in a case dealing with a State's infringement of a fundamental right. While the Ninth Amendment—and indeed the entire Bill of Rights—originally concerned restrictions upon federal power, the subsequently enacted Fourteenth Amendment prohibits the States as well from abridging fundamental personal liberties. And, the Ninth Amendment, in indicating that not all such liberties are specifically mentioned in the first eight amendments, is surely relevant in showing the existence of other fundamental personal rights, now protected from state, as well as federal, infringement.

In determining which rights are fundamental, judges are not left at large to decide cases in light of their personal and private notions. Rather, they must look to the "traditions and [collective] conscience of our people" to determine whether a principle is "so rooted [there]. . .as to be ranked as fundamental." *Snyder v. Massachusetts*, 291 U.S. 97, 105. The inquiry is whether a right involved "is of such a character that it cannot be denied without violating those 'fundamental principles of liberty and justice which lie at the base of all our civil and political institutions'. . . ." *Powell v. Alabama*, 287 U.S. 45, 65. . . .

The Connecticut statutes here involved deal with a particularly important and sensitive area of privacy—that of the marital relation and the marital home. This Court recognized in *Meyer v. Nebraska*, that the right "to marry, establish a home and bring up children" was an essential part of the liberty guaranteed by the Fourteenth Amendment, 262 U.S., at 399. In *Pierce v. Society of Sisters*, 268 U.S. 510, the Court held unconstitutional an Oregon Act which forbade parents from sending their children to private schools because such an act "unreasonably interferes with the liberty of parents and guardians to direct the upbringing and education of children under their control." 268 U.S., at 534–35. As this Court said in *Prince v. Massachusetts*, 321 U.S. 158, at 166, the *Meyer* and *Pierce* decisions "have respected the private realm of family life which the state cannot enter.". . .

The logic of the dissents would sanction federal or state legislation that seems to me even more plainly unconstitutional than the statute before us. Surely the Government, absent a showing of a compelling subordinating state interest, could not decree that all husbands and wives must be sterilized after two children have been born to them. Yet by their reasoning such an invasion of marital privacy would not be subject to constitutional challenge because, while it might be "silly," no provision of the Constitution specifically prevents the Government from curtailing the marital right to bear children and raise a family. . . .

MR. JUSTICE HARLAN, concurring in the judgment.

I fully agree with the judgment of reversal, but find myself unable to join the Court's opinion. The reason is that it seems to me to evince an approach to this case very much like that taken by my Brothers BLACK and STEWART in dissent, namely: The Due Process Clause of the Fourteenth Amendment does not touch this Connecticut statute unless the enactment is found to violate some right assured by the letter or penumbra of the Bill of Rights. . . .

In my view, the proper constitutional inquiry in this case is whether this Connecticut statute infringes the Due Process Clause of the Fourteenth Amendment because the enactment violates basic values "implicit in the concept of ordered liberty," *Palko v. Connecticut*, 302 U.S. 319, 325. For reasons stated at length in my dissenting opinion in *Poe v. Ullman*, I believe that it does.

[In *Poe*, J. HARLAN said, in part: "Certainly the safeguarding of the home does not follow merely from the sanctity of property rights. The home derives its pre-eminence as the seat of family life. And the integrity of that life is something so fundamental that it has been found to draw to its protection the principles of more than one explicitly granted Constitutional right. . . .Of this whole 'private realm of family life' it is difficult to imagine what is more private or more intimate than a husband and wife's marital relations. . . .

"Adultery, homosexuality and the like are sexual intimacies which the State forbids. . . but the intimacy of husband and wife is necessarily an essential and accepted feature of the institution of marriage, an institution which the State not only must allow, but which always and in every age it has fostered and protected. It is one thing when the State exerts its power either to forbid extra-marital sexuality. . .or to say who may marry, but it is quite another when, having acknowledged a marriage and the intimacies inherent in it, it undertakes to regulate by means of the criminal law the details of that intimacy."]

MR. JUSTICE WHITE, concurring in the judgment.

In my view this Connecticut law as applied to married couples deprives them of "liberty" without due process of law, as that concept is used in the Fourteenth Amendment. I therefore concur in the judgment of the Court reversing these convictions under Connecticut's aiding and abetting statute.

. . .[T]his is not the first time this Court has had occasion to articulate that the liberty entitled to protection under the Fourteenth Amendment includes the right "to marry, establish a home and bring up children," *Meyer v. Nebraska*, 262 U.S. 390, 399, and "the liberty. . .to direct the upbringing and education of children," *Pierce v. Society of Sisters*, 268 U.S. 510, 534–35, and that these are among "the basic civil rights of man." *Skinner v. Oklahoma*, 316 U.S. 535, 541. These decisions affirm that there is a "realm of family life which the state cannot enter" without substantial justification. *Prince v. Massachusetts*, 321 U.S. 158, 166. Surely the right invoked in this case, to be free of regulation of the intimacies of the marriage relationship, "come[s] to this Court with a momentum for respect lacking when appeal is made to liberties which derive merely from shifting economic arrangements." *Kovacs v. Cooper*, 336 U.S. 77, 95 (opinion of FRANKFURTER, J.).

The Connecticut anti-contraceptive statute deals rather substantially with this relationship. For it forbids all married persons the right to use birth-control devices, regardless of whether their use is dictated by considerations of family planning, health, or indeed even of life itself. In my view, a statute with these effects bears a substantial burden of justification when attacked under the Fourteenth Amendment. *Yick Wo v. Hopkins*, 118 U.S. 356; *Skinner v. Oklahoma*, 316 U.S. 535; *Schware v. Board of Bar Examiners*, 353 U.S. 232; *McLaughlin v. Florida*, 379 U.S. 184, 192.

An examination of the justification offered, however, cannot be avoided by saying that the Connecticut anti-use statute invades a protected area of privacy and association or that it demeans the marriage relationship. The nature of the right invaded is pertinent, to be sure, for statutes regulating sensitive areas of liberty do, under the cases of this Court, require "strict scrutiny," *Skinner v. Oklahoma*, 316 U.S. 535, 541, and "must be viewed in the light of less drastic means for achieving the same basic purpose." *Shelton v. Tucker*, 364 U.S. 479, 488. "Where there is a significant encroachment upon personal liberty, the State may prevail only upon showing a subordinating interest which is compelling." *Bates v. Little Rock*, 361 U.S. 516, 524. See also *McLaughlin v. Florida*, 379 U.S. 184. But such statutes, if reasonably necessary for the effectuation of a legitimate and substantial state interest, and not arbitrary or capricious in application, are not invalid under the Due Process Clause. *Zemel v. Rusk*, 381 U.S. 1. . . . [The] State claims but one justification for its anti-use statute. There is no serious contention that Connecticut thinks the use of artificial or external methods of contraception immoral or unwise in itself, or that the anti-use statute is founded upon any policy of promoting population expansion. Rather, the statute is said to serve the State's policy against all forms of promiscuous or illicit sexual relationships, be they premarital or extramarital, concededly a permissible and legitimate legislative goal.

Without taking issue with the premise that the fear of conception operates as a deterrent to such relationships in addition to the criminal proscriptions

Connecticut has against such conduct, I wholly fail to see how the ban on the use of contraceptives by married couples in any way reinforces the State's ban on illicit sexual relationships. . . . Perhaps the theory is that the flat ban on use prevents married people from possessing contraceptives and without the ready availability of such devices for use in the marital relationship, there will be no or less temptation to use them in extramarital ones. This reasoning rests on the premise that married people will comply with the ban in regard to their marital relationship, notwithstanding total nonenforcement in this context and apparent nonenforcibility, but will not comply with criminal statutes prohibiting extramarital affairs and the anti-use statute in respect to illicit sexual relationships, a premise whose validity has not been demonstrated and whose intrinsic validity is not very evident. . . . A statute limiting its prohibition on use to persons engaging in the prohibited relationship would serve the end posited by Connecticut in the same way, and with the same effectiveness or ineffectiveness, as the broad anti-use statue under attack in this case. I find nothing in this record justifying the sweeping scope of this statute, with its telling effect on the freedoms of married persons, and therefore conclude that it deprives such persons of liberty without due process of law.

MR. JUSTICE BLACK, with whom MR. JUSTICE STEWART joins, dissenting.

I agree with my Brother STEWART'S dissenting opinion. And like him I do not to any extent whatever base my view that this Connecticut law is constitutional on a belief that the law is wise or that its policy is a good one. In order that there may be no room at all to doubt why I vote as I do, I feel constrained to add that the law is every bit as offensive to me as it is to my Brethren of the majority and my Brothers HARLAN, WHITE and GOLDBERG who, reciting reasons why it is offensive to them, hold it unconstitutional. There is no single one of the graphic and eloquent strictures and criticisms fired at the policy of this Connecticut law either by the Court's opinion or by those of my concurring Brethren to which I cannot subscribe— except their conclusion that the evil qualities they see in the law make it unconstitutional.

Had the doctor defendant here, or even the nondoctor defendant, been convicted for doing nothing more than expressing opinions to persons coming to the clinic that certain contraceptive devices, medicines or practices would do them good and would be desirable, or for telling people how devices could be used, I can think of no reasons at this time why their expressions of views would not be protected by the First and Fourteenth Amendments, which guarantee freedom of speech. But speech is one thing; conduct and physical activities are quite another. The two defendants here were active participants in an organization which gave physical examinations to women, advised them what kind of contraceptive devices or medicines would most likely be satisfactory for them, and then supplied the devices themselves, all for a graduated scale of fees, based on the family income. Thus these defendants admittedly engaged with others in a planned course of conduct to help people violate the Connecticut law. Merely because some speech was used in carrying on that conduct—just as in ordinary life some speech accompanies most kinds of conduct—we are not in my view justified in holding that the First Amendment forbids the State to punish their conduct. . . .

The Court talks about a constitutional "right of privacy" as though there is some constitutional provision or provisions forbidding any law ever to be passed which might abridge the "privacy" of individuals. But there is not. There are, of course, guarantees in certain specific constitutional provisions which are designed in part to protect privacy at certain times and places with respect to certain activities. Such, for example, is the Fourth Amendment's guarantee against "unreasonable searches and seizures." But I think it belittles that Amendment to talk about it as though it protects nothing but "privacy." To treat it that way is to give it a niggardly interpretation, not the kind of liberal reading I think any Bill or Rights provision should be given. The average man would very likely not have his feelings soothed any more by having his property seized openly than by having it seized privately and by stealth. He simply wants his property left alone. And a person can be just as much, if not more irritated, annoyed and injured by an unceremonious public arrest by a policeman as he is by a seizure in the privacy of his office or home.

One of the most effective ways of diluting or expanding a constitutionally guaranteed right is to substitute for the crucial word or words of a constitutional guarantee another word or words, more or less flexible and more or less restricted in meaning. This fact is well illustrated by the use of the term "right of privacy" as a comprehensive substitute for the Fourth Amendment's guarantee against "unreasonable searches and seizures." "Privacy" is a broad, abstract and ambiguous concept which can easily be shrunken in meaning but which can also, on the other hand, easily be interpreted as a constitutional ban against many things other than searches and seizures. . . . I like my privacy as well as the next one, but I am nevertheless compelled to admit that government has a right to invade it unless prohibited by some specific constitutional provision. For these reasons I cannot agree with the Court's judgment and the reasons it gives for holding this Connecticut law unconstitutional.

This brings me to the arguments made by my Brothers HARLAN, WHITE and GOLDBERG for invalidating the Connecticut law.... I think that if properly construed neither the Due Process Clause nor the Ninth Amendment, nor both together, could under any circumstances be a proper basis for invalidating the Connecticut law. I discuss the due process and Ninth Amendment arguments together because on analysis they turn out to be the same thing—merely using different words to claim for this Court and the federal judiciary power to invalidate any legislative act which the judges find irrational, unreasonable or offensive.

The due process argument which my Brothers HARLAN and WHITE adopt here is based, as their opinions indicate, on the premise that this Court is vested with power to invalidate all state laws that it considers to be arbitrary, capricious, unreasonable, or oppressive, or on this Court's belief that a particular state law under scrutiny has no "rational or justifying" purpose, or is offensive to a "sense of fairness and justice." If these formulas based on "natural justice," or others which mean the same thing, are to prevail, they require judges to determine what is or is not constitutional on the basis of their own appraisal of what laws are unwise or unnecessary. The power to make such decisions is of course that of a legislative body. Surely it has to be admitted that no provision of the Constitution specifically gives such blanket power to courts to exercise such a supervisory veto over the wisdom and value of legislative policies and to hold unconstitutional those laws which they believe unwise or dangerous. I readily admit that no legislative body, state or national, should pass laws that can justly be given any of the invidious labels invoked as constitutional excuses to strike down state laws. But perhaps it is not too much to say that no legislative body ever does pass laws without believing that they will accomplish a sane, rational, wise and justifiable purpose.... Such an appraisal of the wisdom of legislation is an attribute of the power to make laws, not of the power to interpret them. The use by federal courts of such a formula or doctrine or whatnot to veto federal or state laws simply takes away from Congress and States the power to make laws based on their own judgment of fairness and wisdom and transfers that power to this Court for ultimate determination—a power which was specifically denied to federal courts by the convention that framed the Constitution.

Of the cases on which my Brothers WHITE and GOLDBERG rely so heavily, undoubtedly the reasoning of two of them supports their result here—

as would that of a number of others which they do not bother to name, e.g., *Lochner v. New York*, 198 U.S. 45, *Coppage v. Kansas*, 236 U.S. 1, *Jay Burns Baking Co. v. Bryan*, 264 U.S. 504, and *Adkins v. Children's Hospital*, 261 U.S. 525. [All are economic substantive due process cases.—AU.] The two they do cite and quote from, *Meyer v. Nebraska*, 262 U.S. 390, and *Pierce v. Society of Sister*, 268 U.S. 510, were both decided in opinions by Mr. Justice McReynolds which elaborated the same natural law due process philosophy found in *Lochner v. New York*, one of the cases on which he relied in Meyer, along with such other long-discredited decisions as, e.g., *Adams v. Tanner*, 244 U.S. 590, and *Adkins v. Children's Hospital*. . . .Without expressing an opinion as to whether either of those cases reached a correct result in light of our later decisions applying the First Amendment to the States through the Fourteenth, I merely point out that the reasoning stated in *Meyer* and *Pierce* was the same natural law due process philosophy which many later opinions repudiated, and which I cannot accept. . . .My Brother GOLDBERG. . .states, without proof satisfactory to me, that in making decisions on this basis judges will not consider "their personal and private notions." One may ask how they can avoid considering them. Our Court certainly has no machinery with which to take a Gallup Poll. And the scientific miracles of this age have not yet produced a gadget which the Court can use to determine what traditions are rooted in the "[collective] conscience of our people." . . . [T]his Court does have power, which it should exercise, to hold laws unconstitutional where they are forbidden by the Federal Constitution. My point is that there is no provision of the Constitution which either expressly or impliedly vests power in this Court to sit as a supervisory agency over acts of duly constituted legislative bodies and set aside their laws because of the Court's belief that the legislative policies adopted are unreasonable, unwise, arbitrary, capricious or irrational. The adoption of such a loose, flexible, uncontrolled standard for holding laws unconstitutional, if it is ever finally achieved, will amount to a great unconstitutional shift of power to the courts which I believe and am constrained to say will be bad for the courts and worse for the country. . . .

[W]hat my concurring Brethren urge today . . .would reinstate the *Lochner*, *Coppage*, *Adkins*, *Burns* lines of cases, cases from which this Court recoiled after the 1930's, and which had been I thought totally discredited until now. Apparently my Brethren have less quarrel with state economic regulations than former Justices of their persuasion had. But any limitation upon their using the natural law due process philosophy to strike down any state law, dealing with any activity whatever, will obviously be only self-imposed.

> **MR. JUSTICE STEWART, whom MR. JUSTICE BLACK joins, dissenting.**
>
> Since 1879 Connecticut has had on its books a law which forbids the use of contraceptives by anyone. I think this is an uncommonly silly law. As a practical matter, the law is obviously unenforceable, except in the oblique context of the present case. As a philosophical matter, I believe the use of contraceptives in the relationship of marriage should be left to personal and private choice, based upon each individual's moral, ethical, and religious beliefs. As a matter of social policy, I think professional counsel about methods of birth control should be available to all, so that each individual's choice can be meaningfully made. But we are not asked in this case to say whether we think this law is unwise, or even asinine. We are asked to hold that it violates the United States Constitution. And that I cannot do.
>
> In the course of its opinion the Court refers to no less than six Amendments to the Constitution: the First, the Third, the Fourth, the Fifth, the Ninth, and the Fourteenth. But the Court does not say which of these Amendments, if any, it thinks is infringed by this Connecticut law. . . .
>
> What provision of the Constitution, then, does make this state law invalid? The Court says it is the right of privacy "created by several fundamental constitutional guarantees." With all deference, I can find no such general right of privacy in the Bill of Rights, in any other part of the Constitution, or in any case ever before decided by this Court. . . . We are here to decide cases "agreeably to the Constitution and laws of the United States." It is the essence of judicial duty to subordinate our own personal views, our own ideas of what legislation is wise and what is not. If, as I should surely hope, the law before does not reflect the standards of the people of Connecticut, the people of Connecticut can freely exercise their true Ninth and Tenth Amendment rights to persuade their elected representatives to repeal it. That is the constitutional way to take this law off the books.

Case Questions

1. Does the right of privacy protected in this decision apply to unmarried persons? Do any of the justices think so?

2. Did the Supreme Court invent the right of privacy? Is the right to use birth control a reasonable inference from any particular passage of the Constitution? Does "due process of law" imply protection for all rights deemed "basic" by the Supreme Court? How is the Supreme Court to decide which rights are so basic that they justify overriding legislatures' decisions to the contrary?

3. If American "traditions" indicate the direction by which to find those rights that are "basic," how can the Court claim that an 86-year-old statute violates a "basic" (in the sense of "traditional") right?

4. Justice Black is willing to accept a substantive due process approach (including its corollary strict scrutiny) to protect the substance of liberties mentioned, or at least alluded to, in the Constitution. He objects, however, to *any* substantive due process approach (whether the minimal "reasonableness" one or a strict scrutiny one) for a specific liberty not at least implicitly protected by some words of the Constitution. Should the phrase "shall not deprive any person of liberty without due process of law" be read as implying that every law (because all laws infringe on someone's liberty) must bear a reasonable relationship to the public interest? Would any honest legislative majority adopt a law that did not promote *their* view of the public interest? What justifies the Supreme Court's assumption that it is better able to discern "rationality" than a legislature is?

5. What if Connecticut (agreeing with the Pope) had proffered the "serious contention that...the use of artificial or external methods of contraception [is] immoral.... in itself"? The principle that states have the power and duty to promote morality is thoroughly accepted in American jurisprudence. Could the Supreme Court announce that Connecticut's view of morality was misguided and that the judges knew better? Even if they do know better, is there not an important difference between (1) a system in which judges enforce the *written* law of the land (as adopted by the people in the form of the Constitution) and (2) one in which judges enforce the judges' own views of the national moral code? Can the latter system still be considered a democracy? Can it be considered a democracy if the people have purposely delegated that power to judges (through the due process clause, or the privileges or immunities clause)? If the people have unwittingly so delegated it?

Eisenstadt v. Baird (1972)

All the justices of the *Griswold* majority mentioned the special status of the marriage institution as a sector of our society in which the right to privacy has peculiarly strong claims. It is almost impossible to find statements in the *Griswold* opinion with any direct implications that unmarried persons might have a comparable right. In fact, Justices Harlan, White, and Goldberg (the latter in a section omitted from the excerpt), for a total of five justices, expressly indicated that the suppression of extramarital sexual activity is a legitimate legislative goal.

Within seven years, however, when the Court actually confronted, in *Eisenstadt v. Baird*, the question of whether unmarried persons have a "right of privacy" that protects the use of birth control, the Court majority had crossed sides on this question. More precisely, Brennan (who had concurred in the

Goldberg opinion in *Griswold*) changed sides. Douglas had expressed no view on the subject in *Griswold* (although he, like everyone else, had stressed the importance of the marriage relationship). Stewart had lined up against any right of privacy in *Griswold*, but evidently, when he finally did accept it (as he would explain later in *Roe v. Wade*), he believed it would logically apply to the unmarried as well as the married, for he did side with the majority in *Eisenstadt*. By the time of the *Eisenstadt* decision, Clark, Harlan, Black, Goldberg, and Warren had all left the Court, to be replaced by Burger, Blackmun, Marshall, Powell, and Rehnquist. Because the latter two arrived on the Court too late to participate in *Eisenstadt*, it is the four-justice majority of Brennan, Douglas, Stewart, and Marshall who produced the groundbreaking Court opinion for that case.

That opinion not only extends to unmarried persons a right to use birth control; it goes considerably further. Brennan's majority opinion in *Eisenstadt v. Baird* forges the logical link in the chain between a right to use contraceptive devices and a right to have an abortion. Once *Eisenstadt v. Baird* was announced, the abortion decisions of 1973 were predictable. The link that clinched the judicial future was forged by a single sentence written by Justice Brennan: "If the right of privacy means anything, it is the right of the individual...to be free from unwarranted governmental intrusion into *matters so fundamentally affecting a person as the decision whether to bear or beget a child*" (emphasis added).

The situation provoking this statement began when Bill Baird, a pro-birth-control activist, in the midst of a lecture on contraception at Boston University in 1969, handed a package of Emko vaginal foam (a spermicidal contraceptive) to an unmarried young woman. He performed this act in deliberate contravention of Massachusetts law, which prohibited the giving away of any contraceptive devices, except by registered physicians prescribing for married persons or by registered pharmacists filling such prescriptions. This statute, like the *Griswold* statute, did not address the distribution of implements of birth control for the purpose of preventing disease; distributing them for the prevention of conception was the sole target of the statute. In accordance with this law (1) no one could distribute contraceptives except on medical prescriptions, and (2) no one could give even medically prescribed contraceptives to unmarried persons. Either of these acts was punishable by up to five years in prison.

Bill Baird, a nonphysician, was convicted of the felony of distributing a nonprescribed contraceptive. His conviction was sustained upon appeal to the Massachusetts Supreme Court, and his further appeal was dismissed by the federal District Court. In his next appeal, the Circuit Court of Appeals sided with Baird, ordering him discharged. Eisenstadt, the sheriff of Suffolk County, Massachusetts, then appealed to the U.S. Supreme Court. Their response follows.

EISENSTADT V. BAIRD
405 U.S. 438 (1972)

MR. JUSTICE BRENNAN delivered the opinion of the Court.

The legislative purposes that the statute is meant to serve are not altogether clear. In *Commonwealth v. Baird*, the Supreme Judicial Court noted only the State's interest in protecting the health of its citizens: "[T]he prohibition in § 21," the court declared, "is directly related to" the State's goal of "preventing the distribution of articles designed to prevent conception which may have undesirable, if not dangerous, physical consequences." 247 N.E. 2d, at 578. In a subsequent decision, *Sturgis v. Attorney General*, 260 N.E. 2d 687, 690 (1970), the court, however, found "a second and more compelling ground for upholding the statute"—namely, to protect morals through "regulating the private sexual lives of single persons."[3] The Court of Appeals, for reasons that will appear, did not consider the promotion of health or the protection of morals through the deterrence of fornication to be the legislative aim. Instead, the court concluded that the statutory goal was to limit contraception in and of itself—a purpose that the court held conflicted "with fundamental human rights" under *Griswold v. Connecticut*, 381 U.S. 479 (1965), where this Court struck down Connecticut's prohibition against the use of contraceptives as an unconstitutional infringement of the right of marital privacy. 429 F. 2d, at 1401–2.

We agree that the goals of deterring premarital sex and regulating the distribution of potentially harmful articles cannot reasonably be regarded as legislative aims of § 21 and 21A. And we hold that the statute, viewed as a prohibition on contraception *per se*, violates the rights of single persons under the Equal Protection Clause of the Fourteenth Amendment.

I

... We address at the outset appellant's contention that Baird does not have standing to assert the rights of unmarried persons denied access to contraceptives because he was neither an authorized distributor under § 21A nor a single person unable to obtain contraceptives. There can be no question, of course, that Baird has sufficient interest in challenging the statute's validity to satisfy the "case or controversy" requirement of Article III of the Constitution. . . . [Our] self-imposed rule against the assertion of third-party rights must be relaxed in this case just as in *Griswold v. Connecticut*. . . .[H]ere the relationship between Baird and those whose rights he seeks to assert is not simply that between a distributor and potential distributees, but that between an advocate of the rights of persons to obtain contraceptives and those desirous of doing so. The very point of Baird's giving away the vaginal foam was to challenge the Massachusetts statute that limited access to contraceptives.

In any event, more important than the nature of the relationship between the litigant and those whose rights he seeks to assert is the impact of the litigation on the third party interests. In *Griswold*, 381 U.S., at 481, the Court stated: "The rights of husband and wife, pressed here, are likely to be diluted or adversely affected unless those rights are considered in a suit involving those who have this kind of confidential relation to them." A similar situation obtains here. Enforcement of the Massachusetts statute will materially impair the ability of single persons to obtain contraceptives. In fact, the case for according standing to assert third-party rights is stronger in this regard here than in *Griswold* because unmarried persons denied access to contraceptives in Massachusetts, unlike the users of contraceptives in Connecticut, are not themselves subject to prosecution and, to that extent, are denied a forum in which to assert their own rights. . . .

II

The basic principles governing application of the Equal Protection Clause of the Fourteenth Amendment are familiar. As the CHIEF JUSTICE only recently explained in *Reed*:

> In applying that clause, this Court has consistently recognized that. . . .[a] classification "must be reasonable, not arbitrary, and must rest upon some ground of difference having a fair and substantial relation to the object of the legislation, so that all persons similarly circumstanced shall be treated alike." (*Royster Guano Co. v. Virginia*, 253 U.S. 412, 415 [1920])

The question for our determination in this case is whether there is some ground of difference that rationally explains the different treatment accorded married and unmarried persons under [these laws].[7] For the reasons that follow, we conclude that no such ground exists.

First. . . .The Massachusetts Supreme Judicial Court. . . .reiterated in *Sturgis v. Attorney General* that the object of the legislation is to discourage premarital sexual intercourse. Conceding that the State could, consistently with the Equal Protection Clause, regard the problems of extramarital and premarital sexual relations as "[e]vils...of different dimensions and proportions, requiring different remedies," *Williamson, v. Lee Optical Co.*, 348 U.S. 483, 489 (1955), we cannot agree that the deterrence of premarital sex may reasonably be regarded as the purpose of the Massachusetts law.

It would be plainly unreasonable to assume that Massachusetts has prescribed pregnancy and the birth of an unwanted child as punishment for fornication, which is a misdemeanor under Massachusetts [law]. Aside from the scheme of values that assumption would attribute to the State, it is abundantly clear that the effect of the ban on distribution of contraceptives to unmarried persons has at best a marginal relation to the proffered objectives. What Mr. Justice Goldberg said in *Griswold v. Connecticut*, at 498 (concurring opinion), concerning the effect of Connecticut's prohibition on the use of contraceptives in discouraging extramarital sexual relations, is equally applicable here. "The rationality of this justification is dubious, particularly in light of the admitted widespread availability to all persons in the State of Connecticut, unmarried as well as married, of birth-control devices for the prevention of disease, as distinguished from the prevention of conception." See also *id.*, at 505–507 (WHITE, J., concurring in judgment). Like Connecticut's laws, § 21 and § 21A do not at all regulate the distribution of contraceptives when they are to be used to prevent, not pregnancy, but the spread of disease. Nor, in making contraceptives available to married persons without regard to their intended use, does Massachusetts attempt to deter married persons engaging in illicit sexual relations with unmarried persons. Even on the assumption that the fear of pregnancy operates as a deterrent to fornication, the Massachusetts statute is thus so riddled with exceptions that deterrence of premarital sex cannot reasonably be regarded as its aim.

Moreover, § 21 and § 21A on their face have a dubious relation to the State's criminal prohibition on fornication. As the Court of Appeals explained, "Fornication is a misdemeanor [in Massachusetts], entailing a thirty dollar fine, or three months in jail.... Violation of the present statute is a felony, punishable by five years in prison. We find it hard to believe that the legislature adopted a statute carrying a five-year penalty for its possible, obviously by no means fully effective, deterrence of the commission of a ninety-day misdemeanor." 429 F. 2d, at 1401....[We] cannot believe that in this instance Massachusetts has chosen to expose the aider and abetter who simply gives away a contraceptive to 20 times the 90-day sentence of the offender himself....

Second. . . . If health were the rationale of § 21A, the statute would be both discriminatory and overbroad. If there is need to have a physician prescribe (and a pharmacist dispense) contraceptives, that need is as great for unmarried persons as for married persons. . .[8] Furthermore, we must join the Court of Appeals in noting that not all contraceptives are potentially dangerous.[9] As a result, if the Massachusetts statute were a health measure, it would not only invidiously discriminate against the unmarried, but also be overbroad with respect to the married. . . . We conclude, accordingly, that, despite the statute's superficial earmarks as a health measure, health, on the face of the statute, may no more reasonably be regarded as its purpose than the deterrence of premarital sexual relations.

Third. If the Massachusetts statute cannot be upheld as a deterrent to fornication or as a health measure, may it, nevertheless, be sustained simply as a prohibition on contraception? The Court of Appeals analysis "led inevitably to the conclusion that, so far as morals are concerned, it is contraceptives *per se* that are considered immoral—to the extent that *Griswold* will permit such a declaration." 429 F. 2d, at 1401–2. The Court of Appeals went on to hold, *id.*, at 1402:

> To say that contraceptives are immoral as such, and are to be forbidden to unmarried persons who will nevertheless persist in having intercourse, means that such persons must risk for themselves an unwanted pregnancy, for the child, illegitimacy, and for society, a possible obligation of support. Such a view of morality is not only the very mirror image of sensible legislation; we consider that it conflicts with fundamental human rights. In the absence of demonstrated harm, we hold it is beyond the competency of the state.

We need not and do not, however, decide that important question in this case because, whatever the rights of the individual to access to contraceptives may be, the rights must be the same for the unmarried and the married alike.

If under *Griswold* the distribution of contraceptives to married persons cannot be prohibited, a ban on distribution to unmarried persons would be equally impermissible. It is true that in *Griswold* the right of privacy in question inhered in the marital relationship. Yet the marital couple is not an independent entity with a mind and heart of its own, but an association of two individuals each with a separate intellectual and emotional makeup. If the right of privacy means anything, it is the right of the *individual*, married or single, to be free from unwarranted governmental intrusion into matters so fundamentally affecting a person as the decision whether to bear or beget a child. See *Stanley v. Georgia*,

394 U.S. 557 (1969). See also *Skinner v. Oklahoma*, 316 U.S. 535 (1942); *Jacobson v. Massachusetts*, 197 U.S. 11, 29 (1905).

On the other hand, if *Griswold* is no bar to a prohibition on the distribution of contraceptives, the State could not, consistently with the Equal Protection Clause, outlaw distribution to unmarried but not to married persons. In each case the evil, as perceived by the State, would be identical, and the underinclusion would be invidious. MR. JUSTICE JACKSON, concurring in *Railway Express Agency v. New York*, 336 U.S. 106, 112–13 (1949), made the point:

> The framers of the Constitution knew. . .that there is no more effective practical guaranty against arbitrary and unreasonable government than to require that the principles of law which officials would impose upon a minority must be imposed generally. Conversely, nothing opens the door to arbitrary action so effectively as to allow those officials to pick and choose only a few to whom they will apply legislation and thus to escape the political retribution that might be visited upon them if larger numbers were affected. Courts can take no better measure to assure that laws will be just than to require that laws be equal in operation.

Although MR. JUSTICE JACKSON'S comments had reference to administrative regulations, the principle he affirmed has equal application to the legislation here. We hold that by providing dissimilar treatment for married and unmarried persons who are similarly situated, [these statutes] violate the Equal Protection Clause. The judgment of the Court of Appeals is

Affirmed.

Opinion Footnotes

3 Appellant suggests that the purpose of the Massachusetts statute is to promote marital fidelity as well as to discourage premarital sex. Under § 21A, however, contraceptives may be made available to married persons without regard to whether they are living with their spouses or the uses to which the contraceptives are to be put. Plainly the legislation has no deterrent effect on extramarital sexual relations.

7 Of course, if we were to conclude that the Massachusetts statute impinges upon fundamental freedoms under *Griswold*, the statutory classification would have to be not merely rationally related to a valid public purpose but necessary to the achievement of a compelling state interest. E.g., *Shapiro v. Thompson*, 394 U.S. 618 (1969); *Loving v. Virginia*, 388 U.S. 1 (1967). But just as in *Reed v. Reed*, 404 U.S. 71 (1971), we do not have to address the statute's validity under that test because the law fails to satisfy even the more lenient equal protection standard.

8 Appellant insists that the unmarried have no right to engage in sexual intercourse and hence no health interest in contraception that needs to be served. The short answer to this contention is that the same devices the distribution of which the State purports to regulate when their asserted purpose is to forestall pregnancy are available without any controls whatsoever so long as their asserted purpose is to

prevent the spread of disease. It is inconceivable that the need for health controls varies with the purpose for which the contraceptive is to be used when the physical act in all cases is one and the same.

9   The Court of Appeals stated, 429 F. 2d, at 1401: "[W]e must take notice that not all contraceptive devices risk 'undesirable...[or] dangerous physical consequences.'...[W]e have never heard criticism [of condoms] on the side of health. We cannot think that the legislature was unaware of it, or could have thought that it needed a medical prescription. We believe the same could be said of certain other products."

MR. JUSTICE POWELL and MR. JUSTICE REHNQUIST took no part in the consideration or decision of this case.

MR. JUSTICE DOUGLAS, concurring.

While I join the opinion of the Court, there is for me a narrower ground for affirming .... This to me is a simple First Amendment case, that amendment being applicable to the State by reason of the Fourteenth. *Stromberg v. California*, 283 U.S. 359.

Baird addressed an audience of students and faculty at Boston University on the subject of birth control and overpopulation. His address was approximately one hour in length and consisted of a discussion of various contraceptive devices; overpopulation in the world; ...and the potential harm to women resulting from abortions performed by quack abortionists. Baird also urged members of the audience to petition the Massachusetts Legislature.... At the close of the address Baird invited members of the audience to come to the stage and help themselves to the contraceptive articles....Baird personally handed one woman a package of Emko Vaginal Foam. He was then arrested....

"[T]his Court has repeatedly stated, [First Amendment] rights are not confined to verbal expression. They embrace appropriate types of action...." *Brown v. Louisiana*, 383 U.S. 131, 141–42.

...[A]s an aid to understanding the ideas which he was propagating he handed out one sample of one of the devices whose use he was endorsing....There is no evidence or finding that Baird intended that the young lady take the foam home with her when he handed it to her or that she would not have examined the article and then returned it to Baird, had he not been placed under arrest immediately...Handing out the article was not even a suggestion that the lady use it. At most it suggested that she become familiar with the product line....

MR. JUSTICE WHITE, with whom MR. JUSTICE BLACKMUN joins, concurring in the result.

Appellee Baird was indicted for giving away Emko Vaginal Foam, a "medicine and article for the prevention of conception...." The State did not purport to charge or convict Baird for distributing to an unmarried person. No proof was offered as to the marital status of the recipient. The gravamen of the offense charged was that Baird had no license and therefore no authority to distribute to anyone. As the Supreme Judicial Court of Massachusetts noted, the constitutional validity of Baird's conviction rested upon his lack of status as a "distributor and not. . .the marital status of the recipient." *Commonwealth v. Baird*, 247 N.E. 2d 574, 578 (1969). The Federal District Court was of the same view.

I assume that a State's interest in the health of its citizens empowers it to restrict to medical channels the distribution of products whose use should be accompanied by medical advice. I also do not doubt that various contraceptive medicines and articles are properly available only on prescription, and I therefore have no difficulty with the Massachusetts court's characterization of the statute at issue here as expressing "a legitimate interest in preventing the distribution of articles designed to prevent conception which may have undesirable, if not dangerous, physical consequences." 247 N.E. 2d, at 578. Had Baird distributed a supply of the so-called "pill," I would sustain his conviction under this statute. Requiring a prescription to obtain potentially dangerous contraceptive material may place a substantial burden upon the right recognized in *Griswold*, but that burden is justified by a strong state interest and does not, as did the statute at issue in *Griswold*, sweep unnecessarily broadly or seek "to achieve its goals by means having a maximum destructive impact upon" a protected relationship. *Griswold v. Connecticut*, 381 U.S., at 485.

Baird, however, was found guilty of giving away vaginal foam. Inquiry into the validity of this conviction does not come to an end merely because some contraceptives are harmful and their distribution may be restricted. Our general reluctance to question a State's judgment on matters of public health must give way where, as here, the restrictions at issue burdens the constitutional rights of married persons to use contraceptives. In these circumstances we may not accept on faith the State's classification of a particular contraceptive as dangerous to health. Due regard for protecting constitutional rights requires that the record contain evidence that a restriction on distribution of vaginal foam is essential to achieve the statutory purpose, or the relevant facts concerning the product must be such as to fall within the range of judicial notice.

Neither requirement is met here. Nothing in the record even suggests that the distribution of vaginal foam should be accompanied by medical advice in order to protect the user's health. Nor does the opinion of the Massachusetts court or the State's brief filed here marshal facts demonstrating that the hazards of using vaginal foam are common knowledge or so incontrovertible that they may be noticed judicially. On the contrary, the State acknowledges that Emko is a product widely available without prescription. Given *Griwold v. Connecticut*, and absent proof of the probable hazards of using vaginal foam, we could not sustain appellee's conviction had it been for selling or giving away foam to a married person. . . .

That Baird could not be convicted for distributing Emko to a married person disposes of this case. Assuming, *arguendo*, that the result would be otherwise had the recipient been unmarried, nothing has been placed in the record to indicate her marital status. The state has maintained that marital status is irrelevant because an unlicensed person cannot legally dispense vaginal foam either to married or unmarried persons. This approach is plainly erroneous and requires the reversal of Baird's conviction; for on the facts of this case, it deprives us of knowing whether Baird was in fact convicted for making a constitutionally protected distribution of Emko to a married person. . . .

Because this case can be disposed of on the basis of settled constitutional doctrine, I perceive no reason for reaching the novel constitutional question whether a State may restrict or forbid the distribution of contraceptives to the unmarried. Cf. *Ashwander v. Tennessee Valley Authority*, 297 U.S. 288, 345–48 (1936) (BRANDEIS, J., concurring).

MR. CHIEF JUSTICE BURGER, dissenting.

The judgment of the Supreme Judicial Court of Massachusetts in sustaining appellee's conviction for dispensing medicinal material without a license seems eminently correct to me and I would not disturb it. It is undisputed that appellee is not a physician or pharmacist and was prohibited under Massachusetts law from dispensing contraceptives to anyone, regardless of marital status. To my mind the validity of this restriction on dispensing medicinal substance is the only issue before the Court, and appellee has no standing to challenge that part of the statute restricting the persons to whom contraceptives are available. There is no need to labor this point, however, for everyone seems to agree that if Massachusetts has validly required, as a health measure, that all contraceptives be dispensed by a physician or pursuant to a physician's prescription, then the statutory distinction based on marital status has no bearing on this case. *United States v. Raines*, 362 U.S. 17, 21 (1960).

The opinion of the Court today brushes aside appellee's status as an unlicensed layman by concluding that the Massachusetts Legislature was not really concerned with the protection of health when it passed this statute. MR. JUSTICE WHITE acknowledges the statutory concern with the protection of health, but finds the restriction on distributors overly broad because the State has failed to adduce facts showing the health hazards of the particular substance dispensed by appellee as distinguished from other contraceptives....

[T]he opinion of the Court and that of MR. JUSTICE WHITE ...seriously invade the constitutional prerogatives of the States and regrettably hark back to the heyday of substantive due process.

In affirming appellee's conviction, the highest tribunal in Massachusetts held that the statutory requirement that contraceptives be dispensed only through medical channels served the legitimate interest of the State in protecting the health of its citizens. The Court today blithely hurdles this authoritative state pronouncement and concludes that the statute has no such purpose...because, "[i]f there is need to have a physician prescribe ...contraceptives, that need is as great for unmarried persons as for married persons." 247 N.E. 2d 574, 581. This argument confuses the validity of the restriction on distributors with the validity of the further restriction on distributees, a part of the statute not properly before the Court. Assuming the legislature too broadly restricted the class of persons who could obtain contraceptives, it hardly follows that it saw no need to protect the health of all persons to whom they are made available.

...

MR. JUSTICE WHITE ... grants that appellee's conviction would be valid if he had given away a potentially harmful substance, but rejects the State's placing this particular contraceptive in that category. So far as I am aware, this Court has never before challenged the police power of a State to protect the public from the risks of possibly spurious and deleterious substances sold within its borders....[T]he opinion invokes *Griswold v. Connecticut*, 381 U.S. 479 (1965), and puts the statutory classification to an unprecedented test: either the record must contain evidence supporting the classification or the health hazards of the particular contraceptive must be judicially noticeable. This is indeed a novel constitutional doctrine....

The actual hazards of introducing a particular foreign substance into the human body are frequently controverted, and I cannot believe that unanimity of expert opinion is a prerequisite to a State's exercise of its police power, no matter what the subject matter of their regulation. Even assuming no present dispute among medical authorities, we cannot ignore that it has become commonplace for a drug or food additive to be universally regarded as harmless on one day and to be condemned as perilous on the next. It is inappropriate for this Court to overrule a legislative classification by relying on the present consensus among leading authorities. The commands of the Constitution cannot fluctuate with the shifting tides of scientific opinion.

Even if it were conclusively established once and for all that the product dispensed by appellee is not actually or potentially dangerous in the somatic sense, I would still be unable to agree that the restriction on dispensing it falls outside the State's power to regulate in the area of health. The choice of a means of birth control, although a highly personal matter, is also a health matter in a very real sense, and I see nothing arbitrary in a requirement of medical supervisions. It is generally acknowledged that contraceptives vary in degree of effectiveness and potential harmfulness. There may be compelling health reasons for certain women to choose the most effective means of birth control available, no matter how harmless the less effective alternatives. Others might be advised not to use a highly effective means of contraception because of their peculiar susceptibility to an adverse side effect. . . .

I do not challenge *Griswold v. Connecticut*, despite its tenuous moorings to the text of the Constitution, but I cannot view it as controlling authority for this case. The Court was there confronted with a statute flatly prohibiting the use of contraceptives, not one regulating their distribution. I simply cannot believe that the limitation on the class of lawful distributors has significantly impaired the right to use contraceptives in Massachusetts. . . .

Case Questions

1. Justice Brennan (for the majority) claims to be rejecting this statute not by means of the compelling interest test but rather by means of the reasonableness test. Because the statute does not regulate the uses to which married persons put contraceptives (see footnote 3), he alleges that it cannot reasonably be viewed as a deterrent to fornication (out-of-wedlock sex). Suppose that Massachusetts *tightened* its regulations on contraceptives, allowing them to be prescribed by physicians only on receiving a signed oath from married persons to the effect that the devices would be used only with the marriage partner. If the state were also to ban all other distribution of contraceptives (e.g., for the purpose of preventing disease) and were to bring the penalties for contraceptive distribution into line with the penalties for fornication, would the Court majority's objections to this statute dissolve? After the Court

majority's description of the right of privacy of the unmarried individual in this case, is Massachusetts still free to impose on fornicators a $30 fine or 30 days in jail?

    2.   The Court majority informs the American public that "not all contraceptives are potentially dangerous." Justice Burger objects that judges are not supposed to be telling legislatures what objects they may and may not consider dangerous or needful of medical advice. Is the Court overstepping its bounds on this point? Is this decision comprehensible without reference to the compelling interest test? Is that the difference between Justice White's opinion and the majority opinion?

    3.   Are married and unmarried persons in fact, "similarly situated" for purposes of this case? Even in light of the majority's concession that a state could constitutionally "regard the problems of extramarital and premarital sexual relations as 'evils of different dimensions and proportions' "?

    4.   Brennan asserts that he does not have to answer the "important question" whether a state may, on the grounds that contraception itself is immoral, constitutionally aim to abolish contraceptive practices as such. His reason for this assertion is not easy to follow. He seems to say there are two all-inclusive possibilities, and either one vitiates the need to answer the question. One is that *Griswold* implicitly prohibited statutes forbidding the distribution (as well as the use) of contraceptives for married persons. And if married persons' "rights of privacy" includes the right to receive contraceptives, then unmarried persons must have the same right. His grounds for this conclusion is that the "right of privacy" acknowledged in *Griswold* "is the right of the *individual*, married or single, to be free from unwarranted governmental intrusion into matters so fundamentally affecting a person as the decision whether to bear or beget a child." Does this follow from *Griswold*? Does it, in fact, contradict much of the logic of *Griswold*? The other possibility, as Brennan sees it, is that the equal protection clause itself bars making such a distinction between the married and the unmarried if contraception per se is viewed as the evil to be attacked. He claims that in the light of the purpose of the statute, such a distinction would be sheerly arbitrary. Is that conclusion really plausible after the Court in *Griswold* asserted that the married couple has a constitutional right to use birth control?

    5.   Would Justice Douglas's argument apply equally to a lecturer who, as part of a lecture advocating legalization of all drugs, handed out a few samples of heroin, cocaine, and Ecstasy?

    6.   Besides contraception and abortion, what other matters are "so fundamentally affecting a person as the decision whether to bear or beget a child"? Would they include the decision to engage in private, consensual sodomy? In a 1986 decision, *Bowers v. Hardwick* (478 U.S. 186), Justice White, writing for a majority of five, said,

None of the rights announced in [cases like *Griswold* and *Eisenstadt*] bears any resemblance to the claimed constitutional right of homosexuals to engage in sodomy.... [A]ny claim that these cases ... stand for the proposition that any kind of private sexual conduct between consenting adults is constitutionally insulated from state proscription is insupportable.

Justice Blackmun, writing for the four dissenters, asserted to the contrary, "The right of an individual to conduct intimate relationships in the intimacy of his or her own home seems to me to be at the heart of the Constitution's protection of privacy." Which is a more accurate depiction of the theme of these precedents?

7. Does the right to privacy cover commercial prostitution?

CASE NOTE: EXTENSIONS OF THE RIGHT OF SEXUAL PRIVACY

In a follow-up 1977 case, *Carey v. Population Services International* (431 U.S. 678), the Supreme Court reaffirmed the basic intent of the *Eisenstadt* decision and extended its reasoning to the situation of unmarried minors under the age of 16. Justices White and Stevens provided the crucial votes in declaring void a New York statute that prohibited the distribution of contraceptives to single persons under sixteen years of age. Justices Brennan, Stewart, Marshall, and Blackmun would have held the statute void on somewhat more sweeping grounds (and Justice Powell would have concurred on more narrow grounds). But the decisive opinions of White and Stevens maintained that the law was unconstitutional essentially because, as Brennan had put it in *Eisenstadt*, "It would be plainly unreasonable to assume that [the state] has prescribed pregnancy and the birth of an unwanted child as punishment for fornication...." The statute thus failed even the "rationality" test.

In 2003 in *Lawrence v. Texas* the Supreme Court overruled *Bowers v. Hardwick* (mentioned in Q.6 above) and put intimate relations within same-sex couples into the right of privacy.

LEGALIZING ABORTION

The years 1971 to 1973 witnessed an explosion of women's rights developments at the Supreme Court level. The year 1971 began slowly with *Ida Phillips v. Martin-Marietta* (see Chapter 3) in January. The 1971–72 term accelerated the pace, with *Reed v. Reed* (Chapter 2), *Eisenstadt v. Baird*, and *Stanley v. Illinois* (Chapter 5) in quick succession. The 1972–73 term continued the fast pace as the Court decided *Frontiero v. Richardson* (Chapter 2) and two abortion cases, *Roe v. Wade* and *Doe v. Bolton*.

The two abortion decisions were handed down together on January 22, 1973. That event was indisputably the most powerful single blast of this series, whether measured by the number of lives affected,[37] the intensity with which they were affected, or the political aftermath of the decisions. None of the other women's rights decisions has produced the political backlash that the double-barreled abortion decision produced. None has aroused a comparable intensity of political debate. None single-handedly invalidated so many state laws.

The judicial decision to legalize abortion did not occur in a political vacuum. Political activism on behalf of the legalization of abortion, spearheaded by such women's rights groups as NOW (the National Organizatgion for Women) and the National Women's Political Caucus, reached its peak a year before the Supreme Court's flurry of activity in behalf of women began.

The calendar year of 1970 seems to have been both a turning point and a stopping point for the effort to achieve the legalization of abortion by pressing for legislative action. That year witnessed the legalization of abortion in four states (Hawaii, Alaska, New York, and Washington), two of those involving highly dramatic battles in which legalization was nearly defeated. In Alaska, the legislative decision to legalize was vetoed by the governor. His veto was overridden with one vote to spare. In New York State, the pro-legalization forces, having barely lost in the assembly on previous votes, believed that they were facing defeat until Assemblyman George Michaels rose to his feet with the announcement that although he knew this would end his political career, he was going to change his vote from negative to positive.[38] His shift provided the winning margin in the legislature.

In addition to those victories, the pro-legalization forces attained a number of near-misses in 1970. The Arizona House approved a legalization statute in February, only to have it defeated in the Arizona Senate. The Maryland legislature approved legalization in April, only to have the bill vetoed by Governor Marvin Mandel in May. And the lower house in Vermont approved a legalization bill, only to have it rebuffed in Vermont's Senate. Although the legislative effort succeeded in only four states, the impact of those changes should not be underestimated. These four states were breaking radically with a century-old tradition of harshly punitive treatment of abortion. Naturally, such a dramatic break with the past aroused strong feelings on both sides of the controversy. The issue did not disappear in these four states after legislation.

Judicial activity in the direction of legalization of abortion also took a great leap forward around this time. The abortion laws of California, Texas, Wisconsin, Georgia, and the District of Columbia were declared unconstitutional in lower courts in late 1969 and in 1970, on the basis of *Griswold*. In 1970 the U.S. Supreme Court refused to accept jurisdiction to review the California and Wisconsin decisions, thereby leaving those states without valid abortion statutes. The Court did agree to review the Washington, D.C., decision, which had ruled that the District of Columbia's statute was void because of vagueness. That statute permitted abortions when the mother's "health" required, and the District Court held that the word "health" was so vague that it did not give fair warning to the physician about what was and was not punishable. (Lack of such warning constitutes denial of "due process of law.")

While the years 1971 and 1972 saw an acceleration of activity on the judicial front, legislative momentum slowed to a standstill. The latter can perhaps be explained by the fact that the vigorous lobbying activity—picketing, demonstrating, letter writing, testifying—of the pro-legalization groups eventually stimulated an equally active counter-lobby of anti-abortion groups. For example, on April 15, 1972, 10,000 people (mostly women) marched down Fifth Avenue in New York City to demand repeal of New York's permissive abortion law.[39] This counter-lobby succeeded in the New York State legislature, but Governor Nelson Rockefeller vetoed their repeal bill.

Meanwhile, the judiciary was proving a more fruitful lobbying target for the proponents of legalization. In January 1971, a federal District Court in Illinois declared that state's abortion law to be an unconstitutional invasion of the right to privacy (following *Griswold*). In 1972, the abortion laws of Florida, New Jersey, and Connecticut met a similar fate. The Connecticut case had been launched, in almost classic interest-group fashion, by a total of 838 women of childbearing age. By the end of 1972, then, eight states had lost their abortion laws at the hands of judges.

The U.S. Supreme Court by this time had entered the fray. In April 1971 it decided the District of Columbia case,[40] but at that point the signals the Court was emitting about its future direction were ambiguous. The Court held that the District of Columbia statute prohibiting abortion except where necessary for the mother's life or "health" was not void for vagueness. In interpreting "health," however, the Court said that the statute obviously included considerations of mental and emotional health. And the Court seemed to imply that the word "necessary" should be read as "medically appropriate" rather than as "essential." Thus, although the Court *did* uphold an anti-abortion statute, it did so with an interpretation that substantially liberalized the statutory permission for abortions.

Roe v. Wade (1973) and *Doe v. Bolton* (1973)

In May 1971 the Supreme Court docketed for the fall calendar the appeals of the 1970 abortion cases from Texas and Georgia (*Roe v. Wade* and *Doe v. Bolton*). In December 1971 it heard the arguments from counsel in those cases. In March 1972 the Court handed down *Eisenstadt v. Baird* in words, as we have noted, that foreshadowed the legalization of abortion.[41] In June 1972 the Court announced that the abortion cases would be scheduled for reargument the following fall. Because of the loss of Justices Black and Harlan, the Court had had only seven members at the time of the first arguments. In a decision as momentous as the abortion one was going to be, the Court did not want to appear shorthanded. With Justices Rehnquist and Powell filling out the Court, the abortion cases were reargued on October 11, 1972.

The two abortion cases treated challenges to anti-abortion statutes by two women using pseudonyms, Jane Roe and Mary Doe. Each challenged the statute on behalf of herself "and others similarly situated"; thus, these were class-action suits.

Jane Roe was an unmarried pregnant woman who desired an abortion in Texas, where all abortions were forbidden except "for the purpose of saving the life of the mother." The majority of states had abortion laws that followed the Texas pattern. She initiated her lawsuit in March 1970. Roe gave birth before the protracted court process yielded a decision, and placed the child up for adoption.[42] In later years, Roe revealed her name to be Norma McCorvey, and decided her pro-choice involvement had been a mistake. She became an evangelical Christian, and later converted to Catholicism. Due to her newfound faith, McCorvey became a prominent advocate for pro-life groups until her death in 2017.[43]

Mary Doe was a 22-year-old married resident of Georgia who already had three children and was once again pregnant, and has since disputed that she sought to terminate her fourth pregnancy. Revealed as Sandra Cano, she, too, became a vocal supporter and advocate for pro-life groups prior to her death. The *Doe* case challenged a Georgia law that permitted abortions only for Georgia residents, in an accredited hospital, upon the decision of three licensed physicians and a hospital staff abortion committee that determined that (1) continued pregnancy would endanger the pregnant woman's life or "seriously and permanently" injure her health; (2) the fetus would "very likely be born with a grave, permanent, and irremediable mental or physical defect"; or (3) the pregnancy resulted from rape or incest.[44] This law was modeled after the American Legal Institute's recommended abortion code.

Both women had prevailed at the district court level against the attorney general of the state in question. The basis of the district courts' decisions had been the *Griswold* right of privacy, and each district court had issued a declaratory judgment to the effect that the statutes in question were unconstitutional. But both women nonetheless appealed to the Supreme Court, because in each case the district court had declared the particular statutes unconstitutional but had refused to grant the women's request that all future criminal sanctions on abortion be enjoined.

By January 1973, when the Supreme Court handed down its decisions, naturally neither woman was still pregnant. For that reason, nothing that the Court could say would change the outcome for them. A situation such as this is ordinarily considered "moot," and the Court, as a rule, refuses to decide moot cases (because they do not present a concrete "controversy" but are closer to disputes of opinion). Here the Supreme Court made an exception and held that both Roe and Doe had standing to challenge the statutes. Justice Blackmun, writing for the majority, explained this decision as follows:

> The usual rule in federal cases is that an actual controversy must exist at stages of appellate or certiorari review, and not simply at the date the action is initiated. [Case citations omitted.]
>
> But when, as here, pregnancy is a significant fact in the litigation, the normal 266-day human gestation period is so short that the pregnancy will come to term before the usual appellate process is complete. If that termination makes a case moot, pregnancy litigation seldom will survive much beyond the trial stage and appellate review will be effectively denied. Our law should not be that rigid. Pregnancy often comes more than once to the same woman....Pregnancy provides a classic justification for a conclusion of nonmootness. It truly could be "capable of repetition, yet evading review...." (*Roe v. Wade*, 410 U.S. 113, 125)

Although Blackmun, writing for the Court majority (consisting of Burger, Douglas, Brennan, Stewart, Marshall, Powell, and himself), issued a separate opinion for each of the two cases, Douglas, Burger, and White (the latter dissenting on behalf of Rehnquist and himself) wrote additional opinions that applied to the combination of the two cases. For this reason, we have consolidated the two cases. The two majority opinions appear together first, and these are followed by the concurring opinions and the dissents.

ROE V. WADE
AND
DOE V. BOLTON
410 U.S. 113 (1973);
410 U.S. 179 (1973)

MR. JUSTICE BLACKMUN delivered the opinion of the Court [for *Roe v. Wade*].

* * *

We forthwith acknowledge our awareness of the sensitive and emotional nature of the abortion controversy, of the vigorous opposing views, even among physicians, and of the deep and seemingly absolute convictions that the subject inspires. One's philosophy, one's experiences, one's religious training, one's attitudes toward life and family and their values, and the moral standards one establishes and seeks to observe, are all likely to influence and to color one's thinking and conclusions about abortion.

In addition, population growth, pollution, poverty, and racial overtones tend to complicate and not to simplify the problem.

Our task, of course, is to resolve the issue by constitutional measurement, free of emotion and of predilection. We seek earnestly to do this, and, because we do, we have inquired into, and in this opinion place some emphasis upon, medical and medical-legal history and what that history reveals about man's attitudes toward the abortion procedure over the centuries. . . .

V

The principal thrust of appellant's attack on the Texas statutes is that they improperly invade a right, said to be possessed by the pregnant woman, to choose to terminate her pregnancy. Appellant would discover this right in the concept of personal "liberty" embodied in the Fourteenth Amendment's Due Process Clause; or in personal, marital, familial, and sexual privacy said to be protected by the Bill of Rights or its penumbras, see *Griswold v. Connecticut*, 381 U.S. 479 (1965); *Eisenstadt v. Baird*, 405 U.S. 438 (1972); *id.*, at 460 (WHITE, J., concurring in result); or among those rights reserved to the people by the Ninth Amendment, *Griswold v. Connecticut*, 381 U.S., at 486 (GOLDBERG, J., concurring). Before addressing this claim, we feel it desirable briefly to survey, in several aspects, the history of abortion, for such insight as that history may afford us, and then to examine the state purposes and interests behind the criminal abortion laws.

VI

It perhaps is not generally appreciated that the restrictive criminal abortion laws in effect in a majority of States today are of relatively recent vintage. Those laws, generally proscribing abortion or its attempt at any time during pregnancy except when necessary to preserve that pregnant woman's life, are not of ancient or even of common-law origin. Instead, they derive from statutory changes effected, for the most part, in the latter half of the 19th century.

1. *Ancient attitudes.* These are not capable of precise determination. . . .[A]bortion was practiced in Greek times as well as in the Roman Era,[9] and. . ."it was resorted to without scruple."[10] . . .If abortion was prosecuted in some places, it seems to have been based on a concept of a violation of the father's right to his offspring. Ancient religion did not bar abortion.[12]

2. *The Hippocratic Oath.* What then of the famous Oath that has stood so long as the ethical guide of the medical profession and that bears the name of the great Greek (460(?)–377(?) B.C.), who has been described as the Father of Medicine. . .? The Oath was not uncontested even in Hippocrates' day; only the Pythagorean school of philosophers frowned upon the related act of suicide. Most Greek thinkers, on the other hand, commended abortion, at least prior to viability. See Plato, *Republic*, V. 461; Aristotle, *Politics*, VII, 1335b 25. For the Pythagoreans, however, it was a matter of dogma. For them the embryo was animate from the moment of conception, and abortion meant destruction of a living being. The abortion clause of the Oath, therefore, "echoes Pythagorean doctrines," and "[i]n no other stratum of Greek opinion were such views held or proposed in the same spirit of uncompromising austerity."[17] . . .But with the end of antiquity a decided change took place. Resistance against suicide and against abortion became common. The Oath came to be popular. The emerging teachings of Christianity were in agreement with the Pythagorean ethic. The Oath "became the nucleus of all medical ethics" and "was applauded as the embodiment of truth.". . .[19]

This. . .enables us to understand, in historical context, a long-accepted and revered statement of medical ethics.

3. *The common law.* It is undisputed that at common law, abortion performed *before* "quickening"—the first recognizable movement of the fetus *in utero*, appearing usually from the 16th to the 18th week of pregnancy—was not an indictable offense. . .Christian theology and the canon law came to fix the point of animation at 40 days for a male and 80 days for a female, a view

that persisted until the 19th century, [but] there was otherwise little agreement about the precise time of formation or animation. There was agreement, however, that prior to this point the fetus was to be regarded as part of the mother, and its destruction, therefore, was not homicide. . . . Bracton focused upon quickening as the critical point. The significance of quickening was echoed by later common-law scholars and found its way into the received common law in this country.

Whether abortion of a *quick* fetus was a felony at common law, or even a lesser crime, is still disputed. . . . A recent review of the common-law precedents argues. . .that those precedents contradict Coke and that even post-quickening abortion was never established as a common-law crime[26]. . . . [I]t now appear[s] doubtful that abortion was ever firmly established as a common-law crime even with respect to the destruction of a quick fetus.

4. *The English statutory law*. England's first criminal abortion statute. Lord Ellenborough's Act, 43 Geo.3, c.58, came in 1803. It made abortion of a quick fetus, § 1, a capital crime, but in § 2 it provided lesser penalties for the felony of abortion before quickening, and thus preserved the "quickening" distinction. . . . [J. BLACKMUN traces British abortion law up to the present. As of 1967 British law was similar to the Georgia statute treated in *Doe v. Bolton*.]

5. *The American law*. In this country, the law in effect in all but a few States until mid-19th century was the pre-existing English common law. Connecticut, the first State to enact abortion legislation, adopted in 1821 that part of Lord Ellenborough's Act that related to a woman "quick with child." The death penalty was not imposed. Abortion before quickening was made a crime in that State only in 1860. In 1828, New York enacted legislation that, in two respects, was to serve as a model for early anti-abortion statutes. First, while barring destruction of an unquickened fetus as well as a quick fetus, it made the former only a misdemeanor, but the latter second-degree manslaughter. Second, it incorporated a concept of therapeutic abortion by providing that an abortion was excused if it "shall have been necessary to preserve the life of such mother, or shall have been advised by two physicians to be necessary for such purpose." By 1840, when Texas had received the common law, only eight American States had statutes dealing with abortion. It was not until after the War Between the States that legislation began generally to replace the common law. Most of these initial statutes dealt severely with abortion after quickening but were lenient with it before quickening. Most punished attempts equally with completed abortions. While many statutes included the exception for an abortion thought by one or more physicians to

be necessary to save the mother's life, that provision soon disappeared and the typical law required that the procedure actually be necessary for that purpose.

Gradually, in the middle and late 19th century the quickening distinction disappeared from the statutory law of most States and the degree of the offense and the penalties were increased. By the end of the 1950's, a large majority of the jurisdictions banned abortion, however and whenever performed, unless done to save or preserve the life of the mother. . . .In the past several years, however, a trend toward liberalizaton of abortion statutes has resulted in adoption, by about one-third of the States, of less stringent laws, most of them patterned after the ALI Model Penal Code. . . .

It is thus apparent that at common law, at the time of the adoption of our Constitution, and throughout the major portion of the 19th century, abortion was viewed with less disfavor than under most American statutes currently in effect. Phrasing it another way, a woman enjoyed a substantially broader right to terminate a pregnancy than she does in most States today. At least with respect to the early stage of pregnancy, and very possibly without such a limitation, the opportunity to make this choice was present in this country well into the 19th century. Even later, the law continued for some time to treat less punitively an abortion procured in early pregnancy.

6. *The position of the American Medical Association.* [This section reviews AMA committee reports of 1857 and 1871 condemning abortion and calling "the attention of the clergy of all denominations to the perverted views of morality entertained by a large class of females—aye, and men also, on this important question." It then describes the liberalizaton of AMA positions in 1967 and 1970.]

7. *The position of the American Public Health Association.* In October 1970, the Executive Board of the APHA adopted Standards for Abortion Services. These [urged:] "Rapid and simple abortion referral must be readily available through state and local public health departments, medical societies, or other nonprofit organizations. . . ."(Recommended Standards for Abortion Services, 61 *Am. J. Pub. Health* 396 [1971]). . .It was said that at present abortions should be performed by physicians or osteopaths who are licensed to practice and who have "adequate training." *Id.*, at 398.

8. *The position of the American Bar Association.* At its meeting in February 1972 the ABA House of Delegates approved, with 17 opposing votes, the Uniform Abortion Act. . . .We set forth the Act in full in the margin . . . [This model ordinance, the full version of which is omitted here, limited abortions

to the first twenty weeks of pregnancy, and to operations performed by licensed physicians in licensed facilities. After twenty weeks they would be permitted only if there were "substantial risk" (i) to the mother's life or of "grave impair(ment)" to the "physical or mental health of the mother" or (ii) "of grave physical or mental defect" to the child, or (iii) "that the pregnancy resulted from rape or incest, or illicit intercourse with a girl under the age of 16 years." Violations would be a felony punishable by five years in prison.—AU.]

VII

Three reasons have been advanced to explain historically the enactment of criminal abortion laws in the 19th century and to justify their continued existence.

It has been argued occasionally that these laws were the product of a Victorian social concern to discourage illicit sexual conduct. Texas, however, does not advance this justification in the present case, and it appears that no court or commentator has taken the argument seriously. The appellants and *amici* contend, moreover, that this is not a proper state purpose at all and suggest that, if it were, the Texas statutes are overbroad in protecting it since the law fails to distinguish between married and unwed mothers.

A second reason is concerned with abortion as a medical procedure. When most criminal abortion laws were first enacted, the procedure was a hazardous one for the woman. This was particularly true prior to the development of antisepsis. Antiseptic techniques. . .were not generally accepted and employed until about the turn of the century. Abortion mortality was high. Even after 1900, and perhaps until as late as the development of antibiotics in the 1940's, standard modern techniques such as dilation and curettage were not nearly so safe as they are today. Thus, it has been argued that a State's real concern in enacting a criminal abortion law was to protect the pregnant woman, that is, to restrain her from submitting to a procedure that placed her life in serious jeopardy.

Modern medical techniques have altered this situation. Appellants and various *amici* refer to medical data indicating that abortion in early pregnancy, that is, prior to the end of the first trimester, although not without its risk, is now relatively safe. Mortality rates for women undergoing early abortions, where the procedure is legal, appear to be as low as or lower than the rates for normal childbirth. Consequently, any interest of the State in protecting the woman from an inherently hazardous procedure, except when it would be equally dangerous for her to forgo it, has largely disappeared. Of course, important state interests in the areas of health and medical standards do remain. The State has a legitimate interest in seeing to it that abortion, like any other medical procedure, is performed under circumstances that insure maximum safety for the patient. This interest obviously extends at least to the performing physician and his staff, to the facilities involved, to the availability of after-care, and to adequate provision for any complication or emergency that might arise....Moreover, the risk to the woman increases as her pregnancy continues. Thus, the State retains a definite interest in protecting the woman's own health and safety when an abortion is proposed at a late stage of pregnancy.

The third reason is the State's interest—some phrase it in terms of duty—in protecting prenatal life. Some of the argument for this justification rests on the theory that a new human life is present from the moment of conception. The State's interest and general obligation to protect life then extends, it is argued, to prenatal life.... Logically, of course, a legitimate state interest in this area need not stand or fall on acceptance of the belief that life begins at conception or at some other point prior to live birth. In assessing the State's interest, recognition may be given to the less rigid claim that as long as at least *potential* life is involved, the State may assert interests beyond the protection of the pregnant woman alone.

Parties challenging state abortion laws have sharply disputed in some courts the contention that a purpose of these laws, when enacted, was to protect prenatal life....[and] they claim that most state laws were designed solely to protect the woman. Because medical advances have lessened this concern, at least with respect to abortion in early pregnancy, they argue that with respect to such abortions the laws can no longer be justified by any state interest. There is some scholarly support for this view of original purpose. The few state courts called upon to interpret their laws in the late 19th and early 20th centuries did focus on the State's interest in protecting the woman's health rather than in preserving the embryo and fetus. Proponents of this view point out that in many States, including Texas, by statute or judicial interpretation, the pregnant woman herself could not be prosecuted for self-abortion or for cooperating in an abortion performed upon her by another. They claim that adoption of the "quickening" distinction through received common law and state statutes tacitly recognizes the greater health hazards inherent in the late abortion and impliedly repudiates the theory that life begins at conception....

VIII

The Constitution does not explicitly mention any right of privacy. In a line of decisions, however, going back perhaps as far as *Union Pacific R. Co. v. Botsford*, 141 U.S. 250, 251 (1891), the Court has recognized that a right of personal privacy, or a guarantee of certain areas or zones of privacy, does exist under the Constitution. In varying contexts, the Court or individual Justices have, indeed, found at least the roots of that right in the First Amendment, *Stanley v. Georgia*, 394 U.S. 557, 564 (1969); in the Fourth and Fifth Amendments, *Terry v. Ohio*, 392 U.S. 1, 8–9 (1968), *Katz v. United States*, 389 U.S. 347, 350 (1967), *Boyd v. United States*, 116 U.S. 616 (1886), see *Olmstead v. United States*, 277 U.S. 438, 478 (1928) (Brandeis, J., dissenting); in the penumbras of the Bill of Rights, *Griswold v. Connecticut*, 381 U.S., at 484–885: in the Ninth Amendment, *id.*, at 486 (GOLDBERG, J., concurring); or in the concept of liberty guaranteed by the first section of the Fourteenth Amendment, see *Meyer v. Nebraska*, 262 U.S. 390, 399 (1923). These decisions made it clear that only personal rights that can be deemed "fundamental" or "implicit in the concept of ordered liberty," *Palko v. Connecticut*, 302 U.S. 319, 325 (1937), are included in this guarantee of personal privacy. They also make it clear that the right has some extension to activities relating to marriage, *Loving v. Virginia*, 388 U.S. 1, 12 (1967); procreation, *Skinner v. Oklahoma*, 316 U.S. 535, 541–42 (1942); contraception, *Eisenstadt v. Baird*, 405 U.S., at 453–54; id., at 460, 463–65 (WHITE, J., concurring in result); family relationships, *Prince v. Massachusetts*, 321 U.S. 158, 166 (1944); and child rearing and education, *Pierce v. Society of Sisters*, 268 U.S. 510, 535 (1925), *Meyer v. Nebraska*.

This right of privacy, whether it be founded in the Fourteenth Amendment's concept of personal liberty and restrictions upon state action, as we feel it is, or, as the District Court determined, in the Ninth Amendment's reservation of rights to the people, is broad enough to encompass a woman's decision whether or not to terminate her pregnancy. The detriment that the State would impose upon the pregnant woman by denying this choice altogether is apparent. Specific and direct harm medically diagnosable even in early pregnancy may be involved. Maternity, or additional offspring, may force upon the woman a distressful life and future. Psychological harm may be imminent. Mental and physical health may be taxed by child care. There is also the distress, for all concerned, associated with the unwanted child, and there is the problem of bringing a child into a family already unable, psychologically and otherwise, to care for it. In other cases, as in this one, the additional difficulties and continuing stigma of unwed motherhood may be involved. All these are factors the woman and her responsible physician necessarily will consider in consultation.

On the basis of elements such as these, appellant and some *amici* argue that the woman's right is absolute and that she is entitled to terminate her pregnancy at whatever time, in whatever way, and for whatever reason she alone chooses. With this we do not agree. Appellant's arguments that Texas either has no valid interest at all in regulating the abortion decision, or no interest strong enough to support any limitation upon the woman's sole determination, are unpersuasive. The Court's decisions recognizing a right of privacy also acknowledge that some regulation in areas protected by that right is appropriate. As noted above, a State may properly assert important interests in safeguarding health, in maintaining medical standards, and in protecting potential life. At some point in pregnancy, these respective interests become sufficiently compelling to sustain regulation of the factors that govern the abortion decision. The privacy right involved, therefore, cannot be said to be absolute. In fact, it is not clear to us that the claim asserted by some *amici* that one has an unlimited right to do with one's body as one pleases bears a close relationship to the right of privacy previously articulated in the Court's decisions. The Court has refused to recognize an unlimited right of this kind in the past. *Jacobson v. Massachusetts*, 197 U.S. 11 (1905) (vaccination); *Buck v. Bell*, 274 U.S. 200 (1927) (sterilization).

We, therefore, conclude that the right of personal privacy includes the abortion decision, but that this right is not unqualified and must be considered against important state interests in regulation. . . .[This] right, nonetheless, is not absolute and is subject to some limitations; and. . .at some point the state interests as to protection of health, medical standards, and prenatal life, become dominant. . . .

Where certain "fundamental rights" are involved, the Court has held that regulation limiting these rights may be justified only by a "compelling state interest," *Kramer v. Union Free School District*, 395 U.S. 621, 627 (1969); *Shapiro v. Thompson*, 394 U.S. 618, 634 (1969); *Sherbert v. Verner*, 374 U.S. 398, 406 (1963), and that legislative enactments must be narrowly drawn to express only the legitimate state interests at stake. *Griswold v. Connecticut*, 381 U.S., at 485; *Aptheker v. Secretary of State*, 378 U.S. 500, 508 (1964); *Cantwell v. Connecticut*, 310 U.S. 296, 307–8 (1940); see *Eisenstadt v. Baird*, 405 U.S., at 460, 463–64 (WHITE, J., concurring in result).

In the recent abortion cases . . . courts have recognized these principles. Those striking down state laws have generally scrutinized the State's interests in protecting health and potential life, and have concluded that neither interest justified broad limitations on the reasons for which a physician and his pregnant patient might decide that she should have an abortion in the early stages of pregnancy. Courts sustaining state laws have held that the State's determinations to protect health or prenatal life are dominant and constitutionally justifiable.

IX

The District Court held that the appellee failed to meet his burden of demonstrating that the Texas statute's infringement upon Roe's rights was necessary to support a compelling state interest, and that, although the appellee presented "several compelling justifications for state presence in the area of abortions," the statutes outstripped these justifications and swept "far beyond any areas of compelling state interest." 314 F. Supp., at 1222–23. Appellant and appellee both contest that holding. Appellant, as has been indicated, claims an absolute right that bars any state imposition of criminal penalties in the area. Appellee argues that the State's determination to recognize and protect prenatal life from and after conception constitutes a compelling state interest. As noted above, we do not agree fully with either formulation.

A. The appellee and certain *amici* argue that the fetus is a "person" within the language and meaning of the Fourteenth Amendment. In support of this, they outline at length and in detail the well-known facts of fetal development. If this suggestion of personhood is established, the appellant's case, of course, collapses, for the fetus' right to life would then be guaranteed specifically by the Amendment. . .[but] no case [can] be cited that holds that a fetus is a person within the meaning of the Fourteenth Amendment.

The Constitution does not define "person" in so many words. Section 1 of the Fourteenth Amendment contains three references to "person." The first, in defining "citizens," speaks of "persons born or naturalized in the United States.". . ."Person" is used in other places in the Constitution. . . .But in nearly all these instances, the use of the word is such that it has application only postnatally. None indicates, with any assurance, that it has any possible prenatal application.

All this, together with our observation, that throughout the major portion of the 19th century prevailing legal abortion practices were far freer than they are today, persuades us that the word "person," as used in the Fourteenth Amendment, does not include the unborn. This is in accord with the results reached in those few cases where the issue has been squarely presented. [He cites seven lower court cases and one Supreme Court case of indirect reference, *U.S. v. Vuitch*, 402 U.S. 62 (1971).]

B. The pregnant woman cannot be isolated in her privacy. She carries an embryo and, later, a fetus....The situation therefore is inherently different from marital intimacy, or bedroom possession of obscene material, or marriage, or procreation, or education, with which *Eisenstadt* and *Griswold*, *Stanley*, *Loving*, *Skinner*, and *Pierce* and *Meyer* were respectively concerned. As we have intimated above, it is reasonable and appropriate for a State to decide that at some point in time another interest, that of health of the mother or that of potential human life, becomes significantly involved. The woman's privacy is no longer sole and any right of privacy she possesses must be measured accordingly.

Texas urges that, apart from the Fourteenth Amendment, life begins at conception and is present throughout pregnancy, and that, therefore, the State has a compelling interest in protecting that life from and after conception. We need not resolve the difficult question of when life begins. When those trained in the respective disciplines of medicine, philosophy, and theology are unable to arrive at any consensus, the judiciary, at this point in the development of man's knowledge, is not in a position to speculate as to the answer.

It should be sufficient to note briefly the wide divergence of thinking on this most sensitive and difficult question. There has always been strong support for the view that life does not begin until live birth. This was the belief of the Stoics. It appears to be the predominant, though not the unanimous, attitude of the Jewish faith. It may be taken to represent also the position of a large segment of the Protestant community, insofar as that can be ascertained; organized groups that have taken a formal position on the abortion issue have generally regarded abortion as a matter for the conscience of the individual and her family. As we have noted, the common law found greater significance in quickening. Physicians and their scientific colleagues have regarded that event with less interest and have tended to focus either upon conception, upon live birth, or upon the interim point at which the fetus becomes "viable," that is, potentially able to live outside the mother's womb, albeit with artificial aid. Viability is usually placed at about seven months (28 weeks) but may occur earlier, even at 24 weeks....[The Roman Catholic Church] would recognize the existence of life from the moment of conception....As one brief *amicus* discloses, this is a view strongly held by many non-Catholics as well, and by many physicians. Substantial problems for precise definition of this view are posed, however, by new embryological data that purport to indicate that conception is a "process" over time, rather than an event, and by new medical techniques such as menstrual extraction, the "morning-after" pill, implantation of embryos, artificial insemination, and even artificial wombs.

In areas other than criminal abortion, the law has been reluctant to endorse any theory that life, as we recognize it, begins before live birth or to accord legal rights to the unborn except in narrowly defined situations and except when the rights are contingent upon live birth. For example, the traditional rule of tort law denied recovery for prenatal injuries even though the child was born alive. That rule has been changed in almost every jurisdiction. In most States, recovery is said to be permitted only if the fetus was viable, or at least quick, when the injuries were sustained, though few courts have squarely so held. In a recent development, generally opposed by the commentators, some States permit the parents of a stillborn child to maintain an action for wrongful death because of prenatal injuries. Such an action, however, would appear to be one to vindicate the parents' interest and is thus consistent with the view that the fetus, at most, represents only the potentiality of life. . . .

X

In view of all this, we do not agree that, by adopting one theory of life, Texas may override the rights of the pregnant woman that are at stake. We repeat, however, that the State does have an important and legitimate interest in preserving and protecting the health of the pregnant woman, whether she be a resident of the State or a nonresident who seeks medical consultation and treatment there, and that it has still *another* important and legitimate interest in protecting the potentiality of human life. These interests are separate and distinct. Each grows in substantiality as the woman approaches term and, at a point during pregnancy, each becomes "compelling."

With respect the State's important and legitimate interest in the health of the mother, the "compelling" point, in the light of present medical knowledge, is at approximately the end of the first trimester. This is so because of the now-established medical fact, referred to above, that until the end of the first trimester mortality in abortion may be less than mortality in normal childbirth. It follows that, from and after this point, a State may regulate the abortion procedure to the extent that the regulation reasonably relates to the preservation and protection of maternal health. Examples of permissible state regulation in this area are requirements as to the qualifications of the person who is to perform the abortion; as to the licensure of that person; as to the facility in which the procedure is to be performed, that is, whether it must be a hospital or may be a clinic or some other place of less-than-hospital status; as to the licensing of the facility; and the like.

This means, on the other hand, that, for the period of pregnancy prior to this "compelling" point, the attending physician, in consultation with his patient, is free to determine, without regulation by the State, that, in his medical judgment, the patient's pregnancy should be terminated. If that decision is reached, the judgment may be effectuated by an abortion free of interference by the State.

With respect to the State's important and legitimate interest in potential life, the "compelling" point is at viability. This is so because the fetus then presumably has the capability of meaningful life outside the mother's womb. State regulation protective of fetal life after viability thus has both logical and biological justifications. If the State is interested in protecting fetal life after viability, it may go so far as to proscribe abortion during that period, except when it is necessary to preserve the life or health of the mother.

Measured against these standards, Art. 1196 of the Texas Penal Code, in restricting legal abortions to those "procured or attempted by medical advice for the purpose of saving the life of the mother," sweeps too broadly. The statute made no distinction between abortions performed early in pregnancy and those performed later, and it limits to a single reason, "saving" the mother's life, the legal justification for the procedure. The statute, therefore, cannot survive the constitutional attack made upon it here. . . .

XI

To summarize and to repeat:

1. A state criminal abortion statute of the current Texas type, that excepts from criminality only a *life-saving* procedure on behalf of the mother, without regard to pregnancy stage and without recognition of the other interests involved, is violative of the Due Process Clause of the Fourteenth Amendment.

(a) For the stage prior to approximately the end of the first trimester, the abortion decision and its effectuation must be left to the medical judgment of the pregnant woman's attending physician.

(b) For the stage subsequent to approximately the end of the first trimester, the State, in promoting its interest in the health of the mother, may, if it chooses, regulate the abortion procedure in ways that are reasonably related to maternal health.

(c) For the stage subsequent to viability, the State in promoting its interest in the potentiality of human life may, if it chooses, regulate, and even proscribe, abortion except where it is necessary, in appropriate medical judgment, for the preservation of the life or health of the mother.

2. The State may define the term "physician," as it has been employed in the preceding paragraphs of this Part XI of this opinion, to mean only a physician currently licensed by the State, and may proscribe any abortion by a person who is not a physician as so defined.

In *Doe v. Bolton* procedural requirements contained in one of the modern abortion statutes are considered. That opinion and this one, of course, are to be read together. . . .

Opinion Footnotes

9 J. Ricci, *The Genealogy of Gynaecology* 52, 84, 113, 149 (2d ed. 1950) (hereinafter Ricci); L. Lader, *Abortion* 75–77 (1966) (hereinafter Lader); K. Niswander, *Medical Abortion Practices in the United States in Abortion and the Law* 37, 38–40 (D. Smith ed. 1967); G. Williams, *The Sanctity of Life and the Criminal Law* 148 (1957) (hereinafter Williams); J. Noonan, *An Almost Absolute Value in History, in The Morality of Abortion* 1, 3–7 (J. Noonan ed. 1970) (hereinafter Noonan); Quay, *Justifiable Abortion—Medical and Legal Foundations* (pt. 2), 49 Geo. L. J. 395, 406–442 (1961) (hereinafter Quay).

10 L. Edelstein, *The Hippocratic Oath* 10 (1943) (hereinafter Edelstein).

12 Edelstein 13–14.

17 *Id.*, at 18; Lader 76.

19 *Id.*, at 64.

26 Means, "The Phoenix of Abortional Freedom: Is a Penumbral or Ninth-Amendment Right About to Arise from the Nineteenth-Century Legislative Ashes of a Fourteenth-Century Common-Law Liberty?" 17 *N.Y.L.F.* 335 (1971) (hereinafter Means II). . . .

MR. JUSTICE BLACKMUN delivered the opinion of the Court [for *Doe v. Bolton*].

* * *

A. . . .What is said [in *Roe*] is applicable here and need not be repeated.

B. . . .Appellants argue that . . .because it would be physically and emotionally damaging to Doe to bring a child into her poor, "fatherless" family, and because advances in medicine and medical techniques have made it safer for a woman to have a medically induced abortion than for her to bear a child,. . ."a statute that requires a woman to carry an unwanted pregnancy to term infringes not only on a fundamental right of privacy but on the right to life itself.". . . .

C. . . .The net result of the District Court's decision is that the abortion determination, so far as the physician is concerned, is made in the exercise of his professional, that is, his "best clinical," judgment in the light of all the attendant circumstances. . .

We agree with the District Court, 319 F. Supp., at 1058, that the medical judgment may be exercised in the light of all factors—physical, emotional, psychological, familial, and the woman's age—relevant to the well-being of the patient. All these factors may relate to health. This allows the attending physician the room he needs to make his best medical judgment. . . .

D. The appellants next argue that the District Court should have declared unconstitutional three procedural demands of the Georgia statute: (1) that the abortion be performed in a hospital accredited by the Joint Commission on Accreditation of Hospitals: (2) that the procedure be approved by the hospital staff abortion committee; and (3) that the performing physician's judgment be confirmed by the independent examinations of the patient by two other licensed physicians. . . .The physician-appellants also argue that, by subjecting a doctor's individual medical judgment to committee approval and to confirming consultations, the statute impermissibly restricts the physician's right to practice his profession and deprives him of due process.

1. *JCAH accreditation.* . . . In Georgia, there is no restriction on the performance of non-abortion surgery in a hospital not yet accredited by the JCAH [Joint Commission on the Accreditation of Hospitals] so long as other requirements imposed by the State, such as licensing of the hospital and of the operating surgeon, are met.

We hold that the JCAH-accreditation requirement does not withstand constitutional scrutiny in the present context. It is a requirement that simply is not "based on differences that are reasonably related to the purposes of the Act in which it is found." *Morey v. Doud,* 354 U.S. 457, 465 (1957).

This is not to say that Georgia may not or should not, from and after the end of the first trimester, adopt standards for licensing all facilities where abortions may be performed so long as those standards are legitimately related to the objective the State seeks to accomplish. The appellants contend that such a relationship would be lacking even in a lesser requirement that an abortion be performed in a licensed hospital, as opposed to a facility, such as a clinic, that may be required by the State to possess all the staffing and services necessary to perform an abortion safely (including those adequate to handle serious complications or other emergency, or arrangements with a nearby hospital to provide such services). Appellants and various *amici* have presented us with a mass of data purporting to demonstrate that some facilities other than hospitals are entirely adequate to perform abortions. . . . The State, on the other hand, has not presented persuasive data to show that only hospitals meet its acknowledged interest in insuring [safety]. . . . We hold that the hospital requirement of the Georgia law, because it fails to exclude the first trimester of pregnancy, see *Roe v. Wade*, is also invalid. . . .

2. *Committee approval.* The second aspect of the appellants' procedural attack relates to the hospital abortion committee. . . . Viewing the Georgia statute as a whole, we see no constitutionally justifiable pertinence in the structure for the advance approval . . . . We are not cited to any other surgical procedure made subject to committee approval as a matter of state criminal law. . . .

3. *Two-doctor concurrence.* Appellants' attack centers on the . . . required confirmation by two Georgia-licensed physicians in addition to the recommendation of the pregnant woman's own consultant (making under the statute, a total of six physicians involved, including the three on the hospital's abortion committee). We conclude that this provision, too, must fall.

. . . Again, no other voluntary medical or surgical procedure for which Georgia requires confirmation by two other physicians has been cited to us. If a physician is licensed by the State, he is recognized by the State as capable of exercising acceptable clinical judgment. . . .

E. The appellants attack the residency requirement of the Georgia law . . . as violative of the right to travel stressed in *Shapiro v. Thompson*, 394 U.S. 618, 629–31 (1969), and other cases. A requirement of this kind, of course, could be deemed to have some relationship to the availability of post-procedure medical care for the aborted patient.

Nevertheless, we do not uphold the constitutionality of the residence requirement. It is not based on any policy of preserving state-supported facilities for Georgia residents, for the bar also applies to private hospitals and to privately retained physicians. There is no intimation, either, that Georgia facilities are utilized to capacity in caring for Georgia residents. Just as the Privileges and Immunities Clause, Const. Art. IV, § 2, protects persons who enter other States to ply their trade, *Ward v. Maryland*, 12 Wall. 418, 430 (1871); *Blake v. McClung*, 172 U.S. 239, 248–56 (1898), so must it protect persons who enter Georgia seeking the medical services that are available there. See *Toomer v. Witsell*, 334 U.S. 385, 396–97 (1948). A contrary holding would mean that a State could limit to its own residents the general medical care available within its borders. This we could not approve. . . .

In summary, we hold that [these challenged provisions] . . .are all violative of the Fourteenth Amendment. . . .

MR. JUSTICE STEWART, concurring [in *Roe v. Wade*].

In 1963, this Court, in *Ferguson v. Skrupa*, 372 U.S. 726, purported to sound the death knell for the doctrine of substantive due process, a doctrine under which many state laws had in the past been held to violate the Fourteenth Amendment. As MR. JUSTICE BLACK'S opinion for the Court in *Skrupa* put it: "We have returned to the original constitutional proposition that courts do not substitute their social and economic beliefs for the judgment of legislative bodies, who are elected to pass laws." *Id.*, at 730.[1]

Barely two years later, in *Griswold v. Connecticut*, 381 U.S. 479, the Court held a Connecticut birth control law unconstitutional. In view of what had been so recently said in *Skrupa*, the Court's opinion in *Griswold* understandably did its best to avoid reliance on the Due Process Clause of the Fourteenth Amendment as the ground for decision. Yet, the Connecticut law did not violate any provision of the Bill of Rights, nor any specific provision of the Constitution.[2] So it was clear to me then, and it is equally clear to me now, that the *Griswold* decision can be rationally understood only as a holding that the Connecticut statute substantively invaded the "liberty" that is protected by the Due Process Clause of the Fourteenth Amendment. As so understood, *Griswold* stands as one in a long line of pre-*Skrupa* cases decided under the doctrine of substantive due process, and I now accept it as such. . . .The Constitution nowhere mentions a specific right of personal choice in matters of marriage and family life, but the "liberty" protected by the Due Process Clause of the Fourteenth Amendment covers more than those freedoms explicitly named in the Bill of Rights. See *Schware v. Board of Bar Examiners*, 353 U.S. 232, 238–39; *Pierce v. Society of Sisters*, 268 U.S. 510, 534–35; *Meyer v. Nebraska*, 262 U.S. 390, 399–400. Cf. *Shapiro v. Thompson*, 394 U.S. 618, 629–30; *United States v. Guest*, 383 U.S. 745, 757–58; *Carrington v. Rash*, 380 U.S. 89, 96; *Aptheker v. Secretary of State*, 378 U.S. 500, 505; *Kent v. Dulles*, 357 U.S. 116, 127; *Bolling v. Sharpe*, 347 U.S. 497, 499–500; *Truax v. Raich*, 239 U.S. 33, 41.

As MR. JUSTICE HARLAN once wrote: "[T]he full scope of the liberty guaranteed by the Due Process Clause cannot be found in or limited by the precise terms of the specific guarantees elsewhere provided in the Constitution. This 'liberty' is not a series of isolated points pricked out in terms of the taking of property; the freedom of speech, press, and religion; the right to keep and bear arms; the freedom from unreasonable searches and seizures; and so on. It is a rational continuum which, broadly speaking, includes a freedom from all substantial arbitrary impositions and purposeless restraints. . .and which also recognizes, what a reasonable and sensitive judgment must, that certain interests require particularly careful scrutiny of the state needs asserted to justify their abridgment." *Poe v. Ullman,* 367 U.S. 497, 543 (opinion dissenting from dismissal of appeal). In the words of MR. JUSTICE FRANKFURTER, "Great concepts like. . . 'liberty'. . . were purposely left to gather meaning from experience. For they relate to the whole domain of social and economic fact, and the statesmen who founded this Nation knew too well that only a stagnant society remains unchanged." *National Mutual Ins. Co. v. Tidewater Transfer Co.,* 337 U.S. 582, 646 (dissenting opinion).

Several decisions of this Court make clear that freedom of personal choice in matters of marriage and family life is one of the liberties protected by the Due Process Clause of the Fourteenth Amendment. *Loving v. Virginia,* 388 U.S. 1, 12; *Griswold v. Connecticut; Pierce v. Society of Sisters; Meyer v. Nebraska.* See also *Prince v. Massachusetts,* 321 U.S. 158, 166; *Skinner v. Oklahoma,* 316 U.S. 535, 541. As recently as last Term, in *Eisenstadt v. Baird,* 405 U.S. 438, 453, we recognized "the right of the *individual,* married or single, to be free from unwarranted governmental intrusion into matters so fundamentally affecting a person as the decision whether to bear or beget a child." That right necessarily includes the right of a woman to decide whether or not to terminate her pregnancy. "Certainly the interests of a woman in giving of her physical and emotional self during pregnancy and the interests that will be affected throughout her life by the birth and raising of a child are of a far greater degree of significance and personal intimacy than the right to send a child to private school protected in *Pierce v. Society of Sisters,* or the right to teach a foreign language protected in *Meyer v. Nebraska," Abele v. Markle,* 351 F. Supp. 224, 227 (Conn. 1972).

Clearly, therefore, the Court today is correct in holding that the right asserted by Jane Roe is embraced within the personal liberty protected by the Due Process Clause of the Fourteenth Amendment.

It is evident that the Texas abortion statute infringes that right directly. Indeed, it is difficult to imagine a more complete abridgment of a constitutional freedom than that worked by the inflexible criminal statute now in force in Texas. The question then becomes whether the state interests advanced to justify this abridgment can survive the "particularly careful scrutiny" that the Fourteenth Amendment here requires.

The asserted state interests are protection of the health and safety of the pregnant woman, and protection of the potential future human life within her. These are legitimate objectives, amply sufficient to permit a State to regulate abortions as it does other surgical procedures, and perhaps sufficient to permit a State to regulate abortions more stringently or even to prohibit them in the late stages of pregnancy. But such legislation is not before us, and I think the Court today has thoroughly demonstrated that these state interests cannot constitutionally support the broad abridgment of personal liberty worked by the existing Texas law. Accordingly, I join the Court's opinion holding that the law is invalid under the Due Process Clause of the Fourteenth Amendment.

Opinion Footnotes

1 Only MR. JUSTICE HARLAN failed to join the Court's opinion, 372 U.S., at 733.

2 There is no constitutional right of privacy, as such. "[The Fourth] Amendment protects individual privacy against certain kinds of governmental intrusion, but its protections go further, and often have nothing to do with privacy at all. Other provisions of the Constitution protect personal privacy from other forms of governmental invasions. But the protection of a person's general right to privacy—his right to be let alone by other people—is, like the protection of his property and of his very life, left largely to the law of the individual States." *Katz v. United States,* 389 U.S. 347, 350–51.

MR. CHIEF JUSTICE BURGER, concurring [for both *Roe* and *Doe*].

I agree that, under the Fourteenth Amendment to the Constitution, the abortion statutes of Georgia and Texas impermissibly limit the performance of abortions necessary to protect the health of pregnant women, using the term health in its broadest medical context. See *United States v. Vuitch,* 402 U.S. 62, 71–72 (1971). I am somewhat troubled that the Court has taken notice of various scientific and medical data in reaching its conclusion; however, I do not believe that the Court has exceeded the scope of judicial notice accepted in other contexts.

In oral argument, counsel for the State of Texas informed the Court that early abortion procedures were routinely permitted in certain exceptional cases, such as nonconsensual pregnancies resulting from rape and incest. In the face of a rigid and narrow statute, such as that of Texas, no one in these circumstances should be placed in a posture of dependence on a prosecutorial policy or prosecutorial discretion. Of course, States must have broad power, within the limits indicated in the opinion, to regulate the subject of abortions, but where the consequences of state intervention are so severe, uncertainty must be avoided as much as possible. For my part, I would be inclined to allow a State to require the certification of two physicians to support an abortion, but the Court holds otherwise. I do not believe that such a procedure is unduly burdensome, as are the complex steps of the Georgia statutes, which require as many as six doctors and the use of a hospital certified by the JCAH.

I do not read the Court's holdings today as having the sweeping consequences attributed to them by the dissenting Justices; the dissenting views discount the reality that the vast majority of physicians observe the standards of their profession, and act only on the basis of carefully deliberated medical judgments relating to life and health. Plainly, the Court today rejects any claim that the Constitution requires abortions on demand.

[Concurrence of JUSTICE DOUGLAS for both *Roe* and *Doe* omitted.]

MR. JUSTICE REHNQUIST, dissenting [in *Roe v. Wade*].

The Court's opinion brings to the decision of this troubling question both extensive historical fact and a wealth of legal scholarship. While the opinion thus commands my respect, I find myself nonetheless in fundamental disagreement with those parts of it that invalidate the Texas statute in question, and therefore dissent.

I

The Court's opinion decides that a State may impose virtually no restriction on the performance of abortions during the first trimester of pregnancy. Our previous decisions indicate that a necessary predicate for such an opinion is a plaintiff who was in her first trimester of pregnancy at some time during the pendency of her lawsuit. While a party may vindicate his own constitutional rights, he may not seek vindication for the rights of others. *Moose Lodge v. Irvis*, 407 U.S. 163 (1972); *Sierra Club v. Morris*, 405 U.S. 727 (1972). The Court's statement of facts in this case makes clear, however, that the record in no way indicates the presence of such a plaintiff. We know only that plaintiff Roe at the time of filing her complaint was a pregnant woman; for aught that appears in this record, she may have been in her *last* trimester of pregnancy as of the date the complaint was filed.

Nothing in the Court's opinion indicates that Texas might not constitutionally apply its proscription of abortion as written to a woman in that stage of pregnancy. Nonetheless, the Court uses her complaint against the Texas statute as a fulcrum for deciding that States may impose virtually no restrictions on medical abortions performed during the *first* trimester of pregnancy. In deciding such a hypothetical lawsuit, the Court departs from the longstanding admonition that it should never "formulate a rule of constitutional law broader than is required by the precise facts to which it is to be applied." *Liverpool, New York & Philadelphia S. S. Co. v. Commissioners of Emigration*, 113 U.S. 33, 39 (1885). See also *Ashwander v. TVA*, 297 U.S. 288, 345 (1936) (BRANDEIS, J., concurring).

II

Even if there were a plaintiff in this case capable of litigating the issue which the Court decides, I would reach a conclusion opposite to that reached by the Court. I have difficulty in concluding, as the Court does, that the right of "privacy" is involved in this case. Texas, by the statute here challenged, bars the performance of a medical abortion by a licensed physician on a plaintiff such as *Roe*. A transaction resulting in an operation such as this is not "private" in the ordinary usage of that word. Nor is the "privacy" that the Court finds here even a distant relative of the freedom from searches and seizures protected by the Fourth Amendment to the Constitution, which the Court has referred to as embodying a right to privacy. *Katz v. United States*, 389 U.S. 347 (1967).

If the Court means by the term "privacy" no more than that the claim of a person to be free from unwanted state regulation of consensual transactions may be a form of "liberty" protected by the Fourteenth Amendment, there is no doubt that similar claims have been upheld in our earlier decisions on the basis of that liberty. I agree with the statement of MR. JUSTICE STEWART in his concurring opinion that the "liberty," against deprivation of which without due process the Fourteenth Amendment protects, embraces more than the rights found in the Bill of Rights. But that liberty is not guaranteed absolutely against deprivation, only against deprivation without due process of law. The test traditionally applied in the area of social and economic legislation is whether or not a law such as that challenged has a rational relation to a valid state objective. *Williamson v. Lee Optical Co.*, 348 U.S. 483, 491 (1955). The Due Process Clause of the Fourteenth Amendment undoubtedly does place a limit, albeit a broad one, on legislative power to enact laws such as this. If the Texas statute were to prohibit an abortion even where the mother's life is in jeopardy, I have little doubt that such a statute would lack a rational relation to a valid state objective under the test stated in *Williamson*. But the Court's sweeping invalidation of any restrictions on abortion during the first trimester is impossible to justify under that standard, and the conscious weighing of competing factors that the Court's opinion apparently substitutes for the established test is far more appropriate to a legislative judgment than to a judicial one. . . .

As in *Lochner* and similar cases applying substantive due process standards to economic and social welfare legislation, the adoption of the compelling state interest standard will inevitably require this Court to examine the legislative policies and pass on the wisdom of these policies in the very process of deciding whether a particular state interest put forward may or may not be "compelling." The decision here to break pregnancy into three distinct terms and to outline the permissible restrictions the State may impose in each one, for example, partakes more of judicial legislation than it does of a determination of the intent of the drafters of the Fourteenth Amendment.

The fact that a majority of the States reflecting, after all, the majority sentiment in those States, have had restrictions on abortions for at least a century is a strong indication, it seems to me, that the asserted right to an abortion is not "so rooted in the traditions and conscience of our people as to be ranked as fundamental," *Snyder v. Massachusetts*, 291 U.S. 97, 105 (1934). Even today, when society's views on abortion are changing, the very existence of the debate is evidence that the "right" to an abortion is not so universally accepted as the appellant would have us believe.

To reach its result, the Court necessarily has had to find within the scope of the Fourteenth Amendment a right that was apparently completely unknown to the drafters of the Amendment. . . .By the time of the adoption of the Fourteenth Amendment in 1868, there were at least 36 laws enacted by state or territorial legislatures limiting abortion. While many States have amended or updated their laws, 21 of the laws on the books in 1868 remain in effect today. . . .

There apparently was no question concerning the validity of this provision or of any of the other state statutes when the Fourteenth Amendment was adopted. The only conclusion possible from this history is that the drafters did not intend to have the Fourteenth Amendment withdraw from the States the power to legislate with respect to this matter.

III

Even if one were to agree that the case that the court decides were here, and that the enunciation of the substantive constitutional law in the Court's opinion were proper, the actual disposition of the case by the Court is still difficult to justify. The Texas statute is struck down in *toto*, even though the Court apparently concedes that at later periods of pregnancy Texas might impose these selfsame statutory limitations on abortion. My understanding of past practice is that a statute found to be invalid as applied to a particular plaintiff, but not unconstitutional as a whole, is not simply "struck down" but is, instead, declared unconstitutional as applied to the fact situation before the Court. *Yick Wo v. Hopkins*, 118 U.S. 356 (1886); *Street v. New York*, 394 U.S. 576 (1969).

For all of the foregoing reasons, I respectfully dissent.

MR. JUSTICE REHNQUIST, dissenting [in *Doe v. Bolton*].

The holding in *Roe v. Wade*, that state abortion laws can withstand constitutional scrutiny only if the State can demonstrate a compelling state interest, apparently compels the Court's close scrutiny of the various provisions in Georgia's abortion statute. Since, as indicated by my dissent in *Wade*, I view the compelling-state-interest standard as an inappropriate measure of the constitutionality of state abortion laws, I respectfully dissent from the majority's holding.

MR. JUSTICE WHITE, with whom MR. JUSTICE REHNQUIST joins, dissenting [for both cases].

At the heart of the controversy in these cases are those recurring pregnancies that pose no danger whatsoever to the life or health of the mother but are, nevertheless, unwanted for any one or more of a variety of reasons—convenience, family planning, economics, dislike of children, the embarrassment of illegitimacy, etc. The common claim before us is that for any one of such reasons, or for no reason at all, and without asserting or claiming any threat to life or health, any woman is entitled to an abortion at her request if she is able to find a medical advisor willing to undertake the procedure.

The Court for the most part sustains this position: During the period prior to the time the fetus becomes viable, the Constitution of the United States values the convenience, whim, or caprice of the putative mother more than the life or potential life of the fetus. . .

With all due respect, I dissent. I find nothing in the language or history of the Constitution to support the Court's judgment. The Court simply fashions and announces a new constitutional right for pregnant mothers and, with scarcely any reason or authority for its action, invests that right with sufficient substance to override most existing state abortion statutes. The upshot is that the people and the legislatures of the 50 States are constitutionally disentitled to weigh the relative importance of the continued existence and development of the fetus, on the one hand, against a spectrum of possible impacts on the mother, on the other hand. As an exercise of raw judicial power, the Court perhaps has authority to do what it does today; but in my view its judgment is an improvident and extravagant exercise of the power of judicial review that the Constitution extends to this Court.

. . .I find no constitutional warrant for imposing such an order of priorities on the people and legislatures of the States. . . .

Case Questions

1. In *Griswold, Eisenstadt,* and the *Roe* and *Doe* cases, the Supreme Court went out of its way to extend standing to the litigants; in *Griswold* and *Eisenstadt* the litigants were permitted to base their case on the constitutional rights of *other* people. In *Roe* and *Doe* the Court overlooked the problem of mootness, because pregnancy is a short-term, easily repeatable condition. The Court could have held to its standing rules and refused to decide these cases. Would that choice have done less harm to democratic processes than these decisions did? Less harm to the constitutional structure? Was the furtherance of the women's cause worth these costs? Are these "costs" imaginary?

2. The appellees in *Roe v. Wade* argued that the Constitution (which says that neither life, liberty, nor property may be taken without due process of law) implies an inviolable "right to be born." What kinds of analysis did the Court use to decide that the Constitution implies the right to have an abortion and that it does not imply a right to be born?

3. What connection do you think Justice Blackmun perceives between the history of abortion beliefs, practices and legality, on the one hand, and "constitutional measurement" on the other?

4. Blackmun cites *Buck v. Bell* as a valid precedent in section VII of the Court opinion. Is *Buck v. Bell* compatible with this decision? Which invades the dignity of the "person" more: (1) compulsion by the state that forces someone (irrespective of the cause of the pregnancy or justifiability of the abortion) to endure nine months of pregnancy and the travail of childbirth, or (2) compulsion by the state that forces someone to undergo a surgical operation that will forever deprive that person of the chance to bear children?

5. The Court grants that a compelling state interest could justify a blanket prohibition on abortions. Would a severe depletion of the population as a result of war constitute a sufficiently compelling interest?

6. Doctors are already able to implant embryos conceived in a petri dish into the womb of someone not the genetic mother. Should states be allowed to mandate that "extras" of such embryos may not be destroyed but have to be allowed to be "adopted" by parents who want them or used for medical (e.g., stem cell) research if the genetic parents do not want them? If not, why not, exactly?

7. Is Justice White treating the situation too lightly when he refers to a nine-month pregnancy and the difficulties of bearing a child as interferences with the "convenience" or "whim" of the putative mother? Is the Court majority treating the situation too lightly when it confidently asserts that concerned communities are not free to protect a six-month or five-month fetus? Who, within our governmental structure, is best suited to decide these questions?

Post-*Roe* Restrictions on Abortion

The right-to-life counteroffensive did not lie down and play dead after the enormous setback imposed by this Supreme Court decision. The immediate strategy of the pro-life movement was to secure legislation, in as many states as possible, to hem in the impending outbreak of abortions. The basic approach of such legislation was to forbid abortions in a variety of specified circumstances. These efforts achieved success in a great many states, but most of that success was to be short-lived.

Constitutional Framework

In July 1976 the Supreme Court examined two examples of such legislation and handed down decisions that set the basic contours of abortion regulation for the next three decades. One, *Planned Parenthood v. Danforth*, limited abortion in several ways, and the Court declared unconstitutional its most stringent provisions. The second, *Bellotti v. Baird*, decided the same day, concerned parental consent for abortions performed on minors (i.e. persons under 18), and yielded mixed results from the Court.

Planned Parenthood v. Danforth (1976)

This first statute came from Missouri. John Danforth, the state's attorney general (later elected to the U.S. Senate; still later appointed U.S. Ambassador to the United Nations by President George W. Bush) defended it. The appellant was Planned Parenthood of Central Missouri, which brought suit in conjunction with two licensed physicians actively involved in abortion work, David Hall and Michael Freiman. Hall and Freiman were challenging the legislative intrusions into their professional practice.

The statute at issue contained nine provisions under attack:

1. The physicians challenged the statute's definition of "viability" as "that stage of fetal development when the life of the unborn child may be continued indefinitely outside the womb by natural or artificial life-supportive systems"; they argued instead for the fixed definition of viability proffered in *Roe v. Wade*—namely, the last three months of fetal life.

2. The physicians challenged the statutory requirement that a woman desiring an abortion must indicate in writing, during the first 12 weeks of pregnancy, that her decision is "informed and freely given and is not the result of coercion." The challenge to this requirement asserted that *Roe* had prohibited *all*

restrictions on abortion during that first trimester and that even this restriction was thereby unconstitutional.

 3. On similar grounds, the physicians challenged the requirement that to perform a first-trimester abortion, the physician must obtain written consent of a woman's spouse unless the abortion is needed to save the woman's life.

 4. Also on similar grounds, they challenged the requirement that unmarried women under the age of 18 obtain written consent from a parent for a first trimester abortion.

 5. These doctors attacked the mandate that persons who perform abortions shall "exercise that degree of professional skill, care, and diligence to preserve the . . . fetus which such person would be required to exercise. . .to preserve. . .any fetus intended to be born." Because this section did not make an explicit exception for nonviable fetuses, the physicians felt that it violated the law established in *Roe*.

 6 & 7. The statute also ordered that records be kept, for statistical and public health purposes, of every abortion performed in the state, and that these records be held for at least seven years. The appellants claimed that these provisions placed an undue burden on their practice of medicine, and they challenged, in particular, the application of these regulations to abortions within the first 12 weeks of pregnancy.

 8. After the first 12 weeks of pregnancy the statute flatly prohibited abortion by the technique of saline amniocentesis, the most popular method of post-first-trimester abortions. (For medical reasons, saline abortions are performed only after the sixteenth week of pregnancy.) This restriction was attacked on the grounds of unreasonableness.

 9. The statute declared that an infant who survived an attempted abortion would become an "abandoned" ward of the state and that his/her biological parents would lose legal rights to him/her (unless the abortion had been performed to preserve the mother's life or health).

The District Court had upheld every provision except the one that required the physician to make an effort to keep alive every aborted fetus. The Supreme Court ruled that the physicians did not have standing to challenge the ninth provision listed above, for it did not affect them directly. Thus, only the first eight challenges were before the Supreme Court. The state prevailed on the requirement of written consent from the would-be mother, on the flexible definition of viability, and on the reporting and recordkeeping provisions. The state lost on parental and spousal consent, the prohibition of saline amniocentesis, and the requirement that an effort be made to preserve the life of every fetus.

The Supreme Court justices aligned in a complex variety of groupings on these issues. We provide each alignment's explanation of its own position.

PLANNED PARENTHOOD V. DANFORTH
428 U.S. 52 (1976)

MR. JUSTICE BLACKMUN delivered the opinion of the Court.

IV

A

The definition of viability. Section 2(2) of the Act defines "viability" as "that stage of fetal development when the life of the unborn child may be continued indefinitely outside the womb by natural or artificial life-supportive systems." Appellants claim that this definition violates and conflicts with the discussion of viability in our opinion in *Roe*. 410 U.S., at 160, 163. In particular, appellants object to the failure of the definition to contain any reference to a gestational time period, to...the three stages of pregnancy, to the presence of the word "indefinitely," and to the extra burden of regulation imposed....

In *Roe*, we used the term "viable," properly we thought, to signify the point at which the fetus is "potentially able to live outside the mother's womb, albeit with artificial aid," and presumably capable of "meaningful life outside the mother's womb," 410 U.S., at 160, 163. We noted that this point "is usually placed" at about seven months or 28 weeks, but may occur earlier. *Id.*, at 160.

We...conclude that the definition of viability in the Act does not conflict with what was said and held in *Roe*....

B

The woman's consent. Under § 3(2) of the Act, a woman, prior to submitting to an abortion during the first 12 weeks of pregnancy, must certify in writing her consent to the procedure and "that her consent is informed and freely given and is not the result of coercion." Appellants argue that this requirement is violative of *Roe v. Wade*, 410 U.S., at 164–65, by imposing extra...regulation on...abortion...

* * *

It is true that *Doe* and *Roe* clearly establish that the State may not restrict the decision of the patient and her physician regarding abortion during the first stage of pregnancy. Despite the fact that apparently no other Missouri statute, with [a few very narrow] exceptions . . .requires a patient's written consent to a surgical procedure, the imposition by § 3(2) of such a requirement . . . even during the first stage, in our view, is not in itself an unconstitutional requirement. The decision to abort, indeed, is an important, and often a stressful one, and it is desirable and imperative that it be made with full knowledge of its nature and consequences. The woman is the one primarily concerned, and her awareness of the decision and its significance may be assured, constitutionally, by the State to the extent of requiring her prior written consent.

We could not say that a requirement imposed by the State that a prior written consent for any surgery would be unconstitutional. As a consequence, we see no constitutional defect in requiring it only for some types of surgery. . .

C

The spouse's consent. Section 3(3) requires the prior written consent of the spouse of the woman seeking an abortion during the first 12 weeks of pregnancy, unless "the abortion is certified by a licensed physician to be necessary in order to preserve the life of the mother."

The appellees defend § 3(3) on the ground that it was enacted in the light of the General Assembly's "perception of marriage as an institution," and that any major change in family status is a decision to be made jointly by the marriage partners. Reference is made to an abortion's possible effect on the woman's childbearing potential. It is said that marriage always has entailed some legislatively imposed limitations: reference made to adultery and bigamy as criminal offenses; to Missouri's general requirement. . ., that for an adoption of a child born in wedlock the consent of both parents is necessary; to similar joint consent requirements imposed by a number of States with respect to artificial insemination and the legitimacy of children so conceived; to the law of two States requiring spousal consent for voluntary sterilization. . . .

The appellants, on the other hand, contend that § 3(3) obviously is designed to afford the husband the right unilaterally to prevent or veto an abortion, whether or not he is the father of the fetus. . . .We now hold that the State may not unconstitutionally require the consent of the spouse, as is specified under § 3 (3) of the Missouri Act, as a condition for abortion during the first 12 weeks of pregnancy. [T]he State cannot "delegate to a spouse a veto power which the state itself is absolutely and totally prohibited from exercising during the first trimester of pregnancy." 393 F. Supp., at 1375. Clearly, since the State cannot regulate or proscribe abortion during the first stage, when the physician and his patient make that decision, the State cannot delegate authority to any particular person, even the spouse, to prevent abortion during the same period.

We are not unaware of the deep and proper concern and interest that a devoted and protective husband has in his wife's pregnancy and in the growth and development of the fetus she is carrying. Neither has this Court failed to appreciate the importance of the marital relationship in our society. See, e.g., *Griswold v. Connecticut*, 381 U.S. 479, 486 (1965); *Maynard v. Hill*, 125 U.S. 190, 211 (1888). Moreover, we recognize that the decision whether to undergo or to forgo an abortion may have profound effects on the future of any marriage, effects that are both physical and mental, and possibly deleterious. Notwithstanding these factors, we cannot hold that the State has the constitutional authority to give the spouse unilaterally the ability to prohibit the wife from terminating her pregnancy, when the State itself lacks that right. See *Eisenstadt v. Baird*, 405 U.S. 438, 453 (1972).

It seems manifest that, ideally, the decision to terminate a pregnancy should be one concurred in by both the wife and her husband. No marriage may be viewed as harmonious or successful if the marriage partners are fundamentally divided on so important and vital an issue. But it is difficult to believe that the goal of fostering mutuality and trust in a marriage, and of strengthening the marital relationship and the marriage institution, will be achieved by giving the husband a veto power exercisable for any reason whatsoever or for no reason at all. . . .[I]t is not at all likely that such action would further, as the District Court majority phrased it, the "interest of the state in protecting the mutuality of decisions vital to the marriage relationship." 392 F. Supp., at 1370.

. . .The obvious fact is that when the wife and the husband disagree on this decision, the view of only one of the two marriage partners can prevail. Since it is the woman who physically bears the child and who is the more directly and immediately affected by the pregnancy, as between the two, the balance weighs in her favor. Cf. *Roe v. Wade*, 410 U.S., at 153.

We conclude that § 3(3) of the Missouri Act is inconsistent with the standards enunciated in *Roe v. Wade*, 410, U.S., at 164–65, and is unconstitutional. . . .

D

Parental consent. Section 3(4) requires, with respect to the first 12 weeks of pregnancy, where the woman is unmarried and under the age of 18 years, the written consent of a parent or person in *loco parentis* unless, again, "the abortion is certified by a licensed physician as necessary in order to preserve the life of the mother.". . .

The appellees defend the statute in several ways. They point out that the law properly may subject minors to more stringent limitations than are permissible with respect to adults. . . .Missouri law, it is said, "is replete with provisions reflecting the interest of the state in assuring the welfare of minors." Certain decisions are considered by the State to be outside the scope of a minor's ability to act in his own best interest or in the interest of the public, citing statutes proscribing the sale of firearms and deadly weapons to minors without parental consent, and other statutes . . . .It is pointed out that the record contains testimony to the effect that children of tender years (even ages 10 and 11) have sought abortions. Thus, a State's permitting a child to obtain an abortion without the counsel of an adult "who has responsibility or concern for the child would constitute an irresponsible abdication of the State's duty to protect the welfare of minors.". . .

We agree with appellants. . .that the State may not impose a blanket provision, such as § 3(4), requiring the consent of a parent or person in *loco parentis* as a condition for abortion of an unmarried minor during the first 12 weeks of her pregnancy. Just as with the requirement of consent from the spouse, so here, the State does not have the constitutional authority to give a third party an absolute, and possibly arbitrary, veto over the decision of the physician and his patient to terminate the patient's pregnancy, regardless of the reason for withholding the consent.

Constitutional rights do not mature and come into being magically only when one attains the state-defined age of majority. Minors, as well as adults, are protected by the Constitution and possess constitutional rights. See, e.g., *Breed v. Jones*, 421 U.S. 519 (1975); *Goss v. Lopez*, 419 U.S. 565 (1975); *Tinker v. Des Moines School District*, 393 U.S. 503 (1969); *In re Gault*, 387 U.S. 1 (1957). The Court indeed, however, long has recognized that the State has somewhat broader authority to regulate the activities of children than of adults. *Prince v. Massachusetts*, 321 U.S., at 170; *Ginsberg v. New York*, 390 U.S. 629 (1968). It remains, then, to examine whether there is any significant state interest in conditioning an abortion on the consent of a parent or person in *loco parentis* that is not present in the case of an adult.

One suggested interest is the safeguarding of the family unit and of parental authority. 392 F. Supp., at 1370. It is difficult, however, to conclude that providing a parent with absolute power to overrule a determination, made by the physician and his minor patient, to terminate the patient's pregnancy will serve to strengthen the family unit. Neither is it likely that such veto power will enhance parental authority or control where the minor and the nonconsenting parent are so fundamentally in conflict and the very existence of the pregnancy already has fractured the family structure. . . .

We emphasize that our holding that § 3(4) is invalid does not suggest that every minor, regardless of age or maturity, may give effective consent for termination of her pregnancy. . . .The fault with § 3(4) is that it imposes a special consent provision, . . .without a sufficient justification for the restriction.

E

Saline amniocentesis. Section 9 of the statute prohibits the use of saline amniocentesis, as a method or technique of abortion, after the first 12 weeks of pregnancy. . . .The statute imposes this proscription on the ground that the technique "is deleterious to maternal health," and places it in the form of a legislative finding. Appellants challenge this provision on the ground that it operates to preclude virtually all abortions after the first trimester. This is so, it is claimed, because a substantial percentage, in the neighborhood of 70% according to the testimony, of all abortions performed in the United States after the first trimester are effected through the procedure of saline amniocentesis. . . .

The District Court's majority . . . .[r]eferring to such methods as hysterotomy, hysterectomy, "mechanical means of inducing abortion," and prostaglandin injection, . . .said that at least the latter two techniques were safer than saline. Consequently, the majority concluded, the restriction in § 9 could be upheld as reasonably related to maternal health.

We feel that the majority, in reaching its conclusion, failed to appreciate and to consider several significant facts. First, it did not recognize the prevalence, as the record conclusively demonstrates, of the use of saline amniocentesis as an accepted medical procedure in this country; the procedure, as noted above, is employed in a substantial majority (the testimony from both sides ranges from 68% to 80%) of all post-first trimester abortions. Second, it failed to recognize that at the time of trial, there were severe limitations on the availability of the prostaglandin technique, which, although promising, was used only on an experimental basis until less than two years before. See *Wolf v. Schroering*, 388 F. Supp., at 637, where it was said that at that time (1974), "there are no physicians in Kentucky competent in the technique of prostaglandin amnio infusion." And the State offered no evidence that prostaglandin abortions were available in Missouri.[12] Third, the statute's reference to the insertion of "a saline or other fluid" appears to include within its proscription the intra-amniotic injection of prostaglandin itself and other methods that may be developed in the future and that may prove highly effective and completely safe. Finally, the majority did not consider the anomaly inherent in § 9 when it proscribes the use of saline but does but does not prohibit techniques that are many times more likely to result in maternal death. See 392 F. Supp., at 1378 n. 8 (dissenting opinion).

These unappreciated or overlooked factors place the State's decision to bar use of the saline method in a completely different light. The State, through § 9, would prohibit the use of a method which the record shows is the one most commonly used nationally by physicians after the first trimester and which is safer, with respect to maternal mortality, than even continuation of the pregnancy until normal childbirth. Moreover, as a practical matter, it forces a woman and her physician to terminate her pregnancy by methods more dangerous to her health than the method outlawed.

And so viewed, particularly in the light of the present unavailability—as demonstrated by the record—of the prostaglandin technique, the outright legislative proscription of saline fails as a reasonable regulation for the protection of maternal health. It comes into focus, instead, as an unreasonable or arbitrary regulation designed to inhibit, and having the effect of inhibiting, the vast majority of abortions after the first 12 weeks. As such, it does not withstand constitutional challenge.

F

Recordkeeping. Section 10 and 11 of the Act impose recordkeeping requirements for health facilities and physicians concerned with abortions irrespective of the pregnancy stage. Under § 10, each such facility and physician is to be supplied with forms "the purpose and function of which shall be the preservation of maternal health and life by adding to the sum of medical knowledge through the compilation of relevant maternal health and life data and to monitor all abortions performed to assure that they are done only under and in accordance with the provisions of the law." The statute states that the information on the forms "shall be confidential and shall be used only for statistical purposes." The "records, however, may be inspected and health data acquired by local, state, or national public health officers." Under § 11 the records are to be kept for seven years in the permanent files of the health facility where the abortion was performed.

Appellants object to these reporting and recordkeeping provisions on the ground that they, too, impose an extra layer and burden of regulation, and that they apply throughout all stages of pregnancy. . . .

Recordkeeping and reporting requirements that are reasonably directed to the preservation of maternal health and that properly respect a patient's confidentiality and privacy are permissible. . . . As to the first stage [of pregnancy], one may argue forcefully that the State should not be able to impose any recordkeeping requirements that significantly differ from those imposed with respect to other, and comparable, medical or surgical procedures. We conclude, however, that the provisions of § 10 and § 11, while perhaps approaching permissible limits, are not constitutionally offensive in themselves. Record-keeping of this kind, if not abused or overdone, can be useful to the State's interest in protecting the health of its female citizens, and may be a resource that is relevant to decisions involving medical experience and judgment. The added requirements for confidentiality. . . and for retention for seven years, a period not unreasonable in length, assist and persuade us in our determination of the constitutional limits. As so regarded, we see no legally significant impact or consequence on the abortion decision or on the physician-patient relationship. . . .

G

Standard of care. Appellee Danforth [in a companion case] appeals from the unanimous decision of the District Court that § 6(1) of the Act is unconstitutional. That section provides:

> No person who performs or induces an abortion shall fail to exercise that degree of professional skill, care and diligence to preserve the life and health of the fetus which such person would be required to exercise in order to preserve the life and health of any fetus intended to be born and not aborted. Any physician or person assisting in the abortion who shall fail to take such measures to encourage or to sustain the life of the child, and the death of the child results, shall be deemed guilty of manslaughter. . . . Further, such physician or other person shall be liable in an action for damages.

The District Court held that the first sentence was unconstitutionally overbroad because it failed to exclude from its reach the stage of pregnancy prior to viability. 392 F. Supp., at 1371.

The Attorney General argues that the District Court's interpretation is erroneous and unnecessary. He claims that the first sentence of § 6(1) establishes only the general standard of care that applies to the person who performs the abortion, and that the second sentence describes the circumstances when that standard of care applies, namely, when a live child results from the procedure. Thus, the first sentence, it is said, despite its reference to the fetus, has no application until a live birth results. . . .

[W]e are unable to accept the appellee's sophisticated interpretation of the statute. Section 6(1) requires the physician to exercise the prescribed skill, care, and diligence to preserve the life and health of the *fetus*. It does not specify that such care need be taken only after the stage of viability has been reached. As the provision now reads, it impermissibly requires the physician to preserve the life and health of the fetus, whatever the stage of pregnancy. The fact that the second sentence of § 6(1) refers to a criminal penalty where the physician fails "to take such measures to encourage or to sustain the life of the *child*, and the death of the *child* results" (emphasis supplied), simply does not modify the duty imposed by the previous sentence or limit that duty to pregnancies that have reached the stage of viability.

We conclude, as did the District Court, that § 6(1) must stand or fall as a unit. Its provisions are inextricably bound together. And a physician's or other person's criminal failure to protect a liveborn infant surely will be subject to prosecution in Missouri under the State's criminal statutes.

The judgment of the District Court is affirmed in part and reversed in part. . . .

Opinion Footnote

12 In response to MR. JUSTICE WHITE'S criticism that the prostaglandin method of inducing abortion was available in Missouri, either at the time the Act was passed or at the time of trial, we make the following observations. First, there is no evidence in the record. . .that demonstrates that the prostaglandin method was or is available in Missouri. Second, the evidence presented to the District Court does not support such a view. Until January 1974 prostaglandin was used only on an experimental basis in a few medical centers. And, at the time the Missouri General Assembly proscribed saline, the sole distributor of prostaglandin "restricted sales to around twenty medical centers from coast to coast."

It is clear, therefore, that at the time the Missouri General Assembly passed the Act, prostaglandin was not available in any meaningful sense of that term. Because of this undisputed fact, it was incumbent upon the State to show that at the time of trial in 1974 prostaglandin was available. It failed to do so. . . .

MR. JUSTICE STEWART, with whom MR. JUSTICE POWELL joins, concurring.

While joining the Court's opinion, I write separately to indicate my understanding of some of the constitutional issues raised by this case....

I agree with the Court that the patient consent provision in § 3(2) is constitutional....

As to the provision of the law that requires a husband's consent to an abortion, § 3(3), the primary issue that it raises is whether the State may constitutionally recognize and give effect to a right on his part to participate in the decision to abort a jointly conceived child. This seems to me a rather more difficult problem than the Court acknowledges. Previous decisions have recognized that a man's right to father children and enjoy the association of his offspring is a constitutionally protected freedom. See *Stanley v. Illinois*, 405 U.S. 645; *Skinner v. Oklahoma*, 316 U.S. 535. But the Court has recognized as well that the Constitution protects "a *woman's* decision whether or not to terminate her pregnancy." 410 U.S., at 153 (emphasis added). In assessing the constitutional validity of § 3(3) we are called upon to choose between these competing rights. I agree with the Court, that since "it is the woman who physically bears the child and who is the more directly and immediately affected by the pregnancy...the balance weighs in her favor."

With respect to the state law's requirement of parental consent, § 3(4), I think it clear that its primary constitutional deficiency lies in its imposition of an absolute limitation on the minor's right to obtain an abortion...[A] materially different constitutional issue would be presented under a provision requiring parental consent or consultation in most cases but providing for prompt (i) judicial resolution of any disagreement between the parent and the minor, or (ii) judicial determination that the minor is mature enough to give an informed consent without parental concurrence or that abortion in any event is in the minor's best interest. Such a provision would not impose parental approval as an absolute condition upon the minor's right but would assure in most instances consultation between the parent and child.

...[This] is a grave decision, and a girl of tender years, under emotional stress, may be ill-equipped to make it without mature advice and emotional support. It seems unlikely that she will obtain adequate counsel and support from the attending physician at an abortion clinic, where abortions for pregnant minors frequently take place.

MR. JUSTICE STEVENS, concurring in part and dissenting in part.

With the exception of Parts **IV-D** and **IV-E**, I join the Court's opinion. . . .

In my opinion. . .the parental consent requirement is consistent with the holding in *Roe*. The State's interest in the welfare of its young citizens justifies a variety of protective measures. Because he may not foresee the consequences of his decision, a minor may not make an enforceable bargain. He may not lawfully work or travel where he pleases, or even attend exhibitions of constitutionally protected adult motion pictures. Persons below a certain age may not marry without parental consent. Indeed, such consent is essential even when the young woman is already pregnant. The State's interest in protecting a young person from harm justifies the imposition of restraints on his or her freedom even though comparable restraints on adults would be constitutionally impermissible. Therefore, the holding in *Roe v. Wade* that the abortion decision is entitled to constitutional protection merely emphasizes the importance of the decision; it does not lead to the conclusion that the state legislature has no power to enact legislation for the purpose of protecting a young pregnant woman from the consequences of an incorrect decision.

The abortion decision is, of course, more important than the decision to attend or to avoid an adult motion picture, or the decision to work long hours in a factory. It is not necessarily any more important than the decision to run away from home or the decision to marry. But even if it is the most important kind of a decision a young person may ever make, that assumption merely enhances the quality of the State's interest in maximizing the probability that the decision be made correctly and with full understanding of the consequences of either alternative.

The Court recognizes that the State may insist that the decision not be made without the benefit of medical advice. But since the most significant consequences of the decision are not medical in character, it would seem to me that the State may, with equal legitimacy, insist that the decision be made only after other appropriate counsel has been had as well. Whatever choice a pregnant young woman makes—to marry, to abort, to bear her child out of wedlock—the consequences of her decision may have a profound impact on her entire future life. A legislative determination that such a choice will be made more wisely in most cases if the advice and moral support of a parent play a part in the decisionmaking process is surely not irrational. Moreover, it is perfectly clear that the parental consent requirement will necessarily involve a parent in the decisional process.

If there is no parental consent requirement, many minors will submit to the abortion procedure without ever informing their parents. An assumption that the parental reaction will be hostile, disparaging or violent no doubt persuades many children simply to bypass parental counsel which would in fact be loving, supportive and, indeed, for some indispensable. It is unrealistic, in my judgment, to assume that every parent-child relationship is either (a) so perfect that communication and accord will take place routinely or (b) so imperfect that the absence of communication reflects the child's correct prediction that the parent will exercise his or her veto arbitrarily to further a selfish interest rather than the child's interest. A state legislature may conclude that most parents will be primarily interested in the welfare of their children, and further, that the imposition of a parental consent requirement is an appropriate method of giving the parents an opportunity to foster that welfare.... [E]ven doctors are not omniscient; specialists in performing abortions may incorrectly conclude that the immediate advantages of the procedure outweigh the disadvantages which a parent could evaluate in better perspective. In each individual case factors much more profound than a mere medical judgment may weigh heavily in the scales. The overriding consideration is that the right to make the choice be exercised as wisely as possible.

The Court assumes that parental consent is an appropriate requirement if the minor is not "capable of understanding the procedure and of appreciating its consequences and those of available alternatives." This assumption is, of course, correct and consistent with the predicate which underlies all State legislation seeking to protect minors from the consequences of decisions they are not yet prepared to make. In all such situations chronological age has been the basis for imposition of a restraint on the minor's freedom of choice even though it is perfectly obvious that such a yardstick is imprecise and perhaps even unjust in particular cases. The Court seems to assume that the capacity to conceive a child and the judgment of the physician are the only constitutionally permissible yardsticks for determining whether a young woman can independently make the abortion decision. I doubt the accuracy of the Court's empirical judgment. Even if it were correct, however, as a matter of constitutional law I think a State has power to conclude otherwise and to select a chronological age as its standard.

In short, the State's interest in the welfare of its young citizens is sufficient, in my judgment, to support the parental consent requirement.

[On **IV-E**, STEVENS, J., agrees with the Court's result, but he explains the reasons differently.]

MR. JUSTICE WHITE, with whom THE CHIEF JUSTICE and MR. JUSTICE REHNQUIST join, concurring in the judgment in part and dissenting in part.

...[E]ven accepting *Roe v. Wade*, there is nothing in the opinion in that case and nothing articulated in the Court's opinion in this case which justifies the invalidation of [these] five provisions....Accordingly, I dissent, in part.

I

Roe v. Wade, 410 U.S. 113, 163, holds that until a fetus becomes viable, the interest of the State in the life or potential life it represents is outweighed by the interest of the mother in choosing "whether or not to terminate her pregnancy." *Id.*, at 153. Section 3(3) of the Act provides that a married woman may not obtain an abortion without her husband's consent. The Court strikes down this statute in one sentence. It says that "since the State cannot....proscribe abortion...the State cannot delegate authority to any particular person, even the spouse, to prevent abortion...." But the State is not—under § 3 (3)—delegating to the husband the power to vindicate the *State*'s interest in the future life of the fetus. It is instead recognizing that the husband has an interest of his own in the life of the fetus which should not be extinguished by the unilateral decision of the wife. It by no means follows, from the fact that the mother's interest in deciding "whether or not to terminate her pregnancy" outweighs the *State*'s interest in the potential life of the fetus, that the husband's interest is also outweighed and may not be protected by the State. A father's interest in having a child—perhaps his only child—may be unmatched by any other interest in his life. See *Stanley v. Illinois*, 405 U.S. 645, 651, and cases there cited. It is truly surprising that the majority finds in the United States Constitution, as it must in order to justify the result it reaches, a rule that the State must assign a greater value to a mother's decision to cut off a potential human life by abortion than to a father's decision to let it mature into a live child. Such a rule cannot be found there, nor can it be found in *Roe v. Wade*. These are matters which a State should be able to decide free from the suffocating power of the federal judge, purporting to act in the name of the Constitution.

In describing the nature of a mother's interest in terminating a pregnancy, the Court in *Roe v. Wade* mentioned only the post-birth burdens of rearing a child, *id.*, at p. 153, and rejected a rule based on her interest in controlling her own body during pregnancy. *Id.*, at 154. Missouri has a law which prevents a woman from putting a child up for adoption over her husband's objection.... This law represents a judgment by the State that the mother's interest in avoiding the burdens of child rearing do not outweigh or snuff out the father's interest in participating in bringing up his own child. That law is plainly valid, but no more so than § 3(3) of the Act now before us....

II

Section 3(4) requires that an unmarried woman under 18 years of age obtain the consent of a parent or a person in *loco parentis* as a condition to an abortion....Missouri is entitled to protect the minor unmarried woman from making the decision in a way which is not in her own best interests, and it seeks to achieve this goal by requiring parental consultation and consent. This is the traditional way by which States have sought to protect children from their own immature and improvident decisions...

III

Section 9 of the Act prohibits abortion by the method known as saline amniocentesis—a method used at the time the Act was passed for 70% of abortions performed after the first trimester. Legislative history reveals that the Missouri Legislature viewed saline amniocentesis as far less safe a method of abortion than the so-called prostaglandin method....

The District Court also cited considerable evidence establishing that the prostaglandin method is safer. In fact, the Chief of Obstetrics at Yale University, Dr. Anderson, suggested that "physicians should be liable for malpractice if they chose saline over prostaglandin after having been given all the facts on both methods." The Court nevertheless reverses the decision of the District Court sustaining § 9 against constitutional challenge. It does so apparently because saline amniocentesis was widely used before the Act was passed; because the prostaglandin method was seldom used and was not generally available; and because other abortion techniques more dangerous than saline amniocentesis were not banned. At bottom the majority's holding—as well as the concurrence—rests on this *factual* finding that the prostaglandin method is unavailable to the women of Missouri. It therefore concludes that the ban on the saline method is "an unreasonable or arbitrary regulation designed to inhibit, and having the effect of inhibiting, the vast majority of abortions after the first 12 weeks." This factual finding was not made either by the majority or by the dissenting judge below.... In fact the record below does not support such a finding. There is *no* evidence in the record that women in

Missouri will be unable to obtain abortions by the prostaglandin method. . . . The record discloses that the prostaglandin method of abortion was the country's second most common method of abortion during the second trimester, that although the prostaglandin method had previously been available only on an experimental basis, it was, at the time of trial available in "small hospitals all over the country," that in another year or so the prostaglandin method would become—even in the absence of legislation on the subject—the most prevalent method. Moreover, one doctor quite sensibly testified that if the saline method were banned, hospitals would quickly switch to the prostaglandin method.

The majority relies on the testimony of one doctor that—as already noted—prostaglandin had been available on an experimental basis only until January 1, 1974; and that its manufacturer, the Upjohn Company, restricted its sales to large medical centers for the following six months, after which sales were to be unrestricted. In what manner this evidence supports the proposition that prostaglandin is unavailable to the women of Missouri escapes me. The statute involved in this case was passed on June 14, 1974; evidence was taken in July 1974; the District Court's decree sustaining the ban on the saline method which this Court overturns was entered in January 1975; and this Court declares the statute unconstitutional in July of 1976. There is simply no evidence in the record that prostaglandin was or is unavailable at any time relevant to this case.

In any event, the point of § 9 is to change the practice under which most abortions were performed under the saline amniocentesis method generally available. It promises to achieve that result, if it remains operative, and the evidence discloses that the result is a desirable one or at least that the legislature could have so viewed it.

IV

Section 6(1) of the Act provides:

No person who performs or induces an abortion shall fail to exercise that degree of professional skill, care and diligence to preserve the life and health of the fetus which such person would be required to exercise in order to preserve the life and health of any fetus intended to be born and not aborted. Any physician or person assisting in the abortion who shall fail to take such measures to encourage or to sustain the life of the child, and the death of the child results, shall be deemed guilty of manslaughter. . . . Further, such physician or other person shall be liable in an action for damages.

If this section is read in any way other than through a microscope, it is plainly intended to require that, where a "fetus...[may have] the capability of meaningful life outside the mother's womb," *Roe v. Wade*, at 163, the abortion be handled in a way which is designed to preserve that life notwithstanding the mother's desire to terminate it. Indeed, even looked at through a microscope the statute seems to go no further. It requires a physician to exercise "that degree of professional skill...to preserve the fetus," which he would be required to exercise if the mother wanted a live child. Plainly, if the pregnancy is to be terminated at a time when there is no chance of life outside the womb, a physician would not be required to exercise any care or skill to preserve the life of the fetus during abortion no matter what the mother's desires. The statute would appear then to operate only in the gray area after the fetus *might* be viable but while the physician is still able to certify "with reasonable medical certainty that the fetus is not viable." See § 5 of the Act which flatly prohibits abortions absent such a certification. Since the State has a compelling interest, sufficient to outweigh the mother's desire to kill the fetus, when the "fetus...has the capability of meaningful life outside the mother's womb," *Roe v. Wade*, at 163, the statute is constitutional.

Incredibly, the Court reads the statute instead to require "the physician to preserve the life and health of the fetus, whatever the stage of pregnancy," thereby attributing to the Missouri Legislature the strange intention of passing a statute with absolutely no chance of surviving constitutional challenge under *Roe v. Wade*.

* * *

V

I join the judgment of the Court insofar as it upholds the other portions of the Act...

Case Questions

1. Is this decision consistent with the Court's statement in *Stanley v. Illinois* that a father's right to enjoy the care and comfort of his children is "fundamental" and is protected by the Constitution?

2. The Court majority notes that two states require a wife's consent before her husband can get surgically sterilized. Does this decision suggest that these laws are unconstitutional?

Bellotti v. Baird (1976)

Although the Court majority in *Danforth* rejected Missouri's *absolute* requirement of parental consent for abortions performed on unmarried minors, they did qualify their rejection with the proviso that "not. . .every minor. . .may give effective consent." Justice Stewart (joined by Justice Powell) elaborated this qualification in his concurring opinion: a nonabsolute requirement of parental consent—one that in unusual circumstances could be superseded by a judicial hearing—would, he believed, pass constitutional muster. The Court majority itself, in nonbinding dicta, announced a similar principle in another case handed down on the same day as *Danforth, Bellotti v. Baird*.[45]

Bellotti v. Baird involved a Massachusetts parental consent ordinance. For technical reasons, the Supreme Court did not decide the "merits" of the case but remanded it back to the lower courts for another decision. In so doing, however, the Supreme Court indicated that it *would* uphold the law if Massachusetts were to interpret its statute as imposing only a flexible parental consent requirement—one permitting a judge to override parental vetoes in cases of mature and "informed" minors or in other cases where the best interest of the minor would be served thereby. Such a statute would ensure parental *consultation* for unmarried minors without endowing those parents with an absolute veto power over their daughter's abortion decision. This arrangement, known as a "judicial bypass" option, seems to be the point at which the Supreme Court has located the balance between the state's concern for the welfare of minor women and their constitutional freedoms.

Refinements of the Framework: 1979–1989

In 1981 the Supreme Court clarified a related issue concerning minors' abortion rights. In *H.L. v. Matheson*,[46] the Court upheld a statute from Utah that required notification (as distinguished from consent) "if possible, [of] the parents or guardian of the woman upon whom the abortion is to be performed, if she is a minor." The plaintiff was a 15-year-old residing with her parents, and the Court sustained the law specifically with regard to these facts, indicating that its holding would not necessarily apply to a mature or emancipated minor or to one presenting mitigating evidence concerning her relationship with her parents. Justices Blackmun, Brennan, and Marshall dissented.

An earlier clarification of *Danforth* came about in 1979 with regard to viability. In *Colautti v. Franklin*,[47] the Court declared void for vagueness a Pennsylvania provision that rendered physicians criminally liable if they failed to "exercise that degree of professional . . .diligence to preserve the life and health of the fetus which [they]. . .would be required to exercise [for]. . .any fetus intended to be born" and to choose the abortion technique most likely to produce a live fetus as long as it did not endanger the mother's health. These provisions applied to instances when the fetus was viable or when there was "sufficient reason to believe that the fetus may be viable." Blackmun writing for the majority found the standard of care provision "impermissibly vague" and the section on viability "ambiguous" and lacking in protection for the physician who makes an honest error of judgment. He defined viability as the point "when, in the judgment of the attending physician on the particular facts of the case before him, there is a reasonable likelihood of the fetus' sustained survival outside the womb, with or without artificial support." Justice White wrote a dissent joined by Rehnquist and Burger claiming that the Court was backtracking on permission for abortion regulations it had granted in *Roe* and *Danforth*, and he emphasized that under *Roe* viability had been defined as *potential* ability to survive outside the womb, as distinguished from *actual* ability to do so. He felt the Court majority was now moving toward the latter definition.

In the election campaign of 1980, Ronald Reagan promised to appoint pro-life judges, and his first appointment to the Court was a woman, Sandra Day O'Connor. Her first opinion on the abortion question turned out to be a dissent in the 1983 case *Akron v. Akron Center for Reproductive Health* (later referred to as *Akron I*),[48] in which she argued, in an opinion joined by Justices White and Rehnquist (the *Roe* dissenters) that the *Roe* three-stage, or trimester, framework should be abandoned because it was "on a collision course with itself," since medical technology would steadily move the date of viability to earlier in the pregnancy and steadily extend to a later point in the pregnancy that stage during which abortion was safer for a woman than childbirth. Strangely, Chief Justice Burger (who had concurred in *Roe* but who had been dissenting in favor of upholding abortion restrictions ever since *Planned Parenthood*) did not align with O'Connor's dissent, so the vote in *Akron I* was not the expected 5–4 but rather 6–3 on behalf of following *Roe v. Wade*. In addition to her "collision with itself" reasoning, O'Connor criticized *Roe* for failing to acknowledge that the state's interest in protecting "the potentiality of human life" in the fetus amounted to a compelling interest not just in the third trimester but "*throughout* pregnancy" (her italics). She argued, "At any stage in pregnancy, there is the *potential* for human life" (her italics).[49] By this logic, it appeared that Justice O'Connor would vote to uphold virtually all abortion restrictions, for every abortion prohibition furthers the state's interest in the potentiality of life and is arguably necessary for that potential life to become actual.[50]

But at this point, Justice O'Connor complicated her argument by adding a second consideration; she explained that "not every regulation that the state imposes must be measured against the state's compelling interests and examined with strict scrutiny." She quoted an earlier precedent to the effect that "the right in *Roe v. Wade* . . . protects the woman from *unduly burdensome interference* with her freedom to decide whether to terminate her pregnancy."[51] She characterized the concept of "undue burden" with phrases such as "state action 'drastically limiting the availability and safety of the desired service,' " "the imposition of an 'absolute obstacle' on the abortion decision," and " 'official interference' and 'coercive restraint' imposed on the abortion decision." She then added that, if there were no undue burden, the statute need satisfy only the very minimal "reasonableness" test; the state needed to show at least a rational connection between the law and some legitimate governmental goal. (Protecting potential life would always count as a legitimate purpose.)

Justice O'Connor did not make clear the relation between her two lines of reasoning. If potential life were not just a legitimate interest but even a "compelling interest" warranting state protection throughout pregnancy, it was not clear where the "unduly burdensome" test would come into play, because it would seem, for the sake of potential life, that states could totally prohibit abortion throughout pregnancy, and an outright prohibition is as burdensome as a regulation ever becomes. She closed this section of her reasoning with the rather cryptic remark, "[S]tate action 'encouraging childbirth except in the most urgent circumstances' is 'rationally related to the legitimate government objective of protecting potential life.' "[52] This left the impression that in "the most urgent" circumstances—say, threat to a mother's life, or perhaps grave threat to physical or mental health—the mother's right to choose against childbirth could be protected (i.e., an abortion prohibition would be ruled "unduly burdensome"), but absent such circumstances O'Connor would be willing to uphold absolute prohibitions on abortion as in furtherance of the compelling interest in potential life. At this point it appeared that if one or two (depending on the unreliable vote of Justice Burger) justices were to join the O'Connor group, the abortion freedom secured by *Roe v. Wade* would become a thing of the past, and the United States would return to the pre-*Roe* status quo.

The six-judge majority in *Akron I* all concurred in an opinion drafted by Justice Powell. This opinion devoted its lengthy first footnote to rebutting the proposition of Justice O'Connor that *Roe* should be abandoned. The footnote documented the number of justices and the number of precedents that had concurred with *Roe*'s "basic principle that a woman has a fundamental right to make the highly personal choice whether or not to terminate her pregnancy" and pointedly insisted, "We respect [the doctrine of following precedent, 'stare decisis'] today, and reaffirm *Roe v. Wade*."

The majority (in Section II of Powell's opinion) reiterated the precedents that underlay the logic of *Roe* and recapitulated the law of abortion as it had evolved up until 1983: (1) During "approximately the first trimester" the state is forbidden to restrict a woman's freedom, in consultation with her [licensed] physician, to decide to have an abortion, with the qualification that "regulations [e.g., mandating confidential recordkeeping] that have no significant impact on the woman's exercise of her right may be permissible where justified by important state health objectives." (2) From approximately the end of the first trimester until the point of viability the state may adopt regulations reasonably tailored to the goal of promoting maternal health. (3) After viability, abortion may be forbidden except for purposes of preserving the life or health of the mother.

After this summary, Powell proceeded to acknowledge that abortion technology had changed since *Roe*. In 1973 it had been medically reasonable to require (because of techniques then prevalent) that second trimester abortions be limited to full-service hospitals. Now, however, throughout the fourth month of pregnancy, abortions could safely be, and were routinely, performed in (much less expensive and more widely available) clinics. Because of this change in medical reality, Akron's statute, which restricted *all* second-trimester abortions to full-service hospitals, was not truly "reasonably related" to promoting maternal health. Such a statute could be constitutional only if it kicked in after the fourth (not third) month of pregnancy, when such a restriction was now medically reasonable. So, as written, the statute was declared unconstitutional.[53]

Moreover, the majority declared unconstitutional on vagueness grounds its mandate that every aborted fetus be "disposed of in a humane and sanitary manner."

Finally, Akron's elaborate requirements ostensibly aiming at informed consent of the abortion-seeking patient were ruled unconstitutional by the Supreme Court. These included a 24-hour waiting period between her signing a consent form and the performance of an abortion and requirements that prior to obtaining her signature, her physician inform her of a number of things, including the date when her fetus would become viable and what its approximate stage of development was; the statement that "the unborn child is a human life from the moment of conception"; the statement that a number of abortion risks and complications are possible (whether they were likely in her case or not); the statement that state agencies were available to help her with birth control, adoption, and childbirth; and, finally, in accordance with his/her own medical judgment, the particular risks that might be likely with respect to her particular pregnancy and the particular abortion techniques the physician planned to use. With respect to the last item on the list, the Court ruled that while a state might reasonably require that this information be provided to a patient, it was not reasonable to insist that the only qualified person to give this information was the attending physician. Therefore, the Court struck it down as reaching more broadly than necessary into the area of protected freedom. As to the other provisions—a 24-hour wait, a litany of state-alleged risks, and a mandated assertion by the doctor that life begins at conception—the Supreme Court struck them down as not reasonably related to promoting maternal health.[54]

On the same day that *Akron I* was decided, the Supreme Court decided *Planned Parenthood v. Ashcroft*.[55] Five justices—Burger, Powell, O'Connor, Rehnquist, and White—formed a majority to rule constitutional Missouri's parental consent with judicial bypass provision for unmarried minors and also two new sorts of abortion regulations. The first required a pathology report for all abortions. The majority reasoned that this was a minimally burdensome regulation, similar to recordkeeping requirements. The dissenters argued that this could add as much as $40 to the price of every abortion and that pathology reports were not routine medical practice for comparable surgery (in other words, that the requirement amounted to an unreasonable burden on abortion). Second, the majority upheld a rule that for all post-viability abortions (i.e., those done to preserve a mother's life or health), a second physician be on hand to care for the fetus. The majority, interpreting the statute to imply an exception if delay of the second physician endangered the mother's life, reasoned that this rule was acceptable because it was closely related to the state's compelling interest in the life of the viable fetus. The dissent objected on the grounds that sometimes a mother's health necessitated use of an abortion technique that inevitably destroys the fetus, and for these procedures the second physician requirement is simply irrational.

The *Ashcroft* decision made clear that the lines on permissible regulations of abortion had shifted slightly since *Roe*, but the *Akron I* decision, handed down on the same day, indicated that *Roe* still had the support of a six-justice majority.

Within three years, with no personnel change on the Court, that support of six for *Roe* was to dwindle to five in the case of *Thornburgh v. American College of Obstetricians and Gynecologists* (ACOG);[56] Chief Justice Burger joined the dissenters' camp arguing that the Court "should re-examine *Roe*." He explained that what provoked him to change sides was the now-prevailing Court understanding of *Roe v. Wade,* which he claimed was a more extreme version than was really warranted by *Roe*. If this extreme version of *Roe* was going to continue, then Burger would now be willing to abandon the *Roe v. Wade* precedent.

The particular actions that drove Burger into the anti-*Roe* camp were the majority's declarations of unconstitutionality of several Pennsylvania statutes. These had mandated the following:

1. Twenty-four hours prior to obtaining a woman's written consent to abortion, her physician was required to tell her (a) his/her own name, (b) the "fact that there may be detrimental physical and psychological effects [of the abortion] which are not accurately foreseeable," (c) the "particular medical risks associated with the particular abortion procedure to be employed," (d) the probable gestational age of the fetus, and (e) the "medical risks associated with carrying her child to term."

2. By the same deadline, the law also required that the woman be informed "that medical assistance benefits may be available for prenatal care, childbirth and neonatal care," that the father "is liable to assist" in the child's support even if the father has offered to pay for the abortion, and that the state has available printed materials that describe the fetus (detailing "probable anatomical and physiological characteristics for the unborn child at two-week increments") and a list of agencies offering alternatives to abortion. If she could not read the material, she could choose to have it read to her and if she had any questions, they were to be answered in her own language. Her written consent was supposed to indicate that all this had been done prior to the 24-hour limit.

3. Records were to be kept specifying the performing and referring physicians, the facility, the probable age of gestation, the basis for determination of nonviability, the method of payment for the abortion, the woman's political subdivision and state of residence, plus her age, race, marital status, number of previous pregnancies, and date of last menstrual period. This material was to be available to the public except for the woman's name and the physicians' names.

4. For post-viability abortions, three rules applied: (a) A second physician had to be on hand to preserve the life and health of the fetus. (b) The abortion performer had to exercise the same degree of care for the fetus as he or she would for a fetus intended to be born. (c) The abortion technique selected had to be one that maximized the chances of fetal survival unless, in the

physician's good faith judgment, this technique "would present a significantly greater medical risk to the life or health of the pregnant woman."

The (five-justice) majority declared all of these provisions unconstitutional. Blackmun reasoned, for the majority, that the information-mandating provisions were not aimed at truly informed consent, because the physician was required to present the information whether or not his or her medical judgment viewed it as relevant to the particular patient. To the degree that the mandated information was irrelevant, these provisions were not truly promotive of health and therefore were unconstitutional. Moreover, by superimposing government views where professional medical judgment should prevail, the state was unconstitutionally interfering with the privacy of the doctor-patient relationship. As to the recordkeeping provisions, the Court reasoned that the detailed level of specificity of the information gathered and the fact that it was to be available to the public presented a specter of intimidation and harassment of abortion patients and abortion providers that threatened the right of privacy. Finally, the post-viability abortion rules were struck down because, despite the statutory language protecting women against selection of a pro-fetus abortion technique that "would present a significantly greater risk" to her health, the majority nonetheless reasoned that the statute mandated some degree of "trade-off" of maternal health for fetal survival and that this government choice violated the Constitution. The rule for a second physician was struck down because the statute contained no exception, implied or expressed, for an emergency situation where physician delay might pose a threat to the woman's life.

In addition to Burger, Justices O'Connor and White contributed dissents to the *Thornburgh* decision, and Rehnquist joined both dissents. Justice O'Connor made it a point to reiterate her views of *Akron I*, particularly her explication of the analysis that ought to replace the *Roe* framework. White, an appointee of President John F. Kennedy, wrote a lengthy dissent, forthrightly urging, "[T]he time has come to recognize that *Roe v. Wade*, no less than the cases overruled by the Court in the past . . . 'departs from a proper understanding' of the Constitution and to overrule it." He granted that the Court properly protected as fundamental a right to privacy "in connection with family life, the rearing of children, marital privacy and the use of contraceptives, and the preservation of the individual's capacity to procreate," but insisted that the issues involved with abortion are different because it involves the destruction of a fetus which is "an entity that bears in its cells all the genetic information that characterizes a member of the species *homo sapiens* and distinguishes an individual member of that species from all others, and . . . there is no nonarbitrary line separating a fetus from a child or, indeed, an adult human being."[57] These facts rendered abortion unique and thus not properly classed with matters like contraception or childrearing. Nor should freedom to choose abortion be viewed as part of the liberty protected by "due process" because it was not a liberty traditional to our society. Legal prohibition of it date to early American history.[58] Thus, White concluded, *Roe* was wrongly decided. Moreover, even if the right were somehow fundamental, it would be outweighed by the compelling governmental interest of "protecting those who will be citizens if their lives are not ended in the womb."[59]

Finally, White argued that even without abandoning *Roe* all of these statutes should be found constitutional: The recordkeeping requirements did mandate confidentiality as to names and thus would not produce harassment and intimidation; the post-viability rules served the compelling interest in the life of a viable fetus, forbade any significant risk to the mother's health, and (contrary to the majority reading) were worded in such a way as to encourage the inference that any maternal health emergency would justify an abortion before waiting for a second physician to arrive; and the 24-hour waiting period and informational requirements did further health, mental and physical, by assuring that consent was truly informed. He called the Court's reasoning on the last topic "nonsensical" because even if abortion freedom is a constitutional right, the practice of medicine is not, and government has always heavily regulated it in the United States.

Justice White's dissent provoked a special concurrence from majority-justice Stevens, which focused specifically on why *Roe v. Wade* should not be overruled. In effect, Justice Stevens presented a new rationale for *Roe*, evidently concerned that Justice Blackmun's original opinion had not been adequately cogent or powerful. Justice Stevens's starting point was the right of privacy; he reminded readers that White and other justices in the minority by now pretty routinely conceded that it did cover contraception. Stevens then wrote:

> For reasons that are not entirely clear ... Justice White abruptly announces that the interest in "liberty" that is implicated by a decision not to bear a child that is made a few days after conception is less fundamental than a comparable decision made before conception. There may, of course, be a difference in the strength of the countervailing state interest, but I fail to see how a decision on childbearing becomes *less* important the day after conception than the day before. Indeed, if one decision is more fundamental to the individual's freedom than the other, surely it is the postconception decision that is the more serious. Thus it is difficult for me to understand how Justice White reaches the conclusion that restraints upon this

aspect of a woman's liberty do not "call into play anything more than the most minimal scrutiny."

* * *

Justice White is also surely wrong in suggesting that the government interest in protecting fetal life is equally compelling during the entire period from the moment of conception until the moment of birth.... I should think it obvious that the state's interest in the protection of an embryo—even if that interest is defined as "protecting those who will become citizens,"—increases progressively and dramatically as the organism's capacity to feel pain, to experience pleasure, to survive, and to react to its surroundings increases day by day. The development of a fetus—and pregnancy itself—are not static conditions, and the assertion that the government's interest is static simply ignores this reality.... [I]t seems to me quite odd to argue that distinctions may not be drawn between the state interest in protecting the freshly fertilized egg and the state interest in protecting the nine-month-gestated, fully sentient fetus on the eve of birth. Recognition of this distinction is supported not only by logic, but also by history and by our shared experiences.[60]

Shifting Judicial Consensus, 1989–1991

After the *Thornburgh* decision, the judicial battle lines around *Roe v. Wade* appeared to be very close indeed; only five justices out of nine still maintained support for *Roe*. At this point, two justices left the Court, one from each contingent: Chief Justice Burger and Justice Powell. President Reagan moved Rehnquist up into the role of Chief Justice and filled the former Rehnquist slot with Antonin Scalia, an Italian Catholic and a very conservative jurist. Reagan filled the Powell vacancy with Anthony Kennedy, who was generally viewed as a moderate.[61] If Kennedy were to vote as Powell had, and Scalia as the recently anti-*Roe* Burger, the close balance on the Court would not change. However, the next major abortion decision, *Webster v. Reproductive Services*[62] was to reveal an inclination on the part of both Scalia and Kennedy to scrap *Roe v. Wade*.

The *Webster* case presented a challenge to a group of statutes that contained a mixture of restrictions concerning abortion funding and abortion itself. A recapitulation of the precedents concerning the public funding of abortion will therefore be helpful at this point for providing the legal context that surrounded the justices' discussion of the abortion funding aspects of *Webster*.

Background: Restrictions on Abortion Funding, 1977–1980

In states where popular antagonism toward the Supreme Court's 1973 abortion decision was intense, legislative reaction extended beyond the overt restrictions of the sort discussed above. In addition, these states prohibited the use of state Medicaid funds for "nontherapeutic" abortions or for abortions not "medically necessary." Statutory definition of these terms varied from state to state. (It is worth noting, however, that the Supreme Court had made clear in the 1971 case of *U.S. v. Vuitch*, described above, that references to the mother's "health" in such statutes would be interpreted to include mental and emotional health.)

Challenges to these refusals to fund abortions arose from two directions. One line of attack on denials of Medicaid funds for abortion rested on statutory interpretation, and it was presented in the case of *Beal v. Doe*.[63] Federal law establishes the Medicaid program (Title XIX of the Social Security Act), and this program provides federal funds for medical services to the "medically needy" (persons too poor to pay for medical care who are not already on welfare). State participation in the program is optional. But if states do participate, they must abide by any federal regulations that are part of the program. This follows from the basic principle of our legal system that federal law always overrides state law in case of a conflict.[64] This line of attack maintained that the wording of the federal Medicaid law implied that abortions had to be funded by all states participating in the Medicaid program.

The precise wording at issue was the following federal statutory requirement: "A state plan for medical assistance must...include *reasonable standards...for determining eligibility* for and *the extent of medical assistance* under the plan which . . . are consistent with the objectives of this [Title]"[65] (emphasis added).

The wording by which the statute described its own "objective" included the phrase "to meet the costs of necessary medical services."[66] Thus, this decision hinged on whether the Supreme Court were willing to view certain abortions as "unnecessary" medical services. As of 1977 six members of the Court were. (The dissenters were Blackmun, Brennan, and Marshall. They argued that an abortion was the medically necessary service for an unwanted pregnancy.)

The particular Pennsylvania statute at issue refused Medicaid funds to any abortions not "medically necessary" as the statute itself defined that term. "Medically necessary," as Pennsylvania viewed it, included abortions only (1) when continued pregnancy threatened the mother's health, (2) when the infant faced a probability of being born with a physical or mental deficiency, or (3) when the pregnancy resulted from rape or incest and constituted a threat to the mother's "mental or physical health." The U.S. Supreme Court majority interpreted Title XIX of the Social Security Act to permit the imposition of these three conditions as a "not unreasonable" interpretation of federal law. They also permitted other states to read the law as allowing funding for all abortions for the needy. In other words, they permitted a diversity of state approaches under this law.

The second line of challenge rested on the Constitution itself, using a combination of the equal protection clause and the right to privacy. This approach maintained that the right of privacy required the state to treat equally the decision to give birth and the decision to abort, because it was a right to be free of government interference in making the choice. For the state to fund one (childbirth) but not the other (abortion) was to rig the scales in the case of indigent women, thus unconstitutionally interfering with what ought to be an unfettered private choice.

On the same day that it handed down *Beal v. Doe*, the Supreme Court handed down two more decisions affecting the availability of abortions, and these addressed this second approach. In the first of these, *Maher v. Roe*,[67] the Court faced squarely the constitutional attack on a state's denial of Medicaid funds for abortions not "medically necessary."[68] And the Supreme Court had to address this equal protection argument because the District Court below had reasoned that indigent pregnant women needing Medicaid funds for abortions had a constitutional right to such funds. Six other lower federal courts had announced decisions agreeing with this reasoning of the District Court in *Maher*.[69]

In sustaining the constitutional attack on this denial of abortion funds by the state of Connecticut, the District Court had been acting within a complex legal environment. A substantial series of cases had announced that the Constitution forbids the government to condition the exercise of fundamental civil rights on wealth or on the payment of a fee. This rule of law had been used to strike down a state law forbidding entry into the state by indigents,[70] state laws requiring even impoverished convicts to pay fees for various trial records needed to appeal their own convictions,[71] state laws that refused to supply free attorneys to impoverished criminal defendants,[72] state laws imposing poll taxes on the privileges of voting,[73] state laws imposing a property ownership requirement on people running for public office,[74] and state laws requiring even the impoverished to pay filing fees before they could sue for divorce.[75] These cases involved, respectively, the right to travel freely among the states, the right to due process of law, the right to counsel, the right to vote and run for office, and the right of marital freedom. Although the Court had announced in the poll-tax case that "lines drawn on the basis of wealth or property, like those of race, are traditionally disfavored,"[76] the Court has nonetheless never invalidated a law *solely* because it drew a line on the basis of poverty. To do that would imply that all our welfare laws and many of our tax laws are unconstitutional. And even the conditioning of certain legal procedures on the payment of a fee has not always been held unconstitutional. In 1973 the Court held that the Bankruptcy Act's requirement of a $500 filing fee was not unconstitutional because (among other reasons) "bankruptcy is not a 'fundamental right.' "[77]

Neither the combination of poverty with the fundamental right of privacy, which the *Maher* case presented, nor the equal protection reasoning of the District Court, persuaded the U.S. Supreme Court to rule for Susan Roe. Having just rejected in *Beal* the statutory attack on denials of Medicaid for abortion, the Supreme Court in *Maher* rejected this constitutional attack. Justice Powell's basic argument for the majority was that the district (and other) court(s) had misconceived the nature of the right to privacy described in *Roe v. Wade*. It was a right to be free of "government compulsion" in making certain kinds of decisions. Since this Connecticut law placed no obstacle in front of a woman who wanted an abortion, the law in no way impinged on the right of privacy. Her poverty predated the statute and was simply unaltered by it. Justice Powell went on to distinguish between "direct state interference with a protected activity" (which is generally unconstitutional) and "state encouragement of an alternate activity," for which the state has much more leeway. He concluded, "[A] state is not required to show a compelling interest for its policy choice to favor normal childbirth any more than a state must justify its decision to fund public but not private education [even though, similarly, there is a constitutionally protected right of the individual to choose to attend private school]."

Finally, on the same day that it announced *Beal* and *Maher*, the Court majority, in a third case, sustained another variety of a state effort to limit the availability of abortions. St. Louis had issued an outright prohibition on "nontherapeutic" abortions within its two city-owned hospitals. The city defined "nontherapeutic" as covering any abortion not needed to save the mother's life or to save her from "grave physiological injury." Since this amounted to an outright governmental prohibition, although one of limited extent because private hospitals did function in St. Louis, it is somewhat surprising that the court majority devoted less effort to settling this case, *Poelker v. Doe*,[78] than to either *Beal* or *Maher*. The Court majority issued only a brief *per curiam* opinion for this case, treating the city's decision not as a limited prohibition on abortions but rather as a refusal to provide a government subsidy (via its subsidy of the hospital facilities) for abortion services. The same three justices as in *Beal* dissented in both *Maher* and *Poelker*, endorsing for the latter two the equal protection line of reasoning described in the text above.

Even before *Beal*, *Maher*, and *Poelker* were handed down (on June 20, 1977), Congress, in an effort orchestrated by Rep. Henry Hyde (R-IL) had added its voice to the chorus opposing public financing of abortions. In a series of amendments to annual appropriations bills, each called a Hyde Amendment, Congress began in September 1976 to forbid the use of federal funds to reimburse the cost of abortions for Medicaid recipients, with a very narrow range of permitted exceptions. The 1977 fiscal year appropriation made an exception only for those pregnancies that endangered the life of the mother. The Hyde Amendments for '78 and '79 additionally exempted abortions to end pregnancies that were the result of "promptly reported" rape or incest or that would cause "severe and long-lasting health damage" to the mother. The 1980 Hyde Amendment removed the health damage exemption but retained the exemptions for rape or incest or life-threatening pregnancies.

On September 30, 1976, the day the first Hyde Amendment was enacted, Cora McRae, a pregnant Medicaid recipient in New York, brought suit with a number of other plaintiffs to enjoin the enforcement of the funding restriction on the grounds that it was unconstitutional. The Secretary of Health, Education and Welfare (HEW) was joined on the defendant side by Senators James Buckley and Jesse Helms and by Rep. Hyde. The District Court certified the suit as a class-action suit on behalf of all pregnant or potentially pregnant women eligible for Medicaid in New York State who choose to seek an abortion and all abortion service providers, and it granted an injunction against enforcing the law, pending a full hearing. Then *Beal* and *Maher* were decided and the Supreme Court vacated the injunction and remanded the case to the District Court for reconsideration in light of the reasoning in those decisions.

The plaintiffs argued along both statutory and constitutional lines. First, they claimed that Title XIX of the Social Security Act even with the Hyde Amendments still obliged the states to pay for medically necessary abortions, for they were necessary medical services within the meaning of the act. The District Court rejected this argument, and none of the Supreme Court justices quarreled with that statutory interpretation.

The plaintiffs' constitutional arguments, on the other hand, met with more success at the District Court. They claimed that the Hyde Amendment violated the First Amendment clauses forbidding laws "respecting an establishment of religion" or prohibiting the free exercise of religion, and also violated the equal protection concept implied in the Fifth Amendment due process clause.[79] They succeeded in convincing the District Court of both the free exercise and the Fifth Amendment arguments. The District Court then enjoined the Secretary of HEW (again) from enforcing the Hyde Amendment. The Secretary appealed to the Supreme Court for a stay of the injunction pending appeal, but the Supreme Court refused to grant it. After hearing the appeal, however, in the case of *Harris v. McRae*[80] the Supreme Court did (on June 24, 1980) overturn the District Court's order and permit the Hyde Amendment to take effect.[81]

The decision was 5–4, because Justice Stevens joined the *Maher* dissent group of Brennan, Marshall, and Blackmun. He made a point of arguing that there was a difference of constitutional dimension between denying a medically needed, in the sense of needed for the woman's health, abortion, as this law did, and merely denying funds for nontherapeutic abortions, as the laws treated in earlier decisions had done. Stevens argued that, contrary to the disclaimers of the majority, the outcome of this ordinance *was* to place a special burden on the woman who needed a therapeutic abortion. *Roe v. Wade* had established the legal principle that a woman "has a constitutional right to place a higher value on avoiding serious harm to her own health . . . than on protecting potential life," (indeed, even as to a viable fetus) and "the exercise of that right cannot provide the basis for the denial of a benefit [medically needed services] to which she would otherwise be entitled."

The Court majority reiterated its reasoning of the earlier cases: This law impinged on no fundamental right, because it did not add any new obstacle that would not have been there, were the government refusing to pay for all medical services. Since it impinged on no protected right, the law needed to have only some rational relation to a legitimate government interest, and protecting potential life was at least a legitimate (even if not at all stages "compelling") government interest. Encouraging childbirth, by funding it for the poor, was rationally related to the goal of protecting potential life.

Obituary for *Roe v. Wade*? *Webster v. Reproductive Health Services* (1989)

After *Harris v. McRae*, no major new public funding issues came before the Court until *Webster v. Reproductive Health Services* (492 U.S. 490) in 1989. And in that case, for the first time since 1973, a majority of the Supreme Court appeared to go on record as favoring the overruling of *Roe v. Wade*. For that reason, *Webster* appeared to initiate a new phase of abortion litigation.

The new anti-*Roe* majority consisted of the three Reagan appointees, O'Connor, Scalia, and Kennedy, plus the original *Roe* dissenters, White and Rehnquist. One justice, Scalia, wrote an opinion urging an immediate overruling of *Roe*; three justices (Rehnquist, White, and Kennedy) concurred in the view, expressed in an opinion authored by Rehnquist, that "the rigid trimester framework" of *Roe* had to be rejected, although the statute at issue in *Webster* did not conflict with the specific holding of *Roe v. Wade*. In addition, this Rehnquist plurality opinion quoted a fifth justice, O'Connor, to the effect that the state has a compelling interest in protecting the potential life of the fetus not only after viability—*contra* what *Roe v. Wade* established—but "*throughout* pregnancy." Justice O'Connor refused to concur with the group who quoted her, on the grounds that the rule of *Roe v. Wade* did not have to be disturbed in order to uphold the statute at issue in *Webster*, although she did acknowledge that she continues "to consider problematic" the "trimester framework" of *Roe*. Thus, the *Webster* array of opinions looked like five opponents of *Roe* and four defenders (Marshall, Brennan, Blackmun, and Stevens). It finally appeared that the thin 5–4 majority who in 1986, in *Thornburgh v. ACOG,* endorsed the survival of *Roe*, had eroded by 1989 (with the appointment of Kennedy) to a 4–5 minority.

The *Webster* case involved a multipart anti-abortion statute from the state of Missouri, which blended funding restrictions with direct abortion regulations and with a proclamation of belief and an interpretive guideline. The brief proclamation said (in the statutory preamble), "The life of each human being begins at conception," and "unborn children have protectable interests in life, health, and well-being" (without any more concrete specification of the interests). The interpretive guideline said that state laws should be interpreted "to acknowledge on behalf of the unborn child at every stage of development, all the rights, privileges and immunities available to other persons . . . of this state, *subject only to the Constitution of the United States, and decisional interpretations thereof by the U.S. Supreme Court . . .*" (emphasis added). The regulation of abortion practice in the statute was a rule that, before performing an abortion on a woman whom he or she believes to be 20 or more weeks pregnant, the physician must ascertain whether the fetus is viable by "using and exercising that degree of care, skill, and proficiency commonly exercised by the ordinarily skillful, careful, and prudent physician" and by performing "such medical examinations and tests as are necessary to make a finding of the gestational age, weight, and lung maturity" and must record "such findings and determination of viability." Finally, the public funding restrictions had three aspects: (1) "Public facilities" (defined as facilities "owned, leased, or controlled" by the state) could not be used to perform abortions not necessary for the mother's survival; (2) public employees could not "within the scope of [their] employment" perform abortions not necessary for saving a woman's life; and (3) public funds could not be expended for "encouraging or counseling abortions."

In addition, the statute had originally prohibited public employees from doing any abortion counseling and had prohibited professional abortion counseling on the premises of legally defined "public facilities." In response to a challenge brought by a group of abortion providers that included five medical professionals employed at a state-owned hospital, the District Court and the Circuit Court of Appeals had declared these last two provisions an unconstitutional restriction of a woman's constitutional right to receive medical information needed for an informed exercise of the right to choose whether to bear a child. The state of Missouri decided to accept those decisions as to the last two provisions and did not appeal them to the U.S. Supreme Court.

Moreover, Missouri explained to the U.S. Supreme Court that it interpreted the prohibition on using public funds for abortion counseling to be a restriction simply on the fiscal officers of the state against spending money specifically for abortion counseling. In response to this interpretation, the attorneys for the various abortion providers withdrew their challenge to this section of the law, indicating that with this reading it no longer directly affected them. As to this single section of the law the Supreme Court managed a unanimous response: The issue was moot because the challenge had been withdrawn.

The rest of the statute, however, produced a confusing disarray on the Court, a bare majority of five (Rehnquist, White, Kennedy, O'Connor, and Scalia) concurred in Rehnquist's opinion upholding the belief declarations (and interpretive guideline) in the statute (on the grounds that they did not per se restrict anybody's freedom) and the restrictions on performance of abortions by on-the-job public employees and in publicly funded facilities (on the grounds of the public funding precedents reviewed above). On the remaining piece of the statute, this majority held together as to the result only: The viability testing requirement was not void.

Three justices, through Rehnquist, said it required only tests for viability that a normally prudent physician would do but that since these tests aimed to protect the fetus and not the mother's health, there was a conflict with the *Roe* trimester approach, so that approach had to go. O'Connor pointed out statements in earlier precedents that noted that viability is an individual matter, that it does not necessarily fall exactly at the end of the second trimester, and that states may act to protect potential life of a viable fetus. Therefore, she saw no conflict between viability testing and the rules derived from *Roe*. Scalia agreed with Rehnquist's arguments on the viability testing provision but added that this provision "effectively" conflicted with *Roe* and that, under the circumstances described below, this fact led him to favor an immediate overruling.

The majority dissolved into utter ambiguity on the doctrinal issue of the decade: was *Roe v. Wade* still to be followed? One of the five, Scalia, would simply overrule *Roe*. Three of the five, Rehnquist, Kennedy, and White, urged an immediate abandonment of what they called "key elements of the *Roe* framework—trimesters and viability." They specifically endorsed replacing these key elements with the rule that states have a compelling interest in the protection of potential life throughout pregnancy, not just after viability, and they quoted Justice O'Connor's opinions from both *Akron I* and *Thornburgh* endorsing the same point. The three, speaking through Rehnquist, urged that the Court "modify and narrow *Roe*" by this new doctrine—namely, that states may regulate abortion "throughout pregnancy" to protect potential life.

The ambiguity as to *Roe* was introduced by the fact that Justice O'Connor now pointedly refused to concur in this portion of the Rehnquist opinion, which quoted her own words, and she argued instead that this Missouri statute does not conflict "in any way" with prior decisions of the Court, including *Roe v. Wade*, and that therefore the Court was behaving improperly in reconsidering *Roe* (something she had herself urged in both *Akron I* and *Thornburgh*). Her apparent waffling evidently infuriated Scalia, for the tone of his opinion is not only unusually strident, but he goes out of his way to mock Justice O'Connor's reasoning in a lengthy footnote. Here, in part, is what Scalia wrote.

> **JUSTICE SCALIA, concurring in part and concurring as to the result [in *Webster*]:**
>
> The real question, then, is whether there are valid reasons to go beyond the most stingy possible holding today. It seems to me there are not only valid but compelling ones. Ordinarily, speaking no more broadly than is absolutely required avoids throwing settled law into confusion; doing so today preserves a chaos that is evident to anyone who can read and count. Alone sufficient to justify a broad holding is the fact that our retaining control, through *Roe*, of what I believe to be, and many of our citizens recognize to be, a political issue, continuously distorts the public perception of the role of this Court. We can now look forward to at least another Term with carts full of mail from the public, and streets full of demonstrators, urging us—their unelected and life-tenured judges who have been awarded those extraordinary, undemocratic characteristics precisely in order that we might follow the law despite the popular will—to follow the popular will. Indeed, I expect we can look forward

to even more of that than before, given our indecisive decision today. And if these reasons for taking the unexceptional course of reaching a broader holding are not enough, then consider the nature of the constitutional question we avoid: In most cases, we do no harm by not speaking more broadly than the decision requires. Anyone affected by the conduct that the avoided holding would have prohibited will be able to challenge it himself and have his day in court to make the argument. Not so with respect to the harm that many States believed, pre-*Roe*, and many may continue to believe, is caused by largely unrestricted abortion. That will continue to occur if the States have the constitutional power to prohibit it, and would do so, but we skillfully avoid telling them so. Perhaps those abortions cannot constitutionally be proscribed. That is surely an arguable question, the question that reconsideration of *Roe v. Wade* entails. But what is not at all arguable, it seems to me, is that we should decide now and not insist that we be run into a corner before we grudgingly yield up our judgment. The only sound reason for the latter course is to prevent a change in the law—but to think that desirable begs the question to be decided.

It was an arguable question today whether § 188.029 of the Missouri law contravened this Court's understanding of *Roe v. Wade*,* and I would have examined *Roe* rather than examining the contravention. Given the Court's newly contracted abstemiousness, what will it take, one must wonder, to permit us to reach that fundamental question? The result of our vote today is that we will not reconsider that prior opinion, even if most of the Justices think it is wrong, unless we have before us a statute that in fact contradicts it—and even then (under our newly discovered "no-broader-than-necessary" requirement) only minor problematical aspects of *Roe* will be reconsidered, unless one expects state legislatures to adopt provisions whose compliance with *Roe* cannot even be argued with a straight face. It thus appears that the mansion of constitutionalized abortion law, constructed overnight in *Roe v. Wade*, must be disassembled doorjamb by doorjamb, and never entirely brought down, no matter how wrong it may be.

Of the four courses we might have chosen today—to reaffirm *Roe*, to overrule it explicitly, to overrule it *sub silentio*, or to avoid the question—the last is the least responsible. On the question of the constitutionality of § 188.029, I concur in the judgment of the Court and strongly dissent from the manner in which it has been reached.

Opinion Footnote

* That question, compared with the question whether we should reconsider and reverse *Roe*, is hardly worth a footnote, but I think JUSTICE O'CONNOR answers that incorrectly as well. In *Roe v. Wade*, 410 U.S. 113, 165–166 (1973), we said that "the physician [has the right] to administer medical

> treatment according to his professional judgment up to the points where important state interests provide compelling justifications for intervention." We have subsequently made clear that it is also a matter of medical judgment when viability (one of those points) is reached. "The time when viability is achieved may vary with each pregnancy, and the determination of whether a particular fetus is viable is, and must be, a matter for the judgment of the responsible attending physician." *Planned Parenthood of Central Mo. v. Danforth*, 428 U.S. 52, 64 (1976). Section 188.029 conflicts with the purpose and hence the fair import of this principle because it will sometimes require a physician to perform tests that he would not otherwise have performed to determine whether a fetus is viable. It is therefore a legislative imposition on the judgment of the physician, and one that increases the cost of an abortion.
>
> JUSTICE O'CONNOR would nevertheless uphold the law because it "does not impose an undue burden on a woman's abortion decision." This conclusion is supported by the observation that the required tests impose only a marginal cost on the abortion procedure, far less of an increase than the cost-doubling hospitalization requirement invalidated in *Akron v. Akron Center for Reproductive Health*. . . .The fact that the challenged regulation is less costly than what we struck down in *Akron* tells us only that we cannot decide the present case on the basis of that earlier decision. It does not tell us whether the present requirement is an "undue burden," and I know of no basis for determining that this particular burden (or any other for that matter) is "due." One could with equal justification conclude that it is not. To avoid the question of *Roe v. Wade*'s validity, with the attendant costs that this will have for the Court and for the principles of self-governance, on the basis of a standard that offers "no guide but the Court's own discretion," *Baldwin v. Missouri*, 281 U.S. 586, 595 (1930) (Holmes, J., dissenting), merely adds to the irrationality of what we do today.
>
> Similarly irrational is the new concept that JUSTICE O'CONNOR introduces into the law in order to achieve her result, the notion of a State's "interest in potential life when viability is possible." Since "viability" means the mere possibility (not the certainty) of survivability outside the womb, "possible viability" must mean the possibility of a possibility of survivability outside the womb. Perhaps our next opinion will expand the third trimester into the second even further, by approving state action designed to take account of "the chance of possible viability."

Strangely enough, had the [pro-*Roe*] dissenters agreed with the majority's reading of the viability-testing provision of the statute, they would have upheld it as completely consistent with *Roe v. Wade*. In other words, they interpreted *Roe* as less hostile to this abortion restriction than did the anti-*Roe* group of Rehnquist, White, Kennedy, and Scalia. However, the *Webster* dissenters believed the majority erred in reading the statute as less harsh than its language seems; the four dissenters believed (with two lower courts) that the statute required doctors to perform certain medical tests even for cases where the doctors honestly and correctly believed the tests to be both unhelpful in determining viability and dangerous to the woman's health. On this reading, the statute turns out to be unconstitutional on the grounds of sheer irrationality. (It takes away liberty "without due process of law," since it bears no reasonable relation to any legitimate government interest.)

All four dissenters also disputed the majority's contentions as to the declarative parts of the statute and its rules for the use of "public facilities." With the exception of Justice Stevens, however, they devoted the bulk of their attention to the issue of the continued force of *Roe v. Wade*. As to their fears that the law of

Women and Reproductive Freedom

Roe v. Wade was about to become a dead letter, here, in part, is what they said, through the pen of Justice Blackmun.

> **JUSTICE BLACKMUN, dissenting in Webster:**
>
> ### I-D
>
> Thus, "not with a bang, but a whimper," the plurality discards a landmark case of the last generation, and casts into darkness the hopes and visions of every woman in this country who had come to believe that the Constitution guaranteed her the right to exercise some control over her unique ability to bear children. The plurality does so either oblivious or insensitive to the fact that millions of women, and their families, have ordered their lives around the right to reproductive choice, and that this right has become vital to the full participation of women in the economic and political walks of American life. The plurality would clear the way once again for government to force upon women the physical labor and specific and direct medical and psychological harms that may accompany carrying a fetus to term. The plurality would clear the way again for the State to conscript a woman's body and to force upon her a "distressful life and future." *Roe*, 410 U.S., at 153.
>
> The result, as we know from experience, see Cates & Rochat, "Illegal Abortions in the United States: 1972–1974," 8 *Family Planning Perspectives* 86, 92 (1976), would be that every year hundreds of thousands of women, in desperation, would defy the law, and place their health and safety in the unclean and unsympathetic hands of back-alley abortionists, or they would attempt to perform abortions upon themselves with disastrous results. Every year, many women, especially poor and minority women, would die or suffer debilitating physical trauma, all in the name of enforced morality or religious dictates or lack of compassion, as it may be.
>
> Of the aspirations and settled understandings of American women, of the inevitable and brutal consequences of what it is doing, the tough-approach plurality utters not a word. This silence is callous. It is also profoundly destructive of this Court as an institution. To overturn a constitutional decision is a rare and grave undertaking. To overturn a constitutional decision that secured a fundamental personal liberty to millions of persons would be unprecedented in our 200 years of constitutional history.... [The requirement of strong] justification [for overruling precedent] applies with unique force where, as here, the Court's abrogation of precedent would destroy people's

> firm belief, based on past decisions of this Court, that they possess an unabridgeable right to undertake certain conduct.
>
> As discussed at perhaps too great length above, the plurality makes no serious attempt to carry "the heavy burden of persuading ... that changes in society or in the law dictate" the abandonment of *Roe* and its numerous progeny, *Vasquez v. Hillery*, 474 U.S. 254, 266, much less the greater burden of explaining the abrogation of a fundamental personal freedom. Instead, the plurality pretends that it leaves *Roe* standing, and refuses even to discuss the real issue underlying this case: whether the Constitution includes an unenumerated right to privacy that encompasses a woman's right to decide whether to terminate a pregnancy....
>
> This comes at a cost. The doctrine of *stare decisis* "permits society to presume that bedrock principles are founded in the law rather than in the proclivities of individuals, and thereby contributes to the integrity of our constitutional system of government, both in appearance and in fact." 474 U.S., at 265–266. Today's decision involves the most politically divisive domestic legal issue of our time. By refusing to explain or to justify its proposed revolutionary revision in the law of abortion, and by refusing to abide not only by our precedents, but also by our canons for reconsidering those precedents, the plurality invites charges of cowardice and illegitimacy to our door. I cannot say that these would be undeserved.
>
> **II**
>
> For today, at least, the law of abortion stands undisturbed. For today, the women of this Nation still retain the liberty to control their destinies. But the signs are evident and very ominous, and a chill wind blows.[82]

Justice Stevens's dissent for *Webster* zeroed in on a difference of opinion between the Missouri legislature and "standard medical texts" as to the meaning of "conception." While the statute equated "conception" with "fertilization" of ovum by sperm (which, in fact, takes several hours, not a "moment"), Stevens noted that the "standard medical texts now define 'conception' as including implantation in the uterine wall," which is completed about a week after sperm meets egg. Thus, it still would make sense to use the term "contraception" to describe medications (or intrauterine devices—IUDs) that operate post-fertilization but pre-implantation. He also lists as a "method of contraception" the medication RU-486, which could be given to women with confirmed pregnancies during the first six weeks following their last menstrual period, and he quotes the

Association of Reproductive Health Professionals to the effect that this is "the indeterminate period between contraception and abortion."[83]

The advent of RU-486 as a medical alternative to surgical abortion was approved by the Food and Drug Administration (FDA) in 2000.[84] RU-486, a combination of hormones that induces an abortion, is often referred to as "medical abortion" or "medication abortion" (or "chemical abortion" by anti-abortion activists). It calls for women to take two different types of pills 24–48 hours apart. The first pills are ingested in a medical setting such as a doctor's office or Planned Parenthood center. The second type of pills are provided to the patient when she is in the medical setting taking the first pills, but this second type is to be taken later in the privacy of her own home. The first ingested pills are mifepristone, a hormone that blocks the production of progesterone, which is a hormone that supports pregnancy. The second ingested pills are misoprostol, a hormone that expels the embryo from the uterus. One to two weeks after taking the pills, the woman is supposed to be checked by her physician to be sure the pills have worked.

Because RU-486 is a two-step process, it can be interrupted and reversed. In 2010, a small group of doctors started to give large doses of progesterone to women who changed their minds about having the abortion after taking the mifepristone but before taking the misoprostol. These doctors argued that the large doses of progesterone, administered over several weeks, reversed the effects of the mifepristone, and thereby allowed live births at full term. Other doctors have found that not taking the misoprostol has the same effect as taking progesterone would, because the pregnant woman's body eventually reproduces progesterone after a short time.[85]

When RU-486 was first approved by the FDA in 2000, it was considered effective for six weeks after conception. The FDA ruled in March 2016 that RU-486 can be used effectively for ten weeks after conception. The ease and privacy associated with using RU-486 as an alternative to surgical abortion has fostered the belief that RU-486 would make up 30–40% of all abortions within five years after FDA approval. This prediction was not realized. The Centers for Disease Control and Prevention (CDC) reports that, as of 2014, medical abortions comprise 23% of all abortions.[86]

The change in FDA rules is likely to increase this percentage dramatically. One can draw this conclusion because the state of Texas, in an effort to reduce abortions, legislated in 2013 that all women doing medical abortion had to follow the (at the time) strict FDA guidelines *and* take all the medication within a clinic. This law then caused an enormous drop in the number of medical abortions provided in Texas within the first year after the law took effect, because it would require three separate visits to a clinic. After the FDA liberalized its own guidelines on taking the abortion medication, permitting the pills to be taken at home and in smaller doses and also later into the pregnancy, the number of such abortions in Texas immediately rose sharply. Whole Woman's Health, which ran three abortion-providing clinics in Texas, reported a jump from ten percent to "more than half" of their patients who requested medical abortions under the new rules. Planned Parenthood, which operates five clinics in Texas, reported that the number of patients seeking abortion via these drugs quadrupled under the new FDA rules.[87]

The relative ease and privacy associated with medical abortions have changed how anti-abortion activists frame their abortion opposition. Of particular concern to anti-abortion activists is that the opportunity to influence women's decisions via protests outside abortion clinics would be reduced if there were fewer women seeking surgical abortions. For example, Republican presidential nominee George W. Bush stated that he was worried that RU-486 would contribute to more women having abortions in 2000.[88]

Overall, the number of women seeking abortions increased between the *Roe v. Wade* decision in 1973 and 1981, after which the number of abortions performed (whether surgical or medical abortions) declined. The Guttmacher Institute tracked abortions among women 15–44. It reports that, in 1973, the number of abortions performed was 16.3 per 1000 women. That number increased to 29.3 abortions per 1000 women in 1981, and declined to 14.6 abortions per 1000 women in 2014.[89] In fact, the number of abortions performed in the United States fell below one million for the first time since 1975.[90] These figures do not count as abortions those fertilized eggs prevented from developing into full-blown pregnancies by the "morning after pill," more technically known as emergency contraception.

Emergency contraception too was embroiled in the controversy surrounding RU-486 as a surgical abortion alternative. Emergency contraception like RU-486 is a combination of hormones that women take in the privacy of their homes. In contrast to RU-486, emergency contraception (which must be taken within 72 hours of unprotected sex) acts to prevent pregnancy, whereas RU-486 terminates an existing pregnancy. Emergency contraception is taken in a single dose of 1.5 mg. of levonorgestrel (synthetic progestin and estrogen). Its purpose is to prevent or delay ovulation, interfere with fertilization, prevent the implantation of a fertilized egg or alter the uterine lining. Emergency contraception is most effective

Women and Reproductive Freedom

the sooner that it is taken. About 11% of the time, emergency contraception fails to prevent the fertilized egg from being implanted in the uterine wall.

These advances in medical technology further complicate the politics of contraception and abortion and have the potential to inform the legal debates as well. Apart from the matter of the politically motivated distortion of language that seems to be omnipresent in the abortion debates, these considerations would seem to lend credence to the view that if the Scalia-Rehnquist group had developed into a solidly anti-*Roe* majority, they might have had trouble drawing a clear line between the protected contraceptive freedom of *Griswold* and *Eisenstadt* and what they would treat as the unprotected practice of abortion.

Six Votes Against *Roe*? *Rust v. Sullivan* (1991)

Alignment on the Court appeared to shift even further against *Roe* in 1991 when Justice Brennan left the Court, to be replaced by David Souter, appointed by President George H. W. Bush, or Bush I. Justice Souter's first Supreme Court case implicating abortion rights was *Rust v. Sullivan*[91] in 1991. At stake was a set of new federal regulations, adopted as presidential "executive orders" forbidding medical and other staff at federally assisted family planning clinics to discuss the abortion option with pregnant patients. The regulations made no explicit exception for abortions that might be needed to preserve a woman's health. The Supreme Court upheld these regulations in a 5–4 vote. The newest justice, Souter, aligned with the majority, but Sandra Day O'Connor placed herself in dissent, not on the grounds that the choice of abortion was a fundamental right but rather on the grounds that courts are obliged to construe laws in a way that avoids serious constitutional doubts. Because these executive branch regulations imposed a "content-based restriction on speech," they raised precisely such doubts concerning the First Amendment and thus should be viewed as not permitted by the federal statute being claimed as their implicit authorization by the Reagan/Bush administrations. Because of the First Amendment side issue in *Rust v. Sullivan* and the absence of a direct clash with *Roe* in *Webster*, O'Connor had given no indication since her *Akron I* and *Thornburgh* dissents of any change in her view, expressed there, that the reasoning of *Roe v. Wade* was "on a collision course with itself" and thus should be abandoned or that she in any way had altered her view, also expressed in both those cases, that a state's interest in protecting fetal life was important enough to be considered "compelling" not just after viability but also "*throughout* pregnancy." Justice Kennedy had aligned with the Rehnquist opinion in *Webster* rejecting the *Roe* framework, and again in *Rust* he did so to uphold this federal "gag rule" on abortion. The new Justice Souter also went along with the gag rule in *Rust*. With the addition of these to the original and still persistent *Roe* dissenters Rehnquist and White, plus the vociferously anti-*Roe* Scalia, then, by 1992 it appeared that the anti-*Roe* majority on the Supreme Court had reached the level of 6–3.

Rust v. Sullivan took up the public funding issues with which the Court had dealt in the *Webster* case, but with a new twist. What was new in *Rust* was that it added First Amendment, freedom of speech complications to the general question of a refusal to provide governmental funding for abortion.

In 1970 Congress had adopted Title X of the Public Service Health Act, which authorized federal subsidies to family planning clinics. The title contained § 1008 which stated, "None of the funds appropriated under this title shall be used in programs where abortion is a method of family planning."[92] Originally, in implementing the law, the Secretary of Health, Education and Welfare, had adopted a regulation stating that projects receiving federal funds under this title simply had to comply with the rule, "The project will not provide abortions as a method of family planning."[93] In February 1988, however, the Reagan administration added a number of regulations that focused specifically on *discussing*, as contrasted with performing, abortions. These new regulations were ostensibly in furtherance of the 18-year-old law, which Congress had not amended. The new regulations had three elements:

First, "Title X project[s could] not provide counseling concerning the use of abortion as a method of family planning or provide referral for abortion as a method of family planning."[94] Title X projects were to provide preventive, preconception care and counseling but had to refer a pregnant client elsewhere "for appropriate prenatal and/or social services by furnishing a list of available providers that promote the welfare of the mother and unborn child." The list could not be indirectly used to promote abortion

> such as by weighing the list of referrals in favor of health care providers which perform abortions, by including on the list ... health care providers whose principal business is the provision of abortions, by excluding available providers who do not provide abortions, or by steering clients to providers who offer abortion as a method of family planning.[95]

Even if a woman specifically requested information on how to locate a medically qualified abortion provider, Title X projects were forbidden to give the information. The regulations suggested the reply of "[This] project does not consider abortion an appropriate method of family planning and therefore does not counsel or refer for abortion."[96]

Second, Title X projects were forbidden to advocate abortion in any manner, including lobbying for its legalization, taking legal action to make abortion more widely available, or providing public speakers who would promote abortion "as a method of family planning."[97]

And third, Title X projects now had to be rendered "physically and financially separate" from facilities that did provide abortion counseling or abortion services.[98]

Prior to the adoption of these new regulations, the understanding of agencies subsidized under Title X had been that they might provide various reproductive health services, including counseling about contraception but also including counseling about the handling of unexpected pregnancies. While the agencies did not perform abortions, they understood their function to include referrals of pregnant women to a health care provider suitable to the wishes and needs of the woman herself. These new regulations drastically altered that counseling function.

Several family planning clinics immediately challenged the new regulations in federal courts, requesting declaratory judgments that they were unconstitutional (before the rules were put into effect), so that the clinics would not have the painful choice of either forgoing what they believed to be their, and their employees', constitutional right to freedom of speech or else forgoing the federal subsidy that enabled them to operate. Two federal circuit courts of appeal[99] did rule that the regulations were an unconstitutional infringement on the First Amendment right of freedom of speech, but another upheld them.[100]

The appeal of the latter decision was the one the Supreme Court addressed in *Rust v. Sullivan*. By the time of even the first of the circuit court decisions, Reagan was no longer president. President Bush I, however, kept the regulations in force, and his Secretary of Health and Human Services, Louis Sullivan, was officially the other party in the case, responding to the petitioner, Dr. Irving Rust, director of a family planning clinic. As it had in *Akron I*, *Thornburgh*, and *Webster*, the U.S. Department of Justice (presenting Sullivan's case) again asked the Supreme Court to overturn *Roe v. Wade*, but in this decision the Supreme Court ignored the issue of *Roe*'s continuing validity.[101] As in *Webster* (1989) and in *Hodgson v. Minnesota* (1990)[102] (a case presenting a requirement for notifying both parents of an unemancipated minor desiring an abortion but allowing a judicial bypass), but despite personnel changes—Justice Souter having replaced Justice Brennan—the Supreme Court again divided 5–4 to uphold these abortion restrictions in *Rust*.

The Court addressed three separate questions challenging the executive branch regulations in this case: (1) Did they exceed the authority of the Title X statute or conflict with its intent? (2) Did they violate the First Amendment rights of subsidized healthcare providers, such as Irving Rust; or (3) Did the regulations violate the right to privacy (secured at the federal level by the Fifth Amendment due process clause) of women seeking competent pregnancy counseling at these public clinics? The majority (Rehnquist, White, Scalia, Kennedy and Souter) answered "no" to each of these challenges. The dissents varied: All four answered "yes" on statutory invalidity of the regulations, with O'Connor and Stevens making the additional argument that the Court majority should not have proceeded to the constitutional questions. Stevens, Blackmun, and Marshall all agreed with the two other circuit courts in the conclusion that these new regulations did violate both the First Amendment and the constitutional right to privacy.

Basically, the majority ruled that the new regulations followed from one plausible reading of a statute whose language and legislative history were ambiguous. This Court opinion rejected the First Amendment and right to privacy claims on the grounds that this program was similar to a refusal to fund abortions, not a penalty on seeking one.

Political reaction to *Rust v. Sullivan* came quickly. Congress promptly adopted an amendment to Title X that made explicit its intent that the full range of pregnancy counseling, including abortion referrals when desired by the pregnant patient, be permitted at funded clinics. Just as promptly, President Bush I vetoed the amendment (which action allowed his regulations to stand). The Senate voted 76–26 to override the veto. But the House vote, which came in early October 1992, just one month before the 1992 elections, was 266–148, ten votes short of the two-thirds majority needed for an override.

Bush's solicitor general (the official in the Justice Department responsible for arguing the executive branch position in court cases) had already argued both in his *Rust* written brief and orally in the Supreme Court that the regulations did *not* permit referrals of pregnant patients for abortion even when the abortion is needed to prevent serious damage to the woman's health. When pressed hard by several justices in oral argument, he had finally conceded that if the woman were threatened with death within a matter of hours, yes, the statute did provide an exception for genuine emergencies.[103] The opinion of the Court majority for *Rust* had then strongly hinted that the Court would view with disfavor an actual application of the regulations that negatively sanctioned a doctor for giving a referral for a medically needed (as distinguished from a family planning method) abortion. Probably in response to this cue from the Court, President Bush I, in lieu of Congress's amendment, amended the regulations on his own, to permit physicians to refer patients for abortions when the abortions were needed to prevent serious damage to the patients' health. But his administration rushed these regulations into place (perhaps with an eye to the 1992 election) without following the detailed procedures required for new administrative regulations. As a consequence of this procedural irregularity, the federal court for the D.C. Circuit declared the new regulations void. Since the new regulations had been a replacement of the old, it now appeared that there were no formal regulations in place that specified counseling policy under Title X.

Before any new policy could be adopted, the voters spoke, electing Democratic Arkansas Governor Bill Clinton to replace President Bush I. Clinton had made clear during the campaign that his administration would eliminate this "gag rule." Between the November defeat and his exit from office in January 1993, President Bush I did not reenact the gag rule. Still, the *Rust v. Sullivan* precedent stands as the current guideline as to federal government leeway in utilizing funding policy to restrict the discussion of disfavored topics.

President George W. Bush (Bush II) chose not to reenact the gag rule upon taking office in 2001, but he did, on January 22, two days into his term, enact a so-called "global gag rule" (more formally known as the "Mexico City Policy") on abortion counseling for organizations in other parts of the world that offer family planning services and that receive financial assistance from the U.S. government. This "global gag rule" had been put in place in 1984 by President Reagan but was lifted by President Clinton in 1993.[104] One can speculate that the decision by President Bush II to refrain from reenacting this gag rule for Americans (although he did reenact the one for foreign groups operating outside the U.S., which are not protected by the First Amendment) suggests that he sides with one or more of the dissents in *Rust*.

The "back and forth" between presidents of the two different parties continued into the Obama and Trump administrations. On January 23, 2009, three days into his presidency and one day after the anniversary of the *Roe v. Wade* decision, Democratic President Barack Obama overturned the "global gag rule" while also committing his support for the United Nations Population Fund, which "...is the lead UN agency for delivering a world where every pregnancy is wanted, every childbirth is safe and every young person's potential is fulfilled."[105] These actions affirmed Obama's belief in women's right to choose in both domestic and international spheres.

Eight years later Republican President Donald Trump reinstated a "global gag rule" on January 23, 2017. President Trump's version of the gag rule not only prohibited foreign organizations that provide health care from receiving U.S. funds for advocating abortion as a family planning method, but also cut off U.S. funding if the organization used funds from any other source for such advocacy.[106]

The patterns that have developed since Ronald Reagan established the "Mexico City Policy" show that the party of the chief executive determines whether or not this policy will be enforced. Democratic presidents have established that the policy will not be implemented while Republican presidents have supported its enforcement through presidential memoranda.

Reprieve and Reset on *Roe v. Wade*: *Planned Parenthood v. Casey* (1992)

It came as no small surprise to observers when in June 1992 six justices in *Planned Parenthood v. Casey* announced *support* for the "essential holding of *Roe v. Wade*." That unexpected announcement unfolded as follows.

As the issues raised in *Rust* were winding their way through the courts, legislatures below the federal level began reacting to the Supreme Court's apparent signal in the June 1989 *Webster* decision that five justices were now prepared to scrap *Roe v. Wade*. That signal intensified when two of the justices who had dissented in the *Webster* case, William Brennan and Thurgood Marshall, left the Court, to be replaced by Bush appointees, David Souter and Clarence Thomas. Souter's vote in *Rust* then made him appear to be the sixth anti-abortion vote on the Court—or fifth if Sandra Day O'Connor was abandoning the opposition to *Roe* that she had expressed in *Akron I* and *Thornburgh*. Thomas did not appear a likely supporter of *Roe*, since he claimed during his 1991 Senate confirmation hearings that he had never discussed *Roe v. Wade* in his entire life. If Souter, O'Connor, and Thomas were to join Rehnquist, White, Scalia, and Kennedy (the *Webster* plurality who had argued for abandoning "the key elements of the *Roe* framework"), seven of the nine justices would be willing to abandon the rules established in *Roe v. Wade*.

The first legislature to respond to the apparent *Webster* invitation to contravene *Roe* was that of the territory Guam. In March 1990, the governor of Guam signed into law a prohibition on all abortions except those needed, as confirmed by two doctors, to save a pregnant woman's life or to end a pregnancy posing grave risk to her health. By January 1991, Utah had followed suit, adopting a ban on all abortions except those needed to save the woman's life or when pregnancy posed grave danger to her physical health, those needed because of grave defect in the fetus, or those needed as a result of rape or incest. (For the latter category, the abortion had to be performed during the first 20 weeks of the pregnancy.) By June 1991, Louisiana had passed into law a ban on all abortions except those needed to save a woman's life or those resulting from a rape reported to the police within seven days or of incest reported to the police. The time limit for rape or incest victims to procure the abortion was the first 13 weeks of pregnancy. Each of these laws was declared void by federal judges on the grounds that *Roe v. Wade* had not yet been formally overruled and was thus still the law of the land. In each case, the government (state or territorial, respectively) appealed the decision.

Before any of these direct floutings of the law of *Roe v. Wade* reached the Supreme Court, the Court delivered its *Planned Parenthood v. Casey* surprise. The *Casey* decision did not even necessitate a reconsideration of *Roe*; it involved a variety of abortion regulations but no sweeping prohibitions. Still, the executive branch once again presented a brief requesting that *Roe* be overruled, and, in contrast to its silence in *Rust v. Sullivan*, the Supreme Court decided to respond (albeit negatively) to that request.

The Court issued its decision in *Casey* with striking drama, as the three pivotal justices—O'Connor, Kennedy, and Souter—announced a jointly authored, jointly signed opinion. The joint authoring of opinions is extraordinarily rare on the U.S. Supreme Court—indeed, nearly unprecedented.[107] It created an impression of unusually strong unity (at least among those three justices). The case itself produced no majority opinion. The three-justice pivotal plurality agreed on some of the results with a four-justice group led by Rehnquist and Scalia (each of whom wrote an opinion and concurred with the other, and with whose opinions White and Thomas concurred), who were still advocating an overruling of *Roe*, and on the other results with the staunchly pro-*Roe* Justices Stevens and Blackmun (who both agreed with part but not all of the plurality opinion). The three-justice plurality staked out a position endorsing "the essential holding" of *Roe v. Wade* but admittedly modifying some of its particulars. The reader will be able to assess the degree to which *Roe* does or does not endure after reading the *Casey* opinion of the three-justice plurality, its restatements by Stevens and Blackmun, and its critiques by Rehnquist and Scalia.

Casey examines the constitutionality of several abortion regulations adopted by the state of Pennsylvania (whose governor, Robert Casey, a pro-life Democrat, appears in the case title.) The regulations (the lengthy list of which took up several pages of the Court opinion) essentially required the following:

1. Women seeking abortions, except in the case of medical emergencies, had to provide written "informed consent" at least 24 hours before the abortion. Informed consent meant that the woman had to be told by the physician the probable gestational age of the fetus; the proposed abortion procedure and "those risks and alternatives to the procedure . . . that a reasonable patient would consider material to the decision whether or not to undergo the abortion" (unless the physician "reasonably believe[s] that furnishing the information would . . . result[ ] in a severely adverse effect on the physical or mental health of the patient"); and the medical risks associated with continuing the pregnancy to term. Also the woman had to be informed by a counselor that free printed materials were available that describe fetal development and that list agencies that offer alternatives to abortion, that medical assistance benefits for pregnancy and childbirth and neonatal care may be available and that the printed material contains more details, and that the father of the "unborn child" is liable to assist in its support, even if he offered to pay for the abortion. The last point need not be mentioned to victims of rape.

2. An unemancipated minor wanting an abortion needed to obtain the "informed consent" (as described in #1 above) of a parent or guardian or go to court and obtain an order either that the abortion is in her best interest or that she is mature enough to make her own decision.

3. Before performing an abortion on a married woman for a fetus fathered by her husband—except in the case of an abortion necessitated by medical emergency—the physician had to receive a statement signed by the woman indicating that her husband has been notified of the pending abortion or else (a) that she is unable to locate the father, (b) that the fetus resulted from spousal sexual assault, or (c) that she fears bodily injury as a result of notifying her husband.

4. Facilities providing abortions that received public funds had to file publicly available reports indicating who owned the facility and how many abortions—broken down by trimester of pregnancy—were performed there each quarter year. Also, confidential reports had to be filed by all abortion providers specifying the names of the abortion performer and the referring physician for each abortion and data on the woman receiving the abortion: name, age, county of residence, number of previous pregnancies, type of procedure used, and nature of medical complications. If the physician performed the abortion as a response to a medical emergency, the grounds

for the physician's judgment had to be specified and, if her husband were not notified, the grounds for the decision not to notify him.

The federal District Court had obliged Planned Parenthood's request for a declaratory judgment that all of these provisions were "on their face" unconstitutional because they violated a strict reading of the rules established in *Roe v. Wade* (utilizing reasoning very similar to what shows up in Justice Blackmun's partially dissenting opinion below). The Circuit Court of Appeals decided that the prevailing rule of law since *Akron II* (*Ohio v. Akron Center for Reproductive Health*, 497 U.S. 502 [1990]) and *Hodgson* was an "undue burden" test grafted on to the basic framework of *Roe*. This conclusion was derived from the facts that (1) in *Akron II* and *Hodgson* (both concerning laws that demanded parental notification prior to abortions on an unemancipated minor, but that included a judicial bypass option), a majority (for the first time) supported the "undue burden" test, and (2) in *Webster* support for the "undue burden" test was the tipping point that, added to either plurality, made a majority. Applying this test, the Circuit Court upheld all of these provisions except husband notification. The U.S. Supreme Court, with varying groups of justices dissenting on particular results, affirmed the judgment of the court of appeals. The issues of *Casey* engendered the following several opinions at the Supreme Court level:

PLANNED PARENTHOOD OF SOUTHEASTERN PA. V. CASEY
505 U.S. 833 (1992)

JUSTICE O'CONNOR, JUSTICE KENNEDY, and JUSTICE SOUTER announced the judgment of the Court and delivered the opinion of the Court with respect to Parts I, II, III, V-A, V-C, and VI, an opinion with respect to Part V-E, in which JUSTICE STEVENS joins, and an opinion with respect to Parts IV, V-B, and V-D.

I

Liberty finds no refuge in a jurisprudence of doubt. Yet, 19 years after our holding that the Constitution protects a woman's right to terminate her pregnancy in its early stages, *Roe v. Wade*, 410 U.S. 113 (1973), that definition of liberty is still questioned. Joining the respondents as *amicus curiae*, the United States, as it has done in five other cases in the last decade, again asks us to overrule *Roe*.

At issue in these cases are five provisions of the Pennsylvania Abortion Control Act of 1982, as amended in 1988 and 1989. 18 Pa. Cons. Stat. 3203–3220 (1990). . . . [Here followed a summary of the Act.—AU.]

. . . After considering the fundamental constitutional questions resolved by *Roe*, principles of institutional integrity, and the rule of stare decisis, we are led to conclude this: the essential holding of *Roe v. Wade* should be retained and once again reaffirmed.

It must be stated at the outset and with clarity that *Roe*'s essential holding, the holding we reaffirm, has three parts. First is a recognition of the right of the woman to choose to have an abortion before viability and to obtain it without undue interference from the State. Before viability, the State's interests are not strong enough to support a prohibition of abortion or the imposition of a substantial obstacle to the woman's effective right to elect the procedure. Second is a confirmation of the State's power to restrict abortions after fetal viability if the law contains exceptions for pregnancies which endanger the woman's life or health. And third is the principle that the State has legitimate interests from the outset of the pregnancy in protecting the health of the woman and the life of the fetus that may become a child. These principles do not contradict one another; and we adhere to each.

II

Constitutional protection of the woman's decision to terminate her pregnancy derives from the Due Process Clause of the Fourteenth Amendment. It declares that no State shall "deprive any person of life, liberty, or property, without due process of law." The controlling word in the cases before us is "liberty." Although a literal reading of the Clause might suggest that it governs only the procedures by which a State may deprive persons of liberty, for at least 105 years, since *Mugler v. Kansas*, 123 U.S. 623, 660–661 (1887), the Clause has been understood to contain a substantive component as well, one "barring certain government actions regardless of the fairness of the procedures used to implement them." *Daniels v. Williams*, 474 U.S. 327, 331 (1986). As Justice Brandeis (joined by Justice Holmes) observed, "[d]espite arguments to the contrary which had seemed to me persuasive, it is settled that the due process clause of the Fourteenth Amendment applies to matters of substantive law as well as to matters of procedure. Thus all fundamental rights comprised within the term liberty are protected by the Federal Constitution from invasion by the States." *Whitney v. California*, 274 U.S. 357, 373 (1927) (Brandeis, J., concurring). . . .

...It is tempting, as a means of curbing the discretion of federal judges, to suppose that liberty encompasses no more than those rights already guaranteed to the individual against federal interference by the express provisions of the first eight amendments to the Constitution. See *Adamson v. California*, 332 U.S. 46, 68–92 (1947) (Black, J., dissenting). But ... this Court has never accepted that view.

It is also tempting, for the same reason, to suppose that the Due Process Clause protects only those practices, defined at the most specific level, that were protected against government interference by other rules of law when the Fourteenth Amendment was ratified. See *Michael H. v. Gerald D.*, 491 U.S. 110, 127–128, n. 6 (1989) (opinion of SCALIA, J.). But such a view would be inconsistent with our law. It is a promise of the Constitution that there is a realm of personal liberty which the government may not enter. We have vindicated this principle before. Marriage is mentioned nowhere in the Bill of Rights, and interracial marriage was illegal in most States in the 19th century, but the Court was no doubt correct in finding it to be an aspect of liberty protected against state interference by the substantive component of the Due Process Clause in *Loving v. Virginia*, 388 U.S. 1, 12 (1967) (relying, in an opinion for eight Justices, on the Due Process Clause). . . .

Neither the Bill of Rights nor the specific practices of States at the time of the adoption of the Fourteenth Amendment marks the outer limits of the substantive sphere of liberty which the Fourteenth Amendment protects. See U.S. Const., Amdt. 9. As the second Justice Harlan recognized:

> [T]he full scope of the liberty guaranteed by the Due Process Clause. . . recognizes. . .that certain interests require particularly careful scrutiny of the state needs asserted to justify their abridgment. *Poe v. Ullman*, 367 U.S., at 543 (dissenting from dismissal on jurisdictional grounds).

. . . It is settled now, as it was when the Court heard arguments in *Roe v. Wade*, that the Constitution places limits on a State's right to interfere with a person's most basic decisions about family and parenthood, see *Carey v. Population Services International*; *Moore v. East Cleveland*, 431 U.S. 494 (1977); *Eisenstadt v. Baird*; *Loving v. Virginia*; *Griswold v. Connecticut*; *Skinner v. Oklahoma*; *Pierce v. Society of Sisters*; *Meyer v. Nebraska* as well as bodily integrity, see, *e.g., Washington v. Harper*, 494 U.S. 210, 221–222 (1990); *Winston v. Lee*, 470 U.S. 753 (1985); *Rochin v. California*, 342 U.S. 165 (1952).

The inescapable fact is that adjudication of substantive due process claims may call upon the Court in interpreting the Constitution to exercise that same capacity which, by tradition, courts always have exercised: reasoned judgment. Its boundaries are not susceptible of expression as a simple rule. That does not mean we are free to invalidate state policy choices with which we disagree; yet neither does it permit us to shrink from the duties of our office.

. . .

Men and women of good conscience can disagree . . . about the profound moral and spiritual implications of terminating a pregnancy, even in its earliest stage. Some of us as individuals find abortion offensive to our most basic principles of morality, but that cannot control our decision. Our obligation is to define the liberty of all, not to mandate our own moral code. The underlying constitutional issue is whether the State can resolve these philosophic questions in such a definitive way that a woman lacks all choice in the matter, except perhaps in those rare circumstances in which the pregnancy is itself a danger to her own life or health, or is the result of rape or incest. . . .

Our law affords constitutional protection to personal decisions relating to marriage, procreation, contraception, family relationships, child rearing, and education. *Carey v. Population Services International*, 431 U.S., at 685. Our cases recognize the right of the *individual*, married or single, to be free from unwarranted governmental intrusion into matters so fundamentally affecting a person as the decision whether to bear or beget a child. *Eisenstadt v. Baird*, 405 U.S., at 453 (emphasis in original). Our precedents "have respected the private realm of family life which the state cannot enter." *Prince v. Massachusetts*, 321 U.S. 158, 166 (1944). These matters, involving the most intimate and personal choices a person may make in a lifetime, choices central to personal dignity and autonomy, are central to the liberty protected by the Fourteenth Amendment. At the heart of liberty is the right to define one's own concept of existence, of meaning, of the universe, and of the mystery of human life. Beliefs about these matters could not define the attributes of personhood were they formed under compulsion of the State.

These considerations begin our analysis . . . but cannot end it. . . . Abortion is . . . fraught with consequences for others: for the woman who must live with the implications of her decision; for the persons who perform and assist in the procedure; for the spouse, family, and society which must confront the knowledge that these procedures exist, procedures some deem nothing short of an act of violence against innocent human life; and, depending on one's beliefs, for the life or potential life that is aborted. Though abortion is conduct, it does not follow that the State is entitled to proscribe it in all instances. That is because the liberty of the woman is at stake in a sense unique to the human condition, and so, unique to the law. The mother who carries a child to full term is subject to anxieties, to physical constraints, to pain that only she must bear. That these sacrifices have from the beginning of the human race been endured by woman with a pride that ennobles her in the eyes of others and gives to the infant a bond of love cannot alone be grounds for the State to insist she make the sacrifice. Her suffering is too intimate and personal for the State to insist, without more, upon its own vision of the woman's role, however dominant that vision has been in the course of our history and our culture. The destiny of the woman must be shaped to a large extent on her own conception of her spiritual imperatives and her place in society.

It should be recognized, moreover, that in some critical respects, the abortion decision is of the same character as the decision to use contraception, to which *Griswold v. Connecticut*, *Eisenstadt v. Baird*, and *Carey v. Population Services International* afford constitutional protection..... The same concerns are present when the woman confronts the reality that, perhaps despite her attempts to avoid it, she has become pregnant.

It was this dimension of personal liberty that *Roe* sought to protect, and its holding invoked the reasoning and the tradition of the precedents we have discussed, granting protection to substantive liberties of the person. *Roe* was, of course, an extension of those cases and, as the decision itself indicated, the separate States could act in some degree to further their own legitimate interests in protecting prenatal life. The extent to which the legislatures of the States might act to outweigh the interests of the woman in choosing to terminate her pregnancy was a subject of debate both in *Roe* itself and in decisions following it.

[T]he reservations any of us may have in reaffirming the central holding of Roe are outweighed by the explication of individual liberty we have given, combined with the force of *stare decisis*. We turn now to that doctrine.

III

A

The obligation to follow precedent begins with necessity, and a contrary necessity marks its outer limit. With Cardozo, we recognize that no judicial system could do society's work if it eyed each issue afresh in every case that raised it. See B. Cardozo, *The Nature of the Judicial Process* 149 (1921). Indeed, the very concept of the rule of law underlying our own Constitution requires such continuity over time that a respect for precedent is, by definition, indispensable. See Powell, "Stare Decisis and Judicial Restraint," 1991 *Journal of Supreme Court History* 13, 16. At the other extreme, a different necessity would make itself felt if a prior judicial ruling should come to be seen so clearly as error that its enforcement was, for that very reason, doomed.

Even when the decision to overrule a prior case is not, as in the rare, latter instance, virtually foreordained, it is common wisdom that the rule of *stare decisis* is not an "inexorable command," and certainly it is not such in every constitutional case [precedents here omitted—AU.] Rather, when this Court reexamines a prior holding, its judgment is customarily informed by a series of prudential and pragmatic considerations designed to test the consistency of overruling a prior decision with the ideal of the rule of law, and to gauge the respective costs of reaffirming and overruling a prior case. Thus, for example, we may ask [1]whether the rule has proven to be intolerable simply in defying practical workability, *Swift & Co. v. Wickham*, 382 U.S. 111, 116 (1965); [2]whether the rule is subject to a kind of reliance that would lend a special hardship to the consequences of overruling and add inequity to the cost of repudiation, *e.g., United States v. Title Ins. & Trust Co.*, 265 U.S. 472, 486 (1924); [3]whether related principles of law have so far developed as to have left the old rule no more than a remnant of abandoned doctrine, see *Patterson v. McLean Credit Union*, 491 U.S. 164, 173–174 (1989); or [4] whether facts have so changed, or come to be seen so differently, as to have robbed the old rule of significant application or justification, *e.g., Burnet*, 285 U.S. at 412 (Brandeis, J., dissenting).

So in this case, we may enquire whether *Roe*'s central rule has been found unworkable; whether the rule's limitation on state power could be removed without serious inequity to those who have relied upon it or significant damage to the stability of the society governed by it; whether the law's growth in the intervening years has left *Roe*'s central rule a doctrinal anachronism discounted by society; and whether Roe's premises of fact have so far changed in the ensuing two decades as to render its central holding somehow irrelevant or unjustifiable in dealing with the issue it addressed.

1

Although *Roe* has engendered opposition, it has in no sense proven "unworkable," representing as it does a simple limitation beyond which a state law is unenforceable. . . .

2

The inquiry into reliance counts the cost of a rule's repudiation as it would fall on those who have relied reasonably on the rule's continued application.

... [F]or two decades of economic and social developments, people have organized intimate relationships and made choices that define their views of themselves and their places in society, in reliance on the availability of abortion in the event that contraception should fail. The ability of women to participate equally in the economic and social life of the Nation has been facilitated by their ability to control their reproductive lives. See, *e.g.*, R. Petchesky, *Abortion and Woman's Choice* 109, 133, n. 7 (rev. ed. 1990). The Constitution serves human values, and while the effect of reliance on *Roe* cannot be exactly measured, neither can the certain cost of overruling *Roe* for people who have ordered their thinking and living around that case be dismissed.

3

No evolution of legal principle has left Roe's doctrinal footings weaker than they were in 1973. No development of constitutional law since the case was decided has implicitly or explicitly left Roe behind as a mere survivor of obsolete constitutional thinking.

It will be recognized, of course, that *Roe* stands at an intersection of two lines of decisions, but in whichever doctrinal category one reads the case, the result for present purposes will be the same. The *Roe* Court itself placed its holding in the succession of cases most prominently exemplified by *Griswold v. Connecticut*, 381 U.S. 479 (1965). See *Roe*, 410 U.S., at 152–153. When it is so seen, *Roe* is clearly in no jeopardy, since subsequent constitutional developments have neither disturbed, nor do they threaten to diminish, the scope of recognized protection accorded to the liberty relating to intimate relationships, the family, and decisions about whether or not to beget or bear a child.

Roe, however, may be seen not only as an exemplar of *Griswold* liberty but as a rule (whether or not mistaken) of personal autonomy and bodily integrity, with doctrinal affinity to cases recognizing limits on governmental power to mandate medical treatment or to bar its rejection. If so, our cases since *Roe* accord with *Roe*'s view that a State's interest in the protection of life falls short of justifying any plenary override of individual liberty claims. *Cruzan v. Director, Mo. Dept. of Health*, 497 U.S. 261, 278 (1990); *cf., e.g., Riggins v. Nevada*, 504 U.S. 127, 135 (1992); *Washington v. Harper*, 494 U.S. 210 (1990); see also, *e.g., Rochin v. California*, 342 U.S. 165 (1952); *Jacobson v. Massachusetts*, 197 U.S. 11, 24–30 (1905).

Finally, one could classify *Roe* as *sui generis*. If the case is so viewed, then there clearly has been no erosion of its central determination. The original holding resting on the concurrence of seven Members of the Court in 1973 was expressly affirmed by a majority of six in 1983, see *Akron v. Akron Center for Reproductive Health, Inc.* (1983) (Akron I), and by a majority of five in 1986, see *Thornburgh v. American College of Obstetricians and Gynecologists* (1986), expressing adherence to the constitutional ruling despite legislative efforts in some States to test its limits. More recently, in *Webster v. Reproductive Health Services* (1989), although two of the present authors questioned the trimester framework in a way consistent with our judgment today, see *id.*, at 518 (REHNQUIST, C.J., joined by WHITE and KENNEDY, JJ.); *id.*, at 529 (O'CONNOR, J., concurring in part and concurring in judgment), a majority of the Court either decided to reaffirm or declined to address the constitutional validity of the central holding of *Roe*. See *Webster* [opinions/votes of Rehnquist, White, Kennedy, O'Connor, Blackmun, Brennan, Marshall, and Stevens]. . . .

The soundness of this prong of the *Roe* analysis is apparent from a consideration of the alternative. If indeed the woman's interest in deciding whether to bear and beget a child had not been recognized as in *Roe*, the State might as readily restrict a woman's right to choose to carry a pregnancy to term as to terminate it, to further asserted state interests in population control, or eugenics, for example. Yet *Roe* has been sensibly relied upon to counter any such suggestions. *E.g., Arnold v. Board of Education of Escambia County, Ala.*, 880 F.2d 305, 311 (CA11 1989) (relying upon *Roe* and concluding that government officials violate the Constitution by coercing a minor to have an abortion); *Avery v. County of Burke*, 660 F.2d 111, 115 (CA4 1981) ([reinstating lawsuit against] county agency [for] inducing teenage girl to undergo unwanted sterilization on the basis of misrepresentation that she had sickle cell trait); see also *In re Quinlan*, 70 N. J. 10, 355 A.2d 647, cert. denied *sub nom. Garger v. New Jersey*, 429 U.S. 922 (1976) (relying on *Roe* in finding a right to terminate medical treatment). In any event, because *Roe*'s scope is confined by the fact of its concern with postconception potential life, a concern otherwise likely to be implicated only by some forms of contraception protected independently under *Griswold* and later cases, any error in *Roe* is unlikely to have serious ramifications in future cases.

4

We have seen how time has overtaken some of *Roe*'s factual assumptions: advances in maternal health care allow for abortions safe to the mother later in pregnancy than was true in 1973, see *Akron I*, 462 U.S. at 429, n. 11, and advances in neonatal care have advanced viability to a point somewhat earlier. Compare *Roe*, 410 U.S., at 160, with *Webster*, 492 U.S., at 515–516 (opinion of REHNQUIST, C.J.); see *Akron I*, 462 U.S., at 457, and n. 5 (O'CONNOR, J., dissenting). But these facts go only to the scheme of time limits on the realization of competing interests, and the divergences from the factual premises of 1973 have no bearing on the validity of *Roe*'s central holding, that viability marks the earliest point at which the State's interest in fetal life is constitutionally adequate to justify a legislative ban on nontherapeutic abortions.... Whenever it may occur, the attainment of viability may continue to serve as the critical fact, just as it has done since *Roe* was decided....

5

The sum of the precedential enquiry to this point shows *Roe*'s underpinnings unweakened in any way affecting its central holding. While it has engendered disapproval, it has not been unworkable. An entire generation has come of age free to assume *Roe*'s concept of liberty in defining the capacity of women to act in society, and to make reproductive decisions; [nor have the other conditions that call for overruling been met.] ... Within the bounds of normal *stare decisis* analysis, then, and subject to the considerations on which it customarily turns, the stronger argument is for affirming Roe's central holding, with whatever degree of personal reluctance any of us may have, not for overruling it.

B

In a less significant case, *stare decisis* analysis could, and would, stop at the point we have reached. But the sustained and widespread debate Roe has provoked calls for some comparison between that case and others of comparable dimension that have responded to national controversies and taken on the impress of the controversies addressed. Only two such decisional lines from the past century present themselves for examination, and in each instance the result reached by the Court accorded with the principles we apply today.

...To overrule prior law for no other reason than [a present doctrinal disposition to come out differently from the Court of 1973] ... would run counter to the view, repeated in our cases, that a decision to overrule should rest on some special reason over and above the belief that a prior case was wrongly decided. See, *e.g., Mitchell v. W.T. Grant Co.*, 416 U.S. 600, 636 (1974) (Stewart, J., dissenting) ("A basic change in the law upon a ground no firmer than a change in our membership invites the popular misconception that this institution is little different from the two political branches of the Government. . . .").

C

. . . [O]verruling *Roe*'s central holding would not only reach an unjustifiable result under principles of *stare decisis*, but would seriously weaken the Court's capacity to exercise the judicial power and to function as the Supreme Court of a Nation dedicated to the rule of law. To understand why this would be so, it is necessary to understand the source of this Court's authority, the conditions necessary for its preservation, and its relationship to the country's understanding of itself as a constitutional Republic.

. . . The Court's power lies . . . in its legitimacy, a product of substance and perception that shows itself in the people's acceptance of the Judiciary as fit to determine what the Nation's law means, and to declare what it demands.

. . . The Court must take care to speak and act in ways that allow people to accept its decisions on the terms the Court claims for them, as grounded truly in principle, not as compromises with social and political pressures having, as such, no bearing on the principled choices that the Court is obliged to make. Thus, the Court's legitimacy depends on making legally principled decisions. . .perceived as such. . . .

In two circumstances . . . the Court would almost certainly fail to receive the benefit of the doubt in overruling prior cases. There is, first, a point beyond which frequent overruling would overtax the country's belief in the Court's good faith. Despite the variety of reasons that may inform and justify a decision to overrule, we cannot forget that such a decision is usually perceived (and perceived correctly) as, at the least, a statement that a prior decision was wrong. There is a limit to the amount of error that can plausibly be imputed to prior Courts. If that limit should be exceeded, disturbance of prior rulings would be taken as evidence that justifiable reexamination of principle had given way to drives for particular results in the short term. The legitimacy of the Court would fade with the frequency of its vacillation.

. . .Where, in the performance of its judicial duties, the Court decides a case in such a way as to resolve the sort of intensely divisive controversy reflected in *Roe* and those rare, comparable cases, its decision has a dimension that the resolution of the normal case does not carry. It is the dimension present whenever the Court's interpretation of the Constitution calls the contending sides of a national controversy to end their national division by accepting a common mandate rooted in the Constitution.

The Court is not asked to do this very often, having thus addressed the Nation only twice in our lifetime, in the decisions of *Brown* [v. Bd. of Education (1954)] and *Roe*. But when the Court does act in this way, its decision requires an equally rare precedential force to counter the inevitable efforts to overturn it and to thwart its implementation. Some of those efforts may be mere unprincipled emotional reactions; others may proceed from principles worthy of profound respect.... [O]nly the most convincing justification under accepted standards of precedent could suffice to demonstrate that a later decision overruling the first was anything but a surrender to political pressure and an unjustified repudiation of the principle on which the Court staked its authority in the first instance. So to overrule under fire in the absence of the most compelling reason to reexamine a watershed decision would subvert the Court's legitimacy beyond any serious question. Cf. *Brown v. Board of Education*, 349 U.S. 294, 300 (1955) (*Brown II*) ("[I]t should go without saying that the vitality of th[e] constitutional principles [announced in *Brown I*,] cannot be allowed to yield simply because of disagreement with them").

The country's loss of confidence in the Judiciary would be underscored by an equally certain and equally reasonable condemnation for another failing in overruling unnecessarily and under pressure. Some cost will be paid by anyone who approves or implements a constitutional decision where it is unpopular.... The price may be criticism or ostracism, or it may be violence. An extra price will be paid by those who themselves disapprove of the decision's results when viewed outside of constitutional terms, but who nevertheless struggle to accept it, because they respect the rule of law. To all those who will be so tested by following, the Court implicitly undertakes to remain steadfast, lest in the end a price be paid for nothing. The promise of constancy, once given, binds its maker for as long as the power to stand by the decision survives and the understanding of the issue has not changed so fundamentally as to render the commitment obsolete. From the obligation of this promise, this Court cannot and should not assume any exemption when duty requires it to decide a case in conformance with the Constitution.

... If the Court's legitimacy should be undermined, then, so would the country be in its very ability to see itself through its constitutional ideals. The Court's concern with legitimacy is not for the sake of the Court, but for the sake of the Nation to which it is responsible.

... A decision to overrule *Roe*'s essential holding under the existing circumstances would address error, if error there was, at the cost of both profound and unnecessary damage to the Court's legitimacy, and to the Nation's commitment to the rule of law. It is therefore imperative to adhere to the essence of *Roe*'s original decision, and we do so today.

IV

From what we have said so far, it follows that it is a constitutional liberty of the woman to have some freedom to terminate her pregnancy. We conclude that the basic decision in *Roe* was based on a constitutional analysis which we cannot now repudiate. The woman's liberty is not so unlimited, however, that, from the outset, the State cannot show its concern for the life of the unborn and, at a later point in fetal development, the State's interest in life has sufficient force so that the right of the woman to terminate the pregnancy can be restricted.

That brings us, of course, to the point where much criticism has been directed at *Roe*, a criticism that always inheres when the Court draws a specific rule from what in the Constitution is but a general standard. . . .

We conclude the line should be drawn at viability, so that, before that time, the woman has a right to choose to terminate her pregnancy. We adhere to this principle for two reasons. First, as we have said, is the doctrine of *stare decisis*. Any judicial act of line-drawing may seem somewhat arbitrary, but *Roe* was a reasoned statement, elaborated with great care. We have twice reaffirmed it in the face of great opposition. See *Thornburgh*, 476 U.S., at 759; *Akron I*, 462 U.S., at 419–420. Although we must overrule those parts of *Thornburgh* and *Akron I* which, in our view, are inconsistent with *Roe*'s statement that the State has a legitimate interest in promoting the life or potential life of the unborn, the central premise of those cases represents an unbroken commitment by this Court to the essential holding of *Roe*. . . . [T]hat premise . . . we reaffirm today.

The second reason is that the concept of viability, as we noted in *Roe*, is the time at which there is a realistic possibility of maintaining and nourishing a life outside the womb, so that the independent existence of the second life can, in reason and all fairness, be the object of state protection that now overrides the rights of the woman. See *Roe v. Wade*, 410 U.S., at 163. Consistent with other constitutional norms, legislatures may draw lines which appear arbitrary without the necessity of offering a justification. But courts may not. We must justify the lines we draw. And there is no line other than viability which is more workable. To be sure, as we have said, there may be some medical developments that affect the precise point of viability, but this is an imprecision within tolerable limits . . . . The viability line also has, as a practical matter, an element of fairness. In some broad sense, it might be said that a woman who fails to act before viability has consented to the State's intervention on behalf of the developing child.

The woman's right to terminate her pregnancy before viability is the most central principle of *Roe v. Wade*. It is a rule of law and a component of liberty we cannot renounce.

On the other side of the equation is the interest of the State in the protection of potential life. The *Roe* Court recognized the State's "important and legitimate interest in protecting the potentiality of human life." *Roe*, at 162. . . .We do not need to say whether each of us, had we been Members of the Court when the valuation of the state interest came before it as an original matter, would have concluded, as the *Roe* Court did, that its weight is insufficient to justify a ban on abortions prior to viability even when it is subject to certain exceptions. The matter is not before us in the first instance, and, coming as it does after nearly 20 years of litigation in *Roe*'s wake we are satisfied that the immediate question is not the soundness of Roe's resolution of the issue, but the precedential force that must be accorded to its holding. And we have concluded that the essential holding of Roe should be reaffirmed.

Yet it must be remembered that *Roe v. Wade* speaks. . .also [of] the State's "important and legitimate interest in potential life." *Roe*, at 163. That portion of the decision in *Roe* has been given too little acknowledgment and implementation by the Court in its subsequent cases. Those cases decided that any regulation touching upon the abortion decision must [face] strict scrutiny [and] be sustained only if drawn in narrow terms to further a compelling state interest. Not all of the cases decided under that formulation can be reconciled with the holding in *Roe* itself that the State has legitimate interests in the health of the woman and in protecting the potential life within her. In resolving this tension, we choose to rely upon *Roe*, as against the later cases.

Roe established a trimester framework to govern abortion regulations. Under this elaborate but rigid construct, almost no regulation at all is permitted during the first trimester of pregnancy; regulations designed to protect the woman's health, but not to further the State's interest in potential life, are permitted during the second trimester; and, during the third trimester, when the fetus is viable, prohibitions are permitted provided the life or health of the mother is not at stake. *Roe*, at 163–166. Most of our cases since *Roe* have involved the application of rules derived from the trimester framework. . . . We do not agree, however, that the trimester approach is necessary to accomplish this objective. A framework of this rigidity was unnecessary. . . .

Though the woman has a right to choose to terminate or continue her pregnancy before viability, it does not at all follow that the State is prohibited from taking steps to ensure that this choice is thoughtful and informed. Even in the earliest stages of pregnancy, the State may enact rules and regulations designed to encourage her to know that there are philosophic and social arguments of great weight that can be brought to bear in favor of continuing the pregnancy to full term, and that there are procedures and institutions to allow adoption of unwanted children as well as a certain degree of state assistance if the mother chooses to raise the child herself. "[T]he Constitution does not forbid a State or city, pursuant to democratic processes, from expressing a preference for normal childbirth." *Webster v. Reproductive Health Services*, 492 U.S., at 511 (opinion of the Court) (quoting *Poelker v. Doe*, 432 U.S. 519, 521 (1977)). It follows that States are free to enact laws to provide a reasonable framework for a woman to make a decision that has such profound and lasting meaning. This, too, we find consistent with *Roe*'s central premises, and indeed the inevitable consequence of our holding that the State has an interest in protecting the life of the unborn.

We reject the trimester framework, which we do not consider to be part of the essential holding of *Roe*. See *Webster v. Reproductive Health*, at 518 (opinion of REHNQUIST, C.J.); id., at 529 (O'CONNOR, J., concurring in part and concurring in judgment) (describing the trimester framework as "problematic"). Measures aimed at ensuring that a woman's choice contemplates the consequences for the fetus do not necessarily interfere with the right recognized in *Roe*, although those measures have been found to be inconsistent with the rigid trimester framework announced in that case. A logical reading of the central holding in Roe itself, and a necessary reconciliation of the liberty of the woman and the interest of the State in promoting prenatal life, require, in our view, that we abandon the trimester framework as a rigid prohibition on all pre-viability regulation aimed at the protection of fetal life.

As our jurisprudence relating to all liberties save perhaps abortion has recognized, not every law which makes a right more difficult to exercise is, *ipso facto*, an infringement of that right. An example clarifies the point. We have held that not every ballot access limitation amounts to an infringement of the right to vote. Rather, the States are granted substantial flexibility in establishing the framework within which voters choose the candidates for whom they wish to vote. *Anderson v. Celebrezze*, 460 U.S. 780, 788 (1983); *Norman v. Reed*, 502 U.S. 279 (1992).

The abortion right is similar. Numerous forms of state regulation might have the incidental effect of increasing the cost or decreasing the availability of medical care, whether for abortion or any other medical procedure. The fact that a law which serves a valid purpose, one not designed to strike at the right itself, has the incidental effect of making it more difficult or more expensive to procure an abortion cannot be enough to invalidate it. Only where state regulation imposes an undue burden on a woman's ability to make this decision does the power of the State reach into the heart of the liberty protected by the Due Process Clause. [Citations omitted.]

For the most part, the Court's early abortion cases adhered to this view. In *Maher v. Roe*, 432 U.S. 464, 473–474 (1977), the Court explained: Roe did not declare an unqualified "constitutional right to an abortion," as the District Court seemed to think. Rather, the right protects the woman from unduly burdensome interference with her freedom to decide whether to terminate her pregnancy. See also *Doe v. Bolton*, 410 U.S. 179, 198 (1973) ("[T]he interposition of the hospital abortion committee is unduly restrictive of the patient's rights"); *Bellotti I*, 428 U.S., at 147 (State may not "impose undue burdens upon a minor capable of giving an informed consent"); *Harris v. McRae*, 448 U.S. 297, 314 (1980).

... [D]espite the protestations contained in the original *Roe* opinion to the effect that the Court was not recognizing an absolute right, 410 U.S., at 154–155, the Court's experience applying the trimester framework has led to the striking down of some abortion regulations which in no real sense deprived women of the ultimate decision. Those decisions went too far, because the right recognized by *Roe* is a right to be free from unwarranted governmental intrusion into matters so fundamentally affecting a person as the decision whether to bear or beget a child. *Eisenstadt v. Baird*, 405 U.S., at 453. Not all governmental intrusion is, of necessity, unwarranted, and that brings us to the other basic flaw in the trimester framework: even in *Roe*'s terms, in practice, it undervalues the State's interest in the potential life within the woman.

... Before viability, *Roe* and subsequent cases treat all governmental attempts to influence a woman's decision on behalf of the potential life within her as unwarranted. This treatment is, in our judgment, incompatible with the recognition that there is a substantial state interest in potential life throughout pregnancy. Cf. *Webster*, 492 U.S., at 519 (opinion of REHNQUIST, C.J.); *Akron I*, 462 U.S., at 461 (O'CONNOR, J., dissenting).

The very notion that the State has a substantial interest in potential life leads to the conclusion that not all regulations must be deemed unwarranted. Not all burdens on the right to decide whether to terminate a pregnancy will be undue. In our view, the undue burden standard is the appropriate means of reconciling the State's interest with the woman's constitutionally protected liberty.

. . . [I]t is important to clarify what is meant by an undue burden.

A finding of an undue burden is a shorthand for the conclusion that a state regulation has the purpose or effect of placing a substantial obstacle in the path of a woman seeking an abortion of a nonviable fetus. A statute with this purpose is invalid because the means chosen by the State to further the interest in potential life must be calculated to inform the woman's free choice, not hinder it. And a statute which, while furthering the interest in potential life or some other valid state interest, has the effect of placing a substantial obstacle in the path of a woman's choice cannot be considered a permissible means of serving its legitimate ends. To the extent that the opinions of the Court or of individual Justices use the undue burden standard in a manner that is inconsistent with this analysis, we set out what, in our view, should be the controlling standard. . . . In our considered judgment, an undue burden is an unconstitutional burden. See *Akron II*, 497 U.S., at 519–520 (opinion of KENNEDY, J.). Understood another way, we answer the question, left open in previous opinions discussing the undue burden formulation, whether a law designed to further the State's interest in fetal life which imposes an undue burden on the woman's decision before fetal viability could be constitutional. See, *e.g., Akron I*, 462 U.S. at 462–463 (O'CONNOR, J., dissenting). The answer is no.

. . . Regulations which do no more than create a structural mechanism by which the State, or the parent or guardian of a minor, may express profound respect for the life of the unborn are permitted, if they are not a substantial obstacle to the woman's exercise of the right to choose. See [discussion below of] Pennsylvania's parental consent requirement. Unless it has that effect on her right of choice, a state measure designed to persuade her to choose childbirth over abortion will be upheld if reasonably related to that goal. Regulations designed to foster the health of a woman seeking an abortion are valid if they do not constitute an undue burden.

.... We give this summary:

(a) To protect the central right recognized by *Roe v. Wade* while at the same time accommodating the State's profound interest in potential life, we will employ the undue burden analysis as explained in this opinion. An undue burden exists, and therefore a provision of law is invalid, if its purpose or effect is to place a substantial obstacle in the path of a woman seeking an abortion before the fetus attains viability.

(b) We reject the rigid trimester framework of *Roe v. Wade*. . . .[T]hroughout pregnancy, the State may take measures to ensure that the woman's choice is informed, and measures designed to advance th[e] interest [in potential life] will not be invalidated as long as their purpose is to persuade the woman to choose childbirth over abortion. These measures must not be an undue burden on the right.

(c) As with any medical procedure, the State may enact regulations to further the health or safety of a woman seeking an abortion. Unnecessary health regulations that have the purpose or effect of presenting a substantial obstacle to a woman seeking an abortion impose an undue burden on the right.

(d) Our adoption of the undue burden analysis does not disturb the central holding of *Roe v. Wade*, and we reaffirm that holding. . . . [A] State may not prohibit any woman from making the ultimate decision to terminate her pregnancy before viability.

(e) We also reaffirm *Roe*'s holding that, subsequent to viability, the State, in promoting its interest in the potentiality of human life, may, if it chooses, regulate, and even proscribe, abortion except where it is necessary, in appropriate medical judgment, for the preservation of the life or health of the mother. *Roe v. Wade*, 410 U.S., at 164–165.

These principles control our assessment of the Pennsylvania statute, and we now turn to the issue of the validity of its challenged provisions.

V

The Court of Appeals applied what it believed to be the undue burden standard, and upheld each of the provisions except for the husband notification requirement. We agree generally with this conclusion. . . .

A

[We follow the Circuit Court in construing the statutory definition of "medical emergency" so that it is constitutional.]

B

We next consider the informed consent requirement. 18 Pa. Cons.Stat. Ann. 3205 (1990)....

Our prior decisions establish that, as with any medical procedure, the State may require a woman to give her written informed consent to an abortion. See *Planned Parenthood of Central Mo. v. Danforth*, 428 U.S., at 67. In this respect, the statute is unexceptional. Petitioners challenge the statute's definition of informed consent because it includes the provision of specific information by the doctor and the mandatory 24-hour waiting period. The conclusions reached by a majority of the Justices in the separate opinions filed today and the undue burden standard adopted in this opinion require us to overrule in part some of the Court's past decisions, decisions driven by the trimester framework....

. . .

To the extent *Akron I* and *Thornburgh* find a constitutional violation when the government requires, as it does here, the giving of truthful, nonmisleading information about the nature of the procedure, the attendant health risks and those of childbirth, and the "probable gestational age" of the fetus, those cases go too far, are inconsistent with *Roe*'s acknowledgment of an important interest in potential life, and are overruled....If the information the State requires to be made available to the woman is truthful and not misleading, the requirement may be permissible.

We also see no reason why the State may not require doctors to inform a woman seeking an abortion of the availability of materials relating to the consequences to the fetus, even when those consequences have no direct relation to her health. An example illustrates the point. We would think it constitutional for the State to require that, in order for there to be informed consent to a kidney transplant operation, the recipient must be supplied with information about risks to the donor as well as risks to himself or herself.... [W]e depart from the holdings of *Akron I* and *Thornburgh* to the extent that we permit a State to further its legitimate goal of protecting the life of the unborn by enacting legislation aimed at ensuring a decision that is mature and informed, even when, in so doing, the State expresses a preference for childbirth over abortion. In short, requiring that the woman be informed of the availability of information relating to fetal development and the assistance available should she decide to carry the pregnancy to full term is a reasonable measure to ensure an informed choice, one which might cause the woman to choose childbirth over abortion. This requirement cannot be considered a substantial obstacle to obtaining an abortion, and, it follows, there is no undue burden.

Our prior cases also suggest that the "straitjacket," *Thornburgh*, at 762 (quoting *Danforth*, at 67, n. 8), of particular information which must be given in each case interferes with a constitutional right of privacy between a pregnant woman and her physician. As a preliminary matter, it is worth noting that the statute now before us does not require a physician to comply with the informed consent provisions if he or she can demonstrate by a preponderance of the evidence that he or she reasonably believed that furnishing the information would have resulted in a severely adverse effect on the physical or mental health of the patient. 18 Pa. Cons.Stat. § 3205 (1990). In this respect, the statute does not prevent the physician from exercising his or her medical judgment.

... [A] requirement that a doctor give a woman certain information as part of obtaining her consent to an abortion is, for constitutional purposes, no different from a requirement that a doctor give certain specific information about any medical procedure.

... [T]he practice of medicine [is] subject to reasonable licensing and regulation by the State cf. *Whalen v. Roe*, 429 U.S. 589, 603 (1977). We see no constitutional infirmity...here.

The Pennsylvania statute also requires us to reconsider the holding in *Akron I* that the State may not require that a physician, as opposed to a qualified assistant, provide information relevant to a woman's informed consent. 462 U.S., at 448. Since there is no evidence on this record that requiring a doctor to give the information as provided by the statute would amount, in practical terms, to a substantial obstacle to a woman seeking an abortion, we conclude that it is not an undue burden. Our cases reflect the fact that the Constitution gives the States broad latitude to decide that particular functions may be performed only by licensed professionals....See *Williamson v. Lee Optical of Okla., Inc.*, 348 U.S. 483 (1955). Thus, we uphold the provision....

Our analysis of Pennsylvania's 24-hour waiting period between the provision of the information deemed necessary to informed consent and the performance of an abortion under the undue burden standard requires us to reconsider the premise behind the decision in *Akron I* invalidating a parallel requirement. In *Akron I* we said: "Nor are we convinced that the State's legitimate concern that the woman's decision be informed is reasonably served by requiring a 24-hour delay as a matter of course." 462 U.S., at 450. We consider that conclusion to be wrong. The idea that important decisions will be more informed and deliberate if they follow some period of reflection does not strike us as unreasonable.... The statute, as construed by the Court of Appeals, permits avoidance of the waiting period in the event of a medical emergency, and the record evidence shows that, in the vast majority of cases, a 24-hour delay does not create any appreciable health risk. In theory, at least, the waiting period is a reasonable measure to implement the State's interest in protecting the life of the unborn ... [and] does not amount to an undue burden.

Whether the mandatory 24-hour waiting period is nonetheless invalid because, in practice, it is a substantial obstacle to a woman's choice to terminate her pregnancy is a closer question. The findings of fact by the District Court indicate that, because of the distances many women must travel to reach an abortion provider, the practical effect will often be a delay of much more than a day because the waiting period requires that a woman seeking an abortion make at least two visits to the doctor. The District Court also found that, in many instances, this will increase the exposure of women seeking abortions to "the harassment and hostility of anti-abortion protesters demonstrating outside a clinic." 744 F.Supp., at 1351.

These findings are troubling in some respects, but they do not demonstrate that the waiting period constitutes an undue burden. We do not doubt that, as the District Court held, the waiting period has the effect of "increasing the cost and risk of delay of abortions," *id.*, at 1378, but ... we cannot say that the waiting period imposes a real health risk.

We also disagree with the District Court's conclusion that the "particularly burdensome" effects of the waiting period on some women require its invalidation. A particular burden is not, of necessity, a substantial obstacle. Whether a burden falls on a particular group is a distinct inquiry from whether it is a substantial obstacle even as to the women in that group. And the District Court did not conclude that the waiting period is such an obstacle even for the women who are most burdened by it. Hence, on the record before us, and in the context of this facial challenge, we are not convinced that the 24-hour waiting period constitutes an undue burden.

... [T]he right protected by *Roe* is a right to decide to terminate a pregnancy free of undue interference by the State. Because the informed consent requirement facilitates the wise exercise of that right, it cannot be classified as an interference with the right *Roe* protects. The informed consent requirement is not an undue burden on that right.

C

Section 3209 of Pennsylvania's abortion law provides, except in cases of medical emergency, that no physician shall perform an abortion on a married woman without receiving a signed statement from the woman that she has notified her spouse that she is about to undergo an abortion [or that she fits into one of the statute's exceptions.]. . .

The District Court heard the testimony of numerous expert witnesses, and made detailed findings of fact regarding the effect of this statute. These included:

273. The vast majority of women consult their husbands prior to deciding to terminate their pregnancy.

. . .

279. The "bodily injury" exception could not be invoked by a married woman whose husband, if notified, would, in her reasonable belief, threaten to (a) publicize her intent to have an abortion to family, friends or acquaintances; (b) retaliate against her in future child custody or divorce proceedings; (c) inflict psychological intimidation or emotional harm upon her, her children or other persons; (d) inflict bodily harm on other persons such as children, family members or other loved ones; or (e) use his control over finances to deprive her of necessary monies for herself or her children.

. . .

281. Studies reveal that family violence occurs in two million families in the United States. This figure, however, is a conservative one that substantially understates (because battering is usually not reported until it reaches life-threatening proportions) the actual number of families affected by domestic violence. In fact, researchers estimate that one of every two women will be battered at some time in their life. . . .

282. A wife may not elect to notify her husband of her intention to have an abortion for a variety of reasons, including the husband's illness, concern about her own health, the imminent failure of the marriage, or the husband's absolute opposition to the abortion.

. . .

288. In a domestic abuse situation, it is common for the battering husband to also abuse the children in an attempt to coerce the wife....

289. Mere notification of pregnancy is frequently a flashpoint for battering and violence within the family. The number of battering incidents is high during the pregnancy, and often the worst abuse can be associated with pregnancy.... The battering husband may deny parentage and use the pregnancy as an excuse for abuse....

290. Secrecy typically shrouds abusive families. Family members are instructed not to tell anyone, especially police or doctors, about the abuse and violence. Battering husbands often threaten their wives or her children with further abuse if she tells an outsider of the violence, and tells her that nobody will believe her. A battered woman, therefore, is highly unlikely to disclose the violence against her for fear of retaliation by the abuser.... 744 F.Supp., at 1360–1362.

These findings are supported by studies of domestic violence.... Thus, on an average day in the United States, nearly 11,000 women are severely assaulted by their male partners....

Other studies fill in the rest of this troubling picture. Physical violence is only the most visible form of abuse. Psychological abuse, particularly forced social and economic isolation of women, is also common. L. Walker, *The Battered Woman Syndrome* 27–28 (1984).... Thirty percent of female homicide victims are killed by their male partners. *Domestic Violence: Terrorism in the Home, Hearing before the Subcommittee on Children, Family, Drugs and Alcoholism of the Senate Committee on Labor and Human Resources*, 101st Cong., 2d Sess., 3 (1990).

... This information and the District Court's findings reinforce what common sense would suggest. In well-functioning marriages, spouses discuss important intimate decisions such as whether to bear a child. But there are millions of women in this country who are the victims of regular physical and psychological abuse at the hands of their husbands. Should these women become pregnant, they may have very good reasons for not wishing to inform their husbands of their decision to obtain an abortion. Many may have justifiable fears of physical abuse, but may be no less fearful of the consequences of reporting prior abuse to the Commonwealth of Pennsylvania. Many may have a reasonable fear that notifying their husbands will provoke further instances of child abuse; these women are not exempt from § 3209's notification requirement. Many may fear devastating forms of psychological abuse from their husbands, including verbal harassment, threats of future violence, the destruction of possessions, physical confinement to the home, the withdrawal of financial support, or the disclosure of the abortion to family and friends. These methods of psychological abuse may act as even more of a deterrent to notification than the possibility of physical violence, but women who are the victims of the abuse are not exempt from § 3209's notification requirement. And many women who are pregnant as a result of sexual assaults by their husbands will be unable to avail themselves of the exception for spousal sexual assault, § 3209(b) (3), because the exception requires that the woman have notified law enforcement authorities within 90 days of the assault, and her husband will be notified of her report once an investigation begins, § 3128(c)....

The spousal notification requirement is thus likely to prevent a significant number of women from obtaining an abortion. It does not merely make abortions a little more difficult or expensive to obtain; for many women, it will impose a substantial obstacle. We must not blind ourselves to the fact that the significant number of women who fear for their safety and the safety of their children are likely to be deterred from procuring an abortion as surely as if the Commonwealth had outlawed abortion in all cases.

...Respondents argue that, since some of these women will be able to notify their husbands without adverse consequences or will qualify for one of the exceptions, the statute affects fewer than one percent of women seeking abortions. For this reason, it is asserted, the statute cannot be invalid on its face. We disagree....

The analysis does not end with the one percent of women upon whom the statute operates; it begins there.... The proper focus of constitutional inquiry is the group for whom the law is a restriction, not the group for whom the law is irrelevant.... [The target of § 3209] is married women seeking abortions who do not wish to notify their husbands of their intentions and who do not qualify for one of the statutory exceptions to the notice requirement. The unfortunate yet persisting conditions we document above will mean that, in a large fraction of the cases in which § 3209 is relevant, it will operate as a substantial obstacle to a woman's choice to undergo an abortion. It is an undue burden, and therefore invalid.

This conclusion is in no way inconsistent with our decisions upholding parental notification or consent requirements. See, *e.g., Akron II*, 497 U.S., at 510–519; *Bellotti v. Baird*, 443 U.S. 622 (1979) (*Bellotti II*); *Planned Parenthood of Central Mo. v. Danforth*, 428 U.S., at 74. Those enactments, and our judgment that they are constitutional, are based on the quite reasonable assumption that minors will benefit from consultation with their parents and that children will often not realize that their parents have their best interests at heart. We cannot adopt a parallel assumption about adult women.

We recognize that a husband has a deep and proper concern and interest . . . in his wife's pregnancy and in the growth and development of the fetus she is carrying. *Danforth,* at 69. With regard to the children he has fathered and raised, the Court has recognized his "cognizable and substantial" interest in their custody. *Stanley v. Illinois,* 405 U.S. 645, 651–652 (1972); see also *Quilloin v. Walcott; Caban v. Mohammed; Lehr v. Robertson.* If this case concerned a State's ability to require the mother to notify the father before taking some action with respect to a living child raised by both, therefore, it would be reasonable to conclude, as a general matter, that the father's interest in the welfare of the child and the mother's interest are equal.

Before birth, however, the issue takes on a very different cast. It is an inescapable biological fact that state regulation with respect to the child a woman is carrying will have a far greater impact on the mother's liberty than on the father's. The effect of state regulation on a woman's protected liberty is doubly deserving of scrutiny in such a case, as the State has touched not only upon the private sphere of the family, but upon the very bodily integrity of the pregnant woman. Cf. *Cruzan v. Director, Mo. Dept. of Health,* 497 U.S., at 281. The Court has held that, when the wife and the husband disagree on this decision, the view of only one of the two marriage partners can prevail. Inasmuch as it is the woman who physically bears the child and who is the more directly and immediately affected by the pregnancy, as between the two, the balance weighs in her favor. *Danforth,* at 71. This conclusion rests upon the basic nature of marriage and the nature of our Constitution:

> [T]he marital couple is not an independent entity with a mind and heart of its own, but an association of two individuals, each with a separate intellectual and emotional makeup. If the right of privacy means anything, it is the right of the *individual,* married or single, to be free from unwarranted governmental intrusion into matters so fundamentally affecting a person as the decision whether to bear or beget a child. *Eisenstadt v. Baird,* 405 U.S., at 453 (emphasis in original). . . .

There was a time, not so long ago, when a different understanding of the family and of the Constitution prevailed. In *Bradwell v. State,* 16 Wall. 130 (1873), three Members of this Court reaffirmed the common law principle that a woman had no legal existence separate from her husband, who was regarded as her head and representative in the social state . . . . *Id.*, at 141 (Bradley, J., joined by Swayne and Field, JJ.). Only one generation has passed since this Court observed that "woman is still regarded as the center of home and family life," with attendant "special responsibilities" that precluded full and independent legal status under the Constitution. *Hoyt v. Florida*, 368 U.S. 57, 62 (1961). These views, of course, are no longer consistent with our understanding of the family, the individual, or the Constitution.

In keeping with our rejection of the common law understanding of a woman's role within the family, the Court held in *Danforth* that the Constitution does not permit a State to require a married woman to obtain her husband's consent before undergoing an abortion. 428 U.S., at 69. The principles that guided the Court in *Danforth* should be our guides today. For the great many women who are victims of abuse inflicted by their husbands, or whose children are the victims of such abuse, a spousal notice requirement enables the husband to wield an effective veto over his wife's decision. . . .

. . . If a husband's interest in the potential life of the child outweighs a wife's liberty, the State could require a married woman to notify her husband before she uses a post-fertilization contraceptive. Perhaps next in line would be a statute requiring pregnant married women to notify their husbands before engaging in conduct causing risks to the fetus. After all, if the husband's interest in the fetus' safety is a sufficient predicate for state regulation, the State could reasonably conclude that pregnant wives should notify their husbands before drinking alcohol or smoking. Perhaps married women should notify their husbands before using contraceptives or before undergoing any type of surgery that may have complications affecting the husband's interest in his wife's reproductive organs. And if a husband's interest justifies notice in any of these cases, one might reasonably argue that it justifies exactly what the *Danforth* Court held it did not justify—a requirement of the husband's consent as well. A State may not give to a man the kind of dominion over his wife that parents exercise over their children.

. . .Women do not lose their constitutionally protected liberty when they marry. . . . [Section] 3209 is invalid.

D

[As to parental consent w]e have been over most of this ground before. Our cases establish, and we reaffirm today, that a State may require a minor seeking an abortion to obtain the consent of a parent or guardian, provided that there is an adequate judicial bypass procedure. [Citations omitted.]. . . [T]he one-parent consent requirement and judicial bypass procedure are constitutional. . . .

E

[Here appeared a summary of the reporting requirement.—AU.] In *Danforth*, 428 U.S., at 80, we held that recordkeeping and reporting provisions that are reasonably directed to the preservation of maternal health and that properly respect a patient's confidentiality and privacy are permissible. We think that, under this standard, all the provisions at issue here except that relating to spousal notice are constitutional . . . [as] . . . relate[d] to health. The collection of information with respect to actual patients is a vital element of medical research, and so it cannot be said that the requirements serve no purpose other than to make abortions more difficult. Nor do we find that the requirements impose a substantial obstacle to a woman's choice. At most, they might increase the cost of some abortions by a slight amount. While at some point increased cost could become a substantial obstacle, there is no such showing on the record before us. . . .

. . .

The judgment [of the Circuit Court] is affirmed. . . .

JUSTICE STEVENS, concurring in part and dissenting in part.

The portions of the Court's opinion that I have joined are more important than those with which I disagree. I shall therefore first comment on significant areas of agreement, and then explain the limited character of my disagreement.

I

The Court is unquestionably correct in concluding that the doctrine of *stare decisis* has controlling significance in a case of this kind, notwithstanding an individual Justice's concerns about the merits.[1] The central holding of *Roe v. Wade*, 410 U.S. 113 (1973), has been a "part of our law" for almost two decades. It was a natural sequel to the protection of individual liberty established in *Griswold v. Connecticut*, 381 U.S. 479 (1965). See also *Carey v. Population Services International*, 431 U.S. 678, 687, 702 (1977) (WHITE, J., concurring in part and concurring in result). The societal costs of overruling Roe at this late date would be enormous. *Roe* is an integral part of a correct understanding of both the concept of liberty and the basic equality of men and women. . . .

I also accept what is implicit in the Court's analysis, namely, a reaffirmation of *Roe*'s explanation of *why* the State's obligation to protect the life or health of the mother must take precedence over any duty to the unborn. The Court in *Roe* carefully considered, and rejected, the State's argument "that the fetus is a 'person' within the language and meaning of the Fourteenth Amendment." 410 U.S., at 156. After analyzing the usage of "person" in the Constitution, the Court concluded that that word "has application only postnatally." *Id.*, at 157. . . . [T]he unborn have never been recognized in the law as persons in the whole sense. *Id.*, at 162. Accordingly, an abortion is not "the termination of life entitled to Fourteenth Amendment protection." *Id.*, at 159. From this holding, there was no dissent, see *id.*, at 173; indeed, no Member of the Court has ever questioned this fundamental proposition. Thus, as a matter of federal constitutional law, a developing organism that is not yet a "person" does not have what is sometimes described as a "right to life." This has been and, by the Court's holding today, remains, a fundamental premise of our constitutional law governing reproductive autonomy.

II

My disagreement with the joint opinion begins with its understanding of the trimester framework established in *Roe*. Contrary to the suggestion of the joint opinion, it is not a "contradiction" to recognize that the State may have a legitimate interest in potential human life and, at the same time, to conclude that that interest does not justify the regulation of abortion before viability (although other interests, such as maternal health, may). The fact that the State's interest is legitimate does not tell us when, if ever, that interest outweighs the pregnant woman's interest in personal liberty. It is appropriate, therefore, to consider more carefully the nature of the interests at stake. . . .

Identifying the State's interests—which the States rarely articulate with any precision—makes clear that the interest in protecting potential life is not grounded in the Constitution. It is, instead, an indirect interest supported by both humanitarian and pragmatic concerns. Many of our citizens believe that any abortion reflects an unacceptable disrespect for potential human life, and that the performance of more than a million abortions each year is intolerable; many find third-trimester abortions performed when the fetus is approaching personhood particularly offensive. The State has a legitimate interest in minimizing such offense. The State may also have a broader interest in expanding the population, believing society would benefit from the services of additional productive citizens—or that the potential human lives might include the occasional Mozart or Curie. These are the kinds of concerns that comprise the State's interest in potential human life. . . .

Weighing the State's interest in potential life and the woman's liberty interest, I agree with the joint opinion that the State may "expres[s] a preference for normal childbirth," that the State may take steps to ensure that a woman's choice "is thoughtful and informed," and that States are free to enact laws to provide a reasonable framework for a woman to make a decision that has such profound and lasting meaning. Serious questions arise, however, when a State attempts to "persuade the woman to choose childbirth over abortion." Decisional autonomy must limit the State's power to inject into a woman's most personal deliberations its own views of what is best. The State may promote its preferences by funding childbirth, by creating and maintaining alternatives to abortion, and by espousing the virtues of family; but it must respect the individual's freedom to make such judgments. . . .

In my opinion, the principles established in [a] long line of cases and the wisdom reflected in Justice Powell's opinion for the Court in *Akron* (and followed by the Court just six years ago in *Thornburgh*) should govern our decision today. Under these principles, Pa. Cons. Stat. §§ 3205(a) (2)(i)–(iii) (1990) of the Pennsylvania statute are unconstitutional. Those sections require a physician or counselor to provide the woman with a range of materials clearly designed to persuade her to choose not to undergo the abortion. While the Commonwealth is free, pursuant to § 3208 of the Pennsylvania law, to produce and disseminate such material, the Commonwealth may not inject such information into the woman's deliberations just as she is weighing such an important choice.

Under this same analysis, §§ 3205(a) (1)(i) and (iii) of the Pennsylvania statute are constitutional. Those sections, which require the physician to inform a woman of the nature and risks of the abortion procedure and the medical risks of carrying to term, are neutral requirements comparable to those imposed in other medical procedures. . . .

III

The 24-hour waiting period required by 3205(a) (1)–(2) of the Pennsylvania statute raises even more serious concerns. . . .

. . . [I]t can . . . be argued that the 24-hour delay furthers the Commonwealth's interest in ensuring that the woman's decision is informed and thoughtful. But there is no evidence that the mandated delay benefits women, or that it is necessary to enable the physician to convey any relevant information to the patient. The mandatory delay thus appears to rest on outmoded and unacceptable assumptions about the decisionmaking capacity of women. . . .

No person undertakes such a decision lightly—and States may not presume that a woman has failed to reflect adequately merely because her conclusion differs from the State's preference. . . .

IV

In my opinion, a correct application of the "undue burden" standard leads to the same conclusion concerning the constitutionality of these requirements. A state-imposed burden on the exercise of a constitutional right is measured both by its effects and by its character: a burden may be "undue" either because the burden is too severe or because it lacks a legitimate, rational justification. . . .[6]

The counseling provisions are similarly infirm. Whenever government commands private citizens to speak or to listen, careful review of the justification for that command is particularly appropriate. In this case, the Pennsylvania statute directs that counselors provide women seeking abortions with information concerning alternatives to abortion, the availability of medical assistance benefits, and the possibility of child support payments. §§ 3205(a)(2)(i)–(iii). The statute requires that this information be given to *all* women seeking abortions, including those for whom such information is clearly useless, such as those who are married, those who have undergone the procedure in the past and are fully aware of the options, and those who are fully convinced that abortion is their only reasonable option. Moreover, the statute requires physicians to inform all of their patients of "[t]he probable gestational age of the unborn child." § 3205(a) (1)(ii). This information is of little decisional value in most cases, because 90% of all abortions are performed during the first trimester, when fetal age has less relevance than when the fetus nears viability. Nor can the information required by the statute be justified as relevant to any "philosophic" or "social" argument either favoring or disfavoring the abortion decision in a particular case. In light of all of these facts, I conclude that the information requirements in § 3205(a)(1)(ii) and §§ 3205(a)(2)(i)–(iii) do not serve a useful purpose, and thus constitute an unnecessary—and therefore undue—burden on the woman's constitutional liberty to decide to terminate her pregnancy.

Accordingly, while I disagree with Parts **IV**, **V-B**, and **V-D** of the joint opinion, I join the remainder of the Court's opinion.

> **Opinion Footnotes**
>
> 1 It is sometimes useful to view the issue of *stare decisis* from a historical perspective. In the last 19 years, 15 Justices have confronted the basic issue presented in *Roe*. Of those, 11 have voted as the majority does today: Chief Justice Burger, Justices Douglas, Brennan, Stewart, Marshall, and Powell, and Justices BLACKMUN, O'CONNOR, KENNEDY, SOUTER, and myself. Only four—all of whom happen to be on the Court today—have reached the opposite conclusion.
>
> 6 The meaning of any legal standard can only be understood by reviewing the actual cases in which it is applied. For that reason, I discount both JUSTICE SCALIA's comments on past descriptions of the standard, and the attempt to give it crystal clarity in the joint opinion.

JUSTICE BLACKMUN, concurring in part, concurring in the judgment in part, and dissenting in part.

I join Parts **I, II, III, V-A, V-C, and VI** of the joint opinion of JUSTICES O'CONNOR, KENNEDY, and SOUTER.

I do not underestimate the significance of today's joint opinion. Yet I remain steadfast in my belief that the right to reproductive choice is entitled to the full protection afforded by this Court before *Webster*. And I fear for the darkness as four Justices anxiously await the single vote necessary to extinguish the light.

I

Make no mistake, the joint opinion of Justices O'CONNOR, KENNEDY, and SOUTER is an act of personal courage and constitutional principle. In contrast to previous decisions in which Justices O'CONNOR and KENNEDY postponed reconsideration of *Roe v. Wade*, 410 U.S. 113 (1973), the authors of the joint opinion today join JUSTICE STEVENS and me in concluding that "the essential holding of *Roe v. Wade* should be retained and once again reaffirmed." In brief, five Members of this Court today recognize that "the Constitution protects a woman's right to terminate her pregnancy in its early stages."

. . .

In striking down the Pennsylvania statute's spousal notification requirement, the Court has established a framework for evaluating abortion regulations that responds to the social context of women facing issues of reproductive choice. In determining the burden imposed by the challenged regulation, the Court inquires whether the regulation's "*purpose or effect* is to place a substantial obstacle in the path of a woman seeking an abortion before the fetus attains viability" (emphasis added). The Court reaffirms: The proper focus of constitutional inquiry is the group for whom the law is a restriction, not the group for whom the law is irrelevant." . . . And in applying its test, the Court remains sensitive to the unique role of women in the decisionmaking process....

Lastly, while I believe that the joint opinion errs in failing to invalidate the other regulations, I am pleased that the joint opinion has not ruled out the possibility that these regulations may be shown to impose an unconstitutional burden.... I am confident that, in the future, evidence will be produced to show that, "in a large fraction of the cases in which [these regulations are] relevant, [they] will operate as a substantial obstacle to a woman's choice to undergo an abortion."

II

Today, no less than yesterday, the Constitution and decisions of this Court require that a State's abortion restrictions be subjected to the strictest of judicial scrutiny. Our precedents and the joint opinion's principles require us to subject all non-de-minimis abortion regulations to strict scrutiny. Under this standard, the Pennsylvania statute's provisions requiring content-based counseling, a 24-hour delay, informed parental consent, and reporting of abortion-related information must be invalidated.

. . .

In my view, application of [*Roe*'s trimester] analytical framework is no less warranted than when it was approved by seven Members of this Court in *Roe*.... No majority of this Court has ever agreed upon an alternative approach. The factual premises of the trimester framework have not been undermined, see *Webster*, 492 U.S., at 553 (BLACKMUN, J., dissenting), and the *Roe* framework is far more administrable, and far less manipulable, than the "undue burden" standard adopted by the joint opinion.

... *Roe*'s requirement of strict scrutiny as implemented through a trimester framework should not be disturbed....

Application of the strict scrutiny standard results in the invalidation of all the challenged provisions...[7]

III

....THE CHIEF JUSTICE's criticism of *Roe* follows from his stunted conception of individual liberty. While recognizing that the Due Process Clause protects more than simple physical liberty, he then goes on to construe this Court's personal liberty cases as establishing only a laundry list of particular rights, rather than a principled account of how these particular rights are grounded in a more general right of privacy. This constricted view is reinforced by THE CHIEF JUSTICE's exclusive reliance on tradition as a source of fundamental rights. He argues that the record in favor of a right to abortion is no stronger than the record in *Michael H. v. Gerald D.*, 491 U.S. 110 (1989), where the plurality found no fundamental right to visitation privileges by an adulterous father, or in *Bowers v. Hardwick*, 478 U.S. 186 (1986), where the Court found no fundamental right to engage in homosexual sodomy, or in a case involving the " 'firing [of] a gun . . . into another person's body.' " In THE CHIEF JUSTICE's world, a woman considering whether to terminate a pregnancy is entitled to no more protection than adulterers, murderers, and so-called sexual deviates. Given THE CHIEF JUSTICE's exclusive reliance on tradition, people using contraceptives seem the next likely candidate for his list of outcasts.

. . .

But, we are reassured, there is always the protection of the democratic process. While there is much to be praised about our democracy, our country, since its founding, has recognized that there are certain fundamental liberties that are not to be left to the whims of an election. A woman's right to reproductive choice is one of those fundamental liberties. Accordingly, that liberty need not seek refuge at the ballot box.

IV

In one sense, the Court's approach is worlds apart from that of THE CHIEF JUSTICE and JUSTICE SCALIA. And yet, in another sense, the distance between the two approaches is short—the distance is but a single vote.

I am 83 years old. I cannot remain on this Court forever, and when I do step down, the confirmation process for my successor well may focus on the issue before us today. That, I regret, may be exactly where the choice between the two worlds will be made.

Opinion Footnote

7 While I do not agree with the joint opinion's conclusion that [the informational] provisions should be upheld, the joint opinion has remained faithful to principles this Court previously has announced in examining counseling provisions. For example, the joint opinion concludes that the "information the State requires to be made available to the woman" must be "truthful and not misleading." Because the State's information must be "calculated to inform the woman's free choice, not hinder it," the measures must be designed to ensure that a woman's choice is "mature and informed," not intimidated, imposed, or impelled. To this end, when the State requires the provision of certain information, the State may not alter the *manner* of presentation in order to inflict "psychological abuse," designed to shock or unnerve a woman seeking to exercise her. . . right. This, for example, would appear to preclude a State from requiring a woman to view graphic literature or films detailing the performance of an abortion operation. Just as a visual preview of an operation to remove an appendix plays no part in a physician's securing informed consent to an appendectomy, a preview of scenes appurtenant to any major medical intrusion into the human body does

not constructively inform the decision of a woman of the State's interest in the preservation of the woman's health or demonstrate the State's "profound respect for the life she carries within her."

CHIEF JUSTICE REHNQUIST, with whom JUSTICE WHITE, JUSTICE SCALIA, and JUSTICE THOMAS join, concurring in the judgment in part and dissenting in part.

The joint opinion, following its newly minted variation on *stare decisis*, retains the outer shell of *Roe v. Wade*, but beats a wholesale retreat from the substance of that case. We believe that *Roe* was wrongly decided, and that it can and should be overruled consistently with our traditional approach to *stare decisis* in constitutional cases. We would adopt the approach of the plurality in *Webster v. Reproductive Health Services*, and uphold the challenged provisions of the Pennsylvania statute in their entirety.

I

...

...Justices O'CONNOR, KENNEDY, and SOUTER adopt a revised undue burden standard to analyze the challenged regulations. We conclude, however, that such an outcome is an unjustified constitutional compromise, one which leaves the Court in a position to closely scrutinize all types of abortion regulations despite the fact that it lacks the power to do so under the Constitution.

...

...[W]hen confronted with State regulations of this type in past years, the Court has become increasingly more divided: The three most recent abortion cases have not commanded a Court opinion. See *Ohio v. Akron Center for Reproductive Health*, 497 U.S. 502 (1990); *Hodgson v. Minnesota*, 497 U.S. 417 (1990); *Webster v. Reproductive Health Services*.

...This state of confusion and disagreement warrants reexamination of the "fundamental right" accorded to a woman's decision to abort a fetus in *Roe*, with its concomitant requirement that any state regulation of abortion survive "strict scrutiny." See *Payne v. Tennessee*, 501 U.S. 808, 827–828 (1991) (observing that reexamination of constitutional decisions is appropriate when those decisions have generated uncertainty and failed to provide clear guidance, because "correction through legislative action is practically impossible"); *Garcia v. San Antonio Metropolitan Transit Authority*, 469 U.S. 528, 546–547, 557 (1985).

We have held that a liberty interest protected under the Due Process Clause of the Fourteenth Amendment will be deemed fundamental if it is "implicit in the concept of ordered liberty." *Palko v. Connecticut*, 302 U.S. 319, 325 (1937). Three years earlier, in *Snyder v. Massachusetts*, 291 U.S. 97 (1934), we referred to a "principle of justice so rooted in the traditions and conscience of our people as to be ranked as fundamental." *Id.*, at 105. These expressions are admittedly not precise, but our decisions implementing this notion of "fundamental" rights do not afford any more elaborate basis on which to base such a classification.

In construing the phrase "liberty" incorporated in the Due Process Clause of the Fourteenth Amendment, we have recognized that its meaning extends beyond freedom from physical restraint. In *Pierce v. Society of Sisters* (1925), we held that it included a parent's right to send a child to private school; in *Meyer v. Nebraska* (1923), we held that it included a right to teach a foreign language in a parochial school. Building on these cases, we have held that the term "liberty" includes a right to marry, *Loving v. Virginia* (1967); a right to procreate, *Skinner v. Oklahoma ex rel. Williamson* (1942); and a right to use contraceptives, *Griswold v. Connecticut* (1965); *Eisenstadt v. Baird* (1972).

In *Roe v. Wade*, the Court recognized a "guarantee of personal privacy" which "is broad enough to encompass a woman's decision whether or not to terminate her pregnancy." 410 U.S., at 152–153. We are now of the view that, in terming this right fundamental, the Court in *Roe* read the earlier opinions upon which it based its decision much too broadly. Unlike marriage, procreation, and contraception, abortion "involves the purposeful termination of a potential life." *Harris v. McRae*, 448 U.S. 297, 325 (1980). . . . One cannot ignore the fact that a woman is not isolated in her pregnancy, and that the decision to abort necessarily involves the destruction of a fetus.

Nor do the historical traditions of the American people support the view that the right to terminate one's pregnancy is . . . [a] deeply rooted tradition . . .[and therefore a] "fundamental" [right] under the Due Process Clause of the Fourteenth Amendment.

We think. . . the Court was mistaken in *Roe* when it classified a woman's decision to terminate her pregnancy as a "fundamental right" that could be abridged only in a manner which withstood "strict scrutiny.". . .

. . .The Court in *Roe* reached too far when it analogized the right to abort a fetus to the rights involved in *Pierce*, *Meyer*, *Loving*, and *Griswold*, and thereby deemed the right to abortion fundamental.

II

...

In our view, authentic principles of *stare decisis* do not require that any portion of the reasoning in *Roe* be kept intact. "Stare decisis is not ... a universal, inexorable command," especially in cases involving the interpretation of the Federal Constitution. *Burnet v. Coronado Oil & Gas Co.,* 285 U.S. 393, 405 (1932) (Brandeis, J., dissenting).... It is... our duty to reconsider constitutional interpretations that "depar[t] from a proper understanding" of the Constitution. *Garcia v. San Antonio Metropolitan Transit Authority,* 469 U.S., at 557

...And surely there is no requirement, in considering whether to depart from *stare decisis* in a constitutional case, that a decision be more wrong now than it was at the time it was rendered. If that were true, the most outlandish constitutional decision could survive forever, based simply on the fact that it was no more outlandish later than it was when originally rendered.

...

[T]he simple fact that a generation or more had grown used to [longstanding but erroneous] major decisions [such *as Plessy v. Ferguson*] did not prevent the Court from correcting its errors in those cases, nor should it prevent us from correctly interpreting the Constitution here. See *Brown v. Board of Education* (1954) (rejecting the "separate but equal" doctrine)...

...

... In terms of public protest ... *Roe*, so far as we know, was unique. But just as the Court should not respond to that sort of protest by retreating from the decision simply to allay the concerns of the protesters, it should likewise not respond by determining to adhere to the decision at all costs, lest it *seem* to be retreating under fire....

...

...The Judicial Branch derives its legitimacy not from following public opinion, but from deciding by its best lights whether legislative enactments of the popular branches of Government comport with the Constitution. The doctrine of *stare decisis* is an adjunct of this duty, and should be no more subject to the vagaries of public opinion than is the basic judicial task.

...

...The joint opinion's message to...protesters [against our opinions] appears to be that they must cease their activities in order to serve their cause, because their protests will only cement in place a decision which, by normal standards of *stare decisis*, should be reconsidered.

The end result of the joint opinion's paeans of praise for legitimacy is the enunciation of a brand new standard for evaluating state regulation of a woman's right to abortion—the "undue burden" standard. As indicated above, *Roe v. Wade* adopted a "fundamental right" standard under which state regulations could survive only if they met the requirement of "strict scrutiny." While we disagree with that standard, it at least had a recognized basis in constitutional law at the time *Roe* was decided. The same cannot be said for the "undue burden" standard, which is created largely out of whole cloth by the authors of the joint opinion. It is a standard which even today does not command the support of a majority of this Court....

In evaluating abortion regulations under that standard, judges will have to decide whether they place a "substantial obstacle" in the path of a woman seeking an abortion. In that this standard is based even more on a judge's subjective determinations than was the trimester framework, the standard will do nothing to prevent "judges from roaming at large in the constitutional field," guided only by their personal views. *Griswold v. Connecticut*, 381 U.S., at 502 (Harlan, J., concurring in judgment).

. . .

We have stated above our belief that the Constitution does not subject state abortion regulations to heightened scrutiny. Accordingly, we think that the correct analysis is that set forth by the plurality opinion in *Webster*. A woman's interest in having an abortion is a form of liberty protected by the Due Process Clause, but States may regulate abortion procedures in ways rationally related to a legitimate state interest. *Williamson v. Lee Optical of Oklahoma, Inc.*, 348 U.S. 483, 491 (1955); cf. *Stanley v. Illinois*, 405 U.S. 645, 651–65 (1972). With this rule in mind, we examine each of the challenged provisions.

. . .

[The dissent agrees with the plurality on all the upheld provisions, and says this about the spousal notice provision:]

III-C

... [As to the spousal notice provision, petitioners contend] that the real effect of such a notice requirement is to give the power to husbands to veto a woman's abortion choice. The District Court indeed found that the notification provision created a risk that some woman who would otherwise have an abortion will be prevented from having one. 947 F.2d, at 712. For example, petitioners argue, many notified husbands will prevent abortions through physical force, psychological coercion, and other types of threats. But Pennsylvania has incorporated exceptions in the notice provision in an attempt to deal with these problems. For instance, a woman need not notify her husband if the pregnancy is the result of a reported sexual assault, or if she has reason to believe that she would suffer bodily injury as a result of the notification. 18 Pa.Cons.Stat. § 3209(b) (1990). Furthermore, because this is a facial challenge to the Act, it is insufficient for petitioners to show that the notification provision "might operate unconstitutionally under some conceivable set of circumstances." *United States v. Salerno*, 481 U.S. 739, 745 (1987). Thus, it is not enough for petitioners to show that, in some "worst case" circumstances, the notice provision will operate as a grant of veto power to husbands. *Ohio v. Akron Center for Reproductive Health*, 497 U.S., at 514. Because they are making a facial challenge to the provision, they must "show that no set of circumstances exists under which the [provision] would be valid." *Ibid*. This they have failed to do.

The question before us is therefore whether the spousal notification requirement rationally furthers any legitimate state interests. We conclude that it does. First, a husband's interests in procreation within marriage and in the potential life of his unborn child are certainly substantial ones. See *Planned Parenthood of Central Mo. v. Danforth*, 428 U.S., at 69 .... The State itself has legitimate interests both in protecting these interests of the father and in protecting the potential life of the fetus, and the spousal notification requirement is reasonably related to advancing those state interests. By providing that a husband will usually know of his spouse's intent to have an abortion, the provision makes it more likely that the husband will participate in deciding the fate of his unborn child, a possibility that might otherwise have been denied him. This participation might in some cases result in a decision to proceed with the pregnancy....

The State also has a legitimate interest in promoting "the integrity of the marital relationship." 18 Pa.Cons.Stat. § 3209(a) (1990). This Court has previously recognized "the importance of the marital relationship in our society." *Planned Parenthood of Central Mo. v. Danforth,* at 69. In our view, the spousal notice requirement is a rational attempt by the State to improve truthful communication between spouses and encourage collaborative decisionmaking, and thereby fosters marital integrity. . . . [I]n our view, it is unrealistic to assume that every husband-wife relationship is either (1) so perfect that this type of truthful and important communication will take place as a matter of course, or (2) so imperfect that, upon notice, the husband will react selfishly, violently, or contrary to the best interests of his wife. See *Planned Parenthood of Central Mo. v. Danforth,* at 103–104 (STEVENS, J., concurring in part and dissenting in part) (making a similar point in the context of a parental consent statute). The spousal notice provision will admittedly be unnecessary in some circumstances, and possibly harmful in others, but the existence of particular cases in which a feature of a statute performs no function (or is even counterproductive) ordinarily does not render the statute unconstitutional or even constitutionally suspect. *Thornburgh,* 476 U.S., at 800 (WHITE, J., dissenting). The Pennsylvania Legislature was in a position to weigh the likely benefits of the provision against its likely adverse effects, and presumably concluded, on balance, that the provision would be beneficial. Whether this was a wise decision or not, we cannot say that it was irrational. We therefore conclude that the spousal notice provision comports with the Constitution.

. . .

JUSTICE SCALIA, with whom THE CHIEF JUSTICE, JUSTICE WHITE, and JUSTICE THOMAS join, concurring in the judgment in part and dissenting in part.

My views on this matter are unchanged from those I set forth in my separate opinions in *Webster v. Reproductive Health Services,* 492 U.S. 490, 532 (1989) (opinion concurring in part and concurring in judgment), and *Ohio v. Akron Center for Reproductive Health,* 497 U.S. 502, 520 (1990) (Akron II) (concurring opinion). The States may, if they wish, permit abortion on demand, but the Constitution does not require them to do so. The permissibility of abortion, and the limitations upon it, are to be resolved like most important questions in our democracy: by citizens trying to persuade one another and then voting. . . . Laws against bigamy, for example—with which entire societies of reasonable people disagree—intrude upon men and women's liberty to marry and live with one another. But bigamy happens not to be a liberty specially "protected" by the Constitution.

That is, quite simply, the issue in this case: not whether the power of a woman to abort her unborn child is a "liberty" in the absolute sense; or even whether it is a liberty of great importance to many women. Of course it is both. The issue is whether it is a liberty protected by the Constitution of the United States. I am sure it is not. I reach that conclusion...for the same reason I reach the conclusion that bigamy is not constitutionally protected—because of two simple facts: (1) the Constitution says absolutely nothing about it, and (2) the longstanding traditions of American society have permitted it to be legally proscribed.[1] *Akron II*, at 520 (SCALIA, J., concurring)....

Beyond that brief summary of the essence of my position, I will not swell the United States Reports with repetition of what I have said before; and applying the rational basis test, I would uphold the Pennsylvania statute in its entirety. I must, however, respond to a few of the more outrageous arguments in today's opinion, which it is beyond human nature to leave unanswered. I shall discuss each of them under a quotation from the Court's opinion to which they pertain.

The inescapable fact is that adjudication of substantive due process claims may call upon the Court, in interpreting the Constitution, to exercise that same capacity which, by tradition, courts always have exercised: reasoned judgment. [Emphasis in original.—AU.]

... But "reasoned judgment" does not begin by begging the question, as *Roe* and subsequent cases unquestionably did by assuming that what the State is protecting is the mere "potentiality of human life." See, *e.g., Roe*, at 162.... The whole argument of abortion opponents is that what the Court calls the fetus and what others call the unborn child *is a human life*....

[In the majority's]exhaustive discussion of all the factors that go into the determination of when *stare decisis* should be observed and when disregarded, they never mention "how wrong was the decision on its face?" Surely, if "[t]he Court's power lies ... in its legitimacy, a product of substance and perception," the "substance" part of the equation demands that plain error be acknowledged and eliminated. *Roe* was plainly wrong...

... [A]fter more than 19 years of effort by some of the brightest (and most determined) legal minds in the country, after more than 10 cases upholding abortion rights in this Court, and after dozens upon dozens of *amicus* briefs submitted in this and other cases, the best the Court can do to explain how it is that the word "liberty" *must* be thought to include the right to destroy human fetuses is to rattle off a collection of adjectives that simply decorate a value judgment and conceal a political choice. . . . It is not reasoned judgment that supports the Court's decision; only personal predilection. . . .

. . .

[Justice Scalia's dissent went on for many pages in a similar tone.]

. . .[B]efore *Roe v. Wade* was decided[ ] [p]rofound disagreement existed among our citizens over the issue—as it does over other issues, such as the death penalty—but that disagreement was being worked out at the state level. As with many other issues, the division of sentiment within each State was not as closely balanced as it was among the population of the Nation as a whole, meaning not only that more people would be satisfied with the results of state-by-state resolution, but also that those results would be more stable. Pre-*Roe*, moreover, political compromise was possible.

. . .

I cannot agree with, indeed I am appalled by, the Court's suggestion that the decision whether to stand by an erroneous constitutional decision must be strongly influenced—*against* overruling, no less—by the substantial and continuing public opposition the decision has generated. . . .

But whether it would "subvert the Court's legitimacy" or not, the notion that we would decide a case differently from the way we otherwise would have in order to show that we can stand firm against public disapproval is frightening. It . . . acquires a character of almost czarist arrogance. . . .

Opinion Footnote

1 The Court's suggestion, that adherence to tradition would require us to uphold laws against interracial marriage is entirely wrong. Any tradition in that case was contradicted by a text—an Equal Protection Clause that explicitly establishes racial equality as a constitutional value. See *Loving v. Virginia*, 388 U.S. 1, 9 (1967). . . .The enterprise launched in *Roe v. Wade,* by contrast, sought to establish—in the teeth of a clear, contrary tradition—a value found nowhere in the constitutional text. . . .

There is, of course, no comparable tradition barring recognition of a "liberty interest" in carrying one's child to term free from state efforts to kill it. For that reason, it does not follow that the Constitution does not protect childbirth simply because it does not protect abortion.

Case Questions

1. Justice Stevens asserts (in part **II** of his opinion) that it is constitutional for Pennsylvania to "produce and disseminate" printed material such as the kind at issue here but that it is unconstitutional for the state to ordain that women contemplating abortion be told of the availability of this printed material. What in the Constitution convinces him that disseminating to the general public is acceptable but to particular groups at particular times, not acceptable?

2. Justice Stevens (in part **IV**) insists that information as to gestational age of the fetus is not "justified as relevant to any philosophic or social argument . . . favoring or disfavoring the abortion decision." Is gestational age really separate from viability, on which Stevens hinges his own "philosophic or social argument" concerning the point at which legislation may interfere with the private freedom to choose abortion?

3. Is Justice Stevens being overly optimistic in asserting (in part **III**) that no woman "undertakes [an abortion] decision lightly"?

4. Justice Blackmun praises the plurality for their acknowledgment that our Constitution places certain "fundamental liberties" beyond the reach of majorities hostile to them. Does either Blackmun or the plurality explain what guidelines they use to decide which liberties are or are not "fundamental" for Americans?

5. In explaining his own guideline for that question, Justice Scalia specifies the constitutional text and tradition. He justifies going against the tradition forbidding interracial marriage, because, he says, the (textual) equal protection clause "explicitly establishes racial equality as a constitutional value" (footnote 1). (Note that the word race is not "explicit" in the equal protection clause.) However, he opposes the Court's then-recent decision[108] that the First Amendment ban on any "law respecting an establishment of religion" was violated by official school prayers at graduation ceremonies of state-run high schools. Despite the explicitness of the establishment clause, Justice Scalia calls it an "ambiguous text" that was "clarif[ied]" by the "clear tradition" of the graduation prayers. Is the equal protection clause really less ambiguous than the establishment clause or the anti-miscegenation tradition (which endured under the equal protection clause for more than one hundred years) any less clear than the prayer tradition?

6. Both Rehnquist (in part **II**) and Scalia express concern about the plurality's new rule that those "watershed" decisions of the Court that are the most "intensely divisive" should be overruled only when the Court has "the most compelling reason" to do so, to avoid the appearance of "overruling under fire." The Rehnquist/Scalia concern is that this rule runs afoul of the First Amendment rights of people who wish to protest the decision: The more they protest, the more the decision will appear "divisive," so the new rule looks like a threat that the decision will be maintained as a kind of punishment for the protest. (It is perhaps worth noting that in 1992 the Court was facing a case, *Bray v. Alexander*,[109] that dealt with the punishment of violent protests at abortion clinics, so the question of abortion protests was highly salient for the justices.) Should the plurality's reasoning have been more attentive to this First Amendment concern?

7. When Justice Rehnquist states (in part **I**) that abortion is a "liberty interest protected by the due process clause" that may be restricted whenever the state has a rational basis for doing so, he is saying that abortion is protected *not* as a fundamental

right but only as much as any other liberty, such as, say, walking down the street or driving an automobile. On the other hand, the Rehnquist group continues to view contraception as a fundamental right. Abortion, Rehnquist says, is different because it "involves the purposeful termination of potential life." When an IUD or a birth control pill causes a fertilized egg to fail to nest in the uterine wall, is this, too, a "purposeful termination of potential life"? Does the Rehnquist opinion mean that only prefertilization birth control techniques are now protected by the Constitution? Would this be a strange principle of constitutional law?

8. Justice Scalia argues that a larger number of people would be content with abortion policy if it were allowed to vary from state to state. Is he correct? Could the same argument be made about the meaning of, say, an "unreasonable search and seizure" or what is a "law respecting an establishment of religion"? Both of these clauses, and most other parts of the Bill of Rights, have been applied to state governments, nationwide, through the due process clause of the Fourteenth Amendment. Would there be a greater number of contented Americans if state variation on all these matters were allowed?

9. Who is the proper group to consider in assessing the constitutionality of the spousal notice provision: married pregnant women in general, the vast majority of whom would discuss any consideration of abortion with their husbands, or only those married pregnant women who feel burdened by the law, in which group a large fraction will experience the law as an "effective veto"?

Case note: Within months, the Supreme Court added clarity to the import of the *Casey* precedent by its action in refusing to grant review to two federal circuit court decisions. While the Court never writes explanations of a refusal to grant review and may have any number of reasons for one, certain inferences may sometimes plausibly be drawn. For instance, in the first of these actions, on November 30, 1992, the Court let stand a ruling that the Guam statute described above (in the introduction to the *Casey* case) was unconstitutional on the grounds that it clashed directly with *Roe v. Wade*. Three justices—Scalia, Rehnquist, and White—dissented, with the latter two joining in Scalia's argument that the Court should consider whether, instead of declaring the entire statute void, the lower court should instead have tried to uphold it as constitutional in part, because it would be constitutional if applied only to viable fetuses.[110] One cannot know why Clarence Thomas, who had concurred with them in *Casey*, left their ranks this time. For now, laws of the Guam type—sweeping prohibitions of abortion that did not respect the viability threshold—remain unconstitutional.

On the other side of the abortion policy scale, just one week later, the Supreme Court refused, without dissent, to review a decision upholding a 24 hour waiting period statute of the state of Mississippi that was virtually identical to the clause the

Supreme Court upheld in *Casey*.[111] Pro-choice attorneys had hoped that a fact-based argument emphasizing how different Pennsylvania is from Mississippi, where approximately 50% of women live more than 100 miles from an abortion clinic, would convince the Court that a 24-hour waiting period in the southern state in fact amounted to an undue burden, because it often necessitated either a second, arduous journey, or the extra cost of an overnight stay. One difficulty with their argument was that they were asking for a declaratory judgment that the law was unconstitutional "on its face." Such a declaration is supposed to rest on the premise that there are no circumstances where the law can be applied constitutionally. This law obviously did not place such an extra burden on women living near the clinics. Thus, while the Court officially left open in *Casey* the possibility that attorneys might be able to demonstrate circumstances where a 24 hour waiting period is unconstitutional, the justices evidently are willing to be so convinced only with regard to particular applications of the law, not with a declaratory judgment *before* the law is ever applied.

RESTRICTING ABORTION TECHNIQUE

Stenberg v. Carhart (2000)

Pro-life activists in the wake of the *Casey* decision did not limit themselves to 24-hour waiting periods. Their main offensive was to promote legislative bans on what they call "partial birth abortion," a particular abortion technique employed for abortions after the 15th week of pregnancy. This legislative initiative really took off in 1995 when the Republicans became a majority of both houses of Congress for the first time in decades.[112] The federal bill forbade "intentionally delivering into the vagina a living unborn child, or a substantial portion thereof, for the purpose of performing a procedure that the person knows will kill the unborn child." Twice this ban passed in Congress, only to be vetoed by President Clinton.

President Clinton explained his veto by noting that the bill did not allow for a health exception, such that a physician would be free to choose this otherwise forbidden medical technique if he or she believed it necessary to safeguard the patient's health. *Roe v. Wade* had ruled that exceptions to safeguard a woman's health had to be permitted even in laws forbidding the abortion of a viable fetus. *Casey v. Planned Parenthood* had reiterated this rule of law. The Presidential Oath prescribed in the Constitution obliges the president to "preserve, protect, and defend the Constitution of the United States." Clinton said repeatedly that he would happily sign the bill if it included an exception for the mother's health. Congress refused to oblige, hoping to pass the bill over his veto. The bill's supporters in the House of Representatives did muster the two-thirds needed for an override, but the Senate didn't follow. Senate votes were held shortly before the national elections, in 1996 and 1998.[113]

After the defeat of the national bill, 30 states on their own (by the year 2000) adopted duplicate versions of the ban, most of which drew court challenges.[114] In 2000 the first of those challenges reached the U.S. Supreme Court, in the case *Stenberg, Attorney General of Nebraska, v. Carhart* (a physician who performed abortions). Researchers looking into the question of the frequency of this abortion technique estimated that 2,200 intact D&E or D&X procedures (the official medical labels—i.e., "intact dilation and evacuation" or "dilation and extraction") were performed in the United States in 2000, accounting for about 0.17% of abortions performed.[115]

The Supreme Court's 5–4 ruling rendered 29 of the 31 extant bans unconstitutional.[116] In this case, the District Court, responding to a lawsuit from Dr. Carhart, had issued an injunction staying enforcement of the ban, on the grounds that it was unconstitutional (11 F. Supp. 2d 1099 [Neb. 1998]). The Eighth Circuit Court of Appeals had affirmed this conclusion (192 F. 3d 1142 [1999]).[117] The U.S. Supreme Court agreed.

The Nebraska law in question had stated: "No partial birth abortion shall be performed in this state, unless such procedure is necessary to save the life of the mother whose life is endangered by a physical disorder, physical illness, or physical injury, including a life-endangering physical condition caused by or arising from the pregnancy itself" (Neb. Rev. Stat. Ann. § 28–328[1] [Supp. 1999]. The bill had defined "partial birth abortion" as "an abortion procedure in which the person performing the abortion partially delivers vaginally a living unborn child before killing the unborn child and completing the delivery" (§ 28–326[9]), and then defined "partially delivers vaginally a living unborn child before killing the unborn child" to mean "deliberately and intentionally delivering into the vagina a living unborn child, or a substantial portion thereof, for the purpose of performing a procedure that the person performing such procedure knows will kill the unborn child and does kill the unborn child" (ibid.).

By the time of this decision, pro-choice Justice Blackmun and pro-life Justice White had been replaced by two Clinton appointees: Ruth Bader Ginsburg, who had successfully argued many important sex equality cases at the Supreme Court in the 1970s and was at the time of appointment already a federal judge, and Stephen Breyer, also a sitting federal judge. While a total of five justices did concur in the majority opinion of Justice Breyer, feelings in the case ran so high that eight of the nine justices expressed themselves in separate opinions. Of these, three— the Court opinion, Thomas's dissent (joined by Rehnquist and Scalia) and

Kennedy's dissent—provide detailed, graphic descriptions not just of the technique that is known politically as "partial birth abortion" (medically, "dilation and extraction" or D&X or "intact D&E") but also of its main competitor, D&E (dilation and evacuation), the dominant, or "mainstream" abortion technique for late-term abortion (i.e., 16 weeks of pregnancy or later).

The Breyer majority noted that 90% of abortions are performed during the first trimester of pregnancy with a procedure that essentially vacuums out the uterine contents and that "mortality rates for first trimester abortion are . . . 5 to 10 times lower than those associated with carrying the fetus to term."[118] For weeks 12–15 a modified version of this vacuum method is used. After that, for later term abortions the previously dominant method, saline amniocentesis, which basically induced labor, causing expulsion of the dead fetus, has now been largely abandoned in favor of safer techniques that, instead, dilate the cervix and then use instruments to remove the fetus and other uterine contents.[119]

There are two basic ways to do the dilation and removal. In D&E, which partial birth ban advocates say they would permit, the doctor pulls a foot or arm through the cervical opening, which is not big enough to let the rest of the body through, so the limb tears off and the fetus bleeds to death. The doctor continues, removing the fetus piece by piece, and eventually needs to collapse the skull of the (dead) fetus to remove it all. This procedure is *not*, at least according to testimony in the *Stenberg v. Carhart* case and also in Congress, intended to be forbidden by "partial birth abortion laws." This is the prevalent, standard method of late term abortions in the United States.

With D&X, or "intact D&E," the fetus is extracted from the uterus whole, or "intact." If the fetus is in the normal, headfirst, birth position, the doctor uses a scissors to puncture the skill until there is a hole big enough for a vacuuming instrument to remove the cranial contents in order to shrink the head so that it will fit through the cervix. This method kills the fetus prior to its passage through the cervix, so it, too, is *not* forbidden by "partial birth abortion" (PBA) laws. The only version that is forbidden as "partial birth abortion" is used when the fetus presents feet first. In this situation, the doctor pulls the legs and torso out of the uterus, such that some of it is in the vaginal cavity and the rest is outside the woman's body. The head remains in the uterus because of its size. (Justice Thomas noted in his dissent that a 16-week fetus averages 6 inches in length and a 20-week fetus averages 8 inches.) The doctor then punctures the head, and proceeds as described for the head-first version. Because so much of the fetus is visible outside the woman's body, PBA-ban advocates find the process exceptionally morally repugnant and wish to ban it, that is, D&X of a feet-first fetus.

In 2000 in *Stenberg v. Carhart*, 530 U.S. 914, the U.S. Supreme Court by a 5–4 vote struck down the partial birth abortion ban (i.e. the ban on intact D&E, also known as D&X). Justice Breyer wrote for the majority, beginning with:

> ...Three established principles determine the issue before us. We shall set them forth in the language of the joint opinion in *Casey*. First, before "viability . . . the woman has a right to choose to terminate her pregnancy." *Id.*, at 870 (joint opinion of O'Connor, Kennedy, and Souter, JJ.).
>
> Second, "a law designed to further the State's interest in fetal life which imposes an undue burden on the woman's decision before fetal viability" is unconstitutional. *Id.*, at 877. An "undue burden is . . . shorthand for the conclusion that a state regulation has the purpose or effect of placing a substantial obstacle in the path of a woman seeking an abortion of a nonviable fetus." *Ibid.*
>
> Third, " 'subsequent to viability, the State in promoting its interest in the potentiality of human life may, if it chooses, regulate, and even proscribe, abortion except where it is necessary, in appropriate medical judgment, for the preservation of the life or health of the mother.' " *Id.*, at 879 (quoting *Roe v. Wade*, at 164–165).

Applying these three rules, the Court majority then concluded that the ban on intact D&E did not measure up because there was substantial testimony in the record to the effect that for certain pregnancies this was the safest abortion technique for avoiding serious injury to the pregnant woman. Under the constitutional right of privacy, a pregnant woman has a right to attempt to preserve her own health.

On separate grounds (at 938–940), the Court majority also concluded that the statute was unconstitutional due to its vagueness. The law's wording did not make clear that its prohibitions left doctors free to perform regular D&E abortions. These are the vast majority of late-term abortions.

The four dissenters were Rehnquist, Scalia, Thomas and Kennedy. Kennedy broke with his *Casey* allies, arguing here that in light of the shocking impact of seeing so much of the fetus outside of the woman's body before its life is terminated, "Nebraska was entitled to find the existence of a consequential moral difference between the procedures." Since Nebraska, according to the dissenters, was still allowing late term abortions to be performed using the generally safe and widely accepted alternative D&E method, he and the other dissenters believed the law passed muster even under the *Casey* rules. The three other dissenters still insisted that *Roe v. Wade* should be overruled.

CONSTITUTIONAL LAW CHANGES WITH JUDICIAL PERSONNEL

President George W. Bush (Bush II) took office in January 2001. Congress in 2003 adopted a revised version of the partial birth abortion ban and Bush II signed it into law on November 5, 2003. The new law did describe with more precision the procedure being banned in order to avoid the constitutional problem of vagueness.

This newer version of the federal law also mentions *Stenberg v. Carhart* and states several times that the District Court findings of fact on which the Supreme Court relied were "erroneous" and states as Congressional "findings" the following:

1. A moral, medical, and ethical consensus exists that the practice of performing a partial-birth abortion—an abortion in which a physician deliberately and intentionally vaginally delivers a living, unborn child's body until either the entire baby's head is outside the body of the mother, or any part of the baby's trunk past the navel is outside the body of the mother and only the head remains inside the womb, for the purpose of performing an overt act (usually the puncturing of the back of the child's skull and removing the baby's brains) that the person knows will kill the partially delivered infant, performs this act, and then completes delivery of the dead infant—is a gruesome and inhumane procedure **that is never medically necessary** and should be prohibited.

2. Rather than being an abortion procedure that is embraced by the medical community, particularly among physicians who routinely perform other abortion procedures, partial-birth abortion remains a disfavored **procedure that is** not only **unnecessary to preserve the health of the mother**, but in fact poses serious risks to the long-term health of women and in some circumstances, their lives. . . . (Emphases added.)

After lengthy "findings" along these lines, the law imposes fines and/or imprisonment for up to two years as a penalty on performers of such abortions, as limited by the statement: "This subsection does not apply to a partial-birth abortion that is necessary to save the life of a mother." Congress appears to believe that partial birth abortions are never necessary to prevent serious damage to a woman's health but may sometimes be necessary to save a woman's life. The bill does not explain this puzzle.[120]

The law was challenged immediately in three federal district courts, and U.S. District Judge Phyllis Hamilton ruled the law unconstitutional, largely on the grounds of conflict with *Stenberg v. Carhart*, and issued a permanent injunction against enforcement of the ban with respect to the groups that filed that lawsuit (primarily affiliates of Planned Parenthood Federation of America).[121] The federal government appealed. By the time this case reached the Court as *Gonzales v. Carhart*, 550 U.S. 124 (2007), two justices left the Court, one of whom (O'Connor) had been part of the *Casey* majority.

Associate Justice Sandra Day O'Connor announced on July 1, 2005 that she would be retiring once her successor was confirmed. Fifty-year old U.S. Court of Appeals for the District of Columbia Circuit Judge John Roberts was nominated just over two weeks later to replace O'Connor on the Court. Less than two months after that, on September 3, Chief Justice William Rehnquist died at age 80 leaving that position open. President Bush withdrew Roberts' nomination as Associate Justice after which he nominated Roberts as Chief Justice. Roberts was confirmed by the Senate in a 78–22 vote, and assumed office on September 29, 2005.

Bush then nominated Harriet Miers, the White House Counsel, to replace O'Connor. After a political uproar in which both Democrats and Republicans opposed Miers as unqualified, Bush withdrew her nomination. On November 10, 2005, Bush nominated U.S. Court of Appeals for the Third Circuit Judge Samuel Alito. Alito's nomination was confirmed on January 31, 2006 with a mostly party line vote, and he took office that same day.

In their confirmation hearings, both Roberts and Alito were grilled intensively on their views about the hot button issue of abortion. Below is an excerpt from an exchange between U.S. Senator Arlen Specter (R-PA)[122] and Judge Roberts during his confirmation hearings regarding Roberts' interpretation of abortion rights in the context of the right of privacy during the second day of his nomination hearings, on September 13, 2005:

SPECTER: Judge Roberts, in your confirmation hearing for the circuit court, your testimony read to this effect, and it's been widely quoted: *Roe* is the settled law of the land. Do you mean settled for you, settled only for your capacity as a circuit judge, or settled beyond that?

ROBERTS: Well, beyond that, it's settled as a precedent of the court, entitled to respect under principles of stare decisis. And those principles, applied in the *Casey* case, explain when cases should be revisited and when they should not. And it is settled as a precedent of the court, yes.

SPECTER: You went on then to say, quote, "It's a little more than settled. It was reaffirmed in the face of a challenge that it should be overruled in the *Casey* decision. So it has that added precedential value."

ROBERTS: I think the initial question for the judge confronting an issue in this area, you don't go straight to the *Roe* decision; you begin with *Casey*, which modified the *Roe* framework and reaffirmed its central holding.

SPECTER: And you went on to say, accordingly: It is the settled law of the land, using the term settled again. Then your final statement as to this quotation: There is nothing in my personal views that would prevent me from fully and faithfully applying the precedent, as well as *Casey*. There have been questions raised about your personal views. And let me digress from *Roe* for just a moment because I think this touches on an issue which ought to be settled. When you talk about your personal views and, as they may relate to your own faith, would you say that your views are the same as those expressed by John Kennedy when he was a candidate (in 1960), when he spoke to the Greater Houston Ministerial Association in September of 1960, quote, I do not speak for my church on public matters and the church does not speak for me, close quote?

ROBERTS: I agree with that, Senator. Yes.

SPECTER: And did you have that in mind when you said, "There's nothing in my personal views that would prevent me from fully and faithfully applying the precedent, as well as *Casey*?"

ROBERTS: Well, I think people's personal views on this issue derive from a number of sources. And there's nothing in my personal views based on faith or other sources that would prevent me from applying the precedents of the court faithfully under principles of stare decisis.

SPECTER: Judge Roberts, the change in positions have been frequently noted. Early on, in one of your memoranda, you had made a comment on the so-called right to privacy.

SPECTER: This was a 1981 memo to Attorney General Smith, December 11th, 1981. You were referring to a lecture which Solicitor General Griswold had given six years earlier and you wrote, quote, that, Solicitor General Griswold devotes a section to the so-called right to privacy; acquiring, as we have—that such an amorphous arguing, as we have, that such an amorphous right was not to be found in the Constitution. Do you believe today that the right to privacy does exist in the Constitution?

ROBERTS: Senator, I do. The right to privacy is protected under the Constitution in various ways. It's protected by the Fourth Amendment which provides that the right of people to be secure in their persons, houses, effects and papers is protected. It's protected under the First Amendment dealing with prohibition on establishment of a religion and guarantee of free exercise. It protects privacy in matters of conscience. It was protected by the framers in areas that were of particular concern to them. It may not seem so significant today: the Third Amendment, protecting their homes against the quartering of troops. And in addition, the court has—it was a series of decisions going back 80 years—has recognized that personal privacy is a component of the liberty protected by the due process clause. The court has explained that the liberty protected is not limited to freedom from physical restraint and that it's protected not simply procedurally, but as a substantive matter as well. And those decisions have sketched out, over a period of 80 years, certain aspects of privacy that are protected as part of the liberty in the due process clause under the Constitution.[123]

* * *

One year after Alito's appointment, in *Gonzales v. Carhart* (2007), the Court was asked to evaluate the constitutionality of the new federal Partial-Birth Abortion Act of 2003. The majority opinion authored by Justice Kennedy distinguished the congressional legislation from the recently struck-down Nebraska version. As the excerpt below demonstrates, one of the central questions for the Court was whether Congress' decision to exclude an explicit protection for a D&X procedure that might be needed to protect against a grave threat to the pregnant woman's health constituted a constitutional violation. Roberts and Alito voted with the new majority to answer in the negative.

GONZALES V. CARHART
550 U.S. 124 (2007)

JUSTICE KENNEDY delivered the opinion of the Court.

These cases require us to consider the validity of the Partial-Birth Abortion Ban Act of 2003 (Act), 18 U.S.C. § 1531 (2000 ed., Supp. IV), a federal statute regulating abortion procedures. In recitations preceding its operative provisions the Act refers to the Court's opinion in *Stenberg* v. *Carhart*, 530 U.S. 914 (2000), which also addressed the subject of abortion procedures used in the later stages of pregnancy. Compared to the state statute at issue in *Stenberg*, the Act is more specific concerning the instances to which it applies and in this respect more precise in its coverage. We conclude the Act should be sustained against the objections lodged by the broad, facial attack brought against it.

. . .

II

. . .

We assume the following principles for the purposes of this opinion. Before viability, a State "may not prohibit any woman from making the ultimate decision to terminate her pregnancy." 505 U.S., at 879 (plurality opinion). It also may not impose upon this right an undue burden, which exists if a regulation's "purpose or effect is to place a substantial obstacle in the path of a woman seeking an abortion before the fetus attains viability." *Id.,* at 878. On the other hand, "[r]egulations which do no more than create a structural mechanism by which the State, or the parent or guardian of a minor, may express profound respect for the life of the unborn are permitted, if they are not a substantial obstacle to the woman's exercise of the right to choose." *Id.,* at 877. *Casey*, in short, struck a balance. The balance was central to its holding. We now apply its standard to the cases at bar.

III

We begin with a determination of the Act's operation and effect. A straightforward reading of the Act's text demonstrates its purpose and the scope of its provisions: It regulates and proscribes, with exceptions or qualifications to be discussed, performing the intact D&E procedure.

Respondents agree the Act encompasses intact D&E, but they contend its additional reach is both unclear and excessive. Respondents assert that, at the least, the Act is void for vagueness because its scope is indefinite. In the alternative, respondents argue the Act's text proscribes all D&Es. Because D&E is the most common second-trimester abortion method, respondents suggest the Act imposes an undue burden. In this litigation the Attorney General does not dispute that the Act would impose an undue burden if it covered standard D&E.

We conclude that the Act is not void for vagueness, does not impose an undue burden from any overbreadth, and is not invalid on its face.

. . .

C

We next determine whether the Act imposes an undue burden, as a facial matter, because its restrictions on second-trimester abortions are too broad. A review of the statutory text discloses the limits of its reach. The Act prohibits intact D&E; and, notwithstanding respondents' arguments, it does not prohibit the D&E procedure in which the fetus is removed in parts.

. . .

IV

. . .

A

The Act's purposes are set forth in recitals preceding its operative provisions. A description of the prohibited abortion procedure demonstrates the rationale for the congressional enactment. The Act proscribes a method of abortion in which a fetus is killed just inches before completion of the birth process. Congress stated as follows: "Implicitly approving such a brutal and inhumane procedure by choosing not to prohibit it will further coarsen society to the humanity of not only newborns, but all vulnerable and innocent human life, making it increasingly difficult to protect such life." Congressional Findings (14)(N), in notes following 18 U.S.C. § 1531 (2000 ed., Supp. IV), p. 769. The Act expresses respect for the dignity of human life.

. . .

The Act's ban on abortions that involve partial delivery of a living fetus furthers the Government's objectives. No one would dispute that, for many, D&E is a procedure itself laden with the power to devalue human life. Congress could nonetheless conclude that the type of abortion proscribed by the Act requires specific regulation because it implicates additional ethical and moral concerns that justify a special prohibition. Congress determined that the abortion methods it proscribed had a "disturbing similarity to the killing of a newborn infant," Congressional Findings (14)(L), in notes following 18 U.S.C. § 1531 (2000 ed., Supp. IV), p. 769, and thus it was concerned with "draw[ing] a bright line that clearly distinguishes abortion and infanticide." Congressional Findings (14)(G), *ibid.* The Court has in the past confirmed the validity of drawing boundaries to prevent certain practices that extinguish life and are close to actions that are condemned. *Glucksberg* found reasonable the State's "fear that permitting assisted suicide will start it down the path to voluntary and perhaps even involuntary euthanasia." 521 U.S., at 732–735, and n. 23.

Respect for human life finds an ultimate expression in the bond of love the mother has for her child. The Act recognizes this reality as well. Whether to have an abortion requires a difficult and painful moral decision. *Casey, supra*, at 852–853 (opinion of the Court). While we find no reliable data to measure the phenomenon, it seems unexceptionable to conclude some women come to regret their choice to abort the infant life they once created and sustained. See Brief for Sandra Cano [the Doe of *Doe v. Bolton* (1973)—AU.]et al. as *Amici Curiae*. . . . Severe depression and loss of esteem can follow. See *ibid*.

. . .

It is a reasonable inference that a necessary effect of the regulation and the knowledge it conveys will be to encourage some women to carry the infant to full term, thus reducing the absolute number of late-term abortions. The medical profession, furthermore, may find different and less shocking methods to abort the fetus in the second trimester, thereby accommodating legislative demand. The State's interest in respect for life is advanced by the dialogue that better informs the political and legal systems, the medical profession, expectant mothers, and society as a whole of the consequences that follow from a decision to elect a late-term abortion.

. . .

B

The Act's furtherance of legitimate government interests bears upon, but does not resolve, the next question: whether the Act has the effect of imposing an unconstitutional burden on the abortion right because it does not allow use of the barred procedure where " 'necessary, in appropriate medical judgment, for [the] preservation of the . . . health of the mother.' " *Ayotte*, 546 U.S., at 327–328 (quoting *Casey, supra*, at 879 (plurality opinion)). The prohibition in the Act would be unconstitutional, under precedents we here assume to be controlling, if it "subject[ed] [women] to significant health risks." *Ayotte, supra*, at 328; see also *Casey, supra*, at 880 (opinion of the Court). In *Ayotte* the parties agreed a health exception to the challenged parental-involvement statute was necessary "to avert serious and often irreversible damage to [a pregnant minor's] health." 546 U.S., at 328. Here, by contrast, whether the Act creates significant health risks for women has been a contested factual question. The evidence presented in the trial courts and before Congress demonstrates both sides have medical support for their position.

Respondents presented evidence that intact D&E may be the safest method of abortion, for reasons similar to those adduced in *Stenberg*. See 530

U.S., at 932. Abortion doctors testified, for example, that intact D&E decreases the risk of cervical laceration or uterine perforation because it requires fewer passes into the uterus with surgical instruments and does not require the removal of bony fragments of the dismembered fetus, fragments that may be sharp. Respondents also presented evidence that intact D&E was safer both because it reduces the risks that fetal parts will remain in the uterus and because it takes less time to complete. Respondents, in addition, proffered evidence that intact D&E was safer for women with certain medical conditions or women with fetuses that had certain anomalies. See, *e.g., Carhart*, 331 F. Supp. 2d, at 923–929; *Nat. Abortion Federation, supra*, at 470–474; *Planned Parenthood*, 320 F. Supp. 2d, at 982–983.

These contentions were contradicted by other doctors who testified in the District Courts and before Congress. They concluded that the alleged health advantages were based on speculation without scientific studies to support them. They considered D&E always to be a safe alternative. See, *e.g., Carhart, supra*, at 930–940; *Nat. Abortion Federation*, 330 F. Supp. 2d, at 470–474; *Planned Parenthood*, 320 F. Supp. 2d, at 983.

There is documented medical disagreement whether the Act's prohibition would ever impose significant health risks on women. See, *e.g., id.,* at 1033 ("[T]here continues to be a division of opinion among highly qualified experts regarding the necessity or safety of intact D & E"); see also *Nat. Abortion Federation, supra,* at 482. The three District Courts that considered the Act's constitutionality appeared to be in some disagreement on this central factual question. The District Court for the District of Nebraska concluded "the banned procedure is, sometimes, the safest abortion procedure to preserve the health of women." *Carhart, supra,* at 1017. The District Court for the Northern District of California reached a similar conclusion. *Planned Parenthood, supra,* at 1002 (finding intact D&E was "under certain circumstances . . . significantly safer than D & E by disarticulation"). The District Court for the Southern District of New York was more skeptical of the purported health benefits of intact D&E. It found the Attorney General's "expert witnesses reasonably and effectively refuted [the plaintiffs'] proffered bases for the opinion that [intact D&E] has safety advantages over other second-trimester abortion procedures." *Nat. Abortion Federation*, 330 F. Supp. 2d, at 479. In addition it did "not believe that many of [the plaintiffs'] purported reasons for why [intact D&E] is medically necessary [were] credible; rather [it found them to be] theoretical or false." *Id.,* at 480. The court nonetheless invalidated the Act because it determined "a significant body of medical opinion . . . holds that D & E has safety advantages over induction and that [intact D&E] has some safety advantages (however hypothetical and unsubstantiated by scientific evidence) over D & E for some women in some circumstances." *Ibid.*

The question becomes whether the Act can stand when this medical uncertainty persists. The Court's precedents instruct that the Act can survive this facial attack. The Court has given state and federal legislatures wide discretion to pass legislation in areas where there is medical and scientific uncertainty. See *Kansas* v. *Hendricks*, 521 U.S. 346, 360, n. 3 (1997); *Jones* v. *United States*, 463 U.S. 354, 364–365, n. 13, 370 (1983); *Lambert* v. *Yellowley*, 272 U.S. 581, 597 (1926); *Collins* v. *Texas*, 223 U.S. 288, 297–298 (1912); *Jacobson* v. *Massachusetts*, 197 U.S. 11, 30–31 (1905); see also *Stenberg, supra*, at 969–972 (Kennedy, J., dissenting); *Marshall* v. *United States*, 414 U.S. 417, 427 (1974) ("When Congress undertakes to act in areas fraught with medical and scientific uncertainties, legislative options must be especially broad").

This traditional rule is consistent with *Casey*, which confirms the State's interest in promoting respect for human life at all stages in the pregnancy. Physicians are not entitled to ignore regulations that direct them to use reasonable alternative procedures. The law need not give abortion doctors unfettered choice in the course of their medical practice, nor should it elevate their status above other physicians in the medical community. In *Casey* the controlling opinion held an informed-consent requirement in the abortion context was "no different from a requirement that a doctor give certain specific information about any medical procedure." 505 U.S., at 884 (joint opinion). The opinion stated "the doctor-patient relation here is entitled to the same solicitude it receives in other contexts." *Ibid.;* see also *Webster* v. *Reproductive Health Services*, 492 U.S. 490, 518–519 (1989) (plurality opinion) (criticizing *Roe*'s trimester framework because, *inter alia*, it "left this Court to serve as the country's *ex officio* medical board with powers to approve or disapprove medical and operative practices and standards throughout the United States" (internal quotation marks omitted)); *Mazurek* v. *Armstrong*, 520 U.S. 968, 973 (1997) *(per curiam)* (upholding a restriction on the performance of abortions to licensed physicians despite the respondents' contention "all health evidence contradicts the claim that there is any health basis for the law" (internal quotation marks omitted)).

Medical uncertainty does not foreclose the exercise of legislative power in the abortion context any more than it does in other contexts. See *Hendricks, supra*, at 360, n. 3. The medical uncertainty over whether the Act's prohibition creates significant health risks provides a sufficient basis to conclude in this facial attack that the Act does not impose an undue burden.

The conclusion that the Act does not impose an undue burden is supported by other considerations. Alternatives are available to the prohibited procedure. As we have noted, the Act does not proscribe D&E. One District Court found D&E to have extremely low rates of medical complications. *Planned Parenthood, supra*, at 1000. Another indicated D&E was "generally the safest method of abortion during the second trimester." *Carhart*, 331 F. Supp. 2d, at 1031; see also *Nat. Abortion Federation, supra*, at 467–468 (explaining that "[e]xperts testifying for both sides" agreed D&E was safe). In addition the Act's prohibition only applies to the delivery of "a living fetus." 18 U.S.C. § 1531(b)(1)(A) (2000 ed., Supp. IV). If the intact D&E procedure is truly necessary in some circumstances, it appears likely an injection that kills the fetus is an alternative under the Act that allows the doctor to perform the procedure.

The instant cases, then, are different from *Planned Parenthood of Central Mo. v. Danforth*, 428 U.S. 52, 77–79 (1976), in which the Court invalidated a ban on saline amniocentesis, the then-dominant second-trimester abortion method. The Court found the ban in *Danforth* to be "an unreasonable or arbitrary regulation designed to inhibit, and having the effect of inhibiting, the vast majority of abortions after the first 12 weeks." *Id.,* at 79. Here the Act allows, among other means, a commonly used and generally accepted method, so it does not construct a substantial obstacle to the abortion right.

In reaching the conclusion the Act does not require a health exception we reject certain arguments made by the parties on both sides of these cases. On the one hand, the Attorney General urges us to uphold the Act on the basis of the congressional findings alone. Brief for Petitioner in No. 05–380, at 23. Although we review congressional factfinding under a deferential standard, we do not in the circumstances here place dispositive weight on Congress' findings. The Court retains an independent constitutional duty to review factual findings where constitutional rights are at stake. See *Crowell* v. *Benson*, 285 U.S. 22, 60 (1932) ("In cases brought to enforce constitutional rights, the judicial power of the United States necessarily extends to the independent determination of all questions, both of fact and law, necessary to the performance of that supreme function").

As respondents have noted, and the District Courts recognized, some recitations in the Act are factually incorrect. See *Nat. Abortion Federation*, 330 F. Supp. 2d, at 482, 488–491. Whether or not accurate at the time, some of the important findings have been superseded. Two examples suffice. Congress determined no medical schools provide instruction on the prohibited procedure. Congressional Findings (14)(B), in notes following 18 U.S.C. § 1531 (2000 ed., Supp. IV), p. 769. The testimony in the District Courts, however, demonstrated intact D&E is taught at medical schools. *Nat. Abortion Federation, supra*, at 490; *Planned Parenthood*, 320 F. Supp. 2d, at 1029. Congress also found there existed a medical consensus that the prohibited procedure is never medically necessary. Congressional Findings (1), in notes following 18 U.S.C. § 1531 (2000 ed., Supp. IV), p. 767. The evidence presented in the District Courts contradicts that conclusion. See, *e.g., Carhart, supra*, at 1012–1015; *Nat. Abortion Federation, supra*, at 488–489; *Planned Parenthood, supra*, at 1025–1026. Uncritical deference to Congress' factual findings in these cases is inappropriate.

On the other hand, relying on the Court's opinion in *Stenberg*, respondents contend that an abortion regulation must contain a health exception "if 'substantial medical authority supports the proposition that banning a particular procedure could endanger women's health.'" Brief for Respondents... (quoting 530 U.S., at 938); see also Brief for Respondent Planned Parenthood et al.... (same). As illustrated by respondents' arguments and the decisions of the Courts of Appeals, *Stenberg* has been interpreted to leave no margin of error for legislatures to act in the face of medical uncertainty. *Carhart*, 413 F. 3d, at 796; *Planned Parenthood*, 435 F. 3d, at 1173; see also *Nat. Abortion Federation*, 437 F. 3d, at 296 (Walker, C. J., concurring) (explaining the standard under *Stenberg* "is a virtually insurmountable evidentiary hurdle").

A zero tolerance policy would strike down legitimate abortion regulations, like the present one, if some part of the medical community were disinclined to follow the proscription. This is too exacting a standard to impose on the legislative power, exercised in this instance under the Commerce Clause, to regulate the medical profession. Considerations of marginal safety, including the balance of risks, are within the legislative competence when the regulation is rational and in pursuit of legitimate ends. When standard medical options are available, mere convenience does not suffice to displace them; and if some procedures have different risks than others, it does not follow that the State is altogether barred from imposing reasonable regulations. The Act is not invalid on its face where there is uncertainty over whether the barred procedure is ever necessary to preserve a woman's health, given the availability of other abortion procedures that are considered to be safe alternatives.

V

***

Respondents have not demonstrated that the Act, as a facial matter, is void for vagueness, or that it imposes an undue burden on a woman's right to abortion based on its overbreadth or lack of a health exception. For these reasons the judgments of the Courts of Appeals for the Eighth and Ninth Circuits are reversed.

It is so ordered.

JUSTICE THOMAS, with whom JUSTICE SCALIA joins, concurring.

I join the Court's opinion because it accurately applies current jurisprudence, including *Planned Parenthood of Southeastern Pa.* v. *Casey*, 505 U.S. 833 (1992). I write separately to reiterate my view that the Court's abortion jurisprudence, including *Casey* and *Roe* v. *Wade*, 410 U.S. 113 (1973), has no basis in the Constitution. . .

JUSTICE GINSBURG, with whom JUSTICE STEVENS, JUSTICE SOUTER, and JUSTICE BREYER join, dissenting.

In *Planned Parenthood of Southeastern Pa.* v. *Casey*, 505 U.S. 833, 844 (1992), the Court declared that "[l]iberty finds no refuge in a jurisprudence of doubt." There was, the Court said, an "imperative" need to dispel doubt as to "the meaning and reach" of the Court's 7-to-2 judgment, rendered nearly two decades earlier in *Roe* v. *Wade*, 410 U.S. 113 (1973). 505 U.S., at 845. Responsive to that need, the Court endeavored to provide secure guidance to "[s]tate and federal courts as well as legislatures throughout the Union," by defining "the rights of the woman and the legitimate authority of the State respecting the termination of pregnancies by abortion procedures." *Ibid*.

. . .

Seven years ago, in *Stenberg* v. *Carhart*, 530 U.S. 914 (2000), the Court invalidated a Nebraska statute criminalizing the performance of a medical procedure that, in the political arena, has been dubbed "partial-birth abortion." With fidelity to the *Roe-Casey* line of precedent, the Court held the Nebraska statute unconstitutional in part because it lacked the requisite protection for the preservation of a woman's health. *Stenberg*, 530 U.S., at 930; cf. *Ayotte* v. *Planned Parenthood of Northern New Eng.*, 546 U.S. 320, 327 (2006).

Today's decision is alarming. It refuses to take *Casey* and *Stenberg* seriously. It tolerates, indeed applauds, federal intervention to ban nationwide a procedure found necessary and proper in certain cases by the American College of Obstetricians and Gynecologists (ACOG). It blurs the line, firmly drawn in *Casey*, between pre-viability and post-viability abortions. And, for the first time since *Roe*, the Court blesses a prohibition with no exception safeguarding a woman's health.

I dissent from the Court's disposition. Retreating from prior rulings that abortion restrictions cannot be imposed absent an exception safeguarding a woman's health, the Court upholds an Act that surely would not survive under the close scrutiny that previously attended state-decreed limitations on a woman's reproductive choices.

I

A

As *Casey* comprehended, at stake in cases challenging abortion restrictions is a woman's "control over her [own] destiny.". . .

In keeping with this comprehension of the right to reproductive choice, the Court has consistently required that laws regulating abortion, at any stage of pregnancy and in all cases, safeguard a woman's health. . .

We have thus ruled that a State must avoid subjecting women to health risks not only where the pregnancy itself creates danger, but also where state regulation forces women to resort to less safe methods of abortion. See *Planned Parenthood of Central Mo.* v. *Danforth*, 428 U.S. 52, 79 (1976) (holding unconstitutional a ban on a method of abortion that "force[d] a woman . . . to terminate her pregnancy by methods more dangerous to her health"). See also *Stenberg*, 530 U.S., at 931 ("[Our cases] make clear that a risk to . . . women's health is the same whether it happens to arise from regulating a particular method of abortion, or from barring abortion entirely."). Indeed, we have applied the rule that abortion regulation must safeguard a woman's health to the particular procedure at issue here—intact dilation and evacuation (D&E).[3]

In *Stenberg*, we expressly held that a statute banning intact D&E was unconstitutional in part because it lacked a health exception. 530 U.S., at 930, 937. We noted that there existed a "division of medical opinion" about the relative safety of intact D&E, *id.*, at 937, but we made clear that as long as "substantial medical authority supports the proposition that banning a particular abortion procedure could endanger women's health," a health exception is required, *id.*, at 938. . .

B

In 2003, a few years after our ruling in *Stenberg*, Congress passed the Partial-Birth Abortion Ban Act—without an exception for women's health. See 18 U. S. C. § 1531(a) (2000 ed., Supp. IV). The congressional findings on which the Partial-Birth Abortion Ban Act rests do not withstand inspection, as the lower courts have determined and this Court is obliged to concede. *Ante.* See *National Abortion Federation* v. *Ashcroft*, 330 F. Supp. 2d 436, 482 (SDNY 2004) ("Congress did not ... carefully consider the evidence before arriving at its findings."), aff'd *sub nom. National Abortion Federation* v. *Gonzales*, 437 F. 3d 278 (CA2 2006). See also *Planned Parenthood Federation of Am.* v. *Ashcroft*, 320 F. Supp. 2d 957, 1019 (ND Cal. 2004) ("[N]one of the six physicians who testified before Congress had ever performed an intact D&E. Several did not provide abortion services at all; and one was not even an obgyn. ... [T]he oral testimony before Congress was not only unbalanced, but intentionally polemic."), ...

. . .

More important, Congress claimed there was a medical consensus that the banned procedure is never necessary. Congressional Findings (1), in notes following 18 U.S.C. § 1531 (2000 ed., Supp. IV), p. 767. But the evidence "very clearly demonstrate[d] the opposite." *Planned Parenthood*, 320 F. Supp. 2d, at 1025. See also *Carhart*, 331 F. Supp. 2d, at 1008–1009 ("[T]here was no evident consensus in the record that Congress compiled. There was, however, a substantial body of medical opinion presented to Congress in opposition. If anything ... the congressional record establishes that there was a 'consensus' in favor of the banned procedure."); *National Abortion Federation*, 330 F. Supp. 2d, at 488 ("The congressional record itself undermines [Congress'] finding" that there is a medical consensus that intact D&E "is never medically necessary and should be prohibited." (internal quotation marks omitted)).

Similarly, Congress found that "[t]here is no credible medical evidence that partial-birth abortions are safe or are safer than other abortion procedures." Congressional Findings (14)(B), in notes following 18 U.S.C. § 1531 (2000 ed., Supp. IV), p. 769. But the congressional record includes letters from numerous individual physicians stating that pregnant women's health would be jeopardized under the Act, as well as statements from nine professional associations, including ACOG, the American Public Health Association, and the California Medical Association, attesting that intact D&E carries meaningful safety advantages over other methods. See *National Abortion Federation*, 330 F. Supp. 2d, at 490. See also *Planned Parenthood*, 320 F. Supp. 2d, at 1021 ("Congress in its findings . . . chose to disregard the statements by ACOG and other medical organizations."). No comparable medical groups supported the ban. In fact, "all of the government's own witnesses disagreed with many of the specific congressional findings." *Id.,* at 1024.

C

In contrast to Congress, the District Courts made findings after full trials at which all parties had the opportunity to present their best evidence. The courts had the benefit of "much more extensive medical and scientific evidence . . . concerning the safety and necessity of intact D&Es." *Planned Parenthood,* 320 F. Supp. 2d, at 1014; cf. *National Abortion Federation,* 330 F. Supp. 2d, at 482 (District Court "heard more evidence during its trial than Congress heard over the span of eight years.").

During the District Court trials, "numerous" "extraordinarily accomplished" and "very experienced" medical experts explained that, in certain circumstances and for certain women, intact D&E is safer than alternative procedures and necessary to protect women's health. *Carhart,* 331 F. Supp. 2d, at 1024–1027; see *Planned Parenthood,* 320 F. Supp. 2d, at 1001 ("[A]ll of the doctors who actually perform intact D&Es concluded that in their opinion and clinical judgment, intact D&Es remain the safest option for certain individual women under certain individual health circumstances, and are significantly safer for these women than other abortion techniques, and are thus medically necessary."); cf. *ante* ("Respondents presented evidence that intact D&E may be the safest method of abortion, for reasons similar to those adduced in *Stenberg.*").

According to the expert testimony plaintiffs introduced, the safety advantages of intact D&E are marked for women with certain medical conditions, for example, uterine scarring, bleeding disorders, heart disease, or compromised immune systems. See *Carhart,* 331 F. Supp. 2d, at 924–929, 1026–1027; *National Abortion Federation,* 330 F. Supp. 2d, at 472–473; *Planned Parenthood,* 320 F. Supp. 2d, at 992–994, 1001. Further, plaintiffs' experts testified that intact D&E is significantly safer for women with certain pregnancy-related conditions, such as placenta previa and accreta, and for women carrying fetuses with certain abnormalities, such as severe hydrocephalus. See *Carhart,* 331 F. Supp. 2d, at 924, 1026–1027; *National Abortion Federation,* 330 F. Supp. 2d, at 473–474; *Planned Parenthood,* 320 F. Supp. 2d, at 992–994, 1001. See also *Stenberg,* 530 U.S., at 929; Brief for ACOG as *Amicus Curiae.*

Intact D&E, plaintiffs' experts explained, provides safety benefits over D&E by dismemberment for several reasons: *First*, intact D&E minimizes the number of times a physician must insert instruments through the cervix and into the uterus, and thereby reduces the risk of trauma to, and perforation of, the cervix and uterus—the most serious complication associated with nonintact D&E. See *Carhart*, 331 F. Supp. 2d, at 923–928, 1025; *National Abortion Federation*, 330 F. Supp. 2d, at 471; *Planned Parenthood*, 320 F. Supp. 2d, at 982, 1001. *Second*, removing the fetus intact, instead of dismembering it *in utero*, decreases the likelihood that fetal tissue will be retained in the uterus, a condition that can cause infection, hemorrhage, and infertility. See *Carhart*, 331 F. Supp. 2d, at 923–928, 1025–1026; *National Abortion Federation*, 330 F. Supp. 2d, at 472; *Planned Parenthood*, 320 F. Supp. 2d, at 1001. *Third*, intact D&E diminishes the chances of exposing the patient's tissues to sharp bony fragments sometimes resulting from dismemberment of the fetus. See *Carhart*, 331 F. Supp. 2d, at 923–928, 1026; *National Abortion Federation*, 330 F. Supp. 2d, at 471; *Planned Parenthood*, 320 F. Supp. 2d, at 1001. *Fourth*, intact D&E takes less operating time than D&E by dismemberment, and thus may reduce bleeding, the risk of infection, and complications relating to anesthesia. See *Carhart*, 331 F. Supp. 2d, at 923–928, 1026; *National Abortion Federation*, 330 F. Supp. 2d, at 472; *Planned Parenthood*, 320 F. Supp. 2d, at 1001. See also *Stenberg*, 530 U.S., at 928–929, 932; Brief for ACOG as *Amicus Curiae*.

Based on thoroughgoing review of the trial evidence and the congressional record, each of the District Courts to consider the issue rejected Congress' findings as unreasonable and not supported by the evidence. See *Carhart*, 331 F. Supp. 2d, at 1008–1027; *National Abortion Federation*, 330 F. Supp. 2d, at 482, 488–491; *Planned Parenthood*, 320 F. Supp. 2d, at 1032. The trial courts concluded, in contrast to Congress' findings, that "significant medical authority supports the proposition that in some circumstances, [intact D&E] is the safest procedure." *Id.,* at 1033 (quoting *Stenberg*, 530 U.S., at 932); accord *Carhart*, 331 F. Supp. 2d, at 1008–1009, 1017–1018; *National Abortion Federation*, 330 F. Supp. 2d, at 480–482; cf. *Stenberg*, 530 U.S., at 932 ("[T]he record shows that significant medical authority supports the proposition that in some circumstances, [intact D&E] would be the safest procedure.").

The District Courts' findings merit this Court's respect. See, *e.g.*, Fed. Rule Civ. Proc. 52(a); *Salve Regina College* v. *Russell*, 499 U.S. 225, 233 (1991). Today's opinion supplies no reason to reject those findings. Nevertheless, despite the District Courts' appraisal of the weight of the evidence, and in undisguised conflict with *Stenberg*, the Court asserts that the Partial-Birth Abortion Ban Act can survive "when . . . medical uncertainty persists." *Ante*. This assertion is bewildering. Not only does it defy the Court's longstanding precedent affirming the necessity of a health exception, with no carve-out for circumstances of medical uncertainty, see *supra*; it gives short shrift to the records before us, carefully canvassed by the District Courts. Those records indicate that "the majority of highly-qualified experts on the subject believe intact D&E to be the safest, most appropriate procedure under certain circumstances." *Planned Parenthood*, 320 F. Supp. 2d, at 1034. See *supra*.

The Court acknowledges some of this evidence, *ante*, but insists that, because some witnesses disagreed with the ACOG and other experts' assessment of risk, the Act can stand. *Ante*. In this insistence, the Court brushes under the rug the District Courts' well-supported findings that the physicians who testified that intact D&E is never necessary to preserve the health of a woman had slim authority for their opinions. They had no training for, or personal experience with, the intact D&E procedure, and many performed abortions only on rare occasions. See *Planned Parenthood*, 320 F. Supp. 2d, at 980; *Carhart*, 331 F. Supp. 2d, at 1025; cf. *National Abortion Federation*, 330 F. Supp. 2d, at 462–464. Even indulging the assumption that the Government witnesses were equally qualified to evaluate the relative risks of abortion procedures, their testimony could not erase the "significant medical authority support[ing] the proposition that in some circumstances, [intact D&E] would be the safest procedure." *Stenberg*, 530 U.S., at 932.[6]

II

A

The Court offers flimsy and transparent justifications for upholding a nationwide ban on intact D&E *sans* any exception to safeguard a women's health. Today's ruling, the Court declares, advances "a premise central to [*Casey*'s] conclusion"—*i.e.*, the Government's "legitimate and substantial interest in preserving and promoting fetal life." *Ante*. See also *ante* ("[W]e must determine whether the Act furthers the legitimate interest of the Government in protecting the life of the fetus that may become a child."). But the Act scarcely furthers that interest: The law saves not a single fetus from destruction, for it targets only a *method* of performing abortion. See *Stenberg*, 530 U.S., at 930. And surely the statute was not designed to protect the lives or health of pregnant women. *Id.*, at 951 (Ginsburg, J., concurring); cf. *Casey*, 505 U.S., at 846 (recognizing along with the State's legitimate interest in the life of the fetus, its "legitimate interes[t] . . . in protecting the *health of the woman*" (emphasis added)). In short, the Court upholds a law that, while doing nothing to "preserv[e] . . . fetal life," *ante*, bars a woman from choosing intact D&E although her doctor "reasonably believes [that procedure] will best protect [her]." *Stenberg*, 530 U.S., at 946 (Stevens, J., concurring).

As another reason for upholding the ban, the Court emphasizes that the Act does not proscribe the nonintact D&E procedure. See *ante*. But why not, one might ask. Nonintact D&E could equally be characterized as "brutal," *ante*, involving as it does "tear[ing] [a fetus] apart" and "ripp[ing] off" its limbs, *ante*. "[T]he notion that either of these two equally gruesome procedures . . . is more akin to infanticide than the other, or that the State furthers any legitimate interest by banning one but not the other, is simply irrational." *Stenberg*, 530 U.S., at 946–947 (Stevens, J., concurring).

Delivery of an intact, albeit nonviable, fetus warrants special condemnation, the Court maintains, because a fetus that is not dismembered resembles an infant. *Ante*. But so, too, does a fetus delivered intact after it is terminated by injection a day or two before the surgical evacuation, *ante*, 34–35, or a fetus delivered through medical induction or cesarean, *ante*. Yet, the availability of those procedures—along with D&E by dismemberment—the Court says, saves the ban on intact D&E from a declaration of unconstitutionality. *Ante*. Never mind that the procedures deemed acceptable might put a woman's health at greater risk. See *supra*, and n. 6. . . .

Ultimately, the Court admits that "moral concerns" are at work, concerns that could yield prohibitions on any abortion. See *ante* ("Congress could . . . conclude that the type of abortion proscribed by the Act requires specific regulation because it implicates additional ethical and moral concerns that justify a special prohibition."). Notably, the concerns expressed are untethered to any ground genuinely serving the Government's interest in preserving life. By allowing such concerns to carry the day and case, overriding fundamental rights, the Court dishonors our precedent. See, *e.g.*, *Casey*, 505 U.S., at 850 ("Some of us as individuals find abortion offensive to our most basic principles of morality, but that cannot control our decision. Our obligation is to define the liberty of all, not to mandate our own moral code."); *Lawrence* v. *Texas*, 539 U.S. 558, 571 (2003) (Though "[f]or many persons [objections to homosexual conduct] are not trivial concerns but profound and deep convictions accepted as ethical and moral principles," the power of the State may not be used "to enforce these views on the whole society through operation of the criminal law." (citing *Casey*, 505 U.S., at 850)).

Revealing in this regard, the Court invokes an antiabortion shibboleth for which it concededly has no reliable evidence: Women who have abortions come to regret their choices, and consequently suffer from "[s]evere depression and loss of esteem." Because of women's fragile emotional state and because of the "bond of love the mother has for her child," the Court worries, doctors may withhold information about the nature of the intact D&E procedure. *Ante*. The solution the Court approves, then, is *not* to require doctors to inform women, accurately and adequately, of the different procedures and their attendant risks. Cf. *Casey*, 505 U.S., at 873 (plurality opinion) ("States are free to enact laws to provide a reasonable framework for a woman to make a decision that has such profound and lasting meaning."). Instead, the Court deprives women of the right to make an autonomous choice, even at the expense of their safety.[9]

This way of thinking reflects ancient notions about women's place in the family and under the Constitution—ideas that have long since been discredited. Compare, *e.g.*, *Muller* v. *Oregon*, 208 U.S. 412, 422–423 (1908); *Bradwell* v. *State*, 16 Wall. 130, 141 (1873) (Bradley, J., concurring), with *United States* v. *Virginia*, 518 U.S. 515, 533, 542, n. 12 (1996); *Califano* v. *Goldfarb*, 430 U.S. 199, 207 (1977)).[Quotations from these cases omitted—AU.]

Though today's majority may regard women's feelings on the matter as "self-evident," *ante*, this Court has repeatedly confirmed that "[t]he destiny of the woman must be shaped ... on her own conception of her spiritual imperatives and her place in society." *Casey*, 505 U.S., at 852. See also *id.*, at 877 (plurality opinion) ("[M]eans chosen by the State to further the interest in potential life must be calculated to inform the woman's free choice, not hinder it."); *supra*.

B

In cases on a "woman's liberty to determine whether to [continue] her pregnancy," this Court has identified viability as a critical consideration. See *Casey*, 505 U.S., at 869–870 (plurality opinion). "[T]here is no line [more workable] than viability," the Court explained in *Casey*, for viability is "the time at which there is a realistic possibility of maintaining and nourishing a life outside the womb, so that the independent existence of the second life can in reason and all fairness be the object of state protection that now overrides the rights of the woman. . . . In some broad sense it might be said that a woman who fails to act before viability has consented to the State's intervention on behalf of the developing child." *Id.*, at 870.

Today, the Court blurs that line, maintaining that "[t]he Act [legitimately] appl[ies] both previability and postviability because ... a fetus is a living organism while within the womb, whether or not it is viable outside the womb." *Ante*. Instead of drawing the line at viability, the Court refers to Congress' purpose to differentiate "abortion and infanticide" based not on whether a fetus can survive outside the womb, but on where a fetus is anatomically located when a particular medical procedure is performed. See *ante* (quoting Congressional Findings (14)(G), in notes following 18 U.S.C. § 1531 (2000 ed., Supp. IV), p. 769).

One wonders how long a line that saves no fetus from destruction will hold in face of the Court's "moral concerns." See *supra*; cf. *ante* (noting that "[i]n this litigation" the Attorney General "does not dispute that the Act would impose an undue burden if it covered standard D&E"). The Court's hostility to the right *Roe* and *Casey* secured is not concealed. Throughout, the opinion refers to obstetrician-gynecologists and surgeons who perform abortions not by the titles of their medical specialties, but by the pejorative label "abortion doctor." *Ante*. A fetus is described as an "unborn child," and as a "baby," *ante*; second-trimester, previability abortions are referred to as "late-term," *ante*; and the reasoned medical judgments of highly trained doctors are dismissed as "preferences" motivated by "mere convenience," *ante*. Instead of the heightened scrutiny we have previously applied, the Court determines that a "rational" ground is enough to uphold the Act, *ante*. And, most troubling, *Casey*'s principles, confirming the continuing vitality of "the essential holding of *Roe*," are merely "assume[d]" for the moment, *ante*, rather than "retained" or "reaffirmed," *Casey*, 505 U.S., at 846.

. . .

In sum, the notion that the Partial-Birth Abortion Ban Act furthers any legitimate governmental interest is, quite simply, irrational. The Court's defense of the statute provides no saving explanation. In candor, the Act, and the Court's defense of it, cannot be understood as anything other than an effort to chip away at a right declared again and again by this Court—and with increasing comprehension of its centrality to women's lives. See *supra*. When "a statute burdens constitutional rights and all that can be said on its behalf is that it is the vehicle that legislators have chosen for expressing their hostility to those rights, the burden is undue." *Stenberg*, 530 U.S., at 952 (Ginsburg, J., concurring) (quoting *Hope Clinic* v. *Ryan*, 195 F. 3d 857, 881 (CA7 1999) (Posner, C. J., dissenting)).

* * *

For the reasons stated, I dissent from the Court's disposition and would affirm the judgments before us for review.

Opinion Footnotes

3 Dilation and evacuation (D&E) is the most frequently used abortion procedure during the second trimester of pregnancy; intact D&E is a variant of the D&E procedure. See *ante*; *Stenberg*, 530 U.S., at 924, 927; *Planned Parenthood*, 320 F. Supp. 2d, at 966. Second-trimester abortions (*i.e.*, midpregnancy, previability abortions) are, however, relatively uncommon. Between 85 and 90 percent of all abortions performed in the United States take place during the first three months of pregnancy. See *ante*. See also *Stenberg*, 530 U.S., at 923–927; *National Abortion Federation* v. *Ashcroft*, 330 F. Supp. 2d 436, 464 (SDNY 2004), aff'd *sub nom. National Abortion Federation* v. *Gonzales*, 437 F. 3d 278 (CA2 2006); *Planned Parenthood*, 320 F. Supp. 2d, at 960, and n. 4.

Adolescents and indigent women, research suggests, are more likely than other women to have difficulty obtaining an abortion during the first trimester of pregnancy. Minors may be unaware they are pregnant until relatively late in pregnancy, while poor women's financial constraints are an obstacle to timely receipt of services. See Finer et al., "Timing of Steps and Reasons for Delays in Obtaining Abortions in the United States," 74 *Contraception* 334, 341–343 (2006). See also Drey et al., "Risk Factors Associated with Presenting for Abortion in the Second Trimester," 107 *Obstetrics & Gynecology* 128, 133 (Jan. 2006) (concluding that women who have second-trimester abortions typically discover relatively late that they are pregnant). Severe fetal anomalies and health problems confronting the pregnant woman are also causes of second-trimester abortions; many such conditions cannot be diagnosed or do not develop until the second trimester. See, *e.g.*, Finer, *supra*, at 344; F. Cunningham et al., Williams *Obstetrics* 242, 290, 328–329 (22d ed. 2005); cf. Schechtman, et al. "Decision-Making for Termination of Pregnancies with Fetal Anomalies: Analysis of 53,000 Pregnancies," 99 *Obstetrics & Gynecology* 216, 220–221 (Feb. 2002) (nearly all women carrying fetuses with the most serious central nervous system anomalies chose to abort their pregnancies).

6 The majority contends that "[i]f the intact D&E procedure is truly necessary in some circumstances, it appears likely an injection that kills the fetus is an alternative under the Act that allows the doctor to perform the procedure." *Ante*. But a "significant body of medical opinion believes that inducing fetal death by injection is almost always inappropriate to the preservation of the health of women undergoing abortion because it poses tangible risk and provides no benefit to the woman." *Carhart* v. *Ashcroft*, 331 F. Supp. 2d 805, 1028 (Neb. 2004) (internal quotation marks omitted), aff'd, 413 F. 3d 791 (CA8 2005). In some circumstances, injections are "absolutely [medically] contraindicated." 331 F. Supp. 2d, at 1027.See also *id.*, at 907–912; *National Abortion Federation*, 330 F. Supp. 2d, at 474–475; *Planned Parenthood*, 320 F. Supp. 2d, at 995–997. The Court also identifies medical induction of labor as an alternative. See *ante*. That procedure, however, requires a hospital stay, *ibid.*, rendering it inaccessible to patients who lack financial resources, and it too is considered less safe for many women, and impermissible for others. See *Carhart*, 331 F. Supp. 2d, at 940–949, 1017; *National Abortion Federation*, 330 F. Supp. 2d, at 468–470; *Planned Parenthood*, 320 F. Supp. 2d, at 961, n. 5, 992–994, 1000–1002.

9 Eliminating or reducing women's reproductive choices is manifestly *not* a means of protecting them. When safe abortion procedures cease to be an option, many women seek other means to end unwanted or coerced pregnancies. See, *e.g.*, World Health Organization, *Unsafe Abortion: Global and Regional Estimates of the Incidence of Unsafe Abortion and Associated Mortality in 2000*, pp. 3, 16 (4th ed. 2004) ("Restrictive legislation is associated with a high incidence of unsafe abortion" worldwide; unsafe abortion represents 13% of all "maternal" deaths); Henshaw, *Unintended Pregnancy and Abortion: A Public Health Perspective, in A Clinician's Guide to Medical and Surgical Abortion* 11, 19 (M. Paul et al., eds. 1999) ("Before legalization, large numbers of women in the United States died from unsafe abortions."); H. Boonstra et al., *Abortion in Women's Lives* 13, and fig. 2.2 (2006) ("as late as 1965, illegal abortion still accounted for an estimated . . . 17% of all officially reported pregnancy-related deaths"; "[d]eaths from abortion declined dramatically after legalization").

Case Questions

1. Justice Kennedy states, "It is a reasonable inference that a necessary effect of the regulation and the knowledge it conveys will be to encourage some women to carry the infant to full term, thus reducing the absolute number of late-term abortions." He concludes from this that the regulation serves Congress's goal in promoting respect for life. He is describing a prohibition on a technique that doctors, prior to the law, used for only 0.17% of abortions. For a woman in a rare situation where her doctor would, but for this law, have advised that her medical condition makes this type of now-forbidden abortion (D&X) the safest type, but who now hears from her doctor that another type of abortion (D&E) is still generally safe, is it plausible that knowing that D&X is now forbidden will cause her to decide to have the baby?

2. The Court majority maintains that it continues to honor the principle of *Casey* and related precedents, that prohibitions on abortion are unconstitutional, if it "subjects [women] to significant health risks." Despite a substantial degree of medical opinion that this prohibition does exactly that for a number of women (albeit, a tiny number), the Court decides to accept Congress's rejection of this conclusion because a smaller number of doctors disagrees with that opinion. Under the logic of *Roe* and of *Casey*, should Congress be granted this leeway to pick and choose among doctors where it finds disagreement? Is Congress showing disrespect for the lives of women whose health it may be putting at additional risk by this new law?

SECURING ACCESS TO ABORTION: RICO LAWSUITS AND BUFFER ZONES

The pro-life movement after *Roe v. Wade* did not limit itself to seeking legislative restrictions on abortion. In addition, private groups organized a variety of measures to persuade women not to seek abortions and to dissuade abortion provision professionals from continuing their work. These anti-abortion efforts ranged from silent vigils, to pregnancy counseling, to preaching to individuals attempting to enter abortion clinics, to burning down or bombing abortion facilities, to outright kidnapping and murder of abortion providers.

Even the peaceful efforts at unrequested "sidewalk counseling" at the entrances to abortion clinics typically were perceived as harassing by clinic staffers and, especially, clients—many of whom had agonized for weeks over their decisions and were not looking for last-minute "advice." To deal with such harassment, pro-choice groups sought and obtained protective policies from both legislatures and judges.

As early as 1983 pro-choice activists successfully invoked federal court jurisdiction under the RICO (Racketeering Influenced and Corrupt Organizations) statute against anti-abortion militants who had kidnapped a doctor and his wife and threatened them with death until the doctor promised to cease performing abortions.[124] RICO essentially aims at keeping organized crime from interfering with commerce among the states, and since abortion clinics engage in commerce (by selling abortion services), they can claim coverage from the act. RICO authorizes the assessment of extremely heavy civil damage awards as well as stiff fines and prison sentences.

In addition to RICO, pro-choice attorneys invoked the Ku Klux Klan Act of 1871, which prohibits "conspiracies to deprive any person or class of persons of the equal protection of the laws, or of equal privileges and immunities under the laws" (42 U.S.C. § 1985[3]). Attorneys for the National Organization for Women, Planned Parenthood, and operators of abortion clinics in Washington, DC persuaded judges on the federal district and circuit courts, beginning in 1989, that organized blockades of such clinics amounted to a conspiracy to interfere with women's right to travel freely across state lines (to obtain abortions in DC), of which the right of travel is one of the "privileges or immunities of citizenship."[125] On this basis, the federal District Court permanently enjoined Operation Rescue and similar organizations from "physically impeding access to, and egress from, premises that offer and provide legal abortion services and related medical and psychological counseling." Someone who disobeys a court order can be immediately imprisoned for contempt of court, so this injunction greatly facilitated the arrest and incarceration of blockaders of clinics. By January 1993, however, the U.S. Supreme Court, in *Bray v. Alexandria Women's Health*, threw out this injunction on the grounds that the blockade activists were not targeting interstate travelers as such but were simply blocking anyone who happened to want to enter the clinic.[126] While this ruling precluded use of the KKK Act, state laws were still available for the basis of court injunctions, and efforts to obtain such orders continued.

Meanwhile, the National Organization for Women (NOW) along with two clinics that provided abortion services, the National Women's Health Organization of Summit and the National Women's Health Organization of Delaware, began a lawsuit under RICO in 1986 against a group of militant anti-abortion activists, including Operation Rescue, the Pro-Life Action Network (or PLAN) a pro life coalition—and named individuals, including Joseph Scheidler, Andrew Scholberg, and Timothy Murphy. Their plan was to deploy the RICO statute in a systematic way, nationwide, to provide security for abortion providers against vandals, arsonists, kidnappers, and persons who threatened violence. Because many ideologically motivated pro-life activists were letting themselves get repeatedly arrested and convicted and were serving short jail terms for trespassing or vandalism in order to gain publicity for their cause, the pro-choice organizations decided that laws designed to deal with petty crime were not adequate to the task of securing safe access to abortion. The turn to RICO was an attempt to have such heavy fines imposed on groups like Operation Rescue that they would be bankrupted out of existence. In the early nineties this lawsuit encountered obstacles at the federal district and circuit court levels in their effort to have RICO applied in this way, but then, at least at first (i.e., in 1994), received encouragement from the U.S. Supreme Court.[127]

Initially, the lower courts dismissed on the grounds that the extortion prohibited by RICO had to proceed from an economic motive (since RICO was a regulation aimed at protecting commerce). The Supreme Court rejected this restrictive interpretation of the word "extortion" and sent the case back for evidentiary hearings. In 1998, Randall Terry, the founder of Operation Rescue, agreed to accept a nationwide permanent injunction from the federal District Court in Chicago against his anti-abortion activities, and he dissolved his organization.[128] Joseph Scheidler, head of PLAN, continued the lawsuit. The case came back to the U.S. Supreme Court in 2003 (see below) with a less favorable result for the applicability of RICO.

While this series of cases was winding its way through the courts, the abortion-provider security problem reached crisis proportions. On March 10, 1993, nine months after the Supreme Court reaffirmed in *Casey* its commitment to women's fundamental right to seek an abortion, and two months after the Court (in *Bray*) lifted an injunction aimed at clinic safety, the first murder in the name of a "right to life" was committed. Michael Griffin, a regular participant in anti-abortion protests outside the Pensacola (Florida) Women's Medical Services, walked up behind Dr. David Gunn, who was heading into the rear entrance to the clinic from his car, and at "point blank range" shot him three times in the back.[129]

The city of Pensacola had become a focal point of militant anti-abortion activism ever since the firebombing of all three of its abortion clinics on Christmas Day 1984. While by no means the first act of arson or bombing against clinics, this obviously coordinated action had drawn much national publicity, which then attracted a steady stream of anti-abortion extremists to Pensacola's two reopened clinics. The protesters carried signs that, in addition to showing gigantically enlarged photos of aborted fetuses, declared Dr. David Gunn a murderer who would burn in hell. Gunn's murderer proudly claimed responsibility upon being arrested and insisted he was "acting in God's name."

His "success" evidently inspired two more "pro-life" murders in the same city at its other abortion clinics one year later, in July 1994. A clinic doctor, John B. Britton, and his 74-year-old escort were shot to death while attempting to enter. This murderer, Paul Hill, claimed the defense of justifiable homicide and urged pro-life groups to support his effort. Instead, many publicly condemned the murder, with Cardinal John J. O'Connor of New York taking the occasion to announce, "If anyone has an urge to kill an abortionist, let him kill me instead."

Right in the midst of this peak of turmoil around abortion clinic safety, three and a half months after the first of these murders and days before the second and third, the U.S. Supreme Court handed down its second case dealing with a court injunction on the subject, *Madsen v. Women's Health Center* (of Melbourne, Florida).[130] The Madsen case concerned a court injunction issued under state law on April 8, 1993 (one month after the Gunn murder in Pensacola).[131] This order swept broadly and was issued in explicit response to a history of disobedience to a more limited injunction of September 1992 from the same court. This one prohibited, among other things, "congregating, picketing, patrolling, demonstrating or entering that portion of public right-of-way or private property within thirty-six feet of the property line of the Clinic" at any time; "singing, chanting, whistling, shouting, yelling, use of bullhorns, auto horns, sound amplification equipment or other sounds or images observable to or within earshot of the patients inside the Clinic" from 7:30 A.M. to noon, the hours of surgery and recovery periods, Monday through Saturday; "physically approaching any person seeking the services of the Clinic unless such person indicates a desire to communicate by approaching [the protester]" at any place within 300 feet of the clinic; or "congregating, picketing ... or using bullhorns or other sound amplification equipment within three-hundred feet of the residence of any of the" clinic staff or owners.

In choosing how to deal with this injunction, the Court majority treated it as content- and viewpoint-neutral (even though it targeted specifically anti-abortion protests) on the grounds that it was designed to deal with the problem of disobedience of a prior injunction, not designed to suppress anti-abortion speech in general, and with this categorization the Court refused to apply the strict scrutiny test (of suppressing no more speech than is necessary for attaining a compelling government interest). Instead the Court ruled that the injunction needed to be narrowly tailored to suppress "no more speech than necessary to serve a significant government interest."[132] Using this guideline, the Court identified as adequately "significant" interests, "the combination of . . .protecting a pregnant woman's freedom to seek lawful medical or counseling services, ensuring public safety and order, promoting the free flow of traffic on public streets and sidewalks, protecting citizens' property rights, and assuring residential privacy"[133] and then upheld the 36-foot "buffer" zone around the clinic entrances and driveway and the quiet hours for surgical patients. The Court struck down the ban on displaying "observable images" (explaining that if patients felt bothered by these, the clinic could just close its curtains, and the ban could be more narrowly drawn to cover only signs that implied threats of violence) and struck down the 300-foot "no approach" zone for patients and the 300-foot buffer zone around residences as sweeping too broadly into freedom of expression. For the "no approach" zone, the Court majority suggested a ban that limited itself to intimidating speech rather than suppression of all efforts at persuasion, however mild; and for the private residences, the Court recommended smaller buffer zones or time limits or restrictions on the size of protest groups that could congregate.

Madsen was followed by a similar case in 1997, *Schenck v. Pro-Choice Network of Western N.Y.*, in which the Court reaffirmed the ruling from *Madsen* as to a reasonably sized fixed buffer zone to protect entrance to and egress from pregnancy-related clinics but declared invalid a "floating" buffer zone around moving individuals that caused "sidewalk counselors" to have to stay at least 15 feet away from people trying to enter clinics.[134] The Court majority reasoned that such a large distance simply cut off so much peaceful communication that it violated the First Amendment. The Court's opinion in *Schenck* is useful because it provides a graphic description of what actually goes on in these demonstrations:

> [T]he clinics were subjected to numerous large scale blockades in which protesters would march, stand, kneel, sit, or lie in parking lot driveways and in doorways. This conduct blocked or hindered cars from entering clinic parking lots, and patients, doctors, nurses, and other clinic employees from entering the clinics.
>
> In addition to these large scale blockades, smaller groups of protesters consistently attempted to stop or disrupt clinic operations. Protesters trespassed onto clinic parking lots and even entered the clinics themselves. Those trespassers who remained outside the clinics crowded around cars or milled around doorways and driveway entrances in an effort to block or hinder access to the clinics. Protesters sometimes threw themselves on top of the hoods of cars or crowded around cars as they attempted to turn into parking lot driveways. Other protesters on clinic property handed literature and talked to people entering the

clinics—especially those women they believed were arriving to have abortions—in an effort to persuade them that abortion was immoral. Sometimes protesters used more aggressive techniques, with varying levels of belligerence: getting very close to women entering the clinics and shouting in their faces; surrounding, crowding, and yelling at women entering the clinics; or jostling, grabbing, pushing, and shoving women as they attempted to enter the clinics. Male and female clinic volunteers who attempted to escort patients past protesters into the clinics were sometimes elbowed, grabbed, or spit on. Sometimes the escorts pushed back. Some protesters remained in the doorways after the patients had entered the clinics, blocking others from entering and exiting. . . .[Sidewalk c]ounselors would walk alongside targeted women headed toward the clinics, handing them literature and talking to them in an attempt to persuade them not to get an abortion. Unfortunately, if the women continued toward the clinics and did not respond positively to the counselors, such peaceful efforts at persuasion often devolved into "in your face" yelling, and sometimes into pushing, shoving, and grabbing. Men who accompanied women attempting to enter the clinics often became upset by the aggressive sidewalk counseling and sometimes had to be restrained (not always successfully) from fighting with the counselors.[135]

Meanwhile, after the first murder of a physician who performed abortions, both state and federal legislatures responded to the escalating violence by promptly enacting protective legislation even before *Madsen* was decided by the Court. On January 25, 1994, Congress enacted the Freedom of Access to Clinic Entrances Act (or FACE) 18 U.S.C. § 248. Its key provisions make it a federal crime to "by force or threat of force or by physical obstruction, intentionally injure, intimidate or interfere with . . . any person because that person is or has been, or in order to intimidate such person or any other person or any class of persons from, obtaining or providing reproductive health services . . .or a place of worship. . ." or to attempt to do so, or to damage or destroy a reproductive health facility or place of worship, or attempt to do so. It imposes tough criminal penalties, including the death penalty if someone is killed, hefty criminal fines— e.g. up to $25,000 for a second, and for *each*, offense of "nonviolent obstruction"—and also makes available generous civil damage awards ($5,000 for *each* offense). Paul Hill, the double murderer described above, was the first person prosecuted under FACE, and he was executed shortly after 6:00 P.M. on September 3, 2003. In his final statement, after thanking his family and thanking Jesus, he again exhorted opponents of abortion to follow his example.[136]

Hill v. Colorado (2000)

Although the Supreme Court has not taken up any challenge to FACE, it has dealt with one of the state laws enacted during this period. Colorado in 1993 enacted a criminal law that set up a 100-foot buffer zone around abortion clinics and prohibited approaching within 8 feet of anyone in that zone to offer them undesired counseling. Two women, Leila Jeanne Hill and Audrey Himmelmann, and one man, Everitt W. Simpson, with the support of the American Center for Law and Justice, a group formed in the 1980s to support conservative cause litigation, brought a lawsuit requesting a court injunction against enforcement of this law on the grounds that it violated the First Amendment. The lawsuit wound its way up to the Colorado Court of Appeals and then to the U.S. Supreme Court, which sent it back down, requesting the Colorado courts to reconsider it in light of their recent *Schenck* decision. Both the Colorado Court of Appeals and the Colorado Supreme Court ruled that their law differed significantly from the provision thrown out in *Schenck*. Six members of the U.S. Supreme Court agreed.

LEILA JEANNE HILL ET AL. V. COLORADO ET AL.
530 U.S. 703 (2000)

JUSTICE STEVENS delivered the opinion of the Court.

.... Although the [challenged] statute [Colo. Rev. Stat. § 18–9–122(3) (1999)] prohibits speakers from approaching unwilling listeners, it does not require a standing speaker to move away from anyone passing by. Nor does it place any restriction on the content of any message that anyone may wish to communicate to anyone else, either inside or outside the regulated areas. It does, however, make it more difficult to give unwanted advice, particularly in the form of a handbill or leaflet, to persons entering or leaving medical facilities.

The question is whether the First Amendment rights of the speaker are abridged by the protection the statute provides for the unwilling listener....

I

... [P]etitioners ... stated that prior to the enactment of the statute, they had engaged in "sidewalk counseling" on the public ways and sidewalks within 100 feet of the entrances to facilities where human abortion is practiced. "Sidewalk counseling" consists of efforts "to educate, counsel, persuade, or inform passersby about abortion and abortion alternatives by means of verbal or written speech, including conversation and/or display of signs and/or distribution of literature." They further alleged that such activities frequently entail being within eight feet of other persons and that their fear of prosecution under the new statute caused them "to be chilled in the exercise of fundamental constitutional rights."

[They allege the statute violates freedom of speech and of the press]...

...[D]emonstrations in front of abortion clinics impeded access to those clinics and were often confrontational. Indeed, it was a common practice to provide escorts for persons entering and leaving the clinics both to ensure their access and to provide protection from aggressive counselors who sometimes used strong and abusive language in face-to-face encounters.[7] There was also evidence that emotional confrontations may adversely affect a patient's medical care....

[Here followed a review of the case history.]

...

We now affirm.

II

Before confronting the question whether the Colorado statute reflects an acceptable balance between the constitutionally protected rights of law-abiding speakers and the interests of unwilling listeners, it is appropriate to examine the competing interests at stake. A brief review of both sides of the dispute reveals that each has legitimate and important concerns.

The First Amendment interests of petitioners are clear and undisputed. As a preface to their legal challenge, petitioners emphasize three propositions. First, they accurately explain that the areas protected by the statute encompass all the public ways within 100 feet of every entrance to every health care facility everywhere in the State of Colorado. There is no disagreement on this point, even though the legislative history makes it clear that its enactment was primarily motivated by activities in the vicinity of abortion clinics. Second, they correctly state that their leafletting, sign displays, and oral communications are protected by the First Amendment. The fact that the messages conveyed by those communications may be offensive to their recipients does not deprive them of constitutional protection. Third, the public sidewalks, streets, and ways affected by the statute are "quintessential" public forums for free speech. Finally, although there is debate about the magnitude of the statutory impediment to their ability to communicate effectively with persons in the regulated zones, that ability, particularly the ability to distribute leaflets, is unquestionably lessened by this statute.

On the other hand, petitioners do not challenge the legitimacy of the state interests that the statute is intended to serve. It is a traditional exercise of the States' "police powers to protect the health and safety of their citizens." *Medtronic, Inc.* v. *Lohr,* 518 U.S. 470, 475 (1996). That interest may justify a special focus on unimpeded access to health care facilities and the avoidance of potential trauma to patients associated with confrontational protests. See *Madsen* v. *Women's Health Center, Inc.,* 512 U.S. 753 (1994); *NLRB* v. *Baptist Hospital, Inc.,* 442 U.S. 773 (1979). Moreover, as with every exercise of a State's police powers, rules that provide specific guidance to enforcement authorities serve the interest in even-handed application of the law. Whether or not those interests justify the particular regulation at issue, they are unquestionably legitimate.

It is also important when conducting this interest analysis to recognize the significant difference between state restrictions on a speaker's right to address a willing audience and those that protect listeners from unwanted communication. This statute deals only with the latter.

The right to free speech, of course, includes the right to attempt to persuade others to change their views, and may not be curtailed simply because the speaker's message may be offensive to his audience. But the protection afforded to offensive messages does not always embrace offensive speech that is so intrusive that the unwilling audience cannot avoid it. *Frisby* v. *Schultz,* 487 U.S. 474, 487 (1988). Indeed, "[i]t may not be the content of the speech, as much as the deliberate 'verbal or visual assault,' that justifies proscription." *Erznoznik* v. *Jacksonville,* 422 U.S. 205, 210–211, n. 6 (1975)....

The recognizable privacy interest in avoiding unwanted communication varies widely in different settings. It is far less important when "strolling through Central Park" than when "in the confines of one's own home," or when persons are "powerless to avoid" it. *Cohen* v. *California,* 403 U.S. 15, 21–22. But even the interest in preserving tranquility in "the Sheep Meadow" portion of Central Park may at times justify official restraints on offensive musical expression. *Ward,* 491 U.S., at 784, 792. More specific to the facts of this case, we have recognized that "[t]he First Amendment does not demand that patients at a medical facility undertake Herculean efforts to escape the cacophony of political protests." *Madsen,* 512 U.S., at 772–773.

The unwilling listener's interest in avoiding unwanted communication has been repeatedly identified in our cases. It is an aspect of the broader "right to be let alone" that one of our wisest Justices characterized as "the most comprehensive of rights and the right most valued by civilized men." *Olmstead*

v. *United States*, 277 U.S. 438, 478 (1928) (Brandeis, J., dissenting).24 The right to avoid unwelcome speech has special force in the privacy of the home, *Rowan* v. *Post Office Dept.*, 397 U.S. 728, 738 (1970), and its immediate surroundings, *Frisby* v. *Schultz*, 487 U.S., at 485, but can also be protected in confrontational settings. Thus, this comment on the right to free passage in going to and from work applies equally—or perhaps with greater force—to access to a medical facility:

> How far may men go in persuasion and communication, and still not violate the right of those whom they would influence? In going to and from work, men have a right to as free a passage without obstruction as the streets afford, consistent with the right of others to enjoy the same privilege. We are a social people, and the accosting by one of another in an inoffensive way and an offer by one to communicate and discuss information with a view to influencing the other's action, are not regarded as aggression or a violation of that other's rights. If, however, the offer is declined, as it may rightfully be, then persistence, importunity, following and dogging, become unjustifiable annoyance and obstruction which is likely soon to savor of intimidation. From all of this the person sought to be influenced has a right to be free, and his employer has a right to have him free. *American Steel Foundries* v. *Tri-City Central Trades Council*, 257 U.S. 184, 204 (1921).

We have since recognized that the "right to persuade" discussed in that case is protected by the First Amendment, *Thornhill* v. *Alabama*, 310 U.S. 88 (1940), as well as by federal statutes. Yet we have continued to maintain that "no one has a right to press even 'good' ideas on an unwilling recipient." *Rowan*, 397 U.S., at 738. None of our decisions has minimized the enduring importance of "the right to be free" from persistent "importunity, following and dogging" after an offer to communicate has been declined. While the freedom to communicate is substantial, "the right of every person 'to be let alone' must be placed in the scales with the right of others to communicate." *Id.*, at 736. It is that right, as well as the right of "passage without obstruction," that the Colorado statute legitimately seeks to protect. The restrictions imposed by the Colorado statute only apply to communications that interfere with these rights rather than those that involve willing listeners.

. . .

III

All four of the state court opinions upholding the validity of this statute concluded that it is a content-neutral time, place, and manner regulation. Moreover, they all found support for their analysis in *Ward* v. *Rock Against Racism,* 491 U.S. 781 (1989). It is therefore appropriate to comment on the "content neutrality" of the statute. As we explained in *Ward:* "The principal inquiry in determining content neutrality, in speech cases generally and in time, place, or manner cases in particular, is whether the government has adopted a regulation of speech because of disagreement with the message it conveys." *Id.,* at 791.

The Colorado statute passes that test for three independent reasons. First, it is not a "regulation of speech." Rather, it is a regulation of the places where some speech may occur. Second, it was not adopted "because of disagreement with the message it conveys." . . . [T]he statute's "restrictions apply equally to all demonstrators, regardless of viewpoint, and the statutory language makes no reference to the content of the speech." Third, the State's interests in protecting access and privacy, and providing the police with clear guidelines, are unrelated to the content of the demonstrators' speech. As we have repeatedly explained, government regulation of expressive activity is "content neutral" if it is justified without reference to the content of regulated speech.

Petitioners nevertheless argue that the statute is not content neutral insofar as it applies to some oral communication. . . . With respect to persons who are neither leafletters nor sign carriers, however, the statute does not apply unless their approach is "for the purpose of . . . engaging in oral protest, education, or counseling." Petitioners contend that an individual near a health care facility who knowingly approaches a pedestrian to say "good morning" . . . would not be subject to the statute's restrictions. Because the content of the oral statements made by an approaching speaker must sometimes be examined . . . [to apply the statute], petitioners argue that the law is "content-based" under our reasoning in *Carey* v. *Brown,* 447 U.S. 455, 462 (1980).

. . .

It is common in the law to examine the content of a communication to determine the speaker's purpose. Whether a particular statement constitutes a threat, blackmail, an agreement to fix prices, a copyright violation, a public offering of securities, or an offer to sell goods often depends on the precise content of the statement. We have never held, or suggested, that it is improper to look at the content of an oral or written statement in order to determine whether a rule of law applies to a course of conduct. With respect to the conduct that is the focus of the Colorado statute, it is unlikely that there would often be any need to know exactly what words were spoken in order to determine whether "sidewalk counselors" are engaging in "oral protest, education, or counseling" rather than pure social or random conversation.

Theoretically, of course, cases may arise in which it is necessary to review the content of the statements made by a person approaching within eight feet of an unwilling listener to determine whether the approach is covered by the statute. . . .Nevertheless, we have never suggested that the kind of cursory examination that might be required to exclude casual conversation from the coverage of a regulation of picketing would be problematic.[30]

. . .

The Colorado statute's regulation of the location of protests, education, and counseling. . . simply establishes a minor place restriction on an extremely broad category of communications with unwilling listeners. Instead of drawing distinctions based on the subject that the approaching speaker may wish to address, the statute applies equally to used car salesmen, animal rights activists, fundraisers, environmentalists, and missionaries. Each can attempt to educate unwilling listeners on any subject, but without consent may not approach within eight feet to do so.

. . .

The Colorado courts correctly concluded that § 18–9–122(3) is content neutral.

IV

We also agree with the state courts' conclusion that § 18–9–122(3) is a valid time, place, and manner regulation under the test applied in *Ward* because it is "narrowly tailored." We already have noted that the statute serves governmental interests that are significant and legitimate and that the restrictions are content neutral. We are likewise persuaded that the statute is "narrowly tailored" to serve those interests and that it leaves open ample alternative channels for communication. As we have emphasized on more than one occasion, when a content-neutral regulation does not entirely foreclose any means of communication, it may satisfy the tailoring requirement even though it is not the least restrictive or least intrusive means of serving the statutory goal.[32]

The three types of communication regulated by § 18–9–122(3) are the display of signs, leafletting, and oral speech. The 8-foot separation between the speaker and the audience should not have any adverse impact on the readers' ability to read signs displayed by demonstrators. In fact, the separation might actually aid the pedestrians' ability to see the signs by preventing others from surrounding them and impeding their view. Furthermore, the statute places no limitations on the number, size, text, or images of the placards. And, as with all of the restrictions, the 8-foot zone does not affect demonstrators with signs who remain in place.

With respect to oral statements, the distance certainly can make it more difficult for a speaker to be heard, particularly if the level of background noise is high and other speakers are competing for the pedestrian's attention. Notably, the statute places no limitation on the number of speakers or the noise level, including the use of amplification equipment, although we have upheld such restrictions in past cases. See, *e.g., Madsen,* 512 U.S., at 772–773. More significantly, this statute does not suffer from the failings that compelled us to reject the "floating buffer zone" in *Schenck,* 519 U.S., at 377. Unlike the 15-foot zone in *Schenck,* this 8-foot zone allows the speaker to communicate at a "normal conversational distance." *Ibid.* Additionally, the statute allows the speaker to remain in one place, and other individuals can pass within eight feet of the protester without causing the protester to violate the statute. Finally, here there is a "knowing" requirement that protects speakers "who thought they were keeping pace with the targeted individual" at the proscribed distance from inadvertently violating the statute. *Id.,* at 378, n. 9.

It is also not clear that the statute's restrictions will necessarily impede, rather than assist, the speakers' efforts to communicate their messages. The statute might encourage the most aggressive and vociferous protesters to moderate their confrontational and harassing conduct, and thereby make it easier for thoughtful and law-abiding sidewalk counselors like petitioners to make themselves heard. But whether or not the 8-foot interval is the best possible accommodation of the competing interests at stake, we must accord a measure of deference to the judgment of the Colorado Legislature. . . .

The burden on the ability to distribute handbills is more serious because it seems possible that an 8-foot interval could hinder the ability of a leafletter to deliver handbills to some unwilling recipients. The statute does not, however, prevent a leafletter from simply standing near the path of oncoming pedestrians and proffering his or her material, which the pedestrians can easily accept.[33] And, as in all leafletting situations, pedestrians continue to be free to decline the tender. In *Heffron* v. *International Soc. for Krishna Consciousness, Inc.,* 452 U.S. 640 (1981), we upheld a state fair regulation that required a religious organization desiring to distribute literature to conduct that activity only at an assigned location—in that case booths. As in this case, the regulation primarily burdened the distributors' ability to communicate with unwilling readers. We concluded our opinion by emphasizing that the First Amendment protects the right of every citizen to " 'reach the minds of willing listeners and to do so there must be opportunity to win their attention.' *Kovacs* v. *Cooper,* 336 U.S. 77, 87 (1949)." *Id.,* at 655. The Colorado statute adequately protects those rights.

Finally, in determining whether a statute is narrowly tailored, we have noted that "[w]e must, of course, take account of the place to which the regulations apply in determining whether these restrictions burden more speech than necessary." *Madsen,* 512 U.S., at 772. States and municipalities plainly have a substantial interest in controlling the activity around certain public and private places. For example, we have recognized the special governmental interests surrounding schools,[34] courthouses,[35] polling places,[36] and private homes.[37] Additionally, we previously have noted the unique concerns that surround health care facilities:

> " 'Hospitals, after all, are not factories or mines or assembly plants. They are hospitals, where human ailments are treated, where patients and relatives alike often are under emotional strain and worry, where pleasing and comforting patients are principal facets of the day's activity, and where the patient and [her] family . . . need a restful, uncluttered, relaxing, and helpful atmosphere.' " *Ibid.* (quoting *NLRB* v. *Baptist Hospital, Inc.,* 442 U.S., at 783–784, n. 12).

Persons who are attempting to enter health care facilities—for any purpose—are often in particularly vulnerable physical and emotional conditions. The State of Colorado has responded to its substantial and legitimate interest in protecting these persons from unwanted encounters, confrontations, and even assaults by enacting an exceedingly modest restriction on the speakers' ability to approach.

. . .

As we explained above, the 8-foot restriction on an unwanted physical approach leaves ample room to communicate a message through speech. Signs, pictures, and voice itself can cross an 8-foot gap with ease. If the clinics in Colorado resemble those in *Schenck,* demonstrators with leaflets might easily stand on the sidewalk at entrances (without blocking the entrance) and, without physically approaching those who are entering the clinic, peacefully hand them leaflets as they pass by.

Finally, the 8-foot restriction occurs only within 100 feet of a health care facility—the place where the restriction is most needed. The restriction interferes far less with a speaker's ability to communicate than did the total ban on picketing on the sidewalk outside a residence (upheld in *Frisby* v. *Schultz*, 487 U.S. 474 (1988)), the restriction of leafletting at a fairground to a booth (upheld in *Heffron* v. *International Society for Krishna Consciousness, Inc.*, 452 U.S. 640 (1981)), or the "silence" often required outside a hospital. Special problems that may arise where clinics have particularly wide entrances or are situated within multipurpose office buildings may be worked out as the statute is applied.

This restriction is thus reasonable and narrowly tailored.

. . .

VII

Finally, petitioners argue that § 18–9–122(3)'s consent requirement is invalid because it imposes an unconstitutional "prior restraint" on speech. We rejected this argument previously in *Schenck,* 519 U.S., at 374, n. 6, and *Madsen,* 512 U.S., at 764, n. 2. Moreover, the restrictions in this case raise an even lesser prior restraint concern than those at issue in *Schenck* and *Madsen* where particular speakers were at times completely banned within certain zones. Under this statute, absolutely no channel of communication is foreclosed. No speaker is silenced. And no message is prohibited. . . .

Furthermore, our concerns about "prior restraints" relate to restrictions imposed by official censorship. The regulations in this case, however, only apply if the pedestrian does not consent to the approach. Private citizens have always retained the power to decide for themselves what they wish to read, and within limits, what oral messages they want to consider. This statute simply empowers private citizens entering a health care facility with the ability to prevent a speaker, who is within eight feet and advancing, from communicating a message they do not wish to hear. Further, the statute does not authorize the pedestrian to affect any other activity at any other location or relating to any other person. These restrictions thus do not constitute an unlawful prior restraint.

* * *

The judgment of the Colorado Supreme Court is affirmed.

Opinion Footnotes

7 A nurse practitioner testified that some antiabortion protesters "yell, thrust signs in faces, and generally try to upset the patient as much as possible, which makes it much more difficult for us to provide care in a scary situation." *Hill v. Thomas*, 973 P. 2d 1246, 1250 (Colo. 1999). A volunteer who escorts patients into and out of clinics testified that the protestors "are flashing their bloody fetus signs. They are yelling, 'you are killing your baby.' [T]hey are talking about fetuses and babies being dismembered, arms and legs torn off . . . a mother and her daughter . . . were immediately surrounded and yelled at and screamed at . . ."

30 In *United States v. Grace*, 461 U.S. 171 (1983), after examining a federal statute that was "interpreted and applied" as "prohibit[ing] picketing and leafletting, but not other expressive conduct" within the Supreme Court building and grounds, we concluded that "it is clear that the prohibition is facially content-neutral." Id., at 181, n. 10. Similarly, we have recognized that statutes can equally restrict all "picketing." See, e.g., *Police Dept. of Chicago v. Mosley*, 408 U.S. 92, 98 (1972) ("This is not to say that all picketing must always be allowed. We have continually recognized that reasonable 'time, place, and manner' regulations of picketing may be necessary to further significant governmental interests"), and cases cited. See also *Frisby v. Schultz*, 487 U.S. 474 (1988) (upholding a general ban on residential picketing). And our decisions in *Schenck* and *Madsen* both upheld injunctions that also prohibited "demonstrating." *Schenck v. Pro-Choice Network of Western N. Y.*, 519 U.S. 357, 366, n. 3 (1997); *Madsen*, 512 U.S., at 759.

32 "Lest any confusion on the point remain, we reaffirm today that a regulation of the time, place, or manner of protected speech must be narrowly tailored to serve the government's legitimate, content-neutral interests but that it need not be the least restrictive or least intrusive means of doing so." *Ward v. Rock Against Racism*, 491 U.S., at 798.

33 Justice Kennedy states that the statute "forecloses peaceful leafleting." This is not correct. All of the cases he cites in support of his argument involve a total ban on a medium of expression to both willing and unwilling recipients. Nothing in this statute, however, prevents persons from proffering their literature, they simply cannot approach within eight feet of an unwilling recipient.

34 See *Grayned v. City of Rockford*, 408 U.S. 104, 119 (1972).

35 See *Cox v. Louisiana*, 379 U.S. 559, 562 (1965).

36 See *Burson v. Freeman*, 504 U.S. 191, 206–208 (1992) (plurality opinion); Id., at 214–216 (Scalia, J., concurring in judgment).

37 See *Frisby v. Schultz*, 487 U.S., at 484–485.

JUSTICE SOUTER, with whom JUSTICE O'CONNOR, JUSTICE GINSBURG, and JUSTICE BREYER join, concurring.

I join the opinion of the Court and add this further word. The key to determining whether Colo. Rev. Stat. § 18–9–122(3) (1999), makes a content-based distinction between varieties of speech lies in understanding that content-based discriminations are subject to strict scrutiny because they place the weight of government behind the disparagement or suppression of some messages, whether or not with the effect of approving or promoting others. *United States* v. *Playboy Entertainment Group, Inc.*, 529 U.S. 803, 815 (2000)); *R. A. V.* v. *St. Paul*, 505 U.S. 377, 382 (1992); cf. *Police Dept. of Chicago* v. *Mosley*, 408 U.S. 92, 95–96 (1972). Thus the government is held to a very exacting and rarely satisfied standard when it disfavors the discussion of particular subjects, *Simon & Schuster, Inc.* v. *Members of N. Y. State Crime Victims Bd.*, 502 U.S. 105, 116 (1991), or particular viewpoints within a given subject matter, *Carey* v. *Brown*,

447 U.S. 455, 461–463 (1980) (citing *Chicago, supra,* at 95–96); cf. *National Endowment for Arts* v. *Finley,* 524 U.S. 569, 601–602 (1998) (*Souter,* J., dissenting).

Concern about employing the power of the State to suppress discussion of a subject or a point of view is not, however, raised in the same way when a law addresses not the content of speech but the circumstances of its delivery. The right to express unpopular views does not necessarily immunize a speaker from liability for resorting to otherwise impermissible behavior meant to shock members of the speaker's audience, see *United States* v. *O'Brien,* 391 U.S. 367, 376 (1968) (burning draft card), or to guarantee their attention, see *Kovacs* v. *Cooper,* 336 U.S. 77, 86–88 (1949) (sound trucks); *Frisby* v. *Schultz,* 487 U.S. 474, 484–485 (1988) (residential picketing); *Heffron* v. *International Soc. for Krishna Consciousness, Inc.,* 452 U.S. 640, 647–648 (1981) (soliciting). Unless regulation limited to the details of a speaker's delivery results in removing a subject or viewpoint from effective discourse (or otherwise fails to advance a significant public interest in a way narrowly fitted to that objective), a reasonable restriction intended to affect only the time, place, or manner of speaking is perfectly valid. See *Ward* v. *Rock Against Racism,* 491 U.S. 781, 791 (1989)...

. . .

JUSTICE SCALIA, with whom JUSTICE THOMAS joins, dissenting.

The Court today concludes that a regulation requiring speakers on the public thoroughfares bordering medical facilities to speak from a distance of eight feet is "not a 'regulation of speech,'" but "a regulation of the places where some speech may occur"; and that a regulation directed to only certain categories of speech (protest, education, and counseling) is not "content-based." For these reasons, it says, the regulation is immune from the exacting scrutiny we apply to content-based suppression of speech in the public forum. The Court then determines that the regulation survives the less rigorous scrutiny afforded content-neutral time, place, and manner restrictions because it is narrowly tailored to serve a government interest—protection of citizens' "right to be let alone"—that has explicitly been disclaimed by the State, probably for the reason that, as a basis for suppressing peaceful private expression, it is patently incompatible with the guarantees of the First Amendment.

None of these remarkable conclusions should come as a surprise. What is before us, after all, is a speech regulation directed against the opponents of abortion, and it therefore enjoys the benefit of the "ad hoc nullification machine" that the Court has set in motion to push aside whatever doctrines of constitutional law stand in the way of that highly favored practice. *Madsen* v. *Women's Health Center, Inc.,* 512 U.S. 753, 785 (1994) (*Scalia,* J., concurring in judgment in part and dissenting in part). Having deprived abortion opponents of the political right to persuade the electorate that abortion should be restricted by law, the Court today continues and expands its assault upon their individual right to persuade women contemplating abortion that what they are doing is wrong. Because, like the rest of our abortion jurisprudence, today's decision is in stark contradiction of the constitutional principles we apply in all other contexts, I dissent.

I

. . .[T]he regulation as it applies to oral communications is obviously and undeniably content-based. A speaker wishing to approach another for the purpose of communicating *any* message except one of protest, education, or counseling may do so without first securing the other's consent. Whether a speaker must obtain permission before approaching within eight feet—and whether he will be sent to prison for failing to do so—depends entirely on *what he intends to say* when he gets there. I have no doubt that this regulation would be deemed content-based *in an instant* if the case before us involved antiwar protesters, or union members seeking to "educate" the public about the reasons for their strike. "[I]t is," we would say, "the content of the speech that determines whether it is within or without the statute's blunt prohibition," *Carey* v. *Brown,* 447 U.S. 455, 462 (1980). But the jurisprudence of this Court has a way of changing when abortion is involved.

. . .

. . . As for the Court's appeal to the fact that we often "examine the content of a communication" to determine whether it "constitutes a threat, blackmail, an agreement to fix prices, a copyright violation, a public offering of securities, or an offer to sell goods," the distinction is almost too obvious to bear mention: Speech of a certain content is constitutionally proscribable. The Court has not yet taken the step of consigning "protest, education, and counseling" to that category.

Finally, the Court is not correct in its assertion that the restriction here is content-neutral because it is "*justified* without reference to the content of regulated speech," in the sense that "the State's interests in protecting access and privacy, and providing the police with clear guidelines, are unrelated to the content of the demonstrators' speech." (emphasis added). That is not an accurate statement of our law. . . . An ordinance directed at the suppression of noise (and therefore "justified without reference to the content of regulated speech") cannot be applied only to sound trucks delivering messages of "protest." Our very first use of the "justified by reference to content" language made clear that it is a prohibition *in addition to*, rather than in place of, the prohibition of facially content-based restrictions. "Selective exclusions from a public forum" we said, "may not be based on content alone, *and* may not be justified by reference to content alone." *Police Dept. of Chicago* v. *Mosley,* 408 U.S. 92, 96 (1972) (emphasis added).

. . .[I]t is clear that the regulation is *both* based on content *and* justified by reference to content. . . .

. . . As such, it must survive that stringent mode of constitutional analysis our cases refer to as "strict scrutiny," which requires that the restriction be narrowly tailored to serve a compelling state interest. See *United States* v. *Playboy Entertainment Group, Inc.,* 529 U.S. ___, ___ (2000); *Perry Ed. Assn.* v. *Perry Local Educators' Assn.,* 460 U.S. 37, 45 (1983). Since the Court does not even attempt to support the regulation under this standard, I shall discuss it only briefly. Suffice it to say that if protecting people from unwelcome communications (the governmental interest the Court posits) is a compelling state interest, the First Amendment is a dead letter. And if (as I shall discuss at greater length below) forbidding peaceful, nonthreatening, but uninvited speech from a distance closer than eight feet is a "narrowly tailored" means of preventing the obstruction of entrance to medical facilities (the governmental interest the State asserts) narrow tailoring must refer not to the standards of Versace, but to those of Omar the tentmaker. . . .

II

As the Court explains, under our precedents even a content-neutral, time, place, and manner restriction must be narrowly tailored to advance a significant state interest, and must leave open ample alternative means of communication. *Ward,* 491 U.S., at 802. It cannot be sustained if it "burden[s] substantially more speech than is necessary to further the government's legitimate interests." *Id.,* at 799.

This requires us to determine, first, what *is* the significant interest the State seeks to advance? Here there appears to be a bit of a disagreement between the State of Colorado (which should know) and the Court (which is eager to speculate). Colorado has identified in the text of the statute itself the interest it sought to advance: to ensure that the State's citizens may "obtain medical counseling and treatment in an unobstructed manner" by "preventing the willful obstruction of a person's access to medical counseling and treatment at a health care facility." Colo. Rev. Stat. § 18–9–122(1) (1999). In its brief here, the State repeatedly confirms the interest squarely identified in the statute under review. . . .

Indeed, the situation is even more bizarre than that. The interest that the Court makes the linchpin of its analysis . . . was explicitly *disclaimed* by the State in its brief before this Court. . . . We may thus add to the lengthening list of "firsts" generated by this Court's relentlessly proabortion jurisprudence, the first case in which, in order to sustain a statute, the Court has relied upon a governmental interest . . . positively repudiated [by the State]. . . .

A

. . .

To support the legitimacy of its self-invented state interest, the Court relies upon a bon mot in a 1928 dissent (which we evidently overlooked in *Schenck*). It characterizes the "unwilling listener's interest in avoiding unwanted communication" as an "aspect of the broader 'right to be let alone' " Justice Brandeis coined in his dissent in *Olmstead* v. *United States*, 277 U.S. 438, 478. The amusing feature is that even this slim reed contradicts rather than supports the Court's position. The right to be let alone that Justice Brandeis identified was a right the Constitution "conferred, *as against the government*"; it was *that* right, not some generalized "common-law right" or "interest" to be free from hearing the unwanted opinions of one's fellow citizens, which he called the "most comprehensive" and "most valued by civilized men." *Ibid.* (emphasis added). To the extent that there can be gleaned from our cases a "right to be let alone" in the sense that Justice Brandeis intended, it is the right of the *speaker* in the public forum to be free from government interference of the sort Colorado has imposed here.

In any event, the Court's attempt to disguise the "right to be let alone" as a "governmental interest in protecting the right to be let alone" is unavailing for the simple reason that this is not an interest that may be legitimately weighed against the speakers' First Amendment rights (which the Court demotes to the status of First Amendment "interests.") We have consistently held that "the Constitution does not *permit* the government to decide which types of otherwise protected speech are sufficiently offensive to require protection *for the unwilling listener or viewer*." *Erznoznik* v. *Jacksonville*, 422 U.S. 205, 210 (1975) (emphasis added). And as recently as in *Schenck*, the Court reiterated that "[a]s a general matter, we have indicated that in public debate our own citizens must tolerate insulting, and even outrageous, speech in order to provide adequate breathing space to the freedoms protected by the First Amendment." 519 U.S., at 383 (internal quotation marks omitted).

. . .We have upheld limitations on a speaker's exercise of his right to speak on the public streets *when that speech intrudes into the privacy of the home. Frisby*, 487 U.S., at 483. " '[W]e are often 'captives' *outside* the sanctuary of the home and subject to objectionable speech.' " *Frisby, supra*, at 484 (quoting *Rowan,*, at 738) (emphasis added). . . .³

There is apparently no end to the distortion of our First Amendment law that the Court is willing to endure in order to sustain this restriction upon the free speech of abortion opponents. . .

B

I turn now to the real state interest at issue here—the one set forth in the statute and asserted in Colorado's brief: the preservation of unimpeded access to health care facilities. We need look no further than subsection (2) of the statute to see what a provision would look like that is narrowly tailored to serve *that* interest. Under the terms of that subsection, any person who "knowingly obstructs, detains, hinders, impedes, or blocks another person's entry to or exit from a health care facility" is subject to criminal and civil liability. It is possible, I suppose, that subsection (2) of the Colorado statute will leave unrestricted some expressive activity that, if engaged in from within eight feet, may be sufficiently harassing as to have the effect of impeding access to health care facilities. In subsection (3), however, the State of Colorado has prohibited a vast amount of speech that cannot possibly be thought to correspond to that evil.

To begin with, the 8-foot buffer zone attaches to *every* person on the public way or sidewalk within 100 feet of the entrance of a medical facility, regardless of whether that person is seeking to enter or exit the facility. In fact, the State acknowledged at oral argument that the buffer zone would attach to any person within 100 feet of the entrance door of a skyscraper in which a single doctor occupied an office on the 18th floor. . . .The sweep of this prohibition is breathtaking.

The Court makes no attempt to justify on the facts this blatant violation of the narrow-tailoring principle. Instead, it flirts with the creation of yet a new constitutional "first" designed for abortion cases: "[W]hen," it says, "a content-neutral regulation does not entirely foreclose any means of communication, it may satisfy the tailoring requirement even though it is not the least restrictive or least intrusive means of serving the statutory goal." The implication is that the availability of alternative means of communication permits the imposition of the speech restriction upon more individuals, or more types of communication, than narrow tailoring would otherwise demand...

The burdens this law imposes upon the right to speak are substantial...I have certainly held conversations at a distance of eight feet seated in the quiet of my chambers, but I have never walked along the public sidewalk—and have not seen others do so—"conversing" at an 8-foot remove. The suggestion is absurd.... The availability of a powerful amplification system will be of little help to the woman who hopes to forge, in the last moments before another of her sex is to have an abortion, a bond of concern and intimacy that might enable her to persuade the woman to change her mind and heart. The counselor may wish to walk alongside and to say, sympathetically and as softly as the circumstances allow, something like: "My dear, I know what you are going through. I've been through it myself. You're not alone and you do not have to do this. There are other alternatives. Will you let me help you? May I show you a picture of what your child looks like at this stage of her human development?" The Court would have us believe that this can be done effectively—yea, perhaps even *more* effectively—by shouting through a bullhorn at a distance of eight feet.

. . .

In contrast to the laws approved in [our precedents] . . ., the law before us here enacts a broad prophylactic restriction which does not "respon[d] precisely to the substantive problem which legitimately concern[ed]" the State,—namely (the only problem asserted by Colorado), the obstruction of access to health facilities..... "Broad prophylactic rules in the area of free expression are suspect.... Precision of regulation must be the touchstone in an area so closely touching our most precious freedoms." *NAACP* v. *Button*, 371 U.S. 415, 438 (1963). In *United States* v. *Grace*, 461 U.S. 171 (1983), we declined to uphold a ban on certain expressive activity on the sidewalks surrounding the Supreme Court. The purpose of the restriction was the perfectly valid interest in security, just as the purpose of the restriction here is the perfectly valid interest in unobstructed access; and there, as here, the restriction furthered that interest—but it furthered it with insufficient precision and hence at excessive cost to the freedom of speech....

. . .

...I cannot improve upon the Court's conclusion in *Madsen* that "it is difficult, indeed, to justify a prohibition on all uninvited approaches of persons seeking the services of the clinic, regardless of how peaceful the contact may be, without burdening more speech than necessary to prevent intimidation and to ensure access to the clinic. Absent evidence that the protestors' speech is independently proscribable (*i.e.,* 'fighting words' or threats), or is so infused with violence as to be indistinguishable from a threat of physical harm, this provision cannot stand." 512 U.S., at 774. The foregoing discussion of overbreadth was written before the Court, in responding to JUSTICE KENNEDY abandoned any pretense at compliance with that doctrine, and acknowledged—indeed, boasted—that the statute it approves "takes a prophylactic approach," and adopts "[a] bright-line prophylactic rule."[5] I scarcely know how to respond to such an unabashed repudiation of our First Amendment doctrine. Prophylaxis is the antithesis of narrow tailoring. . . . So one can add to the casualties of our whatever-it-takes proabortion jurisprudence the First Amendment doctrine of narrow tailoring and overbreadth. R. I. P.

. . .For those who share an abiding moral or religious conviction (or, for that matter, simply a biological appreciation) that abortion is the taking of a human life, there is no option but to persuade women, one by one, not to make that choice. And as a general matter, the most effective place, if not the only place, where that persuasion can occur, is outside the entrances to abortion facilities. By upholding these restrictions on speech in this place the Court ratifies the State's attempt to make even that task an impossible one.

Those whose concern is for the physical safety and security of clinic patients, workers, and doctors should take no comfort from today's decision. Individuals or groups intent on bullying or frightening women out of an abortion, or doctors out of performing that procedure, will not be deterred by Colorado's statute; bullhorns and screaming from eight feet away will serve their purposes well. But those who would accomplish their moral and religious objectives by peaceful and civil means, by trying to persuade individual women of the rightness of their cause, will be deterred; and that is not a good thing in a democracy. This Court once recognized, as the Framers surely did, that the freedom to speak and persuade is inseparable from, and antecedent to, the survival of self-government. The Court today rotates that essential safety valve on our democracy one-half turn to the right, and no one who seeks safe access to health care facilities in Colorado or elsewhere should feel that her security has by this decision been enhanced.

It is interesting to compare the present decision, which *upholds* an utterly bizarre proabortion "request to approach" provision of Colorado law, with *Stenberg v. Carhart*, also announced today, which *strikes down* a live-birth abortion prohibition adopted by 30 States and twice passed by both Houses of Congress (though vetoed both times by the President)....

Does the deck seem stacked? You bet. As I have suggested throughout this opinion, today's decision ...is one of many aggressively proabortion novelties announced by the Court in recent years. See, *e.g., Madsen* v. *Women's Health Center, Inc.,* 512 U.S. 753 (1994); *Schenck* v. *Pro-Choice Network of Western N. Y.,* 519 U.S. 357 (1997); *Thornburgh* v. *American College of Obstetricians and Gynecologists,* 476 U.S. 747 (1986). Today's distortions, however, are particularly blatant.... "Uninhibited, robust, and wide open" debate is replaced by the power of the state to protect an unheard-of "right to be let alone" on the public streets. I dissent.

Opinion Footnotes

3 I do not disagree with the Court that "our cases have repeatedly recognized the interests of unwilling listeners" in locations, such as public conveyances, where " 'the degree of captivity makes it impractical for the unwilling viewer or auditor to avoid exposure,' " (*Erzoznick* v. *City of Jacksonville,* 422 U.S. 205 (1975)). But we have never made the absurd suggestion that a pedestrian is a "captive" of the speaker who seeks to address him on the public sidewalks, where he may simply walk quickly by.

5 Of course the Court greatly understates the scope of the prophylaxis, saying that "the statute's prophylactic aspect is justified by the great difficulty of protecting, say, a pregnant woman from physical harassment with legal rules that focus exclusively on the individual impact of each instance of behavior." But the statute prevents the "physically harassing" act of (shudder!) approaching within closer than eight feet not only when it is directed against pregnant women, but also (just to be safe) when it is directed against 300-pound, male, and unpregnant truck drivers—surely a distinction that is not "difficult to make accurately."

JUSTICE KENNEDY, dissenting.

The Court's holding contradicts more than a half century of well-established First Amendment principles. For the first time, the Court approves a law which bars a private citizen from passing a message, in a peaceful manner and on a profound moral issue, to a fellow citizen on a public sidewalk. If from this time forward the Court repeats its grave errors of analysis, we shall have no longer the proud tradition of free and open discourse in a public forum. In my view, Justice Scalia's First Amendment analysis is correct and mandates outright reversal. In addition to undermining established First Amendment principles, the Court's decision conflicts with the essence of the joint opinion in *Planned Parenthood of Southeastern Pa.* v. *Casey,* 505 U.S. 833 (1992). It seems appropriate in these circumstances to reinforce Justice Scalia's correct First Amendment conclusions and to set forth my own views.

I

...The Court wields the categories of *Ward* v. *Rock Against Racism* so that what once were rules to protect speech now become rules to restrict it....Colorado's statute is a textbook example of a law which is content based.

A

...The law is a prime example of a statute inviting screening and censoring of individual speech; and it is serious error to hold otherwise.

The Court errs in asserting the Colorado statute is no different from laws sustained as content neutral in earlier cases. The prohibitions against "picketing" and/or "leafleting" upheld in [our precedents] ...the Court says, see n. 30, are no different from the restrictions on "protest, education, or counseling" imposed by the Colorado statute. The parallel the Court sees does not exist. No examination of the content of a speaker's message is required to determine whether an individual is picketing, or distributing a leaflet, or impeding free access to a building. Under the Colorado enactment, however, the State must review content to determine whether a person has engaged in criminal "protest, education, or counseling." When a citizen approaches another on the sidewalk in a disfavored-speech zone, an officer of the State must listen to what the speaker says. If, in the officer's judgment, the speaker's words stray too far toward "protest, education, or counseling"—the boundaries of which are far from clear—the officer may decide the speech has moved from the permissible to the criminal. The First Amendment does not give the government such power.

...

After the Court errs in finding the statute content neutral, it compounds the mistake by finding the law viewpoint neutral. Viewpoint-based rules are invidious speech restrictions, yet the Court approves this one. The purpose and design of the statute—as everyone ought to know and as its own defenders urge in attempted justification—are to restrict speakers on one side of the debate: those who protest abortions. The statute applies only to medical facilities.... The testimony to the Colorado Legislature consisted, almost in its entirety, of debates and controversies with respect to abortion, a point the majority acknowledges. The legislature's purpose to restrict unpopular speech should be beyond dispute.

... Under the most reasonable interpretation of Colorado's law, if a speaker approaches a fellow citizen within any one of Colorado's thousands of disfavored-speech zones and chants in praise of the Supreme Court and its abortion decisions, . . . there is neither protest, nor education, nor counseling. If the opposite message is communicated, however, a prosecution to punish protest is warranted. . . . Colorado is now allowed to punish speech because of its content and viewpoint.

The Court time and again has held content-based or viewpoint-based regulations to be presumptively invalid. . . . I would hold the statute invalid from the very start.

. . .

II

The Colorado statute . . .is a law more vague and overly broad than any criminal statute the Court has sustained as a permissible regulation of speech. The statute's imprecisions are so evident that this, too, ought to have ended the case without further discussion.

The law makes it a criminal offense to "knowingly approach another person within eight feet of such person, unless such other person consents, for the purpose of passing a leaflet or handbill to, displaying a sign to, or engaging in oral protest, education, or counseling with such other person in the public way or sidewalk area within a radius of one hundred feet from any entrance door to a health care facility." Colo. Rev. Stat. § 18–9–122(3) (1999). The operative terms and phrases of the statute are not defined. . . .

In the context of a law imposing criminal penalties for pure speech, "protest" is an imprecise word; "counseling" is an imprecise word; "education" is an imprecise word. . . . I simply disagree with the majority's estimation that it is "quite remote" that "anyone would not understand any of those common words.". . .

. . .

There runs through our First Amendment theory a concept of immediacy, the idea that thoughts and pleas and petitions must not be lost with the passage of time. In a fleeting existence we have but little time to find truth through discourse. No better illustration of the immediacy of speech, of the urgency of persuasion, of the preciousness of time, is presented than in this case. Here the citizens who claim First Amendment protection seek it for speech which, if it is to be effective, must take place at the very time and place a grievous moral wrong, in their view, is about to occur. The Court tears away from the protesters the guarantees of the First Amendment when they most need it. . . .

I dissent.

Case Questions

1. The majority reads this law as securing not only safe access to medical care but also "the right to be free from persistent importunity, following, and dogging." The dissent characterizes it as closing off people in the vicinity of health-care facilities from exposure to disagreeable ideas. Are there attributes of the statute that help one resolve this stark contrast of perceptions?

2. Justice Kennedy views the law as a total ban on distributing an unwanted leaflet in the vicinity of abortion clinics. The Court majority views it as permitting such distribution if the leafleteer is stationary, say, next to a clinic entrance, and simply refrains from walking up to people or following them. Who is right?

3. To argue that the law is not content-neutral, Scalia cites the preamble to the statute, which says in part, "The general assembly recognizes that . . . the exercise of a person's right to protest or counsel against certain medical procedures must be balanced against another person's right to obtain medical counseling and treatment in an unobstructed manner." To argue that the law is content neutral, the majority looks at the wording of what is actually prohibited. Who has the better case?

4. Is Justice Scalia correct in his perception that this law renders "impossible" the task of persuading a woman "outside the entrance to abortion facilities" (the "most effective place" to reach her) that she may be making the mistake of her life?

Scheidler v. NOW (2003)

Seventeen years after it began, the RICO lawsuit mentioned above reached the U.S. Supreme Court, for the second time in 2003 as *Scheidler v. NOW*, 537 U.S. 393. RICO authorizes not only severe criminal penalties but also property forfeitures, injunctive relief and triple the damages that a jury awards. PLAN and Operation Rescue leaders had often served jail time for their various unlawful protest activities, such as trespass and destruction of clinic property, but this RICO-based litigation by NOW (representing a certified class of all women who have used or would use the services of an abortion clinic in the United States) and the two women's health clinics (representing a certified class of all clinics in the United States that, among other services, perform abortions) was an attempt to shut PLAN down by making its rough, illegal, and threatening tactics simply too expensive.

The RICO law had been amended in 1970 as a chapter of the Organized Crime Control Act (18 USC §§ 1961–1968). It prohibits in 18 USC § 1962(c) "any person associated with an enterprise engaged in, or the activities of which affect, interstate or foreign commerce, from conducting the affairs of the enterprise through a pattern of racketeering activity." RICO (in 18 USC § 1961) provides a long and diverse list of the activities that count as racketeering:

> "(1) racketeering activity" means (A) any act or threat involving murder, kidnapping, gambling, arson, robbery, bribery, extortion, dealing in obscene matter, or dealing in a controlled substance or listed chemical (as defined in § 102 of the Controlled Substances Act), which is chargeable under State law and punishable by imprisonment for more than one year; [or] (B) any act which is indictable under any of the following provisions of title 18, United States Code: [here follows a long list that ranged from prohibitions on forging passports, to witness-tampering, to counterfeiting, to fraud, and to peonage, and which list includes] § 1951 [relating to interference with commerce, robbery, or extortion]...
>
> Section 1951, known as the Hobbs Act, contained the following language:
>
> (a) Whoever in any way or degree obstructs, delays, or affects commerce or the movement of any article or commodity in commerce, by robbery or extortion or attempts or conspires so to do, or commits or threatens physical violence to any person or property in furtherance of a plan or purpose to do anything in violation of this section shall be fined under this title or imprisoned not more than twenty years, or both.

The National Organization for Women had sued in federal district court alleging many acts of extortion by PLAN, Operation Rescue, and their leaders. Thus, the statutory definition of extortion was central to their case. The Hobbs Act defines extortion as: "the obtaining of property from another, with his consent, induced by wrongful use of actual or threatened force, violence, or fear, or under color of official right."

At first these suits had been dismissed on the grounds that these anti-abortion groups had no economic motive for what they did. When the Supreme Court had sent this case, *NOW v. Scheidler*, back down to the lower courts in 1994, after the first murder of an abortion provider but before Congress enacted the FACE law, the Court had ruled unanimously in an opinion written by Justice Rehnquist (no fan of *Roe v. Wade*) that the word "extortion" did not imply the necessity of an economic motive. With that guideline, both the federal district, in a jury trial, and the federal circuit court of appeals, this time ruled in NOW's favor. The jury found Scheidler, leader of PLAN, and his allies guilty of 21 violations of the Hobbs Act; 25 violations of state extortion law; 25 instances of attempting or conspiring to commit either federal or state extortion; 23 violations of the Travel Act;[137] and 23 instances of attempting to violate the Travel Act. The jury awarded damages of $31,455.64 to the Delaware women's clinic and $54,471.28 to the Summit clinic, and pursuant to § 1964(c), the District Court judge, following the statute, tripled the size of the damages. (See discussion above, prior to the description of *Hill v. Colorado* (2000), for how the FACE Act penalties would compare.) This judge also issued a permanent nationwide injunction prohibiting the involved parties from "obstructing access to the clinics, trespassing on clinic property, damaging clinic property, or using violence of threats of violence against the clinics, their employees, or their patients."[138] The circuit court upheld these rulings.[139] Scheidler then went again to the Supreme Court.

This time, however, in *Scheidler v. NOW* (2003), Scheidler and his allies emerged victorious. Even the most firmly pro-choice of the justices, except for Justice Stevens, joined Chief Justice Rehnquist's opinion. Rehnquist zeroed in on the meaning of "extortion" and argued that the predecessor to the Hobbs Act (the Anti-Racketeering Act of 1934) had forbidden two different crimes, "extortion" and "coercion." Extortion classically involved the use by someone of threats, force, or violence to induce someone else to "consent" (out of fear) to one's "obtaining property" from that person. Coercion, by contrast, involved the same tactics simply to limit someone else's freedom of action. The Court majority ruled that the pro-lifers were engaging in the lesser crime of coercion, not the crime of extortion, since they did not "obtain" property (even with the understanding that "property" included, for instance, such things as the doctor's right to carry on his or her business of the sale of professional medical services). The Court acknowledged that some doctors might have been literally driven out of business, but since the pro-lifers did not in any meaningful sense "obtain" that business, their action was not extortion. Justice Ginsburg wrote a concurrence for herself and Justice Breyer, expressing concern that interpreting the law the way the lower courts had would open up the use of the law to prosecute such peaceful dissenters as people who had engaged in sit-ins for civil rights.

Scheidler v. NOW (2003) did not end here, because the Supreme Court remanded to the circuit court for further action. There, NOW argued that even if "extortion" allegations were eliminated, the RICO injunction needed to stay in force because of the threats and actual instances of violence. At this point the circuit court remanded to the District Court for a factual determination on the question of violence. Then Scheidler and his anti-abortion allies appealed for review to the U.S. Supreme Court. Justice Stevens had left the Court, and this time the Court's decision, written by Justice Breyer, was unanimous.

Scheidler v. NOW, 547 U.S. 9 (2006) again rejected NOW's reading of the Hobbs Act, ruling that its relevant language imposed criminal liability only on persons who used, threatened to use or conspired to use violence to affect interstate commerce via robbery or extortion. Because abortion provision takes place nationwide and people purchase and ship supplies for it and travel to obtain it and so forth, its effect on commerce was not in dispute. Nonetheless, since the violent opponents of abortion neither aimed their violence at committing robbery nor were using violence to further economically motivated extortion, the Court judged that the Hobbs Act could not be applied against them. The Court concluded its reasoning with specific reference to the FACE Act, as follows:

> And in 1994, Congress enacted a specific statute aimed directly at the type of abortion clinic violence and other activity at issue in this litigation, thereby suggesting it did not believe that the Hobbs Act already addressed that activity. See Freedom of Access to Clinic Entrances Act, 18 U.S.C. § 248(a)(3) (imposing criminal liability on anyone who "intentionally damages or destroys the property of a facility, or attempts to do so, because such facility provides reproductive health services").

This law is described above just prior to the discussion of the *Hill v. Colorado* (2000) case. The Supreme Court's complete turnabout on the appropriateness of applying the Hobbs Act against the violent wing of the anti-abortion movement appears to have been strongly influenced by Congress's adoption of the FACE Act during this long litigation process.

Legislation Against Abortion Clinics: *Whole Woman's Health v. Hellerstedt* (2016)

Besides protests at abortion clinics, the prolife movement has also tried using legislation that would restrict the type of clinics that could perform abortions. State legislators, activists and others have argued that *Roe* does not speak to the precautions needed to protect the health of women seeking abortions. Arguably addressing such a question the Texas legislature passed House Bill 2 in 2013. Among other provisions, the bill required that physicians have admitting privileges at a hospital no more than 30 miles away from abortion clinics where they were performing abortions. A second aspect of the law required that abortion clinics comply with the same minimum standards as those required of ambulatory surgical centers.

Whole Woman's Health is a chain of women's health centers in five states that provide gynecological and other women's health services including abortion.

Of the eight clinic locations, four are in Texas. Whole Woman's Health sought to invalidate these provisions as they related to two of the Texas-based facilities in McAllen and El Paso on the grounds that the law violated the 14th Amendment's equal protection guarantees in a manner that was unreasonable and arbitrary, and placed a substantial burden on women seeking abortions in violation of *Casey*.

The District Court agreed with Whole Woman's Health, that requiring physicians to have admitting privileges at a nearby hospital "imposes an undue burden on the right of women throughout Texas to seek a pre-viability abortion." The Court of Appeals overturned the District Court's decision on June 9, 2015 finding that the Texas statutory provisions were constitutional and could take effect.[140]

The Supreme Court granted cert in late 2015 and decided the case in late June 2016. During the interval between these two events, 79 year-old Associate Justice Antonin Scalia, a staunch conservative, died in his sleep on February 13, 2016. Thus, the Court that decided to grant cert (which requires only four votes) differed from the Court that decided the case. Senate Majority Leader Mitch McConnell and other Senate Republicans stated on the day of Scalia's death that they would not consider any appointments put forward by President Obama who was leaving office the following January at the end of his second term, per constitutionally-mandated term limits. McConnell stated that the Senate would wait until the next president took office in January 2017 before acting on a potential replacement. Still, President Obama nominated Chief Judge of the United States Court of Appeals for the District of Columbia Circuit Merrick Garland to replace Scalia on March 16, 2016. True to their word, the Republican Senate leadership held "no hearings, no votes, no action whatsoever" on Garland's nomination.[141] As a result, the U.S. Supreme Court that decided *Whole Woman's Health v. Hellerstedt* included only eight members, not the usual nine. Justice Breyer wrote the opinion for the majority (joined by Justices Kennedy, Ginsburg, Sotomayor and Kagan). Justice Ginsburg filed a brief concurring opinion, and Justices Thomas, Alito, and Roberts dissented.

WHOLE WOMAN'S HEALTH V. HELLERSTEDT
136 S.Ct. 2292 (2016)

JUSTICE BREYER delivered the opinion of the Court.

. . .

III

Undue Burden—Legal Standard

We begin with the standard, as described in *Casey*. We recognize that the "State has a legitimate interest in seeing to it that abortion, like any other medical procedure, is performed under circumstances that insure maximum safety for the patient." *Roe* v. *Wade*, 410 U.S. 113, 150 (1973). But, we added, "a statute which, while furthering [a] valid state interest, has the effect of placing a substantial obstacle in the path of a woman's choice cannot be considered a permissible means of serving its legitimate ends." *Casey,* 505 U.S., at 877 (plurality opinion). Moreover, "[u]nnecessary health regulations that have the purpose or effect of presenting a substantial obstacle to a woman seeking an abortion impose an undue burden on the right." *Id.*, at 878.

. . .

IV

Undue Burden—Admitting-Privileges Requirement

Turning to the lower courts' evaluation of the evidence, we first consider the admitting-privileges requirement. Before the enactment of H. B. 2, doctors who provided abortions were required to "have admitting privileges *or* have a working arrangement with a physician(s) who has admitting privileges at a local hospital in order to ensure the necessary back up for medical complications." Tex. Admin. Code, tit. 25, § 139.56 (2009) (emphasis added). The new law changed this requirement by requiring that a "physician performing or inducing an abortion . . . must, on the date the abortion is performed or induced, have active admitting privileges at a hospital that . . . is located not further than 30 miles from the location at which the abortion is performed or induced." Tex. Health & Safety Code Ann. § 171.0031(a). The District Court held that the legislative change imposed an "undue burden" on a woman's right to have an abortion. We conclude that there is adequate legal and factual support for the District Court's conclusion.

The purpose of the admitting-privileges requirement is to help ensure that women have easy access to a hospital should complications arise during an abortion procedure. Brief for Respondents. But the District Court found that it brought about no such health-related benefit. The court found that "[t]he great weight of evidence demonstrates that, before the act's passage, abortion in Texas was extremely safe with particularly low rates of serious complications and virtually no deaths occurring on account of the procedure." 46 F. Supp. 3d, at 684. Thus, there was no significant health-related problem that the new law helped to cure.

. . .

We have found nothing in Texas' record evidence that shows that, compared to prior law (which required a "working arrangement" with a doctor with admitting privileges), the new law advanced Texas' legitimate interest in protecting women's health.

We add that, when directly asked at oral argument whether Texas knew of a single instance in which the new requirement would have helped even one woman obtain better treatment, Texas admitted that there was no evidence in the record of such a case. See Tr. of Oral Arg. This answer is consistent with the findings of the other Federal District Courts that have considered the health benefits of other States' similar admitting-privileges laws. See *Planned Parenthood of Wis., Inc.* v. *Van Hollen*, 94 F. Supp. 3d 949, 953 (WD Wis. 2015), aff'd sub nom. *Planned Parenthood of Wis., Inc.* v. *Schimel*, 806 F. 3d 908 (CA7 2015); *Planned Parenthood Southeast, Inc.* v. *Strange*, 33F. Supp. 3d 1330, 1378 (MD Ala. 2014).

At the same time, the record evidence indicates that the admitting-privileges requirement places a "substantial obstacle in the path of a woman's choice." *Casey*, 505 U.S., at 877 (plurality opinion). The District Court found, as of the time the admitting-privileges requirement began to be enforced, the number of facilities providing abortions dropped in half, from about 40 to about 20. 46 F. Supp. 3d, at 681. Eight abortion clinics closed in the months leading up to the requirement's effective date. See App.; cf. Brief for Planned Parenthood Federation of America et al. as *Amici Curiae* (noting that abortion facilities in Waco, San Angelo, and Midland no longer operate because Planned Parenthood is "unable to find local physicians in those communities with privileges who are willing to provide abortions due to the size of those communities and the hostility that abortion providers face"). Eleven more closed on the day the admitting-privileges requirement took effect. See App.; Tr. of Oral Arg.

Other evidence helps to explain why the new requirement led to the closure of clinics. We read that other evidence in light of a brief filed in this

Court by the Society of Hospital Medicine. That brief describes the undisputed general fact that "hospitals often condition admitting privileges on reaching a certain number of admissions per year." Brief for Society of Hospital Medicine et al. as *Amici Curiae*. Returning to the District Court record, we note that, in direct testimony, the president of Nova Health Systems, implicitly relying on this general fact, pointed out that it would be difficult for doctors regularly performing abortions at the El Paso clinic to obtain admitting privileges at nearby hospitals because "[d]uring the past 10 years, over 17,000 abortion procedures were performed at the El Paso clinic [and n]ot a single one of those patients had to be transferred to a hospital for emergency treatment, much less admitted to the hospital." App. In a word, doctors would be unable to maintain admitting privileges or obtain those privileges for the future, because the fact that abortions are so safe meant that providers were unlikely to have any patients to admit.

. . .

In our view, the record contains sufficient evidence that the admitting-privileges requirement led to the closure of half of Texas' clinics, or thereabouts. Those closures meant fewer doctors, longer waiting times, and increased crowding. Record evidence also supports the finding that after the admitting-privileges provision went into effect, the "number of women of reproductive age living in a county . . . more than 150 miles from a provider increased from approximately 86,000 to 400,000 . . . and the number of women living in a county more than 200 miles from a provider from approximately 10,000 to 290,000." 46 F. Supp. 3d, at 681. We recognize that increased driving distances do not always constitute an "undue burden." See *Casey*, 505 U.S., at 885–887 (joint opinion of O'Connor, Kennedy, and Souter, JJ.). But here, those increases are but one additional burden, which, when taken together with others that the closings brought about, and when viewed in light of the virtual absence of any health benefit, lead us to conclude that the record adequately supports the District Court's "undue burden" conclusion. Cf. *id.*, at 895 (opinion of the Court) (finding burden "undue" when requirement places "substantial obstacle to a woman's choice" in "a large fraction of the cases in which" it "is relevant").

. . .

V

Undue Burden—Surgical-Center Requirement

The second challenged provision of Texas' new law sets forth the surgical-center requirement. Prior to enactment of the new requirement, Texas law required abortion facilities to meet a host of health and safety requirements. Under those pre-existing laws, facilities were subject to annual reporting and recordkeeping requirements, see Tex. Admin. Code, tit. 25, §§ 139.4, 139.5, 139.55, 139.58; a quality assurance program, see § 139.8; personnel policies and staffing requirements, see §§ 139.43, 139.46; physical and environmental requirements, see § 139.48; infection control standards, see § 139.49; disclosure requirements, see § 139.50; patient-rights standards, see § 139.51; and medical- and clinical-services standards, see § 139.53, including anesthesia standards, see § 139.59. These requirements are policed by random and announced inspections, at least annually, see §§ 139.23, 139.31; Tex. Health & Safety Code Ann. § 245.006(a) (West 2010), as well as administrative penalties, injunctions, civil penalties, and criminal penalties for certain violations, see Tex. Admin. Code, tit. 25, § 139.33; Tex. Health & Safety Code Ann. § 245.011 (criminal penalties for certain reporting violations).

H. B. 2 added the requirement that an "abortion facility" meet the "minimum standards . . . for ambulatory surgical centers" under Texas law. § 245.010(a) (West Cum. Supp. 2015). The surgical-center regulations include, among other things, detailed specifications relating to the size of the nursing staff, building dimensions, and other building requirements. . . .

There is considerable evidence in the record supporting the District Court's findings indicating that the statutory provision requiring all abortion facilities to meet all surgical-center standards does not benefit patients and is not necessary. The District Court found that "risks are not appreciably lowered for patients who undergo abortions at ambulatory surgical centers as compared to nonsurgical-center facilities." 46 F. Supp. 3d, at 684. The court added that women "will not obtain better care or experience more frequent positive outcomes at an ambulatory surgical center as compared to a previously licensed facility." *Ibid.* And these findings are well supported.

The record makes clear that the surgical-center requirement provides no benefit when complications arise in the context of an abortion produced through medication. [This Texas law also required that all medication-induced, i.e. non-surgical, abortions also be performed only in licensed clinics.—AU.] That is because, in such a case, complications would almost always arise only after the patient has left the facility. See *supra*; App. The record also contains evidence indicating that abortions taking place in an abortion facility are safe—indeed, safer than numerous procedures that take place outside hospitals and to which Texas does not apply its surgical-center requirements. See, *id.* The total number of deaths in Texas from abortions was five in the period from 2001 to 2012, or about one every two years (that is to say, one out of about 120,000 to 144,000 abortions). *Id.* Nationwide, childbirth is 14 times more likely than abortion to result in death, *ibid.*, but Texas law allows a midwife to oversee childbirth in the patient's own home. Colonoscopy, a procedure that typically takes place outside a hospital (or surgical center) setting, has a mortality rate 10 times higher than an abortion. *Id*; see ACOG Brief (the mortality rate for liposuction, another outpatient procedure, is 28 times higher than the mortality rate for abortion). Medical treatment after an incomplete miscarriage often involves a procedure identical to that involved in a nonmedical abortion, but it often takes place outside a hospital or surgical center. App.; see ACOG Brief. And Texas partly or wholly grandfathers (or waives in whole or in part the surgical-center requirement for) about two-thirds of the facilities to which the surgical-center standards apply. But it neither grandfathers nor provides waivers for any of the facilities that perform abortions. 46 F. Supp. 3d, at 680–681; see App. These facts indicate that the surgical-center provision imposes "a requirement that simply is not based on differences" between abortion and other surgical procedures "that are reasonably related to" preserving women's health, the asserted "purpos[e] of the Act in which it is found." *Doe*, 410 U.S., at 194 (quoting *Morey* v. *Doud*, 354 U.S. 457, 465 (1957); internal quotation marks omitted).

. . .

The upshot is that this record evidence, along with the absence of any evidence to the contrary, provides ample support for the District Court's conclusion that "[m]any of the building standards mandated by the act and its implementing rules have such a tangential relationship to patient safety in the context of abortion as to be nearly arbitrary." 46 F. Supp. 3d, at 684. That conclusion, along with the supporting evidence, provides sufficient support for the more general conclusion that the surgical-center requirement "will not [provide] better care or . . . more frequent positive outcomes." *Ibid.* The record evidence thus supports the ultimate legal conclusion that the surgical-center requirement is not necessary.

At the same time, the record provides adequate evidentiary support for the District Court's conclusion that the surgical-center requirement places a substantial obstacle in the path of women seeking an abortion. The parties stipulated that the requirement would further reduce the number of abortion facilities available to seven or eight facilities, located in Houston, Austin, San Antonio, and Dallas/Fort Worth. See App. In the District Court's view, the proposition that these "seven or eight providers could meet the demand of the entire State stretches credulity." 46 F. Supp. 3d, at 682. We take this statement as a finding that these few facilities could not "meet" that "demand."

. . .

More fundamentally, in the face of no threat to women's health, Texas seeks to force women to travel long distances to get abortions in crammed-to-capacity superfacilities. Patients seeking these services are less likely to get the kind of individualized attention, serious conversation, and emotional support that doctors at less taxed facilities may have offered. Healthcare facilities and medical professionals are not fungible commodities. Surgical centers attempting to accommodate sudden, vastly increased demand, see 46 F. Supp. 3d, at 682, may find that quality of care declines. Another commonsense inference that the District Court made is that these effects would be harmful to, not supportive of, women's health. See *id.,* at 682–683.

Finally, the District Court found that the costs that a currently licensed abortion facility would have to incur to meet the surgical-center requirements were considerable, ranging from $1 million per facility (for facilities with adequate space) to $3 million per facility (where additional land must be purchased). *Id.,* at 682. This evidence supports the conclusion that more surgical centers will not soon fill the gap when licensed facilities are forced to close.

We agree with the District Court that the surgical-center requirement, like the admitting-privileges requirement, provides few, if any, health benefits for women, poses a substantial obstacle to women seeking abortions, and constitutes an "undue burden" on their constitutional right to do so.

. . .

For these reasons the judgment of the Court of Appeals is reversed, and the case is remanded for further proceedings consistent with this opinion.

It is so ordered.

JUSTICE GINSBURG, concurring.

The Texas law called H. B. 2 inevitably will reduce the number of clinics and doctors allowed to provide abortion services. Texas argues that H. B. 2's restrictions are constitutional because they protect the health of women who experience complications from abortions. In truth, "complications from an abortion are both rare and rarely dangerous." *Planned Parenthood of Wis., Inc.* v. *Schimel*, 806 F. 3d 908, 912 (CA7 2015) [Additional citations omitted.—AU.] Many medical procedures, including childbirth, are far more dangerous to patients, yet are not subject to ambulatory-surgical-center or hospital admitting-privileges requirements. [Citations omitted.—AU.] Given those realities, it is beyond rational belief that H. B. 2 could genuinely protect the health of women, and certain that the law "would simply make it more difficult for them to obtain abortions." *Planned Parenthood of Wis.*, 806 F. 3d, at 910.

JUSTICE THOMAS, dissenting.

. . . .I remain fundamentally opposed to the Court's abortion jurisprudence. . . Even taking *Casey* as the baseline, however, the majority radically rewrites the undue-burden test in three ways. First, today's decision requires courts to "consider the burdens a law imposes on abortion access together with the benefits those laws confer." *Ante*. Second, today's opinion tells the courts that, when the law's justifications are medically uncertain, they need not defer to the legislature, and must instead assess medical justifications for abortion restrictions by scrutinizing the record themselves. *Ibid*. Finally, even if a law imposes no "substantial obstacle" to women's access to abortions, the law now must have more than a "reasonabl[e] relat[ion] to . . . a legitimate state interest." *Ibid*. (internal quotation marks omitted). These precepts are nowhere to be found in *Casey* or its successors, and transform the undue-burden test to something much more akin to strict scrutiny. . . .

JUSTICE ALITO, with whom THE CHIEF JUSTICE and JUSTICE THOMAS join, dissenting.

. . .

III

[W]hat matters for present purposes is not the effect of the H. B. 2 provisions on petitioners but the effect on their patients. Under our cases, petitioners must show that the admitting privileges and ASC requirements impose an "undue burden" on women seeking abortions. *Gonzales* v. *Carhart*, 550 U.S. 124, 146 (2007). And in order to obtain the sweeping relief they seek— facial invalidation of those provisions—they must show, at a minimum, that these provisions have an unconstitutional impact on at least a "large fraction" of Texas women of reproductive age. *Id.,* at 167–168. Such a situation could result if the clinics able to comply with the new requirements either lacked the requisite overall capacity or were located too far away to serve a "large fraction" of the women in question.

Petitioners did not make that showing. Instead of offering direct evidence, they relied on two crude inferences. First, they pointed to the number of abortion clinics that closed after the enactment of H. B. 2, and asked that it be inferred that all these closures resulted from the two challenged provisions. See Brief for Petitioners. They made little effort to show why particular clinics closed. Second, they pointed to the number of abortions performed annually at [ambulatory surgical centers, or] ASCs before H. B. 2 took effect and, because this figure is well below the total number of abortions performed each year in the State, they asked that it be inferred that ASC-compliant clinics could not meet the demands of women in the State. See App. Petitioners failed to provide any evidence of the actual capacity of the facilities that would be available to perform abortions in compliance with the new law—even though they provided this type of evidence in their first case to the District Court at trial and then to this Court in their application for interim injunctive relief. Appendix, *infra*.

A

I do not dispute the fact that H. B. 2 caused the closure of some clinics. Indeed, it seems clear that H. B. 2 was intended to force unsafe facilities to shut down. The law was one of many enacted by States in the wake of the Kermit Gosnell scandal, in which a physician who ran an abortion clinic in Philadelphia was convicted for the first-degree murder of three infants who were born alive and for the manslaughter of a patient. Gosnell had not been actively supervised by state or local authorities or by his peers, and the Philadelphia grand jury that investigated the case recommended that the Commonwealth adopt a law requiring abortion clinics to comply with the same regulations as ASCs. If Pennsylvania had had such a requirement in force, the Gosnell facility may have been shut down before his crimes. And if there were any similarly unsafe facilities in Texas, H. B. 2 was clearly intended to put them out of business.

While there can be no doubt that H. B. 2 caused some clinics to cease operation, the absence of proof regarding the reasons for particular closures is a problem because some clinics have or may have closed for at least four reasons other than the two H. B. 2 requirements at issue here. These are:

1. *H. B. 2's restriction on medication abortion*. In their first case, petitioners challenged the provision of H. B. 2 that regulates medication abortion, but that part of the statute was upheld by the Fifth Circuit and not relitigated

in this case. The record in this case indicates that in the first six months after this restriction took effect, the number of medication abortions dropped by 6,957 (compared to the same period the previous year). App.

2. *Withdrawal of Texas family planning funds.* In 2011, Texas passed a law preventing family planning grants to providers that perform abortions and their affiliates. In the first case, petitioners' expert admitted that some clinics closed "as a result of the defunding," and as discussed below, this withdrawal appears specifically to have caused multiple clinic closures in West Texas. See *infra* and n. 18.

3. *The nationwide decline in abortion demand.* Petitioners' expert testimony relies on a study from the Guttmacher Institute which concludes that " '[t]he national abortion rate has resumed its decline, and *no evidence was found that the overall drop in abortion incidence was related to the decrease in providers or to restrictions implemented between 2008 and 2011.*' " App. (direct testimony of Dr. Peter Uhlenberg) (quoting R. Jones & J. Jerman, *Abortion Incidence and Service Availability In the United States*, 2011, 46 *Perspectives on Sexual and Reproductive Health* 3 (2014); emphasis in testimony). Consistent with that trend, "[t]he number of abortions to residents of Texas declined by 4,956 between 2010 and 2011 and by 3,905 between 2011 and 2012." App.

4. *Physician retirement (or other localized factors).* Like everyone else, most physicians eventually retire, and the retirement of a physician who performs abortions can cause the closing of a clinic or a reduction in the number of abortions that a clinic can perform. When this happens, the closure of the clinic or the reduction in capacity cannot be attributed to H. B. 2 unless it is shown that the retirement was caused by the admitting privileges or surgical center requirements as opposed to age or some other factor.

At least nine Texas clinics may have ceased performing abortions (or reduced capacity) for one or more of the reasons having nothing to do with the provisions challenged here. For example, in their first case, petitioners alleged that the medication-abortion restriction would cause at least three medication-only abortion clinics to cease performing abortions, and they predicted that "[o]ther facilities that offer both surgical and medication abortion will be unable to offer medication abortion," presumably reducing their capacity. It also appears that several clinics (including most of the clinics operating in West Texas, apart from El Paso) closed in response to the unrelated law restricting the provision of family planning funds.[18] And there is reason to question whether at least two closures (one in Corpus Christi and one in Houston) may have been prompted by physician retirements.

Neither petitioners nor the District Court properly addressed these complexities in assessing causation—and for no good reason. The total number of abortion clinics in the State was not large. Petitioners could have put on evidence (as they did for 27 individual clinics in their first case, see Appendix, *infra*) about the challenged provisions' role in causing the closure of each clinic, and the court could have made a factual finding as to the cause of each closure.

Precise findings are important because the key issue here is not the number or percentage of clinics affected, but the effect of the closures on women seeking abortions, *i.e.*, on the capacity and geographic distribution of clinics used by those women. To the extent that clinics closed (or experienced a reduction in capacity) for any reason unrelated to the challenged provisions of H. B. 2, the corresponding burden on abortion access may not be factored into the access analysis. Because there was ample reason to believe that some closures were caused by these other factors, the District Court's failure to ascertain the reasons for clinic closures means that, on the record before us, there is no way to tell which closures actually count. Petitioners—who, as plaintiffs, bore the burden of proof—cannot simply point to temporal correlation and call it causation.

B

Even if the District Court had properly filtered out immaterial closures, its analysis would have been incomplete for a second reason. Petitioners offered scant evidence on the capacity of the clinics that are able to comply with the admitting privileges and ASC requirements, or on those clinics' geographic distribution. Reviewing the evidence in the record, it is far from clear that there has been a material impact on access to abortion.

On clinic capacity, the Court relies on petitioners' expert Dr. Grossman, who compared the number of abortions performed at Texas ASCs before the enactment of H. B. 2 (about 14,000 per year) with the total number of abortions per year in the State (between 60,000–70,000 per year). *Ante*.[21] Applying what the Court terms "common sense," the Court infers that the ASCs that performed abortions at the time of H. B. 2's enactment lacked the capacity to perform all the abortions sought by women in Texas.

The Court's inference has obvious limitations. First, it is not unassailable "common sense" to hold that current utilization equals capacity; if all we know about a grocery store is that it currently serves 200 customers per week, *ante*, that fact alone does not tell us whether it is an overcrowded minimart or a practically empty supermarket. Faced with increased demand, ASCs could potentially increase the number of abortions performed without prohibitively expensive changes. Among other things, they might hire more physicians who perform abortions, utilize their facilities more intensively or efficiently, or shift the mix of services provided. Second, what matters for present purposes is not the capacity of just those ASCs that performed abortions prior to the enactment of H. B. 2 but the capacity of those that would be available to perform abortions after the statute took effect. And since the enactment of H. B. 2, the number of ASCs performing abortions has increased by 50%—from six in 2012 to nine today.

The most serious problem with the Court's reasoning is that its conclusion is belied by petitioners' own submissions to this Court. In the first case, when petitioners asked this Court to vacate the Fifth Circuit's stay of the District Court's injunction of the admitting privileges requirement pending appeal, they submitted a chart previously provided in the District Court that detailed the capacity of abortion clinics after the admitting privileges requirement was to take effect. This chart is included as an Appendix to this opinion. Three of the facilities listed on the chart were ASCs, and their capacity was shown as follows:

Southwestern Women's Surgery Center in Dallas was said to have the capacity for 5,720 abortions a year (110 per week);

Planned Parenthood Surgical Health Services Center in Dallas was said to have the capacity for 6,240 abortions a year (120 per week); and

Planned Parenthood Center for Choice in Houston was said to have the capacity for 9,100 abortions a year (175 per week). See Appendix, *infra*.

The average capacity of these three ASCs was 7,020 abortions per year. If the nine ASCs now performing abortions in Texas have the same average capacity, they have a total capacity of 63,180. Add in the assumed capacity for two other clinics that are operating pursuant to the judgment of the Fifth Circuit (over 3,100 abortions per year), and the total for the State is 66,280 abortions per year. That is comparable to the 68,298 total abortions performed in Texas in 2012, the year before H. B. 2 was enacted, App. and well in excess of the abortion rate one would expect—59,070—if subtracting the apparent impact of the medication abortion restriction, see n. 21, *supra*.

To be clear, I do not vouch for the accuracy of this calculation. . . . The important point is that petitioners put on evidence of actual clinic capacity in their earlier case, and there is no apparent reason why they could not have done the same here. Indeed, the Court asserts that, after the admitting privileges requirement took effect, clinics "were not able to accommodate increased demand," *ante*, but petitioners' own evidence suggested that the requirement had *no* effect on capacity, see n. 21, *supra*. On this point, like the question of the reason for clinic closures, petitioners did not discharge their burden, and the District Court did not engage in the type of analysis that should have been conducted before enjoining an important state law.

So much for capacity. The other potential obstacle to abortion access is the distribution of facilities throughout the State. This might occur if the two challenged H. B. 2 requirements, by causing the closure of clinics in some rural areas, led to a situation in which a "large fraction" of women of reproductive age live too far away from any open clinic. Based on the Court's holding in *Planned Parenthood of Southeastern Pa.* v. *Casey*, 505 U.S. 833, it appears that the need to travel up to 150 miles is not an undue burden, and the evidence in this case shows that if the only clinics in the State were those that would have remained open if the judgment of the Fifth Circuit had not been enjoined, roughly 95% of the women of reproductive age in the State would live within 150 miles of an open facility (or lived outside that range before H. B. 2). Because the record does not show why particular facilities closed, the real figure may be even higher than 95%.

We should decline to hold that these statistics justify the facial invalidation of the H. B. 2 requirements. The possibility that the admitting privileges requirement *might* have caused a closure in Lubbock is no reason to issue a facial injunction exempting Houston clinics from that requirement. I do not dismiss the situation of those women who would no longer live within 150 miles of a clinic as a result of H. B. 2. But under current doctrine such localized problems can be addressed by narrow as-applied challenges.

IV

Even if the Court were right to hold that . . . H. B. 2 imposes an undue burden on abortion access—it is, in fact, wrong . . .—it is still wrong to conclude that the admitting privileges and surgical center provisions must be enjoined in their entirety. H. B. 2 has an extraordinarily broad severability clause that must be considered before enjoining any portion or application of the law. Both challenged provisions should survive in substantial part if the Court faithfully applies that clause. Regrettably, it enjoins both in full. . .

A

Applying H. B. 2's severability clause to the admitting privileges requirement is easy. Simply put, the requirement must be upheld in every city in which its application does not pose an undue burden. It surely does not pose that burden anywhere in the eastern half of the State, where most Texans live and where virtually no woman of reproductive age lives more than 150 miles from an open clinic. See App. (petitioners' expert testimony that 82.5% of Texas women of reproductive age live within 150 miles of open clinics in Austin, Dallas, Fort Worth, Houston, and San Antonio). (Unfortunately, the Court does not address the State's argument to this effect. See Brief for Respondents) And petitioners would need to show that the requirement caused specific West Texas clinics to close (but see *supra* and n. 18) before they could be entitled to an injunction tailored to address those closures.

B

Applying severability to the surgical center requirement calls for the identification of the particular provisions of the ASC regulations that result in the imposition of an undue burden. These regulations are lengthy and detailed, and while compliance with some might be expensive, compliance with many others would not. And many serve important health and safety purposes. Thus, the surgical center requirements cannot be judged as a package. But the District Court nevertheless held that all the surgical center requirements are unconstitutional in all cases, and the Court sustains this holding on grounds that are hard to take seriously.

When the Texas Legislature passed H. B. 2, it left no doubt about its intent on the question of severability. . . . The full provision is reproduced below:

"If any application of any provision in this Act to any person, group of persons, or circumstances is found by a court to be invalid, the remaining applications of that provision to all other persons and circumstances shall be severed and may not be affected. All constitutionally valid applications of this Act shall be severed from any applications that a court finds to be invalid, leaving the valid applications in force, because it is the legislature's intent and priority that the valid applications be allowed to stand alone." *Ibid.*

This provision indisputably requires that all surgical center regulations that are not themselves unconstitutional be left standing. Requiring an abortion facility to comply with any provision of the regulations applicable to surgical centers is an "application of the provision" of H. B. 2 that requires abortion clinics to meet surgical center standards. Therefore, if some such applications are unconstitutional, the severability clause plainly requires that those applications be severed and that the rest be left intact.

How can the Court possibly escape this painfully obvious conclusion? Its main argument is that it need not honor the severability provision because doing so would be too burdensome. See *ante*. This is a remarkable argument.

. . .Federal courts have no authority to carpet-bomb state laws, knocking out provisions that are perfectly consistent with federal law, just because it would be too much bother to separate them from unconstitutional provisions.

In any event, it should not have been hard in this case for the District Court to separate any bad provisions from the good. Petitioners should have identified the particular provisions that would entail what they regard as an undue expense, and the District Court could have then concentrated its analysis on those provisions. In fact, petitioners *did* do this in their trial brief, in *Lakey* (Aug. 12, 2014) ("It is the construction and nursing requirements that form the basis of Plaintiffs' challenge"), but they changed their position once the District Court awarded blanket relief, see 790 F. 3d, at 582 (petitioners told the Fifth Circuit that they "challenge H. B. 2 broadly, with no effort whatsoever to parse out specific aspects of the ASC requirement that they find onerous or otherwise infirm"). In its own review of the ASC requirement, in fact, the Court follows petitioners' original playbook and focuses on the construction and nursing requirements as well. See *ante* (detailed walkthrough of Tex. Admin. Code, tit. 25, §§ 135.15 (2016) (nursing), 135.52 (construction)). I do not see how it "would inflict enormous costs on both courts and litigants," *ante* to single out the ASC regulations that this Court and petitioners have both targeted as the core of the challenge.

By forgoing severability, the Court strikes down numerous provisions that could not plausibly impose an undue burden. For example, surgical center patients must "be treated with respect, consideration, and dignity." Tex. Admin. Code, tit. 25, § 135.5(a). That's now enjoined. Patients may not be given misleading "advertising regarding the competence and/or capabilities of the organization." § 135.5(g). Enjoined. Centers must maintain fire alarm and emergency communications systems, §§ 135.41(d), 135.42(e), and eliminate "[h]azards that might lead to slipping, falling, electrical shock, burns, poisoning, or other trauma," § 135.10(b). Enjoined and enjoined. When a center is being remodeled while still in use, "[t]emporary sound barriers shall be provided where intense, prolonged construction noises will disturb patients or staff in the occupied portions of the building." § 135.51(b)(3)(B)(vi). Enjoined. Centers must develop and enforce policies concerning teaching and publishing by staff.

§§ 135.16(a), (c). Enjoined. They must obtain informed consent before doing research on patients. § 135.17(e). Enjoined. And each center "shall develop, implement[,] and maintain an effective, ongoing, organization-wide, data driven patient safety program." § 135.27(b). Also enjoined. These are but a few of the innocuous requirements that the Court invalidates with nary a wave of the hand.

Any responsible application of the H. B. 2 severability provision would leave much of the law intact. . . .Moreover, as even the District Court found, the surgical center requirement is clearly constitutional as to new abortion facilities and facilities already licensed as surgical centers. *Whole Woman's Health v. Lakey*, 46 F. Supp. 3d 673, 676 (WD Tex. 2014). And we should uphold every application of every surgical center regulation that does not pose an undue burden—at the very least, all of the regulations as to which petitioners have never made a specific complaint supported by specific evidence. . . .

If the Court is unwilling to undertake the careful severability analysis required, that is no reason to strike down all applications of the challenged provisions. The proper course would be to remand to the lower courts for a remedy tailored to the specifics shown in this case, to "try to limit the solution to the problem." *Ayotte v. Planned Parenthood of Northern New Eng.*, 546 U.S. 320, 328 (2006).

V

When we decide cases on particularly controversial issues, we should take special care to apply settled procedural rules in a neutral manner. The Court has not done that here.

I therefore respectfully dissent.

Opinion Footnotes

18 In the first case, petitioners apparently did not even believe that the abortion clinics in Abilene, Bryan, Midland, and San Angelo were made to close because of H. B. 2. In that case, petitioners submitted a list of 15 clinics they believed would close (or have severely limited capacity) because of the admitting privileges requirement—and those four West Texas clinics are *not* on the list. And at trial, a Planned Parenthood executive specifically testified that the Midland clinic closed because of the funding cuts and because the clinic's medical director retired. Petitioners' list and Planned Parenthood's testimony both fit with petitioners' expert's admission in the first case that some clinics closed "as a result of the defunding."

21 In the first case, petitioners submitted a report that Dr. Grossman coauthored with their testifying expert, Dr. Potter. That report predicted that "the shortfall in capacity due to the admitting privileges requirement will prevent at least 22,286 women" from accessing abortion. The methodology used was questionable. As Dr. Potter admitted: "There's no science there. It's just evidence." And in this case, in fact, Dr. Grossman admitted that their prediction turned out to be wildly inaccurate. Specifically, he provided a new figure (approximately 9,200) that was less than half of his earlier prediction. And he then admitted that he had not proven any causal link between the admitting privileges requirement and that

> smaller decline. (quoting Grossman et al., "Change in Abortion Services After Implementation of a Restrictive Law in Texas," 90 *Contraception* 496, 500 (2014)).

Case Questions

Preface to questions: Apart from the issue whether the Court properly accepted jurisdiction, of which the discussion is omitted here, the basic disagreement between dissenters and majority is over whether the rules of the *Casey* precedent are being followed or silently replaced. Justice Kennedy (who votes with the majority here) at this point is the sole co-author of the pivotal *Casey* plurality opinion remaining on the Court. This plurality opinion had established that while reproductive freedom is a constitutionally protected fundamental right, laws restricting it or burdening it but that rationally relate to protecting potential fetal life, respect for fetal life, pregnant women's health, or other valid governmental interest, *and* that do not impose a substantial obstacle on women's reproductive freedom will be upheld. If they do impose a substantial obstacle pre-viability, they will be adjudged to impose an "undue" or unconstitutional burden on women's protected freedom. On this ground, the *Casey* Court (among other things) had upheld a 24-hour waiting period plus written informed consent, which combination was understood by the majority of *Casey* justices to promote a woman's psychological health by assuring her time to mull over the abortion choice to be certain that it is right for her. Those justices had reasoned that whereas the waiting period might "incidentally" increase the cost of an abortion (by necessitating an overnight stay by women who live far from an abortion-providing facility), it did not place a "substantial obstacle" on the woman's freedom.

Under Texas law current when the Court heard oral argument in *Hellerstedt*, even women obtaining a medical abortion (i.e. one brought about simply through taking pills) had to obtain all of the pills while in the clinic and visit the clinic at least three times. (All these measures at the time were following FDA guidelines.) Prior to the Texas law challenged here, some clinics affected by this law had provided only these medical abortions not surgical ones.

Who has the better argument and why on the following issues about the *Casey* precedent:

1. Is this hospital privileges provision for every abortion clinic rationally related to promoting the health of women seeking an abortion in Texas? Why or why not?

2. Is the imposition of rules for ambulatory surgical centers on all abortion-providing clinics rationally related to promoting women's health? Why or why not?

3. If the answers to the first two questions are "yes," would the extra expenses and extra licensing requirements count as unconstitutionally burdensome if they

caused one entire (otherwise problem-free) abortion-providing clinic to shut down? One third of the abortion-providing clinics? Why or why not?

4. Is Justice Alito being unfair in his charge that the majority's treatment of the application of ASC rules to all abortion-providing clinics or to some of them amounts to "carpet-bomb[ing]" the state law?

On January 31, 2017, newly inaugurated president Donald Trump nominated 49-year-old Judge Neil Gorsuch of the United States Court of Appeals for the Tenth Circuit to replace the deceased Justice Scalia. Gorsuch was confirmed on a 54–45, mostly party-line vote and joined the Court on April 8, 2017.

RELIGIOUS FREEDOM VERSUS REPRODUCTIVE RIGHTS

More recently, the First Amendment's guarantees of free exercise of religion, as contrasted to free speech guarantees, have been implicated in litigation involving women's reproductive rights. In 2010, President Obama signed the Patient Protection and Affordable Care Act (ACA) into law. This legislation did a number of things including imposing certain obligations on health care plans offered by employers. Under the ACA, these group health insurance plans are required to cover the cost of contraceptives approved by the Food and Drug Administration for their female employees. Hobby Lobby, a privately-owned national chain of craft stores, sued on the grounds that providing contraceptive coverage to their female employees violated the religious beliefs of the company's owners. David Green, principal owner of Hobby Lobby, argued that consistent with their religious beliefs any form of contraception that interferes with the implantation of a fertilized egg constitutes an abortion because life begins immediately at conception.

In 2014, in *Burwell v. Hobby Lobby Stores*, 134 S.Ct. 2751, a majority of Supreme Court justices ruled that the Religious Freedom Restoration Act (RFRA)—a 1993 federal law that is intended to protect individuals' religious freedom from government interference—applied to privately-owned for-profit corporations. They then proceeded to evaluate whether or not RFRA enabled Hobby Lobby and other "closely held"—privately owned—companies to opt out of the contraceptive mandate of the ACA because certain types of birth control run counter to the religious beliefs of their owners.

BURWELL V. HOBBY LOBBY STORES
134 S.Ct. 2751 (2014)

JUSTICE ALITO delivered the opinion of the Court.

. . .

Since RFRA [the Religious Freedom Restoration Act] applies in these cases, we must decide whether the challenged [Health and Human Services Department, or] HHS regulations substantially burden the exercise of religion, and we hold that they do. The owners of the businesses have religious objections to abortion, and according to their religious beliefs the four contraceptive methods at issue are abortifacients. If the owners comply with the HHS mandate, they believe they will be facilitating abortions, and if they do not comply, they will pay a very heavy price—as much as $1.3 million per day, or about $475 million per year, in the case of one of the companies. If these consequences do not amount to a substantial burden, it is hard to see what would.

Under RFRA, a Government action that imposes a substantial burden on religious exercise must serve a compelling government interest, and we assume that the HHS regulations satisfy this requirement. But in order for the HHS mandate to be sustained, it must also constitute the least restrictive means of serving that interest, and the mandate plainly fails that test. There are other ways in which Congress or HHS could equally ensure that every woman has cost-free access to the particular contraceptives at issue here and, indeed, to all FDA-approved contraceptives.

In fact, HHS has already devised and implemented a system that seeks to respect the religious liberty of religious nonprofit corporations while ensuring that the employees of these entities have precisely the same access to all FDA-approved contraceptives as employees of companies whose owners have no religious objections to providing such coverage. The employees of these religious nonprofit corporations still have access to insurance coverage without cost sharing for all FDA-approved contraceptives; and according to HHS, this system imposes no net economic burden on the insurance companies that are required to provide or secure the coverage.

Although HHS has made this system available to religious nonprofits that have religious objections to the contraceptive mandate, HHS has provided no reason why the same system cannot be made available when the owners of for-profit corporations have similar religious objections. We therefore conclude that this system constitutes an alternative that achieves all of the Government's aims while providing greater respect for religious liberty. And under RFRA, that conclusion means that enforcement of the HHS contraceptive mandate against the objecting parties in these cases is unlawful.

As this description of our reasoning shows, our holding is very specific. We do not hold, as the principal dissent alleges, that for-profit corporations and other commercial enterprises can "opt out of any law (saving only tax laws) they judge incompatible with their sincerely held religious beliefs." *Post* (opinion of Ginsburg, J.). Nor do we hold, as the dissent implies, that such corporations have free rein to take steps that impose "disadvantages . . . on others" or that require "the general public [to] pick up the tab." *Post*. And we certainly do not hold or suggest that "RFRA demands accommodation of a for-profit corporation's religious beliefs no matter the impact that accommodation may have on . . . thousands of women employed by Hobby Lobby." *Post*. The effect of the HHS-created accommodation on the women employed by Hobby Lobby and the other companies involved in these cases would be precisely zero. Under that accommodation, these women would still be entitled to all FDA-approved contraceptives without cost sharing.

I

. . .

B

At issue in these cases are HHS regulations promulgated under the Patient Protection and Affordable Care Act of 2010 (ACA), 124Stat. 119. ACA generally requires employers with 50 or more full-time employees to offer "a group health plan or group health insurance coverage" that provides "minimum essential coverage." 26 U.S.C. § 5000A(f)(2); §§ 4980H(a), (c)(2). Any covered employer that does not provide such coverage must pay a substantial price. Specifically, if a covered employer provides group health insurance but its plan fails to comply with ACA's group-health-plan requirements, the employer may be required to pay $100 per day for each affected "individual." §§ 4980D(a)–(b). And if the employer decides to stop providing health insurance altogether and at least one full-time employee enrolls in a health plan and qualifies for a subsidy on one of the government-run ACA exchanges, the employer must pay $2,000 per year for each of its full-time employees. §§ 4980H(a), (c)(1).

Unless an exception applies, ACA requires an employer's group health plan or group-health-insurance coverage to furnish "preventive care and screenings" for women without "any cost sharing requirements." 42 U.S.C. § 300gg–13(a)(4). Congress itself, however, did not specify what types of preventive care must be covered. Instead, Congress authorized the Health Resources and Services Administration (HRSA), a component of HHS, to make that important and sensitive decision. *Ibid.* The HRSA in turn consulted the Institute of Medicine, a nonprofit group of volunteer advisers, in determining which preventive services to require. See 77 Fed. Reg. 8725–8726 (2012).

In August 2011, based on the Institute's recommendations, the HRSA promulgated the Women's Preventive Services Guidelines. See *id.*, at 8725–8726, and n. 1. The Guidelines provide that nonexempt employers are generally required to provide "coverage, without cost sharing" for "[a]ll Food and Drug Administration [(FDA)] approved contraceptive methods, sterilization procedures, and patient education and counseling." 77 Fed. Reg. 8725 (internal quotation marks omitted). Although many of the required, FDA-approved methods of contraception work by preventing the fertilization of an egg, four of those methods (those specifically at issue in these cases) may have the effect of preventing an already fertilized egg from developing any further by inhibiting its attachment to the uterus. See Brief for HHS in No. 13–354, pp. 9–10, n. 4, FDA, Birth Control: Medicines to Help You.

HHS also authorized the HRSA to establish exemptions from the contraceptive mandate for "religious employers." 45 CFR § 147.131(a). That category encompasses "churches, their integrated auxiliaries, and conventions or associations of churches," as well as "the exclusively religious activities of any religious order." See *ibid* (citing 26 U.S.C. §§ 6033(a)(3)(A)(i), (iii)). In its Guidelines, HRSA exempted these organizations from the requirement to cover contraceptive services.

In addition, HHS has effectively exempted certain religious nonprofit organizations, described under HHS regulations as "eligible organizations," from the contraceptive mandate. See 45 CFR § 147.131(b); 78 Fed. Reg. 39874 (2013). An "eligible organization" means a nonprofit organization that "holds itself out as a religious organization" and "opposes providing coverage for some or all of any contraceptive services required to be covered . . . on account of religious objections." 45 CFR § 147.131(b). To qualify for this accommodation, an employer must certify that it is such an organization. § 147.131(b)(4). When a group-health-insurance issuer receives notice that one of its clients has invoked this provision, the issuer must then exclude contraceptive coverage from the employer's plan and provide separate payments for contraceptive services for plan participants without imposing any cost-sharing requirements on the eligible organization, its insurance plan, or its employee beneficiaries. § 147.131(c).[8] Although this procedure requires the issuer to bear the cost of these services, HHS has determined that this obligation will not impose any net expense on issuers because its cost will be less than or equal to the cost savings resulting from the services. 78 Fed. Reg. 39877.[9]

. . .

II

A

Norman and Elizabeth Hahn and their three sons are devout members of the Mennonite Church, a Christian denomination. The Mennonite Church opposes abortion and believes that "[t]he fetus in its earliest stages . . . shares humanity with those who conceived it."

Fifty years ago, Norman Hahn started a wood-working business in his garage, and since then, this company, Conestoga Wood Specialties, has grown and now has 950 employees. Conestoga is organized under Pennsylvania law as a for-profit corporation. The Hahns exercise sole ownership of the closely held business; they control its board of directors and hold all of its voting shares. One of the Hahn sons serves as the president and CEO.

The Hahns believe that they are required to run their business "in accordance with their religious beliefs and moral principles." 917 F. Supp. 2d 394, 402 (ED Pa. 2013). To that end, the company's mission, as they see it, is to "operate in a professional environment founded upon the highest ethical, moral, and Christian principles." *Ibid.*(internal quotation marks omitted). The company's "Vision and Values Statements" affirms that Conestoga endeavors to "ensur[e] a reasonable profit in [a] manner that reflects [the Hahns'] Christian heritage." App.

As explained in Conestoga's board-adopted "Statement on the Sanctity of Human Life," the Hahns believe that "human life begins at conception." 724 F. 3d 377, 382, and n. 5 (CA3 2013) (internal quotation marks omitted). It is therefore "against [their] moral conviction to be involved in the termination of human life" after conception, which they believe is a "sin against God to which they are held accountable." *Ibid.* (internal quotation marks omitted). The Hahns have accordingly excluded from the group-health-insurance plan they offer to their employees certain contraceptive methods that they consider to be abortifacients. *Id.*, at 382.

The Hahns and Conestoga sued HHS and other federal officials and agencies under RFRA and the Free Exercise Clause of the First Amendment, seeking to enjoin application of ACA's contraceptive mandate insofar as it requires them to provide health-insurance coverage for four FDA-approved contraceptives that may operate after the fertilization of an egg. These include two forms of emergency contraception commonly called "morning after" pills and two types of intrauterine devices.

In opposing the requirement to provide coverage for the contraceptives to which they object, the Hahns argued that "it is immoral and sinful for [them] to intentionally participate in, pay for, facilitate, or otherwise support these drugs." *Ibid.* The District Court denied a preliminary injunction, see 917 F. Supp. 2d, at 419, and the Third Circuit affirmed in a divided opinion, holding that "for-profit, secular corporations cannot engage in religious exercise" within the meaning of RFRA or the First Amendment. 724 F. 3d, at 381. The Third Circuit also rejected the claims brought by the Hahns themselves because it concluded that the HHS "[m]andate does not impose any requirements on the Hahns" in their personal capacity. *Id.*, at 389.

B

David and Barbara Green and their three children are Christians who own and operate two family businesses. Forty-five years ago, David Green started an arts-and-crafts store that has grown into a nationwide chain called Hobby Lobby. There are now 500 Hobby Lobby stores, and the company has more than 13,000 employees. 723 F. 3d, at 1122. Hobby Lobby is organized as a for-profit corporation under Oklahoma law.

One of David's sons started an affiliated business, Mardel, which operates 35 Christian bookstores and employs close to 400 people. *Ibid.* Mardel is also organized as a for-profit corporation under Oklahoma law.

Though these two businesses have expanded over the years, they remain closely held, and David, Barbara, and their children retain exclusive control of both companies. *Ibid.* David serves as the CEO of Hobby Lobby, and his three children serve as the president, vice president, and vice CEO. See Brief for Respondents.

Hobby Lobby's statement of purpose commits the Greens to "[h]onoring the Lord in all [they] do by operating the company in a manner consistent with Biblical principles." App. Each family member has signed a pledge to run the businesses in accordance with the family's religious beliefs and to use the family assets to support Christian ministries. 723 F. 3d, at 1122. In accordance with those commitments, Hobby Lobby and Mardel stores close on Sundays, even though the Greens calculate that they lose millions in sales annually by doing so. *Id.*, at 1122; App. The businesses refuse to engage in profitable transactions that facilitate or promote alcohol use; they contribute profits to Christian missionaries and ministries; and they buy hundreds of full-page newspaper ads inviting people to "know Jesus as Lord and Savior." *Ibid.*

Like the Hahns, the Greens believe that life begins at conception and that it would violate their religion to facilitate access to contraceptive drugs or devices that operate after that point. 723 F. 3d, at 1122. They specifically object to the same four contraceptive methods as the Hahns and, like the Hahns, they have no objection to the other 16 FDA-approved methods of birth control. *Id.*, at 1125. Although their group-health-insurance plan predates the enactment of ACA, it is not a grandfathered plan because Hobby Lobby elected not to retain grandfathered status before the contraceptive mandate was proposed. *Id.*, at 1124.

The Greens, Hobby Lobby, and Mardel sued HHS and other federal agencies and officials to challenge the contraceptive mandate under RFRA and the Free Exercise Clause. The District Court denied a preliminary injunction, see 870 F. Supp. 2d 1278 (WD Okla. 2012), and the plaintiffs appealed, moving for initial en banc consideration. The Tenth Circuit granted that motion and reversed in a divided opinion. Contrary to the conclusion of the Third Circuit, the Tenth Circuit held that the Greens' two for-profit businesses are "persons" within the meaning of RFRA and therefore may bring suit under that law.

The court then held that the corporations had established a likelihood of success on their RFRA claim. 723 F. 3d, at 1140–1147. The court concluded that the contraceptive mandate substantially burdened the exercise of religion by requiring the companies to choose between "compromis[ing] their religious beliefs" and paying a heavy fee—either "close to $475 million more in taxes every year" if they simply refused to provide coverage for the contraceptives at issue, or "roughly $26 million" annually if they "drop[ped] health-insurance benefits for all employees." *Id.*, at 1141.

The court next held that HHS had failed to demonstrate a compelling interest in enforcing the mandate against the Greens' businesses and, in the alternative, that HHS had failed to prove that enforcement of the mandate was the "least restrictive means" of furthering the Government's asserted interests. *Id.*, at 1143–1144 (emphasis deleted...) After concluding that the companies had "demonstrated irreparable harm," the court reversed and remanded for the District Court to consider the remaining factors of the preliminary-injunction test. *Id.*, at 1147.

We granted certiorari.

III

. . .

2

The principal argument advanced by HHS and the principal dissent regarding RFRA protection for Hobby Lobby, Conestoga, and Mardel focuses not on the statutory term "person," but on the phrase "exercise of religion." According to HHS and the dissent, these corporations are not protected by RFRA because they cannot exercise religion. Neither HHS nor the dissent, however, provides any persuasive explanation for this conclusion.

IV

Because RFRA applies in these cases, we must next ask whether the HHS contraceptive mandate "substantially burden[s]" the exercise of religion. 42 U.S.C. § 2000bb–1(a). We have little trouble concluding that it does.

A

As we have noted, the Hahns and Greens have a sincere religious belief that life begins at conception. They therefore object on religious grounds to providing health insurance that covers methods of birth control that, as HHS acknowledges, see Brief, may result in the destruction of an embryo. By requiring the Hahns and Greens and their companies to arrange for such coverage, the HHS mandate demands that they engage in conduct that seriously violates their religious beliefs.

If the Hahns and Greens and their companies do not yield to this demand, the economic consequences will be severe. If the companies continue to offer group health plans that do not cover the contraceptives at issue, they will be taxed $100 per day for each affected individual. 26 U.S.C. § 4980D. For Hobby Lobby, the bill could amount to $1.3 million per day or about $475 million per year; for Conestoga, the assessment could be $90,000 per day or $33 million per year; and for Mardel, it could be $40,000 per day or about $15 million per year. These sums are surely substantial.

It is true that the plaintiffs could avoid these assessments by dropping insurance coverage altogether and thus forcing their employees to obtain health insurance on one of the exchanges established under ACA. But if at least one of their full-time employees were to qualify for a subsidy on one of the government-run exchanges, this course would also entail substantial economic consequences. The companies could face penalties of $2,000 per employee each year. § 4980H. These penalties would amount to roughly $26 million for Hobby Lobby, $1.8 million for Conestoga, and $800,000 for Mardel.

. . .

C

In taking the position that the HHS mandate does not impose a substantial burden on the exercise of religion, HHS's main argument (echoed by the principal dissent) is basically that the connection between what the objecting parties must do (provide health-insurance coverage for four methods of contraception that may operate after the fertilization of an egg) and the end that they find to be morally wrong (destruction of an embryo) is simply too attenuated. Brief for HHS; *post*. HHS and the dissent note that providing the coverage would not itself result in the destruction of an embryo; that would occur only if an employee chose to take advantage of the coverage and to use one of the four methods at issue. *Ibid*.

This argument dodges the question that RFRA presents (whether the HHS mandate imposes a substantial burden on the ability of the objecting parties to conduct business in accordance with *their religious beliefs*) and instead addresses a very different question that the federal courts have no business addressing (whether the religious belief asserted in a RFRA case is reasonable). The Hahns and Greens believe that providing the coverage demanded by the HHS regulations is connected to the destruction of an embryo in a way that is sufficient to make it immoral for them to provide the coverage. . . . Arrogating the authority to provide a binding national answer to this religious and philosophical question, HHS and the principal dissent in effect tell the plaintiffs that their beliefs are flawed. For good reason, we have repeatedly refused to take such a step. See, *e.g.*, *Smith*, 494 U.S., at 887 ("Repeatedly and in many different contexts, we have warned that courts must not presume to determine . . . the plausibility of a religious claim"); *Hernandez* v. *Commissioner*, 490 U.S. 680, 699 (1989); *Presbyterian Church in U.S.* v. *Mary Elizabeth Blue Hull Memorial Presbyterian Church*, 393 U.S. 440, 450 (1969).

. . .

Similarly, in these cases, the Hahns and Greens and their companies sincerely believe that providing the insurance coverage demanded by the HHS regulations lies on the forbidden side of the line, and it is not for us to say that their religious beliefs are mistaken or insubstantial. Instead, our "narrow function . . . in this context is to determine" whether the line drawn reflects "an honest conviction," *id.*, at 716, and there is no dispute that it does.

. . .

V

Since the HHS contraceptive mandate imposes a substantial burden on the exercise of religion, we must move on and decide whether HHS has shown that the mandate both "(1) is in furtherance of a compelling governmental interest; and (2) is the least restrictive means of furthering that compelling governmental interest." 42 U.S.C. § 2000bb–1(b).

A

. . .

. . . We will assume that the interest in guaranteeing cost-free access to the four challenged contraceptive methods is compelling within the meaning of RFRA, and we will proceed to consider the final prong of the RFRA test, *i.e.*, whether HHS has shown that the contraceptive mandate is "the least restrictive means of furthering that compelling governmental interest." § 2000bb–1(b)(2).

B

The least-restrictive-means standard is exceptionally demanding, see *City of Boerne*, 521 U.S., at 532, and it is not satisfied here. HHS has not shown that it lacks other means of achieving its desired goal without imposing a substantial burden on the exercise of religion by the objecting parties in these cases. See §§ 2000bb–1(a), (b) (requiring the Government to "demonstrat[e] that application of [a substantial] burden to *the person* . . . is the least restrictive means of furthering [a] compelling governmental interest" (emphasis added)).

. . . HHS itself has demonstrated that it has at its disposal an approach that is less restrictive than requiring employers to fund contraceptive methods that violate their religious beliefs. As we explained above, HHS has already established an accommodation for nonprofit organizations with religious objections. See *supra* and nn. 8–9. Under that accommodation, the organization can self-certify that it opposes providing coverage for particular contraceptive services. See 45 CFR §§ 147.131(b)(4), (c)(1); 26 CFR §§ 54.9815–2713A(a)(4), (b). If the organization makes such a certification, the organization's insurance issuer or third-party administrator must "[e]xpressly exclude contraceptive coverage from the group health insurance coverage provided in connection with the group health plan" and "[p]rovide separate payments for any contraceptive services required to be covered" without imposing "any cost-sharing requirements . . . on the eligible organization, the group health plan, or plan participants or beneficiaries." 45 CFR § 147.131(c)(2); 26 CFR § 54.9815–2713A(c)(2).

We do not decide today whether an approach of this type complies with RFRA for purposes of all religious claims. At a minimum, however, it does not impinge on the plaintiffs' religious belief that providing insurance coverage for the contraceptives at issue here violates their religion, and it serves HHS's stated interests equally well.

The principal dissent identifies no reason why this accommodation would fail to protect the asserted needs of women as effectively as the contraceptive mandate, and there is none. Under the accommodation, the plaintiffs' female employees would continue to receive contraceptive coverage without cost sharing for all FDA-approved contraceptives, and they would continue to "face minimal logistical and administrative obstacles," *post*, because their employers' insurers would be responsible for providing information and coverage, see, *e.g.*, 45 CFR §§ 147.131(c)–(d); cf. 26 CFR §§ 54.9815–2713A(b), (d). Ironically, it is the dissent's approach that would "[i]mped[e] women's receipt of benefits by 'requiring them to take steps to learn about, and to sign up for, a new government funded and administered health benefit,'" *post*, because the dissent would effectively compel religious employers to drop health-insurance coverage altogether, leaving their employees to find individual plans on government-run exchanges or elsewhere. This is indeed "scarcely what Congress contemplated." *Ibid.*

C

HHS and the principal dissent argue that a ruling in favor of the objecting parties in these cases will lead to a flood of religious objections regarding a wide variety of medical procedures and drugs, such as vaccinations and blood transfusions, but HHS has made no effort to substantiate this prediction. HHS points to no evidence that insurance plans in existence prior to the enactment of ACA excluded coverage for such items. Nor has HHS provided evidence that any significant number of employers sought exemption, on religious grounds, from any of ACA's coverage requirements other than the contraceptive mandate. . . .

* * *

The contraceptive mandate, as applied to closely held corporations, violates RFRA. Our decision on that statutory question makes it unnecessary to reach the First Amendment claim raised by Conestoga and the Hahns.

The judgment of the Tenth Circuit in No. 13-354 is affirmed; the judgment of the Third Circuit in No. 13-356 is reversed, and that case is remanded for further proceedings consistent with this opinion.

It is so ordered.

Opinion Footnotes

8 In the case of self-insured religious organizations entitled to the accommodation, the third-party administrator of the organization must "provide or arrange payments for contraceptive services" for the organization's employees without imposing any cost-sharing requirements on the eligible organization, its insurance plan, or its employee beneficiaries. 78 Fed. Reg. 39893 (to be codified in 26 CFR § 54.9815–2713A(b)(2)). The regulations establish a mechanism for these third-party administrators to be compensated for their expenses by obtaining a reduction in the fee paid by insurers to participate in the federally facilitated exchanges. See 78 Fed. Reg. 39893 (to be codified in 26 CFR § 54.9815–2713A (b)(3)). HHS believes that these fee reductions will not materially affect funding of the exchanges because "payments for contraceptive services will represent only a small portion of total [exchange] user fees." 78 Fed. Reg. 39882.

9 In a separate challenge to this framework for religious nonprofit organizations, the Court recently ordered that, pending appeal, the eligible organizations be permitted to opt out of the contraceptive mandate by providing written notification of their objections to the Secretary of HHS, rather than to their insurance issuers or third-party administrators. See *Little Sisters of the Poor* v. *Sebelius*, 571 U.S. ___ (2014).

JUSTICE KENNEDY concurring.

It seems to me appropriate, in joining the Court's opinion, to add these few remarks. At the outset it should be said that the Court's opinion does not have the breadth and sweep ascribed to it by the respectful and powerful dissent. The Court and the dissent disagree on the proper interpretation of the Religious Freedom and Restoration Act of 1993 (RFRA), but do agree on the purpose of that statute. It is to ensure that interests in religious freedom are protected.

In our constitutional tradition, freedom means that all persons have the right to believe or strive to believe in a divine creator and a divine law. For those who choose this course, free exercise is essential in preserving their own dignity and in striving for a self-definition shaped by their religious precepts. . . .

JUSTICE GINSBURG, with whom JUSTICE SOTOMAYOR joins, and with whom JUSTICE BREYER and JUSTICE KAGAN join as to all but Part III-C-1, dissenting.

. . .

I

"The ability of women to participate equally in the economic and social life of the Nation has been facilitated by their ability to control their reproductive lives." *Planned Parenthood of Southeastern Pa.* v. *Casey*, 505 U.S. 833, 856 (1992). Congress acted on that understanding when, as part of a nationwide insurance program intended to be comprehensive, it called for coverage of preventive care responsive to women's needs. Carrying out Congress' direction, the Department of Health and Human Services (HHS), in consultation with public health experts, promulgated regulations requiring group health plans to cover all forms of contraception approved by the Food and Drug Administration (FDA). The genesis of this coverage should enlighten the Court's resolution of these cases.

A

The Affordable Care Act (ACA), in its initial form, specified three categories of preventive care that health plans must cover at no added cost to the plan participant or beneficiary. Particular services were to be recommended by the U.S. Preventive Services Task Force, an independent panel of experts. The scheme had a large gap, however; it left out preventive services that "many women's health advocates and medical professionals believe are critically important." 155 Cong. Rec. 28841 (2009) (statement of Sen. Boxer). To correct this oversight, Senator Barbara Mikulski introduced the Women's Health Amendment, which added to the ACA's minimum coverage requirements a new category of preventive services specific to women's health.

. . .

As altered by the Women's Health Amendment's passage, the ACA requires new insurance plans to include coverage without cost sharing of "such additional preventive care and screenings . . . as provided for in comprehensive guidelines supported by the Health Resources and Services Administration [(HRSA)]," a unit of HHS. 42 U.S.C. § 300gg–13(a)(4). Thus charged, the HRSA developed recommendations in consultation with the Institute of Medicine (IOM). See 77 Fed. Reg. 8725–8726 (2012). The IOM convened a group of independent experts, including "specialists in disease prevention [and] women's health"; those experts prepared a report evaluating the efficacy of a number of preventive services. IOM, *Clinical Prevention Services for Women: Closing the Gaps* 2 (2011) (hereinafter IOM Report). Consistent with the findings of "[n]umerous health professional associations" and other organizations, the IOM experts determined that preventive coverage should include the "full range" of FDA-approved contraceptive methods. *Id.,* at 10. See also *id.,* at 102–110.

In making that recommendation, the IOM's report expressed concerns similar to those voiced by congressional proponents of the Women's Health Amendment. The report noted the disproportionate burden women carried for comprehensive health services and the adverse health consequences of excluding contraception from preventive care available to employees without cost sharing. See, *e.g., id.,* at 19 ("[W]omen are consistently more likely than men to report a wide range of cost-related barriers to receiving . . . medical tests and treatments and to filling prescriptions for themselves and their families."); *id.,* at 103–104, 107 (pregnancy may be contraindicated for women with certain medical conditions, for example, some congenital heart diseases, pulmonary hypertension, and Marfan syndrome, and contraceptives may be used to reduce risk of endometrial cancer, among other serious medical conditions); *id.,* at 103 (women with unintended pregnancies are more likely to experience depression and anxiety, and their children face "increased odds of preterm birth and low birth weight").

In line with the IOM's suggestions, the HRSA adopted guidelines recommending coverage of "[a]ll [FDA-]approved contraceptive methods, sterilization procedures, and patient education and counseling for all women with reproductive capacity." Thereafter, HHS, the Department of Labor, and the Department of Treasury promulgated regulations requiring group health plans to include coverage of the contraceptive services recommended in the HRSA guidelines, subject to certain exceptions, described *infra*. This opinion refers to these regulations as the contraceptive coverage requirement.

. . .

II

. . .

The exemption sought by Hobby Lobby and Conestoga would override significant interests of the corporations' employees and covered dependents. It would deny legions of women who do not hold their employers' beliefs access to contraceptive coverage that the ACA would otherwise secure. See *Catholic Charities of Sacramento, Inc.* v. *Superior Court,* 32 Cal. 4th 527, 565, 85 P. 3d 67, 93

(2004) ("We are unaware of any decision in which . . . [the U.S. Supreme Court] has exempted a religious objector from the operation of a neutral, generally applicable law despite the recognition that the requested exemption would detrimentally affect the rights of third parties."). In sum, with respect to free exercise claims no less than free speech claims, " '[y]our right to swing your arms ends just where the other man's nose begins.' " Chafee, "Freedom of Speech in War Time," 32 *Harv. L. Rev.* 932, 957 (1919).

III

. . .

C . . . 1

. . .

Until this litigation, no decision of this Court recognized a for-profit corporation's qualification for a religious exemption from a generally applicable law, whether under the Free Exercise Clause or RFRA. . . .

. . .

The reason why is hardly obscure. Religious organizations exist to foster the interests of persons subscribing to the same religious faith. Not so of for-profit corporations. Workers who sustain the operations of those corporations commonly are not drawn from one religious community. Indeed, by law, no religion-based criterion can restrict the work force of for-profit corporations. See 42 U.S.C. §§ 2000e(b), 2000e–1(a), 2000e–2(a); cf. *Trans World Airlines, Inc.* v. *Hardison*, 432 U.S. 63–81 (1977) (Title VII requires reasonable accommodation of an employee's religious exercise, but such accommodation must not come "at the expense of other [employees]"). The distinction between a community made up of believers in the same religion and one embracing persons of diverse beliefs, clear as it is, constantly escapes the Court's attention. One can only wonder why the Court shuts this key difference from sight.

. . .

The Court's determination that RFRA extends to for-profit corporations is bound to have untoward effects. Although the Court attempts to cabin its language to closely held corporations, its logic extends to corporations of any size, public or private. Little doubt that RFRA claims will proliferate, for the Court's expansive notion of corporate personhood—combined with its other errors in construing RFRA—invites for-profit entities to seek religion-based exemptions from regulations they deem offensive to their faith.

2

. . .

The Court barely pauses to inquire whether any burden imposed by the contraceptive coverage requirement is substantial. Instead, it rests on the Greens' and Hahns' "belie[f] that providing the coverage demanded by the HHS regulations is connected to the destruction of an embryo in a way that is sufficient to make it immoral for them to provide the coverage." *Ante.* I agree with the Court that the Green and Hahn families' religious convictions regarding contraception are sincerely held. See *Thomas*, 450 U.S., at 715 (courts are not to question where an individual "dr[aws] the line" in defining which practices run afoul of her religious beliefs). See also 42 U.S.C. §§ 2000bb–1(a), 2000bb–2(4), 2000cc–5(7)(A). But those beliefs, however deeply held, do not suffice to sustain a RFRA claim. RFRA, properly understood, distinguishes between "factual allegations that [plaintiffs'] beliefs are sincere and of a religious nature," which a court must accept as true, and the "legal conclusion . . . that [plaintiffs'] religious exercise is substantially burdened," an inquiry the court must undertake. *Kaemmerling* v. *Lappin*, 553 F. 3d 669, 679 (CADC 2008).

. . .

Undertaking the inquiry that the Court forgoes, I would conclude that the connection between the families' religious objections and the contraceptive coverage requirement is too attenuated to rank as substantial. The requirement carries no command that Hobby Lobby or Conestoga purchase or provide the contraceptives they find objectionable. Instead, it calls on the companies covered by the requirement to direct money into undifferentiated funds that finance a wide variety of benefits under comprehensive health plans. Those plans, in order to comply with the ACA, see *supra*, must offer contraceptive coverage without cost sharing, just as they must cover an array of other preventive services.

Importantly, the decisions whether to claim benefits under the plans are made not by Hobby Lobby or Conestoga, but by the covered employees and dependents, in consultation with their health care providers. Should an employee of Hobby Lobby or Conestoga share the religious beliefs of the Greens and Hahns, she is of course under no compulsion to use the contraceptives in question. But "[n]o individual decision by an employee and her physician—be it to use contraception, treat an infection, or have a hip replaced—is in any meaningful sense [her employer's] decision or action." *Grote* v. *Sebelius*, 708 F. 3d 850, 865 (CA7 2013) (Rovner, J., dissenting). It is doubtful that Congress, when it specified that burdens must be "substantia[l]," had in mind a linkage thus interrupted by independent decisionmakers (the woman and her health counselor) standing between the challenged government action and the religious exercise claimed to be infringed. Any decision to use contraceptives made by a woman covered under Hobby Lobby's or Conestoga's plan will not be propelled by the Government, it will be the woman's autonomous choice, informed by the physician she consults.

3

Even if one were to conclude that Hobby Lobby and Conestoga meet the substantial burden requirement, the Government has shown that the contraceptive coverage for which the ACA provides furthers compelling interests in public health and women's well being. Those interests are concrete, specific, and demonstrated by a wealth of empirical evidence. To recapitulate, the mandated contraception coverage enables women to avoid the health problems unintended pregnancies may visit on them and their children. See IOM Report 102–107. The coverage helps safeguard the health of women for whom pregnancy may be hazardous, even life threatening. See Brief for American College of Obstetricians and Gynecologists et al. as *Amici Curiae*. And the mandate secures benefits wholly unrelated to pregnancy, preventing certain cancers, menstrual disorders, and pelvic pain. Brief for Ovarian Cancer National Alliance et al. as *Amici Curiae*; 78 Fed. Reg. 39872 (2013); IOM Report 107.

That Hobby Lobby and Conestoga resist coverage for only 4 of the 20 FDA-approved contraceptives does not lessen these compelling interests. Notably, the corporations exclude intrauterine devices (IUDs), devices significantly more effective, and significantly more expensive than other contraceptive methods. See *id.,* at 105.[22] Moreover, the Court's reasoning appears to permit commercial enterprises like Hobby Lobby and Conestoga to exclude from their group health plans all forms of contraceptives. (Counsel for Hobby Lobby acknowledged that his "argument . . . would apply just as well if the employer said 'no contraceptives' ").

Perhaps the gravity of the interests at stake has led the Court to assume, for purposes of its RFRA analysis, that the compelling interest criterion is met in these cases. See *ante*. It bears note in this regard that the cost of an IUD is nearly equivalent to a month's full-time pay for workers earning the minimum wage, Brief for Guttmacher Institute et al. as *Amici Curiae*; that almost one-third of women would change their contraceptive method if costs were not a factor, Frost & Darroch, *Factors Associated With Contraceptive Choice and Inconsistent Method*

Use, United States, 2004, 40 Perspectives on Sexual & Reproductive Health 94, 98 (2008); and that only one-fourth of women who request an IUD actually have one inserted after finding out how expensive it would be, Gariepy et al., "The Impact of Out-of-Pocket Expense on IUD Utilization Among Women With Private Insurance," 84 Contraception e39, e40 (2011)...

. . .

The Court ultimately acknowledges a critical point: RFRA's application "*must* take adequate account of the burdens a requested accommodation may impose on nonbeneficiaries." *Ante* (quoting *Cutter* v.*Wilkinson*, 544 U.S. 709, 720 (2005); emphasis added). No tradition, and no prior decision under RFRA, allows a religion-based exemption when the accommodation would be harmful to others—here, the very persons the contraceptive coverage requirement was designed to protect. Cf. *supra,* at 7–8; *Prince* v. *Massachusetts*, 321 U.S. 158, 177 (1944) (Jackson, J., dissenting) ("[The] limitations which of necessity bound religious freedom . . . begin to operate whenever activities begin to affect or collide with liberties of others or of the public.").

4

After assuming the existence of compelling government interests, the Court holds that the contraceptive coverage requirement fails to satisfy RFRA's least restrictive means test. But the Government has shown that there is no less restrictive, equally effective means that would both (1) satisfy the challengers' religious objections to providing insurance coverage for certain contraceptives (which they believe cause abortions); and (2) carry out the objective of the ACA's contraceptive coverage requirement, to ensure that women employees receive, at no cost to them, the preventive care needed to safeguard their health and well being. A "least restrictive means" cannot require employees to relinquish benefits accorded them by federal law in order to ensure that their commercial employers can adhere unreservedly to their religious tenets. See *supra*.

. . .[Considering that the religious corporate owners do pay taxes, one could ask,] Does it rank as a less restrictive alternative to require the government to provide the money or benefit to which the employer has a religion-based objection? Because the Court cannot easily answer that question, it proposes something else: Extension to commercial enterprises of the accommodation already afforded to nonprofit religion-based organizations. . . . I have already discussed the "special solicitude" generally accorded nonprofit religion-based organizations that exist to serve a community of believers, solicitude never before accorded to commercial enterprises comprising employees of diverse faiths. See *supra*.

. . .

IV

. . .

No doubt the Greens and Hahns and all who share their beliefs may decline to acquire for themselves the contraceptives in question. But that choice may not be imposed on employees who hold other beliefs. Working for Hobby Lobby or Conestoga, in other words, should not deprive employees of the preventive care available to workers at the shop next door, at least in the absence of directions from the Legislature or Administration to do so.

. . .

Would the exemption the Court holds RFRA demands for employers with religiously grounded objections to the use of certain contraceptives extend to employers with religiously grounded objections to blood transfusions (Jehovah's Witnesses); antidepressants (Scientologists); medications derived from pigs, including anesthesia, intravenous fluids, and pills coated with gelatin (certain Muslims, Jews, and Hindus); and vaccinations (Christian Scientists, among others)? According to counsel for Hobby Lobby, "each one of these cases . . . would have to be evaluated on its own . . . apply[ing] the compelling interest-least restrictive alternative test." Not much help there for the lower courts bound by today's decision.

The Court, however, sees nothing to worry about. Today's cases, the Court concludes, are "concerned solely with the contraceptive mandate. Our decision should not be understood to hold that an insurance-coverage mandate must necessarily fall if it conflicts with an employer's religious beliefs. Other coverage requirements, such as immunizations, may be supported by different interests (for example, the need to combat the spread of infectious diseases) and may involve different arguments about the least restrictive means of providing them." *Ante*. But the Court has assumed, for RFRA purposes, that the interest in women's health and well being is compelling and has come up with no means adequate to serve that interest, the one motivating Congress to adopt the Women's Health Amendment.

There is an overriding interest, I believe, in keeping the courts "out of the business of evaluating the relative merits of differing religious claims," *Lee*, 455 U.S., at 263, n. 2 (Stevens, J., concurring in judgment), or the sincerity with which an asserted religious belief is held. Indeed, approving some religious claims while deeming others unworthy of accommodation could be "perceived as favoring one religion over another," the very "risk the Establishment Clause was designed to preclude." *Ibid.* The Court, I fear, has ventured into a minefield, cf. *Spencer* v. *World Vision, Inc.*, 633 F. 3d 723, 730 (CA9 2010) (O'Scannlain, J., concurring), by its immoderate reading of RFRA. I would confine religious exemptions under that Act to organizations formed "for a religious purpose," "engage[d] primarily in carrying out that religious purpose," and not "engaged . . . substantially in the exchange of goods or services for money beyond nominal amounts." See *id.*, at 748 (Kleinfeld, J., concurring).

* * *

For the reasons stated, I would reverse the judgment of the Court of Appeals for the Tenth Circuit and affirm the judgment of the Court of Appeals for the Third Circuit.

Opinion Footnote

22 IUDs, which are among the most reliable forms of contraception, generally cost women more than $1,000 when the expenses of the office visit and insertion procedure are taken into account. See Eisenberg, McNicholas, & Peipert, Cost as a Barrier to Long-Acting Reversible Contraceptive (LARC) Use in Adolescents, 52 J. Adolescent Health S59, S60 (2013). See also Winner et al., Effectiveness of Long-Acting Reversible Contraception, 366 New Eng. J. Medicine 1998, 1999 (2012).

JUSTICE BREYER and JUSTICE KAGAN, dissenting.

We agree with Justice Ginsburg that the plaintiffs' challenge to the contraceptive coverage requirement fails on the merits. We need not and do not decide whether either for-profit corporations or their owners may bring claims under the Religious Freedom Restoration Act of 1993. Accordingly, we join all but Part III-C-1 of Justice Ginsburg's dissenting opinion.

Case Questions

1. Should RFRA be amended to say that its references to legislation that burdens religious freedom applies to the religious freedom of human beings rather than corporate entities? To human beings plus corporations that are closely held and employ no more than fifty people?

2. One of the facts noted in the Ginsburg dissent is that, wholly apart from the risk of death posed by childbirth, pregnancy itself can pose a grave, even lethal, threat to women with certain medical conditions. How should this fact affect the reasoning in this case, if at all?

3. The core dispute between the majority and the dissent is over the degree of attenuation between the religious corporation-owners and the actual support for implantation-preventing drugs or devices. Under the ACA the owners had to pay an insurance company that would provide comprehensive benefit options. Whether any particular employees then purchased an abortifacient under the plan would not be known to the employer. The Court majority says that what matters is not the dissenters' views on how attenuated this connection is, but rather whether the objector's religious belief against participating with this degree of connection to abortion is sincere. Suppose that these companies' owners had claimed that even the degree of separation provided to anti-abortion churches-as-employers by the ACA was too much connection; suppose they wanted to be able to buy insurance from a company that provided these specific benefits to no one (such that none of their employees could then obtain employer-provided health insurance for specific contraceptives for which they might have a health-based need). Does the majority's logic mean under this hypothetical that the U.S. government would have to approve health insurance plans that denied some contraception coverage? Would this then deny the women employees of those companies equal protection of the laws?

4. RFRA applies to federal laws, but many states have their own RFRA laws. If such a state law did not provide a tax-law-exception, could a childless Muslim couple legitimately refuse to pay property taxes on the grounds that these taxes support public schools which require attendance on Fridays, the Muslim Sabbath? How does their situation differ, if at all, from that of the owners of *Hobby Lobby*?

Soon after the *Hobby Lobby* decision, HHS announced that it would begin to provide contraception for free to employees of closely-held for-profit corporations that had religious objections to such coverage, just as the Court majority had proposed could be done.[142] The Supreme Court was forced to revisit many of the issues left unresolved by the Hobby Lobby case two years later in *Zubik v. Burwell*, 136 S.Ct. 1557 (2016). This case involved religious non-profits seeking an exemption from the ACA's contraceptive mandate on the grounds that the government's "work around" solution—structured so that the insurance companies and not the non-profits paid for contraceptive coverage—still implicated religious groups in the commission of sinful behavior that runs counter to their religious beliefs. The eight-person Supreme Court issued a per curiam opinion, and remanded the seven consolidated cases back to the circuit courts to consider alternative mechanisms that would accommodate both the religious beliefs of the non-profit organizations and the women's full and equal access to health care coverage.

In 2017, the Trump Administration took action to expand the religious exemption to the ACA. The Department of Health and Human Services issued rules allowing an employer to opt out of the birth control mandate if they wish to do so on the basis of sincere moral or religious beliefs.[143] The rules took effect immediately and would limit female employees' abilities to procure birth control via employer insurance plans. The attorneys general of Massachusetts and California initiated litigation challenging the Trump Administration rules as violations of the First Amendment's prohibitions on government establishment of religion and the Fourteenth Amendment's equal protection guarantees, and additional states quickly joined the lawsuits.[144] In December 2017, two U.S. district courts filed preliminary injunctions halting the implementation of the new rules.[145] The Trump Administration appealed and litigation is ongoing as this book goes to press.

PREGNANT WOMEN'S PRIVACY

Coerced Caesareans: *In re A.C.* (1990)

The right to privacy has applications beyond the contexts of abortion and contraception, and one of its dimensions is the right to bodily integrity. This right has not always prevailed in cases where it competed with other interests. For instance, early in the twentieth century the Supreme Court upheld the power of the state to compel even unwilling persons to get a smallpox vaccination.[146] In that case the interest in protecting public health outweighed the right of bodily integrity. But typically the right is respected; persons with religious objections to direly needed medicine or surgery are not forced to accept either, despite the general public policy against suicide.

In a parallel way, the right of parental control combines with the child's right of bodily integrity to require in normal circumstances parental consent for a medically needed intrusion on the body of a child. On the other hand, the state does intervene (against the fundamental right of parental control) to protect children who need things like surgery or a blood transfusion when the parents, who normally have to give consent, object to such life-saving measures on religious grounds. This exception is founded on the societal obligation to protect the welfare of children.

The principles from these two lines of cases can come into conflict on the site of the body of a (willingly) pregnant woman when her fetus needs some medical intervention to which the mother is opposed. In certain prominent cases, appellate courts have ordered life-saving blood transfusions for a fetus against the wishes of a pregnant woman.[147] The question of a coerced caesarean delivery greatly intensifies this conflict. The woman's right to bodily integrity would seem to preclude the government's coercing her to permit the massive intrusion of caesarean surgery. On the other hand, the state's policy to protect children against abusive or destructive decisions of their parents would seem to call for protection of a near-term, viable fetus, especially in cases where the parents did not opt for abortion and fully intend for the child to be born.

A case presenting a dramatic clash of these principles was decided by the D.C. Court of Appeals (similar to a state court of appeals, but situated in the District of Columbia) in 1990. Even though the reach of the decision as a binding precedent was quite tiny geographically, the issues in the case were so compelling that several national-level interest groups participated in writing briefs, including the AMA, the American College of Obstetricians and Gynecologists (ACOG),[148] NOW, the ACLU (American Civil Liberties Union), Americans United for Life, and the United States Catholic Conference.

The name of the case was *In re: A.C.*[149] The woman in the case, A.C., was 26½ weeks pregnant and had had cancer for several years. At the point where her story reached its crisis, her doctors diagnosed her as having only 24 to 48 hours left to live, and her fetus, if delivered immediately, a 50–60 percent chance of survival and a less than 20 percent chance of substantial impairment. With each passing hour the fetal chances of survival diminished and likelihood of substantial impairment rose.

The court order that was being appealed had been issued on a day on which two hearings were held to determine the wishes of A.C. concerning the caesarean. During the first, convened at the hospital in response to the hospital's request for a declaratory judgment as to how to proceed, her doctors testified that in earlier discussions with A.C., caesarean delivery had been discussed as an option for a 28-week fetus and that she had clearly consented to it, if it would enhance fetal survival, even if for her it would be "a terminal event." Her mother claimed that these earlier discussions should be discounted because A.C. never understood that caesarean surgery might cause her to die before she could hold her baby. Her husband was too distraught to testify. One of her doctors testified that he had heard nothing from A.C. that indicated that she would refuse permission for the caesarean. Another of her doctors testified that A.C., in the earlier discussions of a caesarean, had never seriously considered the possibility that she might not survive the operation. In response to a judicial query whether A.C. could presently be questioned as to her wishes, her doctors testified that A.C. was at that time heavily sedated—too sedated for her consent to count as "informed consent" for legal purposes—and that any reduction in her sedation to intensify her level of consciousness would hasten her death.

After this hearing the trial court entered findings to the effect that one could not clearly know the views of A.C., that the state has an important and legitimate interest in protecting the potentiality of life in the viable fetus, that any delay would greatly increase risk to the fetus, and that the operation "may very well" hasten the death of A.C. Relying on a precedent, *In re Madyun*,[150] the court then ordered the surgery.

At this point A.C.'s doctors had gone to her bedside and informed her of the court order. One of them explained the situation, including the point that a caesarean was the fetus's only chance for survival, and asked if she would agree to the operation. She said yes. He asked if she understood that she might not survive the procedure. She said yes again. He then repeated both questions and asked if she understood them and she again said yes.

The court reconvened later in the day and received this testimony from the doctor. Next, the court recommended moving the hearing to A.C.'s bedside, but the doctors prevailed against that idea. Instead, two doctors and A.C.'s mother and husband went to her bedside to confirm her consent. At this point in response to similar questions but, as the doctors described it, "flanked by a weeping husband and mother," A.C. said of the procedure, "I don't want it done. I don't want it done." Both doctors testified that her level of sedation had worn off enough by this time that she was conscious of what she was hearing and saying but that they believed the circumstances—intensive care intubation, blatantly distraught family members' presence, and the stress of the situation—made informed consent impossible. The court ruled that it was "still not clear" what A.C.'s intent was and again ordered the surgery. A request for a stay to the appeals court was denied, the surgery took place, and a few hours later the baby died. Two days later A.C. died of cancer.

A.C.'s estate then sued the hospital. Meanwhile, the hospital asked the appeals court for a declaratory judgment so that it would have guidance for future, similar cases. The appeals court accepted the hospital's request, explaining that this was one of those situations "capable of repetition but [if mootness rules were strictly applied] evading review."

At the appeals court, the A.C. estate attorneys maintained that "A.C. was competent and that she made an informed choice not to have the caesarean performed" and that therefore "it was error for the trial court to weigh the state's interest in preserving the potential life of a viable fetus against A.C.'s interest in having her decision respected." They argued that, even if the trial court had tried to discern A.C.'s wishes and followed them, it would have concluded that A.C. would not have wanted the caesarean. Counsel for the hospital and for L.M.C. (the baby) contended the contrary: that A.C. was incompetent to make her own medical decisions and that the substituted judgment procedure (i.e., discerning her wishes) would have established that A.C. would have consented to the caesarean. Also, counsel for L.M.C. argued that even if L.M.C.'s interests and those of the state were in conflict with A.C.'s wishes, it was proper for the trial court to balance their interests and resolve the conflict in favor of surgical intervention. The appeals court rejected all of these positions on the grounds that the evidence did not support any of them. The court of appeals produced a 7–1 decision. Both the majority opinion and the partial dissent follow:

> # IN RE A.C.
> 573 A.2d 1235 (1990 D.C. App)
>
> **JUDGE TERRY delivered the opinion of the court.**
>
> We are confronted here with two profoundly difficult and complex issues. First, we must determine who has the right to decide the course of medical treatment for a patient who, although near death, is pregnant with a viable fetus. Second, we must establish how that decision should be made if the patient cannot make it for herself—more specifically, how a court should proceed when faced with a pregnant patient, *in extremis*, who is apparently incapable of making an informed decision regarding medical care for herself and her fetus. We hold that in virtually all cases the question of what is to be done is to be decided by the patient—the pregnant woman—on behalf of herself and the fetus. If the patient is incompetent or otherwise unable to give an informed consent to a proposed course of medical treatment, then her decision must be ascertained through the procedure known as substituted judgment. Because the trial court did not follow that procedure, we vacate its order and remand . . .for further proceedings.[2]
>
> . . .
>
> ## IV
>
> A. *Informed Consent and Bodily Integrity*
>
> From a recent national survey, it appears that over the five years preceding the survey there were thirty-six attempts to override maternal refusals of proposed medical treatment, and that in fifteen instances where court orders

were sought to authorize caesarean interventions, thirteen such orders were granted. Kolder, Gallagher & Parsons, *Court-Ordered Obstetrical Interventions,* 316 NEW ENG. J. MED. at 1192–1193. *Compare* Goldberg, *Medical Choices During Pregnancy: Whose Decision Is It Anyway?* 41 RUTGERS L. REV. 591, 609 (1989) (finding twelve such cases). Nevertheless, there is only one published decision from an appellate court that deals with the question of when, or even whether, a court may order a caesarean section: *Jefferson v. Griffin Spalding County Hospital Authority,* 274 S.E.2d 457 (1981).

Jefferson is of limited relevance, if any at all, to the present case. In *Jefferson* there was a competent refusal by the mother to undergo the proposed surgery, but the evidence showed that performance of the caesarean was in the medical interests of both the mother and the fetus.[7] In the instant case, by contrast, the evidence is unclear as to whether A.C. was competent when she mouthed her apparent refusal of the caesarean ("I don't want it done"), and it was generally assumed that while the surgery would most likely be highly beneficial to the fetus, it would be dangerous for the mother. Thus there was no clear . . . competent decision by the mother to forego a procedure for the benefit of the fetus. The procedure may well have been against A.C.'s medical interest, but if she was competent and given the choice, she may well have consented to an operation of significant risk to herself in order to maximize her fetus' chance for survival. From the evidence, however, we simply cannot tell whether she would have consented or not.

Thus our analysis of this case begins with the tenet common to all medical treatment cases: that any person has the right to make an informed choice, if competent to do so, to accept or forego medical treatment. The doctrine of informed consent, based on this principle and rooted in the concept of bodily integrity, is ingrained in our common law. [Citations omitted.] Under the doctrine of informed consent, a physician must inform the patient, "at a minimum," of "the nature of the proposed treatment, any alternative treatment procedures, and the nature and degree of risks and benefits inherent in undergoing and in abstaining from the proposed treatment." *Crain v. Allison,* 443 A.2d at 562. To protect the right of every person to bodily integrity, courts uniformly hold that a surgeon who performs an operation without the patient's consent may be guilty of a battery, *Canterbury v. Spence,* 464 F.2d at 783, or that if the surgeon obtains an insufficiently informed consent, he or she may be liable for negligence. *Crain v. Allison,* 443 A.2d at 561–562. Furthermore, the right to informed consent "also encompasses a right to informed refusal." *In re Conroy,* 486 A.2d 1209, 1222 (1985).

In the same vein, courts do not compel one person to permit a significant intrusion upon his or her bodily integrity for the benefit of another person's health. [Here court cites cases rejecting judicial coercion for either a skin graft or bone marrow donation, each to save a cousin.] . . .

It has been suggested that fetal cases are different because a woman who "has chosen to lend her body to bring [a] child into the world" has an enhanced duty to assure the welfare of the fetus, sufficient even to require her to undergo caesarean surgery. Robertson, *Procreative Liberty*, 69 VA. L. REV. at 456. Surely, however, a fetus cannot have rights in this respect superior to those of a person who has already been born.[8]

This court has recognized as well that, above and beyond common law protections, the right to accept or forego medical treatment is of constitutional magnitude. [Citations omitted.] Other courts also have found a basis in the Constitution for refusing medical treatment. [Citations omitted.]

Decisions of the Supreme Court, while not explicitly recognizing a right to bodily integrity, seem to assume that individuals have the right, depending on the circumstances, to accept or refuse medical treatment or other bodily invasion. *See, e.g., Winston v. Lee*, 470 U.S. 753 (1985); *Schmerber v. California*, 384 U.S. 757 (1966); *Rochin v. California*; *cf. Union Pacific Ry. v. Botsford*, 141 U.S. 250, 251 (1891) . . . [referring to it as a common law right]). In *Winston v. Lee* a robbery suspect challenged the state's right to compel him to submit to surgery for the removal of a bullet which was lodged in a muscle in his chest. The Court noted that the proposed surgery, which would require a general anesthetic, "would be an 'extensive' intrusion on respondent's personal privacy and bodily integrity" and a "virtually total divestment of respondent's ordinary control over surgical probing beneath his skin," 470 U.S. at 764–765, and held that, without the patient-suspect's consent, the surgery was constitutionally impermissible. Nevertheless, even in recognizing a right to refuse medical treatment or state-imposed surgery, neither *Winston* nor any other Supreme Court decision holds that this right of refusal is absolute. Rather, in discussing the constitutional "reasonableness of surgical intrusions beneath the skin," the Court said in *Winston* that the Fourth Amendment "neither forbids nor permits all such intrusions. . . ." *Id.* at 760 (citing *Schmerber v. California*; *see also Jacobson v. Massachusetts*, 197 U.S. 11 (1905).[9]

This court and others, while recognizing the right to accept or reject medical treatment, have consistently held that the right is not absolute. . . . In some cases, especially those involving life-or-death situations or incompetent patients, the courts have recognized four countervailing interests that may involve the state as *parens patriae:* preserving life, preventing suicide, maintaining the ethical integrity of the medical profession, and protecting third parties. Neither the prevention of suicide nor the integrity of the medical profession has any bearing on this case. Further, the state's interest in preserving life must be truly compelling to justify overriding a competent person's right to refuse medical treatment.

In those rare cases in which a patient's right to decide her own course of treatment has been judicially overridden, courts have usually acted to vindicate the state's interest in protecting third parties, even if in fetal state. *See Jefferson v. Griffin Spalding County Hospital Authority* (ordering that caesarean section be performed on a woman in her thirty-ninth week of pregnancy to save both the mother and the fetus); *Raleigh Fitkin-Paul Morgan Memorial Hospital v. Anderson,* 201 A.2d 537 (ordering blood transfusions over the objection of a Jehovah's Witness, in her thirty-second week of pregnancy, to save her life and that of the fetus), *cert. denied,* 377 U.S. 985 (1964); *In re Jamaica Hospital,* 491 N.Y.S.2d 898 (Sup. Ct. 1985) (ordering the transfusion of blood to a Jehovah's Witness eighteen weeks pregnant, who objected on religious grounds, and finding that the state's interest in the not-yet-viable fetus outweighed the patient's interests); *Crouse Irving Memorial Hospital, Inc. v. Paddock,* 485 N.Y.S.2d 443 (Sup. Ct. 1985) (ordering transfusions as necessary over religious objections to save the mother and a fetus that was to be prematurely delivered); *cf. In re President & Directors of Georgetown College, Inc.,* 331 F.2d at 1008, *cert. denied,* 377 U.S. 978 (ordering a transfusion, *inter alia,* because of a mother's parental duty to her living minor children). *But see Taft v. Taft,* 446 N.E.2d 395 (1983) (vacating an order which required a woman in her fourth month of pregnancy to undergo a "purse-string" operation, on the ground that there were no compelling circumstances to justify overriding her religious objections and her constitutional right of privacy).

What we distill from the cases discussed in this section is that every person has the right, under the common law and the Constitution, to accept or refuse medical treatment. This right of bodily integrity belongs equally to persons who are competent and persons who are not. Further, it matters not what the quality of a patient's life may be; the right of bodily integrity is not extinguished simply because someone is ill, or even at death's door. To protect that right against intrusion by others—family members, doctors, hospitals, or anyone else, however well-intentioned—we hold that a court must determine the patient's wishes by any means available, and must abide by those wishes unless there are truly extraordinary or compelling reasons to override them. When the patient is incompetent, or when the court is unable to determine competency, the substituted judgment procedure must be followed.

From the record before us, we simply cannot tell whether A.C. was ever competent, after being sedated, to make an informed decision one way or the other regarding the proposed caesarean section. The trial court never made any finding about A.C.'s competency to decide. Undoubtedly, during most of the proceedings below, A.C. was incompetent to make a treatment decision. . . .

We think it is incumbent on any trial judge in a case like this, unless it is impossible to do so, to ascertain whether a patient is competent to make her own medical decisions. Whenever possible, the judge should personally attempt to speak with the patient and ascertain her wishes directly, rather than relying exclusively on hearsay evidence, even from doctors. . . . We have no reason to believe that, if competent, A.C. would or would not have refused consent to a caesarean. We hold, however, that without a competent refusal from A.C. to go forward with the surgery, and without a finding through substituted judgment that A.C. would not have consented to the surgery, it was error for the trial court to proceed to a balancing analysis, weighing the rights of A.C. against the interests of the state.

There are two additional arguments against overriding A.C.'s objections to caesarean surgery. First, as the American Public Health Association cogently states in its *amicus curiae* brief:

> Rather than protecting the health of women and children, court-ordered caesareans erode the element of trust that permits a pregnant woman to communicate to her physician—without fear of reprisal—all information relevant to her proper diagnosis and treatment. An even more serious consequence of court-ordered intervention is that it drives women at high risk of complications during pregnancy and childbirth out of the health care system to avoid coerced treatment.

Second, and even more compellingly, any judicial proceeding in a case such as this will ordinarily take place—like the one before us here—under time constraints so pressing that it is difficult or impossible for the mother to communicate adequately with counsel, or for counsel to organize an effective factual and legal presentation in defense of her liberty and privacy interests and bodily integrity. Any intrusion implicating such basic values ought not to be lightly undertaken when the mother not only is precluded from conducting pre-trial discovery (to which she would be entitled as a matter of course in any controversy over even a modest amount of money) but also is in no position to prepare meaningfully for trial. . . .

In this case A.C.'s court-appointed attorney was unable even to meet with his client before the hearing. By the time the case was heard, A.C.'s condition did not allow her to be present, nor was it reasonably possible for the judge to hear from her directly. The factual record, moreover, was significantly flawed because A.C.'s medical records were not before the court. . . . Finally, the time for legal preparation was so minimal that neither the court nor counsel mentioned the doctrine of substituted judgment, which—with benefit of briefs, oral arguments, and above all, time—we now deem critical to the outcome of this case. We cannot be at all certain that the trial judge would have reached the same decision if . . . the abundant legal scholarship filed in this court had been meaningfully available to him, and if there had been enough time for him to . . . reflect on these matters as a judge optimally should do.

B. *Substituted Judgment*

In the previous section we . . . concluded that if a patient is competent and has made an informed decision regarding the course of her medical treatment, that decision will control in virtually all cases. Sometimes, however, as . . . here, a once competent patient will be unable to render an informed decision. In such a case, we hold that the court must make a substituted judgment on behalf of the patient, based on all the evidence. This means that the duty of the court, "as surrogate for the incompetent, is to determine as best it can what choice that individual, if competent, would make with respect to medical procedures." *In re Boyd,* 403 A.2d at 750.

Under the substituted judgment procedure, the court. . .must "substitute itself as nearly as may be for the incompetent, and . . . act upon the same motives and considerations as would have moved her . . . ." *City Bank Farmers Trust Co. v. McGowan*, 323 U.S. 594, 599 (1945). . . .

We have found no reported opinion applying the substituted judgment procedure to the case of an incompetent pregnant patient whose own life may be shortened by a caesarean section, and whose unborn child's chances of survival may hang on the court's decision. Despite this precedential void, we conclude that substituted judgment is the best procedure to follow in such a case because it most clearly respects the right of the patient to bodily integrity. Thus we reaffirm our holding in *In re Boyd*, in which we discussed how a substituted judgment should be made when a patient, although incompetent, has previously expressed objections to treatment, and we observe that many of the factors found relevant to discerning the patient's choice in *Boyd* are relevant here.

We begin with the proposition that the substituted judgment inquiry is primarily a subjective one: as nearly as possible, the court must ascertain what the patient would do if competent [citations omitted]. Due process strongly suggests (and may even require) that counsel or a guardian *ad litem* should be appointed for the patient unless the situation is so urgent that there is no time to do so.

Because it is the patient's decisional rights which the substituted judgment inquiry seeks to protect, courts are in accord that the greatest weight should be given to the previously expressed wishes of the patient. This includes prior statements, either written or oral, even though the treatment alternatives at hand may not have been addressed.... The court should also consider previous decisions of the patient concerning medical treatment, especially when there may be a discernibly consistent pattern of conduct or of thought. Thus in a case such as this it would be highly relevant that A.C. had consented to intrusive and dangerous surgeries in the past, and that she chose to become pregnant and to protect her pregnancy by seeking treatment at the hospital's high-risk pregnancy clinic. It would also be relevant that she accepted a plan of treatment which contemplated caesarean intervention at the twenty-eighth week of pregnancy, even though the possibility of a caesarean during the twenty-sixth week was apparently unforeseen. On the other hand, A.C. agreed to a plan of palliative treatment which posed a greater danger to the fetus than would have been necessary if she were unconcerned about her own continuing care. Further, when A.C. was informed of the fatal nature of her illness, she was equivocal about her desire to have the baby.

Courts in substituted judgment cases have also acknowledged the importance of probing the patient's value system as an aid in discerning what the patient would choose. We agree with this approach.... Most people do not foresee what calamities may befall them; much less do they consider, or even think about, treatment alternatives in varying situations. The court in a substituted judgment case, therefore, should pay special attention to the known values and goals of the incapacitated patient, and should strive, if possible, to extrapolate from those values and goals what the patient's decision would be.

Although treating physicians may be an invaluable source of such information about a patient, the family will often be the best source. Family members or other loved ones will usually be in the best position to say what the patient would do if competent. The court should be mindful, however, that while in the majority of cases family members will have the best interests of the patient in mind, sometimes family members will rely on their own judgments or predilections rather than serving as conduits for expressing the patient's wishes. This is why the court should endeavor, whenever possible, to make an in-person appraisal "of the patient's personal desires and ability for rational choice. In this way the court can always know, to the extent possible, that the judgment is that of the individual concerned and not that of those who believe, however well-intentioned, that they speak for the person whose life is in the balance." *In re Osborne*, 294 A.2d at 374...

In short, to determine the subjective desires of the patient, the court must consider the totality of the evidence, focusing particularly on written or oral directions concerning treatment to family, friends, and health-care professionals. The court should also take into account the patient's past decisions regarding medical treatment, and attempt to ascertain from what is known about the patient's value system, goals, and desires what the patient would decide if competent.

After considering [all these]..., the court may still be unsure what course the patient would choose. In such circumstances the court may supplement its knowledge about the patient by determining what most persons would likely do in a similar situation. [Citations omitted.] When the patient is pregnant, however, she may not be concerned exclusively with her own welfare. Thus it is proper for the court, in a case such as this, to weigh ... the mother's prognosis, the viability of the fetus, the probable result of treatment or non-treatment for both mother and fetus, and the mother's likely interest in avoiding impairment for her child together with her own instincts for survival.

Additionally, the court should consider the context in which prior declarations, treatment decisions, and expressions of personal values were made, including whether statements were made casually or after contemplation, or in accordance with deeply held beliefs. Finally, in making a substituted judgment, the court should become as informed about the patient's condition, prognosis, and treatment options as one would expect any patient to become before making a treatment decision. Obviously, the weight accorded to all of these factors will vary from case to case.

C. *The Trial Court's Ruling*

...The trial court, faced with an issue affecting life and death, was forced to make a decision with almost no time for deliberation.... [I]t is clear to us that the trial court did not follow the substituted judgment procedure....

Instead, the court undertook to balance the state's and L.M.C.'s interests in surgical intervention against A.C.'s perceived interest in not having the caesarean performed....

It is that order which we must now set aside. What a trial court must do in a case such as this is to determine, if possible, whether the patient is capable of making an informed decision about the course of her medical treatment. If [so] . . ., her wishes will control in virtually all cases. If the court finds that the patient is incapable of making an informed consent (and thus incompetent), then the court must make a substituted judgment. This means that the court must ascertain as best it can what the patient would do if faced with the particular treatment question. Again, in virtually all cases the decision of the patient, albeit discerned through the mechanism of substituted judgment, will control. We do not quite foreclose the possibility that a conflicting state interest may be so compelling that the patient's wishes must yield,[22] but we anticipate that such cases will be extremely rare and truly exceptional. This is not such a case.

Having said that, we go no further. We need not decide whether, or in what circumstances, the state's interests can ever prevail over the interests of a pregnant patient. We emphasize, nevertheless, that it would be an extraordinary case indeed in which a court might ever be justified in overriding the patient's wishes and authorizing a major surgical procedure such as a caesarean section. Throughout this opinion we have stressed that the patient's wishes, once they are ascertained, must be followed in "virtually all cases," unless there are "truly extraordinary or compelling reasons to override them." Indeed, some may doubt that there could ever be a situation extraordinary or compelling enough to justify a massive intrusion into a person's body, such as a caesarean section, against that person's will. Whether such a situation may someday present itself is a question that we need not strive to answer here. We see no need to reach out and decide an issue that is not presented on the record before us; this case is difficult enough as it is. We think it sufficient for now to chart the course for future cases resembling this one, and to express the hope that we shall not be presented with a case in the foreseeable future that requires us to sail off the chart into the unknown.

[The court then vacated the order and remanded not for the normally needed "additional findings," but, since it judged such a procedure now "futile," simply for "such further proceedings as may be appropriate."—AU.]

Opinion Footnotes

2 We observe nevertheless that it would be far better if judges were not called to patients' bedsides and required to make quick decisions on issues of life and death. Because judgment in such a case involves complex medical and ethical issues as well as the application of legal principles, we would urge the establishment—through legislation or otherwise—of another tribunal to make these decisions, with limited opportunity for judicial review. . . . Although we conclude that [the emergency decision of the trial judge] . . . must be set aside, we nevertheless commend him for the painstaking and conscientious manner in which he performed the task before him.

7 [I]n *Jefferson* . . . [t]he mother was unquestionably competent to make her own treatment decisions, but refused a caesarean because of her religious beliefs. . .

8 There are also practical consequences to consider. What if A.C. had refused to comply with a court order that she submit to a caesarean? Under the circumstances, she obviously could not have been held in civil contempt and imprisoned or required to pay a daily fine until compliance. Enforcement could be accomplished only through physical force or its equivalent. A.C. would have to be fastened with restraints to the operating table, or perhaps involuntarily rendered unconscious by forcibly injecting her with an anesthetic, and then subjected to unwanted major surgery. Such actions would surely give one pause in a civilized society, especially when A.C. had done no wrong. *Cf. Rochin v. California*, 342 U.S. 165, 169 (1952).

9 We think it appropriate here to reiterate and emphasize a point that the motions division made in its opinion: "that this case is not about abortion." . . . A.C. sought to become pregnant, she wanted to bear her child as close to term as possible, and neither she nor anyone associated with her at any time sought to terminate her pregnancy. The issue [is]. . . who should decide how that child should be delivered. That decision involves the right of A.C. (or any woman) to accept or forego medical treatment. . .

22 Absolutes like "never" should generally be avoided because "the future may bring scenarios which prudence counsels our not resolving anticipatorily." *Florida Star v. B.J.F.*, 491 U.S. 524 (1989).

BELSON, ASSOCIATE JUDGE, concurring in part and dissenting in part:

I agree with much of the majority opinion, but I disagree with its ultimate ruling that the trial court's order must be set aside, and with the narrow view it takes of the state's interest in preserving life and the unborn child's interest in life.

More specifically, I agree with the guidance the opinion affords trial judges as to how to approach a case like this [(1) determine the patient's competency to decide; (2) if she is incompetent, make a substituted judgment; (3) follow it unless there are compelling reasons to the contrary]. . . .

I disagree, however, with the majority's holding that the trial judge erred in failing to determine competency. I think it quite clear from the record that Judge Sullivan found A.C. incompetent. . . . I submit that the most reasonable reading of the record is that the judge found her incompetent when he stated: "The Court is of the view that it does not clearly know what [A.C.'s] present views are with respect to the issue of whether or not the child should live or die." . . . [And later,] "The Court is still not clear what her intent is.". . . It is clear that the trial judge, at the very least, made a finding that was, under the majority's explanation of appropriate procedures, sufficient to move the inquiry forward to the substituted judgment stage.

...I disagree with the holding of the majority that Judge Sullivan erred in proceeding to a balancing analysis, weighing the rights of A.C. against those of the state and the unborn child without first having found either a competent refusal or a finding of nonconsent through substituted judgment....

...[T]he majority...opine[s], in dictum, that this particular case is not one of those "extremely rare and truly exceptional" cases in which a patient's wishes regarding the proposed medical treatment can be overruled by reason of a compelling state interest (here, the interest in protecting the life of the viable unborn child). This is dictum because, as the majority points out, "we have no reason to believe that, if competent, A.C. would or would not have refused consent to a caesarean."[2]...

I think it appropriate, nevertheless, to state my disagreement with the very limited view the majority opinion takes of the circumstances in which the interests of a viable unborn child can afford such compelling reasons. The state's interest in preserving human life and the viable unborn child's interest in survival are entitled, I think, to more weight than I find them assigned by the majority when it states that "in virtually all cases the decision of the patient ...will control." I would hold that in those instances, fortunately rare, in which the viable unborn child's interest in living and the state's parallel interest in protecting human life come into conflict with the mother's decision to forgo a procedure such as a caesarean section, a balancing should be struck in which the unborn child's and the state's interests are entitled to substantial weight.

It was acknowledged in *Roe v. Wade* that the state's interest in potential human life becomes compelling at the point of viability. Even before viability, the state has an "important and legitimate interest in protecting the potentiality of human life." 410 U.S. at 162. When approximately the third trimester of pregnancy is reached (roughly the time of viability, although with advances in medical science the time of viability is being reached sooner and sooner), the state's interest becomes sufficiently compelling to justify what otherwise would be unduly burdensome state interference with the woman's constitutionally protected privacy interest. Once that stage is reached, the state "may, if it chooses, regulate, and even proscribe, abortion except where it is necessary, in appropriate medical judgment, for the preservation of the life or health of the mother." *Roe,* at 165. In addressing this issue, it is important to emphasize, as does the majority opinion, that this case is not about abortion[3].... Rather, we are dealing with the situation that exists when a woman has carried an unborn child to viability. When the unborn child reaches the state of viability, the child becomes a party whose interests must be considered. *See* King, *The Juridical Status of the Fetus: A Proposal for Legal Protection of the Unborn*, 77 MICH. L. REV. 1647, 1687 (1979) (viability, not birth, the determinative moment in development for purpose of determining when fetus is entitled to legal protection).

Turning to the rights of the child, tort law has long recognized the right of a living child to recover for injuries suffered when she was a viable unborn child, [and it has recognized this] in "every jurisdiction in the United States." [Citations omitted.] . . .

[This legal principle is]. . .sufficient to indicate the need for a balancing process in which the rights of the viable unborn child are assigned substantial weight. . . .

. . .

The balancing test should be applied in instances in which women become pregnant and carry an unborn child to the point of viability. This is not an unreasonable classification because, I submit, a woman who carries a child to viability is in fact a member of a unique category of persons. Her circumstances differ fundamentally from those of other potential patients for medical procedures that will aid another person, for example, a potential donor of bone marrow for transplant. This is so because she has undertaken to bear another human being, and has carried an unborn child to viability. Another unique feature of the situation we address arises from the singular nature of the dependency of the unborn child upon the mother. A woman carrying a viable unborn child is not in the same category as a relative, friend, or stranger called upon to donate bone marrow or an organ for transplant. Rather, the expectant mother has placed herself in a special class of persons who are bringing another person into existence, and upon whom that other person's life is totally dependent. Also, uniquely, the viable unborn child is literally captive within the mother's body. No other potential beneficiary of a surgical procedure on another is in that position.

For all of these reasons, a balancing becomes appropriate in those few cases where the interests we are discussing come into conflict. To so state is in no sense to fail to recognize the extremely strong interest of each individual person, including of course the expectant mother, in her bodily integrity, her privacy, and, where involved, her religious beliefs.

Thus, I cannot agree with the conclusion of the majority opinion that while we "do not quite foreclose the possibility that a conflicting state interest may be so compelling that the patient's wishes must yield . . . we anticipate that such cases will be extremely rare and truly exceptional." While it is, fortunately, true that such cases will be rare in the sense that such conflicts between mother and viable unborn child are rare,[7] I cannot agree that in cases where a viable unborn child is in the picture, it would be extremely rare, within that universe, to require that the mother accede to the vital needs of the viable unborn child.[8] . . .

I next address the sensitive question of how to balance the competing rights and interests of the viable unborn child and the state against those of the rare expectant mother who elects not to have a caesarean section necessary to save the life of her child. The indisputable view that a woman carrying a viable child has an extremely strong interest in her own life, health, bodily integrity, privacy, and religious beliefs necessarily requires that her election be given correspondingly great weight in the balancing process. In a case, however, where the court in an exercise of a substituted judgment has concluded that the patient would probably opt against a caesarean section, the court should vary the weight to be given this factor in proportion to the confidence the court has in the accuracy of its conclusion. Thus, in a case where the indicia of the incompetent patient's judgment are equivocal, the court should accord this factor correspondingly less weight. The appropriate weight to be given other factors will have to be worked out by the development of law in this area, and cannot be prescribed in a single court opinion. Some considerations obviously merit special attention in the balancing process. [These include]. . .any danger to the mother's life or health, physical or mental . . . [and t]he mother's religious beliefs as they relate to the operation. . . .

On the other side of the analysis, it is appropriate to look to the relative likelihood of the unborn child's survival. . . . The child's interest in being born with as little impairment as possible should also be considered. This may weigh in favor of a delivery sooner rather than later. The most important factor on this side of the scale, however, is life itself, because the viable unborn child that dies because of the mother's refusal to have a caesarean delivery is deprived, entirely and irrevocably, of the life on which the child was about to embark. . . .

. . . I think this court cannot on this record hold that the trial judge abused his discretion in striking the balance he did. . . .

Opinion Footnotes

2 In view of this statement, I find puzzling the majority's discussion of "two additional arguments against overriding A.C.'s objections to caesarean surgery." No such objections were found to exist.

3 The majority opinion, however, oversimplifies matters [in its note 9]. . . The cruel realities of the situation made the issue far more difficult. It could better be stated as whether the unborn child should face a greatly reduced chance of survival upon *post mortem* delivery occasioned by a decision to forgo a caesarean procedure or whether, instead, the child should be afforded a probability of living as a result of a surgical procedure that involved both some risk to A.C. and an invasion of her bodily integrity.

7 The majority opinion at n.21 quotes Opinion No. 55 of the Ethics Committee of the ACOG as follows: "the welfare of the fetus is of the utmost importance to the majority of women; thus only rarely will a conflict arise." Another observer described the attitude of most expectant mothers more graphically: "The vast majority of women will accept significant risk, pain, and inconvenience to give their babies the best chance possible. One obstetrician who performs innovative fetal surgery stated that most of the women he sees 'would cut off their heads to save their babies.' " Rhoden, *The Judge in the Delivery Room: The Emergence of Court-Ordered Cesareans*, 74 CALIF. L. REV. 1951, 1959 (1986).

8 To the contrary, it appears that a majority of courts faced with this issue have found that the state's compelling interest in protection of the unborn child should prevail. *See* Noble-Allgire, *Court-Ordered Cesarean Sections*, 10 J. LEGAL MED. 211, 236 (1989). I add that in mapping this uncharted area of the law, we can draw lines, and a line I would draw would be to preclude the use of physical force to perform an operation. The force of the court order itself as well as the use of the contempt power would, I think, be adequate in most cases. *See id.* at 243.

Case Questions

1. If you had to come up with a substituted judgment as to A.C., following the majority's guidelines, which way would you decide? Would your decision change if you followed the dissent's guidelines? Does either side in your judgment give adequate guidance for future cases?

2. Do you believe that a judge constructing a "substituted judgment" in a situation where the evidence of the woman's wishes is truly ambiguous will really be able to separate his or her own views of right and wrong from what the patient would want?

3. Compare footnote 8 of the majority to footnote 8 of the dissent. Does the dissenter's guideline precluding the use of governmental force to compel surgery amount to an invitation to civil disobedience on the part of refusers? Is the judge not promising in advance that if the patient cares enough to resist, the government will oblige? Does this guideline amount to discrimination against the unconscious (who are unable to resist)?

4. Is the dissenter being fair in construing a woman's decision to carry a fetus past the point of viability as putting her in a legal position regarding a compelled caesarean that gives her less autonomy than other persons who might be called upon to take medical risks for others, such as organ donors?

5. Do you read the majority decision as disapproving or not of the Jehovah's Witness blood transfusion cases it describes?

Criminalizing Pregnant Behavior: *Ferguson v. Charleston, S.C.* (2001)

During the 1980s epidemic of "crack" (smokable cocaine) use, a number of states experimented with new legal approaches to attempt to prevent the birth of "crack babies," who suffered numerous medical problems as the result of being born addicted to crack. In 1988, staff members at the (public) hospital of the Medical University of South Carolina (MUSC) began discussing how to cope with the increasing number of patients for prenatal care who were using cocaine. In April 1989 the hospital began ordering drug tests on urine samples from suspected maternity patients. If one tested positive, the MUSC staff then referred her to the county substance abuse commission for counseling and treatment. This policy failed to check the increase in births of crack babies.

The nurse who managed cases in the obstetrics department, Shirley Brown, heard on the news a few months later that Greenville, South Carolina had begun arresting and prosecuting (third-trimester) pregnant cocaine users for the crime of child abuse. (This policy was later sustained by the South Carolina Supreme Court, in a case where the pregnant mother had received an eight-year prison sentence, and the U.S. Supreme Court refused to review the decision.[151]) This MUSC nurse then met with the hospital's attorney, who in late August contacted the Charleston city solicitor to offer MUSC's help in prosecuting mothers who tested positive for cocaine at time of birth. The solicitor, Charles Condon, then organized a committee of hospital representatives, police, Substance Abuse Commission members, and Department of Social Services members, and this committee produced a 12-page document describing Policy M-7, which set forth hospital procedures for identifying and/or assisting pregnant patients suspected of drug abuse. The policy was implemented by October 1989.

Among the criteria that the policy listed as grounds to suspect drug abuse was, for example, "no prenatal care."[152] Any patient exhibiting any of the listed grounds for suspicion was to have her urine tested for cocaine. The urine was to be handled under correct police procedures aimed at protecting the "chain of custody" for prosecution purposes. The policy aimed to counsel drug abusers and place them in substance abuse clinics for treatment. Threats of prosecution were to be used to motivate these women to stay in treatment during pregnancy, so their babies would be born drug-free. At first, the policy had two parts. Police would be notified if the pregnant woman, after receiving a warning, either tested positive for cocaine use a *second* time or failed to show up for substance abuse counseling. This part of the policy differed from the one toward women who tested positive for drug use immediately after labor. These women were simply arrested for child abuse. Early in 1990 the city solicitor modified the policy regarding these women so that they too would receive a warning the first time and be able to avoid arrest if they received substance abuse treatment.

The policy outlined a number of prosecution options. If the pregnancy were 27 weeks or fewer, the woman was to be charged with possession; if it were 28 or more weeks, the charge would be delivery of drugs to a minor; and if she gave birth while testing positive, she would be charged additionally with child neglect. Moreover, the policy document instructed police to interrogate the mother "to ascertain the identity of [whoever] provided illegal drugs to the suspect."[153] The document made no mention of medical care of the suspect, apart from recommending substance abuse programs.

The appellants in the case were ten women arrested as a result of the MUSC policy: four were arrested during the first phase, when they received no reform opportunity after the first incriminating urine test; the other six were arrested in phase two, having produced a second incriminating test after receiving a warning, or having failed to show up for treatment. These ten women had sued the hospital on the grounds (among others) that the urine tests violated their Fourth Amendment right to be free of "unreasonable searches" and their constitutional right of privacy. Their case was argued by Priscilla Smith, an attorney for the Center for Reproductive Law and Policy in New York.[154]

At the District Court, the judge ruled that these urine tests for prosecutorial use fit into the category of a "search or seizure" under the Fourth Amendment and therefore required consent in order to be found constitutional. Only if the jury found that the women had consented to the search could the hospital win the case. The jury did find in favor of the hospital, and the District Court therefore so ruled. The women appealed on the grounds that the evidence did not support this jury verdict. The circuit court of appeals affirmed, on the grounds that there were "special needs" justifying the searches such that even if there had been no consent the searches were constitutional.[155]

At the U.S. Supreme Court, the justices divided 6–3 to overturn the Circuit Court decision.

FERGUSON ET AL. V. CITY OF CHARLESTON ET AL.
532 U.S. 67 (2001)

JUSTICE STEVENS delivered the opinion of the Court.

In this case, we must decide whether a state hospital's performance of a diagnostic test to obtain evidence of a patient's criminal conduct for law enforcement purposes is an unreasonable search if the patient has not consented to the procedure. More narrowly, the question is whether the interest in using the threat of criminal sanctions to deter pregnant women from using cocaine can justify a departure from the general rule that an official nonconsensual search is unconstitutional if not authorized by a valid warrant.

I

. . . .

The last six pages of the policy [See above—AU.] contained forms for the patients to sign, as well as procedures for the police to follow when a patient was arrested. The policy also prescribed in detail the precise offenses with which a woman could be charged, depending on the stage of her pregnancy. . . .

II

. . .

Petitioners' complaint challenged the validity of the policy under various theories, including the claim that warrantless and nonconsensual drug tests conducted for criminal investigatory purposes were unconstitutional searches. Respondents advanced two principal defenses to the constitutional claim: (1) that, as a matter of fact, petitioners had consented to the searches; and (2) that, as a matter of law, the searches were reasonable, even absent consent, because they were justified by special non-law-enforcement purposes. The District Court rejected the second defense because the searches in question "were not done by the medical university for independent purposes. [Instead,] the police came in and there was an agreement reached that the positive screens would be shared with the police." [Still, Ferguson lost because . . .] the jury found consent . . . .

Petitioners appealed, arguing that the evidence was not sufficient to support the jury's consent finding. The Court of Appeals for the Fourth Circuit affirmed, but without reaching the question of consent. [The circuit court] majority . . . held that the searches were reasonable as a matter of law under our line of cases recognizing that "special needs" may, in certain exceptional circumstances, justify a search policy designed to serve non-law-enforcement ends. On the understanding "that MUSC personnel conducted the urine drug screens for medical purposes wholly independent of an intent to aid law enforcement efforts," at 477, the majority applied the balancing test used in *Treasury Employees* v. *Von Raab*, 489 U.S. 656 (1989), and *Vernonia School Dist. 47J* v. *Acton*, 515 U.S. 646 (1995), and concluded that the interest in curtailing the pregnancy complications and medical costs associated with maternal cocaine use outweighed what the majority termed a minimal intrusion on the privacy of the patients. . . .

We . . . review the appellate court's holding on the "special needs" issue. Because we do not reach the question of the sufficiency of the evidence with respect to consent, we necessarily assume for purposes of our decision—as did the Court of Appeals—that the searches were conducted without the informed consent of the patients. We conclude that the judgment should be reversed and the case remanded for a decision on the consent issue.

III

Because MUSC is a state hospital, the members of its staff are government actors, subject to the strictures of the Fourth Amendment. *New Jersey* v. *T. L. O.*, 469 U.S. 325, 335–337 (1985). Moreover, the urine tests conducted by those staff members were indisputably searches within the meaning of the Fourth Amendment. *Skinner* v. *Railway Labor Executives' Assn.*, 489 U.S. 602, 617 (1989).[9] Neither the District Court nor the Court of Appeals concluded that any of the nine criteria used to identify the women to be searched provided either probable cause to believe that they were using cocaine, or even the basis for a reasonable suspicion of such use. Rather, the District Court and the Court of Appeals viewed the case as one involving MUSC's right to conduct searches without warrants or probable cause. Furthermore, given the posture in which the case comes to us, we must assume for purposes of our decision that the tests were performed without the informed consent of the patients.

Because the hospital seeks to justify its authority to conduct drug tests and to turn the results over to law enforcement agents without the knowledge or consent of the patients, this case differs from the four previous cases in which we have considered whether comparable drug tests "fit within the closely guarded category of constitutionally permissible suspicionless searches." *Chandler* v. *Miller*, 520 U.S. 305, 309 (1997). In three of those cases, we sustained drug tests for railway employees involved in train accidents, *Skinner* v. *Railway Labor Executives' Assn.*, 489 U.S. 602 (1989), for United States Customs Service employees seeking promotion to certain sensitive positions, *Treasury Employees*

v. *Von Raab*, 489 U.S. 656 (1989), and for high school students participating in interscholastic sports, *Vernonia School Dist. 47J* v. *Acton*, 515 U.S. 646 (1995). In the fourth case, we struck down such testing for candidates for designated state offices as unreasonable. *Chandler* v. *Miller*, 520 U.S. 305 (1997).

In each of those cases, we employed a balancing test that weighed the intrusion on the individual's interest in privacy against the "special needs" that supported the program. As an initial matter, we note that the invasion of privacy in this case is far more substantial than in those cases. In the previous four cases, there was no misunderstanding about the purpose of the test or the potential use of the test results, and there were protections against the dissemination of the results to third parties. The use of an adverse test result to disqualify one from eligibility for a particular benefit, such as a promotion or an opportunity to participate in an extracurricular activity, involves a less serious intrusion on privacy than the unauthorized dissemination of such results to third parties. The reasonable expectation of privacy enjoyed by the typical patient undergoing diagnostic tests in a hospital is that the results of those tests will not be shared with nonmedical personnel without her consent. In none of our prior cases was there any intrusion upon that kind of expectation.[14]

The critical difference between those four drug-testing cases and this one, however, lies in the nature of the "special need" asserted as justification for the warrantless searches. In each of those earlier cases, the "special need" that was advanced as a justification for the absence of a warrant or individualized suspicion was one divorced from the State's general interest in law enforcement.[15] [They served needs such as preventing train accidents or keeping drugs from contaminating interscholastic sports.]... In this case, however, the central and indispensable feature of the policy from its inception was the use of law enforcement to coerce the patients into substance abuse treatment. This fact distinguishes this case from circumstances in which physicians or psychologists, in the course of ordinary medical procedures aimed at helping the patient herself, come across information that under rules of law or ethics is subject to reporting requirements, which no one has challenged here. See, *e.g.,* Council on Ethical and Judicial Affairs, American Medical Association, Policy Finder, Current Opinions E-5.05 (2000) (requiring reporting where "a patient threatens to inflict serious bodily harm to another person or to him or herself and there is a reasonable probability that the patient may carry out the threat")....

Respondents argue in essence that their ultimate purpose—namely, protecting the health of both mother and child—is a beneficent one. In *Chandler*, however, we did not simply accept the State's invocation of a "special need." Instead, we carried out a "close review" of the scheme at issue before concluding that the need in question was not "special," as that term has been defined in our cases. 520 U.S., at 322. In this case, a review of the M-7 policy plainly reveals that the purpose actually served by the MUSC searches "is ultimately indistinguishable from the general interest in crime control." *Indianapolis* v. *Edmond*, 531 U.S. 32 (2000).

In looking to the programmatic purpose, we consider all the available evidence in order to determine the relevant primary purpose. In this case, as Judge Blake put it in her dissent below, "it . . . is clear from the record that an initial and continuing focus of the policy was on the arrest and prosecution of drug-abusing mothers . . ." 186 F. 3d, at 484. Tellingly, the document codifying the policy incorporates the police's operational guidelines. It devotes its attention to the chain of custody, the range of possible criminal charges, and the logistics of police notification and arrests. Nowhere, however, does the document discuss different courses of medical treatment for either mother or infant, aside from treatment for the mother's addiction.

Moreover, throughout the development and application of the policy, the Charleston prosecutors and police were extensively involved in the day-to-day administration of the policy. Police and prosecutors decided who would receive the reports of positive drug screens and what information would be included with those reports. Law enforcement officials also helped determine the procedures to be followed when performing the screens.[19] In the course of the policy's administration, they had access to Nurse Brown's medical files on the women who tested positive, routinely attended the substance abuse team's meetings, and regularly received copies of team documents discussing the women's progress. Police took pains to coordinate . . . the arrests with MUSC staff, and, in particular, Nurse Brown.

While the ultimate goal of the program may well have been to get the women in question into substance abuse treatment and off of drugs, the immediate objective of the searches was to generate evidence *for law enforcement* purposes[20] in order to reach that goal. The threat of law enforcement may ultimately have been intended as a means to an end, but the direct and primary purpose of MUSC's policy was to ensure the use of those means. In our opinion, this distinction is critical. Because law enforcement involvement always serves some broader social purpose or objective, under respondents' view, virtually any nonconsensual suspicionless search could be immunized under the special needs doctrine by defining the search solely in terms of its ultimate, rather than immediate, purpose. Such an approach is inconsistent with the Fourth Amendment. Given the primary purpose of the Charleston program, which was to use the threat of arrest and prosecution in order to force women into treatment, and given the extensive involvement of law enforcement officials at every stage of the policy, this case simply does not fit within the closely guarded category of "special needs."

. . . While state hospital employees, like other citizens, may have a duty to provide the police with evidence of criminal conduct that they inadvertently acquire in the course of routine treatment, when they undertake to obtain such evidence from their patients *for the specific purpose of incriminating those patients*, they have a special obligation to make sure that the patients are fully informed about [and give knowing waivers of] their constitutional rights. . .[24] Cf. *Miranda* v. *Arizona*, 384 U.S. 436 (1966).

As respondents have repeatedly insisted, their motive was benign rather than punitive. Such a motive, however, cannot justify a departure from Fourth Amendment protections, given the pervasive involvement of law enforcement with the development and application of the MUSC policy. The stark and unique fact that characterizes this case is that Policy M-7 was designed to obtain evidence of criminal conduct by the tested patients that would be turned over to the police and that could be admissible in subsequent criminal prosecutions. . .

Opinion Footnotes

9 In arguing that the urine tests at issue were not searches, the dissent attempts to disaggregate the taking and testing of the urine sample from the reporting of the results to the police. However, in our special needs cases, we have routinely treated urine screens taken by state agents as searches within the meaning of the Fourth Amendment even though the results were not reported to the police, see, *e.g.*, *Chandler* v. *Miller*, 520 U.S. 305 (1997); *Vernonia School Dist. 47J* v. *Acton*, 515 U.S. 646 (1995); *Skinner* v. *Railway Labor Executives' Assn.*, 489 U.S. 602, 617 (1989); *Treasury Employees* v. *Von Raab*, 489 U.S. 656 (1989), and respondents here do not contend that the tests were not searches. Rather, they argue that the searches were justified by consent and/or by special needs.

14 In fact, we have previously recognized that an intrusion on that expectation may have adverse consequences because it may deter patients from receiving needed medical care. *Whalen* v. *Roe*, 429 U.S. 589, 599–600 (1977).

15 The dissent, . . . relying on *Griffin* v. *Wisconsin*, 483 U.S. 868 (1987), argues that the special needs doctrine "is ordinarily employed, precisely to enable searches *by law enforcement* officials who, of course, ordinarily have a law enforcement objective. . . *Griffin* does not support the proposition for which the dissent invokes it. . ."

19 Accordingly, the police organized a meeting with the staff of the police and hospital laboratory staffs, as well as Nurse Brown, in which the police went over the concept of a chain of custody system with the MUSC staff.

20 We italicize those words lest our reasoning be misunderstood. See KENNEDY, J., concurring in judgment. In none of our previous special needs cases have we upheld the collection of evidence for criminal law enforcement purposes. Our essential point is the same as Justice Kennedy's—the extensive entanglement of law enforcement cannot be justified by reference to legitimate needs.

According to the dissent, the fact that MUSC performed tests prior to the development of Policy M-7 should immunize any subsequent testing policy despite the presence of a law enforcement purpose and extensive law enforcement involvement. To say that any therapeutic purpose did not disappear is simply to miss the point. What matters is that under the new policy developed by the solicitor's office and MUSC, law enforcement involvement was the means by which that therapeutic purpose was to be met. . . .

24 . . .The dissent . . . mischaracterizes our opinion as holding that "material which a person voluntarily entrusts to someone else cannot be given by that person to the police and used for whatever evidence it may contain." But, as we have noted elsewhere, given the posture of the case, we must assume for purposes of decision that the patients did *not* consent to the searches, and we leave the question of consent for the Court of Appeals to determine.

JUSTICE KENNEDY, concurring in the judgment.

I agree that the search procedure in issue cannot be sustained under the Fourth Amendment. My reasons for this conclusion differ somewhat from those set forth by the Court. . .

The Court does not dispute that the search policy at some level serves special needs, beyond those of ordinary law enforcement, such as the need to protect the health of mother and child when a pregnant mother uses cocaine. Instead, the majority characterizes these special needs as the "ultimate goal[s]" of the policy, as distinguished from the policy's "immediate purpose," the collection of evidence of drug use, which, the Court reasons, is the appropriate inquiry for the special needs analysis.

The majority views its distinction between the ultimate goal and immediate purpose of the policy as critical to its analysis. . .

. . .I agree with the Court that the search policy cannot be sustained [, but not because of this distinction.] As the majority demonstrates and well explains, there was substantial law enforcement involvement in the policy from its inception. None of our special needs precedents has sanctioned the routine inclusion of law enforcement, both in the design of the policy and in using arrests, either threatened or real, to implement the system designed for the special needs objectives. The special needs cases we have decided do not sustain the active use of law enforcement, including arrest and prosecutions, as an integral part of a program which seeks to achieve legitimate, civil objectives. The traditional warrant and probable-cause requirements are waived in our previous cases on the explicit assumption that the evidence obtained in the search is not intended to be used for law enforcement purposes. . . .

In my view, it is necessary and prudent to be explicit in explaining the limitations of today's decision. The beginning point ought to be to acknowledge the legitimacy of the State's interest in fetal life and of the grave risk to the life and health of the fetus, and later the child, caused by cocaine ingestion. Infants whose mothers abuse cocaine during pregnancy are born with a wide variety of physical and neurological abnormalities. . . . There can be no doubt that a mother's ingesting this drug can cause tragic injury to a fetus and a child. *There should be no doubt that South Carolina can impose punishment upon an expectant mother who has so little regard for her own unborn that she risks causing him or her lifelong damage and suffering.* [Emphasis added.—AU.] The State, by taking special measures to give rehabilitation and training to expectant mothers with this tragic addiction or weakness, acts well within its powers and its civic obligations.

The holding of the Court, furthermore, does not call into question the validity of mandatory reporting laws such as child abuse laws which require teachers to report evidence of child abuse to the proper authorities, even if arrest and prosecution is the likely result. That in turn highlights the real difficulty. . . . [R]eputable sources confirm. . . the premise that the medical profession can adopt acceptable criteria for testing expectant mothers for cocaine use in order to provide prompt and effective counseling to the mother and to take proper medical steps to protect the child. If prosecuting authorities then adopt legitimate procedures to discover this information and prosecution follows, that ought not to invalidate the testing. One of the ironies of the case, then, may be that the program now under review, which gives the cocaine user a second and third chance, might be replaced by some more rigorous system. We must, however, take the case as it comes to us; and the use of handcuffs, arrests, prosecutions, and police assistance in designing and implementing the testing and rehabilitation policy cannot be sustained under our previous cases concerning mandatory testing.

An essential, distinguishing feature of the special needs cases is that the person searched has consented, though the usual voluntariness analysis is altered because adverse consequences (*e.g.*, dismissal from employment or disqualification from playing on a high school sports team), will follow from refusal. The person searched has given consent . . . . The consent, and the circumstances in which it was given, bear upon the reasonableness of the whole special needs program.

Here, on the other hand, the question of consent, even with the special connotation used in the special needs cases, has yet to be decided. . . .

JUSTICE SCALIA, with whom THE CHIEF JUSTICE and JUSTICE THOMAS join as to Part II, dissenting.

There is always an unappealing aspect to the use of doctors and nurses, ministers of mercy, to obtain incriminating evidence against the supposed objects of their ministration—although here, it is correctly pointed out, the doctors and nurses were ministering not just to the mothers but also to the children whom their cooperation with the police was meant to protect. But whatever may be the correct social judgment concerning the desirability of what occurred here, that is not the issue in the present case. . . . The question before us is a narrower one: whether . . . this police conduct . . . violates the Fourth Amendment's prohibition of unreasonable searches and seizures. In my view, it plainly does not.

I

The first step in Fourth Amendment analysis is to identify the search or seizure at issue. What petitioners, the Court, and to a lesser extent the concurrence really object to is not the urine testing, but the hospital's reporting of positive drug-test results to police. But the latter is obviously not a search. . . . There is only one act that could conceivably be regarded as a search of petitioners in the present case: the *taking* of the urine sample. I suppose the *testing* of that urine for traces of unlawful drugs could be considered a search of sorts, but the Fourth Amendment protects only against searches of citizens' "persons, houses, papers, and effects"; and it is entirely unrealistic to regard urine as one of the "effects" (*i.e.*, part of the property) of the person who has passed and abandoned it. Cf. *California* v. *Greenwood,* 486 U.S. 35 (1988) (garbage left at curb is not property protected by the Fourth Amendment). Some would argue, I suppose, that testing of the urine is prohibited by some generalized privacy right "emanating" from the "penumbras" of the Constitution (a question that is not before us); but it is not even arguable that the testing of urine that has been lawfully obtained is a Fourth Amendment search. . .

It is rudimentary Fourth Amendment law that a search which has been consented to is not unreasonable. There is no contention in the present case that the urine samples were extracted forcibly. The only conceivable bases for saying that they were obtained without consent are the contentions (1) that the consent was coerced by the patients' need for medical treatment, (2) that the consent was uninformed because the patients were not told that the tests would include testing for drugs, and (3) that the consent was uninformed because the patients were not told that the results of the tests would be provided to the police. (When the court below said that it was reserving the factual issue of consent, see 186 F. 3d 469, 476 (CA4 1999), it was referring at most to these three—and perhaps just to the last two.)

Under our established Fourth Amendment law, the last two contentions would not suffice, even without reference to the special-needs doctrine. The Court's analogizing of this case to *Miranda* v. *Arizona,* 384 U.S. 436 (1966), and its claim that "standards of knowing waiver" apply, are flatly contradicted by our jurisprudence, which shows that using lawfully (but deceivingly) obtained material for purposes other than those represented, and giving that material or information derived from it to the police, is not unconstitutional. In *Hoffa* v. *United States,* 385 U.S. 293 (1966), "[t]he argument [was] that [the informant's] failure to disclose his role as a government informant vitiated the consent that the petitioner gave" for the agent's access to evidence of criminal wrongdoing, *id.*, at 300. We rejected that argument, because "the Fourth Amendment [does not protect] a wrongdoer's misplaced belief that a person to whom he voluntarily confides his wrongdoing will not reveal it." *Id.*, at 302. Because the defendant had voluntarily provided access to the evidence, there was no reasonable expectation of privacy to invade...

Until today, we have *never* held—or even suggested—that material which a person voluntarily entrusts to someone else cannot be given by that person to the police, and used for whatever evidence it may contain. Without so much as discussing the point, the Court today opens a hole in our Fourth Amendment jurisprudence, the size and shape of which is entirely indeterminate. and (like the South Carolina law relevant here, see S. C. Code Ann. § 20–7–510 (2000)) evidence of child abuse....

II

I think it clear, therefore, that there is no basis for saying that obtaining of the urine sample was unconstitutional. The special-needs doctrine is thus quite irrelevant, since it operates only to validate searches and seizures that are otherwise unlawful. In the ensuing discussion, however, I shall assume [for the sake of argument] ... that the taking of the urine sample was ... coerced. Indeed, I shall even assume (contrary to common sense) that the testing of the urine constituted an unconsented search of the patients' effects. On those assumptions, the special-needs doctrine *would* become relevant; and, properly applied, would validate what was done here.

The conclusion of the Court that the special-needs doctrine is inapplicable rests upon its contention that respondents "undert[ook] to obtain [drug] evidence from their patients" not for any medical purpose, but *"for the specific purpose of incriminating those patients."* [I disagree.] . . .

The cocaine tests started in April 1989, *neither at police suggestion nor with police involvement*. Expectant mothers who tested positive were referred by hospital staff for substance-abuse treatment, . . . an obvious health benefit to both mother and child. . . .[Later the police became involved in improving the hospital policy.] Why would there be any reason to believe that, once this policy of using the drug tests for their "ultimate" health benefits had been adopted, use of them for their original, *immediate*, benefits somehow disappeared, and testing somehow became in its entirety nothing more than a "pretext" for obtaining grounds for arrest? On the face of it, this is incredible. The only evidence of the exclusively arrest-related purpose of the testing adduced by the Court is that the police-cooperation policy *itself* does not describe how to care for cocaine-exposed infants. But *of course* it does not, since that policy, adopted months after the cocaine testing was initiated, had as its only health object the "ultimate" goal of inducing drug treatment through threat of arrest. Does the Court really believe (or even *hope*) that, once invalidation of the program challenged here has been decreed, drug testing will cease? . . .

Petitioners seek to distinguish *Griffin* by observing that probationers enjoy a lesser expectation of privacy than does the general public. That is irrelevant to the point I make here, which is that the presence of a law enforcement purpose does not render the special-needs doctrine inapplicable. In any event, I doubt whether Griffin's reasonable expectation of privacy in his home was any less than petitioners' reasonable expectation of privacy in their urine taken, or in the urine tests performed, in a hospital—especially in a State such as South Carolina, which recognizes no physician-patient testimonial privilege and requires the physician's duty of confidentiality to yield to public policy; and which requires medical conditions that indicate a violation of the law to be reported to authorities, see, *e.g.*, S. C. Code Ann. § 20–7–510 (2000) (child abuse). Cf. *Whalen* v. *Roe,* 429 U.S. 589, 597–598 (1977) (privacy interest does not forbid government to require hospitals to provide, for law enforcement purposes, names of patients receiving prescriptions of frequently abused drugs).

The concurrence makes essentially the same basic error as the Court, though it puts the point somewhat differently. . .

* * *

> As I indicated at the outset, it is not the function of this Court—at least not in Fourth Amendment cases—to weigh petitioners' privacy interest against the State's interest in meeting the crisis of "crack babies" that developed in the late 1980's. I cannot refrain from observing, however, that the outcome of a wise weighing of those interests is by no means clear. The initial goal of the doctors and nurses who conducted cocaine-testing in this case was to refer pregnant drug addicts to treatment centers, and to prepare for necessary treatment of their possibly affected children. When the doctors and nurses agreed to the program providing test results to the police, they did so because (in addition to the fact that child abuse was required by law to be reported) they wanted to use the sanction of arrest as a strong incentive for their addicted patients to undertake drug-addiction treatment. And the police themselves used it for that benign purpose, as is shown by the fact that only 30 of 253 women testing positive for cocaine were ever arrested, and only 2 of those prosecuted. It would not be unreasonable to conclude that today's judgment, authorizing the assessment of damages against the county solicitor and individual doctors and nurses who participated in the program, proves once again that no good deed goes unpunished.
>
> But as far as the Fourth Amendment is concerned: There was no unconsented search in this case. And if there was, it would have been validated by the special-needs doctrine. For these reasons, I respectfully dissent.

Case Questions

1. Is Justice Kennedy correct in his (italicized) assertion that "there should be no doubt that South Carolina can impose punishment upon an expectant mother who has so little regard for her own unborn that she risks causing him or her lifelong damage and suffering"? Is there a meaningful difference between in utero child abuse and postbirth child abuse? Should women who knowingly abuse alcohol during the early months of pregnancy, when fetal alcohol syndrome is most likely to occur, be prosecutable?

2. What exactly does the Court majority see as the legal difference between a doctor coming upon the information that a patient is abusing cocaine in the normal course of medical examination, including medically indicated tests, and a doctor purposely looking for cocaine abuse without having come upon medical symptoms indicating the need for such tests?

3. If you leave a backpack at a friend's house for several hours, with the understanding that the friend, if she needs to, can go into the pack to borrow money, would you consider her authorized to give the police permission to search your pack

for evidence of drug dealing? Is this hypothetical situation different from your confiding to the friend that you are a drug dealer and her turning around and telling the police what you said? What exactly distinguishes the situations?

Update on Criminalizing Behavior During Pregnancy

The opioid addiction epidemic of the twenty-first century has brought intensified attention to drug use by pregnant women. As this book goes to press, 24 states and the District of Columbia define the ingestion of any illegal substance during pregnancy as child abuse. In three states, South Dakota, Minnesota, and Wisconsin, it is grounds for court-ordered civil commitment into an institution, such as a hospital with a drug treatment program, irrespective of whether the pregnant woman is in fact addicted. Early in 2018 Oklahoma and Montana announced new initiatives to prosecute pregnant women (as criminals) for using drugs *or* alcohol during pregnancy. Between 2006 and 2015, the state of Alabama, deploying a law originally targeted at parents who risk family safety by cooking amphetamines inside the home, prosecuted and sometimes imprisoned 479 pregnant women for "chemical endangerment" of their fetus.[156]

Lawmakers continue to face challenges in developing adequate treatment programs for pregnant women who would like to wean themselves from addiction for the sake of giving birth to a healthy infant (nineteen states currently publicly fund such programs), and also in developing policies for luring women into the programs that do exist and into obtaining adequate prenatal care. Babies born to opioid-ingesting mothers typically do endure a range of withdrawal symptoms that are encompassed under the label "neonatal abstinence syndrome" (or NAS).[157]

REPRODUCTIVE TECHNOLOGY AND THE LAW

When the twentieth century began, technology had not yet separated sex from procreation. As the century ended, technology was well on its way toward separating procreation from sex. Artificial insemination, in vitro fertilization, embryo implantation, and the preservation of ova, sperm, and zygotes have generated litigation and raised difficult legal and moral questions.

The *Baby M* Case (1988)

As in *A.C.*, the coerced caesarean case discussed above, *Baby M* had only a small geographic reach as a binding precedent, the state of New Jersey, yet it presented such compelling issues that it attracted *amicus curiae* briefs from a number of prominent national organizations (e.g., the American Adoption

Congress, the National Emergency Civil Liberties Union, the Eagle Forum, the Catholic League for Religious and Civil Rights) and even prominent, interested persons (e.g., authors the late Betty Friedan and Gloria Steinem). Unlike *A.C.*, it concerned not a brief and intensely private episode but a drawn-out, public melodrama. Thus, it also attracted weeks of national media attention.

Prior to this New Jersey Supreme Court decision, a number of other state courts had dealt with the legality of so-called surrogacy contracts—i.e., contracts between a man and a woman not married to each other that stipulate a sum of money to be paid to the woman in exchange for her conceiving (by artificial insemination) and bearing his child, and then agreeing to a termination of her own maternal rights so that his wife can adopt the baby. Courts in both New York[158] and Kentucky[159] had ruled that such contracts did not violate existing laws that prohibited baby selling or the payment of excessive fees in connection with adoption. Both courts stated that if the legislature wished to prohibit for-pay surrogacy contracts, it would have to do so explicitly. By contrast, the Michigan Supreme Court had ruled that state laws against excessive fees in connection with an adoption forbade a man to pay a woman for conceiving and bearing his child and for transferring the child to him and his wife.[160] All of these cases differed from the *Baby M* case in that they involved three willing parties—the husband, the wife, and the mother—and a challenge by government officials to the exchange of money.

The *Baby M* case began when the previously willing party, Mary Beth Whitehead, turned unwilling. Under a contract set up in February 1985 with her husband, Richard Whitehead, and with William Stern (and with regard to his wife, Elizabeth Stern), Mary Beth Whitehead agreed to conceive a child through artificial insemination using Stern's sperm, carry the child, deliver it at birth to the Sterns, and then do whatever was necessary to terminate her parental rights so that Mrs. Stern could adopt the baby. The Sterns agreed to pay nothing if the pregnancy did not proceed past four months, to pay $1,000 if the child were stillborn, and to pay $10,000 upon completion of Mrs. Whitehead's surrender of custody and termination of parental rights. (Stern also paid $7,500 to the Infertility Center of New York for arrangements in connection with the surrogacy contract.)

The motives of the parties were described in court as follows: Mrs. Stern had been diagnosed as possibly having multiple sclerosis and therefore feared serious risk to her health if she became pregnant. Mr. Stern wanted to continue his biological bloodline because most of his family had been destroyed in the Holocaust and he was the only survivor. Mrs. Whitehead's motives were that she wanted to give another couple "the gift of life" and that her own family (she had two children with Mr. Whitehead) needed the $10,000. On March 27, 1986, a baby girl was born to Mary Beth Whitehead, and on March 30 she delivered her to the Sterns, who took her home and named her Melissa. By this time Mrs. Whitehead had already cried when the Sterns mentioned naming the baby and expressed uncertainty about giving up the child. On March 31, she went to the Sterns' home and told them that she had become unable to eat, sleep, or concentrate on anything other than her need to have the baby back. She said she could not survive without the baby and that she had to have her, even if just for a week, after which she would return her. Fearing a potential suicide, the Sterns did relinquish the baby upon a promise of her return one week hence.

Mrs. Whitehead refused to return the baby, and she fled the state when Mr. Stern obtained a court order for custody of the child. She hid out with the baby in Florida until the Florida police tracked her down and enforced a second custody order that Stern had obtained from the Florida judiciary. From time to time during Mrs. Whitehead's fugitive sojourn in Florida, she would telephone the Sterns and plead her case, eventually turning to a variety of desperate threats (she would kill herself, kill the child, or falsely accuse William Stern of having sexually molested her other daughter). After the child was back in New Jersey, the trial court ruled that the surrogacy contract was enforceable, ordered termination of Whitehead's parental rights, granted sole custody to William Stern; and then, after a few minutes of testimony from Mrs. Stern, ordered that Mrs. Stern be allowed to adopt Melissa, her husband's daughter. Mary Beth Whitehead appealed the decision to the New Jersey Supreme Court, which handed down the following decision in February 1988, by which time Baby M was almost two years old.

IN THE MATTER OF BABY M
109 N.J 396; 537 A2d 1227 (1988)

CHIEF JUSTICE ROBERT WILENTZ:

...We invalidate the surrogacy contract because it conflicts with the law and public policy of this State. While we recognize the depth of the yearning of infertile couples to have their own children, we find the payment of money to a "surrogate" mother illegal, perhaps criminal, and potentially degrading to women. Although in this case we grant custody to the natural father, the evidence having clearly proved such custody to be in the best interests of the infant, we void both the termination of the surrogate mother's parental rights and the adoption of the child by the wife/stepparent. We thus restore the "surrogate" as the mother of the child. We remand the issue of the natural mother's visitation rights to the trial court, since that issue was not reached below and the record before us is not sufficient to permit us to decide it *de novo*.

We find no offense to our present laws where a woman voluntarily and without payment agrees to act as a "surrogate" mother, provided that she is not subject to a binding agreement to surrender her child. Moreover, our holding today does not preclude the Legislature from altering the current statutory scheme, within constitutional limits, so as to permit surrogacy contracts. Under current law, however, the surrogacy agreement before us is illegal and invalid....

II

Invalidity and Unenforceability of Surrogacy Contract

We have concluded that this surrogacy contract is invalid. Our conclusion has two bases: direct conflict with existing statutes and conflict with the public policies of this State, as expressed in its statutory and decisional law....

A. Conflict with Statutory Provisions

The surrogacy contract conflicts with: (1) laws prohibiting the use of money in connection with adoptions; (2) laws requiring proof of parental unfitness or abandonment before termination of parental rights is ordered or an adoption is granted; and (3) laws that make surrender of custody and consent to adoption revocable in private placement adoptions.

(1) Our law prohibits paying or accepting money in connection with any placement of a child for adoption.... Excepted are fees of an approved agency ... and certain expenses in connection with childbirth....

Considerable care was taken in this case to structure the surrogacy arrangement so as not to violate this prohibition. The arrangement was structured as follows: the adopting parent, Mrs. Stern, was not a party to the surrogacy contract; the money paid to Mrs. Whitehead was stated to be for her services—not for the adoption; the sole purpose of the contract was stated as being that "of giving a child to William Stern, its natural and biological father"; the money was purported to be "compensation for services and expenses and in no way ... a fee for termination of parental rights or a payment in exchange for consent to surrender a child for adoption"; the fee to the Infertility Center ($ 7,500) was stated to be for legal representation, advice, administrative work, and other "services." Nevertheless, it seems clear that the money was paid and accepted in connection with an adoption.... Mr. Stern knew he was paying for the adoption of a child; Mrs. Whitehead knew she was accepting money so that a child might be adopted; the Infertility Center knew that it was being paid for assisting in the adoption of a child. The actions of all three worked to frustrate the goals of the statute. It strains credulity to claim that these arrangements...really amount to something other than a private placement adoption for money.

... Baby-selling potentially results in the exploitation of all parties involved. Conversely, adoption statutes seek to further humanitarian goals, foremost among them the best interests of the child. H. Witmer, E. Herzog, E. Weinstein, & M. Sullivan, *Independent Adoptions: A Follow-Up Study* 32 (1967). The negative consequences of baby-buying are potentially present in the surrogacy context, especially the potential for placing and adopting a child without regard to the interest of the child or the natural mother.

(2) The termination of Mrs. Whitehead's parental rights called for by the surrogacy contract...fails to comply with the stringent requirements of New Jersey law. Our law, recognizing the finality of any termination of parental rights, provides for such termination only where there has been a voluntary surrender of a child to an approved agency or to the Division of Youth and Family Services ("DYFS"), accompanied by a formal document acknowledging termination of parental rights, ... or where there has been a showing of parental abandonment or unfitness.

[A] contractual agreement to abandon one's parental rights, or not to contest a termination action, will not be enforced in our courts. The Legislature would not have so carefully, so consistently, and so substantially restricted termination of parental rights if it had intended to allow termination to be achieved by one short sentence in a contract.

Since the termination was invalid, it follows, as noted above, that adoption of Melissa by Mrs. Stern could not properly be granted.

(3) The provision in the surrogacy contract stating that Mary Beth Whitehead agrees to "surrender custody . . . and terminate all parental rights" contains no clause giving her a right to rescind. It is intended to be an irrevocable consent to surrender the child for adoption. . . . The trial court required a "best interests" showing as a condition to granting specific performance of the surrogacy contract. 217 *N.J. Super.* at 399-400. Having decided the "best interests" issue in favor of the Sterns, that court's order included, among other things, specific performance of this agreement to surrender custody and terminate all parental rights.

...Such a provision, however, making irrevocable the natural mother's consent to surrender custody of her child in a private placement adoption, clearly conflicts with New Jersey law.

...Requirements for a voluntary surrender to an approved agency [state that] the surrender must be in writing,...and...must "be such as to declare that the person executing the same desires to relinquish the custody of the child, acknowledge the termination of parental rights as to such custody in favor of the approved agency, and acknowledge full understanding of the effect of such surrender as provided by this act."

If the foregoing requirements are met, the consent, the voluntary surrender of custody "shall be valid whether or not the person giving same is a minor and shall be irrevocable except at the discretion of the approved agency...."

The importance of that irrevocability is that the surrender itself gives the agency the power to obtain termination of parental rights...leading in the ordinary case to an adoption....

This statutory pattern, providing for a surrender in writing and for termination of parental rights by an approved agency, is generally followed in connection with adoption proceedings and proceedings by DYFS to obtain permanent custody of a child. Our adoption statute...speaks of such surrender as constituting "relinquishment of such person's parental rights in...the child *named therein* and consent by such person to adoption... We emphasize "named therein," for we construe the statute to allow a surrender only after the birth of the child.... [T]he Legislature severely limited the circumstances under which such consent would be irrevocable. The legislative goal is furthered by regulations requiring approved agencies, prior to accepting irrevocable consents, to provide advice and counseling to women, making it more likely that they fully understand and appreciate the consequences of their acts.

B. Public Policy Considerations

... The surrogacy contract's invalidity, resulting from its direct conflict with the above statutory provisions, is further underlined when its goals and means are measured against New Jersey's public policy....

... The surrogacy contract guarantees permanent separation of the child from one of its natural parents. Our policy, however, has long been that to the extent possible, children should remain with and be brought up by both of their natural parents....

... The surrogacy contract violates the policy of this State that the rights of natural parents are equal concerning their child, the father's right no greater than the mother's. "The parent and child relationship extends equally to every child and to every parent, regardless of the marital status of the parents." *N.J.S.A.* 9:17–40. . . . The whole purpose and effect of the surrogacy contract was to give the father the exclusive right to the child by destroying the rights of the mother.

The[se]. . . policies. . .stand in stark contrast to the surrogacy contract and what it implies. Here there is no counseling, independent or otherwise, of the natural mother, no evaluation, no warning. . .Under the contract, the natural mother is irrevocably committed before she knows the strength of her bond with her child. She never makes a totally voluntary, informed decision, for quite clearly any decision prior to the baby's birth is, in the most important sense, uninformed, and any decision after that, compelled by a pre-existing contractual commitment, the threat of a lawsuit, and the inducement of a $10,000 payment, is less than totally voluntary. . .

Although the interest of the natural father and adoptive mother is certainly the predominant interest, realistically the *only* interest served, even they are left with less than what public policy requires. They know little about the natural mother, her genetic makeup, and her psychological and medical history. Moreover, not even a superficial attempt is made to determine their awareness of their responsibilities as parents.

Worst of all, however, is the contract's total disregard of the best interests of the child. There is not the slightest suggestion that any inquiry will be made at any time to determine the fitness of the Sterns as custodial parents, of Mrs. Stern as an adoptive parent, their superiority to Mrs. Whitehead, or the effect on the child of not living with her natural mother.

This is the sale of a child, or, at the very least, the sale of a mother's right to her child, the only mitigating factor being that one of the purchasers is the father. Almost every evil that prompted the prohibition on the payment of money in connection with adoptions exists here.

. . .That the unwanted pregnancy is unintended while the situation of the surrogate mother is voluntary and intended, is really not significant. Initially, it produces stronger reactions of sympathy for the mother whose pregnancy was unwanted than for the surrogate mother, who "went into this with her eyes wide open." On reflection, however, it appears that the essential evil is the same, taking advantage of a woman's circumstances (the unwanted pregnancy or the need for money) in order to take away her child, the difference being one of degree.

...The point is made that Mrs. Whitehead *agreed* to the surrogacy arrangement, supposedly fully understanding the consequences. Putting aside the issue of how compelling her need for money may have been, and how significant her understanding of the consequences, we suggest that her consent is irrelevant. There are, in a civilized society, some things that money cannot buy.

...The surrogacy contract is based on principles that are directly contrary to the objectives of our laws. It guarantees the separation of a child from its mother; it looks to adoption regardless of suitability; it totally ignores the child; it takes the child from the mother regardless of her wishes and her maternal fitness; and it does all of this, it accomplishes all of its goals, through the use of money.

III

Termination

...Nothing in this record justifies a finding that would allow a court to terminate Mary Beth Whitehead's parental rights under the statutory standard. It is not simply that obviously there was no "intentional abandonment or very substantial neglect of parental duties without a reasonable expectation of reversal of that conduct in the future," *N.J.S.A.* 9:3–48c(1), quite the contrary, but furthermore that the trial court never found Mrs. Whitehead an unfit mother and indeed affirmatively stated that Mary Beth Whitehead had been a good mother to her other children. 217 *N.J. Super.* at 397...

IV

Constitutional Issues

Both parties argue that the Constitutions—state and federal—mandate approval of their basic claims. The source of their constitutional arguments is essentially the same: the right of privacy, the right to procreate, the right to the companionship of one's child, those rights flowing either directly from the fourteenth amendment or by its incorporation of the Bill of Rights, or from the ninth amendment, or through the penumbra surrounding all of the Bill of Rights. They are the rights of personal intimacy, of marriage, of sex, of family, of procreation. Whatever their source, it is clear that they are fundamental rights protected by both the federal and state Constitutions. [Here followed a string of U.S. Supreme Court parental rights/privacy case citations.] The right asserted by the Sterns is the right of procreation; that asserted by Mary Beth Whitehead is the right to the companionship of her child. We find that the right of procreation does not extend as far as claimed by the Sterns. As for the right asserted by Mrs. Whitehead, since we uphold it on other grounds (*i.e.*, we have restored her as mother and recognized her right, limited by the child's best interests, to her companionship), we need not decide that constitutional issue. . . .

We conclude that the right of procreation is best understood and protected if confined to its essentials, and that when dealing with rights concerning the resulting child, different interests come into play. There is nothing in our culture or society that even begins to suggest a fundamental right on the part of the father to the custody of the child as part of his right to procreate when opposed by the claim of the mother to the same child. We therefore disagree with the trial court: there is no constitutional basis whatsoever requiring that Mr. Stern's claim to the custody of Baby M be sustained. Our conclusion may thus be understood as illustrating that a person's rights of privacy and self-determination are qualified by the effect on innocent third persons of the exercise of those rights. . .

Mr. Stern also contends that he has been denied equal protection of the laws by the State's statute granting full parental rights to a husband in relation to the child produced, with his consent, by the union of his wife with a sperm donor. *N.J.S.A.* 9:17–44. The claim really is that of Mrs. Stern. It is that she is in precisely the same position as the husband in the statute: she is presumably infertile, as is the husband in the statute; her spouse by agreement with a third party procreates with the understanding that the child will be the couple's child. The alleged unequal protection is that the understanding is honored in the statute when the husband is the infertile party, but no similar understanding is honored when it is the wife who is infertile.

It is quite obvious that the situations are not parallel. A sperm donor simply cannot be equated with a surrogate mother. The State has more than a sufficient basis to distinguish the two situations—even if the only difference is between the time it takes to provide sperm for artificial insemination and the time invested in a nine-month pregnancy—so as to justify automatically divesting the sperm donor of his parental rights without automatically divesting a surrogate mother. Some basis for an equal protection argument might exist if Mary Beth Whitehead had contributed her egg to be implanted, fertilized or otherwise, in Mrs. Stern, resulting in the latter's pregnancy. That is not the case here, however.

V.

Custody

Having decided that the surrogacy contract is illegal and unenforceable, we now must decide the custody question without regard to the provisions of the surrogacy contract that would give Mr. Stern sole and permanent custody. . . . With the surrogacy contract disposed of, the legal framework becomes a dispute between two couples over the custody of a child produced by the artificial insemination of one couple's wife by the other's husband. Under the Parentage Act the claims of the natural father and the natural mother are entitled to equal weight, *i.e.*, one is not preferred over the other solely because he or she is the father or the mother. N.J.S.A. 9:17–40. The applicable rule given these circumstances is clear: the child's best interests determine custody.

Our custody conclusion is based on strongly persuasive testimony contrasting both the family life of the Whiteheads and the Sterns and the personalities and characters of the individuals. The stability of the Whitehead family life was doubtful at the time of trial. Their finances were in serious trouble (foreclosure by Mrs. Whitehead's sister on a second mortgage was in process). Mr. Whitehead's employment, though relatively steady, was always at risk because of his alcoholism, a condition that he seems not to have been able to confront effectively. Mrs. Whitehead had not worked for quite some time, her last two employments having been part-time. One of the Whiteheads' positive attributes was their ability to bring up two children, and apparently well, even in so vulnerable a household. Yet substantial question was raised even about that aspect of their home life. The expert testimony contained criticism of Mrs. Whitehead's handling of her son's educational difficulties. Certain of the experts noted that Mrs. Whitehead perceived herself as omnipotent and omniscient concerning her children. She knew what they were thinking, what they wanted, and she spoke for them. As to Melissa, Mrs. Whitehead expressed the view that she alone knew what that child's cries and sounds meant. Her inconsistent stories about various things engendered grave doubts about her ability to explain honestly and sensitively to Baby M—and at the right time—the nature of her origin. Although faith in professional counseling is not a *sine qua non* of parenting, several experts believed that Mrs. Whitehead's contempt for professional help, especially professional psychological help, coincided with her feelings of omnipotence in a way that could be devastating to a child who most likely will need such help. In short, while love and affection there would be, Baby M's life with the Whiteheads promised to be too closely controlled by Mrs. Whitehead. The prospects for wholesome, independent psychological growth and development would be at serious risk.

The Sterns have no other children, but all indications are that their household and their personalities promise a much more likely foundation for Melissa to grow and thrive. There *is* a track record of sorts—during the one-and-a-half years of custody Baby M has done very well, and the relationship between both Mr. and Mrs. Stern and the baby has become very strong. The household is stable, and likely to remain so. Their finances are more than adequate, their circle of friends supportive, and their marriage happy. Most important, they are loving, giving, nurturing, and open-minded people. They have demonstrated the wish and ability to nurture and protect Melissa, yet at the same time to encourage her independence. Their lack of experience is more than made up for by a willingness to learn and to listen, a willingness that is enhanced by their professional training, especially Mrs. Stern's experience as a pediatrician. They are honest; they can recognize error, deal with it, and learn from it. They will try to determine rationally the best way to cope with problems in their relationship with Melissa. When the time comes to tell her about her origins, they will probably have found a means of doing so that accords with the best interests of Baby M. All in all, Melissa's future appears solid, happy, and promising with them.

Based on all of this we have concluded, independent of the trial court's identical conclusion, that Melissa's best interests call for custody in the Sterns.

We remand to the trial court so that it may determine an appropriate visitation arrangement for Mrs. Whitehead. . .

Case Questions

1. What exactly is the societal harm in allowing adoptive parents to pay a birth mother for her child? Does New Jersey Chief Justice Wilentz convince you that this was a "baby selling" contract rather than a contract for services rendered? Can a father somehow "buy" his own child?

2. If this is more sensibly viewed as a contract for services rendered, might the state nonetheless forbid it, just as it forbids prostitution? Is payment for the use of a uterus (and "donation" of an egg) significantly different from payment for the use of a vagina? If it is unconscionable for the state to allow payment for these services, should the state not also forbid payment to sperm "donors," as well as egg

"donors"? Are donations of sperm and eggs for pay different in significant respects from selling one's parental rights to an actual child?

3. Should the right to privacy cover the right to exchange money for procreative services? Does the very exchange of money take the transaction out of the realm of the private and put it in the realm of the public? Would it be consistent with the Constitution for a state to ban the payment of money for abortion services? If a state were to set a minimum fee for surrogacy contracts in order to prevent economic exploitation of poor women, say, at $25,000, might someone who wanted to negotiate a contract for less—say, $22,000—plausibly claim an infringement of the right to privacy? Should the right to privacy mean that parenthood is so fundamental that mothers may not divest themselves of parental rights in advance of childbirth, and even after that must be given a substantial waiting period for further reflection? Does this question insult the maturity of women?

4. Suppose that in the judge's consideration of the custody issue, the two families had seemed approximately equal in quality of temperament, sensitivity to children's needs, and emotional and financial stability. (And suppose further that the two families were intensely hostile to each other, as these had become, so that joint custody was out of the question.) Would it be appropriate for the judge to count against the mother her written agreement to give up all rights to her child? To give the mother an automatic preference as a way of diminishing the incentives for fathers to hire "surrogate mothers" in the future?

5. As of 2016 the median annual wage for female full-time wage-earners is $38,948, 82% of the median for full-time wage-earning men ($47,580). In light of these figures, is it unconstitutionally discriminatory for judges awarding custody in divorce suits to consider the issue of "financial stability"? Is it unfair to the child not to consider it?

Policy Issues on Surrogate Motherhood

Challenges surrounding surrogacy remain. The ethical concerns continue. The power dynamics between surrogate mothers and the state, between surrogate mothers and the biological fathers of the children born through surrogacy arrangements and between the surrogate mothers and their husbands or partners continue. Questions about the economic and class-based circumstances that make surrogacy an attractive option for women to become surrogates also continue. Information on all aspects of surrogacy and other assisted reproductive technologies is widely available on the World Wide Web. The following excerpts are representative:

Surrogacy Perspectives

A surrogate mother:

I knew that I could carry a baby and I knew that I could go through a delivery again and my family was very supportive but I just could not imagine what it was like to have to find someone to do that for you. I spent many hours asking myself what made me think I was that kind of person and why someone should trust me.

I met my first couple in July of 99. We were made for each other. My IM was like a sister to me....When she held my hand during the transfer and I saw the tears well up in her eyes I realized that I was the one being given the gift of life. What an extraordinary opportunity I was being blessed with!

An intended parent:

Surrogacy is a wonderful thing, I know because it has provided me with two beautiful children and an extended family for life. Please do not let misunderstandings or half truths mar the miracle of surrogacy. It is stories like Baby M that make surrogacy so difficult for everyone. Please don't let another Baby M story set us back.

An egg donor:

It was the spring of 93 when my daughter was born at 35 weeks....We almost lost her. She battled pneumonia 4 times before her first birthday. It was this that made my mind up to do egg donation. I saw all the couples who wanted children so badly and couldn't have them and then I saw the couples who had unplanned pregnancies and unwanted children that they took for granted. I wanted to do anything I could to take this hurt away from the childless couples. I decided I would give them this gift, my eggs....

All in all, I have done 5 egg donations and there have been 5 pregnancies. I get up everyday and look at my own children and know I did something right.

The husband of a surrogate mother:

When Bobbi first laid it on my heart that she felt that she was being called to give the gift of a child to another couple, I was at first appalled at the thought, but then I realized that God had given her a gift that should be shared. It is not every woman who would go through so much pain and discomfort for someone else's benefit....If she has this special gift, how can I as a husband

> not want to support her—even if it means sacrifice on my part. The thing is, Bobbi is not doing this miracle on her own. We are both doing it together.
>
> I do not deny that one of the reasons that my wife and I agreed upon this course of action was financial gain. . . .But the fact remains that Jesus Christ came to serve and not be served, and my wife is using a special gift that she has to serve another couple—to give them the gift of a child that they have been denied because of medical reasons.[161]

Policy Issues on Surrogate Motherhood

Despite the negative press that accrued to the *Baby M* case, surrogacy remains a viable option for many individuals and families capable of covering the costs associated with hiring a surrogate. Today, individuals and couples contract with women as traditional surrogates—when the surrogate is artificially inseminated—as well as gestational surrogates—when a fertilized embryo (or embryos) are implanted in the surrogate. In these ways, surrogacy provides an opportunity to a broad array of individuals—including same-sex couples—to have a child that is genetically connected to one or both of the parents. As of 2016, New Jersey remains one of four states that expressly prohibit paid surrogacy, fourteen states and the District of Columbia expressly allow surrogacy, and in the remaining states the ". . .legality of surrogacy is not addressed by statute."[162] Payment to a surrogate mother averages between $45,000–$60,000 depending on the state and the possible circumstances of the pregnancy (e.g., whether the surrogate has birthed other children for the couple or whether the surrogate is working for a celebrity). Prices may be lower or higher for international surrogacy depending on the home country of the surrogate mother.

After *Baby M*

Muñoz v. Haro (1986) exemplifies Chief Justice Wilentz's fears. Nineteen-year-old Alejandra Muñoz became the victim of a scheme carried out by her relatives. Nettie and Mario Haro invited Alejandra and her daughter to their home in San Diego and helped the two cross the border from Mexico illegally. They asked her to sign a contract she later claimed she could not read and did not understand. The contract promised Alejandra $1,500 if she were inseminated with Mario's sperm, delivered a baby, and surrendered it to the couple. She signed it because her vulnerable status and her inability to speak English limited her alternatives. She consulted a lawyer only after the boy was born and Nettie signed her own name to the birth certificate. The trial court ruled that the contract was unenforceable, but ordered an arrangement similar to that in *Baby M*: the couple got custody, and the birth mother got visitation rights.[163]

The technology involved in *Baby M* and *Muñoz* is not new; artificial insemination has existed for more than 100 years. Gestational surrogacy, however, is a type of in vitro fertilization; it requires the implantation into one woman's body of the product of another woman's ovum and a man's sperm. *Johnson v. Calvert* (1993) presented a classic conflict between ownership and labor. Crispina Calvert had undergone a hysterectomy, but her ovaries still functioned. She and her husband, Mark, conceived a child *in vitro*. Anna Johnson agreed to have the embryo implanted in her body, carry the child to term, and surrender it to the Calverts. The relationship between the surrogate and the intended parents soured, and both sides sued. The California Supreme Court awarded child custody to the genetic parents, Mark and Crispina, with no visitation rights for Anna. Conceding that the state "recognizes both genetic consanguinity and giving birth as means of establishing a mother and child relationship, when the two means do not coincide in one woman, she who intended to procreate the child—that is, she who intended to bring about the birth of a child that she intended to raise as her own—is the natural mother under California law" (851 P.2d 776, 5 Cal. 4th 87, 93).

Nearly 20 years later. California Governor Jerry Brown signed Assembly Bill 1217 "Surrogacy agreements." The focus of the bill was to codify the case law established through several surrogacy cases including *Johnson v. Calvert*. The bill requires the intended surrogate mother and the intended parent(s) "to be represented by separate independent counsel. . . .prior to executing an assisted reproduction agreement for gestational carriers."[164] The bill also requires that specific information be included in surrogacy contracts and that embryos not be transferred until those contracts were fully executed. The law also allows parentage to be established before birth.

WHOSE PROPERTY ARE FROZEN EMBRYOS?

Davis v. Davis (1992)

Zygotes produced by in vitro fertilization need not be implanted in the uterus immediately; they can be stored for future use. When Mary Sue Davis and Junior Davis divorced, they had nine zygotes harvested "during a happier period in their relationship," stored at the Fertility Center of Eastern Tennessee in Knoxville.[165] Mary Sue wanted custody of them, but Junior wanted them destroyed. By the time the case reached the state supreme court, both had remarried, and Mary Sue no longer wanted the embryos for her own use; she wanted to donate them to a childless couple. The Tennessee Supreme Court ruled as follows in Junior's favor:

> Refusal to permit donation of the pre-embryos would impose on her the burden of knowing that the lengthy IVF procedures she underwent were futile, and that the pre-embryos to which she contributed genetic material would never become children. While this is not an insubstantial emotional burden, we can only conclude that Mary Sue Davis's interest in donation is not as significant as the interest Junior Davis has in avoiding parenthood. If she were allowed to donate these pre-embryos, he would face a lifetime of either wondering about his parental status or knowing about his parental status but having no control over it. He testified quite clearly that if these pre-embryos were brought to term he would fight for custody of his child or children. Donation, if a child came of it, would rob him twice—his procreational autonomy would be defeated and his relationship with his offspring would be prohibited (842 S.W. 2d 588, 603–04.).

A.Z. v. B.Z. (2000)

Partly as a result of cases like *Davis*, regulations and contracts for cryogenic preservation typically stipulate the disposition of frozen zygotes: They may be destroyed, donated, or distributed between the partners. Most court decisions honor these agreements, but *A.Z. v. B.Z.* (2000) was an exception. The Z's, a military couple, had married in 1977, conceived twin daughters through IVF, and stored several zygotes. The consent form signed by the couple and the storage facility stipulated that any unimplanted zygotes would be returned to the wife, A.Z. The marriage deteriorated to the extent that the wife obtained a restraining order against her husband. When they divorced, B.Z. asked the court to issue an order prohibiting A.Z. from having the pre-embryos implanted. The Massachusetts' Supreme Judicial Court upheld the ruling: "In this case, we are asked to decide whether the law of the Commonwealth may compel an individual to become a parent over his or her contemporaneous objection. The husband signed this consent form in 1991. Enforcing the form against him would require him to become a parent over his present objection to such an undertaking. We decline to do so."[166]

POSTHUMOUS PROCREATION: *WOODWARD V. COMMISSIONER OF SOCIAL SECURITY* (2002)

Two years later, also in Massachusetts, Lauren Woodward faced a different legal problem. Her husband, Warren, banked his sperm after he was diagnosed with leukemia and told that treatment might make him sterile. Inseminated with his sperm, Lauren gave birth to twins two years after his death. The Social Security Administration rejected Lauren's claim to survivor benefits for herself and the children on the grounds that she had failed to establish that Warren was the children's father. The state's highest court, whose rules for each state prevail under Social Security law, ruled in Lauren's favor.[167] The case was *Woodward v. Commissioner of Social Security*, 435 Mass. 536, 760 N.E.2d 257 (2002), and the court basically settled it by outlining those conditions that would permit, in its words,

> posthumously conceived children [to] enjoy the inheritance rights of "issue" under our intestacy law. These limited circumstances exist where, as a threshold matter, the surviving parent or the child's other legal representative demonstrates a genetic relationship between the child and the decedent. The survivor or representative must then establish both that the decedent affirmatively consented to posthumous conception and to the support of any resulting child. Even where such circumstances exist, time limitations may preclude commencing a claim for succession rights on behalf of a posthumously conceived child. In any action brought to establish such inheritance rights, notice must be given to all interested parties. . . .

CONCLUSION

The case with which this chapter began, *Buck v. Bell*, revealed the Supreme Court of the 1920s displaying what might reasonably be called an alarming insensitivity to the importance of the value of procreative freedom as against compulsory sterilization by government. Perhaps increased awareness of Nazi excesses moved the Court when it declared in 1942 in *Skinner* that procreation is a "basic civil right of man," one that is "fundamental."

This right evolved as litigation pressed attention to new circumstances on the Supreme Court. First, contraceptive freedom, then freedom to obtain abortions, then same-sex intimacy, and eventually same-sex marriage joined this umbrella right, now known as the right of privacy (see Chapter 5 for discussion of same-sex marriage). The U.S. Supreme Court, never far from any vortex of significance in U.S. politics, may soon confront new frontiers on questions of innovative reproductive technologies.

Meanwhile, many legislators at the state and national level continue to fight to overturn *Roe* by adopting laws that seek either to chip away at or blatantly undermine the right to obtain an abortion. The right to life movement, emboldened by its victory in gaining a national prohibition on partial birth abortion, has pushed Congress to pass a national prohibition on abortions performed after the twentieth week of pregnancy. The so-called Pain-Capable Unborn Child Protection Act has yet to pass Congress, but similar measures have passed in twenty states.[168] These laws run counter to the *Roe* and *Casey* decisions because they prohibit abortions pre-viability and do not include any exemptions for when the health and/or life of the pregnant woman would be jeopardized by a continued pregnancy. It is only a matter of time before the Justices of the Supreme Court will be asked to weigh in on one of these laws and revisit the *Roe* precedent yet again, and the October 2018 confirmation of Associate Justice Brett Kavanaugh is likely to accelerate this development.

---

[1] This earliest "strict scrutiny" test was formulated by the Court majority as follows: "The mere assertion that the [law's] subject relates though but in a remote degree to the public health does not necessarily render the enactment valid. The act *must have a more direct relation, as a means to an end, and the end itself must be appropriate and legitimate,* before an act can be held to be valid which interferes with the general right of an individual to be free. . .in his power to contract in relation to his own labor." (*Lochner v. New York*, 198 U.S. 45 [1905]; emphasis added) (Chapter 1.)

[2] *Lochner*; see Chapter 1.

[3] See note 1 above for the *Lochner* majority's statement of the level of scrutiny to be applied to infringements on the "right of contract." By contrast, three of the *Lochner* dissenters explained the rule of ordinary due process scrutiny as follows: "[If] the question [of the public welfare value of a statute] is one about which there is room for debate and for an honest difference of opinion. . .that ought to be the end of the case, for the State is not amenable to the judiciary, in respect of its legislative enactments, unless such enactments are plainly, palpably, beyond all question, inconsistent with the Constitution. . . ."

[4] 268 U.S. 510.

[5] *Gitlow v. New York*, 268 U.S. 652 (1925).

[6] *Near v. Minnesota*, 283 U.S. 697 (1931).

[7] *DeJonge v. Oregon*, 299 U.S. 353 (1937).

[8] *Meyer v. Nebraska*.

[9] *Cantwell v. Connecticut*, 310 U.S. 296 (1940). Interestingly, in adding freedom from the establishment of religion to the other First Amendment freedoms protected by the Fourteenth Amendment, the Supreme Court cites only one precedent (*Schneider v. State*, 308 U.S. 147), one which nowhere mentions that particular freedom.

[10] *West Coast Hotel v. Parrish*, 300 U.S. 379 (1937).

[11] This is a summary of the "Carolene Products footnote," note 4 of *United States v. Carolene Products*, 304 U.S. 144 (1938).

[12] Even when it did become clear in 1965 that they were live precedents, Justices Stewart and Black dissented vehemently, insisting that the substantive due process reasoning that undergirded the *Meyer* and *Pierce* cases had been "repudiated" by "many later opinions."

[13] *Reynolds v. Sims*, 377 U.S. 533 (1964) asserted for the first time that the right to vote is "constitutionally protected," that it is "one of the basic civil rights of man," and that it "is. . .fundamental. . .in a free and

democratic society." The right in question involved suffrage in state legislative elections, a matter which the Constitution implicitly (Art. I, sec. 2) left to state discretion. Of course, the Fifteenth, Nineteenth, and (later) Twenty-sixth Amendments do protect the right to vote for certain groups (Blacks, women, and 18–20-year olds), but no part of the Constitution explicitly addresses general suffrage rights in state elections. The Supreme Court in 1964 asserted that the equal protection clause implicitly does protect such a right.

14   *NAACP v. Alabama*, 357 U.S. 449 (1959). The right of political association is all but spelled out in the First Amendment's protection of the "right of the people peaceably to assemble and petition the government for redress of grievances."

15   *Crandall v. Nevada*, 6 Wall. 35.

16   Art. I, sec. 8, cl. 3. Its explicit statement is that "Congress shall have the power. . .to regulate commerce with foreign nations and among the states."

17   The first of these rules dates back at least to 1824, *Gibbons v. Ogden*, 9 Wheat 1. This reasoning formed the basis of the concurring opinions of Justice Clifford and Chief Justice Chase in *Crandall*. The latter rationale was the basis of the Court opinion in *Crandall*, authored by Justice Miller.

18   *Edwards v. California*, 314 U.S. 160 (1941).

19   *Kent v. Dulles*, 357 U.S. 116 (1958).

20   *Aptheker v. Secretary of State*, 378 U.S. 500 (1964).

21   Ibid., at 508.

22   Ibid., at 517. Justice Douglas, in a lone concurring opinion wrote at some length on why the freedom to travel was important in a free society. But he too had only a brief comment on the constitutional basis of the right: "Freedom of movement is kin to the rights of assembly and the right of free association. These rights may not be abridged." Ibid., at 520.

23   Reprinted in *The Flamingo's Smile* (New York: W. W. Norton, 1985), pp. 307–313.

24   In fact, the Supreme Court declared unconstitutional legislative mandates for this sort of equality of penalty in first degree murder cases in 1976. See *Woodson v. North Carolina*, 428 U.S. 280 and *Roberts v. Louisiana*, 428 U.S. 325.

25   Justice Holmes, author of the *Buck v. Bell Court* opinion, had written the dissenting opinion (for a group of four justices) in *Meyer v. Nebraska*.

26   Nilda Flores-Gonzalez, "Sterilization Abuse," in Judith A. Baer, ed., *Historical and Multicultural Encyclopedia of Women's Reproductive Rights in the United States* (Westport, Conn: Greenwood Publishing Company, 2002), p. 195. See also Anne Waters, "Native American Women and Reproductive Rights," Ibid., pp.143–47.

27   Judith A. Baer, *Women in American Law: The Struggle for Equality from the New Deal to the Present,* 3rd ed. (New York: Holmes and Meier, Inc., 2002), p. 125.

28   Boston Women's Health Collective, *Our Bodies, Ourselves for the New Century* (New York: Simon & Schuster, 1998), pp. 331–332.

29   See Susan Davis, ed., *Women Under Attack:* (Boston: South End Press, 1988); Susan M. Olson, "Government Sterilization Guidelines (1979)," in Baer, ed., *Encyclopedia*, pp. 83–84, above note 26.

30   See Linda Gordon, "Why Nineteenth-Century Feminists Did Not Support Birth Control and Twentieth-Century Feminists Do: Feminism, Reproduction, and the Family," in Barrie Thorne and Marilyn Yalom, eds., *Rethinking the Family: Some Feminist Questions* (New York: Longman, 1982). However, the danger that fertility control can increase women's sexual vulnerability has been recognized by some contemporary feminists. See, for example, Andrea Dworkin, *Right Wing Women* (Berkeley, Calif.: Berkeley Publication Group, 1983); Catharine A. Mackinnon, *Feminism Unmodified* (Cambridge, Mass: Harvard University Press, 1987) and *Toward a Feminist Theory of the State* (Ibid., 1989).

31   Margaret Sanger, *An Autobiography* (New York: W.W. Norton, 1938), pp. 90–91.

32   See Ellen Chesler, "Margaret Sanger," in Baer, ed., *Encyclopedia*, pp. 189–90.

33   *Poe v. Ullman*, 367 U.S. 497 (1961); *Tileston v. Ullman*, 318 U.S. 44 (1943).

34   In *Poe* the Court claimed that there was not yet a "controversy" (as required in Art. III) because no one had been arrested under it and it taxed the judicial credibility to expect that this outdated law would ever be enforced. Griswold later provoked enforcement by opening up a public birth control clinic. In *Tileston* the Supreme Court said that Dr. Tileston (a physician) did not have standing (see discussion of *Taylor v. Louisiana*

Women and Reproductive Freedom 713

in Chapter 2) to claim that his patients' lives were being threatened by the statute in violation of "due process of law." Only his patients, said the Court, could raise that claim.

35 The Bill of Rights applies only to the federal government. But the Supreme Court, in the post-World War II period, has held that most of those commands are implied in the Fourteenth Amendment's requirement that states observe "due process of law." For example, "due process of law" at the state level now includes the right to a lawyer, the right to trial by jury, the right against unreasonable searches, and the right against compulsory self-incrimination. It did not include any of these before the 1940s.

36 Justice Douglas, like Justice Black, was appointed by President Franklin Delano Roosevelt.

37 On the day after the abortion decision, January 23, 1973, *The New York Times* reported that the number of women intending to terminate their pregnancies at the time was estimated at 1.6 million.

38 Michaels was from a small town in a rural section of the state. He explained in interviews that conversations with his teen aged children had caused him to change his mind on the issue. He was, as he had predicted, defeated in the next election. See "Man Proud of Abortion Vote That Ended Career," Hilary Appelman, *Los Angeles Times*, July 5, 1992.

39 *The New York Times*, April 16, 1972.

40 *United States v. Vuitch*, 402 U.S. 62 (1971).

41 Thus, it is not sheer accident that in March 1972, in handing down the *Eisenstadt* decision, the Court spoke in terms not of contraception but of the choice "*whether to bear* or beget a child." The Court had just been listening to arguments to the effect that the right of privacy extended to such a choice.

42 Norma McCorvey, with Andy Meisler, *I am Roe: My Life, Roe v. Wade, and Freedom of Choice* (New York: HarperCollins, 1995).

43 Norma McCorvey with Gary Thomas, *Won by Love* (Nashville, TN: Thomas Nelson Publishers, 1997). Robert D. McFadden, "Norma McCorvey, 'Roe' in *Roe v. Wade*, is Dead at 69." *The New York Times*, February 18, 2017 Available at: https://www.nytimes.com/2017/02/18/obituaries/norma-mccorvey-dead-roe-v-wade.html?rref=collection®sectioncollection®obituaries (accessed April 12, 2018).

44 410 U.S. 179, 183.

45 428 U.S. 132. Because this case returned to the Court later, this version of it is referred to as *Bellotti I*.

46 450 U.S. 398.

47 439 U.S. 379.

48 462 U.S. 416 (1983).

49 O'Connor dissent, Section II.

50 Abortions needed to save a mother's life further the compelling interest in preserving *actual* lives; O'Connor, Rehnquist, and White would presumably acknowledge this to be even more compelling than preserving "potential" life.

51 O'Connor dissent, Section III, quoting *Maher v. Roe*, 432 U.S. 464, at 473–74 (1977); emphasis added.

52 Ibid.

53 *Akron v. Akron Center for Reproductive Health* (*Akron I*), 462 U.S. 416 (1983), Section III of Powell opinion.

54 Justice O'Connor dissented on this point as on the others, but she added a footnote (number 16) indicating that physicians may present persuasive First Amendment objections to this part of the statute, but that none had done so in this case. Her (and the other dissenters') views on the other regulations were that, except for parental consent, none imposed an undue burden on the abortion decision, and thus, since there was some reason for them, they were constitutional. She argued that reviewing the constitutionality of the parental consent provision was premature because it had yet to be authoritatively construed by state judges.

55 462 U.S. 476.

56 476 U.S. 747 (1986).

57 White dissent, Section I, A.

58 Ibid.

59 White dissent, Section I, B.

60 476 U.S. 747, 776–9.

⁶¹ This appointment was made on the heels of two failed nominations. The first was that of Robert Bork, a highly regarded, strongly conservative judge, who was rejected by the Senate on the grounds that his views were too extreme, or outside the American mainstream. The second was that of Douglas Ginsburg, a Harvard law professor (also very conservative in his politics), who withdrew his name from consideration after the press carried reports that he smoked marijuana with his students at Harvard (as well as some other rumors of impropriety in terms of judicial ethics).

⁶² 492 U.S. 490.

⁶³ 432 U.S. 438 (1977).

⁶⁴ See "supremacy clause," Art. VI, sec. 2, U.S. Constitution.

⁶⁵ 52 U.S.C. § 1396 (a) (17).

⁶⁶ 42 U.S.C. § 1396.

⁶⁷ 432 U.S. 464 (1977).

⁶⁸ All that this Connecticut statute said about the phrase "medically necessary" is that it included psychiatric necessity and that it should be determined by the attending physician.

⁶⁹ *Doe v. Rose*, 499 F. 2d 1112; *Wulff v. Singleton*, 508 F.2d 1211; *Doe v. Westby*, 383 F.Supp. 1143 and 402 F.Supp. 140; *Doe v. Wohlgemuth*, 376 F.Supp. 173 (this case became *Beal v. Doe*); *Doe v. Rampton*, 366 F.Supp. 189; and *Klein v. Nassau County Medical Center*, 347 F.Supp. 496 and 409 F.Supp. 731.

⁷⁰ *Edwards v. California*, 314 U.S. 160 (1941).

⁷¹ *Griffin v. Ill.,* 351 U.S. 12 (1956); *Burns v. Ohio*, 360 U.S. 252 (1959); *Smith v. Bennett*, 365 U.S. 708 (1961); *Long v. District Court*, 385 U.S. 192 (1966); *Roberts v. LaVallee*, 389 U.S. 40 (1967); *Mayer v. Chicago*, 404 U.S. 189 (1971).

⁷² *Gideon v. Wainwright*, 372 U.S. 335 (1963); *Douglas v. California*, 372 U.S. 353 (1963); *Argersinger v. Hamlin*, 407 U.S. 25 (1972).

⁷³ *Harper v. Virginia Board of Elections*, 383 U.S. 663 (1966).

⁷⁴ *Turner v. Fouche*, 396 U.S. 346 (1969).

⁷⁵ *Boddie v. Connecticut*, 401 U.S. 371 (1971).

⁷⁶ *Harper v. Virginia Board of Elections*, 383 U.S. 663 (1966).

⁷⁷ *United States v. Kras*, 409 U.S. 434 (1973).

⁷⁸ 432 U.S. 519 (1977).

⁷⁹ The Fourteenth Amendment restricts only the states, so parties wanting to claim that a national law violates equal protection of the law typically argue that this idea is implied in the Fifth Amendment phrase "due process of law." This strategy was first endorsed by the Supreme Court in *Korematsu v. U.S.*, 323 U.S. 214 (1944).

⁸⁰ 448 U.S. 297 (1980).

⁸¹ Nonetheless, 14 states continued to finance Medicaid abortions with their own state funds.

⁸² 492 U.S. 490, 557–560.

⁸³ Excerpted from Justice John Paul Stevens dissenting in part and concurring in part, *Webster v. Reproductive Health Services* (1989), 563–572.

⁸⁴ "Mifeprex (mifepristone) Information," U.S. Food and Drug Administration, U.S. Department of Health and Human Services, March 30, 2016, updated February 5, 2018. Available at https://www.fda.gov/Drugs/DrugSafety/ucm111323.htm (accessed May 9, 2018).

⁸⁵ Ibid.

⁸⁶ "Abortion Surveillance—United States, 2014," Tara C. Jatlaoui et.al., *Surveillance Summaries*, Centers for Disease Control, November 24, 2017, Volume 66(24); 1–48. https://www.cdc.gov/mmwr/volumes/66/ss/ss6624a1.htm (accessed May 27, 2018). "Mifeprex (mifepristone) Information," U.S. Food and Drug Administration, above note 84.

⁸⁷ John Burnett, "Legal Medical Abortions Are Up In Texas, But So Are DIY Pills From Mexico," National Public Radio. Available at https://www.npr.org/sections/health-shots/2016/06/09/481269789/legal-medical-abortions-are-up-in-texas-but-so-are-diy-pills-from-mexico (accessed May 9, 2018). Sabrina Tavernise, "New F.D.A. Guidelines Ease Access to Abortion Pill," *The New York Times*, March 30 and 31,

2016. Available at https://www.nytimes.com/2016/03/31/health/abortion-pill-mifeprex-ru-486-fda.html (accessed May 9, 2018).

[88] "Why George W. Bush's Position on RU486 is in Tension with his Position on Partial Birth Abortion," Sherry Colb, *Legal Commentary*, U.S. Supreme Court Center, October 23, 2000. Available at: https://supreme.findlaw.com/legal-commentary/why-george-w-bushs-position-on-ru486-is-in-tension-with-his-position-on-partial-birth abortion.html (accessed May 27, 2018).

[89] Guttmacher results reported here: "U.S. Abortion Rate Falls to Lowest Level since *Roe v. Wade*," Sarah McCammon, *National Public Radio, Inc.*, January 17, 2017. Available at: https://www.npr.org/sections/thetwo-way/2017/01/17/509734620/u-s-abortion-rate-falls-to-lowest-level-since-roe-v-wade (accessed May 27, 2018).

[90] "A New Front in the War Over Reproductive Rights: 'Abortion-Pill Reversal'," Ruth Graham, *The New York Times*, July 18, 2017.

[91] 500 U.S. 173.

[92] 42 U.S.C. Par. 300a–6.

[93] 42 CFR Par. 59.5(a)(9) (1972).

[94] 42 CFR Par. 59.8(a)(1) (1989).

[95] 42 CFR Par. 59.8(a)(2) and 59.8(a)(3).

[96] 42 CFR Par. 59.8(b)(5).

[97] 42 CFR Par. 59.10(a).

[98] 42 CFR Par. 59.9.

[99] *Massachusetts v. Secretary of Health and Human Services*, 899 F. 2d 53 (CA1 1990); *Planned Parenthood Federation of America v. Sullivan*, 913 F. 2d 1492 (CA10 1990).

[100] *Rust v. Sullivan* and *New York v. Sullivan*, 889 F. 2d 401 (CA2 1989).

[101] The question is not discussed by any of the justices, but the dissenting views of Justices Stevens, Blackmun, and Marshall implicitly assume the continuing validity of *Roe v. Wade*.

[102] 497 U.S. 417 (1990).

[103] 59 U.S.L.W. 3338.

[104] Kaiser Family Foundation, "The Mexico City Policy: An Explainer," 2018. www.kff.org/global-health-policy/fact-sheet/mexico-city-policy-explainer/ (accessed October 6, 2018) .

[105] "About Us," United Nations Population Fund. Available at: www.unfpa.org/about-us (accessed February 26, 2018).

[106] Kaiser Family Foundation, "The Mexico City Policy," above note 104; "Presidential Memorandum Regarding the Mexico City Policy," Donald J. Trump, January 23, 2017. Available at: https://www.whitehouse.gov/presidential-actions/presidential-memorandum-regarding-mexico-city-policy/ (accessed May 27, 2018).

[107] The only other jointly authored U.S. Supreme Court opinion known to the authors of this book is *Cooper v. Aaron*, 358 U.S. 1 (1958), in which all nine justices signed the opinion, responding to a request for slowing school desegregation in Little Rock with the reply that widespread and intense community opposition can never be valid grounds for denying people their constitutional rights. The co-authoring of an opinion by all nine justices is unique in U.S. history.

[108] *Lee v. Weisman*, 505 U.S. 577 (1992).

[109] *Bray v. Alexandria Women's Health Clinic*, 506 U.S. 263. After argument in October 1991 and re-argument in October 1992, the case was decided on January 13, 1993. In a 5–4 vote, the Supreme Court interpreted abortion clinic blockades as not violating any current federal statute, thus leaving their punishment to state and local authorities.

[110] *Ada v. Guam*, 506 U.S. 1011 (1992).

[111] *Barnes v. Moore*, 506 U.S. 1013 (1992).

[112] According to the dissent of Justice Thomas, use of the "partial birth abortion" method achieved prominence as a national issue after it was publicly described by Dr. Martin Haskell in a paper, "Dilation and Extraction for Late Second Trimester Abortion," at the National Abortion Federation's September 1992 Risk Management Seminar. See *Stenberg v. Carhart*, at 987.

113 Julie Rovner of NPR, " 'Partial-Birth Abortion': Separating Fact From Spin," Feb.21, 2006, https://www.npr.org/2006/02/21/5168163/partial-birth-abortion-separating-fact-from-spin (accessed Oct.7, 2018).

114 Ibid.

115 David Brown, "Data Lacking on Abortion Method: Statistics on Late-Term Procedure Among Most Contested," *The Washington Post*, April 19, 2007. Available at: http://www.washingtonpost.com/wp-dyn/content/article/2007/04/18/AR2007041802428_pf.html (accessed May 27, 2018).

116 Rover, note 113 above.

117 Meanwhile, the Seventh Circuit Court of Appeals had ruled to the contrary on a similar law in *Hope Clinic* v. *Ryan*, 195 F.3d 857 (CA7 1999).

118 *Stenberg v. Carhart*, at 923–24.

119 Ibid., at 985, note 3, citing *The Developing Human: Clinically Oriented Embryology 6th Edition* (Ann Arbor, MI: Saunders, 1998).

120 PUBLIC LAW 108–105—NOV. 5, 2003.

121 Mark Kaufman, "Ban on Type of Abortion Reversed: 'Partial Birth' Law Faces Challenges," *The Washington Post*, June 2, 2004, p. A01. Available at: http://www.washingtonpost.com/wp-dyn/articles/A6694-2004Jun1.html (accessed May 27, 2018).

122 Specter was a Democrat pre-1965 and 2009–2012, and a Republican from 1965–2009.

123 "Confirmation Hearing on the Nomination of John G. Roberts, Jr. to be Chief Justice of the United States. Hearing Before the Committee on the Judiciary," United States Senate, 109th Congress, First Session, September 12–15, 2005. Serial No. J-109-37, Government Printing Office, Washington, DC.

124 *U.S. v. Anderson*, 716 F.2d 446 (1983). The kidnappers happened to steal $300 from the doctor while they held him.

125 *National Organization for Women (NOW) et al. v. Operation Rescue et al.*, 914 F. 2d 582 (1990); *Nat'l Org. For Women (NOW) et al. v. Operation Rescue et al.*, 726 F. Supp. 1483 (E.D. Va. 1989).

126 *Jayne Bray et al. v. Alexandria Women's Health Clinic et al.*, 506 U.S. 263 (1993).

127 *National Organization for Women, et al. v. Joseph Scheidler et al.*, 510 U.S. 249 (1994), reversing the dismissal in the lower courts and ordering a hearing; 765 F.Supp 937 (1991), dismissing the complaint; 968 F2d 612 (1992), upholding the dismissal.

128 "Highlights 1996–2006." Available at: https://now.org/about/history/highlights/#1996 (accessed May 18, 2018). Joe Scheidler, head of PLAN, continued the lawsuit. The case came back to the U.S. Supreme Court in 2003 (see below) with a less favorable result for the applicability of RICO.

129 These facts and those in the next two paragraphs come from Gregg Ivers, *American Constitutional Law, Power and Politics, Vol. Two Civil Rights and Liberties* (Boston: Houghton Mifflin, 2002), pp. 110–111.

130 512 U.S. 753 (1994).

131 *Operation Rescue, et al v. Women's Health Center et al.*, 626 So. 2d 664, 667.

132 *Madsen v. Women's Health Center*, 512 U.S. 753.

133 Ibid., at 764–8.

134 519 U.S. 357.

135 Ibid., at 362–363.

136 "Threats over Abortion Execution," Lloyd Vries, CBS News, September 3, 2003. Available at: https://www.cbsnews.com/news/threats-over-abortion-execution/ (accessed May18, 2018), *American Constitutional Law*, 110–111; "Anti-Abortion Activist Executed," Phillip Davis, NPR All Things Considered, September 3, 2003. Available at: https://www.npr.org/templates/story/story.php?storyId=1419472 (accessed May 20, 2018).

137 18 U.S.C. § 1952. This act forbids, among other things, traveling in interstate commerce in order to commit extortion.

138 *Scheidler v. National Organization for Women*, 123 S. Ct. 1057 (2003), at 1062–1063.

139 *National Organization for Women et al. v. Scheidler et. al.*, 267 F.3d 687 (2001).

140 *Whole Woman's Health v. Hellerstedt*, 136 S.Ct. 2292, 2297 (2016).

141 "US Supreme Court Nomination: When is it Announced, and Who Will Donald Trump Pick?" Max Benwell, *Independent*, January 31, 2017. Available at: https://www.independent.co.uk/news/world/americas/

donald-trump-supreme-court-nomination-when-is-it-how-can-i-watch-video-latest-a7555086.html (accessed May 27, 2018).

142 Kimberly Leonard, "After Hobby Lobby Ruling, a Way to Cover Birth Control" *U.S. News and World Report*, July 10, 2015 https://www.usnews.com/news/articles/2015/07/10/after-hobby-lobby-ruling-hhs-announces-birth-control-workaround (accessed Oct.7, 2018).

143 Robert Pear, Rebecca R. Ruiz and Laurie Goodstein, "Trump Administration Rolls Back Birth Control Mandate." *The New York Times*, October 6, 2017. Available at: https://www.nytimes.com/2017/10/06/us/politics/trump-contraception-birth-control.html (accessed on May 11, 2018).

144 Ibid.

145 American Civil Liberties Union, "Federal Court Blocks Implementation of Trump Administration Birth Control Rule in California." Available at: https://www.aclu.org/news/federal-court-blocks-implementation-trump-administration-birth-control-rule-california (accessed on April 22, 2018).

146 *Jacobson v. Massachusetts*, 197 U.S. 11 (1905).

147 *Raleigh-Fitkin Paul Morgan Hospital v. Anderson*, 201 A. 2d 537 (1964) (ordering a transfusion to a woman in her 32nd week of pregnancy); *Crouse Irving Memorial Hospital v. Paddock*, 485 N.Y.S. 2d 443 (ordering a transfusion for a fetus that was to be prematurely delivered); *In re Jamaica Hospital*, 491 N.Y.S. 2d 898 (1985) (ordering a transfusion to a woman 18 weeks pregnant). In a somewhat different situation, *In re President and Directors of Georgetown College*, 331 F. 2d 1000, 1008 (D.C.Cir.), cert. den., 377 U.S. 978 (1964), upheld the order of a transfusion to a woman on the grounds that she had a "responsibility to the community to care for her infant."

148 This is the group that brought the suit in the 1986 Supreme Court abortion case *Thornburgh v. American College of Obstetricians and Gynecologists*.

149 573 A.2d 1235 (1990).

150 Reprinted at 573 A.2d 1259. In that case, the woman had been in labor for two and a half days and refused on religious grounds to allow a caesarean. A blockage made birth canal delivery dangerous to both mother and child; the child faced serious danger of death or brain damage and the mother faced risk of serious infection. The mother's (and father's) religious claim was that Muslims believe that a mother may choose to avoid a risk to her own health even if it means a threat to her fetus. Doctors had placed the risk to the woman of undergoing a caesarean at 0.25% but the risk of fatality to the fetus from attempting vaginal delivery at 50–75%. Caesarean delivery took place, pursuant to court order and a healthy child was born, without injury to the mother's health.

151 *Whitner v. South Carolina*, 492 S.E.2d 777 (1995), cert. denied, 523 U.S. 1145 (1998). At least eight other states, all cited by the South Carolina Supreme Court in this decision, have contrary policies, forbidding such prosecutions.

152 *Ferguson v. Charleston*, 532 U.S. 67 (2001), at 71, note 4.

153 Ibid., at 73.

154 This center is a nonprofit legal advocacy organization formed in 1992. In January 2003 it changed its name to the Center for Reproductive Rights. See "About Us." Available at: www.crlp.org/about.html (accessed August 21, 2003).

155 *Ferguson et al. v. Charleston*, 186 F.3d 469 (1999).

156 Jennifer Egan, "Children of the Epidemic," *The New York Times Sunday Magazine* (May 13, 2018), 34–41 and 59–61 at 38.

157 Ibid., at 37–38.

158 *In the matter of Baby Girl, L.J.*, 505 N.Y.S.2d 813 (1986).

159 *Surrogate Parenting v. Commonwealth ex rel. Armstrong*, 704 S.W.2d 209 (1986). The judge in this case allowed revocation of the mother's promise to give up the child for until five days after birth, just as with ordinary adoption in that state.

160 *Doe v. Kelley*, 307 N.W.2d 438 (1981), cert.denied, 459 U.S. 1183 (1983).

161 Surrogate Mothers Online (Available at: http://www.surromomsonline.com, accessed May 20, 2018).

162 "Surrogacy Law and Policy in the U.S.," Alex Finkelstein et al., *Columbia Law School Sexuality & Gender Law Clinic*, May 2016, Appendix A, p. 55. Available at: https://web.law.columbia.edu/sites/default/files/

microsites/gender-sexuality/files/columbia_sexuality_and_gender_law_clinic_-_surrogacy_law_and_policy_report_-_june_2016.pdf (accessed May 27, 2018).

163 Nikki Graves, "*Muñoz v. Haro,*" in Baer, ed., *Encyclopedia,* pp. 137–38, above note 26.

164 California Assembly Bill 1217, Chapter 466, "An act to amend Section 7960 of, to amend the heading of Part 7 (commencing with Section 7960) of Division 12 of, and to add Section 7962 to, the Family Code, relating to surrogacy agreements," September 2012. Available at: http://leginfo.legislature.ca.gov/faces/billNavClient.xhtml?bill_id=201120120AB1217 (accessed May 27, 2018).

165 842 S.W.2d 588, 589.

166 725 N.E.2d 1051, 1059 (2000).

167 Although federal law preempts state law, Social Security Administration regulations follow the applicable state law in determining who qualifies for survivors' benefits. Therefore, the state court's determination was dispositive in this case.

168 Sheryl Gay Stolberg, "Senate Rejects Bill to Ban Abortions after 20 Weeks," (January 30, 2018), *The New York Times*, A14.

CHAPTER 5

Gender and Family Law

WHAT IS MARRIAGE?

"Marriage, while from its very nature a sacred obligation, is nevertheless, in most civilized nations, a civil contract, and usually regulated by law. Upon it society may be said to be built, and out of its fruits spring social relations and social obligations."[1] Thus said the U.S. Supreme Court in *Reynolds v. United States* (1878), upholding the government's power to forbid plural marriage against a First Amendment challenge based on free exercise of religion. While this case involved a federal law over Utah Territory, states regulate marriage and family law through their police powers.[2]

Once, every jurisdiction in the U.S. restricted marriage to one woman and one man who were above a minimum age (usually younger than the age of majority), legally competent, and not married to anyone else, and also forbidding various degrees of consanguinity (e.g., brother-sister, first cousins). Laws against "miscegenation"—interracial marriage—were once common, especially those prohibiting marriages between whites and non-whites. The Supreme Court struck down one of the 16 remaining anti-miscegenation statutes in *Loving v. Virginia* (1967) as an instance of "the racial discrimination which it was the object of the Fourteenth Amendment to eliminate,"[3] but also determined that it was a violation of the fundamental right to marry.[4] In doing so, the Court harked back to the anti-sterilization case *Skinner v. Oklahoma* (1942) (see Chapter 4) to declare that marriage itself is a constitutionally protected, fundamental right. "Marriage is one of the 'basic civil rights of man,' fundamental to our very existence and survival (*Skinner v. Oklahoma,* 316 U.S. 535, 541 (1942))."[5]

Gay Rights and Marriage

When the gay rights movement began in the 1960s, homosexual behavior was being treated as grounds for criminal incarceration and/or as mental illness warranting institutionalization. By the second decade of the twenty-first century LGBTQ political, legal, and cultural activism had brought wide acceptance of homosexuality. As of 2017, nearly two-thirds of the public agree that homosexuality is morally acceptable, up from 38% fifteen years earlier.[6]

Court rulings both reflected and molded these changes. *Romer v. Evans,* 517 U.S. 620 (1996) ruled that an amendment to Colorado's constitution prohibiting local-level or future state-level governmentally-protected (anti-discrimination) status for gays and lesbians violated the equal protection clause.[7] In *Lawrence v. Texas,* 539 U.S. 558 (2003), the Supreme Court ruled that laws prohibiting oral or anal sex between two persons of the same sex violated the liberty and privacy rights implied in the due process clause of the Fourteenth Amendment—over Justice Scalia's protest that this decision posed a threat to "laws against bigamy, same-sex marriage, adult incest, prostitution, masturbation[!], adultery, fornication, bestiality, and obscenity."[8] *Lawrence* overturned a 1986 decision, *Bowers v. Hardwick* (478 U.S. 186), which had held that sodomy (statutorily defined in both cases as oral or anal sex) was not included in the right of privacy (see Chapter 4).[9]

At the same time, U.S. Supreme Court decisions recognized the right of private groups and organizations to discriminate against LGBTQ persons based on the First Amendment guarantees of free association. In *Boy Scouts of America v. Dale,* 530 U.S. 640 (2000), a majority of the Court determined that the Boy Scouts could legally prohibit gay males from joining the organization as members or leaders because homosexuality ran counter to the group's organizational values. (The Boy Scouts of America have since abandoned this position, admitting gay scouts in 2013, gay leaders in 2015, transgender boys in 2017, and girls in 2018, with a large exemption for religious groups to continue their discrimination.)[10] This case is significant because it licenses private groups to exclude LGBTQ individuals if their presence runs counter to the organization's message.

In sum, the Supreme Court has prohibited state laws that single out gays and lesbians for negative treatment as violations of the 14th Amendment guarantees of equal protection and/or privacy while allowing private organizations' acts of discrimination to be protected under the First Amendment. With these precedents on the record, the Supreme Court, after some twenty years of litigation at the state level, eventually confronted the question whether state laws restricting marriage to one man and one woman violated the Fourteenth Amendment.

Before 1991 gay couples did not have the right to marry. They could will their property to each other or sign advance directives making each other legal guardian in the event of incapacity, but without these interventions their relationships had no legal status. In 1983, when Sharon Kowalski of St. Cloud, Minnesota was badly injured in a collision with a drunk driver, the hospital forbade her partner, Karen Thompson, to see her because she was not "family." Kowalski's parental family cut off contact with Thompson. It took eight years and two court decisions for Thompson to become Kowalski's guardian.[11] Thompson finally won guardianship in December of 1991, and this itself was lauded as a major gay rights victory, but by then constitutional protection for same-sex marriage had already been asserted in the state courts of Hawaii.

In 1991, three same-sex couples sued the state of Hawaii to force the Director of Health, John C. Lewin, to issue them marriage licenses. The trial court in *Baehr v. Lewin,* 74 Haw. 645, 852 P.2d 44, rejected the same-sex marriage claim, and the parties appealed to the Hawaii Supreme Court which ruled that the denial of marriage licenses to same-sex couples should be evaluated using strict scrutiny under the state constitution. The plurality opinion explained that allowing heterosexual marriages but prohibiting same-sex marriages might violate the state constitution's equal protection guarantees, and remanded the case to the trial court so the state could adduce compelling interests necessitated by limiting marriage to heterosexual couples. The trial court then ruled that the state failed to meet its compelling interest test but stayed the injunction opening up marriage, pending Hawaiian Supreme Court review. By this point, it was December 1996, and national attention was focused on Hawaii.

Article IV, Section 1 of the U.S. Constitution includes the Full Faith and Credit Clause which states that, "Full Faith and Credit shall be given in each State to the public Acts, Records, and judicial Proceedings of every other State. And the Congress may by general Laws prescribe the Manner in which such Acts, Records and Proceedings shall be proved, and the Effect thereof." Under this clause, states generally do recognize the validity of marriages performed out of state, but have traditionally retained a right to make exceptions against marriages that violate the strong policy commitments of the state.[12] Opponents of same-sex marriage worried that marriage licenses issued to same-sex couples in Hawaii might be legally enforceable if and when those couples moved to another state. Opponents of such marriages implemented a two-prong strategy to stop its legalization. First, they focused attention on influencing the outcome within the state of Hawaii by lobbying for a state constitutional amendment that would prohibit same-sex marriage. Second, they took proactive steps to restrict the effects of marriage equality should their attempts to sway the situation in Hawaii fail, by lobbying Congress to pass legislation that would exempt states from recognizing same-sex marriage licenses of Hawaii. The mobilization against marriage equality was so strong that Lambda Legal characterized it as "one of the most profound examples of backlash in our movement's history."[13]

Although Hawaii was then by referendum to adopt a constitutional amendment allowing marriage to remain as exclusively a one-male-one-female arrangement before its Supreme Court could take final action, these state judicial innovations provoked Congress into adopting the federal Defense of Marriage Act (DOMA), and President Clinton signed it into law in 1996. It stated, "The word 'marriage' means only a legal union between one man and one woman as husband and wife, and the word 'spouse' refers only to a person of the opposite sex who is a husband or a wife."[14] This language meant that all federal benefits associated with marriage would be available only to marriages of a female plus male couple. DOMA also stated that "No State, territory, or possession of the United States, or Indian tribe, shall be required to give effect to any public act, record, or judicial proceeding of any other State, territory, possession, or tribe respecting a relationship between persons of the same sex that is treated as a marriage under the laws of such other State, territory, possession, or tribe, or a right or claim arising from such relationship."[15] This exempted states from having to recognize same-sex marriages from other states. In addition to the federal DOMA, thirty states passed "little DOMAs" by 2000.

The backlash against marriage equality catalyzed liberal gay rights groups. They prioritized this issue despite the long standing disagreements within LGBTQ communities about this approach. While liberal gay rights groups believed that marriage equality would convey important cultural recognition and material benefits on married LGBTQ couples, others within LGBTQ communities argued that gaining access and assimilating into heteronormative institutions would privilege homonormative gays and lesbians at the expense of others and undermine the goal of a queer liberation from traditional heterosexist constraints. (Despite these disagreements, however, the doubters among LBGTQ groups did not actively oppose legal reforms of marriage.)

Proponents and opponents of marriage equality engaged in a number of heated political and legal battles across the states. In the immediate aftermath of DOMA, proposals that granted same-sex couples the right to form civil unions or domestic partnerships, as distinguished from governmentally-recognized marriages, made headway in the states. In fact, Hawaii adopted a domestic partnership statute in 1997 in order to provide legal recognition to same-sex Hawaiian couples who could not marry.[16] According to the National Conference of State Legislatures, as of 2014 seven states plus DC had enacted domestic partnership laws and four states allowed civil unions. Five states which had at one time allowed civil unions converted those civil unions to marriage.[17]

Prior to 2015, the protections within each category varied across the states. Some states, for example, required employers to extend health benefits to domestic partners while others did not. In contrast, states with civil unions extended nearly all of the benefits of marriage to same-sex couples in legally recognized relationships. The path to extending these rights in some states was more contentious than others; e.g., some states, such as Nevada, enacted civil unions over a governor's veto. Other states, such as Wisconsin, established domestic partnership registries as a means to protect same sex couples where the state constitution defined marriage as between a man and a woman only. There were also regional differences. States in the southeastern U.S. were slower to adopt any protections for same-sex unions. Most of these states enacted constitutional amendments defining marriage as between a man and a woman.[18]

In 1999, the Supreme Court of Vermont declared the state's prohibition on same-sex marriage to be a violation of the state constitution and demanded that the legislature either allow gays and lesbians to marry or form legally equivalent same sex unions. Thus, in 2000, the Vermont legislature created domestic partnerships with all of the legal benefits of marriage.

In 2003, Massachusetts became the first state in the U.S. to legalize same-sex marriages when the Massachusetts Supreme Judicial Court decided *Goodridge v. Department of Public Health*.[19] Marriage licenses were issued to same-sex couples in Massachusetts the following May. Efforts to amend the state constitution to reverse this decision (as Hawaii had done) failed there. Emboldened by these developments, local-level officials in a number of states granted same-sex marriage licenses in 2004 that were later challenged.[20] At the same time, however, in November 2004, eleven of the eleven state ballot initiatives to prohibit marriage equality prevailed at the ballot box. It was increasingly clear that marriage equality was one of the most hotly contested political issues of the early twenty-first century.

As increased public attention was focused on the issue of marriage equality, polling began to reveal a change in public opinion: Americans were becoming more accepting of gays and lesbians.[21] Some states chose to follow the innovative path of Hawaii's Supreme Court. By the time the U.S. Supreme Court took up the same sex marriage question in 2015, thirty-seven states had legalized same-sex marriage either by court action or by legislation. Of these, twenty-five had same-sex marriage imposed by court decision: three states, between 2004 and 2009 (generally by state courts) and the remainder, between 2013 and 2015 (largely by federal courts after the pivotal *Windsor* decision of June 2013, excerpted below). Eight had done so by state legislation between 2009 and 2014, and three by popular vote in 2012–2013. Washington, DC legalized same-sex marriage in 2010.[22] According to Chief Justice Roberts' dissent in *Obergefell v. Hodges*, 576 U.S. ___ (2015), at the time of that decision, five of the court-imposed changes in marriage law came at the hands of state supreme courts; the other twenty came from federal courts. Plainly, the U.S. Supreme Court's decision in *U.S. v. Windsor*, 570 U.S. 744 (2013), changed the calculus moving forward, especially accelerating movement in the lower federal courts that struck down state discrimination against same-sex marriage. Two years after *Windsor*, the U.S. Supreme Court acted to recognize the right of two persons of marriageable age (per state law) to marry each other without regard to sexual orientation or gender identity.

The U.S. Supreme Court Changes the Definition of Marriage

Although the U.S. Constitution includes no explicit language protecting marriage, the Fifth and the Fourteenth amendments have been used by advocates to argue that marriage should be recognized as a fundamental right whether the partners are members of the same or different sexes.

The Fifth Amendment due process clause states that "No person shall . . .be deprived of life, liberty, or property, without due process of law." After DOMA passed in 1996, the federal government defined marriage as being solely between a man and a woman as did several state constitutions. Defining marriage as being solely between a man and a woman at the federal level excluded same-sex couples from collecting the numerous federal benefits that are extended to married couples. DOMA denied to same-sex couples who succeeded in getting married under state law any eligibility for the *federal* marriage benefits. Some of these benefits are sizable: spouses who did not pay into the Social Security system and who are legally married for at least ten years (whether the marriage ends by divorce or death) may receive a portion of their spouse's monthly Social Security benefit. Individuals earning significantly less than their spouses may receive higher Social Security benefits than if based on their own income history, provided that they were married to their spouse for at least 10 years. Such benefits are denied to individuals who are not legally married no matter the length of their relationship or domestic partnership.

Federal inheritance laws also apply differently to married couples compared with individuals. For instance, property transfers are tax free between spouses, including upon the death of one spouse. This means that surviving spouses do not need to pay an estate tax in order to take ownership of their spouse's property. Individuals may also transfer unlimited amounts of money to their spouses, and these recipients do not need to pay a gift tax. Individuals in domestic partnerships or civil unions or those who are not married are subject to estate and gift taxes should property be transferred between partners.

U.S. v. Windsor (2013)

U.S. v. Windsor focused on whether a same-sex marriage performed in Canada and recognized by the State of New York would be recognized by the U.S. government for the purpose of a surviving spouse avoiding estate taxes. Thea Clara Spyer and Edith Windsor, two women, were married in Toronto, Canada in 2007. Spyer died in 2009 naming Windsor as the sole executor and beneficiary of her estate. The couple resided in New York, which enacted a same-sex marriage statute in 2011. As such, Spyer and Windsor were legally married under state law, but their marriage was not recognized by U.S. federal law. Because DOMA established that the federal government would recognize marriages only between one man and one woman, the estate incurred inheritance taxes when it otherwise would not have. The inheritance tax to transfer Spyer's estate to Windsor exceeded $350,000.

On November 9, 2010 Windsor filed suit in the U.S. District Court for the Southern District of New York seeking a declaration that the Defense of Marriage Act was unconstitutional. At the time the suit was filed, the government's position was that DOMA must be defended, but on February 23, 2011, the President and the Attorney General announced that the Obama Administration would no longer defend DOMA. On April 18, 2011, the Bipartisan Legal Advisory Group of the House of Representatives (BLAG) filed a petition to intervene in defense of DOMA and moved to dismiss the case. The district court denied the motion and ruled DOMA unconstitutional and ordered the tax refund. The U.S. Court of Appeals for the Second Circuit affirmed the district court decision. BLAG appealed to the U.S. Supreme Court. In a 5–4 decision, the U.S. Supreme Court refused to dismiss the case and ruled that Section 3 of DOMA was unconstitutional on Fifth Amendment due process grounds.

U.S. v. Windsor
570 U.S. 744 (2013)

Justice Kennedy delivered the opinion of the Court.

II.

The decision of the Executive not to defend the constitutionality of § 3 in court while continuing to deny refunds and to assess deficiencies does introduce a complication. . . .

The *amicus* submits that once the President agreed with Windsor's legal position and the District Court issued its judgment, the parties were no longer adverse. From this standpoint the United States was a prevailing party below, just as Windsor was. Accordingly, the *amicus* reasons, it is inappropriate for this Court to grant certiorari and proceed to rule on the merits; for the United States seeks no redress from the judgment entered against it. . . .

[We disagree.] In this case the United States retains a stake sufficient to support Article III jurisdiction on appeal and in proceedings before this Court. The judgment in question orders the United States to pay Windsor the refund she seeks. An order directing the Treasury to pay money is a real and immediate economic injury, indeed as real and immediate as an order directing an individual to pay a tax. That the Executive may welcome this order to pay the refund if it is accompanied by the constitutional ruling it wants does not eliminate the injury to the national Treasury if payment is made, or to the taxpayer if it is not. . . .

[T]hese principles suffice to show that this case presents a justiciable controversy under Article III,. . .

. . .And the capable defense of the law by BLAG ensures that . . . prudential issues do not cloud the merits question, which is one of immediate importance to the Federal Government and to hundreds of thousands of persons. These circumstances support the Court's decision to proceed to the merits. . . .

III.

When at first Windsor and Spyer longed to marry, neither New York nor any other State granted them that right. After waiting some years, in 2007 they traveled to Ontario to be married there. It seems fair to conclude that, until recent years, many citizens had not even considered the possibility that two persons of the same sex might aspire to occupy the same status and dignity as that of a man and woman in lawful marriage. For marriage between a man and a woman no doubt had been thought of by most people as essential to the very definition of that term and to its role and function throughout the history of civilization. That belief, for many who long have held it, became even more urgent, more cherished when challenged. For others, however, came the beginnings of a new perspective, a new insight. Accordingly some States concluded that same-sex marriage ought to be given recognition and validity in the law for those same-sex couples who wish to define themselves by their commitment to each other. The limitation of lawful marriage to heterosexual couples, which for centuries had been deemed both necessary and fundamental, came to be seen in New York and certain other States as an unjust exclusion.

...[T]he laws of New York came to acknowledge the urgency of this issue for same-sex couples who wanted to affirm their commitment to one another before their children, their family, their friends, and their community. And so New York recognized same-sex marriages performed elsewhere; and then it later amended its own marriage laws to permit same-sex marriage. New York, in common with, as of this writing, 11 other States and the District of Columbia, decided that same-sex couples should have the right to marry and so live with pride in themselves and their union and in a status of equality with all other married persons. . . .

Against this background of lawful same-sex marriage in some States, the design, purpose, and effect of DOMA should be considered as the beginning point in deciding whether it is valid under the Constitution. By history and tradition the definition and regulation of marriage, as will be discussed in more detail, has been treated as being within the authority and realm of the separate States. Yet it is further established that Congress, in enacting discrete statutes, can make determinations that bear on marital rights and privileges. . . .[Here the court gave examples of federal laws that gave priority, counter to state law, to a former wife over a recent wife in life insurance benefits; that gave priority to federal rules as against state rules for deciding what kind of marriages qualify an alien to enter the U.S. as an immigrant; and that made common law marriage valid for Social Security benefit purposes even in states that do not allow common law marriage.—AU.]. . .

Though these discrete examples establish the constitutionality of limited federal laws that regulate the meaning of marriage in order to further federal policy, DOMA has a far greater reach; for it enacts a directive applicable to over 1,000 federal statutes and the whole realm of federal regulations. And its operation is directed to a class of persons that the laws of New York, and of 11 other States, have sought to protect. . . .

. . .

. . . "[T]he states, at the time of the adoption of the Constitution, possessed full power over the subject of marriage and divorce . . . [and] the Constitution delegated no authority to the Government of the United States on the subject of marriage and divorce." *Haddock v. Haddock,* 201 U.S. 562, 575 (1906); see also *In re Burrus,* 136 U.S. 586, 593–594 (1890). . .

Consistent with this allocation of authority, the Federal Government, through our history, has deferred to state-law policy decisions with respect to domestic relations. . . . In order to respect this principle, the federal courts, as a general rule, do not adjudicate issues of marital status even when there might otherwise be a basis for federal jurisdiction. See *Ankenbrandt v. Richards,* 504 U.S. 689, 703 (1992). Federal courts will not hear divorce and custody cases even if they arise in diversity because of "the virtually exclusive primacy. . . of the States in the regulation of domestic relations." *Id.,* at 714 (Blackmun, J., concurring in judgment).

. . . Against this background DOMA rejects the long-established precept that the incidents, benefits, and obligations of marriage are uniform for all married couples within each State, though they may vary, subject to constitutional guarantees, from one State to the next. . . .[Moreover t]he State's power in defining the marital relation is of central relevance in this case quite apart from principles of federalism. Here the State's decision to give this class of persons the right to marry conferred upon them a dignity and status of immense import. When the State used its historic and essential authority to define the marital relation in this way, its role and its power in making the decision enhanced the recognition, dignity, and protection of the class in their own community. DOMA, because of its reach and extent, departs from this history and tradition of reliance on state law to define marriage. "Discriminations of an unusual character especially suggest careful consideration to determine whether they are obnoxious to the constitutional provision." *Romer v. Evans,* 517 U.S. 620, 633 (1996). . . .

The Federal Government uses this state-defined class for the opposite purpose—to impose restrictions and disabilities. That result requires this Court now to address whether the resulting injury and indignity is a deprivation of an essential part of the liberty protected by the Fifth Amendment. . . .

The States' interest in defining and regulating the marital relation, subject to constitutional guarantees, stems from the understanding that marriage is more than a routine classification for purposes of certain statutory benefits. Private, consensual sexual intimacy between two adult persons of the same sex may not be punished by the State, and it can form "but one element in a personal bond that is more enduring." *Lawrence v. Texas,* 539 U.S. 558, 567 (2003). By its recognition of the validity of same-sex marriages performed in other jurisdictions and then by authorizing same-sex unions and same-sex marriages, New York sought to give further protection and dignity to that bond.... [New York's giving this bond lawful status] is a far-reaching legal acknowledgment of the intimate relationship between two people, a relationship deemed by the State worthy of dignity in the community equal with all other marriages. It reflects both the community's considered perspective on the historical roots of the institution of marriage and its evolving understanding of the meaning of equality.

IV

DOMA seeks to injure the very class New York seeks to protect. By doing so it violates basic due process and equal protection principles applicable to the Federal Government....*Bolling v. Sharpe,* 347 U.S. 497 (1954). The Constitution's guarantee of equality "must at the very least mean that a bare congressional desire to harm a politically unpopular group cannot" justify disparate treatment of that group. *Department of Agriculture v. Moreno,* 413 U.S. 528, 534 (1973).... DOMA cannot survive under these principles. The responsibility of the States for the regulation of domestic relations is an important indicator of the substantial societal impact the State's classifications have in the daily lives and customs of its people. DOMA's unusual deviation from the usual tradition of recognizing and accepting state definitions of marriage here operates to deprive same-sex couples of the benefits and responsibilities that come with the federal recognition of their marriages. This is strong evidence of a law having the purpose and effect of disapproval of that class. The avowed purpose and practical effect of the law here in question are to impose a disadvantage, a separate status, and so a stigma upon all who enter into same-sex marriages made lawful by the unquestioned authority of the States. The history of DOMA's enactment and its own text demonstrate that interference with the equal dignity of same-sex marriages, a dignity conferred by the States in the exercise of their sovereign power, was more than an incidental effect of the federal statute. It was its essence....

...DOMA writes inequality into the entire United States Code.... Among the over 1,000 statutes and numerous federal regulations that DOMA controls are laws pertaining to Social Security, housing, taxes, criminal sanctions, copyright, and veterans' benefits.

DOMA's principal effect is to identify a subset of state-sanctioned marriages and make them unequal. The principal purpose is to impose inequality... This places same-sex couples in an unstable position of being in a second-tier marriage. The differentiation demeans the couple, whose moral and sexual choices the Constitution protects, see *Lawrence,* 539 U.S. 558 and whose relationship the State has sought to dignify. And it humiliates tens of thousands of children now being raised by same-sex couples....

* * *

... [T]he principal purpose and the necessary effect of this law are to demean those persons who are in a lawful same-sex marriage. This requires the Court to hold, as it now does, that DOMA is unconstitutional as a deprivation of the liberty of the person protected by the Fifth Amendment of the Constitution.

The liberty protected by the Fifth Amendment's Due Process Clause contains within it the prohibition against denying to any person the equal protection of the laws....

The federal statute is invalid, for *no legitimate purpose* overcomes the purpose and effect to disparage and to injure those whom the State, by its marriage laws, sought to protect in personhood and dignity. [Emphasis added.—AU.] By seeking to displace this protection and treating those persons as living in marriages less respected than others, the federal statute is in violation of the Fifth Amendment. This opinion and its holding are confined to those lawful marriages.

The judgment of the Court of Appeals for the Second Circuit is affirmed....

CHIEF JUSTICE ROBERTS, dissenting.

I agree with Justice SCALIA that this Court lacks jurisdiction to review the decisions of the courts below. On the merits of the constitutional dispute the Court decides to decide, I also agree with Justice SCALIA that Congress acted constitutionally in passing the Defense of Marriage Act (DOMA). Interests in uniformity and stability amply justified Congress's decision to retain the definition of marriage that, at that point, had been adopted by every State in our Nation. . . .

The majority sees a more sinister motive, pointing out that the Federal Government has generally (though not uniformly) deferred to state definitions of marriage in the past. That is true, of course, but none of those prior state-by-state variations had involved differences over something—as the majority puts it—"thought of by most people as essential to the very definition of [marriage] and to its role and function throughout the history of civilization." *Ante.* That the Federal Government treated this fundamental question differently than it treated variations over consanguinity or minimum age is hardly surprising—and hardly enough to support a conclusion that the "principal purpose," *ante,* of the 342 Representatives and 85 Senators who voted for it, and the President who signed it, was a bare desire to harm. . . . At least without some more convincing evidence that the Act's principal purpose was to codify malice, and that it furthered *no* legitimate government interests, I would not tar the political branches with the brush of bigotry.

But while I disagree with the result to which the majority's analysis leads it in this case, I think it more important to point out that its analysis leads no further. The Court does not have before it, and the logic of its opinion does not decide, the distinct question whether the States, in the exercise of their "historic and essential authority to define the marital relation," *ante,* may continue to utilize the traditional definition of marriage. . . .

JUSTICE SCALIA, with whom JUSTICE THOMAS joins, and with whom THE CHIEF JUSTICE joins as to Part I, dissenting.

This case is about power in several respects. It is about the power of our people to govern themselves, and the power of this Court to pronounce the law. Today's opinion aggrandizes the latter, with the predictable consequence of diminishing the former. We have no power to decide this case. And even if we did, we have no power under the Constitution to invalidate this democratically adopted legislation. The Court's errors on both points spring forth from the same diseased root: an exalted conception of the role of this institution in America.

[Dissent on the standing argument is omitted—AU.]

. . .

II-A

...The opinion does not resolve and indeed does not even mention what had been the central question in this litigation: whether, under the Equal Protection Clause, laws restricting marriage to a man and a woman are reviewed for more than mere rationality....

...The sum of all the Court's nonspecific hand-waving is that this law is invalid (maybe on equal-protection grounds, maybe on substantive-due process grounds, and perhaps with some amorphous federalism component playing a role) because it is motivated by a " 'bare . . . desire to harm' " couples in same-sex marriages. *Ante*. It is this proposition with which I will therefore engage.

B

As I have observed before, the Constitution does not forbid the government to enforce traditional moral and sexual norms. See *Lawrence v. Texas*, 539 U.S. 558, 599 (2003) (SCALIA, J., dissenting). I will not swell the U.S. Reports with restatements of that point. It is enough to say that the Constitution neither requires nor forbids our society to approve of same-sex marriage, much as it neither requires nor forbids us to approve of no-fault divorce, polygamy, or the consumption of alcohol.

However, even setting aside traditional moral disapproval of same-sex marriage (or indeed same-sex sex), there are many perfectly valid—indeed, downright boring—justifying rationales for this legislation. Their existence ought to be the end of this case. For they give the lie to the Court's conclusion that only those with hateful hearts could have voted "aye" on this Act. And more importantly, they serve to make the contents of the legislators' hearts quite irrelevant: "It is a familiar principle of constitutional law that this Court will not strike down an otherwise constitutional statute on the basis of an alleged illicit legislative motive." *United States v. O'Brien*, 391 U.S. 367, 383 (1968). Or at least it *was* a familiar principle. By holding to the contrary, the majority has declared open season on any law that (in the opinion of the law's opponents and any panel of like-minded federal judges) can be characterized as mean-spirited.

The majority concludes that the only motive for this Act was the "bare . . . desire to harm a politically unpopular group." *Ante*. Bear in mind that the object of this condemnation is not the legislature of some once-Confederate Southern state. . ., but our respected coordinate branches, the Congress and Presidency of the United States. Laying such a charge against them should require the most extraordinary evidence, and I would have thought that every attempt would be made to indulge a more anodyne explanation for the statute. The majority does the opposite—affirmatively concealing from the reader the arguments that exist in justification. It makes only a passing mention of the "arguments put forward" by the Act's defenders, and does not even trouble to paraphrase or describe them. See *ante*. I imagine that this is because it is harder to maintain the illusion of the Act's supporters as unhinged members of a wild-eyed lynch mob when one first describes their views as *they* see them.

To choose just one of these defenders' arguments, DOMA avoids difficult choice-of-law issues that will now arise absent a uniform federal definition of marriage. See, *e.g.,* Baude, Beyond DOMA: Choice of State Law in Federal Statutes, 64 Stan. L.Rev. 1371 (2012). Imagine a pair of women who marry in Albany and then move to Alabama, which does not "recognize as valid any marriage of parties of the same sex." Ala.Code § 30–1–19(e) (2011). When the couple files their next federal tax return, may it be a joint one? Which State's law controls, for federal-law purposes: their State of celebration (which recognizes the marriage) or their State of domicile (which does not)? (Does the answer depend on whether they were just visiting in Albany?) Are these questions to be answered as a matter of federal common law, or perhaps by borrowing a State's choice-of-law rules? If so, *which* State's? And what about States where the status of an out-of-state same-sex marriage is an unsettled question under local law? See *Godfrey v. Spano,* 13 N.Y.3d 358, 892 N.Y.S.2d 272, 920 N.E.2d 328 (2009). DOMA avoided all of this uncertainty by specifying which marriages would be recognized for federal purposes. That is a classic purpose for a definitional provision.

Further, DOMA preserves the intended effects of prior legislation against then-unforeseen changes in circumstance. When Congress provided (for example) that a special estate-tax exemption would exist for spouses, this exemption reached only *opposite-sex* spouses—those being the only sort that were recognized in *any* State at the time of DOMA's passage. When it became clear that changes in state law might one day alter that balance, DOMA's definitional section was enacted to ensure that state-level experimentation did not automatically alter the basic operation of federal law, unless and until Congress made the further judgment to do so on its own. That is not animus—just stabilizing prudence. Congress has hardly demonstrated itself unwilling to make such further, revising judgments upon due deliberation. See, *e.g.,* Don't Ask, Don't Tell Repeal Act of 2010, 124 Stat. 3515.

The Court mentions none of this. Instead, it accuses the Congress that enacted this law and the President who signed it of something much worse than, for example, having acted in excess of enumerated federal powers—or even having drawn distinctions that prove to be irrational. Those legal errors may be made in good faith, errors though they are. But the majority says that the supporters of this Act acted with *malice*—with *the "purpose"* (*ante*) "to disparage and to injure" same-sex couples. It says that the motivation for DOMA was to "demean," *ibid.;* to "impose inequality," *ante*; to "impose. . . a stigma," *ante*; to deny people "equal dignity," *ibid.;* to brand gay people as "unworthy," *ante*; and to "*humiliat*[*e*]" their children, *ibid.* (emphasis added).

I am sure these accusations are quite untrue. To be sure (as the majority points out), the legislation is called the Defense of Marriage Act. But to defend traditional marriage is not to condemn, demean, or humiliate those who would prefer other arrangements, any more than to defend the Constitution of the United States is to condemn, demean, or humiliate other constitutions. To hurl such accusations so casually demeans *this institution*. In the majority's judgment, any resistance to its holding is beyond the pale of reasoned disagreement. To question its high-handed invalidation of a presumptively valid statute is to act (the majority is sure) with *the purpose* to "disparage," "injure," "degrade," "demean," and "humiliate" our fellow human beings, our fellow citizens, who are homosexual. All that, simply for supporting an Act that did no more than codify an aspect of marriage that had been unquestioned in our society for most of its existence. . . .

* * *

The penultimate sentence of the majority's opinion is a naked declaration that "[t]his opinion and its holding are confined" to those couples "joined in same-sex marriages made lawful by the State." *Ante.* I have heard such "bald, unreasoned disclaimer[s]" before. *Lawrence,* 539 U.S., at 604. When the Court declared a constitutional right to homosexual sodomy, we were assured that the case had nothing, nothing at all to do with "whether the government must give formal recognition to any relationship that homosexual persons seek to enter." *Id.,* at 578. Now we are told that DOMA is invalid because it "demeans the couple, whose moral and sexual choices the Constitution protects," *ante*—with an accompanying citation of *Lawrence.* It takes real cheek for today's majority to assure us, as it is going out the door, that a constitutional requirement to give formal recognition to same-sex marriage is not at issue here—when what has preceded that assurance is a lecture on how superior the majority's moral judgment in favor of same-sex marriage is to the Congress's hateful moral judgment against it. I promise you this: The only thing that will "confine" the Court's holding is its sense of what it can get away with.

I do not mean to suggest disagreement with THE CHIEF JUSTICE's view, *ante* (dissenting opinion), that lower federal courts and state courts can distinguish today's case when the issue before them is state denial of marital status to same-sex couples—or even that this Court could *theoretically* do so. . . .

In my opinion, however, the view that *this* Court will take of state prohibition of same-sex marriage is indicated beyond mistaking by today's opinion. As I have said, the real rationale of today's opinion. . . is that DOMA is motivated by " 'bare . . . desire to harm' " couples in same-sex marriages. *Supra*. How easy it is, indeed how inevitable, to reach the same conclusion with regard to state laws denying same-sex couples marital status. . . .

. . .

By formally declaring anyone opposed to same-sex marriage an enemy of human decency, the majority arms well every challenger to a state law restricting marriage to its traditional definition. Henceforth those challengers will lead with this Court's declaration that there is "no legitimate purpose" served by such a law, and will claim that the traditional definition has "the purpose and effect to disparage and to injure" the "personhood and dignity" of same-sex couples, see *ante*. The majority's limiting assurance will be meaningless in the face of language like that, as the majority well knows. That is why the language is there. The result will be a judicial distortion of our society's debate over marriage—a debate that can seem in need of our clumsy "help" only to a member of this institution.

. . .Since DOMA's passage, citizens on all sides of the question have seen victories and they have seen defeats. There have been plebiscites, legislation, persuasion, and loud voices—in other words, democracy. Victories in one place for some . . . are offset by victories in other places for others. . . . Even in a *single State,* the question has come out differently on different occasions. . . .

In the majority's telling, this story is black-and-white: Hate your neighbor or come along with us. The truth is more complicated.

. . .Some will rejoice in today's decision, and some will despair at it; that is the nature of a controversy that matters so much to so many. But the Court has cheated both sides, robbing the winners of an honest victory, and the losers of the peace that comes from a fair defeat. . . . I dissent.

[JUSTICE ALITO dissented both as to jurisdiction and on the merits. JUSTICE THOMAS joined his dissent on the merits. ALITO dissent omitted.]

Case Questions

1. Justice Scalia claims in dissent that the majority opinion does not address the issue whether legislation discriminating against same-sex marriages need only meet the rational basis test, as compared to perhaps the test for sex discrimination (intermediate scrutiny) or the test for infringing a fundamental right (strict scrutiny). What would you say is the import of the majority's statement that this legislation served "no legitimate purpose" (see italics)?

2. Justice Scalia lists some legitimate purposes that DOMA serves, whereas the majority opinion mentions none of them. What do you make of this fact?

3. Do you agree with Justice Scalia that the reasoning of the majority makes inevitable a declaration that same-sex marriage is constitutionally protected in every state? Why or why not?

Obergefell v. Hodges (2015)

The *Windsor* case focused solely on DOMA and federal-level rights, but left unaddressed the question of state-level refusal to recognize same-sex marriage. The effect of *Windsor* was to prohibit the federal government from denying all federal legal benefits (both concrete and dignitary) to same-sex marriages lawful in given states while permitting them to heterosexual marriages in those states. Still, people who resided in states that did not recognize marriage equality gained no marriage opportunity directly from *Windsor*.

In the aftermath of *Windsor*, however, as described above, things changed rapidly at the state level. In particular, numerous litigants for marriage equality attained success in federal courts, which repeatedly struck down laws that disallowed same-sex marriage.[23] In June 2015, the Supreme Court directly addressed state-level prohibitions on same-sex marriage in *Obergefell v. Hodges,* 135 S.Ct. 2584 (2015), and declared them unconstitutional on both due process and equal protection grounds.

Residents in Ohio, Michigan, Kentucky and Tennessee brought suit against these states because same-sex marriage was banned in their state constitutions, the states refused to recognize same-sex marriages performed in other states, or both. The individuals bringing the suits included 14 same-sex couples, two men whose same-sex partners had died, and others including children of some of the couples, an adoption agency and a funeral director. In denying these couples the right to marry, they argued, the states were denying them the due process and equal protection of laws that the Fourteenth Amendment guarantees.

All six federal district court rulings found in favor of the same-sex couples and other claimants. On appeal, the cases were consolidated, and the Sixth Circuit Court of Appeals heard the combined cases. The Circuit Court reversed the earlier decisions and held that neither state-level bans on same-sex marriage nor state-level refusals to acknowledge same-sex marriages performed in other jurisdictions violate the Fourteenth Amendment's due process or equal protection guarantees. After the Sixth Circuit Court of Appeals decision, claimants from each of the six cases appealed to the U.S Supreme Court.

The U.S. Supreme Court granted certiorari in January 2015 to four of the same-sex marriage cases appealed from the Sixth Circuit Court of Appeals. The consolidated case was named for James Obergefell, whose marriage to John Arthur performed in Maryland in 2013 was not recognized by the state of Ohio, and Richard Hodges who served as director of the Ohio Department of Health at the time.

In a 5–4 decision, the U.S. Supreme Court ruled on June 26, 2015 that the Fourteenth Amendment due process clause protects marriage rights as a fundamental part of liberty; moreover, denying this liberty to same-sex couples while permitting it to heterosexual couples violates equal protection of the law. The same five justices favoring Windsor in 2013 ruled for Obergefell in 2015 (Kennedy, Breyer, Ginsburg, Sotomayor and Kagan) while the same four justices dissenting against the *Windsor* ruling also dissented against the *Obergefell* ruling (Roberts, Thomas, Alito, Scalia).

Chief Justice Roberts read his dissent aloud from the bench, a rare occurrence. Each dissenter wrote his own dissent; Scalia and Thomas each also concurred in all of the other three. The only dissenter who did not concur with Roberts was Alito, and Roberts alone did not join Alito's dissent. Neither of them explains this pattern.

In the course of his opinion for the Court, Justice Kennedy recounted the circumstances confronting three of the petitioning couples. James Obergefell and John Arthur had lived together in a committed relationship for twenty years. After John Arthur became mortally ill, they traveled from Ohio to Maryland so that they could be lawfully married while both were alive. Three months later John died. Ohio refused to allow James Obergefell's name to go on the death certificate as surviving spouse. Obergefell described this denial as "hurtful for the rest of time."[24]

April DeBoer and Jayne Rowse were a committed couple, both professional nurses, who had adopted and were raising three special needs children. Under the law of their state, Michigan, only one of them could be listed as a legal parent for each child, and if the legal parent of one child were to die, the other parent would have no legal right to the child she had been co-raising.

Ijpe DeKoe was an Army reservist who married his partner Thomas Kostura in New York state, where Kostura lived, just before DeKoe was deployed to Afghanistan. After a year overseas, DeKoe began work full time for the Army Reserve in the state of Tennessee. When they resided in Tennessee, the law viewed them as unmarried. Their legal status shifted depending on which state they inhabited.

OBERGEFELL V. HODGES

135 S.Ct. 2584 (2015)

JUSTICE KENNEDY delivered the opinion of the Court.

The Constitution promises liberty to all within its reach, a liberty that includes certain specific rights that allow persons, within a lawful realm, to define and express their identity. The petitioners in these cases seek to find that liberty by marrying someone of the same sex and having their marriages deemed lawful on the same terms and conditions as marriages between persons of the opposite sex.

. . .

II.

A.

From their beginning to their most recent page, the annals of human history reveal the transcendent importance of marriage. The lifelong union of a man and a woman always has promised nobility and dignity to all persons, without regard to their station in life. Marriage is sacred to those who live by their religions and offers unique fulfillment to those who find meaning in the secular realm. Its dynamic allows two people to find a life that could not be found alone, for a marriage becomes greater than just the two persons. Rising from the most basic human needs, marriage is essential to our most profound hopes and aspirations.

. . . It is fair and necessary to say these references [to marriage in past history] were based on the understanding that marriage is a union between two persons of the opposite sex.

That history is the beginning of these cases. The respondents say it should be the end as well. To them, it would demean a timeless institution if the concept and lawful status of marriage were extended to two persons of the same sex. Marriage, in their view, is by its nature a gender-differentiated union of man and woman. This view long has been held—and continues to be held—in good faith by reasonable and sincere people here and throughout the world.

The petitioners acknowledge this history but contend that these cases cannot end there. Were their intent to demean the revered idea and reality of marriage, the petitioners' claims would be of a different order. But that is neither their purpose nor their submission. To the contrary, it is the enduring importance of marriage that underlies the petitioners' contentions. This, they say, is their whole point. Far from seeking to devalue marriage, the petitioners seek it for themselves because of their respect—and need—for its privileges and responsibilities.

. . .

B.

The ancient origins of marriage confirm its centrality, but it has not stood in isolation from developments in law and society. The history of marriage is one of both continuity and change. That institution—even as confined to opposite-sex relations—has evolved over time.

For example, marriage was once viewed as an arrangement by the couple's parents based on political, religious, and financial concerns; but by the time of the Nation's founding it was understood to be a voluntary contract between a man and a woman. [References omitted in this paragraph—AU.] As the role and status of women changed, the institution further evolved. Under the centuries-old doctrine of coverture, a married man and woman were treated by the State as a single, male-dominated legal entity. As women gained legal, political, and property rights, and as society began to understand that women have their own equal dignity, the law of coverture was abandoned. These and other developments in the institution of marriage over the past centuries were not mere superficial changes.

. . . [C]hanged understandings of marriage are characteristic of a Nation where new dimensions of freedom become apparent to new generations. . . .

This dynamic can be seen in the Nation's experiences with the rights of gays and lesbians. Until the mid-20th century, same-sex intimacy long had been condemned as immoral by the state itself in most Western nations, a belief often embodied in the criminal law. . . . Same-sex intimacy remained a crime in many States. Gays and lesbians were prohibited from most government employment, barred from military service, excluded under immigration laws, targeted by police, and burdened in their rights to associate. . . .

For much of the 20th century, moreover, homosexuality was treated as an illness. . . . Only in more recent years have psychiatrists and others recognized that sexual orientation is both a normal expression of human sexuality and immutable. See Brief for American Psychological Association et al. as *Amici Curiae.*

In the late 20th century, following substantial cultural and political developments, same-sex couples began to lead more open and public lives and to establish families. This development was followed by a quite extensive discussion of the issue in both governmental and private sectors and by a shift in public attitudes toward greater tolerance. As a result, questions about the rights of gays and lesbians soon reached the courts. . .

. . .[I]n 2003, the Court overruled *Bowers* [*v. Hardwick*, 478 U.S. 186 (1986)], holding that laws making same-sex intimacy a crime "demea[n] the lives of homosexual persons." *Lawrence v. Texas*, 539 U.S. 558, 575.

Against this background, the legal question of same-sex marriage arose. [Here the Court reviewed same-sex marriage history beginning with Hawaii in 1993 and going through *Windsor*.]. . .

III.

Under the Due Process Clause of the Fourteenth Amendment, no State shall "deprive any person of life, liberty, or property, without due process of law." The fundamental liberties protected by this Clause include most of the rights enumerated in the Bill of Rights. See *Duncan v. Louisiana*, 391 U.S. 145, 147-149 (1968). In addition these liberties extend to certain personal choices central to individual dignity and autonomy, including intimate choices that define personal identity and beliefs. See, e.g., *Eisenstadt v. Baird*, 405 U.S. 438, 453 (1972); *Griswold v. Connecticut*, 381 U.S. 479, 484-486 (1965). The identification and protection of fundamental rights is an enduring part of the judicial duty to interpret the Constitution. That responsibility, however, "has not been reduced to any formula." *Poe v. Ullman*, 367 U.S. 497, 542 (1961) (Harlan, J., dissenting). Rather, it requires courts to exercise reasoned judgment in identifying interests of the person so fundamental that the State must accord them its respect. See *ibid.* . . . History and tradition guide and discipline this inquiry but do not set its outer boundaries. See *Lawrence, supra*, at 572. That method respects our history and learns from it without allowing the past alone to rule the present.

... When new insight reveals discord between the Constitution's central protections and a received legal stricture, a claim to liberty must be addressed.

Applying these established tenets, the Court has long held the right to marry is protected by the Constitution. In *Loving v. Virginia*, 388 U.S. 1, 12 (1967), which invalidated bans on interracial unions, a unanimous Court held marriage is "one of the vital personal rights essential to the orderly pursuit of happiness by free men." The Court reaffirmed that holding in *Zablocki v. Redhail*, 434 U.S. 374, 384 (1978), which held the right to marry was burdened by a law prohibiting fathers who were behind on child support from marrying. The Court again applied this principle in *Turner v. Safley*, 482 U.S. 78, 95 (1987), which held the right to marry was abridged by regulations limiting the privilege of prison inmates to marry....

It cannot be denied that this Court's cases describing the right to marry presumed a relationship involving opposite-sex partners. The Court, like many institutions, has made assumptions defined by the world and time of which it is a part. This was evident in *Baker v. Nelson*, 409 U.S. 810, a one-line summary decision issued in 1972, holding the exclusion of same-sex couples from marriage did not present a substantial federal question.

Still, there are other, more instructive precedents. This Court's cases have expressed constitutional principles of broader reach. In defining the right to marry these cases have identified essential attributes of that right based in history, tradition, and other constitutional liberties inherent in this intimate bond. See, e.g., *Lawrence*, 539 U.S., at 574; *Turner, supra*, at 95; *Zablocki, supra*, at 384; *Loving, supra*, at 12; *Griswold, supra*, at 486. And in assessing whether the force and rationale of its cases apply to same-sex couples, the Court must respect the basic reasons why the right to marry has been long protected. See, e.g., *Eisenstadt, supra*, at 453-454; *Poe, supra*, at 542-553 (Harlan, J., dissenting). This analysis compels the conclusion that same-sex couples may exercise the right to marry. The four principles and traditions to be discussed demonstrate that the reasons marriage is fundamental under the Constitution apply with equal force to same-sex couples.

A first premise of the Court's relevant precedents is that the right to personal choice regarding marriage is inherent in the concept of individual autonomy.... Like choices concerning contraception, family relationships, procreation, and childrearing, all of which are protected by the Constitution, decisions concerning marriage are among the most intimate that an individual can make. . . .

Choices about marriage shape an individual's destiny. . . .

The nature of marriage is that, through its enduring bond, two persons together can find other freedoms, such as expression, intimacy, and spirituality. This is true for all persons, whatever their sexual orientation. . . .

A second principle in this Court's jurisprudence is that the right to marry is fundamental because it supports a two-person union unlike any other in its importance to the committed individuals. . . . The right to marry thus dignifies couples who "wish to define themselves by their commitment to each other." *Windsor, supra*. Marriage responds to the universal fear that a lonely person might call out only to find no one there. It offers the hope of companionship and understanding and assurance that while both still live there will be someone to care for the other.

A third basis for protecting the right to marry is that it safeguards children and families and thus draws meaning from related rights of childrearing, procreation, and education. See *Pierce v. Society of Sisters*, 268 U.S. 510 (1925); *Meyer*, 262 U.S., at 399. The Court has recognized these connections by describing the varied rights as a unified whole: "[T]he right to 'marry, establish a home and bring up children' is a central part of the liberty protected by the Due Process Clause." *Zablocki*, 434 U.S., at 384. . . . By giving recognition and legal structure to their parents' relationship, marriage allows children "to understand the integrity and closeness of their own family and its concord with other families in their community and in their daily lives." *Windsor, supra*. Marriage also affords the permanency and stability important to children's best interests. . . .

As all parties agree, many same-sex couples provide loving and nurturing homes to their children, whether biological or adopted. . . . Most States have allowed gays and lesbians to adopt, either as individuals or as couples, and many adopted and foster children have same-sex parents. . .

Excluding same-sex couples from marriage thus conflicts with a central premise of the right to marry. Without the recognition, stability, and predictability marriage offers, their children suffer the stigma of knowing their families are somehow lesser. . . .

That is not to say the right to marry is less meaningful for those who do not or cannot have children. An ability, desire, or promise to procreate is not and has not been a prerequisite for a valid marriage in any State. In light of precedent protecting the right of a married couple not to procreate, it cannot be said the Court or the States have conditioned the right to marry on the capacity or commitment to procreate.

Fourth and finally, this Court's cases and the Nation's traditions make clear that marriage is a keystone of our social order. . . . In *Maynard v. Hill*, 125 U.S. 190, 211 (1888), the Court . . . explain[ed] that marriage is "the foundation of the family and of society, without which there would be neither civilization nor progress." Marriage, the Maynard Court said, has long been " 'a great public institution, giving character to our whole civil polity.' " Id., at 213. This idea has been reiterated even as the institution has evolved in substantial ways over time, superseding rules related to parental consent, gender, and race once thought by many to be essential. See generally N. Cott, Public Vows. Marriage remains a building block of our national community.

For that reason. . . society pledge[s] to support the couple, offering symbolic recognition and material benefits to protect and nourish the union. Indeed, while the States are in general free to vary the benefits they confer on all married couples, they have throughout our history made marriage the basis for an expanding list of governmental rights, benefits, and responsibilities. These aspects of marital status include: taxation; inheritance and property rights; rules of intestate succession; spousal privilege in the law of evidence; hospital access; medical decisionmaking authority; adoption rights; the rights and benefits of survivors; birth and death certificates; professional ethics rules; campaign finance restrictions; workers' compensation benefits; health insurance; and child custody, support, and visitation rules. . . .

There is no difference between same- and opposite-sex couples with respect to this principle. Yet by virtue of their exclusion from that institution, same-sex couples are denied the constellation of benefits that the States have linked to marriage. This harm results in more than just material burdens. Same-sex couples are consigned to an instability many opposite-sex couples would deem intolerable in their own lives. . . . [E]xclusion from [the status of marriage] has the effect of teaching that gays and lesbians are unequal in important respects. It demeans gays and lesbians for the State to lock them out of a central institution of the Nation's society. Same-sex couples, too, may aspire to the transcendent purposes of marriage and seek fulfillment in its highest meaning.

The limitation of marriage to opposite-sex couples may long have seemed natural and just, but its inconsistency with the central meaning of the fundamental right to marry is now manifest. . . . Laws excluding same-sex couples from the marriage right impose stigma and injury of the kind prohibited by our basic charter.

. . .

Many who deem same-sex marriage to be wrong reach that conclusion based on decent and honorable religious or philosophical premises, and neither they nor their beliefs are disparaged here. But when that sincere, personal opposition becomes enacted law and public policy, the necessary consequence is to put the imprimatur of the State itself on an exclusion that soon demeans or stigmatizes those whose own liberty is then denied. Under the Constitution, same-sex couples seek in marriage the same legal treatment as opposite-sex couples, and it would disparage their choices and diminish their personhood to deny them this right.

. . .

Rights implicit in liberty and rights secured by equal protection may rest on different precepts and are not always coextensive, yet in some instances each may be instructive as to the meaning and reach of the other.

The Court's cases touching upon the right to marry reflect this dynamic. In *Loving* [*v. Virginia*] the Court invalidated a prohibition on interracial marriage under both the Equal Protection Clause and the Due Process Clause. . . .

The synergy between the two protections is illustrated further in *Zablocki*. There the Court invoked the Equal Protection Clause as its basis for invalidating the challenged law, which, as already noted, barred fathers who were behind on child-support payments from marrying without judicial approval. The equal protection analysis depended in central part on the Court's holding that the law burdened a right "of fundamental importance." 434 U.S., at 383. . . .

. . .

Other cases confirm this relation between liberty and equality. [Court described many cases declaring legal equality of spouses covered in this volume.]

. . . Here the marriage laws enforced by the respondents are in essence unequal: same-sex couples are denied all the benefits afforded to opposite-sex couples and are barred from exercising a fundamental right. . . . The imposition of this disability on gays and lesbians serves to disrespect and subordinate them. And the Equal Protection Clause, like the Due Process Clause, prohibits this unjustified infringement of the fundamental right to marry. See, e.g., *Zablocki, supra*, at 383–388; *Skinner*, 316 U.S., at 541.

These considerations lead to the conclusion that the right to marry is a fundamental right inherent in the liberty of the person, and under the Due Process and Equal Protection Clauses of the Fourteenth Amendment couples of the same-sex may not be deprived of that right and that liberty. The Court now holds that same-sex couples may exercise the fundamental right to marry. No longer may this liberty be denied to them. *Baker v. Nelson* must be and now is overruled, and the State laws challenged by Petitioners in these cases are now held invalid to the extent they exclude same-sex couples from civil marriage on the same terms and conditions as opposite-sex couples.

IV.

[We respond now to Respondents argument that this issue should have been left for decision by democratically elected legislators.]

. . .

Of course, the Constitution contemplates that democracy is the appropriate process for change, so long as that process does not abridge fundamental rights. . . .

. . .

The idea of the Constitution "was to withdraw certain subjects from the vicissitudes of political controversy, to place them beyond the reach of majorities and officials and to establish them as legal principles to be applied by the courts." *West Virginia Bd. of Ed. v. Barnette*, 319 U.S. 624, 638 (1943). This is why "fundamental rights may not be submitted to a vote; they depend on the outcome of no elections." *Ibid.* . . .

. . .

The respondents also argue allowing same-sex couples to wed will harm marriage as an institution by leading to fewer opposite-sex marriages. This may occur, the respondents contend, because licensing same-sex marriage severs the connection between natural procreation and marriage. That argument, however, rests on a counterintuitive view of opposite-sex couple's decisionmaking processes regarding marriage and parenthood. Decisions about whether to marry and raise children are based on many personal, romantic, and practical considerations; and it is unrealistic to conclude that an opposite-sex couple would choose not to marry simply because same-sex couples may do so. See *Kitchen v. Herbert*, 755 F. 3d 1193. . . .

V.

...

The Court, in this decision, holds same-sex couples may exercise the fundamental right to marry in all States. It follows that the Court also must hold—and it now does hold—that there is no lawful basis for a State to refuse to recognize a lawful same-sex marriage performed in another State on the ground of its same-sex character. . . .

The judgment of the Court of Appeals for the Sixth Circuit is reversed.

CHIEF JUSTICE ROBERTS, with whom JUSTICE SCALIA and JUSTICE THOMAS join, dissenting:

Petitioners make strong arguments rooted in social policy and considerations of fairness. They contend that same-sex couples should be allowed to affirm their love and commitment through marriage, just like opposite-sex couples. That position has undeniable appeal; over the past six years, voters and legislators in eleven States and the District of Columbia have revised their laws to allow marriage between two people of the same sex.

But this Court is not a legislature. Whether same-sex marriage is a good idea should be of no concern to us. . . . Although the policy arguments for extending marriage to same-sex couples may be compelling, the legal arguments for requiring such an extension are not. The fundamental right to marry does not include a right to make a State change its definition of marriage. And a State's decision to maintain the meaning of marriage that has persisted in every culture throughout human history can hardly be called irrational. In short, our Constitution does not enact any one theory of marriage. The people of a State are free to expand marriage to include same-sex couples, or to retain the historic definition.

Today, however, the Court takes the extraordinary step of ordering every State to license and recognize same-sex marriage. Many people will rejoice at this decision, and I begrudge none their celebration. But for those who believe in a government of laws, not of men, the majority's approach is deeply disheartening. Supporters of same-sex marriage have achieved considerable success persuading their fellow citizens—through the democratic process—to adopt their view. That ends today. Five lawyers have closed the debate and enacted their own vision of marriage as a matter of constitutional law. Stealing this issue from the people will for many cast a cloud over same-sex marriage, making a dramatic social change that much more difficult to accept. . . .

I.

Petitioners and their amici base their arguments on the "right to marry" and the imperative of "marriage equality." There is no serious dispute that, under our precedents, the Constitution protects a right to marry and requires States to apply their marriage laws equally. The real question in these cases is what constitutes "marriage," or—more precisely—who decides what constitutes "marriage"? The majority largely ignores these questions...

A.

As the majority acknowledges, marriage "has existed for millennia and across civilizations." *Ante*. For all those millennia, across all those civilizations, "marriage" referred to only one relationship: the union of a man and a woman. See ante; Tr. of Oral Arg. on Question 1 (petitioners conceding that they are not aware of any society that permitted same-sex marriage before 2001). . . .

This universal definition of marriage as the union of a man and a woman is no historical coincidence. . . . It arose in the nature of things to meet a vital need: ensuring that children are conceived by a mother and father committed to raising them in the stable conditions of a lifelong relationship. [References omitted.]

The premises supporting this concept of marriage are so fundamental that they rarely require articulation. The human race must procreate to survive. Procreation occurs through sexual relations between a man and a woman. When sexual relations result in the conception of a child, that child's prospects are generally better if the mother and father stay together rather than going their separate ways. Therefore, for the good of children and society, sexual relations that can lead to procreation should occur only between a man and a woman committed to a lasting bond.

Society has recognized that bond as marriage. And by bestowing a respected status and material benefits on married couples, society encourages men and women to conduct sexual relations within marriage rather than without. . . .

II.

The majority . . . resolves these cases for petitioners based almost entirely on the Due Process Clause. . . . Stripped of its shiny rhetorical gloss, the majority's argument is that the Due Process Clause gives same-sex couples a fundamental right to marry because it will be good for them and for society. . . .

A.

Petitioners ...argue ... that the laws violate a right implied by the Fourteenth Amendment's requirement that "liberty" may not be deprived without "due process of law."... Allowing unelected federal judges to select which unenumerated rights rank as "fundamental"—and to strike down state laws on the basis of that determination—raises obvious concerns about the judicial role. Our precedents have accordingly insisted that judges "exercise the utmost care" in identifying implied fundamental rights, "lest the liberty protected by the Due Process Clause be subtly transformed into the policy preferences of the Members of this Court." *Washington v. Glucksberg*, 521 U.S. 702, 720 (1997).

. . .

The only way to ensure restraint in this delicate enterprise is "continual insistence upon respect for the teachings of history, solid recognition of the basic values that underlie our society, and wise appreciation of the great roles [of] the doctrines of federalism and separation of powers." *Griswold v. Connecticut*, 381 U.S. 479, 501 (1965) (Harlan, J., concurring in judgment). The majority acknowledges none of this doctrinal background, and it is easy to see why: Its aggressive application of substantive due process breaks sharply with decades of precedent and returns the Court to the unprincipled approach of *Lochner*.

1

The majority's driving themes are that marriage is desirable and petitioners desire it. The opinion describes the "transcendent importance" of marriage and repeatedly insists that petitioners do not seek to "demean," "devalue," "denigrate," or "disrespect" the institution. Ante. Nobody disputes those points. . . .

As a matter of constitutional law, however, the sincerity of petitioners' wishes is not relevant. When the majority turns to the law, it relies primarily on precedents discussing the fundamental "right to marry." *Turner v. Safley*, 482 U.S. 78, 95 (1987); *Zablocki*, 434 U.S., at 383; see *Loving*, 388 U.S., at 12. These cases. . . require a State to justify barriers to marriage as that institution has always been understood. . . .

None of the laws at issue in those cases purported to change the core definition of marriage as the union of a man and a woman. . . . Removing racial barriers to marriage [, for instance,] did not change what a marriage was any more than integrating schools changed what a school was.

In short, the "right to marry" cases stand for the important but limited proposition that particular restrictions on access to marriage as traditionally defined violate due process. These precedents say nothing at all about a right to make a State change its definition of marriage, which is the right petitioners actually seek here.... Neither petitioners nor the majority cites a single case or other legal source providing any basis for such a constitutional right. None exists, and that is enough to foreclose their claim.

[T]he marriage laws at issue here ... create no crime and impose no punishment. Same-sex couples remain free to live together, to engage in intimate conduct, and to raise their families as they see fit. No one is "condemned to live in loneliness" by the laws challenged in these cases—no one...

...[A]lthough the right to privacy recognized by our precedents certainly plays a role in protecting the intimate conduct of same-sex couples, it provides no affirmative right to redefine marriage and no basis for striking down the laws at issue here.

3

The truth is that today's decision rests on nothing more than the majority's own conviction that same-sex couples should be allowed to marry because they want to, and that "it would disparage their choices and diminish their personhood to deny them this right." *Ante*. Whatever force that belief may have as a matter of moral philosophy, it has no more basis in the Constitution than did the naked policy preferences adopted in *Lochner*.

One immediate question invited by the majority's position is whether States may retain the definition of marriage as a union of two people. Cf. Brown v. Buhman, 947 F. Supp. 2d 1170 (Utah 2013), appeal pending, No. 14-4117 (CA10). Although the majority randomly inserts the adjective "two" in various places, it offers no reason at all why the two-person element of the core definition of marriage may be preserved while the man-woman element may not. Indeed, from the standpoint of history and tradition, a leap from opposite-sex marriage to same-sex marriage is much greater than one from a two-person union to plural unions, which have deep roots in some cultures around the world. If the majority is willing to take the big leap, it is hard to see how it can say no to the shorter one.

. . .

4

. . . There is indeed a process due the people on issues of this sort—the democratic process. Respecting that understanding requires the Court to be guided by law, not any particular school of social thought. . . .

. . .The purpose of insisting that implied fundamental rights have roots in the history and tradition of our people is to ensure that when unelected judges strike down democratically enacted laws, they do so based on something more than their own beliefs. The Court today not only overlooks our country's entire history and tradition but actively repudiates it, preferring to live only in the heady days of the here and now. . . .

III.

In addition to their due process argument, petitioners contend that the Equal Protection Clause requires their States to license and recognize same-sex marriages. The majority does not seriously engage with this claim. Its discussion is, quite frankly, difficult to follow. . . .

. . .[T]he majority fails to provide even a single sentence explaining how the Equal Protection Clause supplies independent weight for its position. . . . In any event, the marriage laws at issue here do not violate the Equal Protection Clause, because distinguishing between opposite-sex and same-sex couples is rationally related to the States' "legitimate state interest" in "preserving the traditional institution of marriage." *Lawrence*, 539 U.S., at 585 (O'Connor, J., concurring in judgment).

It is important to note with precision which laws petitioners have challenged. Although they discuss some of the ancillary legal benefits that accompany marriage, such as hospital visitation rights and recognition of spousal status on official documents, petitioners' lawsuits target the laws defining marriage generally rather than those allocating benefits specifically. The equal protection analysis might be different, in my view, if we were confronted with a more focused challenge to the denial of certain tangible benefits. . . .

IV.

The legitimacy of this Court ultimately rests "upon the respect accorded to its judgments." Republican Party of Minn. v. White, 536 U.S. 765, 793 (2002) (KENNEDY, J., concurring). That respect flows from the perception—and reality—that we exercise humility and restraint in deciding cases according to the Constitution and law. The role of the Court envisioned by the majority today, however, is anything but humble or restrained. Over and over, the majority exalts the role of the judiciary in delivering social change...

. . .

The Court's accumulation of power does not occur in a vacuum. It comes at the expense of the people. And they know it...

When decisions are reached through democratic means, some people will inevitably be disappointed with the results. But those whose views do not prevail at least know that they have had their say, and accordingly are—in the tradition of our political culture—reconciled to the result of a fair and honest debate. In addition, they can gear up to raise the issue later, hoping to persuade enough on the winning side to think again....

But today the Court puts a stop to all that....

Federal courts are blunt instruments when it comes to creating rights. They...do not have the flexibility of legislatures to address concerns of parties not before the court or to anticipate problems that may arise from the exercise of a new right. Today's decision, for example, creates serious questions about religious liberty....

Hard questions arise when people of faith exercise religion in ways that may be seen to conflict with the new right to same-sex marriage—when, for example, a religious college provides married student housing only to opposite-sex married couples, or a religious adoption agency declines to place children with same-sex married couples. Indeed, the Solicitor General candidly acknowledged that the tax exemptions of some religious institutions would be in question if they opposed same-sex marriage. See Tr. of Oral Arg. on Question 1. There is little doubt that these and similar questions will soon be before this Court.

* * *

If you are among the many Americans—of whatever sexual orientation—who favor expanding same-sex marriage, by all means celebrate today's decision. Celebrate the achievement of a desired goal. Celebrate the opportunity for a new expression of commitment to a partner. Celebrate the availability of new benefits. But do not celebrate the Constitution. It had nothing to do with it.

I respectfully dissent.

JUSTICE SCALIA with JUSTICE THOMAS, dissenting:

I join THE CHIEF JUSTICE's opinion in full. I write separately to call attention to this Court's threat to American democracy.

The substance of today's decree is not of immense personal importance to me. The law can recognize as marriage whatever sexual attachments and living arrangements it wishes. . . . It is of overwhelming importance, however, who it is that rules me. Today's decree says that my Ruler, and the Ruler of 320 million Americans coast-to-coast, is a majority of the nine lawyers on the Supreme Court. . . . [This opinion represents the Court's creating] "liberties" that the Constitution and its Amendments neglect to mention. This practice of constitutional revision by an unelected committee of nine, always accompanied (as it is today) by extravagant praise of liberty, robs the People of the most important liberty they asserted in the Declaration of Independence and won in the Revolution of 1776: the freedom to govern themselves.

Until the courts put a stop to it, public debate over same-sex marriage displayed American democracy at its best. . . .

. . .

[W]hat really astounds is the hubris reflected in today's judicial Putsch. The five Justices who compose today's majority are entirely comfortable concluding that every State violated the Constitution for all of the 135 years between the Fourteenth Amendment's ratification and Massachusetts' permitting of same-sex marriages in 2003. They have discovered in the Fourteenth Amendment a "fundamental right" overlooked by every person alive at the time of ratification, and almost everyone else in the time since. . . . They are certain that the People ratified the Fourteenth Amendment to bestow on them the power to remove questions from the democratic process when that is called for by their "reasoned judgment." These Justices know that limiting marriage to one man and one woman is contrary to reason; they know that an institution as old as government itself, and accepted by every nation in history until 15 years ago, cannot possibly be supported by anything other than ignorance or bigotry. And they are willing to say that any citizen who does not agree with that, who adheres to what was, until 15 years ago, the unanimous judgment of all generations and all societies, stands against the Constitution.

The opinion is couched in a style that is as pretentious as its content is egotistic. . . .

Dissent by JUSTICE THOMAS, with whom JUSTICE SCALIA joins, dissenting.

The Court's decision today is at odds not only with the Constitution, but with the principles upon which our Nation was built. Since well before 1787, liberty has been understood as freedom from government action, not entitlement to government benefits. . . .

JUSTICE ALITO, with whom JUSTICE SCALIA and JUSTICE THOMAS join, dissenting.

. . .The question in these cases, however, is not what States should do about same-sex marriage but whether the Constitution answers that question for them. It does not. The Constitution leaves that question to be decided by the people of each State. . . .

I.

To prevent five unelected Justices from imposing their personal vision of liberty upon the American people, the Court has held that "liberty" under the Due Process Clause should be understood to protect only those rights that are " 'deeply rooted in this Nation's history and tradition.' " *Washington v. Glucksberg*, 521 U.S. 701, 720–721 (1997). And it is beyond dispute that the right to same-sex marriage is not among those rights. See *United States v. Windsor*, 570 U.S. ___, ___ (2013) (ALITO, J., dissenting) Indeed:

"In this country, no State permitted same-sex marriage until the Massachusetts Supreme Judicial Court held in 2003 that limiting marriage to opposite-sex couples violated the State Constitution. See *Goodridge v. Department of Public Health*, 440 Mass. 309, 798 N. E. 2d 941. Nor is the right to same-sex marriage deeply rooted in the traditions of other nations. No country allowed same-sex couples to marry until the Netherlands did so in 2000.

"What [those arguing in favor of a constitutional right to same sex marriage] seek, therefore, is not the protection of a deeply rooted right but the recognition of a very new right, and they seek this innovation not from a legislative body elected by the people, but from unelected judges. . . ." *Id.*

II.

Attempting to circumvent the problem presented by the newness of the right found in these cases, the majority claims that the issue is the right to equal treatment. Noting that marriage is a fundamental right, the majority argues that a State has no valid reason for denying that right to same-sex couples. This reasoning is dependent upon a particular understanding of the purpose of civil marriage. Although the Court expresses the point in loftier terms, its argument is that the fundamental purpose of marriage is to promote the well-being of those who choose to marry. Marriage provides emotional fulfillment and the promise of support in times of need. And by benefiting persons who choose to wed, marriage indirectly benefits society because persons who live in stable, fulfilling, and supportive relationships make better citizens. It is for these reasons, the argument goes, that States encourage and formalize marriage, confer special benefits on married persons, and also impose some special obligations. This understanding of the States' reasons for recognizing marriage enables the majority to argue that same-sex marriage serves the States' objectives in the same way as opposite-sex marriage. This understanding of marriage, which focuses almost entirely on the happiness of persons who choose to marry, is shared by many people today, but it is not the traditional one. For millennia, marriage was inextricably linked to the one thing that only an opposite-sex couple can do: procreate.

....Here, the States defending their adherence to the traditional understanding of marriage have explained their position using the pragmatic vocabulary that characterizes most American political discourse. Their basic argument is that States formalize and promote marriage, unlike other fulfilling human relationships, in order to encourage potentially procreative conduct to take place within a lasting unit that has long been thought to provide the best atmosphere for raising children. They thus argue that there are reasonable secular grounds for restricting marriage to opposite-sex couples. If this traditional understanding of the purpose of marriage does not ring true to all ears today, that is probably because the tie between marriage and procreation has frayed. Today, for instance, more than 40% of all children in this country are born to unmarried women. This development undoubtedly is both a cause and a result of changes in our society's understanding of marriage.

....States that do not want to recognize same-sex marriage have not yet given up on the traditional understanding. They worry that by officially abandoning the older understanding, they may contribute to marriage's further decay. It is far beyond the outer reaches of this Court's authority to say that a State may not adhere to the understanding of marriage that has long prevailed, not just in this country and others with similar cultural roots, but also in a great variety of countries and cultures all around the globe.... The long-term consequences of this change are not now known and are unlikely to be ascertainable for some time to come. There are those who think that allowing

> same-sex marriage will seriously undermine the institution of marriage. Others think that recognition of same-sex marriage will fortify a now-shaky institution.
>
> At present, no one—including social scientists, philosophers, and historians—can predict with any certainty what the long-term ramifications of widespread acceptance of same-sex marriage will be....
>
> ### III.
>
> ...If the issue of same-sex marriage had been left to the people of the States, it is likely that some States would recognize same-sex marriage and others would not. It is also possible that some States would tie recognition to protection for conscience rights. The majority today makes that impossible...
>
> ...If a bare majority of Justices can invent a new right and impose that right on the rest of the country, the only real limit on what future majorities will be able to do is their own sense of what those with political power and cultural influence are willing to tolerate. Even enthusiastic supporters of same-sex marriage should worry about the scope of the power that today's majority claims.

Case Questions

1. The opinions on both sides state that across cultures of the world and for millennia marriage has involved a "lifelong" union between one man and woman. Occasional passages admit that in many cultures, the union has not been one plus one, but one man plus several women. This permission for polygamy was true of Judaism until the year 1000 C.E., and characterizes Islam into the present. Also, both of these religions that derive from the Old Testament have always allowed divorce, rather than insisting on a "lifelong" commitment. In short, the justices describe marriage in a particularly Christian way. Does this matter?

2. The dissenters all accuse the majority of inventing a new right—the right to have one's emotional commitment to another person considered a marriage irrespective of biological sex. Is Justice Roberts correct that the majority's reasoning makes likely the judicial legalization of polygamy soon? How about the potential future voiding of laws against adult incest? Against bestiality (sex with non-human animals)? Can an argument be developed that these laws should be treated differently because they prevent actual harm?

3. This single decision struck down the laws of the thirteen states that continued to ban same-sex marriages in 2015. Is this problematic?

4. All four dissenters treat this decision as elevating judicial power over and against the democratic lawmaking process. Is it your perception that members of the

general public worry about such a development, as contrasted with opposing or favoring the decision based on its policy result? Do judges make too much of this issue of undermining democracy?

Case note: In June 2018, in *Masterpiece Cakeshop v. Colorado Civil Rights, Commission* 138 S.Ct. 1719, the U.S. Supreme Court issued a narrow decision in favor of Jack Phillips, a baker and owner of the Masterpiece Cakeshop, who refused to make a wedding cake for a gay couple because same-sex marriage ran counter to his religious beliefs. While the case implicated questions related to public accommodation laws and states' abilities to prohibit discrimination on the basis of sexual orientation in public establishments, free exercise of religion, free speech, and gay rights, the Court's ruling is of limited applicability. Rather than engage in an evaluation of the competing constitutional claims—the civil rights of gays and lesbians as protected by Colorado law versus the free exercise and free speech rights of the baker—a majority of the justices focused attention on procedural issues and determined that the Colorado Civil Rights Commission exhibited hostility towards Phillips' religious beliefs. Specifically, Justice Kennedy's majority opinion determined that the commissioners failed to evaluate Phillips' religious objection to making the wedding cake consistent with the neutral treatment of religion required by the Constitution. While this was a victory for Phillips, it is unclear what this case means for future litigation. Kennedy's majority opinion simultaneously reiterated support for state public accommodation laws that prohibit discrimination against gays and lesbians and recognized that some individuals may have sincere religious objections to providing wedding services for same-sex marriages. As such, while *Masterpiece Cakeshop* appears to leave the competing civil liberties and rights claims for a future court to evaluate, it is likely to embolden individuals who provide wedding services—bakers, caterers, photographers, and so on—and oppose same-sex marriage for (actual and asserted) religious reasons to refuse services to gay and lesbian couples. Thus, there is little doubt that these issues will return to the Supreme Court in short order, but with the retirement of Justice Kennedy, and the confirmation of Justice Brett Kavanaugh as his replacement, it is quite possible that the Court will favor the religious freedoms of some individuals over the civil rights of gays and lesbians in the years ahead.

The Future Family?

While *Obergefell* has been celebrated for legalizing same-sex marriages, it also enabled transgender men and women to enter into legal marriages with one another regardless of their sexes assigned at birth. Prior to the Court's decision, marriages involving a transgender spouse or spouses were vulnerable to the policing of individuals' gender or sex by the state.[25] As such, transgender individuals who sought to marry individuals whose at-birth sex was the same as their own at-birth sex risked legal difficulties as long as "same-sex" marriages were prohibited by law. This is demonstrated by the *Littleton* case in which the Texas Court of Appeals invalidated the seven-year marriage of Christie Lee and Jonathan Littleton because Mrs. Littleton was a transgender woman. Specifically, in *Littleton v. Prange* (9 S.W.3d 223), the Court reasoned that sex is determined by one's chromosomes regardless of one's gender as recorded on identity documents or the state of one's transition including sex reassignment surgery or hormone treatments.[26] Therefore, the fact that Christie Lee Littleton identified and lived as a woman for decades was irrelevant to the Court's evaluation of her marriage. The fact that Littleton had been assigned the male sex at birth meant that she could not enter into a legal marriage with a male in the state of Texas as long as same-sex marriage was prohibited. This case exemplifies how discrimination against transgender individuals intersected with prohibitions on same-sex marriage in problematic ways. Marriage equality, however, enables two individuals of legal age (and appropriate absence of consanguinity) to marry one another without regard to their birth sex or gender identity.

While the *Obergefell* decision applies only to two-person couples, Justice Roberts' dissent raises questions about the viability of legal challenges to prohibitions on plural marriages. Plural marriage is illegal throughout the United States, but the dissident Mormons who founded the Fundamentalist Latter-Day Saints (FLDS) have continued to practice polygamy under the threat of criminal prosecution. *Cleveland v. United States* (1946) upheld the conviction of several FLDS men for violating the Mann Act of 1910, which prohibited the transportation of women across state lines "for prostitution, debauchery, or any other immoral purpose." The Court concluded there "that polygamous practices are not excluded from the Act" even though these trips were "voluntary actions bereft of sex commercialism." Justice Frank Murphy, the lone dissenter, pointed out that plural marriage had existed throughout human history and that the Court's likening it to prostitution and promiscuity did "violence to the anthropological factors involved."[27] This chapter began with a passage from the Supreme Court's reasoning for *Reynolds v. United States* (1878). In upholding prohibitions on polygamy, the reasoning also had included this passage: "[P]olygamy leads to the patriarchal principle, ...which, when applied to large communities, fetters the people in stationary despotism, while that principle cannot long exist in connection with monogamy."[28] In this view, marriages of one man and a plurality of wives, go distinctly against women's rights as co-equal citizens.

Popular 21st-century television series like *Big Love* and *Sister Wives* have presented a sympathetic view of polygyny. The modern feminist controversy over plural marriage is similar to the disputes over pornography and prostitution (described in Chapter 7). Plural wife and lawyer Elizabeth Joseph, a member of the Confederations of Israel, a small Mormon sect, insists that the marriages are consensual and that they promote a feminist lifestyle.[29] But this view has little feminist support because women in polygynous marriages are often economically and legally vulnerable and therefore more susceptible to abuse. In addition, in insular polygynous communities, the demand for wives often subjects relatively young girls to sexual exploitation. Warren Jeffs, a former FLDS leader, was sentenced to life plus 20 years in prison for sexually assaulting teenage girls and forcing them to marry FLDS men. Elissa Wall was 14 years old when Jeffs forced her to marry a young man against her will.[30]

Can institutionalized polygyny exist in the absence of coercion? Was it ever consensual to begin with? Is it intrinsically anti-egalitarian? Apart from these ongoing questions, many consenting adults currently enter into committed polyamorous relationships, which challenge traditional assumptions about monogamy and marriage.

Monogamy, whether heterosexual or homosexual, creates what law professor Martha Albertson Fineman has called a "sexual family." The partners are presumed to have sex, whether they do or not. Polygamy and polyamory, too, could be characterized this way. Fineman also proposes equal legal recognition for a "caring family," in which one or more adults are bound to children or dependent people by agreeing to care for them. Such a family could consist of three or more generations, or of siblings, but the partners need not be related by blood or adoption. Family members could be granted the privileges that married people have vis-à-vis each other.[31] Some scholars argue that legal recognition of these relationships would benefit both men and women by allowing them to choose to separate romantic relationships from family relationships.

LEGAL HISTORY OF MARRIAGE

The idea of marriage has evolved over several centuries of Anglo-American law. Under common law, the nuclear family was a patriarchal institution. The husband was the head of the household. He controlled the family property, and his wife owed him obedience. Married women could not make contracts or buy and sell property. Their wages, if any, belonged to their husbands. A wife was legally obliged to live where her husband chose, to submit to his sexual demands, to bear his children, to maintain his home, and to take his name. A husband could "correct" his wife with physical punishment. A husband was obligated to support his wife and family, and he was responsible for his wife's debts, but these obligations extended only to necessities.

However, the marriage relationship was often more symmetrical than the law declared. Many factors combined to limit the authority of husbands and increase the autonomy of wives. Both parties to the marriage had to be old enough to consent to it; children could not be married off by their parents or the government, although the official age of consent by modern standards was often shockingly low—e.g. in the late nineteenth century the age of sexual and marital consent for girls in Delaware was 7.[32] Although husbands were often older than their wives, the age discrepancy was not great. Most people married their social and economic equals.

Descriptions of early American married life gleaned from fiction, biography, letters, and diaries indicate that reality was not quite as grim as the law suggested. Some husbands and wives had reasonable parity, and the domineering wife was not unknown. Several factors ameliorated the situation of married women. The husband was master of the house, but at least most women could choose their own husbands from the local pool of suitable men. The choice of spouse was assumed to be the result of compatibility, if not romantic love. A marriage was a contract between equals who then assumed unequal roles. Husband and wife were usually about the same age; the husband lacked the advantage of seniority. There was more equality within many marriages than the law supposed.[33] But when things got very bad—when a wife was abused, deserted, neglected, terrorized, or bullied—she had no recourse. Divorce was rare and hard to get, and the father got custody of the children unless proven unfit. The following readings illustrate a common disjunction between legal doctrine and reality.

Eighteenth- and Nineteenth-Century Perspectives

WILLIAM BLACKSTONE, *COMMENTARIES ON THE LAWS OF ENGLAND* (1776)

Effect of Marriage on Status

By marriage, the husband and wife are one person in law: that is, the very being or legal existence of the woman is suspended during the marriage, or at least is incorporated and consolidated into that of the husband: under whose wing, protection, and cover, she performs everything; and is therefore called in our law-french a feme-covert; is said to be covert-baron, or under the protection and influence of her husband, her baron, or lord; and her condition during her marriage is called her coverture. Upon this principle, of a union of person in husband and wife, depend almost all the legal rights, duties, and disabilities, that either of them acquire by the marriage. I speak not at present of the rights of property, but of such as are merely personal. For this reason, a man cannot grant anything to his wife, or enter into covenant with her: for the grant would be to suppose her separate existence; and to covenant with her, would be only to covenant with himself: and therefore it is also generally true, that all compacts made between husband and wife, when single, are void...And a husband may also bequeath anything to his wife by will; for that cannot take effect till the end of the coverture is determined by his death. The husband is bound to provide his wife with necessaries by law, as much as himself; and if she contracts debts for them, he is obliged to pay them: but for anything besides necessaries, he is not chargeable . . .

The Husband's Authority

The husband also (by the old law) might give his wife moderate correction. For, as he is to answer for her misbehaviour, the law thought it reasonable to intrust him with this power of restraining her, by domestic chastisement, in the same moderation that a man is allowed to correct his servants or children; for whom the master or parent is also liable in some cases to answer. But this power of correction was confined within reasonable bounds. . . .With us, in the politer reign of Charles the second, this power of correction began to be doubted, and a wife may now have security of the peace against her husband, or, in return, a husband against his wife. Yet the lower rank of people, who were always fond of the old common law, still claim and exert their ancient privilege, and the courts of law will still permit a husband to restrain a wife of her liberty, in case of any gross misbehaviour.

These are the chief legal effects of marriage during the coverture; upon which we may observe, that even the disabilities, which the wife lies under, are for the most part intended for her protection and benefit. So great a favourite is the female sex of the laws of England. (Book I, Chapter 15, Section 442)

CHARLES DICKENS, *OLIVER TWIST*, CHAPTER 51 (1837)

[Mr. Bumble is the parish beadle. His wife has been accused of stealing jewelry belonging to Oliver's dead mother.]

"It was all Mrs. Bumble. She WOULD do it," urged Mr. Bumble; first looking round to ascertain that his partner had left the room.

> "That is no excuse," replied Mr. Brownlow. "You were present on the occasion of the destruction of these trinkets, and indeed are the more guilty of the two, in the eye of the law, for the law supposes that your wife acts under your direction."
>
> "If the law supposes that," said Mr. Bumble, squeezing his hat emphatically in both hands, "the law is a ass—a idiot. If that's the eye of the law, the law is a bachelor; and the worst I wish the law is, that his eye may be opened by experience—by experience."
>
> Laying great stress on the repetition of these two words, Mr. Bumble fixed his hat on very tight, and putting his hands in his pockets, followed his helpmate downstairs.

Remnants of Coverture: *U.S. v. Yazell* (1966)

By the end of the nineteenth century, most states had abolished married women's legal disabilities. However, the states did not reform their laws at the same rate, and coverture lingered in American law for a long time. Texas still had the doctrine in 1957, when a flood destroyed Yazell's Little Ages, Delbert and Ethel Mae Yazell's children's clothing store in Lampasas. The couple applied for and received a $12,000 disaster loan from the federal Small Business Administration (SBA). Unfortunately, the business failed and the Yazells defaulted on the loan. When the SBA sued them, Ethel Mae Yazell claimed that she was not liable because, at the time she signed the loan, the law of coverture (since repealed), made her incompetent to sign contracts relating to jointly held property. The Supreme Court agreed, and, in the course of doing so, surveyed state coverture laws as of 1966.

> ### UNITED STATES V. YAZELL
> 382 U.S. 341 (1966)
>
> **JUSTICE FORTAS delivered the opinion of the Court:**
>
> ...The SBA chose its contractors with knowledge of the limited office of Mrs. Yazell's signature under Texas law. That knowledge did not deter them. If they had "chosen" Mrs. Yazell as their contractor in the sense that her separate property would be liable for the loan, presumably they would have said so, and they would have proceeded with the formalities necessary under Texas law to have her disability removed. This case is not a call to strike the shackles of an obsolete law from the hands of a beneficent Federal

> Government, nor is it a summons to do battle to vindicate the rights of women. It is much more mundane and commercial than either of these. The issue is whether the Federal Government may voluntarily and deliberately make a negotiated contract with knowledge of the limited capacity and liability of the persons with whom it contracts, and thereafter insist, in disregard of such limitation, upon collecting (a) despite state law to the contrary relating to family property rights and liabilities, and (b) in the absence of federal statute, regulation or even any contract provision indicating that the state law would be disregarded.
>
> The institution of coverture is peculiar and obsolete. It was repealed in Texas after the events of this case. It exists, in modified form, in Michigan. But the Government's brief tells us that there are 10 other States which limit in some degree the capacity of married women to contract. In some of these States, such as California, the limitations upon the wife's capacity and responsibility are part of an ingenious, complex, and highly purposeful distribution of property rights between husband and wife, geared to the institution of community property and designed to strike a balance between efficient management of joint property and protection of the separate property of each spouse.
>
> ...We do not here consider the question of the constitutional power of the Congress to override state law in these circumstances...We decide only that this Court, in the absence of specific congressional action, should not decree in this situation that implementation of federal interests requires overriding the particular state rule involved here.

CASE NOTE: THE EVOLUTION OF MARITAL UNITY

In the context of the criminal law, the legal fiction of the unity of husband and wife meant that the wife could not be charged with a crime of conspiracy with her husband and that the spouses could testify neither for nor against each other. In 1933, in its role as supervisor of the court system for *federal* crimes, the Supreme Court dropped the rule against favorable spousal testimony (*Funk v. U.S.*, 290 U.S. 371). In 1960, in the same role (in *U.S. v. Dege*, 364 U.S. 51) it dropped the prohibition on criminal conspiracy charges. And in 1980 (*Trammel v. U.S.*, 445 U.S. 40), the Court dropped the ban on letting a spouse testify against her (or his) marital partner, except regarding matters of private, marital confidences—for these, the accused can bar adverse testimony by a spouse. None of these new rules affected *state* criminal processes; they applied only in the context of trials for federal crimes. For state crimes each state had its own rules in these matters. These reforms of the federal criminal process were typically accompanied by progressive-sounding rhetoric, as when Justice Frankfurter, the author of the majority opinion in *Goesaert v. Cleary* (see Chapter 1), wrote in *Dege* in 1960 that the idea that, in marital teams committing crimes, women act under their husband's direction "implies a view of American womanhood offensive to the ethos of our society." Despite the rich possibilities of such rhetoric, and despite its modest reforms at the edges, the Court did little to alter the traditional institution of marriage until *Orr v. Orr* in 1979 (see below).

Sex Discrimination: *Stanton v. Stanton* (1975)

In the early seventies, many challenges to discriminatory aspects of marriage law went to the courts. Alabama's regulation that a married woman must use her husband's last name on her driver's license, was upheld by the U.S. Supreme Court as recently as 1972, even after *Reed*, but in a memorandum decision with no written opinion.[34] Another of the challenges that reached the Supreme Court dealt with sex discrimination with respect to rules governing how long children could receive child support payments after a divorce. The case was *Thelma Stanton v. James Stanton*. This case illustrates that the old common law assumptions about family responsibilities have ramifications well beyond family law, affecting beliefs and practices, for instance, about who needs to go to college and who does not.

Unlike *Taylor v. Louisiana* (involving trial by jury) or *Weinberger v. Wiesenfeld* (involving the companionship of one's children), this case involved no established fundamental right. Thus it presented a purely equal protection challenge to a gender-based discrimination in Utah law.

Thelma Stanton divorced her husband, James, in Utah in 1960. Their two children remained with Thelma, and James was ordered to pay child support for them on a monthly basis. When the daughter, Sherri (the elder child), reached 18, her father halted his support payments for her. When Thelma sued for the money in court, she was told that because her daughter, according to Utah statutes, lost her legal status as a "minor" when she turned 18, the father no longer had to support her. He would have to support Sherri's younger brother, Rick, until Rick turned 21, because under Utah law males kept their minor status until the age of 21. Thelma claimed that this arrangement denied Sherri equal protection of the laws, because it cost her three years of support from her father, money she would have received had she been male.

STANTON V. STANTON
421 U.S. 7 (1975)

MR. JUSTICE BLACKMUN delivered the opinion of the Court:

This case presents the issue whether a state statute specifying for males a greater age of majority than it specifies for females denies, in the context of a parent's obligation for support payments for his children, the equal protection of the laws guaranteed by § 1 of the Fourteenth Amendment.

I

...The appellant appealed to the Supreme Court of Utah. She contended, among other things, that § 15–2–1, Utah Code Ann. 1953, to the effect that the period of minority for males extends to age 21 and for females to age 18, is invidiously discriminatory and serves to deny due process and equal protection of the laws, in violation of the Fourteenth Amendment... On this issue, the Utah court affirmed [the divorce court's rejection of Thelma's claim]. 517 P.2d 1010 (1974). The court acknowledged, "There is no doubt that the questioned statute treats men and women differently," but said that people may be treated differently "so long as there is a reasonable basis for the classification, which is related to the purposes of the act, and it applies equally and uniformly to all persons within the class." The court referred to what it called some "old notions," namely, "that generally it is the man's primary responsibility to provide a home and its essentials"; that "it is a salutary thing for him to get a good education and/or training before he undertakes those responsibilities"; that "girls tend generally to mature physically, emotionally and mentally before boys"; and that "they generally tend to marry earlier." It concluded that "it is our judgment that there is no basis upon which we would be justified in concluding that the statute is so beyond a reasonable doubt in conflict with constitutional provisions that it should be stricken down as invalid." If such a change were desirable, the court said, "that is a matter... [for] ...the legislature." The appellant, thus, was held not entitled to support for Sherri for the period after she attained 18, but was entitled to support for Rick "during his minority" unless otherwise ordered by the trial court.

III

We turn to the merits. The appellant argues that Utah's statutory prescription establishing different ages of majority for males and females denies equal protection; that it is a classification based solely on sex and affects a child's "fundamental right" to be fed, clothed, and sheltered by its parents; that no compelling state interest supports the classification; and that the statute can withstand no judicial scrutiny, "close" or otherwise, for it has no relationship to any ascertainable legislative objective. The appellee contends that the test is that of rationality and that the age classification has a rational basis and endures any attack based on equal protection.

We find it unnecessary in this case to decide whether a classification based on sex is inherently suspect. See *Weinberger v. Wiesenfeld* (1975); *Schlesinger v. Ballard* (1975); *Geduldig v. Aiello* (1974); *Kahn v. Shevin* (1974); *Frontiero v. Richardson* (1973); *Reed v. Reed* (1971).

Reed, we feel, is controlling here. That case presented an equal protection challenge to a provision of the Idaho probate code which gave preference to males over females when persons otherwise of the same entitlement applied for appointment as administrator of a decedent's estate. No regard was paid under the statute to the applicants' respective individual qualifications. In upholding the challenge, the Court reasoned that the Idaho statute accorded different treatment on the basis of sex and that it "thus establishes a classification subject to scrutiny under the Equal Protection Clause." *Id.*, at 75. The clause, it was said, denies to States "the power to legislate that different treatment be accorded to persons placed by a statute into different classes on the basis of criteria wholly unrelated to the objective of that statute." *Id.*, at 75-76. "A classification 'must be reasonable, not arbitrary, and must rest upon some ground of difference having a fair and substantial relation to the object of the legislation, so that all persons similarly circumstanced shall be treated alike.' *Royster Guano Co. v. Virginia*, 253 U.S. 412, 415 (1920)." *Id.*, at 76. It was not enough to save the statute that among its objectives were the elimination both of an area of possible family controversy and of a hearing on the comparative merits of petitioning relatives.

The test here, then, is whether the difference in sex between children warrants the distinction in the appellee's obligation to support that is drawn by the Utah statute. We conclude that it does not. It may be true, as the Utah court observed and as is argued here, that it is the man's primary responsibility to provide a home and that it is salutary for him to have education and training before he assumes that responsibility; that girls tend to mature earlier than boys; and that females tend to marry earlier than males. The last mentioned factor, however, under the Utah statute loses whatever weight it otherwise might have, for the statute states that "all minors obtain their majority by marriage"; thus minority, and all that goes with it, is abruptly lost by marriage of a person of either sex. . . .

Notwithstanding the "old notions" to which the Utah court referred, we perceive nothing rational in the distinction drawn by § 15–2–1 which, when related to the divorce decree, results in the appellee's liability for support for Sherri only to age 18 but for Rick to age 21. This imposes "criteria wholly unrelated to the objective of that statute." A child, male or female, is still a child. No longer is the female destined solely for the home and the rearing of the family, and only the male for the marketplace and the world of ideas. See *Taylor v. Louisiana,* n. 17 (1975). Women's activities and responsibilities are increasing and expanding. Coeducation is a fact, not a rarity. The presence of women in business, in the professions, in government and, indeed, in all walks of life where education is a desirable, if not always a necessary antecedent, is apparent and a proper subject of judicial notice. If a specified age of minority is required for the boy in order to assure him parental support while he attains his education and training, so, too, it is for the girl. To distinguish between the two on educational grounds is to be self-serving: if the female is not to be supported so long as the male, she hardly can be expected to attend school as long as he does, and bringing her education to an end earlier coincides with the role-typing society has long imposed. And if any weight remains in this day in the claim of earlier maturity of the female, with a concomitant inference of absence of need for support beyond 18, we fail to perceive its unquestioned truth or its significance, particularly when marriage, as the statute provides, terminates minority for a person of either sex.

Only Arkansas, so far as our investigation reveals, remains with Utah in fixing the age of majority for females at 18 and for males at 21.... Furthermore, Utah itself draws the 18–21 distinction only in § 15–2–1 defining minority, and in § 30–1–9 relating to marriage without the consent of parent or guardian. See also § 30–1–2(4) making void a marriage where the male is under 16 or the female under 14. Elsewhere, in the State's present constitutional and statutory structure, the male and the female appear to be treated alike. [Here the Court cites many Utah statutes and sections of the state constitution.]...

We therefore conclude that under any test—compelling state interest, or rational basis, or something in between—§ 15–2–1, in the context of child support, does not survive an equal protection attack. In that context, no valid distinction between male and female may be drawn.

IV

Our conclusion that in the context of child support the classification effectuated by § 15–2–1 denies the equal protection of the laws, as guaranteed by the Fourteenth Amendment, does not finally resolve the controversy as between this appellant and this appellee. . . . The appellant asserts that [now the common law applies and that at common law the age of majority for both males and females is 21. The appellee claims that any unconstitutional inequality. . .is to be remedied by treating males as adults at age 18, rather than by withholding the privileges of adulthood from women until they reach 21. This plainly is an issue of state law to be resolved by the Utah courts on remand. . . .

The judgment of the Supreme Court of Utah is reversed and the case is remanded for further proceedings not inconsistent with this opinion.

It is so ordered.

MR. JUSTICE REHNQUIST, dissenting:

The Court views this case as requiring a determination of whether the Utah statute specifying that males must reach a higher age than females before attaining their majority denies females the equal protection of the laws guaranteed by § 1 of the Fourteenth Amendment to the United States Constitution. . . . But . . . This Court is bound by the rule, "to which it has rigidly adhered. . . . never to formulate a rule of constitutional law broader than is required by the precise facts to which it is to be applied." *Liverpool N.Y. & Phil. S.S. Co. v. Commissioners of Emigration,* 113 U.S. 33, 39 (1885). . .

. . . The parties concede that the Stantons could have provided in their property settlement agreement that appellee's obligation to support Sherri and Rick would terminate when both turned 18, when both turned 21, or when one turned 18 and the other turned 21. This case arises only because appellant and appellee made no provision in their property settlement agreement fixing the age at which appellee's obligation to support his son or daughter would terminate. The Supreme Court of Utah, faced with the necessity of filling in this blank, referred to the State's general age of majority statute in supplying the terms which the parties had neglected to specify . . . .

Had the Supreme Court of Utah relied upon the statute only insofar as it cast light on the intention of the parties regarding the child support obligations contained in the divorce decree, there would be no basis for reaching the constitutionality of the statute. In supplying the missing term in an agreement executed between two private parties, a court ordinarily looks to the customs, mores, and practice of the parties in an attempt to ascertain what was intended. If, upon consideration of these factors, including the age of majority statute, the Utah Supreme Court had concluded that the Stantons intended to bestow more of their limited resources upon a son than a daughter, perhaps for the

> reasons stated in the opinion of the Supreme Court of Utah, that strikes me as an entirely permissible basis upon which to construe the property settlement agreement.
>
> On the other hand, the Supreme Court of Utah may have concluded that, the parties having failed to specify this term of the agreement, the question became one of Utah statutory law rather than one of determining the intent of the parties. If that were its determination, the constitutionality of § 15–2–1, Utah Code Ann. 1953, would indeed be implicated in this case.
>
> I do not think it possible to say with confidence which of these two approaches was taken by the Supreme Court of Utah in this case. . . . [T]he issue which the Court says is presented by this case, and which it decides, cannot properly be decided on these facts if we are to adhere to our established policy of avoiding unnecessary constitutional adjudication. I would dismiss the appeal for that reason. . . .

Case Questions

1. How relevant is it, for setting the age of majority, whether females mature earlier than males? Would the answer vary by whether the Court is using the "reasonable basis" test, compelling interest, or something in between? What is the "legislative objective" of a law setting the age of adulthood? Is this statute still valid in contexts other than child support?

2. How important to this decision was the fact that 48 other states did not make a sex distinction in defining minors? That women's societal role had changed in recent decades? How important should each of these be in interpreting the equal protection clause?

3. How plausible is Justice Rehnquist's suggestion that this different treatment of the children resulted from an earlier voluntary agreement by both parents?

Revolutionizing Marriage

Orr v. Orr (1979)

In 1979, the justices handed down a decision that revolutionized the law of marriage. The legal core of marriage in Anglo-American law has been that the wife has the duties of conjugal (i.e., sexual) and domestic (i.e., household) service. The husband has the duty of financial support. These duties were reciprocal rather than equal. Thus, even if a wife came from wealthy parents and the husband did not, it was his duty to support her, and not the reverse. Or if he were a prize-winning chef, it was still her legal duty to (among other things) cook their home meals. Of course, these duties were not typically enforced by the state in ongoing marriages; they became relevant in such contexts as divorce or in lawsuits for loss of wifely services ("consortium") when a wife was seriously injured. (The lawsuit would be against the party causing the injury.) *Orr v. Orr* seismically altered this basic arrangement of the legal structure of marriage.

William H. Orr upon his divorce from Lillian Orr challenged the rule (a rule at the time still operative in a substantial number of states) that only husbands and not wives may be ordered to pay alimony. To abrogate this husbands-only rule of alimony would seem to imply a demolishing of the age-old common law rule that it was the husband's, and not the wife's, duty to support the family. The Supreme Court, went ahead and abrogated the traditional alimony rule.

Mr. Orr lost at both the trial and appeals levels in Alabama. He won overwhelmingly at the U.S. Supreme Court. Three justices (Rehnquist, Burger and Powell) dissented not on the merits but on the question of whether the Court should have jurisdiction.

ORR V. ORR
440 U.S. 268 (1979)

Mr. Justice Brennan delivered the opinion of the Court:

The question presented is the constitutionality of Alabama alimony statutes which provide that husbands, but not wives, may be required to pay alimony upon divorce.

[First we address Mrs. Orr's preliminary argument that we should not hear this case since Mr. Orr's earnings are greater, and therefore she would not be ordered to pay him alimony in any event. We reply to that as follows:] . . .There is no question but that Mr. Orr bears a burden he would not bear were he female. The issue is highlighted, although not altered, by transposing it to the sphere of race. There is no doubt that a state law imposing alimony obligations on blacks but not whites could be challenged by a black who was required to pay. The burden alone is sufficient to establish standing. Our resolution of a statute's constitutionality often does "not finally resolve the controversy as between th[e] appellant and th[e] appellee," *Stanton v. Stanton*, 421 U.S., at 17. We do not deny standing simply because the "appellant, although prevailing here on the federal constitutional issue, may or may not ultimately win [his] lawsuit." *Id.*, at 18. . . .[H]is constitutional attack holds the only promise of escape from the burden that derives from the challenged statutes. He has therefore "alleged such a personal stake in the outcome of the controversy as to assure that concrete adverseness which sharpens the presentation of issues upon which th[is] court so largely depends for illumination of difficult constitutional questions," *Linda R. S. v. Richard D.*, 410 U.S. 614, 616 (1973), quoting *Baker v. Carr*, 369 U.S. 186, 204 (1962) . . . .

. . .[W]e now turn to the merits.

In authorizing the imposition of alimony obligations on husbands, but not on wives, the Alabama statutory scheme "provides that different treatment be accorded . . . on the basis of . . . sex; it thus establishes a classification subject to scrutiny under the Equal Protection Clause," *Reed v. Reed*, 404 U.S. 71, 75 (1971). The fact that the classification expressly discriminates against men rather than women does not protect it from scrutiny. *Craig v. Boren*, 429 U.S. 190 (1976). "To withstand scrutiny" under the Equal Protection Clause, " 'classifications by gender must serve important governmental objectives and must be substantially related to achievement of those objectives.' " *Califano v. Webster*, 430 U.S. 313, 316-317 (1977). We shall, therefore, examine the three governmental objectives that might arguably be served by Alabama's statutory scheme.

Appellant views the Alabama alimony statutes as effectively announcing the State's preference for an allocation of family responsibilities under which the wife plays a dependent role, and as seeking for their objective the reinforcement of that model among the State's citizens. . . . Prior cases settle that this purpose cannot sustain the statutes. *Stanton v. Stanton*, 421 U.S. 7, 10 (1975), held that the "old notio[n]" that "generally it is the man's primary responsibility to provide a home and its essentials," can no longer justify a statute that discriminates on the basis of gender. "No longer is the female destined solely for the home and the rearing of the family, and only the male for the marketplace and the world of ideas," id., at 14-15. If the statute is to survive constitutional attack, therefore, it must be validated on some other basis.

The opinion of the Alabama Court of Civil Appeals suggests. . . that the Alabama statutes were "designed" for "the wife of a broken marriage who needs financial assistance," 351 So.2d, at 905. This may be read as asserting either of two legislative objectives. One is a legislative purpose to provide help for needy spouses, using sex as a proxy for need. The other is a goal of compensating women for past discrimination during marriage, which assertedly has left them unprepared to fend for themselves in the working world following divorce. We concede, of course, that assisting needy spouses is a legitimate and important governmental objective. We have also recognized "[r]eduction of the disparity in economic condition between men and women caused by the long history of discrimination against women . . . as . . . an important governmental objective," *Califano v. Webster*, at 317. It only remains, therefore, to determine whether the classification at issue here is "substantially related to achievement of those objectives." *Ibid.*

Ordinarily, we would begin the analysis of the "needy spouse" objective by considering whether sex is a sufficiently "accurate proxy," *Craig v. Boren*, at 204, for dependency to establish that the gender classification rests " 'upon some ground of difference having a fair and substantial relation to the object of the legislation,' " *Reed v. Reed*, at 76. Similarly, we would initially approach the "compensation" rationale by asking whether women had in fact been significantly discriminated against in the sphere to which the statute applied a sex-based classification, leaving the sexes "not similarly situated with respect to opportunities" in that sphere, *Schlesinger v. Ballard*, 419 U.S. 498, 508 (1975). Compare *Califano v. Webster*, at 318, and *Kahn v. Shevin*, 416 U.S. 351, 353 (1974), with *Weinberger v. Wiesenfeld*, 420 U.S. 636, 648 (1975).[11]

But in this case, even if sex were a reliable proxy for need, and even if the institution of marriage did discriminate against women, these factors still would "not adequately justify the salient features of" Alabama's statutory scheme, *Craig v. Boren*, at 202–203. Under the statute, individualized hearings at which the parties' relative financial circumstances are considered already occur. See *Russell v. Russell*, 247 Ala. 284, 286, 24 So.2d 124, 126 (1945); *Ortman v. Ortman*, 203 Ala. 167, 82 So. 417 (1919). There is no reason, therefore, to use sex as a proxy for need. Needy males could be helped along with needy females with little if any additional burden on the State. In such circumstances, not even an administrative convenience rationale exists to justify operating by generalization or proxy. Similarly, since individualized hearings can determine which women were in fact discriminated against vis-a-vis their husbands, as well as which family units defied the stereotype and left the husband dependent on the wife, Alabama's alleged compensatory purpose may be effectuated without placing burdens solely on husbands. Progress toward fulfilling such a purpose would not be hampered, and it would cost the State nothing more, if it were to treat men and women equally by making alimony burdens independent of sex. "Thus, the gender-based distinction is gratuitous; without it, the statutory scheme would only provide benefits to those men who are in fact similarly situated to the women the statute aids," *Weinberger v. Wiesenfeld*, at 653, and the effort to help those women would not in any way be compromised.

Moreover, use of a gender classification actually produces perverse results in this case. As compared to a gender-neutral law placing alimony obligations on the spouse able to pay, the present Alabama statutes give an advantage only to the financially secure wife whose husband is in need. Although such a wife might have to pay alimony under a gender-neutral statute, the present statutes exempt her. . . A gender-based classification which, as compared to a gender-neutral one, generates additional benefits only for those it has no reason to prefer cannot survive equal protection scrutiny.

Legislative classifications which distribute benefits and burdens on the basis of gender carry the inherent risk of reinforcing stereotypes about the "proper place" of women and their need for special protection. Thus, even statutes purportedly designed to compensate for and ameliorate the effects of past discrimination must be carefully tailored. Where, as here, the State's compensatory and ameliorative purposes are as well served by a gender-neutral classification as one that gender classifies and therefore carries with it the baggage of sexual stereotypes, the State cannot be permitted to classify on the basis of sex. And this is doubly so where the choice made by the State appears to redound—if only indirectly—to the benefit of those without need for special solicitude.

Having found Alabama's alimony statutes unconstitutional, we reverse the judgment below and remand the cause for further proceedings not inconsistent with this opinion. . . .[I]t is open to the Alabama courts on remand to consider whether Mr. Orr's stipulated agreement to pay alimony, or other grounds of gender-neutral state law, bind him to continue his alimony payments.

Reversed and remanded.

Opinion Footnote

11 We would also consider whether the purportedly compensatory "classifications in fact penalized women," and whether "the statutory structure and its legislative history revealed that the classification was not enacted as compensation for past discrimination." *Califano v. Webster*, 430 U.S., at 317.

MR. JUSTICE REHNQUIST, with whom THE CHIEF JUSTICE joins, dissenting.

[T]he Court holds that Alabama's alimony statutes may be challenged in this Court by a divorced male who has never sought alimony, who is demonstrably not entitled to alimony even if he had, and who contractually bound himself to pay alimony to his former wife and did so without objection for over two years. I think the Court's eagerness to invalidate Alabama's statutes has led it to deal too casually with the "case and controversy" requirement of Art. III of the Constitution. . . .

MR. JUSTICE POWELL, dissenting.

I agree with MR. JUSTICE REHNQUIST that the Court, in its desire to reach the equal protection issue in this case, has dealt too casually with the difficult Art. III problems which confront us. Rather than assume the answer to questions of state law on which the resolution of the Art. III issue should depend, and which well may moot the equal protection question in this case, I would abstain from reaching either of the constitutional questions at the present time. . . .

Case Questions

1. Does the Court majority appear to be reaching out to settle cases it need not have dealt with? Does the Court appear to be trying to compensate for the anticipated demise of the ERA? (Discussed in Chapter 2.)

2. Has this decision implicitly buried the separate roles within marriage of traditional Anglo-American law?

Kirchberg v. Feenstra (1981)

While one might suppose, along with Blackstone, that Ethel Mae Yazell benefited from coverture because it shielded her from certain negative consequences of her actions, Joan Feenstra's experience with Louisiana law eight years later was different. By the time her case got to the Supreme Court, the legislature had repealed the "head and master" statute that gave the husband complete control over marital property, the Supreme Court had adopted the intermediate scrutiny standard of *Craig v. Boren*, and it had decided *Orr v. Orr*. The stage was set for a confrontation between traditional marriage law and the Burger Court's equal protection doctrine.

KIRCHBERG V. FEENSTRA
450 U.S. 455 (1981)

JUSTICE MARSHALL delivered the opinion of the Court:

In this appeal we consider the constitutionality of a now superseded Louisiana statute that gave a husband, as "head and master" of property jointly owned with his wife, the unilateral right to dispose of such property without his spouse's consent. Concluding that the provision violates the Equal

Protection Clause of the Fourteenth Amendment, we affirm the judgment of the Court of Appeals for the Fifth Circuit . . .

In 1974, appellee Joan Feenstra filed a criminal complaint against her husband, Harold Feenstra, charging him with molesting their minor daughter. While incarcerated on that charge, Mr. Feenstra retained appellant Karl Kirchberg, an attorney, to represent him. Mr. Feenstra signed a $3,000 promissory note in prepayment for legal services to be performed by appellant Kirchberg. As security on this note, Mr. Feenstra executed a mortgage in favor of appellant on the home he jointly owned with his wife. Mrs. Feenstra was not informed of the mortgage, and her consent was not required because a state statute, former Art. 2404 of the Louisiana Civil Code Ann. gave her husband exclusive control over the disposition of community property. This provision has been repealed.

Mrs. Feenstra eventually dropped the charge against her husband. He did not return home, but instead obtained a legal separation from his wife and moved out of the State. Mrs. Feenstra first learned of the existence of the mortgage in 1976, when appellant Kirchberg threatened to foreclose on her home unless she paid him the amount outstanding on the promissory note executed by her husband. . . .

Anticipating Mrs. Feenstra's defense to the foreclosure action, Kirchberg in March 1976 filed this action in the United States District Court for the Eastern District of Louisiana. . . Mrs. Feenstra challeng[ed] the constitutionality of the statutory scheme that empowered her husband unilaterally to execute a mortgage on their jointly owned home. The State of Louisiana and its Governor were joined as third-party defendants on the constitutional counterclaim. The governmental parties, joined by appellant, moved for summary judgment on this claim. The District Court, characterizing Mrs. Feenstra's counterclaim as an attack on "the bedrock of Louisiana's community property system," granted the State's motion for summary judgment. 430 F.Supp. 642, 644 (1977).

Because this provision explicitly discriminated on the basis of gender, the Court of Appeals properly inquired whether the statutory grant to the husband of exclusive control over disposition of community property was substantially related to the achievement of an important governmental objective. The court noted that the State had advanced only one justification for the provision—that "[one] of the two spouses has to be designated as the manager of the community." The court agreed that the State had an interest in defining the manner in which community property was to be managed, but found that the

State had failed to show why the mandatory designation of the husband as manager of the property was necessary to further that interest. The court therefore concluded that Art. 2404 violated the Equal Protection Clause. However, because the court believed that a retroactive application of its decision "would create a substantial hardship with respect to property rights and obligations within the State of Louisiana," the decision was limited to prospective application, 609 F.2d 727, 735–736 (1979). Only Kirchberg appealed the judgment of the Court of Appeals to this Court.... By granting the husband exclusive control over the disposition of community property, Art. 2404 clearly embodies the type of express gender-based discrimination that we have found unconstitutional absent a showing that the classification is tailored to further an important governmental interest....[A]ppellant attempts to distinguish this Court's decisions in cases such as *Craig* v. *Boren* and *Orr* v. *Orr*, 440 U.S. 268 (1979), which struck down similar gender-based statutory classifications, by arguing that appellee Feenstra, as opposed to the disadvantaged individuals in those cases, could have taken steps to avoid the discriminatory impact of Art. 2404. Appellant notes that under Art. 2334 of the Louisiana Civil Code, in effect at the time Mr. Feenstra executed the mortgage, Mrs. Feenstra could have made a "declaration by authentic act" prohibiting her husband from executing a mortgage on her home without her consent. By failing to take advantage of this procedure, Mrs. Feenstra, in appellant's view, became the "architect of her own predicament" and therefore should not be heard to complain of the discriminatory impact of Art. 2404....

[This Court has ruled that] "absence of an insurmountable barrier" will not redeem an otherwise unconstitutionally discriminatory law. *Trimble* v. *Gordon*, 430 U.S. 762, 774 (1977). Instead the burden remains on the party seeking to uphold a statute that expressly discriminates on the basis of sex to advance an "exceedingly persuasive justification" for the challenged classification. *Personnel Administrator of Mass.* v. *Feeney*, 442 U.S. 256, 273 (1979)....[A]ppellant has failed to offer such a justification. [W]e affirm the judgment of the Court of Appeals invalidating Art. 2404.

Case Questions

1. What is the impact of *Kirchberg v. Feenstra* as precedent? After this decision, could any law reinforcing traditional gender roles within marriage survive constitutional scrutiny?

2. Has the relationship between doctrine and reality changed since the days of Blackstone and Dickens? If so, how and why?

THE TRADITIONAL FAMILY

The changes in the constitutional law of marriage in the 1970s and 1980s paralleled the changes in the constitutional law of gender equality examined in Chapter 2. As the last two cases show, the *Craig v. Boren* test of substantial relationship to important purpose essentially invalidates the common law of marriage. But the vast majority of marriage cases are decided on the basis of family law, not constitutional doctrine. Family law is the province of each individual state. Reform efforts in both the nineteenth and twentieth centuries affected changes in the marriage laws long before the Supreme Court revisited the constitutional issues, but the pace varied from state to state.

The Wife as Husband's Property—*Tinker v. Colwell* (1904)

In 1897, Frederick Colwell sued Charles Tinker for criminal conversation: that is, for having sexual intercourse with Colwell's wife. Colwell was awarded $50,000 in damages by a New York trial court in Manhattan. The judgment was still unpaid when Tinker declared bankruptcy two years later. He claimed that the federal Bankruptcy Act of 1898 released him from his debt to Colwell. This law provided that "a discharge in bankruptcy shall release a bankrupt from all his provable debts, except such as ... (2) are judgments in actions for frauds, or obtaining property by false pretenses or false representations, or for willful and malicious injuries to the person or property of another." The Supreme Court had to decide whether a judgment for criminal conversation fit within the last exception.

TINKER V. COLWELL
193 U.S. 473 (1904)

MR. JUSTICE PECKHAM delivered the opinion of the Court:

We are of opinion that [Tinker's debt] was not released. We think the authorities show the husband had certain personal and exclusive rights with regard to the person of his wife which are interfered with and invaded by criminal conversation with her; that such an act on the part of another man constitutes an assault even when, as is almost universally the case as proved, the wife in fact consents to the act; because the wife is in law incapable of giving any consent to affect the husband's rights as against the wrongdoer, and that an assault of this nature may properly be described as an injury to the personal rights and property of the husband, which is both malicious and willful. A judgment upon such a cause of action is not released by the defendant's discharge in bankruptcy.

The assault...is a fiction of the law, assumed at first, in early times, to give jurisdiction of the cause of action as a trespass, to the courts, which then proceeded to permit the recovery of damages by the husband for his wounded feelings and honor, the defilement of the marriage bed, and for the doubt thrown upon the legitimacy of children.

Blackstone, in referring to the rights of the husband, says

Injuries that may be offered to a person, considered as a husband, are principally three: abduction, or taking away a man's wife; adultery, or criminal conversation with her; and beating or otherwise abusing her .... Adultery, or criminal conversation with a man's wife, though it is, as a public crime, left by our laws to the coercion of the spiritual courts; yet, considered as a civil injury (and surely there can be no greater), the law gives a satisfaction to the husband for it by action of trespass against the adulterer, wherein the damages recovered are usually very large and exemplary.

[Analysis of nineteenth century cases omitted.]

Many of the cases hold that the essential injury to the husband consists in the defilement of the marriage bed, in the invasion of his exclusive right to marital intercourse with his wife and to beget his own children. This is a right of the highest kind, upon the thorough maintenance of which the whole social order rests, and in order to the maintenance of the action it may properly be described

...We think such an act is also a willful and malicious injury to the person or property of the husband, within the meaning of the exception in the statute.

There may be cases where the act has been performed without any particular malice towards the husband, but we are of opinion that, within the meaning of the exception, it is not necessary that there should be...personal malevolence toward the husband, but that the act itself necessarily implies that degree of malice which is sufficient to bring the case within the exception stated in the statute. The act is willful, of course, in the sense that it is intentional and voluntary...

In *Bromage v. Prosser*, 4 Barn. & C. 247, which was an action of slander, Mr. Justice Bayley, among other things, said:

> Malice, in common acceptance, means ill will against a person; but in its legal sense it means a wrongful act, done intentionally, without just cause or excuse. If I give a perfect stranger a blow likely to produce death, I do it of malice, because I do it intentionally and without just cause or excuse. If I maim cattle, without knowing whose they are, if I poison a fishery, without knowing the owner, I do it of malice, because it is a wrongful act, and done intentionally. . . .If I traduce a man, whether I know him or not and whether I intend to do him an injury or not, I apprehend the law considers it as done of malice, because it is wrongful and intentional. It equally works an injury, whether I meant to produce an injury or not. . .

We cite the case as good definition of the legal meaning of the word malice. . . .

In Re Freche (U.S. district court, district of New Jersey, 1901) 109 Fed. 620, it was held that a judgment for the father in an action to recover damages for the seduction of his daughter was for a willful and malicious injury to the person and property of another, within the meaning of § 17 of the bankrupt act, and was not released by a discharge in bankruptcy. Kirkpatrick, District Judge, in the course of his opinion, said:

> From the nature of the case, the act of the defendant Freche which caused the injury was willful, because it was voluntary. That act was unlawful, wrongful, and tortious, and, being willfully done, it was, in law, malicious. . . .'Malice,' in law, simply means a depraved inclination on the part of a person to disregard the rights of others, which intent is manifested by his injurious acts. . . .

In *Leicester v. Hoadley*, supreme court of Kansas, 1903, 66 Kan. 172, 71 Pac. 318, it was held that a judgment obtained by a wife against another woman for damages sustained by the wife by reason of the alienation of the affections of her husband is not released by the discharge of the judgment debtor under proceedings in bankruptcy, where such alienation has been accomplished by schemes and devices of the judgment debtor, and resulted in the loss of support and impairment of health to the wife.

The judgment here. . .comes. . . within the language of the statute, reasonably construed. The injury for which it was recovered is one of the grossest which can be inflicted upon the husband, and the person who perpetrates it knows it is an offense of the most aggravated character; that it is a wrong for which no adequate compensation can be made, and hence personal

> and particular malice towards the husband as an individual need not be shown, for the law implies that there must be malice in the very act itself, and we think Congress did not intend to permit such an injury to be released by a discharge in bankruptcy. . . .
>
> For the reasons stated, we think the order of the Court of Appeals of New York must be affirmed.
>
> **MR. JUSTICE BROWN, MR. JUSTICE WHITE, and MR. JUSTICE HOLMES** dissent [without opinion].

Case Questions

1. The Court discusses cases involving three types of injuries: to a husband whose wife has sex with another man, to a wife whose husband has sex with another woman, and to a father whose unmarried daughter has sex with a man. In these cases, who are the injured parties, who are the guilty parties, and what is the role of the third party? What specific injuries are being done? What is the relative importance of the similarities and differences between the three situations?

2. We learn virtually nothing about Colwell's wife, not even her first name. Consider this decision from her point of view. What does it say about her character, her situation, and her relationship to her husband?

A Married Woman's Surname: *Rago* and *Palermo* Cases

Antonia Rago of Chicago and Rosary Palermo of Nashville were both lawyers. Each women was married; both used their original surnames; and both were denied the right to register to vote unless they used their husbands' last names. These two decisions, 30 years apart, provide evidence of the effect of the feminist movement on judicial decision-making.

In 1944, Antonia Rago, a Chicago lawyer, married William C. MacFarland. She then took the City's Board of Election Commissioners to court to get permission to register under her own surname. When she won, the board appealed. The state supreme court reversed, relying on common law, and finding no constitutional issue in the case.[35]

Rosary Palermo's court saw things differently. Under Tennessee's compulsory registration law, she had listed her surname as Palermo on a change of address form, rather than adopting her new husband's surname, Cheatham. She was warned that her name would be purged from the voter registration list if she did not list herself as Cheatham; she refused, her name was purged, and she went to court in 1975 seeking a declaratory judgment that this interpretation of the relevant statute was either erroneous or violated the Nineteenth Amendment or the due process or equal protection clause of the Fourteenth Amendment. Ultimately, the case reached the Tennessee Supreme Court, which ruled that in Tennessee a woman's change to her husband's surname at marriage was customary rather than legally obligatory, and that so long as no fraud was involved, Tennessee law permitted people to use any name they liked.[36]

Asymmetrical Reciprocity: *McGuire v. McGuire* (1953) and *Borelli v. Brousseau* (1993)

The first case below, *McGuire v. McGuire* (1953), gives the reader an opportunity to assess the state of marriage law when the second wave women's movement began in the late 1960s. The case following *McGuire* takes us up to the modern era of marriage law, governed by cases such as *Orr* and *Feenstra*. It offers a chance to judge how far-reaching, or not, the reform has been.

McGuire v. McGuire
157 Neb. 226; 59 N.W.2d 336 (Neb. Supreme Court 1953)

Opinion of Court (Messmore, J.):

The plaintiff, Lydia McGuire, brought this action in equity in the district court for Wayne County against Charles W. McGuire, her husband, as defendant, to recover suitable maintenance and support money, and for costs and attorney's fees. [She prevailed.]

The district court decreed that the plaintiff was legally entitled to use the credit of the defendant and obligate him to pay for certain items in the nature of improvements and repairs, furniture, and appliances for the household in the amount of several thousand dollars; required the defendant to purchase a new automobile with an effective heater within 30 days; ordered him to pay travel expenses of the plaintiff for a visit to each of her daughters at least once a year; that the plaintiff was entitled in the future to pledge the credit of the defendant for what may constitute necessaries of life; awarded a personal allowance to the plaintiff in the sum of $50 a month; awarded $800 for services for the plaintiff's attorney; and as an alternative to part of the award so made, defendant was permitted, in agreement with plaintiff, to purchase a modern home elsewhere.

The record shows that the plaintiff and defendant were married in Wayne, Nebraska, on August 11, 1919. At the time of the marriage the defendant was a bachelor 46 or 47 years of age and had a reputation for more than ordinary frugality, of which the plaintiff was aware. She had visited in his home and had known him for about 3 years prior to the marriage. After the marriage the couple went to live on a farm of 160 acres located in Leslie precinct, Wayne County, owned by the defendant and upon which he had lived and farmed since 1905. The parties have lived on this place ever since. The plaintiff [was previously widowed and had] two daughters...Both of these daughters are married and have families of their own.

At the time of trial plaintiff was 66 years of age and the defendant nearly 80 years of age. No children were born to these parties. The defendant had no dependents except the plaintiff.

The plaintiff testified that she was a dutiful and obedient wife, worked and saved, and cohabited with the defendant until the last 2 or 3 years. She worked in the fields, did outside chores, cooked, and attended to her household duties such as cleaning the house and doing the washing. For a number of years she raised as high as 300 chickens, sold poultry and eggs, and used the money to buy clothing, things she wanted, and for groceries. She further testified that the defendant was the boss of the house and his word was law; that he would not tolerate any charge accounts and would not inform her as to his finances or business; and that he was a poor companion. The defendant did not complain of her work, but left the impression to her that she had not done enough. On several occasions the plaintiff asked the defendant for money. He would give her very small amounts, and for the last 3 or 4 years he had not given her any money nor provided her with clothing, except a coat about 4 years previous. The defendant had purchased the groceries the last 3 or 4 years, and permitted her to buy groceries, but he paid for them by check. There is apparently no complaint about the groceries the defendant furnished. The defendant had not taken her to a motion picture show during the past 12 years. For the past 4 years or more, the defendant had not given the plaintiff money to purchase furniture or other household necessities. Three years ago he did purchase an electric, wood-and-cob combination stove which was installed in the kitchen, also linoleum floor covering for the kitchen. The plaintiff further testified that the house is not equipped with a bathroom, bathing facilities, or inside toilet. The kitchen is not modern. She does not have a kitchen sink. Hard and soft water is obtained from a well and cistern.

It appears that the defendant owned 398 acres of land with 2 acres deeded to a church, the land being of the value of $83,960; that he has bank deposits in the sum of $12,786.81 and government bonds in the amount of $104,500;

and that his income, including interest on the bonds and rental for his real estate, is $8,000 or $9,000 a year.

The facts are not in dispute.

While there is an allegation in the plaintiff's petition to the effect that the defendant was guilty of extreme cruelty towards the plaintiff, and also an allegation requesting a restraining order be entered against the defendant for fear he might molest plaintiff or take other action detrimental to her rights, the plaintiff made no attempt to prove these allegations and the fact that she continued to live with the defendant is quite incompatible with the same.

The plaintiff relies upon the following cases from this jurisdiction which are clearly distinguishable from the facts in the instant case as will become apparent.

In the case of *Earle v. Earle*, 27 Neb. 277, 43 N.W. 118, the plaintiff's petition alleged, in substance, the marriage of the parties, that one child was born of the marriage, and that the defendant sent his wife away from him, did not permit her to return, contributed to her support and maintenance separate and apart from him, and later refused and ceased to provide for her support and the support of his child. The wife instituted a suit in equity against her husband for maintenance and support without a prayer for divorce or from bed and board. The court stated that it was a well-established rule of law that it is the duty of the husband to provide his family with support and means of living—the style of support, requisite lodging, food, clothing, etc., to be such as fit his means, position, and station in life—and for this purpose the wife has generally the right to use his credit for the purchase of necessaries. The court held that if a wife is abandoned by her husband, without means of support, a bill in equity will lie to compel the husband to support the wife without asking for a decree of divorce.

[Additional cases omitted.—AU.]

In *Sinn v. Sinn*, 138 Neb. 621, 294 N.W. 381, the court said that a wife living apart from her husband generally becomes entitled to alimony or separate maintenance when she offers in good faith to return to him and he refuses to accept the offer and receive his wife. The plaintiff left the defendant's home due to violent and indecent language he used, then subsequently made a bona fide offer to return, which he rejected. This court held that she had a right to maintain a suit for separate maintenance and support without seeking a divorce, in line with the previous cases here referred to.

It becomes apparent that there are no cases cited by the plaintiff and relied upon by her from this jurisdiction or other jurisdictions that will sustain the action such as she has instituted in the instant case.

There are also several cases, under statutes of various states, in which separate maintenance was refused the wife, where the husband and wife were living in the same house. These cases are to the effect that it is an indispensable requirement of a maintenance statute that the wife should be living separate and apart from her husband without her fault, and that therefore, a wife living in the same house with her husband, occupying a different room and eating at a different time, was not entitled to separate maintenance. See *Lowe v. Lowe*, 213 Ill. App. 607.

In the instant case the marital relation has continued for more than 33 years, and the wife has been supported in the same manner during this time without complaint on her part. The parties have not been separated or living apart from each other at any time. In the light of the cited cases it is clear, especially so in this jurisdiction, that to maintain an action such as the one at bar, the parties must be separated or living apart from each other.

The living standards of a family are a matter of concern to the household, and not for the courts to determine, even though the husband's attitude toward his wife, according to his wealth and circumstances, leaves little to be said in his behalf. As long as the home is maintained and the parties are living as husband and wife it may be said that the husband is legally supporting his wife and the purpose of the marriage relation is being carried out. Public policy requires such a holding. It appears that the plaintiff is not devoid of money in her own right. She has a fair-sized bank account and is entitled to use the rent from the 80 acres of land left by her first husband, if she so chooses.

For the reasons given in this opinion, the judgment rendered by the district court is reversed and the cause remanded with directions to dismiss...

YEAGER, J., dissenting:

I respectfully dissent. In doing so I do not question the correctness of the statement of facts [but I note below] some important considerations [de-emphasized by the majority.]...

At the time of the marriage plaintiff had a one-third interest in 80 acres of land left by her former husband. Later this interest was transferred to her two daughters. At the time of trial she had a bank account jointly with one of her daughters in the amount of $5,960.22.

This accumulated amount did not come from any contributions made by the defendant. It doubtless came in large part, if not entirely, from eggs and chickens produced and sold by plaintiff and from the income from the 80-acre farm. It appears that she was in general charge of this farm for her daughters and was permitted to use the proceeds.

From the beginning of the married life of the parties the defendant supplied only the barest necessities and there was no change thereafter. He did not even buy groceries until the last 3 or 4 years before the trial, and neither did he buy clothes for the plaintiff.

As long as she was able plaintiff made a garden, raised chickens, did outside chores, and worked in the fields. From the sale of chickens and eggs she provided groceries, household necessities, and her own clothing. These things she is no longer able to do, but notwithstanding this the defendant does no more than to buy groceries. He buys her no clothing and does not give her any money at all to spend for her needs or desires. Only one incident is mentioned in the record of defendant ever buying plaintiff any clothing. He bought her a coat over 3 years before the trial.

The house in which the parties live is supplied with electricity and there is a gas refrigerator, otherwise it is decidedly not modern.

[Here the dissent restated the district court decree—AU.]

There is and can be no doubt that, independent of statutes relating to divorce, alimony, and separate maintenance, if this plaintiff were living apart from the defendant she could in equity and on the facts as outlined in the record be awarded appropriate relief. . .

In the light of what the decisions declare to be the basis of the right to maintain an action for support, is there any less reason for extending the right to a wife who is denied the right to maintenance in a home occupied with her husband than to one who has chosen to occupy a separate abode?

If the right is to be extended only to one who is separated from the husband equity and effective justice would be denied where a wealthy husband refused proper support and maintenance to a wife physically or mentally incapable of putting herself in a position where the rule could become available to her.

It is true that in all cases examined which uphold the right of a wife to maintain an action in equity for maintenance the parties were living apart, but no case has been cited or found which says that separation is a condition precedent to the right to maintain action in equity for maintenance. . .[or]that it is not.

. . .Can a principle of equity which requires a wife to leave her home before becoming able to enforce the obligation of her husband to support and maintain her receive in reason a higher commendation than [a rule applying it to their shared dwelling]. . .? I think not.

I conclude therefore that the district court had the power to entertain the action [but. . .] that the court was without proper power to make any of the awards contained in the decree for the support and maintenance of the plaintiff except the one of $50 a month.

From the cases cited herein it is clear that a husband has the obligation to furnish to his wife the necessaries of life. These decisions make clear that for failure to furnish them the wife may seek allowances for her support and maintenance. However neither these decisions nor any others cited or found support the view contended for by plaintiff that the court may go beyond this and impose obligations other than that of payment of money for the proper support and maintenance of the wife. . .

As pointed out the district court made an allowance of $ 50 a month. In the light of generally well-known present day economy the conclusion is inevitable that this award is insufficient for the maintenance of the plaintiff. The record before us however does not supply adequate information upon which this court could make a finding as to what would be sufficient.

The decree of the district court should be affirmed as to the award of a fee of $ 800 for plaintiff's attorney and as to costs. Otherwise it should be reversed and the cause remanded with directions to the district court to take evidence and to determine and make such allowances to plaintiff for her suitable support and maintenance as may appear proper in the light of such evidence and appropriate rules of law as set forth herein.

BORELLI V. BROUSSEAU
12 Cal App. 4th 647 (1993)

Opinion of Court (PERLEY, J.):

[When Michael Borelli suffered a disabling stroke, he made an agreement with Hildegard, his wife of eight years. If she would care for him at home instead of placing him in a care facility, he would increase his bequest to her. Hildegard fulfilled her part of the agreement, but Michael did not; instead, he willed the bulk of his estate to his daughter, Grace Brousseau. Hildegard filed suit to enforce the agreement she had made with Michael.]

[Note: Many case citations have been omitted.—AU.]

..."The laws relating to marriage and divorce have been enacted because of the profound concern of our organized society for the dignity and stability of the marriage relationship. This concern relates primarily to the status of the parties as husband and wife. The concern of society as to the property rights of the parties is secondary and incidental to its concern as to their status" (*Sapp v. Superior Court* (1953) 119 Cal.App.2d 645, 650; 260 P.2d 119).

...In accordance with these concerns the following pertinent legislation has been enacted: Civil Code § 242—"Every individual shall support his or her spouse ...." Civil Code § 4802—"[A] husband and wife cannot, by any contract with each other, alter their legal relations, except as to property...." Civil Code § 5100—"Husband and wife contract toward each other obligations of mutual respect, fidelity, and support." Civil Code § 5103—"[E]ither husband or wife may enter into any transaction with the other ... respecting property, which either might if unmarried." Civil Code § 5132—"[A] married person shall support the person's spouse while they are living together...."

The courts have stringently enforced and explained the statutory language. "Although most of the cases, both in California and elsewhere, deal with a wife's right to support from the husband, in this state a wife also has certain obligations to support the husband." ...Moreover, interspousal mutual obligations have been broadly defined. "[Husband's] duties and obligations to [wife] included more than mere cohabitation with her. It was his duty to offer [wife] his sympathy, confidence, and fidelity." When necessary, spouses must "provide uncompensated protective supervision services for" each other.

Estate of Sonnicksen (1937) 23 Cal.App.2d 475, 479 [73 P.2d 643] and *Brooks v. Brooks* (1941) 48 Cal.App.2d 347, 349–350 [119 P.2d 970], each hold that under the above statutes and in accordance with the above policy a wife is obligated by the marriage contract to provide nursing-type care to an ill husband. Therefore, contracts whereby the wife is to receive compensation for providing such services are void as against public policy; and there is no consideration for the husband's promise.

Appellant argues that *Sonnicksen* and *Brooks* are no longer valid precedents because they are based on outdated views of the role of women and marriage. She further argues that the rule of those cases denies her equal protection because husbands only have a financial obligation toward their wives, while wives have to provide actual nursing services for free. We disagree.

...[More recent precedents] indicate that the marital duty of support under Civil Code §§ 242, 5100, and 5132 includes caring for a spouse who is ill. They also establish that support in a marriage means more than the physical care someone could be hired to provide. Such support also encompasses sympathy, comfort, love, companionship and affection. Thus, the duty of support can no more be "delegated" to a third party than the statutory duties of fidelity and mutual respect (Civ. Code, § 5100). Marital duties are owed by the spouses personally. This is implicit in the definition of marriage as "a personal relation arising out of a civil contract between a man and a woman." (Civ. Code, § 4100.)

We therefore adhere to the long-standing rule that a spouse is not entitled to compensation for support, apart from rights to community property and the like that arise from the marital relation itself. Personal performance of a personal duty created by the contract of marriage does not constitute a new consideration supporting the indebtedness, alleged in this case.

We agree with the dissent that no rule of law becomes sacrosanct by virtue of its duration, but we are not persuaded that the well-established rule that governs this case deserves to be discarded. If the rule denying compensation for support originated from considerations peculiar to women, this has no bearing on the rule's gender-neutral application today. There is as much potential for fraud today as ever, and allegations like appellant's could be made every time any personal care is rendered. This concern may not entirely justify the rule, but it cannot be said that all rationales for the rule are outdated.

Speculating that appellant might have left her husband but for the agreement she alleges, the dissent suggests that marriages will break up if such agreements are not enforced. While we do not believe that marriages would be fostered by a rule that encouraged sickbed bargaining, the question is not whether such negotiations may be more useful than unseemly. The issue is whether such negotiations are antithetical to the institution of marriage as the Legislature has defined it. We believe that they are.

The dissent maintains that mores have changed to the point that spouses can be treated just like any other parties haggling at arm's length. Whether or not the modern marriage has become like a business, and regardless of whatever else it may have become, it continues to be defined by statute as a personal relationship of mutual support. Thus, even if few things are left that cannot command a price, marital support remains one of them.

The judgment is affirmed.

POCHE, J. (dissenting):

A very ill person wishes to be cared for at home personally by his spouse rather than by nurses at a health care facility. The ill person offers to pay his spouse for such personal care by transferring property to her. The offer is accepted, the services are rendered and the ill spouse dies. . .[T]his court holds that the contract was not enforceable because—as a matter of law—the spouse who rendered services gave no consideration. Apparently, in the majority's view she had a preexisting or precontract nondelegable duty to clean the bedpans herself. Because I do not believe she did, I respectfully dissent.

The majority correctly read *Estate of Sonnicksen* (1937) and *Brooks v. Brooks* (1941) as holding that a wife cannot enter into a binding contract with her husband to provide "nursing-type care" for compensation. It reasons that the wife, by reason of the marital relationship, already has a duty to provide such care, thus she offers no new consideration to support an independent contract to the same effect. (See Civ. Code, § 1550, 1605.) The logic of these decisions is ripe for reexamination.

Sonnicksen and *Brooks* are the California Court of Appeal versions of a national theme. [Citations omitted—AU.]

. . .Statements in two of these [out-of-state] cases to the effect that a husband has an entitlement to his wife's "services" (e.g., *In re Callister's Estate*, 47 N.E. 268 at pp. 269–270; *Ritchie v. White*, 35 S.E.2d 414 at pp. 416–417) smack of the common law doctrine of coverture which treated a wife as scarcely more than an appendage to her husband.

. . .One of the characteristics of coverture was that it deemed the wife economically helpless and governed by an implicit exchange: " 'The husband, as head of the family, is charged with its support and maintenance in return for which he is entitled to the wife's services in all those domestic affairs which pertain to the comfort, care, and well-being of the family. Her labors are her contribution to the family support and care.' " (*Ritchie v. White*, at pp. 416–417.) But coverture has been discarded in California.

Not only has this doctrinal base for the authority underpinning the majority opinion been discarded long ago, but modern attitudes toward marriage have changed almost as rapidly as the economic realities of modern society. The assumption that only the rare wife can make a financial contribution to her family has become badly outdated in this age in which many married women have paying employment outside the home. A two-income family can no longer be dismissed as a statistically insignificant aberration. Moreover today husbands are increasingly involved in the domestic chores that make a house a home. Insofar as marital duties and property rights are not governed by positive law, they may be the result of informal accommodation or formal agreement. (See Civ. Code, § 5200 et seq.) If spouses cannot work things out, there is always the no longer infrequently used option of divorce. For better or worse, we have to a great extent left behind the comfortable and familiar gender-based roles evoked by Norman Rockwell paintings. No longer can the marital relationship be regarded as "uniform and unchangeable." (*In re Callister's Estate,* 47 N.E. 268 at p. 270.)

...[T]he recognition that marriage is "intimate to the degree of being sacred" (*Griswold v. Connecticut* [1965]) does not mean that the law is oblivious to what occurs within that relationship. Solicitude for domestic harmony is no longer synonymous with blindness to crimes spouses commit against each other (see *People v. Pierce* (1964) 61 Cal.2d 879; 395 P.2d 893), even when those crimes involve the previously sacrosanct realm of sexual relations. (See Pen. Code, § 262.) Similarly, civil actions are allowed for intentional or negligent torts committed by one spouse against the other. (See Civ. Code, § 5113....) The same is true for breached contracts. Thus, when the simple justice of redressing obvious wrongs is involved, the arguments for domestic harmony have been rejected and are now in full retreat, not only in California (see *Gibson v. Gibson,* 3 Cal.3d 914 at pp. 917–920 and authorities cited), but throughout the entire nation.

Restraints on interspousal litigation are almost extinct. With the walls supposedly protecting the domestic haven from litigation already reduced to rubble, it hardly seems revolutionary to topple one more brick. Furthermore, in situations such as this, where one spouse has died, preserving " 'domestic life [from] discord and mischief' " (*Brooks v. Brooks,* 48 Cal.App.2d 347 at p. 350) seems an academic concern that no modern academic seems concerned with.

...Reduced to its essence, the alleged contract at issue here was an agreement to transmute Mr. Borelli's separate property into the separate property of his wife. Had there been no marriage and had they been total strangers, there is no doubt Mr. Borelli could have validly contracted to receive her services in exchange for certain of his property. The mere existence of a marriage certificate should not deprive competent adults of the "utmost freedom of contract" they would otherwise possess.

. . .No one doubts that spouses owe each other a duty of support or that this encompasses "the obligation to provide medical care." There is nothing found in *Sonnicksen* and *Brooks,* or cited by the majority, which requires that this obligation be *personally* discharged by a spouse except the decisions themselves. However, at the time *Sonnicksen* and *Brooks* were decided—before World War II—it made sense for those courts to say that a wife could perform her duty of care only by doing so personally. That was an accurate reflection of the real world for women years before the exigency of war produced substantial employment opportunities for them. For most women at that time there was no other way to take care of a sick husband except personally. So to the extent those decisions hold that a contract to pay a wife for caring personally for her husband is without consideration they are correct only because at the time they were decided there were no other ways she could meet her obligation of care. Since that was the universal reality, she was giving up nothing of value by agreeing to perform a duty that had one and only one way of being performed.

However the real world has changed in the 56 years since *Sonnicksen* was decided. . . . [I]n the present day husbands and wives who work outside the home have alternative methods of meeting this duty of care to an ill spouse. Among the choices would be: (1) paying for professional help; (2) paying for nonprofessional assistance; (3) seeking help from relatives or friends; and (4) quitting one's job and doing the work personally.

A fair reading of the complaint indicates that Mrs. Borelli initially chose the first of these options, and that this was not acceptable to Mr. Borelli, who then offered compensation if Mrs. Borelli would agree to personally care for him at home. To contend in 1993 that such a contract is without consideration means that if Mrs. Clinton becomes ill, President Clinton must drop everything and personally care for her.

According to the majority, Mrs. Borelli had nothing to bargain with so long as she remained in the marriage. This assumes that an intrinsic component of the marital relationship is the *personal* services of the spouse, an obligation that cannot be delegated or performed by others. The preceding discussion has attempted to demonstrate many ways in which what the majority terms "nursing-type care" can be provided without either husband or wife being required to empty a single bedpan. It follows that, because Mrs. Borelli agreed to supply this personal involvement, she was providing something over and above what would fully satisfy her duty of support. That personal something—

> precisely because it was something she was not required to do—qualifies as valid consideration sufficient to make enforceable Mr. Borelli's reciprocal promise to convey certain of his separate property.
>
> Not only does the majority's position substantially impinge upon couples' freedom to come to a working arrangement of marital responsibilities, it may also foster the very opposite result of that intended. For example, nothing compelled Mr. Borelli and plaintiff to continue living together after his physical afflictions became known. Moral considerations notwithstanding, no legal force could have stopped plaintiff from leaving her husband in his hour of need. Had she done so, and had Mr. Borelli promised to give her some of his separate property should she come back, a valid contract would have arisen upon her return. Deeming them contracts promoting reconciliation and the resumption of marital relations, California courts have long enforced such agreements as supported by consideration. Here so far as we can tell from the face of the complaint, Mr. Borelli and plaintiff reached largely the same result without having to endure a separation. There is no sound reason why their contract, which clearly facilitated continuation of their marriage, should be any less valid. It makes no sense to say that spouses have greater bargaining rights when separated than they do during an unruptured marriage.

DIVORCE

The law of divorce in the United States has had a history similar to that of family law in general. Male supremacy gave way to asymmetrical reciprocity, which in turn gave way to formal equality. When the Constitution was adopted, divorce was rare and was easier for husbands to obtain than wives. The dissolution of a marriage was an adversary process: one party sued the other on the basis of grounds that were defined by each state. The Seneca Falls Declaration of Sentiments (1848) declared that man "has so framed the law of divorce. . .as to be wholly regardless of the happiness of women."[37]

A century later, the typical divorce involved a wife suing a husband. The recognized grounds were often asymmetrical; for example, a wife could get a divorce if her husband failed to support her, but not vice versa. Grounds varied from adultery (in every state) to "incompatibility" or "irreconcilable differences." Laws about the post-divorce disposition of marital property varied from state to state. Wives who were innocent parties were entitled to ask for alimony from their ex-husbands; wives who retained custody of minor children could ask for child support. Judges did not always grant these awards, nor did ex-husbands necessarily fulfill their obligations.[38] Enforcement powers were negligible.

The spouse most disadvantaged by the adversary system was financially independent, eager to end the marriage, and confronted with a spouse who refused to sue. This group was predominantly male, but included increasing numbers of women by the 1960s and 1970s. By the twenty-first century, divorce law served the interests of this group. "Divorce" was renamed "dissolution," "alimony" is now "spousal support," and the adversary system has been replaced in every state by "no-fault divorce." One spouse can divorce the other without cooperation. Support awards are no longer given on the basis of culpability.

Feminists are divided on the issue of divorce reform, especially no-fault divorce. Some divorce reform activists in the 1970s identified themselves as feminists, seeing change as a welcome step toward equality. But other feminists argue that, since husbands and wives are not equally situated, gender-neutral rules disadvantage ex-wives. No-fault divorce got much of the blame for the "feminization of poverty" discovered by social scientists in the 1980s: the fact that women and children are disproportionately represented among poor Americans. The feminist controversy over divorce is similar to that over pregnancy leaves examined in Chapter 3: Is taking gender differences into account a wise accommodation to social reality, or does it reinforce traditional gender roles?

Yet the text of contemporary divorce statutes does not do either of these things. The Uniform Marriage and Divorce Act of 1974 (UMDA), intended by Congress as a guide to state lawmakers, is written in gender-neutral language but accommodates the interests of ex-wives. Only eight states—Arizona, Colorado, Illinois, Kentucky, Minnesota, Missouri, Montana, and Washington—have adopted this law in its entirety, but the UMDA has to some degree influenced most state legislatures.

ARIZONA REVISED STATUTES

25–319. Maintenance; computation factors

A. In a proceeding for dissolution of marriage or legal separation, or a proceeding for maintenance following dissolution of the marriage by a court that lacked personal jurisdiction over the absent spouse, the court may grant a maintenance order for either spouse for any of the following reasons if it finds that the spouse seeking maintenance:

1. Lacks sufficient property, including property apportioned to the spouse, to provide for that spouse's reasonable needs.

2. Is unable to be self-sufficient through appropriate employment or is the custodian of a child whose age or condition is such that the custodian

> should not be required to seek employment outside the home or lacks earning ability in the labor market adequate to be self-sufficient.
>
> 3. Contributed to the educational opportunities of the other spouse.
>
> 4. Had a marriage of long duration and is of an age that may preclude the possibility of gaining employment adequate to be self-sufficient.
>
> B. The maintenance order shall be in an amount and for a period of time as the court deems just, without regard to marital misconduct, and after considering all relevant factors, including:
>
> 1. The standard of living established during the marriage.
>
> 2. The duration of the marriage.
>
> 3. The age, employment history, earning ability and physical and emotional condition of the spouse seeking maintenance.
>
> 4. The ability of the spouse from whom maintenance is sought to meet that spouse's needs while meeting those of the spouse seeking maintenance.
>
> 5. The comparative financial resources of the spouses, including their comparative earning abilities in the labor market.
>
> 6. The contribution of the spouse seeking maintenance to the earning ability of the other spouse.
>
> 7. The extent to which the spouse seeking maintenance has reduced that spouse's income or career opportunities for the benefit of the other spouse.

These provisions allow judges to accommodate circumstances in which divorcing wives often find themselves. The laws maintain gender equality by allowing support awards for atypical situations as well as women in typical ones. Both wives and husbands are protected against awards that retaliate for misconduct. No-fault divorce law as such does not require that women be disadvantaged; but, somehow, the result of thousands of courts making thousands of decisions lowers the post-divorce standard of living for many women. Nonpayment of maintenance awards is another important factor, although federal and state governments have made it harder to ignore these obligations.[39]

Two important child support enforcement laws were enacted during the 1990s during the Bush I and Clinton administrations. The Child Support Recovery Act, or CSRA, was passed in 1992. The purpose of the CSRA was "to deter nonpayment of State ordered support obligations through prosecution of the most egregious offenders." The U.S. Department of Justice reports that local law enforcement agencies experience some frustration with the CSRA because misdemeanor penalties that are reserved for less-egregious CSRA violations fail to deter perpetrators. To address these concerns, Congress passed the Deadbeat Parents Punishment Act in 1998 (DPPA), which created new categories of federal felonies so that the worst violators would be proportionally punished.[40]

Under the CSRA (1992), it is a federal crime if one "willfully" fails to pay child support for:

1. Children living in another state

2. The support obligations have been determined by a court or administrative order

3. The support owed is overdue by at least one year

4. The unpaid amount must exceed $5000 per child[41]

Section 2 of the DPPA (1998) establishes felony violations for persons who fail to pay their child support under the following circumstances:

(a) OFFENSE—Any person who—

(1) willfully fails to pay a support obligation with respect to a child who resides in another State, if such obligation has remained unpaid for a period longer than 1 year, or is greater than $5,000;

(2) travels in interstate or foreign commerce with the intent to evade a support obligation, if such obligation has remained unpaid for a period longer than 1 year, or is greater than $5,000; or

(3) willfully fails to pay a support obligation with respect to a child who resides in another State, if such obligation has remained unpaid for a period longer than 2 years, or is greater than $10,000;

. . .

(c) PUNISHMENT—The punishment for an offense under this section is—

(1) in the case of a first offense under subsection (a)(1), a fine under this title, imprisonment for not more than 6 months, or both; and

(2) in the case of an offense under paragraph (2) or (3) of subsection (a), or a second or subsequent offense under subsection (a)(1), a fine under this title, imprisonment for not more than 2 years, or both.

(d) MANDATORY RESTITUTION—Upon a conviction under this section, the court shall order restitution under section 3663A in an amount equal to the total unpaid support obligation as it exists at the time of sentencing.

The primary entity responsible for enforcing federal child support enforcement laws is the Office of Child Support Enforcement (OCSE), an office within the Department of Health and Human Services Administration for Children and Families. The OCSE reports to have served 15.6 million children in 2016 representing one in five children in the United States. Three-fourths of child support payments are collected through income withholding from paychecks.[42]

PARENTS' RIGHTS AND CHILD CUSTODY

Under common law, a divorcing father received custody of any minor children unless he was proven unfit. By the twentieth century, paternal preference had been replaced by the "tender years" doctrine, which held that young children belonged with their mothers unless a mother was proven unfit. This effective maternal preference was replaced by a facially neutral standard that awarded custody according to "the best interests of the child." While this remains the prevailing rule in most jurisdictions, two innovations have emerged in child custody law: a preference for the parent who has been the primary caregiver, and a preference for joint custody. The following readings and cases illustrate this portion of legal history.

Paternal Custody and Its Limits

> #### JAMES KENT, *COMMENTARIES ON AMERICAN LAW*, 4TH ED. (1840)
>
> ...The father, says Blackstone, has the benefit of his children's labour while they live with him, and are maintained by him, and this is no more than he is entitled to from his apprentices or servants.
>
> The father may obtain the custody of his children by the writ of *habeas corpus*, when they are improperly detained from him; but the courts, of both law and equity, will investigate the circumstances, and act according to sound discretion, and will not always, and of course, interfere upon *habeas corpus*, and take a child, under fourteen years of age, from the possession of a third person, and deliver it over to the father against the will of the child. They will consult the inclination of an infant, if it be of a sufficiently mature age to judge for itself, and even control the right of the father to the possession and education of his child, when the nature of the case appears to warrant it. The father may also

> maintain trespass for a tort to an infant child, provided he can show a loss of service, for that is the gist of the action by the father (pp. 193–95).

American law has long recognized parents' rights and duties toward their minor children. Today, parents' rights include making decisions about discipline, education, medical treatment, and virtually every aspect of their children's lives. Parental autonomy is subject to such limitations as prohibitions on child abuse and neglect, compulsory education laws, regulations allowing minors to get medical care for sexually transmitted diseases without parental notification, and "judicial bypasses" for abortion.[43] The early nineteenth century version of these limits is detailed by Joseph Story as follows:

> ### JOSEPH STORY, *COMMENTARIES ON EQUITY JURISPRUDENCE*, SEC. 1341 (1836)
>
> The jurisdiction of the Court of Chancery extends to the care of the person of the infant, so far as is necessary for his protection and education. . . . [On this ground] the Court interferes with the ordinary right of parents, as guardians by nature, or by nurture, in regard to the custody and care of their children. For, though in general parents are entrusted with the custody of the persons and the education of their children, yet this is done upon the natural presumption, that the children will be properly taken care of, and brought up with a due education in literature, in morals and religion; and that they will be treated with kindness and affection. But whenever this presumption is removed, and it is found that a father (for example) is guilty of gross ill treatment or cruelty towards his infant children; or that he is in constant habits of drunkenness and blasphemy, or low and gross debauchery; or that he professes atheistical, or irreligious principles; or that his domestic associations are such, as tend to the corruption and contamination of his children; or that he otherwise acts in a manner injurious to their morals or interests; in every such case, the Court of Chancery will interfere, and deprive him of the custody of his children, and appoint a suitable person to act as guardian, and take care of them, and superintend their education.

"Tender Years" Doctrine: *Long v. Long* (1955)

The stormy marriage of Ethel and Herbert Long lasted three years. The combined stress of financial problems, difficulties with in-laws, and the birth of two sons in 16 months led to frequent separations, two withdrawn divorce petitions, and Ethel's suit for divorce and child custody in 1953. Ethel accused her husband of general indignities and failure to support the family, while his countersuit accused her of being an unfit mother. The trial court granted the divorce to Herbert and custody of the children to Ethel. Herbert appealed the decision.

ETHEL LONG V. HERBERT LONG
280 S.W.2d 690 (Missouri 1955)

RUARK, J.

The parties were married on June 15, 1950. Defendant testified he was twenty-four years of age at date of trial (February 27, 1954). Plaintiff's age is not shown, but it is evident she also was young.

...[I]t appears this sorry affair has resulted because the two of them were not sufficiently mature to assume the obligations and burdens of married life rather than because of any viciousness inherent in either of them. Immediately after the marriage they went to live with defendant's parents. Plaintiff testified that prior to the marriage it was agreed that the residence with defendant's parents was to be for two weeks only but that it continued for a considerable portion of their married life. At some later time, date not shown, plaintiff and defendant moved to themselves on a rented farm. During the year 1951 defendant bought and sold (nine) automobiles and he said they lived off the profits from these ventures. For some period, date also not clear but probably in the years 1951 and 1952, defendant farmed in partnership with his father. Early in 1953 he went to work at the Vickers plant in Joplin, Missouri, where he received $400 per month. He continued at this work until October 1953. He was drafted into the Army in December 1953. A son, Robert Lee, was born in May 1952 and another son, Michael, was born September 4, 1953. It is these children who are the subject of the controversy.

In the week immediately preceding the birth of his second child the defendant went to where plaintiff was staying with her mother (the parties were again separated at that time) and, according to plaintiff's testimony, he there assaulted both plaintiff and her mother in an attempt to take the older child, Robert Lee, away by force. This affair graduated to the police court. Defendant denied having assaulted either plaintiff or her mother but admitted he was attempting to take the child. Plaintiff testified he took the child away from the house by force, but whether by force or otherwise he did secure the infant against the consent of the plaintiff and took the child to the home of his parents near Sarcoxie, where such child has since remained.

Defendant's evidence in the main was directed to alleged neglect of the children on the part of the plaintiff and alleged incidents of misconduct and improper correspondence, or correspondence indicating improprieties, with other men. As to neglect of the children, defendant testified that plaintiff kept a filthy house, that she would accumulate stacks of dirty dishes and dirty diapers and that she fed the (older) baby cold milk. His testimony in this regard was largely unsupported.... Plaintiff also produced witnesses who testified that from their observation plaintiff kept the children clean and healthy...

Defendant sought to establish plaintiff's unfitness by three incidents. The first occurred in April 1951 .... while the parties were separated. Plaintiff was working at a cafe and at its closing, sometime after nine o'clock, got into an automobile with three boys and rode off. The defendant sighted them and followed, and they in turn sighted defendant and ran off and left him. Defendant hid in the bushes near where plaintiff was staying at that time and later in the evening one of the boys brought her home. The only conflict in their evidence concerning this incident is the time plaintiff got home.... For another incident defendant called a witness Staley, his relative by marriage, who lived in Kansas City and visited overnight at the home where plaintiff and defendant were then living. This witness testified that early the next morning when plaintiff arose she came from her and her husband's bedroom through the room where he, the witness, was sleeping, and while in the room where he was in bed said, 'What would you do if I got in bed with you?' ....Plaintiff denied having made such statement.

....The only letter which we regard as of any considerable importance was one written by the plaintiff. It was dated December 24, 1952, and addressed to 'My dearest darling Don.' It stated, 'I was in town today and tried to see you, but you were not to be found,' and 'I guess you let me make a fool of myself, or rather that is the way I take it.' The letter contained some terms of endearment and the statement, 'I guess I did the wrong thing the last to (sic) times I was with you. I should have known better, but I guess you got the best of me. Well, I guess there is no sense crying over spilled milk now, because it was my fault anyhow, but I am not sorry and I know I never will be.' Plaintiff's explanation of this letter was that 'I wrote it because I wanted to make him jealous, think he was losing me, so he would have more affection than he had the years we had been married.' She said that she copied portions of the letter quoted out of a True Story magazine, that she left it in an open, unsealed envelope in her purse where, to use her words, 'he would find it because he was looking for loose change that Mother and Daddy might have give me.' He found it.

...[W]here the evidence is conflicting and a determination of the truth involves credibility of witnesses great deference is paid to the judgment of the trial court, who had the advantage of seeing and hearing the witnesses. His determination is not lightly to be disregarded and should not be set aside unless clearly erroneous. This rule is especially applicable where, as here, the order and sequence of events and some of the specific items or incidents under discussion between the attorney and witness are not entirely clear in the record.

Custody of the child or children is usually awarded to the person adjudged to be the innocent and injured party in a divorce case, but this is not always true and it has long been held that although the divorce may be awarded to one party circumstances affecting the welfare of the child may require the placing of care and custody in the other. The cases are innumerable in which part-time custody is awarded to the so-called guilty party in a divorce action. Where there is evidence to support a finding by the trial court that plaintiff was guilty of various indignities other than those which unfit her for custody, the court having awarded her the custody, we will assume his award of the divorce was on those grounds and because of those indignities which do not necessarily disqualify her from such custody.

In determining the question of custody the guiding star which the court must follow is the welfare and best interests of the child. And the custody will not be awarded simply to meet the wishes of either parent nor with any idea of punishment or vengeance.

It has been declared many times that, all other things being equal, custody of the child or children of tender years should be awarded to the mother. With all his technological and social advances, man has found no substitute for the care and affection of a mother.

Plaintiff is living with her parents in a reasonably comfortable home. Defendant is in the Army. He testified that if he received custody of the children they would be kept at his parents' home while he was in service, and both his parents testified as to their willingness to keep and care for the children. Defendant did not relate his plans beyond this arrangement except that he had applied for and expected to obtain a hardship discharge from the Army because of (a) the necessity for care of his children and (b) the physical disability of his father. However, his father testified that he, the father, was in good health and did all the work that was done around the farm. It appears, therefore, that the question here...is in reality a conflict over whether the actual custody, care and training of the children will be lodged in the mother or the paternal grandparents. The reputation of the grandparents (on both sides) is not questioned in any respect. Defendant's parents have a comfortable modern home and no doubt they would do their very utmost to guide their grandchildren in the correct way of life. However, the courts have said many times that the first right (and responsibility) is in the natural parent, and in event of contest between the parent and the grandparents the courts will, unless prevented by circumstances inimical to the welfare of the children, disregard the wishes of the grandparents and award custody to the parent. . . .

The trial court, who saw and heard the witnesses and was in a better position to judge as to their credibility, could well have determined that plaintiff was the guilty party in so far as the termination of the marriage was concerned because of her frequent separations, her evident lack of affection for defendant, and perhaps because of her indiscretions, without determining that she was in any way unfit as a [mother]. As a matter of fact, with the exception of the controversial letter which she wrote, the imputations against her character are more conjectural than actual. As to such letter the court no doubt believed her explanation. As to the testimony of the witness Staley, the court could have believed the words were spoken in jest or he could well have disbelieved the witness in toto. On the other hand, there was evidence concerning defendant's irresponsibility and perhaps willingness to substitute suspicion for facts, which may not have recommended him as one qualified to receive the custody of two children of tender years. It is our opinion that the court acted well within his discretion. . . .

Case Questions

1. Why is Ethel Long the "guilty" party in this divorce? Why is Herbert "innocent?" What relative weight does the trial judge give to the wife's behavior vis-à-vis the husband's?

2. The opinion mentions no fewer than three guiding principles in child custody cases: innocent party preference; maternal preference when the child is of "tender years;" and best interests of the child. How does the appeals court use each of these guidelines here?

The primary criterion employed when courts make custody decisions in divorce situations is the "best interests of the child" standard. Each state decides how to determine what is in a child's best interest; there is no nation-wide standard. The Children's Bureau of the U.S. Department of Health and Human Services notes that " 'Best interests' determinations are generally made by considering a number of factors related to the child's circumstances and the parent or caregiver's circumstances and capacity to parent, with the child's ultimate safety and well-being the paramount concern."[44] Twenty-two states plus the District of Columbia have identified specific factors for courts to consider; eight of these 22 states, plus DC, have adopted the same eight factors focusing on emotional ties and relationships between the parent and child, the child's mental and physical needs, the ability to provide basic necessities of food, clothing and shelter, and whether there is domestic violence in the home. Other states mandate that the child's developmental needs be considered while some states have established that specific criteria may not be considered, such as socio-economic status.[45]

The Best Interests of the Child: Gender-Neutral? *Salk v. Salk* (1975)

This well-publicized case provides a classic example of the elasticity of contemporary child custody law.

> ### KERSTIN SALK V. LEE SALK
> 393 N.Y.S.2d 841 (Supreme Court of NY, NY County 1975)
>
> **RIBAUDO, J:**
>
> This is an action for a divorce instituted by the plaintiff wife; a counterclaim for divorce was interposed by the defendant husband. Both parties requested custody of the two minor children, aged 14 and 8. Throughout the pendency of this action the parties continued to reside in the marital domicile, a spacious brownstone located in Manhattan. This arrangement provided the parties with separate quarters but created extreme tensions and pressures on the parties and the children.
>
> FACTS
>
> The plaintiff and defendant were married on April 9, 1960. There are two issue of the marriage, Eric, born on August 21, 1961, and Pia, born on December 12, 1967.

At the time the parties were married, the plaintiff, a native of Sweden, was engaged in the fashion industry. Subsequent to the marriage, she was never gainfully employed. The defendant has earned a Ph. D. in psychology, and was in the early stages of establishing his practice and reputation as a child psychologist.

During the marriage, commensurate with the defendant's professional advancement, the parties enjoyed a high standard of living.

FINDINGS: CUSTODY

The most difficult issue presented to the court for disposition is the question of which party shall be awarded permanent custody of the infant issue of this marriage.

The pleadings herein indicated that neither party was seeking custody of the children on the basis that the other spouse was by his or her actions unfit to be the custodian of the children, but rather alleged that each was better fit to rear the children.

Thus the scope of the court's inquiry was not directed at applying the "unfitness theory" as the criterion, but rather the use of an affirmative standard, which parent was "better fit," to guide the development of the children and their future. In applying the "better fit theory" it was inescapable that the "fitness" of the parties, both their negative and positive attributes would be developed and put in issue during the course of the hearing.

Under well-settled statutory and case law, neither parent has a prima facie right to custody of a child. The issue is one of *comparative fitness*, with the paramount and controlling consideration being the best interests and welfare of the child. . .

Plaintiff contends that throughout the marriage she has always taken care of the children from the time they were born without the aid of a nurse or governess. This includes, and is not limited to, the daily routines of raising children and running a household.

Plaintiff further argues that defendant is deeply involved with his professional endeavors, will undoubtedly be unable to raise the children without the services of a third party, whether a relative, hired housekeeper, or governess. To award custody to the father in the instant case is tantamount to awarding custody to the third party. Moreover, the fact that the father has greater means than the mother, although a factor to be considered, is not controlling; the court may require the father to provide the mother with sufficient funds to raise the children properly. Although the courts take into account the expressed preference of a child of sufficient age and understanding as to the parent in whose custody he wishes to be, this factor is also not controlling. The courts refuse to allow the child to be the sole judge of his own best interests; moreover, they have recognized that a child's expressed preference can be induced, coaxed or otherwise influenced.

Defendant contends that plaintiff, by her conduct, has attempted to destroy and prevent any fatherly relationship of the defendant with his children; however, defendant if awarded custody would agree to and encourage liberal visitation rights to the plaintiff.

Defendant argues that he is better fit to have custody of the children in that the children have been happiest when with the defendant rather than the plaintiff; when they were exposed to the environment created by the defendant, his associates and his lifestyle, rather than that of the plaintiff; in that the children's growth and development intellectually, morally and psychologically have been enhanced more when exposed to the defendant and the environment created by him rather than that of the plaintiff.

Defendant further argues that both children love and respect defendant, desire to live together with defendant and defendant is better able to care for and maintain them and give them a wholesome family upbringing.

The court is convinced that both parties exhibit genuine love and affection for the children. Neither parent has been neglectful of their parental duties, nor in any way can be characterized as being an unfit custodian of the children.

However, from all the evidence before the court, it has been clearly established that the best interests of the children would be served if permanent custody is awarded to the one parent that appears to more adequately satisfy the emotional and cultural needs of the children.

It is the judgment of this court that permanent custody of both infant issue is awarded to the father, Dr. Lee Salk, as it is the opinion of this court that he is the parent that can best nurture the complex needs and social development of these children.

The "past conduct of the parents relative to their marital obligations is a factor which may not be disregarded in determining which parent will provide the better home" (*Sheil v. Sheil*, 29 AD2d 950).

The courts have generally taken the position that it is not in the best interests of the child to award custody to a parent, whether mother or father, if such action is tantamount to awarding custody to a grandparent or a third party.

The evidence indicates that the defendant has adjusted his schedule so that his professional commitments do not interfere with his children's activities whenever possible. The defendant maintains his professional office in the lower level of the marital domicile. Furthermore, much of his professional activities include writing which is usually done at home or his hospital office, television and radio appearances, usually during the children's school period. The evidence indicates that the defendant more often than the plaintiff met the children after school, and clearly had more contact with school officials with respect to the children's educational development. The court considers it more important to ascertain the quality, rather than the quantity of time a parent devotes to his or her children, in determining the best interests of the child. . .

The parties are from somewhat similar lower-middle class backgrounds. Neither party came into the marriage with any substantial capital assets. The plaintiff did not work during the marriage. The defendant has through professional achievement, been able to provide material advantages and luxurious living to the family.

The courts, in awarding custody to one parent or the other, may consider a parent's professional achievements and personal associations, although this criteria is not controlling. The court is aware that defendant has earned a high degree of professional esteem in the field of child psychology. However, the court does not base its decision on this factor, but because the defendant has proven himself to be faithful and exceptionally qualified to provide loving paternal influence and guidance to the children.

The court has taken the opportunity of interviewing the children *in camera* on three separate occasions. Once, prior to the commencement of trial, during the trial, and following the summer recess, at which time the trial was almost completed.

The court found Eric and Pia to be bright, intelligent and mature children. Both were very verbal and communicated their thoughts with a high degree of clarity. The children indicated a strong desire to remain together, and although exhibiting a genuine love for their mother, felt, especially Eric, that they would enjoy and be happiest living with their father, provided they could also be with their mother on a frequent basis.

The expressed wishes of a child of sufficient age and discretion are a factor to be considered by the court.

Recent case law would indicate that it may be improper for the court to make a custody determination without making any effort to determine the wishes and desires of the child. The courts must be aware that children can be influenced to state a particular preference.

The court is convinced that the children have expressed their desires freely and with unusual insight and candor. Moreover, the court was convinced from these conversations and the expert psychiatric and psychological reports that consideration should be given to the children's preference. This evidence also was given weight and consideration in the court's determination that it was beneficial for the children to be reared together, as courts are reluctant to separate siblings unless the necessity for split custody is clearly demonstrated by the circumstances of the case.

In preparation of trial, defendant had his children interviewed by both a psychiatrist and psychologist. Dr. Sol Gordon, Ph.D., is a clinical child psychologist. Dr. Gordon currently holds the position of Professor of Child and Family Studies at Syracuse University. Dr. Gordon testified that he interviewed Eric on October 12, 1974. The witness stated that "Eric showed no evidence of insecurity or emotional maladjustment. He appears to be a stable young man with many interests and friends. He is a very good student and seems to enjoy life." Dr. Gordon felt that Eric could handle the ramifications of his parents' divorce and manage the separation from one parent. Eric informed the witness, "that neither parent was applying pressure for him to stay with them, although both expressed preference for him to remain with them. Eric suggested that he would like his sister to be with him, but he was mainly interested in remaining with his father." Dr. Gordon stated that in his expert opinion he would recommend that Eric be permitted to remain with his father. This conclusion was based on Dr. Gordon's judgment that Eric would be happier with his father, because life would be more intellectually stimulating and exciting. Moreover, Eric is an emotionally stable child and appears to be fully capable of stating his preferences. The witness believes these preferences should be respected.

Dr. Lisa Tallal, M. D. is a qualified child psychiatrist. Dr. Tallal was associated with the Mental Health Clinic of the Family Court and New York Hospital. Dr. Tallal testified that she interviewed Eric and Pia on October 5 and 8, 1974. The witness stated that Pia appears to be "bright and solidly established in her latency stage of development. There was no evidence of thought disorder, but much guarding with respect to any discussion of the events at home." Dr. Tallal stated that it was her professional evaluation that

Pia most desperately wants to keep her family and since she knows her mother and father are divorcing, she clings to Eric as her "family."

However, Pia was not willing to leave her future to Eric's wishes, even though she knew he was outspoken in his wish to be with his father. Pia also stated her own wish to live with her father "even though she knew it would make her mother sad." It would probably be in her best interest to not be separated from Eric. It might be better for her to have liberal visiting arrangements with her mother, as often good quality visiting time is preferable to greater quantity with loss of objects.

Dr. Tallal further testified that [Eric]... sadly but philosophically accepts the fact that his mother and father cannot live together. He would rather not have the split take place, but he is definite about the fact that when it happens he wishes to remain with his father. He feels guilty and somehow disloyal toward his mother, but he states, "it is not that she does things that are so bad—it's just that he understands and just does them so much better." Eric is also attached to his sister, Pia, for whom he feels loving protectiveness. Dr. Tallal concluded by stating "There is no question that Eric's self-determination should be respected. His own ego enhancement and self-respect can only be benefitted as he realizes that his wishes are important to the primary people in his life."

Dr. Stein, a duly qualified psychiatrist, testified on behalf of plaintiff. From his interviews with plaintiff over a period of time, he observed that Mrs. Salk exhibited some signs of extreme tensions and anxiety caused by her marital difficulties. She is not, he testified, a violent woman but does have a temper. However, recent interviews indicated that Mrs. Salk's tensions and anxieties have lessened; her immaturity and insecurity have also diminished. She has now matured considerably and is able to make firm decisions. Once the marital difficulties are concluded, it is Dr. Stein's expert opinion that Mrs. Salk will be able to make a better life for herself and for her children.

The court in the interest of justice, and because the adversary process does not lend itself to providing a neutral source for information, directed that the parties and the children be examined by a court-appointed psychologist and psychiatrist....The court-appointed experts submitted in-depth and comprehensive reports on their observations and results of the psychiatric testing of the parties and children. The court has reviewed their reports and recommendations with great care and consideration.

> The court is convinced that the conclusions reached by Dr. Robertiello and Dr. Granofsky confirm and support the findings and decision of this court, that both the children, despite exhausting and frequent interrogation about themselves and their feelings about this highly publicized case seem to be still relatively unaffected by the publicity or other people's persuasions. Because of this their stated preference to see that their father should be awarded custody seems to be a genuine and well-considered choice.
>
> The children's preference is, of course, not the controlling criteria for the court in awarding custody to the defendant father. Since the birth of the children, Dr. Salk has exhibited a vast interest in the various stages of the children's development, his interaction with the children is not due solely to the fact that the father is a child psychologist.
>
> The defendant's successful relationship with his children is based, in part, on his ability to provide positive input into the children's development, specifically, consistent affection, approval, acceptance, guidance, protection and control.
>
> Dr. Salk is indeed a very bright, essentially stable person whose ability to conceptualize accurately and appropriately is quite superior—a fact which is reflected in turn in a high degree of competency to render proper and realistic judgments and skill in mastering effectively problems within himself and his environment, including those related to his children.

Case Questions

1. Can the question "Whose custody is in the children's best interests?" be answered in isolation from considerations of wealth and success? Since husbands usually have more of both commodities than their wives, does Judge Ribaudo's "affirmative standard" build a male bias into custody decisions? Are you convinced by the judge that removal of these children from the custody of their, until now, stay-at-home mother is in fact in their best interest?

2. Did reliance on psychological testimony put Kerstin Salk at a disadvantage because Lee was a psychologist? Did professional courtesy or collegiality work to her disadvantage?

3. Can any gender-neutral standard be fair to mothers in practice? Or is a return to maternal preference the only way of making sure mothers are not at a disadvantage?

Case note: Kerstin Andersson-Salk died in 2012 in her daughter's home.

Race and "Best Interest of the Child": *Palmore v. Sidoti* (1984)

Custody cases rarely present federal questions. *Palmore v. Sidoti* was an exception, because it involved racial discrimination. When Linda Sidoti, a white woman, married Clarence Palmore, a Black man, her white ex-husband, Anthony, won custody of their daughter, Melanie. A Florida court ruled that the best interests of the child would be served by awarding custody to the father: "This Court feels that despite the strides that have been made in bettering relations between the races in this country, it is inevitable that Melanie will, if allowed to remain in her present situation and attains school age and thus becomes more vulnerable to peer pressures, suffer from the social stigmatization that is sure to come."[46] Chief Justice Warren Burger reversed for a unanimous Supreme Court: "The effects of racial prejudice, however real, cannot justify a racial classification removing an infant child from the custody of its natural mother found to be an appropriate person to have such custody."[47]

The Primary Caregiver Standard

There was a time when in West Virginia, "the custody of very young children [wa]s awarded automatically to the primary caretaker parent, if he or she is a fit parent." When a child is old enough to formulate an opinion, but not yet 14, the judge could consider that opinion in making an award. Children over 14 could make their own choice as long as the parent was fit. "The result of our simple, ironclad rule," wrote the state's former chief justice, "is that in West Virginia there is almost no custody litigation."[48] *M. v. M.*, the third case below, was an exception to this rule. At the current time, both West Virginia and Minnesota have abandoned sole reliance on the primary caregiver rule.[49]

Unfaithful Spouses and Child Custody: Comparative Cases

The facts of the next three cases, decided over a 40-year time period, are similar. In each case, the children's mother had a sexual relationship outside of marriage. However, the three cases were decided under different criteria: relative parental fitness in the first; best interests of the child in the second; and primary caregiver preference in the third. Consider the similarities and differences in the reasoning and the results of the decisions. Questions for all three cases follow *M. v. M.*

LOUIS A. BUNIM V. ETHEL BUNIM
298 N.Y. 391; 83 N.E.2d 848 (NY Court of Appeals, 1949)

Opinion: DESMOND, J.

On the trial of this divorce suit the wife admitted numerous deliberate adulteries (with a man who was married and had children), attempted to rationalize and justify those adulteries, denied any repentance therefor, committed perjury in swearing to denials in her answer), and, as found by both courts below, testified to a deliberately false story as to consent by plaintiff (a reputable and successful physician) to the adulteries. With all that in the record, custody of the two children of the marriage (eleven and thirteen years old at the time of the trial) has been, nonetheless, awarded to defendant.

There is an affirmed finding below that the husband is a fit and proper person to have such custody, and no such finding as to the wife, but a finding that "the interests and welfare of the children, the issue of said marriage, will be best served by awarding the custody to the defendant." We see in this record no conceivable basis for that latter finding, unless it be the testimony of the two daughters that, though they love their father, they prefer to live with their mother. Unless that attitude of these adolescent girls be controlling as against every other fact and consideration this judgment, insofar as it deals with custody, is unsupported and unsupportable.

...We hold that there was here such abuse of discretion as to be error of law, with consequent jurisdiction to review, and duty to reverse, in this court.

No decision by any court can restore this broken home or give these children what they need and have a right to—the care and protection of two dutiful parents. No court welcomes such problems, or feels at ease in deciding them. But a decision there must be, and it cannot be one repugnant to all normal concepts of sex, family and marriage. The State of New York has old, strong policies on those subjects, strongly stated by the Legislature. Our whole society is based on the absolutely fundamental proposition that: "Marriage, as creating the most important relation in life," has "more to do with the morals and civilization of a people than any other institution." Defendant here, in open court, has stated her considered belief in the propriety of indulgence, by a dissatisfied wife such as herself, in extramarital sex experimentation. It cannot be that "the best interests and welfare" of those impressionable teen-age girls will be "best served" by awarding their custody to one who proclaims, and lives by, such extraordinary ideas of right conduct.

The judgment should be modified...

FULD, J. (dissenting):

...I hesitate to stamp as an abuse the discretion exercised by the Special Term judge, and affirmed by four justices of the Appellate Division, only after the most painstaking and conscientious consideration...

The primary and paramount concern of the trial judge was the welfare and happiness of the children. Would it better serve their interests and their well-being to place them with their mother or with their father? Bearing directly on that issue was evidence that the father was inordinately preoccupied with his professional duties; that, as a result, he gave little of his time or of himself to the children; and that not infrequently he treated them brusquely, impatiently and even intemperately. Likewise pertinent was proof that the wife was ever a good and devoted mother; that her indiscretions were unknown to the children; that she was deeply devoted to the children and truly concerned with their welfare; and that, for their part, the children returned her affection with an attachment that was, in the language of the trial court, "almost Biblical" in its intensity.

With such evidence—and there was more of like import—in the record, the decision at Special Term and the judgment of the Appellate Division awarding custody to the mother cannot be said to be completely beyond the pale of permissible discretion.

I would affirm the judgment.

JACQUELINE JARRETT V. WALTER JARRETT
78 Ill. 2d 337; 400 N.E.2d 421 (1979)

[Jacqueline Jarrett was granted a divorce from Walter Jarrett in December 1976 on grounds of extreme and repeated mental cruelty. Jacqueline was awarded custody of their three daughters. Five months later, Wayne Hammon, Jacqueline's boyfriend, moved in with them, despite Walter's protests. Walter then sued for custody.]

UNDERWOOD, J:

...The children, who were not "overly enthused" when they first learned that Hammon would move into the family home with them, asked Jacqueline if she intended to marry Hammon, but Jacqueline responded that she did not know. At the modification hearing Jacqueline testified that she did not want to remarry because it was too soon after her divorce; because she did not believe that a marriage license makes a relationship; and because the divorce decree required her to sell the family home within six months after remarriage. She did not want to sell the house because the children did not want to move and she could not afford to do so. Jacqueline explained to the children that some people thought it was wrong for an unmarried man and woman to live together but she thought that what mattered was that they loved each other. Jacqueline testified that she told some neighbors that Hammon would move in with her but that she had not received any adverse comments. Jacqueline further testified that the children seemed to develop an affectionate relationship with Hammon, who played with them, helped them with their homework, and verbally disciplined them. Both Jacqueline and Hammon testified at the hearing that they did not at that time have any plans to marry. . .

Walter Jarrett testified that he thought Jacqueline's living arrangements created a moral environment which was not a proper one in which to raise three young girls. He also testified that the children were always clean, healthy, well dressed and well nourished when he picked them up, and that when he talked with his oldest daughter, Kathleen, she did not object to Jacqueline's living arrangement.

The circuit court found that it was "necessary for the moral and spiritual well-being and development" of the children that Walter receive custody. In reversing, the appellate court reasoned that the record did not reveal any negative effects on the children caused by Jacqueline's cohabitation with Hammon, and that the circuit court had not found Jacqueline unfit. It declined to consider potential future harmful effects of the cohabitation on the children.

Both parties to this litigation have relied on §§ 602 and 610 of the new Illinois Marriage and Dissolution of Marriage Act (Ill. Rev. Stat. 1977, ch. 40, §§ 602, 610), which provide:

> § 602. Best interest of child. (a) The court shall determine custody in accordance with the best interest of the child. The court shall consider all relevant factors including: (1) the wishes of the child's parent or parents as to his custody; (2) the wishes of the child as to his custodian; (3) the interaction and interrelationship of the child with his parent or parents, his siblings and any other person who may significantly affect the child's best interest; (4) the child's adjustment to his home, school and community; and (5) the mental and physical health of all individuals involved. . .

§ 610. Modification. (a) No motion to modify a custody judgment may be made earlier than 2 years after its date, unless the court permits it to be made on the basis of affidavits that there is reason to believe the child's present environment may endanger seriously his physical, mental, moral or emotional health.

(b) The court shall not modify a prior custody judgment unless it finds, upon the basis of facts that have arisen since the prior judgment or that were unknown to the court at the time of entry of the prior judgment, that a change has occurred in the circumstances of the child or his custodian and that the modification is necessary to serve the best interest of the child. In applying these standards the court shall retain the custodian appointed pursuant to the prior judgment unless: . . .(3) the child's present environment endangers seriously his physical, mental, moral or emotional health and the harm likely to be caused by a change of environment is outweighed by its advantages to him. . . .

The chief issue in this case is whether a change of custody predicated upon the open and continuing cohabitation of the custodial parent with a member of the opposite sex is contrary to the manifest weight of the evidence in the absence of any tangible evidence of contemporaneous adverse effect upon the minor children. Considering the principles previously enunciated, and the statutory provisions, and prior decisions of the courts of this State, we conclude that under the facts in this case the trial court properly transferred custody of the Jarrett children from Jacqueline to Walter Jarrett.

The relevant standards of conduct are expressed in the statutes of this State: § 11–8 of the Criminal Code of 1961 (Ill. Rev. Stat. 1977, ch. 38, 11–8) provides that "[a]ny person who cohabits or has sexual intercourse with another not his spouse commits fornication if the behavior is open and notorious." In *Hewitt v. Hewitt* (1979), 77 Ill. 2d 49, 61–62, we emphasized the refusal of the General Assembly in enacting the new Illinois Marriage and Dissolution of Marriage Act (Ill. Rev. Stat. 1977, ch. 40, § 101 *et seq.*) to sanction any nonmarital relationships and its declaration of the purpose to "strengthen and preserve the integrity of marriage and safeguard family relationships" (Ill. Rev. Stat. 1977, ch. 40, § 102(2)).

Jacqueline argues, however, that her conduct does not affront public morality because such conduct is now widely accepted, and cites 1978 Census Bureau statistics that show 1.1 million households composed of an unmarried man and woman, close to a quarter of which also include at least one child.

This is essentially the same argument we rejected last term in *Hewitt v. Hewitt* (1979), 77 Ill. 2d 49, and it is equally unpersuasive here. The number of people living in such households forms only a small percentage of the adult population, but more to the point, the statutory interpretation urged upon us by Jacqueline simply nullifies the fornication statute. The logical conclusion of her argument is that the statutory prohibitions are void as to those who believe the proscribed acts are not immoral, or, for one reason or another, need not be heeded. So stated, of course, the argument defeats itself. The rules which our society enacts for the governance of its members are not limited to those who agree with those rules—they are equally binding on the dissenters. The fornication statute and the Illinois Marriage and Dissolution of Marriage Act evidence the relevant moral standards of this State, as declared by our legislature. The open and notorious limitation on the former's prohibitions reflects both a disinclination to criminalize purely private relationships and a recognition that open fornication represents a graver threat to public morality than private violations. Conduct of that nature, when it is open, not only violates the statutorily expressed moral standards of the State, but also encourages others to violate those standards, and debases public morality. While we agree that the statute does not penalize conduct which is essentially private and discreet (*People v. Cessna* (1976), 42 Ill. App. 3d 746, 749), Jacqueline's conduct has been neither, for she has discussed this relationship and her rationalization of it with at least her children, her former husband and her neighbors. It is, in our judgment, clear that her conduct offends prevailing public policy.

Jacqueline's disregard for existing standards of conduct instructs her children, by example, that they, too, may ignore them, and could well encourage the children to engage in similar activity in the future. That factor, of course, supports the trial court's conclusion that their daily presence in that environment was injurious to the moral well-being and development of the children. . .

Jacqueline also argues, and the appellate court agreed (64 Ill. App. 3d 932, 937), that the trial court's decision to grant custody of the children to Walter Jarrett was an improper assertion by the trial judge of his own personal moral beliefs. She further argues that the assertion of moral values in this case, as in *Hewitt v. Hewitt* (1979), 77 Ill. 2d 49, is a task more appropriately carried out by the legislature. As pointed out earlier, however, it is the legislature which has established the standards she has chosen to ignore, and the action of the trial court merely implemented principles which have long been followed in this State.

The mother argues, too, that § 610 of the Illinois Marriage and Dissolution of Marriage Act requires the trial court to refrain from modifying a prior custody decree unless it finds that the children have suffered actual tangible harm. The statute, however, directs the trial court to determine whether "the child's present environment *endangers* seriously his physical, mental, moral or emotional health." (Emphasis added.) In some cases, particularly those involving physical harm, it may be appropriate for the trial court to determine whether the child is endangered by considering evidence of actual harm. In cases such as this one, however, such a narrow interpretation of the statute would defeat its purpose. At the time of the hearing the three Jarrett children, who were then 12, 10 and 7 years old, were obviously incapable of emulating their mother's moral indiscretions. To wait until later years to determine whether Jacqueline had inculcated her moral values in the children would be to await a demonstration that the very harm which the statute seeks to avoid had occurred. Measures to safeguard the moral well-being of children, whose lives have already been disrupted by the divorce of their parents, cannot have been intended to be delayed until there are tangible manifestations of damage to their character.

While our comments have focused upon the moral hazards, we are not convinced that open cohabitation does not also affect the mental and emotional health of the children. Jacqueline's testimony at the hearing indicated that when her children originally learned that Wayne Hammon would move in with them, they initially expected that she would marry him. It is difficult to predict what psychological effects or problems may later develop from their efforts to overcome the disparity between their concepts of propriety and their mother's conduct. Nor will their attempts to adjust to this new environment occur in a vacuum. Jacqueline's domestic arrangements are known to her neighbors and their children; testimony at the hearing indicated that Wayne Hammon played with the Jarrett children and their friends at the Jarrett home and also engaged in other activities with them. If the Jarrett children remained in that situation, they might well be compelled to try to explain Hammon's presence to their friends and, perhaps, to endure their taunts and jibes. In a case such as this the trial judge must also weigh these imponderables, and he is not limited to examining the children for current physical manifestations of emotional or mental difficulties.

...[T]he trial court recognized that the affection and care of a parent do not alone assure the welfare of the child if other conduct of the parent threatens the child's moral development. Since the evidence indicated that Jacqueline had not terminated the troublesome relationship and would probably continue it in the future, the trial court transferred custody to Walter Jarrett, an equally caring and affectionate parent whose conduct did not contravene the standards established by the General Assembly and earlier judicial decisions. Its action in doing so was not contrary to the manifest weight of the evidence...

Appellate court reversed; circuit court affirmed.

GOLDENHERSH, C.J., dissenting:

The majority states, "The chief issue in this case is whether a change of custody predicated upon the open and continuing cohabitation of the custodial parent with a member of the opposite sex is contrary to the manifest weight of the evidence in the absence of any tangible evidence of contemporaneous adverse effect upon the minor children." An examination of the opinion fails to reveal any other issue, and the effect of the decision is that the plaintiff's cohabitation with Hammon *per se* was sufficient grounds for changing the custody order previously entered. This record shows clearly that the children were healthy, well adjusted, and well cared for, and it should be noted that both the circuit and appellate courts made no finding that plaintiff was an unfit mother. The majority, too, makes no such finding and based its decision on a nebulous concept of injury to the children's "moral well-being and development." I question that any competent sociologist would attribute the increase of "live in" unmarried couples to parental example.

The fragility of its conclusion concerning "prevailing public policy" is demonstrated by the majority's reliance on cases decided by this court in 1852 (*Searls v. People*, 13 Ill. 597) and 1902 (*Lyman v. People*, 198 Ill. 544)...

As the appellate court pointed out, the courts should not impose the personal preferences and standards of the judiciary in the decision of this case. Courts are uniquely equipped to decide legal issues and are well advised to leave to the theologians the question of the morality of the living arrangement into which the plaintiff had entered.

As a legal matter, simply stated, the majority has held that on the basis of her presumptive guilt of fornication, a Class B misdemeanor, plaintiff, although not declared to be an unfit mother, has forfeited the right to have the custody of her children. This finding flies in the face of the established rule that, in order to modify or amend an award of custody, the evidence must show that

> the parent to whom custody of the children was originally awarded is unfit to retain custody, or that a change of conditions makes a change of custody in their best interests. This record fails to show either.

DAVID M. V. MARGARET M.
182 W.Va. 57, 385 S.E.2d 912 (1989)

NEELY, JUSTICE:

Margaret M. appeals from a divorce order entered by the Circuit Court of Wood County that awarded David M. custody of their son, Timothy, age six. Mrs. M. contends that the Circuit Court erred in adopting the findings of the family law master which held that although Mrs. M. was the primary caretaker of the child, she was not a fit and suitable person to have permanent care and custody of the child. We agree with Mrs. M. and reverse the trial court's ruling.

The parties were married on 4 August 1979 and lived together in Wood County until 7 September 1988. Mr. M. filed a complaint alleging cruel and inhuman treatment or, in the alternative, adultery and seeking custody of their son, then age five. In her answer, Mrs. M. denied the allegations, filed a counterclaim alleging irreconcilable differences and sought custody of their son. Mr. M., in his reply to the counterclaim, admitted that irreconcilable differences existed between the parties.

The case was referred to a family law master and by agreement of the parties the case was bifurcated with only the divorce and the custody issues to be heard, reserving all other issues for further proceedings. After a hearing on the matter, the family law master found: (1) irreconcilable differences existed between the parties; (2) Mrs. M. was the primary caretaker; (3) Mrs. M. had committed adultery on two occasions over two years; and (4) Mrs. M. was not a fit and suitable person to have custody of the child. The Circuit Court adopted the findings and conclusions of the family law master, granted the parties a divorce, and awarded Mr. M. custody of their child, subject to reasonable visitation rights.

In the present case, although the primary caretaker parent rule as described in *Garska v. McCoy*, 167 W.Va. 59, 278 S.E.2d 357 (1981), appears to have been followed, the primary caretaker was denied custody through a broad interpretation of the fitness requirement. We have noted that our very narrow exception to the primary caretaker rule has of late developed a voracious appetite which, if left unchecked, will allow it to eat the rule. We write today to reaffirm and clarify the benefits of the primary caretaker parent rule to assist the family law masters and the circuit courts in reaching the best interests of the child by applying the primary caretaker parent presumption and its limited requirement of fitness. When properly applied, the primary caretaker parent presumption reduces sharp practices in custody negotiation, prevents fathers and mothers from being penalized on account of their gender, and avoids custody battles that are so unwieldy and intrusive that they make the lives of a divorcing couple and their children even more miserable than they otherwise would be.

I

In the nineteenth century, and in the early part of this century, the law gave fathers custody of their children after divorce, particularly when mothers were held at fault in breaking up the marriage. That rule was a logical extension of the inferior legal status of women, the husband's property right in his family's labor, and the husband's absolute obligation to support his children. Even a hundred years ago, however, this rule made little sense in light of human emotions and society's expectation that children would be raised by women. Consequently, it was abolished in this century. By 1950, it was almost always the rule that a mother was the preferred custodian of young children if she was a fit parent.

But the behavior that different courts characterized as evidencing "fitness" differed dramatically. In application, the rule of maternal preference allowed judges substantial leeway to take a mother's fault into consideration in the award of custody. It was frequently the case, therefore, that sexual "promiscuity" (a term that tends to mean different things when applied to women than to men, with women getting the short end of the double standard) on the part of the woman would cause a court to declare her "unfit."

Currently, all parental rights in child custody matters are subordinate to the interests of the innocent child. The pole star in child custody cases is the welfare of the child. We have repeatedly acknowledged that the child's welfare is the paramount and controlling factor in all custody matters.

...Today, the presumption in favor of mothers is rapidly eroding because the maternal preference presumption discriminates against fathers on the basis of sex. In the 1980 amendment to W.Va.Code, 48–2–15, the legislature provided in relevant part:

> ... There shall be no legal presumption that, as between the natural parents, either the father or the mother should be awarded

custody of said children but the court shall make an award of custody solely for the best interest of the children based upon the merits of each case.

Although in *Garska, supra*, we abolished the gender-based presumption, we reaffirmed our holding in *J.B. v. A.B.*, "except that wherever the words 'mother,' 'maternal,' or 'maternal preference' [were] used" some variation of the term "primary caretaker parent" should be substituted.

In jurisdictions that retain some type of maternal preference in awarding custody of very young children, the maternal preference has become largely a tie breaker. The emerging rule is that all custody disputes be decided on their individual merits, with the parent whom the judge considers the most competent receiving custody. At first glance, this emerging rule seems to make sense, since some fathers are excellent parents and some mothers are child abusers. Unfortunately, however, this individualized, sex-neutral approach poses serious problems because the welfare of the child is often lost by the distorted incentives created by the divorce settlement process.

Substantial research has confirmed that young children, as a result of intimate interaction, form a unique bond with their primary caretaker. This unique attachment to a primary caretaker is an essential cornerstone of a child's sense of security and healthy emotional development.

. . .Thus, the young child's welfare can be best served by preserving the child's relationship with the primary caretaker parent. Without a presumption in favor of the primary caretaker parent, the process—or even the prospect—of sorting out custody problems in court affects those problems, usually for the worse.

The unpredictability of courts in divorce matters offers many opportunities for a parent (generally the father) to minimize support payments and gain leverage in settlement negotiations. The most effective, and hence the most generally used, tactic is to threaten a custody fight. The effectiveness of the threat increases in direct proportion to the other parent's unwillingness to give up custody. Because women, much more than men, are preeminently interested in custody, seemingly gender-neutral custody rules actually serve to expose women to extortionate bargaining at the hands of their husbands. . .

Fathers are now demanding that courts award custody based on an individualized inquiry into their specific situations. This appears reasonable on its face. But when we understand the costs of such an inquiry, and appreciate as well just how much sinister bargaining is carried out in the shadow of such an unpredictable, case-specific system, we must think again. . .

II

The individualized approach might be ideal if it were costless and if courts actually considered the relative merits of the parents in each case. In fact, however, the individualized approach is intrusive, time-consuming and inherently distortive in its effect. And, because the vast majority of divorces are settled without ever reaching court, very few custody arrangements receive even the dubious benefit of a judicial determination that they are in the "best interests of the child."

Under the individualized approach to the "best interests of the child" standard, custody, when contested, goes to the parent who the court believes will do a better job of child rearing. This standard is a substitute for the maternal preference rule or its gender-neutral successor, the primary caretaker parent rule. It operates as well in those states retaining a weak maternal preference, with that preference being only a tie breaker. In order to assign custody, the court must explore the dark recesses of psychological theory to determine which parent will, in the long run, do a better job.

However, this undertaking inevitably leads to the hiring of expert witnesses—psychologists, psychiatrists, social workers and sociologists. These experts are paid by the parties to demonstrate that one or the other (coincidentally, always the client) is the superior parent in light of his or her personality, experience and aptitude for parenting. The experts will advance the theory that whatever positive aspects of personality their client possesses are preeminently important to successful single-parent child-raising.

Expert witnesses are, after all, very much like lawyers: They are paid to take a set of facts from which different inferences may be drawn and to characterize those facts so that a particular conclusion follows. There are indeed cases in which a mother or father may appear competent on the surface, only to be exposed after perfunctory inquiry as a child abuser. Under truly careful inquiry, such discoveries might be made more often. Such careful inquiry, however, is almost impossible in the real world because it requires experts who combine competence and integrity in a way that is seldom found, at least in courtrooms. The side with the stronger case can afford to hire only competent experts with profound integrity; the side with the weaker case, on the other hand, wants impressively glib experts who are utterly devoid of principles. When both parents are good parents, the battle of the experts can result only in gibberish.

No issue is more subject to personal bias than a decision about which parent is "better." Should children be placed with an "open, empathetic" father or with a "stern but value-supporting" mother? The decision may hinge on the judge's memory of his or her own parents or on his or her distrust of an expert whose eyes are averted once too often. It is unlikely that the decision will be the kind of individualized justice that the system purports to deliver. . .

In the child custody context, children fall into one of three groups, depending on their age. Children under six years of age are called "children of tender years": They are the most dependent on their parents, but they usually cannot articulate an intelligent opinion about their custody. Children between six and fourteen are also dependent on their parents, but they can usually articulate a preference regarding custody arrangements and explain their reasons. By the age of fourteen a child takes on many of the qualities of an adult; in most cases, unless geography interferes, a child over fourteen will decide for himself or herself the parent with whom he or she wants to live, regardless of what a court says.

Children over the age of six might seem to be the best available experts on the subject of how the parents and children get along. Usually, however, children do not want what is best for them; they want what is pleasant. If children are permitted to influence decisions about custody simply by stating a preference, the parents are placed in the position of being competitive bidders in a counterfeit currency. For the children, the results are seldom positive. That is because the litigation process is not neutral, but has its own peculiar and dangerous side effects. Unlike other litigation that sorts out rights and obligations based on facts frozen in time, custody decisions are predictions of what is best for the child—predictions based on facts constantly changing in part as a result of the litigation process. If the divorce drags through the trial and appellate courts for two years, the lawsuit itself may wound or destroy the very children whose welfare is supposed to be at its center. In addition, money that would have been available to ease the transition from joint household to separate households is diverted instead to lawyers, court fees and expert witnesses.

. . .The harms of courtroom custody battles happen only in a relatively small minority of divorces because the vast majority of divorce cases are settled out of court However, the possibility of a courtroom custody battle also causes problems in out-of-court settlement negotiations.

Divorce decrees are typically drafted for the parties after compromises reached through private negotiation. These compromises are then approved by a judge, who generally gives them only the most perfunctory review. The result is that parties (usually husbands) are free to use whatever leverage is available to obtain a favorable settlement. In practice this tends to mean that husbands will threaten custody fights, with all of the accompanying traumas and uncertainties discussed above, as a means of intimidating wives into accepting less child support, alimony or distribution of marital property than is sufficient to allow the mother to live and raise the children appropriately as a single parent. . . .Because women are usually unwilling to accept even a minor risk of losing custody,. . .such techniques, despite the guidelines, are generally successful because the guidelines establish minima and do not apply to alimony or property distribution.

Under any purportedly gender-neutral system, women on statistical average come out of divorce settlements with the worst of all possible results: They get the children, but insufficient money with which to support them. They are forced to scrape along to support their families at inadequate standards of living, and the children are forced to grow up poor, or at least poorer than they should be. Yet the negotiation dynamic is seldom discussed, despite its importance in promoting the growth of a rapidly-expanding class of poor people, the female-headed household.

An important reason that little attention has been given to the effect of in-court rules on out-of-court bargaining is that views on divorce are informed more by wishful thinking than by the facts of life. Many people (especially men) begin with a political conviction that women ought to be equal to men economically, from which they leap to the insupportable conclusion that women are equal to men economically. It then follows that women can support children as well as men can and that whoever wants the children can pay for them.

In the real world, however, women are much poorer than men, and this pattern is highly resistant to change. The cost of child care itself is a major economic burden placed on single mothers. Single mothers, who start with unequal earning power, also provide child care—care that involves great amounts of time that could be spent earning money. But the unfairness only begins there, as so many women are forced to accept lower child support and alimony payments in order to be sure of getting the children (and the accompanying economic burden) at all.

The everyday occurrence of children being traded for money should be sufficient in and of itself to prompt a reevaluation of a system that turns custody awards into bargaining chips. The fact that such trading also has contributed to the impoverishment of women makes the need for change still more urgent. What is needed is a standard for custody awards that assures the welfare of the child without encouraging such pernicious bargaining, but which also does not discriminate by gender.

III

Most of the problems of child custody litigation can be avoided by not litigating the issue in the first place. It is here that the wisdom of the old maternal preference, or its gender-neutral alternative, the "primary caretaker parent presumption," becomes apparent. The primary caretaker presumption severely limits opportunities for using child custody litigation as a bargaining chip.

West Virginia law does not permit a maternal preference. But we do accord an explicit and almost absolute preference to the "primary caretaker parent" of young children, *Garska*, 167 W.Va. at 68, 278 S.E.2d at 362. We have defined the "primary caretaker" as the parent who:

> . . . has taken primary responsibility for, *inter alia*, the performance of the following caring and nurturing duties of a parent: (1) preparing and planning of meals; (2) bathing, grooming and dressing; (3) purchasing, cleaning, and care of clothes; (4) medical care, including nursing and trips to physicians; (5) arranging for social interaction among peers after school, i.e. transporting to friends' houses or, for example, to girl or boy scout meetings; (6) arranging alternative care, i.e. babysitting, day-care, etc.; (7) putting child to bed at night, attending to child in the middle of the night, waking child in the morning; (8) disciplining, i.e. teaching general manners and toilet training; (9) educating, i.e. religious, cultural, social, etc.; and, (10) teaching elementary skills, i.e., reading, writing and arithmetic. *Id.* 167 W.Va. at 69–70, 278 S.E.2d at 363.

This list of criteria usually, but not necessarily, spells "mother." That fact reflects social reality; the rule itself is neutral on its face and in its application. When women pursue lucrative and successful careers while their husbands take care of the children, those husbands receive the benefit of the presumption as strongly as do traditional mothers. Furthermore, where both parents share child-rearing responsibilities equally, our courts hold hearings to determine which parent would be the better single parent. This latter situation is rare, but is evidence of the actual gender-neutrality of the primary caretaker...

Although the primary caretaker parent presumption may appear cut-and-dried and insufficiently sensitive to the needs of individual children, it serves the welfare of the child by achieving stability of care in the child's life, reducing the uncertainty of custody decisions, limiting the invasiveness of the custody determination process and reducing the expense of domestic litigation. Because litigation per se can be the cause of serious emotional damage to children (and to adults), we consider the primary caretaker parent presumption to be in the best interests of children. Even more important, children cannot be used as pawns in fights that are actually about money because a lawyer can tell a primary caretaker parent that, if fit, that parent has absolutely no chance of losing custody of very young children. The result is that questions of alimony, property distribution, and child support are settled on their own merits.

IV

When we adopted the primary caretaker presumption in *Garska,* only one other jurisdiction relied upon a determination of primary caretaker in reaching custody decisions. *Garska, supra,* at 69, n. 10, 278 S.E.2d at 357, n. 10, citing *Matter of Marriage of Derby,* 31 Ore. App. 803, 571 P.2d 562 (1977.) Since then the Supreme Court of Minnesota, citing *Garska,* adopted a primary caretaker parent presumption for custody of young children. *Pikula v. Pikula,* 374 N.W.2d 705 (Minn. 1985). Justice Wahl in *Pikula, id.* at 711, reasoned that the primary caretaker presumption secured the best interests of the child by protecting the psychological bonding [and] also noted that the "uncertainty of other indicia of a child's best interest .... and the pressing need for coherent decision making on the trial court level and for effective appellate review" required the primary caretaker presumption. In order to preserve the presumption in favor of the primary caretaker...a strong showing of parental unfitness was required to grant custody to the other parent. *Tanghe v. Tanghe,* 400 N.W.2d 389 (Minn. App. 1987)...

Other courts have implicitly considered the role of primary caretaker and have awarded custody to the nurturing parent, or the parent who was responsible for the child. *See In re Marriage of Leopando,* 106 Ill. App. 3d 444, 435 N.E.2d 1312, *aff'd,* 96 Ill. 2d 114, 449 N.E.2d 137 (1983); *Anderson v. Anderson,*

121 Ariz. 405, 590 P.2d 944 (Ariz. App. 1979); *Nale v. Nale,* 409 So. 2d 1299 (La. App. 1982.)

. . .Many jurisdictions have turned to joint custody to solve divorce-related custody problems. Under joint custody, divorced parents have equal time with the children and equal say in decisions about their schooling, religious training and lifestyle. Joint custody, however, does not solve the problem of extortion in the settlement process because many mothers find shared custody as unacceptable as complete loss of custody. Joint custody works well when both parents live in the same neighborhood or at least in the same city, and so long as they can cooperate on child-rearing matters. Divorcing couples on their own often agreed to joint custody in the past, long before court-ordered joint custody became a public issue. When joint custody is by agreement, the same cooperative spirit that animated the underlying agreement will usually allow the parents to rear a child with no more antagonism than is experienced in most married households.

Voluntary joint custody, however, must be distinguished from court-ordered joint custody. A court can order that custody be shared, but it cannot order that the parents stop bickering, stop disparaging one another, or accommodate one another in child-care decisions as married persons would. And if parents do not live close to one another, joint custody can place an intolerable strain on a child's social and academic life if one parent is not willing to allow the other to supply a more-or-less permanent home. Furthermore, parents must constantly give permission for one thing or another. Who decides whether the child can have a driver's license at age sixteen? Who decides when the child can date, under what conditions, and with whom? When the parents violently disagree—and particularly when they disagree because there are continuing fights left over from the marriage—the child is likely to be left hopelessly confused as the parents are played off one against the other. We do not authorize court-ordered joint custody today over the objection of a primary caretaker parent, although parents may agree to such an arrangement.

V

In the present case, the record established that Mrs. M. was the primary caretaker parent of the child. Mrs. M. (1) bathed, groomed and dressed the child, (2) purchased, cleaned and cared for his clothes, (3) organized and purchased his food, (4) secured medical attention, when needed, (5) missed work to nurse the child, and (6) put the child to bed, attended to him in the middle of the night and awakened him in the morning. We note that the father assisted in some of the cooking, and both parents were responsible for disciplining, educating and teaching general manners and elementary skills.

...Acts of sexual misconduct by a [primary caretaker], albeit wrongs against an innocent spouse, may not be considered as evidence going to the fitness of the [caretaker] for child custody unless [his or] her conduct is so aggravated, given contemporary moral standards, that reasonable men would find that [his or] her immorality, per se, warranted a finding of unfitness because of the deleterious effect upon the child of being raised by a [primary caretaker] with such a defective character.

Although the record contains evidence of three acts of marital misconduct, two of which were adultery, there is no evidence that Mrs. M.'s marital misconduct was known to the child or damaged the child. We have repeatedly held that a "circuit court may not base a finding of parental unfitness solely on the ground that the parent is guilty of sexual misconduct." [Citation omitted—AU.] Mrs. M. testified that two of the instances occurred about midnight when the child was asleep and the third occurred after the child and his stepbrother left to visit a neighbor and was concluded before the children returned home. Although evidence of marital misconduct, this restrained normal sexual behavior does not make Mrs. M. an unfit parent.

The circuit court was clearly wrong in its position that the three instances of sexual misconduct, occurring over two years, warranted a finding of unfitness, without evidence establishing that the child was harmed or that the conduct per se was so outrageous, given contemporary moral standards, as to call into question her fitness as a parent....Accordingly, for the reasons set forth above, the judgment of the Circuit Court of Wood County with respect to the granting of a divorce is affirmed, but with respect to the award of custody is reversed and this case is remanded with directions to enter an order consistent with this opinion.

Affirmed in part; Reversed in part; and Remanded with directions.

Case Questions

1. What part, if any, does maternal preference play in *Bunim v. Bunim*?

2. Are Ethel Bunim and Jacqueline Jarrett unfit mothers? Why or why not?

3. *Bunim* identifies traditional marriage as "an absolutely fundamental proposition" on which our whole society is based. Is this an empirical statement that can be proved or disproved, or is it an analytical premise? What does it mean? Does religious doctrine play any part in it? If it does, what are the implications?

4. Does the *Jarrett* majority opinion's emphasis on social norms, especially disapproval of unmarried cohabitation, suggest that nonconformity can endanger a divorcing parent's chances of getting child custody? Explain your reasoning.

5. The primary caregiver standard is no longer the primary criterion for custody awards anywhere in the United States. Is this helpful or harmful for women? Why?

The Future of Child Custody

As *M. v. M.* indicates, not all jurisdictions that adopted the primary caregiver preference went so far as to require a showing of unfitness to rebut the presumption. Most states are friendlier to joint custody than West Virginia was here. The following two cases illustrate more recent trends.

LINDA TETREAULT V. MARK TETREAULT
99 Haw. 352; 55 P.3d 845 (Int'med. Ct. App. of Haw. 2002)

BURNS, C. J.

On July 11, 1981, Defendant-Appellant Mark D. Tetreault (Father) and Plaintiff-Appellee Linda J. Tetreault (Mother) were married in Cook, Illinois. . . . [Fourteen years later twins were born to them; four years after that the mother filed for divorce. A judge awarded pre-trial custody to the mother and visiting rights to the father and appointed a Guardian Ad Litem, Marvin Acklin, Ph.D., to speak for the children's interests. Four months later Acklin recommended custody to the mother. Four months after that, the judge expanded the father's visiting rights times. At a hearing three months later, on May 15, 2000 the mother proposed relocating from Hawaii to a suburb of Chicago. The court-appointed investigator, Janice Wolf, reported back to the court on July 12, 2000.]

On August 7, 2000, . . . Father moved for a stay of "the oral ruling after trial on July 31[sic], 2000 which allows [Mother] to leave the City and County of Honolulu, State of Hawaii with the minor children of the marriage." A hearing on this motion was held on August 17, 2000. On August 21, 2000, the family court entered an Order Denying Motion for Stay. . .

On September 14, 2000, the family court entered its [Divorce] Decree awarding. . .legal and physical custody of the children to Mother,. . .and stating,. . ."Mother and the children shall be allowed to relocate to Naperville, Illinois.". . .

> On March 19, 2001 . . . .Father filed his opening brief in which he asserted the following: . . .
>
> 2. The family court erred in awarding custody to Mother who was contemplating moving to another state where both parties are equally fit to have custody and there was no showing that the children's well-being would be better served by such a move.
>
> 3. The family court erred in excluding testimony from Dr. William Wright regarding the effects that Mother's removal of the parties' minor children from Hawaii to Illinois would have on the relationship between the children and Father. . . .
>
> On June 14, 2001, the family court entered its Findings. . .Conclusions. . .and Order. . .
>
> Father contends that the family court erred in awarding physical custody to Mother who was contemplating moving to another state where both parties are equally fit to have physical custody, and there was no showing that the children's well-being would be better served by such a move. . . . [The Findings of Fact state in part:]
>
> 19. This Court believes the testimony of Dr. Acklin, Mother, Mother's friends and Ms. Wolf. Specifically, the unbiased testimony of Dr. Acklin has credibly established that: a) Mother is the primary caregiver for the Children; b) it was in the best interests of the Children to award full custody to Mother, regardless of the move to Naperville; and c) Mother suffers from no mental impairment which detrimentally affects her parenting ability. . . .
>
> 23. This Court also finds that the move to Naperville would serve the best interests of the Children. Based on Mother's testimony as well as the report and testimony of Ms. Wolf, Mother furnished substantial evidence that Naperville contains excellent schools for the Children, possesses good job opportunities for Mother, and is a low-crime, family-friendly, unpolluted environment. . . .
>
> 28. Looking at all the evidence in the record, this Court finds and determines that it is in the best interests of the Children to award full physical and legal custody of the Children to Mother, and that, given the totality of circumstances, Mother's proposed relocation to Naperville is in the best interest of the children. . . .

> We affirm the family court's September 14, 2000 Decree Granting Absolute Divorce and Awarding Child Custody.

IN RE MARRIAGE OF CULBERTSON
2001 Iowa App. Lexis 466 (Iowa Ct. of Appeals 2001)

ZIMMER, J:

Nicola Culbertson appeals from the custody provisions of her dissolution decree. She contends the evidence does not support the trial court's decision to order a joint physical care arrangement. She claims she is best suited to meet the long-term best interests of the children as their primary care provider. Because we find the trial court's order of joint physical care is in the children's best interests, we affirm.

Background Facts and Proceedings. Nicola and Cory were married in 1994. They are the parents of Joseph, born in 1994, and twin sons Joshua and Justin, born in 1997. In October of 1998, the parties separated. The parties later reconciled for a time, but Nicola filed for divorce in July 1999. . . . In September 2000, the trial court issued a dissolution decree incorporating the agreements set forth in the partial stipulation and awarding the parties joint legal custody and joint physical care of the children. Nicola was to have physical care of the children from 10 a.m. Wednesday to 8 p.m. Saturday or 8 a.m. Sunday in alternating weeks. Cory was awarded physical care from 8 p.m. Saturday until 10 a.m. Wednesday, but every other week he would not have the children until 8 a.m. Sunday. Additionally, Nicola was awarded visitation on Mother's Day and her birthday, and Cory was to receive visitation on Father's Day and his birthday. Provisions were also made for holiday and summer visitation. Nicola was ordered to maintain health coverage on the children but neither party was awarded child support. Finally, the decree prohibited either parent from moving the children out of their school district without prior approval from the court.

Nicola appeals. She contends the evidence showed she is best suited to be the primary caregiver of the children. She also claims the physical care provision of the dissolution decree denies her right to play a practicing role in providing for the religious training of her children. She contends the decree's requirement that neither parent shall move the children from the Sentral school district interferes with the parties' right to travel and decide what is in the best interests of their children. Finally, Nicola argues that statements she made to her counselor and her doctor regarding Cory's abusive nature should have been presumed to be truthful and accurate. Cory contends joint primary care is in the best interests of the children, but if the court determines otherwise, he should be given primary physical care. Both parties request an award of appellate attorney fees.

Joint Physical Care. . . . In any custody determination, the primary consideration is the best interests of the children. The court's objective is to place the children in the environment most likely to bring them to healthy physical, mental, and social maturity. We identify numerous factors to help determine which parent should serve as the primary caretaker of the children in a divorce. These include the characteristics of the parents, as well as the capacity and desire of each parent to provide for the needs of the children.

The trial court awarded the parties joint physical care of their children. Joint physical care is defined as

> an award of physical care of a minor child to both joint legal custodial parents under which both parents have rights and responsibilities toward the child including, but not limited to, shared parenting time with the child, maintaining homes for the child, providing routine care for the child and under which neither parent has physical care rights superior to those of the other parent. Iowa Code § 598.1(4).

Although joint physical care was once strongly disfavored by the courts, the Iowa legislature has proclaimed it a viable disposition of a custody dispute. An award of joint physical care is proper where "such action would be in the best interest of the child and would preserve the relationship between each parent and the child. . . ."

Nicola contends she is best suited to meet the long-term best interests of the children as primary care provider. Nicola first argues Cory intentionally withheld funds for child support in July and August of 1999. She claims he did so in an attempt to retaliate against her for forcibly removing him from her home. She believes Cory's action militates against him being awarded shared primary physical care.

During the parties' initial separation, Cory voluntarily gave Nicola $100 per week to help support the children and paid one-half of some of the children's bills. After Nicola filed for divorce, Cory did not make any payments to her, instead waiting for the court to set the amount of temporary child support he was to pay. In its temporary support order of August 16, 1999, the court did not require Cory to make any payments for past child support. Cory was current with respect to all court-ordered child support at the time of trial. As a result, the trial court found Nicola's claim to be a non-issue. We agree.

The principal focus of Nicola's argument on appeal centers on her accusations that Cory has a bad temper, is verbally abusive, and tries to control her. Nicola also accuses Cory of one incident of physical abuse. A history of domestic abuse by one parent is a factor in making child custody determinations under Iowa Code § 598.41(3)(j). In assessing what is sufficient to constitute a history of domestic abuse, we weigh the evidence of abuse, its nature, severity, repetition, and to whom directed, not just count the number of incidents. We first note the allegations of emotional abuse surfaced for the first time during the dissolution proceedings. Earlier medical records contain no evidence of such abuse, and no complaints by Nicola that she was suffering from stress. The single incident of physical abuse alleged by Nicola was never reported to the authorities and is denied by Cory. The trial court found the evidence concerning this allegation inconclusive and concluded Nicola failed to show by a preponderance of the evidence that Cory abused her. Upon our de novo review of the record, we agree.

Nicola also claimed that on one occasion Cory hit Joseph hard enough to leave a purple bruise covering half of his bottom. Cory did admit that in November of 1998 he spanked Joseph's wet bottom, which left a red mark. The trial court found that Nicola exaggerated when describing the mark left on Joseph's bottom when Cory spanked him. Because the trial court had the benefit of observing the parties at trial, we do not disturb this finding. Furthermore, this is the only incident of physical abuse of any of the children that Nicola has ever alleged. We find nothing else in the record to indicate Cory was abusive toward the children.

The trial court did note that Cory has had some problems with anger management. Some people in the community observed this. For example, on July 3, 1999, Cory got into an argument with a friend of Nicola's and some shoving occurred between Cory and Nicola's brother. However, it was Cory who called the police and he agreed to leave Nicola's home at the officer's suggestion. The trial court concluded Nicola's drinking contributed as much to this incident as Cory's anger.

Nicola also cites to one occasion in October of 1999 when Cory attempted to terminate his employment after an argument with his supervisor. However, Cory revoked his termination notice later that same day, citing the difficulties in his personal life as a factor in making such a hasty decision. This one incident did not affect the children as Cory continues to be employed at Murphy Family Farms with some supervisory responsibilities.

While Nicola has a number of complaints concerning Cory, the record reveals that she has also demonstrated some questionable behavior. For example, the record shows that Nicola frequently sleeps late and on many occasions the children have been downstairs unsupervised while she was still in bed. We agree with the district court that such behavior is unacceptable given the age of her children. . . .

While neither party is a model parent, the district court found them both to be competent caretakers of the children. Each party admits the other is a good parent and loves the children. A home study conducted by the Department of Human Services concluded both parties are capable parents.

Nicola is employed by Snap-On-Tools. She works Mondays through Fridays from 3 p.m. until 11 p.m. During the time that Nicola had temporary physical care, the children were left at day care during their mother's shift. Nicola would pick up the sleeping children at approximately 11:15 p.m. and would have to put them back to bed again when they arrived home fifteen minutes later. Meanwhile, Cory is employed by Murphy Family Farms where he works Wednesdays through Saturdays from 7 a.m. until 7 p.m. In reaching its decision to order joint physical care, the trial court considered the parties' unusual work schedules, the finding that both parties were fit parents, and the parties' ability to cooperate with respect to care of the children. The trial court concluded an award of joint physical care would reduce the need for childcare and increase the amount of time the parties could spend with the children. Upon de novo review of the record, we conclude the joint physical care arrangement fashioned by the trial court is in the best interests of the children.

Religious Training. Nicola argues the dissolution decree denies her the right to play a practicing role in providing for the religious training of her children because she rarely has custody of the children on Sundays. We disagree.

Iowa Code § 598.41(5) states that where one parent has physical care of a child, the other parent's rights and responsibilities as a legal custodian are not affected. These rights and responsibilities include equal participation in decisions affecting the children's religious instruction. Iowa Code § 598.41(5). In the case of *In re Marriage of Craig,* 462 N.W.2d 692, 694–95 (Iowa Ct. App. 1990), this court stated: "Under the plain language of [Iowa Code § 598.41(5)],

> both parties are entitled to participate in deciding questions regarding the religious instruction of the children."
>
> The mere fact that Cory typically has physical care of the children on Sunday does not prohibit Nicola from participating in decisions affecting the children's religious instruction in her role as joint custodian and caretaker. In addition, Nicola will have primary care of the children on Sundays during holiday visitation, Mother's Day, and during summer visitation...
>
> ***Statements Regarding Abuse.*** Nicola argues that the statements she made to her therapist and to a health care professional regarding Cory's alleged abuse should be presumed to be truthful and accurate. She reasons these statements are reliable because they were made for the purpose of medical treatment and because she resisted the production of her medical records in pretrial discovery. However, Nicola does not cite any authority in support of her arguments. We find Nicola's failure to cite authority constitutes a waiver of this issue. Iowa R. App. P. 14(a)(3).
>
> **AFFIRMED.**

Case Questions

1. Both cases raise a question that has become important in many custody cases: what happens if one parent wants to move far away? Should the parent's reason for moving make any difference? Are limitations on freedom of movement justified? How do courts resolve these questions?

2. In both cases, the court must decide whom, if anyone, to believe: which expert testimony, which factual accounts, etc. For instance, why might Judge Zimmer have discounted Nicola's testimony while apparently accepting accounts of her behavior at face value? Are there any checks on a judge's power to decide what or whom to believe?

RIGHTS OF UNMARRIED FATHERS

The fathers who have been most disadvantaged under the law have been those who did not marry the mothers of their children. Asserting their rights under the U.S. Constitution and state law, these fathers have achieved a mixed record of success. Their victories have resulted in significant changes in family law.

As illustrated by *Taylor v. Louisiana* (in Chapter 2), in the *Reed-Craig* period the Court sometimes avoided the need to twist the rationality test by invoking, instead, a relevant fundamental constitutional right (such as the right to trial by jury) which would, quite apart from the gender discrimination, trigger the strict scrutiny/compelling interest test (i.e., If the government tries to infringe a fundamental right, it needs to prove a compelling interest for doing so.) Sometimes the right had a textual referent in the Constitution; trial by jury is mentioned in both Article III and the Sixth Amendment. Other times (as in the now discredited "liberty of contract" cases covered in Chapter 1) the Court claimed to locate the fundamental right in American societal and legal traditions. The latter approach was used by the Court to resolve the conflict between Peter Stanley and the State of Illinois in 1972.

Stanley v. Illinois (1972)

Under Illinois law, if the mother of a nonmarital child died, the child automatically became a parent-less ward of the state, to be put up for adoption or placed in foster care. If, however, the parents were married and one parent died, their children could not be taken away from the living parent without a court hearing proving parental unfitness. Also, if the unmarried father of a child died, the unmarried mother would not lose custody of the child (unless she was proved to be an unfit parent in a child custody proceeding). In short, the statute automatically conferred parental rights including child custody on a married father and on a mother, married or unmarried, and it automatically denied it to an unmarried father. Clearly, in treating unmarried mothers differently from unmarried fathers, the law was classifying persons on the basis of gender.

Peter Stanley had lived with Joan Stanley intermittently for 18 years, during which time they had three children. Peter Stanley supported the children. When Joan Stanley died, Illinois declared two of her children[50] wards of the state in a dependency proceeding, and placed them with court-appointed guardians. Peter Stanley appealed the decision, claiming that this process denied him equal protection of the laws in depriving him of a benefit that would be given by law to unmarried mothers or to married fathers. The Illinois Supreme Court rejected his constitutional argument, and he proceeded to the U.S. Supreme Court.

In responding to Stanley's claim, the Court had more to guide it than the early twentieth century precedents that had cavalierly condoned discrimination against men. Besides the very recent *Reed v. Reed* signal that the equal protection clause was more sensitive to sex-based discrimination than formerly, a number of cases involving the constitutional status of family relationships had entered the body of American legal precedent between 1911 and 1972.

Two cases in the 1920s[51] had established that parents' right to guide their child's education is a "fundamental right" of Americans and that the due process clause requires careful scrutiny of laws infringing on that right. One of those cases[52] established that parents may send their children to private schools (subject, however, to appropriate accreditation requirements of the state), and the other[53] established the parental right to have one's child study a foreign language.

A case in the 1940s[54] had established that the right of procreation is one of the "basic civil rights of man" and a "basic liberty," and that legislative classifications that infringe on it would be subject to "strict scrutiny" under the equal protection clause.[55] In that case the Supreme Court had declared unconstitutional a law that established sterilization as the punishment for certain crimes.

Then, in 1965[56] and 1972[57] (the latter just a couple of weeks before the *Stanley* decision), the Supreme Court had handed down two groundbreaking decisions on questions involving the use of contraceptives. Both decisions, in striking down prohibitions on contraceptive use and distribution, had relied on a "right of privacy," which the Court said was implied by several of the Bill of Rights amendments and by the very idea of due process of law within the American tradition. In describing that right of privacy in the 1972 case, the Court majority had said, "If the right of privacy means anything, it is the right of the *individual*, married or single, to be free from unwarranted governmental intrusion into matters so fundamentally affecting a person as the decision whether to bear or beget a child."[58]

Thus, Peter Stanley, when he came before the Supreme Court, had available to him two separate legal threads out of which his attorneys might weave his case. First, there was the long thread reaching all the way back to the 1920s that delineated the special legal sanctity of the parent-child relationship.[59] Second, there was the shorter but perhaps potentially sturdier thread that had begun in 1971 to shape a pattern of Supreme Court opposition to gender-based discrimination. The Court opinion of Justice White selected the first of these threads for its dominant lines, but the second can be found woven into the background of the pattern, strengthening the dominant theme.[60]

PETER STANLEY V. ILLINOIS
405 U.S. 645 (1972)

MR. JUSTICE WHITE delivered the opinion of the Court:

. . .

Stanley presses his equal protection claim here. The State continues to respond that unwed fathers are presumed unfit to raise their children and that it is unnecessary to hold individualized hearings to determine whether particular fathers are in fact unfit parents before they are separated from their children. We granted certiorari to determine whether this ... procedure by presumption could be allowed to stand in light of the fact that Illinois allows married fathers—whether divorced, widowed, or separated—and mothers—even if unwed—the benefit of the presumption that they are fit to raise their children.

I

At the outset we reject any suggestion that we need not consider the propriety of the dependency proceeding that separated the Stanleys because Stanley might be able to regain custody of his children as a guardian or through adoption proceedings.... Surely, in the case before us, if there is delay between the doing and the undoing petitioner suffers from the deprivation of his children, and the children suffer from uncertainty and dislocation.

... Neither can we ignore that in the proceedings from which this action developed, the "probation officer," the assistant state's attorney, and the judge charged with the case, made it apparent that Stanley, unmarried and impecunious as he is, could not now expect to profit from adoption proceedings.

... We must therefore examine the question that Illinois would have us avoid: Is a presumption that distinguishes and burdens all unwed fathers constitutionally repugnant? We conclude that, as a matter of due process of law, Stanley was entitled to a hearing on his fitness as a parent before his children were taken from him and that, by denying him a hearing and extending it to all other parents whose custody of their children is challenged, the State denied Stanley the equal protection of the laws guaranteed by the Fourteenth Amendment.

II

The State's right—indeed, duty—to protect minor children through a judicial determination of their interests in a neglect proceeding is not challenged here. Rather, we are faced with a dependency statute that empowers state officials to circumvent neglect proceedings on the theory that an unwed father is not a "parent" whose existing relationship with his children must be considered. "Parents," says the State, "means the father and mother of a legitimate child..., or the natural mother of an illegitimate child, and includes any adoptive parent," Ill. Rev. Stat., c. 37, § 701–14, but the term does not include unwed fathers.

Under Illinois law, therefore, while the children of all parents can be taken from them in neglect proceedings, that is only after notice, hearing, and proof of such unfitness as a parent as amounts to neglect, an unwed father is uniquely subject to the more simplistic dependency proceeding. By use of this proceeding, the State, on showing that the father was not married to the mother, need not prove unfitness in fact, because it is presumed at law. Thus, the unwed father's claim of parental qualification is avoided as "irrelevant."

In considering this procedure under the Due Process Clause, we recognize, as we have in other cases, that due process of law does not require a hearing "in every conceivable case of government impairment of private interest." *Cafeteria Workers v. McElroy*, 367 U.S. 886, 894 (1961)....

The private interest here, that of a man in the children he has sired and raised, undeniably warrants deference and, absent a powerful countervailing interest, protection. It is plain that the interest of a parent in the companionship, care, custody, and management of his or her children "come[s] to this Court with a momentum for respect lacking when appeal is made to liberties which derive merely from shifting economic arrangements." *Kovacs v. Cooper*, 336 U.S. 77, 95 (1949) (Frankfurter, J., concurring).

The Court has frequently emphasized the importance of the family. The rights to conceive and to raise one's children have been deemed "essential," *Meyer v. Nebraska*, 262 U.S. 390, 399 (1923), "basic civil rights of man," *Skinner v. Oklahoma*, 316 U.S. 535, 541 (1942), and "[r]ights far more precious . . . than property rights," *May v. Anderson*, 345 U.S. 528, 533 (1953). "It is cardinal with us that the custody, care and nurture of the child reside first in the parents, whose primary function and freedom include preparation for obligations the state can neither supply nor hinder." *Prince v. Massachusetts*, 321 U.S. 158, 166 (1944). The integrity of the family unit has found protection in the Due Process Clause of the Fourteenth Amendment, *Meyer v. Nebraska*, at 399, the Equal Protection Clause of the Fourteenth Amendment, *Skinner v. Oklahoma*, at 541, and the Ninth Amendment, *Griswold v. Connecticut*, 381 U.S. 479, 496 (1965) (Goldberg, J., concurring).

Nor has the law refused to recognize those family relationships unlegitimized by a marriage ceremony. The Court has declared unconstitutional a state statute denying natural, but illegitimate, children a wrongful-death action for the death of their mother, emphasizing that such children cannot be denied the right of other children because familial bonds in such cases were often as warm, enduring, and important as those arising within a more formally organized family unit. *Levy v. Louisiana*, 391 U.S. 68, 71–72 (1968). "To say that the test of equal protection should be the 'legal' rather than the biological relationship is to avoid the issue. For the Equal Protection Clause necessarily limits the authority of a State to draw such 'legal' lines as it chooses." *Glona v. American Guarantee Co.*, 391 U.S. 73, 75–76 (1968).

These authorities make it clear that, at the least, Stanley's interest in retaining custody of his children is cognizable and substantial.

For its part, the State has made its interest quite plain: Illinois has declared that the aim of the Juvenile Court Act is to protect "the moral, emotional, mental, and physical welfare of the minor and the best interests of the community" and to "strengthen the minor's family ties whenever possible, removing him from the custody of his parents only when his welfare or safety or the protection of the public cannot be adequately safeguarded without removal. . . ." Ill. Rev. Stat., c. 37, § 701–2. These are legitimate interests, well within the power of the State to implement. . . .

But we are here not asked to evaluate the legitimacy of the state ends, rather, to determine whether the means used to achieve these ends are constitutionally defensible. What is the state interest in separating children from fathers without a hearing designed to determine whether the father is unfit in a particular disputed case? We observe that the State registers no gain towards its declared goals when it separates children from the custody of fit parents. Indeed, if Stanley is a fit father, the State spites its own articulated goals when it needlessly separates him from his family.

In *Bell v. Burson*, 402 U.S. 535 (1971), we found a scheme repugnant to the Due Process Clause because it deprived a driver of his license without reference to the very factor (there fault in driving, here fitness as a parent) that the State itself deemed fundamental to its statutory scheme. Illinois [argues]. . . that Stanley and all other unmarried fathers can reasonably be presumed to be unqualified to raise their children.[5]

It may be, as the State insists, that most unmarried fathers are unsuitable and neglectful parents. It may also be that Stanley is such a parent and that his children should be placed in other hands. But all unmarried fathers are not in this category; some are wholly suited to have custody of their children. This much the State readily concedes, and nothing in this record indicates that Stanley is or has been a neglectful father who has not cared for his children. . . .

[It] may be argued that unmarried fathers are so seldom fit that Illinois need not undergo the administrative inconvenience of inquiry in any case, including Stanley's. The establishment of prompt efficacious procedures to achieve legitimate state ends is a proper state interest worthy of cognizance in constitutional adjudication. But the Constitution recognizes higher values than speed and efficiency.[8] Indeed, one might fairly say of the Bill of Rights in general, and the Due Process Clause in particular, that they were designed to protect the fragile values of a vulnerable citizenry from the overbearing concern for efficiency and efficacy that may characterize praiseworthy government officials no less, and perhaps more, than mediocre ones.

Procedure by presumption is always cheaper and easier than individualized determination. But when, as here, the procedure forecloses the determinative issues of competence and care, when it explicitly disdains present realities in deference to past formalities, it needlessly risks running roughshod over the important interests of both parent and child. It therefore cannot stand.

. . .

. . . The State's interest in caring for Stanley's children is *de minimis* if Stanley is shown to be a fit father. It insists on presuming rather than proving Stanley's unfitness solely because it is more convenient to presume than to prove. Under the Due Process Clause that advantage is insufficient to justify refusing a father a hearing when the issue at stake is the dismemberment of his family.

III

The State of Illinois assumes custody of the children of married parents, divorced parents, and unmarried mothers only after a hearing and proof of neglect. The children of unmarried fathers, however, are declared dependent children without a hearing on parental fitness and without proof of neglect. Stanley's claim in the state courts and here is that failure to afford him a hearing on his parental qualifications while extending it to other parents denied him equal protection of the laws. We have concluded that all Illinois parents are constitutionally entitled to a hearing on their fitness before their children are removed from their custody. It follows that denying such a hearing to Stanley and those like him while granting it to other Illinois parents is inescapably contrary to the Equal Protection Clause.

The judgment of the Supreme Court of Illinois is

Reversed. . . .

Opinion Footnotes

5 Illinois says in its brief: ". . . In effect, Illinois has imposed a statutory presumption that the best interests of a particular group of children necessitates some governmental supervision in certain clearly defined situations. The group of children who are illegitimate are distinguishable from legitimate children

... by the factual differences in their upbringing. While a legitimate child usually is raised by both parents with the attendant familial relationships and a firm concept of home and identity, the illegitimate child normally knows only one parent—the mother....

"... The petitioner has premised his argument upon particular factual circumstances—a lengthy relationship with the mother ... a familial relationship with the two children, and a general assumption that this relationship approximates that in which the natural parents are married to each other.

"... Even if this characterization were accurate (the record is insufficient to support it) it would not affect the validity of the statutory definition of parent...."

Pp. 24–26 (... studies are cited in support of the proposition that men are not naturally inclined to childrearing), and Tr. of Oral Arg. ("We submit that both based on history or [sic] culture the very real differences ... between the married father and the unmarried father, in terms of their interests in children and their legal responsibility for their children, that the statute here fulfills the compelling governmental objective of protecting children....").

8 Cf. *Reed v. Reed,* 404 U.S. 71, 76 (1971). "Clearly the objective of reducing the workload on probate courts by eliminating one class of contests is [legitimate].... [But to] give a mandatory preference to members of either sex over members of the other, merely to accomplish the elimination of hearings on the merits, is to make the very kind of arbitrary legislative choice forbidden by the Equal Protection Clause of the Fourteenth Amendment...."

MR. JUSTICE POWELL and MR. JUSTICE REHNQUIST took no part in the consideration or decision of this case.

MR. JUSTICE DOUGLAS joins in Parts I and II of this opinion.

MR. CHIEF JUSTICE BURGER, with whom MR. JUSTICE BLACKMUN concurs, dissenting:

The only constitutional issue raised and decided in the courts of Illinois in this case was whether the Illinois statute that omits unwed fathers from the definition of "parents" violates the Equal Protection Clause. We granted certiorari to consider whether the Illinois Supreme Court properly resolved that equal protection issue....

No due process issue was raised in the state courts; and no due process issue was decided by any state court.... [T]he Court holds *sua sponte* that the Due Process Clause requires that Stanley, the unwed biological father, be accorded a hearing as to his fitness as a parent before his children are declared wards of the state court; the Court then reasons that since Illinois recognizes such rights to due process in married fathers, it is required by the Equal Protection Clause to give such protection to unmarried fathers. This "method of analysis" is, of course, no more or less than the use of the Equal Protection Clause as a shorthand condensation of the entire Constitution.... The limits on this Court's jurisdiction are not properly expandable by the use of such semantic devices as that.

Not only does the Court today use dubious reasoning in dealing with limitations upon its jurisdiction, it proceeds as well to strike down the Illinois statute here involved by "answering" arguments that are nowhere to be found in the record or in the State's brief—or indeed in the oral argument. . . .

In regard to the only issue that I consider properly before the Court, I agree with the State's argument that the Equal Protection Clause is not violated when Illinois gives full recognition only to those father-child relationships that arise in the context of family units bound together by legal obligations arising from marriage or from adoption proceedings. Quite apart from the religious or quasi-religious connotations that marriage has—and has historically enjoyed—for a large proportion of this Nation's citizens, it is in law an essentially contractual relationship, the parties to which have legally enforceable rights and duties, with respect both to each other and to any children born to them. Stanley and the mother of these children never entered such a relationship. . . .

Where there is a valid contract of marriage, the law of Illinois presumes that the husband is the father of any child born to the wife during the marriage; as the father, he has legally enforceable rights and duties with respect to that child. When a child is born to an unmarried woman, Illinois recognizes the readily identifiable mother, but makes no presumption as to the identity of the biological father. . . .[He may, however,] marry the mother and acknowledge the child as his own; this has the legal effect of legitimating the child and gaining for the father full recognition as a parent. Ill. Rev. Stat., c. 3, § 12-8.

. . .

The Illinois Supreme Court correctly held that the State may constitutionally distinguish between unwed fathers and unwed mothers. . . [as] part of that State's statutory scheme for protecting the welfare of illegitimate children. In almost all cases, the unwed mother is readily identifiable, generally from hospital records, and alternatively by physicians or others attending the child's birth. Unwed fathers, as a class, are not traditionally quite so easy to identify and locate. Many of them either deny all responsibility or exhibit no interest in the child or its welfare; and, of course, many unwed fathers are simply not aware of their parenthood.

Furthermore, I believe that a State is fully justified in concluding, on the basis of common human experience, that the biological role of the mother in carrying and nursing an infant creates stronger bonds between her and the child than the bonds resulting from the male's often casual encounter. This view is reinforced by the observable fact that most unwed mothers exhibit a concern for their offspring either permanently or at least until they are safely placed for adoption, while unwed fathers rarely burden either the mother or the child with their attentions or loyalties. Centuries of human experience buttress this view of the realities of human conditions and suggest that unwed mothers of illegitimate children are generally more dependable protectors of their children than are unwed fathers. While these, like most generalizations, are not without exceptions, they nevertheless provide a sufficient basis to sustain a statutory classification whose objective is not to penalize unwed parents but to further the welfare of illegitimate children in fulfillment of the State's obligations as *parens patriae*.[4]

Stanley depicts himself as a somewhat unusual unwed father, namely, as one who has always acknowledged and never doubted his fatherhood of these children. He alleges that he loved, cared for, and supported these children from the time of their birth until the death of their mother. He contends that he consequently must be treated the same as a married father of legitimate children. Even assuming the truth of Stanley's allegations, I am unable to construe the Equal Protection Clause as requiring Illinois to tailor its statutory definition of "parents" so meticulously as to include such unusual unwed fathers, while at the same time excluding those unwed, and generally unidentified, biological fathers who in no way share Stanley's professed desires.

Indeed, the nature of Stanley's own desires is less than absolutely clear from the record in this case. Shortly after the death of the mother, Stanley turned these two children over to the care of a Mr. and Mrs. Ness; he took no action to gain recognition of himself as a father, through adoption, or as a legal custodian, through a guardianship proceeding. Eventually it came to the attention of the State that there was no living adult who had any legally enforceable obligation for the care and support of the children; it was only then that the dependency proceeding here under review took place and that Stanley made himself known to the juvenile court in connection with these two children. Even then, however, Stanley did not ask to be charged with the legal responsibility for the children. He asked only that such legal responsibility be given to no one else. He seemed, in particular, to be concerned with the loss of the welfare payments he would suffer as a result of the designation of others as guardians of the children.

Not only, then, do I see no ground for holding that Illinois' statutory definition of "parents" on its face violates the Equal Protection Clause; I see no ground for holding that any constitutional right of Stanley has been denied in the application of that statutory definition in the case at bar.

As Mr. Justice Frankfurter once observed, "Invalidating legislation is serious business . . . ." *Morey v. Doud*, 354 U.S. 457, 474 (1957) (dissenting opinion). The Court today . . . invalidates a provision of critical importance to Illinois carefully drawn statutory scheme . . . . And in so [doing, it] embarks on a novel concept of the natural law for unwed fathers that could well have strange boundaries as yet undiscernible.

Opinion Footnote

4 When the marriage between the parents of a legitimate child is dissolved by divorce or separation, the State, of course, normally awards custody of the child to one parent or the other. This is considered necessary for the child's welfare, since the parents are no longer legally bound together. The unmarried parents of an illegitimate child are likewise not legally bound together. Thus, even if Illinois did recognize the parenthood of both the mother and father of an illegitimate child, it would, for consistency with its practice in divorce proceedings, be called upon to award custody to one or the other of them, at least once it had by some means ascertained the identity of the father.

Case Questions

1. How relevant is it, to the legal issues at stake, that Peter Stanley is a "welfare father"? Why do you suppose Justice Burger mentions it?

2. According to this Illinois statute, if Peter Stanley had been married to Joan Stanley at the time of each child's birth, even if he had divorced Joan Stanley within hours after each birth and had never made contact with the children again until Joan Stanley's death, the children would have been lawfully his at that time. Burger argues that the marriage ceremony itself indicates a certain level of responsibility and that it is permissible for the law to take that into account. Is it reasonable that the law gives automatic deference to the marriage ceremony but would give no automatic deference to Peter Stanley's living with and supporting the children throughout their lives and to his informal but continuous acknowledgment of paternity? Do you think the case would have gone differently had Peter Stanley not been living with the children, but only occasionally visited, and had come forward at his wife's death to take custody? Should it have?

3. If the state could demonstrate that 99 out of 100 illegitimate fathers abandon their offspring, and that 99 out of 100 illegitimate mothers either raise their offspring responsibly or else give them up properly for lawful adoption, would this legislative classification be "reasonable"? How about 9,999 out of 10,000? Does this case turn on the reasonableness of Illinois's assumption "that most unmarried fathers are unsuitable and neglectful parents"? On the reasonableness of its assumption that unmarried fathers are less suitable parents than unmarried mothers? On the fact that the state had no compelling interest in depriving unmarried fathers of their own children? If it is the last, what about the state interest in providing for the children's welfare?

4. Does this decision mean that unmarried mothers cannot give up their illegitimate children for adoption without the consent of the father? What if the father refuses to acknowledge paternity? Must there be a paternity suit before the child can be adopted? Does this decision mean that states may legislate a requirement that no fetus may be aborted without its father's consent? (It was not long before each of these issues reached the Court.)

Follow-up to Stanley: *Fiallo v. Bell* and *Quilloin v. Walcott*

Stanley v. Illinois established, in effect, that the right of a natural father to care for, and have the companionship of, his own children, legitimate or illegitimate, is fundamental in our society and that infringements on that right would be subjected to the strict scrutiny test under both the due process clause and the equal protection clause. In our constitutional system, however, two "fundamental" rights may conflict with each other. In those instances, the judicial outcome is not as predictable as when only one fundamental right is at stake. For example, in 1976 in *Planned Parenthood v. Danforth*, the Supreme Court held that a woman's constitutional right to privacy renders void any laws that require her husband's consent as a precondition for allowing her to abort a fetus she is carrying (see Chapter 4). Although the Court acknowledged that the father's concern for his unborn child is "deep and proper" and that the relationship is one of "importance," nonetheless, the Court held that since the mother carries the fetus within her own body, her right over its fate overrides the father's.

Similarly, certain powers of government may be deemed so fundamental by the judiciary that those powers override rights that are also fundamental. In general these powers are those thought to involve the basic survival of our nation (and its constitutional system) or those involving foreign relations. During wartime, for example, governmental powers are interpreted very generously by the courts, and citizen rights tend to be constricted accordingly. In other words, the classic example of a compelling interest that is generally found to satisfy even the strict scrutiny test is the government's need for flexibility in exercising its foreign relations power. The Court acknowledged in 1977 in *Fiallo v. Bell* that not even an unmarried father's fundamental right to the care and companionship of his children was enough to override this compelling need within the specific context of immigration law.[61]

By 1978 the constitutional status of fathers' rights could be described as follows: *Stanley v. Illinois* had posed for the Court the question, "Is a legal presumption that distinguishes and burdens all unwed fathers constitutionally repugnant?" The *Stanley* opinion had seemed to answer "yes" to that question, and then the *Planned Parenthood* and *Fiallo* cases had carved out modest exceptions to that answer, changing it to "Yes, except when there is a conflict with other fundamental rights or when the burden is part of a federal immigration law." In 1978, the Supreme Court further enlarged the category of exceptions in *Quilloin v. Walcott*, 434 U.S. 246, a case that pitted the rights of an unmarried father against those of the unmarried mother.

Under Georgia law, if a child was born out-of-wedlock, the child's mother was recognized as its only legal parent unless the natural father petitioned the local court for a legitimation order. The mother had to be notified, in advance, of the legitimation hearing. If the judge granted the petition, the child would then become "legitimate" and would acquire rights to inherit from its father. Once the child was legitimated, the unwed father then shared with the mother the legal rights of parents. (In contrast, the laws voided in *Stanley* would have required formal adoption proceedings; they technically treated the father as a stranger to the child.) This requirement that an unwed father go through a legitimation hearing to become a legal parent, where no such requirement was imposed on divorced fathers or unwed mothers, was upheld by the Supreme Court, in the context of an adoption proceeding. Mrs. Walcott, for 11 years married to Mr. Walcott, wanted to let him become the adoptive father of her 14-year-old, non-marital son by Leon Quilloin, who was trying to block the adoption. The Court emphasized the factual specifics and concluded as follows: "Whatever might be required in other situations, we cannot say that the State was required in this situation to find anything more than that the adoption, and denial of legitimation, was in the 'best interests of the child'" (p. 255).

Caban v. Mohammed (1979)

Quilloin v. Walcott failed to create any clear rule on laws that distinguish between unwed mothers and unwed fathers in the context of the release of a child for adoption. The Court did so one year later in *Caban v. Mohammed*, but that apparent clarity was to become muddied within a few years in *Lehr v. Robertson*.

Caban v. Mohammed presented the Court with a factual setting of unusual drama. Abdiel Caban and Maria Mohammed had lived together for five years, representing themselves as husband and wife (although in fact they had never married and for some of the time he had been married to another woman). During those years they had two children, and the four lived as a family. Then Maria moved out with the children and married another man (Kazim Mohammed), but the children saw their father every weekend. The children then visited their maternal grandmother in Puerto Rico for a year, during which their mother wrote them letters and their father communicated with them through his parents who also lived there. In November 1975 Caban abducted his children and took them back to New York. The Mohammeds then sought and obtained legal custody, and Caban, with his new wife Nina, received visitation rights. Then in January 1976 the Mohammeds petitioned for Kazin Mohammed to adopt the children; two months later the Cabans cross-petitioned for Nina to adopt them.

Under New York law (§ 111) any unwed mother (like any married parent), unless she had abandoned her child or been judged an unfit parent, retained an absolute right to consent to the adoption of her own child. Unwed fathers had no parallel right; they could appear at the adoption hearing and offer evidence that adoption might not accord with the child's "best interest" but (unlike mothers) could not veto a decision that would terminate their parental rights. Abdiel Caban lost at the hearing, the adoption was ordered, and he appealed to the highest court of New York and then the U.S. Supreme Court. At the adoption hearing the children were ages 4 and 6; by the time the case was resolved, they were 7 and 8. Finally, he prevailed.

ABDIEL CABAN V. KAZIM AND MARIA MOHAMMED
441 U.S. 380 (1979)

MR. JUSTICE POWELL delivered the opinion of the Court:

...Appellant presses [the] claims.... that the distinction drawn under New York law between the adoption rights of an unwed father and those of other parents violates the Equal Protection Clause....

[T]he... decision in the present case, affirmed by the New York Court of Appeals, was based upon the assumption that there was a distinctive difference between the rights of Abdiel Caban, as the unwed father of David and Denise, and Maria Mohammed, as the unwed mother of the children. ...It is clear that § 111 treats unmarried parents differently according to their sex.

III

Gender-based distinctions "must serve important governmental objectives and must be substantially related to achievement of those objectives" in order to withstand judicial scrutiny under the Equal Protection Clause. *Craig v. Boren*, 429 U.S. 190, 197 (1976). *See also Reed v. Reed*, 404 U.S. 71 (1971). The question before us, therefore, is whether the distinction in § 111 between unmarried mothers and unmarried fathers bears a substantial relation to some important state interest. Appellees assert that the distinction is justified by a fundamental difference between maternal and paternal relations—that "a natural mother, absent special circumstances, bears a closer relationship with her child . . . than a father does."

Contrary to appellees' argument and to the apparent presumption underlying § 111, maternal and paternal roles are not invariably different in importance. Even if unwed mothers as a class were closer than unwed fathers to their newborn infants, this generalization concerning parent-child relations would become less acceptable as a basis for legislative distinctions as the age of the child increased. The present case demonstrates that an unwed father may have a relationship with his children fully comparable to that of the mother. Appellant Caban, appellee Maria Mohammed, and their two children lived together as a natural family for several years. As members of this family, both mother and father participated in the care and support of their children. There is no reason to believe that the Caban children—aged 4 and 6 at the time of the adoption proceedings—had a relationship with their mother unrivaled by the affection and concern of their father. We reject, therefore, the claim that the broad, gender-based distinction of § 111 is required by any universal difference between maternal and paternal relations at every phase of a child's development.

As an alternative justification for § 111, appellees argue that the distinction between unwed fathers and unwed mothers is substantially related to the State's interest in promoting the adoption of illegitimate children. Although the legislative history of § 111 is sparse,[8] the New York Court of Appeals identified as the legislature's purpose in enacting § 111 the furthering of the interests of illegitimate children, for whom adoption often is the best course. The court concluded:

> [t]o require the consent of fathers of children born out of wedlock . . ., or even some of them, would have the overall effect of denying homes to the homeless and of depriving innocent children of the other blessings of adoption. The cruel and undeserved out-of-wedlock stigma would continue its visitations. At the very least, the worthy process of adoption would be severely impeded. *In re Malpica-Orsini*, 36 N. Y. 2d 568, at 572 (1975).

The court reasoned that people wishing to adopt a child born out of wedlock would be discouraged if the natural father could prevent the adoption by the mere withholding of his consent. Indeed, the court went so far as to suggest that "[m]arriages would be discouraged because of the reluctance of prospective husbands to involve themselves in a family situation where they might only be a foster parent and could not adopt the mother's offspring." *Id.,* at 573. Finally, the court noted that if unwed fathers' consent were required before adoption could take place, in many instances the adoption would have to be delayed or eliminated altogether, because of the unavailability of the natural father.

The State's interest in providing for the well-being of illegitimate children is an important one. We do not question that the best interests of such children often may require their adoption into new families who will give them the stability of a normal, two-parent home. Moreover, adoption will remove the stigma under which illegitimate children suffer. But the unquestioned right of the State to further these desirable ends by legislation is not in itself sufficient to justify the gender-based distinction of § 111. Rather, under the relevant cases applying the Equal Protection Clause it must be shown that the distinction is structured reasonably to further these ends. . . .

We find that the distinction in § 111 between unmarried mothers and unmarried fathers, as illustrated by this case, does not bear a substantial relation to the State's interest in providing adoptive homes for its illegitimate children. It may be that, given the opportunity, some unwed fathers would prevent the adoption of their illegitimate children. This impediment to adoption usually is the result of a natural parental interest shared by both genders alike; it is not a manifestation of any profound difference between the affection and concern of mothers and fathers for their children. Neither the State nor the appellees have argued that unwed fathers are more likely to object to the adoption of their children than are unwed mothers; nor is there any self-evident reason why as a class they would be.

The New York Court of Appeals in *In re Malpica-Orsini* suggested that the requiring of unmarried fathers' consent for adoption would pose a strong impediment for adoption because often it is impossible to locate unwed fathers when adoption proceedings are brought, whereas mothers are more likely to remain with their children. Even if the special difficulties attendant upon locating and identifying unwed fathers at birth would justify a legislative distinction between mothers and fathers of newborns,[11] these difficulties need not persist past infancy. When the adoption of an older child is sought, the State's interest in proceeding with adoption cases can be protected by means that do not draw such an inflexible gender-based distinction as that made in § 111. In those cases where the father never has come forward to participate in the rearing of his child, nothing in the Equal Protection Clause precludes the State from withholding from him the privilege of vetoing the adoption of that child. Indeed, under the statute as it now stands the surrogate may proceed in the absence of consent when the parent whose consent otherwise would be required never has come forward or has abandoned the child.[13] But in cases such as this, where the father has established a substantial relationship with the child and has admitted his paternity, a State should have no difficulty in identifying the father even of children born out of wedlock.[15] Thus, no showing has been made that the different treatment afforded unmarried fathers and unmarried mothers under § 111 bears a substantial relationship to the proclaimed interest of the State in promoting the adoption of illegitimate children.

In sum, we believe that § 111 is another example of "over-broad generalizations" in gender-based classifications. See *Califano v. Goldfarb* (1977); *Stanton v. Stanton* (1975). The effect of New York's classification is to discriminate against unwed fathers even when their identity is known and they have manifested a significant paternal interest in the child. The facts of this case illustrate the harshness of classifying unwed fathers as being invariably less qualified and entitled than mothers to exercise a concerned judgment as to the fate of their children. Section 111 both excludes some loving fathers from full participation in the decision whether their children will be adopted and, at the same time, enables some alienated mothers arbitrarily to cut off the paternal rights of fathers. We conclude that this undifferentiated distinction between unwed mothers and unwed fathers, applicable in all circumstances where adoption of a child of theirs is at issue, does not bear a substantial relationship to the State's asserted interests.

The judgment of the New York Court of Appeals is

Reversed.

Opinion Footnotes

8 Consent of the unmarried father has never been required for adoption under New York law, although parental consent otherwise has been required at least since the late 19th century.

11 Because the question is not before us, we express no view whether such difficulties would justify a statute addressed particularly to newborn adoptions, setting forth more stringent requirements concerning the acknowledgment of paternity or a stricter definition of abandonment.

13 If the New York Court of Appeals is correct that unmarried fathers often desert their families (a view we need not question), then allowing those fathers who remain with their families a right to object to the termination of their parental rights will pose little threat to the State's ability to order adoption in most cases. For we do not question a State's right to do what New York has done in this portion of § 111: provide that fathers who have abandoned their children have no right to block adoption of those children. . . .

15 States have a legitimate interest, of course, in providing that an unmarried father's right to object to the adoption of a child will be conditioned upon his showing that it is in fact his child.

MR. JUSTICE STEWART, dissenting.

For reasons similar to those expressed in the dissenting opinion of MR. JUSTICE STEVENS, I agree that § 111 (1) (c) . . . is not constitutionally infirm. The State's interest in promoting the welfare of illegitimate children is of far greater importance than the opinion of the Court would suggest. Unlike the children of married parents, illegitimate children begin life with formidable handicaps. They typically depend upon the care and economic support of only one parent—usually the mother. And, even in this era of changing mores, they still may face substantial obstacles simply because they are illegitimate. Adoption provides perhaps the most generally available way of removing these handicaps. See H. Clark, *Law of Domestic Relations* 177 (1968). Most significantly, it provides a means by which an illegitimate child can become legitimate—a fact that the Court's opinion today barely acknowledges.

The New York statute reflects the judgment that, to facilitate this ameliorative change in the child's status, the consent of only one parent should ordinarily be required for adoption of a child born out of wedlock. The mother has been chosen as the parent whose consent is indispensable. A different choice would defy common sense. But the unwed father, if he is the lawful custodian of the child, must under the statute also consent. And, even when he does not have custody, the unwed father who has an established relationship with his illegitimate child is not denied the opportunity to participate in the adoption proceeding. His relationship with the child will be terminated through adoption only if a court determines that adoption will serve the child's best interest. These distinctions represent, I think, a careful accommodation of the competing interests at stake and bear a close and substantial relationship to the State's goal of promoting the welfare of its children. In my view, the Constitution requires no more. . . .

A

The appellant relies primarily on *Stanley v. Illinois*. . . . But it is obvious that the principle established in that case is not offended by the New York law. The Illinois statute invalidated in Stanley employed a stark and absolute presumption that the unwed father was not a fit parent.

. . .

In some circumstances the actual relationship between father and child may suffice to create in the unwed father parental interests comparable to those of the married father. *Cf. Stanley v. Illinois*. But here we are concerned with the rights the unwed father may have when his wishes and those of the mother are in conflict, and the child's best interests are served by a resolution in favor of the mother. It seems to me that the absence of a legal tie with the mother may in such circumstances appropriately place a limit on whatever substantive constitutional claims might otherwise exist by virtue of the father's actual relationship with the children.

B

The appellant's equal protection challenge to the distinction drawn between the unwed father and mother seems to me more substantial. Gender, like race, is a highly visible and immutable characteristic that has historically been the touchstone for pervasive but often subtle discrimination. Although the analogy to race is not perfect and the constitutional inquiry therefore somewhat different, gender-based statutory classifications deserve careful constitutional examination because they may reflect or operate to perpetuate mythical or stereotyped assumptions about the proper roles and the relative capabilities of men and women that are unrelated to any inherent differences between the sexes.... Such laws cannot be defended, as can the bulk of the classifications that fill the statute books, simply on the ground that the generalizations they reflect may be true of the majority of members of the class, for a gender-based classification need not ring false to work a discrimination that in the individual case might be invidious. Nonetheless, gender-based classifications are not invariably invalid. When men and women are not in fact similarly situated in the area covered by the legislation in question, the Equal Protection Clause is not violated. *See, e. g., Schlesinger v. Ballard*, 419 U.S. 498.

In my view, the gender-based distinction drawn by New York falls in this latter category. With respect to a large group of adoptions—those of newborn children and infants—unwed mothers and unwed fathers are simply not similarly situated, as my Brother STEVENS has demonstrated. Our law has given the unwed mother the custody of her illegitimate children precisely because it is she who bears the child and because the vast majority of unwed fathers have been unknown, unavailable, or simply uninterested.... This custodial preference has carried with it a correlative power in the mother to place her child for adoption or not to do so.

The majority of the States have incorporated these basic common-law rules in their statutes identifying the persons whose participation or consent is requisite to a valid adoption.... These common-law and statutory rules of law reflect the physical reality that only the mother carries and gives birth to the child, as well as the undeniable social reality that the unwed mother is always an identifiable parent and the custodian of the child—until or unless the State intervenes. The biological father, unless he has established a familial tie with the child by marrying the mother, is often a total stranger from the State's point of view. I do not understand the Court to question these pragmatic differences. An unwed father who has not come forward and who has established no relationship with the child is plainly not in a situation similar to the mother's. New York's consent distinctions have clearly been made on this basis, and in my view they do not violate the Equal Protection Clause of the Fourteenth Amendment. See *Schlesinger v. Ballard*, 419 U.S. 498.

In this case, of course, we are concerned . . . with an unwed father who has established a paternal relationship with his children. He is thus similarly situated to the mother, and his claim is that he thus has parental interests no less deserving of protection than those of the mother. His contention that the New York law in question consequently discriminates against him on the basis of gender cannot be lightly dismissed. For substantially the reasons expressed by MR. JUSTICE STEVENS in his dissenting opinion, I believe, however, that this gender-based distinction does not violate the Equal Protection Clause as applied in the circumstances of the present case.

. . .There are not two, but three interests at stake: the mother's the father's, and the children's. Concerns humane as well as practical abundantly support New York's provision that only one parent need consent to the adoption of an illegitimate child, though it requires both parents to consent to the adoption of one already legitimate. If the consent of both unwed parents were required, and one withheld that consent, the illegitimate child would remain illegitimate. Viewed in these terms the statute does not in any sense discriminate on the basis of sex. The question, then, is whether the decision to select the unwed mother as the parent entitled to give or withhold consent and to apply that rule even when the unwed father in fact has a paternal relationship with his children constitutes invidious sex-based discrimination.

The appellant's argument would be a powerful one were this an instance in which it had been found that adoption by the father would serve the best interests of the children, and in the face of that finding the mother had been permitted to block the adoption. But this is not such a case. As my Brother STEVENS has observed, under a sex-neutral rule—assuming that New York is free to require the consent of but one parent for the adoption of an illegitimate child—the outcome in this case would have been the same. The appellant has been given the opportunity to show that an adoption would not be in his children's best interests. Implicit in the finding made by the New York courts is the judgment that termination of his relationship with the children will in fact promote their well-being—a judgment we are obligated to accept.

That the statute might permit—in a different context—the unwed mother arbitrarily to thwart the wishes of the caring father as well as the best interests of the child is not a sufficient reason to invalidate it as applied in the present case. For here the legislative goal of the statute—to facilitate adoptions that are in the best interests of illegitimate children after consideration of all other interests involved—has indeed been fully and fairly served by this gender-based classification. Unless the decision to require the consent of only one parent is in itself constitutionally defective, which nobody has argued, the same interests that support that decision are sufficiently profound to overcome the appellant's claim that he has been invidiously discriminated against because he is a male.

I agree that retroactive application of the Court's decision today would work untold harm, and I fully subscribe to Part III of MR. JUSTICE STEVENS' dissent.

MR. JUSTICE STEVENS, with whom THE CHIEF JUSTICE and MR. JUSTICE REHNQUIST join, dissenting.

. . .

I

This case concerns the validity of rules affecting the status of the thousands of children who are born out of wedlock every day.[2] All of these children have an interest in acquiring the status of legitimacy; a great many of them have an interest in being adopted by parents who can give them opportunities that would otherwise be denied; for some the basic necessities of life are at stake. The state interest in facilitating adoption in appropriate cases is strong—perhaps even "compelling."

Nevertheless, it is also true that § 111 (1) (c) gives rights to natural mothers that it withholds from natural fathers. Because it draws this gender-based distinction between two classes of citizens who have an equal right to fair and impartial treatment by their government, it is necessary to determine whether there are differences between the members of the two classes that provide a justification for treating them differently. . . .

Men and women are different, and the difference is relevant to the question whether the mother may be given the exclusive right to consent to the adoption of a child born out of wedlock. Because most adoptions involve newborn infants or very young children,[7] it is appropriate at the outset to focus on the significance of the difference in such cases.

...The differences between the male and the female have an important impact on the child's destiny. Only the mother carries the child; it is she who has the constitutional right to decide whether to bear it or not.[9] In many cases, only the mother knows who sired the child, and it will often be within her power to withhold that fact, and even the fact of her pregnancy, from that person. If during pregnancy the mother should marry a different partner, the child will be legitimate when born, and the natural father may never even know that his "rights" have been affected. On the other hand, only if the natural mother agrees to marry the natural father during that period can the latter's actions have a positive impact on the status of the child; if he instead should marry a different partner during that time, the only effect on the child is negative, for the likelihood of legitimacy will be lessened.

...At birth and immediately thereafter ... the mother and child are together; the mother's identity is known with certainty. The father, on the other hand, may or may not be present; his identity may be unknown to the world and may even be uncertain to the mother.[11] These natural differences between [un]married fathers and mothers make it probable that the mother, and not the father or both parents, will have custody of the new-born infant.

In short, it is virtually inevitable that from conception through infancy the mother will constantly be faced with decisions about how best to care for the child, whereas it is much less certain that the father will be confronted with comparable problems. There no doubt are cases in which the relationship of the parties at birth makes it appropriate for the State to give the father a voice of some sort in the adoption decision.[13] But as a matter of equal protection analysis, it is perfectly obvious that at the time and immediately after a child is born out of wedlock, differences between men and women justify some differential treatment of the mother and father in the adoption process.

Most particularly, these differences justify a rule that gives the mother of the newborn infant the exclusive right to consent to its adoption. Such a rule gives the mother, in whose sole charge the infant is often placed anyway, the maximum flexibility in deciding how best to care for the child. It also gives the loving father an incentive to marry the mother.[14] ... It facilitates the interests of the adoptive parents, the child, and the public at large by streamlining the often traumatic adoption process and allowing the prompt, complete, and reliable integration of the child into a satisfactory new home at as young an age as is feasible.[15] Put most simply, it permits the maximum participation of interested natural parents without so burdening the adoption process that its attractiveness to potential adoptive parents is destroyed.

This conclusion is borne out by considering the alternative rule proposed by appellant. If the State were to require the consent of both parents, or some kind of hearing to explain why either's consent is unnecessary or unobtainable, it would unquestionably complicate and delay the adoption process. Most importantly, such a rule would remove the mother's freedom of choice in her own and the child's behalf without also relieving her of the unshakable responsibility for the care of the child. Furthermore, questions relating to the adequacy of notice to absent fathers could invade the mother's privacy,[17] cause the adopting parents to doubt the reliability of the new relationship, and add to the expense and time required to conclude what is now usually a simple and certain process.[18] While it might not be irrational for a State to conclude that these costs should be incurred to protect the interest of natural fathers, it is nevertheless plain that those costs, which are largely the result of differences between the mother and the father, establish an imposing justification for some differential treatment of the two sexes in this type of situation.

With this much the Court does not disagree; it confines its holding to cases such as the one at hand involving the adoption of an older child against the wishes of a natural father who previously has participated in the rearing of the child and who admits paternity. The Court does conclude, however, that the gender basis for the classification drawn by § 111 (1) (c) makes differential treatment so suspect that the State has the burden of showing not only that the rule is generally justified but also that the justification holds equally true for *all* persons disadvantaged by the rule. In its view, since the justification is not as strong for some indeterminately small part of the disadvantaged class as it is for the class as a whole, the rule is invalid under the Equal Protection Clause insofar as it applies to that subclass. With this conclusion I disagree.

If we assume, as we surely must, that characteristics possessed by all members of one class and by no members of the other class justify some disparate treatment of mothers and fathers of children born out of wedlock, the mere fact that the statute draws a "gender-based distinction," should not, in my opinion, give rise to any presumption that the impartiality principle embodied in the Equal Protection Clause has been violated. Indeed, if we make the further undisputed assumption that the discrimination is justified in those cases in which the rule has its most frequent application—cases involving newborn infants and very young children in the custody of their natural mothers, we should presume that the law is entirely valid and require the challenger to demonstrate that its unjust applications are sufficiently numerous and serious to render it invalid.

In this case, appellant made no such showing; his demonstration of unfairness, assuming he has made one, extends only to himself and by implication to the unknown number of fathers just like him. Further, while appellant did nothing to inform the New York courts about the size of his subclass and the overall degree of its disadvantage under § 111 (1) (c), the New York Court of Appeals has previously concluded that the subclass is small and its disadvantage insignificant by comparison to the benefits of the rule as it now stands.[20]

The mere fact that an otherwise valid general classification appears arbitrary in an isolated case is not a sufficient reason for invalidating the entire rule, nor...for concluding that the application of a valid rule in a hard case constitutes a violation of equal protection principles.[22] We cannot test the conformance of rules to the principle of equality simply by reference to exceptional cases.

Moreover, I am not at all sure that § 111 (1) (c) is arbitrary even if viewed solely in the light of the exceptional circumstances presently before the Court. This case involves a dispute between natural parents over which of the two may adopt the children. If both are given a veto, as the Court requires, neither may adopt and the children will remain illegitimate. If, instead of a gender-based distinction, the veto were given to the parent having custody of the child, the mother would prevail just as she did in the state court.[23] Whether or not it is wise to devise a special rule to protect the natural father who (a) has a substantial relationship with his child, and (b) wants to veto an adoption that a court has found to be in the best interests of the child, the record in this case does not demonstrate that the Equal Protection Clause requires such a rule.

I have no way of knowing how often disputes between natural parents over adoption of their children arise after the father "has established a substantial relationship with the child and is willing to admit his paternity," but has previously been unwilling to take steps to legitimate his relationship. I am inclined to believe that such cases are relatively rare. But whether or not this assumption is valid, the far surer assumption is that in the more common adoption situations, the mother will be the more, and often the only, responsible parent, and that a paternal consent requirement will constitute a hindrance to the adoption process. Because this general rule is amply justified in its normal application, I would therefore require the party challenging its constitutionality to make some demonstration of unfairness in a significant number of situations before concluding that it violates the Equal Protection Clause. . . . [This case presents]. . . what is unquestionably . . . [a] justifiabl[e] . . . gender-based distinction.

II

Although the substantive due process issue is more troublesome, I can briefly state the reason why I reject it.

I assume that, if and when one develops, the relationship between a father and his natural child is entitled to protection against arbitrary state action as a matter of due process. *See Stanley v. Illinois*, 405 U.S. 645, 651. Although the Court has not decided whether the Due Process Clause provides any greater substantive protection for this relationship than simply against official caprice, it has indicated that an adoption decree that terminates the relationship is constitutionally justified by a finding that the father has abandoned or mistreated the child. *See id.*, at 652. In my view, such a decree may also be justified by a finding that the adoption will serve the best interests of the child, at least in a situation such as this in which the natural family unit has already been destroyed, the father has previously taken no steps to legitimate the child, and a further requirement such as a showing of unfitness would entirely deprive the child—and the State—of the benefits of adoption and legitimation. . . .

III

There is often the risk that the arguments one advances in dissent may give rise to a broader reading of the Court's opinion than is appropriate. That risk is especially grave when the Court is embarking on a new course that threatens to interfere with social arrangements that have come into use over long periods of time. Because I consider the course on which the Court is currently embarked to be potentially most serious, I shall explain why I regard its holding in this case as quite narrow.

The adoption decrees that have been entered without the consent of the natural father must number in the millions. An untold number of family and financial decisions have been made in reliance on the validity of those decrees. Because the Court has crossed a new constitutional frontier with today's decision, those reliance interests unquestionably foreclose retroactive application of this ruling. *See Chevron Oil Co. v. Huson*, 404 U.S. 97, 106–107. Families that include adopted children need have no concern about the probable impact of this case on their familial security.

Nor is there any reason why the decision should affect the processing of most future adoptions. . . . The procedure to be followed in cases involving infants who are in the custody of their mothers—whether solely or jointly with the father—or of agencies with authority to consent to adoption, is entirely unaffected by the Court's holding or by its reasoning. In fact, as I read the Court's opinion, the statutes now in effect may be enforced as usual unless "the adoption of an older child is sought," and "the father has established a substantial relationship with the child and is willing to admit his paternity." State legislatures will no doubt promptly revise their adoption laws to comply with the rule of this case, but as long as state courts are prepared to construe their existing statutes to contain a requirement of paternal consent "in cases such as this," I see no reason why they may not continue to enter valid adoption decrees in the countless routine cases that will arise before the statutes can be amended.

In short, this is an exceptional case that should have no effect on the typical adoption proceeding. . . . I respectfully dissent.

Opinion Footnotes

2 Illegitimate births accounted for an estimated 14.7% and 15.5% of all births in the United States during the years 1976 and 1977, respectively. . . . . In total births, this represents 468,100 and 515,700 illegitimate births, respectively. Although statistics for New York State are not available, the problem of illegitimacy appears to be especially severe in urban areas. For example, in 1975, over 50% of all births in the District of Columbia were out of wedlock. . . .

Adoption is an important solution to the problem of illegitimacy. . . .

7 . . . [O]f the children adopted by unrelated parents in New York in 1974 and 1975, respectively, 66% and 62% were under 1 year old, and 90% and 88% were under 6 years old. In 1974, moreover, the median age of the child at the time of adoption was 5 months. . . .

9 See *Planned Parenthood of Central Missouri v. Danforth*, 428 U.S. 52, 67–75.

11 The Court has frequently noted the difficulty of proving paternity in cases involving illegitimate children. E. g., *Trimble v. Gordon*, at 770–771; *Gomez v. Perez*, 409 U.S. 535, 538. . . .

13 *Cf.* Part II, *infra*. Indeed, New York does give unwed fathers ample opportunity to participate in adoption proceedings. In this case, for example, appellant appeared at the adoption hearing with counsel, presented testimony, and was allowed to cross-examine the witnesses offered by appellees. . . . As a substantive matter, the natural father is free to demonstrate, as appellant unsuccessfully tried . . ., that the best interests of the child favor the preservation of existing parental rights and forestall cutting off those rights by way of adoption. Had appellant been able to make that demonstration, the result would have been the same as that mandated by the Court's insistence upon paternal as well as maternal consent in these circumstances: neither parent could adopt the child into a new family with a stepparent; both would have parental rights (*e. g.,* visitation); and custody would be determined by the child's best interests. . . .

14 Marrying the mother would not only legitimate the child but would also assure the father the right to consent to any adoption.

15 These are not idle interests. A survey of adoptive parents registered on the New York State Adoption Exchange as of January 1975 showed that over 75% preferred to adopt children under 3 years old; over half preferred children under 1 year old. . . .

17 To be effective, any such notice would probably have to name the mother and perhaps even identify her further, for example, by address. Moreover, the terms and placement of the notice in, for example, a newspaper, no matter how discreet and tastefully chosen, would inevitably be taken by the public as an announcement of illegitimate maternity. To avoid the embarrassment of such announcements,

> the mother might well be forced to identify the father (or potential fathers)—despite her desire to keep that fact a secret.
>
> **18** In the opinion upon which it relied in dismissing the appeal in this case, the New York Court of Appeals concluded that the "trauma" that would be added to the adoption process by a paternal consent rule is "unpleasant to envision." *In re Malpica-Orsini*, at 574.
>
> **20** "To require the consent of fathers of children born out of wedlock . . . or even some of them, would have the overall effect of denying homes to the homeless and of depriving innocent children of the other blessings of adoption. The cruel and undeserved out-of-wedlock stigma would continue its visitations. At the very least, the worthy process of adoption would be severely impeded. . . ." *In re Malpica-Orsini*, at 572–574. . . .
>
> **22** Even if the exclusive-consent requirement were limited to newborn infants there would still be an occasional case in which the interests of the child would be better served by a responsible paternal veto than by an irresponsible maternal veto.
>
> **23** In fact, although the Court understands it differently, the New York statute apparently does turn consent rights on custody. Thus, § 111 (1) (d) gives consent rights to "any person . . . having lawful custody of the adoptive child.". . . In this light, the allegedly improper impact of the gender-based classification in § 111 (1) (c) as challenged by appellant is even more attenuated than I have suggested because it only disqualifies those few natural fathers of older children who have established a substantial relationship with the child and have admitted paternity, but who nonetheless do not have custody of the children.

Case Questions

1. If you were a state legislator revising adoption provisions to conform to *Caban v. Mohammed*, how would you proceed regarding nonmarital newborns? Regarding, say, a 3-year-old whose father had signed the birth certificate, visited several times and provided occasional gifts? Regarding the offspring of an unwed mother who wishes to place her child for adoption and who knows but refuses to divulge the name of the child's father? An unwed mother who does not know the father's identity? Would a statute requiring adoption consent only from "any natural parent who has retained sole custody of an illegitimate child since its birth" satisfy the majority's concerns?

2. Are the dissenters' concerns about the harms of "illegitimacy" overblown?

3. Is the majority inadequately attentive to the potential mother who wants to give her child up for adoption and is firmly convinced that the biological father should not raise the child? Might this decision scare her into getting an abortion?

Parham v. Hughes (1974)

The five-man majority for the rights of unwed fathers did not endure even for the one day on which *Caban* was handed down. On that same day, the Court divided 5–4 against an unwed father in the decision of *Parham v. Hughes*, 441 U.S 347 (1979). There Justice Powell deserted the fathers' rights bloc to vote to uphold a statute that permitted unmarried mothers but not fathers to bring "wrongful death" lawsuits against persons who had killed their children. Even though Parham had signed the birth certificate of his child, Lemuel, contributed to

Lemuel's support, and visited him regularly, five justices rejected his challenge to this gender discrimination. (The boy's mother had been killed along with the boy in a car accident.)

Justice Stewart (writing also for Stevens, Burger, and Rehnquist) reasoned that this gender distinction was justified by two state concerns. First, it served as an incentive to an unwed father to legitimate his child (and thereby to take on the legal duty of support): "Legitimation would have removed the stigma of bastardy and allowed the child to inherit from the father in the same manner as if born in lawful wedlock" (441 U.S. 353). Second, providing an incentive for the father to go through a legitimation hearing while the child, and presumably the child's mother, were still alive was a rational mechanism for (or in Powell's terms "substantially furthered") "dealing with 'the often difficult problem of proving the paternity of illegitimate children'" (p. 357). Justice Powell, in his solo but pivotal opinion, put much more emphasis than Stewart on the *Craig* rule but said that he felt this second state concern did meet the *Craig* test.

White, writing also for Brennan, Marshall, and Blackmun, in dissent, insisted that the proof-of-paternity concern was frivolous, since in any wrongful death lawsuit the parent would have to offer proof of parenthood in order to win. Moreover, the dissenters believed that any connection between barring unwed fathers from wrongful death actions and promoting legitimation hearings was "far too tenuous to justify the sex discrimination" (p. 363). They did not find it credible that the hope of future recovery in wrongful death actions would actually lure unwed fathers into legitimating their offspring.

While *Parham* made clear that some gender discriminations against unwed fathers would still be tolerated, *Caban* at least had seemed to cast quite a shadow of doubt over their constitutionality in the context of release for adoption. That shadow, however, was partially lifted in the 1983 decision, *Lehr v. Robertson*.

Lehr v. Robertson (1983)

One cannot simply recount the factual background to the *Lehr* case, because the Court divided sharply over which story makes the best sense of the facts. The choice of story shaped the justices' differing views as to the constitutional rights of Jonathan Lehr, the unwed father (or perhaps their feelings about him drove their choice of narrative). Some points were not in dispute. Lehr lived with Lorraine Robertson for two years, at the end of which she gave birth to a daughter, Jessica, on November 9, 1976. Lehr visited mother and daughter at the hospital, but his name was not put on the birth certificate. (Robertson never denied that Lehr was the father.) At this point the Supreme Court majority of six, in the voice of Stevens, says, "He did not live with appellee or Jessica after Jessica's birth, he has never provided them with any financial support, and he has never offered to marry appellee" (463 U.S. 248, 252). Stevens later summarized the facts as follows: "Appellant has never had any significant custodial, personal, or financial relationship with Jessica, and he did not seek to establish a legal tie until after she was two years old" (463 U.S., at 262).

The three dissenters, White, Marshall, and Blackmun, in an opinion by White, detail Lehr's side of the rest of the story, as follows:

> Lehr visited Lorraine and Jessica in the hospital every day during Lorraine's confinement. According to Lehr, from the time Lorraine was discharged from the hospital until August, 1978, she concealed her whereabouts from him. During this time Lehr never ceased his efforts to locate Lorraine and Jessica and achieved sporadic success until August, 1977, after which time he was unable to locate them at all. On those occasions when he did determine Lorraine's location, he visited with her and her children to the extent she was willing to permit it. When Lehr, with the aid of a detective agency, located Lorraine and Jessica in August, 1978, Lorraine was already married to Mr. Robertson. Lehr asserts that at this time he offered to provide financial assistance and to set up a trust fund for Jessica, but that Lorraine refused. Lorraine threatened Lehr with arrest unless he stayed away and refused to permit him to see Jessica. Thereafter Lehr retained counsel who wrote to Lorraine in early December, 1978, requesting that she permit Lehr to visit Jessica and threatening legal action on Lehr's behalf. On December 21, 1978, perhaps as a response to Lehr's threatened legal action, appellees commenced the adoption action at issue here. (463 U.S., at 269)

On January 30, 1979 (a month later) Lehr filed a petition in his home county asking for a determination of paternity, a support order, and reasonable visitation privileges. Robertson received notice of that hearing on February 22, 1979. Four days later her attorney informed her home county's court of the paternity proceeding in Lehr's county. Her county judge stayed the paternity proceeding until he could decide whether that hearing should be moved into the county where the Robertsons resided. On March 3 Lehr was served notice of the motion to move the paternity proceeding and thus learned of the pending adoption proceeding. On March 7, Lehr's attorney telephoned the judge in the Robertsons' county to let him know that he was going to request a stay of the adoption proceeding. The lawyer was told that earlier that day the judge had signed the adoption order. The judge did this in full knowledge of the pending paternity proceeding.

This Supreme Court case then arose out of a petition by Lehr to vacate the adoption order as having resulted from a violation of his constitutional rights to due process and equal protection. Two New York appeals courts upheld the adoption order. New York state law, revised after *Stanley v. Illinois*, required several categories of potential unwed fathers to be given notice of, and a chance to be heard at, any pending adoption proceeding. These included those who had been adjudicated to be the father; those who lived openly with the child and its mother, holding themselves out as the father; those who had been identified by the mother in a sworn written statement; and those who had married the mother before the child reached six months old. In addition, any male could send a postcard to New York's "putative father registry," indicating intent to claim paternity of a child. This registration was revocable at will and would establish a right to receive notice of that child's adoption proceeding. Lehr had failed to send such a postcard, although his intent to claim paternity was both a matter of public record and known to the judge. The New York courts had upheld the judge's refusal to accord him notice of the hearing terminating his parental rights (i.e., the adoption) because he had followed the wrong legal procedures. The U.S. Supreme Court (with Jessica nearly 7 years old) affirmed.

LEHR V. ROBERTSON
463 U.S. 248 (1983)

JUSTICE STEVENS delivered the opinion of the Court:

The question presented is whether New York has sufficiently protected an unmarried father's inchoate relationship with a child whom he has never supported and rarely seen in the two years since her birth. The appellant, Jonathan Lehr, claims that the Due Process and Equal Protection Clauses of the Fourteenth Amendment, as interpreted in *Stanley v. Illinois* and *Caban v. Mohammed*, give him an absolute right to notice and an opportunity to be heard before the child may be adopted. We disagree.

. . .

Appellant . . . offers two alternative grounds for holding the New York statutory scheme unconstitutional. First, he contends that a putative father's actual or potential relationship with a child born out of wedlock is an interest in liberty which may not be destroyed without due process of law; he argues therefore that he had a constitutional right to prior notice and an opportunity to be heard before he was deprived of that interest. Second, he contends that the gender-based classification in the statute, which both denied him the right to consent to Jessica's adoption and accorded him fewer procedural rights than her mother, violated the Equal Protection Clause.

The Due Process Claim.

...We ... first consider the nature of the interest in liberty for which appellant claims constitutional protection and then turn to a discussion of the adequacy of the procedure that New York has provided for its protection.

I

... In the vast majority of cases, state law determines the final outcome. *Cf. United States v. Yazell,* 382 U.S. 341, 351–353 (1966). Rules governing the inheritance of property, adoption, and child custody are generally specified in statutory enactments that vary from State to State. Moreover, equally varied state laws governing marriage and divorce affect a multitude of parent-child relationships. The institution of marriage has played a critical role both in defining the legal entitlements of family members and in developing the decentralized structure of our democratic society. In recognition of that role, and as part of their general overarching concern for serving the best interests of children, state laws almost universally express an appropriate preference for the formal family.

In some cases, however, this Court has held that the Federal Constitution supersedes state law and provides even greater protection for certain formal family relationships. In those cases, as in the state cases, the Court has emphasized the paramount interest in the welfare of children and has noted that the rights of the parents are a counterpart of the responsibilities they have assumed. Thus, the "liberty" of parents to control the education of their children that was vindicated in *Meyer v. Nebraska,* 262 U.S. 390 (1923), and *Pierce v. Society of Sisters,* 268 U.S. 510 (1925), was described as a "right, coupled with the high duty, to recognize and prepare [the child] for additional obligations." *Id.,* at 535. The linkage between parental duty and parental right was stressed again in *Prince v. Massachusetts,* 321 U.S. 158, 166 (1944), when the Court declared it a cardinal principle "that the custody, care and nurture of the child reside first in the parents, whose primary function and freedom include preparation for obligations the state can neither supply nor hinder." *Id.* at 166....[T]he relationship of love and duty in a recognized family unit is an interest in liberty entitled to constitutional protection....

There are also a few cases in which this Court has considered the extent to which the Constitution affords protection to the relationship between natural parents and children born out of wedlock. . . . This Court has examined the extent to which a natural father's biological relationship with his child receives protection under the Due Process Clause in precisely three cases: *Stanley v. Illinois*, *Quilloin v. Walcott*, and *Caban v. Mohammed*. [Summaries of the three followed.]

. . .

[Because in *Caban* this Court upheld the father's] equal protection claim, the majority did not address his due process challenge. The comments on the latter claim by the four dissenting Justices are nevertheless instructive, because they identify the clear distinction between a mere biological relationship and an actual relationship of parental responsibility.

Justice Stewart correctly observed:

Even if it be assumed that each married parent after divorce has some substantive due process right to maintain his or her parental relationship, *cf. Smith v. Organization of Foster Families*, 431 U.S. 816, 862–863 (opinion concurring in judgment), it by no means follows that each unwed parent has any such right. *Parental rights do not spring full-blown from the biological connection between parent and child. They require relationships more enduring.* (441 U.S., at 397 [emphasis added].)

In a similar vein, the other three dissenters in *Caban* were prepared to "assume that, *if and when one develops*, the relationship between a father and his natural child is entitled to protection against arbitrary state action as a matter of due process." *Caban v. Mohammed*, 441 U.S. 380, 414 (emphasis added).

The difference between the developed parent-child relationship that was implicated in *Stanley* and *Caban*, and the potential relationship involved in *Quilloin* and this case, is both clear and significant. When an unwed father demonstrates a full commitment to the responsibilities of parenthood by "com[ing] forward to participate in the rearing of his child," *Caban*, 441 U.S., at 392, his interest in personal contact with his child acquires substantial protection under the Due Process Clause. At that point it may be said that he "act[s] as a father toward his children." *Id.*, at 389, n. 7. But the mere existence of a biological link does not merit equivalent constitutional protection. The actions of judges neither create nor sever genetic bonds. "[T]he importance of the familial relationship, to the individuals involved and to the society, stems from the emotional attachments that derive from the intimacy of daily association, and from the role it plays in 'promot[ing] a way of life' through the instruction of children . . . as well as from the fact of blood relationship." *Smith v. Organization of Foster Families for Equality and Reform*, 431 U.S. 816, 844 (1977) (quoting *Wisconsin v. Yoder*, 406 U.S. 205, 231–233 [1972]).

The significance of the biological connection is that it offers the natural father an opportunity that no other male possesses to develop a relationship with his offspring. If he grasps that opportunity and accepts some measure of responsibility for the child's future, he may enjoy the blessings of the parent-child relationship and make uniquely valuable contributions to the child's development. If he fails to do so, the Federal Constitution will not automatically compel a State to listen to his opinion of where the child's best interests lie.

In this case, we are not assessing the constitutional adequacy of New York's procedures for terminating a developed relationship. Appellant has never had any significant custodial, personal, or financial relationship with Jessica, and he did not seek to establish a legal tie until after she was two years old.[19] We are concerned only with whether New York has adequately protected his opportunity to form such a relationship.

II

The most effective protection of the putative father's opportunity to develop a relationship with his child is provided by the laws that authorize formal marriage and govern its consequences. But the availability of that protection is, of course, dependent on the will of both parents of the child. Thus, New York has adopted a special statutory scheme to protect the unmarried father's interest in assuming a responsible role in the future of his child.

. . . If this scheme were likely to omit many responsible fathers, and if qualification for notice were beyond the control of an interested putative father, it might be thought procedurally inadequate. Yet, as all of the New York courts that reviewed this matter observed, the right to receive notice was completely within appellant's control. By mailing a postcard to the putative father registry, he could have guaranteed that he would receive notice of any proceedings to adopt Jessica. The possibility that he may have failed to do so because of his ignorance of the law cannot be a sufficient reason for criticizing the law itself. The New York Legislature concluded that a more open-ended notice requirement would merely complicate the adoption process, threaten the privacy interests of unwed mothers, create the risk of unnecessary controversy, and impair the desired finality of adoption decrees. Regardless of whether we would have done likewise if we were legislators instead of judges, we surely cannot characterize the State's conclusion as arbitrary.[22]

Appellant argues, however, that even if the putative father's opportunity to establish a relationship with an illegitimate child is adequately protected by the New York statutory scheme in the normal case, he was nevertheless entitled to special notice because the court and the mother knew that he had filed an affiliation proceeding in another court. This argument amounts to nothing more than an indirect attack on the notice provisions of the New York statute. The legitimate state interests in facilitating the adoption of young children and having the adoption proceeding completed expeditiously that underlie the entire statutory scheme also justify a trial judge's determination to require all interested parties to adhere precisely to the procedural requirements of the statute. The Constitution does not require either a trial judge or a litigant to give special notice to nonparties who are presumptively capable of asserting and protecting their own rights. Since the New York statutes adequately protected appellant's inchoate interest in establishing a relationship with Jessica, we find no merit in the claim that his constitutional rights were offended because the Family Court strictly complied with the notice provisions of the statute.

The Equal Protection Claim.

The concept of equal justice under law requires the State to govern impartially. *New York City Transit Authority v. Beazer*, 440 U.S. 568, 587 (1979). The sovereign may not draw distinctions between individuals based solely on differences that are irrelevant to a legitimate governmental objective. *Reed v. Reed.* Specifically, it may not subject men and women to disparate treatment when there is no substantial relation between the disparity and an important state purpose. *Id., Craig v. Boren*, 429 U.S. 190, 197–199 (1976).

The legislation at issue in this case, N. Y. Dom. Rel. Law § 111 and § 111–a, is intended to establish procedures for adoptions. Those procedures are designed to promote the best interests of the child, to protect the rights of interested third parties, and to ensure promptness and finality.[25] To serve those ends, the legislation guarantees to certain people the right to veto an adoption and the right to prior notice of any adoption proceeding. The mother of an illegitimate child is always within that favored class, but only certain putative fathers are included. Appellant contends that the gender-based distinction is invidious.

As we have already explained, the existence or nonexistence of a substantial relationship between parent and child is a relevant criterion in evaluating both the rights of the parent and the best interests of the child. . . .

We have held that these statutes may not constitutionally be applied in that class of cases where the mother and father are in fact similarly situated with regard to their relationship with the child. In *Caban v. Mohammed*, the Court held that it violated the Equal Protection Clause to grant the mother a veto over the adoption of a 4-year-old girl and a 6-year-old boy, but not to grant a veto to their father, who had admitted paternity and had participated in the rearing of the children. The Court made it clear, however, that if the father had not "come forward to participate in the rearing of his child, nothing in the Equal Protection Clause [would] preclud[e] the State from withholding from him the privilege of vetoing the adoption of that child." 441 U.S., at 392.

Jessica's parents are not like the parents involved in *Caban*. If one parent has an established custodial relationship with the child and the other parent has either abandoned or never established a relationship, the Equal Protection Clause does not prevent a State from according the two parents different legal rights.

The judgment of the New York Court of Appeals is

Affirmed.

Opinion Footnotes

19 . . . In denying the putative father relief in *Quilloin*, we made an observation equally applicable here: "Nor is this a case in which the proposed adoption would place the child with a new set of parents with whom the child had never before lived. Rather, the result of the adoption in this case is to give full recognition to a family unit already in existence, a result desired by all concerned, except appellant. Whatever might be required in other situations, we cannot say that the State was required in this situation to find anything more than that the adoption, and denial of legitimation, were in the 'best interests of the child.'" 434 U.S., at 255.

22 Nor can we deem unconstitutionally arbitrary the state courts' conclusion that appellant's absence did not distort their analysis of Jessica's best interests. The adoption does not affect Jessica's relationship with her mother. It gives legal permanence to her relationship with her adoptive father, a relationship they had maintained for 21 months at the time the adoption order was entered. Appellant did not proffer any evidence to suggest that legal confirmation of the established relationship would be unwise; he did not even know the adoptive father.

25 Appellant does not contest the vital importance of those ends to the people of New York. It has long been accepted that illegitimate children whose parents never marry are "at risk" economically, medically, emotionally, and educationally. . . .

JUSTICE WHITE, with whom JUSTICE MARSHALL and JUSTICE BLACKMUN join, dissenting.

The question in this case is whether the State may, consistent with the Due Process Clause, deny notice and an opportunity to be heard in an adoption proceeding to a putative father when the State has actual notice of his existence, whereabouts, and interest in the child.

I

It is axiomatic that "[t]he fundamental requirement of due process is the opportunity to be heard 'at a meaningful time and in a meaningful manner.'" *Mathews v. Eldridge*, 424 U.S. 319, 333 (1976), quoting *Armstrong v. Manzo*, 380 U.S. 545, 552 (1965). As Jessica's biological father, Lehr either had an interest protected by the Constitution or he did not. If the entry of the adoption order in this case deprived Lehr of a constitutionally protected interest, he is entitled to notice and an opportunity to be heard before the order can be accorded finality. [Here followed Lehr's version of facts.]

. . .

The "nature of the interest" at stake here is the interest that a natural parent has in his or her child, one that has long been recognized and accorded constitutional protection. We have frequently "stressed the importance of familial bonds, whether or not legitimized by marriage, and accorded them constitutional protection." *Little v. Streater*, 452 U.S. 1, 13 (1981). If "both the child and the [putative father] in a paternity action have a compelling interest" in the accurate outcome of such a case, *ibid.*, it cannot be disputed that both the child and the putative father have a compelling interest in the outcome of a proceeding that may result in the termination of the father-child relationship. "A parent's interest in the accuracy and justice of the decision to terminate his or her parental status is . . . a commanding one." *Lassiter v. Department of Social Services*, 452 U.S. 18, 27 (1981). It is beyond dispute that a formal order of adoption, no less than a formal termination proceeding, operates to permanently terminate parental rights.

Lehr's version of the "facts" paints a far different picture than that portrayed by the majority. . . . Appellant has never been afforded an opportunity to present his case. The legitimation proceeding he instituted was first stayed, and then dismissed, on appellees' motions. Nor could appellant establish his interest during the adoption proceedings, for it is the failure to provide Lehr notice and an opportunity to be heard there that is at issue here. We cannot fairly make a judgment based on the quality or substance of a relationship without a complete and developed factual record. This case requires us to assume that Lehr's allegations are true....

I reject the peculiar notion that the only significance of the biological connection between father and child is that "it offers the natural father an opportunity that no other male possesses to develop a relationship with his offspring." A "mere biological relationship" is not as unimportant in determining the nature of liberty interests as the majority suggests.

"[T]he usual understanding of 'family' implies biological relationships, and most decisions treating the relation between parent and child have stressed this element." *Smith v. Organization of Foster Families,* at 843. The "biological connection" is itself a relationship that creates a protected interest. Whether Lehr's interest is entitled to constitutional protection does not entail a searching inquiry into the quality of the relationship but a simple determination of the fact that the relationship exists—a fact that even the majority agrees must be assumed to be established.

That is not to say that due process requires actual notice to every putative father or that adoptive parents or the State must conduct an exhaustive search of records or an intensive investigation before a final adoption order may be entered. The procedures adopted by the State, however, must at least represent a reasonable effort to determine the identity of the putative father and to give him adequate notice.

II

In this case, of course, there was no question about either the identity or the location of the putative father. The mother knew exactly who he was and both she and the court entering the order of adoption knew precisely where he was and how to give him actual notice that his parental rights were about to be terminated by an adoption order. Lehr was entitled to due process, and the right to be heard is one of the fundamentals of that right, which " 'has little reality or worth unless one is informed that the matter is pending and can choose for himself whether to appear or default, acquiesce or contest.' " *Schroeder v. City of New York,* 371 U.S. 208, 212 (1962)......

The State concedes this much but insists that Lehr has had all the process that is due to him. It relies on § 111–a, which designates seven categories of unwed fathers to whom notice of adoption proceedings must be given, including any unwed father who has filed with the State a notice of his intent to claim paternity. The State submits that it need not give notice to anyone who has not filed his name, as he is permitted to do, and who is not otherwise within the designated categories, even if his identity and interest are known or are reasonably ascertainable by the State.

I am unpersuaded by the State's position. In the first place, § 111–a defines six categories of unwed fathers to whom notice must be given even though they have not placed their names on file pursuant to the section. Those six categories, however, do not include fathers such as Lehr who have initiated filiation proceedings, even though their identity and interest are as clearly and easily ascertainable as those fathers in the six categories. Initiating such proceedings necessarily involves a formal acknowledgment of paternity, and requiring the State to take note of such a case in connection with pending adoption proceedings would be a trifling burden, no more than the State undertakes when there is a final adjudication in a paternity action. Indeed, there would appear to be more reason to give notice to those such as Lehr who acknowledge paternity than to those who have been adjudged to be a father in a contested paternity action.

The State asserts that any problem in this respect is overcome by the seventh category of putative fathers to whom notice must be given, namely, those fathers who have identified themselves in the putative fathers' register maintained by the State. Since Lehr did not take advantage of this device to make his interest known, the State contends, he was not entitled to notice and a hearing even though his identity, location, and interest were known to the adoption court prior to entry of the adoption order. I have difficulty with this position. First, it represents a grudging and crabbed approach to due process. The State is quite willing to give notice and a hearing to putative fathers who have made themselves known by resorting to the putative fathers' register. It makes little sense to me to deny notice and hearing to a father who has not placed his name in the register but who has unmistakably identified himself by filing suit to establish his paternity and has notified the adoption court of his action and his interest. I thus need not question the statutory scheme on its face. Even assuming that Lehr would have been foreclosed if his failure to utilize the register had somehow disadvantaged the State, he effectively made himself known by other means, and it is the sheerest formalism to deny him a hearing because he informed the State in the wrong manner.

No state interest is substantially served by denying Lehr adequate notice and a hearing. . . .

Because in my view the failure to provide Lehr with notice and an opportunity to be heard violated rights guaranteed him by the Due Process

> Clause, I need not address the question whether § 111–a violates the Equal Protection Clause. . . .
>
> Respectfully, I dissent.

Case Questions

1. Does the combination of *Stanley*, *Quilloin*, *Caban*, and *Lehr* yield the proposition that single mothers who do not want the child's adoption hindered by the father are encouraged to conceal the child from its father until the adoption is complete? If so, is this wise public policy?

2. Does the court majority in cases like *Lehr* and *Quilloin* seem to be largely motivated by a desire to refrain from interfering in an ongoing family (rather than by rules found in the Constitution)? Is the Court well suited to act as a national child welfare agency?

3. Should an unwed mother and an unwed father be given equal veto rights over the adoption of their newly born child? Equal custody rights to the child? Is this a matter of gender discrimination or a matter of dealing with dissimilar situations?

Case note: As this book goes to press New York State's current rules allow the biological fathers of children to whose mothers they are not married to establish legal paternity. Establishing legal paternity allows those children access to various services that they would otherwise not have including medical and life insurance, Social Security, veterans' benefits and child support, as appropriate. Biological fathers may establish paternity by seeking a court order determining paternity or by signing a voluntary "Acknowledgement of Paternity" form.[62]

The "Baby Richard" Case

The role of single fathers in the adoption of newborn children was the issue in two notorious court decisions in the 1990s.[63] The facts in the cases were similar: a mother surrendered a baby for adoption, she reunited with the father soon afterwards, they were married, the father then challenged the adoption on the grounds that he had not consented to it. Both cases ended the same way, with the adoptions nullified and the children removed from their homes and awarded to birth parents who were strangers to them. "Baby Richard" was 4 years old when he was taken from Kimberly and Robert Warburton.

Partly as a result of these cases, many state courts and legislatures have expanded the rights of single fathers to consent to or veto adoptions.

IN RE PETITION OF DOE
159 Ill. 2d 347, 638 N.E. 2d 181 (1994)

JUSTICE HEIPLE delivered the opinion of the court:

John and Jane Doe filed a petition to adopt a newborn baby boy. The baby's biological mother, Daniella Janikova, executed a consent to have the baby adopted four days after his birth without informing his biological father, Otakar Kirchner, to whom she was not yet married.

The mother told the father that the baby had died, and he did not find out otherwise until 57 days after the birth. The trial court ruled that the father's consent was unnecessary because he did not show sufficient interest in the child during the first 30 days of the child's life. The appellate court affirmed (with one justice dissenting.) We granted leave to appeal and now reverse.

Otakar and Daniella began living together in the fall of 1989, and Daniella became pregnant in June of 1990. For the first eight months of her pregnancy, Otakar provided for all of her expenses.

In late January 1991, Otakar went to his native Czechoslovakia to attend to his gravely ill grandmother for two weeks. During this time, Daniella received a phone call from Otakar's aunt saying that Otakar had resumed a former romantic relationship with another woman.

Because of this unsettling news, Daniella left their shared apartment, refused to talk with Otakar on his return, and gave birth to the child at a different hospital than where they had originally planned. She gave her consent to the adoption of the child by the Does, telling them and their attorney that she knew who the father was but would not furnish his name. Daniella and her uncle warded off Otakar's persistent inquiries about the child by telling him that the child had died shortly after birth.

Otakar found out that the child was alive and had been placed for adoption 57 days after the child was born. He then began the instant proceedings by filing an appearance contesting the Does' adoption of his son. As already noted, the trial court ruled that Otakar was an unfit parent under section 1 of the Adoption Act because he had not shown a reasonable degree of interest in the child within the first 30 days of his life. Therefore, the father's consent was unnecessary under section 8 of the Act.

The finding that the father had not shown a reasonable degree of interest in the child is not supported by the evidence. In fact, he made various attempts to locate the child, all of which were either frustrated or blocked by the actions of the mother. Further, the mother was aided by the attorney for the adoptive parents, who failed to make any effort to ascertain the name or address of the father despite the fact that the mother indicated she knew who he was. Under the circumstances, the father had no opportunity to discharge any familial duty.

In the opinion below, the appellate court, wholly missing the threshold issue in this case, dwelt on the best interests of the child. Since, however, the father's parental interest was improperly terminated, there was no occasion to reach the factor of the child's best interests. That point should never have been reached and need never have been discussed.

Unfortunately, over three years have elapsed since the birth of the baby who is the subject of these proceedings. To the extent that it is relevant to assign fault in this case, the fault here lies initially with the mother, who fraudulently tried to deprive the father of his rights, and secondly, with the adoptive parents and their attorney, who proceeded with the adoption when they knew that a real father was out there who had been denied knowledge of his baby's existence. When the father entered his appearance in the adoption proceedings 57 days after the baby's birth and demanded his rights as a father, the petitioners should have relinquished the baby at that time. It was their decision to prolong this litigation through a lengthy, and ultimately fruitless, appeal.

The adoption laws of Illinois. . .place the burden of proof on the adoptive parents in establishing both the relinquishment and/or unfitness of the natural parents and, coincidentally, the fitness and the right to adopt of the adoptive parents. In addition, Illinois law requires a good-faith effort to notify the natural parents of the adoption proceedings. These laws are designed to protect natural parents in their preemptive rights to their own children wholly apart from any consideration of the so-called best interests of the child. If it were otherwise, few parents would be secure in the custody of their own children. If best interests of the child were a sufficient qualification to determine child custody, anyone with superior income, intelligence, education, etc., might challenge and deprive the parents of their right to their own children. The law is otherwise and was not complied with in this case.

Accordingly, we reverse.

Case Questions

1. All the justices agree that parental rights override a child's best interests. Should they? Can you think of explanations of why interests are ranked this way?

2. Like several other fathers' rights cases, this decision assigns equal weight to the interests of both biological parents. Is that good policy in the case of a newborn? Why or why not?

"ADULTEROUS FATHERS": *MICHAEL H. V. GERALD D.* (1989)

This child custody dispute presented drama more typical of television soap operas than of stories about law, whether fictional or newsworthy. The case, *Michael H. v. Gerald D.*, concerned a dispute over fathers' rights that involved a mother who at the time of conception, birth, and thereafter was wed to someone other than the child's father. California, like other states, treats the mother's husband, in general, as the legal father of all children born into the marriage. The statutory exceptions were described (in Calif. Evid. Code Ann. § 621) as follows:

> Except as provided [here] the issue of a wife cohabiting with her husband, who is not impotent or sterile, is conclusively presumed to be a child of the marriage. . . . The notice of a motion for blood tests [to determine paternity]. . . may be raised by the husband not later than two years from the child's date of birth. . . [or] by the mother of the child [under the same deadline] if the child's biological father has filed an affidavit with the Court acknowledging paternity. . .

Michael H., informed by Carole, the mother (who was married to Gerald D.), that he, Michael, was the father of Victoria, the child—information confirmed by blood tests with 98% accuracy—challenged the constitutionality of this statute, asking that he be declared the legal (or one of the two legal) father(s) of Victoria and be accorded visitation rights as such.

Concerning the facts of this case, Justice Scalia (an Italian Catholic then in his early fifties), writing for a plurality of four, who with Stevens' vote produced a majority upholding the law, began his opinion with the statement, "The facts of this case are, we must hope, extraordinary." Justice Brennan (an Irish Catholic then in his eighties) concluded his dissent with the remark that "the situation confronting us here . . . repeat[s] itself every day in every corner of the country."

Carole (an "international model") was married in 1976 to Gerald D. (a "top executive in a French oil company"), and they established a home in Los Angeles. In the summer of 1978 Carole began an affair with Michael H., a neighbor. Carole gave birth to Victoria in May 1981. Gerald was listed on the birth certificate as the father, but soon after the birth Carole confided to Michael that she believed him to be the father. For the first three years of Victoria's life, her mother lived with her in the following circumstances: May-October 1981 with husband Gerald (in October Gerald left for New York, for business; in late October Carole and Michael had blood tests confirming his paternity); January 1982–March 1982 in Michael's home in St. Thomas (his primary business home); March 1982–autumn 1982 with Scott (a third man) in California; periods in spring and summer of 1982 with Gerald in New York City and on vacation in Europe; fall 1982–March 1983 with Scott in California; March 1983–July 1983 with Gerald in New York City; August 1983–April 1984 with Michael in Los Angeles (in Carole's apartment) whenever Michael was not in St. Thomas (in April, 1984 Carole signed a stipulation that Michael was Victoria's father, but she moved out on him in May and ordered her lawyers not to file the stipulation); June 1984–1989 reconciled with Gerald and resided with him in New York (and opposed visits by Michael).

Before the case reached the Supreme Court, during 1983–84, a number of motions and cross motions were filed: Michael asked for filiation hearings to establish his paternity and a right to regular visitation; Carole in some motions supported his request and in others turned against him. Eventually, in October of 1984, the husband Gerald had moved for a summary judgment denying Michael's request, since under California law, he, Gerald, was Victoria's father. Meanwhile a court-appointed guardian *ad litem* for the daughter, Victoria, had filed a request that if Victoria had more than one "psychological or de facto father," she should be allowed "to maintain her filial relationship with all its attendant rights, duties, and obligations, with both" fathers. For the duration of the litigation at the trial court level, pursuant to a recommendation from a court-appointed psychologist, the court ordered limited visitation rights between Michael and Victoria. In January of 1985, the trial court granted Gerald's summary judgment, rejecting Michael's and Victoria's argument[64] for the unconstitutionality of the statute declaring Gerald to be Victoria's father. The judge ruled further that visitation would not be permitted pending the appeal (which visitation the judge was statutorily authorized to allow to any person "having a reasonable interest in the welfare of [a] child"). The judge claimed that "the integrity of the family unit" of Victoria would be "impugned" by further visitation. Michael's and Victoria's lawyers appealed, alleging that constitutional rights of both procedural and substantive due process were violated by this outcome. In addition to its denial of the procedural right to a hearing to demonstrate paternity, Michael claimed that this ruling transgressed the substance of his constitutional right to the care and companionship of his child. The California Court of Appeal affirmed and the

California Supreme Court refused to hear the case. The U.S. Supreme Court then took the appeal, and by the time it decided the case Victoria was already 8 years old. (At the U.S. Supreme Court, the lawyers also challenged the statutes on equal protection grounds, but Michael's lawyer had failed to raise that issue below, so the Supreme Court, as is standard, refused to address it.[65])

The Supreme Court's resolution of this dispute is difficult to summarize because the justices disagreed among themselves even over what the issues of the case were. Scalia, Rehnquist, O'Connor and Kennedy believe that Michael was claiming a constitutional right "to be declared *the* father of Victoria" and to thereby obtain parental rights. They ruled that there is no such fundamental constitutional right for a man in Michael's situation. Justice Stevens concurred in the judgment, stating that there is no constitutional right in the abstract to have paternity merely declared. On the other hand, he believed that since California law did provide for a court to establish visitation rights for *any* person "having an interest in the welfare of the child" when the court believed such visits would serve the best interests of the child, "Michael was given a fair opportunity to show that he is Victoria's natural father, that he had a developed relationship with her, and that her interests would be served by...visitation." Thus, Stevens believed that Michael *had been* accorded his "constitutional right to try to convince a trial judge that Victoria's best interest would be served by granting him visitation rights."

The dissenters (Brennan, Blackmun, Marshall, and White) agreed with Stevens that the issue in the case was a procedural one—the right to a hearing as to parental visitation rights—but they disagreed with his conclusion that California law honored this right by merely allowing others "interested in the welfare of the child" to be accorded, at the discretion of the judge, visitation rights. They believed that Michael had a constitutional right to an opportunity to establish his fatherhood in court because an official declaration of paternity would have a substantial impact on the visitation decision.

The five-justice majority in *Michael H.* broke ranks over a lengthy footnote (#6), in which Scalia tried to limit the right of privacy to what were, in effect, relations within the nuclear family (whether *de jure* or *de facto*). Thus, he viewed the issue as whether the Constitution specifically protects *adulterous* fatherhood (and answered, "No"), whereas the dissenters focused on parenthood as such. Both O'Connor and Kennedy, as well as the four dissenters, noted that Scalia's approach was inconsistent with precedents such as *Eisenstadt v. Baird*. Excerpts follow.

MICHAEL H. v. GERALD D.
491 U.S. 110 (1989)

JUSTICE SCALIA announced the judgment of the Court and delivered an opinion, in which **THE CHIEF JUSTICE** joins, and in all but footnote 6 of which **JUSTICE O'CONNOR** and **JUSTICE KENNEDY** join:

. . .

I

The facts of this case are, we must hope, extraordinary. . . . [Here followed the facts.—AU.]

. . .

III

...California law, like nature itself, makes no provision for dual fatherhood. Michael was seeking to be declared *the* father of Victoria. The immediate benefit he evidently sought to obtain from that status was visitation rights. See Cal. Civ. Code Ann. § 4601 (parent has statutory right to visitation "unless it is shown that such visitation would be detrimental to the best interests of the child"). But if Michael were successful in being declared the father, other rights would follow—most importantly, the right to be considered as the parent who should have custody. . . .

Michael raises two related challenges to the constitutionality of § 621. First, he asserts that requirements of procedural due process prevent the State from terminating his liberty interest in his relationship with his child without affording him an opportunity to demonstrate his paternity in an evidentiary hearing. We believe this claim derives from a fundamental misconception of the nature of the California statute. While § 621 is phrased in terms of a presumption, that rule of evidence is the implementation of a substantive rule of law. California declares it to be, except in limited circumstances, *irrelevant* for paternity purposes whether a child conceived during, and born into, an existing marriage was begotten by someone other than the husband and had a prior relationship with him. As the Court of Appeal phrased it:

> "The conclusive presumption is actually a substantive rule of law based upon a determination by the Legislature as a matter of overriding social policy, that given a certain relationship between the husband and wife, the husband is to be held responsible for the child,

and that the integrity of the family unit should not be impugned." 191 Cal. App. 3d, at 1005. . . .

Of course the conclusive presumption not only expresses the State's substantive policy but also furthers it, excluding inquiries into the child's paternity that would be destructive of family integrity and privacy.[1] . . . We . . . reject Michael's procedural due process challenge and proceed to his substantive claim.

Michael contends as a matter of substantive due process that, because he has established a parental relationship with Victoria, protection of Gerald's and Carole's marital union is an insufficient state interest to support termination of that relationship. This argument is, of course, predicated on the assertion that Michael has a constitutionally protected liberty interest in his relationship with Victoria.

It is an established part of our constitutional jurisprudence that the term "liberty" in the Due Process Clause extends beyond freedom from physical restraint. See, *e.g., Pierce v. Society of Sisters*; *Meyer v. Nebraska*. Without that core textual meaning as a limitation, defining the scope of the Due Process Clause "has at times been a treacherous field for this Court," giving "reason for concern lest the only limits to . . . judicial intervention become the predilections of those who happen at the time to be Members of this Court." *Moore v. East Cleveland*, 431 U.S. 494, 502 (1977). The need for restraint has been cogently expressed by JUSTICE WHITE (dissenting opinion):

> That the Court has ample precedent for the creation of new constitutional rights should not lead it to repeat the process at will. The Judiciary, including this Court, is the most vulnerable and comes nearest to illegitimacy when it deals with judge-made constitutional law having little or no cognizable roots in the language or even the design of the Constitution. Realizing that the present construction of the Due Process Clause represents a major judicial gloss on its terms, as well as on the anticipation of the Framers . . ., the Court should be extremely reluctant to breathe still further substantive content into the Due Process Clause so as to strike down legislation adopted by a State or city to promote its welfare. Whenever the Judiciary does so, it unavoidably pre-empts for itself another part of the governance of the country without express constitutional authority. *Moore*, at 544.

In an attempt to limit and guide interpretation of the Clause, we have insisted not merely that the interest denominated as a "liberty" be "fundamental" (a concept that, in isolation, is hard to objectify), but also that it be an interest traditionally protected by our society.[2] As we have put it, the Due Process Clause affords only those protections "so rooted in the traditions and conscience of our people as to be ranked as fundamental." *Snyder v. Massachusetts*, 291 U.S. 97, 105 (1934)....

This insistence that the asserted liberty interest be rooted in history and tradition is evident, as elsewhere, in our cases according constitutional protection to certain parental rights. Michael reads the landmark case of *Stanley v. Illinois*, and the subsequent cases of *Quilloin v. Walcott*, *Caban v. Mohammed*, and *Lehr v. Robertson*, as establishing that a liberty interest is created by biological fatherhood plus an established parental relationship—factors that exist in the present case as well. We think that distorts the rationale of those cases. As we view them, they rest not upon such isolated factors but upon the historic respect—indeed, sanctity would not be too strong a term—traditionally accorded to the relationships that develop within the unitary family.[3] In *Stanley*, for example, we forbade the destruction of such a family when, upon the death of the mother, the State had sought to remove children from the custody of a father who had lived with and supported them and their mother for 18 years. As Justice Powell stated for the plurality in *Moore v. East Cleveland*, at 503: "Our decisions establish that the Constitution protects the sanctity of the family precisely because the institution of the family is deeply rooted in this Nation's history and tradition."

Thus, the legal issue in the present case reduces to whether the relationship between persons in the situation of Michael and Victoria has been treated as a protected family unit under the historic practices of our society, or whether on any other basis it has been accorded special protection. We think it impossible to find that it has. In fact, quite to the contrary, our traditions have protected the marital family (Gerald, Carole, and the child they acknowledge to be theirs) against the sort of claim Michael asserts.[4]

The presumption of legitimacy was a fundamental principle of the common law. H. Nicholas, *Adulturine Bastardy* 1 (1836). Traditionally, that presumption could be rebutted only by proof that a husband was incapable of procreation or had had no access to his wife during the relevant period. Id., at 9–10 (citing Bracton, *De Legibus et Consuetudinibus Angliae*, bk. i, ch. 9, p. 6; bk. ii, ch. 29, p. 63, ch. 32, p. 70 (1569))....

We have found nothing in the older sources, nor in the older cases, addressing specifically the power of the natural father to assert parental rights over a child born into a woman's existing marriage with another man. Since it is Michael's burden to establish that such a power (at least where the natural father has established a relationship with the child) is so deeply embedded within our traditions as to be a fundamental right, the lack of evidence alone might defeat his case. But the evidence shows that even in modern times—when, as we have noted, the rigid protection of the marital family has in other respects been relaxed—the ability of a person in Michael's position to claim paternity has not been generally acknowledged. . . .

Moreover, even if it were clear that one in Michael's position generally possesses, and has generally always possessed, standing to challenge the marital child's legitimacy, that would still not establish Michael's case. As noted earlier, what is at issue here is not entitlement to a state pronouncement that Victoria was begotten by Michael. It is no conceivable denial of constitutional right for a State to decline to declare facts unless some legal consequence hinges upon the requested declaration. What Michael asserts here is a right to have himself declared the natural father *and thereby to obtain parental prerogatives*. What he must establish, therefore, is not that our society has traditionally allowed a natural father in his circumstances to establish paternity, but that it has traditionally accorded such a father parental rights, or at least has not traditionally denied them. . . . What counts is whether the States in fact award substantive parental rights to the natural father of a child conceived within, and born into, an extant marital union that wishes to embrace the child. We are not aware of a single case, old or new, that has done so. This is not the stuff of which fundamental rights qualifying as liberty interests are made.[6]

. . .In accord with our traditions, a limit is also imposed by the circumstance that the mother is, at the time of the child's conception and birth, married to, and cohabitating with, another man, both of whom wish to raise the child as the offspring of their union. It is a question of legislative policy and not constitutional law whether California will allow the presumed parenthood of a couple desiring to retain a child conceived within and born into their marriage to be rebutted.

We do not accept JUSTICE BRENNAN's criticism that this result "squashes" the liberty that consists of "the freedom not to conform." . . . If Michael has a "freedom not to conform" (whatever that means), Gerald must equivalently have a "freedom to conform." One of them will pay a price for asserting that "freedom"—Michael by being unable to act as father of the child he has adulterously begotten, or Gerald by being unable to preserve the integrity of the traditional family unit he and Victoria have established. . . .

The judgment of the California Court of Appeal is

Affirmed.

Opinion Footnotes

1 In those circumstances in which California allows a natural father to rebut the presumption of legitimacy of a child born to a married woman, *e. g.*, where the husband is impotent or sterile, or where the husband and wife have not been cohabiting, it is more likely that the husband already knows the child is not his, and thus less likely that the paternity hearing will disrupt an otherwise harmonious and apparently exclusive marital relationship.

2 We do not understand what JUSTICE BRENNAN has in mind [when he says] . . . our practice of limiting the Due Process Clause to traditionally protected interests turns the Clause "into a redundancy." Its purpose is to prevent future generations from lightly casting aside important traditional values—not to enable this Court to invent new ones.

3 JUSTICE BRENNAN asserts that only a "pinched conception of 'the family' " would exclude Michael, Carole, and Victoria from protection. We disagree. The family unit accorded traditional respect in our society, which we have referred to as the "unitary family," is typified, of course, by the marital family, but also includes the household of unmarried parents and their children. Perhaps the concept can be expanded even beyond this, but it will bear no resemblance to traditionally respected relationships—and will thus cease to have any constitutional significance—if it is stretched so far as to include the relationship established between a married woman, her lover, and their child, during a 3-month sojourn in St. Thomas, or during a subsequent 8-month period when, if he happened to be in Los Angeles, he stayed with her and the child.

4 JUSTICE BRENNAN insists that in determining whether a liberty interest exists we must look at Michael's relationship with Victoria in isolation, without reference to the circumstance that Victoria's mother was married to someone else when the child was conceived, and that that woman and her husband wish to raise the child as their own. We cannot imagine what compels this strange procedure of looking at the act which is assertedly the subject of a liberty interest in isolation from its effect upon other people—rather like inquiring whether there is a liberty interest in firing a gun where the case at hand happens to involve its discharge into another person's body. . . .

6 Justice Brennan criticized our methodology in using historical traditions specifically relating to the rights of an adulterous natural father, rather than inquiring more generally "whether parenthood is an interest that historically has received our attention and protection." There seems to us no basis for the contention that this methodology is "nove[l]," . . .

Though the dissent has no basis for the level of generality it would select, we do: We refer to the most specific level at which a relevant tradition protecting, or denying protection to, the asserted right can be identified. If, for example, there were no societal tradition, either way, regarding the rights of the natural father of a child adulterously conceived, we would have to consult, and (if possible) reason from, the traditions regarding natural fathers in general. But there is such a more specific tradition, and it unqualifiedly denies protection to such a parent.

One would think that Justice Brennan would appreciate the value of consulting the most specific tradition available, since he acknowledges that "[e]ven if we can agree . . . that 'family' and 'parenthood' are part of the good life, it is absurd to assume that we can agree on the content of those terms and destructive to pretend that we do." Because such general traditions provide such imprecise guidance, they permit judges to dictate rather than discern the society's views. The need, if arbitrary decisionmaking is to be avoided, to adopt the most specific tradition as the point of reference—or at least to announce, as Justice Brennan declines to do, some other criterion for selecting among the innumerable relevant traditions that could be consulted—is well enough exemplified by the fact that in the present case Justice Brennan's opinion and Justice O'Connor's opinion, which disapproves this footnote, both appeal to the tradition, but on the basis of the tradition they select reach opposite results. Although assuredly having the virtue (if it be that) of leaving judges free to decide as they think best when the unanticipated occurs, a rule of law that binds neither by text nor by any particular, identifiable tradition is no rule of law at all.

JUSTICE O'CONNOR, with whom JUSTICE KENNEDY joins, concurring in part.

I concur in all but footnote 6 of JUSTICE SCALIA's opinion. This footnote sketches a mode of historical analysis to be used when identifying liberty interests protected by the Due Process Clause of the Fourteenth Amendment that may be somewhat inconsistent with our past decisions in this area. See *Griswold v. Connecticut, Eisenstadt v. Baird.* On occasion the Court has characterized relevant traditions protecting asserted rights at levels of generality that might not be "the most specific level" available. [Justice Scalia's] n. 6. See *Loving v. Virginia*, 388 U.S. 1, 12 (1967); *Turner v. Safley*, 482 U.S. 78, 94 (1987). . . . I would not foreclose the unanticipated by the prior imposition of a single mode of historical analysis.

JUSTICE STEVENS, concurring in the judgment:

As I understand this case, it raises two different questions about the validity of California's statutory scheme. First, is Cal. Evid. Code Ann. § 621 unconstitutional because it prevents Michael and Victoria from obtaining a judicial determination that he is her biological father—even if no legal rights would be affected by that determination? Second, does the California statute deny appellants a fair opportunity to prove that Victoria's best interests would be served by granting Michael visitation rights?

On the first issue I agree with JUSTICE SCALIA that the Federal Constitution imposes no obligation upon a State to "declare facts unless some legal consequence hinges upon the requested declaration.". . .

On the second issue I do not agree with JUSTICE SCALIA's analysis. He seems to reject the possibility that a natural father might ever have a constitutionally protected interest in his relationship with a child whose mother was married to, and cohabiting with, another man at the time of the child's conception and birth. I think cases like *Stanley v. Illinois*, and *Caban v. Mohammed*, demonstrate that enduring "family" relationships may develop in unconventional settings. I therefore would not foreclose the possibility that a constitutionally protected relationship between a natural father and his child might exist in a case like this. Indeed, I am willing to assume for the purpose of deciding this case that Michael's relationship with Victoria is strong enough to give him a constitutional right to try to convince a trial judge that Victoria's best interest would be served by granting him visitation rights. I am satisfied, however, that the California statute, as applied in this case, gave him that opportunity.

Section 4601 of the California Civ. Code Annot. provides: "[R]easonable visitation rights [shall be awarded] to a parent unless it is shown that the visitation would be detrimental to the best interests of the child. In the discretion of the court, reasonable visitation rights may be granted *to any other person having an interest in the welfare of the child.*" (Emphasis added.)

The presumption established by § 621 denied Michael the benefit of the first sentence of § 4601 because, as a matter of law, he is not a "parent." It does not, however, prevent him from proving that he is an "other person having an interest in the welfare of the child." On its face, therefore, the statute plainly gave the trial judge the authority to grant Michael "reasonable visitation rights."

I recognize that my colleagues have interpreted § 621 as creating an absolute bar that would prevent a California trial judge from regarding the natural father as either a "parent" within the meaning of the first sentence of § 4601 *or* as "any other person" within the meaning of the second sentence. That is not only an unnatural reading of the statute's plain language, but it is also not consistent with the California courts' reading of the statute. [Discussion of California cases followed.—AU.] . . .

[The trial judge found] that "the existence of two (2) 'fathers' as male authority figures will confuse the child and be counter-productive to her best interests." In its opinion, the Court of Appeal also concluded that Michael "is not entitled to rights of visitation under § 4601."

Under the circumstances of the case before us, Michael was given a fair opportunity to show that he is Victoria's natural father, that he had developed a relationship with her, and that her interests would be served by granting him visitation rights. On the other hand, the record also shows that after its rather shaky start, the marriage between Carole and Gerald developed a stability that now provides Victoria with a loving and harmonious family home. In the circumstances of this case, I find nothing fundamentally unfair about the exercise of a judge's discretion that, in the end, allows the mother to decide whether her child's best interests would be served by allowing the natural father visitation privileges. . . . I am satisfied that the California statutory scheme is consistent with the Due Process Clause of the Fourteenth Amendment.

I therefore concur in the Court's judgment of affirmance.

JUSTICE BRENNAN, with whom JUSTICE MARSHALL and JUSTICE BLACKMUN join, dissenting:

In a case that has yielded so many opinions as has this one, it is fruitful to begin by emphasizing the common ground shared by a majority of this Court.

Five Members of the Court refuse to foreclose "the possibility that a natural father might ever have a constitutionally protected interest in his relationship with a child whose mother was married to, and cohabiting with, another man at the time of the child's conception and birth." (STEVENS, J., concurring in judgment). Five Justices agree that the flaw inhering in a conclusive presumption that terminates a constitutionally protected interest without any hearing whatsoever is a *procedural* one. (WHITE, J., dissenting); (STEVENS, J., concurring in judgment). Four Members of the Court agree that Michael H. has a liberty interest in his relationship with Victoria (WHITE, J., dissenting), and one assumes for purposes of this case that he does, see (STEVENS, J., concurring in judgment).

. . .Because the plurality opinion's exclusively historical analysis portends a significant and unfortunate departure from our prior cases and from sound constitutional decisionmaking, I devote a substantial portion of my discussion to it.

I

Once we recognized that the "liberty" protected by the Due Process Clause of the Fourteenth Amendment encompasses more than freedom from bodily restraint, today's plurality opinion emphasizes, the concept was cut loose from one natural limitation on its meaning. This innovation paved the way, so the plurality hints, for judges to substitute their own preferences for those of elected officials. Dissatisfied with this supposedly unbridled and uncertain state of affairs, the plurality casts about for another limitation on the concept of liberty.

It finds this limitation in "tradition." Apparently oblivious to the fact that this concept can be as malleable and as elusive as "liberty" itself, the plurality pretends that tradition places a discernible border around the Constitution. The pretense is seductive; it would be comforting to believe that a search for "tradition" involves nothing more idiosyncratic or complicated than poring through dusty volumes on American history. . . . Indeed, wherever I would begin to look for an interest "deeply rooted in the country's traditions," one thing is certain: I would not stop (as does the plurality) at Bracton, or Blackstone, or Kent, or even the American Law Reports in conducting my search. Because reasonable people can disagree about the content of particular traditions, and because they can disagree even about which traditions are relevant to the definition of "liberty," the plurality has not found the objective boundary that it seeks.

Even if we could agree, moreover, on the content and significance of particular traditions, we still would be forced to identify the point at which a tradition becomes firm enough to be relevant to our definition of liberty and the moment at which it becomes too obsolete to be relevant any longer. The plurality supplies no objective means by which we might make these determinations. Indeed, as soon as the plurality sees signs that the tradition upon which it bases its decision (the laws denying putative fathers like Michael standing to assert paternity) is crumbling, it shifts ground and says that the case has nothing to do with that tradition, after all. "[W]hat is at issue here," the plurality asserts after canvassing the law on paternity suits, "is not entitlement to a state pronouncement that Victoria was begotten by Michael." But that is precisely what is at issue here, and the plurality's last-minute denial of this fact dramatically illustrates the subjectivity of its own analysis.

It is ironic that an approach so utterly dependent on tradition is so indifferent to our precedents. . . .

It is not that tradition has been irrelevant to our prior decisions. Throughout our decisionmaking in this important area runs the theme that certain interests and practices—freedom from physical restraint, marriage, childbearing, childrearing, and others—form the core of our definition of "liberty." Our solicitude for these interests is partly the result of the fact that the Due Process Clause would seem an empty promise if it did not protect them, and partly the result of the historical and traditional importance of these interests in our society. . . .

Today's plurality, however, does not ask whether parenthood is an interest that historically has received our attention and protection; the answer to that question is too clear for dispute. Instead, the plurality asks whether the specific variety of parenthood under consideration—a natural father's relationship with a child whose mother is married to another man—has enjoyed such protection.

If we had looked to tradition with such specificity in past cases, many a decision would have reached a different result. [Here Brennan reviewed *Eisenstadt*, *Griswold*, *Stanley* and others.—AU.] . . .

The plurality's interpretive method is more than novel; it is misguided. It ignores the good reasons for limiting the role of "tradition" in interpreting the Constitution's deliberately capacious language. In the plurality's constitutional universe, we may not take notice of the fact that the original reasons for the conclusive presumption of paternity are out of place in a world in which blood tests can prove virtually beyond a shadow of a doubt who sired a particular child and in which the fact of illegitimacy no longer plays the burdensome and stigmatizing role it once did. . . .By describing the decisive question as whether Michael's and Victoria's interest is one that has been "traditionally *protected* by our society," (emphasis added), rather than one that society traditionally has thought important (with or without protecting it), and by suggesting that our sole function is to "*discern* the society's views," [Justice Scalia], at n. 6 (emphasis added), the plurality acts as if the only purpose of the Due Process Clause is to confirm the importance of interests already protected by a majority of the States. Transforming the protection afforded by the Due Process Clause into a redundancy mocks those who, with care and purpose, wrote the Fourteenth Amendment. . . .

The document that the plurality construes today is unfamiliar to me. It is not the living charter that I have taken to be our Constitution; it is instead a stagnant, archaic, hidebound document steeped in the prejudices and superstitions of a time long past. *This* Constitution does not recognize that times change, does not see that sometimes a practice or rule outlives its foundations. I cannot accept an interpretive method that does such violence to the charter that I am bound by oath to uphold.

II

. . . [W]e confront an interest—that of a parent and child in their relationship with each other—that was among the first that this Court acknowledged in its cases defining the "liberty" protected by the Constitution, see, *e. g., Meyer v. Nebraska*, at 399; *Skinner v. Oklahoma*, at 541; *Prince v. Massachusetts*, at 166 (1944), and I think I am safe in saying that no one doubts the wisdom or validity of those decisions. Where the interest under consideration is a parent-child relationship, we need not ask, over and over again, whether that interest is one that society traditionally protects. . . .

The . . . approach—. . . commanded by our prior cases and by common sense—is to ask whether the specific parent-child relationship under consideration is close enough to the interests that we already have protected to be deemed an aspect of "liberty" as well. On the facts before us, therefore, the question is . . . whether the relationship under consideration is sufficiently substantial to qualify as a liberty interest under our prior cases.

On four prior occasions, we have considered whether unwed fathers have a constitutionally protected interest in *their relationships with their children. See Stanley v. Illinois; Quilloin v. Walcott; Caban v. Mohammed*; and *Lehr v. Robertson*. . . .These cases have produced a unifying theme: although an unwed father's biological link to his child does not, in and of itself, guarantee him a constitutional stake in his relationship with that child, such a link combined with a substantial parent-child relationship will do so. "When an unwed father demonstrates a full commitment to the responsibilities of parenthood by 'com[ing] forward to participate in the rearing of his child,' . . . his interest in personal contact with his child acquires substantial protection under the Due Process Clause. At that point it may be said that he 'act[s] as a father toward his children.' " *Lehr v. Robertson*, at 261, quoting *Caban v. Mohammed*, at 392, 389, n. 7. This commitment is why Mr. Stanley and Mr. Caban won; why Mr. Quilloin and Mr. Lehr lost; and why Michael H. should prevail today. Michael H. is almost certainly Victoria D.'s natural father, has lived with her as her father, has contributed to her support, and has from the beginning sought to strengthen and maintain his relationship with her. . . .

The evidence is undisputed that Michael, Victoria, and Carole did live together as a family; that is, they shared the same household, Victoria called Michael "Daddy," Michael contributed to Victoria's support, and he is eager to continue his relationship with her. Yet they are not, in the plurality's view, a "unitary family," whereas Gerald, Carole, and Victoria do compose such a family. The only difference between these two sets of relationships, however, is the fact of marriage. . . . However, the very premise of *Stanley* and the cases following it is that marriage is not decisive . . . . In *Quilloin*, *Caban*, and *Lehr*. . ., the husband of the child's mother sought to adopt the child over the objections of the natural father. Significantly, our decisions in those cases in no way relied on the need to protect the marital family. Hence the plurality's claim that *Stanley*, *Quilloin*, *Caban*, and *Lehr* were about the "unitary family," as that family is defined by today's plurality, is surprising indeed. . .

. . . In announcing that what matters is not the father's ability to claim paternity, but his ability to obtain "substantive parental rights," the plurality turns procedural due process upside down. Michael's challenge in this Court does not depend on his ability ultimately to obtain visitation rights; it would be strange indeed if, before one could be granted a hearing, one were required to prove that one would prevail on the merits. The point of procedural due process is to give the litigant a fair chance at prevailing, not to ensure a particular substantive outcome. . . .

III

... California's interest, minute in comparison with a father's interest in his relationship with his child, cannot justify its refusal to hear Michael out on his claim that he is Victoria's father.

A

We must first understand the nature of the challenged statute: it is a law that stubbornly insists that Gerald is Victoria's father, in the face of evidence showing a 98 percent probability that her father is Michael. What Michael wants is a chance to show that he is Victoria's father. By depriving him of this opportunity, California prevents Michael from taking advantage of the best-interest standard embodied in § 4601 of California's Civil Code, which directs that parents be given visitation rights unless "the visitation would be detrimental to the best interests of the child." Cal. Civ. Code Ann. § 4601.

... When, as a result of § 621, a putative father may not establish his paternity, neither may he obtain discretionary visitation rights as a "nonparent" under § 4601. JUSTICE STEVENS' assertion to the contrary is mere wishful thinking....

[Here followed a discussion of California cases.—AU.]

... [I]n the case before us, the court's finding that "the existence of two (2) 'fathers' as male authority figures will confuse the child and be counterproductive to her best interests," is not an evaluation of the relationship between Michael and Victoria, but a restatement of the policies underlying § 621 itself. It may well be that the California courts' interpretation of § 4601 as precluding visitation rights for a putative father is "an unnatural reading" of that provision, but it is not for us to decide what California's statute means.

Section 621 as construed by the California courts thus cuts off the relationship between Michael and Victoria—a liberty interest protected by the Due Process Clause—without affording the least bit of process....

B

The question before us, therefore, is whether California has an interest so powerful that it justifies granting Michael no hearing before terminating his parental rights....

... Gerald D. explains that § 621 promotes marriage, maintains the relationship between the child and presumed father, and protects the integrity and privacy of the matrimonial family.... [But a]dmittedly, § 621 does not foreclose inquiry into the husband's fertility or virility—matters that are ordinarily thought of as the couple's private business. In this day and age, however, proving paternity by asking intimate and detailed questions about a couple's relationship would be decidedly anachronistic. Who on earth would choose this method of establishing fatherhood when blood tests prove it with far more certainty and far less fuss? The State's purported interest in protecting matrimonial privacy thus does not measure up to Michael's and Victoria's interest in maintaining their relationship with each other.

Make no mistake: to say that the State must provide Michael with a hearing to prove his paternity is not to express any opinion of the ultimate state of affairs between Michael and Victoria and Carole and Gerald. In order to change the current situation among these people, Michael first must convince a court that he is Victoria's father, and even if he is able to do this, he will be denied visitation rights if that would be in Victoria's best interests. See Cal. Civ. Code Ann. § 4601. It is elementary that a determination that a State must afford procedures before it terminates a given right is not a prediction about the end result of those procedures.

IV

The atmosphere surrounding today's decision is one of make-believe. Beginning with the suggestion that the situation confronting us here does not repeat itself every day in every corner of the country, moving on to the claim that it is tradition alone that supplies the details of the liberty that the Constitution protects, and passing finally to the notion that the Court always has recognized a cramped vision of "the family," today's decision lets stand California's pronouncement that Michael—whom blood tests show to a 98 percent probability to be Victoria's father—is not Victoria's father. When and if the Court awakes to reality, it will find a world very different from the one it expects.

. . .

JUSTICE WHITE, with whom JUSTICE BRENNAN joins, dissenting.

. . .

I

Like JUSTICES BRENNAN, MARSHALL, BLACKMUN, and STEVENS, I do not agree with the plurality opinion's conclusion that a natural father can never "have a constitutionally protected interest in his relationship with a child whose mother was married to, and cohabiting with, another man at the time of the child's conception and birth." (STEVENS, J., concurring in judgment). Prior cases here have recognized the liberty interest of a father in his relationship with his child. In none of these cases did we indicate that the father's rights were dependent on the marital status of the mother or biological father. The basic principle enunciated in the Court's unwed father cases is that an unwed father who has demonstrated a sufficient commitment to his paternity by way of personal, financial, or custodial responsibilities has a protected liberty interest in a relationship with his child. . . .

In the case now before us, Michael H. is not a father unwilling to assume his responsibilities as a parent. To the contrary, he is a father who has asserted his interests in raising and providing for his child since the very time of the child's birth. In contrast to the father in *Lehr*, Michael had begun to develop a relationship with his daughter. There is no dispute on this point. . . . There is a personal and emotional relationship between Michael and Victoria, who grew up calling him "Daddy." Michael held Victoria out as his daughter and contributed to the child's financial support. . . . "When an unwed father demonstrates a full commitment to the responsibilities of parenthood by 'com[ing] forward to participate in the rearing of his child,' *Caban*, at 392, his interest in personal contact with his child acquires substantial protection under the Due Process Clause." *Lehr*, at 261. The facts in this case satisfy the *Lehr* criteria, which focused on the relationship between father and child, not on the relationship between father and mother. Under *Lehr* a "mere biological relationship" is not enough, but in light of Carole's vicissitudes, what more could Michael have done? It is clear enough that Michael . . . has a liberty interest entitled to protection under the Due Process Clause of the Fourteenth Amendment.

II

California plainly denies Michael this protection, by refusing him the opportunity to rebut the State's presumption that the mother's husband is the father of the child. California law not only deprives Michael of a legal parent-child relationship with his daughter Victoria but even denies him the opportunity to introduce blood-test evidence to rebut the demonstrable fiction that Gerald is Victoria's father. . . .

The interest in protecting a child from the social stigma of illegitimacy lacks any real connection to the facts of a case where a father is seeking to establish, rather than repudiate, paternity. . . . It may be true that a child conceived in an extramarital relationship would be considered a "bastard" in the literal sense of the word, but whatever stigma remains in today's society is far less compelling in the context of a child of a married mother, especially

> when there is a father asserting paternity and seeking a relationship with his child. It is hardly rare in this world of divorce and remarriage for a child to live with the "father" to whom her mother is married, and still have a relationship with her biological father.
>
> The State's professed interest in the preservation of the existing marital unit is a more significant concern. To be sure, the intrusion of an outsider asserting that he is the father of a child whom the husband believes to be his own would be disruptive to say the least. On the facts of this case, however, Gerald was well aware of the liaison between Carole and Michael. . . .
>
> . . . I fail to see the fairness in the process established by the State of California and endorsed by the Court today. . . .
>
> . . . I respectfully dissent.

Case Questions

1. Had Carole been the unmarried person and Michael married to another woman, Carole's parental rights would have been unquestioned by the law. With the situation reversed (i.e., Michael the unmarried one) Michael's parental rights are utterly negated by the law. Should this be viewed as unjustified sex discrimination and thus a violation of "equal protection of the laws"? As a necessary accommodation to natural differences in the birth process and thus justified as serving important governmental interests?

2. Under this statute, either partner of the marital couple could mount a legal challenge to "their" child's paternity (although if it were the woman, her challenge had to be accompanied by that of her extramarital partner), but the extramarital biological father had no legal right to bring such a challenge on his own. Is this pattern a violation of equal protection in that it discriminates to an unconstitutional degree between the married and the unmarried?

3. Is this case best understood as presenting a conflict between the familial dimension of the right to privacy of the marital couple and parental dimension of the right to privacy of the biological father? Is such a conflict better left to legislatures or courts for resolution?

4. In interpreting California's § 4601, Justice Stevens read it as authorizing a judge to grant persons in Michael H.'s situation visitation rights if the child's best interest warranted it. (This is a standard similar to that typically applied to noncustodial divorced fathers.) Four justices (in dissent) argue that Stevens misinterprets the statute, that in fact it denies visitation rights to persons in Michael's situation and that, as thus (correctly) interpreted, the statute is unconstitutional. Does

this combination of five votes mean that in the future, to honor the Constitution, California must interpret § 4601 as Justice Stevens has done?

5. Justice Scalia refers snidely to "the relationship established between a married woman, her lover, and their child during a 3-month sojourn in St. Thomas, or during a subsequent 8-month period when, if he happened to be in Los Angeles, he stayed with her and the child." As Justice White describes this father-daughter relationship, the father had lived with his daughter, contributed to her support, held himself out as her father, and was known to her as "Daddy." Is this dramatic difference in describing the same situation more a manifestation of idiosyncratic judicial psychology than of legal analysis?

6. Justice White poses the question, "[I]n light of Carole's vicissitudes what more could Michael H. have done?" Is it wrong to let Michael's constitutional rights turn on "Carole's vicissitudes"? If Gerald and Carole were suddenly to die without a will, would Michael have any legal claim to custody or guardianship? Is his lack of claim a problem?

The Court's decision in this case demonstrates the extent to which assumptions about the traditional family—one father, one mother, and children—inform the law; another example of what Fineman has criticized as the practice of privileging the "sexual family."[66] In practice, however, alternative family arrangements abound. In addition to the longstanding recognition that children are sometimes raised by grandparents,[67] courts have begun to recognize "tri-parenting" relationships among married same-sex couples, their children and a sperm donor, egg donor, or surrogate, and legislatures in some states, such as California and Maine, have also acted to support family arrangements involving more than two parents.[68] State courts also have recognized that individuals who may not be a child's biological parent have rights to take part in raising and supporting those children. These individuals include grandparents, step-parents and men who sign birth certificates claiming parentage of children when they are born even though they are not the biological fathers of those children. There also have been instances when single women facing terminal illness have sought out adoptive parents for their children in preparation for their demise. Tri-parenting has been pursued to cement these arrangements. Non-biological parents who are given formal, legal recognition in children's lives may be referred to as "de-facto" or "psychological" parents by various courts.

The growing legal recognition of tri-parenting has emerged from various factors. Same-sex marriage and same-sex relationships are more widely accepted, and such couples, along with a minority of heterosexual couples, often resort to the kind of assistive technology that gives rise to tri-parenting. Moreover, the rate of voluntary single motherhood has risen sharply since the twentieth century, and such women, too may resort to assistive technology.[69]

In the case of *In re: M.C.*, which arose in California courts in 2011,[70] the biological mother of M.C. was in a domestic partnership with a woman, Irene, when she became pregnant. During a breakup between the two women, one of them, Melissa, lived with a man, Jesus, who impregnated her. Then they broke up and the two women reconciled. During the pregnancy the biological mother, Melissa, legally married her domestic partner, Irene, and gave birth in 2009. The birth mother is the only parent listed on the birth certificate even though her spouse was present at birth. The biological father did not seek visitation or custody after the birth of the child, did pay a small amount of child support and did seek to locate the child, but was thwarted by the mother. The case that unfolded involved domestic violence between the two married women, multiple breakups between them, drug abuse, new relationships and the incarceration of the biological mother, Melissa, for assault on Irene. The biological father of the child had moved to Oklahoma to pursue an employment opportunity and sought custody. In a 2010 jurisdictional hearing, the juvenile court ruled that under California statutes, the biological father was the presumed father, the married partner of the biological mother was the presumed mother and the biological mother to be the actual mother of the child. Since presumed parents were entitled to parental rights, in essence, the juvenile court recognized as a matter of law that the child had three parents. However, California law also limited the number of legal parents to two. In the words of Joanna Grossman, commenting on the case, "Stuck with the two-parent cap, the court in *M.C.* remanded the case for a determination as to whether Jesus or Irene had the stronger claim to parentage."[71]

In October 2013, California Governor Jerry Brown then signed into law a statute addressing the issues that *In re: M.C.* posed. The law lifted the longstanding, judicially-established two-parent limit. Senate Bill 274, Chapter 564:

> . . .would authorize a court to find that more than 2 persons with a claim to parentage, as specified, are parents if the court finds that recognizing only 2 parents would be detrimental to the child. The bill would direct the court, in making this determination, to consider all relevant factors, including, but not limited to, the harm of removing the child from a stable placement with a parent who has fulfilled the child's physical needs and the child's psychological needs for care and affection, and who has assumed that role for a substantial period of time.[72]

While Maine is the only other state to enact legislation recognizing that children may have more than two parents, courts in 10 other states have acknowledged that children may have more than two persons claiming parentage in one or more forms (e.g., biological, psychological, legal).[73]

PARENTS VERSUS GRANDPARENTS

The gender-neutral standards for awarding child custody—best interests of the child, primary caregiver preference, joint custody preference, etc.—formally apply only in cases that involve both parents. In disputes between a parent and a third party, the law has a built-in preference for the parent; in some jurisdictions, the parent can lose custody only if he or she is unfit. But when the third party is a grandparent—one not only older but better off and more settled than the parent—concepts like "interests" and "unfitness" may take on a life of their own.

Painter v. Bannister (1966)[74]

Jeanne Bannister and Harold Painter came from sharply divergent backgrounds. Jeanne grew up on a farm in Iowa. After graduating from college, she got a job with a newspaper in Anchorage, Alaska. Here she met Harold, a college dropout who was raised by foster parents. Married in 1957, they had two children. Jeanne Painter and their daughter were killed in an automobile accident in 1962. Harold struggled to care for Mark and support the family, and in 1963 he asked his former in-laws to take the boy, now 4, and they agreed. A year later Harold remarried and asked for the boy back; Dwight and Margaret Bannister refused to give Mark up. Harold sued and won in the trial court. The Bannisters appealed, Mark remaining with them for the time being by order of the state supreme court.

That court discounted not only the state's parental preference but also an accepted convention of appellate jurisdiction that we have encountered before: A higher court respects the original court's factual findings. Instead, the Iowa Supreme Court judges portrayed the case as a classic 1960s conflict between the bourgeoisie and the counterculture:

> We are not confronted with a situation where one of the contesting parties is not a fit or proper person. There is no criticism of either the Bannisters or their home. There is no suggestion in the record that Mr. Painter is morally unfit. It is obvious the Bannisters did not approve of their daughter's marriage to Harold Painter and do not want their grandchild reared under his guidance. The philosophies of life are entirely different. As stated by the psychiatrist who examined Mr.

Painter at the request of Bannisters' attorneys: "It is evident that there exists a large difference in ways of life and value systems between the Bannisters and Mr. Painter, but in this case there is no evidence that psychiatric instability is involved. Rather, these divergent life patterns seem to represent alternative normal adaptations."

It is not our prerogative to determine custody upon our choice of one of two ways of life within normal and proper limits and we will not do so. However, the philosophies are important as they relate to Mark and his particular needs.

The Bannister home provides Mark with a stable, dependable, conventional, middle-class, middlewestern background and an opportunity for a college education and profession, if he desires it. It provides a solid foundation and secure atmosphere. In the Painter home Mark would have more freedom of conduct and thought with an opportunity to develop his individual talents. It would be more exciting and challenging in many respects, but romantic, impractical and unstable.

We have... concluded that Mark's best interest demands that his custody remain with the Bannisters.....Mark has established a father-son relationship with Mr. Bannister, which he apparently had never had with his natural father. He is happy, well adjusted and progressing nicely in his development. We do not believe it is for Mark's best interest to take him out of this stable atmosphere in the face of warnings of dire consequences from an eminent child psychologist and send him to an uncertain future in his father's home. Regardless of our appreciation of the father's love for his child and his desire to have him with him, we do not believe we have the moral right to gamble with this child's future.[75]

Pamela Kay Bottoms v. Sharon Bottoms (1995)[76]

The case of *Bottoms v. Bottoms* addressed whether a mother's fitness to parent was compromised by her sexual orientation. Virginia resident Sharon Bottoms was sued by her mother Pamela Kay Bottoms in April 1993. Sharon Bottoms gave birth to her son in July 1991 at which time she was separated from the child's biological father to whom she was legally married. Before the child's first birthday, Sharon met April Wade. They soon moved in together and pledged their commitment to each other the following year.

Sharon struggled with parenthood and left her son Tyler with her mother for long periods. Soon before Tyler's second birthday Kay sued her daughter for custody of Tyler. Pamela Kay Bottoms was awarded custody of Tyler on the grounds that Sharon was an unfit parent due to Sharon being a lesbian who was in a committed relationship with another woman. Sharon was allowed to visit Tyler twice per week although Tyler was not allowed to go to his mother's home or have contact with April Wade. Sharon Bottoms appealed the decision. The Virginia Court of Appeals reversed the decision and granted Sharon Bottoms custody of her son. "The fact that a mother is a lesbian and has engaged in illegal sexual acts does not alone justify taking custody of a child from her and awarding the child to a non-parent." Pamela Kay Bottoms appealed the decision to the Virginia Supreme Court which awarded custody of Tyler back to her.

The Virginia Supreme Court denied that it was reinstating a ruling that awarded custody of 4-year-old Tyler Doustou to his maternal grandmother, Pamela Bottoms, because his mother was a lesbian. Other factors militated against Sharon Bottoms: her demonstrated inability to support herself, her frequent moves, her transitory relationships, and the fact that her partner, April Wade, admitted hitting Tyler. But Pamela Bottoms did not sue for custody or accuse Sharon of neglecting Tyler until Sharon moved in with April, her first female lover. (Tyler's father was absent.) The juvenile court gave Pamela custody; the appellate court reversed. The state supreme court accepted Pamela's allegation that Tyler "is currently living in an environment which is harmful to his mental and physical well being," and the recommendation of Tyler's guardian *ad litem*. The law's presumption that the child's best interests would be served by remaining with the parent, said the court, must yield to proof of parental unfitness. "[T]he appellate court should view the facts in the light most favorable to the party prevailing before the trial court. Accordingly, we shall summarize the facts in the light most favorable to the grandmother, resolving all conflicts in the evidence in her favor." From that perspective, the court said this.

> [t]he evidence plainly is sufficient, when applying the clear and convincing standard...to support the trial court's findings that the parental presumption has been rebutted, that the mother is an unfit custodian at this time, and that the child's best interests would be promoted by awarding custody to the grandmother...
>
> In the present case, the record shows a mother who, although devoted to her son, refuses to subordinate her own desires and priorities to the child's welfare. For example, the mother disappears for days without informing the child's custodian of her whereabouts. She moves

her residence from place to place, relying on others for support, and uses welfare funds to "do" her fingernails before buying food for the child. She has participated in illicit relationships with numerous men, acquiring a disease from one, and "sleeping" with men in the same room where the child's crib was located. To aid in her mobility, the mother keeps the child's suitcase packed so he can be quickly deposited at the grandmother's . . .

And, we shall not overlook the mother's relationship with Wade, and the environment in which the child would be raised if custody is awarded the mother. We have previously said that living daily under conditions stemming from active lesbianism practiced in the home may impose a burden upon a child by reason of the "social condemnation" attached to such an arrangement, which will inevitably afflict the child's relationships with its "peers and with the community at large." We do not retreat from that statement. . .[77]

In 1996, Sharon dropped her custody fight but asked for more extensive visitation rights with Tyler. The circuit court granted Sharon more time but ordered her to keep the boy away from April Wade. Since the two women still lived together, Wade had to leave the apartment when Tyler was present.[78]

Troxel v. Granville (2000)

Painter and *Bottoms* suggest that delegating child care to one's parents or in-laws may carry some risks. But custody battles are not the only difficulties inherent in intergenerational relationships. Grandparents run the risk of losing contact with their grandchildren if their child dies or becomes the noncustodial parent after a divorce. Parents, for their part, may want to cut off contact with people they dislike or distrust. It is easy to make a case for either.

After the death of their son, Jenifer and Gary Troxel sued Tommie Granville, the mother of the Troxels' two granddaughters, for visitation rights. Brad, the Troxels' son, had lived with his parents after separating from Tommie in 1991 until he committed suicide in 1993. During this time, he often brought the girls to visit his parents. Five months after Brad's death, Tommie told the Troxels that she wanted to reduce their contact with the girls. The Troxels went to court.

State legislatures, in which grandparents tend to be generously represented, have been solicitous of their interests. Laws allowing grandparents to obtain visitation rights exist in all 50 states. In Washington, where both families lived, the relevant statute provided, "Any person may petition the court for visitation rights at any time including, but not limited to, custody proceedings. The court may order visitation rights for any person when visitation may serve the best interest of the child whether or not there has been any change of circumstances." In response to the Troxels' petition, a state court ruling expanded their visitation time. Tommie Granville appealed. Meanwhile, she married, and her new husband adopted the children. The state supreme court ruled in her favor on the grounds that the visitation law conflicted with parents' constitutional right to raise their children. The U.S. Supreme Court did not go so far, ruling only that the law as applied in this case deprived Granville of her due process rights. The plurality opinion of Justice O'Connor, which allowed Tommie Granville control over this visitation issue, and which announced the judgment of the Court, is presented below. (Her opinion was joined by Rehnquist, Ginsburg and Breyer, with Souter and Thomas concurring in the result. Stevens, Scalia, and Kennedy dissented. All opinions other than O'Connor's are omitted here.)

TROXEL V. GRANVILLE
530 U.S. 57 (2000)

JUSTICE O'CONNOR announced the judgment of the Court and delivered [this] opinion...

Section 26.10.160(3) contains no requirement that a court accord the parent's decision any presumption of validity or any weight whatsoever. Instead, the Washington statute places the best-interest determination solely in the hands of the judge. Should the judge disagree with the parent's estimation of the child's best interests, the judge's view necessarily prevails. Thus, in practical effect, in the State of Washington a court can disregard and overturn *any* decision by a fit custodial parent concerning visitation whenever a third party affected by the decision files a visitation petition, based solely on the judge's determination of the child's best interests...

The problem here is not that the Washington Superior Court intervened, but that when it did so, it gave no special weight at all to Granville's determination of her daughters' best interests. More importantly, it appears that the Superior Court applied exactly the opposite presumption. In reciting its oral ruling after the conclusion of closing arguments, the Superior Court judge explained: "The burden is to show that it is in the best interest of the children to have some visitation and some quality time with their grandparents. I think in most situations a commonsensical approach [is that] it is normally in the best interest of the children to spend quality time with the grandparent,

> unless...there are some issues or problems involved wherein the grandparents, their lifestyles are going to impact adversely upon the children. That certainly isn't the case here from what I can tell."
>
> The judge's comments suggest that he presumed the grandparents' request should be granted unless the children would be "impacted adversely." In effect, the judge placed on Granville, the fit custodial parent, the burden of *disproving* that visitation would be in the best interest of her daughters...
>
> The decisional framework employed by the Superior Court directly contravened the traditional presumption that a fit parent will act in the best interest of his or her child. In that respect, the court's presumption failed to provide any protection for Granville's fundamental constitutional right to make decisions concerning the rearing of her own daughters...
>
> Because we rest our decision on the sweeping breadth of § 26.10.160(3) and the application of that broad, unlimited power in this case, we do not consider the primary constitutional question passed on by the Washington Supreme Court—whether the Due Process Clause requires all nonparental visitation statutes to include a showing of harm or potential harm to the child as a condition precedent to granting visitation. We do not, and need not, define today the precise scope of the parental due process right in the visitation context.[79]

It is likely that the Troxel precedent will remain the federal standard. In 2012, the U.S. Supreme Court refused to grant certiorari in an Alabama case where grandparents sought visitation of their minor grandchildren following the collapse of the relationship between the grandparents and their son, the father of the minor children, and his wife, the children's mother. The father and grandfather had owned a business together that failed after which the relationship between the parents and grandparents disintegrated. The parents denied continued contact between the grandchildren and their grandparents in response to the broken relationship. The Court's decision reinforces the notion that the parents' due process rights are favored while the burden of proof that visitation is in the child's best interest rests with the grandparents.[80]

PARENTS' RIGHTS VERSUS COMMUNITY RIGHTS: NATIVE AMERICANS AND FAMILY LAW

The anomalous constitutional status of Native Americans residing on reservations has given rise to some cases that ask the government to resolve conflicts between parents and their communities. The various tribal governments predated the U.S. Constitution and did not ratify it as their official government. Thus, the Bill of Rights, as such, does not describe the relation between tribal governments and tribe members. The U.S. government, however, intervened in 1968 to give the basic civil liberties set forth in that part of the Constitution to Native Americans by means of a federal law, the Indian Civil Rights Act. The text of this law appears in the case below.

Santa Clara Pueblo v. Martinez (1978)

The Santa Clara Pueblo tribe gave full membership to the children of two Santa Clarans and to children whose fathers were tribe members but not to the children of a Santa Claran mother. Julia Martinez, a Santa Clara Pueblo married since 1941 to a Navajo, had raised her family on the Santa Clara reservation. Her adult children still lived there, but they could not become tribe members, live on the reservation after her death, or inherit her property or her interest in the communal lands. According to Martinez's brief, "in 1968 Julia Martinez's now-deceased daughter Natalie, suffering from strokes associated with her terminal illness, was refused emergency medical treatment by the Indian Health Services. This was solely because her mother had previously been unable to obtain tribal recognition for her."[81] The invidious gender discrimination in the tribal laws was obvious: Fathers could confer membership on their children, but mothers could not. Julia and her daughter, Audrey, sued the tribe under the Indian Civil Rights Act of 1968 (ICRA), which in relevant part applied the equal protection guarantee and the right of habeas corpus to Native American tribes. The district court had ruled in favor of the tribe, but the circuit court had reversed.

SANTA CLARA PUEBLO ET AL. V. MARTINEZ ET AL.
436 U.S. 49 (1978)

MARSHALL, J., delivered the opinion of the Court, in which **BURGER, C. J.,** and **BRENNAN, STEWART, POWELL,** and **STEVENS, JJ.,** joined, and in all but Part III of which **REHNQUIST, J.,** joined:

This case requires us to decide whether a federal court may pass on the validity of an Indian tribe's ordinance denying membership to the children of certain female tribal members.

Petitioner Santa Clara Pueblo is an Indian tribe that has been in existence for over 600 years. Respondents, a female member of the tribe and her daughter . . . [are] seeking declaratory and injunctive relief against enforcement of a tribal ordinance denying membership in the tribe to children of female members who marry outside the tribe, while extending membership to children of male members who marry outside the tribe. Respondents claimed that this rule discriminates on the basis of both sex and ancestry in violation of Title I of the Indian Civil Rights Act of 1968 (ICRA), 25 U.S.C. §§ 1301–1303, which provides in relevant part that "[no] Indian tribe in exercising powers of self-government shall . . . deny to any person within its jurisdiction the equal protection of its laws." § 1302 (8).

Title I of the ICRA does not expressly authorize the bringing of civil actions for declaratory or injunctive relief to enforce its substantive provisions. The threshold issue in this case is thus whether the Act may be interpreted to impliedly authorize such actions, against a tribe or its officers, in the federal courts. For the reasons set forth below, we hold that the Act cannot be so read.

Two years before [Julia Martinez's] marriage, the Pueblo passed the membership ordinance here at issue, which bars admission of the Martinez children to the tribe because their father is not a Santa Claran. . . .

After unsuccessful efforts to persuade the tribe to change the membership rule, respondents filed this lawsuit in the United States District Court for the District of New Mexico, on behalf of themselves and others similarly situated. Petitioners moved to dismiss the complaint on the ground that the court lacked jurisdiction to decide intratribal controversies affecting matters of tribal self-government and sovereignty. The District Court rejected petitioners' contention, finding that jurisdiction was conferred by 28 U.S.C. § 1343 (4) and 25 U.S.C. § 1302 (8). The court apparently concluded, first, that the substantive provisions of Title I impliedly authorized civil actions for declaratory and injunctive relief, and second, that the tribe was not immune from such suit. Accordingly, the motion to dismiss was denied.

Following a full trial, the District Court found for petitioners on the merits. While acknowledging the relatively recent origin of the disputed rule, the District Court nevertheless found it to reflect traditional values of patriarchy still significant in tribal life. The court recognized the vital importance of respondents' interests, but also determined that membership rules were "no more or less than a mechanism of social . . . self-definition," and as such were basic to the tribe's survival as a cultural and economic entity. [402 F.Supp], at 15. In sustaining the ordinance's validity under the "equal protection clause" of the ICRA, 25 U.S.C. § 1302 (8), the District Court concluded that the balance to be struck between these competing interests was better left to the judgment of the Pueblo:

> [The] equal protection guarantee of the Indian Civil Rights Act should not be construed in a manner which would require or authorize this Court to determine which traditional values will promote cultural survival and should therefore be preserved. . . . Such a determination should be made by the people of Santa Clara; not only because they can best decide what values are important, but also because they must live with the decision every day. . . .
>
> . . . To abrogate tribal decisions, particularly in the delicate area of membership, for whatever 'good' reasons, is to destroy cultural identity under the guise of saving it." *Id.*, at 18–19.

On respondents' appeal, the Court of Appeals for the Tenth Circuit. . . found that "since [the ICRA] was designed to provide protection against tribal authority, the intention of Congress to allow suits against the tribe was an essential aspect [of the ICRA]." . . . The Court of Appeals disagreed, however, with the District Court's ruling on the merits. While recognizing that standards of analysis developed under the Fourteenth Amendment's Equal Protection Clause were not necessarily controlling in the interpretation of this statute, the Court of Appeals apparently concluded that because the classification was one based upon sex it was presumptively invidious and could be sustained only if justified by a compelling tribal interest. Because of the ordinance's recent vintage, and because in the court's view the rule did not rationally identify those persons who were emotionally and culturally Santa Clarans, the court held that the tribe's interest in the ordinance was not substantial enough to justify its discriminatory effect.

We granted certiorari, and we now reverse.

II

Indian tribes are "distinct, independent political communities, retaining their original natural rights" in matters of local self-government. *Worcester* v. *Georgia*, 6 Pet. 515, 559 (1832.) ...As separate sovereigns pre-existing the Constitution, tribes have historically been regarded as unconstrained by those constitutional provisions framed specifically as limitations on federal or state authority. Thus, in *Talton* v. *Mayes*, 163 U.S. 376 (1896), this Court held that the Fifth Amendment did not "[operate] upon" "the powers of local self-government enjoyed" by the tribes. *Id.*, at 384. In ensuing years the lower federal courts have extended the holding of *Talton* to other provisions of the Bill of Rights, as well as to the Fourteenth Amendment.

...As the Court in *Talton* recognized, however, Congress has plenary authority to limit, modify or eliminate the powers of local self-government which the tribes otherwise possess. *Ibid.* Title I of the ICRA represents an exercise of that authority. In 25 U.S.C. § 1302, Congress acted to modify the effect of *Talton* and its progeny by imposing certain restrictions upon tribal governments similar, but not identical, to those contained in the Bill of Rights and the Fourteenth Amendment.[8] ...

Petitioners concede that § 1302 modifies the substantive law applicable to the tribe; they urge, however, that Congress did not intend to authorize federal courts to review violations of its provisions except as they might arise on habeas corpus. They argue, further, that Congress did not waive the tribe's sovereign immunity from suit. Respondents, on the other hand, contend that § 1302 not only modifies the substantive law applicable to the exercise of sovereign tribal powers, but also authorizes civil suits for equitable relief against the tribe and its officers in federal courts. We consider these contentions first with respect to the tribe.

. . .

IV

...Although Congress clearly has power to authorize civil actions against tribal officers, and has done so with respect to habeas corpus relief in § 1303, a proper respect both for tribal sovereignty itself and for the plenary authority of Congress in this area cautions that we tread lightly in the absence of clear indications of legislative intent...

A

Two distinct and competing purposes are manifest in the provisions of the ICRA: In addition to its objective of strengthening the position of individual tribal members vis-a-vis the tribe, Congress also intended to promote the well-established federal "policy of furthering Indian self-government.". . .

Where Congress seeks to promote dual objectives in a single statute, courts must be more than usually hesitant to infer from its silence a cause of action that, while serving one legislative purpose, will disserve the other. Creation of a federal cause of action for the enforcement of rights created in Title I, however useful it might be in securing compliance with § 1302, plainly would be at odds with the congressional goal of protecting tribal self-government. . . .

Moreover, contrary to the reasoning of the court below, implication of a federal remedy in addition to habeas corpus is not plainly required to give effect to Congress' objective of extending constitutional norms to tribal self-government. Tribal forums are available to vindicate rights created by the ICRA, and § 1302 has the substantial and intended effect of changing the law which these forums are obliged to apply. Tribal courts have repeatedly been recognized as appropriate forums for the exclusive adjudication of disputes affecting important personal and property interests of both Indians and non-Indians.

B

. . .Congress considered and rejected proposals for federal review of alleged violations of the Act arising in a civil context. . . .[F]loor debates on the bill, indicate[ ] that the ICRA was generally understood to authorize federal judicial review of tribal actions only through the habeas corpus provisions of § 1303. These factors, together with Congress' rejection of proposals that clearly would have authorized causes of action other than habeas corpus, persuade us that Congress, aware of the intrusive effect of federal judicial review upon tribal self-government, intended to create only a limited mechanism for such review, namely, that provided for expressly in § 1303.

V

. . . Congress may also have considered that resolution of statutory issues under § 1302, and particularly those issues likely to arise in a civil context, will frequently depend on questions of tribal tradition and custom which tribal forums may be in a better position to evaluate than federal courts. . . .As is suggested by the District Court's opinion in this case, efforts by the federal judiciary to apply the statutory prohibitions of § 1302 in a civil context may substantially interfere with a tribe's ability to maintain itself as a culturally and politically distinct entity.

A tribe's right to define its own membership for tribal purposes has long been recognized as central to its existence as an independent political community. See *Roff* v. *Burney*, 168 U.S. 218 (1897); *Cherokee Intermarriage Cases*, 203 U.S. 76 (1906). Given the often vast gulf between tribal traditions and those with which federal courts are more intimately familiar, the judiciary should not rush to create causes of action that would intrude on these delicate matters.

...Congress retains authority expressly to authorize civil actions for injunctive or other relief to redress violations of § 1302, in the event that the tribes themselves prove deficient in applying and enforcing its substantive provisions. But unless and until Congress makes clear its intention to permit the additional intrusion on tribal sovereignty that adjudication of such actions in a federal forum would represent, we are constrained to find that § 1302 does not impliedly authorize actions for declaratory or injunctive relief against either the tribe or its officers.

The judgment of the Court of Appeals is, accordingly, *Reversed*.

Opinion Footnote

8 Section 1302 in its entirety provides that:

"No Indian tribe in exercising powers of self-government shall—

"(1) make or enforce any law prohibiting the free exercise of religion, or abridging the freedom of speech, or of the press, or the right of the people peaceably to assemble and to petition for a redress of grievances;

"(2) violate the right of the people to be secure in their persons, houses, papers, and effects against unreasonable search and seizures, nor issue warrants, but upon probable cause, supported by oath or affirmation, and particularly describing the place to be searched and the person or thing to be seized;

"(3) subject any person for the same offense to be twice put in jeopardy;

"(4) compel any person in any criminal case to be a witness against himself;

"(5) take any private property for a public use without just compensation;

"(6) deny to any person in a criminal proceeding the right to a speedy and public trial, to be informed of the nature and cause of the accusation, to be confronted with the witnesses against him, to have compulsory process for obtaining witnesses in his favor, and at his own expense to have the assistance of counsel for his defense;

"(7) require excessive bail, impose excessive fines, inflict cruel and unusual punishments, and in no event impose for conviction of any one offense any penalty or punishment greater than imprisonment for a term of six months or a fine of $500, or both;

"(8) *deny to any person within its jurisdiction the equal protection of its laws* or deprive any person of liberty or property without due process of law; [emphasis supplied]

"(9) pass any bill of attainder or ex post facto law; or

"(10) deny to any person accused of an offense punishable by imprisonment the right, upon request, to a trial by jury of not less than six persons."

Section 1301 is a definitional section, which provides, *inter alia*, that the "powers of self-government" shall include "all governmental powers possessed by an Indian tribe, executive, legislative and judicial, and all offices, bodies, and tribunals by and through which they are executed...." 25 U.S.C. § 1301 (2).

JUSTICE WHITE, dissenting:

The declared purpose of the Indian Civil Rights Act of 1968 (ICRA or Act), 25 U.S.C. §§ 1301–1341, is "to insure that the American Indian is afforded the broad constitutional rights secured to other Americans." S. Rep. No. 841, 90th Cong., 1st Sess., 6 (1967) (hereinafter Senate Report). The Court today, by denying a federal forum to Indians who allege that their rights under the ICRA have been denied by their tribes, substantially undermines the goal of the ICRA and in particular frustrates Title I's purpose of "[protecting] individual Indians from arbitrary and unjust actions of tribal governments." *Ibid.* Because I believe that implicit within Title I's declaration of constitutional rights is the authorization for an individual Indian to bring a civil action in federal court against tribal officials for declaratory and injunctive relief to enforce those provisions, I dissent.

Under 28 U.S.C. § 1343 (4), federal district courts have jurisdiction over "any civil action authorized by law to be commenced by any person ... [to] recover damages or to secure equitable or other relief under any Act of Congress providing for the protection of civil rights, including the right to vote." Because the ICRA is unquestionably a federal Act "providing for the protection of civil rights," the necessary inquiry is whether the Act authorizes the commencement of a civil action for such relief.

...We have previously identified the factors that are relevant in determining whether a private remedy is implicit in a statute not expressly providing one: whether the plaintiff is one of the class for whose especial benefit the statute was enacted; whether there is any indication of legislative intent either to create a remedy or to deny one; whether such a remedy is consistent with the underlying purposes of the statute; and whether the cause of action is one traditionally relegated to state law. *Cort* v. *Ash*, 422 U.S. 66, 78 (1975). Application of these factors in the present context indicates that a private cause of action under Title I of the ICRA should be inferred.

As the majority readily concedes, "respondents, American Indians living on the Santa Clara reservation, are among the class for whose especial benefit this legislation was enacted." In spite of this recognition of the congressional intent to provide these particular respondents with the guarantee of equal protection of the laws, the Court denies them access to the federal courts to enforce this right because it concludes that Congress intended habeas corpus to be the exclusive remedy under Title I. My reading of the statute and the legislative history convinces me that Congress did not intend to deny a private cause of action to enforce the rights granted under § 1302.

The ICRA itself gives no indication that the constitutional rights it extends to American Indians are to be enforced only by means of federal habeas corpus actions. On the contrary, since several of the specified rights are most frequently invoked in noncustodial situations, the natural assumption is that some remedy other than habeas corpus must be contemplated. This assumption is not dispelled by the fact that the Congress chose to enumerate specifically the rights granted under § 1302, rather than to state broadly, as was originally proposed, that "any Indian tribe in exercising its powers of local self-government shall be subject to the same limitations and restraints as those which are imposed on the Government of the United States by the United States Constitution." S. 961, 89th Cong., 1st Sess. (1965). The legislative history reflects that the decision "to indicate in more specific terms the constitutional protections the American Indian possesses in relation to his tribe," was made in recognition of the "peculiarities of the Indian's economic and social condition, his customs, his beliefs, and his attitudes . . . ." Subcommittee on Constitutional Rights of the Senate Committee on the Judiciary, *Constitutional Rights of the American Indian: Summary Report of Hearings and Investigations pursuant to S. Res. 194*, 89th Cong., 2d Sess., 25, 9 (Comm. Print 1966) (hereinafter *Summary Report*). While I believe that the uniqueness of the Indian culture must be taken into consideration in applying the constitutional rights granted in § 1302, I do not think that it requires insulation of official tribal actions from federal-court scrutiny. Nor do I find any indication that Congress so intended.

The inferences that the majority draws from various changes Congress made in the originally proposed legislation are to my mind unsupported by the legislative history. . . .

. . . Several witnesses appearing before the Senate Subcommittee testified concerning deprivations of their rights by tribal authorities and their inability to gain relief. Mr. Frank Takes Gun, President of the Native American Church, for example, stated that "the Indian is without an effective means to enforce whatever constitutional rights he may have in tribal proceedings instituted to deprive him of liberty or property. While I suppose that abstractedly *[sic]* we might be said to enjoy [certain] rights . . ., the blunt fact is that unless the tribal court elects to confer that right upon us we have no way of securing it." 1965

> Hearings 164. Miss Emily Schuler, who accompanied a former Governor of the Isleta Pueblo to the hearings, echoed these concerns. She complained that "[the] people get governors and sometimes they get power hungry and then the people have no rights at all," to which Senator Ervin responded: " 'Power hungry' is a pretty good shorthand statement to show why the people of the United States drew up a Constitution. They wanted to compel their rulers to stay within the bounds of that Constitution and not let that hunger for power carry them outside it." *Id.*, at 264.
>
> Given Congress' concern about the deprivations of Indian rights by tribal authorities, I cannot believe, as does the majority, that it desired the enforcement of these rights to be left up to the very tribal authorities alleged to have violated them. In the case of the Santa Clara Pueblo, for example, both legislative and judicial powers are vested in the same body, the Pueblo Council. To suggest that this tribal body is the "appropriate" forum for the adjudication of alleged violations of the ICRA is to ignore both reality and Congress' desire to provide a means of redress to Indians aggrieved by their tribal leaders.
>
> ...Because I believe that respondents stated a cause of action over which the federal courts have jurisdiction, I would proceed to the merits of their claim. Accordingly, I dissent from the opinion of the Court.

Case Questions

1. Catharine MacKinnon (see Chapter 7) remarked, "I find *Martinez* a difficult case on a lot of levels, and I don't usually find cases difficult."[82] Do you agree that this case is difficult to understand or to resolve? Why or why not?

2. How, and to what extent, would a decision in favor of Julia Martinez and her daughter threaten the tribe's autonomy?

3. Discuss the significance of this case in the context of federal-tribal relations.

Mississippi Choctaw v. Holyfield (1989)

By removing all the rights secured by the ICRA except habeas corpus from the supervision of federal courts, *Martinez* drastically weakened the ICRA. *Mississippi Choctaw Indians v. Holyfield* did not even mention it. *Holyfield* presents a situation in which the mother and father are trying to give up parental rights in circumstances of their own choosing. They were challenged in this attempt by their tribal government, and the Supreme Court ruled that federal law gives the tribe rather than the parents control over this decision. The justices limited their discussion to a federal statute, the 1978 Indian Child Welfare Act, but the constitutional rights[83] implied in the 1968 Indian Civil Rights Act lurk in the background.

The Court's resolution of the case, enabling tribal governments to forbid parents to place their children for adoption with certain kinds of (i.e., non-Native American) parents, would seem to be of dubious constitutionality outside the Native American context. In other words if a pregnant Anglo woman were to travel out of her home state to give up her child for adoption in the second state because she preferred its adoption procedures, her rights of parental privacy would seem to permit her that option. The comparable right to travel 200 miles away from her reservation in order to give up her twins for adoption to a family that was not Native American was denied to "J.B." (and to her companion, the twins' father, "W.J.") by the U.S. Supreme Court in this case.[84]

The Indian Child Welfare Act of 1978 established tribal court jurisdiction over adoptive and foster care placement of reservation Native American children and established a preference for Native American parents against non-Native American parents, and tribal over nontribal, for those placements. For Native Americans living off a reservation, a tribal court is permitted to take jurisdiction away from a state court in a proceeding for either foster care or adoptive placement of the Native American child, "absent objection by either parent."

In the *Choctaw* case both parents (unwed reservation Native Americans) had traveled 200 miles away from the reservation, and stayed there for ten days, so that their twins would be born outside tribal jurisdiction. The parents then intentionally placed the babies for adoption in a non-Native American home. Three years later the tribal court intervened and voided the Mississippi adoption order, claiming that its own jurisdiction followed the parents and covered their children. The Chancery Court that had first placed the children overruled the tribal court on the grounds that the twins, in accord with the wishes of their biological parents, had been born off of the reservation and had been promptly placed for adoption. The Court thus ruled that the twins had never been under the jurisdiction of the tribal court. The Mississippi Supreme Court had affirmed,[85] and the tribal government had then appealed to the U.S. Supreme Court.

The Court majority of six upheld the tribe's reading of the statute. The dissenters (Stevens, Rehnquist, and Kennedy) insisted that the statute was meant to inhibit state removal of Native American children *against* the will of their parents, not to thwart the will of the parents. The Court majority argued that the statute aimed at preserving specifically *tribal* rights over Native American children. Neither group made any reference to any fundamental constitutional right of either the Native American or the adoptive parents, the Holyfields, who for years had been under the impression they had had full parental rights to these twins. No one on the Court raised the question whether this statute denied to Native American mothers and fathers constitutional rights that could be denied to no other Americans.

> ### MISSISSIPPI BAND OF CHOCTAW INDIANS V. HOLYFIELD
> 490 U.S. 30 (1989)
>
> **JUSTICE BRENNAN delivered the opinion of the court.**
>
> This appeal requires us to construe the provisions of the Indian Child Welfare Act that establish exclusive tribal jurisdiction over child custody proceedings involving Indian children domiciled on the tribe's reservation.
>
> **I**
>
> **A**
>
> The Indian Child Welfare Act of 1978 (ICWA), 92 Stat. 3069, 25 U.S.C. §§ 1901–1963 was the product of rising concern in the mid-1970's over the consequences to Indian children, Indian families, and Indian tribes of abusive child welfare practices that resulted in the separation of large numbers of Indian children from their families and tribes through adoption or foster care placement, usually in non-Indian homes. Senate oversight hearings in 1974 yielded numerous examples, statistical data, and expert testimony documenting what one witness called "[t]he wholesale removal of Indian children from their homes, . . . the most tragic aspect of Indian life today." Indian Child Welfare Program, *Hearings before the Subcommittee on Indian Affairs of the Senate Committee on Interior and Insular Affairs*, 93d Cong., 2d Sess., 3 (statement of William Byler) (hereinafter 1974 Hearings). Studies undertaken by the Association on American Indian Affairs in 1969 and 1974, and presented in the Senate hearings, showed that 25 to 35% of all Indian children had been separated from their families and placed in adoptive families, foster care, or institutions. *Id.*, at 15; see also H. R. Rep. No. 95-1386, p. 9 (1978) (hereinafter House Report). Adoptive placements counted significantly in this total: in the State of Minnesota, for example, one in eight Indian children under the age of 18 was in an adoptive home, and during the year 1971–1972 nearly one in every four infants under one year of age was placed for adoption. The adoption rate of Indian children was eight times that of non-Indian children. Approximately 90% of the Indian placements were in non-Indian homes. 1974 Hearings, at 75–83. A number of witnesses also testified to the serious adjustment problems encountered by such children during adolescence, as well as the impact of the

adoptions on Indian parents and the tribes themselves. See generally 1974 Hearings.

Further hearings, covering much the same ground, were held during 1977 and 1978 on the bill that became the ICWA. While much of the testimony again focused on the harm to Indian parents and their children who were involuntarily separated by decisions of local welfare authorities, there was also considerable emphasis on the impact on the tribes themselves of the massive removal of their children. For example, Mr. Calvin Isaac, Tribal Chief of the Mississippi Band of Choctaw Indians and representative of the National Tribal Chairmen's Association, testified as follows:

> "Culturally, the chances of Indian survival are significantly reduced if our children, the only real means for the transmission of the tribal heritage, are to be raised in non-Indian homes and denied exposure to the ways of their People. Furthermore, these practices seriously undercut the tribes' ability to continue as self-governing communities. Probably in no area is it more important that tribal sovereignty be respected than in an area as socially and culturally determinative as family relationships." 1978 Hearings, at 193.

See also *id.*, at 62. Chief Isaac also summarized succinctly what numerous witnesses saw as the principal reason for the high rates of removal of Indian children:

> "One of the most serious failings of the present system is that Indian children are removed from the custody of their natural parents by nontribal government authorities who have no basis for intelligently evaluating the cultural and social premises underlying Indian home life and childrearing. Many of the individuals who decide the fate of our children are at best ignorant of our cultural values, and at worst contemptful of the Indian way and convinced that removal, usually to a non-Indian household or institution, can only benefit an Indian child." *Id.*, at 191-192.

. . . At the heart of the ICWA are its provisions concerning jurisdiction over Indian child custody proceedings. Section 1911 lays out a dual jurisdictional scheme. Section 1911(a) establishes exclusive jurisdiction in the tribal courts for proceedings concerning an Indian child "who resides or is domiciled within the reservation of such tribe." . . . Section 1911(b), on the other hand, creates concurrent but presumptively tribal jurisdiction in the case of children not domiciled on the reservation: on petition of either parent or the tribe, state-court proceedings for foster care placement or termination of parental rights are to be transferred to the tribal court, except in cases of "good cause," objection by either parent, or declination of jurisdiction by the tribal court.

...The most important substantive requirement imposed on state courts is that of § 1915(a), which, absent "good cause" to the contrary, mandates that adoptive placements be made preferentially with (1) members of the child's extended family, (2) other members of the same tribe, or (3) other Indian families.

The ICWA thus, in the words of the House Report accompanying it, "seeks to protect the rights of the Indian child as an Indian and the rights of the Indian community and tribe in retaining its children in its society." House Report, at 23. It does so by establishing "a Federal policy that, where possible, an Indian child should remain in the Indian community," *ibid*, and by making sure that Indian child welfare determinations are not based on "a white, middle-class standard which, in many cases, forecloses placement with [an] Indian family." *Id.*, at 24.

II

...The sole issue in this case is, as the Supreme Court of Mississippi recognized, whether the twins were "domiciled" on the reservation.

A

The meaning of "domicile" in the ICWA is, of course, a matter of Congress' intent. The ICWA itself does not define it. The initial question we must confront is whether there is any reason to believe that Congress intended the ICWA definition of "domicile" to be a matter of state law.

We... think it beyond dispute that Congress intended a uniform federal law of domicile for the ICWA.

B

It remains to give content to the term "domicile" in the circumstances of the present case. The holding of the Supreme Court of Mississippi that the twin babies were not domiciled on the Choctaw Reservation appears to have rested on two findings of fact by the trial court: (1) that they had never been physically present there, and (2) that they were "voluntarily surrendered" by their parents.

"Domicile" is, of course, a concept widely used in both federal and state courts for jurisdiction and conflict-of-laws purposes, and its meaning is generally uncontroverted... "Domicile" is not necessarily synonymous with "residence," and one can reside in one place but be domiciled in another. For adults, domicile is established by physical presence in a place in connection with a certain state of mind concerning one's intent to remain there.

. . . .Since most minors are legally incapable of forming the requisite intent to establish a domicile, their domicile is determined by that of their parents. *Yarborough* v. *Yarborough*, 290 U.S. 202, 211 (1933).

. . .Under these principles, it is entirely logical that "[o]n occasion, a child's domicile of origin will be in a place where the child has never been."

It is undisputed in this case that the domicile of the mother (as well as the father) has been, at all relevant times, on the Choctaw Reservation. Thus, it is clear that at their birth the twin babies were also domiciled on the reservation, even though they themselves had never been there. . .

Nor can the result be any different simply because the twins were "voluntarily surrendered" by their mother. Tribal jurisdiction under § 1911(a) was not meant to be defeated by the actions of individual members of the tribe, for Congress was concerned not solely about the interests of Indian children and families, but also about the impact on the tribes themselves of the large numbers of Indian children adopted by non-Indians.

In addition, it is clear that Congress' concern over the placement of Indian children in non-Indian homes was based in part on evidence of the detrimental impact on the children themselves of such placements outside their culture. Congress determined to subject such placements to the ICWA's jurisdictional and other provisions, even in cases where the parents consented to an adoption, because of concerns going beyond the wishes of individual parents. As the 1977 Final Report of the congressionally established American Indian Policy Review Commission stated, in summarizing these two concerns, "[r]emoval of Indian children from their cultural setting seriously impacts a long-term tribal survival and has damaging social and psychological impact on many individual Indian children." Senate Report, at 52.

These congressional objectives make clear that a rule of domicile that would permit individual Indian parents to defeat the ICWA's jurisdictional scheme is inconsistent with what Congress intended. See *In re Adoption of Child of Indian Heritage*, 111 N. J. 155, 168–171, 543 A. 2d 925, 931–933 (1988). The appellees in this case argue strenuously that the twins' mother went to great lengths to give birth off the reservation so that her children could be adopted by the Holyfields. But that was precisely part of Congress' concern. Permitting individual members of the tribe to avoid tribal exclusive jurisdiction by the simple expedient of giving birth off the reservation would, to a large extent, nullify the purpose the ICWA was intended to accomplish.

III

We are not unaware that over three years have passed since the twin babies were born and placed in the Holyfield home, and that a court deciding their fate today is not writing on a blank slate in the same way it would have in January 1986. Three years' development of family ties cannot be undone, and a separation at this point would doubtless cause considerable pain.

Whatever feelings we might have as to where the twins should live, however, it is not for us to decide that question. We have been asked to decide the legal question of *who* should make the custody determination concerning these children—not what the outcome of that determination should be. The law places that decision in the hands of the Choctaw tribal court. Had the mandate of the ICWA been followed in 1986, of course, much potential anguish might have been avoided, and in any case the law cannot be applied so as automatically to "reward those who obtain custody, whether lawfully or otherwise, and maintain it during any ensuing (and protracted) litigation." [*In re Adoption of*] *Halloway*, 732 P. 2d 962 at 972 [1986]. It is not ours to say whether the trauma that might result from removing these children from their adoptive family should outweigh the interest of the Tribe—and perhaps the children themselves—in having them raised as part of the Choctaw community. Rather, "we must defer to the experience, wisdom, and compassion of the [Choctaw] tribal courts to fashion an appropriate remedy." *Ibid.*

The judgment of the Supreme Court of Mississippi is reversed.

JUSTICE STEVENS, with whom THE CHIEF JUSTICE and JUSTICE KENNEDY join, dissenting:

The parents of these twin babies unquestionably expressed their intention to have the state court exercise jurisdiction over them. J. B. gave birth to the twins at a hospital 200 miles from the reservation, even though a closer hospital was available. Both parents gave their written advance consent to the adoption and, when the adoption was later challenged by the Tribe, they reaffirmed their desire that the Holyfields adopt the two children. As the Mississippi Supreme Court found, "the parents went to some efforts to prevent the children from being placed on the reservation as the mother arranged for their birth and adoption in Gulfport Memorial Hospital, Harrison County, Mississippi." . . .

To preclude parents domiciled on a reservation from deliberately invoking the adoption procedures of state court, the Court gives "domicile" a meaning that Congress could not have intended and distorts the delicate balance between individual rights and group rights recognized by the ICWA.

... The ICWA was passed in 1978 in response to congressional findings that "an alarmingly high percentage of Indian families are broken up by the *removal*, often unwarranted, of their children from them by nontribal public and private agencies," and that "the States, exercising their recognized jurisdiction over Indian child custody proceedings through administrative and judicial bodies, have often failed to recognize the essential tribal relations of Indian people and the cultural and social standards prevailing in Indian communities and families." 25 U.S.C. §§ 1901(4), (5) (emphasis added). The Act is thus primarily addressed to the unjustified removal of Indian children from their families through the application of standards that inadequately recognized the distinct Indian culture.

...The Act gives Indian tribes certain rights, not to restrict the rights of parents of Indian children, but to complement and help effect them. The Indian tribe may petition to transfer an action in state court to the tribal court, but the Indian parent may veto the transfer. § 1911(b). The Act provides for a tribal right of notice and intervention in involuntary proceedings but not in voluntary ones. §§ 1911(c), 1912(a). Finally, the tribe may petition the court to set aside a parental termination action upon a showing that the provisions of the ICWA that are designed to protect parents and Indian children have been violated. § 1914.

....Although parents of Indian children are shielded from the exercise of state jurisdiction when they are temporarily off the reservation, the Act also reflects a recognition that allowing the tribe to defeat the parents' deliberate choice of jurisdiction would be conducive neither to the best interests of the child nor to the stability and security of Indian tribes and families. Section 1911(b), providing for the exercise of concurrent jurisdiction by state and tribal courts when the Indian child is not domiciled on the reservation, gives the Indian parents a veto to prevent the transfer of a state-court action to tribal court. "By allowing the Indian parents to 'choose' the forum that will decide whether to sever the parent-child relationship, Congress promotes the security of Indian families by allowing the Indian parents to defend in the court system that most reflects the parents' familial standards." Jones, 21 *Ariz. L. Rev.*, at 1141....

If J. B. and W. J. had established a domicile off the reservation, the state courts would have been required to give effect to their choice of jurisdiction; there should not be a different result when the parents have not changed their

> own domicile, but have expressed an unequivocal intent to establish a domicile for their children off the reservation. The law of abandonment, as enunciated by the Mississippi Supreme Court in this case, does not defeat, but serves the purposes of, the Act. An abandonment occurs when a parent deserts a child and places the child with another with an intent to relinquish all parental rights and obligations. *Restatement (Second) of Conflict of Laws* § 22, Comment *e* (1971) (hereinafter *Restatement*); *In re Adoption of Halloway*, 732 P. 2d 962, 966 (Utah 1986). If a child is abandoned by his mother, he takes on the domicile of his father; if the child is abandoned by his father, he takes on the domicile of his mother. *Restatement* § 22, Comment *e*. . . .
>
> The ICWA expresses the intent that exclusive tribal jurisdiction is not so frail that it should be defeated as soon as the Indian child steps off the reservation. Similarly, when the child is abandoned by one parent to a person off the reservation, the tribe and the other parent domiciled on the reservation may still have an interest in the exercise of exclusive jurisdiction. That interest is protected by the rule that a child abandoned by one parent takes on the domicile of the other. But when an Indian child is deliberately abandoned by both parents to a person off the reservation, no purpose of the ICWA is served by closing the state courthouse door to them.
>
> . . .The Court concludes its opinion with the observation that whatever anguish is suffered by the Indian children, their natural parents, and their adoptive parents because of its decision today is a result of their failure to initially follow the provisions of the ICWA. By holding that parents who are domiciled on the reservation cannot voluntarily avail themselves of the adoption procedures of state court and that all such proceedings will be void for lack of jurisdiction, however, the Court establishes a rule of law that is virtually certain to ensure that similar anguish will be suffered by other families in the future. Because that result is not mandated by the language of the ICWA and is contrary to its purposes, I respectfully dissent.

Case Questions

1. The Utah Supreme Court, whose reasoning Justice Brennan follows, argues that this statute put Native American tribal rights in children "on a parity" with the interests of the parents in their children. Since the parents' wishes are being overridden by the tribe here, does "parity" seem like an accurate description?

2. Even fundamental constitutional rights can be restricted to the degree that the restriction is necessitated by a "compelling governmental interest." Is this decision best understood as suggesting that tribal preservation and avoiding adjustment

difficulties for the adopted Native American child amount to compelling interests? Ought the biological parents be allowed to choose for their child between these potential adjustment difficulties in non-Native American families and the difficulties of life on the reservation?

3. The federal government enacted the Multi-Ethnic Placement Act in 1994. That law forbids race, color and national origin, or RCNO, from being considered when placing children in foster care and adoptive homes. One exception to that prohibition is when "individualized determination that the facts and circumstances of the specific case require the consideration of RCNO in order to advance the best interests of the specific child. Any placement policy or action that takes RCNO into account is subject to strict scrutiny." In essence, violating RCNO is subject to strict scrutiny. On what grounds do you believe that violating RCNO would pass a strict scrutiny test? For instance, would the argument that placing Black babies with Black adoptive families helps them learn to cope with racism amount to a compelling interest that necessitates such placement?

4. Does the fact that Native Americans who wish to avoid tribal courts can simply establish domicile off the reservation before giving birth mean that the restrictions of the ICWA as now interpreted are only minor obstacles? Consider Justice Stevens's dissent on this point.

Adoptive Couple v. Baby Girl (2013)

More recently, the U.S. Supreme Court was asked to evaluate how the ICWA applies to children born to one Native American parent and one non-Native parent who are then put up for adoption. In *Adoptive Couple v. Baby Girl* (570 U.S. 637, 2013), the Justices had to determine if a non-custodial Native American biological father could invoke the ICWA to block the adoption of his daughter. In this instance, Christina Maldonado, the child's Latina mother, entered into an adoption contract with a non-Native American family. The child's father Dusten Brown, a member of the Cherokee Nation, then sued under the ICWA to stop the adoption and requested full custody. Brown won at the state trial and supreme courts, after which he obtained custody of the child. The adoptive parents appealed to the U.S. Supreme Court. At the time of this decision, "Baby Girl" was three months shy of her fourth birthday.

ADOPTIVE COUPLE V. BABY GIRL
570 U.S. 637 (2013)

JUSTICE ALITO delivered the opinion of the Court.

This case is about a little girl (Baby Girl) who is classified as an Indian because she is 1.2% (3/256) Cherokee. Because Baby Girl is classified in this way, the South Carolina Supreme Court held that certain provisions of the federal Indian Child Welfare Act of 1978 required her to be taken, at the age of 27 months, from the only parents she had ever known and handed over to her biological father, who had [earlier] attempted to relinquish his parental rights and who had no prior contact with the child. The provisions of the federal statute at issue here do not demand this result.

Contrary to the State Supreme Court's ruling, we hold that 25 U.S.C. § 1912(f)—which bars involuntary termination of a parent's rights in the absence of a heightened showing that serious harm to the Indian child is likely to result from the parent's "continued custody" of the child—does not apply when, as here, the relevant parent never had custody of the child. We further hold that § 1912(d)—which conditions involuntary termination of parental rights with respect to an Indian child on a showing that remedial efforts have been made to prevent the "breakup of the Indian family"—is inapplicable when, as here, the parent abandoned the Indian child before birth and never had custody of the child. Finally, we clarify that § 1915(a), which provides placement preferences for the adoption of Indian children, does not bar a non-Indian family like Adoptive Couple from adopting an Indian child when no other eligible candidates have sought to adopt the child. We accordingly reverse the South Carolina Supreme Court's judgment and remand for further proceedings.

. . .

In this case, Birth Mother (who is predominantly Hispanic) and Biological Father (who is a member of the Cherokee Nation) became engaged in December 2008. One month later, Birth Mother informed Biological Father, who lived about four hours away, that she was pregnant. After learning of the pregnancy, Biological Father asked Birth Mother to move up the date of the wedding. He also refused to provide any financial support until after the two had married. The couple's relationship deteriorated, and Birth Mother broke off the engagement in May 2009. In June, Birth Mother sent Biological Father a text message asking if he would rather pay child support or relinquish his parental rights. Biological Father responded via text message that he relinquished his rights.

Birth Mother then decided to put Baby Girl up for adoption. Because Birth Mother believed that Biological Father had Cherokee Indian heritage, her attorney contacted the Cherokee Nation to determine whether Biological Father was formally enrolled. The inquiry letter misspelled Biological Father's first name and incorrectly stated his birthday, and the Cherokee Nation responded that, based on the information provided, it could not verify Biological Father's membership in the tribal records.

Working through a private adoption agency, Birth Mother selected Adoptive Couple, non-Indians living in South Carolina, to adopt Baby Girl. Adoptive Couple supported Birth Mother both emotionally and financially throughout her pregnancy. Adoptive Couple was present at Baby Girl's birth in Oklahoma on September 15, 2009, and Adoptive Father even cut the umbilical cord. The next morning, Birth Mother signed forms relinquishing her parental rights and consenting to the adoption. Adoptive Couple initiated adoption proceedings in South Carolina a few days later, and returned there with Baby Girl. After returning to South Carolina, Adoptive Couple allowed Birth Mother to visit and communicate with Baby Girl.

It is undisputed that, for the duration of the pregnancy and the first four months after Baby Girl's birth, Biological Father provided no financial assistance to Birth Mother or Baby Girl, even though he had the ability to do so. Indeed, Biological Father "made no meaningful attempts to assume his responsibility of parenthood" during this period. App. to Pet. for Cert. (Sealed; internal quotation marks omitted).

Approximately four months after Baby Girl's birth, Adoptive Couple served Biological Father with notice of the pending adoption. (This was the first notification that they had provided to Biological Father regarding the adoption proceeding.) Biological Father signed papers stating that he accepted service and that he was "not contesting the adoption." App. But Biological Father later testified that, at the time he signed the papers, he thought that he was relinquishing his rights to Birth Mother, not to Adoptive Couple.

. . .

It is undisputed that, had Baby Girl not been 3/256 Cherokee, Biological Father would have had no right to object to her adoption under South Carolina law. . . .

Our reading of § 1912(f) comports with the statutory text demonstrating that the primary mischief the ICWA was designed to counteract was the unwarranted *removal* of Indian children from Indian families due to the cultural insensitivity and biases of social workers and state courts. The statutory text expressly highlights the primary problem that the statute was intended to solve: "an alarmingly high percentage of Indian families [were being] broken up by the *removal*, often unwarranted, of their children from them by nontribal public and private agencies.". . . In sum, when, as here, the adoption of an Indian child is voluntarily and lawfully initiated by a non-Indian parent with sole custodial rights, the ICWA's primary goal of preventing the unwarranted removal of Indian children and the dissolution of Indian families is not implicated.

Under our reading of § 1912(f), Biological Father should not have been able to invoke § 1912(f) in this case, because he had never had legal or physical custody of Baby Girl as of the time of the adoption proceedings. As an initial matter, it is undisputed that Biological Father never had *physical* custody of Baby Girl. And as a matter of both South Carolina and Oklahoma law, Biological Father never had *legal* custody either. . . .

In sum, the South Carolina Supreme Court erred in finding that § 1912(f) barred termination of Biological Father's parental rights.

B

Section 1912(d) provides that "[a]ny party" seeking to terminate parental rights to an Indian child under state law "shall satisfy the court that active efforts have been made to provide remedial services and rehabilitative programs designed *to prevent the breakup of the Indian family* and that these efforts have proved unsuccessful.". . .

Consistent with the statutory text, we hold that § 1912(d) applies only in cases where an Indian family's "breakup" would be precipitated by the termination of the parent's rights. The term "breakup" refers in this context to "[t]he discontinuance of a relationship," American Heritage Dictionary 235 (3d ed. 1992), or "an ending as an effective entity," Webster's 273 (defining "breakup" as "a disruption or dissolution into component parts: an ending as an effective entity"). See also Compact OED 1076 (defining "break-up" as, *inter alia*, a "disruption, separation into parts, disintegration"). But when an Indian parent abandons an Indian child prior to birth and that child has never been in the Indian parent's legal or physical custody, there is no "relationship" that would be "discontinu[ed]"—and no "effective entity" that would be "end[ed]"—by the termination of the Indian parent's rights. In such a situation, the "breakup of the Indian family" has long since occurred, and § 1912(d) is inapplicable.

. . .

The Indian Child Welfare Act was enacted to help preserve the cultural identity and heritage of Indian tribes, but under the State Supreme Court's reading, the Act would put certain vulnerable children at a great disadvantage solely because an ancestor—even a remote one—was an Indian. As the State Supreme Court read §§ 1912(d) and (f), a biological Indian father could abandon his child *in utero* and refuse any support for the birth mother—perhaps contributing to the mother's decision to put the child up for adoption—and then could play his ICWA trump card at the eleventh hour to override the mother's decision and the child's best interests. If this were possible, many prospective adoptive parents would surely pause before adopting any child who might possibly qualify as an Indian under the ICWA. Such an interpretation would raise equal protection concerns, but the plain text of §§ 1912(f) and (d) makes clear that neither provision applies in the present context. Nor do § 1915(a)'s rebuttable adoption preferences apply when no alternative party has formally sought to adopt the child. We therefore reverse the judgment of the South Carolina Supreme Court and remand the case for further proceedings not inconsistent with this opinion.

It is so ordered.

JUSTICE SCALIA, dissenting.

I join JUSTICE SOTOMAYOR's dissent. . .

While I am at it, I will add one thought. The Court's opinion, it seems to me, needlessly demeans the rights of parenthood. It has been the constant practice of the common law to respect the entitlement of those who bring a child into the world to raise that child. We do not inquire whether leaving a child with his parents is "in the best interest of the child." It sometimes is not; he would be better off raised by someone else. But parents have their rights, no less than children do. This father wants to raise his daughter, and the statute amply protects his right to do so. There is no reason in law or policy to dilute that protection.

JUSTICE SOTOMAYOR, with whom JUSTICE GINSBURG and JUSTICE KAGAN join, and with whom JUSTICE SCALIA joins in part, dissenting.

A casual reader of the Court's opinion could be forgiven for thinking this an easy case, one in which the text of the applicable statute clearly points the way to the only sensible result. In truth, however, the path from the text of the Indian Child Welfare Act of 1978 (ICWA) to the result the Court reaches is anything but clear, and its result anything but right.

. . .

Beginning its reading with the last clause of § 1912(f), the majority concludes that a single phrase appearing there—"continued custody"—means that the entirety of the subsection is inapplicable to any parent, however committed, who has not previously had physical or legal custody of his child. Working back to front, the majority then concludes that § 1912(d), tainted by its association with § 1912(f), is also inapplicable; in the majority's view, a family bond that does not take custodial form is not a family bond worth preserving from "breakup." Because there are apparently no limits on the contaminating power of this single phrase, the majority does not stop there. Under its reading, § 1903(9), which makes biological fathers "parent[s]" under this federal statute (and where, again, the phrase "continued custody" does not appear), has substantive force only when a birth father has physical or state-recognized legal custody of his daughter.

When it excludes noncustodial biological fathers from the Act's substantive protections, this textually backward reading misapprehends ICWA's structure and scope. Moreover, notwithstanding the majority's focus on the perceived parental shortcomings of Birth Father, its reasoning necessarily extends to *all* Indian parents who have never had custody of their children, no matter how fully those parents have embraced the financial and emotional responsibilities of parenting. The majority thereby transforms a statute that was intended to provide uniform federal standards for child custody proceedings involving Indian children and their biological parents into an illogical piecemeal scheme.

. . .

First, ICWA defines the term "parent" broadly to mean "any biological parent . . . of an Indian child or any Indian person who has lawfully adopted an Indian child." § 1903(9). It is undisputed that Baby Girl is an "Indian child" within the meaning of the statute, see § 1903(4); *ante*, and Birth Father consequently qualifies as a "parent" under the Act. The statutory definition of parent "does not include the unwed father where paternity has not been acknowledged or established," § 1903(9), but Birth Father's biological paternity has never been questioned by any party and was confirmed by a DNA test during the state court proceedings, App. to Pet. for Cert. (Sealed).

. . .

Second, the Act's comprehensive definition of "child custody proceeding" includes not only " 'adoptive placement[s],' " " 'preadoptive placement[s],' " and " 'foster care placement[s],' " but also " 'termination of parental rights' " proceedings. § 1903(1). This last category encompasses "*any* action resulting in the termination of the *parent-child relationship*," § 1903(1)(ii) (emphasis added). So far, then, it is clear that Birth Father has a federally recognized status as Baby Girl's "parent" and that his "parent-child relationship" with her is subject to the protections of the Act.

These protections are numerous. Had Birth Father petitioned to remove this proceeding to tribal court, for example, the state court would have been obligated to transfer it absent an objection from Birth Mother or good cause to the contrary. See § 1911(b). Any voluntary consent Birth Father gave to Baby Girl's adoption would have been invalid unless written and executed before a judge and would have been revocable up to the time a final decree of adoption was entered. . .

. . .

The majority, reaching the contrary conclusion, asserts baldly that "when an Indian parent abandons an Indian child prior to birth and that child has never been in the Indian parent's legal or physical custody, there is no 'relationship' that would be 'discontinu[ed]' . . . by the termination of the Indian parent's rights." *Ante.* Says who? Certainly not the statute. Section 1903 recognizes Birth Father as Baby Girl's "parent," and, in conjunction with ICWA's other provisions, it further establishes that their "parent-child relationship" is protected under federal law. In the face of these broad definitions, the majority has no warrant to substitute its own policy views for Congress' by saying that "no 'relationship' " exists between Birth Father and Baby Girl simply because, based on the hotly contested facts of this case, it views their family bond as insufficiently substantial to deserve protection.[3] *Ibid.*

. . .

On a more general level, the majority intimates that ICWA grants Birth Father an undeserved windfall: in the majority's words, an "ICWA trump card" he can "play . . . at the eleventh hour to override the mother's decision and the child's best interests." *Ante.* The implicit argument is that Congress could not possibly have intended to recognize a parent-child relationship between Birth Father and Baby Girl that would have to be legally terminated (either by valid consent or involuntary termination) before the adoption could proceed.

. . .

Without doubt, laws protecting biological fathers' parental rights can lead—even outside the context of ICWA—to outcomes that are painful and distressing for both would-be adoptive families, who lose a much wanted child, and children who must make a difficult transition. See, *e.g.*, *In re Adoption of Tobias D.*, 2012 Me. 45, ¶ 27, 40 A. 3d 990, 999 (recognizing that award of custody of 2½-year-old child to biological father under applicable state law once paternity is established will result in the "difficult and painful" necessity of "removing the child from the only home he has ever known"). On the other hand, these rules recognize that biological fathers have a valid interest in a relationship with their child. See *supra*. And children have a reciprocal interest in knowing their biological parents. See *Santosky*, 455 U.S., at 760–761, n. 11 (describing the foreclosure of a newborn child's opportunity to "ever know his natural parents" as a "los[s] [that] cannot be measured"). These rules also reflect the understanding that the biological bond between a parent and a child is a strong foundation on which a stable and caring relationship may be built. Many jurisdictions apply a custodial preference for a fit natural parent over a party lacking this biological link. . . .

Balancing the legitimate interests of unwed biological fathers against the need for stability in a child's family situation is difficult, to be sure, and States have, over the years, taken different approaches to the problem. Some States, like South Carolina, have opted to hew to the constitutional baseline established by this Court's precedents and do not require a biological father's consent to adoption unless he has provided financial support during pregnancy. See *Quilloin* v. *Walcott*, 434 U.S. 246, 254–256 (1978); *Lehr*, 463 U.S., at 261. Other States, however, have decided to give the rights of biological fathers more robust protection and to afford them consent rights on the basis of their biological link to the child. At the time that ICWA was passed, as noted, over one-fourth of States did so. See *supra*,

ICWA, on a straightforward reading of the statute, is consistent with the law of those States that protected, and protect, birth fathers' rights more vigorously. This reading can hardly be said to generate an anomaly. ICWA, as all acknowledge, was "the product of rising concern . . . [about] abusive child welfare practices that resulted in the separation of large numbers of Indian children from their families." *Holyfield*, 490 U.S., at 32. It stands to reason that the Act would not render the legal status of an Indian father's relationship with his biological child fragile, but would instead grant it a degree of protection commensurate with the more robust state-law standards.[14]

. . .

The majority opinion turns § 1912 upside down, reading it from bottom to top in order to reach a conclusion that is manifestly contrary to Congress' express purpose in enacting ICWA: preserving the familial bonds between Indian parents and their children and, more broadly, Indian tribes' relationships with the future citizens who are "vital to [their] continued existence and integrity." § 1901(3).

The majority casts Birth Father as responsible for the painful circumstances in this case, suggesting that he intervened "at the eleventh hour to override the mother's decision and the child's best interests," *ante*. I have no wish to minimize the trauma of removing a 27-month-old child from her adoptive family. It bears remembering, however, that Birth Father took action to assert his parental rights when Baby Girl was four months old, as soon as he learned of the impending adoption. As the South Carolina Supreme Court recognized, " '[h]ad the mandate of . . . ICWA been followed [in 2010], . . . much potential anguish might have been avoided[;] and in any case the law cannot be applied so as automatically to "reward those who obtain custody, whether lawfully or otherwise, and maintain it during any ensuing (and protracted) litigation." ' " 398 S. C., at 652, 731 S. E. 2d, at 564 (quoting *Holyfield*, 490 U.S., at 53–54).

The majority's hollow literalism distorts the statute and ignores Congress' purpose in order to rectify a perceived wrong that, while heartbreaking at the time, was a correct application of federal law and that in any case cannot be undone. Baby Girl has now resided with her father for 18 months. However difficult it must have been for her to leave Adoptive Couple's home when she was just over 2 years old, it will be equally devastating now if, at the age of 3½, she is again removed from her home and sent to live halfway across the country. Such a fate is not foreordained, of course. But it can be said with certainty that the anguish this case has caused will only be compounded by today's decision.

I believe that the South Carolina Supreme Court's judgment was correct, and I would affirm it. I respectfully dissent.

Opinion Footnote

3 The majority's discussion of § 1912(d) repeatedly references Birth Father's purported "abandon[ment]" of Baby Girl, ante, at 12, 13, n. 8, 14, and it contends that its holding with regard to this provision is limited to such circumstances, see ante, at 13, n. 8; see also ante, at 1 (Breyer, J., concurring). While I would welcome any limitations on the majority's holding given that it is contrary to the language and purpose of the statute, the majority never explains either the textual basis or the precise scope of its "abandon[ment]" limitation. I expect that the majority's inexact use of the term "abandon[ment]" will sow

> confusion, because it is a commonly used term of art in state family law that does not have a uniform meaning from State to State. See generally 1 J. Hollinger, Adoption Law and Practice § 4.04[1][a][ii] (2012) (discussing various state-law standards for establishing parental abandonment of a child).
>
> 14 It bears emphasizing that the ICWA standard for termination of parental rights of which Birth Father claims the benefit is more protective than, but not out of step with, the clear and convincing standard generally applied in state courts when termination of parental rights is sought. Birth Father does not claim that he is entitled to custody of Baby Girl unless petitioners can satisfy the demanding standard of §1912(f). See Brief for Respondent Birth Father 40, n. 15. The question of custody would be analyzed independently, as it was by the South Carolina Supreme Court. Of course, it will often be the case that custody is subsequently granted to a child's fit parent, consistent with the presumption that a natural parent will act in the best interests of his child. See supra, at 19–20.

Case Questions

1. Describe the reasons that Justice Scalia gives, in his dissent, that, "The Court's opinion, it seems to me, needlessly demeans the rights of parenthood." Why do you suppose Justice Scalia is defending the father's biological tie so much more here than he did in the Michael H. case?

2. The majority weighs heavily the facts that the biological father voluntarily relinquished parental rights (informally) rather than pay child support as a non-custodial father, and that he also consented in writing to the adoption when first notified of it. (Apparently, per Justice Sotomayor, he changed his mind shortly thereafter and sued for custody.) Justice Sotomayor stresses the combination of his biological tie to his daughter and his interest in asserting his parental rights "as soon as he [fully] learned of the impending adoption." Which perspective makes more sense? Why?

PARENTS' RIGHTS VERSUS HUMAN RIGHTS

While parents exercise broad authority over their children, the state also has an interest in protecting children from abuse. These two concepts come into tension, however, when the parents' religious practices and/or cultural beliefs lead them to make decisions on behalf of their minor daughters that may be considered child abuse by the state, e.g. genital mutilation or teen marriages. The nature of these practices has been subject to criticism on the grounds that they violate basic human rights. This raises the question: What are the limits on parental rights if their decisions, consistent with their religious practices and cultural beliefs, violate the human rights of their children?

Female genital mutilation (FGM, or, more neutrally stated, female genital cutting), is the practice of intentionally altering, injuring or cutting female genitalia for cultural purposes. FGM offers no health benefits, and poses its own health risks. FGM often results in severe bleeding, infections, difficulty with urination and childbirth, and increased risk of newborn death. FGM is performed on girls from newborn to age 15, and it is estimated that there are approximately 500,000 women and girls at risk of FGM in the U.S.[86]

The World Health Organization has determined that FGM is a human rights violation. Beginning in the 1990s, various U.S. states and the federal government produced legislation criminalizing FGM. In 1996, Congress included prohibitions on FGM in the Illegal Immigration Reform and Immigrant Responsibility Act, and made it a felony to perform FGM on anyone under age 18. In addition, a number of states not only criminalized FGM but also made it a crime to take a minor female across state lines or out of the state to undergo FGM.[87] In 2013, President Obama signed the Transport for Female Genital Mutilation Act to prohibit individuals from transporting girls outside the United States for the specific purpose of having the procedure performed on those girls. As of 2017, a total of 26 states have passed laws against FGM. The first FGM prosecution occurred in the U.S. in 2017.

Child marriage is defined by the United Nations as "a formal marriage or informal union where one or both parties is under the age of 18."[88] All but two states prohibit marriage before age 18 (Nebraska's marriage age is 19 while Mississippi's is 21) although each state allows for exemptions such as parental consent or pregnancy such that 25 states have no real minimum age requirement. The American Community Survey reports that 55% of all persons married among those ages 15–17[89] are female while the U.S. Census Bureau reports that 57,800 Americans ages 15–17 are married.[90]

Child marriage is of particular concern in that girls marrying before age 18 tend to have children earlier in life compared with unmarried girls. Evidence suggests that individuals marrying as teens demonstrate a lower overall rate of educational achievement whether because of a higher high school dropout rate, a decision not to pursue higher education or suspending college enrollment. Individuals marrying as teenagers tend to earn lower wages and to live in poverty compared with those marrying in their twenties and later.[91] Girls marrying as teens[92] also exhibit higher rates of mental health concerns, and their physical health tends to be worse compared with women marrying later.[93] These factors, individually and taken together, contribute to lower overall income and educational opportunities which have lifelong consequences.

One subset of child marriage is marriage that is compelled between rapists and their victims. Legally, sex before the age of majority, whether consensual or not, is classified as statutory rape. However, getting legally married while younger than the age of consent is one way to make legal the underage sex that would otherwise be unlawful. There are also those parents who compel their daughters who have been raped to marry their rapists; the reasons associated with these compelled marriages is that the marriage removes the perceived stigma of the rape to the family of the victim or to the church to which she belongs, and to the girl who may no longer be deemed attractive and marriageable, or a pregnancy may have resulted from the rape. Rapists may agree to marry their victims if given the choice between doing so or being arrested for the rape.[94]

In each of these cases the girl is denied her autonomy in that it is one or both parents who decide whether she will be subject to childhood FGM, "allowed" to marry before her state's age of consent, or be compelled to marry her rapist. These three issues are receiving increasing attention and focus in the United States: certain subcultures or religious groups promote one or another of these practices even though prominent organizations such as the United Nations, the World Health Organization and the U.S. Department of State have taken stands against them as human rights violations.

CONCLUSION

"The family is the basis of civil society." This cliché is a staple in contemporary discourse. As an axiom—the sense in which Judge Desmond meant the statement in *Bunim v. Bunim*—it is far from what the Declaration of Independence called a "self-evident" truth. Candidates for office proclaim their commitment to "family values." This term is also slippery. A foreigner—or the conveniently naïve hypothetical visitor from Mars—might think it referred to support for family leave, child care, education, health care, and the like; but not in this country at this time. Instead, family values is a term used to signal support for traditional marriage, heterosexual monogamy, and parental authority. This chapter has shown that sometimes these principles can degenerate into homophobia and male supremacy. At the same time, the cases reviewed in this chapter demonstrate how the construction of and role of family in the U.S. is constantly evolving.

For example, marriage has had a complex history in American law. Once a patriarchal institution, marriage in the twenty-first century is a relationship between equal partners. But a gap has always existed between law and practice. When the husband was head of the family, similarities in the social status of husband and wife often tempered his authority. Now that husband and wife are equal before the law, socioeconomic differences (age, education, earning power, etc.) often favor the husband and increase his power within marriage and after divorce. *Salk v. Salk* and *M. v. M.* remind us that gender-neutral rules can become distorted when implemented by people with biased attitudes.

At a minimum, however, the law no longer privileges the male as the head of the household in heterosexual marriages. In addition, the U.S. Supreme Court's *Obergefell v. Hodges* decision broadened the definition of marriage such that individuals may now obtain governmental recognition, state and federal, with all attendant benefits, for marriages to a person of their choice, without restriction as to that person's sex or gender.

Interestingly, while the Court has expanded access to the institution of marriage, the number of individuals getting married has rapidly declined in the U.S. in recent decades. This is not to suggest, however, that these individuals are not in committed relationships. To the contrary, they are entering into relationships but opting out of marriage. In fact, cohabitation has increased, and nearly a quarter of never married adults between the ages of 25 and 34 live with their partner.[95] The Pew Research Center projects that when the young adults of today reach their 40s and 50s, a full quarter of them will not have married at all, and those who do get married are choosing to do so later in life.[96] These developments have implications for broader issues in family law as committed couples opt to have children out of wedlock and more single women choose to have children on their own. According to U.S. Census Bureau data from 2016, 38 percent of unmarried heterosexual couples have a child living with them in the home. In addition, while the majority of children still live in a home with two parents (69 percent in 2016 down from 88 percent in 1960), a full 23 percent lives in homes with single mothers (up from 8 percent in 1960).[97] As such, the relationship between marriage and family is increasingly tenuous as more individuals seek to create family outside of the confines of traditional marriage.

The last sections of this chapter move away from relationships between partners to relationships within the extended family and between the family and society: the parental rights of nonmarital fathers; the rights of children, grandparents, and third parties; and parents' obligation to honor human rights of daughters. The "Baby Richard" case and arguably the *Bottoms* case illustrate the possibility of conflict between parents' and children's interests. *Martinez* and *Holyfield* inquire into the permissible role of historically marginalized communities intervening between the individual and the state. Equality, individual rights, and family law remain sites of creative conflict and controversy.

Yet, the reality is that family has always been more complicated than the nuclear family model would suggest. Formal and informal kinship arrangements are prevalent in a variety of communities and while some are sanctioned by the law (e.g., designating a friend or partner as your legal guardian on a medical directive), many are not. As non-traditional family units become more prevalent, however, it is likely that new legal arrangements will develop to account for these complexities such as the decision by some states to recognize tri-parenting as discussed above. Still, questions about biological versus legal versus psychological parents abound, and the courts will be called on to mitigate disputes among parents and guardians in the future much as they have in the past. While the facts may change, the courts are likely to continue their commitment to putting the best interests of minor children first.

---

[1] 98 U.S. 145, 165 (1878.) Members of the Church of Jesus Christ of Latter-day Saints had challenged this law. The Mormons gave up polygamy in 1896, as a condition of Utah's admission as a state. The Court ruled in *Coyle v. Smith*, 221 U.S. 559 (1911) that Congress lacked the power to impose conditions of admission on new states.

[2] States' power to regulate marriage under their police powers was upheld in *Maynard v. Hill,* 125 U.S. 190 (1888).

[3] 388 U.S. 1, 11.

[4] Ibid., at 12.

[5] *Loving v. Virginia*, 388 U.S. 1, 12 (1967). The full passage at 541 in *Skinner* was this: "We are dealing here with legislation which involves one of the basic civil rights of man. Marriage and procreation are fundamental to the very existence and survival of the race."

[6] "Gay and Lesbian Rights: 'Regardless of whether or not you think it should be legal, for each one, please tell me whether you personally believe that in general it is morally acceptable or morally wrong. How about gay or lesbian relations?' " Available at http://news.gallup.com/poll/1651/gay-lesbian-rights.aspx (accessed May 10, 2018).

[7] 517 U.S. 620.

[8] 539 U.S. 558, 590.

[9] 478 U.S. 186, 187. *Bowers* is discussed in the Case Questions for *Eisenstadt v. Baird* in Chapter 4.

[10] Niraj Chokshi, "Boy Scouts, Reversing Century-Old Stance, Will Allow Transgender Boys," *The New York Times,* January 30, 2017. Available at: https://www.nytimes.com/2017/01/30/us/boy-scouts-reversing-century-old-stance-will-allow-transgender-boys.html (accessed May 18, 2018).

[11] *Guardianship of Kowalski* (Minn. Court of Appeals, 382 N.W. 2nd 861 (1986); *Guardianship of Kowalski* (ibid.), 478 N.W. 2nd 790 (1991).

[12] Patrick Borchers, "The Essential Irrelevance of the Full Faith and Credit Clause to the Same Sex Marriage Debate," *Creighton Law Review* 38: 353–364, 354 and 357.

[13] *Baehr v. Miike*, "Context," Lambda Legal. Available at https://www.lambdalegal.org/in-court/cases/baehr-v-miike (accessed May 8, 2018).

[14] *Defense of Marriage Act*, 1996. Public Law 104–199. Section 2 (a). 1 U.S.C. § 7.3

[15] Ibid.

[16] Jason Pierceson, *Courts, Liberalism and Rights: Gay Law and Politics in the United States and Canada* (Philadelphia, PA: Temple University Press, 2005), p. 121.

[17] "Civil Unions and Domestic Partnership Statutes," National Council of State Legislatures, November 18, 2014. Available at: http://www.ncsl.org/research/human-services/civil-unions-and-domestic-partnership-statutes.aspx (accessed April 26, 2018).

[18] Ibid.

[19] *Goodridge et al. v. Commissioner of Public Health,* 440 Mass. 309, 798 N.E. 2nd 941 (2003). Chief Justice Margaret Marshall wrote for a 4–3 majority on the Supreme Judicial Court that laws against same-sex marriage did not satisfy even the rational basis test.

[20] Robert Kolker, "The Marrying Kind," *New York Magazine,* March 8, 2004; Thomas Crampton, "Issuing Licenses, Quietly, To Couples in Asbury Park," *The New York Times,* March 10, 2004; "Oregon County Issues Same-Sex Marriage Licenses." CNN, March 3, 2004; National Council of State Legislatures, "Civil

Unions and Domestic Partnership Statutes," November 8, 2014. Available at: http://www.ncsl.org/research/human-services/civil-unions-and-domestic-partnership-statutes.aspx (accessed May 10, 2018).

21 Jeremiah J. Garretson, "The How, Why, and Who of LGBTQ 'Victory' A Critical Examination of Change in Public Attitudes Involving LGBTQ People," in *LGBTQ Politics: A Critical Reader*, Marla Brettschneider, Susan Burgess, Christine Keating (eds.) (New York, NY: New York University Press, 2017).

22 National Council of State Legislatures, "Same Sex Marriage Laws," and "State Same-Sex Marriage Laws Prior to 2015 U.S. Supreme Court Ruling: Legislatures and Courts," June 26, 2015. Available at: http://www.ncsl.org/research/human-services/same-sex-marriage-laws.aspx (accessed April 29, 2018).

23 National Council of State Legislatures, "Same Sex Marriage Laws," June 26, 2015. Available at: http://www.ncsl.org/research/human-services/same-sex-marriage-laws.aspx (accessed April 29, 2018).

24 *Obergefell v. Hodges*, 135 S.Ct. 2584, 2594-2595(2015).

25 Phyllis Randolph Frye and Alyson Dodi Meiselman, "Same-Sex Marriages Have Existed Legally in the United States for a Long Time Now," *Albany Law Review* 64, no. 3 (2001): 1031–1071.

26 Ibid.

27 *Cleveland v. U.S.*, 329 U.S. 14, at 18, 17, 26 (1946).

28 98 U.S. 145, 166.

29 "My Husband's Nine Wives," *The New York Times,* May 23, 1991.

30 *Stolen Innocence* (New York: William Morrow, 2008).

31 Marth A. Fineman, *The Neutered Mother, the Sexual Family, and other Twentieth-Century Tragedies* (New York: Routledge, 1995). *See also* Holly Brewer, "The Unfinished Revolution: Children and the American Revolution," The American Revolution, National Park Service, 2003. Available at https://www.nps.gov/revwar/unfinished_revolution/childrens_rights.htm (accessed April 30, 2018).

32 Linda Hirschman and Jane Larson, *Hard Bargains: The Politics of Sex* (New York, NY: Oxford University Press, 1999), 126. See also 14 Del. Laws 105 (1871).

33 Nancy F. Cott, *Public Vows: A History of Marriage and the Nation* (Cambridge, Mass.: Harvard University Press, 2000).

34 *Forbush v. Wallace*, 405 U.S. 970.

35 *People ex rel. Rago v. Lipsky*, 390 Ill. 70; 60 N.E.2d 422 (1945).

36 *Dunn v. Palermo*, 522 S.W. 2d 679 (Tenn 1975).

37 Henry Steele Commager, ed. *Documents in American History,* 7th ed. (New York: Appleton-Century-Crofts, 1963), vol. I, p. 316.

38 See William E. Goode, *Women and Divorce* (New York: Free Press, 1965).

39 See Judith A. Baer, *Women in American Law: The Struggle for Equality from the New Deal to the Present*, 3rd ed. (New York: Holmes & Meier Publishers, Inc., 2002), pp. 134–144.

40 Child Support Enforcement, Federal Child Support Laws, U.S. Department of Justice. (Available at: https://www.justice.gov/criminal-ceos/child-support-enforcement (accessed May 10, 2018).

41 Ibid.

42 "2016 Child Support: More Money for Families," Office of Child Support Enforcement, Administration for Children and Families. See also *Office of Child Support Enforcement Preliminary Report FY 2016*, Office of Child Support Enforcement, Administration for Children and Families. Available at: https://www.acf.hhs.gov/sites/default/files/programs/css/fy_2016_annual_report.pdf (accessed May 21, 2018).

43 Parental rights decisions include *Meyer v. Nebraska*, 262 U.S. 390 (1923), curriculum; *Pierce v. Society of Sisters*, 268 U.S. 510 (1925), choice of school; *Wisconsin v. Yoder*, 406 U.S. 205 (1972), religion-based exemption from compulsory education law; *Parham v. J.R.*, 442 U.S. 584 (1979), commitment of minor child to institution with consent of director; *Planned Parenthood v. Ashcroft*, 462 U.S. 476 (1983), consent from parent or alternatively a judge as condition of abortion on a minor child.

44 Child Welfare Information Gateway, *Determining the Best Interests of the Child* (Washington, DC: U.S. Department of Health and Human Services, Children's Bureau, 2016), 1–2. Available at: https://www.childwelfare.gov/pubPDFs/best_interest.pdf#page=2&view=Guiding%20principlesöf%20bestinterests%20determinations (accessed April 30, 2018).

45 Ibid.

46 App. to Pet. for Cert. 26–27.

47 466 U.S. 429, 434 (1984).

48 Richard Neely, *Why Courts Don't Work* (New York: Mc-Graw-Hill, 1983), pp. 120–21.

49 Kathleen Bartlett, "Prioritizing Past Caretaking in Child-Custody Decisionmaking," *Law & Contemporary Problems* 77, no. 1 (2014): 29–67.

50 The third (and eldest) had been taken from the Stanleys at an earlier date on grounds of neglect. At that time the family court had believed erroneously that the Stanleys were married.

51 *Pierce v. Society of Sisters*, 268 U.S. 510 (1925), and *Meyer v. Nebraska*, 262 U.S. 390 (1923). The "fundamental rights" phrase is from *Meyer*.

52 *Pierce v. Society of Sisters*.

53 *Meyer v. Nebraska*.

54 *Skinner v. Oklahoma*, 316 U.S. 535 (1942). See Chapter 4.

55 316 U.S., at 541.

56 *Griswold v. Connecticut*, 381 U.S. 479. See Chapter 4.

57 *Eisenstadt v. Baird*, 405 U.S. 438. See Chapter 4.

58 405 U.S., at 453.

59 Although the *Eisenstadt* decision was handed down almost two weeks before the *Stanley* decision, oral arguments in *Stanley* predated the oral arguments in *Eisenstadt*. Thus, Stanley's lawyers could not refer to *Eisenstadt*.

60 The Supreme Court relegates *Reed v. Reed* to a footnote in the *Stanley* decision, but the two cases seem to be pieces of a single pattern of increasing Supreme Court hostility to gender-based discrimination.

61 *Fiallo v. Bell*, 430 U.S. 787 (1977).

62 "Paternity Establishment," "Child Support," New York Child Support Online. Available at: https://www.childsupport.ny.gov/dcse/paternity_establishment.html#whatis (accessed May 11, 2018).

63 The "Baby Richard" case, *In re Petition of Doe*, is included in this chapter below. The other notorious decision, known as the "Baby Jessica" case, is discussed in Lucinda Franks, "The War over Baby Clausen," *The New Yorker* 69 (March 22, 1993): 56–73.

64 The argument of "Victoria" was developed and presented by a court-appointed attorney.

65 The Supreme Court saw little merit in Victoria's equal protection argument (concerning the statute's granting to her lawful parents, but not to her, permission to challenge Gerald's paternity), and Scalia's brief discussion of it is omitted from the excerpt here.

66 Fineman, *The Neutered Mother, the Sexual Family, and other Twentieth-Century Tragedies* (New York: Routledge, 1995).

67 *Moore v City of E. Cleveland*, 431 U.S. 494 (1977).

68 Christina Spiezia, "In the Courts: State Views on the Psychological-Parent and De Facto-Parent Doctrines," *Children's Legal Rights Journal*, 33(2), Article 11, Fall 2013. This is the source of material in the rest of this paragraph.

69 Kate Bolick, "Should You Have a Baby on Your Own? Exploring the Growing Ranks of Do-It-Yourself Motherhood," *Cosmopolitan Magazine,* May 11, 2015. Available at: https://www.cosmopolitan.com/lifestyle/a40134/having-a-baby-by-yourself/ (accessed April 30, 2018).

70 *In re M.C., a Person Coming Under the Juvenile Court Law, Los Angeles County Department of Children and Family Resources, v. Irene V.*, 195 Cal.App.4th 197 (Court of Appeal of the State of California, Second Appellate District) (2011).

71 See Joanna L. Grossman, "California Allows Children to Have More Than Two Legal Parents," *Verdict*, October 15, 2013. Available at: https://verdict.justia.com/2013/10/15/california-allows-children-two-legal-parents (accessed April 30, 2018).

72 SB-274 Family law: parentage: child custody and support, An act to amend Sections 3040, 4057, 7601, 7612, and 8617 of, and to add Section 4052.5 to, the Family Code, relating to family law. Available at: https://leginfo.legislature.ca.gov/faces/billNavClient.xhtml?bill_id=201320140SB274 (accessed April 30, 2018).

73 "Modern Family: More Courts Allowing Three Parents of One Child," NBCNews.com, June 19, 2017. Available at: https://www.nbcnews.com/feature/nbc-out/modern-family-more-courts-allowing-three-parents-one-child-n774031 (accessed May 10, 2018).

74 258 Iowa 1390, 140 N.W. 2d 152 (1966).

75 140 N.W. 2d 152, 154–55, 158.

76 249 Va. 410; 457 S.E.2d 102.

77 457 S.E. 2d 102, 104–05, 107–08.

78 "Judge Bars Mother from Seeing Son with Lesbian Lover," *The Virginian Pilot*, August 22, 1996.

79 530 U.S. 57–61.

80 *In re E.H.G. and D.W.G. v. E.R.G. and C.L.G.* (cert. den.)(2011).

81 Martinez brief, pp. 2–3. See Ayelet Shachar, *Multicultural Jurisdictions* (Cambridge: Cambridge University Press, 2001), p. 18.

82 Angela P. Harris, "Race and Essentialism in Feminist Legal Theory," in Katharine T. Bartlett and Rosanne Kennedy, eds., *Feminist Legal Theory: Readings in Law and Gender* (Boulder, Colo.: Westview Press, 1991), p.243.

83 Or more precisely, the statutory rights of Native Americans, which are constitutional rights of other Americans.

84 While the case for brevity's sake is referred to herein as *Mississippi Choctaw v. Holyfield*, the appellees in the case actually included both the adoptive parents, Mr. and Mrs. Holyfield, and the birth parents, J.B. and W.J. Mr. Holyfield died during the litigation.

85 511 So. 2d 918 (1987).

86 Howard Goldberg, Paul Stupp, Ekwutosi Okoroh, Ghenet Besera, David Goodman, and Isabella Danel, "Female Genital Mutilation/Cutting in the United States: Updated Estimates of Women and Girls at Risk, 2012," *Public Health Reports* 131, no. 2 (March-April 2016). Available at: https://www.ncbi.nlm.nih.gov/pmc/articles/PMC4765983/ (accessed May 21, 2018).

87 "Legislation on Female Genital Mutilation in the United States," Briefing Paper, Center for Reproductive Rights, November 2004.

88 UNICEF, "Child Marriage," *Child Protection from Violence, Exploitation and Abuse*, March 5, 2018. Available at: https://www.unicef.org/protection/57929_58008.html (accessed May 21, 2018).

89 David McClendon and Aleksandra Sandstrom, "Child Marriage is Rare in the U.S., Though This Varies by State," *Pew Research Center*, November 1, 2016. Available at: http://www.pewresearch.org/fact-tank/2016/11/01/child-marriage-is-rare-in-the-u-s-though-this-varies-by-state/ (accessed May 21, 2018).

90 David McClendon and Aleksandra Sandstrom, Table: More Girls than Boys are Married at Young Ages, "Child marriage is rare in the U.S., though this varies by state," *Pew Research Center*, November 1, 2016. Available at: http://www.pewresearch.org/fact-tank/2016/11/01/child-marriage-is-rare-in-the-u-s-though-this-varies-by-state/ (accessed May 21, 2018).

91 "Early Teen Marriage and Future Poverty," *Demography* 47, No. 3 (2010): pp. 689–718, pp. 689–691.

92 The U.S. Department of Health and Human Services Office of Adolescent Health reports that, as of 2016, 11% of babies born to teen mothers (age 15–19) are born "outside of marriage." See "Teen Births," Trends in Teen Pregnancy and Childbearing, Office of Adolescent Health, U.S. Department of Health and Human Services. Available at: https://www.hhs.gov/ash/oah/adolescent-development/reproductive-health-and-teen-pregnancy/teen-pregnancy-and-childbearing/trends/index.html (accessed May 11, 2018).

93 Vivian E. Hamilton, "The Act of Marital Capacity: Reconsidering Civil Recognition of Adolescent Marriage," *Boston University Law Review* 92 (2012): 1817–1863, p. 1820.

94 Nicholas Kristof, "11 Years Old, a Mom, and Pushed to Marry Her Rapist in Florida," *The New York Times*, May 26, 2017. Available at: https://www.nytimes.com/2017/05/26/opinion/sunday/it-was-forced-on-me-child-marriage-in-the-us.html (accessed May 21, 2018).

95 Wendy Wang and Kim Parker, "Record Share of Americans Have Never Married As Values, Economics and Gender Patterns Change," *Pew Research Center Social & Demographic Trends*, September 24, 2014. Available at: http://www.pewsocialtrends.org/2014/09/24/record-share-of-americans-have-never-married/ (accessed May 21, 2018).

96 Ibid.

[97] "The Majority of Children Live With Two Parents, Census Bureau Reports," Press Release Number: CB16-192, *United States Census Bureau*, November 17, 2016. (Available at: https://www.census.gov/newsroom/press-releases/2016/cb16-192.html (accessed May 21, 2018).

CHAPTER 6

Women and Education

When the Constitution was adopted, few Americans went to school at all. Most children got their education at home, often while being trained in their parents' occupations. The exceptions were mostly white, mostly affluent, and mostly boys, and the schools available to them were mostly private. In that respect, this country was a typical eighteenth-century agrarian society. Where the United States was atypical was in the fact that the law excluded some children from education—teaching slaves to write was forbidden in both South Carolina and Georgia.[1] The vast system of public education we have now is a by-product of the Industrial Revolution.

By 1900, compulsory public education was the norm. Boys and girls of all races attended elementary school, and four-year secondary schools were available to most white children. Most public schools were coeducational, but racial segregation was common. By convention, though not by constitutional command, education was part of the states' police powers. State governments created boards that set educational standards and requirements; local districts, responsible to the state, operated the schools and hired the teachers. Funds came from local property taxes, often supplemented by the state. This decentralized system remains in place in the twenty-first century, but the federal government now plays at least as important a role in education as do the states.

Two factors have driven this change. First, the federal government has more money; the states lack sufficient resources to educate their children. Congress has conditioned the distribution of federal funds on the states' compliance with federal regulations. Second, federal courts have interpreted the equal protection clause of the Fourteenth Amendment to forbid many kinds of race and sex discrimination, and these decisions inform local education policies. In 1954, when the Supreme Court invalidated legal racial segregation in elementary and secondary schools in *Brown v. Board of Education*,[2] many critics insisted that the federal government had usurped the powers of the states. But by the time George

W. Bush took office, federal involvement in education was so widely accepted that opposition to the No Child Left Behind Act of 2001, which imposed stringent conditions on the state, was based on its content, not its constitutionality.

SINGLE-SEX PUBLIC SCHOOLS: SEPARATE BUT EQUAL?

Even when statutes single out men or women for special treatment, and thus are not gender-neutral on their face, it is not always obvious that the singling out amounts to discriminatory treatment. Statutes that separate men from women, for instance, are not necessarily, at least in principle, providing unequal treatment to the two groups. For litigation challenging legally mandated sex segregation under the equal protection clause, courts have to address two distinct questions: (1) Does the separation amount to unequal treatment? (2) If so, is the unequal treatment nonetheless justified under equal protection standards?

Most Americans are aware that *Brown v. Board of Education* (1954) declared that racially "separate" cannot be "equal" in the field of elementary and secondary public education, thus ending the official legality[3] of law-imposed racial segregation in schools. Not many people are aware of two 1950 cases that set the stage for the *Brown* decision, establishing the legal doctrine that was to bring about the demise of school segregation by race. Only when this doctrine is fully understood can one critically evaluate what the federal courts have been doing in the area of single-sex schooling.

The doctrine that killed racial segregation in public education involved what the Supreme Court called "intangible factors." Once the federal courts began to crack down on Southern school boards and to require something approaching a semblance of actual equality of facilities, certain states developed unusual stratagems for handling their Black students; these stratagems directed the Supreme Court's attention to the phenomenon of "intangible factors" that affect the quality of education.

The first unusual stratagem was adopted by Texas. Under pressure from the federal courts, Texas opened a separate "college of law" for Black individuals rather than admit a Black student to the University of Texas Law School. The state rented a few rooms, ordered ten thousand books, hired a small part-time faculty, and called it equality. In deciding that this treatment was unconstitutional, the Supreme Court, after canvassing the obvious superiority of the University of Texas Law School in such tangible factors as number of faculty, variety in course offerings, scope of the library, and so forth, stated with considerable emphasis:[4]

What is more important, the University of Texas Law School possesses to a far greater degree those qualities which are incapable of objective measurement but which make for greatness in a law school. Such qualities, to name but a few, include reputation of the faculty, experience of the administration, position and influence of the alumni, standing in the community, traditions and prestige. [Moreover, the law school]...cannot be effective in isolation from the individuals and institutions with which the law interacts. Few students and no one who has practiced law would choose to study in an academic vacuum, removed from the interplay of ideas and the exchange of views with which the law is concerned. The law school to which Texas is willing to admit petitioner excludes from its student body members of the racial groups which number 85% of the population of the State and include most of the lawyers, witnesses, jurors, judges and other officials with whom petitioner will inevitably be dealing when he becomes a member of the Texas bar.[5]

The second critical 1950 case[6] involved a Black graduate student who, after a successful court challenge, attained admission into the erstwhile all-white University of Oklahoma graduate school. Oklahoma had created separate four-year colleges for Black students, but had taken no steps to create separate graduate schools. Once admitted, G.W. McLaurin was assigned to sit at a special desk, designated "colored," adjacent to the classroom; he had to eat at a special table in the cafeteria, designated "colored," and had to eat only at specified times; and he had to study at a separate table, designated "colored," outside the library reading room. In declaring that this treatment was unconstitutional, even though the Black student had access to the same physical university as white students, the Supreme Court reasoned once again that intangible as well as tangible factors must be considered in determining whether equality of educational facilities was being provided by the state. The court held that equal protection of the laws had been denied this Black student because of inequality in the intangible factors shaping the education he would receive; those factors included "ability to study, to engage in discussions and exchange views with other students, and in general, to learn his profession."[7]

Once the Supreme Court began to take into account such intangible factors as the reputation of the school, the reputation of the faculty, opportunities to interact with fellow students from different backgrounds, and opportunities to interact with those persons likely to attain positions of political or economic influence, the handwriting on the wall was written in large and clear letters. State-imposed racial segregation in any public school produced inequality in these factors and thus would have to be judged a denial of "equal protection of the law." And so it was, in the next case to come along, in 1954.

The point of including this elaborate background on racial segregation has not been to explain the evolution of *Brown v. Board of Education* but to provide background for assessing the constitutionality of single-sex schooling. The question that must be asked for that assessment is: To what extent do the Court's statements about the intangible but real inequality of educational opportunity offered by racially segregated schools apply to sex-segregated schools?

Although popular in the nineteenth century, in the era of universal compulsory education, single-sex public schools have been limited to these: military colleges for men, state colleges for women (which often emphasized programs to train teachers and nurses), and elite secondary schools modeled on the boarding schools of the Northeast (without the dormitories or religious affiliations.) Generations of bright children from poor families thrived at Stuyvesant (boys), Bronx Science (boys), and Hunter College (girls) high schools in New York, Boston Latin and Girls Latin, and Philadelphia's Central High and Girls High. But this separate education was not necessarily equal for both sexes, as the following excerpt and cases illustrate.

ALICE DE RIVERA, "ON DE-SEGREGATING STUYVESANT HIGH"[8]

The first time it really occurred to me that I was oppressed as a woman was when I...realized I had no real plans for the future—college, maybe, and after that was a dark space in my mind....The boys that I knew all had at least some slight idea in their minds of what career or job they were preparing for....It seemed to me that I should fill the blank spot in my mind as the boys were able to do, and I decided to study science (biology, in particular) much more intensively. It was then that I encountered one of the many blocks which stand in the woman student's way: discrimination against women in the specialized science and math high schools in the city...

Many years before women in New York State had won their right to vote, a school was established for those high-school students who wished to specialize in science and math. Naturally it was not co-ed, for women were not regarded legally or psychologically as people. This school, Stuyvesant High School, was erected in 1903. In 1956,...the school was renovated; yet no provision was made for girls to enter.

There are only two other high schools in New York which specialize in science and math: Brooklyn Technical, a school geared towards engineering, and Bronx High School of Science. Brooklyn Tech moved from the warehouse, where its male-only classes were started, into a modern building in 1933. It was renovated in 1960, yet still no provision was made for girls.

This left only Bronx Science . . . It became [co-ed] in 1946, the year it moved to a new building. However, although it admits girls, it still discriminates against them; it admits only one girl for every two boys. . . Bronx Science is one-and-one-half hours travel time from my home. It presents very stiff competition because of the discriminatory policy which allows only a certain number of girls to enter, and because all the girls who would otherwise be trying out for Stuyvesant or Brooklyn Tech have Bronx Science as their only alternative. I became disgusted with this, not only for my own sake, but for all the girls who hadn't become scientists or engineers because they were a little less than brilliant or had been put down by nobody having challenged those little blank spots in their minds. After talking about it with my parents and friends, I decided to open up Stuyvesant and challenge the. . .policy.

I took my idea to Ramona Ripston, co-director of the National Emergency Civil Liberties Committee, and she accepted it warmly. Pretty soon I became involved in trying to get an application for the entrance exam to Stuyvesant filled out and sent. It was turned down and we—NECLC, my parents, and I—went to court against the principal of Stuyvesant and the Board of Ed. . . .The Board of Ed granted me the privilege of taking the test for Bronx Science (which is the same as the one given for Stuyvesant). . .

[After] we found out that I had passed for entrance into both Stuyvesant and Bronx Science, we went to court again. . .[The judge scheduled] an open hearing for May 13. . .However, on April 30 the New York City Board of Education voted to admit me to Stuyvesant High School in the Fall.

JANICE BRAY ET AL. V. JOSEPH LEE ET AL.
337 F. Supp. 934 (D. Mass. 1972)

CAFFREY, DISTRICT JUDGE.

. . .The plaintiffs. . .are a group of girl students, each of whom took the examination in March 1970 for admission as seventh grade students to the Girls Latin School for the academic year beginning in September 1970. Plaintiffs allege, and I find, that they are representatives of a class with an outside figure of 177 members, all of whom took the same examination for admission to Girls Latin School in September 1970, scored from 120 to 133, and, nevertheless, were not admitted in the fall of 1970. In their complaint plaintiffs allege that the various respondents illegally discriminated against them on the basis of their sex, for the reason that a boy who applied for admission to Latin School for the school year beginning September 1970 was admitted if he made a score on the examination of 120 or better out of a possible 200 points. Plaintiffs further allege that a girl who took the same examination was required to score 133 or better in order to gain admission at the same time to Girls Latin School. The accuracy of these factual representations is conceded by respondents.

...Boys Latin building has a seating capacity for approximately 3,000 students and the Girls Latin building has a seating capacity for approximately 1,500 students. Because of the disparity in the seating capacity of the two buildings, the Boston School Department, in evaluating the results of examinations in the past, first made a determination of how many seats were available in the boys building. They then counted down from the top possible score of 200 until they had accepted a number of boys equal to the number of available seats for the following September. This established the cut-off mark for the admission of boys which, in 1970, turned out to be a mark of 120 out of a possible 200. Any boy who scored 120 or higher was then admitted to Boys Latin school for the school year beginning in September 1970.

Using the same technique with reference to the number of seats available in Girls Latin School, the School Department evaluated the result of the girls' examination by counting down from 200 until they reached a number equal to the number of seats available in September 1970 and thus determined that the cut-off mark for girls, because of the lesser number of seats available, was 133 out of a possible 200.

In response to a direction from the court, the School Department made a computation, the accuracy of which has been stipulated to by counsel for the plaintiffs, that in September 1970 a combined total of 648 seats were filled by incoming seventh grade students at the Boys and Girls Latin schools, and a further determination was made that had the School Department not used separate cut-off marks for boys and girls, but, on the contrary, had used one cut-off mark for both boys and girls measured by the available 648 seats, the cut-off for both boys and girls on a merged basis would have been a score of 127 out of the possible 200.

On February 14, the court directed the School Department to send a letter to the parents of each of the 177 potential plaintiffs asking the parents if they still wished their daughter to be admitted to Latin school in the fall of 1972. At a conference held this date, counsel for the parties stipulated that of the 95 plaintiffs who have responded affirmatively to the questionnaire only 47 received a score of 127 or better. Accordingly, I find that only 47 of the plaintiffs would have been admitted as seventh grade students in September 1970 had the test results been evaluated without using different cut-off marks for boys and for girls, and I find that these are the only plaintiffs presently entitled to relief.

...On the basis of the foregoing, I rule that the use of separate and different standards to evaluate the examination results to determine the admissibility of boys and girls to the Boston Latin schools constitutes a violation of the Equal Protection Clause of the Fourteenth Amendment, the plain effect of which is to prohibit prejudicial disparities before the law between all citizens, including women or girls. I further find that on the basis of the record of this case female students seeking admission to Boston Latin School have been illegally discriminated against solely because of their sex, and that discrimination has denied them their constitutional right to an education equal to that offered to male students at the Latin school.

It should be noted that subsequent to the filing of the instant complaint the Massachusetts Legislature enacted a law captioned "Chapter 622 of the Acts of 1971," which in pertinent part provided:

Section 5. Every child shall have a right to attend the public schools of the town where he actually resides, subject to the following section. No child shall be excluded from or discriminated against in admission to a public school of any town, or in obtaining the advantages, privileges and courses of study of such public school on account of race, color, sex, religion, or national origin.

This bill was signed into law by the Governor on August 6, 1971.

...Respondents are permanently enjoined from hereafter using a different standard to determine the admissibility of boys and girls, and are affirmatively ordered to use the same standard for admission of boys and girls to any school operated by the City of Boston, including the Boston Latin School.

With regard to specific relief herein, it is ordered that all 47 plaintiffs who scored 127 or higher in the March 1970 examination be admitted in September 1972 to the Boston Latin school without the necessity of taking the ninth grade examination... [The two schools became coed in September of 1972, with Girls' Latin taking the new name Boston Latin Academy.—AU.]

SUSAN L. VORCHHEIMER V. SCHOOL DISTRICT OF PHILADELPHIA

532 F. 2d 880 (3rd Circ. 1976)

WEIS, CIRCUIT JUDGE.

Do the Constitution and laws of the United States require that every public school, in every public school system in the Nation, be coeducational? Stated another way, do our Constitution and laws forbid the maintenance by a public school board, in a system otherwise coeducational, of a limited number of single-sex high schools in which enrollment is voluntary and the educational opportunities offered to girls and boys are essentially equal? This appeal presents those questions and, after careful consideration, we answer negatively. Accordingly, we vacate the district court's judgment which held that the school board policy was impermissible.[1]

The Plaintiff is a teen-age girl who graduated with honors from a junior high school in Philadelphia. She then applied to Central High School, a public school in the city, but was refused admission because that institution is restricted to male students. After that setback, she filed this class action in the United States District Court seeking relief under 42 U.S.C. § 1983 from alleged unconstitutional discrimination. After a trial, the district court granted an injunction, ordering that she and other qualified female students be admitted to Central.

The Philadelphia School District offers four types of senior high schools: academic, comprehensive, technical and magnet... Academic high schools have high admission standards and offer only college preparatory courses. There are but two such schools in Philadelphia, and they accept students from the entire city rather than operating on a neighborhood basis. Central is restricted to males, and Girls High School, as the name implies, admits only females.

Central High School was founded in 1836 and has maintained a reputation for academic excellence. For some years before 1939, it was designated a comprehensive rather than an academic high school as it is presently. Its graduates both before and after 1939 have made notable contributions to the professions, business, government and academe.

Girls High has also achieved high academic standing. It was founded in 1848 and became an academic school in 1893. Its alumnae have compiled enviable records and have distinguished themselves in their chosen diverse fields. It now has a faculty of more than 100 and a student body of approximately 2,000, about the same as those of Central.

Enrollment at either school is voluntary and not by assignment. Only 7% of students in the city qualify under the stringent standards at these two schools, and it is conceded that plaintiff met the scholastic requirements of both. The Philadelphia school system does not have a co-ed academic school with similar scholastic requirements for admission.

The courses offered by the two schools are similar and of equal quality. The academic facilities are comparable, with the exception of those in the scientific field where Central's are superior. [The district court also found that two U.S. presidents, the vice-president and the U.S. Attorney General had visited and spoken at Central High over the years; that its alumni Association was influential within Philadelphia; and that its alumni had created for it a substantial private endowment—AU.] The district court concluded "that [generally] the education available to the female students at Girls is comparable to that available to the male students at Central." Moreover, "[graduates] of both Central and Girls High, as well as the other senior high schools of Philadelphia," have been and are accepted by the most prestigious universities.

The plaintiff has stipulated that "the practice of educating the sexes separately is a technique that has a long history and world-wide acceptance." Moreover, she agrees that "there are educators who regard education in a single-sex school as a natural and reasonable educational approach." In addition to this stipulation, the defendants presented the testimony of Dr. J. Charles Jones, an expert in the field of education. Dr. Jones expressed a belief, based on his study of New Zealand's sex-segregated schools, that students in that educational environment had a higher regard for scholastic achievement and devoted more time to homework than those in co-ed institutions. The district judge commented that even had the parties not stipulated to the educational value of the practice, "this Court would probably have felt compelled to validate the sex-segregated school on the basis of Dr. Jones' hypotheses concerning the competition for adolescent energies in a coed school and its detrimental effect on student learning and academic achievement."

Before deciding which school she wished to attend, the plaintiff visited a number of them and developed some definite opinions. As to Girls High, she commented, "I just didn't like the impression it gave me. I didn't think I would be able to go there for three years and not be harmed in any way by it." As to Central, she said, "I liked it there. I liked the atmosphere and also what I heard about it, about its academic excellence." She was somewhat dissatisfied with her education at George Washington High School because of her belief that the standards which the teacher set for the students were not high enough.

The trial judge found the gender based classification of students at the two schools to lack a "fair and substantial relationship to the School Board's legitimate interest" and enjoined the practice.

The court's factual finding that Girls and Central are academically and functionally equivalent establishes that the plaintiff's desire to attend Central is based on personal preference rather than being founded on an objective evaluation. . .

With this factual background, we now turn to a review of the legal issues. We look first to federal statutory law. . . .

In 1972 Congress provided that the benefits of educational programs funded through federal monies should be available to all persons without discrimination based on sex. 20 U.S.C. §§ 1681 *et seq*. The statute applies, however, to only specified types of educational institutions and excludes from its coverage the admission policies of secondary schools.[4] . . .

In 1974, during House debate on HR 69, a bill to extend and amend the Elementary and Secondary Education Act of 1965, Representative Esch, an advocate of the Equal Educational Opportunities Act of 1972, proposed an amendment identical in relevant portions with that Act. The amendment was adopted and HR 69, after modifications in the Senate not pertinent to our discussion, was enacted into law. 20 U.S.C. §§ 1701–1721.

The result is an anomaly. In an early part of the enactment, Congress finds that maintenance of dual school systems in which students are assigned solely on the basis of sex denies equal protection. 20 U.S.C. § 1702(a)(1). Despite that policy pronouncement, however, the statute does not prohibit the states from segregating schools on the basis of sex although there is a specific proscription on segregation based on race, color or national origin. 20 U.S.C. § 1703(a). Insofar, then, that the Equal Educational Opportunities Act of 1974 might have application to established single-sex schools, the legislation is at best ambiguous.

. . .

The Act's policy declaration is that children are entitled to "equal educational opportunity" without regard to race, color, or sex. The finding of the district court discloses no inequality in opportunity for education between

Central and Girls High Schools. We cannot, therefore, find that language applicable here. . . .

We conclude the legislation is so equivocal that it cannot control the issue in this case. . . .

Finding no Congressional enactments which authoritatively address the problem, we must consider the constitutional issues which provided the impetus for issuance of the injunction.

The district court reviewed the line of recent cases dealing with sex discrimination . . . As a result of that analysis, the district judge reasoned that, while the Supreme Court has not held sex to be a suspect classification, a stricter standard than the rational relationship test applies and is denominated "fair and substantial relationship."

In each of the cases cited, however, there was an actual deprivation or loss of a benefit to a female which could not be obtained elsewhere. . . None of the cases was concerned with a situation in which equal opportunity was extended to each sex or in which the restriction applied to both. And, significantly, none occurred in an educational setting.

The nature of the discrimination which the plaintiff alleges must be examined with care. She does not allege a deprivation of an education equal to that which the school board makes available to boys. Nor does she claim an exclusion from an academic school because of a quota system, *cf. Berkelman v. San Francisco Unified School District*, 501 F.2d 1264 (9th Cir. 1974), or more stringent scholastic admission standards. *Cf. Bray v. Lee*, 337 F. Supp. 934 (D. Mass. 1972). Moreover, enrollment at the single-sex schools is applicable only to high schools and is voluntary, not mandatory. The plaintiff has difficulty in establishing discrimination in the school board's policy. If there are benefits or detriments inherent in the system, they fall on both sexes in equal measure.

Plaintiff cites *Sweatt v. Painter*, 339 U.S. 629 (1950), and *Brown v. Board of Education*, 347 U.S. 483 (1954), which prohibit racial segregation in the educational process. Those cases are inapplicable here. Race is a suspect classification under the Constitution, but the Supreme Court has declined to so characterize gender. We are committed to the concept that there is no fundamental difference between races and therefore, in justice, there can be no dissimilar treatment. But there are differences between the sexes which may, in limited circumstances, justify disparity in law. As the Supreme Court has said: "[gender] has never been rejected as an impermissible classification in all instances." *Kahn v. Shevin*, 416 U.S. at 356 n.10.

Equal educational opportunities should be available to both sexes in any intellectual field. However, the special emotional problems of the adolescent years are matters of human experience and have led some educational experts to opt for one-sex high schools. While this policy has limited acceptance on its merits, it does have its basis in a theory of equal benefit and not discriminatory denial.

The only occasion on which the Supreme Court ruled upon a gender classification in school admissions policy was in *Williams v. McNair*, 316 F. Supp. 134 (D.S.C. 1970), *aff'd*, 401 U.S. 951 (1971), a case which was decided many years after *Sweatt* and *Brown*. *Williams* was a summary affirmance of a three-judge district court, and we do not have the benefit of the Supreme Court's reasoning. Yet, the result does have precedential weight for us. The district court's opinion details a fact situation quite similar to that confronting us here, except that the plaintiffs were males who sought admission to a girls' state college. *Reed v. Reed* (1971) had not yet been decided and the district court therefore had no reason to discuss a substantial relationship test. Rather, it applied the traditional rational relationship guidelines. The court said:

"While history and tradition alone may not support a discrimination, the Constitution does not require that a classification 'keep abreast of the latest' in educational opinion, especially when there remains a respectable opinion to the contrary; it only demands that the discrimination not be wholly wanting in reason." 316 F. Supp. at 137.

Believing the problem could not be considered in isolation, the court noted that the school involved was only one in an extensive state system which included several co-ed schools as well as an all male one.

We may not cavalierly disregard *Williams* although it predated *Reed* by a few months. Indeed, the two cases are not inconsistent because the state schools' restrictive admissions policy applied to both sexes, a significant difference from the preferential statutory procedure in *Reed*. This distinction is enough to justify the use of the rational relationship test in *Williams* even though it is likely that the result would have been the same under the substantial relationship formula.

We do not accept *Williams* as being inapplicable merely because males were barred rather than females. . . . We are aware of the suggestion that disparity is likely to be favorably considered when it confers on the female some benefit tending to rectify the effects of past discrimination. . .But we have no such exempting qualification here because there is no evidence of past deprivation of educational opportunities for women in the Philadelphia School District. Indeed, the factual findings establish that, for many years past and at the present, excellent educational facilities have been and are available to both sexes.

Since there is no remedial measure at stake, we see no basis for differentiation between *Williams* and the case at bar. Consequently, we differ with the district court's opinion that *Williams* has only a tenuous applicability here. In our view it is strong, if not controlling authority, for denial of an injunction.

The record does contain sufficient evidence to establish that a legitimate educational policy may be served by utilizing single-sex high schools. The primary aim of any school system must be to furnish an education of as high a quality as is feasible. Measures which would allow innovation in methods and techniques to achieve that goal have a high degree of relevance. Thus, given the objective of a quality education and a controverted, but respected theory that adolescents may study more effectively in single-sex schools, the policy of the school board here does bear a substantial relationship.

We need not decide whether this case requires application of the rational or substantial relationship tests because, using either, the result is the same. We conclude that the regulations establishing admission requirements to Central and Girls High School based on gender classification do not offend the Equal Protection Clause of the United States Constitution...

The judgment of the district court will be reversed.

Opinion Footnotes

1 The district court's opinion is published at 400 F. Supp. 326 (E.D. Pa. 1975).

4 Moreover, there is a specific exclusion of the admissions policies of public colleges which traditionally enrolled only students of one sex. 20 U.S.C. § 1681(a)(5).

GIBBONS, CIRCUIT JUDGE, dissenting.

The majority opinion may be briefly summarized as follows:

The object of the [14th] Amendment was undoubtedly to enforce the... equality of the two [sexes] before the law, but in the nature of things it could not have been intended to abolish distinctions based upon [sex], or to enforce social, as distinguished from political equality, or a commingling of the two [sexes] upon terms unsatisfactory to either. Laws permitting, and even requiring, their separation in places where they are liable to be brought into contact with each other do not necessarily imply the inferiority of either [sex] to the other, and have been generally, if not universally, recognized as within the competency of the state legislatures in the exercise of their police power. The most common instance of this is connected with the establishment of separate schools for [male] and [female] children, which has been held to be a valid exercise of the legislative power even by courts of States where the political rights of [women] have been longest and most earnestly enforced.

The quotation, with appropriate substitutions, will be recognized immediately as the analysis of Justice Brown, for the majority of the Supreme Court, in *Plessy v. Ferguson*, 163 U.S. 537, 544 (1896). No doubt had the issue in this case been presented to the Court at any time from 1896 to 1954, a "separate but equal" analysis would have carried the day. I was under the distinct impression, however, that "separate but equal" analysis, especially in the field of public education, passed from the fourteenth amendment jurisprudential scene over twenty years ago. *See, e.g., Brown v. Board of Education*, 347 U.S. 483 (1954). The majority opinion, in establishing a twentieth-century sexual equivalent to the *Plessy* decision, reminds us that the doctrine can and will be invoked to support sexual discrimination in the same manner that it supported racial discrimination prior to *Brown*.

But the resurrection of the "separate but equal" analysis is not my most serious quarrel with the majority opinion. What I find most disturbing is the majority's deliberate disregard of an express Congressional finding that the maintenance of dual school systems in which students are assigned to schools solely on the basis of sex violates the equal protection clause of the fourteenth amendment. § 203(a)(1), Equal Educational Opportunities Act of 1974, 20 U.S.C. § 1702(a)(1) (Supp. 1976). So long as Congress has acted within the sphere of its legislative competence in making such a finding, I submit, we are not free to substitute a "separate but equal" legislative judgment of our own. Because I conclude that Congress has acted to prohibit the maintenance of single-sex public schools pursuant to its powers under § 5 of the fourteenth amendment, I dissent from the majority's substitution of a "separate but equal" legislative judgment. I would affirm the decision below.

...The majority opinion ironically emphasizes that Vorchheimer's choice of an academic high school was "voluntary." It was "voluntary," but only in the same sense that Mr. Plessy voluntarily chose to ride the train in Louisiana. The train Vorchheimer wants to ride is that of a rigorous academic program among her intellectual peers. Philadelphia, like the state of Louisiana in 1896, offers the service but only if Vorchheimer is willing to submit to segregation.

Her choice, like Plessy's, is to submit to that segregation or refrain from availing herself of the service...

Assuming, as the majority does, that *Williams v. McNair* is authority for a separate but equal treatment of the sexes in public education, one would still have to conclude that the legislative finding of § 203(a)(1)—that separate is not equal for purposes of the fourteenth amendment—has overruled it. Indeed, from an historical perspective, section 5 of the fourteenth amendment would have allowed Congress, had it possessed the decency and will, to overrule *Plessy v. Ferguson* at any time between 1896 and 1954. Had Congress done so, I suggest, it would have carried the Court along with it. There is much to be said, I submit, in favor of congressional initiative rather than judicial activism in the unfolding of the full meaning of the equal protection clause. When Congress, reflecting the democratic processes, concludes that a state classification is unlawful, its conclusion has the advantage of the authority that comes from democratic consensus, while at the same time its conclusion remains subject to judicial review. When the Court acts similarly there is neither the authority of consensus nor the safeguard of review by another branch....Certainly Congress has a greater capacity than the Court to weigh the competing considerations....

...

... The district court concluded, and, I agree, that since *Reed v. Reed* the rational relationship test is regarded by a majority of the court as inapplicable to gender based classifications.

Unlike the majority, I find it particularly difficult to say on the basis of the record in this case that the exclusion of females from Central bears a fair and substantial relationship to any of the Philadelphia School Board's legitimate objectives. Admittedly coeducation at the senior high school level has its supporters and its critics. The majority is also undoubtedly correct in suggesting that a legitimate educational policy may be served by utilizing single-sex high schools. But certainly that observation does not satisfy the substantial relationship test. Some showing must be made that a single-sex academic high school policy advances the Board's objectives in a manner consistent with the requirements of the Equal Protection Clause. *Reed v. Reed,* 404 U.S. at 76.

The Board, as the district court emphasized, did not present sufficient evidence that coeducation has an adverse effect upon a student's academic achievement. Indeed the Board could not seriously assert that argument in view of its policy of assigning the vast majority of its students to coeducational

> schools. Presumably any detrimental impact on a student's scholastic achievement attributable to coeducation would be as evident in Philadelphia's coeducational comprehensive schools which offer college preparatory courses as the Board suggests it would be in its exclusively academic high schools. Thus, the Board's single-sex policy reflects a choice among educational techniques but not necessarily one substantially related to its stated educational objectives. One of those objectives, in fact, is to provide "educational options to students and their parents." The implementation of the Board's policy excluding females from Central actually precludes achievement of this objective because there is no option of a coeducational academic senior high school.
>
> Because I agree with the district court that the Board has not made the required showing of a substantial relationship between its single-sex academic high school policy and its stated educational objectives, I would affirm the decision below even if I were willing to ignore the pertinent provisions of the E.E.O.A.

Case note: Vorchheimer appealed to the Supreme Court; the justices divided 4–4, so no opinion was issued and the Circuit Court opinion stood (but see Question 3 below).

Case Questions

1. What reasons for sex segregation in schools does Judge Weis give in the majority opinion? Can you think of others? Are some of these reasons more valid than others, or are they pretexts entailing the belief that women are inferior to men?

2. *Vorchheimer* was decided before *Craig v. Boren*. Could Philadelphia's single-sex schools have survived intermediate scrutiny? Strict scrutiny?

3. Central High has admitted girls since *MUW v. Hogan* (1982) (see below) was decided, even though that decision explicitly stated that the ruling did not apply to secondary schools. But the Philadelphia High School for Girls has maintained both its name and its single-sex policy. This is obviously sex discrimination. Can all-girls schools be constitutional if all-boys schools are not? If so, why?

Girls' High was one of 283 single-sex public schools in the United States in the 2014–15 academic year.[9] Although Title IX of the Education Amendments Act of 1972 (see below) applies to public elementary and secondary schools, the number of single sex schools increased in the second decade of the twenty-first century as both urban and rural school districts experimented with single sex education as a way to address the needs of at-risk students, particularly Black and

Latino boys.[10] While there are more all-boys public schools in the U.S. than all-girls schools, currently more girls attend such schools than do boys.[11] Only ten percent of students in these public, single-sex schools are white.[12]

In 1991 a plan for such all-boy academies by the Detroit, Michigan school board lost a challenge in federal district court, before they could even open.[13] They were scheduled to offer an "Afro-centric curriculum" and to emphasize "male responsibilities." The federal district court declared the plan unconstitutional because no comparable offerings for Black girls were being made available, even though there were many at-risk female students in the Detroit public schools. Also, the Detroit Board did not successfully demonstrate a substantial relationship between excluding Black girls and attaining educational success for Black boys.[14]

In the No Child Left Behind law, however, the Bush II administration specifically encouraged single-sex academies by making available "federal innovative assistance funds" to support local educational programs for providing single-sex schools "consistent with applicable law."[15] This statute mandated that the Secretary of Education issue, within 120 days, guidelines for local education agencies seeking funding for the programs described.[16] The Office for Civil Rights of the Department of Education then published guidelines on current Title IX requirements related to single-sex classes and schools. These guidelines make clear that the Department believes that Title IX and its regulations permit single-sex schools within a school system, but only if a school district that establishes a single-sex school for one sex with a particular program also establishes for the other sex equal access to a comparable school with that curriculum. The "comparable school" has to be single-sex.[17] On that same day, the Department of Education indicated in the Federal Register its intent to propose regulations providing more flexibility under Title IX for creating single-sex classes and schools.[18]

A highly touted, public high school with a curriculum designed specifically for boys of color in Washington D.C., Ronald Brown College Prep High School, admitted its first class in September 2016. The ACLU immediately announced an intent to challenge the boys-only admission program in court unless the school offered admission to girls or D.C. opened a comparable school for girls. In September of 2016, the ACLU publicly announced that it had received assurance from lawyers from the attorney general's office that girls were as eligible as boys to apply to the new school. The D.C. Public Schools then, along with official spokespersons for the attorney general's office, immediately publicly refuted the ACLU announcement, insisting that it was still a boys-only school.[19] As this book goes to press, neither a court challenge nor admission of a girl to Ronald Brown College Prep has occurred.

HIGHER EDUCATION

As the above discussion demonstrates, girls faced unique obstacles as they sought to gain access to elementary and secondary education and later to integrate boys-only secondary schools. The obstacles to gaining access to institutions of higher education were no less daunting, but often implicated a distinctive set of issues related to women's reproductive capacities and roles as mothers. For example, Dr. Edward Clarke was a prominent American physician whose book *Sex and Education* (1883) was widely read in the late nineteenth century, and he argued that a college education would render female students infertile. Here is an excerpt.

> ### FROM EDWARD H. CLARKE, M.D., *SEX IN EDUCATION; OR, A FAIR CHANCE FOR THE GIRLS*
>
> . . . It has just been said that the educational methods of our schools and colleges for girls are, to a large extent, the cause of "the thousand ills" that beset American women. . . . Those grievous maladies which torture a woman's earthly existence, called leucorrhoea, amenorrhea, dysmenorrhea, chronic and acute ovaritis. There have been instances, and I have seen such, of females in whom the special mechanism we are speaking of remained germinal,— undeveloped. It seemed to have been aborted. They graduated from school or college excellent scholars, but with undeveloped ovaries. Later they married, and were sterile.
>
> Prolapsus uteri, hysteria, neuralgia, and the like. . . are directly and largely affected by the causes that will be presently pointed out, and which arise from a neglect of the peculiarities of a woman's organization. The regimen of our schools fosters this neglect. The regimen of a college arranged for boys, if imposed on girls, would foster it still more.
>
> . . .[At the age] when the divergence of the sexes becomes obvious to the most careless observer, the complicated apparatus peculiar to the female enters upon a condition of functional activity. "The ovaries, which constitute," says Dr. Dalton, "the 'essential parts' of this apparatus, and certain accessory organs, are now rapidly developed." Previously they were inactive. . . At this period they take on a process of rapid growth and development. Coincident with this process, indicating it, and essential to it, are the periodical phenomena which

> characterize woman's physique until she attains the third division of her tripartite life. The growth of this peculiar and marvelous apparatus, in the perfect development of which humanity has so large an interest, occurs during the few years of a girl's educational life. No such extraordinary task, calling for such rapid expenditure of force, building up such a delicate and extensive mechanism within the organism . . .is imposed upon the male physique at the same epoch. . . The importance of having our methods of female education recognize this peculiar demand for growth, and of so adjusting themselves to it, as to allow a sufficient opportunity for the healthy development of the ovaries and their accessory organs, and for the establishment of their periodical functions, cannot be overestimated. . .

Several generations of women college students have proved Dr. Clarke wrong. The female reproductive system functions efficiently most of the time, no matter what activity an individual woman pursues. But the notion of a possible conflict between higher education and women's reproductive function persisted well into the twentieth century, as exemplified in the following excerpt from a 1950 book by Lynn White, president of Mills, a woman's college in Oakland, California, from 1943 to 1958.

> ### FROM LYNN WHITE, *EDUCATING OUR DAUGHTERS: A CHALLENGE TO THE COLLEGES*[20]
>
> On my desk lies a letter from a young mother, a few years out of college: "I have come to realize that I was educated to be a successful man and now must learn by myself how to be a successful woman." The basic irrelevance of what passes as women's education in America could not be more compactly phrased. . .
>
> The pattern of a man's existence is fairly simple. He is born; he is educated partly to become a person and partly to earn a living; he earns a living, gets a wife, begets children, and works until he dies. The pattern of a woman's life today is essentially different. After she graduates from college she is faced with her first major choice: family or career (although "career" is a glamour-word for the kind of jobs most women can get!) If a man marries he must work, harder than ever at his career; there is no conflict. Yet, despite all the brave phrases which are currently fashionable, a married woman who tries to combine the two usually has either a token career or a token family, at least while her children are young. . .

> Incidentally, one of the least forgivable symptoms of the masculine dominance is the notion, widespread not only among men but also among women whose training has led them to accept a masculine scale of values, that if a girl is going to get married there is no use wasting four years of higher education on her. 'Do you send a girl to college to learn how to have babies?' they ask, with a leer. The answer is an emphatic Yes. Motherhood has its spiritual as well as its biological aspects. The balance between the qualities of personality, the breadth of understanding and interest which are the traditional goals of liberal education, are needed by no one more than by a wife and mother....
>
> Would it be impossible to present a beginning course in foods as exciting, and as difficult to work up after college, as a course in post-Kantian philosophy would be?...Why not study the theory and preparation of a Basque paella, of a well-marinated shish kebab, lamb kidneys sautéed in sherry, an authoritative curry, the use of herbs, even such simple sophistications as serving cold artichokes with fresh milk. A girl majoring in history or chemistry could well find time for such a course which, we may be sure, would do much to enliven her own life and that of her family and friends in later years. It is rumored that the divorce rate of home economics majors is greatly below that of college women as a whole.

"We are not educating women to be scholars," President White was fond of saying; "we are educating them to be wives and mothers."[21] This orientation made Mills very different from the first women's colleges in the U.S., founded in the nineteenth century. Vassar, Bryn Mawr, Smith, and the rest of the "Seven Sisters" did educate women to be scholars; these were women's versions of the elite men's colleges founded in the seventeenth and eighteenth centuries, and at least as exclusive. Despite private education opportunities for women, the establishment of public colleges and universities played a significant role in making higher education available to both men and women.

The Morrill Land-Grant Act of 1862 set aside federal lands in each state for a public university and began a democratization of higher education that made college possible for increasing numbers of Americans. The larger states, like California, Texas, and New York, established more than one state institution; even some cities, like New York and Chicago, had their own systems. By 1950, no state denied women access to public higher education. All-female and all-male public colleges did exist, but most institutions of higher education were coeducational. The City College of New York, or CCNY (now City College of the City University of New York), was modeled after the private elite colleges much as Central High and Boston Latin were modeled after exclusive prep schools, and served the similar purpose of making elite education available to a broader array of individuals beyond the affluent and elite. Felix Frankfurter, the future Supreme Court justice (and the third justice who was Jewish), attended CCNY at a time when elite private colleges admitted few Jews. But public colleges for women were not modeled after the Seven Sisters. (Nor were the vast majority of coed or men's colleges modeled after the Ivy League.) Public women's colleges rarely endorsed Lynn White's vision of women's education, but they were often described as places to earn the "Mrs." degree.

Texas A&M Cases: *Heaton v. Bristol* (1958) and *Allred v. Heaton* (1960)

In the 1950s, Lena Bristol of Bryan, Texas wanted to attend the all-male Texas A&M University (in court records, "The Agricultural and Mechanical College of Texas"). Bristol, a 34-year-old wife and mother, could not relocate to any of the 16 coeducational institutions or to the one women's public college in the state. Texas A&M was the only land-grant college in the nation that was not coeducational. When founded in 1876, it was essentially a military college; all students had to belong to the Corps of Cadets. This requirement had been reduced to two years in the Corps by the time Bristol applied, was rejected, and sued, but the military atmosphere remained. When Bristol won in the state trial court, the university appealed. The state appellate court found the case more similar to *Goesaert v. Cleary* (see Chapter 1) than to *Brown v. Board of Education*. Conforming to the prevailing constitutional doctrine in 1958, the judges ruled in the university's favor writing that

> the controlling question... is whether the State, as a matter of public policy, may as a part of its total system of higher education, maintain, for the choice and service of its citizens, one all-male and one all-female institution, along with sixteen institutions which are co-educational. We think undoubtedly the answer is Yes. Such a plan exalts neither sex at the expense of the other, but to the contrary recognizes the equal rights of both sexes to the benefits of the best, most varied system of higher education that the State can supply.[22]

Margaret Allred's situation was somewhat different from Lena Bristol's. The Brazos County resident wanted to major in floriculture. Texas A&M was not only convenient but also the only university in Texas that offered this program. Therefore, much of what the appeals court said in *Bristol* was inapplicable to *Allred v. Heaton.* But the court remained unreceptive to her assertion that she could not get the education she wanted without leaving Texas.

Texas A&M began admitting women on a limited basis in 1963. Not until 1968 did the university open a women's dormitory.

Kirstein v. Rector and Visitors of the University of Virginia (1970)

Like Texas, Virginia had an all-male state-supported military college: the Virginia Military Institute (VMI), which remained a single-sex institution until the 1990s (see *U.S. v. Virginia* below). Unlike in Texas or any other state, Virginia's flagship campus, the University of Virginia (UVA), remained exclusively male until 1970. Unlike Lena Bristol and Margaret Allred, Joanne Kirstein and her fellow plaintiffs took their case to federal court. The three-judge district court disavowed any intention of forcing VMI or any of the other three single-sex institutions in Virginia to change their policies. The opinion declared, however, that UVA was unique among Virginia's 31 public institutions of higher learning and must admit women.

KIRSTEIN V. RECTOR AND VISITORS OF THE UNIVERSITY OF VIRGINIA

309 F. Supp.184 (E.D. Va. 1970)

CRAVEN, CIRCUIT JUDGE:

...It is difficult to evaluate the quality of education. Without attempting to do so, we think it fair to say from the evidence that the most prestigious institution of higher education in Virginia is the University of Virginia at Charlottesville, despite the apparent high quality of education offered at other Virginia institutions. The University of Virginia at Charlottesville is by far the largest educational institution, and its diversity of instruction is not paralleled in Virginia.

At the first hearing of this case we indicated our reluctance to interfere with the internal operation of any Virginia college or university, and particularly that of the University of Virginia at Charlottesville. We expended our best efforts to encourage the litigants to agree upon a consent judgment that might satisfactorily implement the Board of Visitors' contemplated changes in structure and nature of the University of Virginia at Charlottesville. We were impressed with the so-called Woody Commission report and its strong recommendation that sex barriers to admission to any Virginia institution of higher education be removed...

...The pattern of separation by sex of educational institutions is a long established one in America and a system widely and generally accepted until the last decade. Despite this history, it seems clear to us that the Commonwealth of Virginia may not now deny to women, on the basis of sex, educational opportunities at the Charlottesville campus that are not afforded in other institutions operated by the state. Unquestionably the facilities at Charlottesville do offer courses of instruction that are not available elsewhere. Furthermore, as we have noted, there exists at Charlottesville a "prestige" factor that is not available at other Virginia educational institutions. These particular individual plaintiffs are not in a position, without regard to the type of instruction sought, to go elsewhere without harm to themselves and disruption of their lives. Two of the plaintiffs are married to graduate students who must remain at the University of Virginia at Charlottesville. A pattern of continued sex restriction would present these plaintiffs with the dilemma of choosing between the marriage relationship and further education. We think the state may not constitutionally impose upon a qualified young woman applicant the necessity of making such a choice. We hold, and this is all we hold, that on the facts of this case these particular plaintiffs have been... denied their constitutional right to an education equal with that offered men at Charlottesville and that such discrimination on the basis of sex violates the Equal Protection Clause of the Fourteenth Amendment.

Williams v. McNair (1970)

Williams v. McNair, decided six months after *Kirstein*, was the first federal case involving men who wanted to attend a women's college. South Carolina's public higher education system was symmetrical to that of Texas in 1960: one women's college, one all-male military college, and six coeducational institutions.

WILLIAMS V. MCNAIR
316 F. Supp. 134 (D.S.C. 1970)

DONALD RUSSELL, DISTRICT JUDGE:

[T]he State of South Carolina has established a wide range of educational institutions at the college and university level...The several institutions so established vary in purpose, curriculum, and location. Some are limited to undergraduate programs; others extend their offerings into the graduate field.

With two exceptions, such institutions are co-educational. Two, by law, however, limit their student admissions to members of one sex. Thus the Citadel restricts its student admission to males and Winthrop, the college involved in this proceeding, may not admit as a regular degree candidate males. There is an historical reason for these legislative restrictions upon the admission standards of these two latter institutions. The first, the Citadel, while offering a full range of undergraduate liberal arts courses and granting degrees in engineering as well, is designated as a military school, and apparently, the Legislature deemed it appropriate for that reason to provide for an all-male student body. Winthrop, on the other hand, was designed as a school for young ladies, which, though offering a liberal arts program, gave special attention to many courses thought to be specially helpful to female students.

The Equal Protection Clause of the Fourteenth Amendment does not require "identity of treatment" for all citizens, or preclude a state, by legislation, from making classifications and creating differences in the rights of different groups. It is only when the discriminatory treatment and varying standards, as created by the legislative or administrative classification are arbitrary and wanting in any rational justification that they offend the Equal Protection Clause. Specifically, a legislative classification based on sex, has often been held to be constitutionally permissible.

. . .Of course, if there is no rational basis for the classification by sex, the legislation must fall. An instance of such a classification is involved in *United States ex rel. Robinson v. York* (D.C. Conn. 1968) 281 F. Supp. 8, in which it was held that differences in authorized sentences between males and females in a criminal statute was "invidious discrimination" and invalid. However, the Court prefaced its decision with the statement: "This deference to legislative classifications can extend to classifications based on sex."

It is conceded that recognized pedagogical opinion is divided on the wisdom of maintaining "single-sex" institutions of higher education but it is stipulated that there is a respectable body of educators who believe that "a single-sex institution can advance the quality and effectiveness of its instruction by concentrating upon areas of primary interest to only one sex." The idea of educating the sexes separately, the plaintiffs admit, "has a long history" and "is practiced extensively throughout the world." It is no doubt true, as plaintiffs suggest, that the trend in this country is away from the operation of separate institutions for the sexes, but there is still a substantial number of private and public institutions, which limit their enrollment to one sex and do so because they feel it offers better educational advantages. While history and tradition

> alone may not support a discrimination, the Constitution does not require that a classification "keep abreast of the latest" in educational opinion, especially when there remains a respectable opinion to the contrary; it only demands that the discrimination not be wholly wanting in reason.
>
> ...If the State operated only one college and that college was Winthrop, there can be no question that to deny males admission thereto would be impermissible under the Equal Protection Clause. But, as we have already remarked, these plaintiffs have a complete range of state institutions they may attend. They are free to attend either an all-male or, if they wish, a number of co-educational institutions at various locations over the State. There is no suggestion that there is any special feature connected with Winthrop that will make it more advantageous educationally to them than any number of other State-supported institutions. They point to no courses peculiar to Winthrop in which they wish to enroll. It is true that, in the case of some, if not all, of the plaintiffs, Winthrop is more convenient geographically for them than the other State institutions. They...are treated no differently than are other students who reside in communities many miles distant from any State supported college or university.

Case note: The Supreme Court affirmed this decision without opinion in March 1971.

Mississippi University for Women v. Hogan (1982)

Williams v. McNair was the last constitutional case on sex segregation before *Reed v. Reed* (see Chapter 2). The Supreme Court's abandonment of the rational basis test for sex discrimination cases in favor of the *Craig v. Boren* intermediate scrutiny test (substantial relationship to important purpose) encouraged new challenges to public single-sex education. *Mississippi University for Women v. Hogan* was the first majority opinion written by Sandra Day O'Connor, the first woman appointed to the U.S. Supreme Court. The majority ruled that the relationship between Mississippi University for Women's (MUW) single-sex policy and the state's desire to compensate women for disadvantages was not substantial enough to justify excluding a man from the only public nursing education program near his home. The fact that men could already attend classes at MUW (as auditors or as non-degree students) may have made the case easier. Nevertheless, *Hogan* was decided 5–4.

Joe Hogan had found himself in a situation similar to what Margaret Allred had encountered in Texas 30 years earlier. Hogan, a registered nurse employed in the city where MUW was located, wished to pursue a B.A. degree in nursing there. Although otherwise qualified, he was refused admission pursuant to the state laws that maintained MUW as an all-women institution. Hogan argued that the single-sex admission policy violated the equal protection clause. A federal district court had rejected his claims in a summary judgment, but a Circuit Court of Appeals had found in his favor under the *Craig* test (646 F.2d 1116). When Mississippi appealed to the U.S. Supreme Court, Justice Sandra Day O'Connor, the first woman on the Court, wrote for the majority as follows:

MISSISSIPPI UNIVERSITY FOR WOMEN V. HOGAN
458 U.S. 718 (1982)

JUSTICE O'CONNOR delivered the opinion of the Court.

This case presents the narrow issue of whether a state statute that excludes males from enrolling in a state-supported professional nursing school violates the Equal Protection Clause of the Fourteenth Amendment.

The facts are not in dispute. In 1884, the Mississippi Legislature created the Mississippi Industrial Institute and College for the Education of White Girls of the State of Mississippi, now the oldest state-supported all-female college in the United States. 1884 Miss. Gen. Laws, Ch. 30, 6. The school, known today as Mississippi University for Women (MUW), has from its inception limited its enrollment to women.[1]

We . . . now affirm the judgment of the Court of Appeals.[7]

We begin our analysis aided by several firmly established principles. Because the challenged policy expressly discriminates among applicants on the basis of gender, it is subject to scrutiny under the Equal Protection Clause of the Fourteenth Amendment. *Reed v. Reed*, 404 U.S. 71, 75 (1971). That this statutory policy discriminates against males rather than against females does not exempt it from scrutiny or reduce the standard of review.[8] *Caban v. Mohammed*, 441 U.S. 380, 394 (1979); *Orr v. Orr*, 440 U.S. 268, 279 (1979). Our decisions also establish that the party seeking to uphold a statute that classifies individuals on the basis of their gender must carry the burden of showing an "exceedingly persuasive justification" for the classification. *Kirchberg v. Feenstra*, 450 U.S. 455, 461 (1981); *Personnel Administrator of Mass. v. Feeney*, 442 U.S. 256, 273 (1979). The burden is met only by showing at least that the classification serves "important governmental objectives and that the discriminatory means employed" are "substantially related to the achievement of those objectives." *Wengler v. Druggists Mutual Ins. Co.*, 446 U.S. 142, 150 (1980).

Although the test for determining the validity of a gender-based classification is straightforward, it must be applied free of fixed notions concerning the roles and abilities of males and females. Care must be taken in ascertaining whether the statutory objective itself reflects archaic and stereotypic notions. Thus, if the statutory objective is to exclude or "protect" members of one gender because they are presumed to suffer from an inherent handicap or to be innately inferior, the objective itself is illegitimate. See *Frontiero v. Richardson*, 411 U.S. 677, 684–685 (1973) (plurality opinion).[10]

If the State's objective is legitimate and important, we next determine whether the requisite direct, substantial relationship between objective and means is present. The purpose of requiring that close relationship is to assure that the validity of a classification is determined through reasoned analysis rather than through the mechanical application of traditional, often inaccurate, assumptions about the proper roles of men and women. The need for the requirement is amply revealed by reference to the broad range of statutes already invalidated by this Court, statutes that relied upon the simplistic, outdated assumption that gender could be used as a "proxy for other, more germane bases of classification," *Craig v. Boren*, 429 U.S. 190, 198 (1976), to establish a link between objective and classification.

Applying this framework, we now analyze the arguments advanced by the State to justify its refusal to allow males to enroll for credit in MUW's School of Nursing.

The State's primary justification for maintaining the single-sex admissions policy of MUW's School of Nursing is that it compensates for discrimination against women and, therefore, constitutes educational affirmative action.[13] Applied to the School of Nursing, we find the State's argument unpersuasive.

In limited circumstances, a gender-based classification favoring one sex can be justified if it intentionally and directly assists members of the sex that is disproportionately burdened. See *Schlesinger v. Ballard*, 419 U.S. 498 (1975). However, we consistently have emphasized that "the mere recitation of a benign, compensatory purpose is not an automatic shield which protects against any inquiry into the actual purposes underlying a statutory scheme." *Weinberger v. Wiesenfeld*, 420 U.S. 636, 648 (1975). The same searching analysis must be made, regardless of whether the State's objective is to eliminate family controversy, *Reed v. Reed*, 404 U.S. 71 (1971), to achieve administrative efficiency, *Frontiero v. Richardson*, 411 U.S. 677 (1973), or to balance the burdens borne by males and females.

It is readily apparent that a State can evoke a compensatory purpose to justify an otherwise discriminatory classification only if members of the gender benefited by the classification actually suffer a disadvantage related to the classification. We considered such a situation in *Califano v. Webster*, 430 U.S. 313 (1977)...[and] *Schlesinger v. Ballard* [and upheld the compensatory schemes].

In sharp contrast, Mississippi has made no showing that women lacked opportunities to obtain training in the field of nursing or to attain positions of leadership in that field when the MUW School of Nursing opened its door or that women currently are deprived of such opportunities. In fact, in 1970, the year before the School of Nursing's first class enrolled, women earned 94 percent of the nursing baccalaureate degrees conferred in Mississippi and 98.6 percent of the degrees earned nationwide. U.S. Dept. of Health, Education, and Welfare, *Earned Degrees Conferred: 1969–1970, Institutional Data* 388 (1972). That year was not an aberration; one decade earlier, women had earned all the nursing degrees conferred in Mississippi and 98.9 percent of the degrees conferred nationwide. U.S. Dept. of Health, Education, and Welfare, *Earned Degrees Conferred, 1959–1960: Bachelor's and Higher Degrees* 135 (1960). As one would expect, the labor force reflects the same predominance of women in nursing. When MUW's School of Nursing began operation, nearly 98 percent of all employed registered nurses were female. 14 United States Bureau of Census, *1981 Statistical Abstract of the United States* 402 (1981).

Rather than compensate for discriminatory barriers faced by women, MUW's policy of excluding males from admission to the School of Nursing tends to perpetuate the stereotyped view of nursing as an exclusively woman's job.[15] By assuring that Mississippi allots more openings in its state-supported nursing schools to women than it does to men, MUW's admissions policy lends credibility to the old view that women, not men, should become nurses, and makes the assumption that nursing is a field for women a self-fulfilling prophecy. Thus, we conclude that, although the State recited a "benign, compensatory purpose," it failed to establish that the alleged objective is the actual purpose underlying the discriminatory classification.

The policy is invalid also because it fails the second part of the equal protection test, for the State has made no showing that the gender-based classification is substantially and directly related to its proposed compensatory objective. To the contrary, MUW's policy of permitting men to attend classes as auditors fatally undermines its claim that women, at least those in the School of Nursing, are adversely affected by the presence of men.

MUW permits men who audit to participate fully in classes. Additionally, both men and women take part in continuing education courses offered by the School of Nursing, in which regular nursing students also can enroll. The uncontroverted record reveals that admitting men to nursing classes does not affect teaching style, that the presence of men in the classroom would not affect the performance of the female nursing students, and that men in coeducational nursing schools do not dominate the classroom. In sum, the record in this case is flatly inconsistent with the claim that excluding men from the School of Nursing is necessary to reach any of MUW's educational goals.

Thus, considering both the asserted interest and the relationship between the interest and the methods used by the State, we conclude that the State has fallen far short of establishing the "exceedingly persuasive justification" needed to sustain the gender-based classification. Accordingly, we hold that MUW's policy of denying males the right to enroll for credit in its School of Nursing violates the Equal Protection Clause of the Fourteenth Amendment.[17]

In an additional attempt to justify its exclusion of men from MUW's School of Nursing, the State contends that MUW is the direct beneficiary "of specific congressional legislation which, on its face, permits the institution to exist as it has in the past." The argument is based upon the language of 901(a) in Title IX of the Education Amendments of 1972, 20 U.S.C. 1681(a). Although 901(a) prohibits gender discrimination in education programs that receive federal financial assistance, subsection 5 exempts the admissions policies of undergraduate institutions "that traditionally and continually from [their] establishment [have] had a policy of admitting only students of one sex" from the general prohibition. Arguing that Congress enacted Title IX in furtherance of its power to enforce the Fourteenth Amendment, a power granted by Section 5 of that Amendment, the State would have us conclude that § 901(a)(5) is but "a congressional limitation upon the broad prohibitions of the Equal Protection Clause of the Fourteenth Amendment."

The argument requires little comment. Initially, it is far from clear that Congress intended, through § 901(a)(5), to exempt MUW from any constitutional obligation. Rather, Congress apparently intended, at most, to exempt MUW from the requirements of Title IX.

Even if Congress envisioned a constitutional exemption, the State's argument would fail. Section 5 of the Fourteenth Amendment gives Congress broad power indeed to enforce the command of the Amendment and "to secure to all persons the enjoyment of perfect equality of civil rights and the equal protection of the laws against State denial or invasion . . . ." *Ex parte Virginia*, 100 U.S. 339, 346 (1880). Congress' power under Section 5, however, "is limited to adopting measures to enforce the guarantees of the Amendment; Section 5 grants Congress no power to restrict, abrogate, or dilute these guarantees." *Katzenbach v. Morgan*, 384 U.S. 641, 651, n. 10 (1966). . . .

. . .

Opinion Footnotes

1 The charter of MUW, basically unchanged since its founding, now provides: "The purpose and aim of the Mississippi State College for Women is the moral and intellectual advancement of the girls of the state by the maintenance of a first-class institution for their education in the arts and sciences, for their training in normal school methods and kindergarten, for their instruction in bookkeeping, photography, stenography, telegraphy, and typewriting, and in designing, drawing, engraving, and painting, and their industrial application, and for their instruction in fancy, general and practical needlework, and in such other industrial branches as experience, from time to time, shall suggest as necessary or proper to fit them for the practical affairs of life." Miss. Code Ann. 37–117–3 (1972). Mississippi maintains no other single-sex public university or college. Thus, we are not faced with the question of whether States can provide "separate but equal" undergraduate institutions for males and females. Cf. *Vorchheimer v. School District of Philadelphia*, 532 F.2d 880 (CA3 1975), aff'd by an equally divided Court, 430 U.S. 703 (1977).

7 Although some statements in the Court of Appeals' decision refer to all schools within MUW, . . . the Court of Appeals' holding applies only to Hogan's individual claim for relief. 646 F.2d, at 1119–1120. . . . Hogan sought only admission to the School of Nursing. Tr. of Oral Arg. 24. Because Hogan's claim is thus limited, and because we review judgments, not statements in opinions, *Black v. Cutter Laboratories*, 351 U.S. 292 (1956), we decline to address the question of whether MUW's admissions policy, as applied to males seeking admission to schools other than the School of Nursing, violates the Fourteenth Amendment.

8 Without question, MUW's admissions policy worked to Hogan's disadvantage. Although Hogan could have attended classes and received credit in one of Mississippi's state-supported coeducational nursing programs, none of which was located in Columbus, he could attend only by driving a considerable distance from his home. A similarly situated female would not have been required to choose between forgoing credit and bearing that inconvenience. Moreover, since many students enrolled in the School of Nursing hold full-time jobs, Hogan's female colleagues had available an opportunity, not open to Hogan, to obtain credit for additional training. The policy of denying males the right to obtain credit toward a baccalaureate degree thus imposed upon Hogan "a burden he would not bear were he female." *Orr v. Orr*, 440 U.S. 268, 273 (1979).

10 History provides numerous examples of legislative attempts to exclude women from particular areas simply because legislators believed women were less able than men to perform a particular function. In 1873, this Court remained unmoved by Myra Bradwell's argument that the Fourteenth Amendment prohibited a State from classifying her as unfit to practice law simply because she was female. *Bradwell v. Illinois*, 16 Wall. 130 (1873). . . . [This note further discusses *Bradwell*, *Goesaert* and cases that presumed women workers were weaker and needed protection from certain jobs.—AU.]

13 . . . Apparently, the impetus for founding MUW came not from a desire to provide women with advantages superior to those offered men, but rather from a desire to provide white women in Mississippi access to state-supported higher learning. In 1856, Sally Reneau began agitating for a college for white women. Those initial efforts were unsuccessful, and, by 1870, Mississippi provided higher education only for white men and black men and women. In 1882, two years before MUW was chartered, the University of Mississippi opened its doors to women. However, the institution was in those early years not "extensively patronized by females; most of those who come being such as desire to qualify themselves to teach." By 1890, the largest number of women in any class at the University had been 23, while nearly 350 women enrolled in the first session of MUW. Because the University did not solicit the attendance of women until after 1920, and did not accept women at all for a time between 1907 and 1920, most Mississippi women who attended college attended MUW. Thus, in Mississippi, as elsewhere in the country, women's colleges were founded to provide some form of higher education for the academically disenfranchised. [Sources omitted—AU.]

15 Officials of the American Nurses Association have suggested that excluding men from the field has depressed nurses' wages. To the extent the exclusion of men has that effect, MUW's admissions policy actually penalizes [women]. . .

17 JUSTICE POWELL's dissent suggests that a second objective is served by the gender-based classification in that Mississippi has elected to provide women a choice of educational environments. Since any gender-based classification provides one class a benefit or choice not available to the other class, however, that argument begs the question. The issue is not whether the benefited class profits from the classification, but whether the State's decision to confer a benefit only upon one class by means of a discriminatory classification is substantially related to achieving a legitimate and substantial goal.

CHIEF JUSTICE BURGER, dissenting.

I agree generally with JUSTICE POWELL'S dissenting opinion. I write separately, however, to emphasize that the Court's holding today is limited to the context of a professional nursing school. Since the Court's opinion relies heavily on its finding that women have traditionally dominated the nursing profession, it suggests that a State might well be justified in maintaining, for example, the option of an all-women's business school or liberal arts program.

JUSTICE BLACKMUN, dissenting.

Unless Mississippi University for Women wished to preserve a historical anachronism, one only states the obvious when he observes that the University long ago should have replaced its original statement of purpose and brought its corporate papers into the 20th century. It failed to do so and, perhaps in partial consequence, finds itself in this litigation, with the Court's opinion taking full advantage of that failure. . .

Despite that failure, times have changed in the intervening 98 years. What was once an "Institute and College" is now a genuine university, with a 2-year School of Nursing established 11 years ago and then expanded to a 4-year baccalaureate program in 1974. But respondent Hogan "wants in" at this particular location in his home city of Columbus. It is not enough that his State of Mississippi offers baccalaureate programs in nursing open to males at Jackson and at Hattiesburg. Mississippi thus has not closed the doors of its educational system to males like Hogan. Assuming that he is qualified—and I have no reason whatsoever to doubt his qualifications—those doors are open and his maleness alone does not prevent his gaining the additional education he professes to seek.

I have come to suspect that it is easy to go too far with rigid rules in this area of claimed sex discrimination, and to lose—indeed destroy—values that mean much to some people by forbidding the State to offer them a choice while not depriving others of an alternative choice. . . .

While the Court purports to write narrowly, declaring that it does not decide the same issue with respect to "separate but equal" undergraduate institutions for females and males, at n. 1, or with respect to units of MUW other than its School of Nursing, at n. 7, there is inevitable spillover from the Court's ruling today. That ruling, it seems to me, places in constitutional jeopardy any state-supported educational institution that confines its student body in any area to members of one sex, even though the State elsewhere provides an equivalent program to the complaining applicant. The Court's reasoning does not stop with the School of Nursing of the Mississippi University for Women.

I hope that we do not lose all values that some think are worthwhile (and are not based on differences of race or religion) and relegate ourselves to needless conformity. The ringing words of the Equal Protection Clause of the Fourteenth Amendment. . . do not demand that price.

JUSTICE POWELL, with whom JUSTICE REHNQUIST joins, dissenting.

The Court's opinion bows deeply to conformity. Left without honor—indeed, held unconstitutional—is an element of diversity that has characterized much of American education and enriched much of American life. The Court in effect holds today that no State now may provide even a single institution of higher learning open only to women students. It gives no heed to the efforts of the State of Mississippi to provide abundant opportunities for young men and young women to attend coeducational institutions, and none to the preferences of the more than 40,000 young women who over the years have evidenced their approval of an all-women's college by choosing Mississippi University for Women (MUW) over seven coeducational universities within the State. The Court decides today that the Equal Protection Clause makes it unlawful for the State to provide women with a traditionally popular and respected choice of educational environment. It does so in a case instituted by one man, who represents no class, and whose primary concern is personal convenience.

It is undisputed that women enjoy complete equality of opportunity in Mississippi's public system of higher education. Of the State's 8 universities and 16 junior colleges, all except MUW are coeducational. At least two other

Mississippi universities would have provided respondent with the nursing curriculum that he wishes to pursue. No other male has joined in his complaint. The only groups with any personal acquaintance with MUW to file amicus briefs are female students and alumnae of MUW. And they have emphatically rejected respondent's arguments, urging that the State of Mississippi be allowed to continue offering the choice from which they have benefited.

Nor is respondent significantly disadvantaged by MUW's all-female tradition. His constitutional complaint is based upon a single asserted harm: that he must travel to attend the state-supported nursing schools that concededly are available to him. The Court characterizes this injury as one of "inconvenience." At n. 8. This description is fair and accurate, though somewhat embarrassed by the fact that there is, of course, no constitutional right to attend a state-supported university in one's home town. Thus the Court, to redress respondent's injury of inconvenience, must rest its invalidation of MUW's single-sex program on a mode of "sexual stereotype" reasoning that has no application whatever to the respondent or to the "wrong" of which he complains. At best this is anomalous. And ultimately the anomaly reveals legal error—that of applying a heightened equal protection standard, developed in cases of genuine sexual stereotyping, to a narrowly utilized state classification that provides an additional choice for women. Moreover, I believe that Mississippi's educational system should be upheld in this case even if this inappropriate method of analysis is applied.

Coeducation, historically, is a novel educational theory. From grade school through high school, college, and graduate and professional training, much of the Nation's population during much of our history has been educated in sexually segregated classrooms. At the college level, for instance, until recently some of the most prestigious colleges and universities—including most of the Ivy League—had long histories of single-sex education. As Harvard, Yale, and Princeton remained all-male colleges well into the second half of this century, the "Seven Sister" institutions established a parallel standard of excellence for women's colleges....Mount Holyoke, Smith, and Wellesley recently have made considered decisions to remain essentially single-sex institutions.... Barnard retains its independence from Columbia, its traditional coordinate institution. Harvard and Radcliffe maintained separate admissions policies as recently as 1975.[2]

The sexual segregation of students has been a reflection of, rather than an imposition upon, the preference of those subject to the policy. It cannot be disputed, for example, that the highly qualified women attending the leading women's colleges could have earned admission to virtually any college of their choice.³ Women attending such colleges have chosen to be there, usually expressing a preference for the special benefits of single-sex institutions. Similar decisions were made by the colleges that elected to remain open to women only.⁴

The arguable benefits of single-sex colleges also continue to be recognized by students of higher education. The Carnegie Commission on Higher Education has reported that it "favor[s] the continuation of colleges for women. They provide an element of diversity . . . and [an environment in which women] generally . . . speak up more in their classes, . . . hold more positions of leadership on campus, . . . and . . . have more role models and mentors among women teachers and administrators." *Carnegie Report*, quoted in K. Davidson, R. Ginsburg, & H. Kay, *Sex-Based Discrimination* 814 (1975 ed.). A 10-year empirical study by the Cooperative Institutional Research Program of the American Counsel of Education and the University of California, Los Angeles, also has affirmed the distinctive benefits of single-sex colleges and universities. As summarized in A. Astin, *Four Critical Years* 232 (1977), the data established that

> [b]oth [male and female] single-sex colleges facilitate student involvement in several areas: academic, interaction with faculty, and verbal aggressiveness. . . . Men's and women's colleges also have a positive effect on intellectual self-esteem. Students at single-sex colleges are more satisfied than students at coeducational colleges with virtually all aspects of college life . . . . The only area where students are less satisfied is social life.

Despite the continuing expressions that single-sex institutions may offer singular advantages to their students, there is no doubt that coeducational institutions are far more numerous. But their numerical predominance does not establish—in any sense properly cognizable by a court—that individual preferences for single-sex education are misguided or illegitimate, or that a State may not provide its citizens with a choice.

The issue in this case is whether a State transgresses the Constitution when—within the context of a public system that offers a diverse range of campuses, curricula, and educational alternatives—it seeks to accommodate the legitimate personal preferences of those desiring the advantages of an all-women's college. In my view, the Court errs seriously by assuming—without argument or discussion—that the equal protection standard generally applicable to sex discrimination is appropriate here. That standard was designed to free women from "archaic and overbroad generalizations." *Schlesinger v. Ballard*, 419 U.S. 498, 508 (1975). In no previous case have we applied it to invalidate state efforts to expand women's choices. Nor are there prior sex discrimination decisions by this Court in which a male plaintiff, as in this case, had the choice of an equal benefit.

The cases cited by the Court therefore do not control the issue now before us. In most of them women were given no opportunity for the same benefit as men. Cases involving male plaintiffs are equally inapplicable. In *Craig v. Boren*, 429 U.S. 190 (1976), a male under 21 was not permitted to buy beer anywhere in the State.... A similar situation prevailed in *Orr v. Orr*, 440 U.S. 268, 279 (1979), where men had no opportunity to seek alimony from their divorced wives....

By applying heightened equal protection analysis to this case, the Court frustrates the liberating spirit of the Equal Protection Clause. It prohibits the States from providing women with an opportunity to choose the type of university they prefer. And yet it is these women whom the Court regards as the *victims* of an illegal, stereotyped perception of the role of women in our society. The Court reasons this way in a case in which no woman has complained, and the only complainant is a man who advances no claims on behalf of anyone else. His claim, it should be recalled, is not that he is being denied a substantive educational opportunity, or even the right to attend an all-male or a coeducational college. It is *only* that the colleges open to him are located at inconvenient distances.

The Court views this case as presenting a serious equal protection claim of sex discrimination. I do not, and I would sustain Mississippi's right to continue MUW on a rational-basis analysis. But I need not apply this "lowest tier" of scrutiny. I can accept for present purposes the standard applied by the Court: that there is a gender-based distinction that must serve an important governmental objective by means that are substantially related to its achievement. E. g., *Wengler v. Druggists Mutual Ins. Co.*, 446 U.S. 142, 150 (1980). The record in this case reflects that MUW has a historic position in the State's educational system dating back to 1884. More than 2,000 women presently evidence their preference for MUW by having enrolled there. The choice is one that discriminates invidiously against no one. And the State's purpose in preserving that choice is legitimate and substantial. Generations of our finest minds, both among educators and students, have believed that single-sex, college-level institutions afford distinctive benefits....

In arguing to the contrary, the Court suggests that the MUW is so operated as to "perpetuate the stereotyped view of nursing as an exclusively women's job." But as the Court itself acknowledges, MUW's School of Nursing was not created until 1971—about 90 years after the single-sex campus itself was founded. This hardly supports a link between nursing as a woman's profession and MUW's single-sex admission policy. Indeed, MUW's School of Nursing was not instituted until more than a decade after a separate School of Nursing was established at the coeducational University of Mississippi at Jackson. The School of Nursing makes up only one part—a relatively small part—of MUW's diverse modern university campus and curriculum. The other departments on the MUW campus offer a typical range of degrees and a typical range of subjects. There is no indication that women suffer fewer opportunities at other Mississippi state campuses because of MUW's admission policy.

In sum, the practice of voluntarily chosen single-sex education is an honored tradition in our country, even if it now rarely exists in state colleges and universities. Mississippi's accommodation of such student choices is legitimate because it is completely consensual and is important because it permits students to decide for themselves the type of college education they think will benefit them most. Finally, Mississippi's policy is substantially related to its long-respected objective.[17]

A distinctive feature of America's tradition has been respect for diversity. This has been characteristic of the peoples from numerous lands who have built our country. It is the essence of our democratic system. At stake in this case as I see it is the preservation of a small aspect of this diversity. But that aspect is by no means insignificant, given our heritage of available choice between single-sex and coeducational institutions of higher learning. The Court answers that there is discrimination. . . . But, having found "discrimination," the Court finds it difficult to identify the victims. It hardly can claim that women are discriminated against. A constitutional case is held to exist solely because one man found it inconvenient to travel to any of the other institutions made available to him by the State of Mississippi. In essence he insists that he has a right to attend a college in his home community. This simply is not a sex discrimination case. The Equal Protection Clause was never intended to be applied to this kind of case.[18]

Opinion Footnotes

2 The history, briefly summarized above, of single-sex higher education in the Northeast is duplicated in other States. I mention only my State of Virginia, where even today Hollins College, Mary Baldwin College, Randolph Macon Woman's College, and Sweet Briar College remain all women's colleges. Each has a proud and respected reputation of quality education.

3 It is true that historically many institutions of higher education—particularly in the East and South—were single-sex. To these extents, choices were by no means universally available to all men and women. But choices always were substantial, and . . .generations of Americans, including scholars, have thought—wholly without regard to any discriminatory animus—that there were distinct advantages in this type of higher education.

4 In announcing Wellesley's decision in 1973 to remain a women's college, President Barbara Newell said that "[t]he research we have clearly demonstrates that women's colleges produce a disproportionate number of women leaders and women in responsible positions in society; it does demonstrate that the higher proportion of women on the faculty the higher the motivation for women students." *Carnegie Report*, in Babcock et al. *Sex Discrimination and the Law*, at 1014.

17 The Court argues that MUW's means are not sufficiently related to its goal because it has allowed men to audit classes. The extent of record information is that men have audited 138 courses in the last 10 years. On average, then, men have audited 14 courses a year. MUW's current annual catalog lists 913 courses offered in one year. It is understandable that MUW might believe that it could allow men to audit courses without materially affecting its environment. MUW charges tuition but gives no academic credit for auditing. The University evidently is correct in believing that few men will choose to audit under such circumstances. This deviation from a perfect relationship between means and ends is insubstantial.

18 The Court, in the opening and closing sentences and note 7 of its opinion, states the issue in terms only of a "professional nursing school" and "decline[s] to address the question of whether MUW's admissions policy, as applied to males seeking admission to schools other than the School of Nursing, violates the Fourteenth Amendment." This would be a welcome limitation if, in fact, it leaves MUW free to remain an all-women's university in each of its other schools and departments . . .The question the Court does not answer is whether MUW may remain a women's university in every respect except its School of Nursing. This is a critical question for this University and its responsible board and officials. The Court holds today that they have deprived Hogan of constitutional rights because MUW is adjudged guilty of sex discrimination. The logic of the Court's entire opinion, apart from its statements mentioned above, appears to apply sweepingly to the entire University. The exclusion of men from the School of Nursing is repeatedly characterized as "gender-based discrimination," subject to the same standard of analysis applied in previous sex discrimination cases of this Court. Nor does the opinion anywhere deny that this analysis applies to the entire University. The Court nevertheless purports to decide this case "narrow[ly]." Normally and properly we decide only the question presented. It seems to me that in fact the issue properly before us is the single-sex policy of the University, and it is this issue that I have addressed in this dissent. The Court of Appeals so viewed this case, and unambiguously held that a single-sex state institution of higher education no longer is permitted by the Constitution. I see no principled way—in light of the Court's rationale—to reach a different result with respect to other MUW schools and departments. But given the Court's insistence that its decision applies only to the School of Nursing, it is my view that the Board and officials of MUW may continue to operate the remainder of the University on a single-sex basis without fear of personal liability. The standard of such liability is whether the conduct of the official "violate[s] clearly established statutory or constitutional rights of which a reasonable person would have known." *Harlow v. Fitzgerald*, 457 U.S. 800, 818 (1982). The Court today leaves in doubt the reach of its decision.

Case Questions

1. According to Justice O'Connor's majority, Hogan suffers gender discrimination as compared to others who live in his region because they can pursue a nursing degree at a state college within commuting distance if they are female, but he cannot. According to Justices Blackmun, Powell, and Rehnquist, he suffers no gender discrimination because many females in the state share with him the dilemma of not living within commuting distance of a state college where they can pursue a nursing degree. Who is correct?

2. If Mississippi decided to bar males from continuing education classes and from auditing at MUW, could it then overcome the Court's argument that its single-sex policy was not substantially enough related to its objective of providing women with the compensatory educational benefits of single-sex schooling?

Women in the Military Academies: *U.S. v. Virginia* (1996)

After *Hogan*, there remained some ambiguity whether states might retain single-sex admissions policies "for schools other than ... Nursing" (n.7 of O'Connor opinion). Most states had eliminated state-funded single sex colleges by the 1980s,[23] but two prominent cases remained: both South Carolina and Virginia ran all-male military colleges, The Citadel (founded in 1842) and Virginia Military Institute (VMI) (founded in 1839), respectively. Both military colleges became embroiled in litigation, and the version that eventually reached the U.S. Supreme Court was the case of VMI in 1996.[24] The national military academies had admitted women in the 1970s, pursuant to Congressional legislation. West Point, for instance, began taking women in 1976.

U.S. v. Virginia began with a lawsuit in 1990 from the U.S. Department of Justice, prompted by a complaint filed by a female high school student who wanted admission.[25] The U.S. attorney general (under President George Bush I) charged Virginia with violating the equal protection clause in its refusal to consider women for admission to VMI no matter how well qualified they might be. Virginia claimed that its single-sex admission policy served the purpose of "educational diversity." At the district court level, Judge Jackson Kiser reasoned that the military college differed in legally significant ways from MUW:

> The record is replete with testimony that single gender education at the undergraduate level is beneficial to both males and females. Moreover, the evidence establishes that key elements of the adversative VMI educational system, with its focus on barracks life, would be fundamentally altered, and the distinctive ends of the system would be thwarted, if VMI were forced to admit females and to make changes necessary to accommodate their needs and interests.[26]

In short, the district court treated the state's goal of offering a diverse array of educational options as legitimately including the option of maintaining an educational system replete with psychological and physical hardships so as to toughen men up for military and civic leadership, but then went beyond this premise to assume that if women were admitted, the system would for this reason have to be softened up, thus destroying it as a truly distinctive option. In other words, the judge presumed that, "even though some women are capable of all of the individual activities required of VMI cadets," if women were admitted, so many of them would fail to meet the rigorous physical and psychological standards that the school would (for reasons not explained) then be forced to lower the standards.[27] The U.S. government appealed the case and then won a reversal of sorts at the circuit court level.

The circuit court conceded that the educational opportunity afforded to students at VMI was unique and that it would be altered in certain respects if women were admitted. It described the system as follows:

> Focusing primarily on character development and leadership training through a unique and intense process, characterized as an "adversative" educational model drawn from earlier military training and English public schools, VMI's educational method emphasizes physical rigor, mental stress, absolute equality of treatment, absence of privacy, minute regulation of behavior, and indoctrination of values. The process is designed to foster in VMI cadets doubts about previous beliefs and experiences and to instill in cadets new values which VMI seeks to impart. The model employs a hostile, spartan environment that is characterized by six interrelated components—the "rat line," the class system, the "dyke" system, the honor code, the barracks life, and the military system.
>
> The rat line refers to the harsh orientation process to which all new cadets ("rats") are subjected during their first seven months at VMI. Designed to be comparable to the Marine Corps' boot camp in terms of physical rigor and mental stress, the rat line includes indoctrination, minute regulation of individual behavior, frequent punishments, rigorous physical education, and military drills. The class system entails the peer assignment of privileges and responsibilities, including supervisory roles, to classes of cadets based on rank. The dyke system, which is "closely linked" with the rat line, assigns each rat to a first classman, who acts as a mentor ("dyke") to relieve some of the stress generated from the rat line. The dyke system aims to create cross-class bonding and provide a model for leadership and support. The honor code, that a cadet "does not lie, cheat, steal nor tolerate those who do," is a stringently enforced code of conduct applying to all aspects of life at VMI and providing the single penalty of expulsion for its violation. The barracks life, described as important to VMI's ethos of egalitarianism, is dictated by the nature and functioning of the barracks. Each class is assigned to one floor of the four-story barracks structure

and three to five cadets are assigned to a room. The rooms are stark and unattractive. There are no locks on the doors and windows are uncovered. Access to bathrooms is provided by outside corridors visible to the quadrangle, and there is a total lack of privacy in the barracks, where cadets are subjected to constant scrutiny and minute regulation, all intended to foster cadet equality and to induce stress. Finally, the military system, providing regulation, etiquette, and drill, pervades life at VMI. As part of the military system each cadet must participate in an ROTC program throughout his four years.[28]

The circuit court concluded that at least three aspects of the VMI program would definitely be altered if women were admitted: physical training (because not enough women would measure up to the men's standards), the absence of privacy, and the adversative approach. These changes in turn would lead to "a substantial change in the egalitarian ethos that is a critical aspect of VMI's training."[29]

On the other hand, the circuit court saw no good reason why Virginia should offer such a unique educational opportunity only to males. Thus, it declared unconstitutional the current system but gave Virginia three options: create a comparable single-sex educational institution for women, admit women to VMI, or let VMI become a private college unsupported by the state (since the equal protection clause is addressed to state governments, not private actors). Virginia chose the first and created a training program for women that it funded at the otherwise-private Mary Baldwin College. It planned to admit 25–30 women in the first year of the Virginia Women's Institute for Leadership (VWIL) and to substitute for the VMI's "adversative" approach a more psychologically nurturant leadership training program geared to the dispositions characteristic of "most women."[30] The U.S. Justice Dept. immediately challenged this alternative system at both district and circuit court[31] levels, but both courts upheld the planned VWIL as offering Virginia women an educational option substantially equal to what VMI offered men. When the case reached the U.S. Supreme Court, President Clinton's Justice Department changed the legal argument to claim that strict scrutiny, rather than merely intermediate scrutiny, was appropriate for laws imposing gender-based discrimination. The Supreme Court handed down its decision in June 1996 and declared that women had to be admitted to VMI.

The opinion was penned by a Clinton appointee, Justice Ruth Bader Ginsburg. She had attained national prominence as head of the ACLU Women's Rights Project, successfully arguing landmark women's rights cases before her appointment to the D.C. Circuit Court of Appeals in the 1970s. Six other justices joined her judgment; of them, five joined her opinion. Justice Antonin Scalia wrote a lone dissent, and Clarence Thomas recused himself because his son attended VMI.

> ### UNITED STATES V. VIRGINIA
> 518 U.S. 515 (1996)
>
> **JUSTICE GINSBURG delivered the opinion of the Court:**
>
> [T]his case present[s] two ultimate issues. First, does Virginia's exclusion of women from the educational opportunities provided by VMI—extraordinary opportunities for military training and civilian leadership development—deny to women "capable of all of the individual activities required of VMI cadets," the equal protection of the laws guaranteed by the Fourteenth Amendment? Second, if VMI's "unique" situation—as Virginia's sole single-sex public institution of higher education—offends the Constitution's equal protection principle, what is the remedial requirement?
>
> ### IV.
>
> We note . . . the core instruction of this Court's pathmarking decisions in *J.E.B. v. Alabama ex rel. T. B.*, 511 U.S. 127, 136–137, and n. 6 (1994), and *Mississippi Univ. for Women*, 458 U.S., at 724: Parties who seek to defend gender-based government action must demonstrate an "exceedingly persuasive justification" for that action.
>
> Today's skeptical scrutiny of official action denying rights or opportunities based on sex responds to volumes of history. As a plurality of this Court acknowledged a generation ago, "our Nation has had a long and unfortunate history of sex discrimination." *Frontiero v. Richardson*, 411 U.S. 677, 684 (1973). Through a century plus three decades and more of that history, women did not count among voters composing "We the People";[5] not until 1920 did women gain a constitutional right to the franchise. Id., at 685. And for a half century thereafter, it remained the prevailing doctrine that government, both federal and state, could withhold from women opportunities accorded men so long as any "basis in reason" could be conceived for the discrimination. See, e.g., *Goesaert v. Cleary*, 335 U.S. 464, 467 (1948).
>
> In 1971, for the first time in our Nation's history, this Court ruled in favor of a woman who complained that her State had denied her the equal protection of its laws. *Reed v. Reed*, 404 U.S. 71, 73. Since Reed, the Court has repeatedly recognized that neither federal nor state government acts compatibly with the equal protection principle when a law or official policy denies to women, simply

because they are women, full citizenship stature—equal opportunity to aspire, achieve, participate in and contribute to society based on their individual talents and capacities. See, e.g., *Kirchberg v. Feenstra*, 450 U.S. 455, 462-463 (1981); *Stanton v. Stanton*, 421 U.S. 7 (1975).

Without equating gender classifications, for all purposes, to classifications based on race or national origin, the Court, in post-*Reed* decisions, has carefully inspected official action that closes a door or denies opportunity to women (or to men). See *J.E.B.*, 511 U.S., at 152 (Kennedy, J., concurring in judgment) (case law evolving since 1971 "reveal[s] a strong presumption that gender classifications are invalid"). To summarize the Court's current directions for cases of official classification based on gender: Focusing on the differential treatment or denial of opportunity for which relief is sought, the reviewing court must determine whether the proffered justification is "exceedingly persuasive." The burden of justification is demanding and it rests entirely on the State. See *Mississippi Univ. for Women*, 458 U.S., at 724. The State must show "at least that the [challenged] classification serves 'important governmental objectives and that the discriminatory means employed' are 'substantially related to the achievement of those objectives.'" *Ibid.* The justification must be genuine, not hypothesized or invented post hoc in response to litigation. And it must not rely on overbroad generalizations about the different talents, capacities, or preferences of males and females. See *Weinberger v. Wiesenfeld*, 420 U.S. 636, 643, 648 (1975); *Califano v. Goldfarb*, 430 U.S. 199, 223-224 (1977) (Stevens, J., concurring in judgment).

The heightened review standard our precedent establishes does not make sex a proscribed classification. . . . "Inherent differences" between men and women [are not] cause for denigration of the members of either sex or for artificial constraints on an individual's opportunity. Sex classifications may be used to compensate women "for particular economic disabilities [they have] suffered," *Califano v. Webster*, 430 U.S. 313, 320 (1977) (per curiam), to "promot[e] equal employment opportunity," see *California Federal Sav. & Loan Assn. v. Guerra*, 479 U.S. 272, 289 (1987), to advance full development of the talent and capacities of our Nation's people.[7] But such classifications may not be used, as they once were, see *Goesaert*, 335 U.S., at 467, to create or perpetuate the legal, social, and economic inferiority of women.

[Applying] . . . the review standard just described, we conclude that Virginia has shown no "exceedingly persuasive justification" for excluding all women from the citizen-soldier training afforded by VMI. We therefore affirm the Fourth Circuit's initial judgment, which held that Virginia had violated the

Fourteenth Amendment's Equal Protection Clause. Because the remedy proffered by Virginia—the Mary Baldwin VWIL program—does not cure the constitutional violation, i.e., it does not provide equal opportunity, we reverse the Fourth Circuit's final judgment in this case.

V.

...

A.

Single-sex education affords pedagogical benefits to at least some students, Virginia emphasizes, and that reality is uncontested in this litigation. Similarly, it is not disputed that diversity among public educational institutions can serve the public good. But Virginia has not shown that VMI was established, or has been maintained, with a view to diversifying, by its categorical exclusion of women, educational opportunities within the State. In cases of this genre, our precedent instructs that "benign" justifications proffered in defense of categorical exclusions will not be accepted automatically; a tenable justification must describe actual state purposes, not rationalizations for actions in fact differently grounded. See *Wiesenfeld*, 420 U.S., at 648, and n. 16; *Goldfarb*, 430 U.S., at 212–213.

Mississippi Univ. for Women is immediately in point. There the State asserted, in justification of its exclusion of men from a nursing school, that it was engaging in "educational affirmative action" by "compensat[ing] for discrimination against women." 458 U.S., at 727. Undertaking a "searching analysis," *id.*, at 728, the Court found no close resemblance between "the alleged objective" and "the actual purpose underlying the discriminatory classification," *id.*, at 730. Pursuing a similar inquiry here, we reach the same conclusion.

Neither recent nor distant history bears out Virginia's alleged pursuit of diversity through single-sex educational options. In 1839, when the State established VMI, a range of educational opportunities for men and women was scarcely contemplated. Higher education at the time was considered dangerous for women;[9] reflecting widely held views about women's proper place, the Nation's first universities and colleges—for example, Harvard in Massachusetts, William and Mary in Virginia—admitted only men. See E. Farello, *A History of the Education of Women in the United States* 163 (1970). VMI was not at all novel in this respect: In admitting no women, VMI followed the lead of the State's flagship school, the University of Virginia, founded in 1819.

"[N]o struggle for the admission of women to a state university," a historian has recounted, "was longer drawn out, or developed more bitterness, than that at the University of Virginia." 2 T. Woody, *A History of Women's Education in the United States* 254 (1929). In 1879, the State Senate resolved to look into the possibility of higher education for women, recognizing that Virginia " 'has never, at any period of her history,' " provided for the higher education of her daughters, though she " 'has liberally provided for the higher education of her sons.' " *Ibid*. Despite this recognition, no new opportunities were instantly open to women.

Virginia eventually provided for several women's seminaries and colleges. Farmville Female Seminary became a public institution in 1884.... Mary Washington College and James Madison University, were founded [for women] in 1908; another, Radford University, was founded in 1910. By the mid-1970's, all four schools had become coeducational.

Debate concerning women's admission as undergraduates at the main university continued well past the century's midpoint. Familiar arguments were rehearsed. If women were admitted, it was feared, they "would encroach on the rights of men; there would be new problems of government, perhaps scandals; the old honor system would have to be changed; standards would be lowered to those of other coeducational schools; and the glorious reputation of the university, as a school for men, would be trailed in the dust." 2 *History of Women's Education* 255.

Ultimately, ... "the most prestigious institution of higher education in Virginia," the University of Virginia, . . . in 1972, began to admit women on an equal basis with men. A three-judge Federal District Court confirmed: "Virginia may not now deny to women, on the basis of sex, educational opportunities at the Charlottesville campus that are not afforded in other institutions operated by the [S]tate." *Kirstein v. Rector* 309 F. Supp. 184, at 187.

Virginia describes the current absence of public single-sex higher education for women as "an historical anomaly." But the historical record indicates [a pattern]. . .: First, protection of women against higher education; next, schools for women far from equal in resources and stature to schools for men; finally, conversion of the separate schools to coeducation....

In sum, we find no persuasive evidence in this record that VMI's male-only admission policy "is in furtherance of a state policy of 'diversity.' " See 976 F. 2d, at 899. No such policy, the Fourth Circuit observed, can be discerned from the movement of all other public colleges and universities in Virginia away from single-sex education. See *ibid*. That court also questioned "how one institution with autonomy, but with no authority over any other state institution, can give effect to a state policy of diversity among institutions." *Ibid*. A purpose genuinely to advance an array of educational options, as the Court of Appeals recognized, is not served by VMI's historic and constant plan—a plan to "affor[d] a unique educational benefit only to males." *Ibid*. However "liberally" this plan serves the State's sons, it makes no provision whatever for her daughters. That is not *equal* protection.

B.

Virginia next argues that VMI's adversative method of training provides educational benefits that cannot be made available, unmodified, to women. Alterations to accommodate women would necessarily be "radical," so "drastic," Virginia asserts, as to transform, indeed "destroy," VMI's program. Neither sex would be favored by the transformation, Virginia maintains: Men would be deprived of the unique opportunity currently available to them; women would not gain that opportunity because their participation would "eliminat[e] the very aspects of [the] program that distinguish [VMI] from . . . other institutions of higher education in Virginia."

. . .[I]t is uncontested that women's admission would require accommodations, primarily in arranging housing assignments and physical training programs for female cadets. It is also undisputed, however, that "the VMI methodology could be used to educate women." 852 F. Supp., at 481. The District Court even allowed that some women may prefer it to the methodology a women's college might pursue. See ibid. "[S]ome women, at least, would want to attend [VMI] if they had the opportunity," the District Court recognized, 766 F. Supp., at 1414, and "some women," the expert testimony established, "are capable of all of the individual activities required of VMI cadets," id., at 1412. The parties, furthermore, agree that "some women can meet the physical standards [VMI] now impose[s] on men." 976 F. 2d, at 896. In sum, as the Court of Appeals stated, "neither the goal of producing citizen soldiers," VMI's raison d'être, "nor VMI's implementing methodology is inherently unsuitable to women." *Id.*, at 899.

In support of its initial judgment for Virginia, a judgment rejecting all equal protection objections presented by the United States, the District Court made "findings" on "gender-based developmental differences." 766 F. Supp., at 1434–1435. These "findings" restate the opinions of Virginia's expert witnesses, opinions about typically male or typically female "tendencies." *Id.*, at 1434. For example, "[m]ales tend to need an atmosphere of adversativeness," while "[f]emales tend to thrive in a cooperative atmosphere." *Ibid.* "I'm not saying that some women don't do well under [the] adversative model," VMI's expert on educational institutions testified, "undoubtedly there are some [women] who do"; but educational experiences must be designed "around the rule," this expert maintained, and not "around the exception." *Ibid.*

The United States does not challenge any expert witness estimation on average capacities or preferences of men and women. Instead, the United States emphasizes that time and again since this Court's turning point decision in *Reed v. Reed,* 404 U.S. 71 (1971), we have cautioned reviewing courts to take a "hard look" at generalizations or "tendencies" of the kind pressed by Virginia, and relied upon by the District Court. See O'Connor, "Portia's Progress," 66 *N. Y. U. L. Rev.* 1546, 1551 (1991). State actors controlling gates to opportunity, we have instructed, may not exclude qualified individuals based on "fixed notions concerning the roles and abilities of males and females." *Mississippi Univ. for Women,* 458 U.S., at 725; see *J.E.B.,* 511 U.S., at 139, n. 11.

It may be assumed, for purposes of this decision, that most women would not choose VMI's adversative method. As Fourth Circuit Judge Motz observed, however, in her dissent from the Court of Appeals' denial of rehearing en banc, it is also probable that "many men would not want to be educated in such an environment." 52 F. 3d, at 93. (On that point, even our dissenting colleague might agree.) Education, to be sure, is not a "one size fits all" business. The issue, however, is not whether "women—or men—should be forced to attend VMI"; rather, the question is whether the State can constitutionally deny to women who have the will and capacity, the training and attendant opportunities that VMI uniquely affords. *Ibid.*

The notion that admission of women would downgrade VMI's stature, destroy the adversative system and, with it, even the school, is a judgment hardly proved, a prediction hardly different from other "self-fulfilling prophec[ies]," see *Mississippi Univ. for Women,* 458 U.S., at 730, once routinely used to deny rights or opportunities. When women first sought admission to the bar and access to legal education, concerns of the same order were expressed. For example, in 1876, the Court of Common Pleas of Hennepin County, Minnesota, explained why women were thought ineligible for the practice of law. Women train and educate the young, the court said, which "forbids that they shall bestow that time (early and late) and labor, so essential in attaining to the eminence to which the true lawyer should ever aspire. It cannot therefore be said that the opposition of courts to the admission of females to practice . . . is to any extent the outgrowth of . . . 'old fogyism[.]' . . .

[I]t arises rather from a comprehension of the magnitude of the responsibilities connected with the successful practice of law, and a desire to *grade up* the profession." *In re Application of Martha Angle Dorsett to . . . Practice as Attorney . . .(Minn. C. P. Hennepin Cty.*, 1876), in *The Syllabi*, Oct. 21, 1876, pp. 5, 6 (emphasis added).

A like fear, according to a 1925 report, accounted for Columbia Law School's resistance to women's admission, although "[t]he faculty . . . never maintained that women could not master legal learning . . . . No, its argument has been . . . more practical. If women were admitted to the Columbia Law School, [the faculty] said, then the choicer, more manly and red-blooded graduates of our great universities would go to the Harvard Law School!" *The Nation*, Feb. 18, 1925, p. 173.

Medical faculties similarly resisted men and women as partners in the study of medicine. . . . More recently, women seeking careers in policing encountered resistance based on fears that their presence would "undermine male solidarity," see F. Heidensohn, *Women in Control?* 201 (1992); deprive male partners of adequate assistance, see id., at 184–185; and lead to sexual misconduct, see C. Milton et al., *Women in Policing* 32–33 (1974). Field studies did not confirm these fears. See *Women in Control?* at 92–93; P. Bloch & D. Anderson, *Policewomen on Patrol: Final Report* (1974).

Women's successful entry into the federal military academies,[13] and their participation in the Nation's military forces, indicate that Virginia's fears for the future of VMI may not be solidly grounded. . . .VMI's mission [is] to produce "citizen-soldiers," individuals "imbued with love of learning, confident in the functions and attitudes of leadership, possessing a high sense of public service, advocates of the American democracy and free enterprise system, and ready . . . to defend their country in time of national peril." 766 F. Supp., at 1425 (quoting Mission Study Committee of the VMI Board of Visitors, Report, May 16, 1986).

Surely that goal is great enough to accommodate women, who today count as citizens in our American democracy equal in stature to men. Just as surely, the State's great goal is not substantially advanced by women's categorical exclusion, in total disregard of their individual merit, from the State's premier "citizen soldier" corps. Virginia, in sum, "has fallen far short of establishing the 'exceedingly persuasive justification,' " *Mississippi Univ. for Women*, 458 U.S., at 731, that must be the solid base for any gender-defined classification.

VI.

In the second phase of the litigation, Virginia presented its remedial plan—maintain VMI as a male-only college and create VWIL as a separate program for women. . . . The United States challenges this "remedial" ruling as pervasively misguided.

A.

A remedial decree, this Court has said, must closely fit the constitutional violation; it must be shaped to place persons unconstitutionally denied an opportunity or advantage in "the position they would have occupied in the absence of [discrimination]." See *Milliken v. Bradley*, 433 U.S. 267, 280 (1977). The constitutional violation in this case is the categorical exclusion of women from an extraordinary educational opportunity afforded men. A proper remedy for an unconstitutional exclusion, we have explained, aims to "eliminate [so far as possible] the discriminatory effects of the past" and to "bar like discrimination in the future." *Louisiana v. United States*, 380 U.S. 145, 154 (1965).

Virginia chose not to eliminate, but to leave untouched, VMI's exclusionary policy. For women only, however, Virginia proposed a separate program, different in kind from VMI and unequal in tangible and intangible facilities. Having violated the Constitution's equal protection requirement, Virginia was obliged to show that its remedial proposal "directly address[ed] and relate[d] to" the violation, see *Milliken*, 433 U.S., at 282, i.e., the equal protection denied to women ready, willing, and able to benefit from educational opportunities of the kind VMI offers. Virginia described VWIL as a "parallel program," and asserted that VWIL shares VMI's mission of producing "citizen-soldiers" and VMI's goals of providing "education, military training, mental and physical discipline, character . . . and leadership development." Brief. If the VWIL program could not "eliminate the discriminatory effects of the past," could it at least "bar like discrimination in the future"? See *Louisiana*, 380 U.S., at 154. A comparison of the programs said to be "parallel" informs our answer. In exposing the character of, and differences in, the VMI and VWIL programs, we recapitulate facts earlier presented. [Most citations to opinions in the lower courts in rest of **VI. A.** and **B.** are omitted.—AU.]

VWIL affords women no opportunity to experience the rigorous military training for which VMI is famed. Instead, the VWIL program "deemphasize[s]" military education, and uses a "cooperative method" of education "which reinforces self-esteem."

VWIL students participate in ROTC and a "largely ceremonial" Virginia Corps of Cadets, but Virginia deliberately did not make VWIL a military institute. The VWIL House is not a military-style residence and VWIL students need not live together throughout the 4-year program, eat meals together, or wear uniforms during the school day. VWIL students thus do not experience the "barracks" life "crucial to the VMI experience," the spartan living arrangements designed to foster an "egalitarian ethic." "[T]he most important aspects of the VMI educational experience occur in the barracks," the District Court found, at 1423, yet Virginia deemed that core experience nonessential, indeed inappropriate, for training its female citizen-soldiers.

VWIL students receive their "leadership training" in seminars, externships, and speaker series, episodes and encounters lacking the "[p]hysical rigor, mental stress, . . . minute regulation of behavior, and indoctrination in desirable values" made hallmarks of VMI's citizen-soldier training. Kept away from the pressures, hazards, and psychological bonding characteristic of VMI's adversative training, VWIL students will not know the "feeling of tremendous accomplishment" commonly experienced by VMI's successful cadets.

Virginia maintains that these methodological differences are "justified pedagogically," based on "important differences between men and women in learning and developmental needs," "psychological and sociological differences" Virginia describes as "real" and "not stereotypes." Brief. The Task Force charged with developing the leadership program for women, drawn from the staff and faculty at Mary Baldwin College, "determined that a military model and, especially VMI's adversative method, would be wholly inappropriate for educating and training *most women*." 852 F. Supp., at 476 (emphasis added). See also 44 F. 3d, at 1233–1234 (noting Task Force conclusion that, while "some women would be suited to and interested in [a VMI-style experience]," VMI's adversative method "would not be effective for *women as a group*") (emphasis added).

As earlier stated, generalizations about "the way women are," estimates of what is appropriate for most women, no longer justify denying opportunity to women whose talent and capacity place them outside the average description. Notably, Virginia never asserted that VMI's method of education suits most men. It is also revealing that Virginia accounted for its failure to make the VWIL experience "the entirely militaristic experience of VMI" on the ground that VWIL "is planned for women who do not necessarily expect to pursue military careers." By that reasoning, VMI's "entirely militaristic" program would be inappropriate for men in general or as a group, for "[o]nly about 15% of VMI cadets enter career military service."

In contrast to the generalizations about women on which Virginia rests, we note again these dispositive realties: VMI's "implementing methodology" is not "inherently unsuitable to women"; "some women . . . do well under [the] adversarial model"; "some women, at least, would want to attend [VMI] if they had the opportunity"; "some women are capable of all of the individual activities required of VMI cadets" and "can meet the physical standards [VMI] now impose[s] on men." It is on behalf of these women that the United States has instituted this suit, and it is for them that a remedy must be crafted,[19] a remedy that will end their exclusion from a state-supplied educational opportunity for which they are fit, a decree that will "bar like discrimination in the future." *Louisiana*, 380 U.S., at 154.

B.

In myriad respects other than military training, VWIL does not qualify as VMI's equal. VWIL's student body, faculty, course offerings, and facilities hardly match VMI's. Nor can the VWIL graduate anticipate the benefits associated with VMI's 157-year history, the school's prestige, and its influential alumni network.

Mary Baldwin College, whose degree VWIL students will gain, enrolls first-year women with an average combined SAT score about 100 points lower than the average score for VMI freshmen. The Mary Baldwin faculty holds "significantly fewer Ph.D.'s," and receives substantially lower salaries, than the faculty at VMI.

Mary Baldwin does not offer a VWIL student the range of curricular choices available to a VMI cadet. VMI awards baccalaureate degrees in liberal arts, biology, chemistry, civil engineering, electrical and computer engineering, and mechanical engineering. VWIL students attend a school that "does not have a math and science focus"; they cannot take at Mary Baldwin any courses in engineering or the advanced math and physics courses VMI offers.

For physical training, Mary Baldwin has "two multi-purpose fields" and "[o]ne gymnasium." VMI has "an NCAA competition level indoor track and field facility; a number of multi-purpose fields; baseball, soccer and lacrosse fields; an obstacle course; large boxing, wrestling and martial arts facilities; an 11-laps-to-the-mile indoor running course; an indoor pool; indoor and outdoor rifle ranges; and a football stadium that also contains a practice field and outdoor track."

Although Virginia has represented that it will provide equal financial support for in-state VWIL students and VMI cadets, and the VMI Foundation has agreed to endow VWIL with $5.4625 million, the difference between the two schools' financial reserves is pronounced. Mary Baldwin's endowment, currently about $19 million, will gain an additional $35 million based on future commitments; VMI's current endowment, $131 million-the largest per-student endowment in the Nation-will gain $220 million.

The VWIL student does not graduate with the advantage of a VMI degree. Her diploma does not unite her with the legions of VMI "graduates [who] have distinguished themselves" in military and civilian life. "[VMI] alumni are exceptionally close to the school," and that closeness accounts, in part, for VMI's success in attracting applicants. A VWIL graduate cannot assume that the "network of business owners, corporations, VMI graduates and non-graduate employers . . . interested in hiring VMI graduates," will be equally responsive to her search for employment ("the powerful political and economic ties of the VMI alumni network cannot be expected to open" for graduates of the fledgling VWIL program).

Virginia, in sum, while maintaining VMI for men only, has failed to provide any "comparable single-gender women's institution." Instead, the Commonwealth has created a VWIL program fairly appraised as a "pale shadow" of VMI in terms of the range of curricular choices and faculty stature, funding, prestige, alumni support and influence.

Virginia's VWIL solution is reminiscent of the remedy Texas proposed 50 years ago, in response to a state trial court's 1946 ruling that, given the equal protection guarantee, African Americans could not be denied a legal education at a state facility. See *Sweatt v. Painter*, 339 U.S. 629 (1950). Reluctant to admit African Americans to its flagship University of Texas Law School, the State set up a separate school for Herman Sweatt and other black law students. *Id.*, at 632. As originally opened, the new school had no independent faculty or library, and it lacked accreditation. *Id.*, at 633. Nevertheless, the state trial and appellate courts were satisfied that the new school offered Sweatt opportunities for the study of law "substantially equivalent to those offered by the State to white students at the University of Texas." *Id.*, at 632.

Before this Court considered the case, the new school had gained "a faculty of five full-time professors; a student body of 23; a library of some 16,500 volumes serviced by a full-time staff; a practice court and legal aid association; and one alumnus who ha[d] become a member of the Texas Bar." *Id.*, at 633. This Court contrasted resources at the new school with those at the school from which Sweatt had been excluded. The University of Texas Law School had a full-time faculty of 16, a student body of 850, a library containing over 65,000 volumes, scholarship funds, a law review, and moot court facilities. *Id.*, at 632–633.

More important than the tangible features, the Court emphasized, are "those qualities which are incapable of objective measurement but which make for greatness" in a school, including "reputation of the faculty, experience of the administration, position and influence of the alumni, standing in the community, traditions and prestige." *Id.*, at 634. Facing the marked differences reported in the *Sweatt* opinion, the Court unanimously ruled that Texas had not shown "substantial equality in the [separate] educational opportunities" the State offered. Id., at 633. Accordingly, the Court held, the Equal Protection Clause required Texas to admit African Americans to the University of Texas Law School. Id., at 636. In line with *Sweatt*, we rule here that Virginia has not shown substantial equality in the separate educational opportunities the State supports at VWIL and VMI.

C.

When Virginia tendered its VWIL plan, the Fourth Circuit did not inquire whether the proposed remedy, approved by the District Court, placed women denied the VMI advantage in "the position they would have occupied in the absence of [discrimination]." *Milliken*, 433 U.S., at 280. Instead, the Court of Appeals considered whether the State could provide, with fidelity to the equal protection principle, separate and unequal educational programs for men and women.

. . . The Fourth Circuit displaced the standard developed in our precedent, and substituted a standard of its own invention. . . . The Court of Appeals devised another test, a "substantive comparability" inquiry, and proceeded to find that new test satisfied.

The Fourth Circuit plainly erred in exposing Virginia's VWIL plan to a deferential analysis, for "all gender-based classifications today" warrant "heightened scrutiny." See *J.E.B.*, 511 U.S., at 136. Valuable as VWIL may prove for students who seek the program offered, Virginia's remedy affords no cure at all for the opportunities and advantages withheld from women who want a VMI education and can make the grade.[20] In sum, Virginia's remedy does not match the constitutional violation; the State has shown no "exceedingly persuasive justification" for withholding from women qualified for the experience premier training of the kind VMI affords.

VII.

...

VMI ... offers an educational opportunity no other Virginia institution provides, and the school's "prestige"—associated with its success in developing "citizen-soldiers"—is unequaled. Virginia has closed this facility to its daughters and, instead, has devised for them a "parallel program," with a faculty less impressively credentialed and less well paid, more limited course offerings, fewer opportunities for military training and for scientific specialization. Cf. *Sweatt*, 339 U.S., at 633. VMI, beyond question, "possesses to a far greater degree" than the VWIL program "those qualities which are incapable of objective measurement but which make for greatness in a ... school," including "position and influence of the alumni, standing in the community, traditions and prestige." Id., at 634. Women seeking and fit for a VMI-quality education cannot be offered anything less, under the State's obligation to afford them genuinely equal protection.

There is no reason to believe that the admission of women capable of all the activities required of VMI cadets would destroy the Institute rather than enhance its capacity to serve the "more perfect Union."

...

For the reasons stated, the final judgment of the Court of Appeals, is reversed, and the case is remanded for further proceedings consistent with this opinion.

Opinion Footnotes

5 As Thomas Jefferson stated the view prevailing when the Constitution was new: "Were our State a pure democracy ... there would yet be excluded from their deliberations ... women, who, to prevent depravation of morals and ambiguity of issue, should not mix promiscuously in the public meetings of men." Letter from Thomas Jefferson to Samuel Kercheval (Sept. 5, 1816), in 10 *Writings of Thomas Jefferson* 45–46, n. 1 (P. Ford ed. 1899).

7 ....We do not question the State's prerogative evenhandedly to support diverse educational opportunities. We address specifically and only an educational opportunity recognized by the District Court and the Court of Appeals as "unique," see 766 F. Supp., at 1413, 1432; 976 F. 2d, at 892, an opportunity available only at Virginia's premier military institute, the State's sole single-sex public university or college. ...

9 Dr. Edward H. Clarke of Harvard Medical School, whose influential book, *Sex in Education*, went through 17 editions, was perhaps the most well-known speaker from the medical community opposing higher education for women. He maintained that the physiological effects of hard study and academic competition with boys would interfere with the development of girls' reproductive organs. See E. Clarke, *Sex in Education* 38–39, 62–63 (1873); id., at 127 ("identical education of the two sexes is a crime before God and humanity, that physiology protests against, and that experience weeps over"); see also H. Maudsley, *Sex in Mind and in Education* 17 (1874) ("It is not that girls have not ambition, nor that they fail generally to run the intellectual race [in coeducational settings], but it is asserted that they do it at a cost to their strength and health which entails life-long suffering, and even incapacitates them for the adequate

performance of the natural functions of their sex."); C. Meigs, *Females and Their Diseases* 350 (1848) (after five or six weeks of "mental and educational discipline," a healthy woman would "lose . . . the habit of menstruation" and suffer numerous ills as a result of depriving her body for the sake of her mind).

13 Women cadets have graduated at the top of their class at every federal military academy. See Brief for Lieutenant Colonel Rhonda Cornum et al. as *Amici Curiae* 11, n. 25. . . .

19 Admitting women to VMI would undoubtedly require alterations necessary to afford members of each sex privacy from the other sex in living arrangements, and to adjust aspects of the physical training programs. See Brief for Petitioner 27–29; cf. note following 10 U.S.C. Section(s) 4342 (academic and other standards for women admitted to the Military, Naval, and Air Force Academies "shall be the same as those required for male individuals, except for those minimum essential adjustments in such standards required because of physiological differences between male and female individuals"). Experience shows such adjustments are manageable. See *U.S. Military Academy*, A. Vitters, N. Kinzer, & J. Adams, Report of Admission of Women (Project Athena I-IV) (1977–1980) (4-year longitudinal study of the admission of women to West Point); Defense Advisory Committee on Women in the Services, *Report on the Integration and Performance of Women at West Point* 17–18 (1992).

20 Virginia's prime concern, it appears, is that "plac[ing] men and women into the adversative relationship inherent in the VMI program . . . would destroy, at least for that period of the adversative training, any sense of decency that still permeates the relationship between the sexes." 44 F. 3d, at 1239; see supra, at 22–27. It is an ancient and familiar fear. Compare *In re Lavinia Goodell*, 39 Wis. 232, 246 (1875) (denying female applicant's motion for admission to the bar of its court, Wisconsin Supreme Court explained: "Discussions are habitually necessary in courts of justice, which are unfit for female ears. The habitual presence of women at these would tend to relax the public sense of decency and propriety.")

CHIEF JUSTICE REHNQUIST, concurring in the judgment.

The Court holds first that Virginia violates the Equal Protection Clause by maintaining the Virginia Military Institute's (VMI's) all-male admissions policy, and second that establishing the Virginia Women's Institute for Leadership (VWIL) program does not remedy that violation. While I agree with these conclusions, I disagree with the Court's analysis and so I write separately.

I.

Two decades ago in *Craig v. Boren*, 429 U.S. 190, 197 (1976), we announced that "[t]o withstand constitutional challenge, . . . classifications by gender must serve important governmental objectives and must be substantially related to achievement of those objectives." We have adhered to that standard of scrutiny ever since. [String of citations of ch.2 cases omitted here.—AU] While the majority adheres to this test today, [2 mentions cited], it also says that the State must demonstrate an " 'exceedingly persuasive justification' " to support a gender-based classification. [cited 9 mentions]. It is unfortunate that the Court thereby introduces an element of uncertainty respecting the appropriate test.

While terms like "important governmental objective" and "substantially related" are hardly models of precision, they have more content and specificity than does the phrase "exceedingly persuasive justification." That phrase is best confined, as it was first used, as an observation on the difficulty of meeting the applicable test, not as a formulation of the test itself. See, e.g., *Feeney*, at 273

("[T]hese precedents dictate that any state law overtly or covertly designed to prefer males over females in public employment require an exceedingly persuasive justification"). To avoid introducing potential confusion, I would have adhered more closely to our traditional, "firmly established," *Hogan*, at 723; *Heckler*, at 744, standard that a gender-based classification "must bear a close and substantial relationship to important governmental objectives." *Feeney*, at 273.

Our cases dealing with gender discrimination also require that the proffered purpose for the challenged law be the actual purpose.

. . .

Before this Court, Virginia has sought to justify VMI's single-sex admissions policy primarily on the basis that diversity in education is desirable, and that while most of the public institutions of higher learning in the State are coeducational, there should also be room for single-sex institutions. I agree with the Court that there is scant evidence in the record that this was the real reason that Virginia decided to maintain VMI as men only. But, unlike the majority, I would consider only evidence that postdates our decision in *Hogan*, and would draw no negative inferences from the State's actions before that time. . . .

Even if diversity in educational opportunity were the State's actual objective, the State's position would still be problematic. The difficulty with its position is that the diversity benefited only one sex; there was single-sex public education available for men at VMI, but no corresponding single-sex public education available for women. When *Hogan* placed Virginia on notice that VMI's admissions policy possibly was unconstitutional, VMI could have dealt with the problem by admitting women; but its governing body felt strongly that the admission of women would have seriously harmed the institution's educational approach. Was there something else the State could have done to avoid an equal protection violation? Since the State did nothing, we do not have to definitively answer that question.

I do not think, however, that the State's options were as limited as the majority may imply. The Court cites, without expressly approving it, a statement from the opinion of the dissenting judge in the Court of Appeals, to the effect that the State could have "simultaneously opened single-gender undergraduate institutions having substantially comparable curricular and extra-curricular programs, funding, physical plant, administration and support services, and faculty and library resources." If this statement is thought to exclude other possibilities, it is too stringent a requirement. VMI had been in operation for over a century and a half, and had an established, successful and devoted group of alumni. No legislative wand could instantly call into existence a similar institution for women; and it would be a tremendous loss to scrap VMI's history and tradition. In the words of Grover Cleveland's second inaugural address, the State faced a condition, not a theory. And it was a condition that had been brought about, not through defiance of decisions construing gender bias under the Equal Protection Clause, but, until the decision in *Hogan*, a condition which had not appeared to offend the Constitution. Had Virginia made a genuine effort to devote comparable public resources to a facility for women, and followed through on such a plan, it might well have avoided an equal protection violation. I do not believe the State was faced with the stark choice of either admitting women to VMI, on the one hand, or abandoning VMI and starting from scratch for both men and women, on the other.

But, as I have noted, neither the governing board of VMI nor the State took any action after 1982. If diversity in the form of single-sex, as well as coeducational, institutions of higher learning were to be available to Virginians, that diversity had to be available to women as well as to men.

The dissent criticizes me for "disregarding the four all-women's private colleges in Virginia (generously assisted by public funds)." The private women's colleges are treated by the State exactly as all other private schools are treated, which includes the provision of tuition-assistance grants to Virginia residents. Virginia gives no special support to the women's single-sex education. But obviously, the same is not true for men's education. Had the State provided the kind of support for the private women's schools that it provides for VMI, this may have been a very different case. For in so doing, the State would have demonstrated that its interest in providing a single-sex education for men, was to some measure matched by an interest in providing the same opportunity for women.

Virginia offers a second justification for the single-sex admissions policy: maintenance of the adversative method. I agree with the Court that this justification does not serve an important governmental objective. A State does not have substantial interest in the adversative methodology unless it is pedagogically beneficial. While considerable evidence shows that a single-sex education is pedagogically beneficial for some students, and hence a State may have a valid interest in promoting that methodology, there is no similar evidence in the record that an adversative method is pedagogically beneficial or is any more likely to produce character traits than other methodologies.

II.

The Court defines the constitutional violation in this case as "the categorical exclusion of women from an extraordinary educational opportunity afforded to men." By defining the violation in this way, and by emphasizing that a remedy for a constitutional violation must place the victims of discrimination in " 'the position they would have occupied in the absence of [discrimination],' " the Court necessarily implies that the only adequate remedy would be the admission of women to the all-male institution. As the foregoing discussion suggests, I would not define the violation in this way; it is not the "exclusion of women" that violates the Equal Protection Clause, but the maintenance of an all-men school without providing any—much less a comparable—institution for women.

Accordingly, the remedy should not necessarily require either the admission of women to VMI, or the creation of a VMI clone for women. An adequate remedy in my opinion might be a demonstration by Virginia that its interest in educating men in a single-sex environment is matched by its interest in educating women in a single-sex institution. To demonstrate such, the State does not need to create two institutions with the same number of faculty PhD's, similar SAT scores, or comparable athletic fields. Nor would it necessarily require that the women's institution offer the same curriculum as the men's; one could be strong in computer science, the other could be strong in liberal arts. It would be a sufficient remedy, I think, if the two institutions offered the same quality of education and were of the same overall caliber.

If a state decides to create single-sex programs, the state would, I expect, consider the public's interest and demand in designing curricula. And rightfully so. But the state should avoid assuming demand based on stereotypes; it must not assume a priori, without evidence, that there would be no interest in a women's school of civil engineering, or in a men's school of nursing.

In the end, the women's institution Virginia proposes, VWIL, fails as a remedy, because it is distinctly inferior to the existing men's institution and will continue to be for the foreseeable future. VWIL simply is not, in any sense, the institution that VMI is. In particular, VWIL is a program appended to a private college, not a self-standing institution; and VWIL is substantially underfunded as compared to VMI. I therefore ultimately agree with the Court that Virginia has not provided an adequate remedy.

JUSTICE SCALIA, dissenting.

Today the Court shuts down an institution that has served the people of the Commonwealth of Virginia with pride and distinction for over a century and a half. To achieve that desired result, it rejects (contrary to our established practice) the factual findings of two courts below, sweeps aside the precedents of this Court, and ignores the history of our people. As to facts: it explicitly rejects the finding that there exist "gender-based developmental differences" supporting Virginia's restriction of the "adversative" method to only a men's institution, and the finding that the all-male composition of the Virginia Military Institute (VMI) is essential to that institution's character. As to precedent: it drastically revises our established standards for reviewing sex-based classifications. And as to history: it counts for nothing the long tradition, enduring down to the present, of men's military colleges supported by both States and the Federal Government.

Much of the Court's opinion is devoted to deprecating the closed-mindedness of our forebears with regard to women's education, and even with regard to the treatment of women in areas that have nothing to do with education. Closed-minded they were—as every age is, including our own, with regard to matters it cannot guess, because it simply does not consider them debatable. The virtue of a democratic system with a First Amendment is that it readily enables the people, over time, to be persuaded that what they took for granted is not so, and to change their laws accordingly. That system is destroyed if the smug assurances of each age are removed from the democratic process and written into the Constitution. So to counterbalance the Court's criticism of our ancestors, let me say a word in their praise: they left us free to change. The same cannot be said of this most illiberal Court, which has embarked on a course of inscribing one after another of the current preferences of the society (and in some cases only the counter-majoritarian preferences of the society's law-trained elite) into our Basic Law. Today it enshrines the notion that no substantial educational value is to be served by an all-men's military academy—so that the decision by the people of Virginia to maintain such an institution denies equal protection to women who cannot attend that institution but can attend others. Since it is entirely clear that the Constitution of the United States—the old one—takes no sides in this educational debate, I dissent.

I.

I shall devote most of my analysis to evaluating the Court's opinion on the basis of our current equal-protection jurisprudence, which regards this Court as free to evaluate everything under the sun by applying one of three tests: "rational basis" scrutiny, intermediate scrutiny, or strict scrutiny. These tests are no more scientific than their names suggest, and a further element of randomness is added by the fact that it is largely up to us which test will be applied in each case. Strict scrutiny, we have said, is reserved for state "classifications based on race or national origin and classifications affecting fundamental rights," *Clark v. Jeter*, 486 U.S. 456, 461 (1988). It is my position that the term "fundamental rights" should be limited to "interest[s] traditionally protected by our society," *Michael H. v. Gerald D.*, 491 U.S. 110, 122 (1989) (plurality opinion of Scalia, J.); but the Court has not accepted that view, so that strict scrutiny will be applied to the deprivation of whatever sort of right we consider "fundamental." We have no established criterion for "intermediate scrutiny" either, but essentially apply it when it seems like a good idea to load the dice. So far it has been applied to content-neutral restrictions that place an incidental burden on speech, to disabilities attendant to illegitimacy, and to discrimination on the basis of sex. See, e.g., *Turner Broadcasting System, Inc. v. FCC*, 512 U.S. 622(1994); *Mills v. Habluetzel*, 456 U.S. 91, 98–99 (1982); *Craig v. Boren*, 429 U.S. 190, 197 (1976).

I have no problem with a system of abstract tests such as rational-basis, intermediate, and strict scrutiny (though I think we can do better than applying strict scrutiny and intermediate scrutiny whenever we feel like it). Such formulas are essential to evaluating whether the new restrictions that a changing society constantly imposes upon private conduct comport with that "equal protection" our society has always accorded in the past. But in my view the function of this Court is to *preserve* our society's values regarding (among other things) equal protection, not to *revise* them; to prevent backsliding from the degree of restriction the Constitution imposed upon democratic government, not to prescribe, on our own authority, progressively higher degrees. For that reason it is my view that, whatever abstract tests we may choose to devise, they cannot supersede—and indeed ought to be crafted *so as to reflect*—those constant and unbroken national traditions that embody the people's understanding of ambiguous constitutional texts. More specifically, it is my view that "when a practice not expressly prohibited by the text of the Bill of Rights [or a practice asserted to be in violation of, but not expressly prohibited by, the post-Civil War Fourteenth Amendment] bears the endorsement of a long tradition of open, widespread, and unchallenged use that dates back to the beginning of the Republic, we have no proper basis for striking it down." *Rutan v. Republican Party of Ill.*, 497 U.S. 62, 95 (1990) (Scalia, J., dissenting) [more citations to Scalia dissents omitted here—AU].

The all-male constitution of VMI comes squarely within such a governing tradition.... In other words, the tradition of having government-funded military schools for men is as well rooted in the traditions of this country as the tradition of sending only men into military combat. The people may decide to change the one tradition, like the other, through democratic processes; but the assertion that either tradition has been unconstitutional through the centuries is not law, but politics-smuggled-into-law.

. . .

II.

To reject the Court's disposition today, however, it is not necessary to accept my view that the Court's made-up tests cannot displace longstanding national traditions as the primary determinant of what the Constitution means. It is only necessary to apply honestly the test the Court has been applying to sex-based classifications for the past two decades.... We have denominated this standard "intermediate scrutiny" and under it have inquired whether the statutory classification is "substantially related to an important governmental objective." *Ibid.* See, e.g., *Heckler v. Mathews*, 465 U.S. 728, 744 (1984); *Wengler v. Druggists Mutual Ins. Co.*, 446 U.S. 142, 150 (1980); *Craig v. Boren*, 429 U.S., at 197.

Before I proceed to apply this standard to VMI, I must comment upon the manner in which the Court avoids doing so. Notwithstanding our above-described precedents and their " 'firmly established principles,' " *Heckler*, at 744 (quoting *Hogan*, at 723), the ... Court effectively accepts [the new argument of the U.S. Government urging the strict scrutiny test.]

Although the Court in two places recites the test as stated in *Hogan*, which asks whether the State has demonstrated "that the classification serves important governmental objectives and that the discriminatory means employed are substantially related to the achievement of those objectives," the Court never answers the question presented in anything resembling that form. When it engages in analysis, the Court instead prefers the phrase "exceedingly persuasive justification" from *Hogan*. The Court's nine invocations of that phrase,... and even its fanciful description of that imponderable as "the core instruction" of the Court's decisions in *J.E.B. v. Alabama*, 511 U.S. 127 (1994), and *Hogan*, would be unobjectionable if the Court acknowledged that whether a "justification" is "exceedingly persuasive" must be assessed by asking "[whether] the classification serves important governmental objectives and [whether] the discriminatory means employed are substantially related to the achievement of those objectives." Instead, however, the Court proceeds to interpret "exceedingly persuasive justification" in a fashion that contradicts the reasoning of *Hogan* and our other precedents.

That is essential to the Court's result, which can only be achieved by establishing that intermediate scrutiny is not survived if there are *some* women interested in attending VMI, capable of undertaking its activities, and able to meet its physical demands. Thus, the Court summarizes its holding as follows:

> In contrast to the generalizations about women on which Virginia rests, we note again these *dispositive* realities: VMI's implementing methodology is not *inherently* unsuitable to women; *some* women do well under the adversarial model; *some* women, at least, would want to attend VMI if they had the opportunity; *some* women are capable of all of the individual activities required of VMI cadets and can meet the physical standards VMI now imposes on men.

. . .

Only the amorphous "exceedingly persuasive justification" phrase, and not the standard elaboration of intermediate scrutiny, can be made to yield this conclusion that VMI's single-sex composition is unconstitutional because there exist several women (or, one would have to conclude under the Court's reasoning, a single woman) willing and able to undertake VMI's program. Intermediate scrutiny has never required a least-restrictive-means analysis, but only a "substantial relation" between the classification and the state interests that it serves. . . . There is simply no support in our cases for the notion that a sex-based classification is invalid unless it relates to characteristics that hold true in every instance.

[Further,] the Court purports to reserve the question whether, even in principle, a higher standard (i.e., strict scrutiny) should apply. "The Court has," it says, "*thus far* reserved most stringent judicial scrutiny for classifications based on race or national origin . . .," (n.6) (emphasis added); and it describes our earlier cases as having done no more than decline to "equat[e] gender classifications, *for all purposes,* to classifications based on race or national origin," (emphasis added). The wonderful thing about these statements is that they are not actually false [but] the statements are irresponsible, insofar as they are calculated to destabilize current law. Our task is to clarify the law—not to muddy the waters, and not to exact over-compliance by intimidation. The States and the Federal Government are entitled to know before they act the standard to which they will be held, rather than be compelled to guess about the outcome of Supreme Court peek-a-boo.

[Here Scalia argues for dropping intermediate scrutiny and returning to the rational basis test for gender discrimination. Then he turns to the current rule, intermediate scrutiny.—AU.]...

III.

The question to be answered, I repeat, is whether the exclusion of women from VMI is "substantially related to an important governmental objective."

A.

It is beyond question that Virginia has an important state interest in providing effective college education for its citizens. That single-sex instruction is an approach substantially related to that interest should be evident enough from the long and continuing history in this country of men's and women's colleges. But beyond that, as the Court of Appeals here stated: "That single-gender education at the college level is beneficial to both sexes is a *fact established in this case*." 44 F. 3d 1229, 1238 (CA4 1995) (emphasis added).

...

But besides its single-sex constitution, VMI is different from other colleges in another way. It employs a "distinctive educational method," sometimes referred to as the "adversative, or doubting, model of education." 766 F. Supp., at 1413, 1421....No one contends that this method is appropriate for all individuals; education is not a "one size fits all" business. Just as a State may wish to support junior colleges, vocational institutes, or a law school that emphasizes case practice instead of classroom study, so too a State's decision to maintain within its system one school that provides the adversative method is "substantially related" to its goal of good education. Moreover, it was uncontested that "if the state were to establish a women's VMI-type [i.e., adversative] program, the program would attract an insufficient number of participants to make the program work," 44 F. 3d, at 1241; and it was found by the District Court that if Virginia were to include women in VMI, the school "would . . . find it necessary to drop the adversative system," 766 F. Supp., at 1413. Thus, Virginia's options were an adversative method that excludes women or no adversative method at all.

There can be no serious dispute that, as the District Court found, single-sex education and a distinctive educational method "represent legitimate contributions to diversity in the Virginia higher education system." *Id.*, at 1413.

As a theoretical matter, Virginia's educational interest would have been best served (insofar as the two factors we have mentioned are concerned) by six different types of public colleges—an all-men's, an all-women's, and a coeducational college run in the "adversative method," and an all-men's, an all-women's, and a coeducational college run in the "traditional method." But as a practical matter, of course, Virginia's financial resources, like any State's, are not limitless, and the Commonwealth must select among the available options. Virginia thus has decided to fund, in addition to some 14 coeducational 4-year colleges, one college that is run as an all-male school on the adversative model: the Virginia Military Institute.

...It is ... significant that, whereas there are "four all-female private [colleges] in Virginia," there is only "one private all-male college," which "indicates that the private sector is providing for th[e] [former] form of education to a much greater extent that it provides for all-male education." 766 F. Supp., at 1420–1421. In these circumstances, Virginia's election to fund one public all-male institution and one on the adversative model—and to concentrate its resources in a single entity that serves both these interests in diversity—is substantially related to the State's important educational interests.

B.

...

2. The Court suggests that Virginia's claimed purpose in maintaining VMI as an all-male institution—its asserted interest in promoting diversity of educational options—is not "genuin[e]," but is a pretext for discriminating against women.

...

The Court contends that "[a] purpose genuinely to advance an array of educational options ... is not served" by VMI. It relies on the fact that all of Virginia's other public colleges have become coeducational. The apparent theory of this argument is that unless Virginia pursues a great deal of diversity, its pursuit of some diversity must be a sham. This fails to take account of the fact that Virginia's resources cannot support all possible permutations of schools, and of the fact that Virginia coordinates its public educational offerings with the offerings of in-state private educational institutions that the Commonwealth provides money for its residents to attend and otherwise assists—which include four women's colleges.

...

3. In addition to disparaging Virginia's claim that VMI's single-sex status serves a state interest in diversity, the Court finds fault with Virginia's failure to offer education based on the adversative training method to women. It dismisses the District Court's " 'findings' on 'gender-based developmental differences' " on the ground that "[t]hese 'findings' restate the opinions of Virginia's expert witnesses, opinions about typically male or typically female 'tendencies.' " How remarkable to criticize the District Court on the ground that its findings rest on the evidence (i.e., the testimony of Virginia's witnesses)!...

4. ...[VMI's mission is to impart] "learning, leadership, and patriotism." To be sure, those general educational values are described in a particularly martial fashion in VMI's mission statement, in accordance with the military, adversative, and all-male character of the institution. But imparting those values in that fashion—i.e., in a military, adversative, all-male environment—is the distinctive mission of VMI. And as I have discussed (and both courts below found), that mission is not "great enough to accommodate women." The Court's analysis... means that whenever a State's ultimate objective is "great enough to accommodate women" (as it always will be), then the State will be held to have violated the Equal Protection Clause if it restricts to men even one means by which it pursues that objective—no matter how few women are interested in pursuing the objective by that means, no matter how much the single-sex program will have to be changed if both sexes are admitted, and no matter how beneficial that program has theretofore been to its participants.

...

6. Finally, the absence of a precise "all-women's analogue" to VMI is irrelevant....so long as VMI's all-male character is "substantially related" to an important state goal. But VWIL now exists, and the Court's treatment of it shows how far-reaching today's decision is.

VWIL was carefully designed by professional educators who have long experience in educating young women. The program rejects the proposition that there is a "difference in the respective spheres and destinies of man and woman," *Bradwell v. State*, 16 Wall. 130, 141 (1872), and is designed to "provide an all-female program that will achieve substantially similar outcomes [to VMI's] in an all-female environment."...Mary Baldwin College, which runs VWIL, has made the point most succinctly:

> "It would have been possible to develop the VWIL program to more closely resemble VMI, with adversative techniques associated with

the rat line and barracks-like living quarters. Simply replicating an existing program would have required far less thought, research, and educational expertise. But such a facile approach would have produced a paper program with no real prospect of successful implementation."

It is worth noting that none of the United States' own experts in the remedial phase of this case was willing to testify that VMI's adversative method was an appropriate methodology for educating women. This Court, however, does not care. Even though VWIL was carefully designed by professional educators who have tremendous experience in the area, and survived the test of adversarial litigation, the Court simply declares, with no basis in the evidence, that these professionals acted on " 'overbroad' generalizations.' "

C.

A few words are appropriate in response to the concurrence. . . .[First] it is absurd on its face even to *demand* "evidence" to prove that the Commonwealth's reason for maintaining a men's military academy is that a men's military academy provides a distinctive type of educational experience (i. e., fosters diversity). What other purpose *would* the Commonwealth have? . . .

Second,. . .the pedagogical benefits of VMI's adversative approach were not only proved, but were a given in this litigation. The reason the woman applicant who prompted this suit wanted to enter VMI was assuredly not that she wanted to go to an all-male school; it would cease being all-male as soon as she entered. She wanted the distinctive adversative education that VMI provided, and the battle was joined (in the main) over whether VMI had a basis for excluding women from that approach. The Court's opinion recognizes this, and devotes much of its opinion to demonstrating that " 'some women . . . do well under [the] adversative model' " and that "[i]t is on behalf of these women that the United States has instituted this suit." (quoting 766 F. Supp., at1434). Of course, in the last analysis it does not matter whether there are any benefits to the adversative method. The concurrence does not contest that there are benefits to single-sex education, and that alone suffices to make Virginia's case, since admission of a woman will even more surely put an end to VMI's single-sex education than it will to VMI's adversative methodology.

A third reason the concurrence offers in support of the judgment is that . . . .after our decision in *Hogan* (which held a program of the Mississippi University for Women to be unconstitutional—without any reliance on the fact that there was no corresponding Mississippi all-men's program), the

Commonwealth should have known that what this Court expected of it was ...yes!, the creation of a state all-women's program. Any lawyer who gave that advice to the Commonwealth ought to have been either disbarred or committed. (The proof of that pudding is today's 6-Justice majority opinion.) And any Virginia politician who proposed such a step when there were already 4 4-year women's colleges in Virginia (assisted by state support that may well exceed, in the aggregate, what VMI costs) ought to have been recalled.

...

IV.

...

A.

Under the constitutional principles announced and applied today, single-sex public education is unconstitutional. . . .

The Supreme Court of the United States does not sit to announce "unique" dispositions. Its principal function is to establish precedent—that is, to set forth principles of law that every court in America must follow. As we said only this Term, we expect both ourselves and lower courts to adhere to the "rationale upon which the Court based the results of its earlier decisions." *Seminole Tribe of Fla. v. Florida*, 517 U.S. 44(1996) (emphasis added). That is the principal reason we publish our opinions.

And the rationale of today's decision is sweeping: for sex-based classifications, a redefinition of intermediate scrutiny that makes it indistinguishable from strict scrutiny. . . .

In any event,. . .single-sex public education is functionally dead. The costs of litigating the constitutionality of a single-sex education program, and the risks of ultimately losing that litigation, are simply too high to be embraced by public officials. . . . No state official in his right mind will buy such a high-cost, high-risk lawsuit by commencing a single-sex program. The enemies of single-sex education have won; by persuading only seven Justices (five would have been enough) that their view of the world is enshrined in the Constitution, they have effectively imposed that view on all 50 States.

This is especially regrettable. . . . Until quite recently, some public officials have attempted to institute new single-sex programs, at least as experiments. In 1991, for example, the Detroit Board of Education announced a program to establish three boys-only schools for inner-city youth; it was met with a lawsuit, a preliminary injunction was swiftly entered by a District Court that purported to rely on *Hogan*, see *Garrett v. Board of Education of School Dist. of Detroit*, 775 F. Supp. 1004, 1006 (ED Mich. 1991), and the Detroit Board of Education voted to abandon the litigation and thus abandon the plan, see "Detroit Plan to Aid Blacks with All-Boy Schools Abandoned," *Los Angeles Times*, Nov. 8, 1991, p. A4, col. 1. Today's opinion assures that no such experiment will be tried again.

B.

[The principles of today's decision also threaten private single-sex colleges because 19% of their budgets is supplied by state, local, and federal government.] . . .

. . .

The only hope for state-assisted single-sex private schools is that the Court will not apply in the future the principles of law it has applied today. That is a substantial hope, I am happy and ashamed to say. After all, did not the Court today abandon the principles of law it has applied in our earlier sex-classification cases? And does not the Court positively invite private colleges to rely upon our ad-hocery by assuring them this case is "unique"? I would not advise the foundation of any new single-sex college (especially an all-male one) with the expectation of being allowed to receive any government support; but it is too soon to abandon in despair those single-sex colleges already in existence. It will certainly be possible for this Court to write a future opinion that ignores the broad principles of law set forth today, and that characterizes as utterly dispositive the opinion's perceptions that VMI was a uniquely prestigious all-male institution, conceived in chauvinism, etc., etc. I will not join that opinion.

. . . The sphere of self-government reserved to the people of the Republic is progressively narrowed.

Case Questions

1. Justice Ginsburg agrees with Chief Justice Rehnquist, "The constitutional violation in this case is the categorical exclusion of women from an extraordinary educational opportunity afforded men." What he extracts from this term "extraordinary" is the idea of a single-sex, truly educationally rigorous, highly selective, and generously funded undergraduate college, and he would allow Virginia to offer this to women, had Virginia been willing. What the other five majority justices extract is the specific idea of a highly selective, prestigious, rigorous, generously funded, military college. Even though (as acknowledged in the circuit court opinion) Virginia offered coeducational military training at Virginia Tech, Virginia Tech did

not have funding or prestige to match that of VMI, so they ordered women's admission to VMI. Does the equal protection clause enable one to choose between these options: creation by the state of a truly outstanding all-women's college versus female admission to a truly exceptional "adversative system" military college that loses its single-sex character? Should Virginia be allowed to claim, "We wish to offer single-sex military colleges in Virginia, but there is not enough female interest to fill a whole college, so we satisfy equal protection by letting women enroll in ROTC at Virginia Tech until more female interest becomes evident"? What, precisely, is the constitutional flaw in this claim?

2.   Virginia claims that the VWIL program was based on differences between men and women that are "real" and "not stereotypes." Are not some psychological differences between men and women (on average) both "real" and "stereotypes"?

3.   Justice Scalia asserts that when the Court alters what has previously been a consistent tradition of "the people's" constitutional interpretation, the Court is undermining democracy. His approach would seem to allow the government to have continued racial segregation in the 1950s. Other than sheer tradition, or sheer judicial will, is there an alternative standard that can guide the Court when it decides to update a particular constitutional interpretation?

4.   Scalia insists, "There is simply no support in our cases for the notion that a sex-based classification is invalid unless it relates to characteristics that hold true in every case." Is this an accurate characterization of, for instance, *Craig v. Boren*?

5.   Scalia argues that Virginia should be free to provide alternative educational options, such as, for instance, a post-high-school vocational school. By his logic, should Virginia be free to open a men-only vocational college but no college for women only?

TITLE IX AND EDUCATIONAL EQUALITY

Having voted overwhelmingly in 1972 for the ERA, that same year Congress expanded the coverage of federal civil rights law in a number of ways. For instance, the Title VII ban on employment discrimination was extended to cover employees of state and local governments. Another critical expansion of antidiscrimination law was Title IX of the 1972 Education Amendments to the Civil Rights Act of 1964, commonly known simply as "Title IX" (20 U.S.C. § 1681[a] and § 1682). This set of provisions mandated, "No person in the United States shall, on the basis of sex, be excluded from participation in, be denied the benefits of, or be subjected to discrimination under any education program or activity receiving Federal financial assistance. . . ."[32] If a recipient of federal funds were found in violation of this mandate, that recipient was to lose the financial assistance.

In terms of media attention, the spotlight on Title IX first focused on high school and college athletics programs, where its impact was indeed substantial. The number of females participating in intercollegiate sports in the United States went from 16,000 in 1972 to over 150,000 by 1984, and continues to grow.[33] Expansions in athletic programs, however, are only small pieces of the changes wrought by Title IX: high school vocational training programs, once totally sex segregated, had to become nondiscriminatory; co-ed college admission programs (e.g., at Cornell University) that had openly discriminated against females by imposing stiffer admissions standards on them to make more room for males had to stop discriminating. The proportion of women law students nationwide tripled between 1971 and 1974.[34]

Like Title VI of the 1964 Civil Rights Act, Title IX is silent on the question of whether individual victims (of sex discrimination in educational programs that receive federal funds) may sue schools that discriminate against them. But in 1979 the Supreme Court ruled that individual victims may take schools to court for sex discrimination under Title IX[35] (at that point it was not clear whether the suit could ask just for injunctive relief or for damages as well). Then two cases in 1983[36] and 1984[37] established that victims of race discrimination under Title VI could take perpetrators to court, and that monetary damages could be sought under Title VI.

Congress itself followed up by enacting the Civil Rights Remedies Equalization Amendment of 1986,[38] which essentially took away the states' Eleventh Amendment immunity against lawsuits from private citizens when such lawsuits were brought under either Title VI or Title IX (or also the 1973 prohibition on discrimination against the disabled or the 1975 prohibition on age discrimination). (Normally Congress cannot legislate away parts of the Constitution; Congress evidently believes that the Fourteenth Amendment, adopted later than the Eleventh, and which Congress is charged with enforcing, limits the reach of the Eleventh Amendment.) This 1986 act states that under these laws "remedies . . . are available for such a violation to the same extent as . . . are available for such a violation in the suit against any public or private entity other than a State."[39]

Grove City College v. Bell (1984)

The legal force of Title IX was temporarily altered by a Supreme Court decision in February of 1984, *Grove City College v. T.H. Bell, Secretary of Education.*

Prior to that decision, the reference in § 902 to termination of funds for any discriminating recipient in respect to "the particular program, or part thereof, in which noncompliance has been so found" was thought to refer an entire university. That is, it was generally believed that if any part of a university discriminated, the university would lose all of its federal funds. The executive branch had interpreted the law in this way from its passage in 1972, through the district court and court of appeals levels of the *Grove City* case, but by the time the case was argued at the Supreme Court, the Carter administration had become the Reagan administration, and the Department of Education (formerly the Department of Health, Education and Welfare, or HEW) had altered its "own" position in court. At the Supreme Court, the Department of Education argued that the program-specific language of Title IX should be understood as applying to parts of universities, rather than as treating each whole university as an indivisible "program." Thus, a university could take federal aid, say, to construct science buildings but still discriminate in admissions or in sports programs. Six members of the Supreme Court bought this argument. Two (Brennan and Marshall) dissented, and one (Stevens) argued that the Supreme Court did not have jurisdiction to take this case.

This case began when the Department of Education moved in 1977 to declare Grove City College ineligible to receive federal funds in the form of Basic Educational Opportunity Grants (BEOGs) (i.e., need-based scholarships) because the college refused to complete certain obligatory government forms asserting that it refrained from discriminating on the basis of sex (Assurance of Compliance). Grove City was a coed liberal arts college of about 2,200 students, of whom about 140 received BEOGs. The record was clear and undisputed on Grove City's innocence of any racial or sex-based discrimination. But Grove City College as a matter of principle—insisting on its independence from government control—took no money from the government. (The BEOGs went directly to individual students who then used them to pay tuition.) Likewise, on principle, Grove City refused to fill out these bureaucratic forms. The college went to court to block the federal cutoff of funds from its students, arguing that the college was not a recipient of federal funds under the statute and thus should not have to fill out the forms. The Supreme Court was unanimous in rejecting this claim. But six justices stated that Grove City, in order to keep receiving the funds, would have to fill out Assurance of Compliance forms only as to its financial aid program, for it took federal money only for that program. This was the controversial part of the decision because it limited the federal government's ability to utilize financial pressures to gain Title IX compliance across university programs. Justice Brennan insisted that "controlling indicia of Congress's intent" that Title IX applied to entire institutions, not just specific programs, should override "the latest position adopted by the Government."[40]

A bill aimed at overturning this decision (H.R.5490) passed in the House by a vote of 375–32 on June 26, 1984 and its Senate counterpart (S.2568) had 63 co-sponsors as of August 1984. The bill, dubbed at first the Civil Rights Act of 1984, whose coverage would also have extended to laws prohibiting discrimination against the handicapped and the elderly, became entangled in antiabortion politics and in a number of side issues (e.g., would ranchers whose animals drank water from federal water projects have to hire the handicapped)? The campaign against it was led by conservatives such as Orrin Hatch and Jeremiah Benton, and they succeeded in preventing its enactment. But after the Democrats took control of the Senate, the Civil Rights Restoration Act of 1988 was passed over President Reagan's veto. The *Grove City* precedent was dead. Nonetheless, Grove City College still seeks to maintain its independence; it now refuses to participate in federal financial aid programs.[41]

Title IX and College Sports: *Cohen v. Brown U.* (1996)

The controversy over Title IX's application to athletic programs continued. The statute does not literally mandate absolute equality. It allows institutions to maintain separate teams for men and women. However, if there is only one team in a given sport, students previously excluded because of sex must be allowed to try out—except for contact sports (e.g., football, basketball, ice hockey, boxing, etc.). Even this degree of sex equality was a radical enough departure from long-accepted practice to provoke vehement protest. In 1978, the Department of Education (DED) issued regulations that conformed to Congress's intent. The DED announced a three-part test for determining "whether the selection of sports and levels of competition effectively accommodate the interests and abilities of members of both sexes."[42] An institution receiving federal funds was in compliance with Title IX if any one of the following questions could be answered in the affirmative: (1) Are intercollegiate level participation opportunities for male and female students provided in numbers substantially proportionate to their respective enrollments? (2) Where the members of one sex have been and are underrepresented among intercollegiate athletes, can the institution show a history and continuing practice of program expansion that is demonstrably responsive to the developing interests and abilities of the members of that sex? Or (3) where the members of one sex are underrepresented among intercollegiate athletes, and the institution cannot show a continuing practice of program expansion as cited above, can it be demonstrated that the interests and abilities of the members of that sex have been fully and effectively accommodated by the present program?[43] In 1991, Brown University, a private coeducational institution in Providence, Rhode Island, demoted the women's gymnastics and volleyball programs and the men's golf and water polo programs from university-funded to donor-funded status: they could continue only if they raised all their own money. The men's teams, older and more firmly entrenched in the university's culture, had deeper pockets. While the two women's programs needed to raise about $62,000, the men needed about $16,000. Amy Cohen was the named plaintiff in the ensuing class action suit.

Brown University acknowledged that both before and after its budget cuts far more men than women participated in its athletic programs, but the university insisted that a fair standard under Title IX was not numerical equality of participation or percentage equality of participation as percentage of student body, but rather was

> in direct proportion to the comparative levels of interest. . . . Brown . . . argues that an institution satisfactorily accommodates female athletes if it allocates athletic opportunities to women in accordance with the *ratio of interested and able women to interested and able men*, regardless of the number of unserved women or the percentage of the student body that they comprise. (*Cohen II*, 991 F.2d.888, at 899)

In November 1996, a federal appeals court ruled that the demotion of the two women's teams to donor-funded status constituted sex discrimination in violation of Title IX. The panel rejected Brown's "level of interest" argument on the grounds that it was based on stereotypes (*Cohen IV*, 101 F.3rd 155.). The Supreme Court declined Brown's petition to hear the case, and the women's teams were restored to university-funded status.

Other complications for Title IX enforcement are questions about what constitutes a sport and who qualifies as an intercollegiate athlete. In 2009, Quinnipiac University in Hamden, Connecticut cancelled its women's volleyball team in addition to its men's golf and outdoor track and field teams. At the same time it created a new varsity women's cheerleading team. When the volleyball players and the team's coach sued the university for failing to provide female collegiate athletes with equal opportunities to participate in school athletics, the university defended itself by arguing that it had redirected money and resources to the newly created cheerleading team thereby complying with the law. *Biediger v. Quinnipiac University*, 691 F.3d 85 (2 Cir. 2012). In its decision, the appellate court evaluated both the mechanisms by which the university counted male and female athletes and the question of whether or not the members of the cheerleading team should be counted towards the total number of female athletes at Quinnipiac. Ultimately, the court concluded that the university had engaged in some irregularities when counting male and female athletes resulting in an inflated number of female varsity athlete positions, and it excluded the thirty roster slots on the cheerleading team because they did not qualify as "genuine varsity athletic participation" at this time. The court's reasoning followed that of the district court decision: while Quinnipiac was treating the cheerleading team as a competitive intercollegiate varsity team in many ways, the structures of intercollegiate competition for this sport were not yet well enough developed for it to compare to the other varsity sports at Quinnipiac (Id., at 103–106). Once the cheerleading team was eliminated from consideration, Quinnipiac was shown to be providing 3.6 percentage points fewer athletic participation opportunities than women's percentage of the student body, and was therefore ordered to provide more of them than were currently available (id., at 108).

TITLE IX AND SEXUAL HARASSMENT

Franklin v. Gwinnett County (1992)

Title IX has implications for sexual harassment as well as sexual assault in institutions of elementary, secondary and higher education (See Chapter 7 for a discussion of Title IX with respect to sexual assault and rape on college campuses.). While it is understood that Title IX forbids sex discrimination in institutions of education, it was not clear if individuals who sued under Title IX would be able to pursue monetary damages. Congress's rebuff of the *Wards Cove v. Atonio*, *Martin v. Wilks*, and *Patterson v. McLean Credit Union* decisions by the Civil Rights Act of November 1991 (see Chapter 3) was expressed in no uncertain terms. The Supreme Court evidently got the message. In a case argued only one month later, the Court was faced with a choice between a broad and a narrow reading of plaintiff's rights under Title IX. Apparently the Court knew which choice would avoid Congressional ire, for when it handed down its decision on February 26, 1992, it made that choice (despite the fact that the first Bush administration sent its solicitor general to Court to argue for the contrary outcome). Not only did the Court make the interpretive choice that hit harder against sex discrimination; it made the choice unanimously.

Christine Franklin v. Gwinnett County Schools posed the specific issue of whether money damages were permitted in a suit by a victim of sex discrimination under Title IX. Whether a plaintiff in such a lawsuit could ask just for injunctive relief—i.e., a court order to cease the discrimination—or whether monetary damages would also be allowed was not just a narrow, technical question for Christine Franklin. The Court's answer would make a difference in her life.

Her claim was that she had been the victim of sexual harassment by a high school teacher (and sports coach), Andrew Hill, and that despite her complaints, the school administration had done nothing to stop his behavior. She claimed that beginning in 10th grade he engaged her frequently in unwelcome conversation about her sexual tastes and behavior, forcibly kissed her on the mouth in the school parking lot, and three times during her junior year, took her to his private office and subjected her to "coercive intercourse." Despite her complaints, the school, she claimed, did nothing to stop Hill's behavior and in fact discouraged her from pressing criminal charges against him. The school did investigate up to the point that Hill agreed to resign if all matters pending against him were dropped. He did resign and the investigation then ceased. By August 1989, Christine Franklin had graduated from high school, so a corrective injunction would have been useless to her. Thus, she wanted the chance to sue for monetary damages. In a unanimous decision, the Justices ruled that students are eligible to pursue monetary damages under Title IX.

In his opinion for the Court, Justice White cited Title VII sexual harassment cases that applied to supervisors' behavior toward subordinates, and then explained that the same principles apply to teacher-student relations. Should they? Do the two relationships, or the harms done by them differ in any respect that should make a difference in the law? Does it make a difference whether the student is in secondary school or in college?

Gebser v. Lago Vista (1998)

Ninth-grader Alida Gebser of Lago Vista, Texas was already a student in Frank Waldrop's class, and a member of his book discussion club, when *Franklin* was decided. Waldrop often made suggestive remarks to his students and singled out Alida for both verbal and physical attention. A sexual relationship began and continued into the next academic year. Confused, the girl said nothing to authorities. After the principal received complaints about Waldrop from parents of other students, he held a meeting with the teacher and parents—but he did not report the complaints to the superintendent, Lago Vista's Title IX coordinator. Waldrop apologized and promised to mend his ways. Two months later, a police officer discovered the teacher and student having intercourse. He arrested Waldrop, who lost both his job and his license. Alida Gebser and her mother sued the district. The U.S. government joined them as *amicus curiae*. The Court rebuffed the Justice Department again, but this time to limit, rather than facilitate, sexual harassment damages suits. The unanimity of *Franklin* here evolved into a 5–4 split, and produced a new set of rules for a school's liability under Title IX for teacher/employee harassment of a student.

> ### GEBSER V. LAGO VISTA INDEPENDENT SCHOOL DISTRICT
> 524 U.S. 274 (1998)
>
> **JUSTICE O'CONNOR delivered the opinion of the Court.**
>
> The question in this case is when a school district may be held liable in damages in an implied right of action under Title IX of the Education Amendments of 1972, for the sexual harassment of a student by one of the district's teachers. We conclude that damages may not be recovered in those circumstances unless an official of the school district who at a minimum has authority to institute corrective measures on the district's behalf has actual notice of, and is deliberately indifferent to, the teacher's misconduct.
>
> . . .
>
> ### II
>
> . . .In *Franklin*, a high school student alleged that a teacher had sexually abused her on repeated occasions and that teachers and school administrators knew about the harassment but took no action, even to the point of dissuading her from initiating charges. The lower courts dismissed Franklin's complaint against the school district on the ground that the implied right of action under Title IX, as a categorical matter, does not encompass recovery in damages. We reversed the lower courts' blanket rule, concluding that Title IX supports a private action for damages, at least "in a case such as this, in which intentional discrimination is alleged." See 503 U.S. at 74–75. *Franklin* thereby establishes that a school district can be held liable in damages in cases involving a teacher's sexual harassment of a student; the decision, however, does not purport to define the contours of that liability.
>
> We face that issue squarely in this case. Petitioners, joined by the United States as *amicus curiae*, would invoke standards used by the Courts of Appeals in Title VII cases involving a supervisor's sexual harassment of an employee in the workplace. In support of that approach, they point to a passage in *Franklin* in which we stated: "Unquestionably, Title IX placed on the Gwinnett County Public Schools the duty not to discriminate on the basis of sex, and 'when a supervisor sexually harasses a subordinate because of the subordinate's sex, that supervisor "discriminates" on the basis of sex.' We believe the same rule

should apply when a teacher sexually harasses and abuses a student." *Franklin*, at 75.

Specifically, [petitioners and the United States] advance two possible standards under which Lago Vista would be liable for Waldrop's conduct. First, relying on a 1997 "Policy Guidance" issued by the Department of Education, they would hold a school district liable in damages under Title IX where a teacher is " 'aided in carrying out the sexual harassment of students by his or her position of authority with the institution,' " irrespective of whether school district officials had any knowledge of the harassment and irrespective of their response upon becoming aware. That rule is an expression of *respondeat superior* liability, *i.e.*, vicarious or imputed liability, under which recovery in damages against a school district would generally follow whenever a teacher's authority over a student facilitates the harassment. Second, petitioners and the United States submit that a school district should at a minimum be liable for damages based on a theory of constructive notice, *i.e.*, where the district knew or "should have known" about harassment but failed to uncover and eliminate it. Both standards would allow a damages recovery in a broader range of situations than the rule adopted by the Court of Appeals, which hinges on actual knowledge by a school official with authority to end the harassment.

Whether educational institutions can be said to violate Title IX based solely on principles of *respondeat superior* or constructive notice was not resolved by *Franklin*'s citation of *Meritor*. That reference to *Meritor* was made with regard to the general proposition that sexual harassment can constitute discrimination on the basis of sex under Title IX, an issue not in dispute here. In fact, the school district's liability in *Franklin* did not necessarily turn on principles of imputed liability or constructive notice, as there was evidence that school officials knew about the harassment but took no action to stop it. Moreover, *Meritor*'s rationale for concluding that agency principles guide the liability inquiry under Title VII rests on an aspect of that statute not found in Title IX: Title VII, in which the prohibition against employment discrimination runs against "an employer," explicitly defines "employer" to include "any agent." Title IX contains no comparable reference to an educational institution's "agents," and so does not expressly call for application of agency principles. [I.e., the principles governing relations between principals (like the district) and agents (like the teacher).—AU.]

In this case, moreover, petitioners seek not just to establish a Title IX violation but to recover *damages* based on theories of *respondeat superior* and constructive notice. It is that aspect of their action, in our view, which is most critical to resolving the case. Unlike Title IX, Title VII contains an express cause of action, § 2000e–5(f), and specifically provides for relief in the form of monetary damages, § 1981a. Congress therefore has directly addressed the subject of damages relief under Title VII and has set out the particular situations in which damages are available as well as the maximum amounts recoverable. § 1981a(b). With respect to Title IX, however, the private right of action is judicially implied, and there is thus no legislative expression of the scope of available remedies, including when it is appropriate to award monetary damages. In addition, although the general presumption that courts can award any appropriate relief in an established cause of action, coupled with Congress' abrogation of the States' Eleventh Amendment immunity under Title IX, led us to conclude in *Franklin* that Title IX recognizes a damages remedy, we did so in response to lower court decisions holding that Title IX does not support damages relief at all. We made no effort in *Franklin* to delimit the circumstances in which a damages remedy should lie.

III

Because the private right of action under Title IX is judicially implied, we have a measure of latitude to shape a sensible remedial scheme that best comports with the statute.... To guide the analysis, we generally examine the relevant statute to ensure that we do not fashion the parameters of an implied right in a manner at odds with the statutory structure and purpose.

...[W]e conclude that it would "frustrate the purposes" of Title IX to permit a damages recovery against a school district for a teacher's sexual harassment of a student based on principles of *respondeat superior* or constructive notice, *i.e.*, without actual notice to a school district official.... As a general matter, it does not appear that Congress contemplated unlimited recovery in damages against a funding recipient where the recipient is unaware of discrimination in its programs. When Title IX was enacted in 1972, the principal civil rights statutes containing an express right of action did not provide for recovery of monetary damages at all, instead allowing only injunctive and equitable relief. It was not until 1991 that Congress made damages available under Title VII, and even then, Congress carefully limited the amount recoverable in any individual case, calibrating the maximum recovery to the size of the employer. Adopting petitioners' position would amount, then, to allowing unlimited recovery of damages under Title IX where Congress has not spoken on the subject of either the right or the remedy, and in the face of evidence that when Congress expressly considered both in Title VII it restricted the amount of damages available.

Congress enacted Title IX in 1972 with two principal objectives in mind: "to avoid the use of federal resources to support discriminatory practices" and "to provide individual citizens effective protection against those practices." *Cannon*, at 704. The statute was modeled after Title VI of the Civil Rights Act of 1964, which is parallel to Title IX except that it prohibits race discrimination, not sex discrimination, and applies in all programs receiving federal funds, not only in education programs. The two statutes operate in the same manner, conditioning an offer of federal funding on a promise by the recipient not to discriminate, in what amounts essentially to a contract between the Government and the recipient of funds.

That contractual framework distinguishes Title IX from Title VII, which is framed in terms not of a condition but of an outright prohibition. Title VII applies to all employers without regard to federal funding and aims broadly to "eradicate discrimination throughout the economy." [Citation omitted—AU.] Title VII, moreover, seeks to "make persons whole for injuries suffered through past discrimination." Thus, whereas Title VII aims centrally to compensate victims of discrimination, Title IX focuses more on "protecting" individuals from discriminatory practices carried out by recipients of federal funds. *Cannon*, at 704.

...When Congress attaches conditions to the award of federal funds under its spending power, U.S. Const., Art. I, § 8, cl. 1, as it has in Title IX and Title VI, we examine closely the propriety of private actions holding the recipient liable in monetary damages for noncompliance with the condition. Our central concern in that regard is with ensuring "that the receiving entity of federal funds [has] notice that it will be liable for a monetary award." *Franklin*, at 74. . . .

Most significantly, Title IX contains important clues that Congress did not intend to allow recovery in damages where liability rests solely on principles of vicarious liability or constructive notice. Title IX's express means of enforcement—by administrative agencies—operates on an assumption of actual notice to officials of the funding recipient. The statute entitles agencies who disburse education funding to enforce their rules implementing the non-discrimination mandate through proceedings to suspend or terminate funding or through "other means authorized by law." 20 U.S.C. § 1682. Significantly, however, an agency may not initiate enforcement proceedings until it "has advised the appropriate person or persons of the failure to comply with the requirement and has determined that compliance cannot be secured by voluntary means." *Ibid.* The administrative regulations implement that obligation, requiring resolution of compliance issues "by informal means whenever possible," 34 CFR § 100.7(d) (1997), and prohibiting commencement of enforcement proceedings until the agency has determined that voluntary compliance is unobtainable and "the recipient ... has been notified of its failure to comply and of the action to be taken to effect compliance," § 100.8(d); see § 100.8(c).

In the event of a violation, a funding recipient may be required to take "such remedial action as [is] deemed necessary to overcome the effects of [the] discrimination." § 106.3. While agencies have conditioned continued funding on providing equitable relief to the victim, the regulations do not appear to contemplate a condition ordering payment of monetary damages, and there is no indication that payment of damages has been demanded as a condition of finding a recipient to be in compliance with the statute. In *Franklin*, for instance, the Department of Education found a violation of Title IX but determined that the school district came into compliance by virtue of the offending teacher's resignation and the district's institution of a grievance procedure for sexual harassment complaints. 503 U.S. at 64, n. 3.

Presumably, a central purpose of requiring notice of the violation "to the appropriate person" and an opportunity for voluntary compliance before administrative enforcement proceedings can commence is to avoid diverting education funding from beneficial uses where a recipient was unaware of discrimination in its programs and is willing to institute prompt corrective measures. The scope of private damages relief proposed by petitioners is at odds with that basic objective. When a teacher's sexual harassment is imputed to a school district or when a school district is deemed to have "constructively" known of the teacher's harassment, by assumption the district had no actual knowledge of the teacher's conduct. Nor, of course, did the district have an opportunity to take action to end the harassment or to limit further harassment.

It would be unsound, we think, for a statute's *express* system of enforcement to require notice to the recipient and an opportunity to come into voluntary compliance while a judicially *implied* system of enforcement permits substantial liability without regard to the recipient's knowledge or its corrective actions upon receiving notice. Moreover, an award of damages in a particular case might well exceed a recipient's level of federal funding. Where a statute's express enforcement scheme hinges its most severe sanction on notice and unsuccessful efforts to obtain compliance, we cannot attribute to Congress the intention to have implied an enforcement scheme that allows imposition of greater liability without comparable conditions.

IV

Because the express remedial scheme under Title IX is predicated upon notice to an "appropriate person" and an opportunity to rectify any violation, 20 U.S.C. § 1682, we conclude, in the absence of further direction from Congress, that the implied damages remedy should be fashioned along the same lines. An "appropriate person" under § 1682 is, at a minimum, an official of the recipient entity with authority to take corrective action to end the discrimination. Consequently, in cases like this one that do not involve official policy of the recipient entity, we hold that a damages remedy will not lie under Title IX unless an official who at a minimum has authority to address the alleged discrimination and to institute corrective measures on the recipient's behalf has actual knowledge of discrimination in the recipient's programs and fails adequately to respond.

We think, moreover, that the response must amount to deliberate indifference to discrimination. The administrative enforcement scheme presupposes that an official who is advised of a Title IX violation refuses to take action to bring the recipient into compliance. The premise, in other words, is an official decision by the recipient not to remedy the violation. That framework finds a rough parallel in the standard of deliberate indifference. Under a lower standard, there would be a risk that the recipient would be liable in damages not for its own official decision but instead for its employees' independent actions. . .

Applying the framework to this case is fairly straightforward, as petitioners do not contend they can prevail under an actual notice standard. The only official alleged to have had information about Waldrop's misconduct is the high school principal. That information, however, consisted of a complaint from parents of other students charging only that Waldrop had made inappropriate comments during class, which was plainly insufficient to alert the principal to the possibility that Waldrop was involved in a sexual relationship with a student. Lago Vista, moreover, terminated Waldrop's employment upon learning of his relationship with Gebser. JUSTICE STEVENS points out in his dissenting opinion that Waldrop of course had knowledge of his own actions. Where a school district's liability rests on actual notice principles, however, the knowledge of the wrongdoer himself is not pertinent to the analysis.

Petitioners focus primarily on Lago Vista's asserted failure to promulgate and publicize an effective policy and grievance procedure for sexual harassment claims. They point to Department of Education regulations requiring each funding recipient to "adopt and publish grievance procedures providing for prompt and equitable resolution" of discrimination complaints, 34 CFR § 106.8(b) (1997), and to notify students and others "that it does not discriminate on the basis of sex in the educational programs or activities which it operates," § 106.9(a). Lago Vista's alleged failure to comply with the regulations, however, does not establish the requisite actual notice and deliberate indifference. And in any event, the failure to promulgate a grievance procedure does not itself constitute "discrimination" under Title IX. Of course, the Department of Education could enforce the requirement administratively: Agencies generally have authority to promulgate and enforce requirements that effectuate the statute's non-discrimination mandate, 20 U.S.C. § 1682, even if those requirements do not purport to represent a definition of discrimination under the statute. We have never held, however, that the implied private right of action under Title IX allows recovery in damages for violation of those sorts of administrative requirements.

V

The number of reported cases involving sexual harassment of students in schools confirms that harassment unfortunately is an all too common aspect of the educational experience. No one questions that a student suffers extraordinary harm when subjected to sexual harassment and abuse by a teacher, and that the teacher's conduct is reprehensible and undermines the basic purposes of the educational system. The issue in this case, however, is whether the independent misconduct of a teacher is attributable to the school district that employs him under a specific federal statute designed primarily to prevent recipients of federal financial assistance from using the funds in a discriminatory manner. Our decision does not affect any right of recovery that an individual may have against a school district as a matter of state law or against the teacher in his individual capacity under state law or under 42 U.S.C. § 1983. Until Congress speaks directly on the subject, however, we will not hold a school district liable in damages under Title IX for a teacher's sexual harassment of a student absent actual notice and deliberate indifference. We therefore affirm the judgment of the Court of Appeals.

It is so ordered.

JUSTICE STEVENS, with whom JUSTICE SOUTER, JUSTICE GINSBURG, and JUSTICE BREYER join, dissenting.

The question that the petition for certiorari asks us to address is whether the Lago Vista Independent School District (respondent) is liable in damages for a violation of Title IX of the Education Amendments of 1972 (Title IX). The Court provides us with a negative answer to that question because respondent did not have actual notice of, and was not deliberately indifferent to, the odious misconduct of one of its teachers. As a basis for its decision, the majority relies heavily on the notion that because the private cause of action under Title IX is "judicially implied," the Court has "a measure of latitude" to use its own judgment in shaping a remedial scheme. This assertion of lawmaking authority is not faithful either to our precedents or to our duty to interpret, rather than to revise, congressional commands. Moreover, the majority's policy judgment about the appropriate remedy in this case thwarts the purposes of Title IX.

I

[*Cannon* v. *University of Chicago*]... represented our considered judgment about the intent of the Congress that enacted Title IX in 1972. After noting that Title IX had been patterned after Title VI of the Civil Rights Act of 1964, which had been interpreted to include a private right of action, we concluded that Congress intended to authorize the same private enforcement of Title IX. As long as the intent of Congress is clear, an implicit command has the same legal force as one that is explicit.

In *Franklin* v. *Gwinnett County Public Schools,* 503 U.S. 60 (1992), we unanimously concluded that Title IX authorized a high school student who had been sexually harassed by a sports coach/teacher to recover damages from the school district. That conclusion was supported by two considerations. In his opinion for the Court, Justice White first relied on the presumption that Congress intends to authorize "all appropriate remedies" unless it expressly indicates otherwise. He then noted that two amendments to Title IX enacted after the decision in *Cannon* had validated *Cannon*'s holding and supported the conclusion that "Congress did not intend to limit the remedies available in a suit brought under Title IX." JUSTICE SCALIA, concurring in the judgment, agreed that Congress' amendment of Title IX to eliminate the States' Eleventh Amendment immunity, see 42 U.S.C. § 2000d–7(a)(1), must be read "not only 'as a validation of *Cannon*'s holding,' but also as an implicit acknowledgment that damages are available."

Because these constructions of the statute have been accepted by Congress and are unchallenged here, they have the same legal effect as if the private cause of action seeking damages had been explicitly, rather than implicitly, authorized by Congress. We should therefore seek guidance from the text of the statute and settled legal principles rather than from our views about sound policy.

II

...Explaining [in *Franklin*] why Title IX is violated when a teacher sexually abuses a student, we wrote:

> "Unquestionably, Title IX placed on the Gwinnett County Public Schools the duty not to discriminate on the basis of sex, and 'when a supervisor sexually harasses a subordinate because of the subordinate's sex, that supervisor "discriminates" on the basis of sex.' *Meritor*. We believe the same rule should apply when a teacher sexually harasses and abuses a student. *Congress surely did not intend for federal moneys to be expended to support the intentional actions it sought by statute to proscribe.*" 503 U.S. at 75 (emphasis added).

Franklin therefore stands for the proposition that sexual harassment of a student by her teacher violates the duty—assumed by the school district in exchange for federal funds—not to discriminate on the basis of sex, and that a student may recover damages from a school district for such a violation.

Although the opinion the Court announces today is not entirely clear, it does not purport to overrule *Franklin*. Moreover, I do not understand the Court to question the conclusion that an intentional violation of Title IX, of the type we recognized in *Franklin*, has been alleged in this case. During her freshman and sophomore years of high school, petitioner Alida Star Gebser was repeatedly subjected to sexual abuse by her teacher, Frank Waldrop, whom she had met in the eighth grade when she joined his high school book discussion group. Waldrop's conduct was surely intentional and it occurred during, and as a part of, a curriculum activity in which he wielded authority over Gebser that had been delegated to him by respondent. Moreover, it is undisputed that the activity was subsidized, in part, with federal moneys.

The Court nevertheless holds that the law does not provide a damages remedy for the Title IX violation alleged in this case because no official of the school district with "authority to institute corrective measures on the district's behalf" had actual notice of Waldrop's misconduct. That holding is at odds with settled principles of agency law, under which the district is responsible for Waldrop's misconduct because "he was aided in accomplishing the tort by the existence of the agency relation." This case presents a paradigmatic example of a tort that was made possible, that was effected, and that was repeated over a prolonged period because of the powerful influence that Waldrop had over

Gebser by reason of the authority that his employer, the school district, had delegated to him. As a secondary school teacher, Waldrop exercised even greater authority and control over his students than employers and supervisors exercise over their employees. His gross misuse of that authority allowed him to abuse his young student's trust.

. . .The United States Department of Education . . . recently issued a policy "Guidance" stating that a school district is liable under Title IX if one of its teachers "was aided in carrying out the sexual harassment of students by his or her position of authority with the institution." As the agency charged with administering and enforcing Title IX, the Department of Education has a special interest in ensuring that federal funds are not used in contravention of Title IX's mandate. It is therefore significant that the Department's interpretation of the statute wholly supports the conclusion that respondent is liable in damages for Waldrop's sexual abuse of his student, which was made possible only by Waldrop's affirmative misuse of his authority as her teacher.

The reason why the common law imposes liability on the principal in such circumstances is the same as the reason why Congress included the prohibition against discrimination on the basis of sex in Title IX: to induce school boards to adopt and enforce practices that will minimize the danger that vulnerable students will be exposed to such odious behavior. The rule that the Court has crafted creates the opposite incentive. As long as school boards can insulate themselves from knowledge about this sort of conduct, they can claim immunity from damages liability. Indeed, the rule that the Court adopts would preclude a damages remedy even if every teacher at the school knew about the harassment but did not have "authority to institute corrective measures on the district's behalf." It is not my function to determine whether this newly fashioned rule is wiser than the established common-law rule. It is proper, however, to suggest that the Court bears the burden of justifying its rather dramatic departure from settled law, and to explain why its opinion fails to shoulder that burden.

III

The Court advances several reasons why it would "frustrate the purposes" of Title IX to allow recovery against a school district that does not have actual notice of a teacher's sexual harassment of a student. As the Court acknowledges, however, the two principal purposes that motivated the enactment of Title IX were: (1) " 'to avoid the use of federal resources to support discriminatory practices' "; and (2) " 'to provide individual citizens effective protection against those practices.' " It seems quite obvious that both of those purposes would be served—not frustrated—by providing a damages remedy in a case of this kind. . . .

First, the Court observes that at the time Title IX was enacted, "the principal civil rights statutes containing an express right of action did not provide for recovery of monetary damages at all." *Franklin*, however, forecloses this reevaluation of legislative intent. . .

Second, the Court suggests that the school district did not have fair notice when it accepted federal funding that it might be held liable " 'for a monetary award' " under Title IX. The Court cannot mean, however, that respondent was not on notice that sexual harassment of a student by a teacher constitutes an "intentional" violation of Title IX for which damages are available, because we so held shortly before Waldrop began abusing Gebser. Given the fact that our holding in *Franklin* was unanimous, it is not unreasonable to assume that it could have been foreseen by counsel for the recipients of Title IX funds. Moreover, the nondiscrimination requirement set out in Title IX is clear, and this Court held that sexual harassment constitutes intentional sex discrimination long before the sexual abuse in this case began. Normally, of course, we presume that the citizen has knowledge of the law.

The majority nevertheless takes the position that a school district that accepts federal funds under Title IX should not be held liable in damages for an intentional violation of that statute if the district itself "was unaware of the discrimination." The Court reasons that because administrative proceedings to terminate funding cannot be commenced until after the grant recipient has received notice of its noncompliance and the agency determines that voluntary compliance is not possible, see 20 U.S.C. § 1682, there should be no damages liability unless the grant recipient has actual notice of the violation (and thus an opportunity to end the harassment).

The fact that Congress has specified a particular administrative procedure to be followed when a subsidy is to be terminated, however, does not illuminate the question of what the victim of discrimination on the basis of sex must prove in order to recover damages in an implied private right of action. Indeed, in *Franklin*, we noted that the Department of Education's Office of Civil Rights had declined to terminate federal funding of the school district at issue—despite its finding that a Title IX violation had occurred—because "the district had come into compliance with Title IX" after the harassment at issue. That fact did not affect the Court's analysis, much less persuade the Court that a damages remedy was unavailable.

The majority's inappropriate reliance on Title IX's administrative enforcement scheme to limit the availability of a damages remedy leads the Court to require not only actual knowledge on the part of "an official who at a minimum has authority to address the alleged discrimination and to institute corrective measures on the recipient's behalf," but also that official's "refusal to take action," or "deliberate indifference" toward the harassment. Presumably, few Title IX plaintiffs who have been victims of intentional discrimination will be able to recover damages under this exceedingly high standard. The Court fails to recognize that its holding will virtually "render inutile causes of action authorized by Congress through a decision that *no* remedy is available." *Franklin*, 503 U.S. at 74.

IV

...It is not clear to me why the well-settled rules of law that impose responsibility on the principal for the misconduct of its agents should not apply in this case. As a matter of policy, the Court ranks protection of the school district's purse above the protection of immature high school students that those rules would provide. Because those students are members of the class for whose special benefit Congress enacted Title IX, that policy choice is not faithful to the intent of the policymaking branch of our Government.

I respectfully dissent.

JUSTICE GINSBURG, with whom JUSTICE SOUTER and JUSTICE BREYER join, dissenting.

JUSTICE STEVENS' opinion focuses on the standard of school district liability for teacher-on-student harassment in secondary schools. I join that opinion, which reserves the question whether a district should be relieved from damages liability if it has in place, and effectively publicizes and enforces, a policy to curtail and redress injuries caused by sexual harassment. I think it appropriate to answer that question for these reasons: (1) the dimensions of a claim are determined not only by the plaintiff's allegations, but by the allowable defenses; (2) this Court's pathmarkers are needed to afford guidance to lower courts and school officials responsible for the implementation of Title IX.

In line with the tort law doctrine of avoidable consequences, I would recognize as an affirmative defense to a Title IX charge of sexual harassment, an effective policy for reporting and redressing such misconduct. School districts subject to Title IX's governance have been instructed by the Secretary of Education to install procedures for "prompt and equitable resolution" of complaints, 34 CFR § 106.8(b) (1997), and the Department of Education's

> Office of Civil Rights has detailed elements of an effective grievance process, with specific reference to sexual harassment, 62 Fed. Reg. 12034, 12044–12045 (1997).
>
> The burden would be the school district's to show that its internal remedies were adequately publicized and likely would have provided redress without exposing the complainant to undue risk, effort, or expense. Under such a regime, to the extent that a plaintiff unreasonably failed to avail herself of the school district's preventive and remedial measures, and consequently suffered avoidable harm, she would not qualify for Title IX relief.

Case Questions

1. Justice Stevens writes, "To the extent that the Court's reasons for its policy choice have any merit, they suggest that no damages should ever be awarded in a Title IX case." Is his interpretation correct? If you were Justice O'Connor, how might you refute it?

2. If the school district were held responsible for conduct of which it had no knowledge, would that be expecting the impossible? If employers can exercise this responsibility, why can't school officials?

3. *Gebser* and *Franklin* indicate that antidiscrimination laws have two purposes: to end discrimination, and to facilitate redress for victims of discrimination. Yet the *Gebser* majority implies that, while Title VII has both goals, in Title IX the first has priority over the second. Is this reasoning persuasive?

4. The first year that Judith Baer's women and the law class at Texas A&M University discussed Title IX sexual harassment cases, a few students told of faculty-student sexual relationships in their junior and senior high schools. Baer responded, "A teacher who has sex with a student under the age of consent has committed a felony: unlawful sexual intercourse, if not forcible rape. Yet three of you. . ." At least half the class shook their heads and raised their hands to indicate that they, too, had heard of similar cases. Suppose this apparently frequent occurrence were commonly treated as a crime rather than as a tort. Discuss the probable ramifications.

> ### From Stephen Schulhofer, *Unwanted Sex* (1998)[44]
>
> Whether students are in high school, college, or a graduate program, they have—or should have—the right to be educated by their teachers without having to give sexual favors in exchange. Yet existing legal rules and school

> policies leave indefensible gaps in students' right to protection from sexual pressure.
>
> At the high school level, sexual contacts short of intercourse are usually legal if the student is over 13 or 14 years old. And in many states intercourse is legal whenever the student is over 16, regardless of the age or status of the other party. In effect these states focus on maturity (age) as the sole measure of capacity to consent, ignoring the problems of power that arise when an adolescent and her sexual partner are not contemporaries. Federal laws against sexual harassment do not apply unless the student has affirmatively indicated that the contacts are unwelcome, and high school students are often too immature or intimidated to think clearly about how they want to react to sexual invitations from a teacher.

Davis v. Monroe County (1999)

Title IX, like Title VII, prohibits sexual harassment by peers as well as by supervisors. The case of LaShonda Davis, a fifth grader at Hubbard Elementary School in Monroe County, Georgia, offers an egregious example of peer on peer harassment. G.F., a classmate, repeatedly tried to touch her breasts and genitals, rubbed his body against hers, and made such remarks as, "I want to feel your boobs." LaShonda told her mother and her classroom teacher about these incidents. When the harassment continued, the mother spoke to the teacher, who assured her that the principal had been informed. By now, La Shonda was no longer G.F.'s only target. She and several other girls sought an appointment with the principal and were rebuffed. The school took no disciplinary action against the boy. His harassment worsened to the point that LaShonda could not concentrate on her studies and wrote a suicide note. The incidents stopped only after G.F. was charged with sexual battery. LaShonda's mother, Aurelia, sued the school district on her daughter's behalf, alleging that its failure to act constituted a violation of Title IX.

> #### DAVIS V. MONROE COUNTY BOARD OF EDUCATION ET AL.
> 526 U.S. 629 (1999)
>
> [Many citations have been omitted.—AU.]
>
> **JUSTICE O'CONNOR delivered the opinion of the Court.**
>
> . . .We consider here whether a private damages action may lie against the school board in cases of student-on-student harassment. We conclude that it

may, but only where the funding recipient acts with deliberate indifference to known acts of harassment in its programs or activities. Moreover, . . .such an action will lie only for harassment that is so severe, pervasive, and objectively offensive that it effectively bars the victim's access to an educational opportunity or benefit. . . .

II

Title IX provides, with certain exceptions not at issue here, that "no person in the United States shall, on the basis of sex, be excluded from participation in, be denied the benefits of, or be subjected to discrimination under any education program or activity receiving Federal financial assistance."

Congress authorized an administrative enforcement scheme for Title IX. Federal departments or agencies with the authority to provide financial assistance are entrusted to promulgate rules, regulations, and orders to enforce the objectives of § 1681, see § 1682, and these departments or agencies may rely on "any . . . means authorized by law," including the termination of funding, to give effect to the statute's restrictions.

. . .[A]t issue here is the question whether a recipient of federal education funding may be liable for damages under Title IX under any circumstances for discrimination in the form of student-on-student sexual harassment.

A

Petitioner urges that Title IX's plain language compels the conclusion that the statute is intended to bar recipients of federal funding from permitting this form of discrimination in their programs or activities. She emphasizes that the statute prohibits a student from being "*subjected to discrimination* under any education program or activity receiving Federal financial assistance." 20 U.S.C. § 1681 (emphasis supplied). It is Title IX's "unmistakable focus on the benefited class," rather than the perpetrator, that, in petitioner's view, compels the conclusion that the statute works to protect students from the discriminatory misconduct of their peers.

Here, however, we are asked to do more than define the scope of the behavior that Title IX proscribes. We must determine whether a district's failure to respond to student-on-student harassment in its schools can support a private suit for money damages. This Court has indeed recognized an implied private right of action under Title IX, and we have held that money damages are available in such suits. Because we have repeatedly treated Title IX as legislation enacted pursuant to Congress' authority under the Spending Clause, however, private damages actions are available only where recipients of federal funding had adequate notice that they could be liable for the conduct at issue. In interpreting language in spending legislation, we thus "insist that Congress speak with a clear voice," recognizing that "there can, of course, be no knowing acceptance [of the terms of the putative contract] if a State is unaware of the conditions [imposed by the legislation] or is unable to ascertain what is expected of it."

. . .[R]espondents urge that Title IX provides no notice that recipients of federal educational funds could be liable in damages for harm arising from student-on-student harassment. Respondents contend, specifically, that the statute only proscribes misconduct by grant recipients, not third parties. Respondents argue, moreover, that it would be contrary to the very purpose of Spending Clause legislation to impose liability on a funding recipient for the misconduct of third parties, over whom recipients exercise little control.

We agree with respondents that a recipient of federal funds may be liable in damages under Title IX only for its own misconduct. The recipient itself must "exclude [persons] from participation in,. . .deny [persons] the benefits of, or. . .subject [persons] to discrimination under" its "programs or activities" in order to be liable under Title IX. The Government's enforcement power may only be exercised against the funding recipient, see § 1682, and we have not extended damages liability under Title IX to parties outside the scope of this power.

We disagree with respondents' assertion, however, that petitioner seeks to hold the Board liable for G.F.'s actions instead of its own. Here, petitioner attempts to hold the Board liable for its *own* decision to remain idle in the face of known student-on-student harassment in its schools [emphases original—AU.].

. . .[In *Gebser*], we concluded that the district could be liable for damages only where the district itself intentionally acted in clear violation of Title IX by remaining deliberately indifferent to acts of teacher-student harassment of which it had actual knowledge. . . .By employing the "deliberate indifference" theory already used to establish municipal liability. . ., we concluded in *Gebser* that recipients could be liable in damages only where their own deliberate indifference effectively "caused" the discrimination. The high standard imposed in *Gebser* sought to eliminate any "risk that the recipient would be liable in damages not for its own official decision but instead for its employees' independent actions."

Gebser thus established that a recipient intentionally violates Title IX, and is subject to a private damages action, where the recipient is deliberately indifferent to known acts of teacher-student discrimination. . . .

We consider here whether the misconduct identified in *Gebser*—deliberate indifference to known acts of harassment—amounts to an intentional violation of Title IX, capable of supporting a private damages action, when the harasser is a student rather than a teacher. We conclude that, in certain limited circumstances, it does.

. . .This is not to say that the identity of the harasser is irrelevant. On the contrary, both the "deliberate indifference" standard and the language of Title IX narrowly circumscribe the set of parties whose known acts of sexual harassment can trigger some duty to respond on the part of funding recipients. Deliberate indifference makes sense as a theory of direct liability under Title IX only where the funding recipient has some control over the alleged harassment. A recipient cannot be directly liable for its indifference where it lacks the authority to take remedial action.

The language of Title IX itself—particularly when viewed in conjunction with the requirement that the recipient have notice of Title IX's prohibitions to be liable for damages—also cabins the range of misconduct that the statute proscribes. The statute's plain language confines the scope of prohibited conduct based on the recipient's degree of control over the harasser and the environment in which the harassment occurs. If a funding recipient does not engage in harassment directly, it may not be liable for damages unless its deliberate indifference "subjects" its students to harassment.

. . .These factors combine to limit a recipient's damages liability to circumstances wherein the recipient exercises substantial control over both the harasser and the context in which the known harassment occurs. . . .We agree with the dissent that these conditions are satisfied most easily and most obviously when the offender is an agent of the recipient. We rejected the use of agency analysis in *Gebser*, however, and we disagree that the term "under" somehow imports an agency requirement into Title IX. As noted above, the theory in *Gebser* was that the recipient was *directly* liable for its deliberate indifference to discrimination. Liability in that case did not arise because the "teacher's actions [were] treated" as those of the funding recipient; the district was directly liable for its *own* failure to act. . . .

Where, as here, the misconduct occurs during school hours and on school grounds—the bulk of G. F.'s misconduct, in fact, took place in the classroom—the misconduct is taking place "under" an "operation" of the funding recipient. See *Doe* v. *University of Illinois*, 138 F.3d at 661 (finding liability where school fails to respond properly to "student-on-student sexual harassment that takes place while the students are involved in school activities or otherwise under the supervision of school employees"). In these circumstances, the recipient retains substantial control over the context in which the harassment occurs. More importantly, however, in this setting the Board exercises significant control over the harasser. We have observed, for example, "that the nature of [the State's] power [over public schoolchildren] is custodial and tutelary, permitting a degree of supervision and control that could not be exercised over free adults." *Vernonia School Dist. 47J* v. *Acton*, 515 U.S. 646, 655 (1995). On more than one occasion, this Court has recognized the importance of school officials' "comprehensive authority . . ., consistent with fundamental constitutional safeguards, to prescribe and control conduct in the schools." *Tinker* v. *Des Moines Independent Community School Dist.*, 393 U.S. 503, 507 (1969); see also *New Jersey* v. *T. L. O.*, 469 U.S. 325, 342, n. 9 (1985). . . .The common law, too, recognizes the school's disciplinary authority. We thus conclude that recipients of federal funding may be liable for "subjecting" their students to discrimination where the recipient is deliberately indifferent to known acts of student-on-student sexual harassment and the harasser is under the school's disciplinary authority.

At the time of the events in question here, in fact, school attorneys and administrators were being told that student-on-student harassment could trigger liability under Title IX. In March 1993, even as the events alleged in petitioner's complaint were unfolding, the National School Boards Association issued a publication, for use by "school attorneys and administrators in understanding the law regarding sexual harassment of employees and students," which observed that districts could be liable under Title IX for their failure to respond to student-on-student harassment. Drawing on Equal Employment Opportunity Commission guidelines interpreting Title VII, the publication informed districts that, "if [a] school district has constructive notice of severe and repeated acts of sexual harassment by fellow students, that may form the basis of a Title IX claim."

. . .Likewise, although they were promulgated too late to contribute to the Board's notice of proscribed misconduct, the Department of Education's Office for Civil Rights (OCR) has recently adopted policy guidelines providing that student-on-student harassment falls within the scope of Title IX's proscriptions.

We stress that our conclusion here—that recipients may be liable for their deliberate indifference to known acts of peer sexual harassment—does not mean that recipients can avoid liability only by purging their schools of actionable peer harassment or that administrators must engage in particular disciplinary action. We thus disagree with respondents' contention that, if Title IX provides a cause of action for student-on-student harassment, "nothing short of expulsion of every student accused of misconduct involving sexual overtones would protect school systems from liability or damages." . . .

School administrators will continue to enjoy the flexibility they require so long as funding recipients are deemed "deliberately indifferent" to acts of student-on-student harassment only where the recipient's response to the harassment or lack thereof is clearly unreasonable in light of the known circumstances. The dissent consistently mischaracterizes this standard to require funding recipients to "remedy" peer harassment, and to "ensure that . . . students conform their conduct to" certain rules. Title IX imposes no such requirements. On the contrary, the recipient must merely respond to known peer harassment in a manner that is not clearly unreasonable. . . .

Like the dissent, we acknowledge that school administrators shoulder substantial burdens as a result of legal constraints on their disciplinary authority. To the extent that these restrictions arise from federal statutes, Congress can review these burdens with attention to the difficult position in which such legislation may place our Nation's schools. We believe, however, that the standard set out here is sufficiently flexible to account both for the level of disciplinary authority available to the school and for the potential liability arising from certain forms of disciplinary action. A university might not, for example, be expected to exercise the same degree of control over its students that a grade school would enjoy, and it would be entirely reasonable for a school to refrain from a form of disciplinary action that would expose it to constitutional or statutory claims.

While it remains to be seen whether petitioner can show that the Board's response to reports of G. F.'s misconduct was clearly unreasonable in light of the known circumstances, petitioner may be able to show that the Board "subjected" LaShonda to discrimination by failing to respond in any way over a period of five months to complaints of G. F.'s in-school misconduct from LaShonda and other female students.

B

The requirement that recipients receive adequate notice of Title IX's proscriptions also bears on the proper definition of "discrimination" in the context of a private damages action. We have elsewhere concluded that sexual harassment is a form of discrimination for Title IX purposes and that Title IX proscribes harassment with sufficient clarity to satisfy [the] notice requirement and serve as a basis for a damages action. Having previously determined that "sexual harassment" is "discrimination" in the school context under Title IX, we are constrained to conclude that student-on-student sexual harassment, if sufficiently severe, can likewise rise to the level of discrimination actionable under the statute. The statute's other prohibitions, moreover, help give content to the term "discrimination" in this context. Students are not only protected from discrimination, but also specifically shielded from being "excluded from participation in" or "denied the benefits of" any "education program or activity receiving Federal financial assistance." § 1681(a). The statute makes clear that . . . students must not be denied access to educational benefits and opportunities on the basis of gender. We thus conclude that funding recipients are properly held liable in damages only where they are deliberately indifferent to sexual harassment, of which they have actual knowledge, that is so severe, pervasive, and objectively offensive that it can be said to deprive the victims of access to the educational opportunities or benefits provided by the school.

The most obvious example of student-on-student sexual harassment capable of triggering a damages claim would thus involve the overt, physical deprivation of access to school resources. Consider, for example, a case in which male students physically threaten their female peers every day, successfully preventing the female students from using a particular school resource—an athletic field or a computer lab, for instance. District administrators are well aware of the daily ritual, yet they deliberately ignore requests for aid from the female students wishing to use the resource. The district's knowing refusal to take any action in response to such behavior would fly in the face of Title IX's core principles, and such deliberate indifference may appropriately be subject to claims for monetary damages. It is not necessary, however, to show physical exclusion to demonstrate that students have been deprived by the actions of another student or students of an educational opportunity on the basis of sex. Rather, a plaintiff must establish sexual harassment of students that is so severe, pervasive, and objectively offensive, and that so undermines and detracts from the victims' educational experience, that the victim-students are effectively denied equal access to an institution's resources and opportunities.

Whether gender-oriented conduct rises to the level of actionable "harassment" thus "depends on a constellation of surrounding circumstances, expectations, and relationships," *Oncale* v. *Sundowner Offshore Services, Inc.*, including, but not limited to, the ages of the harasser and the victim and the number of individuals involved. Courts, moreover, must bear in mind that schools are unlike the adult workplace and that children may regularly interact in a manner that would be unacceptable among adults. Indeed, at least early on, students are still learning how to interact appropriately with their peers. It is thus understandable that, in the school setting, students often engage in insults, banter, teasing, shoving, pushing, and gender-specific conduct that is upsetting to the students subjected to it. Damages are not available for simple acts of teasing and name-calling among school children, however, even where these comments target differences in gender. Rather, in the context of student-on-student harassment, damages are available only where the behavior is so severe, pervasive, and objectively offensive that it denies its victims the equal access to education that Title IX is designed to protect.

The dissent fails to appreciate these very real limitations on a funding recipient's liability under Title IX. It is not enough to show, as the dissent would read this opinion to provide, that a student has been "teased," or "called . . . offensive names." Comparisons to an "overweight child who skips gym class because the other children tease her about her size," the student "who refuses to wear glasses to avoid the taunts of 'four-eyes,' " and "the child who refuses to go to school because the school bully calls him a 'scaredy-cat' at recess," are inapposite and misleading. Nor do we contemplate, much less hold, that a mere "decline in grades is enough to survive" a motion to dismiss. The drop-off in LaShonda's grades provides necessary evidence of a potential link between her education and G.F.'s misconduct, but petitioner's ability to state a cognizable claim here depends equally on the alleged persistence and severity of G.F.'s actions, not to mention the Board's alleged knowledge and deliberate indifference. We trust that the dissent's characterization of our opinion will not mislead courts to impose more sweeping liability than we read Title IX to require.

. . .The fact that it was a teacher who engaged in harassment in *Franklin* and *Gebser* is relevant. The relationship between the harasser and the victim necessarily affects the extent to which the misconduct can be said to breach Title IX's guarantee of equal access to educational benefits and to have a systemic effect on a program or activity. Peer harassment, in particular, is less likely to satisfy these requirements than is teacher-student harassment.

C

Applying this standard to the facts at issue here, we conclude that the Eleventh Circuit erred in dismissing petitioner's complaint. Petitioner alleges that her daughter was the victim of repeated acts of sexual harassment by G. F. over a 5-month period, and there are allegations in support of the conclusion that G. F.'s misconduct was severe, pervasive, and objectively offensive. The harassment was not only verbal; it included numerous acts of objectively offensive touching, and, indeed, G. F. ultimately pleaded guilty to criminal sexual misconduct. Moreover, the complaint alleges that there were multiple victims who were sufficiently disturbed by G. F.'s misconduct to seek an audience with the school principal. Further, petitioner contends that the harassment had a concrete, negative effect on her daughter's ability to receive an education. The complaint also suggests that petitioner may be able to show both actual knowledge and deliberate indifference on the part of the Board, which made no effort whatsoever either to investigate or to put an end to the harassment.

. . .[T]he judgment of the United States Court of Appeals for the Eleventh Circuit is reversed, and the case is remanded for further proceedings consistent with this opinion.

JUSTICE KENNEDY, with whom THE CHIEF JUSTICE, JUSTICE SCALIA, and JUSTICE THOMAS join, dissenting.

. . .A vital safeguard for the federal balance is the requirement that, when Congress imposes a condition on the States' receipt of federal funds, it "must do so unambiguously." As the majority acknowledges, "legislation enacted . . . pursuant to the spending power is much in the nature of a contract," and the legitimacy of Congress' exercise of its power to condition funding on state compliance with congressional conditions "rests on whether the State voluntarily and knowingly accepts the terms of the 'contract.'" "'There can, of course, be no knowing acceptance [of the terms of the putative contract] if a State is unaware of the conditions [imposed by the legislation] or is unable to ascertain what is expected of it.'" *Pennhurst* v. *Halderman,* 451 U.S. 1. at 17.

Our insistence that "Congress speak with a clear voice" to "enable the States to exercise their choice knowingly, cognizant of the consequences of their participation," . . .is a concrete safeguard in the federal system. Only if States receive clear notice of the conditions attached to federal funds can they guard against excessive federal intrusion into state affairs and be vigilant in policing the boundaries of federal power.... While the majority purports to give effect to these principles, it eviscerates the clear-notice safeguard of our Spending Clause jurisprudence.

...The remedial scheme the majority creates today is neither sensible nor faithful to Spending Clause principles. In order to make its case for school liability for peer sexual harassment, the majority must establish that Congress gave grant recipients clear and unambiguous notice that they would be liable in money damages for failure to remedy discriminatory acts of their students. The majority must also demonstrate that the statute gives schools clear notice that one child's harassment of another constitutes "discrimination" on the basis of sex within the meaning of Title IX, and that—as applied to individual cases—the standard for liability will enable the grant recipient to distinguish inappropriate childish behavior from actionable gender discrimination. The majority does not carry these burdens.

...In the end, the majority not only imposes on States liability that was unexpected and unknown, but the contours of which are, as yet, unknowable. The majority's opinion purports to be narrow, but the limiting principles it proposes are illusory. The fence the Court has built is made of little sticks, and it cannot contain the avalanche of liability now set in motion. The potential costs to our schools of today's decision are difficult to estimate, but they are so great that it is most unlikely Congress intended to inflict them.

The only certainty flowing from the majority's decision is that scarce resources will be diverted from educating our children and that many school districts, desperate to avoid Title IX peer harassment suits, will adopt whatever federal code of student conduct and discipline the Department of Education sees fit to impose upon them. The Nation's schoolchildren will learn their first lessons about federalism in classrooms where the federal government is the ever-present regulator. The federal government will have insinuated itself not only into one of the most traditional areas of state concern but also into one of the most sensitive areas of human affairs. This federal control of the discipline of our Nation's schoolchildren is contrary to our traditions and inconsistent with the sensible administration of our schools. Because Title IX did not give States unambiguous notice that accepting federal funds meant ceding to the federal government power over the day-to-day disciplinary decisions of schools, I dissent.

I. . .

A

. . .[A] plaintiff cannot establish a Title IX violation merely by showing that she has been "subjected to discrimination." Rather, a violation of Title IX occurs only if she is "subjected to discrimination under any education program or activity," 20 U.S.C. § 1681(a), where "program or activity" is defined as "all of the operations of" a grant recipient, § 1687.

Under the most natural reading of this provision, discrimination violates Title IX only if it is authorized by, or in accordance with, the actions, activities, or policies of the grant recipient.

. . .Teacher sexual harassment of students is "under" the school's program or activity in certain circumstances, but student harassment is not. Our decision in *Gebser* recognizes that a grant recipient acts through its agents and thus, under certain limited circumstances, even tortious acts by teachers may be attributable to the school. . . .Where the heightened requirements for attribution are met, the teacher's actions are treated as the grant recipient's actions. In those circumstances, then, the teacher sexual harassment is "under" the operations of the school.

I am aware of no basis in law or fact, however, for attributing the acts of a student to a school and, indeed, the majority does not argue that the school acts through its students. . . .Discrimination by one student against another therefore cannot be "under" the school's program or activity as required by Title IX. The majority's imposition of liability for peer sexual harassment thus conflicts with the most natural interpretation of Title IX's "under a program or activity" limitation on school liability. At the very least, my reading undermines the majority's implicit claim that Title IX imposes an unambiguous duty on schools to remedy peer sexual harassment.

B

1

. . .The majority contends that a school's deliberate indifference to known student harassment "subjects" students to harassment—that is, "causes [students] to undergo" harassment. The majority recognizes, however, that there must be some limitation on the third-party conduct that the school can fairly be said to cause. In search of a principle, the majority asserts, without much elaboration, that one causes discrimination when one has some "degree of control" over the discrimination and fails to remedy it.

To state the majority's test is to understand that it is little more than an exercise in arbitrary line-drawing. The majority does not explain how we are to determine what degree of control is sufficient—or, more to the point, how the States were on clear notice that the Court would draw the line to encompass students.

...One would think that the majority would at least limit its control principle by reference to the long-established practice of the Department of Education (DOE). For the first 25 years after the passage of Title IX—until 1997—the DOE's regulations drew the liability line, at its most expansive, to encompass only those to whom the school delegated its official functions. It is perhaps reasonable to suppose that grant recipients were on notice that they could not hire third parties to do for them what they could not do themselves. For example, it might be reasonable to find that a school was on notice that it could not circumvent Title IX's core prohibitions by, for example, delegating its admissions decisions to an outside screening committee it knew would discriminate on the basis of gender.

Given the state of gender discrimination law at the time Title IX was passed, however, there is no basis to think that Congress contemplated liability for a school's failure to remedy discriminatory acts by students or that the States would believe the statute imposed on them a clear obligation to do so. When Title IX was enacted in 1972, the concept of "sexual harassment" as gender discrimination had not been recognized or considered by the courts. . . .

2

The majority nonetheless appears to see no need to justify drawing the "enough control" line to encompass students. In truth, however, a school's control over its students is much more complicated and limited than the majority acknowledges. A public school does not control its students in the way it controls its teachers or those with whom it contracts. Most public schools do not screen or select students, and their power to discipline students is far from unfettered.

Public schools are generally obligated by law to educate all students who live within defined geographic boundaries. Indeed, the Constitution of almost every State in the country guarantees the State's students a free primary and secondary public education. . . . Schools that remove a harasser from the classroom and then attempt to fulfill their continuing-education obligation by placing the harasser in any kind of group setting, rather than by hiring expensive tutors for each student, will find themselves at continuing risk of

Title IX suits brought by the other students in the alternative education program.

In addition, federal law imposes constraints on school disciplinary actions. This Court has held, for example, that due process requires "at the very minimum," that a student facing suspension "be given some kind of notice and afforded some kind of hearing." *Goss* v. *Lopez*, 419 U.S. 565, 579 (1975).

The Individuals with Disabilities Education Act (IDEA), 20 U.S.C. 1400 *et seq.* (1994 ed., Supp. III), moreover, places strict limits on the ability of schools to take disciplinary actions against students with behavior disorder disabilities, even if the disability was not diagnosed prior to the incident triggering discipline. "Disability," as defined in the Act, includes "serious emotional disturbance," § 1401(3) (A) (i), which the DOE, in turn, has defined as a "condition exhibiting . . . over a long period of time and to a marked degree that adversely affects a child's educational performance" an "inability to build or maintain satisfactory interpersonal relationships with peers and teachers" or "inappropriate types of behavior or feelings under normal circumstances." 34 CFR § 300.7(b)(9) (1998). If, as the majority would have us believe, the behavior that constitutes actionable peer sexual harassment so deviates from the normal teasing and jostling of adolescence that it puts schools on clear notice of potential liability, then a student who engages in such harassment may have at least a colorable claim of severe emotional disturbance within the meaning of IDEA. When imposing disciplinary sanction on a student harasser who might assert a colorable IDEA claim, the school must navigate a complex web of statutory provisions and DOE regulations that significantly limit its discretion.

The practical obstacles schools encounter in ensuring that thousands of immature students conform their conduct to acceptable norms may be even more significant than the legal obstacles. School districts cannot exercise the same measure of control over thousands of students that they do over a few hundred adult employees. The limited resources of our schools must be conserved for basic educational services. Some schools lack the resources even to deal with serious problems of violence and are already overwhelmed with disciplinary problems of all kinds.

Perhaps even more startling than its broad assumptions about school control over primary and secondary school students is the majority's failure to grapple in any meaningful way with the distinction between elementary and secondary schools, on the one hand, and universities on the other. The majority bolsters its argument that schools can control their students' actions by quoting our decision in *Vernonia School Dist. 47J* v. *Acton*, 515 U.S. 646, 655 (1995), for the proposition that " 'the nature of [the State's] power [over public school children] is custodial and tutelary, permitting a degree of supervision and control that could not be exercised over free adults.' " Yet the majority's holding would appear to apply with equal force to universities, which do not exercise custodial and tutelary power over their adult students.

A university's power to discipline its students for speech that may constitute sexual harassment is also circumscribed by the First Amendment. A number of federal courts have already confronted difficult problems raised by university speech codes designed to deal with peer sexual and racial harassment.

The difficulties associated with speech codes simply underscore the limited nature of a university's control over student behavior that may be viewed as sexual harassment. Despite the fact that the majority relies on the assumption that schools exercise a great deal of control over their students to justify creating the private cause of action in the first instance, it does not recognize the obvious limits on a university's ability to control its students as a reason to doubt the propriety of a private cause of action for peer harassment. It simply uses them as a factor in determining whether the university's response was reasonable....

II

...The law recognizes that children—particularly young children—are not fully accountable for their actions because they lack the capacity to exercise mature judgment. It should surprise no one, then, that the schools that are the primary locus of most children's social development are rife with inappropriate behavior by children who are just learning to interact with their peers. The *amici* on the front lines of our schools describe the situation best:

> "Unlike adults in the workplace, juveniles have limited life experiences or familial influences upon which to establish an understanding of appropriate behavior. The real world of school discipline is a rough-and-tumble place where students practice newly learned vulgarities, erupt with anger, tease and embarrass each other, share offensive notes, flirt, push and shove in the halls, grab and offend." Brief for National School Boards Assoc. as *Amici Curiae* (hereinafter school *amici*).

No one contests that much of this "dizzying array of immature or uncontrollable behaviors by students," *ibid*. is inappropriate, even "objectively offensive" at times, and that parents and schools have a moral and ethical responsibility to help students learn to interact with their peers in an appropriate manner. It is doubtless the case, moreover, that much of this inappropriate behavior is directed toward members of the opposite sex, as children in the throes of adolescence struggle to express their emerging sexual identities.

It is a far different question, however, whether it is either proper or useful to label this immature, childish behavior gender discrimination. Nothing in Title IX suggests that Congress even contemplated this question, much less answered it in the affirmative in unambiguous terms.

...[R]espondents have made a cogent and persuasive argument that the type of student conduct alleged by petitioner should not be considered "sexual harassment," much less gender discrimination actionable under Title IX [stating in their brief]:

> "At the time Petitioner filed her complaint, no court, including this Court had recognized the concept of sexual harassment in any context other than the employment context. Nor had any Court extended the concept of sexual harassment to the misconduct of emotionally and socially immature children. The type of conduct alleged by Petitioner in her complaint is not new. However, in past years it was properly identified as misconduct which was addressed within the context of student discipline. The Petitioner now asks this Court to create out of whole cloth a cause of action by labeling childish misconduct as 'sexual harassment,' to stigmatize children as sexual harassers, and have the federal court system take on the additional burden of second guessing the disciplinary actions taken by school administrators in addressing misconduct, something this Court has consistently refused to do."

Likewise, the majority's assertion that *Gebser* and *Franklin* settled the question is little more than *ipse dixit*. *Gebser* and *Franklin* themselves did nothing more than cite *Meritor Savings Bank, FSB* v. *Vinson*, 477 U.S. 57 (1986), a Title VII case, for the proposition that "when a supervisor sexually harasses a subordinate because of the subordinate's sex, that supervisor 'discriminates' on the basis of sex." See *Franklin* at 74; *Gebser*, 524 U.S. at 282-283. To treat that proposition as establishing that the student conduct at issue here is gender discrimination is to erase, in one stroke, all differences between children and adults, peers and teachers, schools and workplaces.

In reality, there is no established body of federal or state law on which courts may draw in defining the student conduct that qualifies as Title IX gender discrimination. Analogies to Title VII hostile environment harassment are inapposite, because schools are not workplaces and children are not adults. The norms of the adult workplace that have defined hostile environment sexual harassment, see, *e.g., Oncale* v. *Sundowner Offshore Services, Inc.*, 523 U.S. 75 (1998), are not easily translated to peer relationships in schools, where teenage romantic relationships and dating are a part of everyday life. Analogies to Title IX teacher sexual harassment of students are similarly flawed. A teacher's sexual overtures toward a student are always inappropriate; a teenager's romantic overtures to a classmate (even when persistent and unwelcome) are an inescapable part of adolescence.

The majority admits that, under its approach, "whether gender-oriented conduct rises to the level of actionable 'harassment' . . . 'depends on a constellation of surrounding circumstances, expectations, and relationships, including, but not limited to, the ages of the harasser and the victim and the number of individuals involved." The majority does not explain how a school is supposed to discern from this mishmash of factors what is actionable discrimination. Its multifactored balancing test is a far cry from the clarity we demand of Spending Clause legislation.

. . .The only guidance the majority gives schools in distinguishing between the "simple acts of teasing and name-calling among school children," said not to be a basis for suit even when they "target differences in gender," and actionable peer sexual harassment is, in reality, no guidance at all. The majority proclaims that "in the context of student-on-student harassment, damages are available only in the situation where the behavior is so serious, pervasive, and objectively offensive that it denies its victims the equal access to education that Title IX is designed to protect." . . .Is equal access denied when a girl who tires of being chased by the boys at recess refuses to go outside? When she cannot concentrate during class because she is worried about the recess activities? When she pretends to be sick one day so she can stay home from school? It appears the majority is content to let juries decide.

The majority's reference to a "systemic effect" does nothing to clarify the content of its standard. The majority appears to intend that requirement to do no more than exclude the possibility that a single act of harassment perpetrated by one student on one other student can form the basis for an actionable claim. That is a small concession indeed.

...On the facts of this case, petitioner has stated a claim because she alleged, in the majority's words, "that the harassment had a concrete, negative effect on her daughter's ability to receive an education." In petitioner's words, the effects that might have been visible to the school were that her daughter's grades "dropped" and her "ability to concentrate on her school work [was] affected." Almost all adolescents experience these problems at one time or another as they mature.

III

The majority's inability to provide any workable definition of actionable peer harassment simply underscores the myriad ways in which an opinion that purports to be narrow is, in fact, so broad that it will support untold numbers of lawyers who will prove adept at presenting cases that will withstand the defendant school districts' pretrial motions. Each of the barriers to run-away litigation the majority offers us crumbles under the weight of even casual scrutiny.

...The majority seems oblivious to the fact that almost every child, at some point, has trouble in school because he or she is being teased by his or her peers. The girl who wants to skip recess because she is teased by the boys is no different from the overweight child who skips gym class because the other children tease her about her size in the locker room; or the child who risks flunking out because he refuses to wear glasses to avoid the taunts of "four-eyes"; or the child who refuses to go to school because the school bully calls him a "scaredy-cat" at recess. Most children respond to teasing in ways that detract from their ability to learn. The majority's test for actionable harassment will, as a result, sweep in almost all of the more innocuous conduct it acknowledges as a ubiquitous part of school life.

...[T]he Court's reliance on the impact on the child's educational experience suggests that the "objective offensiveness" of a comment is to be judged by reference to a reasonable child at whom the comments were aimed. Not only is that standard likely to be quite expansive, it also gives schools—and juries—little guidance, requiring them to attempt to gauge the sensitivities of, for instance, the average seven year old.

...The majority's limitations on peer sexual harassment suits cannot hope to contain the flood of liability the Court today begins. The elements of the Title IX claim created by the majority will be easy not only to allege but also to prove. A female plaintiff who pleads only that a boy called her offensive names, that she told a teacher, that the teacher's response was unreasonable, and that her school performance suffered as a result, appears to state a successful claim.

There will be no shortage of plaintiffs to bring such complaints. Our schools are charged each day with educating millions of children. Of those millions of students, a large percentage will, at some point during their school careers, experience something they consider sexual harassment. A 1993 Study by the American Association of University Women Educational Foundation, for instance, found that "fully 4 out of 5 students (81%) report that they have been the target of some form of sexual harassment during their school lives."

...The prospect of unlimited Title IX liability will, in all likelihood, breed a climate of fear that encourages school administrators to label even the most innocuous of childish conduct sexual harassment. It would appear to be no coincidence that, not long after the DOE issued its proposed policy guidance warning that schools could be liable for peer sexual harassment in the fall of 1996, see 61 Fed. Reg. 42728, a North Carolina school suspended a 6-year-old boy who kissed a female classmate on the cheek for sexual harassment, on the theory that "unwelcome is unwelcome at any age." *Los Angeles Times*, Sept. 25, 1996, p. A11. A week later, a New York school suspended a second-grader who kissed a classmate and ripped a button off her skirt. *Buffalo News*, Oct. 2, 1996, p. A16. The second grader said that he got the idea from his favorite book "Corduroy," about a bear with a missing button. School administrators said only, "We were given guidelines as to why we suspend children. We follow the guidelines."

At the college level, the majority's holding is sure to add fuel to the debate over campus speech codes that, in the name of preventing a hostile educational environment, may infringe students' First Amendment rights. Indeed, under the majority's control principle, schools presumably will be responsible for remedying conduct that occurs even in student dormitory rooms. As a result, schools may well be forced to apply workplace norms in the most private of domains.

...The majority's holding in this case appears to be driven by the image of the school administration sitting idle every day while male students commandeer a school's athletic field or computer lab and prevent female students from using it through physical threats. Title IX might provide a remedy in such a situation, however, without resort to the majority's unprecedented theory of school liability for student harassment. If the school usually disciplines students for threatening each other and prevents them from blocking others' access to school facilities, then the school's failure to enforce its rules when the boys target the girls on a widespread level, day after day, may support an inference that the school's decision not to respond is itself based on gender. That pattern of discriminatory response could form the basis of a Title IX action.

...I fail to see how federal courts will administer school discipline better than the principals and teachers to whom the public has entrusted that task or how the majority's holding will help the vast majority of students, whose educational opportunities will be diminished by the diversion of school funds to litigation. The private cause of action the Court creates will justify a corps of federal administrators in writing regulations on student harassment. It will also embroil schools and courts in endless litigation over what qualifies as peer sexual harassment and what constitutes a reasonable response.

...[T]he majority's decision today says not one word about the federal balance.... The delicacy and immense significance of teaching children about sexuality should cause the Court to act with great restraint before it displaces state and local governments.

... Enforcement of the federal right recognized by the majority means that federal influence will permeate everything from curriculum decisions to day-to-day classroom logistics and interactions. After today, Johnny will find that the routine problems of adolescence are to be resolved by invoking a federal right to demand assignment to a desk two rows away.

...We can be assured that like suits will follow—suits, which in cost and number, will impose serious financial burdens on local school districts, the taxpayers who support them, and the children they serve. Federalism and our struggling school systems deserve better from this Court. I dissent.

Case Questions

1.   Justice Anthony Kennedy employs the time-honored debating technique of *reductio ad absurdum*. Is his critique of the majority's test effective? Was the majority's response to him adequate?

2.   Suppose the principal and school district had told Aurelia Davis, "Boys will be boys. G.F.'s behavior is normal. He'll outgrow it. Learning how to cope with this behavior is a part of growing up. Maybe your daughter needs some help." How might O'Connor's resolution of this case have changed? Kennedy's? Yours?

3.   The cases O'Connor cites to illustrate the Court's endorsement of school authority—*New Jersey v. T.L.O* and *Vernonia v. Acton*—uphold, respectively, student searches and drug testing. How are they similar to *Davis*? How different?

Case note: In *Davis*, the Court used the *Gebser* liability standard that it had developed for sex-based harassment by teachers (or other school employees)—deliberate indifference by school authorities to sex-based harassment of which they were aware—and applied it to the situation of harassment of schoolchildren by other schoolchildren. To be actionable, moreover, the harassment has to be "so severe, pervasive, and objectively offensive that it denies its victims the equal access to education that Title IX is designed to protect." To show that it is not indifferent to the problem, the authorities need to respond in a way that is reasonable for rectifying the discriminatory atmosphere created by the harassment. The four dissenters would have granted no liability until Congress explicitly did so.

Although the combined force of these two decisions provides legal remedies for sexually harassed students, remedies that Congress neglected to provide, some critics argued that Congress should go still further.[45] Under Title VII (in contrast to Title IX), employees could bring lawsuits when employers fail to act against and to correct not just sexual harassment of which they have been made aware, but also sexual harassment that is so pervasive the employer *should have been aware* of it. By 2000, the Office of Civil Rights of the Department of Education had issued guidelines to schools that recommended the same sort of measures from school authorities (to protect students) that Title VII required from employers (to protect employees).[46] Some members of Congress attempted to codify these guidelines into enforceable legislation in a proposed Civil Rights Act of 2008. This bill, however, never passed, and the liability standards for Title VII versus Title IX harassment continue to differ. In recent years, attention has shifted away from elementary and secondary schools to how Title IX prohibitions on sexual discrimination apply to instances of sexual assault on college campuses.

TITLE IX AND RETALIATION

Jackson v. Birmingham [Alabama] Board of Education (2005) presented the Supreme Court with the question of whether third parties may bring charges of retaliation for making complaints. Unlike Title VII, Title IX is silent on the subject of retaliation. Roderick Jackson, an African-American male teacher and basketball coach, did not accuse the board of discriminating against him on the grounds of either race or sex. He alleged that his girls' team got fewer resources than the boys did. Soon after making this complaint, Jackson lost his coaching position (though not his job). The Court ruled that Title IX did allow such a claim and sent Jackson's case back to a lower court.[47] The Birmingham Board of Education ultimately agreed to rename Jackson as head coach and to make his compensation the same as other head coaches in the district. The school board also agreed to take steps to comply with the different requirements of Title IX.[48]

TITLE IX AND GENDER IDENTITY

Under the Obama administration, the Office for Civil Rights in the Department of Education took incremental steps to expand Title IX's prohibitions on sex discrimination to cover gender identity. These efforts included enforcement actions against school districts that discriminated against, and/or refused to provide accommodations to, students on the basis of their gender identities, and culminated in a 2016 "Dear Colleague" letter that explicitly stated that discrimination against a student on the basis of his/her/their transgender status is prohibited as sex discrimination under Title IX. The accompanying guidelines specified that students be allowed to articulate their own gender identity without regard to the sex that is reported on their identity documents, and to access restrooms and locker rooms consistent with their respective gender identity.[49]

Individual students initiated litigation under Title IX as well. Notably, Gavin Grimm, a teenage transgender boy (whose birth assignment had been female), sued the Gloucester County School Board for violating Title IX's prohibitions on sex discrimination when it passed a policy requiring students to use sex-segregated facilities consistent with their sex as assigned at birth and/or unisex accommodations. The Obama Justice Department filed a Statement of Interest in the District Court stating that "Under Title IX, discrimination based on a person's gender identity, a person's transgender status, or a person's nonconformity to sex stereotypes constitutes discrimination based on sex. As such, prohibiting a student from accessing the restrooms that match his gender identity is prohibited sex discrimination under Title IX. There is a public interest in ensuring that all students, including transgender students, have the opportunity to learn in an environment free of sex discrimination."[50] After a lengthy legal process, Grimm won his case, and the school board was ordered to allow him access to the boys facilities at his high school. The Gloucester School Board appealed to the U.S. Supreme Court and the Justices agreed to hear the case, but later reversed this decision. Specifically, after Donald Trump took office as President and before the Justices could hear Grimm's case, the Trump administration issued its own "Dear Colleague" letter that rescinded the Obama administration's Title IX guidelines on gender identity and transgender students.[51] As a result, the Supreme Court vacated the 4th Circuit Court of Appeals' decision that relied on the Obama administration's interpretation of Title IX to substantiate Grimm's right to access male facilities.

Unless and until Congress amends Title IX to explicitly state that discrimination on the basis of gender identity is discrimination on the basis of sex or the U.S. Supreme Court issues an opinion that interprets Title IX in this way, transgender students such as Gavin Grimm may find that their ability to utilize Title IX to challenge discrimination in educational facilities will be contingent upon the ideological predispositions of the current president. As the next chapter makes clear, Title IX's application to sexual assault on college campuses has similarly been contingent on the political leadership of the Department of Education.

CONCLUSION

"Education was long denied" woman, wrote the Supreme Court in *Muller v. Oregon*. As the tense indicates, this was no longer true by 1908: "Now the doors of the schoolroom are opened and her opportunities for acquiring knowledge are great." Nevertheless, the Court included the historical fact among the many conditions that made woman "dependent upon man" while justifying "legislation to protect her from the greed as well as the passion of man."[52] Women's education was a necessary prerequisite for the activism that rendered this prescription obsolete. As women gained access to knowledge, they have asserted their independence and have contributed to changes in laws and attitudes. Little of the progress examined in this casebook could have happened without the kinds of changes examined in this chapter.

But equal education for women was a long time coming. Male supremacist attitudes limited girls' opportunities even after official discrimination was removed. It was not until 1979 that equal numbers of men and women attended college.[53] Policies toward women's education have been and continued to be inextricably linked with attitudes about women's roles. Dr. Edward Clarke's dire warnings about the effect of college on women's health were disproved, only to be followed by Mills College's efforts to educate women for homemaking and gibes about the "Mrs." degree. In the early and mid-1970s, the reinterpretation of the equal protection clause to limit sex discrimination (see Chapter 2) and statutes mandating sexual equality in programs receiving federal funds indicated that law was changing faster than social attitudes. The reach of Title IX has even extended to such entrenched bastions of male privilege as school athletics and has restricted the former tolerance of classroom behavior that would be considered sexual harassment in the workplace. Yet, as the next chapter makes clear, sexual violence continues to plague institutions of higher education and Title IX has been of limited utility in this area. In addition, challenges remain in the quest for gender equity for transgender and gender non-conforming students in elementary, secondary and higher education. In the future, Title IX is likely to be instrumental in these legal and political debates. While the history of gendered education policy displays dramatic progress, there is still much work to be done.

---

[1] Southern laws against teaching slaves to read followed later, after the Nat Turner revolt of 1831. Many slaves before then were taught to read the Scriptures. E.J. Monaghan, *Learning to Read and Write in Colonial America* (Boston: University of Massachusetts Press, 2005), 243.

[2] *Brown v. Board*, 347 U.S. 483 (1954).

[3] Although the official legality of racial segregation ended in 1954, it took more than ten years before schools designated officially as "white" or "colored" were eliminated in Southern states. Most of this elimination took place in the late 1960s after the federal government, under President Lyndon B. Johnson, threatened to withdraw funds from any school district refusing to desegregate.

[4] *Sweatt v. Painter*, 339 U.S. 629, 634 (1950).

[5] Ibid.

[6] *McLaurin v. Oklahoma State Regents*, 339 U.S. 637 (1950).

[7] Ibid. at, 641 (1950).

[8] Robin Morgan, ed., *Sisterhood is Powerful* (New York: Vintage Books, 1970), 366–71.

[9] "Where Are Single-Gender Public Schools?" Single-Gender Public Schools in 5 Charts, *Education Week*, November 2, 2017. Available at: https://www.edweek.org/ew/section/multimedia/single-gender-public-schools-in-5-charts.html (accessed May 12, 2018).

[10] Ibid.

[11] Ibid.

[12] Ibid.

[13] *Garrett v. Board of Education of School District of Detroit*, 775 F.Supp. 1004 (E.D. Mich. 1991).

[14] Ibid.

[15] (Pub. L. 107–110, at § 5131(a)(23), 2001). Donald F. Uerling and Gretchen Hall, "Single-Sex Schools and Classroom: Is 'Separate but Comparable' Legally Permissible?" *Journal of Women in Educational Leadership* 1, no. 2 (April 2003): 17–32, at 17–19. Available at: https://digitalcommons.unl.edu/cgi/viewcontent.cgi?article=1095&context=jwel (accessed May 2, 2018).

[16] Pub.L. 107–110, at § (a)(23) (Id. § 5131 (c), 2001). Uerling and Hall, ibid.

[17] 67 Fed. Reg. 31102, May 8, 2002. Uerling and Hall, ibid.

[18] 67 Fed. Reg. 31098 (2002). Uerling and Hall, ibid.

[19] Greg Toppo, "All-boys' High School Completes First Year; Boasts Wait List for Fall," *USA TODAY*, Published July 5, 2017; Updated July 5, 2017. (Available at: https://www.usatoday.com/story/news/2017/07/05/dc-all-boys-high-school/102898672/, accessed May 2, 2018); Perry Stein, "ACLU Fights D.C. on Its All-male High School's Admission Policy," *The Washington Post*, September 12, 2016. Available at: https://www.washingtonpost.com/local/education/aclu-fights-dc-on-its-all-male-high-schools-admission-policy/2016/09/12/0c21d01c-7902-11e6-beac-57a4a412e93a_story.html?utm_term=.516c087b00b3 (accessed May 2, 2018).

[20] New York: Harper and Brothers, 1950, chaps. 2, 5.

[21] Betty Friedan, *The Feminine Mystique* (New York: W.W. Norton & Company, 1963), 158–59.

[22] *Heaton v. Bristol*, 317 S.W.2d. 86, 99 (Tex. Civ. App. 1958).

[23] E.g., Massachusetts by 1977 eliminated its male-only admissions policy for the Massachusetts Maritime Academy, which trained students for service in the U.S. Merchant Marine, *United States v. Massachusetts Maritime Academy*, 762 F.2d 142 (1985), at n.12.

[24] For the Citadel litigation, see *Faulkner v. Jones*, 10 F.3d 226 (1993); 51 F.3d 440 (1995).

[25] *U.S. v. Virginia*, 766 F. Supp. 1407, 1408 (1991).

[26] Ibid., at 1411.

[27] Ibid., at 1412–1413.

[28] *United States v. Virginia*, 976 F.2d 890, 893–894 (1992).

29 Ibid., at 896–897.

30 *U.S. v. Virginia*, 852 F. Supp. 471, 476 (1994).

31 *U.S. v. Virginia*, 44 F.3d 1229 (1995); 52 F.3d 90 (1995).

32 The statute allows certain exceptions, including an exception for traditionally one-sex colleges that continue to admit only one sex.

33 Kenneth H. Bastian, Jr., "Thank Title IX for Some of That Gold," *The Washington Post*, August 5, 1984.

34 "Different Mix at Law Schools," *The New York Times*, April 5, 1991.

35 *Cannon v. University of Chicago*, 441 U.S. 677 (1979).

36 *Guardians' Assn. v. Civil Service*, 463 U.S. 582 (1983).

37 *Consolidated Rail v. Darrone*, 465 U.S. 624, at 630, n.9 (1984).

38 42 U.S.C. Section 2000d–7.

39 Ibid.

40 *Grove City College v. Bell*, 465 U.S. 555 (1984).

41 Grove City College Catalog 2018–19. http://www.gcc.edu/Portals/0/2018-19-Catalog.pdf#page=22 (accessed October 1, 2018).

42 Title IX, 45 CFR 86.41—Athletics.

43 34 C.F.R. §§ 106.41 et seq., App. 259a ("Title IX regulations").

44 Cambridge, Mass.: Harvard University Press, 1998, pp. 195–196.

45 E.g., Heather D. Redmond, "Davis v. Monroe County Board of Education: Scant Protection for the Student Body," *Law and Inequality* 18 (2000): 393–418, 412–418. Available at: https://scholarship.law.umn.edu/cgi/viewcontent.cgi?article=1016&context=lawineq (accessed May 10, 2018).

46 Ibid, at 417.

47 *Jackson v. Birmingham Board of Education*, 544 U.S. 167 (2005).

48 "Coach in Title IX Case Wins Reinstatement," *Education Week*, December 5, 2006. Available at: https://www.edweek.org/ew/articles/2006/12/06/14law-3.h26.html (accessed on May 11, 2018).

49 Catherine Lhamon and Vanita Gupta, "Dear Colleague Letter on Transgender Students," *U.S. Department of Education* and *U.S. Department of Justice*, May 13, 2016. Available at: https://www.justice.gov/opa/file/850986/download (accessed on May 18, 2018).

50 "Statement of Interest of the United States," Document 28, *Deirdre Grimm v. Gloucester County School Board*, U.S. District Court Eastern District of Virginia, June 29, 2015. Available at: https://www.justice.gov/sites/default/files/crt/legacy/2015/07/09/gloucestersoi.pdf (accessed May 15, 2018).

51 Sandra Battle and T.E. Wheeler, "Dear Colleague Letter," *U.S. Department of Education* and *U.S. Department of Justice*, February 22, 2017. Available at: https://www.justice.gov/opa/press-release/file/941551/download (accessed May 18, 2018).

52 208 U.S. 412, 421–422.

53 Judith A. Baer, *Women in American Law: The Struggle for Equality from the New Deal to the Present*, 3rd ed. (New York: Holmes and Meier Publishers, 2002), 223.

CHAPTER 7

Women and Crime

This chapter is not about women as suspects, criminals, or prisoners. "Women and crime" refers here to gender issues involved in the definition and prosecution of crime. For example, "wife beating" was long an exception to the general rule that doing bodily harm to someone who is not threatening you is a felony called aggravated assault. In common law, a husband could administer "reasonable correction" to his wife. Similarly, marriage created an exception to the rape laws. "Carnal knowledge of a woman, forcibly and without her consent" was impossible within marriage because "by their mutual matrimonial consent and contract the wife hath given up herself in this kind to her husband, which she cannot retract."[1]

In 1961, the American Law Institute's (ALI) Model Penal Code recommended reduced punishments for forcible sex when the victim was the "voluntary social companion" of the accused and/or "had previously permitted him sexual liberties."[2] Today, wife beating has become "domestic violence," rape is "sexual assault," the marital exemption has been abolished, and the behavior described in the ALI's quaint language has been renamed "date rape" or "acquaintance rape." These changes in terminology have been accompanied by increased governmental commitment to deterring and punishing these crimes. The influence of feminism has been particularly strong here. But rape and battering persist. Many perpetrators still escape punishment, and the police are not always held accountable for indifference and neglect.

Pornography, as we shall see, was the subject of vehement controversy among feminists during the 1980s and 1990s. To the extent that pornography fits the definition of obscenity, it is outside the protection of the First Amendment; all states have criminalized it, but in recent decades the criminalization has been focused on showing it to children or using children to produce it. Still, there exists a dissonance between doctrine and practice. Successful obscenity prosecutions are rare. In addition, the advent of the Internet has made it exponentially more difficult for government to regulate sexually explicit speech because the materials available online are transmitted across national and state borders and are downloaded and viewed in the privacy of the home. Thus, while obscenity is not protected by the First Amendment, most pornography is protected by American capitalism. It is a multi-billion-dollar industry. Feminists who regard pornography as degrading to women have proposed civil penalties, so far without success.

Sex bias has resulted not only in the effective decriminalization of much of man's inhumanity to woman, but also the criminalization of women's behavior. "The oldest profession," prostitution, is the acceptance of payment for sexual services, not the purchase of them. Most prostitutes are women (a small minority are men who service other men). Payment for sex is illegal, but it is most often the prostitute, not the client or "john," who is arrested and charged. Procuring sexual services for someone else is also a crime, but pimps, madams, and the like often escape punishment because of their ability to manipulate the legal system.

SPOUSE ABUSE

The Old Days: Three Cases

Joyner v. Joyner (1862)

In the case below, the Court responded to legislative changes that increased the grounds on which divorce could be granted. The Court introduced its opinion with an explanation that it considered itself bound by its own precedents to interpret grounds for divorce "strictly." The Court also explained that according to common law rules, the time and place of an alleged offense are generally required to be specified, although failures to so specify could be permitted except where "time or place entered into the essence of the...fact." The Court then reasoned as follows:

JOYNER V. JOYNER
59 N. C. 322 (1862)

PEARSON, C. J.

The Legislature has deemed it expedient to enlarge the grounds upon which divorces may be obtained; but as a check or restraint on applications for divorces, and to guard against abuses, it is provided that the cause or ground on which the divorce is asked for shall be set forth in the petition "particularly and specially." It is settled by the decisions of this Court that this provision of the statute must be strictly observed, and the cause or causes for which the divorce is prayed must be set forth so "particularly and especially" as to enable the Court to see on the face of the petition that if the facts alleged are true the divorce ought to be granted: *Everton v. Everton*, 50 N.C. 202. The correctness of this construction is demonstrated by the fact that upon appeals from an order allowing alimony pending the suit, like the present, this Court is confined expressly to an examination of the cause or causes of divorce, as set out on the face of the petition, and can look at nothing else in making up the decision; Rev. Code, ch. 40, sec. 15.

By the rules of pleading in actions at the common law every allegation of fact must be accompanied by an allegation of "time and place." This rule was adopted in order to insure proper certainty in pleading, but a variance in the *allegata* and *probata*, that is, a failure to prove the precise time and place as alleged in the pleading, was held not to be fatal, unless time or place entered into the essence and made a material part of the fact relied on in the pleading. . . . But we are of opinion that it was necessary to state the circumstances under which the blow with the horse-whip and the blows with the switch were given; for instance, what was the conduct of the petitioner; what had she done or said to induce such violence on the part of the husband? We are informed by the petitioner that she was a woman "well-bred and of respectable family, and that her husband was not less than a fair match for her." There is no allegation that he was drunk, nor was there any imputation of unfaithfulness on either side (which is the most common ingredient of applications for divorce), so there was an obvious necessity for some explanation, and the cause of divorce could not be set forth "particularly and specially," without stating the circumstances which gave rise to the alleged grievances.

It is said on the argument that the fact that a husband, on one occasion, "struck his wife with a horse-whip, and on another occasion with a switch, leaving several bruises on her person," is, *of itself*, a sufficient cause of divorce, and consequently the circumstances which attended the infliction of these injuries are immaterial, and need not be set forth. This presents the question in the case.

The wife must be subject to the husband. Every man must govern his household, and if by reason of an unruly temper, or an unbridled tongue, the wife persistently treats her husband with disrespect, and he submits to it, he not only loses all sense of self-respect, but loses the respect of the other members of his family, without which he cannot expect to govern them, and forfeits the respect of his neighbors. Such have been the incidents of the marriage relation from the beginning of the human race. Unto the woman it is said, "Thy desire shall be to thy husband, and he shall rule over thee," Genesis, ch. 3, v. 16. It follows that the law gives the husband power to use such a degree of force as is necessary to make the wife behave herself and know her place. Why is it that by the principles of the common law if a wife slanders or assaults and beats a neighbor the husband is made to pay for it? Or if the wife commits a criminal offense, less than felony, in the presence of her husband, she is not held responsible? Why is it that the wife cannot make a will disposing of her land? and cannot sell her land without a privy examination, "separate and apart from her husband," in order to see that she did so voluntarily, and without compulsion on the part of her husband? It is for the reason that the law gives this power to the husband over the person of the wife, and has adopted proper safeguards to prevent an abuse of it.

We will not pursue the discussion further. It is not an agreeable subject, and we are not inclined, unnecessarily, to draw upon ourselves the charge of a want of proper respect for the weaker sex. It is sufficient for our purpose to state that there may be circumstances which will mitigate, excuse and so far justify the husband in striking the wife "with a horse-whip on one occasion and with a switch on another, leaving several bruises on the person," so as not to give her a right to abandon him and claim to be divorced. For instance, suppose a husband comes home and his wife abuses him in the strongest terms—calls him a scoundrel, and repeatedly expresses a wish that he was dead and in torment and being thus provoked in the *furor brevis*, he strikes her with the horse-whip, which he happens to have in his hands, but is afterwards willing to apologize, and expresses regret for having struck her; or suppose a man and his wife get into a discussion and have a difference of opinion as to a matter of fact, she becomes furious and gives way to her temper, so far as to tell him he *lies*, and upon being admonished not to repeat the word, nevertheless does so, and the husband taking up a switch, tells her if she repeat it again he will strike her, and after this notice she again repeats the insulting words, and he thereupon strikes her several blows; these are cases in which, in our opinion, the circumstances attending the act, and giving rise to it, so far justify the conduct of the husband as to take from the wife any ground of divorce for that cause, and authorize the Court to dismiss her petition with the admonition, "if you will amend your manners, you may expect better treatment"; see Shelford on Divorce. So that there are circumstances under which a husband may strike his wife with a horse-whip, or may strike her several times with a switch, so hard as to leave marks on her person, and these acts do not furnish sufficient ground for a divorce. It follows that when such acts are alleged as the causes

> for a divorce, it is necessary in order to comply with the provisions of the statute, to state the circumstances attending the acts and which gave rise to them. [The order that granted the divorce is] PER CURIAM
>
> *Reversed.*

State v. Rhodes (1868)

Mr. Rhodes had been tried by a jury who found "that the defendant struck Elizabeth Rhodes, his wife, three licks, with a switch about the size of one of his fingers (but not as large as a man's thumb), without any provocation except some words uttered by her and not recollected by the witness." But the judge threw out the verdict. "His Honor was of opinion that the defendant had a right to whip his wife with a switch no larger than his thumb, and that upon the facts found in the special verdict he was not guilty in law." The State appealed.³

> ### STATE V. A. B. RHODES
> 61 N.C. 453 (1868)
>
> **JUDGE READE.**
>
> The violence complained of would without question have constituted a battery if the subject of it had not been the defendant's wife. The question is how far that fact affects the case.
>
> The courts have been loath to take cognizance of trivial complaints arising out of the domestic relations—such as master and apprentice, teacher and pupil, parent and child, husband and wife. Not because those relations are not subject to the law, but because the evil of publicity would be greater than the evil involved in the trifles complained of; and because they ought to be left to family government. On the civil side of this Court, under our divorce laws, such cases have been unavoidable and not infrequent. On the criminal side there are but two cases reported. In one the question was, whether the wife was a competent witness to prove a battery by the husband upon her, which inflicted no great or permanent injury. It was decided that she was not. In discussing the subject the Court said, that the abstract question of the husband's right to whip his wife did not arise. The other case was one of a slight battery by the husband upon the wife after gross provocation. He was held not to be punishable. In that case the Court said, that unless some permanent injury be inflicted, or there be an excess of violence, or such a degree of cruelty as shows that it is inflicted to gratify his own bad passions, the law

will not invade the domestic forum, or go behind the curtain. Neither of those cases is like the one before us. The first case turned upon the competency of the wife as a witness, and in the second there was a slight battery upon a strong provocation.

In this case no provocation worth the name was proved. The fact found was that it was "without any provocation except some words which were not recollected by the witness." The words must have been of the slightest import to have made no impression on the memory. We must therefore consider the violence as unprovoked. The question is therefore plainly presented, whether the court will allow a conviction of the husband for moderate correction of the wife without provocation.

Our divorce laws do not compel a separation of husband and wife, unless the conduct of the husband be so cruel as to render the wife's condition intolerable, or her life burdensome. What sort of conduct on the part of the husband would be allowed to have that effect, has been repeatedly considered. And it has not been found easy to lay down any iron rule upon the subject. In some cases it has been held that actual and repeated violence to the person was not sufficient. In others that insults, indignities and neglect without any actual violence, were quite sufficient. So much does each case depend upon its peculiar surroundings.

We have sought the aid of the experience and wisdom of other times and of other countries.

Blackstone says "that the husband, by the old law, might give the wife moderate correction, for as he was to answer for her misbehavior, he ought to have the power to control her; but that in the polite reign of Charles the Second, this power of correction began to be doubted." 1 Black 444. Wharton says, that by the ancient common law the husband possessed the power to chastise his wife; but that the tendency of criminal courts in the present day is to regard the marital relation as no defense to a battery. Cr. L., § 1259–60. Chancellor Walworth says of such correction, that it is not authorized by the law of any civilized country; not indeed meaning that England is not civilized, but referring to the anomalous relics of barbarism which cleave to her jurisprudence. Bish. M. & D., 446, n. The old law of moderate correction has been questioned even in England, and has been repudiated in Ireland and Scotland. The old rule is approved in Mississippi, but it has met with but little favor elsewhere in the United States. *Ibid.*, 485. In looking into the discussions of the other States we find but little uniformity.

From what has been said it will be seen how much the subject is at sea. And, probably, it will ever be so: for it will always be influenced by the habits, manners and condition of every community. Yet it is necessary that we should lay down something as precise and practical as the nature of the subject will admit of, for the guidance of our courts.

Our conclusion is that family government is recognized by law as being as complete in itself as the State government is in itself, and yet subordinate to it; and that we will not interfere with or attempt to control it, in favor of either husband or wife, unless in cases where permanent or malicious injury is inflicted or threatened, or the condition of the party is intolerable. For, however great are the evils of ill temper, quarrels, and even personal conflicts inflicting only temporary pain, they are not comparable with the evils which would result from raising the curtain, and exposing to public curiosity and criticism, the nursery and the bed chamber. Every household has and must have, a government of its own, modeled to suit the temper, disposition and condition of its inmates. Mere ebullitions of passion, impulsive violence, and temporary pain, affection will soon forget and forgive, and each member will find excuse for the other in his own frailties. But when trifles are taken hold of by the public, and the parties are exposed and disgraced, and each endeavors to justify himself or herself by criminating the other, that which ought to be forgotten in a day, will be remembered for life.

It is urged in this case that as there was no provocation, the violence was of course excessive and malicious; that every one in whatever relation of life should be able to purchase immunity from pain, by obedience to authority and faithfulness in duty. And it is insisted that in *S. v. Pendergrass*, 2 D. & B. 365, which was the case of a schoolmistress whipping a child, that doctrine is laid down. It is true that it is there said, that the master may be punishable even when he does not transcend the powers granted; *i. e.,* when he does not inflict permanent injury, if he grossly abuse his powers, and use them as a cover for his malice. But observe, the language is, if he *grossly* abuse his powers. So that everyone would say at once, there was no cause for it, and it was purely malicious and cruel. If this be not the rule then every violence which would amount to an assault upon a stranger, would have to be investigated to see whether there was any provocation. And that would contravene what we have said, that we will punish no case of trifling importance. If in every such case we are to hunt for the provocation, how will the proof be supplied? Take the case before us. The witness said there was no provocation except some slight words. But then who can tell what significance the trifling words may have had to the husband? Who can tell what had happened an hour before, and every hour for a week? To him they may have been sharper than a sword. And so in every case, it might be impossible for the court to appreciate what might be offered as an excuse, or no excuse might appear at all, when a complete justification exists. Or, suppose the provocation could in every case be known, and the court should undertake to weigh the provocation in every trifling family broil, what would be the standard? Suppose a case coming up to us from a hovel, where neither delicacy of sentiment nor refinement of manners is appreciated or known. The parties themselves would be amazed, if they were to be held responsible for rudeness or trifling violence. What do they care for insults and indignities? In such cases what end would be gained by investigation or punishment?

It will be observed that the ground upon which we have put this decision is not that the husband has the *right* to whip his wife much or little; but that we will not interfere with family government in trifling cases. We will no more interfere where the husband whips the wife than where the wife whips the husband; and yet we would hardly be supposed to hold that a wife has a *right* to whip her husband. We will not inflict upon society the greater evil of raising the curtain upon domestic privacy, to punish the lesser evil of trifling violence. Two boys under fourteen years of age fight upon the playground, and yet the courts will take no notice of it, not for the reason that boys have the *right* to fight, but because the interests of society require that they should be left to the more appropriate discipline of the school room and of home. It is not true that boys have a right to fight; nor is it true that a husband has a right to whip his wife. And if he had, it is not easily seen how *the thumb* is the standard of size for the instrument which he may use, as some of the old authorities have said; and in deference to which was his Honor's charge. A light blow, or many light blows, with a stick larger than the thumb, might produce no injury; but a switch half the size might be so used as to produce death. The standard is the *effect produced*, and not the manner of producing it, or the instrument used. There is no error.

State v. Richard Oliver (1874)

Richard Oliver had been convicted of beating his wife "five licks with two switches" because he had not liked the way his bacon looked. He appealed.

> ## STATE V. RICHARD OLIVER
> 70 N.C. 60 (1874)
>
> **SETTLE, J.**
>
> We may assume that the old doctrine, that a husband had a right to whip his wife, provided he used a switch no larger than his thumb, is not law in North Carolina. Indeed, the Courts have advanced from that barbarism until they have reached the position, that the husband has no right to chastise his wife, under any circumstances.
>
> But from motives of public policy,—in order to preserve the sanctity of the domestic circle, the Courts will not listen to trivial complaints.
>
> If no permanent injury has been inflicted, nor malice, cruelty nor dangerous violence shown by the husband, it is better to draw the curtain, shut out the public gaze, and leave the parties to forget and forgive.
>
> No general rule can be applied, but each case must depend upon the circumstances surrounding it.
>
> Without adverting in detail to the facts established by the special verdict in this case, we think that they show both malice and cruelty.
>
> In fact, it is difficult to conceive how a man, who has promised, upon the altar to love, comfort, honor, and keep a woman, can lay rude and violent hands upon her, without having malice and cruelty in his heart.
>
> ...[T]he judgment of the Superior Court is [per curiam] affirmed.

Case Questions

1. In *Joyner*, the judge suggests that the husband's power to "correct" his wife follows logically from his legal responsibility for her actions in some situations. Construct the strongest possible argument for this proposition, and then make the strongest possible counter-argument.

2. Reconsider the Court's explanation of marital privacy in the *Griswold* decision in Chapter 4. Is their thesis similar to that of *Rhodes*? Why or why not?

3. *State v. Oliver* agrees with *Rhodes* that the courts should stay out of the family but reaches a different result from that case. Does the fact that the earlier case was civil and the later case criminal explain the difference? Or is *Oliver* an instance of judicial alteration of law? Of judicial correction of an earlier misconstrual of law? Of a consistent law applied to different facts?

4. Is there a meaningful difference between having a right to beat your wife and having immunity from prosecution for it?

From Wife Beating to Domestic Violence

The number of women who were abused by their husbands in the nineteenth century in the U.S., either in absolute numbers or as a proportion of all wives, is unknown. The three North Carolina women in the cases above were atypical in one important respect: Their battering came to public attention. Even today, when "wife beating" has become "domestic violence" and often gets wide publicity, law enforcement experts believe that wife abuse is a vastly unreported crime in the United States. In the next several cases, the reader will encounter many old myths about domestic violence—and, in the opinion of some commentators, new myths.

Police Responsibility

Police dislike, and sometimes fear, "D.V." calls. Experience has taught responding officers that batterer and victim may turn on them and that victims may not cooperate with criminal prosecution. Police are now required to respond to all complaints, partly as a result of cases like *Thurman v. Torrington*. But the word "response" can denote varying degrees of action. When domestic violence has disastrous results, as in these two cases, police behavior may be subject to civil suits.

Thurman v. Torrington (1984)

In the fall of 1982, Tracey Thurman of Torrington, Connecticut and her young son were living with friends. Tracey's estranged husband, Charles, pursued her there, repeatedly threatened her, removed the boy by force, broke her windshield as she sat in her car, and, in June 1983, stabbed her repeatedly, an attack that left her permanently disabled. Throughout this time, Tracey and her hosts made frequent calls and visits to the police, who arrested Charles only once, in November—an arrest that resulted in a restraining order against him. The police knew Charles as a counterman at a diner they frequented—where they heard him brag that he would kill his wife.

TRACEY THURMAN ET AL. V. CITY OF TORRINGTON ET AL.
595 F. Supp. 1521 (D. Conn. 1984)

MOSHER JOSEPH BLUMENFELD, SENIOR DISTRICT JUDGE.

The plaintiffs have brought this action pursuant to 42 U.S.C. §§ 1983 [a provision of the Civil Rights Act of 1866, making actionable any deprivation of a legal right by a person acting "under color of any statute . . . custom, or usage, of any State"]. . . as well as the fifth, ninth, and fourteenth amendments to the Constitution, alleging that their constitutional rights were violated by the nonperformance or malperformance of official duties by the defendant police officers. In addition, the plaintiffs seek to hold liable the defendant City of Torrington (hereinafter, the "City"). The defendant City has filed a motion to dismiss the plaintiffs' complaint. . . .

I. *Motion to Dismiss the Claims of Tracey Thurman*

The defendant City now brings a motion to dismiss. The City first argues that the plaintiff's complaint should be dismissed for failure to allege the deprivation of a constitutional right. Though the complaint alleges that the actions of the defendants deprived the plaintiff Tracey Thurman of her constitutional right to equal protection of the laws, the defendant City argues that the equal protection clause of the fourteenth amendment "does not guarantee equal application of social services." Rather, the defendant City argues that the equal protection clause "only prohibits intentional discrimination that is racially motivated."

The defendant City's argument is clearly a misstatement of the law. The application of the equal protection clause is not limited to racial classifications or racially motivated discrimination. . . .[For example,] classifications on the basis of gender will be held invalid under the equal protection clause unless they are substantially related to an important governmental objective, *Craig v. Boren*. And lastly, the equal protection clause will be applied to strike down classifications which are not rationally related to a legitimate governmental purpose. *San Antonio School Dist. v. Rodriguez*, 411 U.S. 1, 55 (1973).

In the instant case, the plaintiffs allege that the defendants use an administrative classification that manifests itself in discriminatory treatment violative of the equal protection clause. Police protection in the City of Torrington, they argue, is fully provided to persons abused by someone with whom the victim has no domestic relationship. But the police have consistently afforded lesser protection, plaintiffs allege, when the victim is (1) a woman abused or assaulted by a spouse or boyfriend, or (2) a child abused by a father or stepfather. The issue to be decided, then, is whether the plaintiffs have properly alleged a violation of the equal protection clause of the fourteenth amendment.

Police action is subject to the equal protection clause and § 1983 whether in the form of commission of violative acts or omission to perform required acts pursuant to the police officer's duty to protect. City officials and police officers are under an affirmative duty to preserve law and order, and to protect the personal safety of persons in the community. This duty applies equally to women whose personal safety is threatened by individuals with whom they have or have had a domestic relationship as well as to all other persons whose personal safety is threatened, including women not involved in domestic relationships. If officials have notice of the possibility of attacks on women in domestic relationships or other persons, they are under an affirmative duty to take reasonable measures to protect the personal safety of such persons in the community. Failure to perform this duty would constitute a denial of equal protection of the laws.

Although the plaintiffs point to no law which on its face discriminates against victims abused by someone with whom they have a domestic relationship, the plaintiffs have alleged that there is an administrative classification used to implement the law in a discriminatory fashion. It is well settled that the equal protection clause is applicable not only to discriminatory legislative action, but also to discriminatory governmental action in administration and enforcement of the law. Here the plaintiffs were threatened with assault in violation of Connecticut law. Over the course of eight months the police failed to afford the plaintiffs protection against such assaults, and failed to take action to arrest the perpetrator of these assaults. The plaintiffs have alleged that this failure to act was pursuant to a pattern or practice of affording inadequate protection, or no protection at all, to women who have complained of having been abused by their husbands or others with whom they have had close relations. Such a practice is tantamount to an administrative classification used to implement the law in a discriminatory fashion.

If the City wishes to discriminate against women who are the victims of domestic violence, it must articulate an important governmental interest for doing so. In its memorandum and at oral argument the City has failed to put forward any justification for its disparate treatment of women. Such a practice was at one time sanctioned by law:

English common law during the eighteenth century recognized the right of husbands to physically discipline their wives. Subsequently, American common law in the early nineteenth century permitted a man to chastise his wife " 'without subjecting himself to vexatious prosecutions for assault and battery, resulting in the discredit and shame of all parties concerned.' " Some restrictions on the right of chastisement evolved through cases which defined the type, severity, and timing of permissible wifebeating. . . .B. Finesmith, *Police Response to Battered Women: Critique and Proposals for Reform*, 14 Seton Hall L. Rev. 74, 79 (1983).

In our own country a husband was permitted to beat his wife so long as he didn't use a switch any bigger around than his thumb. . . .

Today, however, any notion of a husband's prerogative to physically discipline his wife is an "increasingly outdated misconception." *Craig v. Boren*, 429 U.S. at 198–99. As such it must join other "archaic and overbroad" premises which have been rejected as unconstitutional. A man is not allowed to physically abuse or endanger a woman merely because he is her husband. Concomitantly, a police officer may not knowingly refrain from interference in such violence, and may not "automatically decline to make an arrest simply because the assaulter and his victim are married to each other." *Bruno v. Codd*, 396 N.Y.S.2d 974, 976 (1976), *rev'd on other grounds*, 407 N.Y.S.2d 165 (1978), *aff'd*, 393 N.E.2d 976 (1979). Such inaction on the part of the officer is a denial of the equal protection of the laws.

In addition, any notion that defendants' practice can be justified as a means of promoting domestic harmony by refraining from interference in marital disputes, has no place in the case at hand. Rather than evidencing a desire to work out her problems with her husband privately, Tracey pleaded with the police to offer her at least some measure of protection. Further, she sought and received a restraining order to keep her husband at a distance. Accordingly, the defendant City of Torrington's motion to dismiss the plaintiff Tracey Thurman's complaint on the basis of failure to allege violation of a constitutional right is denied. . . .

III. *Have the Plaintiffs Properly Alleged a Custom or Policy on the Part of the City of Torrington?*

The plaintiffs have alleged in paragraph 13 of their complaint as follows:

During the period . . . described, and for a long time prior thereto, the defendant City of Torrington acting through its Police Department, condoned a pattern or practice of affording inadequate protection, or no protection at all, to women who have complained of having been abused by their husbands or others with whom they have had close relations. Said pattern, custom or policy, well known to the individual defendants, was the basis on which they ignored said numerous complaints and reports of threats to the plaintiffs with impunity.

While a municipality is not liable for the constitutional torts of its employees on a *respondeat superior* theory, a municipality may be sued for damages under § 1983 when "the action that is alleged to be unconstitutional implements or executes a policy statement, ordinance, regulation, or decision officially adopted and promulgated by the body's officers" or is "visited pursuant to governmental 'custom' even though such a custom has not received formal approval through the body's official decisionmaking channels." *Monell v. New York City Department of Social Services*, 436 U.S. 658 (1978).

[I]n the pleading of a custom or policy on the part of a municipality. . . .A plaintiff must typically point to facts outside his own case to support his allegation of a policy on the part of a municipality. *Appletree v. City of Hartford*, 555 F. Supp. 224, 228 (D. Conn. 1983).

In the instant case, however, the plaintiff Tracey Thurman has specifically alleged in her statement of facts a series of acts and omissions on the part of the defendant police officers and police department that took place over the course of eight months. From this particularized pleading a pattern emerges that evidences deliberate indifference on the part of the police department to the complaints of the plaintiff Tracey Thurman and to its duty to protect her. Such an ongoing pattern of deliberate indifference raises an inference of "custom" or "policy" on the part of the municipality. Furthermore, this pattern of inaction climaxed on June 10, 1983 in an incident so brutal that under the law of the Second Circuit that "single brutal incident may be sufficient to suggest a link between a violation of constitutional rights and a pattern of police misconduct." *Owens v. Haas*, 601 F.2d 1242, 1246 (2d Cir.), *cert. denied*, 444 U.S. 980 (1979). Finally, a complaint of this sort will survive dismissal if it alleges a policy or custom of condoning police misconduct that violates constitutional rights and alleges "that the City's pattern of inaction caused the plaintiffs any compensable injury." *Batista v. Rodriguez*, 702 F.2d 393, 397-98 (2d Cir. 1983). Accordingly, defendant City of Torrington's motion to dismiss the plaintiffs claims against it, on the ground that the plaintiffs failed to properly allege a custom or policy on the part of the municipality, is denied.

> **IV. *The Unidentified Police Officers***
>
> Defendant City of Torrington has moved to dismiss the claims against the unidentified police officers claiming that this court lacks jurisdiction over these parties as they have not been properly served. At this stage of the proceedings, such a dismissal would be inappropriate:
>
>> at this time, before plaintiff has had an opportunity to engage in discovery which could disclose the exact identity of the officers whom plaintiff presently is able to partially identify . . ., the Court discerns no purpose in dismissal of the . . . defendants. *Saffron v. Wilson*, 70 F.R.D. 51, 56 (D.D.C. 1975).
>
> Hence, defendant's motion, to the extent that it suggests dismissal of the unidentified defendants, is denied without prejudice to its renewal . . .

Navarro v. Block (1995)

The surviving relatives of Maria Navarro appeal here against a summary judgment rejecting their 42 U.S.C. § 1983 lawsuit against Los Angeles County for its allegedly discriminatory policy and custom of according lower priority to 911 calls related to domestic violence than to other violence calls.

> ### NAVARRO V. BLOCK, SHERIFF OF LOS ANGELES COUNTY
> 72 F.3d 712 (9th Circ. 1995)
>
> **PREGERSON, CIRCUIT JUDGE.**
>
> . . .We affirm in part, and reverse and remand in part.
>
> FACTS AND PRIOR PROCEEDINGS
>
> At 10:30 p.m. on August 27, 1989, Maria Navarro was celebrating her birthday with her relatives and friends in her home in East Los Angeles when she received a telephone call from the brother of her estranged husband, Raymond Navarro, warning her that Raymond was on his way to her house to kill her and any others present.
>
> Maria immediately dialed 911 to request emergency assistance. She told the 911 dispatcher that she had just received a warning that her estranged husband was on his way to kill her, that she believed that he was in fact on his way to kill her, and that he was under a restraining order.[3]
>
> When Maria stated that her estranged husband had not yet arrived, but that she believed he would definitely come to her house, the dispatcher

responded, "O.K., well, the only thing to do is just call us if he comes over there ... I mean, what can we do? We can't have a unit sit there to wait and see if he comes over."

Fifteen minutes after the 911 call, Raymond Navarro entered through the rear of Maria Navarro's house, shot and killed Maria Navarro and four other people, and injured two others.

On July 13, 1990, the Navarros filed the instant action in the United States District Court for the Central District of California against Los Angeles County and the Sheriff of Los Angeles County. The Navarros claimed that it was the policy and custom of the Sheriff's Department, which administers the 911 emergency system, not to classify requests for assistance relating to domestic violence as an "emergency." The Navarros argued that such a policy and custom, which discriminates against abused women, violates the Fourteenth Amendment to the United States Constitution.

The Navarros also claimed that it was the policy and custom of the Sheriff's Department not to provide adequate assistance to child victims of domestic violence and to residents of minority neighborhoods, thereby denying these respective classes equal protection of the laws. As a third cause of action, the Navarros claimed that the Sheriff's failure to train his dispatchers adequately on how to handle 911 domestic violence calls and on how to respond to 911 calls from residents of minority neighborhoods amounted to deliberate indifference to their constitutional rights.

[The district court granted defendants' motion for summary judgment on the grounds that the Navarros] failed to offer any evidence of a County policy or custom of treating domestic violence 911 calls differently from other violence 911 calls, nor any evidence of a County policy or custom of depriving residents in minority neighborhoods of equal police protection, nor any evidence of the Sheriff's deliberate or conscious indifference to the rights of abused women or residents in minority neighborhoods. . . .

DISCUSSION

. . .

B. *Policy or Practice of Differential Treatment of Domestic Violence Calls.*

1. Existence of a Policy or Practice.

Under *Monell v. Dept. of Social Services,* 436 U.S. 658, 691 (1978), municipalities may not be held liable under 42 U.S.C. § 1983 "unless action pursuant to official municipal policy of some nature caused a constitutional tort." The Supreme Court made clear that in addition to an official policy, a municipality may be sued for "constitutional deprivations visited pursuant to governmental 'custom' even though such custom has not received formal approval through the [governmental] body's official decisionmaking channels." *Id.* at 690–91; *see also Pembaur v. City of Cincinnati,* 475 U.S. 469, 481–82 n.10 (1986).

Proof of random acts or isolated events are insufficient to establish custom. *Thompson v. City of Los Angeles,* 885 F.2d 1439, 1444 (9th Cir. 1989). But a plaintiff may prove "the existence of a custom or informal policy with evidence of repeated constitutional violations for which the errant municipal officials were not discharged or reprimanded." *Gillette v. Delmore,* 979 F.2d 1342, 1348 (9th Cir. 1992), *cert. denied* (1993). Once such a showing is made, a municipality may be liable for its custom "irrespective of whether official policy-makers had actual knowledge of the practice at issue." *Thompson,* 885 F.2d at 1444.

The Navarros claim that the County carried out a policy and practice of not treating 911 requests for assistance relating to domestic violence as "emergency" calls. The Navarros rely primarily on the deposition of Helen Pena, the 911 dispatcher who answered Maria Navarro's call. In her deposition, Helen Pena testified that it was the practice of the Sheriff's Department not to classify domestic violence 911 calls as Code 2 or "emergency procedure" calls.[4] Ms. Pena also testified that dispatchers were not instructed to treat domestic violence calls as emergencies, that there were no clearly delineated guidelines for responding to domestic violence calls, and that as such, the dispatchers were allowed to exercise unbridled discretion.

The County points out that Helen Pena testified that there was no written policy or procedure that precluded dispatchers from sending a patrol car to the scene of an impending domestic violence crime, nor any policy or procedure that accorded domestic violence 911 calls less priority than non-domestic violence calls. However, this testimony does not contradict Ms. Pena's admission that it was the *practice* of the Sheriff's Department not to classify domestic violence calls as an "emergency." Because there was no conclusive evidence that the Sheriff's Department has a policy of refusing to send a squad car to non-domestic crimes not yet in progress, or of only treating crimes in progress as emergencies, a practice of not treating domestic crimes as emergencies may have been the cause of the failure to send a squad car to assist Navarro. The fact that dispatchers readily send patrol cars to crimes "in progress" regardless of their domestic or non-domestic nature also does not refute Ms. Pena's testimony regarding the general practice of the Department not to treat domestic violence calls as an "emergency." Finally, the County's defense that the discretion to send a patrol car rests with each dispatcher is not dispositive of the question whether the dispatchers in practice fail to respond to domestic violence calls unless a crime is in progress.

Fed. R. Civ. P. 56(e) provides that in opposing a motion for summary judgment, "an adverse party may not rest upon the mere allegations or denials of the adverse party's pleadings, but . . . must set forth specific facts showing that there is a genuine issue for trial." The Navarros have satisfied this requirement. Ms. Pena's testimony that dispatchers in practice treat domestic violence calls differently from non-domestic violence calls, if proved, could establish the County's liability under *Monell*. We must view the Navarro's evidence in the light most favorable to them. . . . [T]hus, the district court erred in concluding that there were no genuine issues of material fact as to whether the County had a policy or custom of not classifying domestic violence calls as an "emergency."

2. Equal Protection Violation.

. . .The Equal Protection Clause of the Fourteenth Amendment states: "No State shall . . . deny to any person within its jurisdiction the equal protection of the laws." Gender-based classifications must pass the "intermediate scrutiny" test, *i.e.*, the classification "must serve important governmental objectives and must be substantially related to achievement of those objectives." The Navarros contend that the County's custom of treating domestic violence 911 calls differently from non-domestic violence calls impermissibly discriminates against abused women. The custom of according different treatment to victims of domestic violence is gender-neutral on its face. However, it is well established that discriminatory application of a facially neutral law also offends the Constitution.

Nevertheless, a long line of Supreme Court cases make clear that the Equal Protection Clause requires proof of discriminatory *intent* or *motive*. *See, e.g., Personnel Adm'r of Mass. v. Feeney*, 442 U.S. 256, 279-80 (1979.)

. . .Such evidence includes "the historical background of the decision . . . particularly if it reveals a series of official actions taken for invidious purposes," irregularities in the passage of legislation such as "departures from normal procedural sequence," and "legislative or administrative history" such as "contemporary statements by members of the decisionmaking body, minutes of its meetings, or reports." [*Arlington Heights v. Metro Housing Development Commission*] 429 U.S. at 266–67 [1979].

In *Balistreri v. Pacifica Police Department*, 901 F.2d 696 (9th Cir. 1990), we found that the plaintiff, a victim of domestic violence who sued the police for failing to protect her, alleged sufficient facts to suggest animus against her because she is a woman. We pointed out, for example, that the officer who responded to one of her complaints stated that he did not blame her husband for hitting her because of the way she was "carrying on." *Id.* at 701. In the present case, however, aside from the conclusory allegation that the County's custom of not classifying domestic violence calls as an emergency discriminates against abused women, the Navarros have failed to offer any evidence of such invidious intent or motive.

Nevertheless, even absent evidence of gender discrimination, the Navarros' equal protection claim still survives because they could prove that the domestic violence/non-domestic violence classification fails even the rationality test. Unless a statute employs a classification that is inherently invidious (such as race or gender), or that impinges on fundamental rights, we exercise only limited review. Although we may not substitute our personal notions of good public policy for those of the legislature, the rational-basis standard is "not a toothless one." *Mathews v. Lucas*, 427 U.S. 495, 510 (1976)).

C. *Deliberate Indifference Arising From Failure to Train Dispatchers on Domestic Violence.*

The Navarros also contend that the Sheriff's failure to train dispatchers on how to handle 911 domestic violence calls, and to instruct dispatchers to treat such calls in the same manner as they treat non-domestic violence calls, amounts to deliberate indifference to the equal protection rights of abused women. However, the Navarros fail to offer any evidence to support these claims. Nor have the Navarros offered any evidence to refute Ms. Pena's testimony that she received an eight-hour course on how to handle domestic violence cases. Accordingly, we affirm the district court's conclusion that the Navarros' deliberate indifference claim fails to survive summary judgment.

CONCLUSION

For the foregoing reasons, we (1) affirm the district court's conclusion that the Navarros have failed to provide sufficient evidence to defeat summary judgment on their claim of deliberate indifference to constitutional rights arising from a failure to train 911 dispatchers; and (2) reverse the district court's grant of summary judgment on the Navarros' equal protection claim because

> genuine issues of material fact remain as to whether the County had a custom of not classifying domestic violence 911 calls as "emergencies." AFFIRMED in part, and REVERSED and REMANDED in part for further proceedings consistent with this opinion.
>
> ### Opinion Footnotes
>
> 3 Maria Navarro obtained the restraining order in January 1989. The restraining order expired that same month. However, the fact of the expiration was not known to the 911 dispatcher.
>
> 4 Ms. Pena answered as follows:
>
> Q: So there's certain calls that would fall under the category of emergency procedure calls?
>
> A: Yes.
>
> . . .
>
> Q: Would domestic violence calls come within that category?
>
> A: As emergency procedures?
>
> Q: Yes.
>
> . . .
>
> Q: . . . Let's say, spouse beating up on wife, would it fall under that procedure?
>
> A: Are we speaking of today or are we speaking of . . .
>
> Q: 1989.
>
> A: 1989? No.

The Navarros then lost on the merits at the district court and appealed, alleging that Los Angeles gave lower priority to domestic violence 911 calls than to other violence 911 calls.

> ## FAJARDO, GUARDIAN AD LITEM FOR NAVARRO MINORS [NAVARRO] V. [BLOCK, SHERIFF OF] COUNTY OF LOS ANGELES
>
> 179 F.3d 698 (9th Cir. 1999)
>
> **PREGERSON, CIRCUIT JUDGE:**
>
> . . .In *Navarro I,* we held that the Navarros had established a genuine issue of material fact for trial by offering evidence that 9-1-1 "dispatchers in practice treat domestic violence calls differently from non-domestic violence calls." We also held that the Navarros' equal protection claim survived summary judgment because "they could prove that the domestic violence/non-domestic violence classification fails even the rationality test" under the Equal Protection Clause. *Id.* at 717. Accordingly, we reversed and remanded.
>
> On remand, the district court determined that it did not need to decide whether a custom or policy existed because it had "previously found that such a [policy] meets the rational basis test." Accordingly, the district court granted

Defendants' Rule 12(c) motion for judgment on the pleadings. We again reverse and remand. . . .

ANALYSIS

On remand, the district court ruled that Defendants' practice of treating domestic-violence calls differently from non-domestic-violence calls passed the rational basis test as a matter of law because (1) it is rational to limit emergency response to in-progress calls, and (2) "9-1-1 emergency assistance is provided for individuals who are severely injured and near death and domestic violence *rarely* reaches this level of injury." Defendants argue that these rationales justify discriminating against domestic-violence crimes.

It does not matter whether it is rational to distinguish between in-progress calls and not-in-progress calls because that was not the distinction that Defendants allegedly made. The Navarros allege that Defendants distinguished between domestic-violence 9-1-1 calls and non-domestic-violence 9-1-1 calls regardless of whether the violence was in progress.

Moreover, whether domestic violence "rarely" results in death or severe injury does not, by itself, end the matter. The critical issue is whether domestic-violence crimes result in severe injury or death less frequently than non-domestic-violence crimes that *are* considered 9-1-1 emergencies. Hence, the district court erred by equating domestic violence calls with not-in-progress calls and equating non-domestic violence calls with in-progress calls, and by assuming that domestic-violence crimes are less injurious than non-domestic-violence crimes. Because these assumptions formed the basis of the district court's conclusion, the district court also erred when it concluded, as a matter of law, that Defendants' domestic-violence/non-domestic-violence classification was rational and reasonable under equal-protection analysis.

The separate concurrence reasons that (1) there is no evidence of a domestic violence/non-domestic violence classification, and (2) that even if such a classification were proved, it would not violate equal protection.

The concurrence overlooks the evidence cited in our first opinion. *See Navarro I,* 72 F.3d at 715 & n.4 (noting that a 9-1-1 dispatcher had testified that it was the practice of the Sheriff's department not to classify domestic violence calls as emergency procedure calls). To the extent that the concurrence relies on the lack of any record evidence with regard to a policy or custom that discriminated against *women,* it misses the point. In our earlier decision, we remanded for a hearing on the question whether the County had a policy or custom that discriminated against victims of domestic violence.

Here, the Navarros sued Defendants for allegedly giving lower priority to 9-1-1 domestic-violence calls than to non-domestic-violence calls. Here, there are disputed issues of material fact on the question whether Defendants had such a policy. In our earlier opinion, we reversed the district court's grant of summary judgment on this ground, and we now reverse the district court's grant of judgment on the pleadings.

REVERSED and REMANDED for a hearing to determine first, whether the city had a policy or custom of giving lower priority to domestic-violence calls than to non-domestic-violence calls, and second, if such a policy or custom exists, whether that policy or custom has a rational basis.

KLEINFELD, CIRCUIT JUDGE, concurring:

I reluctantly concur in the result. The majority decision is based on a mistaken reading of the record. It has the unfortunate consequence that we substitute an appellate court's views for the sheriff's views on which 911 calls get priority.

We decided in our prior panel opinion, *Navarro v. Block*, 72 F.3d 712 (9th Cir. 1996), that the plaintiffs had sufficient evidence for their equal protection claim to establish a genuine issue of material fact. Our earlier opinion was, in my view, mistaken. In today's opinion, the majority mistakenly conflates the evidence, relevant to an appeal from summary judgment, with the pleadings, relevant to an appeal from judgment on the pleadings, thereby compounding the previous error.

The complaint alleges an intentional policy of denying protection to abused women who complain of domestic violence. . . .

Plaintiffs' claim can only be based on the Equal Protection Clause. We are reviewing a judgment on the pleadings, and the complaint stated a claim upon which relief could be granted, so that should be the end of the case. The allegation of the complaint necessitates reversal, but not on the expansive rationale used by the majority. If the government were to pick a class of people, by sex, race or some other inappropriate characteristic, and deny people in that class the same protection law enforcement and legal institutions afforded to other people, that classification would implicate the Equal Protection Clause. *DeShaney* [*v. Winnebago Cty. Soc. Servs. Dept.*, 489 U.S. 189 (1989)] says that, "the State may not, of course, selectively deny its protective services to certain disfavored minorities without violating the Equal Protection Clause." *Id.* at 197 The Equal Protection Clause theory asserted in the complaint is that the sheriff provided less police protection to women than others. The assertion is enough to survive judgment on the pleadings, because the issue in an appeal from a judgment on the pleadings is not whether the evidence shows a denial of equal protection, but merely whether the pleadings assert it.

The reason I point out that we erred in our earlier decision, and the district court was right the first time, is that the case really has gone beyond the pleadings, to summary judgment, and there was no evidence submitted on that motion to support a claim of invidious discrimination. The majority opinion says that my concurrence "overlooks the evidence cited in our first opinion." Evidence actually has nothing to do with an appeal of judgment on the pleadings; we are supposed to decide such an appeal based on what the pleadings say. But because of the expansive approach the majority has taken, there is no avoiding a discussion of the evidence. And the majority, in my view, has the evidence wrong.

The majority now seems to concede that there is a lack of record evidence of discrimination against women, but to assert that there is evidence of unconstitutional discrimination against victims of domestic violence ("To the extent that the concurrence relies on the lack of any record evidence with regard to a policy or custom that discriminated against *women*, it misses the point .... we remanded for a hearing on the question whether the County had a policy or custom that discriminated against victims of domestic violence."). Since women, but not victims of domestic violence regardless of sex, are a class of people for whom a higher level of Equal Protection scrutiny is applied, the majority's concession destroys the foundation for its opinion. Without women as the class of persons denied equal protection of the law, there is no serious equal protection claim. The complaint does claim discrimination against women. It alleges a sheriff's policy that "denied abused women—who complained of threatened domestic violence ... equal protection of the laws." The complaint therefore does state an equal protection claim, but evidently the majority concedes that when the case previously came up on summary judgment, there was no evidence for that claim.

The uncontradicted evidence in the record is that there was no policy of denying immediate police response to women. Nor was there any evidence of a policy of denying immediate police response in domestic violence cases. What the evidence showed, and all that it showed, was a policy of giving higher priority to calls reporting violence in progress than to calls reporting threats of violence. So far as the evidence showed, it did not matter whether the threats were of domestic or non-domestic violence. What mattered was whether the violence had already started or whether it was threatened for the future. That is a classification, but it is not invidious. There is a rational basis for treating violence not yet occurring differently from violence already occurring.

The only evidence directly in point was a deposition by the dispatcher, who tragically did not send immediate police assistance to Maria Navarro when she called and reported that her husband was on his way over to kill her. The dispatcher testified that "there's no written policy" for when the dispatcher should send the police. She made the decision in her discretion, "based on my training, my experience, and so forth." In the training, some calls were designated as lights and siren, such as "baby not breathing, shots fired," "when a hospital is in need of a certain type of blood, we're transporting the blood," "felonies in progress, robbery."

The dispatcher testified that the category of "domestic violence" was ambiguous, because it included lights and siren circumstances and discretionary circumstances. She testified that the practice was to distinguish between "where a person has intentionally caused bodily injury to another, intentionally or recklessly caused bodily injury to another or has placed that person in a position where they would be exposed to some type of danger or possibly in danger" from "a threat by an individual." In the first type of domestic violence, "a crime has been committed," and "we would send a police car out there." For the second type, the threat, "they're all very unique. You use your own judgment on what exactly is done, and what exactly the caller is telling you." There was no policy on a threat call other than that the dispatcher was to use her discretion.

The classification for which there was evidence, between threatened violence and violence already taking place, is not a classification by sex. It is also not a classification according to whether the violence is domestic or non-domestic. It has no relationship to a classification by sex. The evidence showed no distinction between the treatment of calls involving a domestic violence threat compared to any other kind of deadly threat. For example, if a person called and said "someone I fired last week is coming over to my store to kill me," the dispatcher's testimony indicates that she would have treated that as a threat call, for which there was no policy other than to use her discretion, as opposed to a felony in progress call, for which she would have necessarily sent a car with lights and siren. She might or might not send a lights and siren car in a threat case, whether domestic or non-domestic, and would have in a felony in progress case, domestic or non-domestic. The distinction was not by sex, or by whether the threat was domestic, but rather by whether the violence was threatened or already occurring.

Based on this uncontradicted evidence, we should have affirmed the summary judgment in the earlier appeal. The evidence established no policy classifying people by sex, and no policy of giving lower priority to domestic violence calls. There was a tragic error, at least in hindsight, in failing to send a lights and siren car to Mrs. Navarro's house immediately, but that is not a denial of equal protection of the laws that entitles a federal court to rearrange sheriff's office policies. The higher priority given to felonies in progress as compared with crimes threatened but not in progress, raises no serious equal protection issue, because the level of scrutiny appropriate to it is rational basis, and there is an obvious rational basis for the different priorities. A threat may not materialize, through failure of will or means by the perpetrator, or avoidance by the prospective victim. "Shots fired" and "felony in progress" have already materialized. Perhaps the sheriff's office should have given threats of deadly violence higher priority than hospital transfer of blood or some felonies in progress, but this is a policy question, not a constitutional question under the Equal Protection Clause.

The First, Third, Fourth, Fifth, Eighth, and Tenth Circuits have rejected the constitutional claims being asserted around the country based on failure of police to prevent domestic violence. These circuits have all held that unless sex discrimination is a motivating factor, there is no constitutional claim. [For example,] see *Soto v. Flores*, 103 F.3d 1056 (1st Cir. 1997)(rejecting equal protection and due process claims where plaintiff failed to show discriminatory intent.) . . .[I]n the case at bar, plaintiffs had the opportunity to prove discriminatory intent, and were unable to do so. What they proved was tragic, and the murder might give rise to a state tort claim of negligence, but it does not give rise to a federal constitutional claim, because *DeShaney* establishes that there is no constitutional right to a bodyguard against a likely threat to life.

The potential harm caused by our decision today, as well as by our prior decision, is that we substitute our judgment for that of the police about how they set priorities for responding to calls. No one has given us the authority to do that. And we do not know enough about police work to do that. So long as the police have a rational basis for the non-invidious classifications they make, the remedies for their mistakes are those afforded by state law in state courts. This kind of question, "to what 911 calls should we automatically send a car with lights and siren," needs experienced police officers around a table arguing about it. They can talk usefully relating their experiences to what needs to be done and what can be done, based on their knowledge of what kinds of calls come in, and what kinds of harms can be averted by an immediate lights and

> siren dispatch, how many officers are available for response, how long the responses will take, and all sorts of other questions that we lack the specialized knowledge to even think of, let alone answer. Nor do our commissions authorize us to make this sort of policy decision.
>
> Our opinion is subject to the reading that police must provide bodyguards against threats of domestic violence, unless they can prove that victims of such threats are less likely to be killed or seriously injured than victims of robberies and "shots fired" crimes. It is unlikely that the police can prove that, because such hypothetical social science propositions are inherently hard to prove. As a practical matter, our decision may simply force police throughout the Ninth Circuit to give at least as high a priority to 911 calls that say "my spouse is coming home and *threatens* to kill me" as to calls that say "someone is *now killing* someone on the street in front of my house." I cannot see why the police have to prove anything to us when they make non-invidious classifications with a rational basis of 911 calls.

Case note: This was the last *Navarro v. Block* case in either the district court or court of appeals. In a different case presenting a similar issue, the U.S. Supreme Court ruled in *Castle Rock, Colorado v. Jessica Gonzalez* (2005)[4] that the mere fact that Ms. Gonzalez had obtained a protective order against her husband that in its own words mandated his arrest if he violated the order (which he had done by kidnapping their three children) did not give her a right to sue the Castle Rock police for failing to arrest him when she told them his whereabouts. He murdered the three children and then drove their bodies to the police station and fired at the police, who then shot and killed him. Prior to the murder (a few hours after he took the children without her knowledge), she had learned of his and the childrens' location by cellphone call, and she had asked the police to arrest him repeatedly—at 8:30 P.M., at 10:10 P.M., at midnight. When no police responded to her requests, she went to the station at 12:50 A.M. and filed an incident report. The officer who took the report, she said, "made no reasonable effort to enforce the [order] or locate the three children. Instead, he went to dinner." Her § 1983 lawsuit claimed that the Castle Rock police had "an official policy or custom of failing to respond properly to complaints of restraining order violations." Her claim was that the "process" "due" to her under the Fourteenth Amendment included the prompt arrest of her husband once he violated the restraining order, especially because the Colorado legislature had recently enacted a law saying that police, upon learning that a restraining order had been violated, "shall arrest" violators of restraining orders as promptly as is reasonably feasible. Justice Scalia (for a majority of seven) rejected her complaint explaining, "A well-established tradition of police discretion has long coexisted with apparently mandatory arrest statutes." Put differently, victims do not have an enforceable legal right to have their perpetrators arrested as immediately as reasonably possible. Still, in 2017 the U.S. Department of Justice reported that from 2006–2015, police responded in ten minutes or less in nearly two-thirds of domestic violence reports.[5] Justice Stevens dissented, joined by Justice Ginsburg, and pointed out, "When Colorado passed its statute in 1994, it joined the ranks of 15 States that mandated arrest for domestic violence offenses and 19 States that mandated arrest for domestic restraining order violations." The dissenters argued that the majority was being insufficiently respectful of these state reforms in its ruling.

Case Questions

1. What reasonable explanation, if any, can you find for the different results in the *Thurman* and *Navarro* cases?

2. Would it be possible to make an argument that treating domestic violence cases differently from other violence cases does in fact constitute a denial of equal protection of the law? Even if as many wives hit husbands as vice versa?

3. Should courts review cases involving police conduct differently from other cases involving government agents? If so, should judges be more respectful or more skeptical of police discretion? If not, why not?

The Victim Who Strikes Back: Wife Abuse and Husband Homicide

Some domestic violence victims turn on their batterers and kill them. These cases are rare but tend to receive wide publicity. When a battered woman stands trial for homicide, her lawyer may use one or both of two common defenses. A verdict of "not guilty by reason of self-defense" may be possible. However, this verdict requires a finding that the defendant perceived imminent danger to herself; as the cases in this chapter show, that scenario does not always fit the facts. Another common defense is the "battered woman syndrome." The next two readings explain and criticize this concept.

From Lenore E. A. Walker, *The Battered Woman Syndrome*[6]

The prevailing viewpoint in the early 1970s, prior to the Battered Woman Syndrome Study was that battered women were poor, uneducated, unable to get a job to support themselves and their children, and from the disadvantaged, minority groups in society. However, once services were established, it became clear that battered women came from all classes and demographic groups—

just like we found in this study. Wealthy Euro-American educated women got beat up just as did poor, young women from the disenfranchised classes...

The theoretical concept of learned helplessness—having lost the ability to predict that what you will do will make a particular outcome occur—was adapted in this research to help explain why women who could develop such intricate and life-saving coping strategies, found it so difficult to escape a battering relationship....It was hypothesized that the women's experiences of the noncontingent nature of their attempts to control the violence would, over time, produce learned helplessness and depression....If a woman is to escape such a relationship, she must overcome the tendency to learned helplessness survival techniques—by, for example, becoming angry rather than depressed and self-blaming; active rather than passive; and more realistic about the likelihood of the relationship continuing on its aversive course rather than improving...The Walker Cycle Theory of Violence...is a tension reduction theory that states that there are three distinct phases associated with a recurring battering cycle: (1) tension building, (2) the acute battering incident, and (3) loving contrition. During the first phase, there is a gradual escalation of tension....The woman attempts to placate the batterer....Phase two is characterized by...a barrage of verbal and physical aggression that can leave the woman severely shaken and injured...In phase three that follows. The batterer may apologize profusely, try to assist his victim, show kindness and remorse, and shower her with gifts and/or promises.

Support was found for both theories tested—the application of learned helplessness to battered women and the Walker cycle theory of violence....A distinct syndrome was found and named "the battered woman syndrome."

From Donald A. Downs, *More Than Victims: Battered Women, the Syndrome Society, and the Law*[7]

[Walker's] cycle theory is key to arguments for self-defense based on justification, for it explains what happens and why it is reasonable from the vantage point of the battered woman to feel danger outside the state of imminent harm and why it is reasonable for her to stay in the relationship....The theory of learned helplessness is the key to incapacity defenses. In the end, Walker's two theories are ingenious efforts to blend the logic of justification and incapacity excuse....

> Learned helplessness reduces battered women to the status of dogs [the subjects of the studies on which the original theory was based]. It denies the very integrity and potential agency that the women wish to attain. When BWS strips battered women of any potential responsibility, it strips them of potential dignity. . . . Walker seems to go back and forth between concluding that learned helplessness entails passivity and that it does not. . . . Although Walker's treatment of helplessness in these passages is somewhat subtle, the image that the concept of learned helplessness conveys in court and in the popular imagination is one of passivity and lack of agency. Interviewees in the shelter movement and related positions in Wisconsin scorned learned helplessness. We did not find a single interviewee involved in the movement who accepted the theory without serious reservations, although several prison interviewees and other interviewees portrayed themselves or their mothers as "largely helpless." . . .
>
> [One battered women's advocate said], "I don't like the phrase 'learned helplessness.' I have seen women in extremely abusive relationships who still scheme after 50 years!"

State v. Kelly (1984)

American judges are divided on how to treat self-defense claims by women who kill their batterers. Here, too, the question has been raised as to whether there should be a "reasonable woman" standard for judging the options available to a woman whose husband may often outweigh her by a hundred pounds and outsize her by several inches. The traditional legal notion of fending off a man's attack with "equal force" may simply not be available to such a woman facing her husband's fists or other weapons. The question might best be posed as, "What should be done by a reasonable person *who finds herself in the same situation as the battered wife?*" (With "same situation" including such particular factors as size and strength differences compared to the husband.)

> ## STATE V. KELLY
> 97 N.J. 178, 478 A.2d 364 (1984)
>
> **WILENTZ, C.J.**
>
> The central issue before us is whether expert testimony about the battered-woman's syndrome is admissible to help establish a claim of self-defense in a homicide case. The question is one of first impression in this state. We hold, based on the limited record before us (the State not having had a full

opportunity to prove the contrary), that the battered-woman's syndrome is an appropriate subject for expert testimony; that the experts' conclusions, despite the relative newness of the field, are sufficiently reliable under New Jersey's standards for scientific testimony; and that defendant's expert was sufficiently qualified. Accordingly, we reverse and remand for a new trial. If on retrial after a full examination of these issues the evidence continues to support these conclusions, the expert's testimony on the battered-woman's syndrome shall be admitted as relevant to the honesty and reasonableness of defendant's belief that deadly force was necessary to protect her against death or serious bodily harm.

I.

On May 24, 1980, defendant, Gladys Kelly, stabbed her husband, Ernest, with a pair of scissors. He died shortly thereafter at a nearby hospital. The couple had been married for seven years, during which time Ernest had periodically attacked Gladys. According to Ms. Kelly, he assaulted her that afternoon, and she stabbed him in self-defense, fearing that he would kill her if she did not act.

Ms. Kelly was indicted for murder. At trial, she did not deny stabbing her husband, but asserted that her action was in self-defense. To establish the requisite state of mind for her self-defense claim, Ms. Kelly called Dr. Lois Veronen as an expert witness to testify about the battered-woman's syndrome. After hearing a lengthy voir dire examination of Dr. Veronen, the trial court ruled that expert testimony concerning the syndrome was inadmissible on the self-defense issue under *State v. Bess*, 53 *N.J.* 10 (1968). Apparently the court believed that the sole purpose of this testimony was to explain and justify defendant's perception of the danger rather than to show the objective reasonableness of that perception.

Ms. Kelly was convicted of reckless manslaughter....We granted certification, 91 *N.J.* 539 (1983), and now reverse....

II.

The Kellys had a stormy marriage. Some of the details of their relationship, especially the stabbing, are disputed. The following is Ms. Kelly's version of what happened—a version that the jury could have accepted and, if they had, a version that would make the proffered expert testimony not only relevant, but critical.

The day after the marriage, Mr. Kelly got drunk and knocked Ms. Kelly down. Although a period of calm followed the initial attack, the next seven years were accompanied by periodic and frequent beatings, sometimes as often as once a week. During the attacks, which generally occurred when Mr. Kelly was drunk, he threatened to kill Ms. Kelly and to cut off parts of her body if she tried to leave him. Mr. Kelly often moved out of the house after an attack, later returning with a promise that he would change his ways. Until the day of the homicide, only one of the attacks had taken place in public.

The day before the stabbing, Gladys and Ernest went shopping. They did not have enough money to buy food for the entire week, so Ernest said he would give his wife more money the next day.

The following morning he left for work. Ms. Kelly next saw her husband late that afternoon at a friend's house. She had gone there with her daughter, Annette, to ask Ernest for money to buy food. He told her to wait until they got home, and shortly thereafter the Kellys left. After walking past several houses, Mr. Kelly, who was drunk, angrily asked "What the hell did you come around here for?" He then grabbed the collar of her dress, and the two fell to the ground. He choked her by pushing his fingers against her throat, punched or hit her face, and bit her leg.

A crowd gathered on the street. Two men from the crowd separated them, just as Gladys felt that she was "passing out" from being choked. Fearing that Annette had been pushed around in the crowd, Gladys then left to look for her. Upon finding Annette, defendant noticed that Annette had defendant's pocketbook. Gladys had dropped it during the fight. Annette had retrieved it and gave her mother the pocketbook.

After finding her daughter, Ms. Kelly then observed Mr. Kelly running toward her with his hands raised. Within seconds he was right next to her. Unsure of whether he had armed himself while she was looking for their daughter, and thinking that he had come back to kill her, she grabbed a pair of scissors from her pocketbook. She tried to scare him away, but instead stabbed him.

III.

The central question in this case is whether the trial court erred in its exclusion of expert testimony on the battered-woman's syndrome. That testimony was intended to explain defendant's state of mind and bolster her claim of self-defense. We shall first examine the nature of the battered-woman's syndrome and then consider the expert testimony proffered in this case and its relevancy.

In the past decade social scientists and the legal community began to examine the forces that generate and perpetuate wife beating and violence in the family. What has been revealed is that the problem affects many more people than had been thought and that the victims of the violence are not only the battered family members (almost always either the wife or the children). There are also many other strangers to the family who feel the devastating impact, often in the form of violence, of the psychological damage suffered by the victims.

Due to the high incidence of unreported abuse (the FBI and other law enforcement experts believe that wife abuse is the most unreported crime in the United States), estimates vary of the number of American women who are beaten regularly by their husband, boyfriend, or the dominant male figure in their lives. One recent estimate puts the number of women beaten yearly at over one million. See *California Advisory Comm'n on Family Law, Domestic Violence* app. F at 119 (1st report 1978). The state police statistics show more than 18,000 *reported* cases of domestic violence in New Jersey during the first nine months of 1983, in 83% of which the victim was female. It is clear that the American home, once assumed to be the cornerstone of our society, is often a violent place.

While common law notions that assigned an inferior status to women, and to wives in particular, no longer represent the state of the law as reflected in statutes and cases, many commentators assert that a bias against battered women still exists, institutionalized in the attitudes of law enforcement agencies unwilling to pursue or uninterested in pursuing wife beating cases.

Another problem is the currency enjoyed by stereotypes and myths concerning the characteristics of battered women and their reasons for staying in battering relationships. Some popular misconceptions about battered women include the beliefs that they are masochistic and actually enjoy their beatings, that they purposely provoke their husbands into violent behavior, and, most critically, as we shall soon see, that women who remain in battering relationships are free to leave their abusers at any time. See L. Walker, *The Battered Woman* at 19–31 (1979).

As these cases so tragically suggest, not only do many women suffer physical abuse at the hands of their mates, but a significant number of women kill (or are killed by) their husbands. In 1978, murders between husband and wife or girlfriend and boyfriend constituted 13% of all murders committed in the United States. Undoubtedly some of these arose from battering incidents.

Federal Bureau of Investigation, Crime in the United States 1978 (1978). Men were the victims in 48% of these killings. *Id*

> ...Dr. Lenore Walker, a prominent writer on the battered-woman's syndrome, defines the battered woman as one
>
>> who is repeatedly subjected to any forceful physical or psychological behavior by a man in order to coerce her to do something he wants her to do without concern for her rights. Battered women include wives or women in any form of intimate relationships with men. Furthermore, in order to be classified as a battered woman, the couple must go through the battering cycle at least twice. Any woman may find herself in an abusive relationship with a man once. If it occurs a second time, and she remains in the situation, she is defined as a battered woman.
>
> [The court then summarized Walker's "cycle theory" of violence. See above—AU.]
>
> ...The cyclical nature of battering behavior helps explain why more women simply do not leave their abusers. The loving behavior demonstrated by the batterer during phase three reinforces whatever hopes these women might have for their mate's reform and keeps them bound to the relationship. R. *Langley & R. Levy, Wife Beating: The Silent Crisis* 112–14 (1977).
>
> Some women may even perceive the battering cycle as normal, especially if they grew up in a violent household. *Battered Women, A Psychosociological Study of Domestic Violence* 60 (M. Roy ed. 1977); D. Martin, *Battered Wives*, 60 (1981). Or they may simply not wish to acknowledge the reality of their situation. *T. Davidson, Conjugal Crime*, at 50 (1978) ("The middle-class battered wife's response to her situation tends to be withdrawal, silence and denial . . .").
>
> Other women, however, become so demoralized and degraded by the fact that they cannot predict or control the violence that they sink into a state of psychological paralysis and become unable to take any action at all to improve or alter the situation. There is a tendency in battered women to believe in the omnipotence or strength of their battering husbands and thus to feel that any attempt to resist them is hopeless. *L. Walker, supra*, at 75.
>
> In addition to these psychological impacts, external social and economic factors often make it difficult for some women to extricate themselves from battering relationships. A woman without independent financial resources who

wishes to leave her husband often finds it difficult to do so because of a lack of material and social resources.

Even with the progress of the last decade, women typically make less money and hold less prestigious jobs than men, and are more responsible for child care. Thus, in a violent confrontation where the first reaction might be to flee, women realize soon that there may be no place to go. Moreover, the stigma that attaches to a woman who leaves the family unit without her children undoubtedly acts as a further deterrent to moving out.

. . .Dr. Walker and other commentators have identified several common personality traits of the battered woman: low self-esteem, traditional beliefs about the home, the family, and the female sex role, tremendous feelings of guilt that their marriages are failing, and the tendency to accept responsibility for the batterer's actions.

Finally, battered women are often hesitant to leave a battering relationship because, in addition to their hope of reform on the part of their spouse, they harbor a deep concern about the possible response leaving might provoke in their mates. They literally become trapped by their own fear. Case histories are replete with instances in which a battered wife left her husband only to have him pursue her and subject her to an even more brutal attack.

The combination of all these symptoms—resulting from sustained psychological and physical trauma compounded by aggravating social and economic factors—constitutes the battered-woman's syndrome. Only by understanding these unique pressures that force battered women to remain with their mates, despite their long-standing and reasonable fear of severe bodily harm and the isolation that being a battered woman creates, can a battered woman's state of mind be accurately and fairly understood.

The voir dire testimony of Dr. Veronen, sought to be introduced by defendant Gladys Kelly, conformed essentially to this outline of the battered-woman's syndrome. Dr. Vernonen, after establishing her credentials, described in general terms the component parts of the battered-woman's syndrome and its effects on a woman's physical and mental health. The witness then documented, based on her own considerable experience in counseling, treating, and studying battered women, and her familiarity with the work of others in the field, the feelings of anxiety, self-blame, isolation, and, above all, fear that plagues these women and leaves them prey to a psychological paralysis that hinders their ability to break free or seek help.

...Dr. Veronen described the various psychological tests and examinations she had performed in connection with her independent research. These tests and their methodology, including their interpretation, are, according to Dr. Veronen, widely accepted by clinical psychologists. Applying this methodology to defendant (who was subjected to all of the tests, including a five-hour interview), Dr. Veronen concluded that defendant was a battered woman and subject to the battered-woman's syndrome.

In addition, Dr. Veronen was prepared to testify as to how, as a battered woman, Gladys Kelly perceived her situation at the time of the stabbing, and why, in her opinion, defendant did not leave her husband despite the constant beatings she endured.

IV.

Whether expert testimony on the battered-woman's syndrome should be admitted in this case depends on whether it is relevant to defendant's claim of self-defense, and, in any event, on whether the proffer meets the standards for admission of expert testimony in this state. We examine first the law of self-defense and consider whether the expert testimony is relevant.

The present rules governing the use of force in self-defense are set out in the justification section of the Code of Criminal Justice...The use of...deadly force is not justifiable "unless the actor reasonably believes that such force is necessary to protect himself against death or serious bodily harm...." [*N.J.S.A.* 2C:3-4(b)(2)].

Self-defense exonerates a person who kills in the reasonable belief that such action was necessary to prevent his or her death or serious injury, even though this belief was later proven mistaken....

While it is not imperative that *actual* necessity exist, a valid plea of self-defense will not lie absent an actual (that is, honest) belief on the part of the defendant in the necessity of using force.

...A defendant claiming the privilege of self-defense must also establish that her belief in the necessity to use force was reasonable....Thus, even when the defendant's belief in the need to kill in self-defense is conceded to be sincere, if it is found to have been unreasonable under the circumstances, such a belief cannot be held to constitute complete justification for a homicide. As with the determination of the existence of the defendant's belief, the question of the reasonableness of this belief "is to be determined by the jury, not the defendant, in light of the circumstances existing at the time of the homicide." *State v. Hipplewith* 33 N.J. at 316. It is perhaps worth emphasizing here that for defendant to prevail, the jury need not find beyond a reasonable doubt that the defendant's belief was honest and reasonable. Rather, if any evidence raising the issue of self-defense is adduced, either in the State's or the defendant's case, then the jury must be instructed that the State is required to prove beyond a reasonable doubt that the self-defense claim does not accord with the facts; acquittal is required if there remains a reasonable doubt whether the defendant acted in self-defense.

With the foregoing standards in mind, we turn to an examination of the relevance of the proffered expert testimony to Gladys Kelly's claim of self-defense.

V.

Gladys Kelly claims that she stabbed her husband in self-defense, believing he was about to kill her. The gist of the State's case was that Gladys Kelly was the aggressor, that she consciously intended to kill her husband, and that she certainly was not acting in self-defense.

The credibility of Gladys Kelly is a critical issue in this case. If the jury does not believe Gladys Kelly's account, it cannot find she acted in self-defense. The expert testimony offered was directly relevant to one of the critical elements of that account, namely, what Gladys Kelly believed at the time of the stabbing, and was thus material to establish the honesty of her stated belief that she was in imminent danger of death.

As can be seen from our discussion of the expert testimony, Dr. Veronen would have bolstered Gladys Kelly's credibility. Specifically, by showing that her experience, although concededly difficult to comprehend, was common to that of other women who had been in similarly abusive relationships, Dr. Veronen would have helped the jury understand that Gladys Kelly could have honestly feared that she would suffer serious bodily harm from her husband's attacks, yet still remain with him. This, in turn, would support Ms. Kelly's testimony about her state of mind (that is, that she honestly feared serious bodily harm) at the time of the stabbing.

On the facts in this case, we find that the expert testimony was relevant to Gladys Kelly's state of mind, namely, it was admissible to show she *honestly* believed she was in imminent danger of death....Moreover, we find that because this testimony was central to the defendant's claim of self-defense, its exclusion, if otherwise admissible, cannot be held to be harmless error.

We also find the expert testimony relevant to the reasonableness of defendant's belief that she was in imminent danger of death or serious injury. . . . [O]ur conclusion is that the expert's testimony, if accepted by the jury, would have aided it in determining whether, under the circumstances, a reasonable person would have believed there was imminent danger to her life.

At the heart of the claim of self-defense was defendant's story that she had been repeatedly subjected to "beatings" over the course of her marriage. . . . [A] juror could infer from the use of the word "beatings," as well as the detail given concerning some of these events (the choking, the biting, the use of fists), that these physical assaults posed a risk of serious injury or death. When that regular pattern of serious physical abuse is combined with defendant's claim that the decedent sometimes threatened to kill her, defendant's statement that on this occasion she thought she might be killed when she saw Mr. Kelly running toward her could be found to reflect a reasonable fear; that is, it could so be found if the jury believed Gladys Kelly's story of the prior beatings, if it believed her story of the prior threats, and, of course, if it believed her story of the events of that particular day.

The crucial issue of fact on which this expert's testimony would bear is why, given such allegedly severe and constant beatings, combined with threats to kill, defendant had not long ago left decedent. Whether raised by the prosecutor as a factual issue or not, our own common knowledge tells us that most of us, including the ordinary juror, would ask himself or herself just such a question. And our knowledge is bolstered by the experts' knowledge, for the experts point out that one of the common myths, apparently believed by most people, is that battered wives are free to leave. To some, this misconception is followed by the observation that the battered wife is masochistic, proven by her refusal to leave despite the severe beatings; to others, however, the fact that the battered wife stays on unquestionably suggests that the "beatings" could not have been too bad for if they had been, she certainly would have left. The expert could clear up these myths, by explaining that one of the common characteristics of a battered wife is her *inability* to leave despite such constant beatings; her "learned helplessness"; her lack of anywhere to go; her feeling that if she tried to leave, she would be subjected to even more merciless treatment; her belief in the omnipotence of her battering husband; and sometimes her hope that her husband will change his ways.

Unfortunately, in this case the State reinforced the myths about battered women. On cross-examination, when discussing an occasion when Mr. Kelly temporarily moved out of the house, the State repeatedly asked Ms. Kelly: "You wanted him back, didn't you?" The implication was clear: domestic life could not have been too bad if she wanted him back.

...Even had the State not taken this approach, however, expert testimony would be essential to rebut the general misconceptions regarding battered women.

The difficulty with the expert's testimony is that it *sounds* as if an expert is giving knowledge to a jury about something the jury knows as well as anyone else, namely, the reasonableness of a person's fear of imminent serious danger. That is not at all, however, what this testimony is *directly* aimed at. It is aimed at an area where the purported common knowledge of the jury may be very much mistaken, an area where jurors' logic, drawn from their own experience, may lead to a wholly incorrect conclusion, an area where expert knowledge would enable the jurors to disregard their prior conclusions as being common myths rather than common knowledge. After hearing the expert, instead of saying Gladys Kelly could not have been beaten up so badly for if she had, she certainly would have left, the jury could conclude that her failure to leave was very much part and parcel of her life as a battered wife. The jury could conclude that instead of casting doubt on the accuracy of her testimony about the severity and frequency of prior beatings, her failure to leave actually reinforced her credibility.

Since a retrial is necessary, we think it advisable to indicate the limit of the expert's testimony on this issue of reasonableness. It would not be proper for the expert to express the opinion that defendant's belief on that day was reasonable, not because this is the ultimate issue, but because the area of *expert* knowledge relates, in this regard, to the reasons for defendant's failure to leave her husband. Either the jury accepts or rejects that explanation and, based on that, credits defendant's stories about the beatings she suffered. No expert is needed, however, once the jury has made up its mind on those issues, to tell the jury the logical conclusion, namely, that a person who has in fact been severely and continuously beaten might very well reasonably fear that the imminent beating she was about to suffer could be either life-threatening or pose a risk of serious injury. What the expert could state was that defendant had the battered-woman's syndrome, and could explain that syndrome in detail, relating its characteristics to defendant, but only to enable the jury better to determine the honesty and reasonableness of defendant's belief. Depending on its content, the expert's testimony might also enable the jury to find that the battered wife, because of the prior beatings, numerous beatings, as often as once a week, for seven years, from the day they were married to the day he died, is particularly able to predict accurately the likely extent of violence in any

> attack on her. That conclusion could significantly affect the jury's evaluation of the reasonableness of defendant's fear for her life.
>
> **VI**
>
> ...We have concluded that the appropriate disposal of this appeal is to reverse and remand for a new trial.

State v. Stewart (1988)

Some battered women have a particularly difficult time invoking a self-defense claim because a woman may kill her husband when he is not in the midst of a battering episode—say, while he sleeps. In these situations, the traditional legal duty to flee, many people would suggest, would seem more appropriate than homicide. A case illustrating the perplexities of these situations is *State of Kansas v. Peggy Stewart*, which is included below. The grisly details of Mike Stewart's long history of battering and otherwise abusing his wife and stepdaughters are presented in full in the majority's opinion. This case was decided by a 5–2 majority in the Supreme Court of Kansas, and the majority was reversing the trial court's verdict of not guilty by reason of self-defense.

> ### STATE V. STEWART
> 763 P.2d 572 (Kan. 1988)
>
> **TYLER C. LOCKETT, JUSTICE.**
>
> A direct appeal by the prosecution upon a question reserved asks whether the statutory justification for the use of deadly force in self-defense provided by K.S.A. 21–3211 excuses a homicide committed by a battered wife where there is no evidence of a deadly threat or imminent danger contemporaneous with the killing. . . .
>
> Peggy Stewart fatally shot her husband, Mike Stewart, while he was sleeping. She was charged with murder in the first degree. Defendant pled not guilty, contending that she shot her husband in self-defense. Expert evidence showed that Peggy Stewart suffered from the battered woman syndrome. Based upon the battered woman syndrome, the trial judge instructed the jury on self-defense. The jury found Peggy Stewart not guilty.
>
> The State stipulates that Stewart "suffered considerable abuse at the hands of her husband," but contends that the trial court erred in giving a self-defense instruction since Peggy Stewart was in no imminent danger when she shot her sleeping husband. We agree that under the facts of this case the giving of the

self-defense instruction was erroneous. We further hold that the trial judge's self-defense instruction improperly allowed the jury to determine the reasonableness of defendant's belief that she was in imminent danger from her individual subjective viewpoint rather than the viewpoint of a reasonable person in her circumstances.

Following an annulment from her first husband and two subsequent divorces in which she was the petitioner, Peggy Stewart married Mike Stewart in 1974. Evidence at trial disclosed a long history of abuse by Mike against Peggy and her two daughters from one of her prior marriages. Laura, one of Peggy's daughters, testified that early in the marriage Mike hit and kicked Peggy, and that after the first year of the marriage Peggy exhibited signs of severe psychological problems. Subsequently, Peggy was hospitalized and diagnosed as having symptoms of paranoid schizophrenia; she responded to treatment and was soon released. It appeared to Laura, however, that Mike was encouraging Peggy to take more than her prescribed dosage of medication.

In 1977, two social workers informed Peggy that they had received reports that Mike was taking indecent liberties with her daughters. Because the social workers did not want Mike to be left alone with the girls, Peggy quit her job. In 1978, Mike began to taunt Peggy by stating that Carla, her 12-year-old daughter, was "more of a wife" to him than Peggy.

Later, Carla was placed in a detention center, and Mike forbade Peggy and Laura to visit her. When Mike finally allowed Carla to return home in the middle of summer, he forced her to sleep in an un-air conditioned room with the windows nailed shut, to wear a heavy flannel nightgown, and to cover herself with heavy blankets. Mike would then wake Carla at 5:30 a.m. and force her to do all the housework. Peggy and Laura were not allowed to help Carla or speak to her.

When Peggy confronted Mike and demanded that the situation cease, Mike responded by holding a shotgun to Peggy's head and threatening to kill her. Mike once kicked Peggy so violently in the chest and ribs that she required hospitalization. Finally, when Mike ordered Peggy to kill and bury Carla, she filed for divorce. Peggy's attorney in the divorce action testified in the murder trial that Peggy was afraid for both her and her children's lives.

One night, in a fit of anger, Mike threw Carla out of the house. Carla, who was not yet in her teens, was forced out of the home with no money, no coat, and no place to go. When the family heard that Carla was in Colorado, Mike refused to allow Peggy to contact or even talk about Carla.

Mike's intimidation of Peggy continued to escalate. One morning, Laura found her mother hiding on the school bus, terrified and begging the driver to take her to a neighbor's home. That Christmas, Mike threw the turkey dinner to the floor, chased Peggy outside, grabbed her by the hair, rubbed her face in the dirt, and then kicked and beat her.

After Laura moved away, Peggy's life became even more isolated. Once, when Peggy was working at a cafe, Mike came in and ran all the customers off with a gun because he wanted Peggy to go home and have sex with him right that minute. He abused both drugs and alcohol, and amused himself by terrifying Peggy, once waking her from a sound sleep by beating her with a baseball bat. He shot one of Peggy's pet cats, and then held the gun against her head and threatened to pull the trigger. Peggy told friends that Mike would hold a shotgun to her head and threaten to blow it off, and indicated that one day he would probably do it.

In May 1986, Peggy left Mike and ran away to Laura's home in Oklahoma. It was the first time Peggy had left Mike without telling him. Because Peggy was suicidal, Laura had her admitted to a hospital. There, she was diagnosed as having toxic psychosis as a result of an overdose of her medication. On May 30, 1986, Mike called to say he was coming to get her. Peggy agreed to return to Kansas. Peggy told a nurse she felt like she wanted to shoot her husband. At trial, she testified that she decided to return with Mike because she was not able to get the medical help she needed in Oklahoma.

When Mike arrived at the hospital, he told the staff that he "needed his housekeeper." The hospital released Peggy to Mike's care, and he immediately drove her back to Kansas. Mike told Peggy that all her problems were in her head and he would be the one to tell her what was good for her, not the doctors. Peggy testified that Mike threatened to kill her if she ever ran away again. As soon as they arrived at the house, Mike forced Peggy into the house and forced her to have oral sex several times.

The next morning, Peggy discovered a loaded .357 magnum. She testified she was afraid of the gun. She hid the gun under the mattress of the bed in a spare room. Later that morning, as she cleaned house, Mike kept making remarks that she should not bother because she would not be there long, or that she should not bother with her things because she could not take them with her. She testified she was afraid Mike was going to kill her.

Mike's parents visited Mike and Peggy that afternoon. Mike's father testified that Peggy and Mike were affectionate with each other during the visit.

Later, after Mike's parents had left, Mike forced Peggy to perform oral sex. After watching television, Mike and Peggy went to bed at 8:00 p.m. As Mike slept, Peggy thought about suicide and heard voices in her head repeating over and over, "kill or be killed." At this time, there were two vehicles in the driveway and Peggy had access to the car keys. About 10:00 p.m., Peggy went to the spare bedroom and removed the gun from under the mattress, walked back to the bedroom, and killed her husband while he slept. She then ran to the home of a neighbor, who called the police.

When the police questioned Peggy regarding the events leading up to the shooting, Peggy stated that things had not gone quite right that day, and that when she got the chance she hid the gun under the mattress. She stated that she shot Mike to "get this over with, this misery and this torment." When asked why she got the gun out, Peggy stated to the police:

> "I'm not sure exactly what . . . led up to it . . . and my head started playing games with me and I got to thinking about things and I said I didn't want to be by myself again. . . . I got the gun out because there had been remarks made about me being out there alone. It was as if Mike was going to do something again like had been done before. He had gotten me down here from McPherson one time and he went and told them that I had done something and he had me put out of the house and was taking everything I had. And it was like he was going to pull the same thing over again."

Two expert witnesses testified during the trial. The expert for the defense, psychologist Marilyn Hutchinson, diagnosed Peggy as suffering from "battered woman syndrome," or post-traumatic stress syndrome. Dr. Hutchinson testified that Mike was preparing to escalate the violence in retaliation for Peggy's running away. She testified that loaded guns, veiled threats, and increased sexual demands are indicators of the escalation of the cycle. Dr. Hutchinson believed Peggy had a repressed knowledge that she was in a "really grave lethal situation."

The State's expert, psychiatrist Herbert Modlin, neither subscribed to a belief in the battered woman syndrome nor to a theory of learned helplessness as an explanation for why women do not leave an abusive relationship. Dr. Modlin testified that abuse such as repeated forced oral sex would not be trauma sufficient to trigger a post-traumatic stress disorder. He also believed Peggy was erroneously diagnosed as suffering from toxic psychosis. He stated that Peggy was unable to escape the abuse because she suffered from schizophrenia, rather than the battered woman syndrome.

At defense counsel's request, the trial judge gave an instruction on self-defense to the jury. The jury found Peggy not guilty.

. . .

Under the common law, the excuse for killing in self-defense is founded upon necessity, be it real or apparent. 40 Am. Jur. 2d, Homicide § 151, p. 439. Early Kansas cases held that killing in self-defense was justifiable when the defendant had reasonable grounds to believe that an aggressor (1) had a design to take the defendant's life, (2) attempted to execute the design or was in an apparent situation to do so, and (3) induced in the defendant a reasonable belief that he intended to do so immediately. *State v. Horne*, 9 Kan. 19, 29 (1872.). . .

These common-law principles were codified in K.S.A. 21–3211, which provides:

"A person is justified in the use of force against an aggressor when and to the extent it appears to him and he reasonably believes that such conduct is necessary to defend himself or another against such aggressor's imminent use of unlawful force."

The traditional concept of self-defense has posited one-time conflicts between persons of somewhat equal size and strength. When the defendant claiming self-defense is a victim of long-term domestic violence, such as a battered spouse, such traditional concepts may not apply. Because of the prior history of abuse, and the difference in strength and size between the abused and the abuser, the accused in such cases may choose to defend during a momentary lull in the abuse, rather than during a conflict. However, in order to warrant the giving of a self-defense instruction, the facts of the case must still show that the spouse was in imminent danger close to the time of the killing.

A person is justified in using force against an aggressor when it appears to that person and he or she reasonably believes such force to be necessary. *State v. Hundley*, 236 Kan. 461, 464, 693 P.2d 475 (1985); *State v. Gray*, 179 Kan. 133, 292 P.2d 698 (1956). A reasonable belief implies both an honest belief and the existence of facts which would persuade a reasonable person to that belief. A self-defense instruction must be given if there is any evidence to support a claim of self-defense, even if that evidence consists solely of the defendant's testimony. *State v. Hill*, 242 Kan. 68, 78, 744 P.2d 1228 (1987).

Where self-defense is asserted, evidence of the deceased's long-term cruelty and violence towards the defendant is admissible. *State v. Hundley*, 236 Kan. 461, 464, 693 P.2d 475 (1985); *State v. Gray*, 179 Kan. 133, 292 P.2d 698 (1956). In cases involving battered spouses, expert evidence of the battered woman syndrome is relevant to a determination of the reasonableness of the defendant's perception of danger. *State v. Hodges*, 239 Kan. 63, 716 P.2d 563 (1986). Other courts which have allowed such evidence to be introduced include those in Florida, Georgia, Illinois, Maine, New Jersey, New York, Pennsylvania, Washington, and Wisconsin. See Johann & Osanka, "I Didn't Mean to Kill Him!" 14 *Barrister* 19, 20 (Fall 1987). However, no jurisdictions have held that the existence of the battered woman syndrome in and of itself operates as a defense to murder.

In order to instruct a jury on self-defense, there must be some showing of an imminent threat or a confrontational circumstance involving an overt act by an aggressor. There is no exception to this requirement where the defendant has suffered long-term domestic abuse and the victim is the abuser. In such cases, the issue is not whether the defendant believes homicide is the solution to past or future problems with the batterer, but rather whether circumstances surrounding the killing were sufficient to create a reasonable belief in the defendant that the use of deadly force was necessary.

. . .Here there is an absence of imminent danger to defendant: Peggy told a nurse at the Oklahoma hospital of her desire to kill Mike. She later voluntarily agreed to return home with Mike when he telephoned her. She stated that after leaving the hospital Mike threatened to kill her if she left him again. Peggy showed no inclination to leave. In fact, immediately after the shooting, Peggy told the police that she was upset because she thought Mike would leave her. Prior to the shooting, Peggy hid the loaded gun. The cars were in the driveway and Peggy had access to the car keys. After being abused, Peggy went to bed with Mike at 8 p.m. Peggy lay there for two hours, then retrieved the gun from where she had hidden it and shot Mike while he slept.

Under these facts, the giving of the self-defense instruction was erroneous. Under such circumstances, a battered woman cannot reasonably fear imminent life-threatening danger from her sleeping spouse. We note that other courts have held that the sole fact that the victim was asleep does not preclude a self-defense instruction. In *State v. Norman*, 89 N.C. App. 384, 366 S.E.2d 586 (1988), cited by defendant, the defendant's evidence disclosed a long history of abuse. Each time defendant attempted to escape, her husband found and beat her. On the day of the shooting, the husband beat defendant continually throughout the day, and threatened either to cut her throat, kill her, or cut off her breast. In the afternoon, defendant shot her husband while he napped. The North Carolina Court of Appeals held it was reversible error to fail to instruct on self-defense. The court found that, although decedent was napping at the time defendant shot him, defendant's unlawful act was closely related in time to an assault and threat of death by decedent against defendant and that the decedent's nap was "but a momentary hiatus in a continuous reign of terror." 89 N.C. App. at 394.

. . .[A]s one court has stated: "To permit capital punishment to be imposed upon the subjective conclusion of the [abused] individual that prior acts and conduct of the deceased justified the killing would amount to a leap into the abyss of anarchy." *Jahnke v. State*, 682 P.2d 991, 997 (Wyo. 1984). Finally, our legislature has not provided for capital punishment for even the most heinous crimes. We must, therefore, hold that when a battered woman kills her sleeping spouse when there is no imminent danger, the killing is not reasonably necessary and a self-defense instruction may not be given. To hold otherwise in this case would in effect allow the execution of the abuser for past or future acts and conduct.

One additional issue must be addressed. . . .We. . .believe it is necessary to clarify certain portions of our opinion in *State v. Hodges*, 239 Kan. 63.

Here, the trial judge gave the instruction approved in *State v. Simon*, 231 Kan. 572, 575, 646 P.2d 1119 (1982), stating:

> The defendant has claimed her conduct was justified as self-defense. A person is justified in the use of force against an aggressor when and to the extent it appears to him and he reasonably believes that such conduct is necessary to defend himself or another against such aggressor's imminent use of unlawful force. Such justification requires both a belief on the part of the defendant and the existence of facts that would persuade a reasonable person to that belief.

The trial judge then added the following:

> You must determine, from the viewpoint of the defendant's mental state, whether the defendant's belief in the need to defend herself was reasonable in light of her subjective impressions and the facts and circumstances known to her.

This addition was apparently encouraged by the following language in *State v. Hodges*, 239 Kan. 63, Syl. para. 4:

Where the battered woman syndrome is an issue in the case, the standard for reasonableness concerning an accused's belief in asserting self-defense is not an objective, but a subjective standard. The jury must determine, from the viewpoint of defendant's mental state, whether defendant's belief in the need to defend herself was reasonable.

The statement that the reasonableness of defendant's belief in asserting self-defense should be measured from the defendant's own individual subjective viewpoint conflicts with prior law. Our test for self-defense is a two-pronged one. We first use a subjective standard to determine whether the defendant sincerely and honestly believed it necessary to kill in order to defend. We then use an objective standard to determine whether defendant's belief was reasonable—specifically, whether a reasonable person in defendant's circumstances would have perceived self-defense as necessary. See *State v. Simon*, 231 Kan. at 573–74. In *State v. Hundley*, 236 Kan. at 467, we stated that, in cases involving battered spouses, "[t]he objective test is how a reasonably prudent battered wife would perceive [the aggressor's] demeanor."

Hundley makes clear that it was error for the trial court to instruct the jury to employ solely a subjective test in determining the reasonableness of defendant's actions. Insofar as the above-quoted language in *State v. Hodges* can be read to sanction a subjective test, this language is disapproved.

The appeal is sustained.

HERD, J., dissenting:

The sole issue before us on the question reserved is whether the trial court erred in giving a jury instruction on self-defense. We have a well-established rule that a defendant is entitled to a self-defense instruction if there is any evidence to support it, even though the evidence consists solely of the defendant's testimony. *State v. Hill*, 242 Kan. 68, 78, 744 P.2d 1228 (1987). It is for the jury to determine the sincerity of the defendant's belief she needed to act in self-defense, and the reasonableness of that belief in light of all the circumstances.

It is not within the scope of appellate review to weigh the evidence. An appellate court's function is to merely examine the record and determine if there is *any* evidence to support the theory of self-defense. If the record discloses any competent evidence upon which self-defense could be based, then the instruction must be given. In judging the evidence for this purpose, all inferences should be resolved in favor of the defendant. *State v. Hill*, 242 Kan. at 79.

. . .It is evident from prior case law appellee met her burden of showing some competent evidence that she acted in self-defense, thus making her defense a jury question. She testified she acted in fear for her life, and Dr. Hutchinson corroborated this testimony. The evidence of Mike's past abuse, the escalation of violence, his threat of killing her should she attempt to leave him, and Dr. Hutchinson's testimony that appellee was indeed in a "lethal situation" more than met the minimal standard of "any evidence" to allow an instruction to be given to the jury. See *State v. Hill*, 242 Kan. at 78.

Appellee introduced much uncontroverted evidence of the violent nature of the deceased and how he had brutalized her throughout their married life. It is well settled in Kansas that when self-defense is asserted, evidence of the cruel and violent nature of the deceased toward the defendant is admissible. The evidence showed Mike had a "Dr. Jekyll and Mr. Hyde" personality. He was usually very friendly and ingratiating when non-family persons were around, but was belligerent and domineering to family members. He had a violent temper and would blow up without reason. Mike was cruel to his two stepdaughters, Carla and Laura, as well as to the appellee. He took pride in hurting them or anything they held dear, such as their pets. Mike's violence toward appellee and her daughters caused appellee to have emotional problems with symptoms of paranoid schizophrenia. He would overdose appellee on her medication and then cut her off it altogether. Mike's cruelty would culminate in an outburst of violence, and then he would suddenly become very loving and considerate. This was very confusing to appellee. She lived in constant dread of the next outburst.

Appellee became progressively more passive and helpless during the marriage but finally became desperate enough to confront Mike and tell him the cruelty to her daughters had to stop. Mike responded by holding a shotgun to her head and threatening to kill her in front of the girls. The violence escalated. At one point, Mike kicked appellee so violently in the chest and ribs that she required hospitalization.

. . .Mike would not let appellee see her daughters and ran Laura off with a shotgun when she tried to visit. Appellee's life became even more isolated. Towards the end, both the phone and utilities were disconnected from the house.

Appellee finally took the car and ran away to Laura's home in Oklahoma. It was the first time she had ever left Mike without telling him. She was suicidal and again hearing voices, and Laura had her admitted to a hospital. She was diagnosed as having toxic psychosis from a bad reaction to her medication. She soon felt better, but was not fully recovered, when Mike found out where she was and called her to say he was coming to get her. She told a nurse she felt like she wanted to shoot him, but the nurse noted her major emotion was one of hopelessness.

The hospital nevertheless released appellee to Mike's care, and he immediately drove her back to Kansas, telling her on the way she was going to have to "settle down now" and listen to him because he was the boss. *He said if she ever ran away again, he would kill her.*

When they reached the house, Mike would not let appellee bring in her suitcases and forced her to have oral sex four or five times in the next 36 hours, with such violence that the inside of her mouth was bruised. The next morning, appellee found a box of bullets in the car that had not been there before. She then discovered a loaded .357 magnum. This frightened her, because Mike had promised to keep his guns unloaded. She did not know how to unload the gun, so she hid it under the mattress of the bed in a spare room. As she cleaned house, Mike remarked she should not bother, because she would not be there long. He told her she should not bother with her things, because she could not take them with her. She took these statements to mean she would soon be dead and she grew progressively more terrified. Throughout the day Mike continued to force her to have oral sex, while telling her how he preferred sex with other women.

The sexual abuse stopped when Mike's parents came to visit. Mike's father testified everything seemed normal during their stay. After the visit, Mike again forced appellee to perform oral sex and then demanded at 8:00 p.m. she come to bed with him. The cumulative effect of Mike's past history, coupled with his current abusive conduct, justified appellee's belief that a violent explosion was imminent. As he slept, appellee was terrified and thought about suicide and heard voices in her head repeating over and over, "kill or be killed." The voices warned her there was going to be killing and to get away.

She went to the spare bedroom and removed the gun from under the mattress, walked back to the bedroom, and fatally shot Mike. After the first shot, she thought he was coming after her so she shot again and fled wildly outside, barefoot, wearing only her underwear. Ignoring the truck and car outside, although she had the keys in her purse inside, she ran over a mile to the neighbors' house and pled with them to keep Mike from killing her. She thought she had heard him chasing her. The neighbor woman took the gun from appellee's hand and gave her a robe while her husband called the sheriff. The neighbor testified appellee appeared frightened for her life and was certain Mike was alive and looking for her.

...The majority implies its decision is necessary to keep the battered woman syndrome from operating as a defense in and of itself. It has always been clear the syndrome is not a defense itself. Evidence of the syndrome is admissible only because of its relevance to the issue of self-defense. The majority of jurisdictions have held it beyond the ordinary jury's understanding why a battered woman may feel she cannot escape, and have held evidence of the battered woman syndrome proper to explain it. The expert testimony explains how people react to circumstances in which the average juror has not been involved. It assists the jury in evaluating the sincerity of the defendant's belief she was in imminent danger requiring self-defense and whether she was in fact in imminent danger.

Dr. Hutchinson explained to the jury at appellee's trial the "cycle of violence" which induces a state of "learned helplessness" and keeps a battered woman in the relationship.... The woman becomes conditioned to trying to make it through one more violent explosion with its battering in order to be rewarded by the "honeymoon phase," with its expressions of remorse and eternal love and the standard promise of "never again." After all promises are broken time after time and she is beaten again and again, the battered woman falls into a state of learned helplessness where she gives up trying to extract herself from the cycle of violence. She learns fighting back only delays the honeymoon and escalates the violence. If she tries to leave the relationship, she is located and returned and the violence increases. She is a captive. She begins to believe her husband is omnipotent, and resistance will be futile at best.

It is a jury question to determine if the battered woman who kills her husband as he sleeps fears he will find and kill her if she leaves, as is usually claimed. Under such circumstances the battered woman is not under actual physical attack when she kills but such attack is imminent, and as a result she believes her life is in imminent danger. She may kill during the tension-building stage when the abuse is apparently not as severe as it sometimes has been, but nevertheless has escalated so that she is afraid the acute stage to come will be fatal to her. She only acts on such fear if she has some survival instinct remaining after the husband-induced "learned helplessness."

It was Dr. Hutchinson's opinion Mike was planning to escalate his violence in retaliation against appellee for running away. She testified that Mike's threats against appellee's life, his brutal sexual acts, and appellee's discovery of the loaded gun were all indicators to appellee the violence had escalated and she was in danger. Dr. Hutchinson believed appellee had a repressed knowledge she was in what was really a gravely lethal situation. She testified appellee was convinced she must "kill or be killed." . . .

The majority claims permitting a jury to consider self-defense under these facts would permit anarchy. This underestimates the jury's ability to recognize an invalid claim of self-defense. Although this is a case of first impression where an appeal by the State has been allowed, there have been several similar cases in which the defendant appealed on other grounds. In each of these cases where a battered woman killed the sleeping batterer, a self-defense instruction has been given when requested by the defendant. . . .

The majority bases its opinion on its conclusion appellee was not in imminent danger, usurping the right of the jury to make that determination of fact. The majority believes a person could not be in imminent danger from an aggressor merely because the aggressor dropped off to sleep. This is a fallacious conclusion. For instance, picture a hostage situation where the armed guard inadvertently drops off to sleep and the hostage grabs his gun and shoots him. The majority opinion would preclude the use of self-defense in such a case.

The majority attempts to buttress its conclusion appellee was not in imminent danger by citing 19th Century law. The old requirement of "immediate" danger is not in accord with our statute on self-defense, K.S.A. 21–3211, and has been emphatically overruled by case law. Yet this standard permeates the majority's reasoning. A review of the law in this state on the requirement of imminent rather than immediate danger to justify self-defense is therefore required. I will limit my discussion to those cases involving battered wives.

The first case, *State v. Hundley*, 236 Kan. 461, 693 P.2d 475 (1985), involved a battered wife who shot her husband when he threatened her and reached for a beer bottle. Hundley pled self-defense. We held it was error for the trial court to instruct that self-defense was justified if a defendant reasonably believed his conduct was necessary to defend himself against an aggressor's *immediate* use of force. We held this instruction improperly excluded from the jury's consideration the effect that Hundley's many years as a battered wife had upon her perception of the dangerousness of her husband's actions. We held the statutory word "imminent" should be used, rather than "immediate."

The next case in which a battered wife claimed self-defense was *State v. Osbey*, 238 Kan. 280, 710 P.2d 676 (1985). The husband had a gun and had threatened to kill Osbey. After an argument while the husband was moving out, Osbey threw a chair towards his van. She shot him when he walked towards her and reached behind some record albums he was carrying. We again held the trial court erred in using the word "immediate" rather than "imminent" in the self-defense instruction to the jury.

In the most recent case, *State v. Hodges*, 239 Kan. 63, 716 P.2d 563 (1986), the battered wife was kicked and beaten before making her way into another room. When her husband ordered her to return to him, she shot him. When her first trial resulted in a hung jury, she was retried and convicted of voluntary manslaughter. K.S.A. 21–3403.

On appeal, we again held the trial court's use of "immediate" in instructing the jury on self-defense was reversible error. Such usage "places undue emphasis on the decedent's immediate conduct and obliterates the build-up of terror and fear the decedent systematically injected into the relationship over a long period of time." 239 Kan. at 74. We also held the trial court erred in not permitting expert testimony on the battered woman syndrome. We found it appropriate that the testimony be offered to prove the reasonableness of the defendant's belief she was in imminent danger. . . .

The majority disapproves *State v. Hodges*, 239 Kan. 63, where we adopted the subjective test for self-defense in battered wife cases. We adopted the subjective test because there is a contradiction in the terms "reasonably prudent battered wife." One battered into "learned helplessness" cannot be characterized as reasonably prudent. Hence, the *Hodges* modification of *State v. Hundley*, 236 Kan. 461, was necessary and properly states the law.

In *State v. Hundley*, we joined other enlightened jurisdictions in recognizing that the jury in homicide cases where a battered woman ultimately kills her batterer is entitled to all the facts about the battering relationship in rendering its verdict. The jury also needs to know about the nature of the cumulative terror under which a battered woman exists and that a batterer's threats and brutality can make life threatening danger imminent to the victim of that brutality even though, at the moment, the batterer is passive. Where a person believes she must kill or be killed, and there is the slightest basis in fact for this belief, it is a question for the jury as to whether the danger was imminent. I

> confess I am an advocate for the constitutional principle that in a criminal prosecution determination of the facts is a function of the jury, not the appellate court.
>
> I would deny this appeal.

Case Questions

1. How is whether or not Gladys Kelly or Peggy Stewart could have left her husband relevant to her claim of self-defense?

2. Was it objectively reasonable for Peggy Stewart to fear that her life was in imminent danger when her husband had just recaptured her after she had run away, had threatened to kill her if she ever ran away again, had a loaded gun in the car, had repeatedly implied that she would soon be dead (e.g., by saying that she would not be around for long), and had previously subjected her to numerous brutal injuries?

3. The majority stresses that she could have taken the car and driven away. Was it reasonable for her to expect that a second escape would be more successful? Might she have simply driven to the police and told them of the threats?

4. In light of Peggy Stewart's history of mental illness and Mike's success at being "friendly and ingratiating to nonfamily persons," might she reasonably expect failure at having the police restrain Mike?

5. Is the phrase "reasonably prudent battered wife" in fact a contradiction in terms? What is the meaning of "reasonable in light of [a given person's] subjective impressions"?

6. Why did the majority not view Dr. Hutchinson's assessment that Peggy was in a "really grave, lethal situation" as indicating that there was "evidence sufficient to create a reasonable belief [that Peggy faced] imminent life-threatening danger"? Why didn't statements like, "You won't be here for long, anyway," count as an "imminent threat"?

7. The majority in *Stewart* warns against "self-defense" rules that would free every battered wife to kill her husband. Why should that be a concern in a case where shortly before the killing, the battering husband had threatened both explicitly and implicitly to kill his wife?

8. Is "learned helplessness" incompatible with "scheming for years"?

Case note: In October 1990, shortly before he left office, Governor Richard Celeste of Ohio issued a mass clemency of 25 battered women who had been convicted of killing or assaulting the man in their lives. This set off what has since been dubbed the "clemency movement." Governor William Schaefer of Maryland granted clemency for 8 similar inmates in 1991. The women who were freed had been convicted in trials where the judge had not permitted testimony presenting the fact that they had been battered. By the end of 1992, governors in a total of seven states had granted clemency to 38 women convicted of assaulting their life partners after having been battered by them.[8]

Resorting to homicide even to alleviate a desperate situation is generally frowned upon in the law. Still, battered women may have a valid perception that they are in imminent danger to their lives, and homicide in self-defense is permitted throughout the United States. A 2017 Centers for Disease Control and Prevention (CDC) report found that, between 2003 and 2014, over half of female homicides were attributed to a male intimate partner.[9]

The U.S. Supreme Court has further broadened the penalties for perpetrators of domestic violence to preclude possession of a firearm. In *United States v. Castleman*, 572 U.S. 157 (2014), the unanimous Court determined that individuals found guilty of "intentionally or knowingly causing bodily injury to a family member" did fit into the category of persons found guilty of "a misdemeanor crime of domestic violence," the category of people Congress had barred from possessing a firearm.[10] Central to this decision was that the causing of bodily harm had to have been committed "knowingly" or "intentionally" to be classified as a misdemeanor.

According to the Court, the decision in *Castleman* "left open whether the same was true of reckless assault."[11] The legal term "reckless" means extreme negligence. Negligence means the absence of a reasonable amount of care. In other words, harm caused accidentally by extremely careless behavior was not an issue present in the *Castleman* case, but might arise in the future. It did indeed arise, reaching the Supreme Court just two years later in *Voisine v. United States*, 136 S.Ct. 2272 (2016). There, in a 6–2 vote, the Court determined that reckless domestic assault also qualified as a "misdemeanor crime of domestic violence."[12] This means that federal law prohibits persons convicted of reckless domestic violence from possessing a firearm. Together, the *Castleman* and *Voisine* rulings prohibit perpetrators of domestic violence from being able to possess a firearm whether the misdemeanor assault was committed knowingly, intentionally, or recklessly.[13]

RAPE

Even women who want to foster women's autonomy have differed publicly in print over how rape should be defined.

FROM CAMILLE PAGLIA, *SEX, ART, AND AMERICAN CULTURE*[14]

Excerpts from interviews, 1991–92.

I think real rape is an outrage. And for me real rape would be either stranger rape or the intrusion of overt sex into a nonsexual situation. I feel that women should take real responsibility for the dating experience.

[Q.] "Is it rape if you don't say no?"

Absolutely not. This kind of thing is turning women into jokes. All the responsibilities [sic] is being shunted onto men. And besides, it's ridiculous to think that saying no always means no. We all know how it goes in the heat of the moment: it's "no" now, it's "maybe" later, and it changes again.

[Q.] "Is it rape if a couple is making out and the girl...doesn't want to go all the way, but the guy forces her to?"

You can't make rules for this type of behavior. These girls don't understand the risks of adulthood and sex. Don't put yourself in that situation and then go crying to authority figures...

[Q.] "Is it rape if she's too drunk to object?"

If she's drunk, she's complicitous.

...What I'm saying is that even in my era, we knew not to go to fraternity parties. We knew fraternity parties were about scoring! I say let's leave fraternity parties to be about scoring. That's what I want....I am radically pro-sex. I think women should have a choice: go to the party or don't go to the party.

...I see a liberated feminism that takes full responsibility for the woman's part in the sexual encounter. You see, in the old days, you did have a system where fathers and brothers protected women, essentially. Men knew that if they devirginized a woman, they could end up dead within twenty-four hours. These controls have been removed.

[Q.] "What I hear is a woman going back into *veils*, in effect."

No, no! I'm encouraging women to *accept* the adventure of sex, *accept* the danger!

> ### FROM SUSAN ESTRICH, *REAL RAPE*[15]
>
> Many women continue to believe that men can force you to have sex against your will and that it isn't rape so long as they know you and don't beat you nearly to death in the process. Many men continue to act as if they have that right. In a very real sense, they do. This is not what the law says. . . .While husbands have always enjoyed the greatest protection, the protection of being excluded from rape prohibitions, even friends and neighbors have been assured sexual access. What the law seems to say and what it has been in practice are two different things. . . .
>
> The distinction between the aggravated and simple case is one commonly drawn in assault. . . .[Legal researchers] defined an aggravated rape as one with extrinsic violence (guns, knives, or beatings) or multiple assailants or no prior relationship between the victim and the defendant. A simple rape was a case in which none of these aggravating circumstances was present: a case of a single defendant who knew his victim and neither beat her nor threatened her with a weapon. They found that juries were four times as willing to convict in the aggravated rape as in the simple rape. And where there was "contributory behavior" on the part of the woman—where she was hitchhiking, or dating the man, or met him at a party, juries were willing to go to extremes in their leniency toward the defendant. . . .
>
> If in the 1980s more women do feel free to say yes, that provides more reason—not less—to credit the word of those who say no. The issue is not chastity or unchastity, but freedom and respect. What the law owes us is a celebration of our autonomy, and an end at long last to the distrust and suspicion of women victims of simple rape. . . .
>
> What makes both the "violent rapist" and the stepfather whose feelings "get out of hand" different and more serious offenders than those who commit assault or robbery is the injury to personal integrity involved in forced sex. That injury is the reason that forced sex should be considered a serious crime even when there is no weapon or beating. . . .Simple rape is real rape.

Rape law has received considerable attention from feminists. For these statutes the bulk of feminists' efforts, in contrast to other areas of the law, has been not toward making these laws gender neutral, but rather toward reforming testimonial aspects of rape law that have rendered rape prosecutions both difficult to win and taxing on the victims. Anglo-American common law long proceeded on the assumption that women might lightly and falsely charge rape.

Consequently, many state jurisdictions, even into the 1970s, required that the victim's word alone, unlike the situation with such crimes as robbery or assault, was not adequate to bring rape charges. Instead, three elements of the crime needed independent corroboration before prosecution could proceed: (1) force, (2) sexual penetration, and (3) the identity of the rapist. Since eyewitnesses were rarely available, these requirements drastically reduced the number of prosecutable rapes.

The feminist movement successfully reformed most such statutes and also achieved some success in sensitizing police and prosecutors' offices to the needs of rape victims. Moreover, a number of states have adopted statutes barring testimony about the sexual history of the rape victim. Additional rape law reforms have included (1) a decision by the U.S. Supreme Court that the death sentence for rape is unconstitutionally harsh (favored by reformers as making conviction more readily obtainable),[16] and (2) making rape by a husband a punishable offense under certain circumstances.

Still, despite these advancements, female rape victims are forced to navigate various stereotypes about rape victims and pervasive rape myths. The 2015 case of "Emily Doe" versus Brock Turner demonstrates these challenges. In this case, Turner was caught sexually assaulting Doe who was unconscious outside of a fraternity house on the Stanford University campus. Two graduate students came upon the scene and intervened, and chased Turner down when he fled. The victim's impact statement demonstrates how myths about consent, alcohol, and the reliability of victims complicate sexual assault and rape prosecutions.

EMILY DOE, *VICTIM IMPACT STATEMENT IN PEOPLE OF THE STATE OF CALIFORNIA V. BROCK ALLEN TURNER* (2016)

The night after it happened, he said he didn't know my name, said he wouldn't be able to identify my face in a lineup, didn't mention any dialogue between us, no words, only dancing and kissing. Dancing is a cute term; was it snapping fingers and twirling dancing, or just bodies grinding up against each other in a crowded room? I wonder if kissing was just faces sloppily pressed up against each other? When the detective asked if he had planned on taking me back to his dorm, he said no. When the detective asked how we ended up behind the dumpster, he said he didn't know. He admitted to kissing other girls at that party, one of whom was my own sister who pushed him away. He admitted to wanting to hook up with someone. I was the wounded antelope of the herd, completely alone and vulnerable, physically unable to fend for myself, and he chose me. Sometimes I think, if I hadn't gone, then this never would've happened. But then I realized, it would have happened, just to somebody else. You were about to enter four years of access to drunk girls and parties, and if this is the foot you started off on, then it is right you did not continue.

The night after it happened, he said he thought I liked it because I rubbed his back. A back rub. Never mentioned me voicing consent, never mentioned us speaking, a back rub.

One more time, in public news, I learned that my ass and vagina were completely exposed outside, my breasts had been groped, fingers had been jabbed inside me along with pine needles and debris, my bare skin and head had been rubbing against the ground behind a dumpster, while an erect freshman was humping my half naked, unconscious body. But I don't remember, so how do I prove I didn't like it.

I thought there's no way this is going to trial; there were witnesses, there was dirt in my body, he ran but was caught. He's going to settle, formally apologize, and we will both move on. Instead, I was told he hired a powerful attorney, expert witnesses, private investigators who were going to try and find details about my personal life to use against me, find loopholes in my story to invalidate me and my sister, in order to show that this sexual assault was in fact a misunderstanding. That he was going to go to any length to convince the world he had simply been confused.

I was not only told that I was assaulted, I was told that because I couldn't remember, I technically could not prove it was unwanted. And that distorted me, damaged me, almost broke me. It is the saddest type of confusion to be told I was assaulted and nearly raped, blatantly out in the open, but we don't know if it counts as assault yet. I had to fight for an entire year to make it clear that there was something wrong with this situation.

When I was told to be prepared in case we didn't win, I said, I can't prepare for that. He was guilty the minute I woke up. No one can talk me out of the hurt he caused me. Worst of all, I was warned, because he now knows you don't remember, he is going to get to write the script. He can say whatever he wants and no one can contest it. I had no power, I had no voice, I was defenseless. My memory loss would be used against me. My testimony was weak, was incomplete, and I was made to believe that perhaps, I am not enough to win this. That's so damaging. His attorney constantly reminded the jury, the only one we can believe is Brock, because she doesn't remember. That helplessness was traumatizing.

Brock Turner was tried on three counts of felonious sexual assault, found guilty, and sentenced to six months in jail to be followed by three years probation and a lifetime of being listed as a sex offender. He was released from jail within three months (for good behavior there). Public outcry at the lightness of his sentence influenced California to recall the sentencing judge and to amend its laws in two ways: the felony of rape, for which years in prison (rather than the option of probation) is mandatory, was extended to include sexual penetration of an unconscious person and also to include penetration by fingers or other foreign object into the vagina or anus.[17]

Force and Consent: *Goldberg v. State of Maryland* (1978)

Well into the twentieth century, the crime of forcible rape in Anglo-American law consisted of carnal knowledge of a woman, not the defendant's wife, forcibly and without her consent. Statutory rape was intercourse with any female below the legally defined "age of consent" (see *Michael M.*, Chapter 2 and below). The influence of the contemporary feminist movement in this area of law has been profound. Since 1969, every state has revised its rape laws, and most have done so more than once. By the twenty-first century, *rape* had become *sexual assault* on the statute books, *statutory rape* had been redefined as *unlawful sexual intercourse*, and the marital exemption had been abolished, formally at least. Sexual contact with an adult who is incapable of giving consent—who is, for example, unconscious, developmentally disabled, drunk, or drugged—is sexual assault (but see above on California's recent refinement of this situation). As a result, both men and women can now be guilty of these crimes.

When cases go to trial, the defendant usually claims that the alleged victim consented. If DNA evidence proves that intercourse took place, consent is the only reasonable defense. The prosecutor in a rape case once had the burden of proving that the defendant used force. Unless the state had compelling forensic evidence that the victim had been injured, the issue of force often became conflated with the issue of consent. To rebut the consent defense, the state had to show either that the woman resisted her attacker or that her resistance was overcome by force or the threat of force. A woman threatened with rape thus faced a classic Catch-22. If she resisted, she increased her risk of injury. If she submitted, she had consented. It was not until rape had been redefined as sexual assault that the law began to distinguish submission from consent. Reconsider in this context the dialogue between "Sharon" and the prosecutor of "Michael M" contained in note * of Justice Blackmun's opinion there (See Chapter 2).

Randy Jay Goldberg v. State of Maryland
41 Md. App. 58; 395 A.2d 1213 (1978)

Melvin, Judge.

On October 18, 1977, Randy Jay Goldberg, the appellant, was found guilty by a jury in the Circuit Court for Baltimore County, of rape in the second degree (Art. 27, Section 463 (a) (1)). The appellant was sentenced to a five year term, of which the first two years were to be served in a work release program at the jail and the remaining three years on probation. [He appeals.]

. . .

I

The eighteen year old prosecuting witness was a high school senior who worked part-time as a sales clerk in the Merry-Go-Round clothing store at Towson Plaza. Around 1:00 P.M., on August 10, 1977, she was at work when the appellant, aged twenty-five, entered the store. The prosecuting witness started out trying to sell the appellant clothing but ended up being sold a story by the appellant that he was a free-lance agent and thought she was an excellent prospect to become a successful model. They arranged to meet at 5 o'clock when she got off from work.

When the appellant returned for her at 5:00 P.M., she asked him for "any ID to show me if you are who you say you are." He showed her his driving license with his picture on it. This satisfied her: "Well, I figured that he wouldn't. . .if he was planning to harm me in any way. . .wouldn't give his name like that, and I figured that, you know, he was who he said he was. I believed him." Despite some cautioning from her employer she drove off with the appellant at 5:10 p.m. in a silver-grey Cadillac Eldorado. The appellant was actually a student at Catonsville Community College and the car belonged to his mother. Appellant told her he was taking her to "a temporary studio" in the Pikesville area. When the "studio" was found to be closed, they drove to a condominium building on Slade Avenue. Upon arrival there, she stayed in the car while appellant went inside. Shortly, he returned to the car and told her he had contacted a friend who said they could use his house for his "studio." When they arrived at the friend's house, she helped appellant find a door that was open. The door led to the kitchen which she described as "very dirty" and she "didn't, you know, understand why we were coming here." From the kitchen they walked into the bedroom which by contrast she described as being "really made up really nice" with "a queen sized bed, real big bed, with a red velvet bedspread, and a big backboard on the back." She was "pretty impressed by the room."

Soon after they entered the bedroom, appellant "motioned" her to sit beside him on the bed. Instead, she sat on a chair at the foot of the bed. Appellant then said it was hot in the room and took his shirt off. When asked her reaction to appellant's removing his shirt she responded: "He told me he was hot, so I figured—so I figured he was hot." She then stood up and appellant "came over to me and he started unbuttoning my blouse. He said this is what I want you to do." She pulled her blouse together and said "no." Asked to describe what happened next she said:

> "He just kept on smooth-talking me and saying I won't hurt you. This is what I do to all the models that I interview. And he, you know, started *motioning* me to take my blouse off and everything, and then I went through the same thing with every piece of clothing. It was like, you know, kept on trying to tell me to take it off, and I didn't want to. And he kept on trying to convince me that—he was still trying to convince me that this was this modeling job, and I knew that it wasn't any more."

She said she removed her clothes because she "was really scared of him." "There was nothing I could do." When asked what caused her fright she said: "Because he was—he was so much bigger than I was, and, you know, I was in a room alone with him, and there was nothing, no buildings around us, or anything, and I mean wouldn't helped if I wouldn't—help me if I didn't. It was like being trapped or something." On cross-examination she said she was "afraid" she was "going to be killed."

After her clothes were removed, the appellant "pushed" her down on the bed and tried "to move [her legs] in different ways, and [she] kept pulling them together, and telling him that [she] didn't want to do it, and just wanted to go home." He kept telling her that he wouldn't hurt her "and just to relax." But she was "just really scared" and she was "shaking and my voice was really shaking" and she "kept on telling him [she] wanted to go home," and that "[she] didn't want to do this"; that she "didn't want to be a model, and [she] didn't want to do it anymore. Just to let [her] alone." When asked, "And what was his reaction?" she testified as follows:

> "A. He was just—he was just really cool about the whole thing, telling me not to worry, and he wouldn't hurt me, and to relax.

Q. All right. Now, after you were on the bed, and he was moving your legs around, what, if anything, occurred next?

A. Well, he kept on trying to make me get in different positions, and kept on telling me to look sexual or something like that. I don't know what the word was.

Q. All right. And what, if anything, occurred after he said that?

A. He laid me down and placed his hands on my vagina and told me he was doing that to make me relax. I told him that it didn't make me relax.

Q. All right. Then what happened after he placed his hands on your vagina?

A. He went into the other room, and I couldn't see him. He wasn't facing me, and had his back to me, and his hands down by his belt buckle. And I realized what he was doing, and I jumped up grabbed my clothes and started putting them on. Then he came in and pulled them away from me and said no.

Q. What did he say?

A. He said don't worry. What are you doing that for. I am not going to hurt you, and he kept telling me just to relax, and not to be nervous. And he laid me down on the bed and tried to get me to that stuff again, and I told him I didn't want to do that.

Q. What happened then?

A. And then he put his arms up on my stomach and his torso was in between my legs. He said just take your time; take a deep breath. And then he moved up on me and placed his penis in my vagina.

Q. What were you doing when this occurred?

A. I squeezed my legs together and got really tense, and I just started crying real hard. And I told him not to do that to me.

Q. And what was his response?

A. He didn't say anything. Just stayed there. And then I felt him move.

. . .

Q. Did the Defendant ejaculate to your knowledge?

> A. Yes, I think he did.
>
> Q. Now, what, if anything, occurred after the Defendant ejaculated?
>
> A. He got up and he said that if I can't enjoy it, then he can't enjoy it."

The appellant then asked her to go to dinner with him but she declined and he drove her to her home where she lived with her parents. On the way home, the appellant gave her his telephone number which she wrote down on a piece of paper. At his request she gave him her telephone number by writing it on a piece of paper with her lipstick. Although she told him she "would never see him again," she said she gave him her correct telephone number because she "didn't want to get him suspicious of me." They had a "general conversation about sex" in which he told her that "girls act like they don't want to, but they really do." She told him that he "had the wrong impression of [her]"; that she "didn't want him to do that." She further testified, somewhat inconsistently, as follows: "I told him I didn't want that. I told him I didn't like him doing that to me, and *didn't let him*. I didn't make him think that I enjoyed all of it, and that I ever wanted to do it again, because *I know I would never do it again*. Never. I know I would never get near him again."

The appellant let her off at her home at 6:25 P. M., 1 1/4 hours after she left her place of employment with him at 5:10 P. M. Before the appellant drove off she told him to "drive home safely . . . I guess I was being more sarcastic than anything." She estimated that they had been at the house where the alleged rape took place for 30 minutes.

When she arrived inside her house she "walked straight pass my parents" to her upstairs room. She said nothing to them because she was "just scared, nervous, just, you know, I wanted to go upstairs and just clean myself up and just forget, you know, about it. Just think." After cleaning herself and using a contraceptive, she called her boyfriend on the telephone and talked to him for "about three minutes." She did not tell him "what happened" because she "didn't know how he would take it." She then called her girlfriend and told her that she "had a problem, and that I was raped today . . . ." She did not relate the details of the "rape." . . .She contemplated calling the police but said she "didn't know who to call," so she called her girlfriend back and asked what she should do. Shortly thereafter the girlfriend and the girlfriend's boyfriend came to her house and after picking up her own boyfriend the four young people eventually went to the police station where the "rape" was reported at approximately 9:00 p.m. According to the girlfriend, the prosecuting witness did not want to report the matter but "[w]e convinced her into going to the police."

After reporting the incident the prosecuting witness was taken to the Greater Baltimore Medical Center for a physical examination. The examining physician's "Impression" was "Recent sexual intercourse," but he found "no evidence of recent trauma" to any part of her body, including the "perineal and genital" areas.

Testifying in his own behalf, the appellant admitted having sexual relations with the prosecuting witness at the time and place alleged, but maintained that it was mutually consensual and that the prosecuting witness did not appear to be frightened at any time.

II

Prior to 1976, the Maryland rape statute was primarily a sentencing law, fixing the penalties without actually defining the crime. The common law definition of rape that has been applied in Maryland is: "the act of a man having unlawful carnal knowledge of a female over the age of ten years by force without the consent and against the will of the victim". *Hazel v. State,* 221 Md. 464, 468–469, 157 A. 2d 922 (1960).

By Chapter 573 of the Laws of 1976, effective July 1, 1976, the Legislature divided the crime of rape into "rape in the first degree" and "rape in the second degree". (sic) See Art. 27, § 462 (first degree rape) and § 463 (second degree rape). Section 463 provides, *inter alia,* that,

> "A person is guilty of rape in the second degree if the person engages in vaginal intercourse with another person:
>
> (1) By force or threat of force against the will and without the consent of the other person...."

Section 464E of the new Act provides that,

> "Undefined words or phrases in this subheading [Sexual Offenses] which describe elements of the common law crime of rape shall retain their judicially determined meaning except to the extent expressly or by implication changed in this subheading."

The terms "force," "threat of force," "against the will" and "without the consent" are not defined by the 1976 Act. We therefore look to the "judicially determined meaning" of these elements of the common law crime of rape. In doing so, we conclude that the evidence was legally insufficient to sustain the conviction and the judgment will be reversed. We reach this conclusion because on the record before us, viewing the evidence in the light most favorable to the State, we find legally insufficient evidence of the requisite element of "force or threat of force."

There was certainly no "threat of force." On the contrary, the prosecuting witness on numerous occasions in her testimony negated that element. As to actual force, the only arguable evidence is the prosecuting witness' testimony that after she herself had removed all her clothes, the appellant put his hands on her shoulders and "pushed" her down on the bed. This is negated, however, by her further testimony on cross-examination that "he didn't push but guided [her] on the bed." She admitted that she was not "injured or anything" by the encounter. This, of course, is consistent with the findings of the physician who subsequently examined her. Those findings so far as they relate to the use of any actual force were completely negative. But *actual physical* force is not an indispensable element of the crime of rape.

As said by the Court of Appeals in *Hazel v. State* [21 Md. 464, 469, 157 A. 2d 922 (1960)],

> "Force is an essential element of the crime and to justify a conviction, the evidence must warrant a conclusion either that the victim resisted and her resistance was overcome by force *or that she was prevented from resisting by threats to her safety*. But no particular amount of force, either actual or constructive, is required to constitute rape. Necessarily that fact must depend upon the prevailing circumstances.... [F]orce may exist without violence. If the acts and threats of the defendant were reasonably calculated to create in the mind of the victim—having regard to the circumstances in which she was placed—a real apprehension, due to fear, of imminent bodily harm, serious enough to impair or overcome her will to resist, then such acts and threats are the equivalent of force.
>
> "With respect to the presence or absence of the element of consent, it is true, of course, that however reluctantly given, consent to the act at any time prior to penetration deprives the subsequent intercourse of its criminal character. There is, however, a wide difference between consent and a submission to the act. Consent may involve submission, but submission does not necessarily imply consent. Furthermore, submission to a compelling force, or as a result of being put in fear, is not consent.

> "The authorities are by no means in accord as to what degree of resistance is necessary to establish the absence of consent. However, *the generally accepted doctrine seems to be that a female—who was conscious and possessed of her natural, mental and physical powers when the attack took place—must have resisted to the extent of her ability at the time, unless it appears that she was overcome by numbers or was so terrified by threats as to overpower her will to resist.* Am. Jur., Rape, § 7....[T]he real test, which must be recognized in all cases, is whether the assault was committed without the consent and against the will of the prosecuting witness.
>
> "The kind of fear which would render resistance by a woman unnecessary to support a conviction of rape includes, but is not necessarily limited to, a fear of death or serious bodily harm, or a fear so extreme as to preclude resistance, or a fear which would well nigh render her mind incapable of continuing to resist, or a fear that so overpowers her that she does not dare resist.
>
> Applying these principles to the present case, we hold that the evidence is legally insufficient to warrant a finding by the jury that the prosecutrix exerted the necessary degree of resistance that was overcome by force or that she was prevented from resisting by fear based upon reasonable apprehension of bodily harm.
>
> The State argues that the "totality of [the] circumstances" caused the prosecutrix's fear of being killed and that the fear was a reasonable fear, thus rendering more resistance than that exerted by her unnecessary. First of all, we find nothing in the record evidencing any real resistance by the prosecutrix to anything the appellant said or did. It is true that she *told* the appellant she "didn't want to do that [stuff]." But the resistance that must be shown involves not merely verbal but *physical* resistance "to the extent of her ability at the time" (*Hazel v. State,* at 460). The State points to her testimony that when penetration occurred she "squeezed [her] legs together and got really tense." Assuming that this was evidence of her reluctance, even unwillingness, to engage in vaginal intercourse, it was not evidence that she resisted "to the extent of her ability" *before* the intercourse occurred.
>
> We are left therefore with the question of whether the prosecutrix's lack of resistance was caused by fear based upon reasonable apprehension of physical harm. We find no legally sufficient evidence warranting an affirmative answer to that question.

> ...The prosecutrix swore that the reasons for her fear of being killed if she did not accede to appellant's advances were two-fold: 1) she was alone with the appellant in a house with no buildings close by and no one to help her if she resisted, and 2) the appellant was much larger than she was. In the complete absence of any threatening words or actions by the appellant, these two factors, as a matter of law, are simply not enough to have created a reasonable fear of harm so as to preclude resistance and be "the equivalent of force." (*Hazel v. State,* at 469.) Without proof of force, actual or constructive, evidenced by words or conduct of the defendant or those acting in consort with him, sexual intercourse is not rape. This is so even though the intercourse may have occurred without the actual consent and against the actual will of the alleged victim. Thus it is that in the absence of actual force, unreasonable subjective fear of resisting cannot convert the conduct of the defendant from that which is non-criminal to that which is criminal.
>
> *Judgment reversed.*

Case Questions

1. Traditionally, the law of rape has conflated consent and the absence of force: intercourse is without consent if and only if the defendant uses or threatens to use force. How might one respond to claims that *Goldberg* reveals defects in this kind of thinking?

2. Two law professors have argued that the behavior Goldberg admitted should be outlawed and punished by a sentence of up to six months if the defendant did not use a condom. Because "unprotected sex can kill and date rapists almost always walk," the authors propose criminalizing "reckless sex," which they define as "penetration, without a condom, in a first sexual encounter."[18] Might such a prohibition act as a general deterrent to nonstranger rape or create a presumption that the use of a condom is a defense to a rape charge?

Resistance

State v. Rusk (1981)

Justice Stevens in footnote 8 of his *Michael M.* opinion refers to the problem of "nonforcible but nonetheless coerced, sexual intercourse" and suggests that states might wish to target a statutory prohibition directly against such conduct, rather than using the roundabout and partial solution of the kind of law applied to Michael M. Indeed, even persons sympathetic to California's approach would have to acknowledge that it would not have been effective if precisely the same incident had taken place when both parties were one and a half years older. Under those hypothetical circumstances, despite the coercive (as well as violent) behavior of punching his victim in the face twice, Michael apparently stood a good chance of being found innocent of rape charges.

These conviction difficulties, typified by Michael M.'s situation, which continue to face prosecutors of rape, have produced a variety of suggestions for reform. Some reformers have endorsed the "reasonable woman" standard, as advocated by the judge in the *Ellison* case from Chapter 3, as a guide to deciding whether consent was denied and whether "force" was either used or threatened.

A much-debated case that illustrates the issues addressed by these reformers is *State v. Rusk*. The rapist, Edward Rusk, was first convicted by a Baltimore jury. On appeal, the Court of Special Appeals in an 8–5 vote reversed his conviction on the grounds that the original trial judge should have ruled that the evidence was insufficient under Maryland law for the charge of rape to go to a jury. Then Maryland's highest court, the Court of Appeals, voted 4–3 to reinstate the conviction. One of those four votes was a woman judge, the only woman out of 21 judges who dealt with the case. (Of the 21, a total of 11 favored releasing the defendant, and only 10 favored conviction. By the luck of the draw, in a sense, Rusk stayed convicted.)

Rusk had been convicted of raping a woman referred to by the judges as "Pat." Pat's story was that she met Rusk in a bar where he appeared to be acquainted with a friend of hers. He asked her for a ride home, and she agreed, although she warned him not to think of it as anything more than a ride. When they reached his house, around 1:00 A.M., he invited her up. She refused. He persisted. She repeatedly refused. He then reached over, grabbed her car keys, pocketed them, got out, and said, "Now will you come up?" Fearing to walk alone in the middle of the night in an unfamiliar urban neighborhood, and already fearing that he might rape her because of a look on his face, Pat followed him up to his one room apartment. She waited a few minutes while he went into the bathroom, and when he returned asked if she could now leave. She reminded him that she had not wanted to come up. He told her to stay and pulled her onto the bed where he then took off her blouse and bra and unzipped her slacks. He asked her to remove her slacks and his pants, and she did so. He then started kissing her as she lay on the bed. Meanwhile she was begging him to let her leave, to return her keys. Then (she reported) she was "really scared" because of the "look in his eyes." She then said to him, "If I do what you want, will you let me go without killing me?" because she had no idea what he might do. She then started to cry. He then placed his hands on her throat and started, (in her description) "lightly to choke" her. She then repeated her question (omitting the "without killing me" phrase) and he said yes, after which she submitted to fellatio and vaginal sex. Immediately after that she again asked if she could leave. He said yes and gave her back her car keys. He also answered her request for directions how to drive home. She went home, thought a bit about the incident, and about an hour later reported it to the police. They picked her up, she led them to his apartment, and he was arrested for rape.

Rusk's story was that she was lying from beginning to end. In his version, she had cuddled with him on route to her car, eagerly petted with him on the way to his home, eagerly followed him in, enthusiastically had sex with him, and only became distraught after the fact. And he had never taken her car keys.

The judges who argued against convicting Rusk *assumed* Pat's story was true and still argued that this was not a rape situation. Maryland law (Article 27, § 463[a][1]) defined rape as "vaginal intercourse with another person by force or threat of force against the will and without the consent of the other person." The Court of Special Appeals majority reasoned that this law required evidence of nonconsent in the form of "resistance" or else evidence that the victim "was prevented from resisting by threats to her safety."[19] As debated on the (higher) Court of Appeals, then, the central question turned out to be whether there had been force or a threat of force against Pat, and if she believed there had, whether her belief itself had to be reasonable. Whether the standard of reasonable fear varied as between women and men was not a question articulated by the judges. The Court of Appeals debate is excerpted below.

STATE V. RUSK

424 A.2d 720 (Maryland 1981)

[ROBERT C.] MURPHY, CHIEF JUDGE.

. . .

On appeal, the Court of Special Appeals, sitting *en banc,* reversed the conviction; it concluded by an 8–5 majority that in view of the prevailing law as set forth in *Hazel v. State,* 221 Md. 464, 157 A.2d 922 (1960), insufficient evidence of Rusk's guilt had been adduced at the trial to permit the case to go to the jury. *Rusk v. State,* 43 Md. App. 476, 406 A.2d 624 (1979).

. . .

In reversing Rusk's second degree rape conviction,. . .Judge Thompson said:

> "In all of the victim's testimony we have been unable to see any resistance on her part to the sex acts and certainly can we see no fear as would overcome her attempt to resist or escape as required by *Hazel*. Possession of the keys by the accused may have deterred her vehicular escape but hardly a departure seeking help in the rooming house or in the street. We must say that 'the way he looked' fails utterly to support the fear required by *Hazel*." 43 Md. App. at 480.

The Court of Special Appeals interpreted *Hazel* as requiring a showing of a reasonable apprehension of fear in instances where the prosecutrix did not resist. It concluded:

> "...We do not believe that 'lightly choking' along with all the facts and circumstances in the case, were sufficient to cause a reasonable fear which overcame her ability to resist. In the absence of any other evidence showing force used by appellant, we find that the evidence was insufficient to convict appellant of rape." Id. at 484.

In argument before us on the merits of the case, the parties agreed that the issue was whether, in light of the principles of *Hazel,* there was evidence before the jury legally sufficient to prove beyond a reasonable doubt that the intercourse was "[b]y force or threat of force against the will and without the consent" of the victim in violation of Art. 27, § 463 (a) (1)....

[*Hazel* established:]

> "Force is an essential element of the crime and to justify a conviction, the evidence must warrant a conclusion either that the victim resisted and her resistance was overcome by force or that she was prevented from resisting by threats to her safety. But no particular amount of force, either actual or constructive, is required to constitute rape. Necessarily that fact must depend upon the prevailing circumstances. As in this case force may exist without violence. If the acts and threats of the defendant were reasonably calculated to create in the mind of the victim—having regard to the circumstances in which she was placed—a real apprehension, due to fear, of imminent bodily harm, serious enough to impair or overcome her will to resist, then such acts and threats are the equivalent of force." Id. at 469.

As to the element of lack of consent, the Court said in *Hazel:*

"[I]t is true, of course, that however reluctantly given, consent to the act at any time prior to penetration deprives the subsequent intercourse of its criminal character. There is, however, a wide difference between consent and a submission to the act. Consent may involve submission, but submission does not necessarily imply consent. Furthermore, submission to a compelling force, or as a result of being put in fear, is not consent." *Id.*

Hazel did not expressly determine whether the victim's fear must be "reasonable.". . . While *Hazel* made it clear that the victim's fear had to be genuine, it did not pass upon whether a real but unreasonable fear of imminent death or serious bodily harm would suffice. The vast majority of jurisdictions have required that the victim's fear be reasonably grounded in order to obviate the need for either proof of actual force on the part of the assailant or physical resistance on the part of the victim. We think that, generally, this is the correct standard.

As earlier indicated, the Court of Special Appeals held that a showing of a reasonable apprehension of fear was essential under *Hazel* to establish the elements of the offense where the victim did not resist. The Court did not believe, however, that the evidence was legally sufficient to demonstrate the existence of "a reasonable fear" which overcame Pat's ability to resist. . . .

We think the reversal of Rusk's conviction by the Court of Special Appeals was in error for the fundamental reason so well expressed in the dissenting opinion by Judge Wilner when he observed that the majority had "trampled upon the first principle of appellate restraint. . . . [because it had] substituted [its] own view of the evidence (and the inferences that may fairly be drawn from it) for that of the judge and jury. . .[and had thereby] improperly invaded the province allotted to those tribunals." 43 Md. App. at 484–85. In view of the evidence adduced at the trial, the reasonableness of Pat's apprehension of fear was plainly a question of fact for the jury to determine. . . . Applying the constitutional standard of review articulated in *Jackson v. Virginia*, 443 U.S. 307, 319 (1979), i.e.—whether after considering the evidence in the light most favorable to the prosecution, any rational trier of fact could have found the essential elements of the crime beyond a reasonable doubt—it is readily apparent to us that the trier of fact could rationally find that the elements of force and non-consent had been established and that Rusk was guilty of the offense beyond a reasonable doubt. Of course, it was for the jury to observe the witnesses and their demeanor, and to judge their credibility and weigh their testimony. Quite obviously, the jury disbelieved Rusk and believed Pat's testimony. From her testimony, the jury could have reasonably concluded that the taking of her car keys was intended by Rusk to immobilize her alone, late at night, in a neighborhood with which she was not familiar; that after Pat had repeatedly refused to enter his apartment, Rusk commanded in firm tones that she do so; that Pat was badly frightened and feared that Rusk intended to rape her; that unable to think clearly and believing that she had no other choice in the circumstances, Pat entered Rusk's apartment; that once inside Pat asked permission to leave but Rusk told her to stay; that he then pulled Pat by the arms to the bed and undressed her; that Pat was afraid that Rusk would kill her unless she submitted, that she began to cry and Rusk then put his hands on her throat and began " 'lightly to choke' " her; that Pat asked him if he would let her go without killing her if she complied with his demands; that Rusk gave an affirmative response, after which she finally submitted.

Just where persuasion ends and force begins in cases like the present is essentially a factual issue, to be resolved in light of the controlling legal precepts. That threats of force need not be made in any particular manner in order to put a person in fear of bodily harm is well established. Indeed, conduct, rather than words, may convey the threat. That a victim did not scream out for help or attempt to escape, while bearing on the question of consent, is unnecessary where she is restrained by fear of violence.

Considering all of the evidence in the case, with particular focus upon the actual force applied by Rusk to Pat's neck, we conclude that the jury could rationally find that the essential elements of second degree rape had been established and that Rusk was guilty of that offense beyond a reasonable doubt.

Judgment of the Court of Special Appeals reversed; case remanded to that court with directions that it affirm the judgment of the Criminal Court of Baltimore; costs to be paid by the appellee.

[HARRY A.] COLE, J. dissenting.

I agree with the Court of Special Appeals that the evidence adduced at the trial of Edward Salvatore Rusk was insufficient to convict him of rape. I, therefore, respectfully dissent.

The standard of appellate review in deciding a question of sufficiency, as the majority correctly notes, is "whether, after viewing the evidence in the light most favorable to the prosecution, *any* rational trier of fact could have found the essential elements of the crime beyond a reasonable doubt." *Jackson v. Virginia* (emphasis in original.). However, it is equally well settled that when one of the essential elements of crime is not sustained by the evidence, the conviction of the defendant cannot stand as a matter of law.

The majority, in applying this standard, concludes that "[i]n view of the evidence adduced at the trial, the reasonableness of Pat's apprehension of fear was plainly a question of fact for the jury to determine." In so concluding, the majority has skipped over the crucial issue. It seems to me that whether the prosecutrix's fear is reasonable becomes a question only after the court determines that the defendant's conduct under the circumstances was reasonably calculated to give rise to a fear on her part to the extent that she was unable to resist. In other words, the fear must stem from his articulable conduct, and equally, if not more importantly, cannot be inconsistent with her own contemporaneous reaction to that conduct. The conduct of the defendant, in and of itself, must clearly indicate force or the threat of force such as to overpower the prosecutrix's ability to resist or will to resist. In my view, there is no evidence to support the majority's conclusion that the prosecutrix was forced to submit to sexual intercourse, certainly not fellatio. . . .

[Fifty years of precedents from rape cases around the country] make plain that *Hazel* intended to require clear and cognizable evidence of force or the threat of force sufficient to overcome or prevent resistance by the female before there would arise a jury question of whether the prosecutrix had a reasonable apprehension of harm. The majority today departs from this requirement and places its imprimatur on the female's conclusory statements that she was in fear, as sufficient to support a conviction of rape.

My examination of the evidence in a light most favorable to the State reveals no conduct by the defendant reasonably calculated to cause the prosecutrix to be so fearful that she should fail to resist and thus, the element of force is lacking in the State's proof.

Here we have a full grown married woman who meets the defendant in a bar under friendly circumstances. They drink and talk together. She agrees to give him a ride home in her car. When they arrive at his house, located in an area with which she was unfamiliar but which was certainly not isolated, he invites her to come up to his apartment and she refuses. According to her testimony he takes her keys, walks around to her side of the car, and says "Now will you come up?" She answers, "yes." The majority suggests that "from her testimony the jury could have reasonably concluded that the taking of her keys was intended by Rusk to immobilize her alone, late at night, in a neighborhood with which she was unfamiliar. . . ." But on what facts does the majority so conclude? There is no evidence descriptive of the tone of his voice; her testimony indicates only the bare statement quoted above. How can the majority extract from this conduct a threat reasonably calculated to create a fear of imminent bodily harm? There was no weapon, no threat to inflict physical injury.

She also testified that she was afraid of "the way he looked," and afraid of his statement, "come on up, come on up." But what can the majority conclude from this statement coupled with a "look" that remained undescribed? There is no evidence whatsoever to suggest that this was anything other than a pattern of conduct consistent with the *ordinary seduction* of a female acquaintance who at first suggests her disinclination. . . (emphasis added—AU).

She then testified that she started to cry and he "started lightly to choke" her, whatever that means. Obviously, the choking was not of any persuasive significance. During this "choking" she was able to talk. She said "If I do what you want will you let me go?" It was at this point that the defendant said yes.

I find it incredible for the majority to conclude that on these facts, without more, a woman was *forced* to commit oral sex upon the defendant and then to engage in vaginal intercourse. [Emphasis in original.] In the absence of any verbal threat to do her grievous bodily harm or the display of any weapon and threat to use it, I find it difficult to understand how a victim could participate in these sexual activities and not be willing.

What was the nature and extent of her fear anyhow?. . . She was afraid because she didn't know him and she was afraid he was going to "rape" her. But there are no acts or conduct on the part of the defendant to suggest that these fears were created by the defendant or that he made any objective, identifiable threats to her which would give rise to this woman's failure to flee, summon help, scream, or make physical resistance.

As the defendant well knew, this was not a child. This was a married woman with children, a woman familiar with the social setting in which these two actors met. It was an ordinary city street, not an isolated spot. He had not forced his way into her car; he had not taken advantage of a difference in years or any state of intoxication or mental or physical incapacity on her part. He did not grapple with her. She got out of the car, *walked with him* across the street and *followed* him up the stairs to his room. She certainly had to realize that they were not going upstairs to play *Scrabble*. . . . [Emphasis original]

The record does not disclose the basis for this young woman's misgivings about her experience with the defendant. The only substantive fear she had was that she would be late arriving home. The objective facts make it inherently

> improbable that the defendant's conduct generated any fear for her physical well-being.
>
> In my judgment the State failed to prove the essential element of force beyond a reasonable doubt and, therefore, the judgment of conviction should be reversed.
>
> Judges Smith and Digges have authorized me to state that they concur in the views expressed herein.

Case Questions

1. If Rusk's actions were not calculated by him to instill enough fear in Pat that she comply with his demands, why did he lie about what happened? If it is Pat who is lying, why wouldn't she just claim that he threatened to kill her?

2. Pat said, "No," several times to Rusk's invitations and even begged for her keys and cried, but she complied with his commands to undress, etc. The dissent concedes that this behavior might be accurately characterized as "unwilling" submission, but says this does not amount to rape. If sex against a person's will is not rape, then what is? Should a reasonable man in Rusk's situation believe that Pat had become willing to have sex? The dissent says that for a rape to be proven, there must be evidence of "resistance beyond mere words." (See italics.) Do you agree? Should weeping count as "beyond mere words"? Does Rusk's behavior strike you as "ordinary seduction"? (See italics.)

3. Does the scenario between Pat and Ed Rusk strike you as materially different from the following hypothetical, and, if so, in what respects?

> A carjacker opens a woman's car door at a red light, grabs her keys, and demands that she get out. (No weapon is displayed.) She tells him she is terrified of being on foot in this neighborhood late at night and she will do anything he asks if he just gives her back her car keys. He says, "OK, come with me." He drives her to his nearby apartment where they go in, have sex, and then he gives her back her car keys, and she leaves. She reports him to the police, who arrest him.

In the Interest of M.T.S. (1992)

Eleven years after *Rusk*, the New Jersey Supreme Court issued a landmark opinion on the issue of resistance. This case involved not a felony trial but a delinquency proceeding. Fifteen-year-old C.G. was living with her mother, three siblings, and two temporary residents, 17-year-old M.T.S. and his girlfriend. One evening, M.T.S. told C.G. that he would visit her in her room that night; she thought he was teasing. According to her testimony, she woke early that morning to find M.T.S. on top of her, penetrating her. She told her mother, who kicked the boy out of the house. Mother and daughter filed a complaint with the police. Charged with sexual assault, M.T.S. claimed that the sex was consensual. The trial court ruled that he was delinquent, but an appeals court reversed on the grounds that the finding of second-degree assault required evidence of force beyond penetration itself, which was lacking here.

IN THE INTEREST OF M.T.S.
129 N.J. 422; 609 A.2d 1266 (1992)

HANDLER, JUSTICE.

Under New Jersey law a person who commits an act of sexual penetration using physical force or coercion is guilty of second-degree sexual assault. The sexual assault statute does not define the words "physical force." The question posed by this appeal is whether the element of "physical force" is met simply by an act of non-consensual penetration involving no more force than necessary to accomplish that result.

That issue is presented in the context of what is often referred to as "acquaintance rape." The record in the case discloses that the juvenile, a seventeen-year-old boy, engaged in consensual kissing and heavy petting with a fifteen-year-old girl and thereafter engaged in actual sexual penetration of the girl to which she had not consented. There was no evidence or suggestion that the juvenile used any unusual or extra force or threats to accomplish the act of penetration. . . .

I

The issues in this case are perplexing and controversial. We must explain the role of force in the contemporary crime of sexual assault and then define its essential features. We then must consider what evidence is probative to establish the commission of a sexual assault. The factual circumstances of this case expose the complexity and sensitivity of those issues and underscore the analytic difficulty of those seemingly-straight-forward legal questions. . . .

At trial, C.G. and M.T.S. offered very different accounts. . .She [C.G.] testified that M.T.S. had attempted to kiss her on numerous other occasions. . .but that she had rejected all of his previous advances. . . .M.T.S. testified that during the three days preceding the incident they had been "kissing and necking" and had discussed having sexual intercourse, and [she had] often encouraged him to "make a surprise visit up in her room." [When she] returned from the bathroom [on the night that he entered her bedroom],... the two began "kissing and all," eventually moving to the bed. Once they were in bed, he said, they undressed each other and continued to kiss and touch for about five minutes [and that for the first three thrusts, she indicated no sign of non-consent to the penetration]....

II

The New Jersey Code of Criminal Justice, *N.J.S.A.* 2C:14–2c(1), defines "sexual assault" as the commission "of sexual penetration" "with another person" with the use of "physical force or coercion." An unconstrained reading of the statutory language indicates that both the act of "sexual penetration" and the use of "physical force or coercion" are separate and distinct elements of the offense. *See Medical Soc. v. Department of Law & Pub. Safety*, 120 N.J. 18, 26, 575 A.2d 1348 (1990) (declaring that no part of a statute should be considered meaningless or superfluous). Neither the definitions section of *N.J.S.A.* 2C:14–1 to –8, nor the remainder of the Code of Criminal Justice provides assistance in interpreting the words "physical force." The initial inquiry is, therefore, whether the statutory words are unambiguous on their face and can be understood and applied in accordance with their plain meaning. The answer to that inquiry is revealed by the conflicting decisions of the lower courts and the arguments of the opposing parties. The trial court held that "physical force" had been established by the sexual penetration of the victim without her consent. The Appellate Division believed that the statute requires some amount of force more than that necessary to accomplish penetration.

The parties offer two alternative understandings of the concept of "physical force" as it is used in the statute. The State would read "physical force" to entail any amount of sexual touching brought about involuntarily. A showing of sexual penetration coupled with a lack of consent would satisfy the elements of the statute. The Public Defender urges an interpretation of "physical force" to mean force "used to overcome lack of consent." That definition equates force with violence and leads to the conclusion that sexual assault requires the application of some amount of force in addition to the act of penetration.

...When a statute is open to conflicting interpretations, the court seeks the underlying intent of the legislature, relying on legislative history and the contemporary context of the statute. *Monmouth County v. Wissell*, 68 N.J. 35, 41–42, 342 A.2d 199 (1975). With respect to a law, like the sexual assault statute, that "alters or amends the previous law or creates or abolishes types of actions, it is important, in discovering the legislative intent, to ascertain the old law, the mischief and the proposed remedy." *Grobart v. Grobart*, 5 N.J. 161, 166, 74 A.2d 294 (1950.) We also remain mindful of the basic tenet of statutory construction that penal statutes are to be strictly construed in favor of the accused. Nevertheless, the construction must conform to the intent of the Legislature.

The provisions proscribing sexual offenses found in the Code of Criminal Justice, *N.J.S.A.* 2C:14–2c(1), became effective in 1979, and were written against almost two hundred years of rape law in New Jersey. The origin of the rape statute that the current statutory offense of sexual assault replaced can be traced to the English common law. Under the common law, rape was defined as "carnal knowledge of a woman against her will." . . .As of 1796, New Jersey statutory law defined rape as "carnal knowledge of a woman, forcibly and against her will." Crimes Act of March 18, 1796 § 8, *N.J.Rev.Laws* (Pennington) 246. Those three elements of rape—carnal knowledge, forcibly, and against her will—remained the essential elements of the crime until 1979. Under traditional rape law, in order to prove that a rape had occurred, the state had to show both that force had been used and that the penetration had been against the woman's will. Force was identified and determined not as an independent factor but in relation to the response of the victim, which in turn implicated the victim's own state of mind. "Thus, the perpetrator's use of force became criminal only if the victim's state of mind met the statutory requirement. The perpetrator could use all the force imaginable and no crime would be committed if the state could not prove additionally that the victim did not consent." National Institute of Law Enforcement and Criminal Justice, *Forcible Rape—An Analysis of Legal Issues* 5 (March 1978) (*Forcible Rape*). Although the terms "non-consent" and "against her will" were often treated as equivalent, see, *e.g., Wilson v. State*, 109 A.2d 381 (Del.1954), *cert. den.*, 348 U.S. 983 (1955), under the traditional definition of rape, both formulations squarely placed on the victim the burden of proof and of action. Effectively, a woman who was above the age of consent had actively and affirmatively to withdraw that consent for the intercourse to be against her will. As a Delaware court stated, "If sexual intercourse is obtained by milder means, or with the consent or silent submission of the female, it cannot constitute the crime of rape." *State v. Brown*, 83 A. 1083, 1084 (O.T. 1912).

The presence or absence of consent often turned on credibility. To demonstrate that the victim had not consented to the intercourse, and also that sufficient force had been used to accomplish the rape, the state had to prove that the victim had resisted. According to the oft-quoted Lord Hale, to be deemed a credible witness, a woman had to be of good fame, disclose the injury immediately, suffer signs of injury, and cry out for help. 1 Matthew Hale, *History of the Pleas of the Crown* 633 (1st ed. 1847). Courts and commentators historically distrusted the testimony of victims, "assuming that women lie about their lack of consent for various reasons: to blackmail men, to explain the discovery of a consensual affair, or because of psychological illness." *Offender's Forceful Conduct*, 56 *Geo. Wash.L.Rev.* at 403. Evidence of resistance was viewed as a solution to the credibility problem; it was the "outward manifestation of nonconsent, [a] device for determining whether a woman actually gave consent." Note, *The Resistance Standard in Rape Legislation*, 18 *Stan.L.Rev.* 680, 689 (1966).

The resistance requirement had a profound effect on the kind of conduct that could be deemed criminal and on the type of evidence needed to establish the crime. Courts assumed that any woman who was forced to have intercourse against her will necessarily would resist to the extent of her ability. In many jurisdictions the requirement was that the woman have resisted to the utmost.... "[A] mere tactical surrender in the face of an assumed superior physical force is not enough. Where the penalty for the defendant may be supreme, so must resistance be unto the uttermost." *Moss v. State*, 208 Miss. 531, 45 *So.*2d 125, 126 (1950). Other states followed a "reasonableness" standard, while some required only sufficient resistance to make non-consent reasonably manifest.

At least by the 1960s courts in New Jersey followed a standard for establishing resistance that was somewhat less drastic than the traditional rule. In *State v. Harris*, 70 *N.J.Super.* 9, 174 *A.*2d 645 (1961), the Appellate Division recognized that the "to the uttermost" test was obsolete. *Id.* at 16. "The fact that a victim finally submits does not necessarily imply that she consented. Submission to a compelling force, or as a result of being put in fear, is not consent." *Id.* at 16-17. Nonetheless, the "resistance" requirement remained an essential feature of New Jersey rape law....

The judicial interpretation of the pre-reform rape law in New Jersey, with its insistence on resistance by the victim, greatly minimized the importance of the forcible and assaultive aspect of the defendant's conduct. Rape prosecutions turned then not so much on the forcible or assaultive character of the defendant's actions as on the nature of the victim's response. Under the prereform law, the resistance offered had to be "in good faith and without pretense, with an active determination to prevent the violation of her person, and must not be merely passive and perfunctory." *State v. Terry*, 89 *N.J.Super.* at 450, 215 *A.*2d 374. That the law put the rape victim on trial was clear.

The resistance requirement had another untoward influence on traditional rape law. Resistance was necessary not only to prove non-consent but also to demonstrate that the force used by the defendant had been sufficient to overcome the victim's will. . . .Resistance, often demonstrated by torn clothing and blood, was a sign that the defendant had used significant force to accomplish the sexual intercourse. Thus, if the defendant forced himself on a woman, it was her responsibility to fight back, because force was measured in relation to the resistance she put forward. Only if she resisted, causing him to use more force than was necessary to achieve penetration, would his conduct be criminalized. *See, e.g., Moss v. State,* 45 *So.*2d at 125. Indeed, the significance of resistance as the proxy for force is illustrated by cases in which victims were unable to resist; in such cases the force incident to penetration was deemed sufficient to establish the "force" element of the offense. . . .

To refute the misguided belief that rape was not real unless the victim fought back, reformers emphasized empirical research indicating that women who resisted forcible intercourse often suffered far more serious injury as a result. . . .The research also helped demonstrate the underlying point of the reformers that the crime of rape rested not in the overcoming of a woman's will or the insult to her chastity but in the forcible attack itself—the assault on her person. Reformers criticized the conception of rape as a distinctly sexual crime rather than a crime of violence. They emphasized that rape had its legal origins in laws designed to protect the property rights of men to their wives and daughters. Although the crime had evolved into an offense against women, reformers argued that vestiges of the old law remained, particularly in the understanding of rape as a crime against the purity or chastity of a woman. The burden of protecting that chastity fell on the woman, with the state offering its protection only after the woman demonstrated that she had resisted sufficiently.

. . .Critics of rape law agreed that the focus of the crime should be shifted from the victim's behavior to the defendant's conduct, and particularly to its forceful and assaultive, rather than sexual, character. Reformers also shared the goals of facilitating rape prosecutions and of sparing victims much of the degradation involved in bringing and trying a charge of rape. There were, however, differences over the best way to redefine the crime. Some reformers advocated a standard that defined rape as unconsented-to sexual intercourse; others urged the elimination of any reference to consent from the definition of rape. Nonetheless, all proponents of reform shared a central premise: that the burden of showing non-consent should not fall on the victim of the crime. In dealing with the problem of consent the reform goal was not so much to purge the entire concept of consent from the law as to eliminate the burden that had been placed on victims to prove they had not consented.

Similarly, with regard to force, rape law reform sought to give independent significance to the forceful or assaultive conduct of the defendant and to avoid a definition of force that depended on the reaction of the victim. Traditional interpretations of force were strongly criticized for failing to acknowledge that force may be understood simply as the invasion of "bodily integrity." In urging that the "resistance" requirement be abandoned, reformers sought to break the connection between force and resistance.

III

The history of traditional rape law sheds clearer light on the factors that became most influential in the enactment of current law dealing with sexual offenses. The circumstances surrounding the actual passage of the current law reveal that it was conceived as a reform measure reconstituting the law to address a widely-sensed evil and to effectuate an important public policy. Those circumstances are highly relevant in understanding legislative intent...

The new statutory provisions covering rape were formulated by a coalition of feminist groups assisted by the National Organization of Women (NOW) National Task Force on Rape. Both houses of the Legislature adopted the NOW bill, as it was called, without major changes and Governor Byrne signed it into law on August 10, 1978. The NOW bill had been modeled after the 1976 Philadelphia Center for Rape Concern Model Sex Offense Statute. The Model Sex Offense Statute in turn had been based on selected provisions of the Michigan Criminal Sexual Conduct Statute, *Mich.Stat.Ann.* § 28.788(4)(b) (Callaghan 1990), [M.C.L.A. § 750.520d] and on the reform statutes in New Mexico, Minnesota, and Wisconsin. The stated intent of the drafters of the Philadelphia Center's Model Statute had been to remove all features found to be contrary to the interests of rape victims. John M. Cannel, *New Jersey Criminal Code Annotated* 279 (1991). According to its proponents the statute would " 'normalize the law. We are no longer saying rape victims are likely to lie. What we are saying is that rape is just like other violent crimes.' " (Roberta Kaufman, New Jersey Coalition Against Rape).

Since the 1978 reform, the Code has referred to the crime that was once known as "rape" as "sexual assault." The crime now requires "penetration," not "sexual intercourse." It requires "force" or "coercion," not "submission" or "resistance." It emphasizes the assaultive character of the offense by defining sexual penetration to encompass a wide range of sexual contacts, going well beyond traditional "carnal knowledge."[2] Consistent with the assaultive character, as opposed to the traditional sexual character, of the offense, the statute also renders the crime gender-neutral: both males and females can be actors or victims. The reform statute defines sexual assault as penetration accomplished by the use of "physical force" or "coercion," but it does not define either "physical force" or "coercion" or enumerate examples of evidence that would establish those elements. Some reformers had argued that defining "physical force" too specifically in the sexual offense statute might have the effect of limiting force to the enumerated examples. The task of defining "physical force" therefore was left to the courts. . . .

The Legislature's concept of sexual assault and the role of force was significantly colored by its understanding of the law of assault and battery. As a general matter, criminal battery is defined as "the unlawful application of force to the person of another." The application of force is criminal when it results in either (a) a physical injury or (b) an offensive touching. . . . Any "unauthorized touching of another [is] a battery." Thus, by eliminating all references to the victim's state of mind and conduct, and by broadening the definition of penetration to cover not only sexual intercourse between a man and a woman but a range of acts that invade another's body or compel intimate contact, the Legislature emphasized the affinity between sexual assault and other forms of assault and battery.

The intent of the Legislature to redefine rape consistent with the law of assault and battery is further evidenced by the legislative treatment of other sexual crimes less serious than and derivative of traditional rape. The Code redefined the offense of criminal sexual contact to emphasize the involuntary and personally-offensive nature of the touching. *N.J.S.A.* 2C:14-1(d). Sexual contact is criminal under the same circumstances that render an act of sexual penetration a sexual assault, namely, when "physical force" or "coercion" demonstrates that it is unauthorized and offensive. *N.J.S.A.* 2C:14-3(b). Thus, just as any unauthorized touching is a crime under traditional laws of assault and battery, so is any unauthorized sexual contact a crime under the reformed law of criminal sexual contact, and so is any unauthorized sexual penetration a crime under the reformed law of sexual assault.

The understanding of sexual assault as a criminal battery, albeit one with especially serious consequences, follows necessarily from the Legislature's decision to eliminate nonconsent and resistance from the substantive definition of the offense. Under the new law, the victim no longer is required to resist and therefore need not have said or done anything in order for the sexual penetration to be unlawful. The alleged victim is not put on trial, and his or her responsive or defensive behavior is rendered immaterial. We are thus satisfied that an interpretation of the statutory crime of sexual assault to require physical force in addition to that entailed in an act of involuntary or unwanted sexual penetration would be fundamentally inconsistent with the legislative purpose to eliminate any consideration of whether the victim resisted or expressed non-consent.

We note that the contrary interpretation of force—that the element of force need be extrinsic to the sexual act—would not only reintroduce a resistance requirement into the sexual assault law, but also would immunize many acts of criminal sexual *contact* short of penetration. The characteristics that make a sexual contact unlawful are the same as those that make a sexual penetration unlawful. An actor is guilty of criminal sexual contact if he or she commits an act of sexual contact with another using "physical force" or "coercion." *N.J.S.A.* 2C:14-3(b). That the Legislature would have wanted to decriminalize unauthorized sexual intrusions on the bodily integrity of a victim by requiring a showing of force in addition to that entailed in the sexual contact itself is hardly possible.

Because the statute eschews any reference to the victim's will or resistance, the standard defining the role of force in sexual penetration must prevent the possibility that the establishment of the crime will turn on the alleged victim's state of mind or responsive behavior. We conclude, therefore, that any act of sexual penetration engaged in by the defendant without the affirmative and freely-given permission of the victim to the specific act of penetration constitutes the offense of sexual assault. Therefore, physical force in excess of that inherent in the act of sexual penetration is not required for such penetration to be unlawful. The definition of "physical force" is satisfied under *N.J.S.A.* 2C:14-2c(1) if the defendant applies any amount of force against another person in the absence of what a reasonable person would believe to be affirmative and freely-given permission to the act of sexual penetration.

Under the reformed statute, permission to engage in sexual penetration must be affirmative and it must be given freely, but that permission may be inferred either from acts or statements reasonably viewed in light of the surrounding circumstances....Permission to engage in an act of sexual penetration can be and indeed often is indicated through physical actions rather than words. Permission is demonstrated when the evidence, in whatever form, is sufficient to demonstrate that a reasonable person would have believed that the alleged victim had affirmatively and freely given authorization to the act.

...The Legislature recast the law of rape as sexual assault to bring that area of law in line with the expectation of privacy and bodily control that long has characterized most of our private and public law. In interpreting "physical force" to include any touching that occurs without permission we seek to respect that goal.

Today the law of sexual assault is indispensable to the system of legal rules that assures each of us the right to decide who may touch our bodies, when, and under what circumstances. The decision to engage in sexual relations with another person is one of the most private and intimate decisions a person can make. Each person has the right not only to decide whether to engage in sexual contact with another, but also to control the circumstances and character of that contact. No one, neither a spouse, nor a friend, nor an acquaintance, nor a stranger, has the right or the privilege to force sexual contact. *See Definition of Forcible Rape*, 61 *Va.L.Rev.* at 1529 (arguing that "forcible rape is viewed as a heinous crime primarily because it is a violent assault on a person's bodily security, particularly degrading because that person is forced to submit to an act of the most intimate nature")....

IV

In a case such as this one, in which the State does not allege violence or force extrinsic to the act of penetration, the factfinder must decide whether the defendant's act of penetration was undertaken in circumstances that led the defendant reasonably to believe that the alleged victim had freely given affirmative permission to the specific act of sexual penetration. Such permission can be indicated either through words or through actions that, when viewed in the light of all the surrounding circumstances, would demonstrate to a reasonable person affirmative and freely-given authorization for the specific act of sexual penetration.

In applying that standard to the facts in these cases, the focus of attention must be on the nature of the defendant's actions. The role of the factfinder is not to decide whether reasonable people may engage in acts of penetration without the permission of others. The Legislature answered that question when it enacted the reformed sexual assault statute: reasonable people do not engage in acts of penetration without permission, and it is unlawful to do so. The role of the factfinder is to decide not whether engaging in an act of penetration without permission of another person is reasonable, but only whether the defendant's belief that the alleged victim had freely given affirmative permission was reasonable.

In these cases neither the alleged victim's subjective state of mind nor the reasonableness of the alleged victim's actions can be deemed relevant to the offense. The alleged victim may be questioned about what he or she did or said only to determine whether the defendant was reasonable in believing that affirmative permission had been freely given. To repeat, the law places no burden on the alleged victim to have expressed non-consent or to have denied permission, and no inquiry is made into what he or she thought or desired or why he or she did not resist or protest.

In short, in order to convict under the sexual assault statute in cases such as these, the State must prove beyond a reasonable doubt that there was sexual penetration and that it was accomplished without the affirmative and freely-given permission of the alleged victim. As we have indicated, such proof can be based on evidence of conduct or words in light of surrounding circumstances and must demonstrate beyond a reasonable doubt that a reasonable person would not have believed that there was affirmative and freely-given permission. If there is evidence to suggest that the defendant reasonably believed that such permission had been given, the State must demonstrate either that defendant did not actually believe that affirmative permission had been freely-given or that such a belief was unreasonable under all of the circumstances. Thus, the State bears the burden of proof throughout the case.

In. . .any defense based on consent [*See N.J.S.A.* 2C:2–10c(3)] [t]he definition of "permission" serves to define the "consent" that otherwise might allow a defendant to avoid criminal liability. Because "physical force" as an element of sexual assault in this context requires the *absence* of affirmative and freely-given permission, . . .a defense based on consent would require the *presence* of such affirmative and freely-given permission. Any lesser form of consent would render the sexual penetration unlawful and cannot constitute a defense.

In this case, the Appellate Division concluded that non-consensual penetration accomplished with no additional physical force or coercion is not criminalized under the sexual assault statute. 247 *N.J.Super.* at 260. It acknowledged that its conclusion was "anomalous" because it recognized that "a woman has every right to end [physically intimate] activity without sexual penetration." *Ibid*. Thus, it added to its holding that "[e]ven the force of penetration might . . . be sufficient if it is shown to be employed to overcome the victim's unequivocal expressed desire to limit the encounter." *Ibid.*

The Appellate Division was correct in recognizing that a woman's right to end intimate activity without penetration is a protectable right the violation of which can be a criminal offense. However, it misperceived the purpose of the statute in believing that the only way that right can be protected is by the woman's unequivocally-expressed desire to end the activity. The effect of that requirement would be to import into the sexual assault statute the notion that an assault occurs only if the victim's will is overcome, and thus to reintroduce the requirement of non-consent and victim-resistance as a constituent material element of the crime. Under the reformed statute, a person's failure to protest or resist cannot be considered or used as justification for bodily invasion.

We acknowledge that cases such as this are inherently fact sensitive and depend on the reasoned judgment and common sense of judges and juries. The trial court concluded that the victim had not expressed consent to the act of intercourse, either through her words or actions. We conclude that the record provides reasonable support for the trial court's disposition.

Accordingly, we reverse the judgment of the Appellate Division and reinstate the disposition of juvenile delinquency for the commission of second-degree sexual assault.

Opinion Footnotes

2 The reform replaced the concept of carnal abuse, which was limited to vaginal intercourse, with specific kinds of sexual acts contained in a broad definition of penetration: "Sexual penetration means vaginal intercourse, cunnilingus, fellatio or anal intercourse between persons or insertion of the hand, finger or object into the anus or vagina either by the actor or upon the actor's instruction." [*N.J.S.A.* 2C:14–1.]

Case Questions

1. New Jersey's legislature and its highest court have determined that verdicts in rape cases must depend on the defendant's behavior, and not the behavior of the alleged victim. Suppose that rule had been in force throughout the United States when *Michael M.*, *Goldberg*, and *Rusk* were decided. How might the decisions have differed? What functions do comments about the victims serve in the opinions we have read?

2. Whether the crime is rape or sexual assault, the concept of "consent" is crucial. What does this reveal about past and present societal attitudes about sex? Does one partner initiate sex and the other partner consent? Can such a rule be gender-neutral?

Rape law is reformed one state at a time. The following essay focuses on the remaining problems in states that have not moved in the reform direction taken by New Jersey.

FROM STEPHEN J. SCHULHOFER, *UNWANTED SEX: THE CULTURE OF INTIMIDATION AND THE FAILURE OF LAW*[20]

...Of all our rights and liberties, few are as important as our right to choose freely whether and when we will become sexually intimate with another person. Yet, as far as the law is concerned, this right—the right to sexual autonomy—doesn't exist. Citizens simply do not have a legally recognized claim to protection of their freedom of sexual choice.

The law of rape suffers from well-known practical limitations. But even under the best of circumstances, its coverage is narrow. It prohibits sex with children or unconscious adults, but in nearly all other situations it protects our sexual freedom *only* against interference by compelling physical force....

When a woman makes a hard choice and accepts sexual intimacy under the pressure of implicit threats or because a doctor or lawyer abused her trust, the law finds valid consent. But legal protection of autonomy is more limited yet, because the law doesn't require evidence that the woman ever made a choice at all; it treats silence and passivity as equivalent to consent. Sometimes, even today, the law finds consent in the face of a woman's explicit protests; "no" doesn't necessarily mean no. And the law doesn't unequivocally prohibit men from using force. The law only prohibits the use of *too much* force, force beyond the physical acts associated with assertive male sexuality. As a result, even when a woman is silent, reluctant, pushing a man back or saying "no," the law doesn't prohibit what it considers "normal" force—hugging, pulling, lifting a woman up, pushing her down, rolling her on her back, pulling off her clothes, and physically penetrating her body. In effect, the law permits men to assume that a woman is always willing to have sex, even with a stranger, even with substantial physical force, unless the evidence shows unambiguously that she was *un*willing....

The interest that law most often devalues or ignores is...the right to choose freely whether to decline a sexual encounter. Law's stinting approach to that facet of autonomy...is the expression of current law's deep commitment to supporting—and never chilling—an interest that seems of overriding importance, especially to men: the freedom to seek sex with any potential partner who might be interested or even reluctant but persuadable....

The costs of this system of unrestricted freedom fall most directly on the many individuals, mostly women, who are the target of sexual advances initiated by their superiors at work or by their teachers, doctors, dentists, psychotherapists, and lawyers....The consequences of law's refusal to protect both facets of autonomy—the right to seek intimacy and the right to refuse it—reach further still, touching flagrant sexual abuse as well. A man can accost a stranger in a remote place, lift her off the ground, carry her into the woods, pull her pants down, and have sex with her. He commits no crime because the woman, paralyzed with fear, never resisted....

Sexual autonomy deserves to be protected directly and for its own sake, not with hesitation or apology, nor with irritation at victims who aren't able to help themselves. It is time to recognize sexual autonomy as an essential component of the freedoms that society properly guarantees and supports for every human being.

Marital Rape

The next two articles discuss the decline, fall, and possible future of the spousal exception.

FROM LISA ESKOW, "THE ULTIMATE WEAPON? DEMYTHOLOGIZING SPOUSAL RAPE..."[21]

Contemporary rape statutes reflect the tenacity of the marital rape exemption. The classic legal definition of rape is: "an act of sexual intercourse accomplished with a person not the spouse of a perpetrator..." In 1981, ten states [still] barred prosecutions of husbands for marital rape. By 1990, no state retained an absolute marital rape exemption, although thirty-five states placed limits on the prosecution of marital rapists. Such prosecutorial restrictions included non-cohabitation or aggravated force requirements, ceilings on punishment, specifications on when—and to whom—marital rape must be reported, and the creation of alternative, frequently misdemeanor, sexual assault statutes that applied when criminal behavior otherwise classifiable as felony rape happened to be perpetrated by a spouse. Within one year, ten of those thirty-five states revoked or revised these provisions. By 1994, twenty-four states had abolished any form of marital rape exemption—either through legislative reform or judicial interpretation of existing statutes. Nevertheless, at least thirteen states still offer preferential or disparate treatment to perpetrators of spousal sexual assault. Marital rape laws are in a constant state of flux; in March 1995, Laura X, Director of the National Clearinghouse on Marital and Date Rape, estimated that marital rape related bills were pending in twenty-eight states.

However, not all recent legislative reform aims to revoke the marital exemption's "raping license." Several states have actually extended their exemptions to include non-married, cohabiting couples. For example, cohabitation is an affirmative defense to rape in Connecticut, regardless of the legal status of the relationship between the victim and the defendant. One of the more egregious examples of a legal "raping license" appears in Delaware, where a "voluntary social companion" exemption impedes prosecution of men who engage in non-consensual sex with "a victim who is in the defendant's company on the occasion of the offense as a result of the victim's exercise of rational intellect and free will, without trick, coercion or duress" and who has engaged in consensual sex with the defendant within the past year. Such expansions of the marital rape exemption into other forms of domestic and social relationships reveal the persistent legal and cultural obstacles to securing women's sexual autonomy, not only in marriage, but also in society generally.

[Note: This "companion exemption" law that Eskow is criticizing was removed from the Delaware code, after this article was published. Delaware formerly defined certain offenses as lesser degrees of "unlawful sexual conduct" if the victim had been a "voluntary social companion" of the perpetrator.—AU.]

KELLY C. CONNERTON, "COMMENT: THE RESURGENCE OF THE MARITAL RAPE EXEMPTION: THE VICTIMIZATION OF TEENS BY THEIR STATUTORY RAPISTS"[22]

...Legally, the [marital] license to rape no longer exists. In practice, however, obstacles remain in the way of enforcing this supposed abolition, and many reforms continue to confer preferential treatment upon rapists who happen to be the husband of their victim. Not all states are aiming to nullify the license to rape that a marriage license has previously conferred. Moreover, if not explicitly aiming to nullify the exemption, implicit sanctioning results when states fail to treat appropriately the marital rape exemption as a crime.

> Failing to criminalize the spousal exemption in some states has extended the exemption to cohabiting couples and voluntary social companions. Such an extension also can be seen in the limits placed on the prosecution of husband rapists, which confer preferential treatment upon husbands, while disparately implementing stringent requirements of proof upon the victims. For instance, South Carolina's criminal sexual conduct statute specifically addresses the situation of the victim as the legal spouse and demonstrates the effects from the exemption. It reads, in relevant part, that "[a] person cannot be guilty of criminal sexual conduct. . .if the victim is the legal spouse unless the couple is living apart . . . ." It also burdens the victim spouse with the requirement of reporting the rape "to appropriate law enforcement authorities within thirty days in order for a person to be prosecuted for these offenses," when the ordinary reporting requirement is usually a year. Thus, remnants of the spousal exemption have survived the recent trend to repeal the exemption.

As of 2018, eight states still have some form of martial rape exemption.[23] Most of these states classify marital rape as distinct from other forms of rape which sends an implicit signal that rapes within marriage are substantively different from "real" rapes. For example, Ohio's marital rape statute requires that there be proof of "force or threat of force" as opposed to coercion in order for the violation to be considered rape.[24] When states establish different standards for marital rape versus rape it not only sanctions coercive sex within marriage that would not be permissible outside of it, but maintains the outdated stereotype that men are free to press sex on their wives as part of the institution of marriage.

FEMINISTS DIVIDE OVER PORNOGRAPHY

Until the (post-1965) second wave of feminism (the first wave having been the suffrage movement), there were two sides to the debate over the censorship of sexually explicit material. The proponents of obscenity laws insisted that limitations on freedom of expression were necessary to preserve sexual morality and insure the welfare of society.[25] The opponents insisted that these concerns were outweighed by the value of free expression.[26] Feminists brought a third argument into the debate: the idea that pornography injured women by legitimating sexual violence toward them, reinforcing male supremacy, and generally limiting their opportunities in life by encouraging men to view them as merely sex objects. But not all feminists agreed—not even all prominent feminist law professors including Catharine MacKinnon and Nadine Strossen who have taken sharply opposed positions. Excerpts from their debate follow.

CATHARINE A. MACKINNON, FROM *ONLY WORDS*[27]

Imagine that...you grow up with your father holding you down covering your mouth so another man can make a horrible, searing pain between your legs. When you are older, your husband ties you to the bed and drips hot wax on your nipples and brings in other men to watch and makes you smile through it. Your doctor will not give you drugs he has addicted you to unless you suck his penis.

You cannot tell anyone. When you try to speak of these things, you are told it did not happen, you imagined it, you wanted it, you enjoyed it. Books say this. No books say what happened to you. Law says this. No law imagines what happened to you, the way it happened...

You hear the camera clicking or whirring as you are being hurt, keeping time to the rhythm of your pain. You always know that the pictures are out there somewhere, sold or traded or shown around or just kept in a drawer. In them, what was done to you is immortal. He has them...What he felt as he watched you as he used you is always being done again and lived again and felt again through the pictures—your violation his arousal, your torture his pleasure ...

Before the invention of the camera, which requires the use of real women; before the rise of a mammoth profitmaking industry of pictures and words acting as pimp; before women spoke out about sexual abuse and were heard, the question of the legal regulation of pornography was framed as a question of the freedom of expression of pornographers and their consumers. The government's interest in censoring the expression of ideas about sex was opposed to publishers' right to express them and readers' right to read and think about them...

Social inequality is substantially created and enforced—that is, *done*—through words and images....Words unproblematically treated as acts in the inequality context include "you're fired," "help wanted—male," "sleep with me and I'll give you an A"...These statements are discriminatory acts and are legally seen as such...Pornography, by contrast, has been legally framed as a vehicle for the expression of ideas...

Pornography contains ideas, like any other social practice. But the way it works is not as a thought or through its ideas as such...[This material] combines the graphic sexually explicit...with activities like hurting, degrading, violating, and humiliating, that is, actively subordinating, treating unequally, as less than human, on the basis of sex . . .

There never has been a fair fight in the United States between equality and speech as two constitutional values, equality supporting a statute or practice, speech challenging it. . . .Nor is equality recognized as legally relevant to the problem of pornography, which is addressed instead under the First Amendment doctrine of obscenity. Obscenity law started with the "deprave and corrupt the morals of consumers" test (*they're* being hurt); moved through the censorship of literature from Joyce through Radclyffe Hall to Henry Miller, making them all bestsellers (*they're* being hurt); winding up with the Supreme Court's devising its own obscenity test, which is so effective that, under it, the pornography industry has quadrupled in size (*they're* being hurt?) . . .What is wrong with pornography is that it hurts women in their equality. What is wrong with obscenity law is that this reality has no role in it.

NADINE STROSSEN, FROM *DEFENDING PORNOGRAPHY*[28]

Since the late 1970s, the traditional conservative and fundamentalist advocates of tighter legal restrictions on sexual expression have been joined by an increasingly vocal and influential segment of the feminist movement. Both groups target the sexual material they would like to curb with the pejorative label "pornography." . . .I share the fears, frustration, and fury about the ongoing problems of violence and discrimination against women, which no doubt have driven many to accept the "quick fix" that censoring pornography is claimed to offer. Who wouldn't welcome an end to the threat of violence that so many women feel every time they venture out alone in the dark? But censoring pornography would not reduce misogynistic violence or discrimination. . .While the procensorship strategy may be superficially appealing, at bottom it reflects, "the defeated, defeatist politics of those who have given up on really altering the basic institutions of women's oppression and instead have decided to slay the messenger.". . .

An increasingly vocal cadre of feminist women who are dedicated to securing equal rights for women and to combating women's continued second-class citizenship in our society strongly opposes any effort to censor sexual expression. We are as committed as any other feminists to eradicating violence and discrimination against women . . .But we believe that suppressing sexual words and images will not advance these crucial causes. To the contrary, we are convinced that censoring sexual expression actually would do more harm than

> good to women's rights and safety. We adamantly oppose any effort to restrict sexual speech not only because it would violate our cherished First Amendment freedoms—our freedoms to read, think speak, sing, write, paint, dance, dream, photograph, film, and fantasize as we wish—but also because it would undermine our equality, our status, our dignity, and our autonomy.
>
> Women should not have to choose between freedom and safety, between speech and equality, between freedom and sexuality. Women can be sexual beings without forsaking other aspects of our identities. We are entitled to enjoy the thrills of sex and sexual expression without giving up our personal security. We can exercise our free speech and our equal rights to denounce any sexist expressions of any sort—including sexist expressions that are also sexual—rather than seek to suppress anyone else's rights.

Obscenity Doctrine: *American Booksellers Association v. Hudnut*

In February 1986, the Supreme Court, without hearing oral argument or issuing an opinion, rejected an innovative antipornography ordinance of Indianapolis. The case was *Hudnut v. American Booksellers Association*, 475 U.S. 1001. The ordinance, typical of those promoted in various parts of the U.S. by Catharine MacKinnon and feminist author Andrea Dworkin, asserted that the sale or production of pornography constituted "sex discrimination" (in that it promoted a climate of opinion that restricted women's opportunities to participate freely and equally in community life), and would be an actionable offense—i.e., women could bring lawsuits for damages to halt such activity.

In contrast to judicial doctrine that removed "obscenity" from First Amendment protection on the grounds that it is not part of the exchange of ideas and lacks serious artistic, literary, political, scientific, or other redeeming value (by court-created legal definition),[29] these ordinances define pornography with reference to its graphicness in the depiction of sex combined with its degrading portrayal of women as either desirous of sexual subjugation or suited to be sexually subjugated and dominated. In the words of the Indianapolis ordinance, one example of "graphic, sexually explicit" depictions of women in words or pictures that would be actionable would be material in which "women are presented as sexual objects for domination, conquest, violation, exploitation, possession, or use, or through postures or positions of servility or submission or display."[30] These ordinances do not exempt from their coverage works of artistic, literary, or other merit. This omission (among other attributes) proved fatal at the circuit court of appeals level (771 F.2d 323), as well as at the district court (598

F.Supp 1316), where the judge happened to be a woman, Sara Evans Barker. The Supreme Court upheld the circuit court decision without comment (although three justices did indicate that they believed oral argument should have been set for the case). Excerpts from the circuit court opinion appear below.

The doctrinal background is as follows: The Supreme Court repeatedly and without exception has ruled that "obscenity" (the Court's legal term for what most people call pornography) is *not* protected by the First Amendment. Since the Supreme Court's earliest exposition of First Amendment law, the Court has consistently held that not all uses of words are included in the phrase "freedom of speech or of the press." If a particular use of words has "the effect of force"—as in, for instance, inciting a murder-prone person to murder—those words in those circumstances are not protected by the First Amendment.[31] More than 75 years ago, the Supreme Court added to this rule, the additional rule that certain *categories* of the use of words are not protected by the First Amendment. The Court explained:

> There are certain well-defined and narrowly limited classes of speech, the prevention and punishment of which have never been thought to raise any Constitutional problem. These include the lewd and obscene, the profane, the libelous, and the insulting or "fighting" words—those which by their very utterance inflict injury or tend to incite an immediate breach of the peace. It has been well observed that such utterances are no essential part of any exposition of ideas, and are of such slight social value as a step to truth that any benefit that may be derived from them is clearly outweighed by the social interest in order and morality. [They] ... are not in any proper sense communication of information or opinion. . . .[32]

Until 1992, when the Court handed down *R.A.V. v. City of St. Paul* (discussed in detail below), it had continued to rule without exception that three categories remained unprotected by the First Amendment: the libelous, the obscene, and "fighting" words (i.e. face-to-face insults aimed at provoking violence.). *R.A.V.* was to muddy what had previously been a clear rule on unprotected speech. As of the mid-1980s, though, when these anti-pornography statutes were being tested in court, the basic legal question was whether what had been legally restricted as "pornography" would be considered close enough to the legal definition of "obscenity" to fit under the shield of the "unprotected speech" category.

In 1973, the Supreme Court produced the currently still valid legal definition of *obscenity*. To be judged obscene a work would have to, "taken as a whole, lack serious literary, artistic, political, or scientific value."[33] In addition, two other tests have to be applied to determine obscenity. First, the judge must determine "whether the average [adult] person applying contemporary community standards would find that the work, taken as a whole, appeals to the prurient interest" [in sex].[34] In an earlier case, the Court had referred readers to a dictionary definition of *prurient*; in part it read: "Itching; longing; uneasy with desire or longing . . ."[35] Second, the judge must decide "whether the work depicts or describes, in a patently offensive way, sexual conduct specifically defined by applicable state law."[36] (One of several examples of "sexual conduct" that the Court listed as possibilities for inclusion in state statutes that itemize what may not be offensively depicted was "lewd exhibition of the genitals".)[37] If a work fails both these tests (colloquially, if it both turns you on and grosses you out) and also lacks "serious importance," then it is legally obscene and may be banned.

In the same pair of cases in which the Court produced this definition, it also elaborated why obscenity was punishable under the First Amendment. It was not, Chief Justice Burger explained, in any meaningful sense "communication of ideas"; rather, it was "crass commercial exploitation of sex." People who buy and sell obscenity are not engaged in the exchange of ideas (or money for the expression of ideas), but rather are simply trafficking in titillation.[38] Moreover, there is an identifiable harm or set of harms attributable to obscenity; it debases the public environment in our commercial centers; one can reasonably believe that it promotes antisocial behavior; and, because what people read and view affects their attitudes, "a sensitive key relationship of human existence [i.e., the intimacy of sexual love] . . . can be debased and distorted," through the prevalence of pornographic works in our society.[39] Thus, it was punishable, despite the First Amendment.

Since it is obvious that virtually all hard-core pornography can be easily judged obscene under the three-part test adopted by this pair of 1973 cases, one may wonder why so much of it is still openly marketed. Basically, most American communities and most prosecutors by the 1970s were not interested in spending scarce public funds to prosecute and imprison pornographers. And many juries were simply unwilling to convict. In the aftermath of the *Miller* decision, production and distribution of pornographic materials did not decrease. While pornography prosecutions remained vigorous throughout the 1970s and 1980s in certain jurisdictions—notably, those geographic regions with strict state and local laws—the industry itself continued to grow.[40] This was the situation that gave rise to the MacKinnon-Dworkin campaign for anti-pornography ordinances. Rather than asking for criminal convictions, the statutes used the weapon of lawsuits to be brought by aggrieved women, thus threatening to hit the multi-billion-dollar pornography industry in its pocketbook.

> ### AMERICAN BOOKSELLERS ASSOC. V. HUDNUT
> 771 F.2d 323 (7th Cir.1985)
>
> **FRANK EASTERBROOK, CIRCUIT JUDGE:**
>
> . . .
>
> ### III
>
> "If there is any fixed star in our constitutional constellation, it is that no official, high or petty, can prescribe what shall be orthodox in politics, nationalism, religion, or other matters of opinion. . ." *West Virginia State Board of Education v. Barnette*, 319 U.S. 624, 642 (1943). Under the First Amendment the government must leave to the people the evaluation of ideas. . . . A belief may be pernicious—the beliefs of Nazis led to the death of millions, those of the Klan to the repression of millions. A pernicious belief may prevail. Totalitarian governments today rule much of the planet, practicing suppression of billions and spreading dogma that may enslave others. One of the things that separates our society from theirs is our absolute right to propagate opinions that the government finds wrong or even hateful.
>
> The ideas of the Klan may be propagated. *Brandenburg v. Ohio*, 395 U.S. 444 (1969). Communists may speak freely and run for office. *DeJonge v. Oregon*, 299 U.S. 353 (1937). The Nazi Party may march through a city with a large Jewish population. *Collin v. Smith*, 578 F.2d 1197 (7th Cir.), *cert. denied*, 439 U.S. 916 (1978). People may criticize the President by misrepresenting his positions, and they have a right to post their misrepresentations on public property. *Lebron v. Washington Metropolitan Area Transit Authority*, 242 U.S. App. D.C. 215, 749 F.2d 893 (D.C. Cir. 1984) (Bork, J.). People may seek to repeal laws guaranteeing equal opportunity. . . They may do this because "above all else, the First Amendment means that government has no power to restrict expression because of its message [or] its ideas . . . ." *Police Department v. Mosley*, 408 U.S. 92, 95 (1972).
>
> Under the ordinance graphic sexually explicit speech is "pornography" or not depending on the perspective the author adopts. Speech that "subordinates" women and also, for example, presents women as enjoying pain, humiliation, or rape, or even simply presents women in "positions of servility or submission or display" is forbidden, no matter how great the literary

or political value of the work taken as a whole. Speech that portrays women in positions of equality is lawful, no matter how graphic the sexual content. This is thought control. It establishes an "approved" view of women, of how they may react to sexual encounters, of how the sexes may relate to each other. Those who espouse the approved view may use sexual images; those who do not, may not.

Indianapolis justifies the ordinance on the ground that pornography affects thoughts. Men who see women depicted as subordinate are more likely to treat them so. Pornography is an aspect of dominance.[1] It does not persuade people so much as change them. It works by socializing, by establishing the expected and the permissible. In this view pornography is not an idea; pornography is the injury.

There is much to this perspective. Beliefs are also facts. People often act in accordance with the images and patterns they find around them. People raised in a religion tend to accept the tenets of that religion, often without independent examination. People taught from birth that black people are fit only for slavery rarely rebelled against that creed; beliefs coupled with the self-interest of the masters established a social structure that inflicted great harm while enduring for centuries. Words and images act at the level of the subconscious before they persuade at the level of the conscious. Even the truth has little chance unless a statement fits within the framework of beliefs that may never have been subjected to rational study.

Therefore we accept the premises of this legislation. Depictions of subordination tend to perpetuate subordination. The subordinate status of women in turn leads to affront and lower pay at work, insult and injury at home, battery and rape on the streets.[2] In the language of the legislature, "pornography is central in creating and maintaining sex as a basis of discrimination. Pornography is a systematic practice of exploitation and subordination based on sex which differentially harms women. The bigotry and contempt it produces, with the acts of aggression it fosters, harm women's opportunities for equality and rights [of all kinds]." Indianapolis Code § 16-1(a)(2).

Yet this simply demonstrates the power of pornography as speech. All of these unhappy effects depend on mental intermediation. Pornography affects how people see the world, their fellows, and social relations. If pornography is what pornography does, so is other speech. Hitler's orations affected how some Germans saw Jews. Communism is a world view, not simply a *Manifesto* by Marx and Engels or a set of speeches. Efforts to suppress communist speech in the United States were based on the belief that the public acceptability of such ideas would increase the likelihood of totalitarian government. . . .Many people believe that the existence of television, apart from the content of specific programs, leads to intellectual laziness, to a penchant for violence, to many other ills. . . .Most governments of the world act on this empirical regularity, suppressing critical speech. In the United States, however, the strength of the support for this belief is irrelevant. Seditious libel is protected speech unless the danger is not only grave but also imminent. See *New York Times Co. v. Sullivan*, 376 U.S. 254 (1964); cf. *Brandenburg v. Ohio, New York Times Co. v. United States*, 403 U.S. 713 (1971).

Racial bigotry, anti-semitism, violence on television, reporters' biases—these and many more influence the culture and shape our socialization. None is directly answerable by more speech, unless that speech too finds its place in the popular culture. Yet all is protected as speech, however insidious. Any other answer leaves the government in control of all of the institutions of culture, the great censor and director of which thoughts are good for us.

Sexual responses often are unthinking responses, and the association of sexual arousal with the subordination of women therefore may have a substantial effect. But almost all cultural stimuli provoke unconscious responses. Religious ceremonies condition their participants. Teachers convey messages by selecting what not to cover; the implicit message about what is off limits or unthinkable may be more powerful than the messages for which they present rational argument. Television scripts contain unarticulated assumptions. People may be conditioned in subtle ways. If the fact that speech plays a role in a process of conditioning were enough to permit governmental regulation, that would be the end of freedom of speech.

It is possible to interpret the claim that the pornography is the harm in a different way. Indianapolis emphasizes the injury that models in pornographic films and pictures may suffer. The record contains materials depicting sexual torture, penetration of women by red-hot irons and the like. These concerns have nothing to do with written materials subject to the statute, and physical injury can occur with or without the "subordination" of women. . . .[A] state may make injury in the course of producing a film unlawful independent of the viewpoint expressed in the film.

The more immediate point, however, is that the image of pain is not necessarily pain. In *Body Double*, a suspense film directed by Brian DePalma, a woman who has disrobed and presented a sexually explicit display is murdered by an intruder with a drill. The drill runs through the woman's body. The film is sexually explicit and a murder occurs—yet no one believes that the actress suffered pain or died. . . .

. . .

We come, finally, to the argument that pornography is "low value" speech, that it is enough like obscenity that Indianapolis may prohibit it. Some cases hold that speech far removed from politics and other subjects at the core of the Farmers' concerns may be subjected to special regulation. E.g., *FCC v. Pacifica Foundation*, 438 U.S. 726 (1978); *Young v. American Mini Theatres, Inc.*, 427 U.S. 50, 67–70 (1976) (plurality opinion); *Chaplinsky v. New Hampshire*, 315 U.S. 568, 571–72 (1942). These cases do not sustain statutes that select among viewpoints, however. In *Pacifica* the FCC sought to keep vile language off the air during certain times. The Court held that it may; but the Court would not have sustained a regulation prohibiting scatological descriptions of Republicans but not scatological descriptions of Democrats, or any other form of selection among viewpoints. See *Planned Parenthood Ass'n v. Chicago Transit Authority*, 767 F.2d 1225 (7th Cir. 1985).

At all events, "pornography" is not low value speech within the meaning of these cases. Indianapolis seeks to prohibit certain speech because it believes this speech influences social relations and politics on a grand scale, that it controls attitudes at home and in the legislature. This precludes a characterization of the speech as low value. . . . Indianapolis left out of its definition any reference to literary, artistic, political, or scientific value. The ordinance applies to graphic sexually explicit subordination in works great and small. The Court sometimes balances the value of speech against the costs of its restriction, but it does this by category of speech and not by the content of particular works. Indianapolis has created an approved point of view and so loses the support of these cases.

Any rationale we could imagine in support of this ordinance could not be limited to sex discrimination. Free speech has been on balance an ally of those seeking change. Governments that want stasis start by restricting speech. Culture is a powerful force of continuity; Indianapolis paints pornography as part of the culture of power. Change in any complex system ultimately depends on the ability of outsiders to challenge accepted views and the reigning institutions. Without a strong guarantee of freedom of speech, there is no effective right to challenge what is.

Opinion Footnotes

1 "Pornography constructs what a woman is in terms of its view of what men want sexually . . . Pornography's world of equality is a harmonious and balanced place. Men and women are perfectly

complementary and perfectly bipolar.... All the ways men love to take and violate women, women love to be taken and violated.... What pornography does goes beyond its content: It eroticizes hierarchy, it sexualizes inequality. It makes dominance and submission sex. Inequality is its central dynamic; the illusion of freedom coming together with the reality of force is central to its working.... Pornography is neither harmless fantasy nor a corrupt and confused misrepresentation of an otherwise neutral and healthy sexual situation. It institutionalizes the sexuality of male supremacy, fusing the erotization of dominance and submission with the social construction of male and female..." Catharine MacKinnon, "Pornography, Civil Rights and Speech," 20 *Harv. Civ. Rts.-Civ. Lib. L.Rev.* 1, at 17–18.... A national commission in Canada recently adopted a similar rationale for controlling pornography. Special Commission on Pornography and Prostitution, 1 *Pornography and Prostitution in Canada* 49–59 (Canadian Government Publishing Centre 1985).

2 MacKinnon's article collects empirical work that supports this proposition. The social science studies are very difficult to interpret, however, and they conflict. Because much of the effect of speech comes through a process of socialization, it is difficult to measure incremental benefits and injuries caused by particular speech. Several psychologists have found, for example, that those who see violent, sexually explicit films tend to have more violent thoughts. But how often does this lead to actual violence? National commissions on obscenity here, in the United Kingdom, and in Canada have found that it is not possible to demonstrate a direct link between obscenity and rape or exhibitionism....In saying that we accept the finding that pornography as the ordinance defines it leads to unhappy consequences, we mean only that there is evidence to this effect, that this evidence is consistent with much human experience, and that as judges we must accept the legislative resolution of such disputed empirical questions.

Case Questions

1. In your judgment, if Indianapolis were to reenact this ordinance but substitute the Supreme Court's definition of obscenity as outlined in *Miller* (offensively explicit depictions of sex, calculated to appeal to prurient interest, and lacking a serious degree of redeeming importance) for the phrase "graphic, sexually explicit," but keeping all the other qualifiers about being degrading to women in one or another way, would the law then be constitutional? In other words, would it be constitutional to ban only some but not all materials that are legally obscene—those that eroticize violence toward women or that eroticize subjugation of women?

2. If it would, why does Easterbrook pay so much attention to the rule that the First Amendment does not allow laws that restrict the expression of particular points of view? Is it because this law included in its proscription material that which was of "serious literary, artistic, political, or scientific value" along with obvious trash?

Hate Speech and the Future of Pornography Laws: *R.A.V. v. St. Paul* (1992)[41]

In June of 1992, a five-justice majority that included the vote of Clarence Thomas, the lone Black justice on the Supreme Court, against heated and lengthy dissents from the other four justices, handed down an implicit answer to Case Question #1 above. According to the four dissenters, this answer contained "serious departures from the teaching of prior cases" and "casts aside long-established First Amendment doctrine."[42]

The legal question directly posed in the *R.A.V.* case involved not pornography but expressive conduct conveying hatred for certain kinds of groups. "R.A.V." was a juvenile who had, along with some other teenagers, burned a cross in the yard of a Black family in violation of St. Paul's law making it a misdemeanor to place on any property "a symbol, object, appellation, characterization or graffiti, including but not limited to, a burning cross or Nazi swastika, which one knows or has reasonable grounds to know arouses anger, alarm or resentment in others on the basis of race, color, creed, religion or gender."[43] The state supreme court of Minnesota in interpreting this law had ruled that it covered only "fighting words," which are not protected by the First Amendment. The U.S. Supreme Court had earlier defined "fighting words" as "words which by their very nature inflict injury or tend to incite an immediate breach of the peace."[44] In the *R.A.V.* case, the Supreme Court majority ruled that even if the statute banned only (unprotected) fighting words, it was unconstitutional for a government to pick and choose among different viewpoints within the unprotected speech category.

According to the *R.A.V.* Court, despite the *Chaplinsky* precedent, which had established that the categories of unprotected speech (obscenity, fighting words, libel) "are no essential part of any exposition of ideas,"[45] it is nonetheless unconstitutional to ban a portion of an unprotected category on the grounds of disapproval of the idea expressed in it.[46] The majority argued that such a ban was an attempt at governmental thought control and therefore disapproved by the First Amendment.

This argument by the *R.A.V.* Court seems to indicate that a statute that banned only those obscene materials showing sexual violence against women or subjugation of women would be unconstitutional (for the sorts of reasons outlined by Judge Easterbrook). On the other hand, the *R.A.V.* opinion left a few loopholes against this inference.

One loophole they described as follows: "When the basis for the content discrimination consists entirely of the very reason the entire class of speech at issue is proscribable, no significant danger of idea or viewpoint discrimination exists. . . . To illustrate: a State might choose to prohibit only that obscenity which is the most patently offensive *in its prurience*—i.e., that which involves the most lascivious displays of sexual activity. But it may not prohibit, for example, only that obscenity which includes offensive *political* messages. . . ."[47] In order to fit into this loophole, an Indianapolis-type ordinance modified along the lines already suggested (making it a partial ban on constitutionally unprotected "obscenity") would have to be defended on the grounds that those types of obscenity (the ones eroticizing violence toward, and subjugation of, women) were the most disruptive of "the social interest in order and morality" (taking "morality" in its broad sense—decent treatment of other people).

A second possible loophole into which modified Indianapolis-type ordinances might be fit was outlined by the Court majority as follows: "[A] particular content-based subcategory of a proscribable class of speech can be swept up incidentally within the reach of a statute directed at conduct rather than speech. . . . Thus, for example, sexually derogatory 'fighting words,' among other words, may produce a violation of Title VII's general prohibition against sexual discrimination in employment practices. Where the government does not target conduct on the basis of its expressive content, acts are not shielded from regulation merely because they express a discriminatory idea or philosophy."[48] Proponents of a modified Indianapolis-type ordinance who wanted to utilize this loophole would need to be able to make a persuasive case that the prevalence of the kinds of obscenity they were banning contributed in a substantial way to employment and educational discrimination against women (both of which are forbidden in federal law.)

Neither of the efforts described here is in principle impossible, but it does appear that the *R.A.V.* decision has thrown new obstacles into the path of proponents of Indianapolis-style anti-pornography laws.

Shortly after handing down *R.A.V.*, the U.S. Supreme Court handed down a decision that seemed to go in a somewhat contrary direction. Whereas *R.A.V.* seemed to create a rule that legislation could not single out particular racial, religious, or gender groups for protection from fighting words, in *Wisconsin v. Mitchell* (1993), the Court ruled that it does not violate the Constitution when a law singles out race-based animus or gender-based animus as grounds for imposing extra penalties on crimes. Even if the only evidence of race-based hostility motivating a crime is the speech of the criminal, such speech can legitimately be used to impose extra time in prison for these "hate crimes."[49]

By the mid-1990s, feminists and legal actors alike began to dedicate less attention to the harms of pornography. The Supreme Court's decision to allow Judge Easterbrook's decision to stand in *American Booksellers Association v. Hudnut*, 771 F.2d 323 (7th Cir.1985), finally was publicly explained by its 1992 decision in *R.A.V. v. City of St. Paul* (505 U.S. 377): legislation cannot single out particular racial, religious, or gender groups for protection from harmful words, even if the words take the form of generally unprotected speech. Thus, the harm to women argument was not a viable route for restricting sexually explicit speech. Pornography prosecutions rapidly declined during the 1990s, a development that reflected both growing public acceptance of sexually explicit speech and decreased interest in pursuing obscenity cases by local, state and federal law enforcement.[50] In addition, the mushrooming of internet porn moved the consumption of pornographic materials into private homes, and such consumption had long been protected by the Supreme Court under the right of privacy.[51]

However, one area where the public harm argument has never abated is with respect to the harm to children associated with pornography. During the late 1990s and early twenty-first century, Congress passed a series of laws intended to protect children from accessing sexually explicit materials on the Internet. The Communications Decency Act of 1996 made it a federal crime to intentionally transmit "obscene or indecent" images to minors, but the Supreme Court declared the prohibition on "indecent" speech to be overly broad because this type of speech falls within the protections of the First Amendment.[52] In response, Congress passed the Child Online Protection Act which made it the responsibility of online content providers to prevent children from accessing "material that is harmful to minors," and the Justices again ruled that Congress' legislation went too far and ran the risk of censoring speech that is protected by the First Amendment.[53] After these initial efforts to protect children from online pornography, Congress moved on to other issues and the government has left it to parents to take precautionary measures to control the content that their children access online.

Prosecutions of child pornographers and consumers of child pornography do, however, remain a priority for law enforcement agents, and the advent of the Internet has added new urgency because this technology makes it so easy to share these materials covertly across national and state boundaries. The U.S. Department of Justice's High Technology Investigative Unit (created in 2002) consists of computer forensic specialists who work the Child Exploitation and Obscenity Section to investigate and prosecute child pornographers as well as find and protect child victims. In addition, Congress passed legislation in 2004 that provides victims of child pornography with the opportunity to seek restitution from both their abusers and the consumers of these depictions.

Restitution for Child Pornography Victims: *Paroline v. United States* (2014)[54]

The federal Justice for All Act of 2004 includes the Crime Victims' Rights Act (CVRA). The CVRA includes specific rights extended to victims of federal crimes. Included among these rights is "The right to full and timely restitution as provided in law."[55] This law allowed for child pornography victims to receive payments from people who had created, distributed or possessed material in which those victims appeared. Questions have arisen as to determining the specific harm or expenses associated with child pornography even though courts have recognized that child pornography victims are harmed by those creating, distributing or possessing materials in which they appear. These questions are illustrated in the events surrounding the "Misty" series.

Beginning at age four, "Amy" was exploited by her uncle who began filming and photographing acts of rape that he committed on her, for videos known as the "Misty" series. These circulated on the Internet for ten years. Amy's uncle continued to sexually abuse her, and to document the abuse on film, until her parents discovered it when Amy was 7 or 8 years old.

Amy began receiving notices at age 15 or 16 that individuals who had downloaded images of her were being prosecuted under federal child pornography laws. Amy was entitled to receive these notices because a provision in the CVRA requires that victims have the "right to reasonable, accurate, and timely notice of any public court proceeding, or any parole proceeding, involving the crime or of any release or escape of the accused." Learning that images of Amy as a young child were being widely distributed via the Internet further traumatized Amy and triggered her feelings of victimization. Amy has contended, then, that she has been victimized twice—once for the repeated rapes that she experienced at the hands of her uncle when she was a young child and again when she learned that these images were being widely distributed online.

Because the CVRA extends victims the right to restitution, Amy sought damages of $3.4 million to pay for counseling, lost wages and legal fees resulting from the exploitation and associated trauma that she experienced both from the sexual abuse and from learning of the wide distribution of images of her being raped.

Central to the discussion of "Amy's" case is whether those persons who downloaded these pornographic images share responsibility in paying these damages. Several individuals have been prosecuted for downloading pornographic images of Amy when she was a child. Questions have arisen as to the degree to which these persons, who were already successfully prosecuted for child pornography because they downloaded and viewed these images, are also responsible for financially compensating victims for the sexual trauma that these victims experienced even though they themselves did not commit sexual abuse on the victims.

The U.S. Supreme Court heard the case of Doyle R. Paroline who had pled guilty to downloading several hundred images of child pornography that included two images of Amy. In addition to being sentenced to 24 months followed by probation, Paroline was sued for $3.4 million restitution, which was challenged in federal district court. That court determined that Paroline did not have to pay restitution because it had not been proven that Paroline's possession of the images of Amy caused her injuries that were eligible for restitution under the CVRA. In essence, the district court determined that a direct connection could not be drawn between Paroline's possession of the two images and Amy's need for therapy, her lost wages and her legal fees. The U.S. Court of Appeals reversed that decision, ordering full restitution according to a payment schedule based on ability to pay, and Paroline appealed to the U.S. Supreme Court.

In a 5–3–1 ruling for Paroline,[56] the U.S. Supreme Court majority determined that Paroline's possession of the two pornographic images did not cause the entirety of the victim's losses and thus, Paroline was not responsible for compensating Amy's losses to the full extent that she sought. The justices sent the case back down to the district court with orders to determine a restitution amount that would be proportional to Paroline's relative role in the overall harm experienced by the victim. Dissenting on behalf of himself, Scalia and Thomas, Chief Justice John Roberts argued that as worded the statute required a degree of proof as to relative role that would always be impossible, so no damages could get awarded until Congress re-wrote the statute. Justice Sotomayor dissented separately to agree with the Circuit Court of Appeals that Paroline should have to pay the full $3.4 million on a schedule graduated to his paying ability.

Although sexual abuse victims are separately victimized when video or photographic images of their abuse are viewed by total strangers through the internet, one key takeaway of the Paroline case is that despite their entitlement to restitution under the CVRA, because the specific amount of harm from any one viewer will usually be relatively tiny, the process of suing viewer after viewer after viewer, with only a small award every time, will discourage victims from seeking the full compensation to which the law in theory entitles them.

THE VIOLENCE AGAINST WOMEN ACT: *UNITED STATES V. MORRISON AND BRZONKALA V. MORRISON* (2000)

In 1994, Congress passed the Violence Against Women Act (VAWA), after a four year effort led by Democratic Senator Joe Biden in his capacity as a member of the Senate Judiciary Committee. This law made it a crime for anyone to "travel across a State line or enter or leave Indian country with the intent to injure, harass, or intimidate that person's spouse or intimate partner, and . . . in the course of or as a result of such travel, intentionally commit a crime of violence and thereby cause bodily injury to such spouse or intimate partner."[57] The law also created a civil right to be free of "gender-motivated violence," which it defined as "a crime of violence committed because of gender or on the basis of gender, and due, at least in part, to an animus based on the victim's gender,"[58] and allowed victims of such crimes to sue for compensatory and punitive damages in civil court at either the state or federal level, even if the state authorities never brought criminal charges against the perpetrator.[59]

This law was enacted against a complicated legal background. The first section of the civil damages portion of the law asserted that Congress was acting "[p]ursuant to the affirmative power of Congress ... under section 5 of the Fourteenth Amendment to the Constitution [to enforce equal protection of the laws], as well as under section 8 of Article I of the Constitution [to regulate commerce among the states]."[60] It seems logical that protecting a group of people against systematic violence aimed at their group would be part of providing "equal protection of the laws," but shortly after the Civil War, the Supreme Court had ruled that Congress's enforcement power under the Fourteenth Amendment was limited to regulations of actions by state governments, and could not reach actions by private persons.[61]

This "state action" limitation on Congress's enforcement powers became discredited toward the end of the twentieth century. In 1966 six of the nine justices indicated clearly in their opinions for the *U.S. v. Guest* case that Congress could regulate activities not themselves outlawed by the Fourteenth Amendment's "no state shall..." language, so long as the Congressional regulation was itself rationally related to securing "equal protection of the laws."[62] The 1964 Civil Rights Act, enacted prior to this shift by the Court on the state action doctrine, was framed with explicit attention to interstate commerce, precisely to avoid any danger of being overturned on state action doctrine grounds. Congress definitely could regulate private behavior involving "commerce among the states," so the act, for instance, where it prohibited discrimination on the basis of sex or race, defined "employer" as "a person engaged in an industry affecting commerce..."[63] This alluded to the Court's longstanding doctrine that if particular local activities, considered in the aggregate, nationwide, had a substantial effect on the commerce of more states than one, then Congress could regulate them.[64]

Supreme Court majorities had during two periods attempted to check the power of Congress over commerce, first from 1895 to 1937 and then from 1976 to 1985. In the first period, the Court had deployed a doctrine of "dual federalism" that simply defined some subjects as outside of "commerce" and therefore within state power rather than federal power. These subjects included manufacturing, mining, agriculture, and other productive enterprises, so even a national manufacturing monopoly was defined by the Court to be outside of the reach of Congress.[65] In 1937, during the pressure of FDR's Court-Packing Plan, the Court abandoned this doctrine[66] (within a few weeks of the time it abandoned the "liberty of contract" doctrine in *West Coast Hotel v. Parrish*) and has never returned to it. But in 1976, a Court majority again put forth a doctrine attempting to hem in Congress's commerce power, this time with the argument that "traditional governmental functions" of the states may not be usurped by Congress's exercise of the commerce power. So, for instance, federal minimum wage laws could regulate a local industry that affects interstate commerce but could not cover state governmental employees, even if it is obvious that the wages of 10 million state employees affect the national economy to a nontrivial degree.[67] This traditional governmental functions doctrine lasted only nine years, openly abandoned in 1985 in *Garcia v. SAMTA*,[68] where the Court announced that finding the line between such functions and state activities properly reachable by the congressional commerce power was really beyond judicial competence and was a political decision to be made in Congress (where all states are represented).

Thus it was that in 1994, the U.S. Congress believed that both the federal commerce power and the federal power to enforce the Fourteenth Amendment served as legitimate bases for the Violence Against Women Act. But in 1995 the Supreme Court moved toward changing the rules of the game. In a decision invalidating the Gun-Free School Zones Act, *U.S. v. Lopez*,[69] a five-justice majority of the Supreme Court purported to be summarizing existing rules of the commerce precedents, in a way that the dissent charged amounted to a changing of the rules. Specifically, the Court majority asserted that the precedents establish that for an activity not itself in interstate commerce to be regulatable by Congress on the grounds that it "affects commerce" of more than one state, the activity itself has to be "economic" or "commercial." This development portended trouble for the Violence Against Women Act, since acts of assault, murder, and rape are not themselves normally thought of as economic activities. On the other hand, the Court had complained in *Lopez* that the legislative history of the Gun-Free School Zones Act lacked "express congressional findings regarding the effects upon interstate commerce of gun possession in a school zone."[70] The Congressional proponents of the VAWA accumulated voluminous legislative findings to demonstrate the impact of violence against women on the national economy, and this fact boded well for the success of VAWA at the Supreme Court. As it turned out, the Court divided over the Violence Against Women Act just as it had in *Lopez*, and *Lopez* figured prominently in the judicial debate.

The court case on the constitutionality of VAWA, *U.S. v. Morrison*, began as *Brzonkala v. Morrison*, initiated by Christy Brzonkala in the aftermath of her experiences at Virginia Polytechnic Institute (Virginia Tech or VPI). In September of her first year there, she met Antonio Morrison and James Crawford, both varsity football players. Brzonkala's account is that within 30 minutes of her meeting them, they assaulted and raped her. Afterwards Morrison boasted openly in the dormitory dining room of enjoying getting girls drunk and taking sexual advantage of them. His boasts were in terms so vulgar that the Supreme Court refused to repeat them, noting only that the "debased remarks" were "vulgar remarks that cannot fail to shock and offend."[71] Brzonkala became severely depressed after the rape, visited the university psychiatrist, received antidepressant medication, stopped attending classes, and eventually dropped out of the university.

Early in 1995 she filed a complaint against both Morrison and Crawford under VPI's sexual assault policy. During the hearing, Morrison admitted that she had twice told him, "No" during the incident but that he had proceeded to have sex with her. The university found insufficient evidence to punish Crawford but ruled Morrison guilty of sexual assault and suspended him for two semesters immediately. In July 1995 Morrison went to court to challenge this ruling of VPI, and this action prompted the university to notify Brzonkala that it had erred procedurally in trying Morrison under the sexual assault policy, since that policy had not been widely publicized among the students. VPI then retried Morrison under its longer-standing Abusive Conduct Policy. He was again found guilty, this time of "using abusive language," and received the identical sentence. He then appealed through university channels and had his sentence set aside by the provost in late August 1995, on the grounds that it was disproportionate to penalties for other abusive conduct convictions. VPI did not bother to notify Christy Brzonkala of this change. She read in a newspaper that he would be returning to school for the fall semester, and she promptly withdrew from the school.

She then went to federal court and sued VPI for violating Title IX of the Education Amendments of 1972 (which forbids sex discrimination in educational programs),[72] and sued Antonio Morrison and James Crawford for violating the Violence Against Women Act.[73] At this point the United States Justice Department intervened to defend the constitutionality of the VAWA, so two cases now were alive, *Brzonkala v. Morrison et al.* and *U.S. v. Morrison et al.*, both involving only the civil provisions of the acts, since no criminal charges were ever filed involving the incident. At the federal district court Brzonkala's suits were both dismissed, but the circuit court reversed both decisions, and the circuit court then met en banc (instead of in a three judge panel) and in a divided decision ruled the VAWA unconstitutional. It remanded the Title IX question to await the Supreme Court ruling in *Davis v. Monroe County*, as to whether there was an individual right to sue for damages under Title IX.[74] Both Christy Brzonkala and the U.S. Department of Justice appealed against the decision that VAWA was unconstitutional. By the time the case was at the circuit court level, 22 feminist and civil liberties organizations (including NOW, the National Coalition against Domestic Violence, Women's Legal Defense Fund, the ACLU's Women's Rights Project, the Anti-Defamation League, the Center for Women's Policy Studies, Jewish Women International, and Women Employed) had joined the case to submit amicus briefs on Christy Brzonkala's behalf.

UNITED STATES V. ANTONIO J. MORRISON ET AL. AND CHRISTY BRZONKALA V. ANTONIO J. MORRISON ET AL.
529 U.S. 598 (2000)

CHIEF JUSTICE REHNQUIST delivered the opinion of the Court.

In these cases we consider the constitutionality of 42 U.S.C. § 13981, which provides a federal civil remedy for the victims of gender-motivated violence. The United States Court of Appeals for the Fourth Circuit, . . . concluded that Congress lacked constitutional authority to enact the section's civil remedy. Believing that these cases are controlled by our decisions in *United States* v. *Lopez*, 514 U.S. 549 (1995), *United States* v. *Harris*, 106 U.S. 629 (1883), and the *Civil Rights Cases*, 109 U.S. 3 (1883), we affirm.

I

[Rehnquist reviewed the facts and continued as follows:]

Every law enacted by Congress must be based on one or more of its powers enumerated in the Constitution. . . . Congress explicitly identified the sources of federal authority on which it relied in enacting § 13981. We address Congress' authority to enact this remedy under each of these constitutional provisions in turn.

II

Due respect for the decisions of a coordinate branch of Government demands that we invalidate a congressional enactment only upon a plain showing that Congress has exceeded its constitutional bounds. With this presumption of constitutionality in mind, we turn to the question whether § 13981 falls within Congress' power under Article I, § 8, of the Constitution.

Brzonkala and the United States rely upon the third clause of the Article, which gives Congress power "[t]o regulate Commerce with foreign Nations, and among the several States, and with the Indian Tribes."

As we discussed at length in *Lopez*, our interpretation of the Commerce Clause has changed as our Nation has developed.... *Lopez* emphasized, however, that even under our modern, expansive interpretation of the Commerce Clause, Congress' regulatory authority is not without effective bounds. *Id.*, at 557.

. . .

As we observed in *Lopez*, modern Commerce Clause jurisprudence has "identified three broad categories of activity that Congress may regulate under its commerce power." 514 U.S., at 558. "First, Congress may regulate the use of the channels of interstate commerce." 514 U.S., at 558 (citing *Heart of Atlanta Motel, Inc. v. United States*, 379 U.S. 241, 256 (1964)...). "Second, Congress is empowered to regulate and protect the instrumentalities of interstate commerce, or persons or things in interstate commerce, even though the threat may come only from intrastate activities." 514 U.S., at 558 (citing *Shreveport Rate Cases*, 234 U.S. 342 (1914); *Southern R. Co. v. United States*, 222 U.S. 20 (1911); *Perez v. U.S.*, 402 U.S. 146, at 150 (1971)). "Finally, Congress' commerce authority includes the power to regulate those activities having a substantial relation to interstate commerce, ... *i.e.*, those activities that substantially affect interstate commerce." 514 U.S., at 558–559 (citing *Jones & Laughlin Steel*, *supra*, at 37).

Petitioners ... seek to sustain § 13981 as a regulation of activity that substantially affects interstate commerce. Given § 13981's focus on gender-motivated violence wherever it occurs (rather than violence directed at the instrumentalities of interstate commerce, interstate markets, or things or persons in interstate commerce), we agree that this is the proper inquiry.

Lopez ... provides the proper framework for conducting the required analysis of § 13981. In *Lopez* [s]everal significant considerations contributed to our decision.

First, we observed that § 922(q) was "a criminal statute that by its terms has nothing to do with 'commerce' or any sort of economic enterprise, however broadly one might define those terms." *Id.*, at 561....

Both petitioners and Justice Souter's dissent downplay the role that the economic nature of the regulated activity plays in our Commerce Clause analysis. But a fair reading of *Lopez* shows that the noneconomic, criminal nature of the conduct at issue was central to our decision in that case. See, *e.g.,* *id.,* at 551 ("The Act [does not] regulat[e] a commercial activity"), 560 ("Even *Wickard,* which is perhaps the most far reaching example of Commerce Clause authority over intrastate activity, involved economic activity in a way that the possession of a gun in a school zone does not"), 561 ("Section 922(q) is not an essential part of a larger regulation of economic activity"), 566 ("Admittedly, a determination whether an intrastate activity is commercial or noncommercial may in some cases result in legal uncertainty. But, so long as Congress' authority is limited to those powers enumerated in the Constitution, and so long as those enumerated powers are interpreted as having judicially enforceable outer limits, congressional legislation under the Commerce Clause always will engender 'legal uncertainty' "), 567 ("The possession of a gun in a local school zone is in no sense an economic activity that might, through repetition elsewhere, substantially affect any sort of interstate commerce"); see also *id.,* at 573–574 (*Kennedy,* J., concurring) (stating that *Lopez* did not alter our "practical conception of commercial regulation" and that Congress may "regulate in the commercial sphere on the assumption that we have a single market and a unified purpose to build a stable national economy"), 577 ("Were the Federal Government to take over the regulation of entire areas of traditional state concern, areas having nothing to do with the regulation of commercial activities, the boundaries between the spheres of federal and state authority would blur"), 580 ("[U]nlike the earlier cases to come before the Court here neither the actors nor their conduct has a commercial character, and neither the purposes nor the design of the statute has an evident commercial nexus." . . .) *Lopez*'s review of Commerce Clause case law demonstrates that in those cases where we have sustained federal regulation of intrastate activity based upon the activity's substantial effects on interstate commerce, the activity in question has been some sort of economic endeavor. See *id.,* at 559–560.[4]

Second the statute contained [did not expressly limit its reach to interstate commerce in some way. . . .]

Third, we noted that neither § 922(q) "nor its legislative history contain[s] express congressional findings regarding the effects upon interstate commerce of gun possession in a school zone." *Ibid.* . . . [T]he existence of such findings may "enable us to evaluate the legislative judgment that the activity in question substantially affect[s] interstate commerce, even though no such substantial effect [is] visible to the naked eye." 514 U.S., at 563.

Finally, our decision in *Lopez* rested in part on the fact that the link between gun possession and a substantial effect on interstate commerce was attenuated. *Id.*, at 563-567. The United States argued that the possession of guns may lead to violent crime, and that violent crime "can be expected to affect the functioning of the national economy in two ways. First, the costs of violent crime are substantial, and, through the mechanism of insurance, those costs are spread throughout the population. Second, violent crime reduces the willingness of individuals to travel to areas within the country that are perceived to be unsafe." *Id.*, at 563-564. The Government also argued that the presence of guns at schools poses a threat to the educational process, which in turn threatens to produce a less efficient and productive workforce, which will negatively affect national productivity and thus interstate commerce. *Ibid.*

We rejected these "costs of crime" and "national productivity" arguments because they would permit Congress to "regulate not only all violent crime, but all activities that might lead to violent crime, regardless of how tenuously they relate to interstate commerce." *Id.*, at 564. We noted that, under this . . . reasoning: "Congress could regulate any activity that it found was related to the economic productivity of individual citizens: family law (including marriage, divorce, and child custody), for example." *Ibid.*

With these principles. . ., the proper resolution of the present cases is clear. Gender-motivated crimes of violence are not, in any sense of the phrase, economic activity. While we need not adopt a categorical rule against aggregating the effects of any noneconomic activity in order to decide these cases, thus far in our Nation's history our cases have upheld Commerce Clause regulation of intrastate activity only where that activity is economic in nature.

Like the Gun-Free School Zones Act at issue in *Lopez*, § 13981 contains[language limiting its reach to movement in interstate commerce]. . . .

In contrast with the lack of congressional findings that we faced in *Lopez*, § 13981 *is* supported by numerous findings regarding the serious impact that gender-motivated violence has on victims and their families. See, *e.g.*, H. R. Conf. Rep. No. 103-711, p. 385 (1994); S. Rep. No. 103-138, p. 40 (1993); S. Rep. No. 101-545, p. 33 (1990). But the existence of congressional findings is not sufficient, by itself, to sustain the constitutionality of Commerce Clause legislation. As we stated in *Lopez*, "[S]imply because Congress may conclude that a particular activity substantially affects interstate commerce does not necessarily make it so." Rather, "[w]hether particular operations affect interstate commerce sufficiently to come under the constitutional power of Congress to regulate them is ultimately a judicial rather than a legislative question, and can be settled finally only by this Court." (*Lopez*, 514 U.S., at 557, n. 2, internal quote marks and citations omitted.)

In these cases, Congress' findings are substantially weakened by the fact that they rely so heavily on a method of reasoning that we have already rejected as unworkable if we are to maintain the Constitution's enumeration of powers. Congress found that gender-motivated violence affects interstate commerce "by deterring potential victims from traveling interstate, from engaging in employment in interstate business, and from transacting with business, and in places involved in interstate commerce; . . . by diminishing national productivity, increasing medical and other costs, and decreasing the supply of and the demand for interstate products." H. R. Conf. Rep. No. 103-711, at 385. Accord, S. Rep. No. 103-138, at 54. Given these findings and petitioners' arguments, the concern that we expressed in *Lopez* that Congress might use the Commerce Clause to completely obliterate the Constitution's distinction between national and local authority seems well founded. The reasoning that petitioners advance seeks to follow the but-for causal chain from the initial occurrence of violent crime (the suppression of which has always been the prime object of the States' police power) to every attenuated effect upon interstate commerce. If accepted, petitioners' reasoning would allow Congress to regulate any crime as long as the nationwide, aggregated impact of that crime has substantial effects on employment, production, transit, or consumption. Indeed, if Congress may regulate gender-motivated violence, it would be able to regulate murder or any other type of violence since gender-motivated violence, as a subset of all violent crime, is certain to have lesser economic impacts than the larger class of which it is a part.

Petitioners' reasoning, moreover, will not limit Congress to regulating violence but may, as we suggested in Lopez, be applied equally as well to family law and other areas of traditional state regulation since the aggregate effect of marriage, divorce, and childrearing on the national economy is undoubtedly significant. . . Under our written Constitution. . . the limitation of congressional authority is not solely a matter of legislative grace.[7]

We accordingly reject the argument that Congress may regulate noneconomic, violent criminal conduct based solely on that conduct's aggregate effect on interstate commerce. The Constitution requires a distinction between what is truly national and what is truly local. *Lopez*, 514 U.S., at 568 (citing *Jones & Laughlin Steel*, 301 U.S., at 30). In recognizing this fact we preserve one of the few principles that has been consistent since the Clause was adopted. The regulation and punishment of intrastate violence that is not directed at the instrumentalities, channels, or goods involved in interstate commerce has always been the province of the States....

III

Because we conclude that the Commerce Clause does not provide Congress with authority to enact § 13981, we address petitioners' alternative argument that the section's civil remedy should be upheld as an exercise of Congress' remedial power under § 5 of the Fourteenth Amendment. As noted above, Congress expressly invoked the Fourteenth Amendment as a source of authority to enact § 13981.

The principles governing an analysis of congressional legislation under § 5 are well settled. Section 5 states that Congress may "enforce," by "appropriate legislation" the constitutional guarantee that no State shall deprive any person of "life, liberty or property, without due process of law," nor deny any person "equal protection of the laws." Section 5 is "a positive grant of legislative power," *Katzenbach* v. *Morgan*, 384 U.S. 641, 651 (1966), that includes authority to "prohibit conduct which is not itself unconstitutional and [to] intrud[e] into 'legislative spheres of autonomy previously reserved to the States.'" *Boerne v. Flores*, 521 U.S. 507, at 518 (quoting *Fitzpatrick* v. *Bitzer*, 427 U.S. 445, 455 (1976)).... However, as broad as the congressional enforcement power is, it is not unlimited...

Petitioners' § 5 argument is founded on an assertion that there is pervasive bias in various state justice systems against victims of gender-motivated violence. This assertion is supported by a voluminous congressional record. Specifically, Congress received evidence that many participants in state justice systems are perpetuating an array of erroneous stereotypes and assumptions. Congress concluded that these discriminatory stereotypes often result in insufficient investigation and prosecution of gender-motivated crime, inappropriate focus on the behavior and credibility of the victims of that crime, and unacceptably lenient punishments for those who are actually convicted of gender-motivated violence. See H. R. Conf. Rep. No. 103-711, at 385–386; S. Rep. No. 103-138, at 38, 41–55; S. Rep. No. 102-197, at 33–35, 41, 43–47. Petitioners contend that this bias denies victims of gender-motivated violence the equal protection of the laws and that Congress therefore acted appropriately in enacting a private civil remedy against the perpetrators of gender-motivated violence to both remedy the States'

bias and deter future instances of discrimination in the state courts. [Emphasis added.—AU.]

As our cases have established, state-sponsored gender discrimination violates equal protection unless it "serves "important governmental objectives and . . . the discriminatory means employed" are "substantially related to the achievement of those objectives." [citations omitted.] However, the language and purpose of the Fourteenth Amendment place certain limitations on the manner in which Congress may attack discriminatory conduct. These limitations are necessary to prevent the Fourteenth Amendment from obliterating the Framers' carefully crafted balance of power between the States and the National Government. See *Flores*, at 520–524 (. . .the Fourteenth . . . Amendment "does not concentrate power in the general government for any purpose of police government within the States") (quoting T. Cooley, *Constitutional Limitations* 294, n. 1 (2d ed. 1871)). Foremost among these limitations is the time-honored principle that the Fourteenth Amendment, by its very terms, prohibits only state action. "[T]he principle has become firmly embedded in our constitutional law that the action inhibited by the first section of the Fourteenth Amendment is only such action as may fairly be said to be that of the States. That Amendment erects no shield against merely private conduct, however discriminatory or wrongful." *Shelley* v. *Kraemer*, 334 U.S. 1, 13, and n. 12 (1948).

Shortly after the Fourteenth Amendment was adopted, we decided two cases interpreting the Amendment's provisions, *United States* v. *Harris*, 106 U.S. 629 (1883), and the *Civil Rights Cases*, 109 U.S. 3 (1883). In *Harris*, the Court considered a challenge to § 2 of the Civil Rights Act of 1871. That section sought to punish "private persons" for "conspiring to deprive any one of the equal protection of the laws enacted by the State." 106 U.S., at 639. We concluded that this law exceeded Congress' § 5 power because the law was "directed exclusively against the action of private persons, without reference to the laws of the State, or their administration by her officers." *Id.,* at 640. In so doing, we reemphasized our statement from *Virginia* v. *Rives*, 100 U.S. 313, 318 (1880), that " 'these provisions of the fourteenth amendment have reference to State action exclusively, and not to any action of private individuals.' " *Harris*, at 639.

We reached a similar conclusion in the *Civil Rights Cases*. In those consolidated cases, we held that the public accommodation provisions of the Civil Rights Act of 1875, which applied to purely private conduct, were beyond the scope of the § 5 enforcement power. 109 U.S., at 11 ("Individual invasion of individual rights is not the subject-matter of the [Fourteenth] [A]mendment"). . . . *United States* v. *Cruikshank*, 92 U.S. 542, 554 (1876) ("The fourteenth amendment prohibits a state from depriving any person of life, liberty, or property, without due process of law; but this adds nothing to the rights of one citizen as against another. It simply furnishes an additional guaranty against any encroachment by the States upon the fundamental rights which belong to every citizen as a member of society").

The force of the doctrine of *stare decisis* behind these decisions stems not only from the length of time they have been on the books, but also from the insight attributable to the Members of the Court at that time. Every Member had been appointed by President Lincoln, Grant, Hayes, Garfield, or Arthur—and each of their judicial appointees obviously had intimate knowledge and familiarity with the events surrounding the adoption of the Fourteenth Amendment.

Petitioners contend that two more recent decisions have in effect overruled this longstanding limitation on Congress' § 5 authority. They rely on *United States* v. *Guest*, 383 U.S. 745 (1966), for the proposition that the rule laid down in the *Civil Rights Cases* is no longer good law. In *Guest*, the Court . . . [said] "we deal here with issues of statutory construction, not with issues of constitutional power." 383 U.S., at 749. Three Members of the Court, in a separate opinion by Justice Brennan, expressed the view that the *Civil Rights Cases* were wrongly decided, and that Congress could under § 5 prohibit actions by private individuals. 383 U.S., at 774 (opinion concurring in part and dissenting in part). Three other Members of the Court, who joined the opinion of the Court, joined a separate opinion by Justice Clark which in two or three sentences stated the conclusion that Congress could "punis[h] all conspiracies—with or without state action—that interfere with Fourteenth Amendment rights." *Id.*, at 762 (concurring opinion). Justice Harlan, in another separate opinion, commented with respect to the statement by these Justices: "The action of three of the Justices who joined the Court's opinion in nonetheless cursorily pronouncing themselves on the far-reaching constitutional questions deliberately not reached in Part II seems to me, to say the very least, extraordinary." *Id.*, at 762, n. 1 (opinion concurring in part and dissenting in part).

Though these three Justices saw fit to opine on matters not before the Court in *Guest*, the Court had no occasion to revisit the *Civil Rights Cases* and *Harris*, having determined "the indictment [charging private individuals with conspiring to deprive blacks of equal access to state facilities] in fact contain[ed] an express allegation of state involvement." 383 U.S., at 756. The Court concluded that the implicit allegation of "active connivance by agents of the State" eliminated any need to decide "the threshold level that state action must attain in order to create rights under the Equal Protection Clause." *Ibid.* All of this Justice Clark explicitly acknowledged. See *id.*, at 762 (concurring opinion) ("The Court's interpretation of the indictment clearly avoids the question whether Congress, by appropriate legislation, has the power to punish private conspiracies that interfere with Fourteenth Amendment rights, such as the right to utilize public facilities").

To accept petitioners' argument, moreover, one must add to the three Justices joining Justice Brennan's reasoned explanation for his belief that the *Civil Rights Cases* were wrongly decided, the three Justices joining Justice Clark's opinion who gave no explanation whatever for their similar view. This is simply not the way that reasoned constitutional adjudication proceeds. We accordingly have no hesitation in saying that it would take more than the naked dicta contained in Justice Clark's opinion, when added to Justice Brennan's opinion, to cast any doubt upon the enduring vitality of the *Civil Rights Cases* and *Harris*.

Petitioners also rely on *District of Columbia* v. *Carter*, 409 U.S. 418 (1973). *Carter* was a case addressing the question whether the District of Columbia was a "State" within the meaning of Rev. Stat. § 1979, 42 U.S.C. § 1983—a section which by its terms requires state action before it may be employed. A footnote in that opinion recites the same litany respecting *Guest* that petitioners rely on. This litany is of course entirely dicta, and in any event cannot rise above its source. We believe that the description of the § 5 power contained in the *Civil Rights Cases* is correct:

> But where a subject has not submitted to the general legislative power of Congress, but is only submitted thereto for the purpose of rendering effective some prohibition against particular [s]tate legislation or [s]tate action in reference to that subject, the power given is limited by its object, any legislation by Congress in the matter must necessarily be corrective in its character, adapted to counteract and redress the operation of such prohibited state laws or proceedings of [s]tate officers. 109 U.S., at 18.

Petitioners alternatively argue that, unlike the situation in the *Civil Rights Cases*, here there has been gender-based disparate treatment by state authorities, whereas in those cases there was no indication of such state action. There is abundant evidence, however, to show that the Congresses that enacted the Civil Rights Acts of 1871 and 1875 had a purpose similar to that of Congress in enacting § 13981: There were state laws on the books bespeaking equality of treatment, but in the administration of these laws there was discrimination against newly freed slaves. The statement of Representative Garfield in the House and that of Senator Sumner in the Senate are representative:

> "[T]he chief complaint is not that the laws of the State are unequal, but that even where the laws are just and equal on their face, yet, by a systematic maladministration of them, or a neglect or refusal to enforce their provisions, a portion of the people are denied equal protection under them." Cong. Globe, 42d Cong., 1st Sess., App. 153 (1871) (statement of Rep. Garfield).

> "The Legislature of South Carolina has passed a law giving precisely the rights contained in your 'supplementary civil rights bill.' But such a law remains a dead letter on her statute-books, because the State courts, comprised largely of those whom the Senator wishes to obtain amnesty for, refuse to enforce it." Cong. Globe, 42d Cong., 2d Sess., 430 (1872) (statement of Sen. Sumner).

See also, *e.g.,* Cong. Globe, 42d Cong., 1st Sess., at 653 (statement of Sen. Osborn); *id.,* at 457 (statement of Rep. Coburn); *id.,* at App. 78 (statement of Rep. Perry); 2 Cong. Rec. 457 (1874) (statement of Rep. Butler); 3 Cong. Rec. 945 (1875) (statement of Rep. Lynch).

But even if that distinction were valid, we do not believe it would save § 13981's civil remedy. For the remedy is simply not "corrective in its character, adapted to counteract and redress the operation of such prohibited [s]tate laws or proceedings of [s]tate officers." *Civil Rights Cases,* 109 U.S., at 18. Or, as we have phrased it in more recent cases, prophylactic legislation under § 5 must have a " 'congruence and proportionality between the injury to be prevented or remedied and the means adopted to that end." *Florida Prepaid Postsecondary Ed. Expense Bd.* v. *College Savings Bank,* 527 U.S. 627, 639 (1999); *Flores,* 521 U.S., at 526. Section 13981 is not aimed at proscribing discrimination by officials which the Fourteenth Amendment might not itself proscribe; it is directed not at any State or state actor, but at individuals who have committed criminal acts motivated by gender bias.

In the present cases, for example, § 13981 visits no consequence whatever on any Virginia public official involved in investigating or prosecuting Brzonkala's assault. The section is, therefore, unlike any of the § 5 remedies that we have previously upheld. . .

Section 13981 is also different from these previously upheld remedies in that it applies uniformly throughout the Nation. Congress' findings indicate that the problem of discrimination against the victims of gender-motivated crimes does not exist in all States, or even most States. By contrast, the § 5 remedy upheld in *Katzenbach* v. *Morgan,* was directed only to the State where the evil found by Congress existed, and in *South Carolina* v. *Katzenbach*, the remedy was directed only to those States in which Congress found that there had been discrimination.

For these reasons, we conclude that Congress' power under § 5 does not extend to the enactment of § 13981.

IV

Petitioner Brzonkala's complaint alleges that she was the victim of a brutal assault. But Congress' effort in § 13981 to provide a federal civil remedy can be sustained neither under the Commerce Clause nor under § 5 of the Fourteenth Amendment. If the allegations here are true, no civilized system of justice could fail to provide her a remedy for the conduct of respondent Morrison. But under our federal system that remedy must be provided by the Commonwealth of Virginia, and not by the United States. The judgment of the Court of Appeals is

Affirmed.

Opinion Footnotes

4 Justice SOUTER's dissent . . . cannot persuasively contradict *Lopez*'s conclusion that, in every case where we have sustained federal regulation under *Wickard*'s aggregation principle, the regulated activity was of an apparent commercial character. See, e.g., *Lopez,* 514 U.S. at 559–560, 580.

7 Justice SOUTER's dissent theory that *Gibbons* v. *Ogden,* 9 Wheat. 1 (1824), *Garcia* v. *San Antonio Metropolitan Transit Authority,* 469 U.S. 528 (1985), and the Seventeenth Amendment provide the answer to these cases is remarkable because it undermines this central principle of our constitutional system. As we have repeatedly noted, the Framers crafted the federal system of government so that the people's rights would be secured by the division of power. . . . It is thus a " 'permanent and indispensable feature of our constitutional system' " that " 'the federal judiciary is supreme in the exposition of the law of the Constitution.' " *Miller* v. *Johnson,* 515 U.S. 900, 922–923 (1995) (quoting *Cooper* v. *Aaron,* 358 U.S. 1, 18 (1958)).

No doubt the political branches have a role in interpreting and applying the Constitution, but ever since *Marbury* this Court has remained the ultimate expositor of the constitutional text.

JUSTICE THOMAS, concurring.

The majority opinion correctly applies our decision in *United States* v. *Lopez,* and I join it in full. I write separately only to express my view that the very notion of a "substantial effects" test under the Commerce Clause is inconsistent with the original understanding of Congress' powers [and the Court should return to that understanding]

JUSTICE SOUTER, with whom JUSTICE STEVENS, JUSTICE GINSBURG, and JUSTICE BREYER join, dissenting.

The Court says both that it leaves Commerce Clause precedent undisturbed and that the Civil Rights Remedy of the Violence Against Women Act of 1994, 42 U.S.C. § 13981, exceeds Congress's power under that Clause. I find the claims irreconcilable and respectfully dissent.[1]

I

Our cases, which remain at least nominally undisturbed, stand for the following propositions. Congress has the power to legislate with regard to activity that, in the aggregate, has a substantial effect on interstate commerce. See *Wickard* v. *Filburn,* 317 U.S. 111, 124-128 (1942); *Hodel* v. *Virginia Surface Mining & Reclamation Assn.,* 452 U.S. 264, 277 (1981). The fact of such a substantial effect is not an issue for the courts in the first instance, *ibid.,* but for the Congress, whose institutional capacity for gathering evidence and taking testimony far exceeds ours. By passing legislation, Congress indicates its conclusion, whether explicitly or not, that facts support its exercise of the commerce power. The business of the courts is to review the congressional assessment, not for soundness but simply for the rationality of concluding that a jurisdictional basis exists in fact.... Applying those propositions in these cases can lead to only one conclusion.

One obvious difference from *United States* v. *Lopez,* is the mountain of data assembled by Congress, here showing the effects of violence against women on interstate commerce.[2] Passage of the Act in 1994 was preceded by four years of hearings, which included testimony from physicians and law professors; from survivors of rape and domestic violence; and from representatives of state law enforcement and private business. The record includes reports on gender bias from task forces in 21 States, and we have the benefit of specific factual findings in the eight separate Reports issued by Congress and its committees over the long course leading to enactment.[8] ...

With respect to domestic violence, Congress received evidence for the following findings:

"Three out of four American women will be victims of violent crimes sometime during their life."

"Violence is the leading cause of injuries to women ages 15 to 44...."

"[A]s many as 50 percent of homeless women and children are fleeing domestic violence."

"Since 1974, the assault rate against women has outstripped the rate for men by at least twice for some age groups and far more for others."

"[B]attering 'is the single largest cause of injury to women in the United States.'"

"An estimated 4 million American women are battered each year by their husbands or partners."

"Over 1 million women in the United States seek medical assistance each year for injuries sustained [from] their husbands or other partners."

"Between 2,000 and 4,000 women die every year from [domestic] abuse."

"[A]rrest rates may be as low as 1 for every 100 domestic assaults."

"Partial estimates show that violent crime against women costs this country at least 3 billion—not million, but billion—dollars a year."

"[E]stimates suggest that we spend $5 to $10 billion a year on health care, criminal justice, and other social costs of domestic violence."

The evidence as to rape was similarly extensive, supporting these conclusions:

"[The incidence of] rape rose four times as fast as the total national crime rate over the past 10 years."

"According to one study, close to half a million girls now in high school will be raped before they graduate."

"[One hundred twenty-five thousand] college women can expect to be raped during this—or any—year."

"[T]hree-quarters of women never go to the movies alone after dark because of the fear of rape and nearly 50 percent do not use public transit alone after dark for the same reason."

"[Forty-one] percent of judges surveyed believed that juries give sexual assault victims less credibility than other crime victims."

"Less than 1 percent of all [rape] victims have collected damages."

"'[A]n individual who commits rape has only about 4 chances in 100 of being arrested, prosecuted, and found guilty of any offense.'"

"Almost one-quarter of convicted rapists never go to prison and another quarter received sentences in local jails where the average sentence is 11 months."

"[A]lmost 50 percent of rape victims lose their jobs or are forced to quit because of the crime's severity."

Based on the data thus partially summarized, Congress found that

crimes of violence motivated by gender have a substantial adverse effect on interstate commerce, by deterring potential victims from traveling interstate, from engaging in employment in interstate business, and from transacting with business, and in places involved, in interstate commerce ...[,] by diminishing national productivity, increasing medical and other costs, and decreasing the supply of and the demand for interstate products .... H. R. Conf. Rep. No. 103-711, p. 385 (1994).

Congress thereby explicitly stated the predicate for the exercise of its Commerce Clause power. Is its conclusion irrational in view of the data amassed? True, the methodology of particular studies may be challenged, and some of the figures arrived at may be disputed. But the sufficiency of the evidence before Congress to provide a rational basis for the finding cannot seriously be questioned. Cf. *Turner Broadcasting System, Inc.* v. *FCC,* 520 U.S. 180, 199 (1997) ("The Constitution gives to Congress the role of weighing conflicting evidence in the legislative process").

Indeed, the legislative record here is far more voluminous than the record compiled by Congress and found sufficient in two prior cases upholding Title II of the Civil Rights Act of 1964 against Commerce Clause challenges. In *Heart of Atlanta Motel, Inc.* v. *United States,* 379 U.S. 241 (1964), and *Katzenbach* v. *McClung,* 379 U.S. 294 (1964), the Court referred to evidence showing the consequences of racial discrimination by motels and restaurants on interstate commerce. Congress had relied on compelling anecdotal reports that individual instances of segregation cost thousands to millions of dollars....Congress also had evidence that the average black family spent substantially less than the average white family in the same income range on public accommodations, and that discrimination accounted for much of the difference.

While Congress did not, to my knowledge, calculate aggregate dollar values for the nationwide effects of racial discrimination in 1964, in 1994 it did rely on evidence of the harms caused by domestic violence and sexual assault, citing annual costs of $3 billion in 1990, see S. Rep. 101-545, and $5 to $10 billion in 1993, see S. Rep. No. 103-138, at 41. Equally important, though, gender-based violence in the 1990's was shown to operate in a manner similar to racial discrimination in the 1960's in reducing the mobility of employees and their production and consumption of goods shipped in interstate commerce. Like racial discrimination, "[g]ender-based violence bars its most likely targets—women—from full partic[ipation] in the national economy." *Id.,* at 54.

If the analogy to the Civil Rights Act of 1964 is not plain enough, one can always look back a bit further. In *Wickard*, we upheld the application of the Agricultural Adjustment Act to the planting and consumption of homegrown wheat. The effect on interstate commerce in that case followed from the possibility that wheat grown at home for personal consumption could ...[affect] supply and demand [, and thereby the price, of wheat] in interstate commerce. Supply and demand for goods in interstate commerce will also be affected by the deaths of 2,000 to 4,000 women annually at the hands of domestic abusers, see S. Rep. No. 101-545, at 36, and by the reduction in the work force by the 100,000 or more rape victims who lose their jobs each year or are forced to quit, see *id.,* at 56, H. R. Rep. No. 103-395, at 25–26. Violence against women may be found to affect interstate commerce and affect it substantially.[10]

II

The Act would have passed muster at any time between *Wickard* in 1942 and *Lopez* in 1995, a period in which the law enjoyed a stable understanding that congressional power under the Commerce Clause, complemented by the authority of the Necessary and Proper Clause, Art. I. § 8 cl. 18, extended to all activity that, when aggregated, has a substantial effect on interstate commerce. As already noted, this understanding was secure even against the turmoil at the passage of the Civil Rights Act of 1964, in the aftermath of which the Court not only reaffirmed the cumulative effects and rational basis features of the substantial effects test, see *Heart of Atlanta,* at 258; *McClung,* at 301–305, but declined to limit the commerce power through a formal distinction between legislation focused on "commerce" and statutes addressing "moral and social wrong[s]," *Heart of Atlanta,* at 257.

The fact that the Act does not pass muster before the Court today is therefore proof, to a degree that *Lopez* was not, that the Court's nominal adherence to the substantial effects test is merely that. Although a new jurisprudence has not emerged with any distinctness, it is clear that some congressional conclusions about obviously substantial, cumulative effects on commerce are being assigned lesser values than the once-stable doctrine would assign them. These devaluations are accomplished not by any express repudiation of the substantial effects test or its application through the aggregation of individual conduct, but by supplanting rational basis scrutiny with a new criterion of review.

Thus the elusive heart of the majority's analysis in these cases is its statement that Congress's findings of fact are "weakened" by the presence of a disfavored "method of reasoning." This seems to suggest that the "substantial effects" analysis is not a factual enquiry, for Congress in the first instance with subsequent judicial review looking only to the rationality of the congressional conclusion, but one of a rather different sort, dependent upon a uniquely judicial competence.

This new characterization of substantial effects has no support in our cases (the self-fulfilling prophecies of *Lopez* aside), least of all those the majority cites. Perhaps this explains why the majority is not content to rest on its cited precedent but...purports to rely on the sensible and traditional understanding that the listing in the Constitution of some powers implies the exclusion of others unmentioned.[11] The majority stresses that Art. I, § 8, enumerates the powers of Congress, including the commerce power, an enumeration implying the exclusion of powers not enumerated. It follows, for the majority, not only that there must be some limits to "commerce," but that some particular subjects arguably within the commerce power can be identified in advance as excluded, on the basis of characteristics other than their commercial effects. Such exclusions come into sight when the activity regulated is not itself commercial or when the States have traditionally addressed it in the exercise of the general police power....

The premise that the enumeration of powers implies that other powers are withheld is sound; the conclusion that some particular categories of subject matter are therefore presumptively beyond the reach of the commerce power is, however, a non sequitur. From the fact that Art. I, § 8, cl. 3 grants an authority limited to regulating commerce, it follows only that Congress may claim no authority under that section to address any subject that does not affect commerce. It does not at all follow that an activity affecting commerce nonetheless falls outside the commerce power, depending on the specific character of the activity, or the authority of a State to regulate it along with Congress. My disagreement with the majority is not, however, confined to logic, for history has shown that categorical exclusions have proven as unworkable in practice as they are unsupportable in theory.

A

Obviously, it would not be inconsistent with the text of the Commerce Clause itself to declare "noncommercial" primary activity beyond or presumptively beyond the scope of the commerce power. That variant of categorical approach is not, however, the sole textually permissible way of defining the scope of the Commerce Clause, and any such neat limitation would at least be suspect in the light of the final sentence of Article I, § 8, authorizing Congress to make "all Laws . . . necessary and proper" to give effect to its enumerated powers such as commerce. See *United States* v. *Darby,* 312 U.S. 100, 118 (1941) ("The power of Congress . . . extends to those activities intrastate which so affect interstate commerce or the exercise of the power of Congress over it as to make regulation of them appropriate means to the attainment of a legitimate end, the exercise of the granted power of Congress to regulate interstate commerce"). Accordingly, for significant periods of our history, the Court has defined the commerce power as plenary, unsusceptible to categorical exclusions, and this was the view expressed throughout the latter part of the 20th century in the substantial effects test. These two conceptions of the commerce power, plenary and categorically limited, are in fact old rivals, and today's revival of their competition summons up familiar history. . .

. . .

Since adherence to these formalistically contrived confines of commerce power in large measure provoked the judicial crisis of 1937, one might reasonably have doubted that Members of this Court would ever again toy with a return to the days before *NLRB* v. *Jones & Laughlin Steel Corp.,* 301 U.S. 1 (1937), which brought the earlier and nearly disastrous experiment to an end. And yet today's decision can only be seen as a step toward recapturing the prior mistakes. Its revival of a distinction between commercial and noncommercial conduct is at odds with *Wickard*, which repudiated that analysis,[13] and the enquiry into commercial purpose, first intimated by the *Lopez* concurrence, see *Lopez,* at 580 (opinion of *Kennedy,* J.), [was] . . . rejected for Commerce Clause purposes in *Heart of Atlanta,* at 257 and *Darby,* at 115.

. . .

. . .The legitimacy of the Court's current emphasis on the noncommercial nature of regulated activity . . . does not turn on any logic serving the text of the Commerce Clause or on the realism of the majority's view of the national economy. The essential issue is rather the strength of the majority's claim to have a constitutional warrant for its current conception of a federal relationship enforceable by this Court through limits on otherwise plenary commerce power. This conception is the subject of the majority's second categorical discount applied today to the facts bearing on the substantial effects test.

B

The Court finds it relevant that the statute addresses conduct traditionally subject to state prohibition under domestic criminal law, a fact said to have some heightened significance when the violent conduct in question is not itself aimed directly at interstate commerce or its instrumentalities. Again, history seems to be recycling, for the theory of traditional state concern as grounding a limiting principle has been rejected previously, and more than once. . . . [See] *Darby,* 312 U.S., at 123–124. . . [and] *Garcia v. San Antonio Metropolitan Transit Authority,* 469 U.S. 528 (1985). . . .[14]

The objection to reviving traditional state spheres of action as a consideration in commerce analysis, however, is compounded by a further defect just as fundamental. The defect, in essence, is the majority's rejection of the Founders' considered judgment that politics, not judicial review, should mediate between state and national interests as the strength and legislative jurisdiction of the National Government inevitably increased through the expected growth of the national economy. Whereas today's majority takes a leaf from the book of the old judicial economists in saying that the Court should somehow draw the line to keep the federal relationship in a proper balance, Madison, Wilson, and Marshall understood the Constitution very differently.

. . . Madison . . . in *The Federalist* No. 46 [wrote that t]he National Government "will partake sufficiently of the spirit [of the States], to be disinclined to invade the rights of the individual States, or the prerogatives of their governments." James Wilson likewise noted that "it was a favorite object in the Convention" to secure the sovereignty of the States, and that it had been achieved through the structure of the Federal Government. 2 *Elliot's Debates* 438–439. . . . In any case, this Court recognized the political component of federalism in the seminal *Gibbons* opinion. After declaring the plenary character of congressional power within the sphere of activity affecting commerce, the Chief Justice spoke for the Court in explaining that there was only one restraint on its valid exercise: "The wisdom and the discretion of Congress, their identity with the people, and the influence which their constituents possess at elections, are, in this, as in many other instances, as that, for example, of declaring war, the sole restraints on which they have relied, to secure them from its abuse. . . ." *Gibbons,* at 197.

. . .

The *Garcia* Court's rejection of "judicially created limitations" in favor of the intended reliance on national politics was all the more powerful owing to the Court's explicit recognition that in the centuries since the framing the relative powers of the two sovereign systems have markedly changed. Nationwide economic integration is the norm, the national political power has been augmented by its vast revenues, and the power of the States has been drawn down by the Seventeenth Amendment, eliminating selection of senators by state legislature in favor of direct election.

The *Garcia* majority recognized that economic growth and the burgeoning of federal revenue have not amended the Constitution, which contains no circuit breaker to preclude the political consequences of these developments. . . .

Amendments that alter the balance of power between the National and State Governments, like the Fourteenth, or that change the way the States are represented within the Federal Government, like the Seventeenth, are not rips in the fabric of the Framers' Constitution, inviting judicial repairs. The Seventeenth Amendment may indeed have lessened the enthusiasm of the Senate to represent the States as discrete sovereignties, but the Amendment did not convert the judiciary into an alternate shield against the commerce power.

C

. . .Today's majority. . .finds no significance whatever in the state support for the Act based upon the States' acknowledged failure to deal adequately with gender-based violence in state courts, and the belief of their own law enforcement agencies that national action is essential.

The National Association of [states'] Attorneys General supported the Act unanimously. . . . It was against this record of failure at the state level that the Act was passed to provide the choice of a federal forum in place of the state-court systems found inadequate to stop gender-biased violence. The Act accordingly offers a federal civil rights remedy aimed exactly at violence against women, as an alternative to the generic state tort causes of action found to be poor tools of action by the state task forces. See S. Rep. No. 101-545, at 45. . . . As the 1993 Senate Report put it, "The Violence Against Women Act is intended to respond both to the underlying attitude that this violence is somehow less serious than other crime and to the resulting failure of our criminal justice system to address such violence. Its goals are both symbolic and practical...." S. Rep. No. 103-138, at 38.

The collective opinion of state officials that the Act was needed continues virtually unchanged, and when the Civil Rights Remedy was challenged in court, the States came to its defense. Thirty-six of them and the Commonwealth of Puerto Rico have filed an *amicus* brief in support of petitioners in these cases, and only one State has taken respondents' side. It is, then, not the least irony of these cases that the States will be forced to enjoy the new federalism whether they want it or not....

III

All of this convinces me that today's ebb of the commerce power rests on error, and at the same time leads me to doubt that the majority's view will prove to be enduring law....

Opinion Footnotes

1 Finding the law a valid exercise of Commerce Clause power, I have no occasion to reach the question whether it might also be sustained as an exercise of Congress's power to enforce the Fourteenth Amendment.

2 It is true that these data relate to the effects of violence against women generally, while the civil rights remedy limits its scope to "crimes of violence motivated by gender"—presumably a somewhat narrower subset of acts. See 42 U.S.C. § 13981(b).... In any event...[h]aving identified the problem of violence against women, Congress may address what it sees as the most threatening manifestation; "reform may take one step at a time." *Williamson* v. *Lee Optical of Okla., Inc.,* 348 U.S. 483, 489 (1955).

8 See S. Rep. No. 101-545 (1990); Majority Staff of Senate Committee on the Judiciary, *Violence Against Women: The Increase of Rape in America*, 102d Cong., 1st Sess. (Comm. Print 1991); S. Rep. No. 102-197 (1991); Majority Staff of Senate Committee on the Judiciary, *Violence Against Women: A Week in the Life of America*, 102d Cong., 2d Sess. (Comm. Print 1992); S. Rep. No. 103-138 (1993); Majority Staff of Senate Committee on the Judiciary, *The Response to Rape: Detours on the Road to Equal Justice*, 103d Cong., 1st Sess. (Comm. Print 1993); H. R. Rep. No. 103-395 (1993); H. R. Conf. Rep. No. 103-711 (1994).

10 It should go without saying that my view of the limit of the congressional commerce power carries no implication about the wisdom of exercising it to the limit. I and other Members of this Court appearing before Congress have repeatedly argued against the federalization of traditional state crimes and the extension of federal remedies to problems for which the States have historically taken responsibility and may deal with today.

11 The claim that powers not granted were withheld was the chief Federalist argument against the necessity of a bill of rights.... The Federalists did not, of course, prevail on this point; most States voted for the Constitution only after proposing amendments and the First Congress speedily adopted a Bill of Rights. While that document protected a range of specific individual rights against federal infringement, it did not, with the possible exception of the Second Amendment, offer any similarly specific protections to areas of state sovereignty.

13 Contrary to the Court's suggestion...[t]he *Wickard* Court admitted that Filburn's activity "may not be regarded as commerce" but insisted that "it may still, whatever its nature, be reached by Congress if it exerts a substantial economic effect on interstate commerce...." 317 U.S., at 125....[I]f substantial effects on commerce are proper subjects of concern under the Commerce Clause, what difference should it make whether the causes of those effects are themselves commercial? Cf., *e.g., National Organization for Women, Inc.* v. *Scheidler,* 510 U.S. 249, 258 (1994) ("An enterprise surely can have a detrimental influence on interstate or foreign commerce without having its own profit-seeking motives").

14 The Constitution of 1787 did, in fact, forbid some exercises of the commerce power. Article I, § 9, cl. 6, barred Congress from giving preference to the ports of one State over those of another. More strikingly, the Framers protected the slave trade from federal interference, see Art. I, § 9, cl. 1, and confirmed the power of a State to guarantee the chattel status of slaves who fled to another State, see Art. IV, § 2, cl. 3. These reservations demonstrate the plenary nature of the federal power; the exceptions prove the rule. Apart from them, proposals to carve islands of state authority out of the stream of commerce power were entirely unsuccessful. Roger Sherman's proposed definition of federal legislative power as excluding "matters of internal police" met Gouverneur Morris's response that "[t]he internal police . . . ought to be infringed in many cases" and was voted down eight to two. 2 *Records of the Federal Convention of 1787*, pp. 25-26 (M. Farrand ed. 1911) (hereinafter Farrand). The Convention similarly rejected Sherman's attempt to include in Article V a proviso that "no state shall . . . be affected in its internal police." 5 *Elliot's Debates* 551-552. Finally, Rufus King suggested an explicit bill of rights for the States, a device that might indeed have set aside the areas the Court now declares off-limits. 1 Farrand 493 ("As the fundamental rights of individuals are secured by express provisions in the State Constitutions; why may not a like security be provided for the Rights of States in the National Constitution"). That proposal, too, came to naught. In short, to suppose that enumerated powers must have limits is sensible; to maintain that there exist judicially identifiable areas of state regulation immune to the plenary congressional commerce power even though falling within the limits defined by the substantial effects test is to deny our constitutional history.

JUSTICE BREYER, with whom JUSTICE STEVENS joins, and with whom JUSTICE SOUTER and JUSTICE GINSBURG join as to Part I-A, dissenting.

No one denies the importance of the Constitution's federalist principles. Its state/federal division of authority protects liberty—both by restricting the burdens that government can impose from a distance and by facilitating citizen participation in government that is closer to home. The question is how the judiciary can best implement that original federalist understanding where the Commerce Clause is at issue.

I

The majority holds that the federal commerce power does not extend to such "noneconomic" activities as "noneconomic, violent criminal conduct" that significantly affects interstate commerce only if we "aggregate" the interstate "effect[s]" of individual instances. Justice Souter explains why history, precedent, and legal logic militate against the majority's approach. I agree and join his opinion. I add that the majority's holding illustrates the difficulty of finding a workable judicial Commerce Clause touchstone—a set of comprehensible interpretive rules that courts might use to impose some meaningful limit, but not too great a limit, upon the scope of the legislative authority that the Commerce Clause delegates to Congress.

A

Consider the problems. The "economic/noneconomic" distinction is not easy to apply. Does the local street corner mugger engage in "economic" activity or "noneconomic" activity when he mugs for money? See *Perez* v.

United States, 402 U.S. 146 (1971) (aggregating local "loan sharking" instances)... Would evidence that desire for economic domination underlies many brutal crimes against women save the present statute?...

The line becomes yet harder to draw given the need for exceptions. The Court itself would permit Congress to aggregate, hence regulate, "noneconomic" activity taking place at economic establishments. See *Heart of Atlanta Motel, Inc.* v. *United States,* 379 U.S. 241 (1964) (upholding civil rights laws forbidding discrimination at local motels); *Katzenbach* v. *McClung,* 379 U.S. 294 (1964) (same for restaurants)... And it would permit Congress to regulate where that regulation is "an essential part of a larger regulation of economic activity, in which the regulatory scheme could be undercut unless the intrastate activity were regulated." *Lopez,* at 561; cf. Controlled Substances Act, 21 U.S.C. § 801 *et seq.* (regulating drugs produced for home consumption). Given the former exception, can Congress simply rewrite the present law and limit its application to restaurants, hotels, perhaps universities, and other places of public accommodation? Given the latter exception, can Congress save the present law by including it, or much of it, in a broader "Safe Transport" or "Workplace Safety" act?

More important, why should we give critical constitutional importance to the economic, or noneconomic, nature of an interstate-commerce-affecting *cause*? If chemical emanations through indirect environmental change cause identical, severe commercial harm outside a State, why should it matter whether local factories or home fireplaces release them? The Constitution itself refers only to Congress' power to "regulate Commerce... among the several States," and to make laws "necessary and proper" to implement that power. Art. I, § 8, cls. 3, 18. The language says nothing about either the local nature, or the economic nature, of an interstate-commerce-affecting cause.

. . .

And in a world where most everyday products or their component parts cross interstate boundaries, Congress will frequently find it possible to redraft a statute using language that ties the regulation to the interstate movement of some relevant object, thereby regulating local criminal activity or, for that matter, family affairs. See, *e.g.,* Child Support Recovery Act of 1992, 18 U.S.C. § 228. Although this possibility does not give the Federal Government the power to regulate everything, it means that any substantive limitation will apply randomly in terms of the interests the majority seeks to protect. How much would be gained, for example, were Congress to reenact the present law in the form of "An Act Forbidding Violence Against Women Perpetrated at Public

Accommodations or by Those Who Have Moved in, or through the Use of Items that Have Moved in, Interstate Commerce"? Complex Commerce Clause rules creating fine distinctions that achieve only random results do little to further the important federalist interests that called them into being...

. . .

Since judges cannot change the world, the "defect" means that, within the bounds of the rational, Congress, not the courts, must remain primarily responsible for striking the appropriate state/federal balance. *Garcia* v. *San Antonio Metropolitan Transit Authority,* 469 U.S. 528, 552 (1985)... Congress is institutionally motivated to do so. Its Members represent state and local district interests. They consider the views of state and local officials when they legislate, and they have even developed formal procedures to ensure that such consideration takes place. Moreover, Congress often can better reflect state concerns for autonomy in the details of sophisticated statutory schemes than can the judiciary, which cannot easily gather the relevant facts and which must apply more general legal rules and categories....

B

I would also note that Congress, when it enacted the statute, followed procedures that help to protect the federalism values at stake. It provided adequate notice to the States of its intent to legislate in an "are[a] of traditional state regulation." And in response, attorneys general in the overwhelming majority of States (38) supported congressional legislation, telling Congress that "[o]ur experience as Attorneys General strengthens our belief that the problem of violence against women is a national one, requiring federal attention, federal leadership, and federal funds."

Moreover, as Justice Souter has pointed out, Congress compiled a "mountain of data" explicitly documenting the interstate commercial effects of gender-motivated crimes of violence....Consequently, the law before us seems to represent an instance, not of state/federal conflict, but of state/federal efforts to cooperate in order to help solve a mutually acknowledged national problem. Cf. §§ 300w–10, 3796gg, 3796hh, 10409, 13931 (providing federal moneys to encourage state and local initiatives to combat gender-motivated violence).

I call attention to the legislative process leading up to enactment of this statute because, as the majority recognizes, it far surpasses that which led to the enactment of the statute we considered in *Lopez*. And even were I to accept

Lopez as an accurate statement of the law, which I do not, that distinction provides a possible basis for upholding the law here. . . .

II

Given my conclusion on the Commerce Clause question, I need not consider Congress' authority under § 5 of the Fourteenth Amendment. Nonetheless, I doubt the Court's reasoning rejecting that source of authority. The Court points out that in *United States* v. *Harris,* 106 U.S. 629 (1883), and the *Civil Rights Cases,* 109 U.S. 3 (1883), the Court held that § 5 does not authorize Congress to use the Fourteenth Amendment as a source of power to remedy the conduct of *private persons.* That is certainly so. The Federal Government's argument, however, is that Congress used § 5 to remedy the actions of *state actors,* namely, those States which, through discriminatory design or the discriminatory conduct of their officials, failed to provide adequate (or any) state remedies for women injured by gender-motivated violence—a failure that the States, and Congress, documented in depth.

Neither *Harris* nor the *Civil Rights Cases* considered this kind of claim. The Court in *Harris* specifically said that it treated the federal laws in question as "directed *exclusively* against the action of private persons, without reference to the laws of the State, or their administration by her officers." 106 U.S., at 640; see also *Civil Rights Cases,* 109 U.S., at 14 (observing that the statute did "not profess to be corrective of any constitutional wrong committed by the States" and that it established "rules for the conduct of individuals in society towards each other, . . . without referring in any manner to any supposed action of the State or its authorities").

The Court responds directly to the relevant "state actor" claim by finding that the present law lacks " 'congruence and proportionality' " to the state discrimination that it purports to remedy. That is because the law. . .is not "directed . . . at any State or state actor."

But why can Congress not provide a remedy against private actors? Those private actors, of course, did not themselves violate the Constitution. But this Court has held that Congress at least sometimes can enact remedial "[l]egislation . . . [that] prohibits conduct which is not itself unconstitutional." *Flores,* 521 U.S. at 518; see also *Katzenbach* v. *Morgan,* at 651; *South Carolina* v. *Katzenbach,* at 308. The statutory remedy . . .restricts private actors only by imposing liability for private conduct that is, in the main, already forbidden by state law. Why is the remedy "disproportionate"? And given the relation between remedy and violation—the creation of a federal remedy to substitute

> for constitutionally inadequate state remedies—where is the lack of "congruence"?
>
> The majority adds that Congress found that the problem of inadequacy of state remedies "does not exist in all States, or even most States." But Congress had before it the task force reports of at least 21 States documenting constitutional violations. And it made its own findings about pervasive gender-based stereotypes hampering many state legal systems, sometimes unconstitutionally so. See, *e.g.,* S. Rep. No. 103-138, pp. 38, 41–42, 44–47 (1993); S. Rep. No. 102-197, pp. 39, 44–49 (1991); H. R. Conf. Rep. No. 103-711, p. 385 (1994). The record nowhere reveals a congressional finding that the problem "does not exist" elsewhere. Why can Congress not take the evidence before it as evidence of a national problem? This Court has not previously held that Congress must document the existence of a problem in every State prior to proposing a national solution.
>
> Despite my doubts about the majority's § 5 reasoning, I need not, and do not, answer the § 5 question, which I would leave for more thorough analysis if necessary on another occasion. Rather, in my view, the Commerce Clause provides an adequate basis for the statute before us. And I would uphold its constitutionality as the "necessary and proper" exercise of legislative power granted to Congress by that Clause. . . .

Case Questions

1. The Court here divides over a number of questions; one is the original understanding of the commerce power (compare Souter's footnotes 11, 13, and 14 with Rehnquist's claim in his footnote 7 that the Framers intended for the Supreme Court to check congressional intrusions onto states' rights). As a practical matter, which institution is more likely to protect diligently the sphere of state authority: Congress members who are obliged to stand for election every two or six years in state and local elections, or justices trained in the law and appointed for life? (Might your selection be different if the question were one of protecting individual rights, such as freedom of speech?)

2. Should we, or the Court, care what the Framers believed in the 1787–1825 period? Should we care what people like Ulysses S. Grant or the justices he appointed in the 1800s believed about the Fourteenth Amendment? Why?

3. Does Justice Souter's logic not imply that Congress could constitutionally, if it chose, replace all state laws about armed robbery with federal laws, since robbery obviously affects the national economy? Does Chief Justice Rehnquist not imply the same thing, since robbery is economic activity? Why is it okay with the Court majority

that Congress regulates mere possession, not just sales, of intoxicating drugs? What is "economic" about possessing marijuana?

4. Consider the portion of the Court opinion that we highlighted in bold. Brzonkala in fact received zero "remedy" from the laws of Virginia, since neither Morrison nor any of his alleged partners in crime were never charged with a crime. Moreover, the Court majority seems to admit that this problem of unremedied criminal violence against women is "pervasive" (even if not documented for every single state), and that the prosecutorial branch in most of the states wants the federal litigation remedy that Congress offered, to supplement the limited resources of the state governments. Do you believe that if Congress were to document a similarly pervasive problem of unprosecuted or unpunished criminal violence against, say, Blacks, or Latinos, the Court would continue to insist that the equal protection clause plus Congress's enforcement powers are not enough to authorize federal power over the situation?

5. Justice Sandra Day O'Connor, the author of the majority opinion in *Davis v. Monroe County BOE* (see Chapter 6), cast the deciding vote in this case. Since *U.S. v. Lopez* (1995), she and the four dissenters in *Davis* usually formed a voting bloc that struck down federal laws that supersede state power, as they do here. Is O'Connor's opinion in *Morrison* consistent with her vote in *Davis* one year earlier? Why or why not?

6. Does *Davis* suggest that schools and colleges could still be liable under Title IX? Or does *Morrison* suggest that *Davis* is obsolete?

While the Court declared § 13981 of the Violence Against Women Act to be an unconstitutional overreach of Congress' commerce authority, other aspects of VAWA remained good law and proved instrumental in facilitating the investigation and prosecution of violent crimes perpetuated against women. VAWA also established the Office on Violence Against Women (OVW) within the U.S. Department of Justice and charged this new executive entity with distributing federal grant money to various state, local and tribal authorities to address and improve their responses for handling violent crimes against women and to organizations that provide services to the victims of domestic violence/abuse, sexual assaults, dating violence and/or stalking.

In 2013, Congress passed the Violence Against Women Reauthorization Act and added a variety of new protections.[75] In addition, this reauthorization is groundbreaking because it includes a nondiscrimination provision which adds protections for individuals who are discriminated against because of their real or perceived sexual orientations or gender identities. In effect, this means that LGBTQ individuals who are the victims of domestic violence/abuse, sexual assaults, dating violence and/or stalking are legally entitled to access and utilize the services of all of the organizations and entities that receive grants from OVW. This development is significant for extending services to individuals in same-sex relationships who may be the victims of domestic and sexual violence. Similarly, the trans-inclusive reauthorized VAWA guarantees that transgender individuals can access programs, and that they must be allowed to utilize sex-segregated and/or sex-specific services that correlate with their articulated gender identities. Furthermore, recognizing that domestic and sexual violence pervades all types of relationships makes LGBTQ individuals and their relationships legible in important ways.

WOMEN AND SEXUAL VIOLENCE ON CAMPUS

Title IX is not limited to students' rights to be free from discrimination in their access to athletics and academics. Sexual misconduct and sexual violence on campus have also limited women's collegiate opportunities. This issue received meaningful attention during the Obama administration. On April 4, 2011, Assistant Secretary for Civil Rights of the Office of Civil Rights at the U.S. Department of Education Russlynn Ali released what became known as the "Dear Colleague" letter. In this 19-page letter, Ali included the directive that "If a school knows or reasonably should know about student-on-student harassment that creates a hostile environment, Title IX requires the school to take immediate action to eliminate the harassment, prevent its recurrence, and address its effects." She stated that sexual violence is a form of sex discrimination thus making sexual violence on campus a Title IX issue. The letter defined sexual violence as "physical sexual acts perpetrated against a person's will or where a person is incapable of giving consent due to the victim's use of drugs or alcohol. An individual also may be unable to give consent due to an intellectual or other disability. A number of different acts fall into the category of sexual violence, including rape, sexual assault, sexual battery, and sexual coercion."[76]

The "Dear Colleague" letter was significant in that it provided guidance as to how all institutions covered by Title IX ("any education program or activity receiving Federal financial assistance") should handle sexual violence on campus. The *Chronicle of Higher Education* indicated that the threat of losing funding for Title IX violations contributed to a significant increase in sexual harassment and sexual violence investigations between 2011 and 2016.[77] Three years later, on April 29, 2014, the DOE Office for Civil Rights issued "Questions and Answers on Title

IX and Sexual Violence" which identified policies and procedures focusing on the sexual harassment complaints and the due process rights of those accused of committing sexual harassment.[78]

The directives outlined in the "Dear Colleague" letter and the "Questions and Answers" that followed were rescinded early on in the Trump Administration by Education Secretary Betsy DeVos on September 22, 2017. DeVos' decision to rescind the directives was largely in response to criticisms levied against the Obama-era directives, with particular concern for protections of persons accused as perpetrators. For example, under the 2011 directive, the accused had to be found guilty if the "preponderance of evidence" standard of proof was met. Once the 2011 directives were rescinded, schools could choose to use the stiffer "clear and convincing evidence" standard to determine the guilt of accused persons. Critics had suggested that the lower "preponderance of evidence" standard denied the accused their due process rights.

According to the September 22, 2017 letter from the U.S. Department of Education Office of Civil Rights rescinding the Obama Adminstration "Letter" of 2011, that 2011 policy letter had created the following due process problems:

> The [Obama policy] Letter insisted that schools with an appeals process allow complainants to appeal not-guilty findings [producing a double jeopardy problem—AU], even though many schools had previously followed procedures reserving appeal for accused students. The Letter discouraged cross-examination by the parties, suggesting that to recognize a right to such cross-examination might violate Title IX. The Letter forbade schools from relying on investigations of criminal conduct by law-enforcement authorities to resolve Title IX complaints, forcing schools to establish policing and judicial systems while at the same time directing schools to resolve complaints on an expedited basis. The Letter provided that any due-process protections afforded to accused students should not "unnecessarily delay" resolving the charges against them.[79]

The 2017 announcement also extends a mediation option between accusers and the accused which was not permitted based on the 2011 directives. Supporters of the DeVos decision argued that it gave to the accused "greater access to evidence and stress[ed] that the identity of their accusers and alleged conduct must be revealed before [the accused are] questioned."[80] Critics of the move, including Fatima Goss Graves of the National Women's Law Center, claimed that the changes would be "devastating" to the victims because they would be discouraged from reporting assaults.[81] Secretary DeVos defended her decision on the grounds that it would balance the rights of victims and the accused.

WOMEN CRIMINALS

Prostitution

Unequal Enforcement—Does It Take Two to Tango?

As of 1968, according to *Black's Law Dictionary* (4th ed. rev., p.1386), and in accord with many centuries of Anglo-American common law, prostitution was a crime that only a female could commit. "Prostitution: common lewdness of a woman for gain. . . .The act or practice of a female. . .offering her body for hire to an indiscriminate intercourse with men for money or its equivalent." In the decade of the seventies, under pressure from the women's movement, prostitution laws were made gender-neutral, such that men or women could each be found guilty for selling sex. But in the view of many an equal-rights feminist, inequity persisted, because the prostitute, generally female, was both more often and more harshly punished than her male partner-in-crime, the customer. This case illustrates that perspective.

> ### IN THE MATTER OF [DORA] P.
> 400 N.Y.S.2d 455 (Family Court, N.Y.County 1977)
>
> **TAYLOR, J.**
>
> Respondent [Dora] P. is a 14-year-old female. She is before this court on the complaint of D. The petition alleges, . . . "Respondent did offer to perform a deviate sexual act for U.S. currency," an act which, if committed by an adult, would constitute the crime of prostitution (Penal Law, § 230.00, a class B misdemeanor) [and, further, that she robbed the petitioner. . .]. The complaining witness was not charged with the violation of patronizing a prostitute (Penal Law, § 230.05). Nor was he charged with any other crime applicable to these facts.
>
> Section 230.00 of the Penal Law reads: "A person is guilty of prostitution when such person engages or agrees or offers to engage in sexual conduct with another person in return for a fee." Respondent. . .has moved to dismiss the prostitution charge on constitutional . . .grounds. . . . [T]he court holds . . .section 230.00. . .unconstitutional under the New York State Constitution [as] . . . a denial of equal protection.

[T]he New York State Constitution guarantees that: "No person shall be denied the equal protection of the laws of this state...." This provision provides at least as broad protection as its Federal counterpart.

The equal protection clause is offended when the State discriminates between classes of citizens similarly situated on arbitrary and unreasonable grounds not related to the objective of the legislation. The selective enforcement of a law against a particular class of individuals on the basis of sex is no less offensive to the equal protection clause of the New York State Constitution than classification by sex on the face of the statute.

Sex is a suspect classification in New York State. Thus, sections 230.00 and 230.05 as applied are subject to strict scrutiny. However, ...[m]odern day theorists ...argue, convincingly we think, that a middle level of review presently exists...[, and it requires that we] examine such factors as the classification involved, the constitutional and societal importance of the interests adversely affected and the relative invidiousness of the basis upon which the classification is drawn.

Prostitution is a class B misdemeanor, carrying a penalty of up to 90 days' imprisonment. A person may be found guilty of prostitution for simply "agreeing" to perform a sexual act, even if the patron is the solicitor. In contrast, patronizing a prostitute is merely a violation carrying a penalty of up to 15 days' imprisonment or up to $250 fine. (Penal Law, § 230.05.) The conduct engaged in by the prostitute and the patron is nearly identical and the wording of the respective statutes is quite similar.

The instant case presents clear evidence of intentional selective enforcement of the prostitution statutes against females. The overwhelming majority of arrests made under section 230.00 of the Penal Law are of female prostitutes. During the first six months of 1977,...[a]lthough 3,219 arrests were made for prostitution, only 62 persons were charged with patronizing a prostitute. Of the 2,944 female prostitutes arrested, only 60 of their male patrons were charged with a violation. This data supports the conclusion that those assigned the task of enforcing the law harbor the attitude that women who supply sex are immoral whereas the men who demand their services are considered blameless.

The methods of enforcement used by the police contribute to the selective enforcement of the prostitution laws against females. Arrests for prostitution are rarely made on the complaint of a private citizen. A police officer must be directly solicited to make an arrest. Male undercover police officers are assigned

> to pose as patrons to entrap streetwalkers. However, female plainclothes officers are not presently assigned to pose as prostitutes to entrap male patrons. Thus, the method of enforcement of the prostitution laws is sex biased, aimed only at punishing the female prostitute.
>
> Thus, the court concludes that even were sex not a "suspect classification," the prostitution statutes nonetheless violate the equal protection clause. There is no, nor has the Corporation Counsel suggested any, reasonable justification for penalizing the conduct of female prostitutes more severely than the conduct of their male patrons. The prostitution laws have undeniably been selectively enforced against females because of their sex. . . . This court can find no real difference between the conduct of the prostitute and the patron. The patron pays and the prostitute receives compensation for her services. Yet, under the wording of the statute and frequently in practice, the patron may be the solicitor. . . . [T]he law as heretofore enforced is an unjust discrimination against women in the matter of an offense which, in its very nature, if completed, requires the participation of men.
>
> . . . The male patron and female prostitute are equal partners in commercial sex. This court can find no legitimate distinction between their conduct. Such intentional and selective enforcement of these laws almost exclusively against females because of their sex violates the equal protection clause of the New York State Constitution. . . .

This decision was reversed on appeal, without much explanation. The appellate court noted simply the judge below erred in that she "lump[ed] together two separate crimes in order to obtain a favorable statistical base. That prostitution and patronizing a prostitute are discrete crimes is apparent when consideration is given to the separate acts necessary to effect their commission."[82] The national pattern of statutes that accord prostitution much harsher penalties than the offense of "patronizing a prostitute" and of police practices that arrest and charge prostitutes in far greater numbers than their purchasers has been typically upheld by courts on the grounds that the prostitute is analogous to the drug dealer, while the buyer of sex is analogous to the drug buyer. The seller in each case is the "profiteer" and commits the crime with far more frequency than the buyer does. See e.g., *People v. Superior Court (Hartway)* 19 Cal.3d 338; 562 P.2d 1315 (Supreme Ct. Calif., 1977).

In recent years many jurisdictions have attempted to deter "johns" (clients), in light of a community reluctance to impose harsh penalties, by shaming them instead, by publicizing their photos and names and addresses. On June 22, 2005,

Chicago, for instance, announced that it would post such information about all persons arrested for soliciting prostitutes on its website for a 30-day period (and updated daily), thereby joining such cities as Durham, Akron, and Denver which already publicize similar information either on local TV or the Internet.[83] Other local governments that have used social media, press conferences and other public forums to shame individuals arrested for purchasing sex from prostitutes include Colorado Springs, Colorado; Albany, New York; Flint, Michigan; Prince George's County, Maryland; and in California: Oakland, Richmond, Fresno and Orange Counties. A more humorous, and early effort to deter clients from purchasing sex occurred when New York City Mayor Ed Koch hosted "The John Hour," when he used public radio to name men who had been convicted for hiring prostitutes. "The John Hour" lasted just two minutes, and happened one time, although it represented a creative effort to shame prostitution clients.[84] Other creative efforts have included Nassau County, New York which, in 2013, conducted several stings over about six weeks using undercover police officers posing as prostitutes. The Nassau County Police Department placed an online advertisement for an escort service. The clients would meet the undercover police officers in hotel rooms. Upon their arrival they were filmed while they made agreements to pay for sex. "Operation Flush the Johns" resulted in the arrest of 104 men who were charged with misdemeanors.[85]

The CEASE program (Cities Empowered Against Sexual Exploitation) is intended to reduce demand for prostitution through education. This national program, implemented in Seattle, Boston, Denver, Portland, Chicago and Phoenix, focuses on both deterrence and accountability. The program seeks to deter clients from pursuing prostitutes through interventions such as messages that are shown as pop-ups when potential "johns" use such Internet search terms as "paying for sex." These pop-up messages are intended to deter "johns" by notifying them of their increased chances of being caught, should they follow up seeking to hire a prostitute, because of their Internet search history. Early successes are noted by increased client arrests and the number of client arrests exceeding the number of prostitute arrests in many of these cities.[86]

Feminists Divide: Modern Remnant of Slavery Versus Just Another Job

There are a few things in America that money cannot (lawfully) buy; one is babies, another is bodily organs, and another is sex.[87] Many feminists endorse the view that the purchase of sex from another human being is peculiarly degrading, that the selling of sex is the selling of oneself in a much more profound sense than the selling of labor is.[88] No one finds it objectionable, for instance, for a parent to force a teenage daughter to work in a restaurant or in retail, in order to make money, yet virtually everyone sees the harm in a parent forcing a child to solicit sex in exchange for money.

One feminist in this camp is Andrea Dworkin, who defines prostitution as follows: "Prostitution . . . is the use of a woman's body for sex by a man, he pays money, he does what he wants. . . . It is the mouth, the vagina, the rectum, penetrated usually by a penis, sometimes hands, sometimes objects, by one man and then another and then another and then another and then another. That's what it is. . . . Prostitution in and of itself is an abuse of a woman's body."[89]

Catharine MacKinnon, too, suggests that prostitution is sensibly viewed as:

sexually exploitative and discriminatory, in need of abolition like slavery. In this view pimps and patrons should be vigorously prosecuted while support and empowering relief should be provided for those used in the industry. This view is informed by the injuries of prostitution to the prostituted, contending that the routine violence of prostitution mocks free choice and the pretense that it is employment feeds on and exacerbates women's second-class status.

She cites research that documents that 90% of street prostitutes are controlled by pimps, through such measures as beatings, rapes and sexual torture (including in a sizable percentage of cases of physical mutilation). One study (in 1982) reported that 66% of prostitutes are beaten by pimps and 65% by customers; another (in 1993) reported 84% are beaten—on average 58 times a year by pimps and 45 times a year by customers. This study added that 53% experienced sexual torture by pimps an average of 49 times a year.[90]

In contrast, other feminists argue that the legalization or decriminalization of prostitution would provide women with protection from exploitation and abuse, and enable women to freely exercise their choice to engage in sex work for any number of reasons including economic pressures and sexual empowerment. As Janet Duran, a sex worker from New Jersey explained, "I have nothing to be ashamed of. It's a real job like every other job."[91] Similarly, the economic argument is summed up by the following comment from a sex worker: "[I]s offering 30 minutes of sex for, say $80, really more awful than working for 8 hours in a sweatshop and earning $4.50 an hour? Some of us don't think so."[92]

In addition, for some marginalized populations who are the targets of intersecting forces of discrimination, sex work is one of the only ways for individuals to make money. As Ceyenne, an activist and former dominatrix in New

York explained, "If you don't want prostitution, or you don't want trans people to solicit, hire them. Simple."[93]

Yet another perspective is presented by Donna Marie Niles, reflecting back after she had left the sex industry:

> I took up work as profitably as I could [at age 19] within a structure that basically offered me either one man in marriage or many men for cash. As a white, educated, feminist hooker, I made more money than I ever expected to see again in life. Because I was an independent contractor, I had lot of time left over to live my life in. . . .[I]t was difficult to leave.
>
> I'll never forget the depression I experienced in my first straight job. . .I was a secretary. . . .As a secretary I was invisible, treated with either disregard or patronizing contempt. My credibility took a sky dive. . .On top of this, I worked a regimented forty hour work week for ridiculously low pay. I was literally earning in two weeks what I had previously made in an evening and paying taxes! It was a shocking welcome back to respectability.
>
> But I have endured, and have not returned for many reasons. One was the constant threat of arrest. It wears you out. . . . However the major reason I left was I simply could no longer justify working in an industry that profited from the sexual objectification of women. Since I felt I could no longer be in collusion with men who make billions from our suffering [I left the industry].[94]

Proponents of decriminalization and legalization argue that this would enable sex workers to act without fear of arrest. The Swedish model—implemented in Sweden in 1999—decriminalized the sale of sex, but continued to criminalize the purchase of sex. The perspective of the Swedish model is to protect the sex worker, but to punish pimps and johns, who are viewed as perpetrating the exploitation of women's bodies. This approach reduced street prostitution by as much as fifty percent, but it has not eliminated sex work. Sex workers themselves criticize the law because many argue that this approach forces them into more secluded locations and makes them more vulnerable to violence and exploitation.[95]

In contrast, legalization of prostitution allows the creation of a legal marketplace for the exchange of sexual services for money. New Zealand and some states in Australia have moved to full legalization in recent years which enables adults to buy and sell sex often via licensed brothels.[96] While there are pros and cons to this approach, legalization does remove the adversarial relationship between sex workers and law enforcement and enables the former to reach out to the latter when they are at risk of or the victims of violence and exploitation. For example, Annah Pickering, who does street outreach for the New Zealand Prostitutes' Collective, describes a more recent dynamic with police [post-legalization] that would be unthinkable almost anywhere else. "We used to wave the police down for help, and they'd keep driving, but now they take sex workers' complaints seriously," she said. . . "One client negotiated with a street worker; she did the act, and he refused to pay. She waved a cop down, and he told the client he had to pay and took him to the A.T.M. to get the money."[97] Furthermore, because legalization removes the ability of police to arrest sex workers and their clients, it eliminates the opportunities for law enforcement to engage in the selective enforcement of solicitation laws on people of color and transgender women. Statistical evidence indicates that those arrested for both sex work and the purchase of sex are overwhelmingly people of color, and that these individuals are racially profiled by police and charged with crimes in numbers that are disproportionate to the actual population of sex workers and individuals who hire them.[98]

While it seems unlikely that either decriminalization of sex work or adoption of the Swedish model will occur in the U.S., the reality remains that the sale of sexual services constitutes a massive underground economy across the country. In recent decades, government enforcement efforts have prioritized the worst offenders: traffickers in sexual slavery.

Sexual Slavery: *U.S. v. Footman* (1999)

We who inhabit twenty-first-century America tend to think of sexual slavery as something that happens to impoverished women of Asia, Africa, or formerly communist Eastern Europe, who have been swindled or abducted and taken across borders, often into Western Europe, and then held there by threats of beatings, killings, or simply deportation. But, as illustrated in the following case (which arose in an action concerning federal sentencing guidelines), it is not limited to faraway places or to abductions across international borders.

U.S. v. TROY FOOTMAN
66 F. Supp. 2d 83 (Dist. Ct. for Mass., 1999)

NANCY GERTNER, JUDGE.

On November 18, 1998, the defendant, Troy Footman (hereinafter "Footman") was found guilty of conspiracy to transport women, including three minors, from Lowell, Massachusetts, to New Castle, Delaware, for prostitution and sexual activity, in violation of 18 U.S.C. §§ 2421 and 2423(a) [the Mann Act] He was also found guilty of a succession of substantive offenses, each count representing a particular trip with a particular minor (A.M., age 17, S.O., age 17, and J-3, age 14, or woman (Rita Boykins [hereinafter "Boykins"]). . . .

18 U.S.C. §§ 2421 and 2423(a) criminalize the transportation of women and girls across state lines for the purpose of prostitution and other sexual activity. To convict, the government does not have to prove that the women were coerced to participate in these activities. It is enough if the defendant "knowingly transports" them for the purpose of prostitution.[3] From one perspective, therefore, §§ 2421 and 2423(a) can simply be viewed as federal versions of standard state statutes prohibiting pimp and prostitution activity. In Massachusetts, for example, the maximum sentence for such acts would be five years; while in federal court, it is ten.

But the facts of this offense go well beyond the barebones statutory outline. What was involved here was much more than "just" an immoral business activity, namely commercial sex conducted across state lines. At least one very young girl—only fourteen years old—was enlisted, while two others were only seventeen. These girls worked as prostitutes at a Delaware truck stop, far away from home. They spent their nights going from truck to truck, driver to driver, engaging in sexual acts in truck cabs or trailers, or occasionally, in a motel room, not because Footman was so charming, or the economic incentives so enticing, but because Footman controlled them. Their compliance was enforced by rape, abduction and beatings. Plainly, these were not just economic crimes, or crimes of immoral conduct. Make no mistake about it, they were crimes of violence. Their analog are the state crimes of rape and kidnaping which provide maximum sentences of ten to twenty years, or possibly life, if a child under 16 years is involved.

The offenses involved here took place between June of 1996, and January of 1997. After spending almost a year in jail awaiting trial on a Suffolk Superior

Court indictment for inducing a minor, A.M., to engage in sex, and deriving support from her prostitution activities, Footman decided that it was "too hot" for him to continue his prostitution operations in Boston, Massachusetts. In an effort to avoid further police attention, he moved the operation to a Delaware truck stop. In so doing, Footman took with him, or arranged for the transportation of, Boykins, another woman Kim You Tes (hereinafter "Tes"), and the three minors, A.M., J-3, and S.O.

While in Delaware, Footman told his "girls" where to stay, and what to charge. At the end of the day, he took the money they earned. The highlights of the testimony follow:

A.M.

A.M. was 16 years old in 1994 when she began working as a prostitute for Footman. In December of that same year she became pregnant by him.

In late July and early August, 1996, Footman directed A.M. to engage in prostitution with truck drivers at a Delaware truck stop. As part of their arrangement, A.M. was to give Footman all of her earnings, except for a small amount to pay for personal hygiene items. Additionally, as the "bottom girl"—a term suggesting that she had worked with Footman the longest—she was also responsible for collecting money from the other "girls," and wiring it to Footman in Boston.

After she returned from this trip to Delaware, A.M. made the first of a number of efforts to leave Footman. She decided that she would rather work for an escort service in Boston than continue to prostitute herself in Delaware. Fearing that this decision would anger Footman, she applied for, and received, a restraining order on September 3, 1996.

On September 6, 1996, when A.M. returned home, Footman was waiting for her on the porch. When she saw him, she ran into the house. He followed her and pushed her up against a wall. She screamed in vain, "Help! Troy's here. He's going to kill me." Footman pulled her out of her house, dragged her into the backyard, and threw her over the fence. At that point, Footman, and two other men, shoved A.M. into a car, and drove her to a bar. There, Footman took all of A.M.'s earnings from her escort work, ostensibly to pay the men who had helped him abduct her, leaving her with nothing.

Later that evening, A.M. bargained with Footman to allow her to have her own place and a boyfriend, if she paid him the money she made prostituting herself. He agreed, but by the next morning, reneged. Instead, their former arrangement would stand: She would work for him and give him all the money she made, while he would give her living expenses.

Before A.M.'s 18th birthday on October 23, 1996, Footman again ordered his "women" to Delaware, providing them with driving directions. On this trip, A.M. drove J-3, and others, while Footman drove S.O. During this, and a subsequent trip before Christmas, A.M. and Boykins wired money to Footman, money which they, and the other girls, had earned as prostitutes.

By mid January of 1997, A.M. tried again to leave Footman by hitching a ride with a truck driver. In February, 1997, she returned, this time working for a different pimp. Footman found her again, and beat her mercilessly. He dragged her from her motel, threw her in his car, and took her to his room. There he yelled, punched her in the face, and kicked her for over 45 minutes. To stop the pain, A.M. agreed to return to work for him; she also believed that she was pregnant at the time. But the beating did not stop. By the time she got back to her motel, she was covered with blood and battered. S.O. confirmed seeing A.M. severely beaten.

After this beating, A.M. again hitched a ride out of Delaware. By April of 1997, however, she was back. When asked why she returned, she testified "I had no place else to go."

S.O.

S.O. met Footman in September of 1996 when she was 17 years old. At the time, she was appearing in court to address issues related to a criminal charge and custody questions concerning her child. During his first solicitation of her, Footman told S.O. that it took money to get her child back, money she could make working for him in an escort and body massage service. S.O. had no place permanent to live at this time. Footman found her the second time at the home of her friend's foster parents, where she was staying temporarily.

After this second solicitation, S.O. began working for Footman as a prostitute in Chinatown; it was the first time she had taken money for sex. Like A.M., she gave Footman all her money, keeping only a small amount for her own expenses. Eventually, as he did with A.M., Footman told S.O. that they would need to move their "work" to the Delaware truck stop, since the police were "on to" him. He also warned her that it was dangerous to work in Boston because she was a juvenile.

As a result, S.O. accompanied Footman for her first trip to Delaware in the October, 1996 trip described above.

But, by late November, 1996, S.O., like A.M., attempted to leave Footman to work for another pimp at the truck stop. Footman made sure she did not succeed. He abducted S.O., put her in the car, and drove her to a motel. S.O. tried to escape, but Footman chased her. When he finally got her back to his motel room, he beat her with "anything in sight," and then raped her both vaginally and anally. After the rape, S.O. escaped and hitched a ride with one of the truck drivers back to the truck stop. Motel records place Footman at a Quality Inn near the truck stop on November 23, 1996. Fifteen days after the rape, S.O. managed to get to a hospital.

J-3

J-3 was only 14 years old, and had recently run away from home when she first accompanied A.M. to the Delaware truck stop, at Footman's direction. Since J-3 was new at "the business," Footman instructed A.M. to have J-3 watch her the first night, and to "show" J-3 the ropes. Since J-3 was so young, he told A.M., "he could get her the way he wanted her."

Thus, J-3 began to work for Footman, giving the money she made to A.M. who wired it back to him.

Rita Boykins

Rita Boykins knew Footman since she was 16, and had worked for him as prostitute in the Chinatown section of Boston, Massachusetts. She was also the mother of two of his children. She confirmed trips to the Delaware truck stop in October of 1996, along with A.M., Tes and J-3, and that money obtained from prostitution activities in Delaware was wired to Footman.

. . .

[Here the judge explains a variety of complexities involving the applying of federal sentencing guidelines to this case]. . . [On the basis of listening to government tapes, she adds] I have no doubt that Footman was threatening and intimidating potential witnesses in this case, and that he was attempting to suborn perjury. The overheard conversations reflect his attempts to enlist the aid of, then co-defendant Tes, Boykins, and others, to find and contact witnesses in order to prevent them from testifying or to influence their testimony. [This increases his sentence.] Finally, there are real threats. In a conversation on November 24, 1997, to Solomon, apparently another pimp, Footman exclaimed . . . ."Well, where's that white bitch Tish at? Your brother got the whore. I'll make sure the whore don't come to court." And then, on December 6, 1997 (second call), in another conversation with Solomon, Solomon relates a conversation between two other pimps about the possibility of a prostitute, known to both, giving information about Footman. According to Solomon, one said "you can't motherfucking let this bitch [referring to Brubeck] go take the stand on my man [apparently Footman], you don't I'm gonna have to hurt this bitch.". . . [The judge refers, further, to tapes revealing Footman bragging that no whores will testify against him and that he will serve little time and be out soon to pimp again. She concludes that the sentence is to be fifteen years in prison.]

Opinion Footnote

3 Prior to 1986, a defendant could be charged under § 2423 if he "knowingly persuade[d], induce[d], entice[d], or coerce[d] any woman or girl who has not attained her eighteenth birthday" to travel in interstate commerce "to engage in prostitution, debauchery or other immoral practice." In addition to extending the statute to minor boys and modernizing the statute in other ways, Congress, in 1986, replaced the persuasion, inducement, enticement, and coercion language, with "transport" of a minor in interstate commerce. This statute also amended similar language in § 2421 in regards to transporting adult women.

Case Questions

1. If prostitution were legalized but pimping (profiteering from prostitution by another person) were kept unlawful, would that reform solve the problems presented in these materials?

2. If prostitution were legalized but pimping kept unlawful and patronizing (i.e. hiring) a prostitute were also kept unlawful (i.e. the Swedish model adopted), would this reform run into constitutional problems under the combination of *Craig v. Boren* and *Massachusetts v. Feeney*?

Human trafficking is a major issue across the globe in the twenty-first century. According to the U.S. Department of Homeland Security, every year millions of men, women and children are trafficked around the world, including the United States, and it is estimated to be a multi-billion dollar industry second only to the international drug trade as the most profitable form of transnational crime.[99] Human trafficking has become a high profile issue for Congress, and members of the House and Senate regularly introduce bills designed to address and combat the issue. In 2000, Congress successfully passed the Victims of Trafficking and Violence Protection Act which made human trafficking a federal crime and implemented numerous programs and policies to target trafficking domestically and internationally, and it has been repeatedly reauthorized. Most recently, it was added as an amendment to the Violence Against Women Reauthorization Act of 2013, and added new protections as well as strategies for reducing the trafficking of children for child marriages. In 2015, Congress passed the Justice for Victims of Trafficking Act which imposes fines on individuals convicted of "(1) peonage, slavery, and trafficking in persons; (2) sexual abuse; (3) sexual exploitation and other abuse of children; (4) transportation for illegal sexual activity; or (5) human smuggling in violation of the Immigration and Nationality Act (exempting any individual involved in the smuggling of an alien who is the alien's spouse, parent, son, or daughter)," and then uses these funds to support the Domestic Trafficking Victims' Fund which provides grants to state and local governments to combat trafficking and provide support to victims.[100] While all individuals are at risk of human trafficking, statistics demonstrate that women and girls are at the greatest risk of being victims of trafficking.[101]

CONCLUSION

Any person can become a victim of crime. All of us whom the law makes accountable for our actions can become offenders, not always deliberately. This chapter has explored the ways in which criminal law is gendered. Traditional Anglo-American law created special categories for certain kinds of harm done to women. Whereas burglary was burglary no matter who the victim was, forced sex was not a subcategory of assault; instead, it was rape, defined to exclude prosecution when the assailant was the woman's husband and regarded with skepticism while reports of other crimes were believed. A similar process of naming has created the offense of prostitution, and stigmatized and punished the prostitute but no effort has been made to punish in any serious way the pimp who lives off her earnings or the customers whose demand keeps the practice alive. The sale and distribution of misogynistic, often violent, pornography although usually forbidden by law as "obscenity," has in fact been protected by consumer demand.

All of these laws have been targets of feminist efforts at change. Feminist activists do not always agree among themselves, as comparison between Estrich and Paglia, or MacKinnon and Strossen, reveal. These authors (as in debates over abortion among women) do not even always agree that their adversaries have a right to claim the title of feminist. This lack of unity may have contributed to the slow progress of legal reform on pornography and prostitution. But feminists have made significant progress in achieving rape law reform all over the country. Although many rape victims are still forced to navigate antiquated assumptions about "real" rape and the predominant rape culture, legal reform in this area has been extensive. While there is still much work to be done to address the prevalence of sexual assaults on college campuses and the evidentiary standards under Title IX remain in flux from one presidential administration to the next, these incidents are now understood by many to be crimes and not simply "morning after" regrets or the exaggerated cries of "rape-crisis feminists."[102] Across the country, laws and statutes have been reformed to account for the experiences of women, but practice all too often lags behind doctrine. As such, while new laws and reforms are in place to recognize the plights of and provide legal recourse to battered women and victims of rape or trafficking, it will require broader socio-cultural reforms to keep these crimes from happening in the first place.

---

[1] Matthew Hale, *History of the Pleas of the Crown* (Philadelphia, PA: R.H. Small, 1847), I, 628.

[2] Subsection 213.

[3] *State v. Rhodes*, 1868 N.C. LEXIS 38, "Prior History."

[4] *Castle Rock v. Gonzalez*, 545 U.S. 748 (2005).

[5] Brian A. Reaves, "Police Response to Domestic Violence, 2006–2015," Bureau of Justice Statistics, Office of Justice Programs, U.S. Department of Justice, p. 1. Available at: https://www.bjs.gov/content/pub/pdf/prdv0615.pdf (accessed May 18, 2018).

[6] 2nd edition (New York: Springer Publishing Company, 2000), pp. 16, 117–18, 126–27, 214.

[7] Chicago: The University of Chicago Press, 1996, pp. 81, 155–57.

[8] Fox Butterfied, "Parole Advised for Women Who Kill Abusive Partner," *New York Times*, January 21, 1993, citing the National Clearinghouse for the Defense of Battered Women, Philadelphia.

[9] Emiko Petrosky et al. "Racial and Ethnic Differences in Homicides of Adult Women and the Role of Intimate Partner Violence—United States, 2003–2014," *Morbidity and Mortality Weekly Report* 66 (July 21, 2017): 741–746. DOI: http://dx.doi.org/10.15585/mmwr.mm6628a1 (accessed May 11, 2018).

[10] *United States v. Castleman*, 572 U.S. 157 (2014), Justice Sonia Sotomayor, Majority Opinion.

[11] *Voisine v. United States*, 136 S.Ct. 2272 (2016), Justice Elena Kagan, Majority Opinion.

[12] Ibid.

[13] See also Melissa Jeltsen, "Supreme Court Affirms That Even 'Reckless' Domestic Abusers Should Lose Gun Rights," *Huffington Post*, June 27, 2016. Available at: https://www.huffingtonpost.com/entry/supreme-court-domestic-violence-gun-rights_us_5771293fe4b0dbb1bbbb0e63 (accessed May 18, 2018).

[14] New York: Vintage Books, 1992, pp. 69–70, 58–59, 67, 71.

[15] Cambridge, MA: Harvard University Press, 1986, pp. 4–5, 102–04.

[16] *Coker v. Georgia*, 433 U.S. 584 (1977).

[17] Jessica Calefati, "Brock Turner Case: Bill to Mandate Prison for Sexually Assaulting Unconscious Victims Clears Assembly," *Mercury News*, August 29, 2016, updated September 14, 2016. Available at: https://www.mercurynews.com/2016/08/29/brock-turner-case-bill-to-mandate-prison-for-sexually-assaulting-unconscious-victims-clears-assembly/ (accessed April 30, 2018). Doug Stanglin, "Calif. Gov Signs Bill Mandating Prison for Sexual Assault," *USA TODAY*, September 30, 2016. Available at: https://www.usatoday.com/story/news/2016/09/30/calif-signs-bill-mandating-prison-sexual-assault/91335410/ (accessed April 30, 2018). "Judge Aaron Persky, Who Gave Brock Turner Lenient Sentence in Rape Case, Recalled from Office," *USA TODAY* June 6, 2018. Available at: https://www.usatoday.com/story/news/2018/06/06/judge-aaron-persky-who-gave-brock-turners-lenient-sentence-sanford-rape-case-recalled/674551002/ (accessed July 14, 2018).

[18] Ian Ayres and Katharine Baker, "The Separate Harms of Reckless Sex," *Balkinization*, September 20, 2004. Available at: http://balkin.blogspot.com/2004/09/separate-harms-of-reckless-sex.html (accessed May 21, 2018); Christopher Shea, "Criminalizing Reckless Sex," *The New York Times Magazine*, December 12, 2004, p. 62.

[19] *State v. Rusk*, 43 Md. App. 476, 480, 406 A.2d 624 (1979).

[20] Cambridge, Mass.: Harvard University Press, 1998, chap. 13.

21 *Stanford Law Review*, Vol.48 (1996), p. 667. [Citations omitted—AU.]

22 *Albany Law Review*, 61 (1997), p. 237.

23 RAINN: Rape, Abuse and Incest National Network.

24 Samantha Allen, "Marital Rape Is Semi-Legal in 8 States," *Daily Beast*, June 9, 2015. Available at: https://www.thedailybeast.com/marital-rape-is-semi-legal-in-8-states (accessed May 18, 2018).

25 See Harry M. Clor, *Obscenity and Public Morality* (Chicago, IL: University of Chicago Press, 1969); Patrick Devlin, *The Enforcement of Morals* (Oxford: Oxford University Press, 1965).

26 See Morris L Ernst and Alan U. Schwartz, *Censorship: The Search for the Obscene* (New York, NY: Macmillan, 1964); Alexander Meikejohn, *Political Freedom: The Constitutional Powers of the People* (New York, NY: Oxford University Press, 1965.)

27 Catharine A. MacKinnon, *Only Words* (Cambridge, MA: Harvard University Press, 1993), pp. 1–2, 8, 13–14, 21–23, 85, 87–88.

28 Nadine Strossen, *Defending Pornography*, (New York: NYU Press, 1995), 12–14.

29 *Miller v. California*, 413 U.S. 15 (1973) and *Paris Adult Theater v. Slaton*, 413 U.S. 49 (1973).

30 Indianapolis Code, Section 16–3(q), cited in *American Booksellers Association v. Hudnut*, 771 F.2d. 324.

31 *Schenck v. U.S.*, 249 U.S. 47 (1919).

32 *Chaplinsky v. New Hampshire*, 315 U.S. 568, 571–72 (1942).

33 *Miller v. California*.

34 Ibid.

35 *Roth v. U.S.*, 354 U.S. 476, n. 2 (1957).

36 *Miller v. California*.

37 Ibid.

38 *Paris Adult Theater*.

39 Ibid.

40 Tim Wu, "American Lawbreaking," *Slate*, October 14, 2007. Available at http://www.slate.com/articles/news_and_politics/jurisprudence/features/2007/american_lawbreaking/introduction.html (accessed May 11, 2018).

41 *R.A.V. v. City of St. Paul, Minnesota*, 505 U.S. 377 (1992).

42 *R.A.V. v. City of St. Paul, Minnesota*, at 398.

43 St. Paul, Minn. Legis. Code Section 292.02 (1990).

44 *Chaplinsky v. New Hampshire*, 315 U.S., at 572.

45 Ibid.

46 The contradiction in assuming that ideas were being expressed in something defined as not part of the exchange of ideas was noted by the dissenters. See *R.A.V. v. City of St. Paul, Minnesota*, Justice White dissenting.

47 *R.A.V. v. City of St. Paul, Minnesota*, at 388.

48 *R.A.V. v. City of St. Paul, Minnesota*, at 390.

49 508 U.S. 476.

50 Tim Wu, "American Lawbreaking," note 40 above.

51 *Stanley v. Georgia*, 394 U.S. 557 (1969).

52 *Reno v. ACLU*, 521 U.S. 844 (1997).

53 *Ashcroft v. ACLU*, 542 U.S. 656 (2004).

54 572 U.S. 434 (2014).

55 18 U.S.C. § 3771 (2004).

56 *Paroline v. United States*, 572 U.S. 434 (2014).

57 18 U.S.C. § 2261(a)(1) (1990).

58 42 U.S.C.§ 13981(d)(1).

59 42 U.S.C. § 13981(b), (c), and (e)(3), § 13981(e)(2).

60 42 U.S.C. § 13981(a).

61 *United States v. Harris,* 106 U.S. 629 (1883); *The Civil Rights Cases,* 109 U.S. 3 (1883).

62 *U.S. v. Guest,* 383 U.S. 745, 762, 774 (1966).

63 42 U.S.C. 2000e (Title VII of the 1964 Civil Rights Act).

64 *Wickard v. Filburn,* 317 U.S. 111 (1942).

65 *U.S. v. E.C. Knight,* 156 U.S. 1 (1895).

66 *NLRB v. Jones & Laughlin Steel,* 301 U.S. 1 (1937); *NLRB v. Friedman-Harry Marks Clothing Co.,* 301 U.S. 58 (1937).

67 *National League of Cities v. Usery,* 426 U.S. 833 (1976).

68 469 U.S. 528.

69 514 U.S. 549.

70 *Lopez,* 514 U.S., 562.

71 *U.S. v. Morrison,* 529 U.S. 598, 602 (2000).

72 86 Stat. 373–375, 20 U.S.C. §§ 1681–1688.

73 *Morrison,* 602–604.

74 *Aurelia Davis v. Monroe County Board of Education,* 526 U.S. 629 (1999). The Supreme Court ruled that there is such a right to sue. Shortly thereafter, Virginia Tech settled with Brzonkala out of court for $75,000. She had sued for over $4 million. Leo Reisberg, "Virginia Tech Settles Lawsuit Over Alleged Rape by Football Players," *Chronicle of Higher Education* (February 28, 2000), https://www.chronicle.com/article/Virginia-Tech-Settles-Lawsuit/106146 (accessed October 13, 2018).

75 Pub. L. No. 113-4, 127 Stat. 54 (March 7, 2013).

76 Russlynn Ali, Assistant Secretary for Civil Rights, "Dear Colleague," United States Department of Education Office for Civil Rights, April 4, 2011. Available at: https://www2.ed.gov/about/offices/list/ocr/letters/colleague-201104.pdf (accessed May 18, 2018).

77 The Chronicle of Higher Education, "Title IX Tracking Sexual Assault Investigations." Available at: https://projects.chronicle.com/titleix/ (accessed January 11, 2018).

78 "Questions and Answers on Title IX and Sexual Violence," U.S. Department of Education Office for Civil Rights, Office of the Assistant Secretary, April 29, 2014. Available at: https://www2.ed.gov/about/offices/list/ocr/docs/qa-201404-title-ix.pdf (accessed May 18, 2018).

79 U.S. Department of Education Office for Civil Rights, Dear Colleague Letter of September 22, 2017. http://www.nicholslawyers.com/Portals/nicholslaw/Dept%20of%20Education%20Letter%209.22.17.pdf?ver=2017-09-26-103901-797 (accessed Oct.13, 2018).

80 Kimberly Hefling and Caitlin Emma, "Obama-era school sexual assault policy rescinded," *Politico,* September 22, 2017. Available at: https://www.politico.com/story/2017/09/22/obama-era-school-sexual-assault-policy-rescinded-243016 (accessed May 18, 2018).

81 Ibid.

82 *In the Matter of Dora P.* (Supreme Court of N. Y., App. Div., 1st Dept.) 418 N.Y.S.2d 597, 604.

83 Gretchen Ruethling, "Chicago Police Put Arrest Photos of Prostitution Suspects Online," *The New York Times,* June 23, 2005, p. A-16.

84 Suzy Khimm, "The Shame Game: The Internet Has Given Us a New Public Square. Now Law Enforcement is Trying to Harness its Power," *The New Republic,* March 9, 2016. Available at: https://newrepublic.com/article/130803/shame-game (accessed May 21, 2018).

85 William Murphy and Ann Givens, "Long Island Prostitution Sting, 'Operation Flush the Johns,' Leads to Arrests of 104 Men," *Newsday,* June 3, 2013.

86 Sara Jean Green, "Tougher Police Tactics Stinging Sex Buyers," *The Seattle Times,* October 15, 2014, updated March 19, 2015. Available at: https://www.seattletimes.com/seattle-news/tougher-police-tactics-stinging-sex-buyers/ (accessed May 21, 2018).

87 Nevada is the sole exception. There, prostitution is legal as a county option.

88 See, e.g. Carole Pateman, *The Sexual Contract* (Stanford, CA: Stanford University Press, 1988), pp. 206–208.

89 "Prostitution and Male Supremacy," *Michigan Journal of Gender & Law* 1 (1993): 2–3.

90 Catharine MacKinnon, *Sex Equality* (New York, NY: Foundation Press, 2001), 1397, 1406, 1416–1417.

91 Emily Bazelon, "Should Prostitution be a Crime?" *The New York Times Magazine*, May 5, 2016. Available at: https://www.nytimes.com/2016/05/08/magazine/should-prostitution-be-a-crime.html (accessed February 9, 2018).

92 Debi Brock and Jennifer Stephen, "Which We Is Who?" *Broadside*, Dec. 1987–Jan.1988, p.4.

93 Emily Bazelon, "Should Prostitution be a Crime?" above note 90.

94 "Confessions of a Priestesstute," in Frédérique *Delacoste* and Priscilla Alexander, eds. *Sex Work: Writings by Women in the Sex Industry* (Pittsburgh, PA: Cleis Press, 1987) pp.148–179, cited in MacKinnon, *Sex Equality* note 89 above, at 1424–5.

95 Emily Bazelon, "Should Prostitution be a Crime?" above note 90.

96 Ibid.

97 Ibid.

98 Ibid.

99 "What is Human Trafficking," Blue Campaign, *U.S. Department of Homeland Security*, 2010. Available at: https://www.dhs.gov/blue-campaign/what-human-trafficking (accessed May 21, 2018).

100 S.178—Justice for Victims of Trafficking Act of 2015, Public Law No: 114–22.

101 "Human Trafficking Cases Reported by State," Annual Report, *National Human Trafficking Resource Center*, 2015. (Available at: https://humantraffickinghotline.org/resources/2015-nhtrc-annual-report, accessed May 21, 2018).

102 Katie Roiphe, *The Morning After: Sex, Fear and Feminism* (Back Bay Books, 1994).

CHAPTER 8

Conclusions

The senior authors of this casebook were born in 1945. Law and society were permeated by male supremacy. When we started elementary school, some districts were still forbidding married women to teach. Employers defended their practice of paying women less than men on the grounds that men had families to support. Job ads were divided by sex. Sixty percent of all employed women were clustered in clerical, service, and teaching jobs.[1] Many of our contemporaries were raised with the expectation that they would become full-time homemakers and were discouraged from training for a profession. Fewer girls than boys went to college,[2] and women faced overt discrimination in admission to graduate and professional schools and in the job market.

The changes in our lifetimes have been little short of revolutionary. Men and women are now equal before the law. Sex discrimination in employment and education is prohibited. The institution of marriage is open to all regardless of sexual orientation, and both spouses share identical legal rights and duties; no longer must wives maintain the home and live where their husbands choose. Sexual assault and domestic violence are crimes. While much work remains to be done to address social and legal biases that continue to work against female victims, the #MeToo and Time's Up movements are public reckonings that have the potential to facilitate real change by drawing attention to ongoing and systemic inequities.

Profound social changes demonstrate the effectiveness of legal changes. The pay gap between the sexes has narrowed. Most coeducational colleges have at least as many women students as men, and some have more; this is also true of medical schools and law schools. Women work alongside men in skilled blue-collar jobs and in the military, including in combat roles. Safe, reliable means of fertility control are far more accessible to most women than they were in the 1950s. These changes have benefited women of every race, age, lifestyle, and economic background.

The junior authors of this casebook are the beneficiaries of many of these changes. Born in 1962 and 1975, we came of age after the passage of the 1964 Civil Rights Act provided women with legal grounds for challenging discriminatory practices in the workforce and in the post-*Reed* world when laws treating men and women differently were open to contestation as violations of the equal protection clause in the courts. In addition, we benefited from Title IX's guarantees of equal access to education and attended college and graduate school surrounded by women. In fact, as undergraduates, Professor Fine and Professor Daum benefited from having strong female role models such as Professor Baer and Professor Goldstein respectively. Thanks to the ground-breaking work of these two women and their peers, it never occurred to either one of us that we should not go on to graduate school to become political scientists ourselves.

Yet, equality on paper does not entail, and has not produced, equality in fact. Our society allots a disproportionate share of freedom to males and responsibility to females. Division of labor within the family and asymmetrical earning opportunities frustrate the attainment of equality in marriage. Women of color, transwomen, lesbians, and disabled women are harmed by social prejudice and incomplete legal protection. Violence against women persists, and rape culture and stereotypes continue to undermine victims of sexual assault. In October 2018, Brett Kavanaugh was confirmed as an Associate Justice of the U.S. Supreme Court after a contentious confirmation battle that included a nationally televised accusation of sexual assault which focused the nation's attention on rape culture and its associated myths and stereotypes.

Despite prohibitions on sexual harassment in the workforce, the surge of women reporting harassment and abuse at the hands of male supervisors and coworkers beginning in 2017 demonstrates that workplace harassment is rampant and that women still fear reporting abuse for fear of retaliation. Women are more likely than men to be poor. The *Burwell v. Hobby Lobby Stores, Inc.* (2014) U.S. Supreme Court decision allowed closely-held private corporations to seek religious exemptions from the Affordable Care Act's mandate to insure the cost of all prescription contraceptives for employees.

Reproductive choice with respect to so-called "partial birth" abortion has been limited, and the reversal of *Roe v. Wade* looms as a present possibility. Indeed several states have legislated specifically to be ready in the event that *Roe v. Wade* gets reversed by the Court: in that event, abortion would stay legal in nine states—California, Connecticut, Delaware, Hawaii, Maine, Maryland, Nevada, Oregon, and Washington—and would become immediately illegal in four—Louisiana,

Mississippi, North Dakota, and South Dakota. As such, law can help reform society, but law alone cannot transform it.[3]

Law's careful neutrality is not always part of the solution to male supremacy; it can be part of the problem. The legal system under which we live was created and, until recently, operated by men; unsurprisingly, it may "authorize the male experience of the world."[4] For example, equal protection doctrine makes no distinction between discrimination against an out-group and distinction against an in-group: compensatory discrimination is viewed as "just as bad" as reverse discrimination. Men have arguably benefited at least as much as women from the changes in equal protection doctrine.

That being said, men's victories may help, and need not harm, women. *Weinberger v. Wiesenfeld* (see Chapter 2) is an obvious example, and *J.E.B. v. Alabama* prevents the use of peremptory challenges to keep either women or men off juries. Although one scholar has written, "*Orr v. Orr* has hurt ordinary mothers and wives,"[5] she advances no evidence to support this statement and it is dubious on its face: Why should permitting men to request spousal support reduce women's chances of getting it? However, in the light of the difficulties women have had in collecting support payments, a ruling extending men's support rights carries a certain irony. The fact that most winners of post-*Reed* equal protection cases are male—after all, more men than women bring cases—need not distress women's rights advocates.

Gender neutrality can work against women's interests in divorce and child custody cases. Although many no-fault divorce laws contain neutral provisions that accommodate women's interests (see the excerpt from Arizona's law in Chapter 5), advocacy and interpretation may result in "neutral" decisions that disadvantage the female partner. Most husbands have more resources than their wives do, and this comparative advantage often allows men to manipulate the system in their favor. With the legalization of marriage equality in all fifty states following *Obergefell v. Hodges* (2015), divorce cases now include same-sex partners. This fact has added new complications to divorce law while potentially challenging long held assumptions about gender roles pertaining to child custody arrangements and spousal and child support.

Feminists disagree about whether and to what extent laws should be gender-neutral or gender-specific. The controversy over *Cal Fed v. Guerra* illustrated the division between those feminists who supported childbearing leaves as recognition of biological reality and those who opposed them as a reinforcement of traditional gender roles. The Supreme Court found no incompatibility between the Pregnancy Discrimination Act's prohibition of discrimination based on pregnancy and California's protection of new mothers' job security. The Family and Medical Leave Act of 1993 (FMLA) accommodated both of these goals in sex-neutral language. Although the United States lags far behind European democracies in reconciling the demands of work and family life, the FMLA indicates that Congress has learned to accommodate gender-specific needs in sex-neutral language.

More recently, disagreements about gender-neutral versus gender-specific legislation have been implicated in discussions about advancing transgender rights. While transgender men and women have benefitted from prohibitions on sex and gender stereotyping consistent with the *Price Waterhouse* case discussed in Chapter 3, these protections are contingent and limited and do not amount to permanent civil rights guarantees for transgender individuals at this time. Litigation has focused on how prohibitions on sex discrimination should be understood to include prohibitions on gender discrimination in a way that incorporates gender identity, as discussed in Chapter 3. Removing sex classifications and moving towards gender-neutral norms would provide even more protections for gender ambiguous and non-conforming individuals as well as transgender men and women. As Heath Fogg Davis explains, "Sex-classification policies are material artifacts that were conceived and codified by people. . . . [M]ore often than not the use of sex on bureaucratic forms or to physically segregate people is habitual rather than the product of strategic thinking about why and how sex is relevant to organizational aims, and why and how the use of sex is discriminatory."[6] At the same time, however, some women are resistant to the idea of eliminating all gender-specific laws, policies, and norms, and, given the extent to which gendered-norms and policies allocate power and resources in the contemporary U.S., it seems unlikely that they will be completely eliminated any time soon. There is little doubt that these issues and debates are going to continue to grow in saliency in the years and decades ahead and will add to the extant case law on sex, gender and the law.

The women who are now entering law school in equal numbers with men will administer, interpret, and make law as attorneys, judges, and legislators. The increasing number of women who become educated, middle-class professionals will be able to use law to their advantage as their male counterparts do. New lawyers can make new law, and new clients can use it. Yet, if recent history has taught us nothing else, it has taught us that no law is self-executing and no legal principle is permanent. The process of updating this casebook (last published in 2006), has impressed all the authors with how much has changed in such a short period of time; we expect that additional change is inevitable in the decades to come.

---

[1] See Judith A. Baer, *Women in American Law: The Struggle Toward Equality from the New Deal to the Present*, 3rd ed. (New York, NY: Holmes and Meier, 2002), chap. 3.

[2] In 1950, 9.4% of American males and 5.6% of females between the ages of 5 and 29 attended or had attended college or professional school. (U.S. Bureau of the Census, *Statistical Abstract of the United States 1952*, Table 125, p. 110).

[3] Meredith Newman, "What Would Happen to Abortions in Delaware?" *Delaware News Journal USA TODAY NETWORK*, July 11, 2018, p.5-A, col.1.

[4] Catharine A. MacKinnon, *Toward a Feminist Theory of the State* (Cambridge, MA: Harvard University Press, 1989), p. 248.

[5] Mary Becker, "Prince Charming: Abstract Equality," in Leslie Friedman Goldstein, ed., *Feminist Jurisprudence: The Difference Debate* (Lanham, MD: Rowman and Littlefield, 1992), p. 111.

[6] Heath Fogg Davis, *Beyond Trans: Does Gender Matter?* (New York, NY: New York University Press, 2017), pp. 142–3.

Glossary

amicus curiae **("friend of the court") brief:** written argument, supplementing the litigants' briefs with arguments presenting a third party's perspective on the case; may be submitted either by permission of both parties or by permission of the Supreme Court.

***ante*:** Latin for "[appearing] earlier."

***arguendo*:** Latin for "for the sake of argument."

BFOQ: bona fide occupational qualification reasonably necessary to the normal operation of a business.

bill of attainder: statute that imposes a penalty on all members of a named group; statute that declares guilt on the basis of who people are rather than on what acts they have committed.

bona fide occupational qualification (BFOQ): An exception to some anti-discrimination provisions in Title VII. Employer may try to show that an employee's sex, religion, or national origin (but never race) is a BFOQ reasonably necessary for the enterprise in question. See *Dothard v. Rawlinson*.

brief: lawyer's written argument presented to an appellate court.

but for causation: degree of causality such that, when many factors contribute to causing an event, if one factor were eliminated that event would not transpire. "But for" this particular factor, the event would not have been caused.

cert: short for certiorari.

certiorari, writ of: Latin term for the writ used to ask the Supreme Court to hear a case. To "grant cert" or to "grant certiorari" is to agree to hear the case.

cisgender: an individual whose sex/gender identity correlate with their sex as assigned at birth.

common law: an old term for case law; decisions made by judges expected to be binding on later judges, in theory articulating a rule embodying the reigning community custom.

comparable worth/pay equity: providing equal (or "comparable") pay for jobs involving comparable overall effort, skill, responsibility, and working conditions, generally targeting gender imbalance in pay.

constructive discharge: a term from labor law meaning mistreatment by employer of an employee that is sufficiently intolerable that a reasonable person would want to quit the job.

ex post facto law: statutes that declare punishments for past actions that, at the time they were committed, were legal.

facial neutrality: silence in the statutory wording about a particular group; statutes may look non-discriminatory on the surface (i.e., "neutral on its face") but may still have a discriminatory impact as applied.

habeas corpus: Latin for "let us have the body"; refers to a judicial order for prison officials to release a prisoner wrongly held.

hostile environment harrassment: conduct that creates am work environment that a reasonable person would consider intimidating, hostile, or abusive.

incorporation: in discussions of U.S. constitutional law, refers to the idea that the phrase "due process" in the Fourteenth Amendment "incorporates" the restraints of the Bill of Rights and applies them to state governments.

infra: Latin for "appearing below."

intersectional identity: this phrase is intended to capture that individuals' different identities—race, sex, gender, disabled/able-bodied, socioeconomic status—intersect with one another to exacerbate the marginalization and oppression of some individuals, as exemplified by the different experiences of Black women in comparison to both white women and Black men.

laches: a defense against a lawsuit for equitable relief that bars recovery by the plaintiff because of the plaintiff's undue delay in seeking relief.

LGBTQ: abbreviation for lesbian, gay, bisexual, transgender, or queer.

minimal scrutiny: see ordinary scrutiny.

miscegenation: marriage or sexual intercourse between members of different races.

mootness: if the passage of time after a case was initiated makes it impossible for the court to grant the requested relief to the initiating party (e.g., a public school child complaining about school prayer graduates high school before case reaches the appeals court), a case is declared moot and jurisdiction is denied because standing is no longer present.

ordinary scrutiny: standard applied for most due process and equal protection challenges to laws: states may restrict liberty and impose classifications, so long as the measures bear a rational relationship to a valid legislative purpose (i.e. promote some aspect of the public good).

per curiam: characterizes a court opinion issued in the name of the Court rather than specific judges.

police power: power of any state to legislate in order to promote any aspect of the public good (health, morality, prosperity, safety, welfare).

polygamy: a marriage with more than one husband or more than one wife.

polygyny: a marriage of one man with multiple wives.

post: Latin for "appearing later."

quid pro quo harassment: "quid pro quo" is Latin for "this for that." This kind of harassment would involve a "do this or else" command (e.g., do this favor for me unrelated to your job requirement, or you won't get a raise.)

solicitor general: the official in the Justice Department responsible for arguing the executive branch position in court cases.

standing: the status of having a personal stake in the outcome of a judicial decision, such that one stands to gain or lose by what the court will say; required for taking a case to federal courts in U.S.

stare decisis: literally, Latin for "let the decision stand." Term refers to the general rule that courts are obliged to follow their own precedents, absent strong reasons to change. *Planned Parenthood v. Casey* reviews these reasons.

statutes: acts passed by a legislative body; what people usually mean by "laws."

summary judgment: judgment issued without a hearing for exploring disputed material facts, because motion has persuaded judge that no material facts are at issue.

supra: Latin for "[appearing] above."

suspect classification: label for a legislative classification that the Supreme Court deems *prima facie* suspicious as likely to have been motivated by group hostility rather than a rational relation to the public good. Can be upheld as constitutional only if proved necessary for a compelling government interest.

transgender: an individual whose gender identity does not correlate with the gender/sex identity assigned at birth. This includes gender-nonconforming and gender-fluid individuals as well as transsexuals and those who seek to transition to their preferred gender but do not seek sexual reassignment surgery.

transsexual: a transgender individual who seeks to permanently transition from their gender/sex identity assigned at birth to their preferred gender identity via sexual reassignment surgery.

void for vagueness: if a statute is so vague that it does not give fair warning of what it forbids and permits, then it denies due process of law and will be declared void.

Index

ABORTION
Generally, 1–2, 9–10, 407, 453–643
Access to abortions, 596–643
Buffer zones at clinics, 596–622
Child custody, rights of unmarried fathers, 843
Federally assisted family planning clinics (gag rule), 521–525
First Amendment, 521–525
Freedom of Access to Clinic Entrances Act, 601
Full service hospitals, 501
Hospital admitting privileges, 625–643
Hyde Amendment, public funding, 510–511
Ku Klux Klan actions, 597
Mexico City Policy (global gag rule), 525–526
Minors, 482–498, 502, 527–571
Parental and spousal consent, 482–498, 527–571
Parental notice, 498
Partial birth abortions, 571–576, 578–596, 1200
Patient consent, 481–497, 501–502, 503–505, 527–571
Public funding, 506–513
Public Service Health Act, 522–525
Reporting and recordkeeping, 482–497, 502, 503–505, 527–571
Restrictions after Roe, 481 et seq.
RICO actions, 596–598, 622–625
RU-486, 518–521
Safety at clinics, 596–625
Spousal consent, 482–498
Spousal notification, 527–571
Standards at clinics, 625–643
Techniques used for abortions, 571–575
Viability of fetus, 481–497, 498–499, 502, 503–505, 512–516
Waiting periods, 527–571

ABUSE
Spousal Abuse, this index

ACCOUNTING FIRMS
Employment, gender stereotyping, 278–293

ADMITTING PRIVILEGES
Abortion, hospitals, 625–643

ADOPTION
Child custody, unmarried fathers, 844–858, 859–873
Native Americans, 907–925

ADULTEROUS FATHERS
Child custody, 873–891

AFFIRMATIVE ACTION
Employment, 360–388

AGENT-TELEGRAPHERS
Employment, Title VII of Civil Rights Act of 1964, 236–240

AGREEMENTS
Contracts, this index

ALCOHOLIC BEVERAGES
Bartenders and Bartending, this index
Beer, intermediate scrutiny, 136–149
Prohibition, 6

ALIMONY
Sex discrimination, 768–773

AMERICAN WOMAN SUFFRAGE ASSOCIATION
Voting rights, 44

APPROVAL
Consent or Approval, this index

ARTISTIC VALUE
Pornography, 1139

ASYMMETRICAL RECIPROCITY
Family law, 780–791

ATHLETICS PROGRAMS
Education, Title IX, 1, 1003, 1005–1007, 1041

ATTORNEYS
Fourteenth Amendment, access to bar, 27–34
Law Firms, this index

BARTENDERS AND BARTENDING
Employment, 221
Equal protection, 98–101

BATTERED WOMAN SYNDROME
Spousal abuse, 1073–1099

BATTERY
Spousal abuse, 1051–1056

BEER
Equal protection, intermediate scrutiny, 136–149

BEST INTERESTS OF CHILD
Child custody, 801–808

BIRTH CONTROL
Generally, 6
Reproductive Freedom, this index

BONA FIDE OCCUPATIONAL QUALIFICATIONS
Employment, this index

BOY SCOUTS
First Amendment, 214–215

BUFFER ZONES
Abortion clinics, 596–622

CASES AND CONTROVERSIES
Jurisdiction, 13–14

CERTIORARI
Supreme Court, 15

CHILD CUSTODY
Generally, 10, 795–898, 1201
Abortion rights, unmarried fathers, 843
Adoption, unmarried fathers, 844–858, 859–873
Adulterous fathers, 873–891
Best interests of child, 801–808
Death of unmarried mother, unmarried fathers, 833–843
De facto parents, 891
Immigration, unmarried fathers, 843
Joint custody, 828–832
Parents *vs.* grandparents, 893–898
Paternal preference, 795–796
Primary caregiver standard, 808

Psychological parents, 891
Race and best interests of child, 808
Relocation of custodial parent, 826–828
Tender years doctrine, 796–800
Tri-parenting relationships, 891–893
Unfaithful spouses, 808–826
Unmarried fathers
    generally, 832–873
    abortion rights, 843
    adoption, 844–858, 859–873
    death of unmarried mother, 833–843
    immigration, 843
    wrongful death actions, 858–859
Wrongful death actions, unmarried fathers, 858–859

CHILDREN AND MINORS
Abortion, 482–498, 502, 527–571
Adoption, this index
Custody. Child Custody, this index
Marriage, 926–927
Pornography, restitution for child pornography victims, 1148–1150
Reproductive freedom, contraception, 453
Support. Child Support, this index

CHILD SUPPORT
Child Support Recovery Act, 793–794
Sex discrimination, 763–768

CITIZENSHIP
Equal protection, nonmarital children of American parents, 187–201

CIVIL RIGHTS
Generally, 5

CIVIL RIGHTS ACT OF 1991
Employment, 298–303

CIVIL RIGHTS REMEDIES EQUALIZATION AMENDMENT OF 1986
Education, Title IX, 1003

CIVIL WAR
Generally, 11

COERCION
Caesarean surgeries, 664–680

COLLEGES AND UNIVERSITIES
Generally, 6, 952–1002
Campus sexual violence, 1180–1182
Fertility of females, 952–953

Male attendance at women's colleges, 957–972
Military academies, 972–1002
Morrill Land-Grant Act of 1862, 954
Texas A&M cases, 955–956
Title IX. Education, this index
University of Virginia, 956–957

COMBAT DUTY
Equal protection, military service, 182–186

COMMERCE CLAUSE
Reproductive freedom, 411–412

COMMISSION ON THE STATUS OF WOMEN
Equal protection, intermediate scrutiny, 113–114

COMMITTEE FOR ABORTION RIGHTS AND AGAINST STERILIZATION ABUSE
Generally, 424

COMMON LAW
Generally, 11–13

COMPARABLE WORTH
Employment, equal pay, 228–230

CONSENT OR APPROVAL
Abortion, patient consent, 481–497, 501–502, 503–505, 527–571
Rape, 1104–1112

CONTEMPORARY COMMUNITY STANDARDS
Pornography, 1140

CONTRACEPTION
Generally, 6
Reproductive Freedom, this index

CONTRACTS
Due process, 49–61
Fourteenth Amendment, 49–61
Maximum hour statutes, 50–66
Minimum wage statutes, 67–81, 84–87
Nineteenth Amendment, 68
Police power, 50–66
Protective legislation, 61–84
Restaurants, 81–84

COVERTURE
Marriage, 761–762

CRIME
Generally, 1047–1198
Campus sexual violence, 1180–1182
Gun-Free School Zones Act, 1152
Pornography, this index
Prostitution, this index
Rape, this index
Spousal Abuse, this index
Violence Against Women Act, 215, 1150–1180

CRIMINAL CONVERSATION
Family law, wife as property of husband, 776–779

CUSTODY OF CHILDREN
Child Custody, this index

DEADBEAT PARENTS PUNISHMENT ACT
Generally, 794–795

DEATH OF UNMARRIED MOTHER
Child custody, unmarried fathers, 833–843

DECEDENTS' ESTATES
Generally, 8
Equal protection, qualifications of administrator, intermediate scrutiny, 115–118

DE FACTO PARENTS
Child custody, 891

DEFENSE OF MARRIAGE ACT
Generally, 722, 725–736

DEFINITIONS
Generally, 1205–1208

DESEGREGATION
School Desegregation, this index

DISPARATE IMPACT
Employment, Title VII of Civil Rights Act of 1964, 303–314

DIVORCE
Generally, 10, 791–795, 1201
Child Custody, this index
Child Support, this index
Spousal abuse, 1051

DOCTRINAL SETTING
Equal protection, intermediate scrutiny, 111–114

DOMESTIC PARTNERSHIPS
Gay rights, 722–723

DOMESTIC VIOLENCE
Spousal abuse, 1056

DRAFT
Equal protection, military service, 180–182

DRUGS
Reproductive freedom, drug use during pregnancy, 681–694

DUE PROCESS
Contracts, 49–61
Marriage, gay rights, 720, 724
Reproductive Freedom, this index

EDUCATION
    Generally, 935–1045
Athletics programs, Title IX, 1, 1003, 1005–1007, 1041
Campus sexual violence, 1180–1182
Civil Rights Remedies Equalization Amendment of 1986, Title IX, 1003
Colleges and Universities, this index
Gender identity, Title IX, 1042–1043
Law schools, Title IX, 1003
No Child Left Behind, 951
Prohibition, 7, 8
Retaliation, Title IX, 1041
School Desegregation, this index
Sexual harassment, Title IX, 1007–1041
Sexual violence, Title IX, 1153–1154, 1180–1182
Single sex public schools, 936–952
Student on student sexual harassment, Title IX, 1022–1041
Termination of federal funds, Title IX, 1003–1005
Title IX
    generally, 1002–1043
    athletics programs, 1003, 1005–1007, 1041
    Civil Rights Remedies Equalization Amendment of 1986, 1003
    college admissions, 1003
    gender identity, 1042–1043
    law schools, 1003
    retaliation, 1041
    sexual harassment, 1007–1041
    sexual violence, 1153–1154, 1180–1182
    student on student sexual harassment, 1022–1041
    termination of federal funds, 1003–1005
    vocational training programs, 1003
Vocational training programs, Title IX, 1003

EMPLOYMENT
    Generally, 5–6, 8–10, 221–406
Accounting firm partners, gender stereotyping, 278–293
Affirmative action based on sex, 360–388
Agent-telegraphers, Title VII of Civil Rights Act of 1964, 236–240
Applicants with pre-school-age children, Title VII of Civil Rights Act of 1964, 241–244
Bartenders, 221
Bona fide occupational qualifications
    mothers, 321–337
    Title VII of Civil Rights Act of 1964, 230–241, 303–314
Civil Rights Act of 1991, 298–303
Comparable worth, equal pay, 228–230
Disparate impact, Title VII of Civil Rights Act of 1964, 303–314
Equal pay
    generally, 9, 224–230
    comparable worth, 228–230
    equal protection, intermediate scrutiny, 113–114
    pensions, 227–228
    shift differentials, 225–227
Equal protection, intermediate scrutiny, 114
Family and Medical Leave Act, mothers, 358–360, 401, 1202
First Amendment, sex designated advertisements, 211–212
Gender stereotyping
    generally, 278–293
    accounting firm partners, 278–293
    law firm partners, 278
Harassment. Sexual harassment, below
Height requirements, Title VII of Civil Rights Act of 1964, 303–314
Intersection of race and sex, 223–224
Laundry workers, 221
Law firm partners, gender stereotyping, 278
Leave and reinstatement for pregnant workers, mothers, 339–358
Lilly Ledbetter Fair Pay Act, 399

Maternity leave as mandatory, mothers, 315–321
Medical benefits for pregnancy, mothers, 338–339
Mothers
    generally, 314–360
    bona fide occupational qualifications, 321–337
    Family and Medical Leave Act, 358–360, 401, 1202
    leave and reinstatement for pregnant workers, 339–358
    maternity leave as mandatory, 315–321
    medical benefits for pregnancy, 338–339
    Pregnancy Discrimination Act, 321–358, 1201–1202
    protection of fetus, 321–337
    protective laws for pregnant workers, 339–358
Pensions, equal pay, 227–228
Pregnancy Discrimination Act, 321–358, 1201–1202
Protection of fetus, mothers, 321–337
Protective legislation
    pregnant workers, 339–358
    Title VII of Civil Rights Act of 1964, 230–240
Psychological wellbeing or injury, sexual harassment, 258–263
Quid pro quo sexual harassment, 244–246
"Reasonable woman" test, sexual harassment, 247–258
Reinstatement for pregnant workers, mothers, 339–358
Same-sex sexual harassment, 263–268
"Sex plus" discrimination, Title VII of Civil Rights Act of 1964, 241–244
Sexual advances, 244–246
Sexual harassment
    generally, 244–277
    psychological wellbeing or injury, 258–263
    quid pro quo harassment, 244–246
    "reasonable woman" test, 247–258
    same-sex harassment, 263–268
    sexual advances, 244–246
    unfulfilled threats, 271–277
    U.S. President, action against, 268–270

Shift differentials, equal pay, 225–227
Slavery, 222
Telephone switchmen, Title VII of Civil Rights Act of 1964, 231–236
Time limits for discrimination actions, 388–399
Title VII of Civil Rights Act of 1964
    generally, 230–244
    agent-telegraphers, 236–240
    applicants with pre-school-age children, 241–244
    bona fide occupational qualification exemption, 230–241, 303–314
    disparate impact, 303–314
    height and weight requirements, 303–314
    protective legislation, 230–240
    "sex plus" discrimination, 241–244
    telephone switchmen, 231–236
    transgender persons, 294–298
Transgender persons, Title VII of Civil Rights Act of 1964, 294–298
Unfulfilled threats, sexual harassment, 271–277
U.S. President, sexual harassment action against, 268–270
Weight requirements, Title VII of Civil Rights Act of 1964, 303–314

EQUAL EMPLOYMENT OPPORTUNITY COMMISSION
Equal protection, intermediate scrutiny, 114

EQUAL PAY
Employment, this index

EQUAL PROTECTION
    Generally, 2–3, 87–107
Bartending, 98–101
Beer, intermediate scrutiny, 136–149
Citizenship, nonmarital children of American parents, 187–201
Combat duty, military service, 182–186
Decedents' estates, qualifications of administrator, intermediate scrutiny, 115–118
Doctrinal setting, intermediate scrutiny, 111–114
Draft, military service, 180–182
Employment, intermediate scrutiny, 114
Hand laundries, 96–97
Immigration, unwed mothers, 180

Intermediate scrutiny
    generally, 111–167
    beer, purchases of, 136–149
    decedents' estates, qualifications of administrator, 115–118
    doctrinal and political setting, 111–114
    military service, promotions, 132–133
    property tax exemptions, 131–132
    Social Security benefits, 134–136, 150
    statutory rape, 150–167
    veterans' benefits, 118–131
Jury duty
    generally, 101–107, 168–179
    peremptory challenges, 179, 187
LGBTQ persons, military service, 184–186
Marriage, gay rights, 720
Military service
    generally, 180–186
    combat duty, 182–186
    draft, 180–182
    intermediate scrutiny, 132–133
    LGBTQ persons, 184–186
    transgender persons, 185–186
    veterans, below
Nationality discrimination, 89
Ordinary scrutiny of sex-based classifications, 96–107
Peremptory challenges, jury duty, 179, 187
Political setting, intermediate scrutiny, 111–114
Poll taxes, 97–98
Poverty discrimination, 89
Property tax exemptions, intermediate scrutiny, 131–132
Protective legislation, 96–98
Racial discrimination, 88–92, 95
Sex and/or gender discrimination, 89–90, 92, 94–95
Social Security benefits, intermediate scrutiny, 134–136, 150
Statutory rape, intermediate scrutiny, 150–167
Transgender persons, military service, 185–186
Veterans
    benefits, intermediate scrutiny, 118–131
    employment preferences, 201–211

EQUAL RIGHTS AMENDMENT
Generally, 1–2, 9, 90
Equal protection, intermediate scrutiny, 114, 118

EUGENICS
Reproductive freedom, contraception, 425

FAMILY AND MEDICAL LEAVE ACT
Generally, 215, 1202
Employment, mothers, 358–360, 401, 1202

FAMILY LAW
Generally, 719–933
Adoption, Native Americans, 907–925
Asymmetrical reciprocity, 780–791
Child Custody, this index
Child Support Recovery Act, 793–794
Criminal conversation, wife as property of husband, 776–779
Deadbeat Parents Punishment Act, 794–795
Divorce, this index
Female genital mutilation, 925–926
Human rights *vs.* parents' right, 925–927
Indian Civil Rights Act of 1968, 899–907
Indian Civil Welfare Act of 1978, 907–925
Maintenance and support, 780–791
Marriage, this index
Native Americans
    generally, 899–925
    adoption, 907–925
    Indian Civil Rights Act of 1968, 899–907
    Indian Civil Welfare Act of 1978, 907–925
    tribal membership, 899–907
No-fault divorce, 792
Surname of married woman, 779–780
Traditional family, generally, 776–791
Tribal membership, Native Americans, 899–907
Uniform Marriage and Divorce Act of 1974, 792–793

FAMILY LEAVE
Generally, 5

FEDERAL SYSTEM
Generally, 11–13
Structure and workload of courts, 14–15

Index

FEEBLE MINDEDNESS
Reproductive freedom, sterilization, 412–416, 423–424

FEMALE GENITAL MUTILATION
Generally, 925–926

FERTILITY OF FEMALES
Colleges and universities, 952–953

FIFTEENTH AMENDMENT
Generally, 11, 21–22

FIRST AMENDMENT
Generally, 211–215
Abortion, 521–525
Boy Scouts, 214–215
Employment advertisements, sex designated, 211–212
Freedom of expression and association, 7
Jaycees organization, 213–214
Law firms, promotion to partner, 212–213
Marriage, gay rights, 720
New York State Club Association, 214
Pornography, 1138–1148
Reproductive freedom, 409–410
Rotary clubs, 214

FORCE
Rape, 1104–1112

FOURTEENTH AMENDMENT
Generally, 11, 21–22
Bar, access to, 27–34
Contracts, 49–61
Privileges and immunities
    generally, 22–34
    bar, access to, 27–34
    Slaughterhouse Cases, 22–27
Slaughterhouse Cases, 22–27
Voting rights, 34–43

FREEDOM OF ACCESS TO CLINIC ENTRANCES ACT
Abortion, 601

FROZEN EMBRYOS
Reproductive freedom, 708–709

FULL FAITH AND CREDIT
Marriage, gay rights, 721

FULL SERVICE HOSPITALS
Abortion, 501

GAG RULE
Abortion, federally assisted family planning clinics, 521–525

GAY RIGHTS
Marriage, this index
Military service, 184–186
Sexual privacy, 452, 560, 720, 729, 730, 740, 744, 929

GENDER DISCRIMINATION
Equal protection, 89–90, 92, 94–95

GENDER IDENTITY
Education, Title IX, 1042–1043

GENDER-MOTIVATED VIOLENCE
Generally, 1

GENDER STEREOTYPING
Employment, this index

GLOBAL GAG RULE
Abortion, Mexico City Policy, 525–526

GRANDPARENTS
Child custody, 893–898

HABITUAL CRIMINALS
Reproductive freedom, sterilization, 416–422

HAND LAUNDRIES
Equal protection, 96–97

HATE SPEECH
Pornography, 1145–1148

HEIGHT REQUIREMENTS
Employment, Title VII of Civil Rights Act of 1964, 303–314

HIGHER EDUCATION
Colleges and Universities, this index

HISTORY
Generally, 7–11

HUMAN TRAFFICKING
Prostitution, 1193–1194

HYDE AMENDMENT
Abortion, public funding, 510–511

IMMIGRATION
Child custody, unmarried fathers, 843
Equal protection, unwed mothers, 180

INCEST
Marriage, 719

INDIAN CIVIL RIGHTS ACT OF 1968
Generally, 899–907

INDIAN CIVIL WELFARE ACT OF 1978
Generally, 907–925

INDUSTRIAL REVOLUTION
Generally, 11

INFANTS
Children and Minors, this index

INHERITANCE LAWS
Marriage, gay rights, 724–736

INTERMEDIATE SCRUTINY
Equal Protection, this index

INTERRACIAL MARRIAGE
Generally, 719

INTIMIDATION
Rape, 1132–1133

INTOXICATING LIQUOR
Bartenders and Bartending, this index
Beer, intermediate scrutiny, 136–149
Prohibition, 6

JAYCEES ORGANIZATION
First Amendment, 213–214

JOINT CUSTODY
Child custody, 828–832

JURISDICTION
Supreme Court, 13–14

JURY DUTY
Equal Protection, this index

KU KLUX KLAN ACTIONS
Abortion, 597

LAUNDRY WORKERS
Employment, 221

LAW ENFORCEMENT OFFICERS
Height requirements, 5
Spousal abuse, police responsibility, 1056–1073

LAW FIRMS
Employment, gender stereotyping, 278

First Amendment, promotion to partner, 212–213

LAW SCHOOLS
Title IX, 1003

LILLY LEDBETTER FAIR PAY ACT
Employment, 399

LIMITATION OF ACTIONS
Employment, discrimination actions, 388–399

LITERARY VALUE
Pornography, 1139

MAINTENANCE AND SUPPORT
Family law, 780–791

MARRIAGE
    Generally, 719–775
Alimony, sex discrimination, 768–773
Child marriage, 926–927
Child support, sex discrimination, 763–768
Coverture, 761–762
Defense of Marriage Act, 722, 725–736
Defined, 719
Domestic partnerships, gay rights, 722–723
Due process, gay rights, 720, 724
English history of marriage, 759–760
Equal protection, gay rights, 720
First Amendment, gay rights, 720
Full faith and credit, gay rights, 721
Gay rights
    generally, 719–756
    Defense of Marriage Act, 722, 725–736
    domestic partnerships, 722–723
    due process, 720, 724
    equal protection, 720
    First Amendment, 720
    full faith and credit, 721
    inheritance laws, 724–736
    privacy, right to, 720
    public accommodation, 756
    state prohibitions, 736–756
History of marriage, generally, 758–775
Incest, 719
Inheritance laws, gay rights, 724–736
Interracial marriage, 719
Oliver Twist, 760–761
Plural marriages, 757–758
Privacy, gay rights, 720

Index

Property rights, sex discrimination, 773–775
Public accommodation, gay rights, 756
Rape
    marital rape, 1133–1135
    marriage of child to rapist, 926–927
Sex discrimination
    generally, 763–775
    alimony, 768–773
    child support, 763–768
    gay rights, above
    property rights, 773–775
State prohibitions, gay rights, 736–756
Transgender persons, 756–758
Unity of husband and wife, 762–763

MATERNITY LEAVE
Employment, mothers, 315–321

MAXIMUM HOURS
Contracts, 50–66

MEDICAID
Abortion, public funding, 507–511

MEDICAL BENEFITS
Employment, pregnancy, 338–339

MEXICO CITY POLICY
Abortion (global gag rule), 525–526

MILITARY ACADEMIES
Colleges and universities, 972–1002

MILITARY SERVICE
Generally, 6
Equal Protection, this index

MINIMUM WAGES
Contracts, 67–81, 84–87

MINORS
Children and Minors, this index

MORRILL LAND-GRANT ACT OF 1862
Colleges and universities, 954

MOTHERS
Employment, this index

NATIONAL AMERICAN WOMAN SUFFRAGE ASSOCIATION
Voting rights, 45–47

NATIONALITY DISCRIMINATION
Equal protection, 89

NATIONAL WOMAN SUFFRAGE ASSOCIATION
Voting rights, 44

NATIVE AMERICANS
Family Law, this index

NEGRO FELLOWSHIP LEAGUE
Voting rights, 45

NEW YORK STATE CLUB ASSOCIATION
First Amendment, 214

NINETEENTH AMENDMENT
Contracts, 68

NO CHILD LEFT BEHIND
Education, 951

NO-FAULT DIVORCE
Generally, 792

OBSCENITY
Pornography, 1138–1150

OLIVER TWIST
Marriage, 760–761

PARENTAL CONSENT
Abortion, 482–498, 527–571

PARENTAL NOTICE
Abortion, 498

PARTIAL BIRTH ABORTIONS
Generally, 571–576, 578–596, 1200

PATERNAL PREFERENCE
Child custody, 795–796

PENSIONS
Employment, equal pay, 227–228

PEREMPTORY CHALLENGES
Equal protection, jury duty, 179, 187

PERMISSION
Consent or Approval, this index

PLURAL MARRIAGES
Generally, 757–758

POLICE OFFICERS
Height requirements, 5
Spousal abuse, police responsibility, 1056–1073

POLICE POWER, 12–13
Contracts, 50–66

POLITICAL SETTING
Equal protection, intermediate scrutiny, 111–114

POLITICAL VALUE
Pornography, 1139

POLL TAXES
Equal protection, 97–98

PORNOGRAPHY
Generally, 1135–1150
Child pornography victims, restitution for, 1148–1150
Contemporary community standards, 1140
First Amendment, 1138–1148
Hate speech, 1145–1148
Literary, artistic, political or scientific value, 1139
Obscenity, 1138–1150
Sexual conduct depicted in patently offensive way, 1140

POSTHUMOUS PROCREATION
Reproductive freedom, 710

POVERTY DISCRIMINATION
Equal protection, 89

PREGNANCY DISCRIMINATION
Generally, 1, 1201–1202
Employment, 321–358, 1201–1202

PRIMARY CAREGIVER STANDARD
Child custody, 808

PRIVACY
Marriage, gay rights, 720
Reproductive Freedom, this index

PRIVILEGES AND IMMUNITIES
Fourteenth Amendment, this index

PROPERTY RIGHTS
Marriage, sex discrimination, 773–775

PROPERTY TAX EXEMPTIONS
Equal protection, intermediate scrutiny, 131–132

PROSTITUTION
Generally, 1182–1194
Human trafficking, 1193–1194
Legalization, 1187–1188
Sexual slavery, 1188–1193
Slavery vs. just another job, 1185–1188

PROTECTION OF FETUS
Employment, mothers, 321–337

PROTECTIVE LEGISLATION
Generally, 2–3, 8–9
Contracts, 61–84
Employment, this index
Equal protection, 96–98

PSYCHOLOGICAL PARENTS
Child custody, 891

PSYCHOLOGICAL WELLBEING OR INJURY
Employment, sexual harassment, 258–263

PUBLIC ACCOMMODATIONS
Marriage, gay rights, 756

PUBLIC FUNDING
Abortion, 506–513

PUBLIC SERVICE HEALTH ACT
Abortion, 522–525

QUID PRO QUO SEXUAL HARASSMENT
Employment, 244–246

RACE
Child custody, best interests of child, 808

RACIAL DISCRIMINATION
Equal protection, 88–92, 95

RAPE
Generally, 1099–1135
Defined, 1100–1101
Force and consent, 1104–1112
Intimidation, 1132–1133
Marital rape, 1133–1135
Marriage of child to rapist, 926–927
Resistance, 1112–1131
Unconscious victims, 1102–1104

"REASONABLE WOMAN" TEST
Employment, sexual harassment, 247–258

REINSTATEMENT
Employment, pregnant workers, 339–358

RELIGIOUS FREEDOM
Reproductive Freedom, this index

RELOCATION OF CUSTODIAL PARENT
Child custody, 826–828

Index

REPORTING AND RECORDKEEPING
Abortion, 482–497, 502, 503–505, 527–571

REPRODUCTIVE FREEDOM
    Generally, 407–718
Abortion, this index
Coercion of Caesarean surgeries, 664–680
Commerce clause, 411–412
Contraception
    generally, 424–453
    due process, 425–440
    eugenics, 425
    minors, 453
    privacy, right to, 425–453
    religious freedom, 643–664, 1200
    RU-486, 518–521
    unmarried persons, 440–453
Drug use during pregnancy, 681–694
Due process
    generally, 408–410
    contraception, 425–440
Eugenics, contraception, 425
Feeble mindedness, sterilization, 412–416, 423–424
First Amendment, 409–410
Frozen embryos, 708–709
Habitual criminals, sterilization, 416–422
Minors, contraception, 453
Posthumous procreation, 710
Privacy, contraception, 425–453
Privacy of pregnant women
    generally, 664–694
    coercion of Caesarean surgeries, 664–680
    drug use during pregnancy, 681–694
Religious freedom
    generally, 643–664
    contraception, 643–664, 1200
Reproductive technology
    generally, 694–710
    frozen embryos, 708–709
    posthumous procreation, 710
    surrogacy contracts, 694–708
RU-486, contraception, 518–521
Sterilization
    generally, 412–424
    feeble mindedness, 412–416, 423–424
    habitual criminals, 416–422
Surrogacy contracts, 694–708
Unmarried persons, contraception, 440–453

RESISTANCE
Rape, 1112–1131

RESTAURANTS
Contracts, 81–84

RETALIATION
Education, Title IX, 1041

RICO
Abortion, 596–598, 622–625

ROTARY CLUBS
First Amendment, 214

RU-486
Reproductive freedom, contraception, 518–521

SAFETY
Abortion clinics, 596–625

SAME-SEX SEXUAL HARASSMENT
Employment, 263–268

SCHOOL DESEGREGATION
Equal protection, racial discrimination, 88–89
Prohibition, 6–7

SCIENTIFIC VALUE
Pornography, 1139

SEX DISCRIMINATION
Equal protection, 89–90, 92, 94–95
Marriage, this index

"SEX PLUS" DISCRIMINATION
Employment, Title VII of Civil Rights Act of 1964, 241–244

SEXUAL ADVANCES
Employment, 244–246

SEXUAL HARASSMENT
Education, Title IX, 1007–1041
Employment, this index

SEXUAL SLAVERY
Prostitution, 1188–1193

SEXUAL VIOLENCE
Education, Title IX, 1153–1154, 1180–1182

SHIFT DIFFERENTIALS
Employment, equal pay, 225–227

SINGLE SEX PUBLIC SCHOOLS
Generally, 936–952

SIXTEENTH AMENDMENT
Generally, 11

SLAUGHTERHOUSE CASES
Fourteenth Amendment, 22–27

SLAVERY
Generally, 8
Employment, 222

SOCIAL SECURITY
Equal protection, intermediate scrutiny, 134–136, 150

SPORTS
Education, Title IX, 1, 1003, 1005–1007, 1041

SPOUSAL ABUSE
Generally, 1048–1099
Battered woman syndrome, 1073–1099
Battery, 1051–1056
Divorce, grounds for, 1051
Domestic violence, 1056
Police responsibility, 1056–1073

STATUTES
Generally, 11–13

STATUTES OF LIMITATION
Employment, discrimination actions, 388–399

STATUTORY RAPE
Equal protection, intermediate scrutiny, 150–167

STERILIZATION
Reproductive Freedom, this index

SUPPORT AND MAINTENANCE
Family law, 780–791

SUPREME COURT
Generally, 13–15
Certiorari, 15
Jurisdiction, 13–14
Proceedings, 15–18
Structure and workload, 14–15

SURNAMES
Married women, 779–780

SURROGACY CONTRACTS
Reproductive freedom, 694–708

TECHNOLOGY
Reproductive Freedom, this index

TELEPHONE SWITCHMEN
Employment, Title VII of Civil Rights Act of 1964, 231–236

TENDER YEARS DOCTRINE
Child custody, 796–800

TEXAS A&M CASES
Colleges and universities, 955–956

THIRTEENTH AMENDMENT
Generally, 11, 21–22

TIME LIMITS
Employment, discrimination actions, 388–399

TITLE IX
Education, this index

TITLE VII OF CIVIL RIGHTS ACT OF 1964
Employment, this index

TRANSGENDER PERSONS
Generally, 4
Employment, Title VII of Civil Rights Act of 1964, 294–298
Equal protection, military service, 185–186
Marriage, 756–758

TRAVEL, RIGHT TO
Generally, 410–412

TRIBAL MEMBERSHIP
Family law, Native Americans, 899–907

TRI-PARENTING RELATIONSHIPS
Child custody, 891–893

UNCONSCIOUS VICTIMS
Rape, 1102–1104

UNFAITHFUL SPOUSES
Child custody, 808–826

UNFULFILLED THREATS
Employment, sexual harassment, 271–277

UNIFORM MARRIAGE AND DIVORCE ACT OF 1974
Generally, 792–793

UNIVERSITIES
Colleges and Universities, this index

UNIVERSITY OF VIRGINIA
Colleges and universities, 956–957

UNMARRIED FATHERS
Child Custody, this index

U.S. PRESIDENTS
Employment, sexual harassment actions, 268–270

VETERANS
Equal Protection, this index

VIABILITY
Abortion, 481–497, 498–499, 502, 503–505, 512–516

VIOLENCE AGAINST WOMEN ACT
Generally, 215, 1150–1180

VOCATIONAL TRAINING PROGRAMS
Education, Title IX, 1003

VOTING RIGHTS
Generally, 43–49
Fourteenth Amendment, 34–43
Nineteenth Amendment, 43–49
Prohibition, 7

WAITING PERIODS
Abortion, 527–571

WEIGHT REQUIREMENTS
Employment, Title VII of Civil Rights Act of 1964, 303–314

WOMEN'S PARTY (CONGRESSIONAL UNION FOR WOMAN SUFFRAGE)
Voting rights, 45–49

WOMEN'S RIGHTS CONVENTION
Generally, 8, 21

WRONGFUL DEATH
Child custody, unmarried fathers, 858–859